ECONOMICS

Principles and Policy   **Second Edition**

William J. Baumol
New York University
and
Princeton University

Alan S. Blinder
Princeton University

Harcourt Brace Jovanovich, Inc.
New York   San Diego   Chicago   San Francisco   Atlanta
London   Sydney   Toronto

To my three children,
Ellen, Daniel,
and now Sabrina

W.J.B.

For William and Scott,
who supply competition
and demand equity

A.S.B.

Printed in the United States of America
Library of Congress Catalog Card Number 81-83083
ISBN: 0-15-518835-6

CREDITS AND ACKNOWLEDGMENTS
p. 11: © Rand McNally & Company, R. L. 78-Y-98; p. 12, top: © 1971, General Drafting Co., Inc.; bottom: Gousha; p. 15: The London School of Economics and Political Science; p. 26: U.S. Geological Survey; p. 48: Brown Brothers; p. 54: The Bettmann Archive, Inc.; p. 81: Brown Brothers; p. 98: From *The Wall Street Journal*, permission—Cartoon Features Syndicate; p. 108: Camera Press—PHOTO TRENDS; p. 148: Brown Brothers; p. 173: UPI; p. 216: B.C. by permission of Johnny Hart and Field Enterprises, Inc.; p. 249: Prepared by the Federal Reserve Bank of St. Louis; p. 299: Art adapted from *Economica*, Nov., 1958; p. 435: Krokodil/Sovfoto; p. 461: Reprinted by permission of *The Wall Street Journal*, © Dow Jones and Co., 1981. All rights reserved.; p. 462: Reprinted by permission of *The Wall Street Journal*, © Dow Jones and Co., 1981. All rights reserved.; p. 547: Gropper, William. "The Senate" (1935). Oil on canvas, 25-1⅛" x 33-⅛". Collection, The Museum of Modern Art, New York. Gift of A. Conger Goodyear.; p. 562: UPI; p. 574: Culver Pictures, Inc.; p. 607: Opinion Research Corporation; p. 628: The Bettmann Archive, Inc.; p. 664: UPI; p. 671: Art adapted from Walter G. Hoffmann, *Das Wachstrum der Deutschen Wirtschafts Seit der Mitte des 19 Jahrhunderts* (Berlin: Springer-Verlag, 1965); p. 688: Photo courtesy of Mobil Oil Corporation; p. 691: Reprinted with permission of American Metal Market/ Metalworking News, © 1981, Fairchild Publications, a Division of Capital Cities Media, Inc.; p. 714: Culver Pictures, Inc.; p. 747: Drawing by Ed Fisher; © 1971, The New Yorker Magazine, Inc.; p. 770: The Bettmann Archive, Inc.; p. 784: UPI; p. 792: Organization for Economic Cooperation and Development; p. 794: Organization for Economic Cooperation and Development; p. 802: Sovfoto; p. 809: UPI; p. 811: UPI.

Preface

For decades, the "principles of economics" book has been expected to codify the entire discipline of economics, to blanket the field, to be encyclopedic. In recent years, this has become at once more imperative and more difficult. On the one hand, the explosion of economic knowledge during the last several decades has made it impossible to put all of economics, even at an introductory level, between two covers. On the other hand, it seems that more and more public policy issues either are basically economic in nature or involve important economic considerations. Intelligent citizens can no longer afford to be innocent of economics.

While the Second Edition represents a rather extensive revision of the First Edition, its preparation has been guided by this dilemma, just as the first volume was. We have studiously avoided the encyclopedic approach and abandoned the fiction, so popular among textbook writers, that literally everything is of the utmost importance. Since students are sufficiently intelligent to see through this ruse in any event, we have tried to highlight those important ideas that are likely to be of lasting significance—principles that you will want to remember long after the course is over because they offer insights that are far from obvious, because they are of practical importance, and because they are widely misunderstood by intelligent laymen. A dozen of the most important of these ideas have been selected as "12 Ideas for Beyond the Final Exam," and are called to your attention when they occur through the use of the book's logo. ◩

All modern economics textbooks abound with "real world" examples, but we have tried to go beyond this, to elevate the examples to preeminence. For in our view, the policy issue or everyday economic problem ought to lead the student naturally to the economic principle, not the other way around. For this reason, many chapters start with a real policy issue or a practical problem that may seem puzzling or paradoxical to noneconomists, and then proceed to describe the economic analysis required to remove the mystery. In doing this, we have tried to utilize technical jargon and diagrams only where there is a clear need, never for their own sake.

Still, economics is a somewhat technical subject and, except for a few rather light chapters, this is a book for the desk, not for the bed. We have, however, made strenuous efforts to simplify the technical level of the discussion as much as we could without sacrificing content. Fortunately, almost every important idea in economics can be explained in plain English, and this, in general, is how we have tried to explain them. Yet, even while reducing the technical difficulty of the book, we have incorporated some elements of economic analysis that have traditionally been left out of introductory books but that are really too important to omit. Foremost among these is our extensive treatment of prices and inflation in Part Two. Introductory (and even intermediate) texts typically devote many chapters to a hypothetical economy in which prices never rise. Here, from the very beginning, we analyze the world as it really is, with prices all too easily driven upward.

Changes from the First Edition

While the philosophy behind the book is unchanged from the First Edition, the implementation of this philosophy is quite different. Most important, the microeconomic portions of the book (Parts Three through Six) have been extensively reorganized, rewritten, and restructured about a central theme that we believe deals with the most significant lessons to be learned in an introductory economics course: what a market system does well, and what it does poorly. Thus, in Part Three we carefully examine the virtues of an idealized system of markets. This helps to explain how the market economy has been able to produce its remarkable accomplishments in terms of efficiency and service to consumers. Then in Parts Four (Big Business and Market Power), Five (Market Failure), and Six (Distribution of Income), we explain some of the things that can go wrong.

In addition to these organizational changes, the following chapters are either all new or have been thoroughly revised since the First Edition: Chapters 3 and 4 (introductory materials), Chapters 20–23 (on the theory of the firm and perfect competition), Chapters 25 and 26 (on monopoly, monopolistic competition, and oligopoly), Chapter 29 (on market failure), Chapters 32 and 33 (on factor markets), and Chapter 36 (on the economics of energy).

Specifically, Chapter 3 now includes expanded discussions of traditional topics such as exchange, specialization, division of labor, and economic efficiency; and a discussion of the role of markets has been added. The new central theme is introduced in Chapter 3 and carries over to Chapter 4's introduction to supply and demand, which features a much more detailed and systematic treatment of shifts in supply and demand curves than did the First Edition.

Chapters 18 and 19, on consumer theory, appear in reverse order from their presentation in the First Edition and have been rewritten in accord with several valuable suggestions from users. For example, there is a much more extensive discussion of elasticity of demand. Chapters 20 and 21, on cost minimization and profit maximization, also have been reversed in order and entirely rewritten. In these chapters especially, and throughout the micro sections, there are longer explanations, more numerical examples, and more graphs than in the First Edition. Also, the discussions have been revised to proceed more deliberately and systematically through the important microeconomic principles. For example, cost curves are explicitly derived from the production function in Chapter 20.

The chapters on market structure (Chapters 22, 25, 26) are also completely reorganized and rewritten. The perfectly competitive firm and the perfectly competitive industry are now treated in the same chapter, and interactions between developments at the level of the firm and developments at the level of the industry are stressed. There is also more material on agriculture. Monopoly occupies a separate chapter; and the discussion of monopolistic competition and oligopoly are greatly expanded. Chapters 32 and 33, on factor pricing, now include a number of new topics, such as critiques of marginal productivity theory, human capital theory, and dual labor markets.

Overall, the macroeconomic section (Part Two) is similar to that of the First Edition, but has been brought up to date to include (a) the most current data available; (b) institutional changes since publication of the First Edition—for example, those that have affected the financial system and the definitions of money; and (c) the economic history of the years 1979–1981—for example, the second oil shock and the Reagan program. In particular, an extended discussion of "supply-side" economics and related matters appears in Chapters 9, 11, and 17. The national income accounting materials (which include 1981 data) no longer constitute a separate chapter; instead, some have been incorporated into the text (especially in Chapters 5 and 7) while most now appear in the appendix to Chapter 7. Several algebraic appendixes have been added (specifically, to Chapters 8, 10, and 11) for courses in which income determination theory is taught with the help of some simple algebra.

Chapter 16, on the trade-off between inflation and unemployment, has been extensively revised. In the First Edition, we treated the *static* trade-off between the *price level* and the *level* of real GNP. In this edition, we apply the same analysis to the *dynamic* trade-off between the *inflation rate* and the *unemployment rate* (which, in a growing economy, is related to the growth rate of real GNP). This alteration permits a much smoother transition from the theoretical model in the text to empirical Phillips curves. The expectational Phillips curve and rational expectations, which are treated only implicitly in the First Edition (that is, the concepts were present, but the terms were not), are now treated explicitly. There is a new chapter, "Coping with Inflation," which pulls together materials from several chapters of the First Edition and adds new material, especially on inflation as a long-run problem and on how productivity growth relates to inflation.

In keeping with our emphasis on current developments, Part Seven now contains an entirely new chapter on energy and natural resources, which replaces the First Edition's chapter on cities. Other chapters in Part Seven have been brought up to date, but are otherwise similar to those of the First Edition.

Studying Principles of Economics

Most courses will begin with Part One, where we have touched most of the traditional bases while keeping the introductory materials briefer than in most texts. Courses concentrating on macroeconomic theory and policy will proceed next to Part Two, while courses specializing in microeconomics will skip to Part Three. Either sort of course may make use of some of the chapters in Part Seven.

Whatever the nature of your course, we would like to offer one suggestion. Unlike some of the other courses you may be taking, principles of economics is cumulative—each week's lesson builds on what you have learned before. You will save yourself a lot of frustration (and also a lot of work) if you keep up on a week to week basis. To help you do this, there is a chapter summary, a list of important terms and concepts, and a selection of discussion questions to help you review at the end of each chapter. In addition to these aids, many students will find the *Study Guide*, designed specifically to accompany this text by Professor Craig Swan, helpful as a self-testing and diagnostic device. When you encounter difficulties in the *Study Guide*, you will know which sections of the text you need to review.

Note to the Instructor

The ordering of chapters in the book is based on courses which treat macro-economics before microeconomics. All of the macroeconomic analysis is found in Part Two. The core micro materials occupy Parts Three through Six, in an order chosen to emphasize the central theme: the working of markets. Part Three describes the theory of the consumer and the theory of the firm and ends with a discussion of perfect competition and the invisible hand at its best. Part Four deals with imperfect competition and policy. Part Five generalizes the discussion of imperfections of the market mechanism. Part Six deals with the theory of distribution. The remaining chapters (Part Seven) contain an assortment of miscellaneous topics that you will use or omit at your discretion. There seems to us no obvious "order" in which to treat these chapters.

What follows is a set of suggested course outlines predicated on the assumptions that (a) a one-semester course will be able to cover about half the book, (b) a one-quarter course will be able to cover about one-third of the book, and (c) the macro course precedes the micro course.

OUTLINE FOR A ONE-SEMESTER COURSE EMPHASIZING
MACROECONOMICS

Chapter Number	Title
1	What Is Economics?
2	The Use and Misuse of Graphs
3	Scarcity and Choice: *The* Economic Problem
4	Supply and Demand: An Initial Look
5	Macroeconomics and Microeconomics
6	Unemployment and Inflation: The Twin Evils of Macroeconomics
7	Aggregate Demand and the Powerful Consumer
8	Demand-Side Equilibrium: Unemployment *or* Inflation?
9	Supply-Side Equilibrium: Unemployment *and* Inflation?
10	Changes on the Demand Side: Multiplier Analysis
11	Managing Aggregate Demand Through Fiscal Policy
12	Banking and the Creation of Money
13	Central Banking and Monetary Policy
14	Money, the National Economy, and the National Debt
15	The Keynesian–Monetarist Debate and Forecasting
16	The Trade-Off Between Inflation and Unemployment
17	Coping with Inflation
35	Economic Growth: Causes, Virtues, and Vices
37	International Trade and Comparative Advantage
38	The International Monetary System: Order or Disorder?
39	Problems of the Less Developed Countries (optional)

OUTLINE FOR A ONE-SEMESTER COURSE EMPHASIZING
MICROECONOMICS

Chapter Number	Title
1	What Is Economics?
2	The Use and Misuse of Graphs

OUTLINE FOR A ONE-SEMESTER COURSE COVERING
BOTH MACRO AND MICRO

OUTLINE FOR A ONE-QUARTER COURSE IN MACROECONOMICS

OUTLINE FOR A ONE-QUARTER COURSE IN MICROECONOMICS

OUTLINE FOR A ONE-QUARTER COURSE ON APPLICATIONS OF BOTH MACRO AND MICRO

With Thanks

Finally, and with great pleasure, we turn to the customary acknowledgments of indebtedness. Ours have been accumulating now through two editions. In these days of specialization, not even a pair of authors can master every subject that an introductory text must cover. Our friends and colleagues Charles Berry, William Branson, Lester Chandler, Stephen Goldfeld, Claudia Goldin, Ronald Grieson, Daniel Hamermesh, Peter Kenen, Arthur Lewis, Burton Malkiel, Edwin Mills, Harvey Rosen, and Laura Tyson have all given generously of their knowledge in particular areas. We have learned much from them, and only wish we had learned more.

Many economists at other colleges and universities, including James Actman of Indiana University, Paul Barkley of Washington State University, George Carter of the University of Southern Mississippi, Tom Cate of Northern Kentucky University, David Denslow of the University of Florida, John Fitts of Carnegie-Mellon University, William Freund of the New York Stock Exchange, Malcolm Getz of Vanderbilt University, Otis Gilley of the University of Texas at Austin, Thomas Holmstrom of Northern Michigan University, Bruce Kaufman of Georgia State University, Ercan Kumcu of Boston College, Patrick Lewis of Otterbein College, Henry McCarl of the University of Alabama at Birmingham, Robert Michaels of California State University at Fullerton, John Powelson of the University of Colorado, John Raisian of the University of Houston, Harry Rosen of the U.S. Air Force Academy, Augustus Shackelford of El Camino College, Paul Sommers of the University of California at San Diego, Charles Staley of the State University of New York at Stony Brook, Lorie Tarshis of the Ontario Economic Council, Robert Thomas of Iowa State University, William

Thweatt of Vanderbilt University, and Bernard Udis of the University of Colorado offered useful suggestions for improvements, many of which we have incorporated into the Second Edition. We thank them all, and also thank the more than 130 economists who responded to our questionnaire. Their responses were invaluable in planning this revision.

Our sanity and survival during the preparation of the Second Edition were assured by the intelligence, ability, and pleasantness of our secretaries, Sue Anne Batey Blackman, Phyllis Durepos, Mary Mateja, and Stephanie Sigall, who did so many things and did them all so well.

And finally there are our wives, Hilda Baumol and Madeline Blinder, who have now participated in this project for six years. Their patience, good judgment, and love have made everything go more smoothly than we had any right to expect. We salute them.

William J. Baumol
Alan S. Blinder

Contents

PART II
Macroeconomics 71

10 Changes on the Demand Side: Multiplier Analysis   176

Appendix: The Simple Algebra of the Multiplier When the Price Level Is Fixed   189

11 Managing Aggregate Demand Through Fiscal Policy   190

Appendix: Algebraic Treatment of Fiscal Policy and Aggregate Demand   211

PART VI
The Distribution of Income   591

32 Pricing the Factors of Production: Interest, Rent, and Profits   592

Appendix A: Discounting and Present Value   612

Appendix B: David Ricardo's Theory of Income Distribution   614

33 The Labor Market and Wages   616

Competitive Labor Markets   617

Unions and Collective Bargaining   627

39 Problems of the Less Developed Countries   751

40 Marxian Economics   768

41 Comparative Economic Systems: What Are the Choices?   782

What Is Economics All About?

I

What Is Economics?

Economics is a broad-ranging discipline, both in the questions it asks and the methods it uses to seek answers. Many definitions of **economics** have been proposed, but we prefer to avoid any attempt to define the discipline in a single sentence or paragraph. Instead, this chapter will introduce you to economics by letting the subject matter speak for itself.

The first part of this chapter is intended to give you some idea of the types of problems that can be approached through economic analysis and the kinds of solutions that economic principles suggest. By the time you finish this course, we can promise you a better understanding of some of the nation's and the world's most pressing problems and of some approaches to solving these problems. This is the real payoff from studying economics.

The second part briefly introduces the methods of economic inquiry, and the tools that economists use. These are tools you may find useful in your life as a citizen, consumer, and worker after the course is over.

Ideas for Beyond the Final Exam

As college professors, we realize it is inevitable that you will forget much of what you learn in this course—perhaps with a sense of relief—very soon after the final exam has been graded. There is not much point bemoaning this fact; elephants may never forget, but people do. Nevertheless, there are a number of economic ideas that are important enough for you to remember well beyond the final exam. You will want to remember them because they offer insights into the workings of the economy, because their significance is enduring, and because you will have shortchanged your own education if you forget them as soon as the course is over.

To help you pick out a few of these crucial ideas, we have selected 12 of them from among the many contained in this book. Some bear on important policy issues that often appear in the newpapers and that may have relevance to your own future decisions. Others point out common misunderstandings that occur among even the most thoughtful lay observers. As the opening quotation of this chapter suggests, many learned judges, politicians, business people, and university administrators who failed to grasp these economic principles could have made far wiser decisions than they did. Each of the **12 Ideas for Beyond the Final Exam** will be discussed in depth as it occurs in the course of the book's narrative. But we think it useful to sketch them briefly here, even though at this point we can only hint at the underlying analyses.

The Illusion of High Interest Rates   IDEA 1

In 1961, banks were happy to lend young families money to build houses at a rate of less than 6 percent annual interest. In 1980, the interest rate had reached 15 percent and more; yet even at these apparently high prices, mortgage money dried up in many parts of the country and housing construction came to a grinding halt. Was this because the banks had grown greedier? Not at all.

Any conclusion based on a direct comparison of the two interest rates is an illusion. In a real sense the 1980 interest rate of 15 percent, despite its appearance, was much *lower* than the 1961 interest rate of 6 percent! Why? In 1961, there was virtually no inflation; prices typically were rising by less than 1 percent a year. But in 1980 inflation was rampant; prices rose over 13 percent in a single year.

What does inflation have to do with interest rates? Consider the position of a person who lends $100 for one year at a rate of 15 percent interest a year when the inflation rate is 13 percent. At the end of the year the lender gets back his $100 plus $15 in interest. But over that same year, because of inflation, his $100 has lost $13 in purchasing power. *Thus he is left only $2 richer in terms of what his money can now buy.* That is, in terms of purchasing power, the lender gains only 2 percent.

Now consider someone who lends $100 at 6 percent interest when prices are rising only 1 percent a year. This lender gets back the original $100 plus $6 in interest, and loses only $1 in purchasing power—for a net gain of $5, or a 5 percent return on his loan.

As we will see in Chapter 6, during the 1970s, policymakers in many states failed to understand this simple principle and so stood steadfastly behind laws and regulations that prohibited interest charges higher than, say, 9 percent a year because they considered such high rates to be evidence of heartless profiteering by the lenders. Yet with inflation sometimes in excess of 9 percent the ceiling on interest rates condemned lenders to lose purchasing power as a reward for their willingness to lend money. As a result, the homebuilding industry languished for lack of funds. As is so often the case, a lack of basic understanding of economic principles led policymakers, despite their good intentions, to make decisions that had serious and unwanted consequences.[1]

Interferences with the   IDEA 2
"Law" of Supply and Demand

In a free market, no one is very surprised if the price of a commodity is relatively high when demand for it is abundant and supply is low. Similarly, we expect the price to be relatively low when supply is abundant and demand scarce. But

---

[1]We will explore this issue in more detail in Chapter 6.

simply because we expect these price fluctuations does not mean we are happy about them.

Politicians from the dawn of history have believed they know what to do to stabilize prices. They pass a law declaring the unpopular price illegal. A ceiling (maximum) may be placed over the price of natural gas or rents, or a floor (minimum) may be placed under the price of wheat or wages.

But the passage of laws does not always make the politicians' wish come true. History shows that price floors and ceilings usually either fail to achieve their aims or, where they do succeed, create other problems that are often more serious than those they were designed to cure. For example, when the Spaniards surrounded Antwerp in 1584, hoping to starve the city into surrender, profiteers found ways to smuggle food into the city at relatively high prices. To end the "exploitation," the city fathers placed price ceilings on food. They succeeded so well that the smugglers were driven out of business—but they also helped the Spaniards achieve their goal! Similarly, when government rules kept energy prices down during the 1970s severe shortages appeared. With deregulation and rising prices in the 1980s the shortage suddenly turned into a "glut" (which may also prove temporary).

As we shall learn in Chapter 4, and indeed throughout this book, such results are no accident. They follow *inescapably* from the nature of price regulations.

IDEA 3 Inflation and Unemployment

Over the past decade, the battle against inflation has probably occupied a higher position on the national agenda than any other social problem. Why has it proven so intractable? Why, despite the best efforts of politicians and economists, is the inflation rate higher today than it was when the battle began?

This is obviously a complex question that defies a short answer. But one element of the answer is clear: Most of the potential cures for inflation are painful. Specifically, there is an agonizing *trade-off between inflation and unemployment*, meaning that most anti-inflation policies cause unemployment to increase. The reasons for this trade-off will be explored in depth in Part Two, especially in Chapter 16. And, in Chapter 17, we will also examine some suggestions for escaping from the trade-off, including "supply-side" economics.

IDEA 4 Increasing Output May Require Sacrificing Equality

"Supply-side" economics has been much in the news in recent years. As just mentioned, it has been offered as an attractive way out of the inflation problem; and other benefits have been claimed for it as well. The basic idea behind supply-side tax cuts (which are discussed in detail in Chapters 9, 11, and 17) is to spur productivity and efficiency by providing greater incentives for working, saving, and investing. This was, for example, one major goal of the large tax cuts of 1981.

Yet there is at least one problem with supply-side economics—a problem that figured prominently in the debate over the tax cut in 1981. In order to provide stronger incentives for success in the economic game, the gaps between the "winners" and the "losers" must necessarily be widened. For it is these gaps that, after all, provide the incentives to work harder, to save more, and to invest productively.

However, some observers feel that the unequal distribution of income in our society is unjust; that it is inequitable for the super rich to sail yachts and give expensive parties while poor people live in slums and eat inadequate diets. People who hold this view are disturbed by the fact that supply-side tax cuts are quite likely to make the distribution of income even more unequal than it already is.

This example illustrates a genuine and pervasive dilemma. There is often a trade-off between the *size* of a nation's output and the degree of *equality* with which that output is distributed. As illustrated by the example of supply-side tax cuts, programs that increase production often breed inequality. And, as we will see in Chapter 34, many policies designed to divide the proverbial economic pie more equally inadvertently cause the size of the pie to shrink.

The Cost Disease of the Service Sector   IDEA 5

There is a distressing phenomenon occurring in cities throughout the industrial-ized world. Many urban services have apparently been growing poorer—fewer police officers on the beat, larger classes in public schools, less reliable garbage pickups—while the public is paying more and more for them. Indeed, the costs have risen substantially and consistently faster than has the rate of inflation. A natural response is to attribute the problem to political corruption and govern-ment inefficiency. But this is certainly not the whole story.

As we shall see in Chapter 29, one of the major causes of the problem is economic. And it has nothing to do with corruption or inefficiency of public employees; rather, it has to do with the dazzling growth in efficiency of private manufacturing industries! Because technological improvements make workers more productive in manufacturing, wages rise. And they rise not only for the manufacturing workers but also for police officers, teachers, and other public employees. But here technology is not easily changed; since it still takes two officers to staff a police cruiser and one teacher to teach a class, the cost of these city services is forced to rise.

The same sort of cost disease affects other services: medical care, university teaching, restaurant cooking, retailing, and automobile repairs, for example; and it explains why their prices have often gone up far faster than the inflation rate.

This is important to understand not because it excuses the financial record of our cities, but because an understanding of the problem suggests what we should expect the future to bring and, perhaps, indicates what policies should be advocated to correct it.

Economic Principles   IDEA 6
to Protect the Environment

Free-market economies have produced an abundance of consumer goods—an achievement that is not inconsequential. But they have been far less successful in their efforts to protect the cleanliness of waterways and streets and the purity of the air. Why is it that our economy serves us so well in providing jeans but so poorly in providing a clean environment?

Economists believe that they know what the trouble is, and they feel that economic analysis can help remedy it as a simple example will illustrate.

When a manufacturer makes jeans he pays all the costs himself—he pays for labor, equipment, raw materials, and energy. These are all expensive resources, so it will pay him to do everything in his power to avoid wasting them. But when a paper mill pours chemical wastes into a nearby river, its owners pay nothing for the resulting damage to the environment. The paper mill uses oxygen to dilute its chemical wastes just as it uses a trucking company to haul away its solid wastes. But there is one important difference—the owners of the mill pay for the trucking services, but they get the oxygen for nothing. Since the oxygen is "free" the firm does not lose anything by using it wastefully. It can pour wastes into the river as if the resulting damage did not matter to anyone.

The basic source of the problem, then, is that the cost of producing jeans is borne internally, and so it pays the firm to avoid waste in the manufacturing process. But the cost of waste disposal—the oxygen that is destroyed—is borne by the general public, not by the paper mill. Consequently, the mill has no incentive to be careful in its use of the waterway, a public resource.

Economists believe there is a straightforward remedy for this problem: Make the paper mill pay for the damage it causes. Specifically, as we shall see in Chapter 31, they recommend that a *tax* be levied on every gallon of chemical waste that the firm spills into the river. In this way, they argue, the firm will be given an incentive to reduce its pollution just as it has an incentive to limit its other costs.

IDEA 7   A New Way to Measure Costs

Economists do not measure costs in the same way that accountants and other people do. Rather than looking only at the monetary costs of purchasing an item, economists ask, *What did you have to give up to acquire this item?*

The costs of a college education provide a vivid example that is probably close to the hearts of all students reading this book. How much do you think it *costs* to go to college? Most likely you would answer this question by adding together your expenditures on tuition, room and board, books, and the like, and then deducting any scholarship funds you may receive. Economists would not. They would first want to know how much you could be earning if you were not attending college. This may sound like an irrelevant question; but because you *give up* these earnings by attending college, they must be added to your tuition bill as a cost of your education. Nor would economists accept the university's bill for room and board as a measure of your living costs. They would want to know by how much this exceeds what it would have cost you to live at home, and only this extra cost would be counted as an expense. On balance, a college education probably costs more than you think.

These costs that economists measure are called **opportunity costs,** a concept we will return to again and again in this volume, beginning in Chapter 3.

IDEA 8   The Surprising Principle of Comparative Advantage

In the period since World War II, the Japanese economy has expanded explosively. Spectacular improvements in the efficiency of its production and in the quality of its products have prompted Americans to buy cars, TV sets, cameras, and other products from Japan in huge quantities. American TV manufacturers, steel producers, and auto makers have complained about the competition and demanded protection against the flood of imports that, in their view, threatens American standards of living. Is this view justified?

The most common argument made in support of protective legislation is entirely fallacious. It runs as follows: What if a combination of higher productivity and lower wages were to permit Japan to produce *everything* more cheaply than we could? Would it not then be true that Americans would have no work and that our nation would be impoverished?

A remarkable result, called the **law of comparative advantage,** shows that even in this extreme event it would still pay the two nations to trade and that both would gain as a result! We will explain this principle fully in Chaper 37, where we will also note some potentially valid arguments in favor of protection; but for now a simple parable will make the reason clear.

Suppose Sam grows up on a farm and is a whiz at plowing, but he is also a successful country singer and gets paid $2000 a performance at hotels and nightclubs. Should Sam refuse some singing engagements to leave time for plowing? Of course not. Instead he should hire Alfie, a much less efficient farmer, to plow for him. Sam is the better farmer, but he earns so much more by specializing in singing that it pays him to leave the farming to Alfie. Alfie, though a poorer farmer than Sam, is an even worse singer. Thus Alfie earns a living by specializing in the job at which he at least has a *comparative* advantage (his farming is not quite as bad as his singing), and both Alfie and Sam gain. The same is true of two countries. Even if one of them is more efficient at everything, both countries can gain by producing the things they do best *comparatively*.

The Importance of Marginal Analysis   IDEA 9

Many pages in this book will be spent explaining, and extolling the virtues of, a type of decision-making process called **marginal analysis** (see especially Chapters 18–21). Here we can best illustrate this process by an example.

Suppose that an airline is told by its accountants that the full cost of transporting one passenger from Los Angeles to New York is $350. Can the airline profit by offering a reduced rate of $250 to students who fly on a standby basis? The surprising answer is: probably yes. The reason is that most of the $350 cost per passenger must be paid whether the plane carries 20 passengers or 120 passengers. Marginal analysis says that full costs—which include costs of maintenance, landing rights, ground crews, and so on—are irrelevant to the decision at hand. The only costs that are relevant in deciding whether to carry standby passengers for reduced rates are the extra costs of writing and processing additional tickets, the food and beverages these passengers consume, the additional fuel required, and so on. These costs are called **marginal costs,** and they are probably quite small in this instance. Any passenger who pays the airline more than its marginal cost will add something to the company's profit, so it probably is more profitable to let the students ride for the reduced fare than to fly the plane with some empty seats.

There are many real cases in which decision makers, not understanding marginal analysis, have rejected advantageous possibilities like the reduced fare in our hypothetical example. These people were misled by calculating in terms of *average* rather than *marginal* cost figures—an error that can be quite costly.

IDEA 10 Stabilizing the Economy Without "Big Government"

Nowadays there is wide agreement that one proper function of government is to regulate the pace of economic activity—restraining the economy when it would otherwise race ahead too quickly and nudging it forward when it would otherwise show signs of sluggishness. Part Two explains why the government may have to take on this responsibility, and how it tries to do the job.

Yet some people worry that frequent government actions to stabilize the economy will lead inevitably to a larger and larger public sector. The slogan "creeping socialism" is sometimes used to describe this alleged phenomenon—with evident disapproval.

Economists argue that this worry arises from confusing two issues that ought to be kept separate. The first issue is how tenacious the government should be in its efforts to promote economic stability. The second issue is how large a government the country should have. As we shall learn in this book, there is plenty of room for disagreement over both issues.

But we shall also see that it is a serious logical error to intertwine the two. Why? Because there are alternative policies that can promote economic stability with either a growing, an unchanged, or even a *shrinking* public sector. For example, as we will see in Chapter 11, when it is advisable to speed up economic activity the size of the public sector can be *expanded* by increasing government spending or *contracted* by reducing taxes. Thus, differences among individuals over how much the government should intervene to promote economic stability ought not to be based on their ideas about how large the government should be.

IDEA 11 The Consequences of Budget Deficits

Most American presidents, including many under whom the national debt has grown very rapidly, have vehemently opposed government budget deficits. President Reagan is only the latest in a long line of chief executives to adopt a balanced budget as a major goal. And during the early 1980s there was even talk of mandating a balanced budget by constitutional amendment.

Economists recognize that government deficits often have undesirable effects. But they emphasize that whether or not a deficit is appropriate depends mainly on the state of the economy. To summarize briefly an argument that will be made at great length in Part Two, most economists believe that deficits are quite desirable when there is high unemployment but quite undesirable when there is high inflation.[2]

They also argue that the fears many people express that the large national debt, which results from budget deficits, will bankrupt the nation or place an intolerable burden upon future generations are entirely without foundation. (The reasons why these fears are groundless will be discussed in Chapter 14.) In sum, economists view the national debt with much less alarm than does the general public.

IDEA 12 Why Speculation Can Be a Good Thing

When the price of a scarce commodity skyrockets, or when stock market prices collapse, or when the value of a nation's money plunges, much of the blame is

---

[2]The issue is far less clear when there is both high unemployment and high inflation. We will examine this question in later chapters.

invariably assigned to evil "speculators." But *how* they cause these things to happen is never quite explained. Perhaps the widespread aversion to speculators stems from a puritanical objection to gambling, for it is true that speculators deliberately deal in risks. But economists believe that speculators fulfill a useful role in society. Once again, an example explains this.

Suppose a bakery signs a contract to deliver bread to the armed forces for a whole year at a prearranged price. Whether that contract will bring profit or loss to the bakery depends on the weather, which will determine the size and price of the wheat crop. No one can eliminate that risk. But a professional speculator may offer to relieve the baker of the risk by assuming it herself.

For example, she may be willing to sign a contract with the bakery guaranteeing to deliver the flour when it is needed, and to do so at some specified mutually agreeable price. Of course, this price will include some fee to the speculator for taking over the risk. If, later on, the market price of flour falls, the speculator will make a tidy profit, for she will buy the flour cheaply and deliver it to the bakery at the price set in their contract. But if the market price of flour rises, it is the speculator, not the baker, who will take the financial beating. She will have to pay the high market price and will receive from the baker only the amount specified in the contract.

In other words, speculators sell an important service—they take over other people's risks (and their worries). In effect, they provide insurance policies to those who engage in unavoidably risky activities. Furthermore, as we shall learn in Chapters 24 and 38, there is good reason to believe that, contrary to popular misconceptions, the activities of professional speculators usually make price fluctuations *smaller* than they would otherwise have been.

Epilogue

These, then, are the dozen fundamental concepts that we hope you will retain beyond the final exam. Do not try to learn them perfectly right now, for you will hear much more about each as the book progresses. Instead, keep them in mind as you read—we will point them out to you as they occur by the use of the book's logo ▨ —and look back over this list at the end of the course. You may be amazed to see how natural, or even obvious, they will seem then.

Inside the Economist's Tool Kit

Now that you have some idea of the kinds of policy issues economists deal with every day, you should know something about how they grapple with these problems. Economics has something of a split personality. Clearly the most rigorous of the social sciences, it nevertheless looks decidedly more "social" than "scientific" when compared with physics. Economists strive to be humanists and scientists simultaneously.

What Economists Do

An economist is, by necessity, a jack of several trades and master of none. Economists borrow modes of investigation from numerous fields, adjusting each to fit the particular problems posed by economic events. Usefulness, not methodological purity, is the criterion for including a technique in the economist's tool kit. Mathematical reasoning is used extensively in economics, but so is historical study. And neither looks quite the same as when practiced by a mathematician or a historian. Statistical inference, too, plays an important role in economic inquiry, but economists have had to modify the standard procedures of statistics to fit the kinds of data they deal with. In 1926, John Maynard Keynes, the great British economist, summed up the many faces of economic inquiry in a statement that still rings true today:

The master-economist . . . must understand symbols and speak in words. He must contemplate the particular in terms of the general, and touch abstract and concrete in the same flight of thought. He must study the present in the light of the past for the purposes of the future. No part of man's nature or his institutions must lie entirely outside his regard. He must be purposeful and disinterested in a simultaneous mood; as aloof and incorruptible as an artist, yet sometimes as near the earth as a politician.[3]

Economics is more easily distinguished by the types of problems it addresses than by the investigative techniques it employs to study them. An introductory course in economics cannot make you an economist, but it should help you approach social problems from a pragmatic and dispassionate point of view. Answers to all society's problems will not be found in this book. But you should learn how to pose the right questions—questions that will help produce answers that are both useful and illuminating.

The Need for Abstraction

Some students find economics unduly abstract and "unrealistic." The stylized world envisioned by economic theory seems only a distant cousin to the world they see around them. There is an old joke about three people—a chemist, a physicist, and an economist—stranded on an isolated island with an ample supply of canned food but no implements to open the cans. In debating what to do, the chemist suggested lighting a fire under the cans, expanding their contents, and thus causing the cans to burst. The physicist doubted that this would work. He advocated building a catapult with which they could smash the cans against some nearby boulders. Then they turned to the economist for his suggestion. He thought for a moment and announced his solution: "Let's assume we have a can opener."

Economists *do* make unrealistic assumptions, and you will encounter many of them in the pages that follow. But this propensity to abstract from reality results from the incredible complexity of the real world, not from any fondness economists have for sounding absurd.

Compare the chemist's task of explaining the interactions of compounds in a chemical reaction with the economist's task of explaining the interactions of people in an economy. Are molecules ever motivated by greed or altruism, by envy or ambition? Do they ever emulate other molecules? Do forecasts about them ever influence their behavior? People, of course, do all these things, and many, many more. It is therefore immeasurably more difficult to predict human behavior than it is to predict chemical reactions. If economists tried to keep track of every aspect of human behavior, they could surely never hope to understand the nature of the economy. Thus:

---

[3] As quoted by Robert Heilbroner in *The Worldly Philosophers*, revised edition (New York: Simon and Schuster, 1972), page 250.

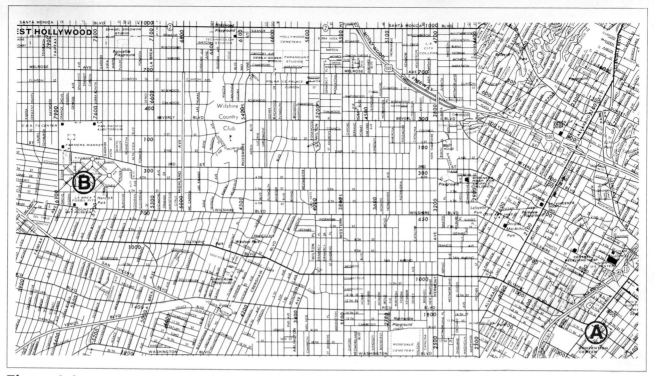

Figure 1-1

Map 1 gives complete details of the road system of Los Angeles. If you are like most people, you will find it hard to read and not very useful for figuring out how to get from the Convention Center (point A) to the La Brea tar pits (point B). For this purpose, the map carries far too much detail, though for some other purposes (for example, locating some very small street in Hollywood) it may be the best map available.

Abstraction from unimportant details is necessary to understand the functioning of anything as complex as the economy.

To appreciate why the economist abstracts from details, put yourself in the following hypothetical situation. You have just arrived, for the first time in your life, in Los Angeles. You are now at the Los Angeles Convention Center. This is the point marked *A* in Figures 1–1 and 1–2, which are alternative maps of part of Los Angeles. You want to drive to the famous La Brea tar pits, marked *B* on each map. Which map would you find more useful? You will notice that Map 1 (Figure 1–1) has the full details of the Los Angeles road system. Consequently, it requires a major effort to read it. In contrast, Map 2 (Figure 1–2) omits many minor roads so that the freeways and major arteries stand out more clearly.

Most strangers to the city would prefer Map 2. With its guidance they are likely to find the tar pits in a reasonable amount of time, even though a slightly shorter route might have been found by careful calculation and planning using Map 1. Map 2 seems to abstract successfully from a lot of confusing details while retaining the essential aspects of the city's geography. Economic theories strive to do the same thing.

Map 3 (Figure 1–3), which shows little more than the major interstate routes that pass through the greater Los Angeles area, illustrates a danger of which all theorists must beware. Armed only with the information provided on this map, you might never find the La Brea tar pits. Instead of a useful idealization of the L.A. road network, the map makers have produced a map that is oversimplified for

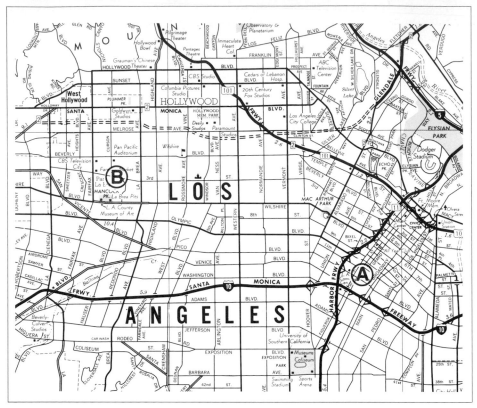

Figure 1–2

Map 2 shows a very different perspective of Los Angeles. Minor roads are eliminated—we might say, *assumed away*—in order to present a clearer picture of where the major arteries and freeways go. As a result of this simplification, several ways of getting from the Convention Center (point *A*) to the La Brea tar pits (point *B*) stand out clearly. For example, we can take the Harbor Freeway north to Wilshire Boulevard, and then follow Wilshire west to the tar pits. While we might find a shorter route by poring over the details of Map 1, most of us will feel more comfortable with Map 2.

Figure 1–3

Map 3 strips away still more details of the Los Angeles road system. In fact, only major trunk roads and freeways remain. This map may be useful for passing through the city or getting around it, but it will not help the tourist who wants to see the sights of Los Angeles. For this purpose, too many details are missing.

our purpose. Too much has been assumed away. Of course, this map was never intended to be used as a guide to the La Brea tar pits, which brings us to a very important point:

There is no such thing as one "right" degree of abstraction for all analytic purposes. The optimal degree of abstraction depends on the objective of the analysis. A model that is a gross oversimplification for one purpose may be needlessly complicated for another.

Economists are constantly treading the thin line between Map 2 and Map 3, between useful generalization about complex issues and gross distortions of the pertinent facts. How can they tell when they have abstracted from reality just enough? There is no objective answer to this question, which is why applied economics is as much art as science. One of the factors distinguishing good economics from bad economics is the degree to which analysts are able to find the factors that constitute the equivalent of Map 2 (rather than Maps 1 or 3) for the problem at hand. It is not always easy to do, as the following examples illustrate.

The Distribution of Income

Suppose you are interested in learning why different people have different incomes, why some are fabulously rich while others are pathetically poor. People differ in many ways, too many to enumerate, much less to study. The economist ignores most of these details in order to focus on a few important facts. The color of a person's hair or eyes probably is not important to the problem at hand, but the color of his skin certainly is. Height and weight may not matter, but his parents' bank balance may. Proceeding in this way, we pare Map 1 down to the manageable dimensions of Map 2. But there is a danger of going too far. To make it easy to analyze a problem we can end up stripping away some of its most crucial features.

The Determination of National Income ✕

Suppose we want to know what factors determine the size of the output of the whole economy. Since the volume of goods and services turned out by the whole economy is affected by literally millions of decisions by investors, business managers, employees, government officials, and others, a complete enumeration of all the factors determining the nation's output clearly makes analysis unworkable (Map 1). Abstraction is necessary. We must prune the list to manageable size. Part Two of this book explains how economists do this; that is, how they draw up a Map 2 of the nation's output.

Several shortcuts to this process have been proposed, but in the opinion of their critics, they have proved on inspection to be like Map 3. For instance, one of the determinants of national output that we will discuss in Part Two is the supply of money, and it is certainly a very important one. For a number of years, a small group of economists thought they could explain the nation's total production almost exclusively from the behavior of the money supply. The critics argued that this would be like making a map of Los Angeles that marked only the Hollywood Freeway.

The Role of Economic Theory

A person "can stare stupidly at phenomena; but in the absence of imagination they will not connect themselves together in any rational way." These words of the renowned American philosopher—scientist C. S. Peirce succinctly express the crucial role of theory in scientific inquiry and help explain why economists are so enamored of it. To the economist or the physical scientist, the word *theory* does not mean what it does in common speech. In scientific usage, a theory is *not* an untested assertion of alleged fact. The statement that saccharine causes cancer is not a theory, it is a *hypothesis*, which will either prove to be true or false after the right sorts of experiments have been completed.

Instead, a theory is a deliberate simplification (abstraction) of factual relationships that attempts to explain how those relationships work. In other words, it is an *explanation* of the mechanism behind observed phenomena. For example, astronomers' data describe the paths of the planets, and gravity forms the basis of theories that are intended to explain these data. Similarly, economists have data suggesting that government policies can affect the degree of a country's prosperity. Keynesian theory (which will be discussed in Part Two) seeks to describe and explain these relationships.

To economists, theorizing is not a luxury; it is a necessity. Economic theory provides a logical structure for organizing and analyzing economic data. Without theory, economists could only "stare stupidly" at the world. With theory, they can attempt to understand it. People who have never studied economics often draw a false distinction between *theory* and *practical policy*. Politicians are particularly guilty of this, scoffing at abstract economic theory as something that is best ignored by "practical" policymakers. The irony of these statements is that:

It is precisely the concern for policy that makes economic theory so necessary and important.

If there were no possibility of changing the economy through public policy, economics might be a historical and descriptive discipline, asking, for example, What happened in the United States during the Great Depression of the 1930s? or How is it that industrial pollution got to be so serious in the 1960s?

But deep concern about public policy forces economists to go beyond such historical and descriptive questions. To formulate rational policy, they are *forced* to deal with possibilities that have not actually occurred. For example, to learn how to prevent depressions, they must investigate whether the Great Depression could have been avoided by more astute management of the nation's money supply. Or to determine what environmental programs will be most effective, they must examine what might happen to pollution in the 1980s if government placed taxes on industrial waste discharges and automobile emissions.

As Peirce pointed out, not even a lifetime of ogling at real-world data will answer such questions. Indeed, the facts can sometimes be highly misleading. Statistics often indicate that two variables behave very similarly: whenever one rises so does the other, and they also both go down simultaneously. But this *correlation* between the data does not prove that either of these variables *causes* the other. For example, in rainy weather, people tend to drive their cars more slowly, and there are also more traffic accidents. But this correlation does not mean that slow driving causes accidents. Rather, both phenomena can be attributed to a common underlying factor (more rain) which leads both to more accidents and to slower driving. Thus, just looking at the degree of correlation (the degree of similarity) between the behavior of two sets of statistics (like accidents and driving speeds) may not tell us much about cause and effect. We need to use theory as part of the analysis.

Because most economic issues hinge on some question of cause and effect, only a combination of theoretical reasoning and data analysis can hope to provide solutions. Simply observing a correlation between data is not enough. We must understand how, if at all, a greater money supply, for example, will lead to a lower unemployment rate or how a tax on emissions will reduce pollution.

What Is an Economic "Model"?

Economists use *models* to describe such cause-and-effect relationships. The notion of a "model" is familiar enough to children, and economists (in common with other scientists) use the term in much the same way that children do.

A child's model automobile or airplane looks and operates much like the real thing, but it is much smaller and much simpler, and so it is much easier to manipulate and understand. Engineers for General Motors and Boeing also build models of cars and planes. While their models are far bigger and much more elaborate than a child's toy, they use them for much the same purposes: to observe the workings of these vehicles "up close," to experiment with them in order to see how they might behave under different circumstances ("What happens if I do this?"). From these experiments, they make educated guesses as to how the real-life version will perform. Often these guesses prove uncannily accurate, as exemplified by the success of the Boeing 747. But sometimes they are wide of the mark: The chronic mechanical problems of General Motors' Corvair prompted Ralph Nader's acclaimed book *Unsafe at Any Speed*, which helped launch the consumer movement.

Economists use models for similar purposes and with similarly mixed results. A. W. Phillips, the famous engineer-turned-economist who discovered the "Phillips curve" (discussed in Chapter 16), was talented enough to construct a working model of the determination of national income in a simple economy, using colored water flowing through pipes. For years this contraption, depicted in Figure 1–4, graced the basement of the London School of Economics. However, most economists lack Phillips's manual dexterity, so economic models are generally built with paper and pencil rather than with hammer and nails.

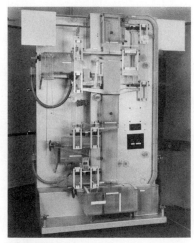

Figure 1–4
THE PHILLIPS MACHINE

The late Professor A. W. Phillips, while teaching at the London School of Economics in the early 1950s, built this machine to illustrate Keynesian theory. This is the same theory that we will explain with words and diagrams later in the book; but Phillips's background as an engineer enabled him to depict the theory with the help of tubes, valves, and pumps. Because economists are not very good plumbers, few of them try to build models of this sort; most rely on paper and pencil instead. But the two sorts of models fulfill precisely the same role. They simplify reality in order to make it understandable.

Because many of the models used in this book are depicted in diagrams, we explain the construction and use of various types of graphs in the next chapter. But sometimes economic models are expressed only in words. The statement "Business people produce the level of output that maximizes their profits," is the basis for a behavioral model whose consequences are explored in some detail in Parts Three and Four. Don't be put off by seemingly abstract models. Think of them as useful road maps, and remember how hard it would be to find your way around Los Angeles without one.

The Concept of "Rational" Behavior

Many economic models rest on a fundamental assumption: namely, that the decision maker—be it a consumer or a business firm—behaves "rationally." What do we mean by *rational* behavior?

First, we do not use the phrase as a term of approval. It is not necessarily "better" to be rational than to be irrational. Some people usually behave rationally and some do not. This is simply a fact, and we are not concerned with judging the virtues of either behavior. Second, and perhaps more important, we use the term **rationality** to characterize *means* rather than *ends*. It is neither more nor less rational to want a pistachio ice-cream cone than to want a mushroom pizza. But once the consumer decides that he wants either the ice cream or the pizza, it is irrational for him to go to the shoe repair shop for it.

Rationality is defined in economics as characterizing those decisions that are most effective in helping the decision maker achieve his own objectives, whatever they may be. The objectives themselves (unless they are self-contradictory) are never considered either rational or irrational.

Reasons for Disagreements: Imperfect Information and Value Judgments

"If all the earth's economists were laid end to end, they could not reach an agreement," or so the saying goes. If economics is a scientific discipline, why do economists seem to quarrel so much? Politicians and reporters are fond of pointing out that economists generally argue both sides of every issue of public policy. Physicists, on the other hand, do not debate whether the earth revolves around the sun or vice versa.

The question reflects a misunderstanding of the nature of science. First of all, the apparently extreme disagreement is attributable in part to the greater visibility of economic discussions. As a matter of fact, physicists formerly did argue over whether the earth revolves around the sun, often with rather grim results for themselves. (Economists, fortunately, are not often burned at the stake!) Nowadays, physicists argue about "black holes," the existence of certain subatomic particles, and other esoteric phenomena. These arguments often go unnoticed by the public because most of us do not understand what they are talking about. In contrast, everyone is eager to join economic debates over inflation, unemployment, pollution, and almost everything else. Because economics is a *social* science, its disputes are aired in public, and almost everyone is personally concerned with the subject matter. Anyone who has ever bought or sold anything, it seems, fancies himself an amateur economist.

Second, there is a much greater area of agreement among economists than most people think. Virtually all economists, regardless of their politics, agree that taxing polluters is one of the best ways to protect the environment (see Chapters 29 and 31), that a negative income tax is superior to most alternative antipoverty programs (see Chapter 34), that free trade among nations is preferable to the erection of barriers through tariffs and quotas (see Chapter 37). The list could go on and on. It is probably true that the issues about which economists agree far exceed the subjects on which they disagree.

Third, many of the disputes among economists are not scientific disputes at all. Economists, like everyone else, come in all political persuasions: conservative, middle-of-the-road, liberal, radical. Each may hold a different view of what is best for society, and so may have a different opinion on what is the "right" solution to any problem of public policy. Public policy issues can rarely be decided on purely scientific and "objective" grounds.

While economists can contribute the best theoretical and factual knowledge there is on a particular issue, the final decision on policy questions often rests either on information that is not currently available, or on tastes and ethical opinions about which people differ (the things we call "value judgments"), or on both.

To illustrate what we mean, consider the following problems.

Taxing Industrial Wastes

As you will learn in Chapter 31, the proper tax to levy on industrial wastes depends on quantitative estimates both of the harm done by the pollutant and the costs of pollution abatement. For most waste products, these numbers are not yet known, although knowledge is accumulating rapidly. So a lack of complete information has made it difficult to reach a decision.

Inflation and Unemployment X

Government policies that succeed in shortening a recession are virtually certain to cause higher inflation for a while. Using tools that we will describe in Part Two, many economists believe they can even measure how much more inflation the economy will suffer as the price of fighting a recession. Is it worth it? An economist cannot answer this any more than a nuclear physicist could have determined whether dropping the atomic bomb on Hiroshima was a good idea. The decision rests on value judgments about the moral trade-off between inflation and unemployment, judgments that can be made only by the citizenry through its elected officials.

These examples underscore something we said earlier in this chapter: Economics cannot provide all the answers, but it can teach you how to ask the right questions. By the time you finish studying this book, you should have a good understanding of when the right course of action turns on disputed facts, when on value judgments, and when on some combination of the two.

The Economist's Odd Vocabulary

George Bernard Shaw once remarked that America and England are two nations separated by a common language. Much the same might be said of economists and the rest of the population, for economists often assign peculiar meanings to words. Here are two examples; you will find many others later on.

1. **Cost** We have already mentioned that when economists speak of "costs" they are normally referring to **opportunity costs.** Accountants, on the other hand, almost always measure costs as the direct monetary expenses involved in any activity. Thus, in calculating the costs of the same activity, the accountant and the economist may arrive at two very different results, as the example of the costs of going to college illustrated. Accountants and economists are indeed divided by a common language.

The **opportunity cost** of some decision is the value of the next-best alternative which you have to give up because of that decision (for example, working instead of going to school).

2. Money Most people work for money, or so they think. Again, the economist disagrees. He will insist that people work to earn *income*, which often happens to be paid—for reasons of convenience—in the form of *money*. What is the difference? To the economist, **money** refers to the amount of cash and bank-account balances you own at any particular moment. Your holdings of money change frequently, often several times in a single day. But **income** refers to the rate at which you earn money over time. A worker would answer the question "What is your income?" by saying "$10,000 a year," or "$200 a week," or something like that. Income probably changes much less frequently than holdings of money, perhaps only once a year. The distinction between money and income is important, and it will occupy our attention in Part Two.

The economist, it would appear, is much like Humpty Dumpty in *Alice in Wonderland* who said imperiously, "When I use a word it means just what I choose it to mean—neither more nor less." Why such obstinacy? Because economists need a *scientific jargon*, just as other scientists do. Any dictionary will testify to the fact that most words in any language have a multiplicity of meanings. Scientists must be more precise than that. And, rather than conjure up entirely new words, as natural scientists frequently do, economists take ordinary words and give them slightly special meanings. One wag pointed out that Canada has a radical group called *separatists* whose members steadfastly refuse to speak English, and that America also has such a group—but calls them *economists*. Who, though, would prefer that we say "phlogiston" instead of "cost" or "nutches" instead of "money"?

Summary

1. To help you get the most out of your first course in economics, we have devised a list of *12 important Ideas* that you will want to remember *Beyond the Final Exam*. Very briefly, they are:
   (1) Interest rates that appear very high may actually be very low if they are accompanied by rapid inflation.
   (2) Lawmakers who try to repeal the "law" of supply and demand are liable to open a Pandora's box of troubles they never expected.
   (3) Most government policies that reduce unemployment are likely to intensify the inflation problem, and vice versa.
   (4) Most policies that equalize income will exact a cost by reducing the nation's output.
   (5) The operation of free markets is likely to lead to rising prices for public and private services.
   (6) The environment can be protected by tax devices that make polluters pay for the cost of their pollution.
   (7) To make a rational decision, the *opportunity cost* of an action must be measured, because only this calculation will tell the decision maker what he has given up.
   (8) Two nations can gain from international trade, even if one is more efficient at making everything.
   (9) Rational decisions often require the use of *marginal analysis* to isolate the costs and benefits of that particular decision.

   (10) Active government policy to stabilize the economy need not imply a large public sector.
   (11) Budget deficits are not nearly so bad as the public thinks, and in some circumstances they are quite advisable.
   (12) Speculation serves a useful social function and may even reduce price fluctuations.

2. Economics is a discipline that uses a variety of approaches, some of them scientific and others humanistic, to address important social questions.

3. Because of the great complexity of human behavior, the economist is forced to abstract from many details, make generalizations that he knows are not quite true, and organize what knowledge he has according to some theoretical structure.

4. Economists use simplified models to understand the real world and predict its behavior, much as a child uses a model railroad to learn how trains work.

5. While these models, if skillfully constructed, can illuminate important economic problems, they rarely can answer the questions that policymakers are confronted with. For this purpose, value judgments are needed, and the economist is no better equipped to make them than is anyone else.

6. A course in economics seeks to teach the student how to formulate the right questions, questions that point to the value judgments or unknown pieces of data that must be obtained in order to make an intelligent decision. It does not try to provide all the answers.

Concepts for Review

Comparative advantage	Abstraction and generalization	Opportunity cost
Marginal analysis	Theory	Money
Marginal costs	Model	Income
Speculation	Rationality	

Questions for Discussion

1. Think about how you would construct a "model" of how your college is governed. Which officers and administrators would you include and exclude from your model if the objective were
   a. to explain how decisions on tuition payments are made?
   b. to explain the quality of the football team?
   Relate this to the map example in the chapter.

2. Relate the process of "abstraction" to the way you take notes in a lecture. Why do you not try to transcribe every word the lecturer utters? Why do you not just write down the title of the lecture and stop there? How do you decide, roughly speaking, on the correct amount of detail?

3. Explain why a government policymaker cannot afford to ignore economic theory.

The Use and Misuse of Graphs

Everything should be made as simple as possible, but not more so.

ALBERT EINSTEIN

In the preceding chapter we pointed out that economic models frequently appear as diagrams. And if you flip through the pages of this book you will see that indeed they are used quite often. Because many of you may not be familiar with diagrams, this chapter explains how some of the simple graphs used by economists are constructed and how they are to be interpreted.

Most readers of this book eventually will encounter graphs quite frequently in everyday life. If you become a doctor, you will see graphs depicting trends in costs of medical care as well as graphs recording the behavior of patients' vital functions. If you are concerned about social problems, you will have to read graphs depicting changes in ethnic composition of the population of a city or those detailing frequency of conviction for a felony and its relation to family income. If you work for a large corporation, you will encounter graphs of sales, profits, and the like. Graphs appear almost daily in the financial pages of the newspaper.

Graphs are invaluable because of the large quantity of data they can display and because of the way they facilitate the interpretation and analysis of the data. They enable the eye to take in at a glance important statistical relationships that would be far less apparent from lengthy prose descriptions or long lists of numbers. It is therefore worth the effort needed to learn how data can be portrayed in graphs. At the very least, you will want to learn to avoid the serious errors into which one can easily be led by graphs that are misleading or distorted.

In this chapter we show, first, how to read a graph that depicts a relationship between two variables. Second, we define the term *slope* and describe how it is measured and interpreted. Third, we explain how the behavior of three variables can be shown on a two-dimensional graph. Fourth, we discuss how misinterpretation is avoided by adjusting many economic graphs to accommodate changes in the purchasing power of the dollar, in the population of the nation, and in other pertinent developments. And finally, we examine several other common ways in which graphs can be misleading if not drawn and interpreted with care.

Graphs Used in Economic Analysis*

Two-Variable Diagrams

Much of the economic analysis to be found in this and other books requires that we keep track of two variables simultaneously. For example, in studying the operation of markets, we will want to keep one eye on the price of a commodity and the other on the quantity that is bought and sold.

For this reason, economists frequently find it useful to display real or imaginary figures in a *two-dimensional graph*, which simultaneously represents the behavior of two economic variables. The numerical value of one variable is measured along the bottom of the graph (called the *horizontal axis*), starting from the **origin** (the point labeled "0"), and the numerical value of the other is measured along the side of the graph (called the *vertical axis*), also starting from the origin.

Figure 2–1 is a typical graph used in economic analysis; it depicts a "demand curve," represented by the heavy blue line. The diagram shows the price of natural gas on the vertical axis and the quantity of gas that people want to buy on the horizontal axis. (Demand curves will be studied in detail in Chapter 4.)

Economic diagrams are generally read as one reads latitudes and longitudes on a map. On the demand curve in Figure 2–1, the point marked *a* represents a hypothetical combination of price and quantity demanded in St. Louis. By drawing a horizontal line leftward from that point to the vertical axis, we learn that the average price for gas in St. Louis is $3 per thousand cubic feet. By dropping a line straight down to the horizontal axis, we find that 80 billion cubic feet are wanted by consumers at this price. The other points on the graph give similar information. For example, point *b* indicates that if natural gas in St. Louis cost only $2 per thousand cubic feet, demand would be higher—it would reach 120 billion cubic feet.

The lower left-hand corner of a graph where the two axes meet is called the **origin.** Both variables are equal to zero at the origin.

*Students who have a nodding acquaintance with geometry and feel quite comfortable with graphs can safely skip the first sections of this chapter and proceed directly to the second part, which begins on page 27.

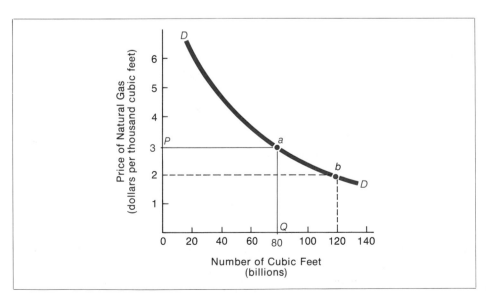

Figure 2–1
A DEMAND CURVE
FOR NATURAL GAS
IN ST. LOUIS
This demand curve shows the relationship between the price of natural gas and the quantity of it that will be demanded. For example, the point labeled *a* indicates that at a price of $3 per thousand cubic feet (point *P*), the quantity demanded will be 80 billion cubic feet (point *Q*).

Notice that information about price and quantity is *all* we can learn from the diagram. The demand curve will not tell us what kinds of people live in St. Louis, how large their homes are, or the condition of their furnaces. It tells us the price and the quantity demanded at that price; no more, no less.

A diagram abstracts from many details, some of which may be quite interesting, in order to focus on the two variables of primary interest—in this case, the price of natural gas and the amount of gas that is demanded at each price. All the diagrams used in this book share this basic feature. They cannot tell the reader the "whole story" any more than a map's latitude and longitude figures for a particular city can make someone an authority on that city.

The Definition and Measurement of Slope

One of the most important features of the diagrams used by economists is the rapidity with which the line, or curve, being sketched runs uphill or downhill as we move to the right. The demand curve in Figure 2–1 clearly slopes downhill (the price falls) as we follow it to the right (that is, as more gas is demanded). In such instances we say that *the curve has a negative slope, or is negatively sloped, because one variable falls as the other one rises.*

The four panels of Figure 2–2 show all the possible slopes for a straight-line relationship between two unnamed variables called Y (measured along the vertical axis) and X (measured along the horizontal axis). Figure 2–2(a) shows a negative slope, much like our demand curve. Figure 2–2(b) shows a positive slope, because variable Y rises (we go uphill) as variable X rises (we move to the right). Figure 2–2(c) shows a *zero* slope, where the value of Y is the same irrespective of the value of X. Figure 2–2(d) shows an *infinite* slope, meaning that the value of X is the same, irrespective of the value of Y.

Slope is a numerical concept, not just a qualitative one. The two panels of Figure 2–3 show two positively sloped straight lines with different slopes. The line in Figure 2–3(b) is clearly steeper. But by how much? The labels should help you compute the answer. In Figure 2–3(a) a horizontal movement, AB, of 10 units $(13 - 3)$ corresponds to a vertical movement, BC, of 1 unit $(9 - 8)$. So the slope is $BC/AB = \frac{1}{10}$. In Figure 2–3(b), the same horizontal movement of 10 units corresponds to a vertical movement of 3 units $(11 - 8)$. So the slope is $\frac{3}{10}$, which is larger.

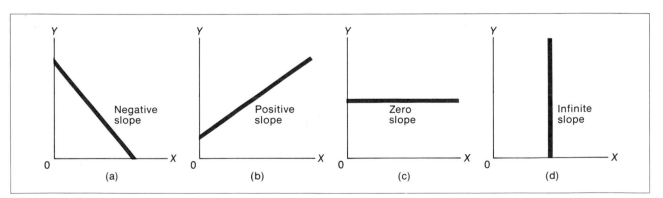

Figure 2–2
DIFFERENT TYPES OF SLOPE OF A STRAIGHT-LINE GRAPH
In Figure 2–2(a), the curve goes downward as we read from left to right, so we say it has a negative slope. The slopes in the other figures can be interpreted similarly.

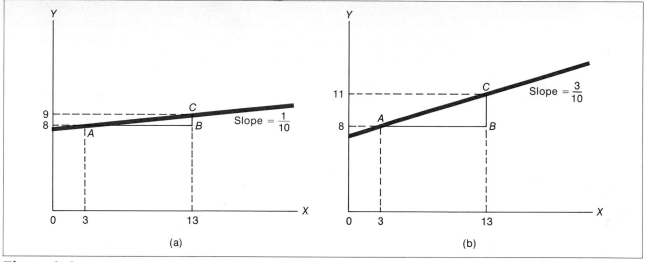

(a)

(b)

Figure 2–3

HOW TO MEASURE SLOPE

Slope indicates how much the graph rises per unit move from left to right. Thus, in Figure 2–3(b), as we go from point A to point B, we go $13 - 3 = 10$ units to the right. But in that interval, the graph rises from the height of point B to the height of point C, that is, it rises 3 units. Consequently, the slope of the line is $BC/AB = 3/10$.

The **slope of any particular straight line** is the same no matter where on that line we choose to measure it. That is why we can pick any horizontal distance, AB, and the corresponding slope triangle, ABC, to measure slope. But this is not true of lines that are curved.

Curved lines also have slopes, but the numerical value of the slope is different at every point.

The four panels of Figure 2–4 provide some examples of **slopes of curved lines.** The curve in Figure 2–4(a) has a negative slope everywhere, while the curve in Figure 2–4(b) has a positive slope everywhere. But these are not the only possibilities. In Figure 2–4(c) we encounter a curve that has a positive slope at first but a negative slope later on. Figure 2–4(d) shows the opposite case: a negative slope followed by a positive slope. It is possible, however, to measure the slope of a smooth curved line numerically *at any particular point.* This is done by drawing a *straight* line that *touches,* but does not *cut,* the curve at the point in question. Such a line is called a **tangent to the curve.** In Figure 2–5 we have

The **slope of a straight line** is the ratio of the vertical change to the corresponding horizontal change as we move to the right along the line, or as it is often said, the ratio of the "rise" over the "run."

The **slope of a curved line** at a particular point is the slope of the straight line that is **tangent to the curve** at that point.

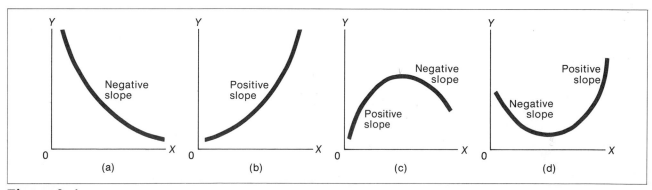

(a)   (b)   (c)   (d)

Figure 2–4

BEHAVIOR OF SLOPES IN CURVED GRAPHS

As Figures 2–4(c) and 2–4(d) indicate, where a graph is not a straight line it may have a slope that starts off as positive but that becomes negative farther to the right, or vice versa.

constructed tangents to a curve at two points. Line *tt* is tangent at point *C*, and line *TT* is tangent at point *F*. We can measure the slope of the curve at these two points by applying the definition in the margin. The calculation for point *C*, then, is the following:

$$\text{Slope at point } C = \text{Slope of line } tt = \frac{\text{Distance } BC}{\text{Distance } AB}$$

$$= \frac{6-2}{10-0} = \frac{4}{10} = +0.4 \ .$$

A similar calculation yields the slope of the curve at point *F*, which, as we can see from Figure 2–5, must be smaller:

$$\text{Slope at Point } F = \text{Slope of line } TT = \frac{14-9}{50-0} = \frac{5}{50} = +0.1 \ .$$

EXERCISE

Show that the slope of the curve at point *D* is between $+0.1$ and $+0.4$.

What would happen if we tried to apply this graphical technique to the high point in Figure 2–4(c) or to the low point in Figure 2–4(d)? Take a ruler and try it. The tangents that you construct should be horizontal, meaning that they should have a slope of exactly zero. It is always true that where the slope of a smooth curve changes from positive to negative, or vice versa, there will be at least a single point with a zero slope.

Curves that have the shape of a hill, such as Figure 2–4(c), have a zero slope at their *highest* point. Curves that have the shape of a valley, such as Figure 2–4(d), have a zero slope at their *lowest* point.

Rays Through the Origin and 45° Lines

The point at which a straight line cuts the vertical (*Y*) axis is called the *Y-intercept*. For example, the Y-intercept of line *tt* in Figure 2–5 is 2, while the

Figure 2–5
HOW TO MEASURE
SLOPE AT A POINT
ON A CURVED GRAPH
To find the slope at point *F*,
draw the line *TT*, which is tangent to the curve at point *F*;
then measure the slope of the
straight-line tangent *TT* as in
Figure 2–3. The slope of the
tangent is the same as the
slope of the curve at point *F*.

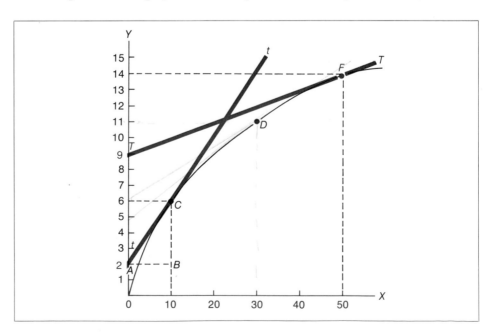

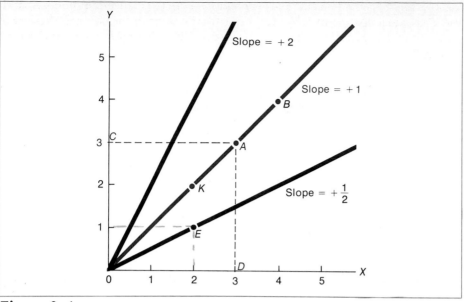

Figure 2–6

RAYS THROUGH THE ORIGIN

Rays are straight lines drawn through the zero point on the graph (*the origin*). Three rays with different slopes are shown. The middle ray, the one with slope = +1, has two properties that make it particularly useful in economics: (1) it makes a 45° angle with either axis, and (2) any point on that ray (for example, point *A*) is exactly equal in distance from the horizontal and vertical axes (length *DA* = length *CA*). So if the items measured on the two axes are in equal units, then at any point on that ray, such as *A*, the number on the *X*-axis (the abscissa) will be the same as the number on the *Y*-axis (the ordinate).

Y-intercept of line *TT* is 9. Lines whose *Y*-intercept is zero have so many special uses that they have been given a special name, a **ray through the origin,** or **ray.**

Figure 2–6 contains three rays through the origin, and the slope of each is indicated in the diagram. The ray in the center—whose slope is 1—is particularly useful in many economic applications because it marks off points where *X* and *Y* are equal (as long as *X* and *Y* are measured in the same units). For example, at point *A* we have *X* = 3 and *Y* = 3, at point *B*, *X* = 4 and *Y* = 4, and a similar relation holds at any other point on that ray. How do we know that this is always true for a ray whose slope is 1? If we start from the origin (where both *X* and *Y* are zero) and the slope of the ray is 1, we know from the definition of slope that:

$$\text{Slope} = \frac{\text{Vertical change}}{\text{Horizontal change}} = 1 \, .$$

This implies that the vertical change and the horizontal change are always equal, so the two variables must always remain equal.

Rays through the origin with a slope of 1 are called **45° lines** because they form an angle of 45° with the horizontal axis. If a point representing some data is above the 45° line, we know that the value of *Y* exceeds the value of *X*. Conversely, whenever we find a point below the 45° line, we know that *X* is larger than *Y*.

A straight line emanating from the origin, or zero point on a graph, is called a **ray through the origin** or, sometimes, just a **ray.**

A **45° line** is a ray through the origin with a slope of +1. It marks off points where the variables measured on each axis have equal values.[2]

[2]The definition assumes that both variables are measured in the same units.

Squeezing Three Dimensions into Two: Contour Maps

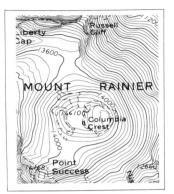

Figure 2–7
A GEOGRAPHIC CONTOUR MAP
All points on any particular contour line represent geographic locations that are at the same height above sea level.
SOURCE: U.S. Geological Survey.

Sometimes, because a problem involves more than two variables, two dimensions just are not enough, which is unfortunate since paper is only two dimensional. When we study the decision-making process of a business firm, for example, we may want to keep track simultaneously of three variables: how much labor it employs, how much machinery it uses, and how much output it creates.

Luckily, there is a well-known device for collapsing three dimensions into two, namely a *contour map*. Figure 2–7 is a contour map of Mount Rainier, the highest peak in the state of Washington. On several of the irregularly shaped "rings" we find a number indicating the height above sea level at that particular spot on the mountain. Thus, unlike the more usual sort of map, which gives only latitudes and longitudes, this contour map exhibits three pieces of information about each point: latitude, longitude, and altitude.

Figure 2–8 looks more like the contour maps one encounters in economics. It shows how some third variable, called Z (think of it as a firm's output, for example), varies as we change either variable X (think of it as a firm's employment) or variable Y (think of it as the use of a firm's machines). Just like the map of Mount Rainier, any point on the diagram conveys three pieces of data. At point A, we can read off the values of X and Y in the conventional way (X is 30 and Y is 40), and we can also note the value of Z by checking to see on which contour line point A falls. (It is on the $Z = 20$ contour.) So point A is able to tell us that 30 hours of labor and 40 hours of machine time produce 20 units of output.

While most of the analyses presented in this book will be based on the simpler two-variable diagrams, contour maps will find their applications, especially in the appendixes to Chapters 18 and 20.

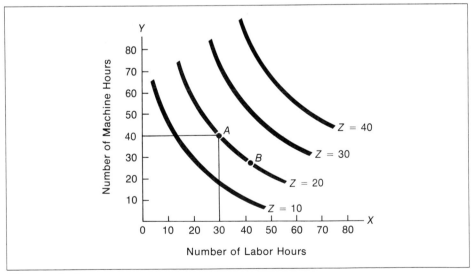

Figure 2–8
A PRODUCTION CONTOUR MAP
In this contour map, all points on a given contour line represent different combinations of labor and capital capable of producing a given output. For example, all points on the curve $Z = 20$ represent input combinations that can produce 20 units of output. Point A on that line means that the 20 units of output can be produced using 30 labor hours and 40 machine hours. Economists call such maps *production indifference maps*.

Perils in the Interpretation of Graphs

The preceding materials contain just about all you will need in order to understand the simple graphics used in economic models. We turn now to the second objective of this chapter: to learn how statistical data are portrayed on graphs and some of the pitfalls to watch out for.

The Interpretation of Growth Trends

Probably the most common form of graph in empirical economics is a year-by-year (or perhaps a month-by-month) depiction of the behavior of some economic variable—the profits of a particular corporation, or its annual sales, or the number of persons unemployed in the U.S. economy, or some measure of consumer prices. For example, Figure 2–9 is this sort of **time series graph** showing the month-by-month unemployment rate in the United States from 1965 to 1981. It shows that the percentage of the labor force that was jobless was relatively low during the first half of the 1970s and particularly high during the recessions of 1975 and 1980. Time series graphs are a type of two-variable diagram in which time is always the variable measured along the horizontal axis.

Such graphs can be quite illuminating, offering an instant visual grasp of the course of the relevant events. *However, if misused, such graphs are very dangerous.* They can easily mislead persons who are not experienced in dealing with them.[3] Perhaps even more dangerous are the lies perpetrated accidentally and unintentionally by people who draw graphs without sufficient care and who may innocently mislead themselves as well as others.

A fine example of this latter occurrence is illustrated in Figure 2–10. Many people felt that there was a "cultural boom" underway in the 1960s that led to an explosion in the demand for tickets to all sorts of artistic performances. This boom, it was thought, accounted for the rapidly rising prices of theater tickets. Figure 2–10 shows the time series graph that formed the basis for this allegation. The growth in spending for theater tickets certainly looks impressive; expenditures rose about 940 percent from 1929 to 1980.

[3]An interesting and informative book on the subject is called *How to Lie with Statistics*, by Darrell Huff and Irving Geis.

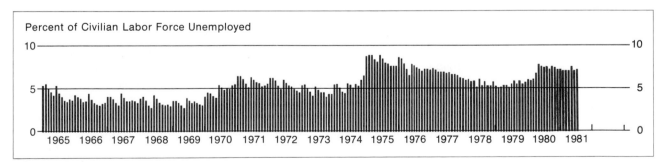

Figure 2–9
TIME SERIES GRAPH
This graph shows the percentage of the labor force that was unemployed in each of the months indicated, from January 1965 through July 1981.

Figure 2–10

INDEX OF EXPENDITURES ON ADMISSIONS TO ARTISTIC PERFORMANCES
This graph, showing expenditures on admissions to artistic performances, seems to indicate that since about 1932 Americans have become much more interested in attending the performing arts.
SOURCE: *Survey of Current Business,* July issues, various years; and *Economic Report of the President,* Washington, D.C.: U.S. Government Printing Office, various years.

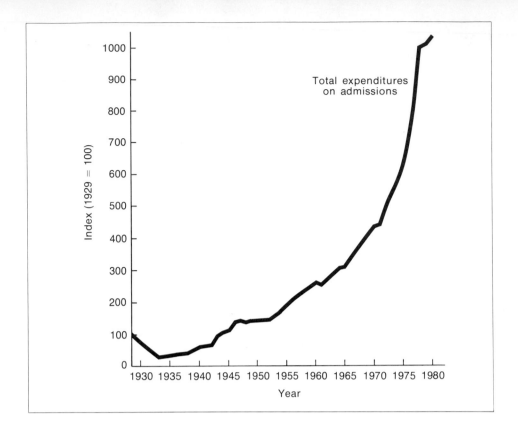

But there is less to this graph than meets the eye—much less. Most of the spectacular growth in spending on theater admissions was a reflection of three rather banal facts. First, there were many more Americans alive in 1980 than in 1929, so spending *per person* rose by much less than Figure 2–10 suggests. Second, the price of almost everything, not just theater tickets, was higher in 1980 than in 1929. In fact, average prices were more than five times their 1929 levels. Third, the average American was richer in 1980 than in 1929, and consequently was more inclined to spend money on everything—not just on cultural activities.

All three of these factors can be accounted for by expressing spending on theater admissions as a *fraction* of total consumer income. The results of this "correction" are shown in Figure 2–11. The explosive growth suggested by the uncorrected data really amounts to a decline in the share of income that the average American spent on theater tickets—from about 15 cents out of each $100 in 1929 to only 7 cents in 1980! How misleading it can be to simply "look at the facts." There is a general lesson to be learned from this example:

The facts, as portrayed in a time series graph, most assuredly do not "speak for themselves." Because almost everything grows in a growing economy, one must use judgment in interpreting growth trends. Depending on what kind of data are being analyzed, it may be essential to correct for population growth, for rising prises, for rising incomes, or for all three.[4]

[4]For a full discussion of how to use a "price index" to correct for rising prices, see the appendix to Chapter 6.

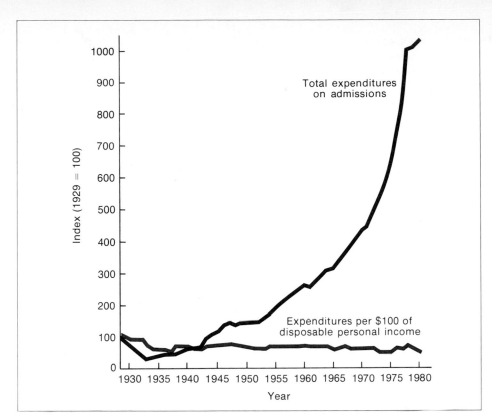

Figure 2–11
APPEARANCE AND REALITY IN ARTS EXPENDITURE
The curve in black shows correctly that the number of *dollars* spent on the arts by Americans rose dramatically since 1932. But because of inflation, a dollar in 1980 was worth much less than in 1929, and there were many more Americans in the latter year, who were also wealthier on the average. After correction for inflation, population changes, and so on, the black line is transformed into the blue line, showing that in 1980 an average American actually spent less of his purchasing power on the arts than in 1929.
SOURCE: *Survey of Current Business,* July issues, various years; and *Economic Report of the President,* Washington D.C., U.S. Government Printing Office, various years.

Distorting Trends by Choice of the Time Period

In addition to possible misinterpretations of growth trends, users of statistical data must be on guard for distortions of trends caused by unskillfully chosen first and last periods for the graph. This is best explained by an example.

Figures 2–12 and 2–13 show the behavior of average stock market prices over the periods 1929–1932 and 1973–1975. They both display a clear downhill movement and would suggest to anyone who does not have other information that stocks are a terrible investment.

However, an unscrupulous seller of stocks could use the same set of stock market statistics to tell exactly the opposite story by carefully selecting another group of years. Figure 2–14 shows the behavior of average stock prices from 1940 through 1965. The persistence and size of the increase is quite dramatic. Stocks now look like a rather good investment.

An even longer and less biased period gives a less distorted picture (Figure 2–15). It indicates that investments in stocks are sometimes profitable and other times unprofitable.

The deliberate or inadvertent distortion resulting from an unfortunate or unscrupulous choice of time period for a graph must constantly be watched for.

There are no rules that can give absolute protection from this difficulty, but several precautions can be helpful.

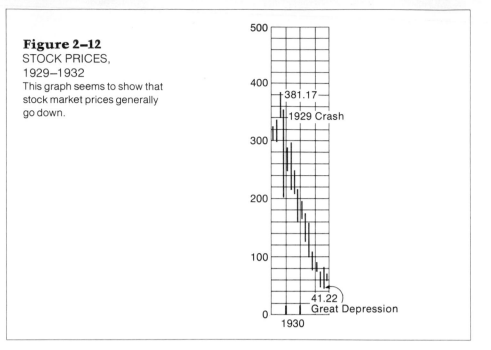

Figure 2–12
STOCK PRICES,
1929–1932
This graph seems to show that
stock market prices generally
go down.

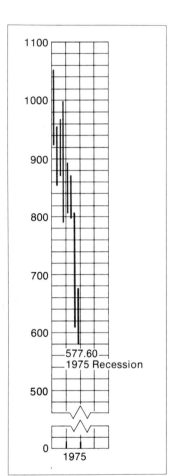

Figure 2–13
STOCK PRICES,
1973–1975
This figure also seems to show
that stock prices generally fall.

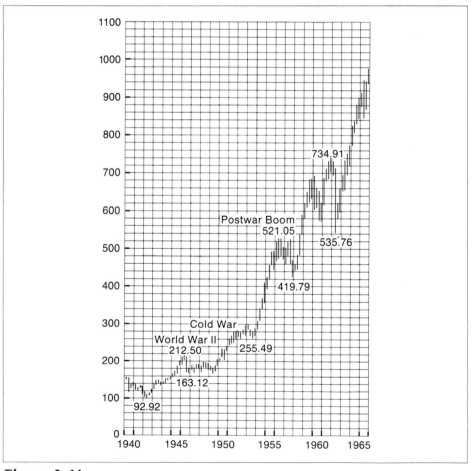

Figure 2–14
STOCK PRICES, 1940–1965
This graph seems to indicate that the value of stocks is on a never-ending climb.

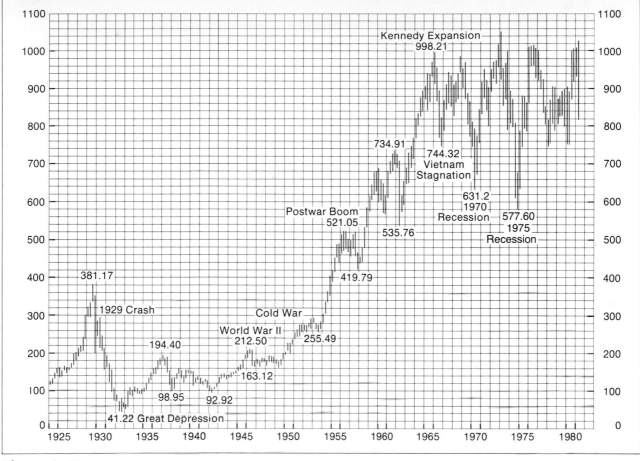

Figure 2-15

THE FULL HISTORY OF STOCK PRICES, 1925–1981

Here we see that stock prices have lots of ups and downs, though they have risen quite a bit on the average.

1. Make sure the first date shown on the graph is not an exceptionally high or low point. In comparison with 1929, a year of unusually high stock market prices, the years immediately following are bound to give the impression of a downward trend.

2. For the same reason, make sure the graph does not end in a year that is extraordinarily high or low (although this may be unavoidable if the graph simply ends with figures that are as up-to-date as possible).

3. Make sure that (in the absence of some special justification) the graph does not depict only a very brief period, which can easily be atypical.

Dangers of Omitting the Origin

Frequently, an economic variable described on a graph will be characterized by very high numbers. For example, this is true of graphs showing gross national product (GNP)—one of the standard measures of the economy's total production, which will be defined and discussed in Chapter 5. In our "three-trillion dollar

Figure 2–16
A GRAPH SHOWING
OMISSION OF THE ORIGIN
A hasty glance at this figure
seems to show that, from 1974
to 1975, gross national product fell from about $1200 bil-
lion almost to zero, and then
shot up again about as fast.

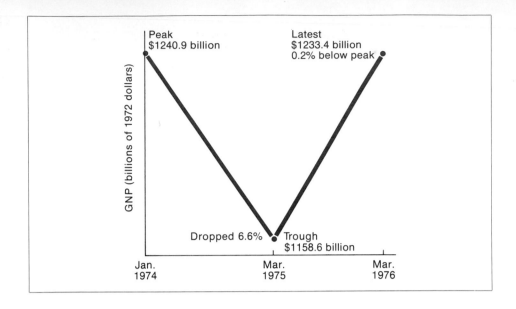

economy," the GNP figure never gets remotely close to zero. It is then tempting to omit all the "wasted space" between the origin and the levels of GNP actually encountered in the period considered. The graph in Figure 2–16, adapted from *The New York Times*, is an example of such an omission—its lowest point (though that is nowhere stated explicitly) is about 1.1 trillion dollars.

What is wrong with the drawing? The answer is that it vastly exaggerates the size of the drop and the rise in GNP that are depicted. It makes the recession of 1975 look like a catastrophic depression in which the bottom dropped out of the economy. The more informative graph, which includes the origin as well as the "wasted space" in between is shown in Figure 2–17. Note how this alternative presentation puts matters into perspective. It shows that in 1975 the economy did indeed experience a drop in GNP, but that it was nowhere nearly as severe as the graph in *The New York Times* would have suggested to the unwary reader.

Figure 2–17
GNP FIGURES INCLUD-
ING POINT OF ORIGIN
Adding the point of zero GNP
to the previous graph shows
that the fall and rise in GNP
from 1974 to 1976 was in fact
not so enormous as the earlier
graph suggests.

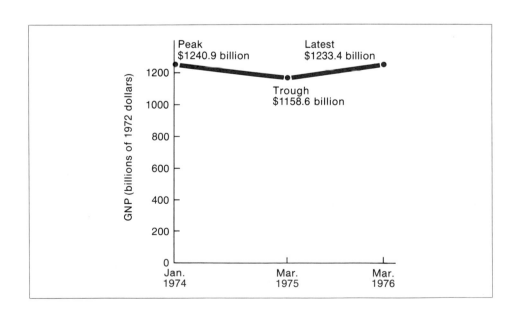

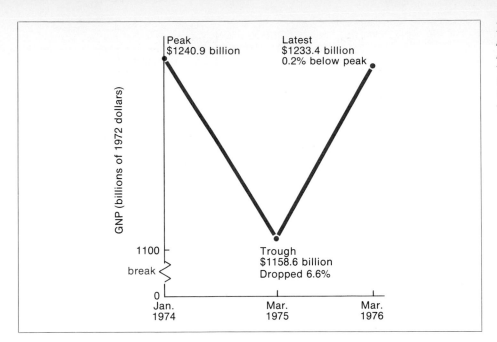

Figure 2–18
A BREAK IN A GRAPH
An alternative way of warning
the reader that the zero point
has been left out is to put a
break in the graph, as illustrated here.

Omitting the origin in a graph is dangerous because it always exaggerates the magnitudes of the changes that have taken place.

Sometimes, it is true, the inclusion of the origin would waste so much space that it is undesirable to include it. In that case, a good practice is to put a very clear warning on the graph to remind the reader that this has been done. Figure 2–18 shows one way of doing so.

Unreliability of Steepness and Choice of Units

The last problem we will consider has conquences very similar to the one we have just discussed. The problem is that we can never trust the impression we get from the steepness of an economic graph. A graph of stock market prices that moves uphill sharply (has a large positive slope) appears to suggest that prices are rising rapidly, while another graph in which the rate of climb is much slower seems to imply that prices are going up sluggishly. Yet, depending on how one draws the graph, exactly the same statistics can produce a graph that is rising very quickly or very slowly.

The reason for this possibility is that in economics there are no fixed units of measurement. Coal production can be measured in hundredweight (hundreds of pounds) or in tons. Prices can be measured in cents or in dollars or in millions of dollars. Time can be measured in days or in months or in years. Any of these choices is perfectly legitimate, but it makes all the difference to the rapidity with which a graph using the resulting figures rises or falls.

An example will bring out the point. Suppose that we have the following (imaginary) figures on daily coal production from a mine, which we measure both in hundredweight and in tons (remembering that 1 ton = 20 hundredweight):

YEAR	PRODUCTION IN TONS	PRODUCTION IN HUNDREDWEIGHT
1970	5000	100,000
1975	5050	101,000
1980	5090	101,800

Look at Figures 2–19(a) and 2–19(b), one graph showing the figures in tons and the other showing the figures in hundredweight. A change in unit of measurement stretches or compresses the axis on which the information is represented, which automatically changes the slope of the graph.

Unfortunately, we cannot solve the problem by agreeing always to stick to the same measurement units. Pounds may be the right unit for measuring demand for beef, but they will not do in measuring demand for cloth or for coal. A penny may be the right monetary unit for postage stamps, but it is not a very convenient unit for the cost of airplanes or automobiles.

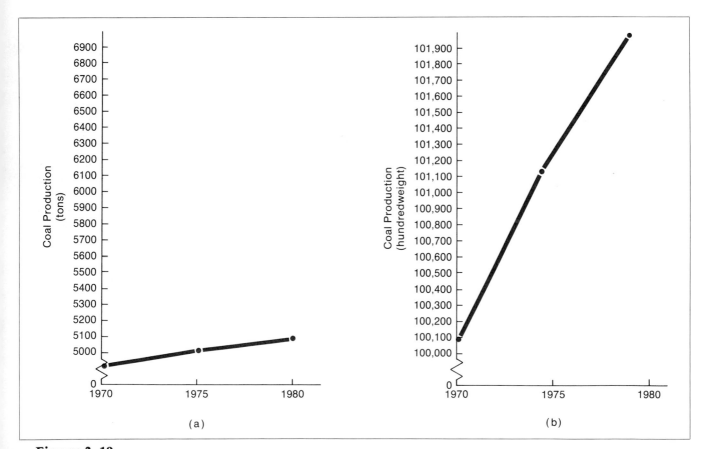

Figure 2–19
SLOPE DEPENDS ON UNITS OF MEASUREMENT
(a) Coal production is measured in tons, and production seems to be rising very slowly. (b) Production is measured in hundredweight (hundred-pound units), so the same facts now seem to say that production is rising spectacularly.

We must never place much faith in the apparent implications of the slope of an ordinary graph in economics.

Later, in Chapter 19 on demand analysis, we will encounter a useful approach economists have adopted to deal with this problem. Instead of calculating changes in "absolute" terms—like millions of tons of coal or millions of barrels of oil—they use as their common unit the *percentage* increase. We will see that by using percentages rather than absolute figures the problem can be avoided. The reason is simple. If we look at our hypothetical figures on coal production again, we see that no matter whether we measure the increase in output from 1970 to 1975 in tons (from 5000 to 5050) or in hundredweight (from 100,000 to 101,000), the *percentage* increase has been the same. Fifty is 1 percent of 5000, and 1000 is 1 percent of 100,000. Since a change in units affects both the numbers *proportionately*, the result is a washout—it does not do anything to the answer of the percentage calculation.

Summary

1. Because graphs are used so often to portray economic models, it is important for students to gain some understanding of their construction and use. Fortunately, the graphics used in economics are not very complex.

2. Most economic models are depicted in two-variable diagrams. We read data from these diagrams just as we read the latitude and longitude on a map: each point represents the values of two variables at the same time.

3. In a few instances, three variables must be shown at once. In these cases, economists use contour maps, which, as the name suggests, show "latitude," "longitude," and "altitude" all at the same time.

4. Often, the most important property of a line or curve drawn on a diagram will be its slope, which is defined as the ratio of the "rise" over the "run," or the vertical change divided by the horizontal change. Curves that go uphill as we move to the right have positive slopes, while curves that go downhill have negative slopes.

5. By definition, a straight line has the same slope wherever we choose to measure it. The slope of a curved line changes, but the slope at any point on the curve can be calculated by measuring the slope of a straight line tangent to the curve at that point.

6. A time series graph is a particular type of two-variable diagram that is useful in depicting statistical data. Time is measured along the horizontal axis, and some variable of interest is measured along the vertical axis.

7. While time series graphs are invaluable in helping us condense a great deal of information in a single picture, they can be quite misleading if they are not drawn and interpreted with care. For example, growth trends can be exaggerated by inappropriate choice of units of measurement or by failure to correct for some obvious source of growth (such as rising population). Omitting the origin can make the ups and downs in a time series appear much more extreme than they actually are. Or, by a clever choice of the starting and ending points for the graphs, the same data can be made to tell very different stories. Readers of such graphs—and this includes anyone who ever reads a newspaper—must be on guard for problems like these or they may find themselves misled by "the facts."

Concepts for Review

Two-variable diagram
Horizontal and vertical axes
Origin (of a graph)
Slope of a straight (or curved) line
Negative, positive, zero, and infinite slope
Tangent to the curve

Y-intercept
Ray through the origin, or ray
45° line
Contour map
Time series graph

Questions for Discussion

1. Look for a graph in your local newspaper, on the financial page or elsewhere. What does the graph try to show? Is someone trying to convince you of something with this graph? Check to see if the graph is distorted in any of the ways mentioned in this chapter.

2. Portray the following hypothetical data on a two-variable diagram:

ENROLLMENT DATA:
UNIVERSITY OF NOWHERE

ACADEMIC YEAR	TOTAL ENROLLMENT	ENROLLMENT IN ECONOMICS COURSES
1977–1978	3000	300
1978–1979	3100	325
1979–1980	3200	350
1980–1981	3300	375
1981–1982	3400	400

Measure the slope of the resulting line, and explain what this number means.

3. From Figure 2–5, calculate the slope of the curve at point D.

4. From Figure 2–6, determine the values of X and Y at point K and at point E. What do you conclude?

5. From Figure 2–8, interpret the economic meaning of points A and B. What do the two points have in common? What is the difference in their economic interpretation?

6. Suppose that between 1981 and 1982 expenditures on dog food rose from $35 million to $70 million and that the price of dog food doubled. What do these facts imply about the popularity of dog food?

7. Suppose that between 1970 and 1980 U.S. population went up 10 percent and that the number of people attending professional wrestling matches rose from 3,000,000 to 3,100,000. What do these facts imply about the growth in popularity of professional wrestling?

Scarcity and Choice: *The Economic Problem*

Our necessities are few
but our wants are endless.
INSCRIPTION FOUND IN A FORTUNE COOKIE

This chapter examines a subject that many economists consider to be *the* fundamental issue of economics: the fact that since virtually no resource is available in unlimited supply, people must consequently make decisions consistent with their limited means. A wild-eyed materialist may dream of a world in which everyone owns a yacht and five automobiles, but the earth almost certainly lacks the resources needed to make that dream come true. The scarcity of resources, both natural and man-made, makes it vital that we stretch our limited resources as far as possible.

The chapter introduces a way to describe the choices available to decision makers, given the resources at their command. The same sort of analysis, based on the concept of *opportunity cost,* will be shown to apply to the decisions of business firms, of governments, and of society as a whole. Many of the most basic ideas of economics—such as *efficiency, division of labor, exchange,* and the *role of markets*—are introduced here for the first time. In particular, we will see that a market system can, if it is functioning properly, promote the efficient use of society's resources without intervention by government planners. The chapter also introduces a broad question that constitutes the central theme of this text: What does the market do well and what does it do poorly?

The "Indispensable Necessity" Syndrome

The late 1970s and early 1980s witnessed an unprecedented belt-tightening in many areas. Tax-cutting initiatives in California, Massachusetts, and other states forced sharp reductions in state and local government spending. President Ronald Reagan, after his inauguration in 1981, pushed through a similarly tight budget for the federal government. Cities like New York, Cleveland, and Boston teetered on the brink of bankruptcy. And formerly affluent universities like Stanford and Yale found themselves under heavy financial pressure as sources of funding dried up.

Budget cuts forced politicians, bureaucrats, and university administrators to make some hard decisions over which services to cut. As they struggled with these decisions, they learned to their dismay that their constituents often were unwilling to accept *any* reductions. Mayors who proposed closing a firehouse or a hospital were confronted by demonstrators decrying the proposed cutback as a "false economy" and describing the firehouse or hospital as "indispensable."

Public Reaction to Budget Cuts

President Reagan's proposed budget cuts in 1981 brought forth the usual protests claiming that each cut was destroying something essential. Here are some examples:

Reduction of Federal Aid to Education
"Will devastate public education in this country."

Statement of Don Cameron, Assistant Executive Director of the National Education Association. Quoted in *The New York Times*, February 22, 1981.

Reduction of Funding for Energy Research
". . . would reduce American national security . . . from its present ravaged state to permanent collapse into third-rate power status."

Mailed promotional piece from Fusion Energy Foundation, Suite 2404, 808 Seventh Avenue, New York, New York.

Reduction of Legal Services for the Poor
". . . poor people are going to be illegally thrown out of their houses, illegally denied Medicare, and they'll have no recourse."

Statement of Dan J. Bradley, President, Legal Services Corporation, Chicago. Quoted in the *Chicago Tribune*, March 17, 1981.

Reduction of Black Lung Disease Program
"Any man who would take benefits from miners would stop at nothing."

Statement of Lane Kirkland, President of the American Federation of Labor and Congress of Industrial Organizations. Quoted in *The New York Times*, March 10, 1981.

Groups marched on Washington to oppose President Reagan's budget cuts. College administrators found their department heads unwilling to set priorities over the different parts of their budgets. Suggestions to eliminate poorly attended courses, cut library hours, or restrict access to the Xerox machine all too frequently were met with the cry that each of these was *absolutely* essential.

Yet, regrettable as it is to have to give up any of these good things, reduced budgets mean that *something* must go. If everyone meets the issue by declaring *everything* to be indispensable, if every department head argues that library hours and student services must *never* be cut but suggests nothing that can be cut instead, the decision maker is in the dark and is likely to end up making cuts that are bad for everyone. When the budget must be reduced, it is critical to determine which cuts are likely to prove *least damaging* to the people affected.

It is nonsense to assign top priority to everything. No one can afford everything. An optimal decision is one that chooses the most desirable alternative *among the possibilities that the available resources permit.*

Scarcity, Choice, and Opportunity Cost

One of the basic themes of economics is that the resources of decision makers, no matter how large they may be, are always limited, and that as a result everyone has some hard decisions to make. Even Philip II, of Spanish Armada fame and one of the most richly endowed kings of history, frequently had to cope with rebellion on the part of his troops, whom he was often unable to pay or to supply with even the most basic provisions.

But far more fundamental than the scarcity of funds is the scarcity of physical resources. The supply of fuel, for example, has never been limitless, and a real scarcity of fuel would force us to make some hard choices. We might have to keep our homes cooler in winter and warmer in summer, live closer to our jobs, or give up such fuel-using conveniences as dishwashers. While energy is the most widely discussed scarcity these days, the general principle of scarcity applies to all the earth's resources—iron, copper, uranium, and so on. Even goods that can be produced are always in limited supply because their production requires fuel, labor, and other limited resources. Wheat and rice can be grown. But nations have nonetheless suffered famines because the land, labor, fertilizer, and water needed to grow these crops were unavailable. We can increase our output of cars, but the increased use of labor, steel, and fuel in auto production will mean that something else, perhaps the production of refrigerators, will have to be cut back. This all adds up to the following fundamental principle of economics, one we will encounter again and again in this text.

Virtually all resources are scarce, meaning that humanity has less of them than it would like. So choices must be made among a *limited* set of possibilities, in full recognition of the inescapable fact that a decision to have more of one thing means we must give up some of another thing.

In fact, one popular definition of economics is "the study of how best to use limited means in the pursuit of unlimited ends." While this definition, like any short statement, cannot possibly cover the sweep of the entire discipline, it does convey the flavor of the type of problem that is the economist's stock in trade.

Economics examines the options left open to households, business firms, governments, and entire societies by the limited resources at their command; and it studies the logic of how **rational decisions** can be made from among the available possibilities. One overriding principle governs this logic—a principle we have already introduced in Chapter 1 as one of the 12 Ideas for Beyond the Final Exam. Because with limited resources, a decision to have more of something is simultaneously a decision to have less of something else, the relevant *cost* of any decision is its **opportunity cost**—the value of the next best alternative that is given up. Rational decision making, be it in industry, government, or households, must be based on opportunity-cost calculations.

To illustrate opportunity cost, we can continue the example in which production of additional cars requires the production of fewer refrigerators. While the production of a car may cost $4000 per vehicle, or some other money amount, its real cost to the community consists of the number of refrigerators it must forgo to get an additional car. If the labor, steel, and fuel needed to make a car are sufficient to make eight refrigerators, we say that the opportunity cost of a car is eight refrigerators. The principle of opportunity cost is of such general applicability that we devote most of this chapter to it.

A **rational decision** is one that best serves the objective of the decision maker, whatever that objective may be. The term "rational" connotes neither approval nor disapproval of the objective itself.

The **opportunity cost** of any decision is the forgone value of the next best alternative that is not chosen.

Opportunity Cost and Money Cost

Since we live in a market economy where (almost) everything "has its price," students often wonder about the connection between the opportunity cost of an item and its market price. What we said above seems to divorce the two concepts: We stressed that the true cost of a car is not the price of the electricity and steel used to make it but the other things (like refrigerators) that the steel or electricity could have been used to make instead. This *opportunity cost* is the true sacrifice the economy must incur to get a car. But isn't the opportunity cost of a car related to its money cost? The answer is that the two are often very closely tied because of the way a market economy sets the prices of the steel and electricity that go into the production of cars. Steel is valuable because it can be used to make other goods. If the items that steel can make are themselves valuable, the price of steel will be high. But if the goods that steel can make have very little value, the price of steel will be low. In sum, if a car has a high opportunity cost, then a well-functioning price system will assign high prices to the resources that are needed to produce a car. The steel and the electricity will cost a good deal of money, and so the car will also command a high price. In sum:

If the market is functioning well, goods that have high opportunity costs will tend to have high money costs, and goods whose opportunity costs are low will tend to have low money costs.

Yet it would be a mistake to treat opportunity costs and price (money cost) as identical. For one thing, there are times when the market does *not* function well, and hence does not assign prices that accurately reflect opportunity costs. Many such examples will be encountered in this book, especially in Chapters 29 and 31. Moreover, some valuable items may not bear explicit price tags at all. We have already encountered one example of this in Chapter 1, where we considered the opportunity cost (as opposed to the explicit money cost) of going to college. We learned that one important item typically omitted from the money-cost calculation is the value of the student's time; that is, the wages he or she could have earned by working instead of attending college. These forgone wages, which are given up by students in order to acquire an education, are part of the opportunity cost of a college education just as surely as are tuition payments.

Scarcity and Choice for a Single Firm

The nature of opportunity cost is perhaps clearest in the case of a single business firm that produces two outputs from a fixed supply of inputs. Given the limited resources at its disposal, the more of one good the firm produces the less of the other it will be able to produce. And unless management carries out an explicit comparison of the available choices, weighing the desirability of each against the others, it is unlikely that it will be able to meet its objectives as effectively as possible.

Consider the specific example of a farmer whose available supplies of land, machinery, labor, and fertilizer are capable of producing various combinations of soybeans and wheat. Obviously, the more land and other resources devoted to the production of soybeans, the less will be available to produce wheat. Table 3–1 summarizes the choices that might be open to such a farmer. It indicates, for example, that if he produces only soybeans, he can harvest 40,000 bushels. If soybean production is reduced to only 30,000 bushels, however, the farmer can also grow 38,000 bushels of wheat. Thus the opportunity cost of obtaining 10,000

Table 3–1
PRODUCTION POSSIBILITIES OPEN TO A FARMER

BUSHELS OF SOYBEANS	BUSHELS OF WHEAT	LABEL IN FIGURE 3–1
40,000	0	A
30,000	38,000	B
20,000	52,000	C
10,000	60,000	D
0	65,000	E

more bushels of soybeans (going from 30,000 up to 40,000) is 38,000 forgone bushels of wheat. Or, put the other way around, the opportunity cost of the 38,000 bushels of wheat is 10,000 bushels of soybeans. The other numbers in Table 3–1 have similar interpretations.

Figure 3–1 is a graphical representation of this same information. Point *A* corresponds to the first line of Table 3–1, point *B* to the second line, and so on. Curves like *AE* will appear frequently in this book; they are called **production possibilities frontiers.** Any point *on or below* the production possibilities frontier is attainable. Points above the frontier cannot be achieved with the available resources. Furthermore, the production possibilities frontier always slopes downward to the right. Why? Because resources are limited. The farmer can *increase* his wheat production (move to the right in Figure 3–1) only by devoting more of his land and labor to growing wheat, meaning that he must simultaneously *reduce* his soybean production (move downward) because less of his land and labor remains available for growing soybeans. Notice that in addition to having a negative slope, our production possibilities frontier, curve *AE*, has another characteristic—it is "bowed outward." Let us consider a little more carefully what this curvature means.

Suppose our farmer is initially producing only soybeans, so that he uses for this purpose even land that is much more suitable for wheat cultivation (point *A*). Now suppose he decides to switch some of his land from soybean production into wheat production. Which part of his land will he switch? Obviously, if he is sensible, the part best suited to wheat growing, or least suited to soybean cultivation. As soybean production falls from 40,000 bushels to 30,000 bushels, wheat production rises from zero to 38,000. A sacrifice of only 10,000 bushels of soybeans "buys" 38,000 bushels of wheat. Imagine now that the farmer wants to switch still more land to wheat production. Figure 3–1 and Table 3–1 tell us that the sacrifice of an additional 10,000 bushels of soybeans (from 30,000 down to 20,000) will yield only 14,000 bushels of wheat. Why? The main reason is that inputs tend to be specialized. As we noted, at point *A* the farmer was using resources for soybean production that were much more suitable for growing wheat. Consequently, their productivity in soybeans was relatively low, and

A **production possibilities frontier** shows the different combinations of various goods that a producer can turn out by reallocating the available resources among different products.

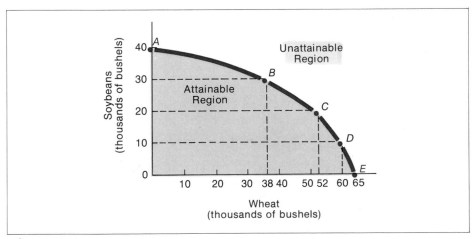

Figure 3–1
PRODUCTION POSSIBILITIES FRONTIER FOR PRODUCTION BY A SINGLE FIRM
With a given set of inputs, the firm can produce only those output combinations given by points in the shaded area. The production possibilities frontier, *AE*, is not a straight line but one that curves more and more as it nears the axes. That is, when the firm specializes in only one product, those inputs that are especially adapted to the production of the other good lose at least part of their productivity.

when they were switched to wheat production the yield was very high. But this cannot continue forever. As more wheat is produced, the farmer must utilize land and machinery that are better suited to producing soybeans and less well-suited to producing wheat. This is why the first 10,000 bushels of soybeans forgone "buys" the farmer 38,000 bushels of wheat while the second 10,000 bushels of soybeans "buys" him only 14,000 bushels of wheat. Figure 3–1 and Table 3–1 show that these returns continue to decline as wheat production expands: the next 10,000-bushel reduction in sobyean production yields only 8000 bushels of additional wheat, and so on.

We can now see that the *slope* of the production possibilities frontier represents graphically the concept of *opportunity cost*. Between points *C* and *B*, for example, the opportunity cost of acquiring 10,000 additional bushels of soybeans is 14,000 bushels of forgone wheat; and between points *B* and *A*, the opportunity cost of 10,000 bushels of soybeans is 38,000 bushels of forgone wheat. In general, as we move upward to the left along the production possibilities frontier (toward more soybeans and less wheat), the opportunity cost of soybeans in terms of wheat increases. Or, putting the same thing differently, as we move downward to the right, the opportunity cost of acquiring wheat by giving up soybeans increases.

The Principle of Increasing Costs

The **principle of increasing costs** states that as the production of one good expands, the opportunity cost of producing yet more of this good generally increases.

We have just described a very general phenomenon, called the **principle of increasing costs,** which is applicable well beyond farming. This principle is not, of course, a universal fact; there can be exceptions to it. But it does seem to be a technological regularity that applies to a wide range of economic activities. It is based, as our example of the farmer suggests, on the fact that resources tend to be specialized, at least in part, so that some of their productivity is lost when they are transferred from doing what they are relatively good at doing to what they are relatively bad at doing. In terms of our production possibilities diagram, the principle simply asserts that the frontier is bowed outward, as in Figure 3–1.

Scarcity and Choice for the Entire Society

Like an individual firm, the entire economy is also constrained by its limited resources. If society wants more aircraft and tanks, it will have to give up some boats and automobiles. If it wants to build more factories and stores, it will have to build fewer homes and sports arenas. In general:

The position and shape of the production possibilities frontier that constrains the choices of the economy are determined by the economy's physical resources, its skills, its willingness to work, and its investment in factories, research, and innovation.

Since the debate over increasing our nation's military strength has been so much on the national agenda in recent years, let us illustrate the nature of society's choices by the example of choosing between military might (represented by missiles) and civilian consumption (represented by milkshakes). Just like a single firm, the economy as a whole has a production possibilities frontier for missiles and milkshakes determined by the available resources of land, labor, capital, and raw materials. This production possibilities frontier may look like curve *BC* in Figure 3–2.

If most workers are employed at soda fountains and dairy farms, the production of milkshakes will be large but the output of missiles will be small. If

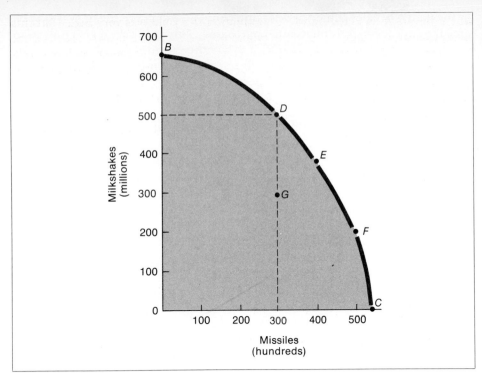

Figure 3–2
THE PRODUCTION POSSI-
BILITIES FRONTIER FOR
THE ENTIRE ECONOMY
This production possibilities
frontier is curved because resources are not perfectly
transferable from milkshake
production to missile production. The limits on available resources place a ceiling, C, on
the output of one product and
a different ceiling, B, on the
output of the other product.

resources are transferred from farms to factories, the mix of output can be shifted toward increased production of missiles at some sacrifice of milkshakes (the move from D to E). However, something is likely to be lost in the transfer process—the hay that helped produce the dairy output will not help in missile production. As summarized in the principle of increasing costs, physical resources tend to be specialized, so the production possibilities frontier probably curves downward toward the axes. We may even reach a point where the only resources left are items that are not very useful outside dairy farms and soda fountains. In that case, even a very large additional sacrifice of milkshakes will enable the economy to produce very few more missiles. That is the meaning of the steep segment, FC, on the frontier. At point C there is very little more output of missiles than at F, even though at C milkshake production has been given up entirely.

The downward slope of society's production possibilities frontier implies that hard choices must be made. Our nation's military strength can be increased only by decreasing civilian consumption ("milkshakes"), not by rhetoric nor by wishing it so. The curvature of the production possibilities frontier implies that, as defense spending increases, it becomes progressively more expensive to "buy" additional military strength ("missiles") by sacrificing civilian consumption.

Scarcity and Choice Elsewhere in the Economy

We have stressed that limited resources force hard choices upon business managers and society as a whole. But the same type of choices arise elsewhere—in households, in universities and other nonprofit organizations, and in the government.

The nature of opportunity cost is perhaps most obvious for a household that must decide how to divide its income among the goods and services that compete for the family's trade. If the Higgins family buys an expensive new car, it may be forced to cut back sharply on its other purchases. This does not make it unwise to buy the car. But it does make it unwise to buy the car until the full implications of the purchase for the family's overall budget are considered. If the Higgins family is to use its limited resources most effectively, it must explicitly acknowledge that the opportunity costs of the car are, say, a shorter vacation and making do with the old TV set.

The situation of charitable foundations is clearly analogous to that of households. Rich as many of them are, they cannot give away more than they have available. When the Ford Foundation, with capital in the neighborhood of $4 billion, decided a decade ago to spend more on the problems of cities and minorities, less was left for other purposes. As a result, the support that the Foundation had formerly provided to the arts, to education, and to other sections of society had to be cut back. Then, when the Foundation ran into financial problems in the mid-1970s, the "philanthropoids" were forced to make even more difficult choices about the distribution of their dwindling support money. Grants were cut back sharply, and many groups that had depended on Ford and other foundations as a continuing source of support suddenly found that their easier days had come to an end.

Even a rich and powerful government like the United States or the Soviet Union must cope with the limitations implied by scarce resources. For the goods and services it buys from others, a government has to prepare a budget similar to that of a very large household. For the items it produces itself—education, police protection, libraries, and so on—it faces a production possibilities frontier much like that of a business firm. Some of the most acrimonious debates between the Reagan administration and its critics in Congress and elsewhere have been over precisely these sorts of issues. How large a share of the government's limited resources should be allocated to the military instead of to public housing, social welfare, and other civilian programs? The necessity for choice imposed on the government by its limited budget is similar in character to the problems faced by business firms, households, and philanthropoids.

Application: Economic Growth

Among the economic choices that any society must make, there is one very important choice that will serve as a good illustration of the opportunity cost concept: This choice is embodied in the question "How fast should the economy grow?" At first, the question may seem ridiculous. Since economic growth means, roughly, that the average citizen has more and more goods and services, is it not self-evident that faster growth is always better?

Again, the fundamental problem of scarcity intervenes. Economies do not grow by magic. Scarce resources must be devoted to the process of growth.[1] Cement and steel that could be used to make swimming pools and stadiums must be diverted to build more machinery and factories. Wood that could make furniture and skis must be used for hammers and ladders instead. Grain that could be eaten must be ploughed back into the soil to increase future yields. By deciding how large a quantity of resources to devote to future needs rather than to current consumption, society in effect *chooses* (within limits) how fast it will grow.

Figure 3–3 illustrates the nature of the choice by depicting production possibilities frontiers for goods that are consumed today (like food and electricity) versus *investment goods* that provide for future consumption (like grocery

---

[1] Economic growth will be studied in detail in Chapters 35 and 39.

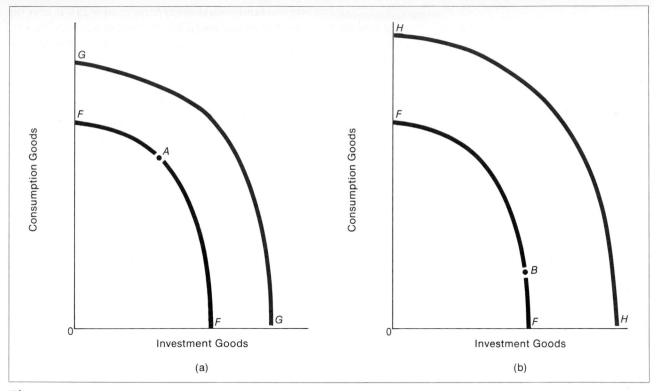

Figure 3–3

GROWTH IN TWO ECONOMIES

Growth shifts the production possibilities frontier *FF* outward to the blue frontiers, *GG* and *HH*, meaning that each economy can produce more of both goods than it could before. If the shift in both economies occurs in the same period of time, then the economy in part (b) is growing faster than the one in part (a). That is because the outward shift in part (b) is much greater than the one in part (a).

stores and generating plants) for two different societies. When the available resources increase, the production possibilities frontier shifts outward over time—meaning that more of both types of goods can be produced. But how fast this happens depends on the choices each society makes. In the example shown in the figure, both societies have the same initial production possibilities frontier, *FF*, but they make different choices. Figure 3–3(a) depicts a society that devotes a relatively small quantity of resources to growth, preferring current consumption instead. That is, it chooses a point like *A*, where consumption is relatively high and investment is relatively low. As a result, its production possibilities frontier shifts only to *GG*. Figure 3–3(b) depicts a society much more enamored of growth. Given the same initial menu of choices, it instead selects a point like *B*, where consumption is much lower and investment is much higher. As a result, its production possibilities frontier moves all the way to *HH*. It grows faster than the other society, but the more rapid growth has a price—an *opportunity cost*. It must give up some current consumption.

The Concept of Efficiency

So far in our discussion of scarcity and choice, we have assumed that either the single firm or the whole economy always operates *on* its production possibilities frontier rather than *below* it. In other words, we have tacitly assumed that, whatever it decides to do, the firm or economy does so efficiently.

Economists define *efficiency* as the absence of waste.[2] To see why any point on the economy's production possibilities frontier in Figure 3–2 (page 43) represents an efficient decision, suppose for a moment that society has decided to produce 300 missiles. According to the production possibilities frontier, if 300 missiles are to be produced, then the maximum number of milkshakes that can be made is 500 million (point *D* in Figure 3–2). The economy is, therefore, operating efficiently if it actually produces 500 million milkshakes rather than some smaller amount, such as 300 million (as at point *G*). Point *D* is efficient while point *G* is not. Note that the concept of efficiency does not tell us which point on the production possibilities frontier is *best*; it only tells us that no point that is *not* on the frontier can be best, because any such point represents wasted resources. For example, should society ever find itself at point *G*, the necessity of making hard choices would (temporarily) disappear. It would be possible to increase production of *both* missiles *and* milkshakes by moving to a point such as *E*.

Why, then, would an economy ever find itself at a point below its production possibilities frontier? There are a number of ways in which resources are wasted in real life. The most important of them, unemployment, is an issue that will take up a substantial part of this book (especially in Part Two). When many workers are unemployed, the economy finds itself at a point like *G*, below the frontier, because by putting the unemployed to work in both industries the economy could produce more missiles *and* more milkshakes. The economy would then move from point *G* to the right (more missiles) and upward (more milkshakes) toward a point like *E* on the production possibilities frontier. Only when no resources are wasted by unemployment or misuse is the economy *on* the frontier. Analogous problems occur in the firm. For example, if a firm uses fertilizer wastefully, it will end up at a point *inside* its production possibilities frontier. It will not be operating efficiently.

Specialization, Division of Labor, and Exchange

Efficiency is one of the basic goals of any economic system. Many features of society contribute toward this goal; others interfere with it. While different societies pursue the goal of economic efficiency in different ways, one source of efficiency is so fundamental that we must single it out for special attention: the tremendous gains in productivity that stem from **specialization** and the consequent **division of labor.**

Adam Smith, the founder of modern economics, first marveled at this mainspring of efficiency and productivity on a visit to a pin factory. In a famous passage near the beginning of his monumental book *The Wealth of Nations* (1776), he described what he saw:

One man draws out the wire, another straightens it, a third cuts it, a fourth points it, a fifth grinds it at the top for receiving the head; to make the head requires two or three distinct operations; to put it on is a peculiar business, to whiten the pins is another; it is even a trade by itself to put them into the paper. . . .[3]

Smith observed that by dividing the work to be done in this way, each worker became quite skilled in his particular specialty, and the productivity of the group of workers as a whole was enhanced enormously. As Smith related it:

[2] A formal definition of *efficiency* is offered in Chapter 23, page 431.
[3] Adam Smith, *The Wealth of Nations*, (New York: Random House, Modern Library Edition 1937), page 4.

*I have seen a small manufactory of this kind where ten men only were employed.
. . . Those ten persons . . . could make among them upwards of forty-eight
thousand pins in a day. . . . But if they had all wrought separately and
independently, . . . they certainly could not each of them have made twenty,
perhaps not one pin in a day. . . .*[4]

In other words, through the miracle of division of labor and specialization, ten
workers accomplished what would otherwise have required thousands. This was
the secret of the Industrial Revolution, which helped lift humanity out of the
abject poverty that had for so long been its lot.

But specialization created a problem. With division of labor, people no
longer produced only what they wanted to consume themselves. The workers in
the pin factory had no use for the thousands of pins they produced each day; they
wanted to trade them for things like food, clothing, and shelter. Specialization
thus made it necessary to have some mechanism by which workers producing
pins could **exchange** their wares with workers producing such things as cloth
and potatoes. Without a system of exchange, the productivity miracle achieved
by the division of labor would have done society little good.

These two principles—specialization and exchange—working in tandem led
to a vast improvement in the well-being of mankind, and they continue to do so
today. But what forces induce workers to join together so that the fruits of the
division of labor can be enjoyed? And what forces establish a smoothly functioning system of exchange so that each person can acquire what he or she wants to
consume? One alternative is to have a central authority telling people what to
do.[5] But Adam Smith explained and extolled another way of organizing and
coordinating economic activity—the use of markets and prices.

Markets, Prices, and Resource Allocation

Smith noted that people were very good at pursuing their own self-interest, and
that a *market system* was a very good way to harness this self-interest. As he put
it, with pretty clear religious overtones, in doing what is best for themselves,
people are "led by an invisible hand" to promote the economic well-being of
society. Let us consider briefly how this works.[6]

In deciding how to use its scarce resources, society must somehow make
three sorts of decisions. First, it must figure out how to utilize its resources
efficiently; that is, find a way to get *on* its production possibilities frontier.
Second, it must decide what combination of goods to produce—how many
missiles, how many milkshakes and so on—that is, it must select one specific
point on the production possibilities frontier. Finally, it must decide how much
of each good to distribute to each person, doing it in a sensible way so that meat
does not go to vegetarians and wine to teetotalers. Certainly, each of these
decisions could be made by a central planner who told people how to produce,
what to produce, and what to consume. But they can also be made without
central direction, through a system of prices and markets.

Since we live in a market economy, the outlines of the process by which this
system works are familiar to all of us. Firms are encouraged by the profit motive to
use inputs efficiently. Exceptionally scarce resources (like energy) will command
high prices, thus causing producers to economize on their use. The price system

---

[4]*Ibid.*, page 5.
[5]This is what takes place under the system of central planning, which we will consider in some detail
in Chapter 41.
[6]This topic is studied in detail in Chapter 23.

Biographical Note:
Adam Smith (1723–1790)

Adam Smith, who was to become the leading advocate of freedom of international trade, was born the son of a customs official in 1723 and ended his career in the well-paid post of collector of customs for Scotland. He received an excellent education at Glasgow College, where, for the first time, some lectures were being given in English rather than Latin. A fellowship to Oxford University followed, and for six years he studied there mostly by himself, since, at that time, teaching at Oxford was virtually nonexistent.

After completing his studies, Smith was appointed professor of logic at Glasgow College and, later, professor of moral philosophy, a field which then included economics as one of its branches. Fortunately, he was a popular lecturer because, in those days, a professor's pay in Glasgow depended on the number of students who chose to attend his lectures. At Glasgow, Smith was responsible for helping young James Watt find a job as an instrument maker. Watt later invented the steam engine, so in this and many other respects, Smith was present virtually at the birth of the Industrial Revolution, whose prophet he was destined to become.

After 13 years at Glasgow, Smith accepted a highly paid post as a tutor to a young Scottish nobleman with whom he spent several years in France, a customary way of educating nobles in the eighteenth century. Primarily because he was bored during these years in France, Smith began working on *The Wealth of Nations*. Several years after his return to England, in 1776, the book was published and rapidly achieved popularity.

The Wealth of Nations contains many brilliantly written passages. It was one of the first systematic treatises in economics, contributing both to theoretical and factual knowledge about the subject. Among the main points made in the book are the importance for a nation's prosperity of freedom of trade and the division of labor permitted by more widespread markets; the dangers of governmental protection of monopolies and imposition of tariffs; and the superiority of self-interest—the instrument of the "invisible hand"—over altruism as a means of improving the economy's service to the general public.

The British government was grateful for the ideas for new tax legislation Smith proposed, and to show its appreciation appointed him to the lucrative sinecure of collector of customs, which, together with the lifetime pension awarded him by his former pupil, left him very well off financially, although he eventually gave away most of his money to charitable causes.

In the eighteenth century, the intellectual world was small, and among the many people with whom Smith was acquainted were David Hume, Samuel Johnson, James Boswell, Benjamin Franklin, and Jean Jacques Rousseau. Smith got along well with everyone except Samuel Johnson, who was noted for his dislike of Scots. Smith was absent-minded and apparently timid with women, being visibly embarrassed by the public attention of the eminent ladies of Paris during his visits there. He never married, and lived with his mother most of his life. When he died, the Edinburgh newspapers recalled only that when Smith was four years old he was kidnapped by gypsies. But thanks to his writings, he is remembered for a good deal more than that.

---

also guides firms' output decisions, and hence those of society. A rise in the price of wheat, for example, will persuade farmers to produce more wheat and fewer soybeans. Finally, a price system determines who gets what goods through a series of voluntary exchanges. Workers with valuable skills and owners of scarce resources will be able to sell what they have at attractive prices. With the incomes they earn, they can then purchase the goods and services they want most, within the limits of their budgets.

This, in broad terms, is how a market economy solves the three basic problems facing any society: how to produce any given combination of goods efficiently, how to select an appropriate combination of goods, and how to distribute these goods sensibly among the people. As we proceed through the following chapters, you will learn much more about these issues. You will see that they constitute the central theme that permeates not only this text, but the work of economists in general. As you progress through the book, keep in mind the following two questions: What does the market do well? What does the market do badly? There are plenty of answers to both questions. As you will learn in coming chapters:

1. Society has many important goals. Some of them, such as producing goods and services with maximum efficiency (minimum waste), can in certain circumstances be achieved extraordinarily well by letting markets operate more or less freely.

2. Free markets will not, however, achieve all of society's goals. In fact, there are some goals—such as protection of the environment—for which the unfettered operation of markets may be positively harmful.

3. But even in cases where the market does not perform at all well, there may be ways of harnessing the power of the market mechanism to remedy its own deficiencies. For example, as we hinted in Chapter 1 and will explain in Chapters 29 and 31, there are ways to use the market mechanism to reduce pollution and protect the environment.

Radicalism, Conservatism, and the Market Mechanism

Since economic debates often have political and ideological overtones, we think it important to close the chapter by stressing that the central theme that we have just outlined is neither a defense of nor an attack upon the capitalist system. Nor is it a "right-wing" position. One does not have to be a conservative to recognize that the market mechanism can be a helpful instrument for the pursuit of economic goals. A number of socialist countries, including Yugoslavia and Hungary, have openly and deliberately organized parts of their economies along market lines, and the People's Republic of China, founded on the principles of communism, is now moving in that direction.

The point is not to confuse means and ends in deciding whether to leave matters to market forces, either with or without suitable modification or constraint. Radicals and conservatives surely have different goals, and they may also differ in the means they advocate to pursue these goals. But means should not be selected for their own sakes; rather, they should be chosen on the basis of how effective they are in achieving the adopted goals. For example, radicals may assign a much higher priority to the elimination of poverty than conservatives do, and they may be willing to accept far greater sacrifices for that purpose. It is then a problem for economic science to determine whether reduction of poverty is promoted or impeded by the market mechanism and, if the market mechanism does turn out to promote it, to determine whether it does so more effectively than the available alternatives. If the answer in both cases is affirmative, then it is sensible for a radical to support the use of the market for this purpose. On the other hand, if the market fails either of the preceding tests—that is, if it does not reduce poverty or does not do it as well as some alternative mechanism—the radical will have valid grounds for opposing the market. Note, however, that in either case the choice is made on the basis of its *consequences*, not on an ideological prejudgment that the market mechanism per se is a "reactionary tool."

We will show in this book that the market mechanism *can* do many useful things, and that it can help both radicals and conservatives to achieve their goals. For example, we suggested above that the market can be used to control pollution. Radicals may favor very tight pollution controls even if controls cut into business profits; conservatives may wish to have things the other way around. Nevertheless, both sides may want to use the market mechanism to achieve their goals. Indeed, each side may conclude that, should it lose the political struggle and the other side's position be adopted, less damage will be done to its own goals if market methods are used.

There certainly are economic problems with which market methods cannot deal. Indeed, we have just noted that the market is the *source* of a number of significant problems. These will be studied in subsequent chapters, where we will also discuss how these problems may be remedied. But the evidence leads economists to believe that there are other economic problems that are best handled by market techniques. The analysis in this book is intended to help you identify the strengths and weaknesses of the market mechanism.

Summary

1. Supplies of all resources are limited. Because resources are scarce, a rational decision is one that chooses the best alternative among the options that are possible with the available resources.

2. It is irrational to assign highest priority to everything. No one can afford everything, and so hard choices must be made.

3. With limited resources, if we decide to obtain more of one item, we must give up some of another item. What we give up is called the *opportunity cost* of what we get; this is the true cost of any decision. The concept of opportunity cost is one of the 12 Ideas for Beyond the Final Exam.

4. When the market is functioning effectively, firms are led to use resources efficiently and to produce the things that consumers want most. In such cases, opportunity costs and money costs (prices) correspond closely. When the market performs poorly, or when important items of cost do not get price tags, opportunity costs and money costs can be quite different.

5. A firm's production possibilities frontier shows the combinations of goods the firm can produce with a given quantity of resources. The frontier usually is not a straight line, but is bowed outward because resources tend to be specialized.

6. The principle of increasing costs states that as the production of one good expands, the opportunity cost of producing yet more of this good generally increases.

7. The economy as a whole has a production possibilities frontier whose position is determined by the available resources of land, labor, capital, and raw materials.

8. If a firm or an economy ends up at a point below its production possibilities frontier, it is using its resources inefficiently or wastefully. This is what happens, for example, when there is unemployment.

9. Economic growth means there is an outward shift in the economy's production possibilities frontier. The faster the growth, the faster this shift will occur. But growth requires a sacrifice of current consumption, and this is its opportunity cost.

10. Efficiency, one of the basic goals of any economic system, is defined by economists as the absence of waste. It is achieved primarily by gains in productivity brought about through specialization, division of labor, and a system of exchange.

11. The market system works very well in solving some of society's basic problems, but it fails to remedy others and may, indeed, create some of its own. Where and how it succeeds and fails constitute the theme of this book and characterize the work of economists in general.

Concepts for Review

Scarcity
Choice
Opportunity cost
Production possibilities frontier

Principle of increasing costs
Investment goods
Efficiency
Specialization

Division of labor
Exchange
Market system

Questions for Discussion

1. Discuss the resource limitations that affect:
   a. the poorest person on earth
   b. the richest person on earth
   c. a firm in Switzerland
   d. a government agency in China
   e. the population of the world
2. If you were president of your college, what would you change if your budget were cut by 5 percent? by 20 percent? by 50 percent?
3. If you were to drop out of college, what things would change in your life? What, then, is the opportunity cost of your education?
4. A person rents a house for which he pays the landlord $3000 a year and keeps money in a bank account that pays 6 percent a year. The house is offered for sale at $70,000. Is this a good deal for the potential buyer? Where does opportunity cost enter the picture?
5. Construct graphically the production possibilities frontier for Lower Slobovia given in the table at the top of the next column.

PRODUCTION POSSIBILITIES FOR LOWER SLOBOVIA, 1984

SOUFFLÉS (millions)	COMPUTERS (thousands)
75	0
60	12
45	22
30	30
15	36
0	40

Does the principle of increasing cost hold in Lower Slobovia?

6. Consider two alternatives for Lower Slobovia in the year 1984. In case (a) its inhabitants eat 60 million soufflés and build only 12,000 computers. In case (b) the population eats only 15 million soufflés but builds 36,000 computers. Which case will lead to a more generous production possibilities frontier for Slobovia in 1985? (*Note:* In Slobovia, computers are used for cooking soufflés.)

Supply and Demand: An Initial Look

4

The free-enterprise system
is absolutely too important to be left
to the voluntary action of the marketplace.
CONGRESSMAN RICHARD KELLY
OF FLORIDA (1979)

I f the issue of scarcity and choice is the basic *problem* of economics, then the mechanism of supply and demand is its basic investigative *tool*. Whether your course concentrates on macroeconomics or microeconomics, you will find that the so-called "law" of supply and demand is the fundamental tool of economic analysis. Supply and demand analysis is used in this book to study issues seemingly as diverse as inflation and unemployment, the international value of the dollar, government regulation of business, and protection of the environment. So careful study of this chapter will pay rich dividends in what follows.

The chapter describes the rudiments of supply and demand analysis in steps. We begin with demand, then add supply, and finally put the two sides together. *Supply and demand curves*—graphs that relate price to quantity supplied and quantity demanded, respectively—are explained and used to show how prices and quantities are determined in a free market. Influences that shift either the demand curve or the supply curve are catalogued briefly, and the analysis is used to explain how Arab sheiks helped make the Netherlands rich in the 1970s. One major theme of the chapter is that governments around the globe and throughout recorded history have attempted to tamper with the price mechanism. We will see that these bouts with Adam Smith's invisible hand often have produced undesired side effects that surprised and dismayed the authorities. And we will show that many of these unfortunate effects were no accidents, but were inherent consequences of interfering with the operation of free markets. The invisible hand fights back!

Finally, a word of caution. This chapter makes heavy use of graphs such as those described in Chapter 2. If you encounter difficulties with these graphs, we suggest you review pages 21–26.

Fighting the Invisible Hand

Adam Smith was a great admirer of the price system. He marveled at its intricacies and extolled its accomplishments. Many people since Smith's time have shared his enthusiasm; but many others have not. His contemporaries in the American colonies, for example, were often unhappy with the prices produced by free markets and thought they could do better by legislative decree.

(They could not, as the boxed insert on page 54 shows.) And there have been countless other instances in which the public's sense of justice was outraged by the prices charged on the open market, particularly when the sellers of the expensive items belonged to a group that did not enjoy great popularity—landlords, moneylenders, and oil companies are good examples.

Attempts to control interest rates (which may be thought of as the price of borrowing money) go back hundreds of years before the birth of Christ, at least to the code of laws compiled under Hammurabi in Babylonia about 1800 B.C. Our historical legacy also includes a rather long list of price ceilings on foods and other products imposed in the reign of Diocletian, emperor of the declining Roman Empire. More recently, Americans have been offered the "protection" of a variety of price controls. Ceilings have been placed on some prices (such as gasoline) to protect buyers, while floors have been placed under other prices (such as farm products) to protect sellers. In New York City, rents have been continuously regulated since World War II—long after every other major city dropped the practice. Many if not most of these measures were adopted in response to popular opinion, and there is a great outcry whenever it is proposed that any one of them be weakened or eliminated. Yet, somehow, everything such regulation touches seems to end up in even greater disarray than it was before. Despite controls, rents in New York City have considerably more than doubled in the last ten years. Tickets for popular shows and sports events sell at tremendous premiums—$40 tickets to the 1981 Super Bowl, for example, reportedly were sold for prices as high as $500. Taxis cost much more in New York City (where they are tightly regulated) than in Washington, D.C., (where they are not). And ceilings on gasoline prices in 1979 forced motorists in several American cities to line up at filling stations for their "ration" of gas.

Still, legislators continue to turn to controls whenever the economy does not work to their satisfaction, just as they did in 1777. Recent years have seen a return to rent controls in many American cities, a brief experiment with overall price controls by a Republican administration that had vowed never to turn to them, determined resistance to abolition of ceilings on interest rates on mortgages, and a web of controls over petroleum prices that has only recently ended.

Public opinion frequently encourages legislative attempts to "repeal the law of supply and demand" by controlling prices. The consequences usually are quite unfortunate, exacting heavy costs from the general public and often aggravating the problem the legislation was intended to cure. This is another of the 12 Ideas for Beyond the Final Exam, and it will occupy our attention throughout this chapter.

To understand what goes wrong when markets are tampered with, we must first learn how they operate when they are unfettered. This chapter takes a first step in that direction by studying the machinery of supply and demand. Then, at the end of the chapter, we return to the issue of price controls, illustrating the problems that can arise by a case study of the market for rental housing in New York City.

The Demand Curve

References in nonprofessional discussions to the "law of supply and demand" imply that it is some sort of vaguely defined but powerful influence affecting the course of economic affairs by raising prices when goods are scarce and lowering prices when goods are abundant. This is true, but to economists the supply–

Price Controls at Valley Forge

George Washington, the history books tell us, was beset by many enemies during the winter of 1777–1778—including the British, their Hessian mercenaries, and the merciless winter weather. But he had another enemy that the history books ignore, an enemy who meant well but almost destroyed his army at Valley Forge. That enemy was the legislature of the Commonwealth of Pennsylvania, as the following excerpt explains.

In Pennsylvania, where the main force of Washington's army was quartered in 1777, . . . the legislature . . . decided to try a period of price control limited to those commodities needed for use by the army. The theory was that this policy would reduce the expense of supplying the army and lighten the burden of the war upon the population. The result might have been anticipated by those with some knowledge of the trials and tribulations of other states. The prices of uncontrolled goods, mostly imported, rose to record heights. Most farmers kept back their produce, refusing to sell at what they regarded as an unfair price. Some who had large families to take care of even secretly sold their food to the British who paid in gold.

After the disastrous winter at Valley Forge when Washington's army nearly starved to death (thanks largely to these well-intentioned but misdirected laws), the ill-fated experiment in price controls was finally ended. The Continental Congress on June 4, 1778, adopted the following resolution:

"Whereas . . . it hath been found by experience that limitations upon the prices of commodities are not only ineffectual for the purposes proposed, but likewise productive of very evil consequences to the great detriment of the public service and grievous oppression of individuals . . . resolved, that it be recommended to the several states to repeal or suspend all laws or resolutions within the said states respectively limiting, regulating or restraining the Price of any Article, Manufacture or Commodity."

SOURCE: Robert L. Schuettinger and Eamonn F. Butler, in their book, *Forty Centuries of Wage and Price Controls*, published by the Heritage Foundation, Washington, D.C., 1979. Reprinted by permission.

demand mechanism is something far more concrete. It is a manifestation of market forces that shows precisely how prices interact with quantities supplied and demanded. We begin our analysis on the demand side of the market.

Noneconomists are apt to think of consumer demands as fixed amounts. For example, when the production of a new type of machine tool is proposed, management asks "What is its market potential? How many will we be able to sell?" Similarly, government bureaus conduct studies to determine just how many skilled workers will be "required" in succeeding years. Economists respond that such questions are not well posed—that there is no *single* number that describes the information required. Rather, they say, the "market potential" for machine tools, or the number of engineers that will be "required," *depends on the price that will be charged for each*. These quantities also depend upon a great many other variables. But, for the moment, let us concentrate on the relationship between the price of a good and the quantity of it that customers demand.

Consider, as an example, natural gas, which is purchased by individuals for heating and cooking, and by industry as a source of energy. If gas is offered at an exorbitant price, its "market potential" may be zero because buyers are apt to find it cheaper to use some other fuel instead. If the price is lowered a bit, gas will attract a few customers who find gas much more convenient than oil or other substitute fuels. If the price is lowered still further, even more gas is likely to be demanded. Thus:

There is no *one* demand figure for natural gas, for machine tools, or for engineers, but rather a series of alternative quantities demanded, each corresponding to a different price.

Table 4–1 displays this information for natural gas in what we call a *demand schedule*. It shows the quantity of natural gas that will be demanded in a year at each possible price ranging from $1 to $8 per thousand cubic feet. We see, for example, that at a relatively low price, like $2 per thousand cubic feet, customers will purchase 70 billion cubic feet per year. But if the price were to raise to, say, $6 per thousand cubic feet, quantity demanded would fall to 23 billion cubic feet. Thus the "market potential" depends on the price. Common sense tells us why this should be so.[1] First, as prices rise, customers will try to economize on their use of natural gas. Second, higher prices will induce some customers to drop out of the market entirely—for example, by switching to oil or electricity. On both counts, quantity demanded will decline as the price rises.

The information contained in Table 4–1 can also be summarized in a graph, which we call a **demand curve,** displayed in Figure 4–1. Each point in the graph corresponds to a line in the table. For example, point *A* corresponds to the second line in the table, indicating that at a price of $7 per thousand cubic feet, 10 billion cubic feet of gas per year will be demanded. Since the quantity demanded declines as the price increases, the demand curve has a negative slope.[2]

Notice the last five words in the definition of the demand curve: "holding all other things constant." Quantity demanded does not depend on price alone. Such "other things" as consumer incomes and preferences, weather, the prices of oil and electricity, and perhaps even advertising by the gas company all influence the quantity of natural gas that is demanded. We will examine these factors in more detail later in the chapter. First, however, let's look at the supply side of the market.

> A **demand curve** is a graph showing how the quantity demanded of some product during a specified period of time will change as the price of that product changes, holding all other things constant.

[1]This common-sense answer is examined more fully in Chapter 18.
[2]If you need to review the concept of *slope*, refer back to Chapter 2, especially pages 22–24.

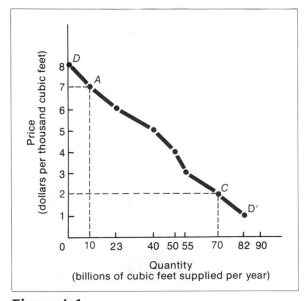

Figure 4–1
DEMAND CURVE FOR NATURAL GAS
This curve shows the relation between price and quantity demanded. To sell 70 billion cubic feet of gas per year, the price must be only $2 (point *C*). If, instead, price is $7, only 10 billion cubic feet will be demanded (point *A*). To sell more gas, the price must be reduced. That is what the negative slope of the demand curve means.

Table 4–1
QUANTITIES OF NATURAL GAS DEMANDED
AT VARIOUS PRICES

PRICE (dollars per thousand cubic feet)	QUANTITY DEMANDED (billions of cubic feet per year)
8	0
7	10
6	23
5	40
4	50
3	55
2	70
1	82

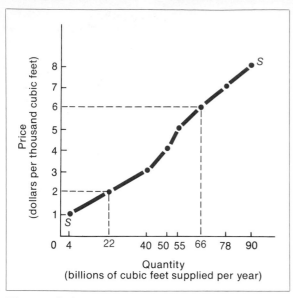

Table 4–2
QUANTITIES OF NATURAL GAS SUPPLIED
AT VARIOUS PRICES

PRICE (dollars per thousand cubic feet)	QUANTITY SUPPLIED (billions of cubic feet per year)
8	90
7	78
6	66
5	55
4	50
3	40
2	22
1	4

Figure 4–2
SUPPLY CURVE FOR NATURAL GAS
This curve shows the relation between the price of natural gas and the quantity supplied. To stimulate a greater quantity supplied, price must be increased. That is the meaning of the positive slope of the supply curve.

The Supply Curve

Price not only influences quantity demanded, it also affects the quantity that will be supplied. If the price of a commodity is so low that it cannot cover the costs of production, nothing will be produced. At higher prices it will pay suppliers to undertake some production, the quantity produced depending on how high the price gets. And at even higher prices, we may expect the firms to produce still more output. Thus to economists, supply, like demand, cannot be considered a single fixed number. Rather there is a relationship between the price and the quantity that is supplied.

Table 4–2 describes this relationship for our natural gas example. This *supply schedule*, as it is called, shows that a low price like $2 per thousand cubic feet will induce suppliers to provide only 22 billion cubic feet, while a higher price, like $6, will induce them to provide much more—66 billion cubic feet. As you might have guessed, when information like this is plotted on a graph, it is called a **supply curve.** Figure 4–2 is the supply curve corresponding to the supply schedule in Table 4–2. It slopes upward because quantity supplied is higher when price is higher.

Notice again the same words in the definition: "holding all other things constant." Like quantity demanded, quantity supplied depends on more than just price. For example, if new firms enter the industry (or if old firms leave) the quantity supplied at any given price will change; that is, the supply curve will shift. Quantity supplied will also be affected by technological breakthroughs that make natural gas cheaper to extract or deliver. We will return to these and other reasons why the supply curve might shift a bit later in the discussion. But first we are ready to put demand and supply together.

A **supply curve** is a graph showing how the quantity supplied of some commodity during a specified period of time will change as the price of that commodity changes, holding all other things constant.

Equilibrium of Supply and Demand

To analyze how price is determined in a free market, it is convenient to utilize a graphic apparatus called the **supply–demand diagram** in which the supply

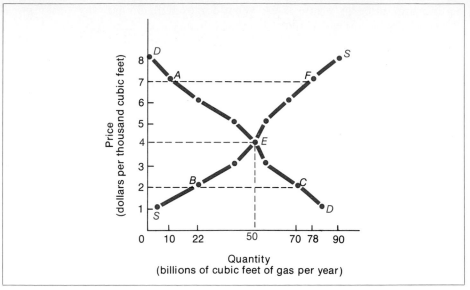

Figure 4–3
SUPPLY–DEMAND
EQUILIBRIUM
In a free market, price and
quantity are determined by the
intersection of the supply curve
and the demand curve. In this
example, the equilibrium price
is $4 and the equilibrium quan-
tity is at 50 billion cubic feet per
year. Any other price is inconsistent with equilibrium. For
example, at a price of $2,
quantity demanded is 70 billion
(point C), while quantity supplied is only 22 billion (point B),
so that price will be driven up
by the unsatisfied demand.

curve and the demand curve are both drawn on the same graph. Figure 4–3 displays the supply and demand curves for our illustrative natural gas market, with curve *DD* the total demand curve of all consumers in the area (reproduced from Figure 4–1) and curve *SS* the supply curve of natural gas by the entire industry (reproduced from Figure 4–2). Curve *DD* has a negative slope while curve *SS* has a positive slope, for reasons we have already explained. Most supply–demand diagrams are drawn with slopes like these.

There is one point in the diagram, point *E*, at which the supply curve and the demand curve intersect. At the price corresponding to point *E*, which is $4 per thousand cubic feet, the quantity supplied is equal to the quantity demanded. For example, at a lower price, such as $2, only 22 billion cubic feet of gas will be supplied (point *B*) whereas 70 billion cubic feet will be demanded (point *C*). Thus, quantity demanded will exceed quantity supplied. Alternatively, at some higher price, such as $7, quantity supplied will be 78 billion cubic feet (point *F*) while quantity demanded will be only 10 billion (point *A*). Quantity supplied will exceed quantity demanded. Since $4 is the price at which quantity supplied and quantity demanded are equal, we say that $4 per thousand cubic feet is the **equilibrium price** in this market. Similarly, 50 billion cubic feet per year is the **equilibrium quantity.**

The term "equilibrium" merits a little explanation, since it arises so fre-
quently in economic analysis. An **equilibrium** is a situation in which there are no inherent forces that produce change; that is, a situation that does not contain the seeds of its own destruction. Think, for example, of a pendulum at rest at its center point. If no outside force (such as a person's hand) comes to push it, the pendulum will remain where it is; it is in *equilibrium*. But, if someone gives the pendulum a shove, its equilibrium will be disturbed and it will start to move upward. When it reaches the top of its arc, the pendulum will, for an instant, be at rest again. But this is not an equilibrium position. A force known as gravity will pull the pendulum downward, and thereafter its motion from side to side will be governed by gravity and friction. Eventually, we know, the pendulum must return to the point at which it started—its only equilibrium position— because at any other point inherent forces will cause the pendulum to move.

The concept of equilibrium in economics is similar, and it can be illustrated by our supply and demand example. Why is no price other than $4 an

An **equilibrium** is a situation in which there are no inherent forces that produce
change. Changes away from
an equilibrium position will
occur only as a result of "outside events" that disturb the
status quo.

equilibrium price in Figure 4–3? What forces will change any other price? Consider first a low price like $2, at which quantity demanded (70 billion) exceeds quantity supplied (22 billion). If the price were this low, there would be many frustrated customers whose demands were not being met. They would compete with one another for the available quantity. Some would offer more than the prevailing price and, as purchasers tried to outbid one another, the market price would be forced up. In other words, a price below the equilibrium price cannot persist in a free market because there are powerful economic forces that would push price upward.

Similar forces operate if the market price is *above* the equilibrium price. If, for example, the price should settle at $7, Figure 4–3 tells us that quantity supplied (78 billion) would far exceed quantity demanded (10 billion). Sellers would be unable to sell their desired quantities of natural gas at the prevailing price, and some would find it in their interest to undercut their competitors by reducing price. This process of competitive price-cutting would continue as long as there were frustrated sellers; that is, as long as quantity supplied exceeded quantity demanded. Thus a price above equilibrium price cannot persist indefinitely.

We are left with only one conclusion. The price $4 per thousand cubic feet and the quantity 50 billion cubic feet is the only price–quantity combination that does not sow the seeds of its own destruction. It is the only *equilibrium*. Any lower price must rise, and any higher price must fall. It is as if natural economic forces place a magnet at point *E* that attracts the market just like gravity attracts the pendulum.

The analogy to a pendulum is worth pursuing further. Most pendulums are more frequently in motion than at rest. However, unless they are repeatedly buffeted by outside forces (which, of course, is exactly what happens to pendulums used in clocks), pendulums gradually return to their resting points. The same is true of price and quantity in a free market.

In principle, in a free market the forces of supply and demand are capable of selecting an equilibrium price and an equilibrium quantity toward which, in practice, we may expect actual price and actual quantity to gravitate.

Markets are not always *in equilibrium*, but, if they are not interfered with, we have good reason to believe that normally they are moving *toward equilibrium*.

The last interesting aspect of the analogy concerns the "outside forces" of which we have spoken. A pendulum that is being blown by the wind or pushed by a hand does not remain in equilibrium. Similarly, many outside forces can disturb a market equilibrium. A frost in Florida will disturb equilibrium in the market for oranges. A strike by miners will disturb equilibrium in the market for coal. Many of these outside influences actually *change the equilibrium price and quantity* by shifting either the supply curve or the demand curve. When this happens, the market must move from its former equilibrium to its new equilibrium. It is to such shifts in supply and demand curves that we now turn.

Shifts in Demand and Supply Curves

The real power of supply and demand analysis comes in its ability to predict the *effects on price and quantity of some prescribed change of circumstances*. If you look again at Figure 4–3 you can see clearly that any event that causes *either* the demand curve *or* the supply curve to shift will also cause the equilibrium price and quantity to change. Such events constitute the "other things" that we held constant in our definitions of supply and demand curves. We are now ready to analyze how these outside forces affect the equilibrium of supply and demand.

Shifts of the Demand Curve

Returning to our example of natural gas, we might expect that in addition to the price of natural gas, the quantity of gas demanded depends on such things as climate, consumer incomes, and the prices of alternative energy sources, like electricity and oil. Should any of these factors change, the quantity of natural gas demanded will also change, *even if the price of gas remains constant.* Graphically, this means that *the entire demand curve will shift.*

A change in the price of a good produces a **movement along a fixed demand curve.** By contrast, a change in any other variable that influences quantity demanded will produce a **shift of the demand curve.** If consumers want to buy *more* at any given price than they wanted previously, the demand curve shifts to the *right* (or *outward*). If they desire *less* at any given price, the demand curve shifts to the *left* (or *inward*).

To make this general principle more concrete, let us consider some specific examples.

1. *Changes in consumer incomes.* If incomes increase, consumers may decide that they can afford to stay warmer in winter, and thus increase their purchases of natural gas even if the price of natural gas remains the same. That is, *increases in income normally shift demand curves outward to the right,* as depicted in Figure 4–4(a). In this example, the quantity demanded at the old equilibrium price of $4 increases from 50 billion cubic feet per year (point E on demand curve DD) to 93 billion (point G on demand curve RR). We know that $4 is no longer the equilibrium price, since at this price quantity demanded (93 billion) exceeds quantity supplied (50 billion). To restore equilibrium, price will have to rise. The diagram shows the new equilibrium as point T, where the price is $6 per thousand cubic feet and the quantity (demanded and supplied) is 66 billion cubic feet per year. This illustrates a general result.

   Any factor that causes the demand curve to shift outward to the right, and does not affect the supply curve, will raise the equilibrium price and the equilibrium quantity.[3]

   Everything works in reverse if consumer incomes fall. Figure 4–4(b) depicts a leftward (inward) shift of the demand curve that results from a decline in consumer incomes. For example, the quantity demanded at the previous equilibrium price ($4) falls from 50 billion cubic feet (point E) to 35 billion (point F on demand curve LL). At the initial $4 price, quantity supplied (50 billion) would now exceed quantity demanded (35 billion), so the price must begin to fall. The new equilibrium will eventually be established at point M, where the price is $3 and both quantity demanded and quantity supplied are 40 billion. In general:

   Any factor that shifts the demand curve to the left, and does not affect the supply curve, will lower both the equilibrium price and the equilibrium quantity.

[3]This statement, like many others in the text, assumes that the demand curve is downward-sloping and the supply curve is upward-sloping.

2. **Consumer preferences.** Some people like to cook with gas while others prefer electricity. Should many families suddenly decide that they like gas better, the demand curve for natural gas would shift to the right, just as shown in Figure 4–4(a). Alternatively, should gas cooking go out of style, the demand curve for natural gas would shift to the left, as in Figure 4–4(b). Again, these are quite general phenomena. *If consumer preferences shift in favor of a particular item, that item's demand curve will shift outward to the right, causing both price and quantity to rise* [Figure 4–4(a)]. *Conversely, if consumer preferences shift against a particular item, that item's demand curve will shift inward to the left, causing price and quantity to fall* [Figure 4–4(b)].

3. **Prices of related goods.** Because oil, electricity, and coal perform many of the same functions as natural gas, a change in the price of any of these competing goods can be expected to shift the demand curve for gas. For example, when the price of home heating oil skyrocketed in the 1970s, many homeowners decided to switch from oil to gas heat. This caused the demand curve for natural gas to shift rightward as in Figure 4–4(a).

But other price changes shift the demand curve for natural gas in the opposite direction. For example, suppose that gas-fired furnaces become more expensive. This may induce some users of gas to switch to oil heat, and thus shift the demand curve for natural gas to the left as in Figure 4–4(b). Common sense normally will tell us in which direction a price change for a related good will shift the demand curve for a good in question. *Increases in the prices of goods that are substitutes for the good in question (as oil is for natural gas) move the demand curve to the right. Increases in the prices of goods that are*

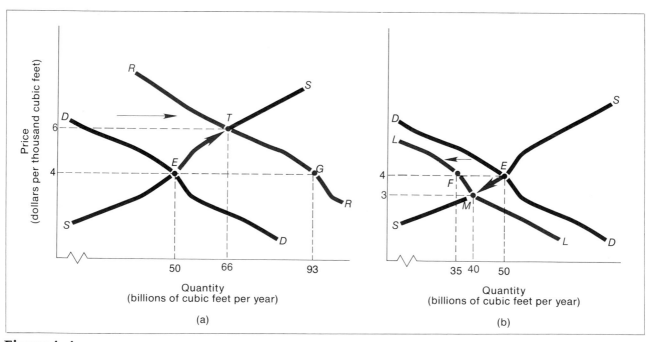

Figure 4–4
THE EFFECTS OF SHIFTS OF THE DEMAND CURVE
A shift of the demand curve will change the equilibrium price and quantity in a free market. In part (a), the demand curve shifts outward from *DD* to *RR*. As a result, equilibrium moves from point *E* to point *T*; both price and quantity rise. In part (b), the demand curve shifts inward from *DD* to *LL*, and equilibrium moves from point *E* to point *M*; both price and quantity fall.

normally used together with the good in question (such as gas furnaces and natural gas) shift the demand curve to the left.[4]

While this does not exhaust the list of possible influences on quantity demanded, enough has been said to indicate the principles involved. We turn our attention next to factors that can shift the supply curve.

Shifts of the Supply Curve

A supply curve indicates how quantity supplied varies as the price of the good in question changes. Thus, a change in the price of the good causes a **movement along a fixed supply curve.** But price is not the only influence on quantity supplied. And, if any of these other influences changes, **the entire supply curve shifts.** Let us consider what some of these factors are, and how they shift the supply curve.

1. *Size of the industry.* We begin with the most obvious factor. If more firms enter the natural gas industry, the quantity supplied at any given price probably will increase. For example, if each firm provides 2 billion cubic feet when the price is $4 per thousand cubic feet, then 25 firms provide 50 billion cubic feet, and 30 firms provide 60 billion. Thus, *the more firms that are attracted to the industry, the greater will be the quantity of gas supplied at any given price, and hence the farther to the right will be the supply curve.* Figure 4–5(a) illustrates the effect of an expansion of the industry from 25 firms to 30 firms—a rightward shift of the supply curve from SS to KK. Notice

[4]Goods that are normally used together are called *complements.* For precise definitions of substitute and complement goods, and further discussion, see Chapter 19, pages 360–361.

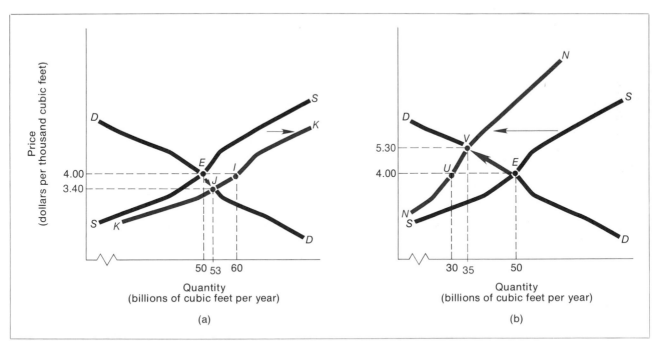

Figure 4–5
EFFECTS OF SHIFTS OF THE SUPPLY CURVE
A shift of the supply curve will change the equilibrium price and quantity in a market. In part (a), the supply curve shifts outward to the right, from SS to KK. As a result, equilibrium moves from point E to point J; price falls as quantity increases. Part (b) illustrates the opposite case—an inward shift of the supply curve from SS to NN. Equilibrium moves from point E to point V, which means that price rises as quantity falls.

that at the initial price of $4, the quantity supplied after the shift is 60 billion cubic feet (point I on supply curve KK), which exceeds the quantity demanded of 50 billion (point E on demand curve DD). We can see in the graph that the price of $4 is too high to be the equilibrium price; so price must fall. The diagram shows the new equilibrium at point J, where the price is $3.40 per thousand cubic feet and the quantity is 53 billion cubic feet. The general point is that:

Any factor that shifts the supply curve outward to the right, and does not affect the demand curve, will lower the equilibrium price and raise the equilibrium quantity.

Figure 4–5(b) illustrates the opposite case: a contraction of the industry from 25 firms to 15 firms. The supply curve shifts inward to the left and equilibrium moves from point E to point V, where price is $5.30 and quantity is 35 billion cubic feet. In general:

Any factor that shifts the supply curve inward to the left, and does not affect the demand curve, will raise the equilibrium price and reduce the equilibrium quantity.

Even if no firms enter or leave the industry, results like those depicted in Figure 4–5 can be produced by expansion or contraction of the existing firms. If firms get larger by drilling more wells, installing larger transmission lines, and so on, the supply curve shifts to the right as in Figure 4–5(a). If firms get smaller (perhaps by not replacing their equipment as it wears out), the supply curve shifts to the left as in Figure 4–5(b).

2. ***Technological progress.*** Suppose someone finds a way to transmit natural gas more cheaply from places where it is found (Texas, Louisiana) to places where it is consumed (Wisconsin, Massachusetts). Then, at any given price, firms in the industry will be encouraged to provide a larger quantity of output; that is, the supply curve will shift outward to the right, as in Figure 4–5(a). This, again, is quite a general influence, applying to almost all industries: *cost-reducing technological progress shifts the supply curve outward to the right.* Thus, as Figure 4–5(a) shows, the usual consequences of technological progress are lower prices and greater output.

3. ***Prices of inputs.*** As a final example, suppose employees in the natural gas industry go on strike and win a raise. Gas companies will find that they have to pay higher wages and consequently can no longer afford to provide 50 billion cubic feet at a price of $4 per thousand cubic feet [point E in Figure 4–5(b)]. Perhaps they will provide only 30 billion (point U on supply curve NN). This example illustrates that *increases in the prices of inputs that suppliers must buy will shift the supply curve inward to the left.*

Application: How the Netherlands Joined OPEC

To see how the supply–demand apparatus works in a real example, consider what happened to the market for natural gas when the Organization of Petroleum Exporting Countries (OPEC) jacked up the price of oil in the 1970s. As noted earlier, oil and natural gas are alternative fuels for heating homes or for firing industrial plants. So when the price of oil leaped upward, many individuals and

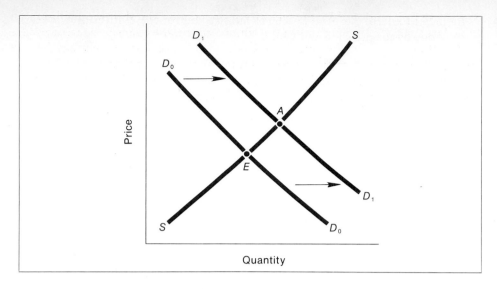

Figure 4–6
THE EFFECTS OF A RISE
IN THE PRICE OF OIL
ON THE MARKET FOR
NATURAL GAS
When the price of oil rose dramatically in the 1970s, this
stimulated demand for alternative fuels. The demand curve
for natural gas shifted to the
right from D_0D_0 to D_1D_1. (SS is
the supply curve.) Equilibrium,
which was initially at point E,
shifted to point A, resulting in a
higher price for natural gas.
Thus, one side effect of
OPEC's decision to raise
prices was a windfall gain for
nations, such as the Netherlands, that produce natural
gas.

businesses reduced their purchases of oil and increased their purchases of natural gas. In a word, *the demand curve for natural gas shifted to the right*, as from D_0D_0 to D_1D_1 in Figure 4–6. As the diagram shows, the result of this shift was that both the quantity and the price of natural gas increased—equilibrium in the natural gas market moved from point E to point A. This created a windfall gain for producers of natural gas, even though they themselves had nothing to do with OPEC's decisions.

Now what does all this have to do with the Netherlands? As it happens, Holland is a net exporter of natural gas; its domestic resources provide more gas than that small country can use. OPEC's actions bestowed a gift upon the Dutch by causing the demand curve for natural gas to shift to the right (as in Figure 4–6) and the price of gas to rise. Though we may assume that the "gift" was unintentional, it led one Dutch economist to quip, "We are now members of OPEC."

Attempts to Restrain the Market Mechanism

As we have noted already, lawmakers and rulers have often been dissatisfied with the outcomes of the operation of the market system. From Rome to Pennsylvania and from biblical times to the space age, they have done battle with the invisible hand. Sometimes, rather than trying to make adjustments in the workings of the market, governments have sought by law either to raise or to lower the prices of specific commodities. In many of these cases, the feeling of those in authority was that the prices set by the market mechanism were, in some sense, immorally low or immorally high. Penalties were therefore imposed on anyone offering the commodities in question at prices lower or higher than those determined by the regulators.

But the market has proven itself a formidable foe that strongly resists attempts to circumvent its workings. In case after case where legal ceilings on prices were imposed, virtually the same set of consequences ensued:

1. A persistent shortage developed of the items whose prices were controlled. Queuing, direct rationing, or any of a variety of other devices, usually inefficient and unpleasant, had to be substituted for the distribution process provided by the price mechanism.

2. An illegal, or "black" market almost invariably arose to supply the commodity at illegal prices. There are, apparently, always some individuals who are willing to take the risks involved in meeting unsatisfied demands illegally, if legal means will not do the job.

3. The prices charged by the black market were almost certainly higher than those that would have prevailed in a free market. After all, black marketeers do expect compensation for the risk of being caught and punished. In many cases, attempts to enforce price controls through stiffer penalties and more vigorous enforcement succeeded only in raising black-market prices to compensate for the greater risks to which black marketeers were consequently exposed.

4. In each case, a substantial portion of the price fell into the hands of the black-market supplier instead of going to those who produced the good or who performed the service. For example, a constant complaint in the series of hearings that have marked the history of theater ticket price controls has been that the "ice" (the illegal excess charge) falls into the hands of "ticket scalpers" rather than going to those who invested in, produced, or acted in the play.

It may be useful to examine a little more closely a current—and very unsuccessful—attempt to circumvent the market mechanism: the case of rent controls in New York City.

Rent Control in New York City: A Case Study*

Most economists are united in their belief that rent control does not help the cities or their inhabitants and that, in the long run, it makes almost everyone worse off. The most extensive effort at rent control in the United States illustrates the problems. As we mentioned earlier in the chapter, New York is the only major city in the United States that has had rent controls continuously since World War II. The objective of rent control is, of course, to protect the consumer from high rents. A supply–demand diagram tells us what in fact happens.

Figure 4–7 is a supply–demand diagram for housing units (apartments and private homes) in New York. Curve DD is the demand curve and curve SS is the supply curve. We know that without controls, equilibrium would be at point E, where rents average $500 per month and 3 million units are occupied. Effective rent controls must set a ceiling price *below* the equilibrium price of $500, because otherwise the rent level would simply settle at the point determined by market forces. But with a low rent ceiling, such as, say, $350, the quantity of housing demanded will be 3.5 million (point B) while the quantity supplied will only be 2.5 million (point C).

In fact, this simple diagram illustrates well what happened in New York City.[5] Every housing market has *some* vacancies because people move or die or new apartments are built. But the vacancy rate in New York City has been abnormally low; in 1979, for example, only 3 percent of rental units were vacant

*The sections on rent control can be omitted in shorter courses.

[5] The information in this section is based mainly on Peter Marcuse, *Rental Housing in the City of New York, 1975–1978* (City of New York, Housing and Development Administration, 1979).

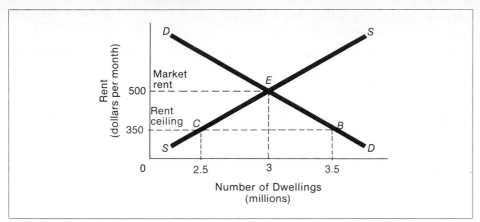

Figure 4–7
SUPPLY–DEMAND
DIAGRAM FOR HOUSING
When market forces are permitted to set rents, the quantity
of dwellings supplied will equal
the quantity demanded. But
when a rent ceiling forces rent
below the market level, the
number of dwellings supplied
(point *C*) will be less than the
number demanded (point *B*).
Thus, rent ceilings induce
housing shortages.

in New York as compared with a nationwide urban average of 5.6 percent. This low vacancy rate is the real-life counterpart of the theoretical concept of an excess of quantity demanded over quantity supplied.

Notice that the supply curve in Figure 4–7 has a positive slope, meaning that the quantity of apartments supplied to the market rises as rental rates rise. For example, higher rents may persuade some homeowners to convert a room in their house into a rental apartment. Conversely, very low rents may lead some landlords to take their properties off the market, because they lose little by doing so. For these and other reasons, controls that reduce rents also decrease the quantity of apartments supplied.

While these initial effects of rent controls are probably not large, the consequences of rent controls do not end here. In fact, in the long run, many economists believe that controls aggravate the very problem they are intended to solve by *shifting the supply curve to the left*. In New York City, this leftward shift of the supply curve can be seen in several ways. Most obviously, controls have discouraged new construction. While private construction did not come to a complete halt (it is still possible to build uncontrolled luxury apartments), the total number of housing units in the city actually fell by about 5 percent during the 1970s.

More immediate was the effect of rent control on the housing already in existence. With rents forced below their equilibrium levels, landlords find that they have no trouble renting apartments even if little or no money is invested in maintenance. With costs rising and rents relatively fixed, landlords also feel that they simply cannot afford the cost of normal upkeep. As a result, housing deteriorates, and the supply curve shifts to the left.

New York is also experiencing an enormous rate of abandonment—houses are simply being left to their fate by landlords seeking to escape deteriorating neighborhoods, high taxes, and rising maintenance and heating costs. It is estimated that New York is losing in this way about 10 percent of its housing stock per decade; an astounding 33,000 housing units per year are being abandoned. In addition, landlords who have been able to get away with it have removed property in good condition from the rental housing market. Many apartment buildings have been converted, illegally, into office space in order to escape controls. Many others have been legally converted to condominiums. All of this suggests that the underlying housing shortage becomes more serious the longer controls remain in effect.

As is usual when there is an attempt to interfere with the market, rent controls have spawned a variety of devices designed to circumvent the law. The

Rent Controls and Off-Campus Living

In 1978, the city of Berkeley, California, passed a rent-control ordinance. Two years later, students at the University of California in Berkeley were learning about the economics of rent controls the hard way, as this newspaper report shows.

"I was told that finding housing here should be pretty bad, but I had no idea it was going to be this bad," said 18-year-old Andy Silberman.

"I've come here four days in a row," added Silberman, who lives in the San Jose suburb of Saratoga, 60 miles south. "I leave around 9 A.M., get here at 10, stay till about 6. I feel like I'm commuting to a job."

It's a job that hasn't paid. Although he's spent two tanks of gas and 32 hours of effort looking for lodging, Silberman still has no place to stay in Berkeley. All he's gotten, he said, is $16 in parking tickets.

A graduate student with an electrical-engineering degree had been walking the streets for four days in search of a home. The brightest prospect so far, he said, is a $135 room with no cooking privileges.

He sat down with a sigh. "I've never been in a position where I have had to sell myself to get an apartment. Before, I only had to look presentable. Now, people want female vegetarians who lean toward socialism and eat dinner promptly at 5 P.M."

SOURCE: Cynthia Kadonaga, *The Los Angeles Times*, September 11, 1980, with special thanks to Professor Robert J. Michaels of California State University, Fullerton, for pointing out the example.

black market in housing operates in a variety of ways: through bribes, "key money" paid to put the prospective tenant higher on the waiting list, or by requiring the purchase of worthless furniture at inflated prices. Often, controls are evaded by reselling the apartments to their tenants (at free-market prices or higher) so that the apartments become owner-occupied dwellings totally exempt from controls. In New York, the fraction of dwellings that are owner occupied increased 40 percent between 1950 and 1980.

Rent Controls: General Conclusions

Several observations sum up the consequences of rent controls:

1. ***Rent controls are likely to have a disastrous effect upon the supply of housing***—leading to deterioration, abandonment, and other forms of removal from the market. One economist (who is, incidentally, politically quite left of center) remarked that rent controls are probably not as effective as wartime bombing in destroying a city but that he would not be surprised if the facts showed things to be the other way around.

2. ***Once adopted, rent controls, like other price controls, are very difficult to eliminate.*** A tenant who has paid thousands of dollars in "key money" for the right to move into a rent-controlled apartment will, with some justice, feel cheated if the controls for which he paid so dearly are suddenly lifted. This example illustrates a very general problem with price controls. Those who benefit from controls usually have had to pay for the privilege; so they will suffer a considerable loss if the controls are eliminated. Such a group typically forms a powerful lobby for retention of the controls.

3. ***Paradoxically, rent controls may in the long run actually increase rents***—even those paid on controlled apartments. When controls cause the supply curve of housing to shift to the left, as they do when buildings are

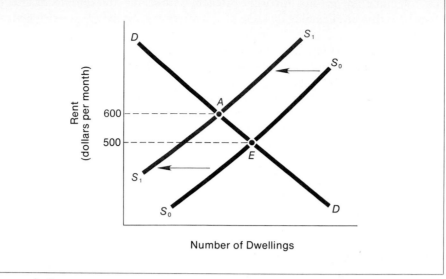

Figure 4–8

THE LONG-RUN EFFECTS OF RENT CONTROLS ON EQUILIBRIUM RENTS

In the long run, rent controls will do more than just decrease quantity supplied; they will shift the entire supply curve to the left. This happens when buildings deteriorate, are abandoned by their owners, or are converted to other uses (such as office space). In this example, when the supply curve shifts inward from S_0S_0 to S_1S_1, the equilibrium level of rent rises from $500 to $600. Thus, even if controls manage to keep actual rents below equilibrium levels, they may nevertheless lead to higher rents.

abandoned or converted to office space, the equilibrium price will rise, as the supply–demand diagram in Figure 4–8 readily confirms. Thus, even if controlled rents are kept, say, at a steady 90 percent of their equilibrium level, tenants end up paying more than they would have in the absence of the controls. For example, suppose that as a result of controls, rent on an apartment that initially had an equilibrium level of $500 a month rises to an equilibrium value of $600. Then, even if controls hold rents 10 percent below equilibrium, the apartment will cost 90 percent of $600, or $540 per month— $40 higher than the original monthly rental.

4. *Because the quantity demanded of rent-controlled apartments exceeds the quantity supplied, some device (or some person) must decide who gets the available apartments.* This can lead to political favoritism, to corruption in government, or to discrimination along racial or religious lines.

We conclude that rent controls cannot suppress the underlying market forces. They only succeed in deflecting these forces, leading to results far from the intentions of the authorities. While it may be desirable to provide inexpensive housing to those who otherwise could not afford it, this should be done by providing the requisite subsidy funds out of taxes. For there is no act of magic that will reduce rents. The market mechanism is a tough bird, which imposes suitable retribution on those who seek to circumvent it by legislative decree.

A Can of Worms

So rent controls cause shortages, are hard to get rid of, and may even drive rents upward rather than downward. These problems also attend other forms of price control; but they are not the only problems. It seems appropriate to end this chapter with a brief catalog of some of the other disadvantages of price controls.

Unenforceability

Attempts to control prices are almost certain to fail in industries with numerous suppliers, simply because the regulating agency must monitor the behavior of so many sellers. Some ways will be found to evade or to violate the law, and something akin to the free-market price will generally reemerge. But there is a difference: since the evasion mechanism, whatever its form, will have some operating costs, those costs must be borne by someone. That someone will be the consumer.

Auxiliary Restrictions

Fears that a system of price controls will break down invariably lead to regulations designed to shore up the shaky edifice. Consumers may be told when and from whom they are permitted to buy. The powers of the police and the courts may be used to prevent the entry of new suppliers. Occasionally, an intricate system of market subdivision is imposed, giving each firm its protected category of operations in which others are not permitted to compete. An example was provided for many years by the regulation of banking in the United States. As part of the process of controlling interest rates, banks were classified into different categories—investment banks, commercial banks, savings banks, and savings and loan associations—each with an assigned set of permissible interest rates and a set of activities at least partly protected from incursion by others. For example, to keep down interest rates, consumers were "protected" by law from receiving interest on checking accounts issued by commercial banks. To prevent these banks from suffering "undue" competition by savings banks, which could pay interest, it was therefore necessary to prevent savings banks from issuing checks. Fortunately, these regulations are now gradually being phased out, and consumers will soon be able to earn reasonable interest rates on their deposits.

Discounts That Take Unwanted Forms

Where prices are controlled, regulation prohibits firms from competing for customers in the way the customers want most—by lowering prices. Hence, firms in regulated industries have often resorted to second-best means of competition. Banks have given away cameras and power tools in lieu of higher interest rates. Airlines have attired their stewardesses in attractive costumes instead of lowering fares. But how many dollars is the display of that Italian designer's outfit really worth to the passenger?

Limitation of Volume of Transactions

To the extent that controls succeed in affecting prices, they can be expected to reduce the volume of transactions. Curiously, this is true whether the regulated price is above or below the free-market's equilibrium price. If it is set above the equilibrium price, quantity demanded will be below the equilibrium quantity. On the other hand, if the imposed price is set below the free-market level, quantity supplied will be cut down. Since sales volume cannot exceed either the quantity supplied or the quantity demanded, a reduction in the volume of transactions is likely to result.

Encouragement of Inefficiency

A price that is above the equilibrium level permits the survival of less-efficient firms whose high operating costs would doom them in an unrestricted market. This invitation to continued inefficiency becomes even more serious if entry of new suppliers is prevented as part of the program of enforcement of price regulations. (This is why deregulation of an industry typically entails a painful "shake out" of the weaker firms.) Moreover, with the penalties for inefficiency severely restricted, the motivation for continued economy of operation by any firm is reduced.

Misallocation of Resources

Economists emphasize that departures from free-market prices are likely to produce misuse of the economy's resources—its fuel, raw materials, and labor supply—because the connection between production costs and prices is broken. For example, shippers use trucks or barges over routes where the resource cost of rail transportation is lower because artificial restrictions impose floors on railroad rates. In addition, just as more complex locks lead to more sophisticated burglary tools, more complex regulations lead to the use of yet more resources for their avoidance. New jobs are created for executives, lawyers, and economists. It may well be conjectured that at least some of the expensive services of these professionals could have been used more productively elsewhere.

Summary

1. The demand for a product cannot be expressed by a fixed number. Rather, there is generally a different quantity demanded at each price at which the product is offered. This relationship is displayed graphically in a demand curve.

2. For most products, the higher the price, the lower the quantity demanded. So the demand curve usually has a negative slope.

3. Price also affects the quantity of a commodity that is supplied, leading to the graphical relationship we call the supply curve. A positively sloping curve for a given product means that an increase in price is necessary to induce suppliers to offer a larger quantity.

4. A market is said to be in equilibrium when quantity supplied is equal to quantity demanded. The equilibrium price and quantity is shown by the point on a graph where the supply and demand curves intersect. In a free market, price and quantity will tend to gravitate to this point.

5. A change in quantity demanded that is caused by a change in price of the good is represented by a movement along a fixed demand curve. A change in quantity demanded that is caused by a change in any other determinant of quantity demanded is represented by a shift of the demand curve.

6. This same distinction applies to the supply curve: Changes in price lead to movements along a fixed supply curve; changes in other determinants of quantity supplied lead to shifts of the whole supply curve.

7. Changes in consumer incomes, tastes, technology, prices of competing products, and many other influences cause shifts in either the demand curve or the supply curve and produce changes in price and quantity that can be determined from supply—demand diagrams.

8. An attempt by government regulations to force prices above or below their equilibrium levels is likely to lead to shortages or oversupplies, black markets in which goods are sold at illegal prices, and to a variety of other problems. This is one of the 12 Ideas for Beyond the Final Exam.

Concepts for Review

Demand curve
Supply curve
Supply—demand diagram

Equilibrium price and quantity
Equilibrium

Shifts in vs. movements along supply and demand curves
Price ceilings and floors

Questions for Discussion

1. How often do you go to the movies? Would you go less often if a ticket cost twice as much? Distinguish between your demand curve for movie tickets and your "quantity demanded" at the current price.

2. What would you expect to be the shape of a demand curve
   a. for a type of medicine that means life or death for a patient?
   b. for the gasoline sold by Sam's gas station, which is surrounded by many other gas stations?

3. The following are the assumed supply and demand schedules for transistor radios:

	DEMAND		SUPPLY
PRICE	QUANTITY DEMANDED	PRICE	QUANTITY SUPPLIED
$30	10,000	$30	110,000
25	50,000	25	50,000
20	90,000	20	40,000
15	110,000	15	25,000
10	150,000	10	0

   a. Plot the supply and demand curves and indicate the equilibrium price and quantity.
   b. What effect will an increase in the price of copper wire (a production input) have on the equilibrium price and quantity of transistor radios (assuming all other things remain constant)? Explain your answer with the help of a diagram.
   c. What effect will a decrease in the price of television sets (a substitute commodity) have on the equilibrium price and quantity of transistor radios (assuming again that all other things are held constant)? Use a diagram in your answer.

4. Assume that the supply and demand schedules for wheat are the following:

PRICE	QUANTITY DEMANDED (millions of bushels)	QUANTITY SUPPLIED (millions of bushels)
$6	3	21
4	12	12
2	21	3

   a. Suppose that the government sets a floor under the price of wheat at $6. Which is greater, the quantity demanded or the quantity supplied? What will be the effect on the wheat market?
   b. Now assume that the government abolishes the minimum price for wheat. What will happen to the price and the quantity of wheat consumed?
   c. Now assume that the government sets a ceiling on the price of wheat at $2. What would be the effect on the wheat market?

5. Show how the following demand curves are likely to shift in response to the indicated changes:
   a. the effect on the demand curve for umbrellas when rainfall increases
   b. the effect on the demand curve for tea when coffee prices rise
   c. the effect on the demand curve for tea when sugar prices rise

6. Discuss the likely effects of
   a. rent ceilings on the supply of apartments
   b. minimum wages on the demand for teen-age workers
   Use supply-demand diagrams to show what may happen in each case.

7. Drinking water is costly to supply. Draw a supply–demand diagram showing how much water would be bought if water were supplied by a private industry controlled by supply and demand. In the same diagram show how much will be consumed if water is supplied by a city government at zero charge. What do you conclude from these results about areas of the country in which water is in short supply?

8. (More difficult) Consider the market for natural gas discussed in this chapter (Tables 4–1 and 4–2, Figures 4–1 through 4–3). Suppose the government decides to promote conservation by levying a tax of $2 per thousand cubic feet on purchases of natural gas. Follow these steps to analyze the effects of the tax:
   a. Construct the new demand curve (to replace Table 4–1) that relates quantity demanded to the price *including tax*. (*Hint:* Before the tax, when producers charged $5, consumers purchased 40 billion cubic feet. With a $2 tax, when producers charge $5 consumers will have to pay $7. Table 4–1 tells us they will purchase only 10 billion cubic feet at this price. This is one point on the new demand curve. The rest of the curve can be constructed in the same way.)
   b. Graph the new demand curve constructed in part (a) on the supply–demand diagram depicted in Figure 4–3. What is the new equilibrium price and quantity?
   c. Does the tax succeed in its goal of promoting conservation?
   d. How much does the equilibrium price increase? Is the price rise greater than, equal to, or less than the $2 tax?
   e. Who actually pays the tax, consumers or producers? (This may be a good question to discuss in class.)

II
Macroeconomics

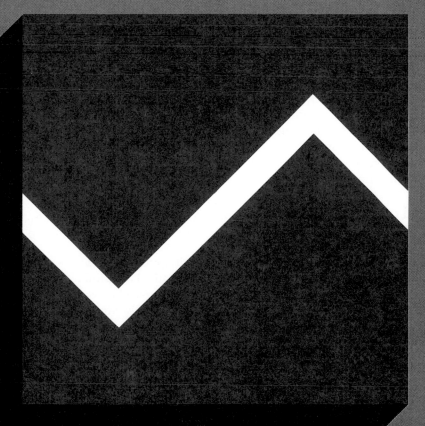

Macroeconomics and Microeconomics

5

"Where the telescope ends,
the microscope begins.
Which of the two has the grander view?"

VICTOR HUGO

Economics traditionally has been divided into two fields: microeconomics and macroeconomics. These rather inelegant words are derived from the Greek—"micro" means something small and "macro" means something large. Although they were not specifically described as such, the basic notions and subject matter of **microeconomics** were introduced in Chapters 3 and 4. This chapter does the same for **macroeconomics.**

We begin the chapter by investigating the dividing line between microeconomics and macroeconomics: How do the two parts of the discipline differ and why? Next, we stress that while the *questions* studied by macroeconomists differ from those addressed by microeconomists, the underlying *tools* each group uses are almost the same. Supply and demand provide the basic organizing framework for constructing macroeconomic models, just as they do for microeconomic models. Third, we define some important macroeconomic concepts, like recession, inflation, and gross national product. Fourth, we look briefly at the broad sweep of American economic history to obtain some evaluation of the prevalence and seriousness of the macroeconomic problems of recession and inflation. And, finally, we preview what is to come in subsequent chapters by introducing the notion of government management of the economy.

Drawing a Line Between Macroeconomics and Microeconomics

In microeconomics *we study the behavior of individual decision-making units.* The landlords and tenants of Chapter 4 are all individual decision-making units; so are the homeowners and firms who purchase natural gas. How do they decide what courses of action are in their own best interests? How are these millions of decisions coordinated by the market mechanism, and with what consequences? Questions like these are the substance of microeconomics and are taken up in Parts Three through Six.

Although Plato and Aristotle might wince at the abuse of their language, microeconomics applies to the decisions of some astonishingly large units. Exxon and the American Telephone and Telegraph Company, for instance, have annual sales that exceed the total production of many nations. Yet someone who studies the pricing policies of AT&T is a microeconomist, whereas someone who studies inflation in Trinidad–Tobago is a macroeconomist. So the micro versus macro distinction in economics is certainly not predicated solely on size.

What, then, is the basis for this time-honored distinction? Whereas microeconomics focuses on the decisions of individual units (no matter how large), *macroeconomics concentrates on the behavior of entire economies* (no matter how small). Rather than looking at the price and output decisions of a single company, macroeconomists study the overall price level, unemployment rate, and other things that we call **economic aggregates.**

Aggregation and Macroeconomics

What is an "economic aggregate?" Nothing but an *abstraction* that people find convenient in describing some salient feature of economic life. For example, while we observe the prices of butter, telephone calls, and movie tickets every day, we never observe "the price level." Yet many people (not only economists) find it both natural and convenient to speak of "the cost of living"—so convenient, in fact, that the Bureau of Labor Statistics' monthly attempts at measuring it are widely publicized by the news media.

Among the most important of these abstract notions is the concept of **national product,** which represents the total production of a nation's economy. The process by which real objects like hairpins, baseballs, cigarettes, and theater tickets get combined into an abstraction called national product is called **aggregation,** and it is one of the foundations of macroeconomics. We can illustrate it by a simple example.

Imagine a nation called Agraria, whose economy is far simpler than the U.S. economy: Business firms in Agraria produce nothing but foodstuffs to sell to consumers. Rather than deal separately with all the markets for pizzas, candy bars, hamburgers, and so on, macroeconomists group them all into a single abstract "market for output." Thus, when macroeconomists in Agraria announce that "firms in Agraria produced 10 percent more output this year than last year," are they referring to more potatoes or hot dogs, more soybeans or green peppers? The answer is: They do not care! In the aggregate measures of macroeconomics, output is output, no matter what form it takes.

Amalgamating the many markets into one means that distinctions among the different products are ignored. Can we really believe that no one cares whether the national output of Agraria consists of $800,000 worth of pickles and $200,000 worth of ravioli rather than $500,000 each of lettuce and tomatoes? Surely this is too much to swallow. Macroeconomists clearly do not believe that no one cares; instead, they rest the case for aggregation on two foundations.

First: While the *composition* of demand and supply in the various markets may be terribly interesting and important for *some* purposes (such as how income is distributed and what kinds of diets the citizens enjoy or endure), it may be of little consequence for the economy-wide issues of inflation and unemployment—the issues that concern macroeconomists.

Second: During economic fluctuations, markets tend to move in unison. When demand in the economy rises, there is more demand for potatoes *and* tomatoes, more demand for artichokes *and* pickles, more demand for ravioli *and* hot dogs.

Though there are exceptions to these two principles, they both seem serviceable enough as approximations. In fact, if they were not, there would be no discipline called macroeconomics, and this book would be only half as long as it is. (Lest this cause you a twinge of regret, bear in mind that unemployment and inflation would be far more difficult to control without macroeconomics, and that would be even more regrettable.)

The Line of Demarcation Revisited

These two principles—that markets normally move together and that the composition of demand and supply may be unimportant for some purposes—enable us to draw a different kind of dividing line between the territories of microeconomics and macroeconomics.

In macroeconomics, we typically assume that most details of resource allocation and income distribution are of secondary importance to the study of the overall rates of inflation and unemployment.

In microeconomics, we typically ignore inflation and unemployment and focus instead on how individual markets allocate resources and distribute income.

To use a well-worn metaphor, the macroeconomist analyzes the determination of the size of the economic "pie," paying scant attention to what is inside it or to how it gets divided among the dinner guests. A microeconomist, on the other hand, assumes that the pie is of the right size and shape, and frets over its ingredients and its division. If you have ever baked or eaten a pie, you will realize that either approach alone is a trifle myopic.

In some chapters of this book (especially in Part Two), macroeconomic issues are discussed as if they could be divorced from questions of resource allocation and income distribution. In other chapters (especially those in Parts Three through Six), microeconomic problems are investigated with scarcely a word about overall inflation and unemployment. Only much later in the book (especially in Part Seven) are the two modes of analysis brought to bear simultaneously on the same social problems. This is done solely for the sake of pedagogical clarity. In reality, the crucial interconnection between macroeconomics and microeconomics is with us all the time. There is, after all, only one economy.

Supply and Demand in Macroeconomics

Some students reading this book will be taking a course that concentrates on macroeconomics while others will be studying microeconomics. The discussion of supply and demand in Chapter 4 serves as an invaluable introduction to both fields because the basic apparatus of supply and demand is just as important in macroeconomics as it is in microeconomics.

Figure 5–1 shows two diagrams that should look familiar from Chapter 4. In Figure 5–1(a), there is a downward-sloping demand curve, labeled DD, and an upward-sloping supply curve, labeled SS. The axes labeled "Price" and "Quantity" do not specify what commodity they refer to because this is a multipurpose diagram. To start on familiar terrain, first imagine that this is a picture of the market for natural gas, so the price axis measures the price of gas while the quantity axis measures the quantity of gas demanded and supplied. As we know, if there are no interferences with the operation of a free market, equilibrium will be at point E with a price P_0 and a quantity of output Q_0.

Next, suppose something happens to shift the demand curve outward. For example, we learned in Chapter 4 that an increase in consumer incomes might do

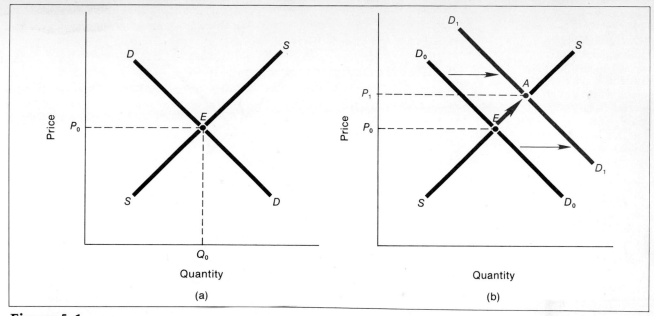

Figure 5–1

TWO INTERPRETATIONS OF A SHIFT IN THE DEMAND CURVE

Part (a) shows an equilibrium at point E, where demand curve DD intersects supply curve SS. Part (b) shows how this equilibrium moves from point E to point A if the demand curve moves outward. If this graph represents the market for natural gas, as it did in the previous chapter, then it shows an increase in the price of gas. But if the graph represents the aggregate market for "national product," then it shows inflation—a rise in the general price level.

this. Figure 5–1(b) shows this shift as a rightward movement of the demand curve from $D_0 D_0$ to $D_1 D_1$. Equilibrium has shifted from E to A, so both price and output have risen.

Now let us reinterpret Figure 5–1 as representing an abstract market for "national product." This is one of those abstractions—an economic aggregate—that we described earlier. No one has ever seen, touched, smelled, or eaten a "unit of national product," but these are the kinds of abstractions upon which macroeconomic analysis is built. Consistent with this reinterpretation, think of the price measured on the vertical axis as being another abstraction—the overall price index, or "cost of living."[1] Then curve DD in Figure 5–1(a) is called an **aggregate demand curve,** and curve SS is called an **aggregate supply curve.**

With this reinterpretation, Figure 5–1(b) can depict the macroeconomic problem of **inflation,** that is, of rising prices. We see from the figure that the outward shift of the aggregate demand curve, whatever its cause, pushes the price level up from P_0 to P_1. If aggregate demand keeps shifting out month after month, the economy will suffer from inflation.

The other principal problems of macroeconomics, recession and unemployment, also can be illustrated on a supply–demand diagram, this time by shifting the demand curve in the opposite direction. Figure 5–2 repeats the supply and demand curves of Figure 5–1(a) and in addition depicts a leftward shift of the aggregate demand curve from $D_0 D_0$ to $D_2 D_2$. Equilibrium now moves from point E to point B so that national product (total output) declines from Q_0 to Q_2. This is what we normally mean by a **recession.**

[1]The appendix to Chapter 6 explains how such price indexes are calculated.

Inflation refers to a sustained *increase* in the general price level. **Deflation** refers to a sustained *decrease* in the general price level.

A **recession** is a period of time during which the total output of the economy declines.

Figure 5–2

AN ECONOMY SLIPPING
INTO A RECESSION
In this aggregate supply–
demand diagram, there is an
initial equilibrium at point E,
where demand curve $D_0 D_0$
intersects supply curve SS.
When the demand curve falls
from $D_0 D_0$ to $D_2 D_2$, equilibrium
moves to point B, and output
falls from Q_0 to Q_2.

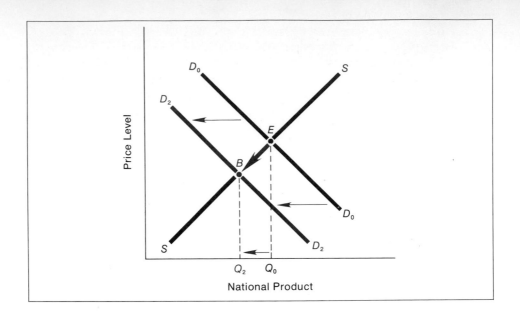

Gross National Product

The economy's total output, we have just seen, is one of the major variables of concern to macroeconomists. While there are several ways to measure it, the most popular choice undoubtedly is the **gross national product,** a term you have probably encountered in the news media. The gross national product, or "GNP" for short, is the most comprehensive measure of the output of all the factories, offices, and shops in the U.S. economy. Several features of the definition of GNP need to be underscored.[2] First, you will notice that:

We add up the *money values* of things.

Gross national product (GNP) is the sum of the money values of all final goods and services produced by the economy during a specified period of time, usually one year.

The GNP consists of a bewildering variety of goods and services: mousetraps and computers, bologna and caviar, ballet performances and rock concerts, tanks and textbooks. How are we to combine all of these into a single number? To an economist, the natural way to do this is first to convert every good and service into *money* terms. If we want to add 10 apples and 20 oranges, we first ask: How much *money* does each cost? If apples cost 20 cents and oranges cost 25 cents, then the apples count for $2 and the oranges for $5, so the sum is $7 worth of "output." The market *price* of each good or service is used as an indicator of its *value* to society simply because *someone* is willing to pay that much money for it.

This decision raises the question of what prices to use in valuing the different outputs. The official data offer two choices. First, we can value each good and service at the price at which it was actually sold during the year. If we do this, the resulting measure is called **nominal GNP,** or *money GNP*, or *GNP in current dollars*. This seems like a perfectly sensible choice. But as a measure of output, it has one serious drawback: nominal GNP rises when prices rise, even if there is no increase in actual production. For example, if hamburgers cost $1 this year but cost only 75 cents last year, then 100 hamburgers will contribute $100 to this year's nominal GNP but only $75 to last year's. But 100 hamburgers are still 100

Nominal GNP is calculated by valuing all outputs at current prices.

---

[2]Certain exceptions to the definition, which are not important here, are noted in the appendix to Chapter 7, especially on pages 130–131.

hamburgers—output has not grown.

For this reason, government statisticians have devised an alternative measure that corrects for inflation by valuing all goods and services at some fixed set of prices. (Currently, the prices of 1972 are used.) For example, if the hamburgers were valued at 75 cents each in both years, $75 worth of hamburger output would be included in GNP in each year. When we treat every output in this way, we obtain the **real GNP** or *GNP in constant dollars.* The news media often refer to it as "GNP corrected for inflation." Throughout most of this book, and certainly when we are discussing the nation's output, it is the real GNP that we shall be concerned with. The distinction between nominal and real GNP leads us to a working definition of a *recession* as a period in which *real* GNP declines. For example, between 1974 and 1975, nominal GNP rose from $1434 billion to $1549 billion; but real GNP *fell* from $1248 billion to $1234 billion.

The next important aspect of the definition of GNP is that:

The GNP for a particular year includes only goods and services produced during that year. Sales of items produced in previous years are explicitly excluded.

For example, suppose you buy a perfectly beautiful 1971 Plymouth next week and are overjoyed by your purchase. The national income statistician will not share your glee because she already counted your car in the GNP in 1971 when it was first produced and sold; the car will never be counted again. The same holds true of houses. An old house (unlike an old car) often will sell for more than its purchasers originally paid, yet the resale value of the house does not count in the GNP since it was already counted in the year it was built. For the same reason, transactions on the stock market and other exchanges of existing assets are not included in the GNP.

Third, you will note the use of the phrase **final goods and services** in the definition. The adjective "final" is the key word here. For example, when the gas company buys gas from an interstate pipeline company, the transaction is not included in the GNP because the gas compay does not want the gas for itself. It buys gas only for resale to homeowners. Only when the gas is sold to homeowners is it considered a final product. When the gas company buys it, economists consider it an **intermediate good.** The GNP does not include sales of intermediate goods or services.

Finally, although the definition does not state this explicitly:

For the most part, only goods and services that pass through organized markets count in the GNP.

This, of course, excludes many economic activities. For example, illegal activities are not included in the GNP. Thus, gambling services in Chicago are not in the GNP, but gambling services in Las Vegas are. The definition reflects the statisticians' confession that they could not hope to measure the value of many of the economy's most important activities, such as housework, do-it-yourself repairs, and leisure time. While these are certainly economic activities that result in currently produced goods or services, they all lack that important measuring rod—a price.

This omission results in certain oddities. For example, suppose that each of two neighboring families hires the other to clean house, generously paying $1000 a week for the services. Each family can easily afford such generosity since it collects an identical salary from its neighbor. Nothing real changes, but GNP goes up by $100,000 a year. If this example seems foolish, consider the effect that the

Real GNP is calculated by valuing all outputs at the prices that prevailed in some agreed-upon year (currently 1972). Therefore, real GNP is a far better measure of changes in national production.

Final goods and services are those that are purchased by their ultimate users.

An **intermediate good** is a good purchased for resale or for use in producing another good.

women's liberation movement might have on the GNP. Presumably, more and more housework will be done by hired men and women (and thus channeled through the market) and less and less will be done by unpaid housewives. Thus more housework will count in the GNP, and billions of dollars may be added to the GNP in this way.

The Economy on a Roller Coaster

We have now defined several of the basic concepts of macroeconomics. To breathe some life into them, let us briefly peruse the economic history of the United States. Figures 5–3 and 5–4 provide a capsule summary of this history since the Civil War. Figure 5–3 charts the behavior of real GNP over a period of approximately 100 years. The pronounced upward slope of the line indicates that the main feature has been economic growth. But the figure also shows that recessions—periods during which the real GNP decreased—have been a persistent feature of America's economic performance.

The history of the price level (Figure 5–4) displays a broadly similar pattern, but one that differs in some important respects. Prices also have been generally rising—that is, inflation has been much more common than deflation—but there have been several periods of marked price stability, such as 1922–1929. And there

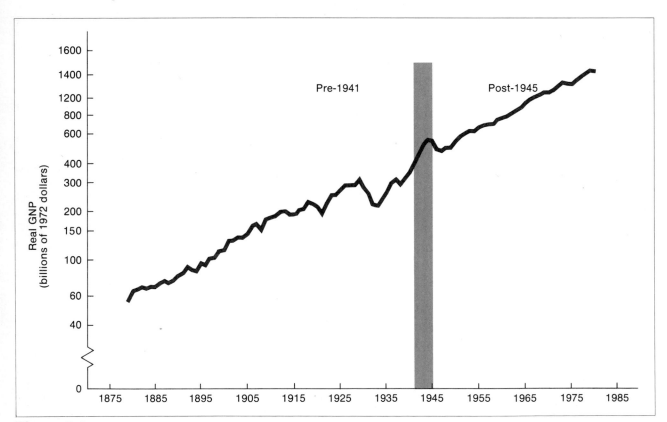

Figure 5–3
REAL GROSS NATIONAL PRODUCT OF THE UNITED STATES, 1879–1981
This time series chart displays the behavior of real gross national product in the United States from 1879 to 1981. (Here real GNP is measured in 1972 prices.) The Great Depression (1929–1933) stands out vividly. The years during World War II are shaded. Does the line look smoother to the right of this shaded area? Notice that the vertical axis is calibrated by what is called a "ratio scale." This means, for example, that the distance between 1000 and 100 is the same as the distance between 100 and 10.
SOURCE: Constructed by the authors from Commerce Department data for 1889–1981. Data for 1879–1888 were kindly furnished by Professor Benjamin Klein.

have also been periods, generally in serious recessions or depressions, in which prices have fallen, such as 1929–1933.

The following exercise may be enlightening. Cover the portions of Figures 5–3 and 5–4 that deal with the period beginning in 1941, the portions to the right of the shaded area in each figure. The picture that emerges for the 1867–1940 period is of an economy on a roller coaster. In Figure 5–3, the ups and downs around the underlying growth trend are frequent and sometimes quite pronounced. In Figure 5–4 we see periods of both inflation and deflation, with hardly any upward trend at all. Indeed, prices at the eve of World War II were not much higher than they were at the close of the Civil War.

Now do the reverse. Cover the data prior to 1946 and look only at the postwar period. There is, indeed, a difference. The upward trend in real GNP predominates more, and the periodic recessions are much less severe. While perfection has not been achieved, things do look much better. When we turn to the price level, however, things look rather worse. Gone are the periods of falling prices that occurred before World War II; even the periods of price stability are rather rare.

This quick inspection of the data suggests that something has happened. The U.S. economy behaved differently in 1946–1981 than it did in 1867–1940. Many economists attribute this shift in the economy's behavior to lessons the government has learned about managing the economy—lessons that we will be learning

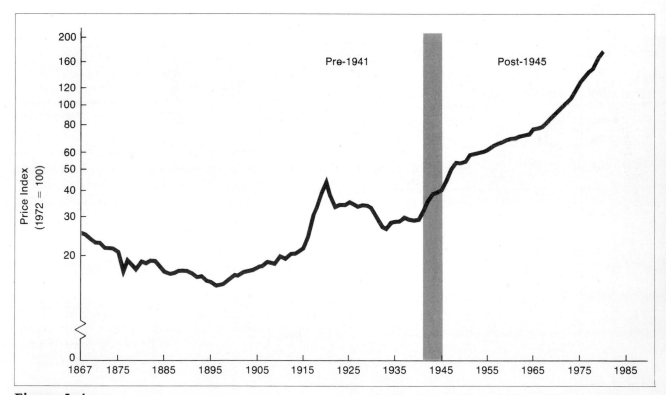

Figure 5–4
THE PRICE LEVEL IN THE UNITED STATES, 1867–1981
This time series chart portrays the behavior of the U.S. price level from 1867 to 1981. (The specific price index used is called the *GNP deflator*, and it is defined as the ratio of nominal GNP divided by real GNP.) Once again, the vertical axis has a ratio scale, and the World War II years are shaded. The difference between the 1867–1940 period and the 1946–1981 period is quite pronounced.
SOURCE: Constructed by the authors from Commerce Department data for 1889–1981. Data for 1867–1888 were kindly furnished by Professor Benjamin Klein.

in Part Two. When you look at the pre-1941 data, you are looking at an unmanaged economy that went through booms and recessions for "natural" economic reasons. The government did little about either. When you examine the post-1945 data, on the other hand, you are looking at an economy that has been increasingly managed by government policy—sometimes successfully and sometimes unsuccessfully. While the recessions are less severe, a cost seems to have been exacted: the economy appears to be more inflation-prone than it was in the more distant past.

The Great Depression of the 1930s

As you look at these graphs, the Great Depression of the 1930s is bound to catch your eye. The decline in economic activity from 1929 to 1933 (see Figure 5–3) was the most severe in our nation's history, and the rapid deflation (see Figure 5–4) was most unusual. The Depression is but a dim memory now, but those who lived through it will never forget it.

While statistics usually conceal the true drama of economic events, this is not so of the Great Depression—they stand here as a bitter testimony to its severity. From its 1929 high to its 1933 low, the production of goods and services dropped 30 percent and the price level fell 23 percent. Business investment almost ceased entirely, and stock market values slumped to less than one-sixth their 1929 level. The unemployment rate rose ominously from about 3 percent in 1929 to 25 percent in 1933—one person in four was jobless. From the data alone, one can virtually conjure up pictures of soup lines, beggars on street corners, closed factories, and homeless families. (See the boxed insert on the next page.) Unlike many earlier and later recessions that plagued the U.S. economy, the Great Depression was a worldwide event. No country was spared its ravages. This traumatic episode literally changed the history of many nations. In Germany, it facilitated the ascendancy of the Nazi party. In the United States, it enabled Franklin Roosevelt's Democratic party to engineer one of the most dramatic political realignments in history and to push through a host of political and economic reforms.

The worldwide depression also caused a much-needed revolution in the thinking of economists. Up until the 1930s, the prevailing economic theory held that a capitalist economy, while it occasionally misbehaved, had a "natural" tendency to cure recessions or inflations by itself. The roller coaster bounced around but did not normally run off the tracks.

This optimistic view was not confined to academia. It characterized the views of most politicians (certainly including President Herbert Hoover) and business leaders as well. As the great American humorist Will Rogers remarked with characteristic sarcasm:

It's almost been worth this depression to find out how little our big men knew. Mayby [sic] this depression is just "normalcy" and we don't know it. It's made a dumb guy as smart as a smart one. . . . Depression used to be a state of mind. Now it's a state of coma, now it's permanent. Last year we said, "Things can't go on like this," and they didn't, they got worse.[3]

The stubbornness of the Great Depression shook almost everyone's faith in the ability of the economy to right itself. In Cambridge, England, this questioning attitude led John Maynard Keynes, one of the world's most respected economists,

[3]From *Sanity Is Where You Find It* by Will Rogers, edited by Donald Day; copyright ©1955 by Rogers Company; reprinted by permission of Houghton Mifflin Company; pages 120–21.

Life in "Hooverville"

During the worst years of the Great Depression, unemployed workers often congregated in shantytowns on the outskirts of many major cities. Conditions in these slums were deplorable. With a heavy dose of irony, these communities were known as "Hoovervilles," in honor of the president of the United States who preached rugged individualism. A contemporary observer described a Hooverville in New York City as follows:

It was a fairly popular "development" made up of a hundred or so dwellings, each the size of a dog house or chickencoop, often constructed with much ingenuity out of wooden boxes, metal cans, strips of cardboard or old tar paper. Here human beings lived on the margin of civilization by foraging for garbage, junk, and waste lumber. I found some splitting or sawing wood with dull tools to make fires; others were picking through heaps of rubbish they had gathered before their doorways or cooking over open fires or battered oilstoves. Still others spent their days improving their rent-free homes, making them sometimes fairly solid and weatherproof. . . . Most of them, according to the police, lived by begging or trading in junk; when all else failed they ate at the soup kitchens or public canteens. They were of all sorts, young and old, some of them rough-looking and suspicious of strangers. They lived in fear of being forcibly removed by the authorities,

A Hooverville in New York City.

though the neighborhood people in many cases helped them and the police tolerated them for the time being.

SOURCE: Mathew Josephson, *Infidel in the Temple* (New York: Alfred A. Knopf, 1967), pages 82–83.

---

to write *The General Theory of Employment, Interest, and Money* (1936). Probably the most important book in economics of the twentieth century, it carried a rather revolutionary message. Keynes discarded the notion that the economy always gravitated toward high levels of employment, replacing it with the assertion that—if a pessimistic outlook led business firms and consumers to curtail their spending plans—the economy might be condemned to stagnation for years and years.

While this doleful prognosis sounded all too realistic at the time, Keynes closed his book on a hopeful note. For he showed how government actions might prod the economy out of its depressed state. The lessons he taught the world then are the lessons we shall be learning in Part Two. They show how governments can manage their economies so that recessions will not turn into depressions and depressions will not last as long as the Great Depression. While Keynes was working on *The General Theory*, he wrote his friend George Bernard Shaw that, "I believe myself to be writing a book on economic theory which will largely revolutionize . . . the way the world thinks about economic problems." In many ways, he was right.

From World War II to the 1970s

The Great Depression finally ended when the country mobilized for war in the early 1940s. With total spending at extraordinarily high levels during the war, mostly because of government expenditures, the economy boomed and the unemployment rate fell as low as 1.2 percent.

Wartime spending of this magnitude usually leads to inflation, but much of the potential inflation during World War II was contained by the legal limitations that were set on prices. With prices held below the levels at which quantity supplied equaled quantity demanded, many goods had to be rationed, and shortages of consumer goods were quite common. All of this ended with the lifting of controls after the war. The shortages, rationing, and black markets were replaced by a burst of inflation.

The period from the end of the war until the early 1960s showed a considerable resemblance to the earlier period of growth with recessions prior to 1929. The main difference was that the four recessions between 1948 and 1961 were noticeably shorter and less severe than their prewar counterparts. Moderate but persistent inflation also became a fact of life.

When the economy emerged from recession in 1961, it entered what proved to be the longest uninterrupted period of expansion in our nation's history. GNP grew smartly and unemployment declined steadily, while the price level, though continuing to rise, showed no tendency to accelerate.

The 1962–1966 boom was credited widely to the success of what came to be called "The New Economics," a term the media created for the policy of economic management prescribed by Keynes in the 1930s. For a while it looked as if we could avoid both unemployment and inflation. But the optimistic verdicts were premature in both cases.

Inflation was the first problem to crop up, beginning in about 1966. Its major cause, as it had been so many times in the past, was high levels of wartime spending—this time for the Vietnam War. Federal defense expenditures skyrocketed from $49 billion in 1965 to $77 billion in 1968, leading to an inflationary boom.

Unemployment was the next problem to arise. The economic expansion ground to a halt in 1969, and a short and mild recession ensued. Despite this, inflation continued at rates that were considered very high at the time—5 to 6 percent a year.

In the face of the persistent inflation, and with the economy beginning to pick up steam once again, President Richard Nixon instituted his "New Economic Policy" in a dramatic radio and television address to the nation in August 1971. This sweeping change in policy included America's first experiment with wage and price controls during peacetime. The controls program, which will be discussed in Chapter 17, held the inflation rate in check for a time as the economic expansion of 1971–1973 progressed. But inflation worsened dramatically in 1973, mainly because of the explosion in food prices caused by poor harvests around the world in 1972 and 1973.

The Great Stagflation, 1973–1975

Then, in October 1973, things began to get much worse, not only for the United States, but for all the oil-importing nations of the world. The war between Israel and the Arab nations led to an embargo on oil shipments to several Western countries and then to a quadrupling of the price of oil by the Organization of Petroleum Exporting Countries (OPEC). The rate of inflation skyrocketed in 1974 to levels not seen in this country since 1947.

While staggering price increases for oil and other energy resources were a principal component of this rapid inflation, they were not the only one.

Continued poor harvests in 1974 in many parts of the globe kept world food prices rising rapidly. Prices of other raw materials also skyrocketed. Naturally, these higher costs of fuel and other materials soon were reflected in the prices of manufactured goods.

By unhappy coincidence, these events coincided with the lifting of wage and price controls. The decontrol process began gradually in the closing months of 1973 and was complete by April 1974. Just as had happened after World War II, the elimination of controls led to an acceleration of inflation as prices that had been held artificially below equilibrium levels were allowed to rise.

For all these reasons, the inflation rate in the United States soared to above 12 percent during 1974. Most other nations suffered a similar inflationary surge—many much worse than ours.

Meanwhile, real GNP, which had stagnated but not declined during 1973, began to slide in 1974. In late 1974 and early 1975, this slide turned into a rout as the U.S. economy plummeted into its longest and most severe recession since the 1930s. In total, real GNP fell by about 5 percent between late 1973 and early 1975. The unemployment rate rose from less than 5 percent to nearly 9 percent over this same period. Thus, both the twin evils of macroeconomics—inflation and unemployment—were unusually virulent in 1974 and 1975. Indeed, a new term—**stagflation**—was coined to refer to the simultaneous occurrence of economic *stag*nation and rapid in*flation*.

Thanks partly to government actions, but mostly to natural economic forces, the economic collapse ended in the spring of 1975, and a gradual, sustained recovery began.

On the price front, three major forces contributed to a remarkably fast diminution of inflation in 1975 and 1976. First, the explosion in food and fuel prices was not repeated. These prices settled down at *levels* far higher than in the early 1970s, but ceased being engines of *inflation*. Second, the adjustment to the end of price controls ended in late 1974, and price behavior returned to normalcy. Third, just as had happened in the past, the severity of the recession put a brake on inflation. The inflation rate tumbled from over 12 percent a year in 1974 to a range of 5 to 7 percent during 1976 and 1977.

Stagflation Again, 1979–1981

But the price of oil began to misbehave again in 1979 when the revolution that deposed the shah of Iran caused a disruption in the flow of Iranian oil, thus sparking chaos in the world oil market. In a series of price increases, OPEC more than doubled the price of oil during 1979, and long lines of motorists waiting at gasoline stations were common in this country during the spring and summer months.

The consequences of OPEC's actions were similar to those of 1973–1975: stagflation returned. Inflation accelerated first—from a 9 percent rate in 1978 to over 13 percent in 1979 and then to an astonishing 16 percent during the first half of 1980. The accompanying recession was unusual both for its severity and its brevity. Output fell at an extraordinarily rapid rate, but the decline lasted for only about the first six months of 1980. During the second half of 1980, output began to recover and inflation receded into the 9–10 percent range. But the economy slipped into recession once again, and as 1981 ended the unemployment rate was near 9 percent though the inflation rate had fallen below 6 percent. Stagflation was with us once again.

The Problem
of Macroeconomic Stabilization

This brief look at the historical record shows that our economy has not generally produced a steady pattern of growth without inflation. Rather, it has been buffeted by periodic bouts of unemployment or inflation, and sometimes has been plagued by both. There was also a hint, in the discussion, that government policies may have had something to do with why macroeconomic performance during the years 1946 to 1973 was so vastly superior to what it had been prior to World War II. Let us now expand upon this hint a little bit.

We can provide a preliminary analysis of **stabilization policy** by using the basic tools of aggregate supply and aggregate demand analysis that were introduced early in this chapter. To facilitate this, we have reproduced as Figures 5–5 and 5–6 two of the diagrams found earlier in this chapter [Figures 5–1(b) and 5–2], but we now give them slightly different interpretations.

Figure 5–5 gives a simplified view of government policy to fight unemployment. We suppose that, in the absence of government intervention, the economy would have reached an equilibrium at point E, where demand curve D_0D_0 crosses supply curve SS. Now if the output corresponding to point E is so low that many workers are unemployed, *the government can reduce unemployment by increasing aggregate demand.* In the diagram, this action shifts the demand curve to D_1D_1, causing equilibrium to move to point A. In general:

Recessions and unemployment are often caused by insufficient aggregate demand. When this is so, government policies that augment demand—such as increases in government spending—can be an effective way to increase output and reduce unemployment.

The opposite type of demand management is often called for when inflation is the main macroeconomic problem. Figure 5–6 illustrates this case. Here again, point E, the intersection of demand curve D_0D_0 and supply curve SS, is the equilibrium that would be reached in the absence of government policy. But now we suppose that the price level corresponding to point E is considered "too high." This means that the *change* in the price level from the previous period to this one

Figure 5–5
STABILIZATION POLICY TO FIGHT UNEM-PLOYMENT
This diagram duplicates Figure 5–1(b), but here we assume that point E—the intersection of demand curve D_0D_0 and supply curve SS—corresponds to high unemployment. With the kind of policy tools that we will study in later chapters the government can shift the aggregate demand curve outward to D_1D_1. This would raise output and lower unemployment.

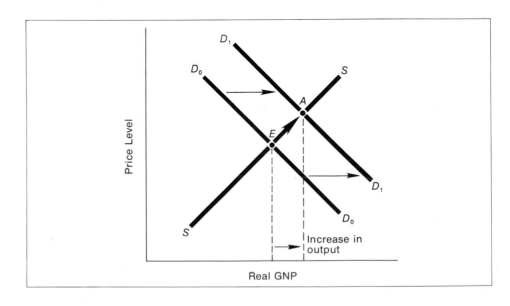

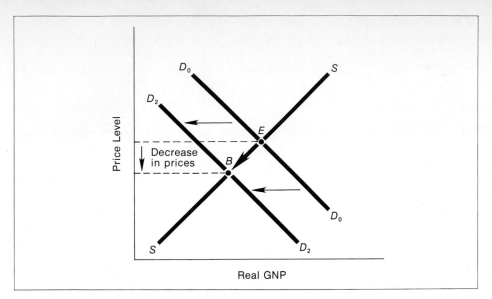

Figure 5–6
STABILIZATION POLICY
TO FIGHT INFLATION
This diagram duplicates Figure
5–2, but here we assume that
point E—the equilibrium the
economy would attain without
government intervention—represents high inflation (that is,
the price level corresponding
to point E is far above last
year's price level). By using its
policy instruments to shift the
aggregate demand curve inward to D_2D_2, the government
can keep this year's price level
lower than it would otherwise
have been; in other words, the
government can reduce inflation.

would be too rapid if the economy moved to point E. Inflation would be too high. A government program that reduces demand from D_0D_0 to D_2D_2 (for example, a reduction in government spending) can keep prices down and thereby reduce inflation. Thus:

Inflation is frequently caused by aggregate demand racing ahead too fast. When this is the case, government policies that reduce aggregate demand can be effective anti-inflationary devices.

This, in brief, summarizes the job of stabilization policy. When demand behavior is the source of economic instability, the government can limit both recessions and inflations by managing aggregate demand, pushing it ahead when it would otherwise lag, and restraining it when it would otherwise grow too quickly.

Sound simple? It's not. In reality, managing aggregate demand is a lot more complicated than shifting around lines on graphs with pencil and paper. We will spend several chapters examining the methods of **demand management** and learning why these methods do not always lead to the results that policymakers hope for. In addition, as we all know, the economy is sometimes plagued by both unemployment and inflation *at the same time*. In this case, the tools of demand management, even if wielded with great precision, are simply not up to the task. In the closing chapters of Part Two we will see why demand management is not enough and study some suggestions for dealing with unemployment and inflation at the same time.

Summary

1. Microeconomics studies the decisions of individuals and firms, how these decisions interact, and how they influence the allocation of society's resources and the distribution of income. Macroeconomics looks at the behavior of entire economies and studies the pressing social problems of inflation and unemployment.

2. While their respective subject matters differ greatly, the basic tools of microeconomics and macroeconomics are virtually identical. Both rely on the supply and demand analysis introduced in Chapter 4.

3. Macroeconomic models use abstract concepts like "the price level" and "national product" that are derived by amalgamating many different markets into one. This process is known as aggregation, and should not be taken literally but should be viewed as a useful approximation.

4. The best specific measure of the abstract concept "national product" is the gross national product (GNP), which is obtained by adding up the money values of all final goods and services produced in a given year. These outputs can be evaluated at current market prices (to get nominal GNP) or the prices of some previous year (to get real GNP). Neither intermediate goods nor transactions that take place outside of organized markets are included in GNP.

5. America's economic history is one of growth punctuated by periodic recessions; that is, periods in which real GNP declined. While the distant past included some periods of falling prices (deflations), more recent history shows only rising prices (inflation).

6. The Great Depression of the 1930s was the worst in our country's history. It had profound effects both on our nation and on countries throughout the world and led also to a revolution in economic thinking, thanks to the work of John Maynard Keynes.

7. From World War II to the early 1970s, the American economy exhibited much steadier growth than it had in the past. Many observers attribute this to the implementation of the economic policies that Keynes suggested. At the same time, however, the price level seems only to rise, never to fall, in the modern economy. The economy seems to have become more "inflation prone."

8. In the mid-1970s, the U.S. economy suffered its worst recession since the Great Depression. At the same time, inflation was unusually virulent. This unhappy combination of economic stagnation with rapid inflation was nicknamed "stagflation." It was this same combination of maladies that plagued us again in 1979–1980.

9. One major cause of inflation is that aggregate demand may grow more quickly than aggregate supply. In such a case, a government policy that reduces aggregate demand may be able to check the inflation.

10. Similarly, recessions often occur because aggregate demand grows too slowly. In this case, a government policy that stimulates demand may be an effective way to fight the recession.

Concepts for Review

Microeconomics	Inflation	Final goods
Macroeconomics	Deflation	Intermediate goods
National product	Recession	Stagflation
Aggregation	Gross national product (GNP)	Stabilization policy
Aggregate demand and aggregate supply curves	Nominal versus real GNP	Demand management

Questions for Discussion

1. Which of the following problems are likely to be studied by a microeconomist and which by a macroeconomist?
   a. the allocation of a university's limited budget
   b. why the Great Depression lasted so long
   c. why Japan's economy grows faster than the United States' economy, while Britain's grows slower
   d. why General Motors sells more cars than Ford Motor Company

2. You probably use "aggregates" quite frequently in everyday discussions. Try to think of some examples. (Here is one: Have you ever said, "The student body at this college generally. . . . "? What, precisely, did you mean?)

3. Use an aggregate supply and demand diagram to study what would happen to an economy in which the aggregate supply curve never moved while the aggregate demand curve shifted outward year after year.

4. Try asking a friend who has not studied economics in which year he or she thinks prices were higher: 1870 or 1900? 1920 or 1940? (You can find the correct answers by referring to Figure 5–4.) Most people your age think that prices have always risen. Why do you think they have this opinion?

5. When were the two worst recessions (or depressions) of the past 60 years?

6. Which of the following transactions are included in the gross national product, and by how much does each raise GNP?
   a. Smith pays a carpenter $4000 to build a garage
   b. Smith purchases $1000 worth of lumber and materials and builds himself a garage, which is worth $4000
   c. Smith goes to the woods, cuts down a tree, and uses the wood to build himself a garage that is worth $4000
   d. the Jones family sells its old house to the Reynolds family for $80,000. The Joneses then buy a newly constructed house from a builder for $130,000.
   e. your university purchases a used computer from another university, paying $500,000.
   f. your university purchases a new computer from IBM, paying $1 million
   g. you lose $100 in a Las Vegas casino
   h. you lose $100 in the stock market

Unemployment and Inflation: The Twin Evils of Macroeconomics

When men are employed,
they are best contented.
BENJAMIN FRANKLIN

Inflation is repudiation.
CALVIN COOLIDGE

Among the many trials faced by Ulysses, the hero of Homer's *Odyssey*, one of the most difficult was to steer his fragile boat through a narrow strait. On one side lay the rock Scylla, which threatened to break his craft into pieces, and on the other was the menacing whirlpool Charybdis. The makers of national economic policy face a similarly difficult task in trying to chart a middle course between the Scylla of unemployment and the Charybdis of inflation. If they steer the economy far from the rocks of unemployment, they run the risk of being swept up in the swift currents of inflation. But if they maintain a safe distance from inflation, they may run aground on the shoals of unemployment.

In Part Two we will explain how economic planners attempt to strike a balance between high employment and low inflation, why these goals cannot be attained with machinelike precision, and why improvement on one front generally spells deterioration on the other. A great deal of attention will be paid to the *causes* of inflation and unemployment. But before getting involved in such important issues of theory and policy, we pause in this chapter to take a rather close look at the twin evils themselves: Why is it that a rise in unemployment is generally considered bad news? Why is inflation so loudly deplored? Can we measure the costs of unemployment and inflation? The answers to some of these questions may at first seem obvious, but we will see that there is more to them than meets the eye.

The chapter is divided into two parts. In the first part we deal with unemployment. After a few words on the human costs of high unemployment, we learn how government statisticians measure unemployment and consider how the concept of "full employment" can be defined. We turn next to our country's system of unemployment insurance, and conclude by investigating—and quantifying—the economic losses associated with unemployment.

In the second part of the chapter we turn to inflation. We begin by exploding some persistent myths about inflation, myths that help explain why inflation is so universally deplored. But the costs of inflation are not all mythical. The first real cost we consider is how and why inflation redistributes income and wealth from one group of people to another. Next, we learn how certain laws cause inflation to have very heavy economic costs that could be avoided if the laws were written differently. This leads us to one of our 12 Ideas for Beyond the Final Exam mentioned in Chapter 1. We shall see that it is the failure to understand the effect of inflation on interest rates that explains the existence of some of these laws and accounts for other costs of inflation as well. Finally, we define and analyze the difference between creeping and galloping inflation and explode a final myth about inflation: the myth that creeping inflation always leads to galloping inflation. In an appendix, we explain how inflation is measured.

The Social Costs of Unemployment

The human costs of unemployment are probably sufficiently obvious. Years ago, loss of a job meant not only enforced idleness and a catastrophic drop in income, it often led to hunger, cold, ill health, and even death. This is the way one unemployed worker during the Great Depression described his family's plight in a mournful letter to the governor of Pennsylvania:

I have six little children to take care of. I have been out of work for over a year and a half. Am back almost thirteen months and the landlord says if I don't pay up before the 1 of 1932 out I must go, and where am I to go in the cold winter with my children? If you can help me please for God's sake and the children's sakes and like please do what you can and send me some help, will you, I cannot find any work. I am willing to take any kind of work if I could get it now. Thanskgiving dinner was black coffee and bread and was very glad to get it. My wife is in the hospital now. We have no shoes to were [sic]; no clothes hardly. Oh what will I do I sure will thank you.[1]

Nowadays, unemployment does not have such dire consequences for most families, although it still holds these terrors for some. Part of the sting has been taken out of temporary unemployment by our system of unemployment insurance (discussed below), and there are other social welfare programs to support the incomes of the poor (see Chapter 34). Yet most families still do suffer a painful loss of income when their breadwinner becomes unemployed.

Even families that are well protected by unemployment compensation suffer when joblessness strikes. Ours is a work-oriented society. A man's "place" has always been in the office or factory or shop, and lately this has become increasingly true for women as well. A worker forced into idleness by a recession endures a psychological cost that is no less real for our inability to measure it. Enforced joblessness is a demoralizing mental burden on the unemployed worker. High unemployment leads to a higher incidence of psychological disorders, divorces, suicides, and the like. (See the boxed insert on the next page.)

Nor are the costs only psychological. Accumulated work experience is a valuable asset. When forced into idleness, workers not only cease accumulating experience, but lengthy periods of unemployment may make them "rusty," and thus less productive when they are reemployed. Short periods of unemployment exact different kinds of costs. A record of steady employment is important in applying for a new job. And a worker who has frequently been laid off will lack this record of reliability.

It is important to realize that these costs, whether large or small in total, are distributed most unevenly across the population. At the bottom of the severe

---

[1]From *Brother, Can You Spare a Dime? The Great Depression 1929—1933*, by Milton Meltzer, page 103. Copyright © 1969 by Milton Meltzer. Reprinted by permission of Alfred A. Knopf, Inc.

Health, Crime, and Unemployment

The social costs of unemployment are by no means limited to narrow economic losses such as reduced incomes and output. It is widely believed, for example, that high unemployment breeds crime, mental anxiety, and ill health. A recent study by a researcher at Johns Hopkins University documented the strong statistical association between unemployment and various measures of mental and physical health and criminal aggression.

Using these statistical relationships, it is possible to estimate how many more cases of various maladies the United States would have if the unemployment rate over a six-year period were one percentage point higher than it actually was. The results are summarized in the accompanying bar chart. For example, such a rise in unemployment would be expected to lead to about 2 percent more deaths from heart disease. The other figures in the chart have similar interpretations.

In looking at these numbers, it should be kept in mind that while the study found a high correlation between unemployment and the various maladies, it does not necessarily imply that unemployment was the *cause* of these ills. Still, the figures are dramatic enough to suggest that there is a real link between unemployment and ill health.

SOURCE: M. Harvey Brenner, "Influence of the Social Environment on Psychopathology: The Historical Perspective" in James E. Barrett *et al.* (eds.), *Stress and Mental Disorder*, Raven Press, New York, 1979.

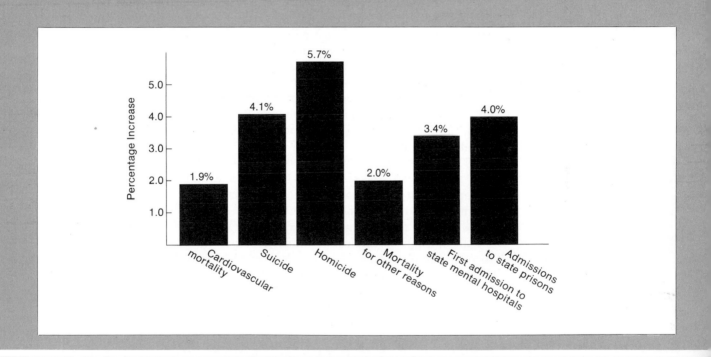

recession of 1973–1975, the unemployment rate among all workers reached 9 percent, a shockingly high figure. But almost 13 percent of blue-collar workers were unemployed, as were more than 14 percent of nonwhite workers. For teen-agers the situation was worse still, with unemployment above 20 percent, and that of nonwhite teen-agers above 37 percent. Married men had the lowest rate—5.7 percent. Although all these rates were unusually high, the relations among them are quite typical:

In good times and bad, married men suffer the least unemployment and teen-agers suffer the most; nonwhites are unemployed much more often than whites; women endure moderately more unemployment than men; and blue-collar workers have above-average rates of unemployment.

Counting the Unemployed: The Official Statistics

The Bureau of Labor Statistics (BLS) of the Department of Labor is responsible for measuring unemployment. How do they do it? How accurate are their measurements?

The BLS's basic method for counting the unemployed is quite direct: it asks people. Specifically, a survey of over 50,000 households is conducted each month. The census-taker asks several questions about the employment status of each member of the household. On the basis of these answers, each person is categorized as being *employed, unemployed,* or *not in the labor force.*

The first category is simplest to define. It includes everybody currently working at a job, including part-time workers. Although some part-time workers work less than a full week because they choose to, others do so only because they cannot find a suitable full-time job. Nevertheless, these workers are not considered "unemployed," though many would consider them "underemployed."

The second category is a bit trickier. For those not currently working, the BLS first determines whether they are temporarily laid off from a job to which they expect to return. If so, they are counted as unemployed. The remaining workers are asked whether they actively sought work during the previous week. If they did, they are also counted as unemployed. But if they did not, they are classified as not in the labor force; that is, since they failed to look for a job they are not considered unemployed.

This seems a reasonable way to draw the distinction—after all, we would not want to count all college students who work during the summer months as unemployed between September and May. Yet, there is a problem: research has shown that many unemployed workers give up looking for jobs after a time. These so-called **discouraged workers** are victims of poor job prospects, just like the officially unemployed. Ironically, when they give up hope, the official unemployment statistics decline! Some critics have therefore argued that an estimate should be made of the number of discouraged workers, and that these people should be added to the roles of the unemployed. In 1980, the BLS estimated that about one million workers fell into this category.

Involuntary part-time work, loss of overtime or shortened work hours, and discouraged workers are all examples of "hidden" or "disguised" unemployment. And those who are concerned about these phenomena argue that we should include them in the official unemployment rate because, if we do not, the magnitude of the problem will be *underestimated.*

There is, however, an opposing school of thought that argues that the official unemployment rate really *overestimates* the unemployment problem. First, they argue, the unemployment rate of 1981 is not directly comparable to the unemployment rate of, say, 1956 because the composition of the labor force has changed dramatically over these years. Specifically, a much higher fraction of all workers are young and female today than was the case 25 years ago. These groups have always had higher rates of unemployment than adult males. Therefore, even if adult men, adult women, and teen-agers each had the *same* unemployment rates in 1981 that they had in 1956 (when overall unemployment was about 4 percent), the unemployment rate for the entire population in 1981 would have been about 5 percent.[2] Second, they argue, to count as unemployed, a person need only *say* that he is looking for work, even if he is not really interested in finding a job. No one knows to what extent the unemployment problem is overstated on account of this, but some think that it may be considerable.

How Much Employment Is "Full Employment"?

Providing jobs for those willing to work is one principal goal of macroeconomic policy. How are we to define this goal? One clearly *incorrect* answer would be "a zero measured unemployment rate." Ours is a dynamic and highly mobile economy. Households move from one state to another. Individuals quit jobs to look for better positions or to "retool" for more attractive occupations. These phenomena, and many more, produce some minimal amount of unemployment—people who literally are *between* jobs. Economists call this the level of **frictional unemployment.**

The critical distinguishing feature of frictional unemployment is that it is short-lived. A frictionally unemployed person has every reason to expect to find a new job soon. People tend to think of frictional unemployment as irreducible, but that is not the case. During World War II, for example, unemployment in this country fell substantially below the frictional level. Frictional unemployment is "irreducible" only in the sense that—under normal circumstances—it is socially undesirable to reduce it.

Geographical and occupational mobility play important roles in our market economy—enabling the "right people" to find the "right jobs." Similarly, waste is avoided by allowing the inefficient firms, or firms producing items no longer desired by consumers, to be replaced by new firms. Inhibition of either of these phenomena must hamper the workings of the market economy. But, when these adjustment mechanisms are allowed to operate, there must be some temporarily unemployed workers looking for jobs just as there must be some firms with unfilled positions looking for workers. This is the genesis of frictional unemployment.

A second type of unemployment is often difficult to distinguish from frictional unemployment, but has very different implications. This is called **structural unemployment.** The crucial difference between frictional and structural unemployment is that, unlike a frictionally unemployed worker, a structurally unemployed worker cannot realistically be considered "between jobs." Instead, he may find his skills and experience unwanted in the changing economy in which he lives. He is thus faced with either a prolonged period of unemployment or the necessity of making a major change in his occupation. For older workers in particular, this may be very difficult.

The remaining type of unemployment, **cyclical unemployment,** will occupy our attention most in this book. Cyclical unemployment is, almost by definition, much more variable than either frictional or structural employment. Whenever the unemployment rate rises ominously or falls precipitously, the data are almost certainly reflecting changes in cyclical unemployment.

Frictional unemployment is unemployment that is due to the normal workings of the labor market. It includes people who are temporarily between jobs because they are moving or changing occupations, or because their old firm went out of business, or for similar reasons.

Structural unemployment refers to workers who have lost their jobs because they have been displaced by automation, because their skills are no longer in demand, or for other similar reasons.

Cyclical unemployment is the portion of unemployment that is attributable to a decline in the economy's total production. Cyclical unemployment rises during recessions and falls as prosperity is restored.

[2] If you do not understand why, consider the following analogy. Suppose your college class contains a mixture of "A" students and "C" students. If, between your freshman year and your senior year, more "C" students enter the class as transfers from other colleges, your class's overall grade point average will decline even if every student earns the same grades as a senior that he or she did as a freshman.

Which of these types of unemployment is considered unavoidable—even under "full employment"? The **Employment Act of 1946,** the landmark piece of legislation in which the U.S. government first explicitly stated its commitment to maintain "conditions under which there will be afforded useful employment opportunities . . . for those able, willing and seeking to work," did not make this entirely clear. However, a common interpretation was that the act called upon the government to hold unemployment close to the frictional level. How much was that? During the prosperous years of the late 1940s and early 1950s, unemployment rates were consistently below 4 percent, dropping as low as 2.9 percent in 1953 during the Korean War. This led President John F. Kennedy, in 1961, to select a 4 percent unemployment rate as an "interim target." The federal government was, for the first time, committed to a numerical goal.

Starting from the high 6.7 percent rate of 1961, unemployment was eroded, more or less steadily, to 3.8 percent in 1966. The interim target was exceeded, but inflation was starting to rear its ugly head. Then the additional military spending for the Vietnam War pushed unemployment down still further. The overall rate reached 3.5 percent in 1969, the lowest rate for a full year since 1953.

During the Nixon and Ford administrations, the 4 percent goal posted by President Kennedy's New Frontier was rejected as being outmoded, although no new numerical target was put in its place. There were several reasons for this rejection of 4 percent.

First, economists of the Nixon–Ford administration argued that the 4 percent target set during the Kennedy administration had to be adjusted upward for the early and middle 1970s because of the changed composition of the labor force. As already mentioned, this alone could raise the unemployment rate compatible with "full employment" to about 5 percent. Second, they suggested, the increased generosity of unemployment compensation had reduced any individual's incentive to get himself off the unemployment rolls. Why work if unemployment benefits and other programs provide an income nearly as large as the salary one could earn on the job? This lack of work incentives made 4 percent unemployment much harder to achieve. Finally, these economists claimed, substantial increases in the federal minimum wage during the 1970s made it harder to employ teen-agers and other workers whose productivity was low. If, for example, their productivity was exceeded by the legal minimum wage, who would hire them?[3]

The last half of the 1970s saw considerable debate, both in government and in academia, over exactly how much measured unemployment corresponded to full employment. As is so often the case, actual events helped to settle the argument. Throughout 1978 and 1979, while the economy was giving every indication that it was operating at approximately normal rates, measured unemployment hovered in the vicinity of 6 percent. Thus, by the beginning of the 1980s there was a fair amount of consensus among economists that **full employment** meant an unemployment rate close to 6 percent, and many economists thought it might even be higher.

These beliefs, however, were not embodied in government policy. Late in 1978, Congress passed and President Carter signed the **Full Employment and Balanced Growth Act,** commonly referred to as the Humphrey–Hawkins Act, partly as a tribute to the late Senator Hubert Humphrey. This law reinstalled President Kennedy's 4 percent figure as the official government definition of full employment—a target so low that most economists view it as attainable only during an extreme boom. Economic policy actions since 1978, however, have

---

[3]For a full discussion of minimum wage laws, including their effect on unemployment, see Chapter 33.

given no reason to believe that the government is serious about pursuing this unrealistic goal.

Unemployment Insurance: The Invaluable Cushion

A surprising feature of the 1980 recession was the equanimity with which the electorate tolerated unemployment rates approaching 8 percent. A major reason for this was our system of **unemployment insurance.**

One of the most valuable pieces of legislation to emerge from the trauma of the Great Depression was the Social Security Act of 1935. Among other things, it established an unemployment insurance system which is now administered by each of the 50 states under federal guidelines. Thanks to this system, many—but, as we shall see, not all—American workers need never experience the complete loss of income that so many suffered during the 1930s.

While the precise amounts vary substantially, the average weekly benefit check to unemployed workers in 1980 was almost $100. This amounted to about 40 percent of average earnings. Though a 60 percent drop in earnings still poses serious problems, the importance of this 40 percent income cushion can scarcely be exaggerated, especially since it is tax free and may be supplemented by funds from other welfare programs. Families covered by unemployment insurance simply do not go hungry when they lose their jobs, and they are only rarely dispossessed from their homes.

Who is eligible to receive these benefits? Precise qualifications vary from state to state, but some stipulations apply quite generally.

1. *Only experienced workers qualify.* The amount of experience necessary to establish eligibility varies state by state; but persons just joining the labor force (for instance, new graduates of high schools or colleges) or reentering after a protracted absence (such as women resuming work after many years of child rearing) are never eligible.

2. *Job quitters are not eligible.* With certain exceptions, people who are unemployed because they quit their last jobs cannot collect benefits.

3. *You must be looking for work to qualify.* People unwilling or unable to work cannot receive unemployment benefits, and a recipient of benefits cannot reject a "suitable" job.

4. *Benefits end after six months of unemployment.* This time limit typically is extended by Congress when there is a recession, but there is always some limit.

Because of all these limitations, only about half the roughly $7\frac{1}{2}$ million persons who were unemployed during 1980 actually received benefits.

The importance of unemployment insurance to those who are or who have been unemployed is obvious. But there are also significant benefits to citizens who never become unemployed. During recession years many billions of dollars are paid out in unemployment benefits, and since recipients probably spend almost all of their benefits, unemployment insurance limits the severity of recessions by providing additional purchasing power when and where it is most needed.

The unemployment insurance system is one of several "cushions" that have been built into our economy since 1933 to prevent the possibility of another Great

Depression. By giving money to those who become unemployed, the system helps prop up aggregate demand during recessions.

While the U.S. economy is now probably "depression proof," this should not be a cause for too much rejoicing, for the recessions of 1973–1975 and 1980 amply demonstrated that we are far from being "recession proof."

The Economic Costs of High Unemployment

The fact that unemployment insurance and other social welfare programs replace a significant fraction of lost income has led some skeptics to claim that unemployment is no longer a serious problem. But the fact is that:

Unemployment insurance is just what the name says—an *insurance* program. And insurance can never prevent a catastrophe from occurring; it can only *spread the costs* of a catastrophe among many people instead of letting them all fall on the shoulders of those few unfortunate souls whom it affects directly.

Fire insurance is an example. If you are covered by fire insurance and your house burns down, you will probably suffer only a small financial loss because the insurance company will pay most of the expenses. Where does it get the money? It cannot create it out of thin air. Rather, it must have collected the funds from the many other families who purchased insurance but did not suffer any fire damages. Thus, one family's loss of perhaps $75,000 is covered by the insurance payments of 500 families each paying $150 a year. In this way, the costs of the catastrophe are spread among hundreds of families, and in the process, made much more bearable.

But despite the insurance, the family whose house is destroyed by fire suffers anguish and inconvenience. No insurance policy can eliminate this. Furthermore, society loses a valuable resource—a house. It will take a great deal of wood, cement, nails, paint, and labor to replace the burnt-out home. *An insurance policy cannot insure society against losses of real resources.*

The case is precisely the same with insurance against unemployment. All workers and employers pay for the insurance policy by a tax that the government levies on wages and salaries. With the funds so collected, the government compensates the victims of unemployment. Thus, instead of letting the costs of unemployment fall entirely on the minority of workers who are out of work, the system of payroll taxes and unemployment benefits *spreads* the costs over the entire population. But it does not eliminate the basic economic cost.

When the economy does not generate enough jobs to employ all those who are willing to work, a valuable resource is lost. Potential goods and services that might have been enjoyed by consumers are lost forever. This is the real economic cost of high unemployment, and no insurance plan can eliminate it.

And these costs are by no means negligible. Table 6–1 summarizes the idleness of workers and machines, and the resulting loss of national output, for some of the years of lowest economic activity since World War II. The first column lists the unemployment rate, and thus measures the unused labor resources. The second lists the fraction of industrial capacity that U.S. manufacturers were actually using, and thus indicates the extent of unused plant and equipment. And the third column shows how much more output (real GNP)

Table 6–1
THE ECONOMIC COSTS OF HIGH UNEMPLOYMENT

YEAR	UNEMPLOYMENT RATE (percent)	CAPACITY UTILIZATION RATE (percent)	REAL GNP LOST DUE TO IDLE RESOURCES (billions of 1972 dollars)
1949	5.9	74.2	23
1954	5.5	80.3	16
1958	6.8	75.2	43
1961	6.7	77.4	45
1971	5.9	78.4	28
1975	8.5	72.9	87
1980	7.1	79.0	68

SOURCES: Bureau of Labor Statistics, Federal Reserve System, and Council of Economic Advisers.

could have been produced if these labor and capital resources had been fully employed.

While these years are extreme examples, the inability to utilize all of the nation's available resources has been a persistent problem for our economy. The blue line in Figure 6–1 shows the actual real GNP in the United States from 1948 to 1980, while the black line shows the real GNP we *could have* produced if "full

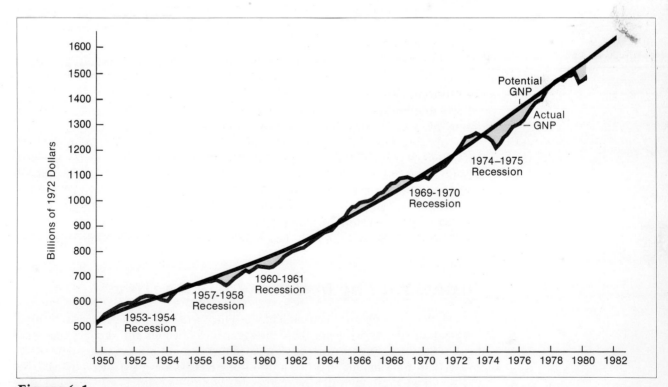

Figure 6–1
ACTUAL AND POTENTIAL GNP IN THE UNITED STATES, 1948–1980
This chart compares the growth of actual GNP (blue line) with that of potential GNP (black line). There have been three lengthy periods during which real GNP remained below its potential (1957–1964, 1969–1972, and 1974 to the present), but only one lengthy period during which GNP remained above potential (1965–1968).

Potential gross national product is the real GNP the economy would produce if its labor and other resources were fully employed.

employment" had been maintained. This last statement defines a concept called **potential GNP.** As our previous discussion of full employment pointed out, it *is* possible to push employment beyond its normal full employment level. This occurs whenever the unemployment rate dips below the "full employment unemployment rate"—a rate now thought to be 6 percent or so. Consequently, it *is* possible for actual GNP to exceed potential GNP. Figure 6–1 shows several instances where this happened. But it also shows that, more typically, actual GNP falls short of potential GNP. The total shortfall of actual GNP below potential GNP since World War II provides some startling information.

The cumulative gap between actual and potential GNP over the years 1948–1980 (all evaluated in 1972 prices), which is shown by the shaded area in Figure 6–1, is an astounding $537 billion. At 1982 levels of output, this loss in output as a result of unemployment would be about four months' worth of production. And there is no way to redeem these losses. The labor wasted in 1980 cannot be utilized in 1982.

Those who argue that unemployment is nothing to worry about today because of unemployment insurance, or because unemployment is concentrated among certain kinds of workers (such as teen-agers), or because many unemployed workers become reemployed within a few weeks, should ponder Figure 6–1. Is the loss of this much output really no cause for worry? Would these optimists react the same way if the government collected a fraction of the output of every factory in America and dumped it into the sea? Waste is waste no matter who ultimately pays the cost.

The Social Costs of Inflation

Both the human and the economic costs of inflation are less obvious than the costs of unemployment. But this does not necessarily make them any less real, for if one thing is crystal clear about inflation, it is that people do not like it.

Public opinion polls consistently show that inflation ranks high on people's list of major national problems, generally even ahead of unemployment. Surveys also find that inflation, like unemployment, causes a deterioration in consumers' sense of well-being—it makes people unhappy. Finally, studies of voting behavior have shown that during congressional elections voters penalize the party that occupies the White House when inflation is high.

The fact is beyond dispute: People consider inflation to be something bad. Why?

Inflation: The Myth and the Reality

At first, the question may seem ridiculous. During times of inflation, people must keep paying higher prices for the same quantities of goods and services they had before. So more and more income is needed just to maintain the same standard of living. Is it not obvious that this erosion of **purchasing power**—that is, the decline in what money will buy—makes everyone worse off?

This would indeed be the case were it not for one very significant fact. The wages people earn are also prices—prices for labor services. During a period of inflation, wages also rise and, in fact, the average wage typically rises more or less in step with prices. Thus, contrary to popular myth, workers as a group are not usually victimized by inflation.

The purchasing power of wages is not systematically eroded by inflation. Sometimes wages rise faster than prices, and sometimes prices rise faster than wages. The fact is that in the long run wages tend to outstrip prices as new capital equipment and innovation increase output per worker.

Figure 6–2 illustrates this simple fact. The blue line shows the annual rate of increase of consumer prices in the United States for each year since 1948, while the black line shows the annual rate of wage increases. Generally, wages rise faster than prices, reflecting the steady advance of technology and of labor productivity. So the black line is usually above the blue line. The years since 1974 stand out as an unusual period in which wages did not generally rise faster than prices. This single fact goes a long way toward explaining why people are so dissatisfied with recent economic performance.

The feature of Figure 6–2 that virtually jumps off the page is the way the two lines seem to dance together. Wages normally rise rapidly when prices rise rapidly, and rise slowly when prices rise slowly. But you should not draw any hasty conclusions from this association. We cannot, for example, learn from this figure whether rising prices cause rising wages or whether rising wages cause rising prices. Remember the warnings given in Chapter 1 about trying to infer causation just by looking at data. But analyzing cause and effect is not our purpose right now. We merely want to explode the myth that inflation inevitably robs workers of their wages.

Why is this myth so widespread? Imagine a world without inflation in which wages are rising 2 percent a year because of the increasing productivity of labor. Now imagine that, all of a sudden, inflation sets in and prices start rising 8 percent a year but that nothing else changes. Figure 6–2 suggests that, with perhaps a small delay, wage increases will accelerate to 2 percent plus 8 percent, or 10 percent a year.

Will workers view this change with equanimity? Probably not. To each worker, the 10 percent wage increase will be seen as something he earned by the sweat of his brow. In his view, he *deserves* every penny of his 10 percent raise.

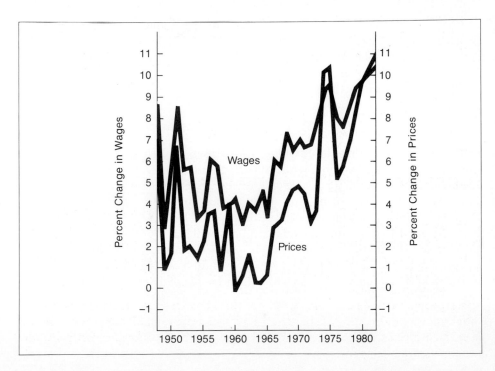

Figure 6–2
RATES OF CHANGE OF WAGES AND PRICES IN THE UNITED STATES, 1948–1980
This chart compares the rate of price inflation (blue line) with the rate of growth of nominal wages in the postwar period. The patterns are clearly quite similar, with wages and prices normally accelerating or decelerating together. Notice that the traditional gap between wage increases and price increases did not prevail in the middle and late 1970s.

And, in a sense, he is right because "the sweat of his brow" earned him a 2 percent increment in purchasing power that, when the inflation rate is 8 percent, can only be achieved by increasing his wages by a total of 10 percent. An economist would divide the wage increase in the following way:

REASON FOR WAGE INCREASE	AMOUNT
Higher productivity	2%
Compensation for higher prices	8%
Total	10%

"Sure, you're raising my allowance. But am I actually gaining any purchasing power?"

But the worker will probably keep score differently. Feeling that he earned the entire 10 percent by his own merits, he will view inflation as having "robbed" him of 8 percent of his just deserts. The higher the rate of inflation, the more of his raise the worker will feel robbed of.

Of course, nothing could be further from the truth. Basically, the economic system is rewarding the worker with *the same 2 percent increment for higher productivity regardless of the rate of inflation.* The "evils of inflation" are often exaggerated because of a failure to understand this mechanism.

A second reason for misunderstanding the effects of inflation is that people are in the habit of thinking in terms of the number of dollars it takes to buy something rather than in terms of the *purchasing power* of these dollars. For example, if inflation doubles both prices and wages, workers will have to labor exactly the same amount of time as before to earn the price of a loaf of bread. But because they now pay $1 a loaf instead of 50 cents, they feel that the price of bread is scandalously high. In fact, nothing really has changed; but people remain stuck with an outmoded idea of what bread *should* cost.

A third misperception results from failure to distinguish between a *rise in the general price level* and a change in **relative prices,** that is, a rise in the price of one commodity relative to that of another. To see the distinction most clearly, imagine first a *pure inflation* in which *every* price rises by 10 percent during the year, so that relative prices do not change. Table 6–2 gives an example in which movie tickets go up from $3 to $3.30, candy bars from 20 cents to 22 cents, and automobiles from $6000 to $6600. After the inflation, just as before, it will still take 15 candy bars to buy a movie ticket, 2000 movie tickets to buy a car, and so on. A person who manufactures candy bars in order to purchase movie tickets is neither helped nor harmed by the inflation. Neither is a car dealer with a sweet tooth.

But real inflations are not like this. When there is 10 percent general inflation—meaning that the "average price" rises by 10 percent[4]—some prices may jump 20 percent or more while others actually fall. Suppose that, instead of the price increases shown in Table 6–2, prices rise as shown in Table 6–3. Movie prices go up by $33\frac{1}{3}$ percent, but candy prices do not change. Surely, candy manufacturers who love movies will be disgruntled because it now costs 20 candy bars instead of 15 to get into the theater. They will blame inflation for raising the price of movie tickets, even though their real problem stems from the *increase in the price of movies relative to candy.* (They would have been hurt just as much if movie tickets had remained at $3 while the price of candy fell to 15 cents.)

[4]The way statisticians figure out "average" price increases is discussed in the appendix to this chapter.

Table 6–2			
ITEM	LAST YEAR'S PRICE	THIS YEAR'S PRICE	PERCENT INCREASE
Candy bar	$ 0.20	$ 0.22	10
Movie ticket	3.00	3.30	10
Automobile	6000	6600	10

Table 6–3			
ITEM	LAST YEAR'S PRICE	THIS YEAR'S PRICE	PERCENT INCREASE
Candy bar	$ 0.20	$ 0.20	0
Movie ticket	3.00	4.00	33.3
Automobile	6000	6400	6.7

Since car prices have risen by less than 7 percent, theater owners in need of new cars will be delighted by the fact that an auto now costs only 1600 movie admissions (just as they would have cheered if car prices had fallen to $4800 while movie tickets remained at $3.) However, they are unlikely to attribute their good fortune to inflation—as indeed they should not. What has actually happened is that *cars became cheaper relative to movies.*

Because real-world inflation proceeds at *uneven* rates, relative prices are constantly changing. There are gainers and losers, just as some would gain and others lose if relative prices changed without any general inflation. Inflation, however, gets a bad name because losers often blame inflation for their misfortune while gainers rarely credit inflation for their good luck. Alas, nobody loves inflation.

These three kinds of misconceptions may go a long way toward explaining why respondents to public opinion polls consistently list inflation as a major national issue, why higher inflation rates depress consumers, and why voters express their ire at the polls when inflation is high.

Inflation does not systematically erode the purchasing power of wages. Nor does it lead to "unfair" prices. Nor is it usually to blame when some goods become more expensive relative to others.

But not all of the costs of inflation are mythical. Let us now turn to some of the real costs.

Inflation as a Redistributor of Income and Wealth

We have just seen that the *average* person is neither helped nor harmed by inflation. But almost no one is exactly average! Some persons gain from inflation and others lose. It is hard to say anything more systematic than this about the effects of inflation on particular prices and wages.

But inflation does have systematic effects on the distribution of income and wealth. Senior citizens trying to scrape by on pensions or other fixed incomes suffer badly from inflation. Since they earn no wages, it is little solace to them that wages are keeping pace with prices. Their pension incomes are not.[5]

This example actually illustrates a much more general problem. We can think of pensioners as people who "lend" money to an organization (the pension fund) when they are young in order to be "paid back" with interest when they are

---

[5]This is not, however, true of recipients of social security. Social security benefits are financed out of tax revenues rather than directly through accumulated savings, and benefit levels are automatically increased to compensate recipients for changes in the price level. For further discussion of the social security system, see Chapter 30.

old. Because of the rise in the price level during the intervening years, the unfortunate pensioners get paid back in less valuable dollars than those they originally loaned. In general:

Those who lend money are usually victimized by inflation.

While lenders lose heavily, borrowers do quite well. For example, home-owners who borrowed money from banks in the form of mortgages back in the 1950s, when interest rates were 3 or 4 percent, gained enormously from the surprisingly virulent inflation of the late 1960s and 1970s. They have paid back dollars of much lower value than those that they borrowed. And the same is true of other borrowers.

Borrowers usually gain from inflation.

Since the redistribution caused by inflation generally benefits borrowers at the expense of lenders, and since both lenders and borrowers can be found at every income level, we must conclude that:

Inflation does not always steal from the rich to aid the poor, nor does it always do the reverse.

Why, then, is the redistribution caused by inflation so widely condemned? Because its victims are selected capriciously. Nobody legislates this redistribution. Nobody enters into it voluntarily. The gainers do not earn their spoils, and the losers do not deserve their fate. Moreover there have been particular classes of people whom inflation has systematically robbed of purchasing power year after year—old-age pensioners, people who have saved money and "loaned" it to banks, and workers on long-term contracts or those whose wages and salaries do not adjust easily for some other reason. Even if people "on the average" suffer no damage from inflation, that offers little consolation to those who are hurt by it persistently and systematically. This is the fundamental indictment of inflation.

Inflation redistributes income in an arbitrary way that distorts society's distribution of income. The actual income distribution should reflect the interplay of the operation of free markets and the deliberate efforts of government to alter the distribution. Inflation interferes with and distorts this process.

Real Versus Nominal Interest Rates

But wait. Must inflation always rob lenders to bestow gifts upon borrowers? If both parties see inflation coming, won't lenders demand that borrowers pay a higher interest rate as compensation for the coming inflation? Indeed they will. For this reason, economists draw a conceptual distinction between inflation that is *expected* and inflation that comes as a surprise.

What happens when inflation is fully expected by both parties? Suppose Diamond Jim wants to borrow $1000 from Scrooge, and both agree that, in the absence of inflation, which erodes the value of money, a fair rate of interest would be 4 percent on a one-year loan. This means that Diamond Jim would pay back $1040 at the end of the year for the privilege of having $1000 now.

If both expect prices to increase by 6 percent, Scrooge may reason as follows, "If Diamond Jim pays me back $1040 a year from today, that money will buy less than what $1000 buys today. Thus I'll really be *paying him* to borrow from me!

I'm no philanthropist. Why don't I charge him 10 percent instead? Then he'll pay back $1100 at the end of the year. With prices 6 percent higher, this will buy roughly what $1040 is worth today. So I'll get the same 4 percent increase in purchasing power that we would have agreed on in the absence of inflation, and won't be any worse off. That's the least I'll accept."

Diamond Jim may follow a similar chain of logic. "With no inflation, I was willing to pay $1040 a year from now for the privilege of having $1000 today, and Scrooge was willing to lend it. He'd be crazy to do the same with a 6 percent inflation. He'll want to charge me more. How much should I pay? If I offer him $1100 a year from now, that will have roughly the same purchasing power as $1040 today, so I won't be any worse off. That's the most I'll pay."

This kind of thinking will lead Scrooge and Diamond Jim to write a contract with a 10 percent interest rate—4 percent as the increase in purchasing power that Diamond Jim pays to Scrooge and 6 percent as compensation for the expected inflation. Then, if the expected 6 percent inflation actually materializes, neither party will have been made better or worse off than was expected at the time the contract was signed.

This example illustrates a very general principle. The 4 percent increase in purchasing power that Diamond Jim agrees to hand over to Scrooge is called the **real rate of interest.** And the 10 percent contractual interest charge that Diamond Jim and Scrooge write into the loan agreement is called the **nominal rate of interest.** The nominal rate of interest is arrived at by adding the *expected rate of inflation* to the real rate of interest. Expected inflation is added to compensate the lender for the loss in purchasing power that he is expected to suffer as a result of inflation. Because of this:

Inflation that is accurately predicted need not redistribute income between borrowers and lenders. If the *expected* rate of inflation that is embodied in the nominal interest rate closely approximates the *actual* rate of inflation, no one gains and no one loses. However, to the extent that expectations prove incorrect, inflation will still redistribute income.[6]

It need hardly be pointed out that errors in predicting the rate of inflation are the norm, not the exception. Published forecasts bear witness to the fact that economists have great difficulty in predicting the rate of inflation. The task is no easier for businesses, consumers, and banks. This is one reason why inflation is so widely condemned as unfair and undesirable. It sets up a guessing game that no one likes.

Usury Laws, Interest Rate Ceilings, and Other Legal Impediments

One major source of the costs of inflation stems from the fact that no one can foresee what the future rate of inflation will be. But there are other costs, perhaps even more serious, that arise from high inflation rates, even when the rates are predicted accurately. These costs are consequences of laws that make it *illegal* for borrowers and lenders to add the expected rate of inflation to their desired real interest rate.

The most obvious example of such legislation is **usury laws.** Usury laws date back to biblical days and command rather widespread popular support. The

The **real rate of interest** is the percentage increase in purchasing power that the borrower pays to the lender for the privilege of borrowing. It indicates the increased ability to purchase goods and services that the lender earns.

The **nominal rate of interest** is the percentage by which the money the borrower pays back exceeds the money that he borrowed, making no adjustment for any fall in the purchasing power of this money that results from inflation.

A **usury law** sets down a maximum permissible interest rate for a particular type of loan. Loans at rates above the usury ceiling are illegal.

[6]EXERCISE: Who gains and who loses if the inflation turns out to be only 4 percent instead of the 6 percent that Scrooge and Diamond Jim expected? What if the inflation rate is 8 percent?

problem is that they place limits on *nominal* interest rates, rather than on *real* interest rates, and thus can have rather perverse effects in an inflationary environment.

Let us recall our previous example in which Scrooge and Diamond Jim both correctly foresee a 6 percent rate of inflation. But now suppose that a usury law sets a maximum rate of 8 percent on consumer loans. Diamond Jim is willing to pay a 10 percent nominal interest rate (4 percent real interest plus 6 percent for expected inflation) in order to get his hands on some money a year earlier, and Scrooge is willing to lend at this rate. But the law intervenes. "Thou shalt not charge usurious interest." The deal cannot be completed, and both Diamond Jim and Scrooge go away disappointed.

The problem is that usury laws were framed in periods of fairly steady prices, when there was no great difference between nominal and real interest rates. If, for example, the usury law had set the legal maximum at an 8 percent *real* rate of interest, it would not have prevented Scrooge from lending to Diamond Jim. As it is, however, a loan carrying a 4 percent real interest rate is perfectly legal at zero inflation but illegal at 6 percent inflation!

This phenomenon helps explain why rapid inflation often has had disastrous consequences for homebuilding. Usury laws in the past have set maximum interest rates on home mortgages. If the usury ceiling is, for example, 10 percent interest, mortgage loans will look like a very bad investment in an inflationary environment when banks can buy bonds of large corporations paying 13 percent interest and more. As a result, banks will stop making mortgage loans, and the housing market will come to a screeching halt. This is precisely what happened in the United States in 1974, and it took several years for the construction industry to recover from the debacle. Much the same thing happened again in 1980, forcing a temporary suspension of usury ceilings on home mortgages by the federal government.

Usury laws are just one example of a general phenomenon:

Many of the laws that govern our financial system become extremely counter-productive in an inflationary environment, causing problems that were never intended by the legislators.

And it is important to note that *these are major costs of inflation that are not purely redistributive.* Society as a whole is the loser when mutually beneficial transactions are prohibited by law, when houses go unbuilt, when loans are not provided to those who need them, and when other useful acts are prevented by obsolete legislation.

The Illusion of High Interest Rates

Why do such laws stay on the books so long?[7] One reason is a general lack of understanding of the difference between real and nominal interest rates. People seem not to understand that it is the *real* rate of interest that matters in an economic transaction because only that rate reveals how much borrowers pay (and lenders receive) *in terms of the goods and services which that money can buy.* They consider high nominal interest rates to be unjustifiable, even if these rates correspond to very low real interest rates. The example of usury ceilings on nominal interest rates has already been given. Here are some others that may help you appreciate how widespread and important this interest rate illusion is.

---

[7]Legislation in 1980 eliminated most usury ceilings on interest rates.

Regulation of Public Utilities

During the period 1959 to 1965, when the rate of inflation averaged about $1\frac{1}{4}$ percent a year, interest rates on high-grade corporate bonds hovered just below $4\frac{1}{2}$ percent, yielding a real rate of interest of just over 3 percent. There were few public complaints suggesting that there was anything scandalous about such earnings rates.

Yet during 1980 when the rate of inflation rose above 12 percent and corporate interest rates rose to perhaps 11 percent (a *negative* real rate of interest!), there was a public uproar. Regulated utilities, which asked the regulatory agencies to permit them a rate of return closer to 11 percent so that they could afford to borrow the money needed to serve expanding public demand, found that their requests were considered exorbitant by the commissions and by the general public. As a result, they failed to increase their capacities sufficiently.

Investment and Profits

Amazingly, even business managers were subject to the same form of illusion. Often they were taken aback by the notion that their investors actually lost out (earned a negative *real* rate of return) when the company was earning a 10 percent profit. The managers noted that 10 percent was the company's highest earnings rate in recent history; but with inflation at 12 percent, it turned out that in real terms it was in fact the firm's lowest.

Interest Rate Regulations

The same illusion is also partly responsible for the regulations that impose ceilings around 5 percent on interest paid on many savings accounts. Thus, *by government decree* small savers are robbed of 5 percent of their purchasing power or more every year during a period of rapid inflation.

Thus, failure to understand that high *nominal* interest rates can signify very low *real* interest rates has been known to impoverish savers during a period of inflation. It has devastated the housing industry. It has sometimes made it impossible for electric companies and other public utilities to raise the capital they need to serve rising consumer demands; and power shortages and failures have been a predictable result.

The difference between real and nominal interest (and profit) rates, and the fact that it is the real rate that matters in terms of economic effects but the nominal rate that is politically significant, are matters that are of the utmost importance and yet are understood by very few people, including many persons who make public policy decisions in these areas.

This concept is one of the 12 Ideas for Beyond the Final Exam, and if you remember it ten years from now you will truly have gotten a great deal out of studying economics.

Other Costs of Inflation

Another cost of inflation is that rapidly changing prices make it risky to enter into long-term contracts. In an extremely severe inflation, the "long term" may be only a few days. But even moderate inflations can have remarkable effects on long-term loans. Suppose a corporation wants to borrow $1 million to finance the purchase of some new equipment and needs the loan for 20 years. If the inflation rate averages 8 percent over this period, the $1 million it repays at the end of 20 years will be worth only $214,548 in today's purchasing power. If inflation averages 4 percent instead, it will be worth $456,387. Lending or borrowing for this long a period is obviously a big gamble. With the stakes this high, the outcome may be that neither lenders nor borrowers want to get involved in long-term contracts. But without long-term loans, business investment becomes impossible. The economy stagnates.

Inflation aso makes life difficult for the shopper. You probably have a group of stores that you habitually patronize because you know they generally carry the items you want to buy at (roughly) the prices you want to pay. This knowledge saves you a great deal of time and energy. But when prices are changing rapidly, your list becomes obsolete very quickly. You return to your favorite clothing store only to find that the price of jeans has risen drastically. Should you buy? Should you shop around at other stores? Will they have also raised their prices? And business firms have precisely the same problem with their suppliers. Rising prices force them to shop around more than they are accustomed to, which imposes costs on the firms and, more generally, reduces the efficiency of the whole economy.

Creeping Versus Galloping Inflation

The preceding litany of costs of inflation alerts us to one very important fact: *predictable inflation is far less burdensome than is unpredictable inflation.* When will an inflation be most predictable? When it proceeds year after year at more or less the same rate. Thus the *variability of the inflation rate* is a crucial factor. Inflation of 9 percent a year for three consecutive years will exact far lower social costs than inflation that is 12 percent in the first year, zero in the second, and 15 percent in the third. In general:

Steady inflation is much more predictable than variable inflation and therefore has much smaller social and economic costs.

But the *average level of the inflation rate* is also important. Partly because of the legal impediments mentioned above and partly because of the more rapid breakdown in normal customer relationships that we have just mentioned, a steady inflation of 10 percent a year is more damaging than a steady inflation of 5 percent a year.

Creeping inflation refers to an inflation that proceeds for a long time at a moderate and fairly steady pace.

Galloping inflation refers to an inflation that proceeds at an exceptionally high rate, perhaps only for a relatively brief period. Galloping inflations are generally characterized by accelerating rates of inflation so that the rate of inflation is higher this month than it was last month.

Economists distinguish between **creeping inflations** and **galloping inflations** partly on their average level and partly on their variability. Postwar Sweden provided a good example of creeping inflation. During the 13-year period from 1954 to 1967, prices climbed a total of 64 percent (compared with only 24 percent in the United States), for an average annual inflation rate of 3.9 percent. And the pace of inflation was remarkably steady, rarely dropping below $2\frac{1}{2}$ percent or rising above 5 percent.

Germany after World War I suffered through one of the more severe inflations in history. Wholesale prices increased about 80 percent during 1920, over 140 percent in 1921, and a colossal 4100 percent during 1922. At this point, what had been a very impressive galloping inflation simply got out of control. Between December 1922 and November 1923, when a hard-nosed reform finally broke the inflationary spiral, wholesale prices in Germany increased by almost 100 million percent! But even this experience was dwarfed by the great Hungarian inflation of 1945–1946, the greatest inflation of them all. For a period of one year, the rate of inflation averaged about 20,000 percent *per month*. And in the final month (July 1946), the price level skyrocketed 42 quadrillion percent!

While the distinction between creeping and galloping inflation is a quantitative one, we refrained from putting any specific numbers into the definitions.

This is because different societies at different points in time have very different conceptions about what rate constitutes creeping inflation and what rate constitutes galloping inflation. For example, in the United States today, annual rates of inflation in the 6 to 9 percent range are generally considered to be "creeping," while rates in the 25 to 30 percent range would surely be construed as "galloping." In most Latin American countries, however, inflation consistently in the 25 to 30 percent range is viewed as "creeping." And in the United States of the 1950s and early 1960s, a 7 percent annual inflation might have been branded "galloping."

These children in Weimar Germany are building a pyramid with cash, worth no more than the sand or sticks used by children elsewhere.

The Costs of Creeping Versus Galloping Inflation

If you review the costs of inflation that have been enumerated in this chapter, you will see why the distinction between creeping and galloping inflation is so fundamental. Many economists feel we can live very nicely, indeed can prosper, in an environment of creeping inflation. No one feels we can survive very well under galloping inflation.

Under creeping inflation, the rate at which prices rise is relatively easy to predict and to take into account in setting interest rates (as long as the law allows this). Under galloping inflation, where prices are rising at ever-increasing rates, this is very difficult, and perhaps impossible, to accomplish. The potential redistributions become monumental, and as a result, lending and borrowing may cease entirely.

Any inflation makes it difficult to write long-term contracts. With creeping inflation, the "long term" may be 20 years, or 10 years, or 5. But with galloping inflation, the "long term" may be measured in weeks or even hours. Restaurant prices may change before you finish your dessert. Railroad fares may go up while you are in the middle of your journey. When it is impossible to enter into contracts of any duration longer than a few minutes, economic activity becomes paralyzed. We conclude that:

The horrors of galloping inflation either are absent in creeping inflation or are present in such muted forms that they can scarcely be considered horrors.

Creeping Inflation Does Not Necessarily Lead to Galloping Inflation

We noted earlier that inflation is surrounded by a mythology that bears precious little relation to reality. It seems appropriate to conclude this chapter by disposing of one particularly persistent myth: that creeping inflation invariably leads to galloping inflation.

There is neither statistical evidence nor theoretical support for the myth that creeping inflation leads to galloping inflation. To be sure, creeping inflations sometimes accelerate. But at other times they slow down.

While creeping inflations have many causes, galloping inflations have occurred only when the government has printed incredible amounts of money, usually to finance wartime expenditures.

In the German inflation of 1923, the government finally found that its printing presses could not produce enough paper money to keep pace with the exploding prices. Not that it did not try. By the end of the inflation, the *daily* output of currency was over 400 quadrillion marks! The Hungarian authorities in 1945–1946 tried even harder. The average growth rate of the money supply was more than 12,000 percent *per month*. Needless to say, these are not the kind of inflation problems that are likely to face the United States in the foreseeable future.

But this should not be interpreted to imply there is nothing wrong with creeping inflation. Much of this chapter has been spent analyzing the very real costs of any inflation, no matter how slow. A case against even moderate inflation can indeed be built, but it does not help this case to shout foolish slogans like "Creeping inflation always leads to galloping inflation." Fortunately, it is simply not true.

Summary

1. Unemployment exacts heavy financial and psychological costs from those who are its victims, costs that are borne quite unevenly by different groups in the population.

2. Unemployment is measured by a government survey. Some critics claim that the survey methods understate the unemployment problem while others contend that the methods overstate the problem.

3. Frictional unemployment arises when people are between jobs for normal reasons. Thus, most frictional unemployment is desirable.

4. Structural unemployment is due to shifts in the pattern of demand or to technological change that results in certain skills becoming more or less obsolete.

5. Cyclical unemployment is the portion of unemployment that rises in recessions and falls when the economy booms.

6. While the Employment Act of 1946 was not terribly specific on this point, it was widely interpreted as committing the government to limiting unemployment to the frictional variety. However, it set no numerical goals.

7. President Kennedy first enunciated the goal of 4 percent unemployment in 1961. Although this goal will be much harder to achieve in the 1980s than it was in the 1960s, the Full Employment and Balanced Growth Act of 1978 once again set 4 percent as an official target.

8. Unemployment insurance replaces nearly one-half the lost income of unemployed persons who are insured. But only about half the unemployed are covered by insurance, and no insurance program can bring back the lost output that could have been produced had these people been working.

9. In recent decades, the U.S. economy typically has produced less output than it could have were it operating at full employment. This shortfall has been particularly large since the mid-1970s.

10. People have many misconceptions about inflation. For example, many people believe that inflation systematically erodes the purchasing power of wages, are appalled by rising prices even when wages are rising just as fast, and blame inflation for any unfavorable changes in relative prices. All of these are myths.

11. Other costs of inflation are very real indeed. For example, inflation often redistributes income from lenders to borrowers.

12. This redistribution can be eliminated by adding the expected rate of inflation to the interest rate, but (a) legal limitations sometimes prevent this, and (b) expectations often prove to be quite inaccurate.

13. The real rate of interest is the nominal rate of interest minus the expected rate of inflation. Since the real rate of interest indicates the command over real resources that the borrower surrenders to the lender, it is of primary economic importance.

14. Yet public attention often is riveted on nominal rates of interest, and this confusion can lead to costly policy mistakes when high inflation converts high nominal interest rates into very low real interest rates. This is one of the 12 Ideas for Beyond the Final Exam.

15. Creeping inflation, which proceeds at moderate and fairly predictable rates year after year, carries far lower social costs than galloping inflation, which proceeds at high and variable rates.

16. The notion that creeping inflation inevitably leads to galloping inflation is a myth with no foundation in economic theory and no basis in historical fact.

Concepts for Review

Discouraged workers
Frictional unemployment
Structural unemployment
Cyclical unemployment
Employment Act of 1946
Full employment

Full Employment and Balanced
  Growth Act of 1978
Unemployment insurance
Potential GNP
Purchasing power
Relative prices

Redistribution by inflation
Real rate of interest
Nominal rate of interest
Expected rate of inflation
Usury laws
Creeping inflation
Galloping inflation

Questions for Discussion

1. Why is it not as terrible to become unemployed nowadays as it was during the Great Depression?
2. "Since unemployed workers receive unemployment benefits and other benefits that make up for most of their lost wages, unemployment is no longer a social problem." Comment.
3. Using what you learned about aggregate demand and aggregate supply in Chapter 5, try to explain why the U.S. economy has failed so frequently to produce up to its potential. (You will be learning much more about this question in chapters to come, so don't worry if you find the question difficult at this stage.)
4. Do you think that the Bureau of Labor Statistics overestimates or underestimates the number of people that are unemployed? Why?
5. Why is it so difficult to define "full employment"? What unemployment rate should the government be shooting for today?
6. Show why each of the following complaints is based on a misunderstanding about inflation:
   a. "Inflation must be stopped because it robs workers of their purchasing power."
   b. "Inflation is a terrible social disease. It leads to unconscionably high prices for basic necessities."
   c. "Inflation makes it impossible for working people to afford many of the things they were hoping to buy."
   d. "Inflation must be stopped today, for if we do not stop it, it will surely accelerate to ruinously high rates and lead to disaster."
7. What is the *real interest rate* paid on a loan bearing 12 percent nominal interest per year, if the rate of inflation is
   a. zero
   b. 2 percent
   c. 7 percent
   d. 12 percent
   e. 14 percent
8. Suppose you agree to lend money to your friend on the day you both enter college, at what you both expect to be a zero *real* rate of interest. Payment is to be made at graduation, with interest at a fixed *nominal* rate. If inflation proves to be *lower* during your four years in college than what you both had expected, who will gain and who will lose?
9. You have lived with inflation all your life. Think about the costs that inflation has imposed on *you* personally. How do these costs relate to the material in this chapter?

Appendix

How Statisticians Measure Inflation

Index Numbers for Inflation

Inflation is generally measured by the change in some index of the general price level. For example, between 1970 and 1980, the Consumer Price Index (CPI), which stood at 100 in 1967, rose from 116.3 to 246.8, an increase of 112 percent. The meaning of the *change* is clear enough. But what is the meaning of the 116.3 figure for 1970 and the 246.8 figure for 1980?

These numbers are **index numbers;** each expresses the cost of a market basket of goods *relative to its cost in some "base" period*. Since the CPI uses 1967 as its base period, the CPI of 246.8 for 1980 means that it cost $246.80 to purchase the same basket of goods and services that cost $100 in 1967.

Now, the particular basket of consumer goods and services under scrutiny really did not cost $100 in 1967. When constructing index numbers, it is conventional to set the index at 100 in the base year. How is this conventional figure used in obtaining index numbers for other years? Very simply. Suppose the budget needed to buy the roughly 250 items included in the CPI was $500 per month in 1967 and $581.50 per month in 1970. Then the index is defined by the following rule:

$$\frac{\text{CPI in 1970}}{\text{CPI in 1967}} =$$

$$\frac{\text{Cost of the 250-item market basket in 1970}}{\text{Cost of the 250-item market basket in 1967}}.$$

Since the CPI in 1967 is set at 100:

$$\frac{\text{CPI in 1970}}{100} = \frac{\$581.50}{\$500} = 1.163$$

or

$$\text{CPI in 1970} = 116.3 .$$

Exactly the same sort of equation enables us to calculate the CPI in any other year. We have the rule:

$$\text{CPI in given year} =$$

$$\frac{\text{Cost of market basket in given year}}{\text{Cost of market basket in base year}} \times 100 .$$

Of course, not every combination of consumer goods that cost $500 in 1967 rose to $581.50 by 1970. For example, a color TV set that cost $500 in 1967 might have sold for $450 in 1970, but a $500 hospital bill in 1967 might have ballooned to $625. Since no two families buy precisely the same bundle of goods and services, no two families suffer precisely the same increase in their cost of living unless all prices rise at the same rate. Economists refer to this phenomenon as the **index number problem.**

When relative prices are changing, there is no such thing as a "perfect price index" that is correct for every consumer. Any statistical index will understate the increase in the cost of living for some families and overstate it for others. At best, the index can represent the situation of an "average" family.

The Consumer Price Index

The most closely watched price index is surely the **Consumer Price Index,** which is calculated and announced each month by the Bureau of Labor Statistics (BLS). When you read in the newspaper or see on television that the "cost of living" rose by 0.8 percent last month, chances are the reporter is referring to the CPI.

The CPI is measured by pricing the items on a list representative of a typical urban household budget. To know what items to include and in what amounts, the BLS conducts an extensive survey of spending habits roughly once every decade (the last one was in 1972). This means that the *same* bundle of goods and services is used as a standard for about 10 years, whether or not spending habits change.[8] A simple example will help us understand how the CPI is constructed. Imagine that college students purchase only three items—hamburgers, jeans, and movie tickets—and that we want to devise a cost-of-living index (call it SPI, for "student price index") for

---

[8]Economists call this a *base-period weight index*, because the relative importance it attaches to each price depends on how much money consumers actually chose to spend on it during the base period.

Table 6–4
RESULTS OF HYPOTHETICAL STUDENT EXPENDITURE SURVEY, 1972

ITEM	AVERAGE PRICE	AVERAGE QUANTITY PURCHASED PER MONTH	AVERAGE EXPENDITURE PER MONTH
Hamburger	$ 0.40	70	$28
Jeans	12.00	1	12
Movie ticket	2.50	4	10
			Total $50

them. First we would conduct a survey of spending habits in the base year (suppose it is 1972). Table 6–4 represents the hypothetical results. You will note that the frugal students of that day spent only $50 per month: $28 on hamburgers, $12 on jeans, and $10 on movies.

Table 6–5 presents hypothetical prices of these same three items in 1982. Each price has risen by a different amount, ranging from only 25 percent for jeans to 150 percent for hamburgers. By how much has the SPI risen? Pricing the 1972 student budget at 1982 prices, we find that what once cost $50 now costs $101, as the following calculation shows:

COST OF 1972 STUDENT BUDGET IN 1982 PRICES

70 hamburgers at $1	$70
1 pair of jeans at $15	15
4 movie tickets at $4	16
Total	$101

Thus the SPI, based on 1972 = 100, is

$$SPI = \frac{\text{Cost of budget in 1982}}{\text{Cost of budget in 1972}} = \frac{\$101}{\$50} \times 100 = 202 .$$

So the SPI in 1982 stands at 202, meaning that students' cost of living has increased 102 percent over the 10 years.

How to Use a Price Index to "Deflate" Monetary Figures

One of the most common uses of price indexes is in the comparison of monetary figures relating to two different points in time. The problem is that, if there has been inflation, the dollar is not a good measuring rod because it is worth less now than it was in the past.

Here is a simple example. Suppose that the average student spent $50 per month in 1972, and that this monthly spending figure had grown to $90 per month in 1982. If there was an outcry that students had become spendthrifts, how would you answer the charge?

The obvious answer is that a dollar in 1982 does not buy what it did in 1972. Specifically, our SPI shows us that it takes $2.02 in 1982 to purchase what $1 would purchase in 1972. To compare the spending habits of students in the two years, we must divide the 1982 spending figure by 2.02. Specifically, *real* spending per student in 1982 (where "real" is defined by 1972 dollars) is:

$$\text{Real spending in 1982} = \frac{\text{Nominal spending in 1982}}{\text{Price index of 1982}} .$$

Table 6–5
HYPOTHETICAL PRICES IN 1982

ITEM	PRICE	PERCENTAGE INCREASE OVER 1972
Hamburger	$ 1	150
Jeans	$15	25
Movie ticket	$ 4	60

Thus,

$$\text{Real spending in 1982} = \frac{\$90}{2.02} = \$44.55 \ .$$

In sum, this calculation shows that, despite appearances to the contrary, the change in nominal spending from $50 to $90 actually represented a *decrease* in real spending.

This calculation procedure is called **deflating by a price index,** and it serves to translate non-comparable monetary figures into more directly comparable real figures.

Deflating is the process of finding the real value of some monetary magnitude by dividing by some appropriate price index.

The GNP Deflator

In macroeconomics, one of the most important of the monetary magnitudes that we have to deflate is the nominal gross national product (GNP). The price index used to do this is called the **GNP deflator.** Our general principle for deflating a nominal magnitude tells us just how to go from nominal GNP to real GNP:

$$\text{Real GNP} = \frac{\text{Nominal GNP}}{\text{GNP deflator}} \ .$$

In fact, this formula is really nothing but the *definition* of the GNP deflator.

Economists often consider the GNP deflator to be a better measure of overall inflation in the economy than the Consumer Price Index. The main reason for this is that the two price indexes are based on different market baskets. As already mentioned, the CPI is based on the budget of a typical urban family. By contrast, the GNP deflator is constructed from a market basket that includes *every* item in the GNP—that is, every final good and service produced by the economy. Thus, in addition to prices of consumer goods, the GNP deflator includes the prices of airplanes, lathes, and other goods purchased by business. It also includes government services. For this reason, the measures of inflation that these two indexes give are rarely the same. Usually their disagreements are minor. But sometimes they can be quite substantial, as in 1979 when the CPI recorded a 13.3 percent inflation rate while the GNP deflator recorded only 8 percent.

Summary

1. Inflation is measured by the percentage increase in an index number of prices, which shows how the cost of some basket of goods has changed over a period of time.
2. Since relative prices are changing all the time, and since all families purchase different items, no price index can represent precisely the change in the cost of living for every family.
3. The Consumer Price Index (CPI) tries to measure the cost of living for an "average" urban household by pricing a "typical" market basket every month.
4. Price indexes like the CPI can be used to *deflate* monetary figures to make them more comparable. This amounts to dividing the monetary magnitude by the appropriate price index.
5. The GNP deflator—defined as the ratio of nominal GNP to real GNP—is a better measure of economy-wide inflation than is the CPI because it includes the price of every good and service in the economy.

Concepts for Review

Index number

Index number problem

Consumer Price Index

Deflating by a price index

GNP deflator

Questions for Discussion

1. Just opposite you will find the amounts (in billions of dollars) that American consumers spent on various items in 1967 and in 1980. The Consumer Price Index in 1980 (on a base of 1967 = 100) was 246.8. Use this to deflate all the 1980 figures and to compare them with the 1967 figures. Which type of spending has grown most rapidly?

YEAR	FOOD	ITEM GASOLINE AND OIL (billions of dollars)	HOUSING
1967	109.6	17.0	74.1
1980	345.7	89.0	272.0

2. Just below you will find nominal GNP and the GNP deflator for 1960, 1970, and 1980.
  a. Compute real GNP for each year.
  b. Compute the percentage change in nominal and real GNP from 1960 to 1970, and from 1970 to 1980.
  c. Compute the percentage change in the GNP deflator over these two periods.

	GNP STATISTICS		
	1960	1970	1980
Nominal GNP (billions of dollars)	506.5	992.7	2626.1
GNP deflator	68.70	91.45	177.36

3. Fill in the blanks in the following table of GNP statistics.

YEAR	1978	1979	1980
Nominal GNP	2156.1	2413.9	
Real GNP	1436.9		1480.7
GNP deflator		162.77	177.36

4. (More difficult) The example in the appendix showed that the Student Price Index (SPI) rose by 102 percent from 1972 to 1982. You can understand the meaning of this better if you:
  a. Use Table 6–4 to compute the fraction of total spending accounted for by each of the three items in 1972. Call these the "expenditure weights."
  b. Compute the weighted average of the percentage increases of the three prices shown in Table 6–5, using the expenditure weights you have just computed.
  c. You should get 102 percent as your answer. This shows that "inflation," as measured by the SPI, is a weighted average of the percentage price increases of all the items that are included in the index.

Aggregate Demand and the Powerful Consumer

7

I n Chapter 5 we saw how the strength of aggregate demand influences the performance of the economy. When aggregate demand is growing briskly, the economy is likely to be booming, though it may also be having trouble with inflation. Similarly, when aggregate demand stagnates, a recession is likely to follow.

This chapter begins our detailed study of the *determination* of aggregate demand, a study that will lead to an understanding of how the government can *manage* aggregate demand. Since consumer spending accounts for the lion's share of total demand, it is natural to begin with the consumer. In the next four chapters we will bring investment spending and government spending into the picture.

We start the chapter with some definitions of alternative concepts of economic activity—distinguishing carefully between total *spending* (aggregate demand), total *output*, and total *income* in the economy. Next, we turn to the interactions among these three concepts, using a convenient pictorial device that shows how they are all interrelated in a market economy. Then we note that government attempts to influence consumer spending have sometimes succeeded and sometimes failed, and we pose the question: Why? The bulk of the chapter is devoted to this question. To answer it, we first describe the important relationship between consumer income and consumer spending, and we use this relationship to show *how* government policies have worked *when* they have been successful. Then we discuss some complications that arise from the fact that consumer income, though crucial, is not the only factor governing consumer spending. One of these complications enables us to understand why the aggregate demand curves of Chapter 5 were drawn with a negative slope. Another holds the clue to why government policies have sometimes failed to influence consumer spending as expected.

Aggregate Demand, National Product, and National Income

Aggregate demand is the total amount that all consumers, business firms, and government agencies are willing to spend on final goods and services.

We begin with some definitions. **Aggregate demand** is a concept that we have been using already, but it is now time for a formal definition. As we noted in Chapter 5, aggregate demand is a schedule, just like any demand curve: The precise quantity demanded depends on the price level. And, like demand curves in microeconomics, it slopes downward. One of the reasons for this negative slope will be explained later in this chapter.

It is convenient to have separate names for the three components of aggregate demand. **Consumer expenditure** (**"consumption"** for short) is simply the total demand for all consumer goods and services. This is the focus of the current chapter, and we shall represent it by the letter C.

Investment spending, which we represent by the letter I, is the amount that firms spend on factories, machinery, and the like, plus the amount that families spend on new houses. Notice that this is a very different usage of the word "investment" from that which is found in common parlance. Most people speak of "investing" in the stock market or in a bank account. This kind of "investment" merely swaps one form of financial asset (such as money) for another form (such as a share of stock). When economists speak of "investment," they mean instead the purchase of some *new physical* asset, like a drill press or an oil rig or a home. It is only this kind of investment that adds directly to the total demand for newly produced goods in the economy.

Finally, the last major component of aggregate demand is **government purchases** of goods and services; that is, things like paper, typewriters, airplanes, ships, and labor that are bought by all levels of government—federal, state, and local. We use the shorthand symbol G to denote this variable. Given all these abbreviations, we have the following shorthand definition of aggregate demand.

Aggregate demand is the sum $C + I + G$.

For the most part, what is demanded gets produced in a market economy. We have already encountered the concept of gross national product as a measure of the total output of the economy.[1]

Last we have the concept of the total *income* of all the individuals in the economy. There are two versions of this: one for before-tax incomes, called **national income,** and one for after-tax incomes, called **disposable income.**[2] The term "disposable income" is meant to be descriptive: it tells us how many dollars consumers actually have available to spend or to save. Because it plays such a prominent role in this chapter, we shall need an abbreviation for it as well; we call it DI.

National income is the sum of the incomes of all the individuals in the economy earned in the forms of wages, interest, rents, and profits. It is calculated before any deductions are taken for income taxes.

Disposable income is the sum of the incomes of all the individuals in the economy after all taxes have been deducted.

The Circular Flow of Spending, Production, and Income

How do these three concepts—aggregate demand, national product, and national income—interact in a market economy? We can answer this best with a rather elaborate diagram (Figure 7–1), which the balance of this section seeks to explain. For obvious reasons, Figure 7–1 is called a **circular flow diagram.** It depicts a large circular tube in which a fluid is circulating in a clockwise direction. There are several breaks in the tube where either some of the fluid leaks out or additional fluid is injected in.

Let us examine this system beginning on the far left. Here, at point 1 on the circle, we find consumers. Disposable income (DI) is flowing into them, and two things are flowing out: consumption (C), which stays in the circular flow, and saving (S), which "leaks" out of the flow. This just says that consumers normally

[1]See Chapter 5, pages 76–78.

[2]More detailed definitions of these and other concepts are provided in an appendix to this chapter.

spend less than they earn and save the balance. The "leakage" to savings, of course, does not disappear, but flows into the financial system. We postpone until Chapters 12 and 13 a consideration of what happens there.

The upper loop of the circular flow represents expenditures, and as we move clockwise to point 2, we encounter the first "injection" into the flow: investment spending (I). The diagram shows this as coming from "investors"—a group that includes both business firms and consumers who buy new homes.[3] As the circular flow moves beyond point 2, it is bigger than it was before. Total spending has increased from C to $C + I$.

At point 3 there is yet another injection. The government adds its demand for goods and services (G) to those of consumers and investors ($C + I$). Thus, by the time we have passed point 3, we have accumulated the full amount of aggregate demand, $C + I + G$.

The circular flow diagram shows this aggregate demand for goods and services arriving at the business firms, which are located at point 4 on the extreme right of the diagram. Responding to this demand, firms produce the national product. As the circular flow emerges from the firms, however, we have renamed it *national income*. Why? The reason is that, except for some complications explained in the appendix:

National income and national product must be equal.

[3]You are reminded of the specific definition of investment on page 113.

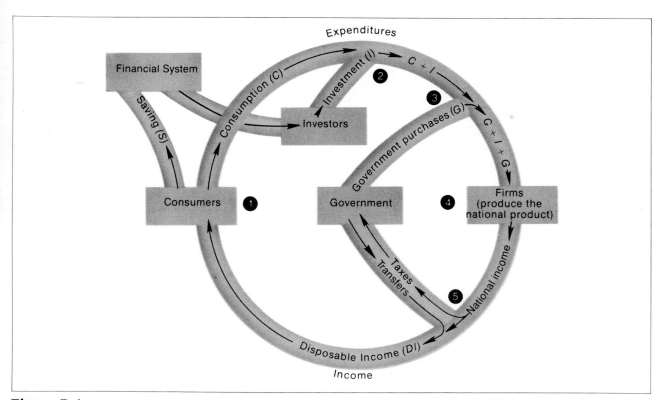

Figure 7–1
THE CIRCULAR FLOW OF EXPENDITURE AND INCOME
The upper half of this circular flow diagram depicts the flow of expenditures on goods and services, which comes from consumers (point 1), investors (point 2), and government (point 3), and goes to the firms that produce the output (point 4). The lower half of the diagram indicates how the income paid out by firms (point 4) flows to consumers (point 1), after some is siphoned off by the government in the form of taxes (point 5) and part of this is replaced by transfer payments.

Why is this the case? When a firm produces and sells $100 worth of output, it pays most of the proceeds to its workers, to people who have lent it money, and to the landlord who owns the property on which it is located. All of these payments become *income* to some individuals. But what about the rest? Suppose, for example, that the wages, interest, and rent that the firm pays add up to $90, while its output is $100. What happens to the remaining $10? The answer is that the owners of the firm receive it as *profits*. But these owners are also citizens of the country, so their incomes count in national income, too. Thus, when we add up all the wages, interest, rents, *and* profits in the economy to obtain the national income, we must arrive at the value of the national output.

The lower loop of the circular flow diagram traces the flow of income by showing national income leaving the firms and heading for consumers. But there is a detour along the way. At point 5, the government does two things: it siphons off a portion of the national income in the form of taxes, and it adds back something called **transfer payments.** These transfer payments include unemployment compensation, social security benefits, and other types of payments. As we can see from the circular flow, the following accounting identity relates GNP and *DI:*[4]

> Government **transfer payments** are sums of money that certain individuals receive as outright *grants* from the government rather than as payments for *services* rendered to employers.

DI = GNP − Taxes + Transfer payments .

Once it has passed point 5, the remaining income—now called disposable income—flows unimpeded to consumers at point 1, and the cycle repeats.

This diagram raises several complicated questions. Although we pose them here, we will not try to answer them at this early stage. The answers will be made clear in subsequent chapters.

1. Is the output that the firms produce at point 4 (the GNP) equal to aggregate demand? If so, what makes these two quantities equal? If not, what happens?

2. Is the flow of spending and income growing larger or smaller as we move clockwise around the circle, and why?

Chapter 8 provides the answers to questions 1 and 2.

3. Are the government's accounts in balance, so that what flows in at point 5 (taxes minus transfers) is equal to what flows out at point 3 (government purchases)? What happens if they are not?

This important question is first addressed in Chapter 11 and then recurs many times.

We cannot discuss these issues profitably now because first we must understand what goes on at point 1 (where consumers make decisions) and point 2 (where investors make decisions). We turn next, therefore, to the determinants of consumer spending.

Demand Management and the Powerful Consumer

As we suggested in Chapter 5, the government sometimes wants to shift the aggregate demand curve. There are a number of ways in which it can try to do so. One direct approach is to alter its own spending (*G*), becoming extravagant when

---

[4]This equation omits a few minor details, which are explained in an appendix to this chapter.

private demand is weak and miserly when private demand is strong. But the government can also take a more indirect route by using taxes and other policy tools to influence *private* spending decisions. A government desiring to change private spending can concentrate its energies either on consumer spending (*C*) or on investment spending (*I*). At various times in our history, the U.S. government has elected to pursue one or the other of these courses of action; sometimes it has endeavored to do both. Since consumer expenditures constitute more than 70 percent of gross national product, *C* presents the most tempting target.

While there are many things it can do to alter consumer spending, the government's principal weapon is the personal income tax. Many of you already have encountered Form 1040, the unwelcome New Year's greeting that every taxpayer receives from the federal government each January. Many more of you probably have been on a payroll and seen a share of your wages deducted and sent to the Internal Revenue Service. It should be no mystery, then, how changes in personal taxes affect consumer spending. Any reduction in personal taxes leaves consumers with more disposable income to spend. Any increase in taxes leaves less. The linkage from taxes to disposable income to consumer spending seems direct and unmistakable, and, in a certain sense, it is. But a look at the recent history of tax changes aimed at altering *C* is sobering. The varying degrees of success both of the measures themselves and of the predictions of their effects explain why economic research into the relationship between taxes and consumption continues.

Case 1: The 1964 Tax Reduction

The year 1964 was a good one for the economy but an even better one for economists. For years economists had been proclaiming that a cut in personal taxes would be an excellent way to stimulate a stagnating economy. But the plea fell on deaf ears until President John F. Kennedy was persuaded of the basic logic of the argument. Under his successor, Lyndon B. Johnson, Congress reduced personal taxes by about $9 billion per year, almost 18 percent of the total personal taxes then being collected. The legislation was designed to spur consumer spending, and it succeeded admirably. Consumers reacted just about as the textbooks of the day predicted, the economic situation improved rapidly and markedly, and economists smiled knowingly.

Case 2: The 1968 Tax Increase

The euphoria of 1964 and 1965 was both unwarranted and short-lived. In 1968–1969 we learned—the hard way—that economists did not have all the answers. Largely because of the massive defense spending associated with the Vietnam War, the macroeconomic problem of 1966–1968 was precisely the opposite of that in 1964: too much demand rather than too little. It appeared logical, then, to prescribe the opposite medicine; and economists were quick to suggest an increase in personal income taxes to force consumers to spend less.

After a considerable delay, President Johnson recommended a temporary tax increase and Congress enacted a 10 percent rise in personal tax payments (calling it a "surcharge"). However, this attempt to cut aggregate demand by reducing *C* enjoyed only modest success. While consumer spending probably was below what it would have been in the absence of the surcharge, it was substantially above what the 1964 experience had led economists to predict.

Case 3: The 1975 Tax Reduction

The next major change in tax laws for stabilization purposes also met with partial success at best. In the spring of 1975, as the economy neared the bottom of its worst postwar recession, President Gerald R. Ford and Congress agreed on a double-edged tax cut amounting to over $20 billion. First, they returned to each taxpayer part of the taxes paid in 1974. Second, they reduced income tax rates for the balance of 1975. (This was subsequently extended.) What happened? Not as much as had been hoped. Consumers confounded the wishes of the president and Congress by saving a good deal of their rebates rather than spending them.

What went wrong in 1968 and 1975 that had not gone wrong in 1964? This chapter will attempt to provide some answers. We begin by exploring the important relationship between consumer income and consumer spending, more or less retracing the chain of logic that led government economists to the right conclusion in 1964. Once this is accomplished, we turn to some of the complications that made things go awry in 1968 and 1975.

Consumer Spending and Income: The Important Relationship

An economist interested in predicting how consumer spending will respond to a change in personal income tax payments must first ask how C is related to income, for an increase in taxes is a decrease in after-tax disposable income (refer to Figure 7–1) and a reduction in taxes is an increase in after-tax income. This section, therefore, will examine what we know about the response of consumer spending to a change in disposable income.

Figure 7–2 depicts the historical paths of C and DI for the United States since 1929. The association is obviously rather close and certainly suggests that consumption will rise whenever disposable income does, and fall whenever income falls. The difference between the two lines is personal saving. Notice how little saving consumers did during the Great Depression of the 1930s, where the two lines are very close together, and how much they did during World War II, when many consumer goods were either unavailable or rationed so there was little on which to spend money.

Of course, knowing that consumer expenditures, C, will move in the same direction as disposable income, DI, is not enough for policy planners. They need to know *how much* one will go up when the other rises a given amount. Figure 7–3 presents the same data that we saw in Figure 7–2 but in a way designed to help answer the "how much" question. Economists call such pictures **scatter diagrams,** and they are very useful in predicting how one economic variable (in this case, consumer spending) will change in response to a change in another economic variable (in this case, disposable income). Each dot in the diagram represents the data on C and DI corresponding to a particular year. For example, the point labeled "1964" shows that real consumer expenditures in 1964 were $528 billion (which we read off the vertical axis), while real disposable incomes amounted to $581 billion (which we read off the horizontal axis). Similarly, each year from 1929 to 1980 is represented by its own dot in Figure 7–3.

How can such a diagram assist the fiscal policy planner? Imagine that this is 1963 and you must decide whether to recommend to Congress a tax cut of $5 billion, $10 billion, or $15 billion. (It has already been decided that a cut smaller than $5 billion is not worth the legislative effort and that a cut of more than $15 billion is politically infeasible.) You have forecasts of what consumer expenditures are expected to be if taxes are not reduced. This, plus other forecasts of investment and government spending, has led you to conclude that aggregate demand in 1964 will be insufficient if taxes are not reduced.

To assist your imagination, another scatter diagram is given in Figure 7–4. This one removes the points for 1964 through 1980, which appeared in Figure 7–3; after all, these would not have been known in 1963. Years prior to 1947 have also been removed because both the Great Depression and wartime rationing seriously disturbed the normal relationship between *DI* and *C*. With no more training in economics than you have right how, what would you do?

One rough-and-ready approach is to get a ruler, set it down on Figure 7–4 and sketch a straight line that comes as close as possible to hitting all the points. Try that now. You will not be able to hit each point exactly, but you will find that you can come remarkably close. The line you have just drawn summarizes, in a very rough way, the consumption–income relationship that is the focus of this chapter. We see at once that it confirms something we might have guessed—that a rise in income is associated with a rise in consumer spending. The slope of the line is certainly positive. The slope of your line is very important.[5] That line has been drawn into Figure 7–5, and we note that its slope is:

$$\text{Slope} = \frac{\text{Vertical change}}{\text{Horizontal change}} = \frac{\$90 \text{ billion}}{\$100 \text{ billion}} = 0.90 \;.$$

[5]To review the concept of *slope*, turn back to page 22.

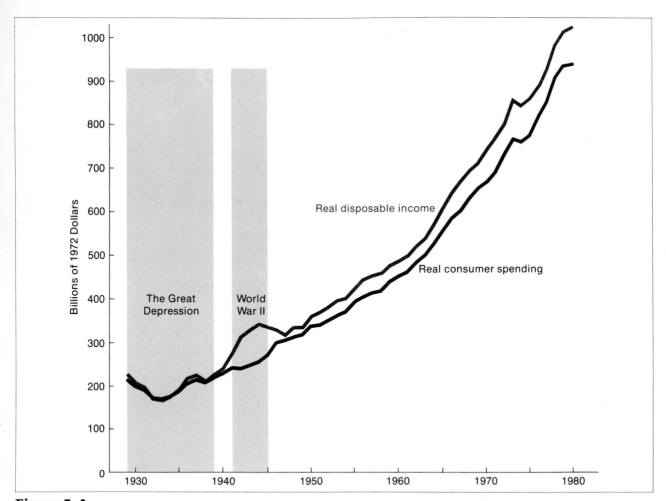

Figure 7–2
CONSUMER SPENDING AND DISPOSABLE INCOME IN THE UNITED STATES SINCE 1929
This time series chart shows the behavior of consumer spending and disposable income in the United States since 1929. Except for the World War II years, the correspondence between the two variables is remarkably close. The distance between the two lines represents consumer saving, which was obviously quite small during the Great Depression of the 1930s and quite large during World War II.
SOURCE: U.S. Department of Commerce.

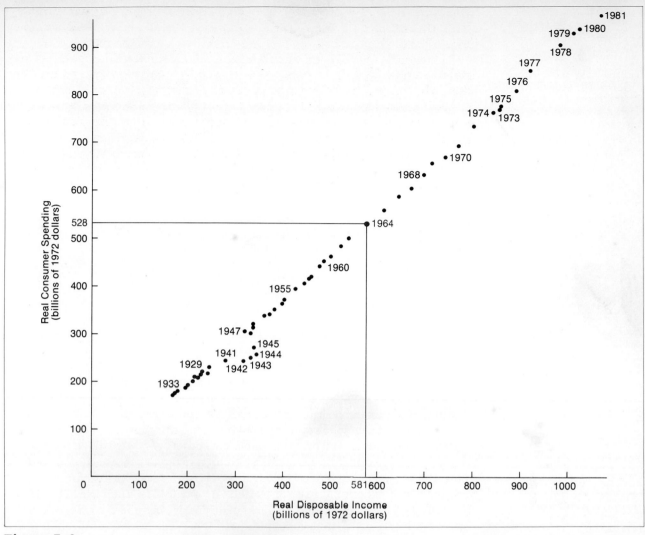

Figure 7–3
SCATTER DIAGRAM OF CONSUMER SPENDING AND DISPOSABLE INCOME IN THE UNITED STATES, 1929–1980
This diagram shows the same data as depicted in Figure 7–2 but in a different manner. Each point on the diagram represents the data for both consumer spending and disposable income during a particular year. For example, the point labeled "1964" indicates that in that year consumer spending was $528 billion while disposable income was $581 billion. Diagrams like this one are called "scatter diagrams."

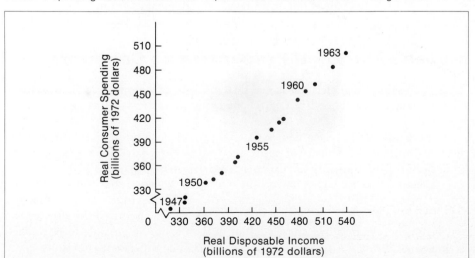

Figure 7–4
SCATTER DIAGRAM OF CONSUMER SPENDING AND DISPOSABLE INCOME IN THE UNITED STATES, 1947–1963
This scatter diagram omits some of the data found in Figure 7–3 and indicates the information that policy planners might have used in deciding upon the size of the 1964 income tax cut.

Figure 7–5
SCATTER DIAGRAM OF
CONSUMER SPENDING
AND DISPOSABLE IN-
COME IN THE UNITED
STATES, 1947–1963
This diagram is the same as
Figure 7–4 except for the addi-
tion of a straight line that
comes about as close as possi-
ble to fitting all the data points.

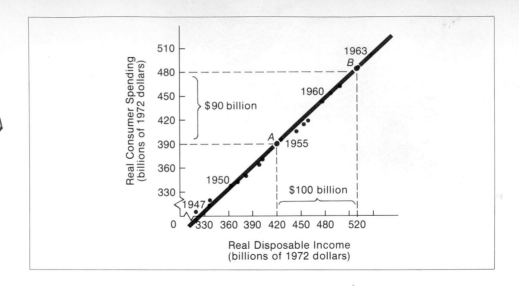

Real Consumer Spending
(billions of 1972 dollars)

Real Disposable Income
(billions of 1972 dollars)

Since the horizontal change involved in the move from *A* to *B* represents a rise in disposable income of $100 billion (from $420 billion to $520 billion), and the corresponding vertical change represents the associated $90 billion rise in consumer spending (from $390 to $480 billion), the slope of the line indicates how spending responds to changes in disposable income. In this case, we see that each additional $1 of income leads to 90 cents of additional spending.

In terms of the policy issue of 1964, this line can therefore help provide an answer to the question: How much more consumer spending will be induced by tax cuts of $5 billion, $10 billion, or $15 billion if the effects are similar to those observed in the past described by the graph? First, we need to keep in mind that each dollar of tax cut increases disposable income by $1. Then, we apply Figure 7–5's finding that each additional dollar of disposable income increases consumer spending by 90 cents, and conclude that proposed tax cuts of $5 billion, $10 billion, or $15 billion would be expected to increase consumer spending by $4.5 billion, $9.0 billion, and $13.5 billion, respectively. Similar questions addressed by economists in 1964 led to a decision to cut taxes by about $9 billion.

Later in this and other chapters, we will encounter several reasons why this procedure, while basically valid, must be used with great caution.

The Consumption Function and the Marginal Propensity to Consume

It has been said that economics is just systematized common sense. Let us, then, try to organize and generalize what has been a completely intuitive discussion thus far.

One thing we have learned is that there is a close and apparently reliable relationship between consumer spending, C, and disposable income, DI. Economists call this relationship the **consumption function.**

A second fact we have picked up from these figures is that the slope of the consumption function is fairly constant. We infer this from the fact that the straight line in Figure 7–5 comes close to touching every point. If the slope of the consumption function had changed a lot, it would not be possible to do so well with a single straight line. Because of its importance in such applications as the

The **consumption function** is the relationship between total consumer expenditure and total disposable income in the economy.

Table 7–1

CONSUMPTION AND INCOME IN MACROLAND

YEAR	(1) CONSUMPTION, C (billions of dollars)	(2) DISPOSABLE INCOME, DI (billions of dollars)	(3) MARGINAL PROPENSITY TO CONSUME, MPC
1977	600	600	
1978	760	800	0.8
1979	920	1000	0.8
1980	1080	1200	0.8
1981	1240	1400	0.8
1982	1400	1600	0.8

tax-cut example, economists have given a special name to this slope—the **marginal propensity to consume.**

This concept is best illustrated by an example, and for this purpose we turn away from U.S. data for a moment and look at the consumption and income data of a hypothetical country called Macroland (see Table 7–1). The data for Macroland resemble those for the United States, except that in Macroland, C and DI figures happen to be nice round numbers, which facilitates computation.

Columns 1 and 2 of Table 7–1 show annual consumer expenditure and disposable income from 1977 to 1982. These two columns constitute Macroland's consumption function and are plotted in Figure 7–6. Column 3 in the table shows the marginal propensity to consume (MPC), which is the slope of the line in Figure 7–6; it is derived from the first two columns. We can see that between 1977 and 1978, DI rose by $200 billion (from $600 to $800) while C rose by $160 billion (from $600 to $760). Thus the MPC was:

$$\frac{\text{Change in consumption}}{\text{Change in disposable income}} = \frac{\$160}{\$200} = 0.80 \ .$$

The **marginal propensity to consume** (or MPC for short) tells us how many more dollars consumers will spend if disposable income rises by $1 billion. On a graph, it appears as the slope of the consumption function. Its formula is:

$$\text{MPC} = \frac{\text{Change in consumption}}{\begin{array}{c}\text{Change in disposable}\\ \text{income that produces}\\ \text{the change in}\\ \text{consumption}\end{array}} \ .$$

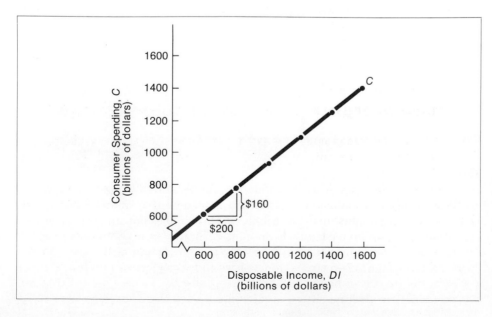

Figure 7–6

THE CONSUMPTION FUNCTION OF MACROLAND

This diagram is similar to Figure 7–4, except that it applies to a hypothetical (and blissfully simple!) economy called Macroland. As can be seen, a straight-line consumption function passes through every point exactly. The slope of this line is 0.8, which is the marginal propensity to consume in Macroland.

As you can easily verify, the MPC between any other pair of years in Macroland was also 0.80. This explains why the slope of the line in Figure 7–5 was so crucial in estimating the effect of a tax cut. This slope, which we found to be 0.90, is nothing but the MPC for the U.S. And it is the MPC that tells us how much *additional* spending will be induced by each dollar *change* in disposable income. For each $1 of tax cut, economists expect consumption to rise by $1 times the marginal propensity to consume. Thus:

To estimate the initial effect of a tax cut on consumer spending, economists must first estimate the MPC and then multiply the amount of the tax cut by the estimated MPC. But since they never know the true MPC with certainty, this prediction is always subject to some margin of error.[6]

In 1963, for example, economists multiplied the anticipated $9 billion tax cut by the estimated MPC of 0.90 and concluded that consumer spending would initially rise by about $8 billion. Their estimate seems to have been remarkably accurate.

Movements Along Versus Shifts of the Consumption Function

Unfortunately, this sort of calculation does not always yield such precise results. Among the most important reasons for this is that the consumption function does not always stand still; sometimes it shifts.

You will recall from Chapter 4 the important distinction between a *movement along* a demand (or supply) curve and a *shift of* the curve. A similar distinction is vital to understanding real-world consumption functions. Any change in disposable income (caused, for example, by a change in the income tax) leads to a **movement along the consumption function.** This is the sort of phenomenon we have been considering in the last two sections. But consumption also has other determinants. And since the consumption schedule relates C to DI, any change in one of these "other determinants" of consumer spending (which we will consider shortly) will **shift the entire consumption function.** It is these unexpected shifts that account for many of the errors in forecasting consumption. To summarize:

Any change in disposable income moves us along a given consumption function. But a change in any of the other variables that influence consumption results in a shift in the entire consumption schedule.

Let us now see what some of these "other variables" are.

Other Determinants of Consumer Spending

The Recent Past
One factor is simple *inertia*, the fact that households normally take some time to adjust to changed economic circumstances. If income rises at an extraordinary pace—as in an economic boom—consumer spending does not surge ahead as fast as income. You can understand why by considering a close-to-home example.

Unless you continue on to graduate study, your income will register a very sharp increase when you graduate from college and get a job. See how long it takes

---

[6]The word "initial" in the first sentence is an important one. Later chapters explain why the effects discussed in this chapter are only the beginning of the story.

until your spending habits have caught up. The same process works in reverse. At the onset of a recession, consumers normally try to maintain their customary spending levels despite losses of income.

Wealth

A second factor is consumers' *wealth*, which is a source of demand in addition to income. Consider two consumers, both earning $20,000 this year. One of them has $100,000 in the bank, while the other has no assets at all. Who do you think will spend more this year? Presumably the one with the big bank account. The general point is that current income is not the only source of funds that households have; they can also finance spending by withdrawals from their bank accounts or by cashing in other forms of wealth. A stock market boom may therefore raise the consumption function, while a collapse of stock prices may lower it.

The Price Level

The next determinant of consumer spending—the *price level*—is related to wealth, and is also important to understanding why the economy's aggregate demand curve slopes downward.

A good deal of consumer wealth is held in forms whose values are fixed in money terms. Money itself is the most obvious example of this, but government bonds, savings accounts, and corporate bonds are all assets with fixed face values in money terms. The *real* values of these **money fixed assets** obviously decline whenever the price level rises, which means that their *purchasing power* (what the assets can buy) falls as the price level rises. For example, if the price level rises by 10 percent, a $1000 government bond will buy about 10 percent less than it could when prices were lower. Consequently:

Higher overall prices, by eroding the purchasing power of consumer wealth, decrease the demand for goods and services.

This is no trivial matter. It has been estimated that the total volume of money fixed assets in the United States is around $3–$4 *trillion*, so that each 1 percent rise in the price level reduces consumer wealth by $30–$40 billion—a tidy sum. The process, of course, operates equally well in reverse. A decline in the price level increases the purchasing power of money fixed assets. So:

Lower overall prices, by enhancing the purchasing power of consumer wealth, increase the demand for goods and services.

Thus the price level is another variable that can shift the entire consumption function. A higher price level leads to less spending *at any given level of real income*, and thus to a lower consumption function. Conversely, a lower price level leads to a higher consumption function. Students are often confused on this point, so it is worth repeating that the depressing effect of the price level on consumer spending works through *wealth*, not *income*. The consumption function is a relationship between real consumer income and real consumer spending. Thus any decline in real income, whether caused by a rise in the price level or by something else, moves the economy *leftward along a fixed consumption function*; it does not shift the consumption function. By contrast, however, any decline in real wealth will *shift the whole consumption function downward*, meaning that there is less spending, even if real income is unchanged.

The fact that a higher price level leads to a lower consumption function is one reason why we drew our aggregate demand schedules in Chapter 5 with negative slopes, indicating that total quantity demanded is lower when prices are higher. Higher prices, we now see, reduce real consumer wealth and therefore lead to lower real spending, C. Since C is a component of aggregate demand (the sum of $C + I + G$), a higher price level leads to a smaller aggregate quantity demanded. Other reasons for the downward slope of the aggregate demand schedule will be encountered in subsequent chapters.

The Inflation Rate

Prices may be high and rising slowly, or they may be low but rising rapidly. Therefore, the depressing effect of a high *price level* on real consumer spending must be distinguished from any effect on spending that the *rate of inflation* (that is, the rate of increase of prices) may have.

Conclusions about the effect the rate of inflation has on spending are not clear; we are not sure whether inflation stimulates or depresses consumer spending. In the past, economists believed that high rates of inflation caused consumers to spend more to "beat" the inflation. That is, people were thought to purchase goods ahead of their needs in order to avoid the higher prices that loomed on the horizon. But behavior during the period of "double-digit" inflation in 1974 belied this contention: consumer spending was actually unusually *low* during this episode of high inflation. However, the opposite happened when inflation returned to double-digit levels in 1979 and early 1980; this time, consumers started spending like mad. Thus, in constructing macroeconomic models in the ensuing chapters, we shall assume that the position of the consumption function is influenced by the *price level*, but not by the *inflation rate*.

Expectations About the Future

It will hardly be considered earth shattering to suggest that consumers' expectations about future income may affect their spending in important ways. This final determinant of consumer spending turns out to hold the key to answering the important question we posed earlier. Why did the tax policy that succeeded so well in 1964 fail to alter consumer spending as much in 1968 and 1975?

Why Tax Policy Failed in 1968 and 1975

To understand how expectations of future incomes affect current consumer expenditures, consider the abbreviated life histories of three consumers given in Table 7–2. The reason for giving our three imaginary individuals such odd names will be apparent shortly.

The consumer named "No Change" earned $100 in each of the four years considered in the table. The consumer named "Temporary Rise" earned $100 in three of the four years, but had a good year in 1975. The consumer named "Permanent Change" enjoyed a permanent rise in income in 1975 and was clearly the richest.

Table 7–2
INCOMES OF THREE CONSUMERS

CONSUMER	INCOMES IN EACH YEAR				TOTAL INCOME
	1974	1975	1976	1977	
No Change	100	100	100	100	400
Temporary Rise	100	120	100	100	420
Permanent Rise	100	120	120	120	460

Now let us use our common sense to figure out how much each of these consumers might have spent in 1975. "Temporary Rise" and "Permanent Rise" had the same income that year. Do you think they spent the same amount? Not if they had some ability to foresee their future incomes, because "Permanent Rise" was richer in the long run.

Now compare "No Change" and "Temporary Rise." Temporary Rise had 20 percent higher income in 1975 ($120 versus $100) but only 5 percent more over the entire four-year period ($420 versus $400). Do you think her spending was closer to 20 percent above No Change's or closer to 5 percent above it? Most people guess the latter.

The point of this example is that it is reasonable for consumers to decide on their *current* consumption spending by looking at their *long-run* income prospects. This should not be a shocking idea to most college students. How many of you are spending only what you earn this year? Probably not very many. And this is not because you are all foolish spendthrifts. On the contrary, you are rational planners. Knowing that your college education gives you a reasonable expectation of future income prospects much greater than those you now have, you are no doubt spending with that in mind.

Now let us see what all this has to do with the failure of the 1975 income tax rebate. For this purpose, imagine that the three rows in Table 7–2 now represent the entire economy under three different government policies. Recall that 1975 was the year of the rebate. The first row ("No Change") shows the unchanged path of disposable income if no tax cut was enacted. The second ("Temporary Rise") shows an increase in disposable income attributable to a tax cut *for one year only*. Finally, the bottom row ("Permanent Rise") shows a policy that increases *DI* in *every future year* by cutting taxes permanently in 1975. Which of the two lower rows do you imagine would have generated more consumer spending in 1975? The bottom row ("Permanent Rise"), of course. What we have concluded, then, is this:

Permanent cuts in income taxes cause greater increases in consumer spending than do temporary cuts of equal magnitude.

The application of this analysis to the case of the 1975 tax cut is immediate. About half the cut was a refund of some of the 1974 taxes that had already been paid. These rebates were clearly one-time increases in income like that experienced by "Temporary Rise" in Table 7–2. No future income was affected. The remaining cuts came in the form of special reduced tax rates announced to apply in 1975 *only*, and thus might reasonably have been expected to be temporary as well. Since the 1975 tax-cut package had little effect on expected future incomes, it is not surprising that its impact on consumer spending was rather mild.

Much the same situation prevailed in 1968, when Congress enacted a temporary 10 percent increase in income taxes to help finance the Vietnam War. Consumers considered the resulting decrease in their disposable income as only a temporary loss and did not curtail their spending as much as government officials had hoped. The general lesson is:

A permanent increase in income taxes provides a greater deterrent to consumer spending than does a temporary increase of equal magnitude.

We have, then, what appears to be a general principle, backed up both by historical evidence and common sense. Permanent changes in income taxes have a more significant impact on consumer spending than do temporary changes.

Though it may now seem obvious, this is not a lesson you would have learned from the introductory textbooks of 1968; it is one that we learned the hard way, through bitter experience. The tax surcharge of 1968 was meant to slow down inflation. Yet consumer prices rose faster in 1968 than they had in 1967, and faster in 1969 than in 1968. The tax reductions of 1975 were meant to halt a precipitous downswing in economic activity. It was subsequently learned that the recession had bottomed out, of its own accord, before the cuts became effective, and the recovery in consumer spending was not all that spectacular.

The Predictability of Consumer Behavior

We have now learned enough to see why the economist's problem in predicting how consumers will react to an increase or decrease in taxes is not quite as simple as suggested earlier in this chapter.

The principal problem seems to be anticipating how taxpayers will view any changes in the income tax law. If the government *says* that a tax cut is permanent, will consumers *believe* it and increase their spending accordingly? Perhaps not, if the government has a history of raising taxes after promising to keep them low. Similarly, when (as in 1968) the government explicitly announces that a tax increase is temporary, will consumers always believe this? Or might they greet such an announcement with a hefty dose of skepticism? This is quite possible if there is a long history of "temporary" tax increases that stayed on the books indefinitely. Thus the effectiveness of any *future* tax policy move may well depend on the government's *past* track record. A government that repeatedly uses a succession of so-called "permanent" tax cuts and tax increases for short-run stabilization purposes may find consumers beginning to ignore the tax changes entirely. The story of the boy who cried wolf is not yet required reading for fiscal policy planners; but someday it might be.

Nor is this the only problem. Economists may underestimate or overestimate the degree of inertia in consumer behavior. Their predictions may fail to take adequate account of large and rapid accumulations of wealth (as happened immediately after World War II, when consumption forecasts were notoriously low) or of sizable losses of wealth (such as the drastic decline in the stock market in 1973–1975, when consumption forecasts were too high). Poor forecasts of future prices may lead consumption forecasts astray. And there are further hazards that we have not even mentioned here. Economic predictions are inexact, and the lesson of predictions based on the consumption function illustrates this well.

There is much more that can be said about the determinants of consumption, but it is best to leave the rest to more advanced courses in macroeconomics. For we are now ready to apply our knowledge of the consumption function to the construction of the first model of the whole economy. While it is true that income determines consumption, the consumption function in turn helps to determine the level of income. If that sounds like circular reasoning, read the next chapter!

Summary

1. Aggregate demand is the total amount of goods and services that consumers, businesses, and government units are willing to purchase. It can be expressed as the sum $C + I + G$, where C is consumer spending, I is investment spending, and G is government spending.

2. Economists reserve the term "investment" to refer to purchases of newly produced factories, machinery, and houses.

3. National product is the total output of final goods and services of the economy. It is most commonly measured by the gross national product.

4. National income is the sum of the before-tax wages, interest, rents, and profits earned by all individuals in the economy. By necessity, it must be equal to national product.

5. Disposable income is the sum of the incomes of all individuals in the economy, after taxes and transfers, and is the chief determinant of consumer expenditure.

6. All of these concepts, and others, can be depicted in a circular flow diagram that shows expenditures on all three sources flowing into business firms and national income flowing out.

7. The government often has tried to manipulate aggregate demand by influencing private consumption decisions, usually through the personal income tax. Although this policy seemed to work very well in 1964, it did not work very well in 1968 and 1975.

8. The close relationship between consumer spending (C) and disposable income (DI) is called the consumption function. Its slope, which is used to predict the change in consumption that will be caused by a change in income taxes, is called the marginal propensity to consume (MPC).

9. Changes in disposable income move us along a given consumption function. Changes in any of the other variables that affect C will shift the entire consumption function. Among the most important of these other variables are total consumer wealth, the price level, and expected future incomes.

10. Because consumers hold so many money fixed assets, they lose out when prices rise, which leads them to reduce their spending. This decline in consumer demand when prices rise helps explain why the aggregate demand curve slopes downward.

11. Future income prospects help explain why tax policy did not affect consumption as much as was hoped in 1968 and 1975. This is because the 1968 tax increase and the 1975 tax cut were both temporary, and therefore left future incomes unaffected. By contrast, the 1964 tax cut was "permanent," and affected future as well as current incomes. It is no surprise, then, that the 1964 actions had stronger effects on spending than did the 1968 or 1975 actions.

Concepts for Review

Aggregate demand
Consumer expenditure, or consumption (C)
Investment spending (I)
Government purchases (G)
$C + I + G$
National income

Disposable income (DI)
Circular flow diagram
Transfer payments
Scatter diagram
Consumption function
Marginal propensity to consume (MPC)

Movements along versus shifts of the consumption function
Money fixed assets
Downward slope of the aggregate demand curve
Temporary versus permanent tax changes

Questions for Discussion

1. What are the three components of aggregate demand? Which of these is the largest?

2. Suppose investment spending were always $100, government spending were always $50, and consumer spending depended on the price level in the following way:

PRICE LEVEL	CONSUMER SPENDING
80	370
90	360
100	350
110	340
120	330

On a piece of graph paper, use these data to construct an aggregate demand curve of the type we used in Chapter 5. Why do you think this example supposes that consumption declines as the price level rises?

3. What is the difference between "investment" as the term is used by most people and "investment" as defined by an economist? Which of the following acts constitute "investment" according to the economist's definition?
   a. General Motors constructs a new assembly line
   b. You buy 100 shares of General Motors stock
   c. A small steel company goes bankrupt, and U.S. Steel purchases its factory and equipment
   d. Your family buys a newly constructed home from a developer
   e. Your family buys an older home from another family (*Hint:* Are any *new* products demanded by this action?)

4. What would the circular flow diagram (Figure 7–1, page 114) look like in an economy with no government? Draw one for yourself.

5. The marginal propensity to consume (MPC) for the nation as a whole is roughly 0.90. Explain in words what this means. What is your personal MPC?

6. Look at the scatter diagram in Figure 7–3 (page 119). What does it tell you about what was going on in this country in the years 1942–1945?

7. What is a "consumption function," and why is it a useful device for government economists planning a tax cut?

8. Explain why permanent tax cuts are likely to lead to bigger increases in consumer spending than are temporary tax cuts.

9. On a piece of graph paper, construct the consumption function for Simpleland from the data given below:

YEAR	CONSUMER SPENDING	DISPOSABLE INCOME
1981	1100	1000
1982	1550	1500
1983	2000	2000
1984	2450	2500
1985	2900	3000

What is the MPC?

Appendix A

The Saving Function and the Marginal Propensity to Save

There is an alternative way of looking at the relationships we have discussed in this chapter. Disposable income that is not spent must be saved. Therefore we can examine the effect of income on *saving* as well as its effect on consumer *spending*.

To see how saving appears on the consumption function diagram, we have repeated the consumption function of Macroland (see Figure 7–6) in Figure 7–7 and added a 45° line. You will recall that a 45° line marks those points where the distances along the horizontal and vertical axes are equal. (If you wish to review, see page 25.) In this case, the 45° line shows where consumer spending equals disposable income; that is, where saving is exactly zero. As can be seen in the diagram, only one point on the consumption function satisfies this requirement—point D, where consumption and disposable income are both $600 billion. When income is above $600 billion, the consumption schedule is below the 45° line. This means that consumer spending is less than income, so some is being saved. Conversely, when income is below $600 billion, the consumption schedule is above the 45° line, so consumer spending exceeds income. Is this impossible? Normally, not. Consumers usually have bank accounts and other sources from which they can obtain funds when their income is low.

To find the amount of saving at each level of income, we need only read the vertical distance (positive or negative) from the consumption function to the 45° line. For example, when income is $1600 billion, saving is the distance AB, or $200

billion. When income is $600 billion, saving must be zero, since the consumption function and the 45°

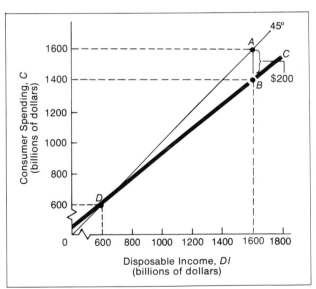

Figure 7–7
THE CONSUMPTION FUNCTION OF MACROLAND
The consumption function of Macroland, which we encountered in Figure 7–6 (page 121), is repeated here, and a 45° line is added for convenience. Since consumption and saving must always add up to disposable income, the vertical distance between the two lines represents saving. For example, points A and B indicate that when disposable income is $1600 billion, saving is $200 billion. The two lines cross at point D (income level $600 billion). Since consumption equals disposable income at this point, there is exactly zero saving.

line intersect.

There is also a more direct way to find saving. Table 7–3 repeats the consumption and disposable income data for Macroland from Table 7–1 (page 121). Then, in column 3, we compute the difference between disposable income and consumption, which gives us **aggregate saving.**

Aggregate saving is the difference between disposable income and consumer expenditure. In symbols, $S = DI - C$.

This subtraction is exactly what we showed graphically in Figure 7–7. Columns 2 and 3 of Table 7–3 constitute what economists call the **saving function.**

The **saving function** is the schedule relating total consumer saving to total disposable income in the economy.

These data are portrayed in Figure 7–8, which is constructed from the numbers in Table 7–3. It could equally well have been constructed as the difference between the 45° line and the C line in Figure 7–7. (Because saving is so much less than consumption, we have stretched the scale of the vertical axis considerably.) Points A, B, and D correspond to the same points in Figure 7–7. The horizontal axis in Figure 7–8 shows all the places where saving is exactly zero, just as the 45° line did in Figure 7–7. When the consumption function is a straight line, and thus has a constant slope, the same will be true of the saving function. In Figure 7–8, we show this slope as the ratio of distance AB to distance DA, or $200/$1000 = 0.2. Economists call this slope the **marginal propensity to save.**

The **marginal propensity to save** (or MPS) is the slope of the saving function. It tells us how much

more consumers will save if disposable income rises by $1 billion.

You may have noticed that the MPS is 0.2 while the MPC for Macroland is 0.8. They add up to 1, and not by accident. Since the portion of each additional dollar of disposable income that is not spent must be saved, the MPC and the MPS always add up to 1. It is a simple fact of accounting.

The MPC and the MPS always add up to 1, meaning that an additional dollar of income must be divided between consumption and saving. In symbols:

$$MPC + MPS = 1.$$

This enables us to compute either one of them from the other.

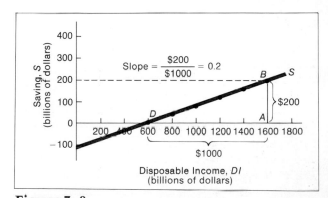

Figure 7–8
THE SAVING FUNCTION OF MACROLAND
The saving function of Macroland, depicted here, can be constructed either from the data in Table 7–3 or from Figure 7–7. This is because when we plot saving against disposable income (as we do here), we are also plotting the difference between consumption and disposable income (the vertical distance between line C and the 45° line in Figure 7–7) against disposable income.

Table 7–3
SAVING IN MACROLAND

YEAR	(1) CONSUMPTION, C	(2) DISPOSABLE INCOME, DI	(3) SAVING, S	(4) MARGINAL PROPENSITY TO SAVE, MPS
1977	600	600	0	0.2
1978	760	800	40	0.2
1979	920	1000	80	0.2
1980	1080	1200	120	0.2
1981	1240	1400	160	0.2
1982	1400	1600	200	

Summary

1. Instead of studying the consumption function, it is possible to study the same data by looking at the saving function, which is defined as the relationship between disposable income and consumer saving.
2. Since consumer saving is merely the difference between disposable income and consumer expenditure, everything we have learned about the consumption function applies to the saving function.
3. The amount of additional saving caused by a growth of $1 in disposable income is called the marginal propensity to save, or MPS.
4. Since each additional $1 of disposable income is either spent or saved, the MPC and the MPS must always add up to 1. Thus, knowledge of one implies knowledge of the other.

Concepts for Review

Aggregate saving
Saving function
Marginal propensity to save

Questions for Discussion

1. Look at the circular flow diagram in Figure 7–1 (page 114). Where does the saving function enter the picture?
2. If the MPC in the U.S. economy is about 0.90, how large is the MPS?
3. Take the data from Simpleland in Question 9 on page 128 and use them to construct a saving function for Simpleland on a piece of graph paper.
4. (More difficult) If taxes are cut *temporarily* and consumer spending does not increase much, what must happen to consumer saving? Ask your instructor what happened to consumer saving immediately after the 1975 tax cuts.

Appendix B

National Income Accounting

The type of macroeconomic analysis presented in this book dates from the publication of John Maynard Keynes's *The General Theory of Employment, Interest, and Money* in 1936. But at that time there was really no way to test Keynes's theories because the necessary data did not exist. It took some years for the theoretical notions used by Keynes to find concrete expression in real-world data. The system of measurement devised for this purpose is called **national income accounting.**

The development of this system of accounts ranks as a great achievement in applied economics, perhaps as important in its own right as Keynes's theoretical work. For, without it, the practical value of Keynesian analysis would be severely limited. Many men and women spent long hours wrestling with the numerous difficult conceptual questions that arose in translating the theory into numbers, but they had one acknowledged leader: Professor Simon Kuznets of Harvard University, who, in 1971, was awarded the Nobel Prize in Economics for his contributions to economic measurement techniques. Along the way some more-or-less arbitrary decisions and conventions had to be made. You may not agree with all of them, but the accounting framework that was devised is eminently serviceable, though, inevitably, it has some limitations that must be understood.

Defining GNP: Exceptions to the Rules

We first encountered the concept of **gross national product** (GNP) in Chapter 5.

Gross national product (GNP) is the sum of the money values of all final goods and services produced during a specified period of time, usually one year.

However, the definition of GNP given there, and repeated above for your convenience, has certain exceptions we have not yet noted. Three major exceptions are discussed here. First, the treatment of government output involves a minor departure from the principle of using market prices. Outputs of private industries are sold on markets, and their prices are measured when this occurs. But "outputs" of government offices are not sold; indeed, it is sometimes even difficult to define what those outputs are. Lacking prices for outputs, national income accountants fall back on the only prices they have: prices for the inputs from which the outputs are produced. Thus:

Government outputs are valued at the cost of the inputs needed to produce them.

This means, for example, that if a clerk at the Department of Motor Vehicles earns $8 an hour and spends one-half hour torturing you with explanations of why you cannot get a driver's license, that particular government "service" is considered as being worth $4, and will increase GNP by that amount.

Second, some goods that are not actually sold on markets during the year are nonetheless counted in that year's GNP. These are the goods that are produced during the year but not sold; that is, goods that firms stockpile as *inventories*. Goods that are added to inventories are part of the GNP even though they do not pass through markets.

National income statisticians treat inventories as if they were "bought" by the firms that produced them, even though this "purchase" never takes place.

Finally, the treatment of investment goods runs slightly counter to the rule that only final goods are to be counted. In a broad sense, factories, generators, machine tools, and the like might be considered as intermediate goods. After all, their owners want them only for use in producing other goods, not for any innate value that they possess. But this would present a real problem, for factories and machines normally are never sold to consumers. So when would we count them in GNP? National income statisticians avoid this problem by defining investment goods as final products demanded by the firms that buy them.

Now that we have a complete definition of just what the GNP is, let us turn to the problem of actually measuring it. National income accountants have devised three ways to perform this task, and we consider each of them in turn.

GNP as the Sum of Final Goods and Services

The first way to measure GNP seems to be the most natural, since it follows so directly from the circular flow diagram in this chapter. It also turns out to be the most useful definition from the point of view of macroeconomics. We simply add up the final demands of all consumers, business firms, and the government. Using the symbol C to denote the final goods and services demanded by *consumers*, the symbol I (for invesment) to denote the final goods demanded by business firms and other *investors*, and the symbol G (for government purchases) to denote the final goods and services demanded by all levels of *government*, we have:

$$GNP = C + I + G.$$

The I that appears in the actual U.S. national accounts is called **gross private domestic investment.** The word "gross" will be explained presently. "Private" indicates that government investment is considered part of G, and "domestic" just means that machinery sold by American firms to foreign companies is not included. Gross private domestic investment in the United States has three components: business investment in plant and equipment, residential construction (home building),[7] and inventory investment. This is perhaps a good place to repeat that *only* these three things are **investment** in national income accounting terminology.

As defined in the national income accounts, **investment** includes only newly produced goods, such as machinery, factories, and new homes. It does not include exchanges of existing assets.

In common parlance, all sorts of activities that are not part of the GNP are often called "investment." People are said to "invest" in the stock market when they purchase shares. Or wealthy individuals "invest" in works of art. But since transactions like these merely exchange one type of asset (money) for another (stock or art works), they are not included in the GNP.

The symbol G, for government purchases, represents the *volume of current goods and services purchased by all levels of government*. Thus, anything the government pays to its employees is counted in G,

[7]Thus purchases of new homes are considered part of I rather than part of C.

as are its purchases of paper, pencils, airplanes, bombs, typewriters, and so forth.

Very few citizens realize that *most of what the federal government spends its money on is not for purchases of goods and services.* Instead, it is on **transfer payments**—literally, giving away money—either to individuals or to other levels of government.

The importance of the conceptual distinction lies in the fact that G represents the part of the national product that government uses up for its own purposes—to pay for armies, bureaucrats, paper, and ink—whereas transfer payments merely represent shuffling of purchasing power from one group of citizens to another group. Except for the administrators needed to run the programs, real economic resources are not used up in this process. Thus in adding up the nation's total output as the sum of $C + I + G$, we are summing the shares of GNP that are used up by consumers, investors, and government, respectively. Since transfer payments merely give someone the capability to spend on C, it is logical to exclude them from our definition of G, including in C only the portion of these transfer payments that is spent. If we included them in G, the same spending would get counted twice: once in G and then again in C.

Table 7–4 shows the GNP for 1980 computed as the sum of $C + I + G$. You will notice that there is an additional item in Table 7–4 beyond the usual $C + I + G$. It is called **net exports,** and is simply defined as our exports *minus* our imports. Why must this be included? GNP is meant to measure *the*

production of the U.S. economy. But any of you who have enjoyed French wine or German beer know that part of C is not produced in the United States but is *imported* from other countries. Similarly, part of I is also imported. Thus, to arrive at a figure for production in the United States, we must *subtract* all imported items. Conversely, part of America's production is not purchased by Americans, but is *exported* to foreigners. These goods are missed when we add up $C + I + G$, and thus must be added back at the end. This is why we *add* exports. On balance, net exports have little effect on the GNP of the United States: Although exports and imports were both very large numbers in 1981, their difference was only about $24 billion—under 1 percent of GNP.

GNP as the Sum of All Factor Payments

There is another way to count up the GNP—*by adding up all the incomes in the economy.* Let's see how this method handles some typical transactions. Suppose General Electric sells a generator to General Motors for a price of $1 million. The first method of calculating GNP simply counts the $1 million as part of I. The second method asks: What incomes resulted from the production of this generator? The answer might be something like this:

Wages of G.E. employees	$400,000
Interest to bondholders	$50,000
Rentals of buildings	$50,000
Profits of G.E. stockholders	$100,000.

The total is $600,000. The remaining $400,000 is accounted for by inputs that G.E. purchased from other companies: steel, circuitry, tubing, rubber, and so on. But if we traced this $400,000 back further, we would find that it is accounted for by the wages, interest, and rentals paid by these other companies, *plus* their profits, *plus* their purchases from other firms. In fact, for *every* firm in the economy, there is an accounting identity that says:

$$\text{Revenues from sales} = \begin{cases} \text{Wages paid } + \\ \text{Interest paid } + \\ \text{Rentals paid } + \\ \text{Profits earned } + \\ \text{Purchases from} \\ \quad \text{other firms .} \end{cases}$$

Why must this always be true? Because profits are the balancing item; they are what is *left over* after the

Table 7–4
GROSS NATIONAL PRODUCT IN 1981
AS THE SUM OF FINAL DEMANDS

ITEM	AMOUNT (billions of dollars)	
Personal consumption expenditures	$1858.1	
Gross private domestic investment	450.6	
Government purchases of goods and services	589.6	
Net exports	23.8	
Exports		366.7
Imports		342.9
Gross national product	$2922.2	

SOURCE: U.S. Department of Commerce.

firm has made all its other payments. In fact, this accounting identity is really just the definition of profits: sales revenue less all costs of production.

Now, when we consider this accounting identity for *all the firms in the economy*, we obtain the following:

$$\text{Total sales revenue} = \begin{cases} \text{Total wages} + \\ \text{Total interest} + \\ \text{Total rents} + \\ \text{Total profits} + \\ \text{Total purchases} \\ \quad \text{from other firms} \, . \end{cases}$$

But the total purchases from other firms are precisely what we call *intermediate goods*. What, then, do we get if we subtract these intermediate transactions from both sides of the equation?

$$\left. \begin{array}{c} \text{Revenues from sales} \\ \text{minus} \\ \text{Purchases from} \\ \text{other firms} \end{array} \right\} = \begin{cases} \text{Wages paid} + \\ \text{Interest paid} + \\ \text{Rentals paid} + \\ \text{Profits earned} \, . \end{cases}$$

On the right-hand side, we have the sum of all factor incomes: payments to labor, land, and capital. On the left-hand side, we have total sales minus sales of intermediate goods. This means that we have only sales of *final* goods, which is precisely our definition of GNP. Thus, the accounting identity for the entire economy can be rewritten as:

$$\text{GNP} = \text{Wages} + \text{Interest} + \text{Rents} + \text{Profits} \, ,$$

and this gives national income accountants another way to measure the GNP.

Table 7–5 shows 1981's GNP measured by the sum of all incomes. Once again, a few details have been omitted in our discussion. The sum of wages, interest, rents, and profits actually adds up to only $2344 billion (whereas GNP was $2922 billion). We call this sum the **national income** because it is the sum of all factor payments. But the actual selling prices of goods include another category of income that we have ignored so far: sales taxes, excise taxes, and the like. National income statisticians call these indirect business taxes, and when we add these to national income we obtain the **net national product (NNP).**

Now we are almost at the GNP. The only difference between GNP and NNP is **depreciation** of the nation's capital stock: GNP includes depreciation while NNP does not.

Table 7–5

GROSS NATIONAL PRODUCT IN 1981 AS THE SUM OF INCOMES

ITEM		AMOUNT (billions of dollars)
Compensation of employees (wages)		$1771.7
plus		
Net interest		215.0
plus		
Rental income		33.6
plus		
Profits		323.4
Corporate profits	189.0	
Proprietors' income	134.4	
equals		
National income		2343.7
plus		
Indirect business taxes and miscellaneous items		
equals		257.0
Net national product		2600.7
plus		
Depreciation		
equals		321.5
Gross national product		$2922.2

SOURCE: U.S. Department of Commerce.

Depreciation is the value of the portion of the nation's capital equipment that is used up within the year. It tells us how much output is needed just to keep the economy's capital stock intact.

Thus, when we add depreciation to the NNP, we obtain the GNP.

The difference between "gross" and "net" simply refers to whether depreciation is included or excluded. That is, GNP is a measure of all final output taking no account of the capital used up in the process (and therefore in need of replacement). NNP deducts the required replacement to arrive at a *net* production figure.

From a conceptual point of view, most economists feel that NNP is a more meaningful indicator of the economy's output than GNP. After all, the depreciation component of GNP represents the output that is needed just to repair and replace worn out factories and machines; it is not available for anybody to consume.[8] So NNP seems to be a better measure of well-being than GNP. But, alas, GNP is

---

[8] If it is used for consumption, the capital stock will decline, and the nation will wind up poorer than before.

much easier to measure because depreciation is a particularly tricky item. What fraction of a tractor does Farmer Jones "use up" this year? How much did the Empire State Building depreciate during 1980? If you ask yourself these difficult questions, you will understand why most economists feel that GNP is measured more accurately than is NNP. For this reason, most economic models are based on GNP.

In Table 7–5 you can hardly help noticing the preponderant share of employee compensation in total national income—about 75 percent. Labor is by far the most important factor of production. The return on land is truly minute—less than 2 percent; and interest accounts for about 9 percent. Profits account for the remaining 14 percent, though the size of corporate profits (less than 8 percent of GNP) is much less than the public thinks. If, by some magic stroke, we could eliminate all corporate profits without upsetting the performance of the economy, the average worker would get a raise of about 11 percent!

GNP as the Sum of Values Added

We come now to the third, and final, way to measure the GNP. But before we explain this method, we must introduce a new concept, called **value added.**

The **value added** by a firm is its revenue from selling a product minus the amounts paid for goods and services purchased from other firms.

The intuitive sense of the concept is clear: If a firm buys some inputs from other firms, does something to them, and sells the resulting product for a price higher than it paid for the inputs, we say that the firm has "added value" to the product. If we sum up the values added in this way by all the firms in the economy, we must get the total value of all final products. Thus:

GNP can be measured as the sum of the values added by all firms.

To verify that this is so, look back at the second accounting identity on page 133. The left-hand side of this equation, sales revenue minus purchases from other firms, is just what we mean by the firm's value added. Thus:

Value added = Wages + Interest + Rents + Profits.

Since the second method we gave for measuring GNP is to add up wages, interest, rents, and profits, we see that the value-added approach must also yield the same answer.

The value-added concept is particularly useful in avoiding double counting. Often it is hard to distinguish intermediate goods from final goods. Paint bought by a painter, for example, is an intermediate good. But paint bought by a do-it-yourselfer is a final good. What happens, then, if the professional painter has some paint left over and uses it to refurbish his own garage? The intermediate good becomes a final good. You can see that the line between intermediate goods and final goods is a fuzzy one in practice.

If we measure GNP by the sum of values added, however, it is not necessary to make such subtle distinctions. In this method, *every* purchase of a new good or service counts, but we do not count the entire selling price, only the part that represents value added.

To illustrate this idea, consider the data in Table 7–6 and how they would affect GNP as the sum of final products. Our example begins when a farmer who grows soybeans sells them to a mill for $3 a bushel. This transaction does *not* count in the GNP, because the miller does not purchase the soybeans for his own use. The miller then grinds up the soybeans and sells the resulting bag of soy meal to a factory that produces soy sauce. The miller receives $4, but GNP still has not increased because the ground beans are also an intermediate product. Next, the factory turns the beans into soy sauce, which it sells to your favorite Chinese restaurant for $8. Still no effect on GNP. But then the big moment arrives: The restaurant sells the sauce to you and other customers as a part of your meals, and you eat it. At this point, the $10 worth of soy sauce becomes a final product and is included in the GNP.

What is the logic of this procedure? Transactions in intermediate goods also have value. So why do we not count these along with transactions in final goods? The reason is that we are interested in measuring the economy's new output, and if we counted all the intermediate goods, we would be double or triple counting by including an item each time it changed hands. We would get an exaggerated impression of the amount of economic activity that is actually going on.

Look again at Table 7–6, which summarizes the four transactions in the life of the soybeans. As we have just noted, only the last transaction counts in the GNP. So all of this activity raises GNP by $10. If we had also counted the three intermediate transactions (farmer to miller, miller to factory, factory to

Table 7–6

AN ILLUSTRATION OF FINAL AND INTERMEDIATE GOODS

ITEM	SELLER	BUYER	PRICE
Bushel of soybeans	Farmer	Miller	$ 3
Bag of soy meal	Miller	Factory	4
Gallon of soy sauce	Factory	Restaurant	8
Gallon of soy sauce used as seasoning	Restaurant	Consumers	10
		Total:	$25
		Addendum: Contribution to GNP:	$10

restaurant), we would have come up with $25—two and one-half times too much.

Why is it too much? The reason is straightforward. Neither the miller nor the factory owner nor the restauranteur value the product we have been considering *for its own sake.* Only the customers who eat the final product (the soy sauce) have had an increase in their material well-being. So only this last transaction counts in the GNP. However, as we shall now see, value-added calculations enable us to come up with the right answer ($10) by counting only part of each transaction. The basic idea is to count at each step only the contribution to the value of the ultimate final product that is made at that step, excluding the values of items produced at earlier steps.

Ignoring the minor items (such as fertilizer) that the farmer purchases from others, the entire $3 selling price of the bushel of soybeans is new output produced by the farmer; that is, the whole $3 is value added. The miller then grinds the beans and sells them for $4. He has added $4 − $3 = $1 to the value of the beans. When the factory turns this soy meal into soy sauce and sells it for $8, it has added $8 − $4 = $4 more in value. And finally, when the restaurant sells it to hungry customers for $10, a

further $2 of value is added.

Table 7–7 shows this chain of creation of value added by appending another column to Table 7–6. We see that the total value added by all four firms is $10, exactly the same as the restaurant's selling price. This is as it must be, for only the restaurant sells the soybeans as a final product.

Alternative Measures of the Income of the Nation

Economists use the term *national income* in two different ways. The most common usage is as a general term indicating the size of the income of the nation as a whole, without being very specific as to exactly how this income is to be measured. This is the sense in which the term "national income" is used in this book. The second, and much more precise, use of the term refers to a very specific concept in national income accounting, which we encountered earlier in Table 7–5 on page 133: that is, the sum of wages, interest, rents, and profits.

Aside from this formal definition of national income, what other accounting concept might be

Table 7–7

AN ILLUSTRATION OF VALUE ADDED

ITEM	SELLER	BUYER	PRICE	VALUE ADDED
Bushel of soybeans	Farmer	Miller	$ 3	$ 3
Bag of soy meal	Miller	Factory	4	1
Gallon of soy sauce	Factory	Restaurant	8	4
Gallon of soy sauce used as seasoning	Restaurant	Consumers	$10	2
		Totals:	$25	$10

Addendum: Contribution to GNP

Final products $10

Sum of values added $10

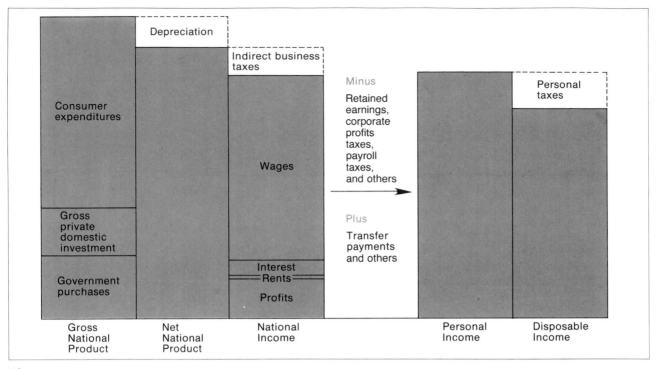

Figure 7–9
ALTERNATIVE MEASURES OF THE INCOME OF THE NATION
This bar chart indicates the relationships among the five alternative measures of the total income of the nation, starting with the largest and most comprehensive measure (GNP) and ranging down to the measure that most closely approximates the spendable income of consumers (disposable income).

used to measure the total income of the nation? The first and most obvious candidate is the GNP itself. GNP, however, is intended to be a measure of *production*, and so has several drawbacks as a measure of *income*. First, it includes some output that represents income to no one—output that simply replaces worn out machinery and buildings (depreciation). When we deduct this depreciation, we obtain the net national product (NNP), as shown in Figure 7–9. Second, because of sales taxes and related items (indirect business taxes), part of the price paid for each good and service does not represent the income of any individual. When we deduct these indirect business taxes from NNP, we arrive at the formal definition of national income (refer again to Figure 7–9). Both these accounting concepts have already been described.

There are, however, two other alternative measures of income. **Personal income** is designed to be superior to national income as a measure of the income that actually accrues to individuals. It is obtained from national income by *subtracting* corporate profits taxes, retained earnings, and payroll taxes (because these items are never received by individuals), and then *adding in* transfer payments (because these sources of income are not part of the wages, interest, rents, or profits that constitute the national income). As Figure 7–9 suggests, this adding and subtracting normally results in a number that is rather close to national income. Finally, if we subtract personal income taxes from personal income, we obtain **disposable income.**

Among all the concepts of the nation's income depicted in Figure 7–9, only two are used frequently in the construction of models of the economy: gross national product (GNP) and disposable income (*DI*). Since the models presented in this book ignore depreciation and indirect business taxes, GNP is basically identical to national income (see Figure 7–9). Similarly, if we ignore retained earnings, GNP and *DI* differ only by the amounts of taxes and transfers (again, see Figure 7–9).

Limitations of the GNP: What GNP Is Not

Having seen in some detail what the GNP *is*, it is worth pausing to expand upon what it *is not*. In particular:

Gross national product is not a measure of the nation's economic well-being.

The GNP is not intended to measure economic well-being, and does not do so for several reasons.

1. Only market activity is included in GNP.

Work done by housewives and do-it-yourselfers certainly contributes to the nation's well-being, but it is not measured in the GNP because it has no price tag.

An important implication of this exclusion is seen when we try to compare the GNPs of developed and less developed countries. Americans are always incredulous to learn that the per capita GNP of the poorest African countries is less than $200 a year. Surely, no one could survive in America on $4 a week. How can Africans do it? One part of the answer, of course, is that these people are incredibly poor. We shall study their plight in Chapter 39. But another part of the answer is that:

International GNP comparisons are vastly misleading when the two countries differ greatly in the fraction of economic activity that each conducts in organized markets.

This fraction is relatively large in the United States and relatively small in the less developed countries, so when we compare their respective measured GNPs we are not comparing the same economic activities at all. Many things that get counted in the U.S. GNP are not counted in the GNPs of less developed nations. So it is ludicrous to think that these people, poor as they are, survive on what to Americans would amount to $4 a week.

2. GNP places no value on leisure even though leisure is so important for well-being.

As a country gets richer, one of the things that happens is that its citizens take more and more leisure time. The steady decrease in the length of the typical workweek in the United States is sufficient evidence for this. This means that the gap is steadily widening between official GNP and some truer measure of national well-being that would include the value of leisure time. For this reason, growth in GNP systematically *understates* the growth in national well-being. But there are also reasons why the GNP *overstates* how well off we are; we consider these next.

3. "Bads" as well as "goods" get counted in GNP.

Suppose there is a natural disaster—as when Mt. St. Helens erupted in the state of Washington in 1980. Surely the well-being of the nation was diminished by this catastrophe. Many homes, businesses, and resorts were destroyed; some people were killed; soot covered cities and towns miles from the blast. Yet the disaster may well have caused GNP to rise. Consumer spending to clean up and replace lost possessions added to C. Rebuilding and repairing the damaged homes, stores, and businesses added to I. Extra government spending for disaster relief and cleanup added to G. Yet no one would think that the nation was better off for its higher GNP.

Wars represent an extreme example of this. Mobilization for outright war always causes a country's GNP to rise rapidly. But men called into the army could be producing civilian output. Factories needed to produce armaments could instead be making cars, washing machines, and televisions. A country at war is surely worse off than a country at peace, but this fact will not be reflected in its GNP accounts.

4. Ecological costs are not netted out of the GNP.

Many of the activities in a modern industrial economy that produce goods and services also have undesirable side effects on the environment. Automobiles provide enjoyment and a means of transportation, but they also despoil the atmosphere. Factories pollute rivers and lakes while manufacturing valuable commodities. Almost everything seems to produce garbage, which creates the problem of what to do with it. None of these ecological costs are deducted from the GNP in an effort to give us a truer measure of the *net* increase in economic welfare that our economy produces. Is this foolishness? Not if we remember the job that national income statisticians are trying to do: They are measuring the economic activity conducted through organized markets, not national welfare.

Summary

1. Gross national product (GNP) is the sum of the money values of all final goods and services produced during a year and sold on organized markets. There are, however, certain exceptions to this definition.

2. One way to measure the GNP is to add up the final demands of consumers, investors, and the government: GNP = $C + I + G$.

3. A second way to measure the GNP is to start with all the

factor payments—wages, interest, rents, and profits—that constitute the national income, and then add indirect business taxes and depreciation.

4. A third way to measure the GNP is to sum up the values added by every firm in the economy (and then once again add indirect business taxes and depreciation).

5. Except for possible bookkeeping and statistical errors, all three methods must give the same answer.

6. The GNP is meant to be a measure of the *production* of the economy, not of the increase in its *well-being*. For example, the GNP places no value on housework and other do-it-yourself activities, nor on leisure time. On the other hand, even commodities that might be considered as "bads" rather than "goods" are counted in the GNP (for example, activities that harm the environment).

Concepts for Review

National income accounting
Gross national product (GNP)
Inventories
Gross private domestic investment
Government purchases

Transfer payments
Net exports
National income
Net national product (NNP)

Depreciation
Value added
Personal income
Disposable income

Questions for Discussion

1. Which of the following transactions are included in the gross national product, and by how much does each raise GNP?
   a. You buy a new refrigerator, paying $400.
   b. You buy a used refrigerator, paying $100.
   c. IBM builds a $10 million factory to make computers.
   d. An unemployed worker receives a government check for $100 in unemployment compensation.
   e. General Motors builds 1000 Cadillacs at a cost of $10,000 each. Unable to sell them, it holds them as inventories.
   f. Mr. Black and Mr. Blue, each out for a Sunday drive, have a collision in which their cars are destroyed. Black and Blue each hire a lawyer to sue the other, paying the lawyers $1000 each for services rendered. The judge throws the case out of court.
   g. You sell $300 of AT&T stock to your roommate.

2. Explain the difference between final goods and intermediate goods. Why is it sometimes difficult to apply this distinction in practice? In this regard, why is the concept of value added useful?

3. Explain the difference between government spending and government purchases of goods and services (*G*). Which is larger?

4. Explain why national income and gross national product would be exactly equal if there were no depreciation and no indirect business taxes.

5. Give some reasons why the gross national product is not a suitable measure of the well-being of the nation. (Have you noticed newspaper accounts in which journalists seem to use GNP for this purpose?)

Demand-Side Equilibrium: Unemployment *or* Inflation?

Investment . . . is a flighty bird,
which needs to be controlled.
J.R. HICKS

In this chapter, we begin a lengthy investigation of the modern economic theory of *income determination*—the theory that explains why the economy sometimes stagnates and sometimes prospers. A simple model of income determination, in which both government and the financial system are mostly ignored, is constructed in this and the next two chapters. Simple as it is, this model teaches us much about the causes of unemployment and inflation. Then, in Chapter 11, we bring the government into the analysis and get a somewhat more complicated picture of how the economy operates. After we acquire some understanding of the financial system and how it works in Chapters 12 and 13, we will be ready to construct and utilize our most complete and realistic model of income determination in Chapter 14.

We learned in Chapter 5 that the interaction of aggregate demand and aggregate supply determines whether the economy will boom or stagnate and whether America's resources of labor and capital will be fully employed or unemployed. This chapter begins our study of how this important process works by describing the aggregate demand side of the economy. The following chapter does the same for aggregate supply.

In the last chapter we examined the largest component of aggregate demand, which is consumer expenditure (C); here, we turn our attention first to the most volatile component, investment (I), and discuss its determinants and the reasons why investment spending is so variable and so difficult to predict.[1] Then, rather than waiting for a full discussion of the third component of aggregate demand, government purchases (G), we construct an abbreviated model of the determination of national income based only on the C and I components. We use this model to provide a preliminary description of how the state of aggregate demand influences the level of the gross national product, and to consider a question of great importance to policymakers: Can the economy be expected to achieve full employment of its resources if the government does not intervene?

---

[1] We repeat the warning given in the previous chapter about the meaning of the word *investment*. It *includes* spending by businesses and individuals on *newly produced* factories, machinery, and houses. But it *excludes* sales of *used* industrial plants, equipment, and homes, and it *also excludes* purely financial transactions, such as the purchase of stocks and bonds.

The Extreme Variability
of Investment

The first thing to be said about investment spending is that it is extraordinarily variable.

Unlike consumer spending, which follows movements in disposable income with great (though not perfect) reliability, investment spending swings from high to low levels with annoying rapidity. During recessions, for example, the decline in investment generally constitutes the vast majority of the total drop in real GNP, despite the fact that investment is only a small portion of GNP—about 10 percent in the postwar United States. What accounts for these movements of investment demand?

Business Confidence
and Expectations About the Future

While many factors influence business people's desires to invest, Keynes himself laid great stress on the *state of business confidence*, which in turn depends on *expectations about the future*.

While tricky to measure, it does seem obvious that businesses will build more factories and purchase more new machines when their expectations are optimistic. Conversely, their investment plans will be very cautious if the economic outlook appears bleak. Keynes pointed out that psychological perceptions like these are subject to abrupt shifts, so that fluctuations in investment can be a major cause of instability in aggregate demand. Thus, we see the logic in Hicks's analogy to a "flighty bird."

Unfortunately, neither economists nor, for that matter, psychologists have any very good ideas about how to *measure* or how to *control* business expectations and confidence. Therefore, economists usually focus on several more objective determinants of investment—determinants that are easy to quantify and that are more easily influenced by government policy.

The Rate of Interest

A good deal of business investment is financed by borrowing, and the interest rate indicates how much firms must pay for that privilege. The higher the interest rate, the more costly it is to borrow. Some investment projects that look profitable at an interest rate of 7 percent will look disastrous if the firm has to pay 12 percent. Thus:

The amount that businesses will want to invest depends on the real interest rate they have to pay on their borrowings. The lower the real rate of interest, the more investment spending there will be.

In Chapter 13 we will study in some detail how the government can influence the rate of interest. Since interest rates affect investment, policymakers have a handle on aggregate demand—a handle they do not hesitate to use. The point is that, unlike business confidence, interest rates are visible and manipulable. Therefore, even if investment responds much more dramatically to changes in confidence than to changes in interest rates, interest rates are nonetheless a more important instrument of government policy.

The State of Demand and Capacity Utilization

There will be a strong incentive to invest when firms find that demand is pressing against their capacity; that is, when existing plant and equipment are straining to produce the amount of goods that consumers wish to buy. Under these circumstances, firms are very likely to feel that any addition to capacity can be employed profitably. By contrast, if there is a great deal of spare capacity (unused machinery, empty factories, and so on), business managers will not find investment attractive even at very low interest rates.

The Growth of Demand

Since it takes a substantial amount of time to order machinery or to build a factory, investment plans are made with an eye toward the future. Even when pressures on current capacity are not particularly severe, a firm experiencing rapid growth in sales is likely to start investing *now* so that it will have adequate capacity when it is needed in the future. In addition, briskly growing sales are likely to make business people more optimistic. Conversely, slow growth of output will discourage investment.

We can summarize these last two points by saying that:

High levels of sales and rapid economic growth create an atmosphere favorable to investment. On the other hand, low levels of sales and slow growth are likely to discourage investment.

Government stabilization policy thus has another handle on investment spending, for by stimulating aggregate demand it can probably persuade business firms to invest more, though the precise amount may be hard to predict.

Tax Provisions

The government has still another important way to influence investment spending—by altering various provisions of the tax law. There is, for example, a federal *tax on corporate profits,* and the government has sometimes reduced it when it wanted firms to invest more and raised it when it wanted firms to invest less. Another incentive is the **investment tax credit,** a device invented by President Kennedy's economists in 1961 and used many times since then. The investment tax credit is, in effect, a bribe to do more investing. The government currently offers to reduce a firm's tax bill by 10 cents for every $1 the firm invests in new industrial equipment. And there are still other tax incentives, which are best left to more advanced courses. To summarize:

The tax law gives the government several ways to influence business spending on investment goods. But its control is quite imperfect. Investment remains a "flighty bird."

A Simplified Circular Flow

Let us now put consumption and investment together and see how they interact, using as our organizing framework the circular flow diagram that we introduced in the last chapter. For this purpose, we simplify the circular flow somewhat by leaving out the government. There are two reasons for doing this. The first is pedagogical: The workings of the model will be much clearer if we strip away some of its complications. But there is a much more important reason. One of the crucial questions surrounding government attempts to stabilize the economy is whether the economy would *automatically* gravitate toward full employment if the government simply left it alone. We can study this issue best by imagining an economy that has no government, so that all the aggregate demand comes from the private sector. This is just what we do in this chapter.

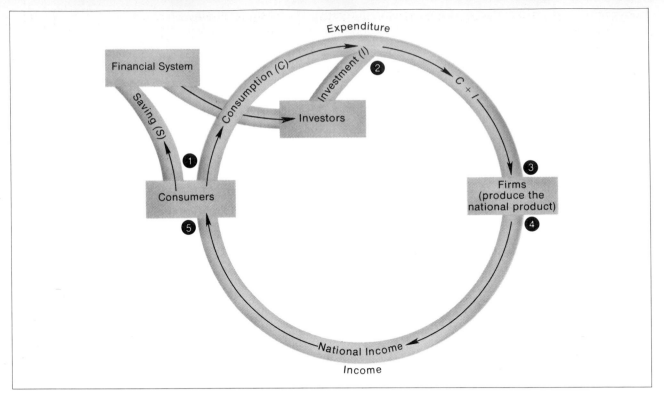

Figure 8–1

A SIMPLIFIED CIRCULAR FLOW

Here we show a simplified version of the circular flow of income and expenditures that we introduced in Chapter 7. The simplification amounts to shutting off the pipes leading into and out of the government. Thus, this circular flow represents an economy with no government. Notice that aggregate demand now has only two components (consumer spending and investment spending) and that the entire national income flows to consumers without taxation.

Look now at Figure 8–1, which is the same as Figure 7–1 of the last chapter except that the government has been omitted. The first thing you may notice is that, with the government out of the picture, there is no longer any leakage out of the national income for taxes (nor are there transfer payments) and there is no important difference between national income and disposable income. Second, there is no government component of total spending; instead, spending is represented by the sum $C + I$.

The Meaning of Equilibrium GNP

We can use Figure 8–1 to begin the construction of a simple model of the determination of national income. A first step is to understand what we mean by "equilibrium income."

As was explained in the last chapter, national *product* and national *income* must of necessity be equal. But the same cannot automatically be said of total *spending*. Look again at Figure 8–1 and imagine that, for some reason, the total expenditures $(C + I)$ that are being made at point 3 are greater than the output that is being produced by the business firms at point 4.

Two things may happen in such a situation. Since consumers and firms together are buying (in the forms of C and I) more than firms are producing, business firms are being forced to take goods out of their warehouses to meet customer demands. Thus, inventory stocks must be falling. These inventory reductions are a signal to retailers of a need to increase their orders, and to manufacturers of a need to step up their production. Thus, production is likely to rise. At some later date, if there is evidence that the high level of aggregate demand is not just a temporary aberration, either manufacturers or retailers (or both) may also respond to the buoyant sales performances by raising their prices. Economists, therefore, say that neither output nor the price level is in **equilibrium** when aggregate demand exceeds the current rate of production.

It is clear from the definition that the economy cannot be in equilibrium when aggregate demand exceeds production, for the falling inventories demonstrate to firms that their production and pricing decisions were not quite appropriate. Thus, since we normally use GNP to measure output:

The equilibrium level of GNP cannot be one at which aggregate demand exceeds output because firms will notice that inventory stocks are being depleted. They may first decide to increase production sufficiently to meet the higher demand. Later they may decide to raise prices as well.

Now imagine the other case, in which the flow of aggregate demand reaching firms falls short of current production. Some output remains unsold, and these unwanted goods wind up as additions to the inventories of some firms. The inventory pile-up acts as a signal to firms that at least one of their decisions was wrong. Once again, they will probably react first by cutting back on production, causing the GNP to fall. If the imbalance persists, they may also lower prices in order to stimulate sales. But they are certainly not likely to be happy with things as they are. Thus:

The equilibrium level of GNP cannot be one at which aggregate demand is less than output because firms will not allow inventories to continue to pile up. They may decide to decrease production, or they may decide to cut prices in order to stimulate demand. Normally, firms are reluctant to cut prices until they are quite certain that the low level of demand is not a temporary phenomenon. So they rely more heavily on reductions in output.

Income Determination: The Equilibrium Level of GNP

You may have noticed that we have now determined, through a process of elimination, the **equilibrium level of national income and product.** We have reasoned that whenever GNP is below aggregate demand ($C + I$) the GNP will rise; and that whenever GNP is above $C + I$, the GNP will fall. Equilibrium can only occur, then, when there is just enough aggregate demand to absorb the existing level of production. Under such circumstances, producers conclude that their price and output decisions are correct, and they have no incentive to change them. We conclude that:

The *equilibrium level of GNP* is the one at which aggregate demand equals production. In such a situation firms find their inventories remaining at desirable levels, and so there is no incentive to change output or prices.

The simple circular flow diagram, then, has helped us to understand the concept of the equilibrium level of GNP, and also how the economy is driven toward it. It leaves unanswered, however, the most important questions that concern us in this chapter:

1. How large is the equilibrium level of GNP?
2. Will the economy suffer from unemployment, inflation, or both?

To deal with these questions we shall need a more specific apparatus.

Constructing the Expenditure Schedule

Our objective now is to determine precisely the equilibrium level of GNP and to see what factors it depends upon. To make the analysis more concrete, we turn to a numerical example. Specifically, we examine the relationship between aggregate demand and GNP in Macroland, the hypothetical economy that was introduced in the last chapter.

Columns 1 and 2 of Table 8–1 incorporate the consumption function of Macroland that we first encountered in Table 7–1. They show how consumer spending, C, depends on national income, which we now begin to symbolize by the letter Y.[2] Column 3 provides the other component of aggregate demand, I, through the simplifying assumption that investment spending is $200 billion in Macroland, regardless of the level of GNP.

By adding together the second and third columns, we calculate $C + I$, or aggregate demand, which is displayed in column 4. Columns 1 and 4, shaded in blue, show how aggregate demand depends on income in Macroland. We call this the **expenditure schedule.**

Figure 8–2 shows the construction of the expenditure schedule graphically. The line labeled C is the consumption function of Macroland and simply duplicates Figure 7–6 of the last chapter. It plots on a graph the numbers given in columns 1 and 2 of Table 8–1. The line labeled $C + I$ in the diagram depicts the total expenditure schedule that we have just derived by plotting the data in columns 1 and 4 of the table. That is, at each level of GNP measured along the horizontal axis, the height of the $C + I$ line indicates the sum of consumption plus investment.

[2]Perceptive students may notice that the consumption function in Chapter 7 related C to *disposable* income, not to *national* income. However, with the government ignored in this chapter, there is no difference between the two income concepts.

Table 8–1
AGGREGATE DEMAND IN MACROLAND (billions of dollars)

(1) INCOME (Y)	(2) CONSUMPTION (C)	(3) INVESTMENT (I)	(4) AGGREGATE DEMAND (C + I)
600	600	200	800
800	760	200	960
1000	920	200	1120
1200	1080	200	1280
1400	1240	200	1440
1600	1400	200	1600
1800	1560	200	1760
2000	1720	200	1920
2200	1880	200	2080
2400	2040	200	2240
2600	2200	200	2400

This table illustrates the derivation of the expenditure schedule, which is shaded in blue. It is derived from the consumption schedule, columns 1 and 2, and from the investment schedule, columns 1 and 3, by simple addition. This is because aggregate demand is the sum $C + I$.

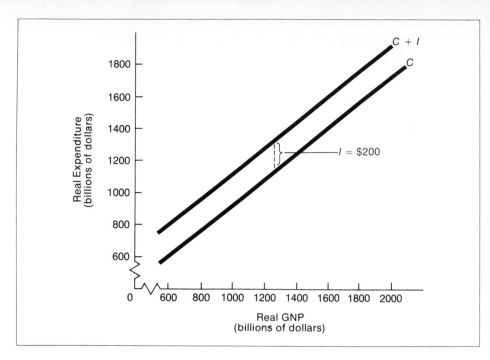

Figure 8–2
CONSTRUCTION OF
THE EXPENDITURE
SCHEDULE
This figure shows in a diagram
what Table 8–1 showed nu-
merically—the construction of
a total expenditure schedule
from its components. Line C is
the consumption function that
we first encountered in Figure
7–6. Line C + I is the expenditure schedule and is obtained
by adding investment (as-
sumed always to be $200 bil-
lion in this example) to the consumption function.

The difference between the two lines, therefore, is investment. In the diagram, the lines are parallel; that is, the distance between them is always the same. This distance is $200 billion—the volume of investment assumed in the example. If investment were not always $200 billion, the two lines would either come closer together (at income levels at which investment was below $200 billion) or grow farther apart (at income levels at which investment was above $200 billion). For example, our list of determinants of investment spending suggested that I might be larger at higher levels of GNP. Because of this added investment—which is called **induced investment**—the resulting C + I schedule would have a steeper slope than the C schedule.

The Mechanics of Income Determination

We are now in a position to determine the equilibrium level of GNP in Macroland. Look first at Table 8–2, which presents the logic of our circular flow argument in tabular form. The first two columns of this table reproduce the expenditure schedule that was constructed in Table 8–1. The other columns explain the process by which equilibrium is approached. Let us see why a GNP of $1600 billion must be the equilibrium level.

Consider first any output level below $1600 billion. For example, at output level Y = $1400 billion, total expenditure is $1440 billion (column 2), which is $40 billion more than production. With sales greater than output (column 3), inventories will be disappearing (column 4). As the table suggests, this will be a signal to producers to raise their output (column 5). Clearly, then, no output level below Y = $1600 billion can be an equilibrium. Output is too low.

A similar line of reasoning can eliminate any output level above $1600 billion. Consider, for example, Y = $1800 billion. The table shows that total spending would be $1760 billion if national income were $1800 billion. So $40 billion of the GNP would go unsold. This would raise producers' inventory stocks and signal them that their rate of production is too high.

Just as we concluded from our circular flow diagram, then, equilibrium will

Table 8–2
THE DETERMINATION OF EQUILIBRIUM OUTPUT

(1) OUTPUT (Y) (billions of dollars)	(2) TOTAL SPENDING (C + I) (billions of dollars)	(3) BALANCE OF SPENDING AND OUTPUT	(4) INVENTORIES ARE:	(5) PRODUCERS WILL RESPOND BY:
600	800	Spending exceeds output	Falling	Producing more
800	960	Spending exceeds output	Falling	Producing more
1000	1120	Spending exceeds output	Falling	Producing more
1200	1280	Spending exceeds output	Falling	Producing more
1400	1440	Spending exceeds output	Falling	Producing more
1600	1600	Spending = output	Constant	Not changing production
1800	1760	Output exceeds spending	Rising	Producing less
2000	1920	Output exceeds spending	Rising	Producing less
2200	2080	Output exceeds spending	Rising	Producing less
2400	2240	Output exceeds spending	Rising	Producing less
2600	2400	Output exceeds spending	Rising	Producing less

Columns 1 and 2 are the expenditure schedule that was derived in the previous table. The remaining columns explain how the equilibrium level of national income can be derived from these data. For example, reading across the first row we see that when GNP is $600 billion, total spending is $800 billion. Thus spending exceeds production (by $200 billion), so that inventories must be falling. Producers are likely to respond to this drop in inventory stocks by raising their rate of production. The other rows are read similarly, and together they show that only $1600 billion can be the equilibrium level of GNP. This is the only output level that firms will not want to change.

be achieved only when total spending $(C + I)$ is equal to GNP (Y). In symbols, our condition for equilibrium GNP is:

$$C + I = Y.$$

The table shows that this occurs only at a GNP of $1600 billion. This, then, must be the equilibrium level of GNP.

Figure 8–3 shows this same conclusion graphically, by adding a 45° line to Figure 8–2. Why a 45° line? Recall that a 45° line marks off all points on a graph

Figure 8–3
INCOME–EXPENDITURE DIAGRAM

This figure adds a 45° line—which marks off points where expenditure and output are equal—to Figure 8–2. Since the condition for equilibrium GNP is that expenditure and output must be equal, this line can be used to determine the equilibrium level of GNP. In this example, equilibrium is at point E, where GNP is $1600 billion—precisely as we found in Table 8–2.

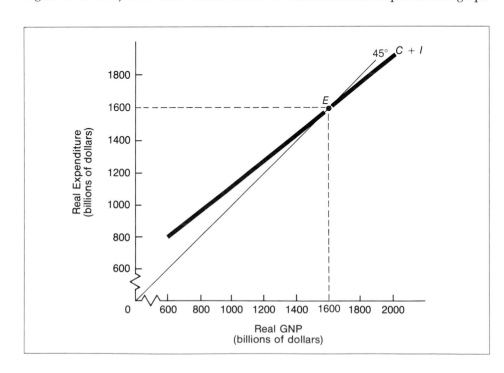

at which the value of the variable measured on the horizontal axis is equal to the value of the variable measured on the vertical axis. In this convenient graph of the expenditure schedule, gross national product (Y) is measured on the horizontal axis and total expenditure ($C + I$) is measured on the vertical axis. So the 45° line shows all the points at which output and spending are equal: that is, where $Y = C + I$. The 45° line therefore displays all the points at which the economy *can possibly* be at equilibrium.

Now we must compare these potential equilibrium points with the actual combinations of spending and output that the economy can attain, given the behavior of consumers and investors. That behavior, as we have seen, is described by the $C + I$ line in Figure 8–3, which shows how total expenditure varies as income changes. Thus, the economy will *always* be on the $C + I$ line; no point in the diagram that is off that $C + I$ line can ever be observed. Similarly, if the economy is in equilibrium, it must be on the 45° line. As Figure 8–3 shows, these two requirements together imply that the only viable equilibrium is at point E, where the $C + I$ line intersects the 45° line. Only this point is consistent both with equilibrium and with the actual propensities to consume and invest.

Notice that to the left of the equilibrium point, E, the $C + I$ line lies above the 45° line. This means that total spending exceeds total output, as we have already noted in words and with numbers. The opposite is true to the right of equilibrium point E; here, spending falls short of output.

Diagrams like this one will recur so frequently in this and the next several chapters that it will be convenient to have a name for them. Let us, therefore, call them **income–expenditure diagrams** since they show how expenditures vary with income. Sometimes we shall also refer to them simply as **45° line diagrams.**

Equilibrium on the Demand Side of the Economy: The Aggregate Demand Curve

Chapter 5 sketched a framework for macroeconomic analysis by introducing aggregate demand and aggregate supply curves which relate aggregate quantities demanded and supplied to the price level. Yet the price level has not even been mentioned so far in our discussion of macroeconomic equilibrium. It is now time to remedy this omission, for only by explicit analysis of the determination of the price level will we be able to deal with important issues relating to inflation.

Fortunately, no further mechanical apparatus is required. The price level can be brought into our income–expenditure analysis by recalling something we learned in the last chapter: At any given level of real income, higher prices lead to lower real consumer spending. The reason, you will recall, is that consumers own many assets whose values are fixed in money terms, and which therefore lose purchasing power when prices rise.[3]

In terms of our 45° line diagram, then, a rise in the price level will lower the consumption function and, hence, lower the total expenditure schedule. Conversely, a fall in the price level will raise both the C and $C + I$ schedules in the diagram. Figure 8–4 illustrates both these sorts of shifts.

What, then, do changes in the price level do to the equilibrium level of real aggregate quantity demanded? The answers can be found in the two parts of Figure 8–5. Part (a) shows that a rise in the price level, by shifting the expenditure

[3]Two warnings issued in Chapter 7 (page 123) are worth repeating: First, the effect referred to here comes from changes in the *price level*, not from changes in the *inflation rate*. Second, a higher price level does *not* reduce spending by reducing real income. Quite to the contrary, real income is held *constant* when we compare consumer expenditures at different price levels.

Figure 8–4
THE EFFECT OF THE
PRICE LEVEL ON THE EX-
PENDITURE SCHEDULE
A higher price level will cause
the $C + I$ schedule to shift
downward, as shown by the
black arrows. A lower price
level will cause the $C + I$
schedule to shift upward, as
shown by the blue arrows.

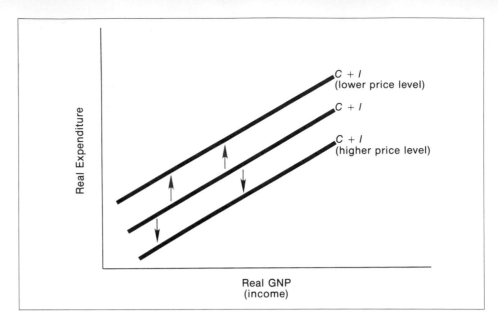

schedule downward from $C_0 + I$ to $C_1 + I$ leads to a reduction in the equilibrium quantity of real GNP demanded from Y_0 to Y_1. Similarly, Figure 8–5(b)
shows that a fall in the price level, by shifting the expenditure schedule upward
from $C_0 + I$ to $C_2 + I$, leads to a rise in the equilibrium quantity of real GNP
demanded from Y_0 to Y_2.

In summary, a rise in the price level leads to a lower equilibrium level of real
aggregate quantity demanded, whereas a fall in the price level leads to a higher
equilibrium quantity demanded. This relationship between the price level and
the equilibrium quantity of real GNP demanded is depicted in Figure 8–6 and is

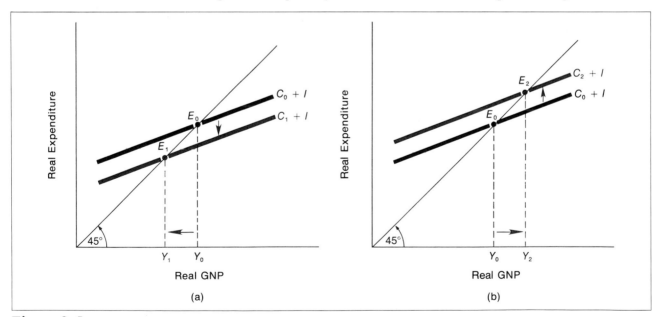

Figure 8–5
THE EFFECT OF THE PRICE LEVEL ON EQUILIBRIUM AGGREGATE QUANTITY DEMANDED
Because a change in the price level causes the expenditure schedule to shift, it changes the equilibrium quantity of real GNP demanded.
Part (a) shows what happens when the price level rises, causing the expenditure schedule to shift downward from $C_0 + I$ to $C_1 + I$.
Equilibrium quantity demanded falls from Y_0 to Y_1. Part (b) shows what happens when the price level falls, causing the expenditure
schedule to shift upward from $C_0 + I$ to $C_2 + I$. Equilibrium quantity demanded rises from Y_0 to Y_2.

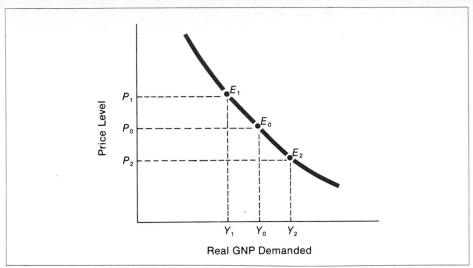

precisely what we called the *aggregate demand curve* in earlier chapters. It comes directly from the 45° line diagrams in Figure 8–5. Thus, points E_0, E_1, and E_2 in Figure 8–6 correspond to the points bearing the same labels in Figure 8–5.

What we have learned so far about the effects of the price level is precisely how the aggregate demand curve is derived and why it slopes downward. We have also been warned that:

An income–expenditure diagram can only be drawn up for a specific price level. At different price levels, the $C + I$ schedule will be different and, hence, the equilibrium quantity of GNP demanded will be different.

As we shall now see, this finding is critical to understanding the genesis of unemployment and inflation.

Demand-Side Equilibrium and Full Employment

The discussion of prices allows us to provide a partial answer to the second major question of this chapter: Will the economy achieve an equilibrium at full employment without inflation, or will there be unemployment, inflation, or both?

In the income–expenditure diagrams used so far, the equilibrium level of GNP demanded has been shown as the intersection of the expenditure schedule and the 45° line, regardless of whatever level of GNP might correspond to full employment. Equilibrium, apparently, can fall either above or below full employment. However, as we will see now, when equilibrium GNP falls above full employment, the economy probably will be plagued by inflation. And when equilibrium falls below full employment, there will be unemployment and recession.

This remarkable fact was one of the principal messages of Keynes's *General Theory of Employment, Interest, and Money*. Writing during the Great Depression, it was natural for him to stress the case in which equilibrium falls short of full employment so that there are unemployed resources. Figure 8–7 illustrates this possibility. A vertical line has been erected at the full-employment level of

Biographical Note: John Maynard Keynes (1883–1946)

It may be one of history's great ironies that the death of Karl Marx, the prophet of capitalism's doom, and the birth of John Maynard Keynes, who many consider capitalism's savior, both occurred in the same year—1883. The son of a prominent upper-class British economist, Keynes was something of a child prodigy. After an outstanding scholastic career at Eton and Cambridge, Keynes took the civil service examination. His second-place score was not good enough to land him the position he wanted and should have had (in the Treasury), so in 1907 he found himself in the India Office. Some years later, reflecting on the fact

that his lowest score on the exam was in the economics section, he suggested with characteristic immodesty that, "The examiners presumably knew less than I did."* He was probably right.

While Keynes disliked his work at the India Office, his time there was not wasted. It was during that period that he wrote his *Treatise on Probability* (1909), which drew the admiration of Bertrand Russell and won Keynes election as a lifetime Fellow of Cambridge's King's College.

During World War I, Keynes was called to the Treasury to assist in planning various financial aspects of the war. There his "unique combination of the guts of a burglar and the intellect of a first-class economist"‡ established him as a dominant figure. At the war's end, though only 36, Keynes represented the British Treasury at the peace conference in Versailles.

The conference was a turning point in Keynes's life, though it was one of his few failures. He sought unsuccessfully to persuade the Allies to take a less punitive attitude toward the vanquished Germans, and then left the conference in protest in June 1919, telling David Lloyd George, the English Prime Minister, "I am slipping way from this scene of nightmare."§ Keynes immediately went to work on his *Economic Consequences of the Peace*, which created a furor when it was published in 1919. In addition to stinging personal portraits of Lloyd George, Georges Clemenceau, and Woodrow Wilson ("the blind and deaf Don Quixote"), Keynes demonstrated with exquisite logic that the Germans could never meet the harsh

GNP (called "potential GNP"), which is assumed to be $2000 billion in the example. We see that the $C + I$ curve cuts the 45° line at point E, which corresponds to a GNP ($Y = 1600 billion) below potential GNP. In this case, the

Figure 8–7

A RECESSIONARY GAP Sometimes equilibrium GNP may fall below potential GNP, so that some workers are unemployed. This diagram illustrates such a case. The horizontal distance *EB* between equilibrium GNP and potential GNP is called the recessionary gap.

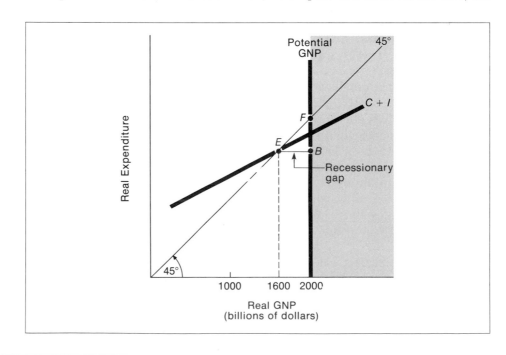

economic terms of the treaty and that its very viciousness posed the threat of continued instability and perhaps another war in Europe. Sadly, his visions were remarkably accurate.

No longer welcome in government, Keynes returned to Cambridge and to his distinguished circle of literary and artistic friends in London's Bloomsbury district—a group that included Virginia Woolf, Lytton Strachey, and E. M. Forster. In 1925 he married the beautiful ballerina Lydia Lopokova, who gave up her stage career for him (though she later acted in a theater that Keynes himself established).

Between the wars, Keynes devoted himself to making money (both for himself and for King's College), to economic theory, and to political economy. Spending about one-half hour each morning with newspapers and financial reports (apparently while still in bed!), Keynes managed to make himself a rich man and increase his college's unrestricted fund from £30,000 to £380,000 by speculating in international currencies and commodities. As a scholar, he wrote the *Tract on Monetary Reform* (1923), a stunning denunciation of the gold standard, which was published two years before Churchill once again tied the pound to gold and, in the view of modern observers, sealed Britain's economic doom. In 1936, he published his masterpiece, *The General Theory of Employment, Interest, and Money*, upon which modern macroeconomics is based. Finally, as a tireless political activist and polemicist, he used newspaper and magazine articles, and visits to Whitehall and Washington, to urge governments to lift their economies out of the Depression (which began for Britain in the 1920s) through policies that we would now call "Keynesian."

A heart attack in 1937 reduced Keynes's activities somewhat, though he maintained careers as both an academic economist and a businessman. He returned to the Treasury during World War II and conducted several delicate financial negotiations with the Americans. Then, as the capstone to a truly remarkable career, he represented the United Kingdom—and by all accounts dominated the proceedings—at the conference in Bretton Woods, New Hampshire, in 1944 that established an international financial system that served the Western world for 27 years. (See Chapter 38.)

He died of a heart attack at his home on Easter Sunday of 1946 as Lord Keynes, Baron of Tilton, a man who had achieved almost everything that he sought, and who had only one regret: He wished he had drunk more champagne.

*Quoted in E. A. G. Robinson, "John Maynard Keynes," in R. Lekachman, ed., *Keynes' General Theory: Reports of Three Decades* (New York: St. Martin's Press, Inc., 1964), page 25.

‡Robert Lekachman, *The Age of Keynes* (New York: Random House, 1966), page 27. This book contains a marvelous biography of Keynes, as does Robert Heilbroner's *The Worldly Philosophers*, 4th edition (New York: Simon and Schuster, 1972).

§Quoted in R. F. Harrod, *The Life of John Maynard Keynes* (New York: Macmillan, 1951), page 253.

$C + I$ curve is too low to lead to full employment. Such a situation might arise because either consumers or investors are unwilling to spend at normal rates, or because the price level is "too high," thereby depressing the $C + I$ curve. Unemployment must occur because not enough output will be demanded to keep the entire labor force busy.

The distance between the equilibrium level of output demanded and the full-employment level of output (that is, potential GNP) is called the **recessionary gap**—and is shown by the horizontal distance from E to B.

It is clear from Figure 8–7 that full employment can be reached only by raising the total spending schedule to eliminate the recessionary gap. Specifically, the $C + I$ schedule must move upward until it cuts the 45° line at point F. Can this happen without government intervention? We shall return to this question in the next chapter; but first let us consider the other case, in which equilibrium GNP exceeds full employment.

Figure 8–8 illustrates this possibility. The expenditure schedule intersects the 45° line at point E, where GNP is $2400 billion. But this exceeds the full-employment level, $Y = \$2000$ billion. A case like this can arise when consumer or investment spending is unusually buoyant or when a "low" price level pushes the $C + I$ curve upward.

To reach an equilibrium at full employment, the price level would have to rise enough to drive the $C + I$ schedule *down* until it passed through point F. The horizontal distance BE—which indicates the amount by which the quantity of GNP demanded exceeds potential GNP—is called the **inflationary gap.** If there is an inflationary gap, a higher price level or some other means of reducing

The **recessionary gap** is the amount by which the equilibrium level of real GNP falls short of potential GNP.

The **inflationary gap** is the amount by which equilibrium real GNP exceeds the full-employment level of GNP.

Figure 8–8

AN INFLATIONARY GAP
Sometimes equilibrium GNP
may lie above potential GNP,
meaning that there are more
jobs than required for full employment. This diagram illustrates such a case. The horizontal distance BE between
potential GNP and equilibrium
GNP is called the inflationary
gap. It is gradually eliminated
by rising prices, which pull the
C + I schedule down until it
passes through point F.

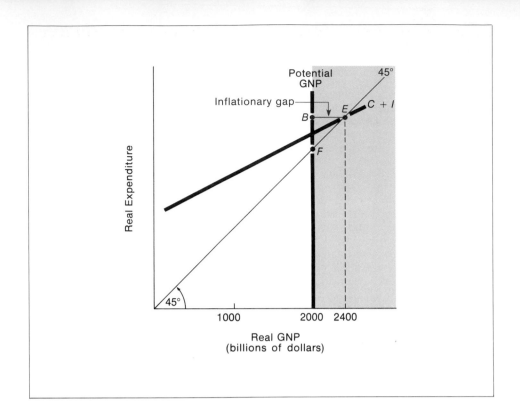

total expenditure is necessary to reach an equilibrium at full employment.

In sum, only if the price level and the spending propensities of consumers and investors are "just right" will the C + I curve intersect the 45° line precisely at full employment, so that neither a recessionary gap nor an inflationary gap occurs. Are there reasons to expect this outcome? Does the economy have a self-correcting mechanism that automatically eliminates recessionary or inflationary gaps and propels it toward full employment? And how is it that inflation and unemployment sometimes occur together? These are questions we are not quite ready to address because we have yet to bring *aggregate supply* into the picture. And, as we learned in Chapter 4, price is determined by the interaction of *both* demand *and* supply. However, it is not too early to get an idea about why things can go wrong, why the economy can find itself far away from full employment.

The Coordination of Saving and Investment

To understand what goes wrong with the economy in a recession, it is useful to restate our equilibrium condition in a slightly different way. To do so, we need to look back at the simplified circular flow diagram (Figure 8–1 on page 142). How can the full-employment level of GNP fail to be an equilibrium? Suppose that firms produce the full-employment level of GNP, and this becomes the national income that emerges at point 4 in the diagram. This full-employment level of income then flows to consumers at point 5, who save some of it and spend the rest. The saving, you will note, "leaks out" of the circular flow at point 1. So, once we pass this point, consumption is less than full-employment GNP. But then at point 2, an additional source of spending enters: investment. Recalling that the condition for equilibrium is that the sum $C + I$ equals the GNP, we have the following conclusion:

The economy will reach an equilibrium at potential GNP only if the amount that consumers wish to save out of full-employment incomes is precisely equal to the amount that investors want to invest. If these two magnitudes happen to be unequal, then full employment will not be an equilibrium for the economy.

Specifically, we can see from the circular flow diagram that if saving exceeds investment at full employment, then the total demand arriving at the firms (point 3) will fall short of total output because the added investment spending is not enough to replace the leakage to saving. With demand inadequate to support production at full employment, we know that the GNP must fall below potential. There will be a recessionary gap. Conversely, if investment exceeds saving when the economy is at full employment, then total demand ($C + I$) will exceed potential GNP and production will rise above the full-employment level. There will be an inflationary gap.

Now this discussion does nothing but restate what we already know in different words.[4] But these words hold the key to understanding why the economy can find itself stuck below full employment (or above it, for that matter), for *the people who do the investing are not the same people who do the saving*. In a modern capitalist economy, most investing is done by corporations, while most saving is done by consumers. It is easy to imagine that their plans may not be well coordinated. If they are not, we have just seen how either unemployment or inflation can arise.

Notice that these problems would never arise if the acts of saving and investing were not separated. Imagine a primitive economy of farmers, each of whom invests only in his own farm. There is no borrowing or lending, and no financial system. In this world, any farmer who wanted to buy a new plow or tractor (that is, wanted to *invest*) would have to refrain from consuming part of his income (that is, would have to *save*). Therefore, the amount that all farmers together planned to save out of full-employment income would of necessity be equal to the amount of planned investment. Total spending and production would always have to be equal at full employment.

Almost the same sequence holds true in a centrally planned economy like that of Soviet Russia. There, the state decides how much will be invested and has a great deal of leverage over how much saving people do. If the planners do their calculations correctly, they can force saving to be equal to investment at full employment. Consequently, business fluctuations are not a major problem in the Soviet Union. (They have plenty of others!)

Keynes observed that modern market economies differ from either primitive societies or centrally planned societies in this fundamental way, and that this flaw in the market mechanism is what leaves them vulnerable to recessions. However, one should not conclude that in order to avoid unemployment and recession the U.S. economy should revert to either a primitive form of capitalism or to rigid central planning. These "remedies" may be far worse than the disease. Fortunately, there are policies the government can follow in an advanced capitalist economy to ease the pain of unemployment and recession—policies that we shall be studying in the following chapters.

---

[4]In symbols, our previous equilibrium condition was $C + I = Y$. If we note that Y is also the sum of consumption plus saving, $Y = C + S$, it follows that $C + I = C + S$, or $I = S$, is a restatement of the equilibrium condition. The saving = investment approach is described in an appendix to this chapter.

Summary

1. Investment is the most volatile component of aggregate demand, largely because it is tied so closely to the state of business confidence and to expectations about the future performance of the economy.
2. Government policy cannot influence business confidence in any reliable way, so policies designed to alter investment spending are aimed at more objective, though possibly less important, determinants of investment. Among these are interest rates, the overall state of aggregate demand, and tax incentives.
3. The equilibrium level of national income and products is the level of income at which aggregate quantity demanded just equals production (GNP). In this chapter we ignore government demand, so aggregate demand is the sum of consumption plus investment. Thus, in symbols, the condition for equilibrium is $Y = C + I$.
4. Income levels below equilibrium are bound to rise because, when spending exceeds output, firms will see their inventory stocks depleted and will react by stepping up production.
5. Income levels above equilibrium are bound to fall because, when total spending is insufficient to absorb total output, inventories will pile up and firms will react by curtailing production.
6. The determination of the equilibrium level of GNP can be portrayed on a convenient "income–expenditure diagram" as the point at which the expenditure schedule—defined as the sum of the consumption and investment schedules—crosses the 45° line. The 45° line is significant because it marks off points at which spending and output are equal (that is, at which $C + I = Y$), and this is the basic condition for equilibrium.
7. An income–expenditure diagram can only be drawn up for a specific price level, however. Thus the equilibrium GNP so determined must depend on the price level.
8. Because higher prices reduce the purchasing power of consumers' wealth, and hence reduce their spending, equilibrium GNP is lower when prices are higher. This downward-sloping relationship is known as the aggregate demand curve.
9. Equilibrium GNP can be above or below potential GNP, which is defined as the GNP that would be produced if the labor force were fully employed.
10. If equilibrium GNP exceeds potential GNP, the difference is called an inflationary gap. If equilibrium GNP falls short of potential GNP, the resulting difference is called a recessionary gap.
11. The reason such gaps can occur is that the saving that consumers want to do at full-employment income levels may differ from the investing that investors want to do. This problem is not likely to arise in a planned economy or in a primitive economy.

Concepts for Review

Investment tax credit
Equilibrium level of GNP
Expenditure schedule
Induced investment
$C + I = Y$

Income–expenditure
(or 45° line) diagram
Aggregate demand curve
Full-employment level of GNP
(or potential GNP)

Recessionary gap
Inflationary gap
Coordination of saving
and investment

Questions for Discussion

1. Why would someone interested in stabilization policy want to study a model of an economy in which there is no government?
2. Since the mid-1970s there have been constant warnings that the rate of business investment in the United States is too low. Does this chapter give you any ideas about what is meant by the phrase "too low"? What factors do you think account for the low level of investment spending? (You may want to discuss this last issue with your instructor.)
3. Why is not any arbitrary level of GNP an equilibrium for the economy? (Do not give a mechanical answer to this question, but explain the economic mechanism involved.)
4. From the following data, construct an expenditure schedule on a piece of graph paper. Then use the income–expenditure (45° line) diagram to determine the equilibrium level of GNP.

INCOME	CONSUMPTION	INVESTMENT
100	80	30
150	125	30
200	170	30
250	215	30
300	260	30

5. From the following data, construct an expenditure schedule on a piece of graph paper. Then use the

income–expenditure (45° line) diagram to determine the equilibrium level of GNP.

INCOME	CONSUMPTION	INVESTMENT
100	110	0
150	140	15
200	170	30
250	200	45
300	230	60

Compare your answer with your answer to Question 4.

6. Does the economy this year seem to have an inflation-ary gap or a recessionary gap? (If you do not know the answer from reading the newspaper, ask your instructor.)
7. Why are there no recessions in the Soviet Union?
8. (More difficult)* Consider an economy in which the consumption function takes the following simple algebraic form:

$$C = 120 + 0.8Y$$

and in which investment (I) is always 200. Find the equilibrium level of GNP from the requirement that $C + I = Y$. Compare your answer to Table 8–2 and Figure 8–3.

*The answer to this question is provided in Appendix B.

Appendix A

The Saving and Investment Approach

As we mentioned in the chapter, there is another way of looking at the determination of the equilibrium level of GNP. Instead of studying the condition that total expenditure ($C + I$) is equal to production (Y), we can study the condition that saving (S) is equal to investment (I). This is what we will do in this appendix.

It must be emphasized at the outset that there is nothing *new* in this approach. It is merely another way of looking at precisely the same phenomenon. The reason is that income (Y) must be either spent on consumer goods (C) or saved (S). Since $Y = C + S$ *always*, and since $Y = C + I$ *when Y is at its equilibrium value*, we can describe equilibrium by the condition that $C + S = C + I$, or simply:

$$S = I.$$

Graphical Analysis

This way of looking at equilibrium has a different graphical representation: It does not use the 45° line diagram, but it contains precisely the same information. Recall that in an appendix to Chapter 7 we constructed the saving schedule, which we repeat here as Figure 8–9. Since the equilibrium condition now under scrutiny is $S = I$, we can complete the story by providing an investment schedule. In the example used in the text, investment was taken to be a fixed number irrespective of income. We again do

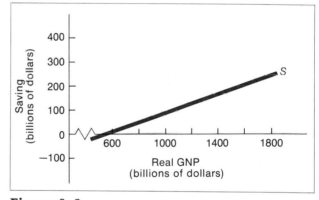

Figure 8–9
THE SAVING SCHEDULE
This diagram shows the relationship between saving and income in Macroland and duplicates Figure 7–8 (page 129).

this here, so the investment schedule is as shown in Figure 8–10 on the next page.

To find the point at which saving and investment are equal, we need only put both curves on the same diagram, which we have done in Figure 8–11. Point E shows the equilibrium level of GNP, which is at an income level of $1600 billion. As must be the case, this is the same answer we obtained with the 45° line diagram.

You will notice that at income levels below $1600 billion, investment exceeds saving, just as

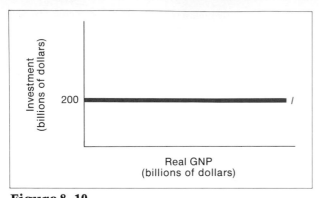

Figure 8–10

THE INVESTMENT SCHEDULE

In this simple example, investment spending is a fixed number—$200 billion—regardless of the level of GNP. Therefore, the investment schedule is a horizontal line at $200 billion.

$C + I$ exceeded output in the 45° line diagram. Similarly, at income levels above $1600 billion, S exceeds I. (In the 45° line diagram, Y exceeded $C + I$ in this range.) This must be the case since the two graphs are alternative depictions of the same phenomena. The economic analyses behind them are precisely the same.

Induced Investment

In the chapter we mentioned the possibility of *induced investment,* that is, of an investment schedule that rises as GNP rises, but we did not examine this possibility in our graphs. (However, this case did arise in Discussion Question 5.) The reason is that what matters in the 45° line diagram is the slope of the *combined* $C + I$ schedule, not the *individual* slopes of the C and I schedules. So an upward-sloping investment schedule does not make much difference to the analysis.

When using the saving and investment approach, however, the slope of the investment schedule becomes more apparent, if not more important. So Figure 8–12 illustrates the case of induced investment. In this diagram, the investment schedule is upward sloping. Equilibrium, however, is still at point E—where the S and I schedules cross. Thus, allowance for induced investment does not change our analysis in any significant way.[5]

[5]Some students may wonder what happens if the slope of the investment schedule exceeds that of the saving schedule. This is a difficult question and one that is best reserved for more advanced courses. Suffice it to say here that the simple model of income determination constructed in this chapter will not work in such a case.

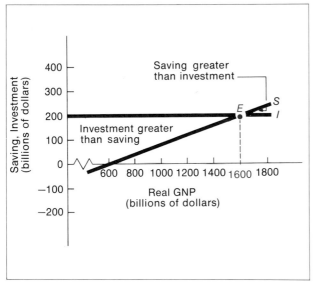

Figure 8–11

DETERMINATION OF EQUILIBRIUM GNP
BY SAVING = INVESTMENT

This diagram, which combines Figures 8–9 and 8–10, depicts the equilibrium of the economy at point E, where the saving and investment schedules intersect. The equilibrium is at a real GNP of $1600 billion, which, as must be the case, is the same conclusion that we reached with the aid of the 45° line diagram (Figure 8–3 on page 146).

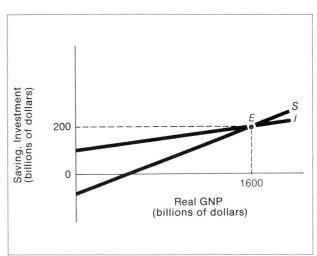

Figure 8–12

INCOME DETERMINATION
WITH INDUCED INVESTMENT

When investment rises with GNP ("induced investment"), the investment schedule acquires a positive slope. Apart from this, the determination of equilibrium output is precisely as it was before. Point E, where the S and I schedules cross, is the equilibrium.

Summary

1. The condition for equilibrium GNP—which we gave in the chapter as the equation of aggregate demand with output $(C + I = Y)$—can be restated as the requirement that saving and investment be equal $(S = I)$. This does not change anything but simply says the same thing in different words.

2. These different words lead to a different graphical presentation, in which we look for equilibrium at the point where the saving schedule crosses the investment schedule.

3. Induced investment—that is, investment that rises as the GNP rises—leads to an upward-sloping investment schedule, but requires no other change in the analysis.

Concepts for Review

$S = I$
Saving schedule
Investment schedule
Induced investment

Questions for Discussion

1. From the data in Discussion Question 4 at the end of the chapter, construct the saving schedule and the investment schedule on a piece of graph paper. (In doing so, remember that any income that is not consumed must have been saved.) Use these constructions to find the equilibrium level of GNP.

2. Do the same thing with the data in Discussion Question 5. (*Hint:* you will find *negative* saving at income level 100. There is nothing wrong with this. You do negative saving any time you draw down your bank account balance.)

Appendix B

The Simple Algebra of Income Determination

The model of demand-side equilibrium that the chapter presented graphically and in tabular form can also be handled with some simple algebra.

Written as an equation, the consumption function in our example is:

$$C = 120 + 0.8Y.$$

This is simply the equation of a straight line with intercept 120 and slope 0.8. Investment in the example was assumed to be 200, regardless of the level of income. So the sum $C + I$ is:

$$C + I = 120 + 0.8Y + 200 = 320 + 0.8Y.$$

This is the equation of the $C + I$ curve found in Figure 8–3.

Since the equilibrium quantity of GNP demanded is defined by:

$$Y = C + I,$$

we can solve for the equilibrium value of Y algebraically by substituting $320 + 0.8Y$ for $C + I$. Thus, we have:

$$Y = C + I = 320 + 0.8Y.$$

To solve this equation for Y, first subtract $0.8Y$ from both sides to get:

$$0.2Y = 320.$$

Then multiply both sides by 5 to obtain the answer:

$$Y = 1600.$$

This, of course, is precisely the solution we found by graphical and tabular methods in the chapter.

The method of solution is easily generalized to

deal with any set of numbers in our equations. Suppose the consumption function is:

$$C = a + bY.$$

(In the example, $a = 120$ and $b = 0.8$.) Then the equilibrium condition that $Y = C + I$ implies:

$$Y = a + bY + I.$$

Subtracting bY from both sides leads to:

$$(1 - b)Y = a + I,$$

and dividing through by $1 - b$ gives:

$$Y = \frac{a + I}{1 - b}.$$

This formula, which is certainly *not* to be memorized, is valid for any numerical values of a, b, and I (so long as b is between zero and one).

Questions for Discussion

1. Find the equilibrium level of GNP demanded in an economy in which investment is always $300 and the consumption function is described by the following algebraic equation:

$$C = 100 + 0.8Y.$$

2. Do the same for an economy in which investment is fixed at $150 and the consumption function is:

$$C = 250 + 0.6Y.$$

3. In each of the above cases, how much saving is there in equilibrium? (*Hint:* Income not consumed must be saved.) Is saving equal to investment?

Supply-Side Equilibrium: Unemployment *and* Inflation?

9

The analysis of the last chapter led to the conclusion that the level of prices, in conjunction with the economy's consumption and investment schedules, governs whether the economy will experience a recessionary or an inflationary gap. If the $C + I$ schedule is "too low," we learned, a *recessionary gap* will arise, while a $C + I$ schedule that is "too high" leads to an *inflationary gap*. Which sort of gap actually occurs is of some importance because, as we shall learn in this chapter, a recessionary gap normally spells unemployment while an inflationary gap means inflation. The tools provided in Chapter 8, however, are not sufficient to determine which sort of gap will actually arise because the position of the $C + I$ schedule depends on the price level. This is the task of the present chapter. To carry it out we have to bring the supply side of the economy into the picture because, as we know from Chapters 4 and 5, prices are determined jointly by *both* supply *and* demand.

After reviewing some puzzling aspects of recent economic history, we explain how the *aggregate supply curve* is derived from business costs. Next we consider the interaction of aggregate supply and aggregate demand, and the joint determination of output and the price level. With this apparatus in hand, we return to the phenomena of recessionary and inflationary gaps, and study how the economy adjusts to each type. Doing this puts us in a position to deal with the crucial question raised in earlier chapters: Does the economy have an efficient self-correcting mechanism? As we shall learn, the economy is better at curing inflationary gaps than recessionary gaps. Finally, we use aggregate supply–aggregate demand analysis to explain the vexing problem of *stagflation*—the simultaneous occurrence of high unemployment *and* high inflation—that has plagued the economy so often since the mid-1970s. The chapter ends with a brief word on "supply-side economics."

The Mystery of Stagflation

The analysis of demand-side equilibrium presented in the preceding chapter seems to suggest that while we can have *either* unemployment (from a recessionary gap) *or* inflation (from an inflationary gap), we should not have both at the same time. And, for many decades, this seemed to be the way things worked out.

The 1930s witnessed severe unemployment and falling prices; World War II led to an inflationary boom; there was very little inflation during the recession-prone 1950s and early 1960s; and so on.

But things started to change in the 1970s, the decade of stagflation. Prices continued to rise rapidly right through the 1970 recession. During the period 1973–1975, the U.S. economy suffered through both its worst inflation and worst recession in many years. The inflationary recession of 1980 was, in many ways, a repeat performance of what happened in 1973–1975. Events made it clear that inflation and unemployment could coexist in unhappy wedlock.

Throughout the 1970s, and right up to the present time, journalists, politicians, and even some economists have proclaimed frequently that the phenomenon of stagflation is a mystery to economists, that somehow it "defies the laws of economics." A *New York Times* article in 1970 was entitled "Impossible! Recession *and* Rising Prices?" Almost eight years later, a Treasury official intoned: "I don't think the President understands why there's high inflation and high unemployment at the same time. But then neither does anyone else."[1]

Despite the many times such claims have been made, the plain fact is that they are false. Standard economic theory *does* provide an explanation of stagflation; and by the end of this chapter, you will be able to explain it yourself. But, unfortunately, *understanding* why stagflation occurs and being able to *cure* it are two very different things. We might as well admit right now that, while some suggestions have been made, no economist has a reliable cure for stagflation. In this respect, stagflation does remain a mystery.

The Aggregate Supply Curve

In earlier chapters we noted that *aggregate demand* is a schedule, not a fixed number. The quantity of real GNP that will be demanded depends on the price level, as summarized in the economy's *aggregate demand curve*. Analogously, the concept of *aggregate supply* does not refer to a fixed number but, rather, to a schedule. The volume of goods and services that will be provided by profit-seeking enterprises depends on the prices they obtain for their outputs. The relationship between the price level and the quantity of real GNP supplied is called the economy's **aggregate supply curve.**

The **aggregate supply curve** shows, for each possible price level, the quantity of goods and services that all the nation's businesses are willing to produce.

A typical aggregate supply curve is drawn in Figure 9–1. It slopes upward, meaning that as prices rise more output is produced, *other things held constant.* (The most important of these "other things" are listed in the following section.) It is not difficult to understand why this curve slopes upward. Producers in the U.S. economy are motivated mainly by profit. Since the profit made by producing a unit of output is simply the difference between the price at which it is sold and the unit costs of production,

$$\text{Profit per unit} = \text{Price} - \text{Cost per unit} ,$$

it is at once clear that the response of production to a rising price level (henceforth, P) depends on the response of costs.[2]

One critical fact affecting this response is that labor and other inputs used by firms normally are available at *relatively fixed prices* for some period of time (though certainly not forever). There are many reasons for this. Some workers

---

[1] *The Wall Street Journal*, September 23, 1977, page 22.
[2] For a full discussion of business output decisions and how they respond to costs, see Chapter 21.

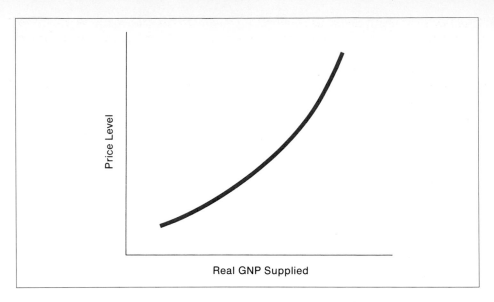

Figure 9–1
AN AGGREGATE SUPPLY
CURVE
This graph shows a typical aggregate supply curve. It has a
positive slope (that is, it rises as
we move to the right), meaning
that the quantity of output supplied rises as the price level
rises.

and firms enter into long-term labor contracts that set money wages up to three years in advance. Even where there are no explicit contracts, employees typically have their wages increased only about once per year. During the interim period, money wages are fixed. Much the same is true of other factors of production. Many firms get deliveries of raw materials under long-term contracts according to which suppliers have agreed to provide the materials at prearranged prices. None of these contracts lasts forever, of course, but many of them last long enough to be of importance.

Why is it significant that firms can purchase inputs like labor and raw materials at fixed prices? Because firms decide how much to produce by comparing selling prices with costs of production; and production costs obviously depend on input prices. If selling prices rise while wages and other factor costs are relatively fixed, this comparison looks more favorable (more profitable), and so firms are persuaded to step up production. Conversely, if selling prices fall while input costs are relatively fixed, profit margins will be squeezed and firms may react by cutting back on production. This behavior is embodied in the upward slope of the aggregate supply curve: production rises when the price level (P) rises, and falls when P falls. In other words:

The aggregate supply curve slopes upward because firms normally can purchase labor and other inputs at fixed costs for some period of time. Thus, higher selling prices make input costs "cheaper" by comparison and therefore make production more attractive.

The clause "for some period of time" alerts us to the possibility that the aggregate supply curve may not stand still. If wages or prices of other inputs change, as they surely will during inflationary times, then the aggregate supply curve will shift.

Shifts of the Aggregate Supply Curve

We have concluded so far that, for any given levels of wages and other input prices, there will be an upward-sloping aggregate supply curve relating the price level to aggregate quantity supplied. But what factors determine the *position* of this curve? What things can make it shift?

Figure 9–2
A SHIFT OF THE AGGREGATE SUPPLY CURVE
This diagram shows what happens to the economy's aggregate supply curve when money wages rise. Higher wages shift the supply curve upward from S_0S_0 to S_1S_1, leading, for example, to a price level of 105 rather than 100 at an output level of $1600 billion. The aggregate supply curve will shift upward in the same manner if the price of any other input (such as energy) increases.

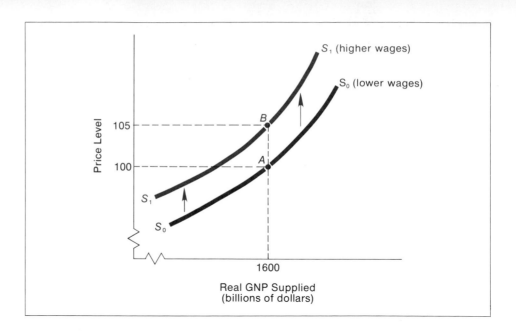

The Wage Rate
Our previous discussion suggests that one obvious determinant of the position of the aggregate supply curve is the wage rate. Wages are the major element of cost for most firms, typically accounting for something like 70 percent of all expenses. Higher wages spell higher costs; and since prices depend fundamentally on costs, this means higher prices as well. Specifically, if the money wage goes up, higher prices must be obtained if production is to remain profitable. This means that the price at which it will be profitable to sell any particular quantity of output, such as $1600 billion in Figure 9–2, must go up. In the graph, firms were willing to supply the quantity $1600 billion at a price level of 100 before wages increased (point A), but are willing to go on providing this quantity of output at the higher price level of 105 (point B) after wages have increased.[3] By similar reasoning, the price level necessary to elicit any given level of production will fall if wages fall. Thus:

A rise in the money wage rate causes the aggregate supply curve to shift upward; a fall in the money wage rate causes the aggregate supply curve to shift downward.

Prices of Other Inputs
In this regard, there is nothing special about wages. An increase in the price of *any* input that firms buy will shift the aggregate supply curve in the same way. That is:

The aggregate supply curve is shifted upward by an increase in the price of any input to the production process, and is shifted downward by a decrease. In plain English, increases in input costs are at least partially "passed on" to consumers.

While there are many inputs other than labor, the one that has attracted the most attention in recent years is energy. We shall have much to say about energy in this book, including further discussion in this chapter and in an entire chapter on the energy problem (Chapter 36). But for present purposes the important thing

[3]Real GNP, it will be recalled, is measured in the prices of the base period (currently 1972). So if the price level rises to 105, the $1600 billion in *real* GNP would correspond to a *nominal* GNP of $1600 × 1.05 = $1680 billion. To review real versus nominal GNP, see Chapter 5, pages 76–77.

to realize is that increases in the price of energy, such as those that took place during 1973–1974 and 1979–1980, push the aggregate supply curve upward more or less as shown in Figure 9–2.

Technology and Productivity

Another factor that determines the position of the aggregate supply curve is the state of technology. Suppose, for example, that there is a technological breakthrough that increases the **productivity** of labor. Such an improvement in productivity will *decrease* business costs, and thus *reduce* the prices that must be charged to make any given level of output profitable. This means that productivity improvements shift the aggregate supply curve in the opposite direction from that shown in Figure 9–2—that is, they will shift it downward. (Figure 9–2 can be viewed as applying to a *decline* in productivity.) As we shall learn in later chapters, slow growth of productivity is one factor that contributed to the inflation of the 1970s, and it remains a source of great concern for the 1980s.

Available Supplies of Labor and Capital

The last determinant of the position of the aggregate supply curve is quite obvious, but we list it anyway for the sake of completeness. The bigger the economy—as measured by its available supplies of labor and capital—the more it is capable of producing. So as the labor force grows, and as the capital stock is increased by investment, the aggregate supply curve will shift outward (to the right), meaning that more output will be produced at any given price level. There is certainly nothing very surprising about this. But, as we shall see in later chapters, sluggish growth of the capital stock (by causing sluggish growth of aggregate supply) has contributed to our recent inflation problem.

These, then, are the "other things" that we hold constant when drawing up an aggregate supply curve: wage rates, prices of other inputs (like energy), technology, labor force, and capital stock. While a change in the price level moves the economy *along a given supply curve*, a change in any of these other determinants of aggregate supply *shifts the entire supply schedule*.

Resource Utilization and the Shape of the Aggregate Supply Curve

One other feature of the aggregate supply curve depicted in Figure 9–1 merits comment. We have drawn our supply curve with a characteristic curvature: it is relatively flat at low levels of output and gets steeper at high levels of output (as we move to the right). There is a reason for this.

When economic activity is weak, product demand slack, and capacity utilization low, firms are likely to respond to an upsurge in demand by bringing their unused capital and labor resources back into production. They will find it neither necessary nor advisable to raise prices very much. The aggregate supply curve, in a word, will be relatively flat. By contrast, if the economy is booming, demand is buoyant, and production is straining capacity, firms will be unable to increase output without increasing costs. Price increases will thus be encouraged by cost developments and, incidentally, will not be resisted very forcefully on the demand side. In this case, the aggregate supply curve will be rather steep. Thus:

The slope of the aggregate supply curve, which tells us the price increase that is associated with a unit increase in quantity supplied, generally rises as the degree of resource utilization rises.

Equilibrium of Aggregate Demand and Supply

In the preceding chapter, we learned that the level of prices is a crucial determinant of whether equilibrium GNP is below full employment (a "recessionary gap"), precisely at full employment, or above full employment (an "inflationary gap"). We are now in a position to analyze which type of gap, if any, will actually occur in any particular case by combining the analysis of aggregate supply just completed with the analysis of aggregate demand from the last chapter to determine *simultaneously* the equilibrium level of real GNP (Y) and the equilibrium prive level (P).

Figure 9–3 shows the mechanics graphically. The aggregate demand curve DD and the aggregate supply curve SS intersect at point E, where real GNP is $1600 billion and the price level is 100. As can be seen in the graph, at any higher price level quantity supplied would exceed quantity demanded, which would put downward pressure on prices. At any lower price level, quantity demanded would exceed quantity supplied, thus putting upward pressure on prices. Only when the price level is 100 are the quantities of real GNP demanded and supplied equal. Hence, only the combination $P = 100$, $Y = $1600 is an equilibrium.

Table 9–1 illustrates this same conclusion in another way, using a tabular analysis similar to that of the last chapter (refer back to Table 8–2). Columns 1 and 2 constitute an aggregate demand schedule corresponding to the aggregate demand curve DD in Figure 9–3. Columns 1 and 3 constitute an aggregate supply schedule with the general shape discussed in this chapter. It corresponds exactly to aggregate supply curve SS in the figure. It is clear from the table that equilibrium occurs only at $P = 100$ and $Y = $1600. At any other price level, aggregate quantities supplied and demanded would be unequal, with consequent upward or downward pressure on prices. For example, at a price level of 80, customers demand $1750 billion worth of goods and services, but firms wish to provide only $1450 billion. The price level is too low and will be forced upward. Conversely, at a price level of, say, 120, quantity supplied ($1700 billion) exceeds quantity demanded ($1500 billion), implying that the price level must fall.

Figure 9–3
EQUILIBRIUM OF REAL GNP AND THE PRICE LEVEL
This diagram shows how the equilibrium levels of real GNP and the price level are simultaneously determined by the intersection of the aggregate demand curve (*DD*) and the aggregate supply curve (*SS*). In this example, equilibrium occurs at point *E*, with a real GNP of $1600 billion and a price level of 100.

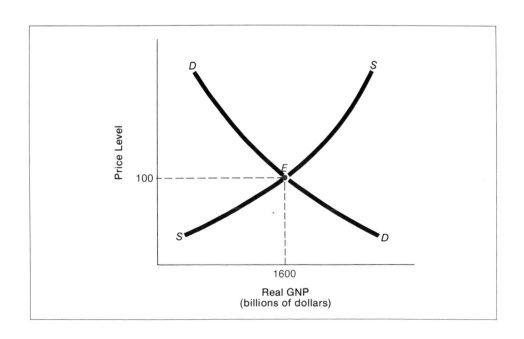

Table 9–1
THE DETERMINATION OF THE EQUILIBRIUM PRICE LEVEL

(1)	(2)	(3)	(4)	(5)
PRICE LEVEL (P)	AGGREGATE QUANTITY DEMANDED (billions of dollars)	AGGREGATE QUANTITY SUPPLIED (billions of dollars)	BALANCE OF SUPPLY AND DEMAND	PRICES WILL:
75	1800	1400	Quantity demanded exceeds quantity supplied	Rise
80	1750	1450	Quantity demanded exceeds quantity supplied	Rise
100	1600	1600	Quantity demanded equals quantity supplied	Remain the same
120	1500	1700	Quantity supplied exceeds quantity demanded	Fall
150	1400	1800	Quantity supplied exceeds quantity demanded	Fall

Let us now reconsider a question we answered in the previous chapter: Will equilibrium occur at, below, or above full employment? The answer is the same as it was there. Nothing in Figure 9–3 tells us where full employment is; it could be above the $1600 billion equilibrium level or below it. Depending on the locations of the aggregate demand and aggregate supply curves, then, we can reach equilibrium above full employment (an inflationary gap), at full employment, or below full employment (a recessionary gap).

These three possibilities are illustrated in the three parts of Figure 9–4. Part (a) simply repeats Figure 9–3, adding the information that full employment GNP

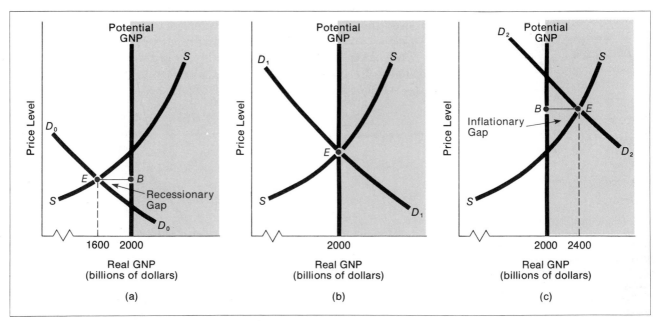

Figure 9–4
RECESSIONARY AND INFLATIONARY GAPS REVISITED
This diagram shows three possible types of equilibrium. In each case, the aggregate supply curve is the same (SS), equilibrium occurs at point E, and full employment GNP is $2000 billion. In part (a), the aggregate demand curve D_0D_0 is relatively low, so that equilibrium falls below full employment. There is a recessionary gap measured by the distance EB, or $400 billion. In part (b), the aggregate demand curve D_1D_1 is higher, and equilibrium occurs precisely at full employment. There is no gap of either kind. In part (c), the aggregate demand curve D_2D_2 is so high that equilibrium occurs beyond full employment. There is an inflationary gap measured by the distance BE, or $400 billion.

is assumed to be $2000 billion. It therefore shows a recessionary gap of $400 billion. This situation corresponds precisely to Figure 8–7 in the previous chapter (page 150). In part (b), the aggregate demand curve is sufficiently high to intersect aggregate supply exactly at full employment. [The aggregate supply curve is exactly the same as in part (a).] Finally, part (c) depicts a case in which the aggregate demand curve is so high that an inflationary gap of $400 billion arises. (Again, the supply curve is the same.) The inflationary gap shown here duplicates that shown in Figure 8–8 in the previous chapter (page 152). However, we have done more than just restate our previous conclusions, because we are now in a position to examine how the economy reacts to either a recessionary gap or an inflationary gap.

Adjusting to an Inflationary Gap: Inflation

We have already suggested that an inflationary gap sets the stage for inflation. As we shall see now, this happens because the economy, if left to its own devices, produces an inflation that eventually eliminates an inflationary gap. In other words, the gap self-destructs, although the process may be slow and painful. Let us see how this works.

When equilibrium GNP is above potential, jobs are plentiful and labor is in great demand. Although some workers are unemployed, this minimal unemployment is less than the frictional level—that is, less than the number we usually expect to be jobless because they are moving, changing occupations, and so on. Many firms, on the other hand, are having trouble finding workers. They may even be having trouble hanging on to their current employees, as other firms try to lure them away with higher wages.

Such a situation is bound to lead to rising wages, and rising wages add to business costs, thus shifting the aggregate supply curve upward. But as the aggregate supply curve shifts upward—eventually moving from $S_0 S_0$ to $S_1 S_1$ in Figure 9–5, for example—the size of the inflationary gap steadily declines. Thus, inflation erodes the inflationary gap, eventually leading the economy to an equilibrium at full employment (point F in Figure 9–5).

Figure 9–5

THE ELIMINATION OF AN INFLATIONARY GAP
When the aggregate supply curve is $S_0 S_0$ and the aggregate demand curve is DD, the economy will initially reach equilibrium (point E) with an inflationary gap. The resulting inflation of wages will push the supply curve upward toward higher prices until it has shifted to the position indicated by curve $S_1 S_1$. Here, with equilibrium at point F, the economy is at normal full employment. But, during the adjustment period from E to F, there will have been inflation.

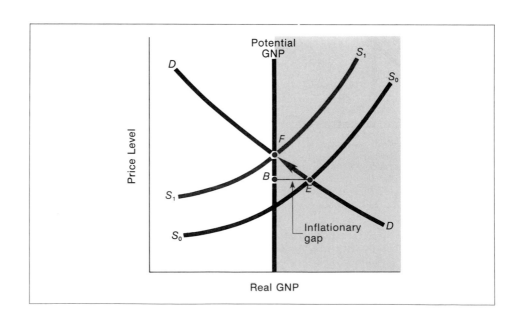

There is a straightforward way of looking at how this self-correcting process works. The trouble arises in the first place because consumers and investors are demanding more output than the economy is capable of producing at normal operating rates. To paraphrase an old cliché, there is too much demand chasing too little supply. Naturally, prices will be rising in such an environment. And the rising prices will eat away at the purchasing power of consumers' wealth, forcing them to cut back on consumption, as explained in Chapter 7. Eventually, consumers' appetites for goods will be scaled down to the economy's capacity to provide those goods; and at this point, the self-correcting process stops. That, in essence, is how the problem cures itself, though the inflationary process may leave many of us unhappy.

One further caveat should be entered. The conclusion that an inflationary gap sows the seeds of its own destruction holds *only* in the absence of further forces propelling the aggregate demand curve outward. As you can see by manipulating the aggregate demand–aggregate supply diagram, if aggregate demand is shifting *out* at the same time that aggregate supply is shifting *in*, there will certainly be inflation, but the inflationary gap may not shrink. (Try this as an exercise, to make sure you understand how to use the apparatus.) So not all inflations come to a natural end. In subsequent chapters we shall study several factors that might shift the aggregate demand curve outward.

Demand Inflation and Stagflation

Simple as it is, this adjustment model teaches us a number of important lessons about inflation in the real world. First of all, Figure 9–5 reminds us that the real culprit in this particular inflation is the excessive level of aggregate demand. The aggregate demand curve is initially so high that it intersects the aggregate supply curve at an output level higher than full employment. The resulting intense demand for workers pushes wages higher; and higher wages spell higher prices. While excessive demand is not the only possible cause of inflation in the real world, it certainly is the cause in our example. However, business managers and journalists are very likely to blame inflation on rising wages.

In a superficial sense, of course, they are correct, because the higher wages do indeed lead firms to raise their prices. But in a deeper sense they are wrong. Both rising wages and rising prices are only symptoms of an underlying malady: too much aggregate demand. Blaming labor for inflation in such a case is a bit like blaming high doctor bills for making you ill.

Second, we see that output falls while prices rise as the economy adjusts from point E to point F in Figure 9–5. This process thus provides our first (but not our last!) explanation of the phenomenon of stagflation. We see that:

A period of stagflation is part of the normal aftermath of a period of excessive aggregate demand.

It is easy enough to understand why stagflation occurs. When aggregate demand is excessive, the economy will (temporarily) produce beyond its normal capacity. Labor markets become very tight and wages rise. Machinery and raw materials may also become scarce and so start rising in price. Faced by higher costs, the natural reaction of business firms is both to produce less and to charge a higher price. This is stagflation.

It may be useful to review what we have learned about inflationary gaps thus far.

If aggregate demand is exceptionally high, the economy may reach an equilibrium above full employment (an inflationary gap). When this occurs, the tight situation in the labor market soon forces wages to rise. Since wages are business costs, prices rise and there is inflation. With cuts in consumer purchasing power, the inflationary gap begins to close. As the inflationary gap is closing, output falls while prices continue to rise, so the economy experiences stagflation until the inflationary gap is eliminated. At this point, a long-run equilibrium is established with a higher price level and with GNP equal to potential GNP.

An Example from Recent History: The United States from 1966 to 1970

Because the years since 1973 have been special in so many respects, one has to go back to the late 1960s to find a "textbook" example of an inflationary gap that extinguished itself in this way.

During 1966–1968, the U.S. economy was booming, unemployment was continually below 4 percent, and jobs were plentiful. According to official estimates, real GNP (measured in 1972 prices) exceeded its potential by an average of $19 billion during those three years. There was an inflationary gap.

Our analysis suggests that wages should have been accelerating, and indeed they were. The bright blue bars in Figure 9–6 illustrate this acceleration. The rate of change of wages rose from less than 3 percent in 1963 and 1964 to more than 6 percent in 1968 before stabilizing. The diagram also shows that, except for a minor dip in 1967, the rate of inflation followed the rate of increase of wages—rising from $1\frac{1}{2}$ percent a year to over 5 percent. This is, again, in line with what our model predicts.

The upsurge in inflation naturally ate away at the inflationary gap, which was gone by the end of 1969. Yet inflation continued unabated through a mild recession in 1969–1970. The U.S. economy was in the stagflation phase. Despite outcries of "excessive" wage demands that "caused" inflation, it is clear that the

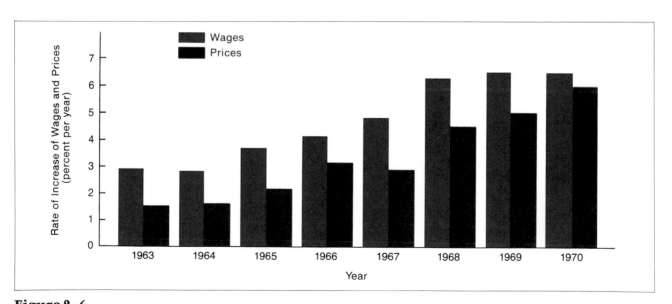

Figure 9–6
GROWTH RATES OF WAGES AND PRICES IN THE UNITED STATES, 1963–1970
These data illustrate what happened when an inflationary gap arose in the United States during the years 1966–1968. Notice the acceleration of both wages and prices beginning in about 1965. By 1969, the gap was eliminated, and wage increases leveled off. There was a minor recession in 1969–1970, but inflation continued.
SOURCE: *Economic Report of the President*, 1981.

ultimate cause of the acceleration in both wages and prices was the excessive aggregate demand of the Vietnam War episode. The economy behaved just as our simple model suggests.

Adjusting to a Recessionary Gap: Deflation or Unemployment?

Let us now consider what can happen when the economy finds itself in equilibrium *below* full employment—that is, when there is a recessionary gap. This might be caused, for example, by inadequate consumer spending or by anemic investment spending.

Figure 9–4(a) on page 165 illustrates such a case and gives an impression of the economic situation inherited by President Reagan when he assumed office in 1981. The unemployment rate, which had been below 6 percent in 1979, stood at 7.4 percent in January 1981.

You might expect that we could just run our previous analysis in reverse: High unemployment leads to falling wages; falling wages reduce business costs and shift the aggregate supply curve downward, so firms cut prices; falling wages and prices eliminate the recessionary gap by propping up consumer spending; and full employment is restored. Very simple. And very irrelevant to our modern economy!

Why is it irrelevant? Our brief review of the historical record in Chapter 5 showed that, while the economy may have operated like this long ago, it certainly does not work that way now. The history of the United States shows many examples of falling wages and prices before World War II but none since then. Not even the Great Recession of 1974–1975, during which unemployment climbed as high as 9 percent, was able to force prices and wages down.

Exactly *why* wages and prices are rigid in the downward direction is not really known. While there are many theories, none of them commands anything like universal assent. For our purposes, we had best just accept it as a fact without trying to explain it. In our modern economy, prices and wages will rise when demand is strong, but they generally will not fall when demand is weak.

The implications of this rigidity are quite serious; for a recessionary gap cannot cure itself without some deflation. And if wages and prices will not fall, deflation cannot occur. This means that *the economy gets stuck at an equilibrium below full employment.* Keynes was the first economist to point out the possibility of a long-lasting equilibrium below full employment and to distinguish it from the full-employment equilibrium that we have just been considering.

When aggregate demand is low, the economy may get stuck in an *unemployment equilibrium.* There is a recessionary gap, but wages and prices refuse to fall; so the gap persists. The economy endures a prolonged period of production below potential GNP.

Does the Economy Have a Self-Correcting Mechanism?

Now a situation like this would, presumably, not last forever. As the recession lengthened, and perhaps deepened, more and more workers would be unable to obtain jobs at the prevailing high wages. Eventually their resistance to wage cuts would be worn down by their need to be employed. Firms, too, would become increasingly willing to cut prices as the period of weak demand lasted longer and longer and managers became convinced that the slump was not merely a temporary aberration. Prices and wages did, in fact, fall during the Great Depression of the 1930s. And they might fall again if a sufficiently drastic depression were allowed to occur.

It was reasoning of precisely this sort that led the Hoover administration to adopt a hands-off attitude toward the deteriorating economy in the dark days of the early 1930s. The reasoning was that if government only showed patience and refrained from tampering with the private economy, wages and prices would fall far enough to restore consumer demand and to re-employ the work force. Americans now consider themselves fortunate that the political activists of the Roosevelt administration did not have such monumental patience!

The same issue arose again during the three recessions of the Eisenhower administration. Rather than take positive actions to end any of these recessions, the Eisenhower economists preferred to wait for the private economy to right itself by wage and price deflation, despite warnings from then Vice-President Richard Nixon that this might cost them the election in 1960. Later, President Kennedy's New Frontiersmen, like the New Dealers, were unwilling to stand by while the economy cured itself of its recessionary illness.

Today a healthy bipartisan attitude prevails. At least since President Nixon said "I am now a Keynesian" in 1970, politicians of both parties believe it is folly to wait for falling wages and prices to eliminate a recessionary gap. But while they agree that *some* government action is both necessary and appropriate under recessionary conditions, there is still vocal—and highly partisan!—debate over *how much* and *what kind* of intervention is warranted. We will discuss these issues in subsequent chapters.

Our overall conclusion about the economy's ability to right itself, then, seems to run something like this:

The economy does indeed have a self-correcting mechanism that tends to eliminate either unemployment or inflation. However, this mechanism is much more efficient at curing inflationary gaps through inflation than at curing recessionary gaps through deflation. In addition, its beneficial effects on inflation are sometimes swamped by strong inflationary forces (such as rapid increases in aggregate demand). Thus the self-correcting mechanism cannot always be relied upon.

Stagflation in the 1970s

We have so far encountered one type of stagflation in this chapter—the stagflation that often follows in the aftermath of an inflationary boom. As we saw, the "mystery" of stagflation in 1969–1970 is solved in this way. However, the same model does not fit the facts of the more serious stagflation episodes of 1973–1975 and 1978–1980 very well. What happened during these more recent "mysteries"?

The Great Stagflation of 1973–1975: A Case Study

The economic boom of 1972–1973 left the U.S. economy with an inflationary gap. While this gap was reported to be very small by official government estimates, many private economists believed it was much larger. Based on our previous analysis, we would expect a period of stagflation to follow. And this, in fact, is what happened. But the magnitudes of the increases in unemployment and inflation, and the speed of the economy's reaction, were simply too large to be accounted for by the normal workings of the self-correcting mechanism.

In 1973, the nation's unemployment rate stood at 4.9 percent—a rate considered to be below the full employment level. In 1974, unemployment crept up to 5.6 percent—very close to full employment. In 1975, however, it skyrocketed to a colossal 8.5 percent—well above even the most pessimistic estimates of the full employment rate. This hardly looks like the workings of a smoothly functioning self-correcting mechanism. On the inflation front, the Consumer Price Index, which had risen only 3.4 percent during 1972, rose 8.8 percent in 1973 and 12.2 percent in 1974. These price increases are much more extreme than those we saw in Figure 9–6.

What was going on during 1973–1975 that caused so much more unemployment and inflation than was expected? What were the causes of this new, more severe, type of stagflation? Several things.

First, the nations constituting the Organization of Petroleum Exporting Countries (OPEC) got together on a collusive agreement to limit production that succeeded in quadrupling the price of crude oil in only a few months. To American consumers, this showed up as a substantial increase in the prices of gasoline and home heating fuels. To American businesses, this action meant that one of the important inputs into the production process—energy—rose drastically in price, thus increasing the cost of doing business.

Second, crop failures in many parts of the world during 1972–1974 sent agricultural prices soaring. Because food prices are an important component of the cost of living, this shortage added directly to inflation. And it also contributed to inflation in two indirect ways. First, since some agricultural products are used as inputs into manufacturing processes, the higher agricultural prices led to higher industrial prices. Second, the accelerating consumer prices encouraged labor to strive for more generous wage increases.

Finally, the U.S. experiment with mandatory wage and price controls—an episode that we will discuss in Chapter 17—came to an end in the spring of 1974. Price and wage increases that had been suppressed by controls suddenly came to the surface in an inflationary bulge.

How do these events fit into our theoretical model of aggregate supply and aggregate demand? Energy prices, we observed earlier, are a cost of doing business. When they increase, as they did in 1974, the economy's aggregate supply curve shifts upward in the manner shown in Figure 9–2 (page 162). Higher agricultural prices have a similar effect on business costs for the two reasons just mentioned, and so they also push the aggregate supply curve upward.

Our analysis predicts that when the aggregate supply curve shifts upward, as it surely did in 1973–1974, production will be reduced. And in order to reduce demand to the available supply, prices will have to rise. The result is the worst of both worlds: falling production and rising prices. This conclusion is shown in Figure 9–7, which superimposes an aggregate demand curve, DD, upon the two aggregate supply curves of Figure 9–2. The economy's equilibrium shifts upward to the left, from point E to point A: thus, output falls while prices rise.

Stagflation is the typical result of adverse supply shifts.

The numbers used in Figure 9–7 are roughly indicative of what happened in the United States between 1973 (represented by supply curve S_0S_0 and point E) and 1975 (represented by supply curve S_1S_1 and point A). Real GNP, in 1972 prices, fell by about $21 billion, while the price level rose almost 20 percent.

Stagflation Again in 1978–1980: Another Case Study

Living through American economic history in 1978–1980 was almost like watching a TV rerun. By 1978 the economy had just about recovered from the severe dislocations of 1973 and 1974, only to be beset by another series of supply shocks. Once again, because of poor weather and other factors, food prices rose first, climbing rapidly during 1978 and early 1979. Then, just as the "food shock"

Figure 9–7
STAGFLATION FROM A SHIFT IN AGGREGATE SUPPLY
This diagram illustrates how stagflation arises if the aggregate supply curve shifts upward to the left (from $S_0 S_0$ to $S_1 S_1$). If the aggregate demand curve does not change, equilibrium moves from point E to point A. Output falls as prices rise, which is what we mean by stagflation. The diagram indicates roughly what happened in the U.S. during 1973–1975, when energy and food price shocks caused stagflation.

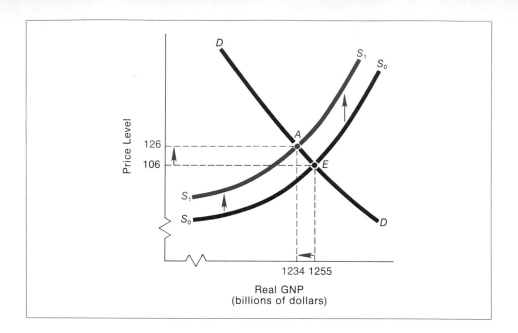

was abating, the ouster of the shah of Iran led to a cutoff of Iranian oil supplies and virtual panic in the world oil market. Oil prices escalated alarmingly as consumers scrambled to secure sources of supply and to build inventories. OPEC was only too happy to follow suit by raising prices, which they did in April, July, and December 1979. The long lines and hot tempers that developed at filling stations during the gasoline-starved summer of 1979 are still clear images in many people's memories.

The results of these supply shocks were much the same as those that occurred earlier in the decade. The inflation rate, which had been a relatively calm 6.8 percent in 1977, rose to 9 percent in 1978, to an astonishing 13.3 percent in 1979, and to a sizzling 18.4 percent in the first three months of 1980. Americans were almost panic-stricken over these unprecedented inflation rates, which dwarfed even the worst months of 1974.

As had been the case during 1973–1975, recession followed inflation. The economy, which had operated near the full employment range (approximately 6 percent unemployment) throughout 1978, began to weaken slightly in 1979. The recession began in earnest in early 1980, and the unemployment rate jumped from only 6.3 percent in March to 7.6 percent in May.

The general lesson to be learned from these two case studies is as important as it is clear:

The typical results of an adverse supply shock are a fall in output and an acceleration in inflation. This is one reason why the world economy was plagued by stagflation in the mid-1970s and early 1980s. And it can happen again if another series of supply-reducing events takes place.

A Word on Supply-Side Economics

It seems appropriate to close this chapter on supply-side equilibrium by mentioning a buzzword that has been much in the news since the late 1970s—**supply-side economics.**

Fighting Inflation from the Supply Side

Herbert Stein, who chaired the Council of Economic Advisers under presidents Nixon and Ford, evaluated supply-side economics in a *Wall Street Journal* column in 1980. His conclusions on the usefulness of supply-side initiatives in the battle against inflation were as follows:

There is a rising tide of literature and talk about supply-side economics. . . . An extreme, and currently very popular, version of supply-side economics is that the way to tackle the inflation problem is from the supply side, especially by cutting taxes. The argument is simply that inflation results from an excess of demand over supply, and there is no sense in correcting that by the painful method of restricting demand when it could be done by the pleasant way of raising supply. The answer is of course equally simple. What we can do on the supply side is not big enough to solve the problem. We have demand growing by about 12% a year and supply growing by about 2% a year, which yields 10% inflation. To increase the rate of growth of supply by 50% from 2% a year to 3% a year, which is a difficult task, would still leave an enormous inflation, especially if the increase of supply is accomplished by means like cutting taxes which at the same time increase demand.

What I have said here is not an argument for or against cutting taxes, or for or against any other policy. It surely is not meant to deny that cutting taxes and expenditures, or restructuring the tax system, can be beneficial in many respects. I am only making a plea for modesty . . .

Despite the tone of much of the current argument, the propositions of supply-side economics are not matters of ideology or principle. They are matters of arithmetic. So far one must say that the arithmetic of any of the "newer" propositions is highly doubtful. Supply-side economics may yet prove to be the irritant which, like the grain of sand in the oyster shell, produces a pearl of new economic wisdom. But up to this point the pearl has not appeared.

SOURCE: Herbert Stein, "Some 'Supply-Side' Propositions," *The Wall Street Journal*, March 19, 1980, page 24.

This phrase, which has been embraced by both President Ronald Reagan and the Joint Economic Committee of Congress, means different things to different people. Like many words that are coined by the media, it defies a concise definition. Yet the basic approach of the "supply siders" is clear enough: they favor government policies that encourage the growth of aggregate supply. Here is a partial list of the possibilities:

1. Reduce taxes on earned income to encourage people to work harder.

2. Reduce taxes on corporations to encourage more investment, and thus faster growth of the capital stock.

3. Reduce taxes on interest and dividends to encourage more saving.

4. Provide greater support for research and development (perhaps through tax incentives) to improve technology and speed up the growth of productivity.

Notice that while these policies span a wide range, they all share the same goal: expansion of aggregate supply.

There is an important element of truth in the supply siders' case. Economic policy in this country has traditionally focused on the demand side, without paying much attention to the supply side. But supply-side effects *do* matter. By running our analysis of aggregate supply shifts (pages 170–172) in reverse, we see clearly that supply-side policy initiatives, *if successful*, will both reduce the price level and raise real output. (To see why, look back at Figure 9–7 and suppose that curve S_1S_1 is the initial aggregate supply curve while S_0S_0 is the supply curve we get after application of a successful supply-side policy.) Lower prices and higher output sound like a good deal, especially in comparison with the demand-side policies we shall consider in the following chapters. As we will see there, demand-side policies cure unemployment only by aggravating inflation, and cure inflation only by causing unemployment.

However, a fair asessment of supply-side economics must recognize that it is no panacea. For one thing, it is far from clear that economic science has identified any supply-side policy that we can really count on to work.[4] For another, even if supply-side policies were to prove successful, they could not be expected to make more than a small dent in the inflation problem. (See the boxed insert on page 173.) The conclusion, then, is that while supply-side economics may possibly play some role in the fight against inflation, particularly in the long run, it cannot be expected to bear the brunt of the battle.

[4]Some specific supply-side policies are considered in Chapters 11 and 17.

Summary

1. The economy's aggregate supply curve relates the quantity of goods and services that will be supplied to the price level. It normally slopes upward to the right because the costs of labor and other inputs are relatively fixed in the short run, meaning that higher selling prices make input costs relatively "cheaper" and therefore encourage greater production.

2. The position of the aggregate supply curve can be shifted by changes in wage rates, prices of other inputs, technology, or quantities of labor and capital available for employment.

3. The aggregate supply curve normally gets steeper as output increases. This means that, as output and capacity utilization rise, any given increase in aggregate demand leads to more inflation and less growth of real output.

4. The equilibrium price level and the equilibrium level of real GNP are jointly determined by the intersection of the economy's aggregate supply and aggregate demand schedules. This intersection may come at full employment, below full employment (a recessionary gap), or above full employment (an inflationary gap).

5. If there is an inflationary gap, the economy has a self-correcting mechanism that erodes the gap through a process of inflation. Specifically, unusually strong job prospects push wages up, which shifts the aggregate supply curve up and reduces the inflationary gap.

6. One consequence of this self-correcting mechanism is that, if a surge in aggregate demand opens up an inflationary gap, part of the economy's natural adjustment to this event will be a period of stagflation; that is, a period in which prices are rising while output is falling.

7. The economy also has a self-correcting mechanism that erodes a recessionary gap. However, this mechanism works much more slowly and less reliably than the inflationary-gap mechanism because it relies on falling wages to pull down the aggregate supply curve.

8. An upward (or leftward) shift of the aggregate supply curve will cause output to fall while prices rise; that is, it will cause stagflation. Among the events that have caused such a shift are the abrupt increases in the price of foreign oil.

9. Adverse supply shifts like this apparently plagued our economy in 1973–1974 and again in 1979, leading to stagflation both times. Thus the stagflation of the 1970s was no mystery at all.

10. Supply-side economics aims to shift the aggregate supply curve outward primarily by cutting taxes. If such policies work, they will indeed be anti-inflationary. However, they can be expected to shoulder only a minor part of the battle against inflation.

Concepts for Review

Aggregate supply curve
Productivity
Equilibrium of real GNP
    and the price level

Inflationary gap
Self-correcting mechanism
Stagflation

Recessionary gap
Supply-side economics

Questions for Discussion

1. In an economy with the following aggregate demand and aggregate supply schedules, find the equilibrium levels of real output and the price level. If full employment comes at $950 billion, is there an inflationary or a recessionary gap?

AGGREGATE QUANTITY DEMANDED (in billions)	PRICE LEVEL	AGGREGATE QUANTITY SUPPLIED (in billions)
975	90	840
950	95	850
925	100	860
900	105	900
875	110	975

2. Suppose a worker receives a wage of $8.50 per hour. Compute the *real* wage (money wage deflated by the price index) corresponding to each of the following possible price levels: 85, 90, 100, 110, 120. What do you notice about the relationship between the real wage and the price level? Relate this to the slope of the aggregate supply curve.

3. In 1973, capacity utilization averaged 88 percent. In 1975, it averaged 73 percent. In which year do you think the economy found itself on a steeper portion of its aggregate supply curve? Explain why.

4. Explain why an increase in the price of foreign oil shifts the aggregate supply curve upward to the left. What are the consequences of such a shift?

5. Comment on the following statement: "Inflationary and recessionary gaps are nothing to worry about because the economy has a built-in mechanism that cures either type of gap automatically."

6. Give *two* different explanations of how the economy can suffer from stagflation.

Changes on the Demand Side: Multiplier Analysis

10

A definite ratio, to be called the *Multiplier*, can be established between income and investment.

JOHN MAYNARD KEYNES

The last two chapters described in some detail how equilibrium output and the equilibrium price level are determined. They also showed how changes in wages and other developments on the supply side of the economy can change that equilibrium. We now return to the demand side to see how equilibrium output and the equilibrium price level are affected by changes in the spending propensities of consumers and investors; that is, by *shifts in aggregate demand.*

The central topic of this chapter is the *multiplier*—the idea that an increase in spending will bring about an *even larger* increase in equilibrium GNP. Just how much larger the increase is, and how this effect works, is the first topic we will discuss. We approach the subject from three different perspectives, each of which provides the reader with different and significant insights into the multiplier process. First, the idea is illustrated graphically using the income–expenditure diagram from Chapter 8. Next, we reach the same conclusion through the use of a numerical example, and finally, we offer an algebraic statement. Each of these is an expression of the remarkable multiplier result.

Once this concept is fully understood, we bring inflation back into the picture, and, with the aid of aggregate supply and demand analysis, we see how inflation affects the multiplier process. Finally, to review what we have learned, we close the chapter by considering how the multiplier process runs in reverse, that is, how *decreases* in spending lead to decreases in both output and prices.

The Magic of the Multiplier

Because it is subject to such abrupt swings, investment spending is often the cause of business fluctuations in the United States and elsewhere. Let us, therefore, ask what would happen to equilibrium income in our fictitious country, Macroland, if firms there suddenly decided to spend more on investment goods. As we shall see, such a decision would have a *multiplied* effect on GNP in Macroland. The same would be true in the U.S. economy.

For simplicity, we begin by assuming that the price level is fixed. (Price level changes will re-enter the picture very shortly.) Refer first to Table 10–1, which looks very much like Table 8–1 (page 144). The only difference is that we assume here that, for some reason, firms in Macroland now want to invest $80

Table 10–1
AGGREGATE DEMAND AFTER THE RISE IN INVESTMENT SPENDING
(billions of dollars)

(1) INCOME (Y)	(2) CONSUMPTION (C)	(3) INVESTMENT (I)	(4) AGGREGATE DEMAND ($C + I$)
600	600	280	880
800	760	280	1040
1000	920	280	1200
1200	1080	280	1360
1400	1240	280	1520
1600	1400	280	1680
1800	1560	280	1840
2000	1720	280	2000
2200	1880	280	2160
2400	2040	280	2320
2600	2200	280	2480

This table shows the construction of a total expenditure schedule for Macroland after investment has risen to $280 billion. As indicated by the numbers shaded in blue, only income level $Y = \$2000$ billion is an equilibrium for the economy because only at this level is aggregate demand ($C + I$) equal to production (Y).

billion more than they previously did—for a total of $280 billion. **The multiplier** principle says that Macroland's GNP will rise by *more* than the $80 billion increased investment. Let us verify that the multiplier is indeed greater than 1.

Table 10–1 shows how to derive a new expenditure schedule by adding up C and I at each level of Y, just as we did in Chapter 8. If you compare the last column of Table 10–1 to that of Table 8–1, you will see that the new expenditure schedule lies uniformly above the old one by $80 billion. Figure 10–1 illustrates this diagrammatically. The schedule marked $C + I_0$ is derived from the last column of Table 8–1, while the higher schedule marked $C + I_1$ is derived from

The multiplier is the ratio of the change in equilibrium GNP (Y) divided by the original change in spending that causes the change in GNP. In shorthand, when we deal with the multiplier for investment (I), the formula is:

$$\text{Multiplier} = \frac{\text{Change in } Y}{\text{Change in } I}$$

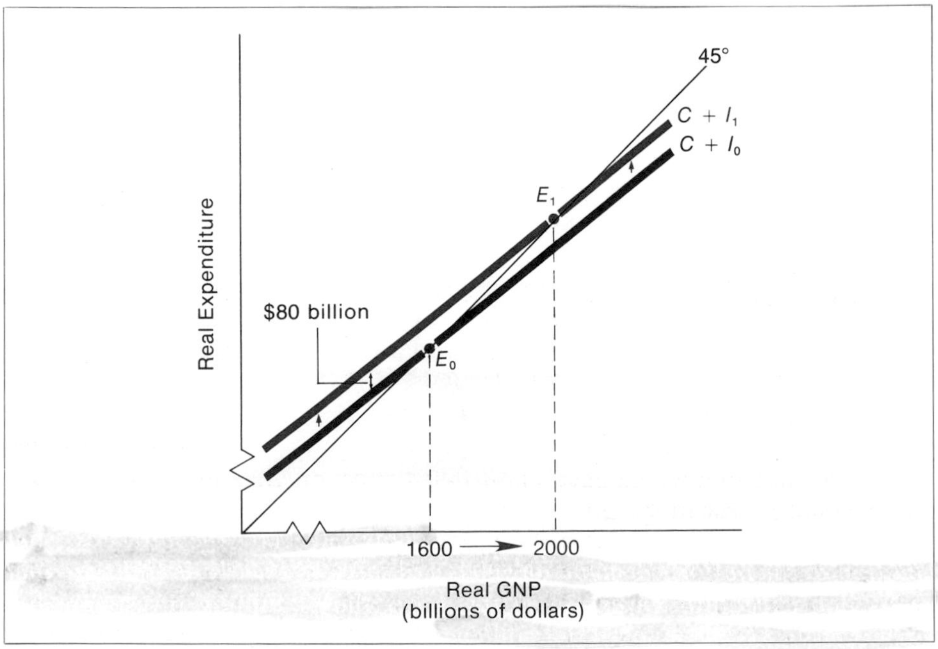

Figure 10–1
ILLUSTRATION OF THE MULTIPLIER
This figure depicts the multiplier effect of a rise in investment spending of $80 billion. The expenditure schedule shifts upward from $C + I_0$ to $C + I_1$, thus moving equilibrium from point E_0 to point E_1. The rise in income is $400 billion, so the multiplier is  $\$400/\$80 = 5$.

the last column of Table 10–1. The two $C + I$ lines are parallel and $80 billion apart.

So far no act of magic has occurred—things look just as you might expect. But one more step will bring the multiplier rabbit out of the hat. Let us see what the upward shift of the $C + I$ line does to equilibrium income. We see in Figure 10–1 that equilibrium moves outward from point E_0 to point E_1, that is, from $1600 billion to $2000 billion. The difference—$2000 billion minus $1600—is an increase in national income of $400 billion. All this from an $80 billion stimulus to investment? That is the magic of the multiplier.

Because the change in I is $80 billion and the change in equilibrium Y is $400 billion, by applying our definition, the multiplier is:

$$\text{Multiplier} = \frac{\text{Change in } Y}{\text{Change in } I} = \frac{\$400}{\$80} = 5.$$

This tells us that, in our example, every additional dollar of investment demand will add $5 to the equilibrium GNP!

This does indeed seem mysterious. Can something be created from nothing? Let us, therefore, check to be sure that the graph has not deceived us. Once we have verified this, we turn to the logic of the multiplier. We shall see that the multiplier loses its mystery once we remember the circular flow of income and expenditure, and the simple fact that one person's spending is another person's income.

The first and last columns of Table 10–1 show in numbers what Figure 10–1 shows in a picture. Notice that, at any income level below $2000, spending ($C + I$) exceeds output ($Y$). As we know, this cannot be an equilibrium situation, because inventories would be disappearing. On the other hand, at any income level above $2000, inventories would be piling up, since $C + I$ is less than Y. Only at $Y = \$2000$ billion are spending and production in balance, as Table 10–1 shows. This is $400 billion higher than the $1600 billion equilibrium GNP obtained in the discussion of Table 8–1, where investment was only $200 billion. Thus an $80 billion rise in investment leads to a $400 billion rise in equilibrium GNP, which goes up from an initial value of $1600 billion to $2000 billion. The multiplier really is 5.

Demystifying the Multiplier: How It Works

We can understand how the multiplier works, and see why it is exactly 5 in our model economy, by looking more closely at what actually happens in the economy if businesses decide to spend an additional $1 million on investment goods.

For the sake of concreteness, suppose that Generous Motors—a major corporation in Macroland—decides to spend $1 million to retool a factory to manufacture pollution-free electronically powered automobiles. Its $1 million expenditure goes to construction workers and owners of construction companies as wages and profits. That is, it becomes their *income*.

But the owners and workers of the construction firms will not simply keep their $1 million in the bank. They will spend some of it. If they are "typical" consumers, their spending will, by definition, be $1 million times the marginal propensity to consume (MPC). In our example, the MPC is 0.8. So let us assume that they spend $800,000 and save the rest. *This $800,000 expenditure is a net addition to the nation's demand for goods and services exactly as GM's original $1 million expenditure was.* So, at this stage, the $1 million investment has already pushed GNP up some $1.8 million.

But the process by no means stops here. Shopkeepers receive the $800,000 spent by construction workers, and these shopkeepers in turn also spend 80 percent of their new income. This accounts for $640,000 (80 percent of $800,000) in additional consumer spending in the "third round." Next follows a fourth round in which the recipients of the $640,000, in their turn, spend 80 percent of this amount, or $512,000, and so on. At each stage in the spending chain, people spend 80 percent of the additional income they receive, and the process continues.

Where does it all end? Does it all end? The answer is that it does, indeed, eventually end—with GNP a total of $5 million higher than it was before Generous Motors spent the original $1 million. The multiplier, as stated, is 5.

Table 10–2 displays the basis for this conclusion. In the table, "round 1" represents GM's initial investment, which creates $1 million in income for construction workers; "round 2" represents the construction workers' spending, which creates $800,000 in income for shopkeepers. The rest of the table proceeds accordingly. Each entry in column 2 is 80 percent of the previous entry, and column 3 tabulates the running sum of column 2. We see that after 10 rounds of spending the initial $1 million investment has mushroomed to nearly $4.5 million, and the sum is still growing. After 20 rounds, the total increase in GNP is over $4.9 million—quite near its eventual value of $5 million. While it takes quite a few rounds of spending before the multiplier chain is near 5, we see from

Table 10–2
THE MULTIPLIER SPENDING CHAIN

(1) ROUND NUMBER	(2) SPENDING IN THIS ROUND	(3) CUMULATIVE TOTAL
1	$1,000,000	$1,000,000
2	800,000	1,800,000
3	640,000	2,440,000
4	512,000	2,952,000
5	409,600	3,361,600
6	327,680	3,689,280
7	262,144	3,951,424
8	209,715	4,161,139
9	167,772	4,328,911
10	134,218	4,463,129
.	.	.
.	.	.
20	14,412	4,942,354
.	.	.
.	.	.
50	18	4,999,929
.	.	.
.	.	.
"Infinity"	0	5,000,000

This table shows how the multiplier unfolds through time. Round 1 is GM's initial spending, which leads to $1 million in additional income to construction workers. Round 2 shows the construction workers spending 80 percent of this amount, since the marginal propensity to consume is 0.8. The other rounds proceed accordingly, with spending in each successive round equal to 80 percent of that in the previous round. Technically, the full multiplier of 5 is reached only after an "infinite" number of rounds. But, as can be seen, we are quite close to the full amount after 20 rounds.

Figure 10–2

HOW THE MULTIPLIER
BUILDS

This diagram portrays the
numbers from Table 10–2 and
shows how the multiplier builds
through time. Notice how the
effect grows quickly at first and
how the full effect is almost
reached after 15 rounds.

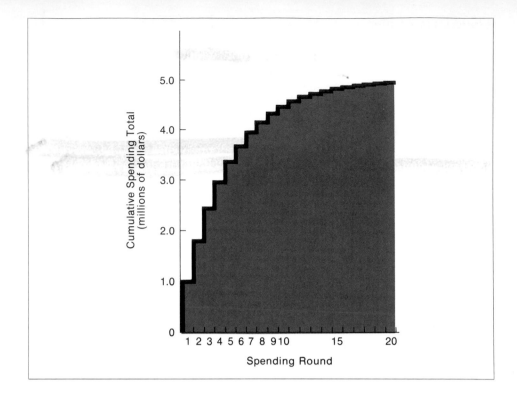

the table that it approaches 4 rather quickly. If each income recipient in the chain waits, say, two months before spending his new income, the multiplier will reach 4 in only about 14 months.

Figure 10–2 provides a graphical presentation of the numbers in the last column of Table 10–2. Notice how the multiplier builds up rapidly at first, and then tapers off to approach its ultimate value (5 in this example) gradually.

Algebraic Statement of the Multiplier

Figure 10–2 and Table 10–2 probably make a persuasive case for the fact that the multiplier eventually reaches 5. But for the remaining skeptics we offer a simple algebraic proof.[1] Most of you learned about an "infinite geometric progression" in high school. This is simply an infinite series of numbers, each one of which is a fixed fraction of the previous one. This fraction is called the "common ratio." A geometric progression beginning with 1 and having a common ratio equal to 0.8 would look like this:

$$1 + 0.8 + (0.8)^2 + (0.8)^3 + \ldots$$

More generally, a geometric progression beginning with 1 and having a common ratio R would be:

$$1 + R + R^2 + R^3 \ldots$$

A simple formula enables us to sum such a progression as long as R is less than 1.[2]

[1] Students who blanch at the sight of algebra should not be put off. Anyone who can balance a checkbook (even many who cannot!) will be able to follow the argument.

[2] If R exceeds 1, nobody can possibly sum it—not even with the aid of a modern computer!

The formula is:[3]

$$\text{Sum of infinite geometric progression} = \frac{1}{1 - R}.$$

Now we can recognize that the multiplier chain in Table 10–2 is just an infinite geometric progression with 0.8 as its common ratio. That is, each $1 spent by GM leads to a $(0.8) \times \$1$ expenditure by construction workers, which in turn leads to a $(0.8) \times (0.8 \times \$1) = (0.8)^2 \times \$1$ expenditure by the shopkeepers, and so on. Thus, for each initial dollar of investment spending, the progression is:

$$1 + 0.8 + (0.8)^2 + (0.8)^3 + (0.8)^4 + \dots .$$

Applying the formula for the sum of such a series, we find that:

$$\text{Multiplier} = \frac{1}{1 - 0.8} = \frac{1}{0.2} = 5.$$

Notice how this result can be generalized. If we did not have a specific numerical value for the marginal propensity to consume, but simply called it "MPC," the geometric progression in Table 10–2 would have been

$$1 + \text{MPC} + (\text{MPC})^2 + (\text{MPC})^3 + \dots ,$$

which has the MPC as its common ratio. Applying the same formula for summing a geometric progression to this more general case gives us the following general result:

Oversimplified Formula for the Multiplier

$$\text{Multiplier} = \frac{1}{1 - \text{MPC}}.$$

We call this formula "oversimplified" because it ignores many factors that are important in the real world. One of them is *inflation*, a complication we will turn to a bit later in this chapter. A second is *income taxation*, a point we will elaborate in the next chapter. A third factor arises from the *financial system* and, after we discuss money and banking in Chapters 12 and 13, we will explain it in Chapter 14. As it turns out, each of these factors *reduces* the size of the multiplier.

We can begin to appreciate just how unrealistic the "oversimplified" formula is by considering some real numbers for the U.S. economy. The marginal propensity to consume (MPC) has been estimated many times, and is about 0.9. From our oversimplified formula, then, it would seem that the multiplier should be:

[3]The proof is simple. Let the symbol S stand for the (unknown) sum of the series:

$$S = 1 + R + R^2 + R^3 + \dots .$$

Then, multiplying by R,

$$RS = R + R^2 + R^3 + \dots .$$

By subtracting RS from S, we obtain:

$$S - RS = 1$$

or

$$S = \frac{1}{1 - R}.$$

$$\text{Multiplier} = \frac{1}{1 - 0.9} = \frac{1}{0.1} = 10 \ .$$

In fact, the actual multiplier for the U.S. economy is believed to be in the neighborhood of 2. This is quite a discrepancy! But it does not mean that anything we have said about the multiplier so far is incorrect. Our story is simply incomplete. As we progress through the following chapters, you will learn why the multiplier is close to 2 even though the MPC is close to 0.9. For now we simply point out that:

While the multiplier is larger than 1 in the real world, it cannot be calculated with any degree of accuracy from the oversimplified formula. The actual multiplier is *lower* than the formula suggests.

The Multiplier Effect of Consumer Spending

Business firms that invest are not the only ones that can work the magic of the multiplier; so can consumers. Before we investigate the complications, let us see how the multiplier works when the process is initiated by an upsurge in consumer spending.

First, we need to distinguish between two types of change in consumer spending. When *C* rises because income rises—that is, when consumers move outward *along a fixed consumption function*—we call the increase in *C* an *induced* increase in consumption. However, if instead *C* rises because the entire consumption function *shifts* up, we call this an **autonomous increase in consumption.** The name indicates that consumption changes independently of income, and Chapter 7's discussion pointed out that a number of events, such as a change in the price level or in the value of the stock market, can initiate such a shift.

Let us suppose that, for some reason, consumer spending rises autonomously by $80 billion. In this case, our table of aggregate demand would have to be revised to look like Table 10–3. Comparing this to Table 10–1 on page 177, we

Table 10–3
AGGREGATE DEMAND AFTER CONSUMERS DECIDE TO SPEND $80 BILLION MORE
(billions of dollars)

(1) INCOME (Y)	(2) CONSUMPTION (C)	(3) INVESTMENT (I)	(4) AGGREGATE DEMAND ($C + I$)
600	680	200	880
800	840	200	1040
1000	1000	200	1200
1200	1160	200	1360
1400	1320	200	1520
1600	1480	200	1680
1800	1640	200	1840
2000	1800	200	2000
2200	1960	200	2160
2400	2120	200	2320
2600	2280	200	2480

This table shows the construction of the total expenditure schedule for Macroland following an autonomous increase of $80 billion in consumption rather than in investment. Notice that columns 2 and 3 differ from the corresponding columns in Table 10–1, but column 4 is the same in both tables. Thus the expenditure schedule in the 45° line diagram is the same as in the earlier example.

note that each entry in column 2 is $80 billion *higher* than the corresponding entry in Table 10–1 (because consumption is higher) and each entry in column 3 is $80 billion *lower* (because investment is lower).

The equilibrium level of income is clearly $Y = \$2000$ billion once again. Indeed, the entire expenditure schedule is the same as it was in Table 10–1. The initial rise of $80 billion in spending leads to an ultimate rise of $400 billion in GNP, just as occurred in the case of higher investment spending. In fact, Figure 10–1 applies to this case without any changes. The multiplier for autonomous changes in consumer spending, then, is also 5 ($400/$80).

The reason is straightforward. It does not matter who injects an additional dollar of spending into the economy, whether it is business investors or consumers. Wherever it comes from, 80 percent of it will be respent if the MPC is 0.8, and the recipients of this second round will in turn spend 80 percent of their additional income, and so on and on. And that is what constitutes the multiplier process. In the next chapter we will learn, not surprisingly, that this same multiplier applies equally well to the third component of aggregate demand—government purchases of goods and services.

Inflation and the Multiplier

Now that we understand the workings of the basic multiplier process, let us turn to the first of the reasons why the multiplier formula is oversimplified—inflation.

This first complication turns out to be nothing more than a restatement of one of the central ideas of economics: that prices are determined by demand *and* supply. In this case, the story we have told about the multiplier so far—whether in words, with numbers, or in an algebraic formula—dealt only with the aggregate demand side of the economy. As we stressed in Chapter 8, the $C + I$ schedule in an income–expenditure diagram is drawn up for a *given* price level. It therefore cannot tell us what the price level will be nor whether prices will change. Let us now consider what is likely to be happening on the supply side of the economy as the multiplier process unfolds. Will this additional demand be taken care of by firms without raising prices?

Often, the answer is no; it will only be provided at higher prices. Thus, as the multiplier chain progresses, raising income and employment, prices will also be rising. And this, as we know from Chapter 7, will dampen consumer spending because rising prices reduce the purchasing power of consumers' wealth. So the multiplier chain will not proceed as far as it would have in the absence of inflation. How much inflation results from the rise in demand? How much of the multiplier chain is cut off by inflation? The answers naturally depend on the economy's aggregate supply curve.

For a concrete example of the analysis, let us return to the $80 billion increase in investment spending with which we began this chapter. As we have learned from our 45° line diagram, this leads—through the multiplier process—to an ultimate increase of $400 billion in the *aggregate quantity demanded at the initial price level*. But to know the actual quantity that will ultimately be produced, and the actual price level, we must bring the aggregate supply curve into the picture.

Figure 10–3 does this. Here we show a *horizontal shift* of the aggregate demand curve, from D_0D_0 to D_1D_1, equal to the $400 billion we calculated from the oversimplified multiplier formula (which ignored rising prices). The aggregate supply curve, SS, then tells us how this expansion of demand is apportioned between higher output and higher prices. We see that as the economy's equilibrium moves from point E_0 to point E_1, real GNP does not rise by $400 billion. Instead, prices rise, which, as we know, tends to discourage part of the rise

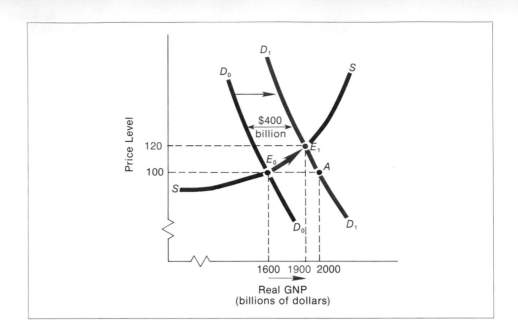

Figure 10–3

INFLATION AND
THE MULTIPLIER

This figure illustrates the complete analysis of the multiplier, including the effect of inflation. The simple multiplier analysis, which ignores changes in the price level, appears here as a *horizontal* shift of $400 billion in the aggregate demand curve, meaning that the multiplier would be $400/$80 = 5 if prices did not rise. However, when aggregate demand shifts from D_0D_0 to D_1D_1, prices rise. In the diagram, the price level increases from 100 to 120 or by 20 percent. Consequently, equilibrium real income increases from $1600 billion to only $1900—for a rise of $300 billion, or a multiplier of $300/$80 = 3.75.

in quantity demanded by consumers. So output increases only from $1600 billion to $1900 billion—an increase of $300 billion. Thus, in our example, inflation has reduced the multiplier from $400/$80 = 5 to $300/$80 = 3.75. In general:

As long as the aggregate supply curve is upward sloping, any increase in aggregate demand will push up the price level. This will, in turn, drain off some of the higher real demand by eroding the purchasing power of consumer wealth. Thus, inflation reduces the multiplier below that suggested by the oversimplified formula.

Notice also that the price level in this example has been pushed up (from 100 to 120, or 20 percent) by the rise in investment demand. This, too, is a general result:

As long as the aggregate supply curve is upward sloping, any upward shift in the aggregate demand curve will cause some rise in prices in the economy.

The economic behavior behind these results certainly cannot be considered surprising. Firms faced with a large increase in aggregate quantity demanded at their original prices respond to these changed circumstances in two natural ways: They raise production (so GNP rises) and they raise prices (so the price level rises). But this rise in the price level reduces the purchasing power of the bank accounts and bonds held by consumers, and they also react in the natural way: they cut down on their spending. Such a reaction amounts to a movement *along* aggregate demand curve D_1D_1 in Figure 10–3 from point A to point E_1. Higher prices thus play their usual dual role in a market economy: they encourage suppliers to produce more and, at the same time, encourage demanders to consume less. In this way, equilibrium is reestablished at higher levels of output and higher prices through the process of inflation.

Figure 10–3 also shows us exactly where the oversimplified multiplier formula goes wrong. By ignoring the effects of the higher price level, the oversimplified formula supposes the economy moves horizontally from point E_0

to point A. As the diagram clearly shows, output does not actually rise this much. Output *would* rise this much *only* if the aggregate supply curve were horizontal. (Verify this for yourself by penciling in an imaginary horizontal aggregate supply curve through points E_0 and A in Figure 10–3.) That is, the oversimplified multiplier formula tacitly assumes that the aggregate supply curve is horizontal. Normally, this is an unrealistic assumption, and that is one reason why the oversimplified formula exaggerates the size of the multiplier.

The Multiplier in Reverse

A good way to check your understanding of the entire multiplier process is to run it in reverse: What happens if, for example, consumers autonomously decide to spend less?

Before trying to trace through the mechanics, it may be useful to sum up the steps of the analysis that we have just completed.

STEPS IN CALCULATING THE MULTIPLIER
1. Shift the expenditure schedule in the 45° line diagram vertically by the amount of the autonomous shift in spending.

2. Use the 45° line diagram, or the oversimplified multiplier formula, to calculate the multiplier effect on GNP that *would* occur *if* the price level did not change.

3. Now move from the 45° line diagram to the aggregate supply and demand diagram to see how the price level will react. Enter the multiplier effect calculated in step 2 as a horizontal shift of the aggregate demand curve in the supply–demand diagram.

4. The supply–demand diagram will now show the actual effect on real output as well as the resulting inflation or deflation.

Let's follow these steps to see what would happen to our hypothetical economy if the consumption function shifted downward. We begin by assuming that a wave of thriftiness comes over the people of Macroland so that, no matter what their total income, they now want to spend $80 billion less than they did previously.

Step 1 tells us to consider first what happens to the expenditure schedule in our 45° line diagram. Now a decision to spend $80 billion less out of any given level of income is, by definition, a downward shift of the total expenditure schedule by $80 billion. This is shown in Figure 10–4, where the $C + I$ schedule falls from $C_0 + I$ to $C_1 + I$. The horizontal distance between these two parallel lines is the $80 billion drop in spending.

Step 2 calls for us to calculate the simple multiplier effect, ignoring any changes in prices. There are two ways of doing this. First, our oversimplified multiplier formula tells us that the multiplier is

$$\frac{1}{1 - \text{MPC}} = \frac{1}{1 - 0.8} = \frac{1}{0.2} = 5 \,.$$

So an $80 billion drop in demand would lead to a full multiplier effect of $400 billion *if* the price level did not change. Alternatively, we can read this conclusion from Figure 10–4. Here the economy's equilibrium point moves down the 45° line from point E_0 to E_1; income drops from $1600 billion to $1200 billion—a decline of $400 billion.

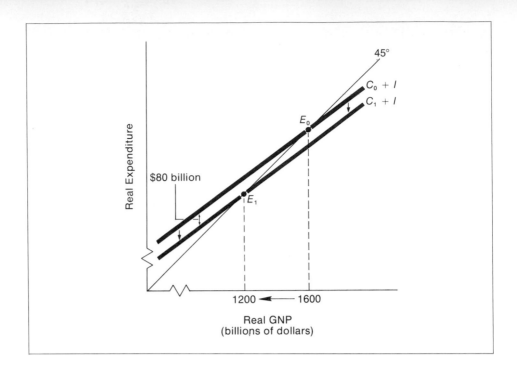

Figure 10–4

THE MULTIPLIER IN REVERSE

This diagram shows the first steps in analyzing the multiplier effect of an autonomous decline in consumer spending of $80 billion. The decline appears as a downward shift of $80 billion in the expenditure schedule, which falls from $C_0 + I$ to $C_1 + I$. Equilibrium, which is always at the intersection of the expenditure schedule and the 45° line, moves from point E_0 to point E_1, and income falls from $1600 billion to $1200 billion.

This completes step 2 and, *if the price level does not fall,* the analysis ends here. We noted in the last chapter that the price level often stubbornly resists falling, so this may be a real possibility. However, to make the analysis complete, let us suppose that prices do fall.

If this happens, we must proceed to step 3 to see how the decline in demand gets divided up between lower output and lower prices. Figure 10–5 is the aggregate supply and demand diagram on which we can portray this division. It shows the initial equilibrium as point E_0, where demand curve D_0D_0 cuts supply curve SS. Our finding from step 2 is transferred to this diagram by shifting the

Figure 10–5

THE MULTIPLIER IN AGGREGATE SUPPLY AND DEMAND ANALYSIS

This figure takes the finding from Figure 10–4—that income would fall by $400 billion if the price level did not change—and transfers it to an aggregate supply and demand diagram. We see that the $400 billion leftward shift of the aggregate demand schedule from D_0D_0 to D_1D_1 leads to a decline in income from $1600 billion to $1300 billion and to a decline in the price level from 100 to 86. The final multiplier, then, is $300/$80 = 3.75.

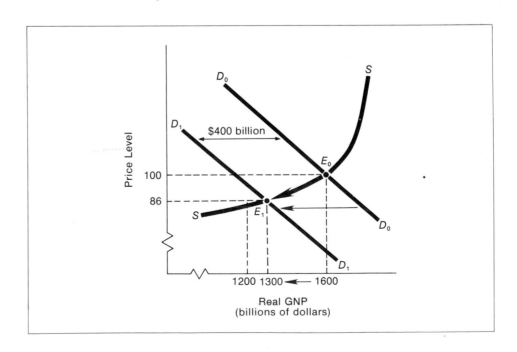

aggregate demand curve to the left by $400 billion—from D_0D_0 to D_1D_1. That is all there is to step 3.

In step 4 we need only read the results of the analysis from Figure 10–5. We see that equilibrium has moved from point E_0 to point E_1, meaning that output has fallen from $1600 billion to $1300 billion. The decline in GNP is, therefore, $300 billion, which is smaller than the initial decline in aggregate quantity demanded of $400 billion. The multiplier, then, is $300/$80 = 3.75.

What has happened to lead us from a multiplier of 5 in Figure 10–4 to a multiplier of 3.75 in Figure 10–5? We see from the figure that the price level has fallen by 14 percent—from 100 to 86. Deflation has augmented the purchasing power of the money and bonds held by consumers, thus persuading them to cut their spending by less than $400 billion.

Now let us compare the analysis of a decline in aggregate demand that is summarized in Figures 10–4 and 10–5 with our previous analysis of an increase in aggregate demand, as shown in Figures 10–1 and 10–3 on pages 177 and 184, respectively. You will see that everything is simply turned in the opposite direction. There is only one minor quantitative difference. Since prices tend to be more resistant to downward movements than to upward movements, the *de*flation caused by a decrease in aggregate demand will be less than the *in*flation caused by an equal increase in aggregate demand. It may even be zero.

This important fact of real-world economic life is reflected in the way we have drawn our aggregate supply curves in this chapter: they get steeper as we move to the right, meaning that supply gets less responsive to price changes as the economy gets closer to its full capacity.

The Paradox of Thrift

This last example of multiplier analysis teaches us an important lesson: it shows that an increase in the desire to save will lead to a cumulative fall in GNP. And the resulting decline in national income will pull saving (and consumption) down. So while saving may pave the road to riches *for an individual,* if *the nation as a whole* decides to save more, the result may be poverty for all! This remarkable result is called the **paradox of thrift.** It is important because it is contrary to most people's thinking and it means that greater saving may be a mixed blessing if it is not accompanied by equally greater investment. We shall have occasion to return to this lesson in the chapter on economic growth (Chapter 35), where it is discussed in greater detail.

Summary

1. Any autonomous increase in expenditure has a multiplier effect on GNP; that is, it increases GNP by more than the original increase in spending.
2. The reason for this multiplier effect is that one person's additional expenditure constitutes a new source of income for another person, and this additional income leads to still more spending, and so on.
3. The multiplier also works in reverse: an autonomous decrease in any component of aggregate demand leads to a multiplied decrease in national income.
4. A simple formula for the multiplier says that its numerical value is $1/(1 - \text{MPC})$. But this formula is too simple to give accurate results.
5. Among the reasons why the oversimplified multiplier formula is wrong is the fact that it ignores any inflation that may be caused by an increase in aggregate demand. Such inflation decreases the multiplier by reducing consumer spending, because consumers as a group suffer a loss of purchasing power when prices rise.
6. Increases in aggregate demand can be apportioned between higher output and higher prices by using an aggregate supply and demand diagram.
7. If the nation as a whole decides to save more, that is, to consume less, the resulting decline in national income may serve to make everyone poorer. This possibility that thriftiness, while a virtue for the individual, may be disastrous for an entire nation, is called the paradox of thrift.

Concepts for Review

The multiplier
Autonomous increase in consumption
Paradox of thrift

Questions for Discussion

1. Try to remember where you last spent a dollar. Explain how this dollar will lead to a multiplier chain of increased income and spending. (Who received the dollar? What will he or she do with it?)

2. Ignoring the complications caused by changes in the price level, use both numerical and graphical methods to find the multiplier effect of the following shift in the consumption function in an economy in which investment is always $100.

INCOME	CONSUMPTION BEFORE SHIFT	CONSUMPTION AFTER SHIFT
$510	$440	$470
540	460	490
570	480	510
600	500	530
630	520	550
660	540	570
690	560	590
720	580	610

(*Hint:* What is the marginal propensity to consume?)

3. Turn back to Discussion Question 4 in Chapter 8 (page 154). Suppose investment spending rises to $40, but the price level is fixed. By how much will the equilibrium GNP increase? Derive the answer both numerically and graphically.

4. Now add the following aggregate supply and demand schedules to the data in Question 3 to see how inflation affects the multiplier.

(1) PRICE LEVEL	(2) AGGREGATE DEMAND (when investment is $30)	(3) AGGREGATE DEMAND (when investment is $40)	(4) AGGREGATE SUPPLY
90	$210	$310	$110
95	205	305	155
100	200	300	200
105	195	295	245
110	190	290	290
115	185	285	335

Draw these schedules on a piece of graph paper. Then:

a. Notice that the difference between columns 2 and 3 (the aggregate demand schedule at two different levels of investment) is always $100. Discuss how this relates to your answer in the previous problem.

b. Find the equilibrium GNP and the equilibrium price level both before and after the increase in investment. What is the value of the multiplier?

5. Explain in words why rising prices reduce the multiplier effect of an autonomous increase in aggregate demand.

6. Use an aggregate supply and demand diagram to show that multiplier effects are smaller when the aggregate supply curve is steeper. Which case gives rise to more inflation—the steep aggregate supply curve or the flat one?

7. Explain the paradox of thrift. Why do you think it is called a paradox?

8. (More difficult) Suppose the consumption function is as given in Discussion Question 8 of Chapter 8 (page 155)

$$C = 120 + 0.8Y$$

and investment (I) rises to 280. Use the equilibrium condition $Y = C + I$ to find the equilibrium level of GNP. (In working out the answer, assume the price level is fixed.) Compare your answer to Table 10–1 and Figure 10–1. Now compare your answer to the answer to Discussion Question 8 of Chapter 8. What do you learn about the multiplier?

Appendix

The Simple Algebra of the Multiplier When the Price Level Is Fixed

In Appendix B to Chapter 8, we worked out a general expression for the equilibrium level of GNP when the price level is fixed, investment is some fixed number, I, and the consumption function is:

$$C = a + bY.$$

The answer obtained there (which can be found on page 158) was:

$$Y = \frac{a + I}{1 - b}.$$

From this formula, it is easy to derive the oversimplified multiplier formula algebraically and to show that it applies equally well to a change in investment or to a change in autonomous consumer spending. To do this, suppose that *either I or a* increased by 1 unit. In either case, the sum $C + I$ would rise from:

$$C + I = a + bY + I,$$

to:

$$C + I = a + bY + I + 1.$$

Using the equilibrium condition that Y must be equal to $C + I$, we can solve for Y just as we did in Appendix B of Chapter 8:

$$Y = C + I$$

so that:

$$Y = a + bY + I + 1$$

and therefore:

$$(1 - b)Y = a + I + 1,$$

or:

$$Y = \frac{a + I + 1}{1 - b}.$$

By comparing this with our previous expression for Y, we see that a 1 unit change in *either a or I* changes equilibrium GNP by:

$$\text{change in } Y = \frac{a + I + 1}{1 - b} - \frac{a + I}{1 - b}$$

$$\text{change in } Y = \frac{a + I + 1 - (a + I)}{1 - b}$$

or:

$$\text{change in } Y = \frac{1}{1 - b}.$$

Recalling that b is the marginal propensity to consume, we see that this is precisely the oversimplified multiplier formula.

Managing Aggregate Demand Through Fiscal Policy

11

I n the last several chapters, we have constructed and analyzed a model of an economy in which there is neither government spending nor taxes. We have seen how equilibrium is determined, and how changes in the consumption and investment components of aggregate demand can change that equilibrium.

But in the U.S. economy, purchases by governments at all levels (federal, state, and local) account for more than 20 percent of gross national product, and the government's budgetary decisions exercise a profound influence over aggregate demand. So to make our model fit the U.S. economy, our task in this chapter is to put the government back into the picture. More than a desire for realism dictates that we bring the government into the model. Without including the government we cannot study what national economic policy can do about inflation and unemployment, and this is perhaps the main purpose of macroeconomic analysis.

We begin by expanding the basic model to allow, first, for government purchases of goods and services as a third component of aggregate demand, and second, for an income tax that makes disposable income less than national income. As we shall see, neither of these complications requires any fundamental change in the way we analyze the determination of GNP and the price level, although taxes do reduce the multiplier. But, while the *model* does not have to change much when the government is introduced, the *policy implications* of the analysis are drastically altered. In fact, the main topic of this chapter is how the government can use its spending and taxing powers to manage the level of aggregate demand.

Once we have mastered some mechanics, we will see why there are always a variety of budgets capable of producing more or less the same effect upon aggregate demand. How, then, does the government decide on the preferred mix of taxing and spending each year? This question will be addressed toward the end of the chapter. In addition, we will take a further look at "supply-side economics," and consider some complications that simple economic models ignore but that policy planners cannot afford to overlook.

How Budget Decisions Are Made

In January of each year, the president of the United States sends to Congress two economic messages that often touch off a vigorous debate—his Budget Message and his Economic Report. The reason for the heated response to these messages is that they outline the administration's proposed **fiscal policy,** a highly volatile issue. In these statements, the president outlines his taxing and spending proposals, explains the effects that government economists expect these proposals to have on aggregate demand, and offers an explanation indicating why this is the right policy at that time.

The government's **fiscal policy** is its plan for spending and taxation. It is designed to steer aggregate demand in some desired direction.

Congress then follows a set procedure for either agreeing or disagreeing with the president's proposals. During the spring, after it has had about three months to consider the president's suggestions, Congress passes its First Concurrent Resolution on the Budget, stating its own notions of how much spending and taxing the government should do. When Congress and the White House are in the hands of different political parties, these two notions may be quite far apart.

A process of either reconciliation or legislative–executive warfare then ensues, during which Congress may pass bills inconsistent with the president's proposed budget, and the president may veto legislation voted by Congress. Then, in the fall, Congress passes its Second Concurrent Resolution on the Budget. Under normal circumstances, this will represent the federal government's budget policy for the fiscal year about to begin.[1]

This chapter is concerned with how these important budget decisions are, or should be, made. If you were a legislator, how would you decide whether to vote for or against one of the concurrent resolutions? How much spending is the right amount? How much taxation is appropriate? Perhaps more to the point, how can you as a voter decide whether your elected representatives have made sound decisions?

Government Purchases and Equilibrium Income

Before attempting to answer questions like these, we must integrate the government into our model of the determination of national income and the price level. We do this in stages, starting first with **government purchases of goods and services (G),** and then adding taxes. Thus, in considering once again the circular flow of income and expenditure (see Figure 11–1), we ignore for the moment the flows of tax revenues and transfer payments at point 5. How would the equilibrium level of GNP be determined in an economy in which the government bought goods but did not levy taxes or make transfers?

The circular flow diagram shows us the answer, just as it did in an economy with no government (Chapter 8). If the size of the circular flow of income and expenditure is to be maintained, then the total amount of new goods and services that firms produce at point 4 (Y) must be equal to the sum of the demands of consumers at point 1 (C), investors at point 2 (I), and government at point 3 (G). We thus obtain the following restatement of the condition for equilibrium on the demand side of the economy:

For any given price level, equilibrium GNP occurs when the sum of consumption demand, investment demand, and government demand for goods and services just equals the GNP. In symbols:

$$Y = C + I + G.$$

The reasoning behind this equilibrium condition is precisely the same as it

[1]The fiscal year for the United States government runs from October of one calendar year through September of the following calendar year. Thus, for example, fiscal year 1983 begins in October 1982 and ends in September 1983.

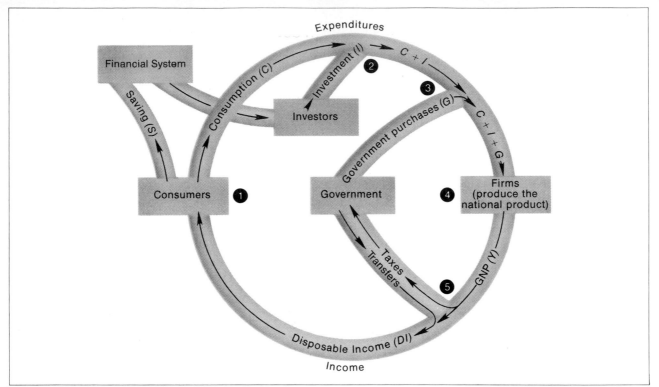

Figure 11–1
THE CIRCULAR FLOW OF EXPENDITURE AND INCOME

was in Chapter 8. At income levels below equilibrium, the sum $C + I + G$ would exceed Y; and so inventories would be disappearing, signaling firms that they should raise their production. Conversely, at income levels above equilibrium, $C + I + G$ would be less than Y, so that unwanted inventories would be accumulating and firms would have incentives to cut back production.

Table 11–1, which may usefully be compared to Table 8–1 in Chapter 8 (page 144), illustrates this process. The first three columns give the same consumption and investment schedules that we worked with there. The fourth column reflects the assumption that government purchases will be $320 billion, irrespective of the level of GNP. Summing these three components gives us our new total expenditure schedule in columns 1 and 5.

What, then, is the equilibrium level of GNP? As the table indicates, only a GNP of $3200 billion can be an equilibrium, for only at this level is aggregate demand in balance with production.

Figure 11–2 shows the same conclusion graphically. The line labeled C is the same consumption function we used in previous chapters. The line labeled $C + I$ adds the fixed $200 billion in investment to this; again, this amount is taken from previous chapters. Finally, the line labeled $C + I + G$ adds an additional $320 billion in government spending to the $C + I$ line, which gives us our new total expenditure schedule.

Just as in previous chapters, the equilibrium of the economy is at point E, where the total expenditure schedule crosses the 45° line. This is because the 45° line includes all the points at which $C + I + G$ add up to Y. The diagram shows that equilibrium is at a GNP of $3200 billion, which consists of $2680 billion in consumption, $200 billion in investment, and $320 billion in government purchases. This agrees precisely with Table 11–1, as must be the case. If all this

Table 11–1

DERIVATION OF AN AGGREGATE DEMAND SCHEDULE WITH GOVERNMENT PURCHASES

(1) NATIONAL INCOME (Y) (billions)	(2) CONSUMPTION (C) (billions)	(3) INVESTMENT (I) (billions)	(4) GOVERNMENT PURCHASES (G) (billions)	(5) AGGREGATE DEMAND (C + I + G) (billions)
$1400	$1240	$200	$320	$1760
1600	1400	200	320	1920
1800	1560	200	320	2080
2000	1720	200	320	2240
2200	1880	200	320	2400
2400	2040	200	320	2560
2600	2200	200	320	2720
2800	2360	200	320	2880
3000	2520	200	320	3040
3200	2680	200	320	3200
3400	2840	200	320	3360
3600	3000	200	320	3520

This table adds government purchases of $320 billion to our model economy. Notice that the equilibrium level of GNP grows to $3200 billion, for this is the level at which output is equal to aggregate demand (the sum of C + I + G).

seems familiar from previous chapters, it should; for the analysis is precisely the same.[2]

In Chapter 10 we stated that when government spending was introduced, the multiplier for G would be the same as the multiplier for autonomous changes in C and I. We can now demonstrate this conclusion.

[2]An algebraic version of this and other topics discussed here can be found in the appendix to this chapter.

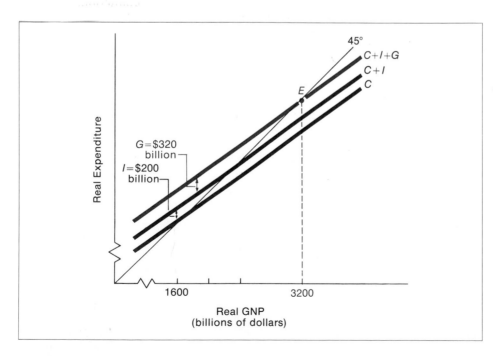

Figure 11–2
INCOME DETERMINATION WITH GOVERNMENT SPENDING
This diagram adds government purchases of goods and services (G) to the income–expenditure diagrams that we have been using. The C + I + G curve is the total expenditure schedule, and the point where it crosses the 45° line (point E) marks the equilibrium level of GNP. The C + I + G line is parallel to the C + I line because of the assumption that whatever the level of GNP, government spending remains at $320 billion.

If you flip back to page 146, you will see that the equilibrium reached there was at a level of output $Y = \$1600$ billion. Now, in an economy that is identical with the one in Chapter 8 except for the $320 billion in government spending, we see that the equilibrium is at $Y = \$3200$ billion. Thus a $320 billion increment in G (from zero to $320 billion) has pushed up GNP by $1600 billion. In this example, then, the multiplier for government spending is $\$1600/\$320 = 5$, which, you will recall, was also the value of the multiplier for autonomous increases in investment or consumption.

The two multipliers are identical because the logic behind them is identical. In the last chapter we studied an example of a multiplier spending chain set in motion when Generous Motors spent $1 million to build a factory. This process could equally well have been kicked off by the federal government buying $1 million worth of new cars from GM. Thereafter, each recipient of additional income would spend 80 percent of it (the assumed marginal propensity to consume), until $5 million in new income had eventually been created.

And the qualification that we placed on the oversimplified multiplier formula in Chapter 10 also applies here. Government spending normally leads to some inflation, which pulls down consumer spending and thus reduces the value of the multiplier below our illustrative figure of 5.

Income Taxes and the Consumption Schedule

You can see, then, that it takes little effort to bring government purchases into our model of income determination. Let us turn our attention next to taxes and, in particular, to the personal income tax.

For our purposes, the most important aspect of taxes is that they create a discrepancy between gross national product (GNP) and disposable income (DI), as can be seen in the circular flow diagram (Figure 11–1). Tax revenues flow out of the circular flow and into the hands of the government. (The effects of the transfer payments, which enter the circular flow at point 5, will be considered presently.)

We learned in Chapter 7 that there is a close and reliable relationship between consumer spending and *disposable* income. Therefore, if we want to construct a relationship between consumer spending and GNP, we first have to allow for the fact that taxes are deducted from GNP before DI is arrived at. The importance of this piece of accounting is that when taxes are increased, disposable income falls—and hence so does consumption—*even if GNP is unchanged.* In other words:

An increase in personal income taxes shifts the consumption schedule in our 45° line diagram downward. Similarly, a reduction in taxes shifts the consumption schedule upward.

The specific manner in which the consumption schedule shifts depends on the nature of the tax change. One way to reduce taxes is to introduce a flat, per person tax credit. The increase in disposable income from this legislation is the *same* regardless of the level of GNP; hence the increase in consumer spending is the same. In a word, the C schedule shifts upward in a parallel manner, as shown in Figure 11–3(a).

But often tax policy is designed to make the change in disposable income depend on the level of income, normally being larger at high income levels than at low ones. This is true, for example, when Congress reduces the bracket rates in

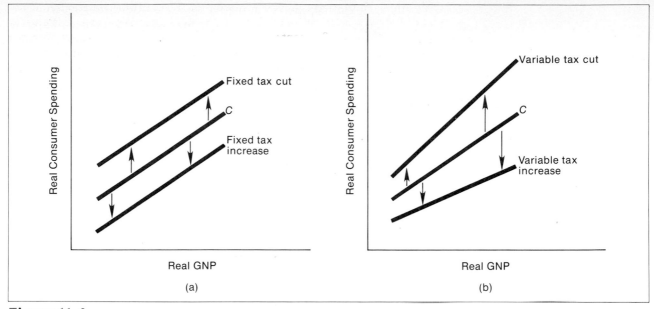

Figure 11–3
HOW TAX POLICY SHIFTS THE CONSUMPTION SCHEDULE
Because consumption depends on disposable income, not GNP, any change in taxes will shift the consumption schedule. Part (a) shows how the curve shifts for changes in taxes of fixed amounts. Part (b) shows how the C curve shifts if the tax cut (or tax increase) is larger at high incomes than at low incomes.

the personal income tax code, as it did in 1981 and several times in the 1970s. Since this sort of tax policy changes disposable income more when GNP is higher, the downward shift in the C schedule is sharper at high income levels than at low ones. Figure 11–3(b) illustrates how this type of tax policy shifts the consumption schedule.

Tax Policy and Equilibrium Income

We are now in a position to put taxes into our model of income determination. To do this, we must first adjust the consumption schedule we have been using to allow for an income tax. Table 11–2 does this on the assumption that taxes are 25

Table 11–2
DERIVATION OF A CONSUMPTION SCHEDULE WITH INCOME TAXATION

(1)	(2)	(3) DISPOSABLE INCOME	(4)
GROSS NATIONAL PRODUCT (billions)	TAXES (billions)	(GNP minus taxes) (billions)	CONSUMPTION (billions)
$1000	$250	$ 750	$ 720
1200	300	900	840
1400	350	1050	960
1600	400	1200	1080
1800	450	1350	1200
2000	500	1500	1320
2200	550	1650	1440

Because taxes (column 2) must be subtracted from gross national product (column 1) to get disposable income (column 3), this table shows how an income tax lowers the consumption schedule (column 4) in a concrete example. (Compare column 4 with the consumption schedule in Table 11–1 to see that the C schedule has indeed fallen.)

percent of GNP. Column 1 shows alternative values of GNP ranging from $1 trillion to $2.2 trillion, and column 2 indicates that taxes are always one-quarter of this amount. Column 3 subtracts column 2 from column 1 to arrive at disposable income (*DI*). Column 4 then shows the amount of consumer spending corresponding to each level of *DI*. Note that columns 3 and 4 just repeat the consumption function that we studied in Chapter 7. But the consumption schedule that we need for our 45° line diagram relates *C* to *Y*, not to *DI*—that is, it relates spending to *total* consumer income, not to income net of taxes—and the schedule is therefore found in columns 1 and 4.

To derive the new expenditure schedule for an economy with taxes, we need only replace the old consumption schedule with this new one—that is, we must replace column 2 of Table 11–1 with column 4 of Table 11–2. This is done numerically in Table 11–3, and the results are shown diagrammatically in Figure 11–4. In particular, the expenditure schedule contained in columns 1 and 5 of Table 11–3 is shown as the *C* + *I* + *G* line in Figure 11–4. Naturally, the inclusion of taxes has lowered the expenditure schedule.

Since the 45° line is given in the diagram, we can immediately locate the equilibrium level of GNP at point *E*. Here, gross national product is $1600 billion, consumption is $1080 billion, investment is $200 billion, and government purchases are $320 billion. As we know, full employment may occur above or below *Y* = $1600 billion. If below, there is an inflationary gap. Prices probably will start to rise, pulling the expenditure schedule down and reducing equilibrium GNP. If above, there is a recessionary gap, and history suggests that prices will not fall. Instead, there will be persistent unemployment.

In a word, once we adjust the expenditure schedule to include the effects of taxes, the determination of national income proceeds exactly as before. The effects of government spending and taxation, therefore, are fairly straightforward, and can be summarized as follows:

Government purchases of goods and services *add* to aggregate demand directly through the *G* component of *C* + *I* + *G*. Taxes indirectly *reduce* aggregate demand by lowering disposable income, and thus reduce the *C* component of *C* + *I* + *G*. On balance, then, the government's actions may raise or lower the equilibrium level of GNP, depending on how much spending and taxing it does.

Table 11–3
THE AGGREGATE DEMAND SCHEDULE WITH TAXES AND GOVERNMENT PURCHASES

(1) GROSS NATIONAL PRODUCT (*Y*) (billions)	(2) CONSUMPTION (*C*) (billions)	(3) INVESTMENT (*I*) (billions)	(4) GOVERNMENT PURCHASES (*G*) (billions)	(5) AGGREGATE DEMAND (*C* + *I* + *G*) (billions)
$ 800	$ 600	$200	$320	$1120
1000	720	200	320	1240
1200	840	200	320	1360
1400	960	200	320	1480
1600	1080	200	320	1600
1800	1200	200	320	1720
2000	1320	200	320	1840
2200	1440	200	320	1960
2400	1560	200	320	2080

This table replaces the previous consumption schedule with a new one that adjusts for the income tax (as shown in Table 11–2) and shows that the equilibrium level of income is $1600 billion.

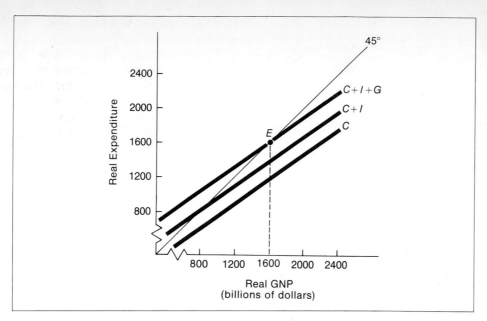

Figure 11-4
INCOME DETERMINATION
WITH GOVERNMENT
SPENDING AND
TAXATION
This diagram adds a 25 percent income tax to the model
economy portrayed in Figure
11-2. Because of this, the C
schedule is shifted down (and
hence the C + I and C + I +
G schedules are also shifted
down). Equilibrium is at point
E, where the C + I + G
schedule crosses the 45° line.
Thus equilibrium GNP is $1600
billion, the same as it was in the
economy with no government.
This, however, is certainly not
a general result; government
actions can either raise or
lower GNP.

Multipliers for Tax Policy

We saw earlier that government purchases (G) have a multiplier effect on GNP. So do changes in tax policy. But because they work indirectly via consumption, the multipliers for tax changes must be worked out in two steps.

Step 1. Before turning to the 45° line diagram, we must figure out what any proposed change in the tax law is likely to do to the consumption schedule.

Step 2. We can then enter this effect as a shift of the $C + I + G$ schedule in the 45° line diagram, and work out the multiplier.

A reduction in income taxes provides a convenient example of this two-step analysis, because we have already done step 1 in an earlier chapter. Specifically, in Chapter 7 we studied how consumer spending would respond to a cut in income taxes. We concluded that if the tax reduction were viewed as permanent, consumers would increase their spending by an amount equal to the tax cut times the marginal propensity to consume. (If you need review, turn back to pages 117–121.)

This is the shift that must be entered in the 45° line diagram to complete step 2, and Figure 11–5 displays such a shift. The tax cut raises the expenditure schedule from $C_0 + I + G$ to $C_1 + I + G$ by raising its C component. The diagram then shows the multiplier effect on GNP, which rises from Y_0 to Y_1.

Government Transfer Payments and Fiscal Policy

Finally, we should mention the last major tool of fiscal policy: **government transfer payments.** How are transfers treated in our models of income determination—like purchases of goods and services (G) or like taxes?

The answer follows readily from the circular flow diagram on page 192 or the accounting identity back on page 115. The important thing to understand about transfer payments is that they intervene between gross national product (Y) and

Figure 11–5
THE MULTIPLIER FOR A
REDUCTION IN INCOME
TAXES
The $C + I + G$ schedule is
shifted upward, from $C_0 + I + G$ to $C_1 + I + G$, by a tax cut
in this example. Equilibrium
GNP therefore increases from
Y_0 to Y_1.

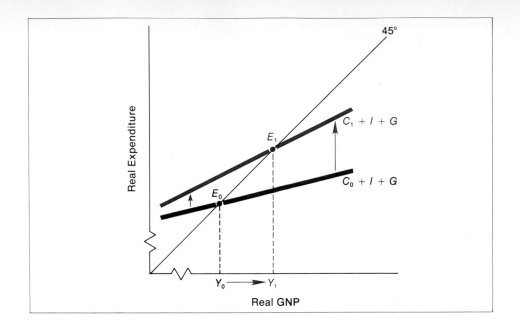

disposable income (*DI*) in precisely the *opposite* way from income taxes. Specifically, starting with the wages, interest, rents, and profits that constitute the national income, we *subtract* income taxes to calculate disposable income. We do so because these taxes represent the portion of incomes that are *earned* but never *received* by consumers. But then we must *add* transfer payments because they represent sources of income that are *received* though they were not *earned* in the process of production. Thus, transfer payments are basically *negative taxes*, and giving a consumer $1 in the form of a transfer payment is equivalent to reducing her taxes by $1.

So to answer our question, in terms of the 45° line diagram, *increases in transfer payments can be treated simply as decreases in taxes*. And we see that Figure 11–5, which we devised to illustrate a tax cut, can also be used to illustrate a rise in unemployment benefits, or in social security benefits, or in any other such transfer payment. Similarly, the analysis of a decrease in transfer payments would proceed exactly like the analysis of an increase in taxes.

The Multiplier Revisited

We now have acquired most of the tools we need to understand how fiscal policy decisions are made. But, before senators or congressmen vote on one of the concurrent resolutions on the budget, they should have an idea of the magnitude of the multiplier. Our figure of 5 is too high, and we can now understand how the income tax works to lower its value. But before getting involved in the mechanics, let us understand the basic reason.

As we learned in Chapter 10, the multiplier works through a chain of spending and responding, as one person's expenditure becomes another's income. But through taxation some of the additional income leaks out of the circular flow at each stage. Specifically, if the income tax rate is 25 percent, when Generous Motors spends $1 million on salaries, workers actually receive only $750,000 in *after-tax* (or disposable) income. If workers spend 80 percent of this amount (based on a marginal propensity to consume of 0.8), spending in the next round will be only $600,000. Notice that this is only *60 percent* of the original expenditure, not *80 percent* as in our earlier example. Thus the multiplier chain for each original dollar of spending shrinks from

$$1 + 0.8 + (0.8)^2 + (0.8)^3 + \ldots = \frac{1}{1 - 0.8} = \frac{1}{0.2} = 5$$

to

$$1 + 0.6 + (0.6)^2 + (0.6)^3 + \ldots = \frac{1}{1 - 0.6} = \frac{1}{0.4} = 2\tfrac{1}{2}.$$

This is clearly a very large reduction in the multiplier. We thus have a second reason why our oversimplified multiplier formula of the previous chapter gives an exaggerated impression of the size of the multiplier:

REASONS WHY THE OVERSIMPLIFIED MULTIPLIER FORMULA IS WRONG

1. It ignores price-level changes, which serve to reduce the size of the multiplier.

2. It ignores income taxes, which serve to reduce the size of the multiplier.

Of the two reasons, the second is much more important in reality. In later chapters, we shall encounter still more reasons.

This conclusion about the multiplier is shown graphically in Figure 11–6, where we have drawn our $C + I + G$ schedules with a slope of 0.6 to reflect an MPC of 0.8, and a tax rate of 25 percent rather than the 0.8 slope that we used previously. The figure depicts the effect of an increase in government purchases of goods and services of $100 billion, which shifts the $C + I + G$ schedule from $C + I + G_0$ to $C + I + G_1$. Equilibrium moves from point E_0 to point E_1—a growth in GNP from $Y = \$1600$ billion to $Y = \$1850$ billion. Thus, if we ignore for the moment any increases in the price level (which would reduce the multiplier shown in Figure 11–6), a $100 billion increment in government spending leads to a $250 billion increment in GNP. So when taxes are included in

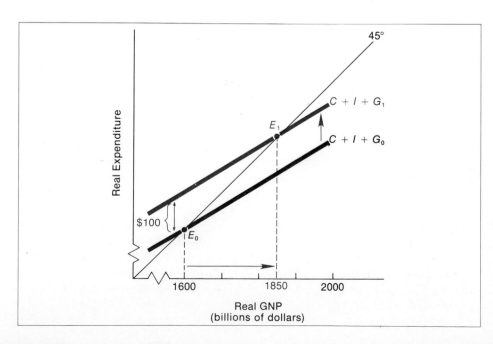

Figure 11–6
THE MULTIPLIER IN THE PRESENCE OF AN INCOME TAX
This diagram illustrates that an economy with an income tax (in this case a 25 percent income tax) has a lower multiplier than an economy without one. Specifically, the $C + I + G$ curve is shifted upward by a $100 billion increase in G, and the diagram shows that equilibrium GNP rises by $250 billion—from $1600 billion to $1850 billion. The multiplier is, therefore, $250/\$100 = 2\tfrac{1}{2}$, whereas without an income tax it is 5.

our model, the multiplier is only $250/$100 = $2\frac{1}{2}$, just as we concluded before.

To test your understanding of the multiplier, consider how the multiplier would work if Congress decided to cut taxes by a fixed amount, such as $125 billion. According to our previous analysis, we should multiply $125 billion by the MPC to arrive at the implied shift in the C schedule ("step 1"). Since the MPC in our example is 0.8, we obtain a figure of $100 billion. Next, we should enter this shift on a 45° line diagram to see how GNP changes ("step 2"). But Figure 11–6 has already done this for us. In showing the effect of an *increase* in government spending of $100 billion, it also shows the effect of a *decrease* in fixed taxes of $125 billion because both policies shift the $C + I + G$ schedule upward by $100 billion. This example illustrates a very general point:

The multiplier for changes in fixed taxes is smaller than the multiplier for changes in government purchases.

The reason is quite straightforward. While G is a direct component of $C + I + G$, taxes are not. Taxes work indirectly, first by changing disposable income and then by changing C. But some of the higher disposable income caused by a tax cut will be saved, not spent, and hence a dollar of tax cut does not have as much effect on spending as does a dollar of G.

Planning Expansive Fiscal Policy

Now, at last, you are ready to pretend that you are a member of Congress deciding how to respond to the president's proposed budget. Suppose that the economy would have a GNP of $1600 billion if last year's budget were simply repeated. Suppose further that your goal is to achieve a fully employed labor force and that staff economists tell you that your goal can be achieved with a GNP of approximately $1850 billion. What budget should you vote for? This question is far from hypothetical. When President Ronald Reagan took office in January 1981, the unemployment rate was 7.4 percent and the gap between actual and potential GNP (in current prices) was estimated to be nearly $70 billion. He immediately scrapped President Carter's proposed budget, and urged Congress to enact an entirely different fiscal policy, including large reductions in both federal spending and taxes. The ensuing debate over the budget occupied the headlines and preoccupied lawmakers for months.

Returning to our hypothetical example, let us suppose—as was certainly *not* the case in 1981—that inflation is not currently considered a major problem, and that Congress wishes to focus its energies squarely on reducing unemployment. Precisely what are the options? This chapter has taught us that Congress can raise government puchases, reduce taxes, or increase transfer payments by enough to close the recessionary gap between actual and potential GNP.

Figure 11–7 illustrates the problem, and its cure through higher government spending, on our 45° line diagram. Figure 11–7(a) shows the equilibrium of the economy if no changes are made in the budget. Except for the full-employment line at $Y = $1850 and the corresponding recessionary gap, it looks just like Figure 11–4. With an expenditure multiplier of $2\frac{1}{2}$, you can figure out that an additional $100 billion of government spending will be needed to push the GNP up $250 billion and eliminate this gap ($250 ÷ $2\frac{1}{2}$ = $100).

So you might vote to raise G from $G_0 = $320 billion to $G_1 = $420 billion, hoping to move the $C + I + G$ curve in Figure 11–7(a) out to the position indicated in Figure 11–7(b), thereby achieving full employment. Of course you

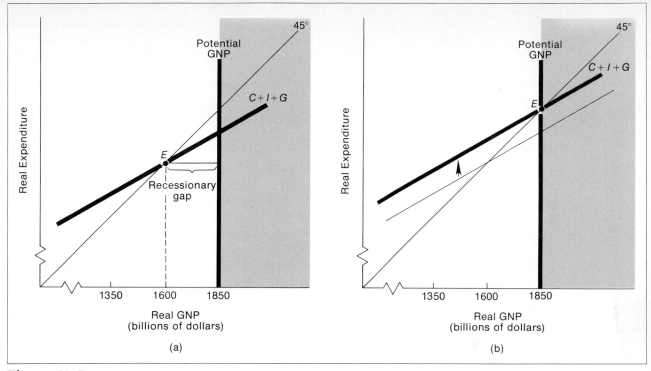

Figure 11–7

FISCAL POLICY TO ELIMINATE A RECESSIONARY GAP

This diagram shows, with more precision than can actually be achieved in practice, how fiscal policy can eliminate a recessionary gap. Part (a) shows the gap: Equilibrium GNP ($1600 billion) falls short of potential GNP ($1850 billion). Part (b) shows how fiscal policy—by moving the $C + I + G$ curve up just enough—can wipe out this gap and restore full employment. With a multiplier of $2\frac{1}{2}$, a rise in G of $100 billion or a cut in taxes large enough to shift C up by $100 billion would do the trick.

might prefer to achieve this fiscal stimulus by lowering income taxes rather than increasing expenditures. Or you might prefer to rely on more generous transfer payments. The point is that there are a variety of budgets capable of pushing the economy up to full employment by increasing GNP by $250 billion. Figure 11–7 applies equally well to any of them.

Planning Restrictive Fiscal Policy

The preceding example assumed that the basic problem of fiscal policy is to overcome a deficiency of aggregate demand, as was the case at the start of the Reagan administration. Often this is so. But at other times—such as after the 1972–1973 boom—the problem is that demand is excessive relative to the economy's capacity to produce. In this case, fiscal policy should assume a restrictive stance in order to reduce inflation.

It does not take much imagination to run our previous analysis in reverse. If, under a continuation of current budget policies, there would be an inflationary gap, there are fiscal policy tools that can eliminate it. Either by cutting spending programs out of the budget, or by raising taxes, or by some combination of these policies, the government can pull the $C + I + G$ schedule down to a noninflationary position and achieve an equilibrium at full employment.

Notice the difference between this way of eliminating an inflationary gap and the natural self-correcting mechanism of the economy that we discussed in Chapter 9. There we observed that if the economy were left to its own devices, a cumulative but self-limiting process of inflation eventually would eliminate the inflationary gap and return the economy to full employment. Here we see that it is not necessary to put the economy through the inflationary wringer. Instead, a restrictive fiscal policy can limit aggregate demand to the level that the economy can produce at full employment.

The Choice Between Spending Policy and Tax Policy

In principle, fiscal policy can nudge the economy in the desired direction equally well by changing government spending (G) or by changing taxes. What, then, are some of the practical considerations that favor one type of policy over the other?

It used to be thought that changes in tax legislation inevitably languished in Congress for such a long time that their usefulness for short-run stabilization policy was dubious. This "fact" was used to argue that the government should rely on increases in G to stimulate demand and decreases in G to restrict demand. However, the legislative record in the case of the Tax Reduction Act of 1975 largely dispelled these doubts. President Gerald Ford recommended a tax cut in January; the Congress, though it changed the president's recommendation substantially, still managed to pass the bill in March. Thus the entire legislative process was compressed into less than three months. (By contrast, 18 months elapsed between President Johnson's request for a tax increase in 1967 and its eventual enactment in 1968.) Clearly, Congress *can* act quickly. Whether or not it actually *will* do so is a question not so easily answered, since it invariably depends more on politics than on economics.

The argument that G is the more flexible instrument is also muddied by the fact that, for both technical and political reasons, it may be hard to start or stop government spending projects on short notice. Public works, for example, may need a long lead time for preparation; and then stopping them when aggregate demand revives may be both wasteful and politically unpopular. Imagine, if you will, trying to explain to people in a community that construction of their local school had to be halted because something as abstract as "aggregate demand" was too high!

Finally, and perhaps most important, each citizen and legislator should ask: How large a public sector should America have?

One point of view, expressed most eloquently in the writings of John Kenneth Galbraith, is that there is something amiss when a country as well endowed with private wealth as the United States has such an impoverished public sector. In Galbraith's view, America's most pressing needs are not for more stereo tape decks, sports cars, and video games, but rather for better schools, more efficient public transportation systems, and cleaner and safer city streets. Those who agree with him believe that we should *increase G* when the economy needs stimulus, and pay for these improved public services by *increasing taxes* when the economy needs to be reined in.

An opposing opinion, whose best-known advocate is President Reagan himself, is that the government sector is already too large; that we are foolish to rely on government to do things that private individuals and businesses could do better on their own; and that the growth of government interferes too much in our everyday lives, and in so doing, circumscribes our freedom. Those who hold this view argue for *tax cuts* when macroeconomic considerations call for expansionary fiscal policy, and for *reductions in public spending* when restrictive policy is required.

This is such an important point, and one on which so many people are confused, that it is one of the 12 fundamental principles that we hope you will remember well Beyond the Final Exam. Too often the active use of fiscal policy for economic stabilization is erroneously associated with a large and growing public sector—that is, with "big government." This need not be the case. Individuals favoring a smaller public sector can advocate an active fiscal policy just as well as those who favor a larger public sector. The dissension between the two groups should arise over the particular *tactics* to employ, not over the basic stabilization *strategy*. Advocates of big government budgets should seek to expand demand (when appropriate) through higher government spending and contract demand (when appropriate) through tax increases. By contrast, advocates of small public budgets should seek to expand demand by cutting taxes and reduce demand by cutting expenditures.

Should the Budget Be Balanced?

There is a belief that runs deep in the American character that there is something inherently wrong with government budget deficits. Using the analogy of an individual who spends more than he earns, the doomsayers argue that calamitous consequences will result if government spending exceeds tax receipts. Should the government balance its budget?

The principles of fiscal policy that we have just been expounding certainly do not lead to this conclusion. Instead, they point to the desirability of budget *deficits* when private demand ($C + I$) is too weak and budget *surpluses* when private demand is too strong. The budget should be balanced, according to these principles, only when $C + I + G$ under a balanced-budget policy approximately equals full-employment levels of output. This may sometimes occur, but it will not necessarily be the norm.

There are a number of fallacies, and some elements of truth, in the argument against deficit spending; and we will consider the subject more fully in Chapter 14. However, the central point is already clear from our present discussion of stabilization policy.

Consider the fiscal policy that would be followed by an administration that believed in balanced budgets and had the votes in Congress to turn its beliefs into reality. If private spending sagged for some reason, the multiplier would pull down GNP. Since personal and corporate taxes are sensitive to GNP, the budget would inevitably swing into the red. To a true budget-balancer, this would be a signal either to reduce spending or to raise taxes—exactly the opposite of the appropriate policy response.

Thus, budget balancing—as was practiced, say, by President Hoover during the Great Depression—will prolong and deepen recessions.

Economists and politicians of both political parties today realize the truth of this judgment. Therefore, actions are rarely taken to eliminate budget deficits during periods of substantial unemployment. President Reagan, for example, has stated time and again that he wishes to balance the budget; yet his important fiscal policy decisions have more often than not led to greater rather than smaller deficits.

Budget balancing can also lead to inappropriate fiscal policy when an economic boom begins. If rising tax receipts induce a budget-balancing government to spend more or cut taxes, fiscal policy will "boom the boom"—with disastrous inflationary consequences. Fortunately, believers in budget balancing usually are not alarmed by surpluses.

The High-Employment Budget

The **high-employment budget** is the hypothetical budget we *would have* if the economy were operating near full employment.

While efforts to keep the budget continually in balance are almost certain to lead to bad economic policy, there surely *is* a case for finding some way to exercise discipline over the budget. Because of the profound effects of the state of the economy on the budget, many economists have suggested that we should replace the idea of balancing the budget with the idea of balancing the **high-employment budget.**

When the economy is below full employment, actual tax receipts will be lower than those counted in the high-employment budget because people have lower incomes. At the same time, expenditures on unemployment compensation and other transfer programs will be higher. Thus, if the high-employment budget is balanced, the actual budget will show more spending than receipts—a budget deficit—during a recession.

When the economy is operating above full employment, the reverse is true. A balanced high-employment budget will mean that there is a surplus in the actual budget in boom periods.

According to this rule, the federal government should decide how much to spend on goods and services and then set tax and transfer laws so that the budget *would be* balanced any time the high-employment level of national income was reached. These policy settings should then be adhered to regardless of the behavior of the economy, except in emergencies. If GNP falls below the high-employment level, falling tax receipts and rising transfer payments provide an automatic cushion for disposable income. And if income booms beyond the high-employment level, the corresponding budget surplus automatically siphons off some of the aggregate demand.

Thus, advocates of this rule *do* recommend deficit spending during recessions, but only the limited kinds of deficits that arise *automatically* from falling tax receipts and rising transfer payments. They *do not* recommend deliberate *discretionary* increases in the deficit through tax cuts or increases in federal spending. But neither do they recommend old-fashioned budget balancing. A quick glance at the postwar record of budget policy shows that the government has certainly *not* adhered to anything like such a rule in practice. Figure 11–8 traces the behavior of both the high-employment budget and the actual budget since 1955. You will notice that the high-employment budget was typically in surplus during the decade 1955–1965, although the actual budget often exhibited a deficit. Then the high-employment budget swung into deficit under pressure from heavy spending on the Vietnam War, only to return (briefly) to a surplus position after the income tax surcharge of 1968. Since 1970, the actual budget has been continually in deficit. The high-employment budget has also typically shown a deficit, though a much smaller one.

Supply-Side Tax Cuts

Increases in government expenditures or any of a variety of tax cuts, we have learned, can close a recessionary gap by increasing aggregate demand. But such expansionary fiscal policies have at least one uncomfortable side effect: they push

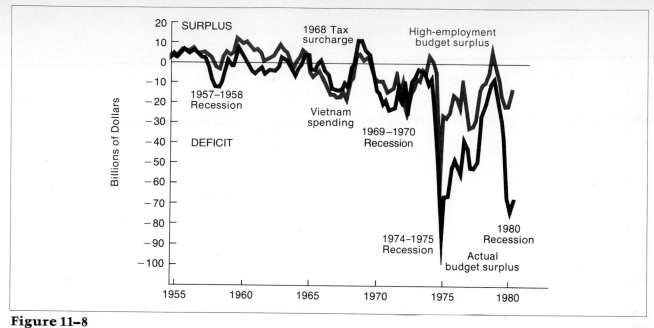

Figure 11–8

HIGH-EMPLOYMENT AND ACTUAL BUDGET SURPLUSES, 1955–1980

The black line charts the behavior of the surplus (positive numbers) or deficit (negative numbers) in the federal government budget. The blue line charts the behavior of the high-employment surplus, which, instead of subtracting actual government spending from actual tax collections, subtracts high-employment spending from high-employment tax receipts. Both budget concepts frequently have shown deficits, though this is much more true of the actual budget than it is of the high-employment budget.

SOURCE: Council of Economic Advisers.

prices higher. Figure 11–9, which is a standard aggregate supply–demand diagram, illustrates this conclusion. Expansionary fiscal policy shifts the aggregate demand curve to the right, from D_0D_0 to D_1D_1, causing the economy's equilibrium to shift from point E to point A. Output expands, as was the intent of the policy; but, in addition, prices rise—an outcome that was not particularly wanted.

This dilemma has led more and more people in recent years to advocate tax cuts aimed at increasing aggregate supply at the same time as they increase

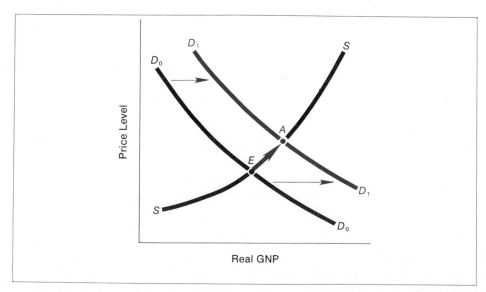

Figure 11–9

EXPANSIONARY FISCAL POLICY

Any of a variety of expansionary fiscal policies will push the aggregate demand curve outward to the right, as depicted by the shift from D_0D_0 to D_1D_1 in this aggregate supply and demand diagram. The economy's equilibrium moves upward to the right along aggregate supply curve SS, from point E to point A. Comparing A with E, we note that output is higher but prices are also higher. The expansionary policy has caused some inflation.

aggregate demand. What kinds of measures are these? Most supply-side tax cuts are aimed at stimulating capital formation. For example:

1. *Raising the Investment Tax Credit.* We have already mentioned (in Chapter 8) the *investment tax credit*—a device invented in 1961 to encourage investment by reducing the taxes of companies and individuals who purchase investment goods. The bigger the tax credit, of course, the more profitable any investment looks, and the greater the incentive to invest. Therefore, many supply siders favor increasing the investment tax credit, which currently allows eligible firms and individuals to reduce their taxes by up to 10 percent of their spending on qualified investment goods.

2. *Accelerated Depreciation.* A company investing in a machine or factory is not permitted to take the entire cost of that asset as a tax write-off in the year it is purchased. Instead, it must spread the cost over the lifetime of the asset in a series of *depreciation allowances*, which are annual tax deductions that in total add up to the value of the asset. Naturally, firms prefer to take their depreciation allowances sooner rather than later, because higher depreciation allowances in the early years of an investment mean lower immediate tax burdens. Many supply siders argue that an effective way to provide greater incentives for investment is to speed up ("accelerate") depreciation allowances. There are many ways to do this, and the details are best left to courses on accounting. However, one very straightforward way, which has attracted many supporters in Congress, is simple enough to explain right here. If Congress reduces the "lifetime" of a machine for tax purposes from, say, seven years to five, then obviously firms will get the tax savings from depreciation faster. This is precisely the course of action advocated by President Reagan, and enacted into law more or less as he suggested, in 1981.

3. *Reducing the Corporation Income Tax.* Another type of tax cut that supply siders often favor is reducing the statutory rates of taxation on corporate income. By letting companies retain more of their pre-tax income, it is argued, government will provide both greater investment incentives (by raising the profitability of investments) and more investable funds (by letting companies keep more of their earnings).

A **capital gain** is an increase in the market value of a piece of property, such as a common stock or a parcel of land, that occurs during the period between when it is bought and when it is sold. A **capital loss** is a decrease in that property's value.

4. *Reducing Taxes on Capital Gains.* Many investments, particularly financial investments such as stocks and bonds, often lead to **capital gains and losses.** For example, if Mr. Cabot purchases 100 shares of IBM stock in 1955 for $10,000 and sells them in 1980 for $100,000, the law says he has reaped a $90,000 *capital gain*, and must pay tax accordingly. Supply siders argue that lower taxes on capital gains would encourage individuals and firms to invest more, and, partly for these reasons, Congress reduced taxes on capital gains in 1979 over President Carter's objections. Currently, individuals must pay tax on only 40 percent of any capital gain that they realize. Thus, in the above example, Mr. Cabot would pay tax only on $36,000 rather than on the whole $90,000.[3]

Not all supply-side tax cuts are aimed at spurring investment. If there is to be more investment, someone must be providing the saving to finance it. Thus, supply siders typically favor:

5. *Reducing Taxes on Income from Savings.* One extreme form of this proposal would simply exempt from taxation all income from interest and

---

[3]More will be said about capital gains taxation, which is viewed by many as a major tax loophole, in Chapter 34.

dividends. Since income must be either consumed or saved, this would, in effect, change our present personal income tax into a tax on consumer spending. While this has not been adopted, the income tax changes introduced in 1981 did contain several significant steps in this direction. They considerably broadened the ability of individuals to establish tax-sheltered retirement accounts, created a new form of tax-free saving certificate (for 1981 and 1982 only), and exempted (beginning in 1985) substantial amounts of interest income from taxation. Supply siders promoted and applauded these changes.

Finally, supply siders recognize that capital is not the only factor of production. Aggregate supply can be expanded by increasing the supply of labor services as well. For this reason, they generally advocate:

6. *Lowering Personal Income Tax Rates.* Such cuts, they argue, will encourage people to work harder and for longer hours, and will induce them to spend more time at productive activities and less time worrying about how to avoid taxes. Sharp cuts in personal taxes have been the cornerstone of President Reagan's economic strategy.

Let us suppose, for the moment, that a successful supply-side tax cut is enacted to help close a recessionary gap. Since *both* aggregate demand *and* aggregate supply increase simultaneously, the economy may be able to avoid the painful inflationary consequences of an expansionary fiscal policy. Figure 11–10 illustrates this conclusion. The two aggregate demand curves and the aggregate supply curve S_0S_0 are carried over directly from Figure 11–9. But we have added an additional supply curve, S_1S_1, to indicate what a successful supply-side tax cut might achieve. The equilibrium of the economy moves from E to B, whereas with a conventional demand-side tax cut it would have moved from E to A. As compared with point A, output is higher and prices are lower at point B. A good deal, you say!

Indeed it is. But at least two problems must be acknowledged. The first is a confession of how little economists know about the determinants of aggregate supply: unusually large uncertainties surround any supply-side initiative. How much more will firms invest if depreciation allowances are liberalized? Will lower taxes on capital gains really induce much additional investment? Will people

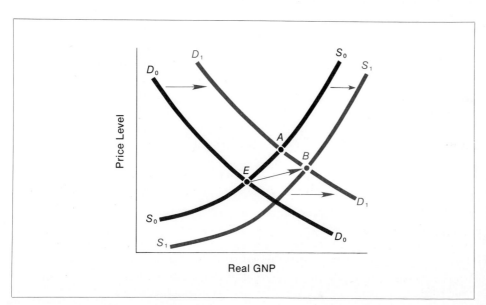

Real GNP

Figure 11–10
A SUCCESSFUL SUPPLY-SIDE TAX REDUCTION
A tax cut specifically aimed at the supply side, if successful, will shift *both* aggregate demand *and* aggregate supply to the right. In this diagram, equilibrium is initially at point E, where demand curve D_0D_0 intersects supply curve S_0S_0. After the supply-side tax cut, the aggregate demand curve is D_1D_1 and the aggregate supply curve is S_1S_1, so equilibrium is at point B. As compared with the results of a tax cut that works only on the demand side (point A), the supply-side tax cut raises output more and prices less.

really save more if their interest income is not taxed, or will they find that their saving goals are easier to achieve and react by saving less? Can we really expect people to work longer hours if we reduce the taxes on their earnings? In each case, an argument can be made that the tax cut will have precious little effect on aggregate supply—and these arguments may be right.

Second, it is noteworthy that most supply-side tax cuts are decidedly tilted in favor of the rich. While raising the incomes of the wealthiest members of our society may not be their primary aim, most supply-side cuts cannot help but concentrate benefits on the rich simply because it is the rich who earn most of the capital gains, interest, and dividends, and who own most of the corporations. Indeed, this tilt toward the rich is almost an inescapable corollary of supply-side logic. The basic aim of supply-side economics is to increase incentives for working and investing; that is, to increase the gap between the rewards of those who succeed in the economic game (by working hard, investing well, and so on) and those who fail. It can hardly be surprising that supply-side policies tend to increase economic inequality.

A Last Word on Some Harsh Realities

The mechanics outlined in this chapter may make the fiscal policy planner's job look rather simple. The elementary diagrams suggest, rather misleadingly, that the authorities can drive GNP to any level they please simply by manipulating their spending and tax programs. It seems as though they should be able to hit the full-employment bull's eye every time.

But, in fact, a better analogy is to shoot through dense fog at an erratically moving target with a gun of uncertain accuracy. The target is moving because, in the real world, the investment schedule (and, to a lesser extent, the consumption schedule) is constantly shifting on account of changes in expectations, new technological breakthroughs, changes in consumers' tastes, and the like. This means that the policies decided upon today, which are to take effect at some future date, may no longer be appropriate by the time that future date rolls around. Policy must be based, to some extent, on *forecasting*, and no one has yet discovered a foolproof method of economic forecasting.[4] Since our forecasting ability is so modest, and because fiscal policy decisions may sometimes take a long time to be carried out, the government may occasionally find itself fighting the last inflation just when the new recession gets under way.

A second misleading feature of our diagrams is that multipliers are not known with as much precision as our examples may suggest. Thus while the "best guess" may be that a $10 billion cut in government purchases will reduce GNP by $20 billion, the actual outcome may be as little as $12 billion or as much as $28 billion. It is therefore impossible to "fine tune" every wrinkle out of the economy's growth path through fiscal policy; economics is simply not that precise a science. The point is even more cogent with respect to tax policy. For example, we get involved in trying to guess whether consumers will view tax changes as permanent or temporary. Some of the analogous complexities that surround supply-side tax cuts were just mentioned.

A third complication is that our target—full-employment GNP—may be only dimly visible, as if through a fog. Especially when the economy's last experience with full employment is very far in the past, economists may have difficulty estimating the GNP level that represents full employment. In fact, as was mentioned in Chapter 6, there is a great deal of controversy over how much unemployment constitutes "full employment" right now.

[4]Some problems and techniques of economic forecasting are considered in Chapter 15.

Finally, in trying to decide whether to push the economy out of a position of unemployment—as was illustrated by Figure 11–7—legislators would like to know what the inflationary costs will be. This crucial *trade-off between unemployment and inflation* is an area of great controversy nowadays. Indeed, it is so important that we will devote an entire chapter to it later (Chapter 16). For the moment, suffice it to say that our knowledge of the trade-off is less than perfect.

As you read this book, government economists in Washington are losing sleep over just these issues. Where will the economy be six months or a year from now? What kinds of policies will be appropriate then? If one of the fiscal policy levers is pushed today, what will be the short- and long-run effects on the economy? How close or far are we from a normal "full employment" level of gross national product? If we stimulate demand to raise GNP, how much inflation will we have to endure? Unfortunately for the policymakers, precise answers to these questions cannot be found in this or any other textbook on economics.

Summary

1. The government's fiscal policy is its plan for managing aggregate demand through its spending and taxing programs. It is made jointly by the president and Congress.

2. Government purchases of goods and services (G) are a direct component of aggregate demand. Therefore, they have the same multiplier as do autonomous changes in consumption or investment.

3. When income taxes are introduced, there is a difference between GNP and disposable income. Since consumer spending (C) depends on disposable income, any change in taxes will shift the consumption schedule on a 45° line diagram.

4. Shifts in the consumption function caused by tax policy are subject to the same multiplier as autonomous shifts in the consumption schedule. However, the income tax reduces the size of this common multiplier just as it reduces the size of the multiplier for G or for I.

5. Government transfer payments are treated like negative taxes, not like government purchases of goods and services, because they influence aggregate demand only indirectly through their effect on consumption.

6. The net effect of the government on aggregate demand—and hence on equilibrium output and prices—depends on whether the expansionary effects of its spending are greater or smaller than the contractionary effects of its taxes.

7. If the multipliers were known precisely, it would be possible to plan any of a variety of fiscal policies to eliminate either a recessionary or an inflationary gap. Recessionary gaps can be cured by raising G, cutting taxes, or increasing transfers. Inflationary gaps can be cured by cutting G, raising taxes, or reducing transfers.

8. Active stabilization policy can be carried out either by means that tend to expand the size of government (by raising either G or taxes when appropriate) or by means that hold back the size of government (by reducing either G or taxes when appropriate). This is one of the 12 Ideas for Beyond the Final Exam.

9. Rigid adherence to budget balancing would make the economy less stable by reducing aggregate demand (via tax rises and reductions in G) when private spending is low, and raising aggregate demand when private spending is high.

10. Because of the inadvisability of keeping the budget balanced, some economists concerned with fiscal discipline have advocated balancing the high-employment budget; that is, adopting tax rates and spending programs that would lead to a balanced budget if the economy were operating near full employment.

11. Expansionary fiscal policy can cure recessions, but it normally exacts a cost in terms of higher inflation. This dilemma has led to a great deal of interest lately in "supply-side" tax cuts designed to stimulate aggregate supply.

12. While supply-side tax cuts have attractive aspects, there are great uncertainties over how well they would actually work; and they would probably lead to greater inequality of incomes.

Concepts for Review

Fiscal policy
Government purchases of
    goods and services (G)

Effect of income taxes
    on the multiplier
Government transfer payments
Budget balancing

High-employment budget
Supply-side tax cuts
Depreciation allowances
Capital gains and losses

Questions for Discussion

1. Where in its annual budget cycle is the federal government right now? (Bring yourself up to date by reading the financial page of your local newspaper.)

2. Consider an economy in which tax collections are always $200 and in which the three components of aggregate demand are as follows:

GNP	TAXES	DI	C	I	G
$480	$200	$280	$210	$100	$200
540	200	340	255	100	200
600	200	400	300	100	200
660	200	460	345	100	200
720	200	520	390	100	200

Find the equilibrium of this economy graphically. What is the marginal propensity to consume? What is the multiplier? What would happen to equilibrium GNP if government purchases were raised by $15 and the price level were unchanged?

3. Now consider a related economy in which investment is also $100, government purchases are also $200, and the price level is also fixed. But taxes now vary with income, and as a result the consumption schedule looks like the following:

GNP	TAXES	DI	C
$480	$160	$320	$240
540	180	360	270
600	200	400	300
660	220	440	330
720	240	480	360

Find the equilibrium graphically. What is the marginal propensity to consume? What is the tax rate? Use your diagram to show the effect of an increase of $15 in government purchases. What is the multiplier?

Compare this answer with your answer to Question 2 above. What do you conclude?

4. Explain why G has the same multiplier as autonomous shifts in C or I, while taxes have a different multiplier.

5. Return to the hypothetical economy in Question 2 and suppose that *both* taxes and government purchases are increased by $60. Find the new equilibrium under the assumption that consumer spending continues to be exactly three-quarters of disposable income (as it is in Question 2).

6. If the government today decides that aggregate demand is excessive and is causing inflation, what options are open to it? What if it decides that aggregate demand is too weak instead?

7. Discuss the difference between a government purchase of a good or service and a government transfer payment.

8. Suppose that you are in charge of the fiscal policy of the economy in Question 2. There is an inflationary gap with income at $600, and you want to reduce income to $540. What specific actions can you take to achieve this goal?

9. Now put yourself in charge of the economy in Question 3, and suppose that full employment comes at a GNP of $720. How can you push income up to that level?

10. Which of the proposed supply-side tax cuts appeals to you most? Draw up a list of arguments for and against enacting such a cut right now.

11. (More difficult) Consider an economy with a horizontal aggregate supply curve. Investment is fixed at $200, government purchases are $320, the consumption function is:

$$C = 120 + 0.8 \, DI,$$

and taxes are one-quarter of GNP—making disposable income (DI) equal to three-quarters of GNP. Find the equilibrium level of GNP. How would this equilibrium change if taxes were abolished? Compare your answer with the examples in this chapter.

Appendix
Algebraic Treatment of Fiscal Policy and Aggregate Demand

In this appendix we explain the simple algebra behind the fiscal policy multipliers discussed in the chapter. In so doing, we deal only with a simplified case in which prices do not change. While it is possible to work out the corresponding algebra for the more realistic aggregate demand–aggregate supply analysis with variable prices, the analysis is rather complicated and is best left to more advanced courses.

We start with the example used in the chapter (especially on pages 195–196 and 198–200). The government spends $320 billion on goods and services ($G = 320$), and levies an income tax equal to 25 percent of GNP. So if the symbol T denotes tax receipts:

$$T = .25\, Y .$$

Since the consumption function we have been working with is

$$C = 120 + 0.8\, DI ,$$

where DI is disposable income, and since disposable income and GNP are related by the accounting identity

$$DI = Y - T ,$$

it follows that the C schedule used in the 45° line diagram is described by the algebraic equation:

$$\begin{aligned} C &= 120 + 0.8\,(Y - T) \\ &= 120 + 0.8\,(Y - .25\,Y) \\ &= 120 + 0.8\,(.75\,Y) \\ &= 120 + 0.6\,Y . \end{aligned}$$

We can now apply the equilibrium condition for an economy with a government, which is:

$$Y = C + I + G .$$

Since investment in this example is $I = 200$, substituting for C, I, and G into this equation gives:

$$\begin{aligned} Y &= 120 + 0.6\,Y + 200 + 320 \\ 0.4\,Y &= 640 \\ Y &= 1600 . \end{aligned}$$

This is all there is to finding equilibrium GNP in an economy with a government.

To find the multiplier for government spending, increase G by 1 and resolve the problem:

$$\begin{aligned} Y &= C + I + G \\ Y &= 120 + 0.6\,Y + 200 + 321 \\ 0.4\,Y &= 641 \\ Y &= 1602.5 . \end{aligned}$$

So the multiplier is $1602.5 - 1600 = 2.5$, as stated in the text.

To find the multiplier for an increase in fixed taxes, change the tax schedule to:

$$T = .25\, Y + 1 .$$

Disposable income is then

$$DI = Y - T = Y - (.25\,Y + 1) = .75\,Y - 1 ,$$

so the consumption function is

$$\begin{aligned} C &= 120 + 0.8\, DI \\ &= 120 + 0.8\,(.75\,Y - 1) \\ &= 119.2 + 0.6\,Y . \end{aligned}$$

Solving for equilibrium GNP as usual gives

$$\begin{aligned} Y &= C + I + G \\ Y &= 119.2 + 0.6\,Y + 200 + 320 \\ 0.4\,Y &= 639.2 \\ Y &= 1598 . \end{aligned}$$

So a $1 increase in fixed taxes lowers Y by $2. The tax multiplier is -2.

Now let us proceed to a more general solution, using symbols rather than specific numbers. The equations of the model are as follows:

(1) $Y = C + I + G$

is the equilibrium condition, as usual;

(2) $C = a + b\,DI$

is the same consumption function we have used in the appendixes of Chapters 8 and 9;

(3) $DI = Y - T$

is the accounting identity relating disposable income to GNP;

(4) $T = T_0 + tY$

is the tax function, where T_0 represents fixed taxes (which were zero in our numerical example) and t represents the tax rate (which was 0.25 in the example). Finally, I and G are just fixed numbers.

We begin the solution by substituting (3) and (4) into (2) to derive the consumption schedule relating C to Y:

$$C = a + b\,DI$$
$$C = a + b(Y - T)$$
$$C = a + b(Y - T_0 - tY)$$
$$(5)\quad C = a - bT_0 + b(1 - t)Y.$$

You will notice that a change in fixed taxes (T_0) shifts the intercept of the C schedule while a change in the tax rate (t) changes its slope, as explained in the text (pages 194–195).

Next substitute (5) into (1) to find equilibrium GNP:

$$Y = C + I + G$$
$$Y = a - bT_0 + b(1 - t)Y + I + G$$
$$(1 - b(1 - t))\,Y = a - bT_0 + I + G$$

or

$$(6)\quad Y = \frac{a - bT_0 + I + G}{1 - b(1 - t)}.$$

Equation (6) shows us that G has the same multiplier as I or a, and that this multiplier is:

$$\text{Multiplier} = \frac{1}{1 - b(1 - t)}.$$

To see that this is in fact the multiplier, raise G or I or a by 1 unit. In each case, equation (6) would be changed to read:

$$Y = \frac{a - bT_0 + I + G + 1}{1 - b(1 - t)}.$$

Subtracting equation (6) from this expression gives the change in Y stemming from a one-unit change in G or I or a:

$$\text{Change in } Y = \frac{1}{1 - b(1 - t)}.$$

We noted in Chapter 10 (page 182) that if there were no income tax $(t = 0)$, a realistic value for b (the marginal propensity to consume) would yield a multiplier of 10, which is much bigger than the true multiplier. Now that we have added taxes to the model, our multiplier formula produces much more realistic numbers. Reasonable values for the parameters for the U.S. economy are $b = \frac{9}{10}$ and $t = \frac{1}{3}$. The multiplier formula then gives:

$$\text{Multiplier} = \frac{1}{1 - \frac{9}{10}\left(1 - \frac{1}{3}\right)} = \frac{1}{1 - \frac{9}{10} \times \frac{2}{3}}$$
$$= \frac{1}{1 - \frac{6}{10}} = \frac{1}{\frac{4}{10}} = 2.5,$$

which is not far from its true value, approximately 2.

Finally, we can see from equation (6) that the multiplier for a change in fixed taxes (T_0) is:

$$\text{Tax multiplier} = \frac{-b}{1 - b(1 - t)}.$$

For the example considered in the text and earlier in this appendix, $b = 0.8$ and $t = 0.25$, so the formula gives:

$$\frac{-.8}{1 - .8(1 - .25)} = \frac{-.8}{1 - .8(.75)}$$
$$= \frac{-.8}{1 - .6} = \frac{-.8}{.4} = -2.$$

According to these figures, each $1 *increase* in T_0 *reduces* Y by $2.

Questions for Discussion

1. In an economy described by the following set of equations:

$$C = 10 + .9\,DI$$
$$I = 140$$
$$G = 255$$
$$T = 50 + (1/3)Y,$$

find the equilibrium level of GNP. Then find the multipliers for government purchases and for fixed taxes. If it is desired to lower GNP by 90, what are some policies that would do the trick?

2. This is a variant of the previous problem that approaches things the way a fiscal policy planner might. In an economy whose consumption function and tax function are as given in Question 1, and with investment fixed at 140, find the value of G that would make GNP equal to 990.

Banking and the Creation of Money

[Money] is a machine for doing quickly and commodiously what would be done, though less quickly and commodiously, without it.

JOHN STUART MILL

The last several chapters have put together a fairly comprehensive model of the factors determining the equilibrium levels of output and prices (Chapters 7 through 9). In studying the factors capable of changing that equilibrium, we have learned that some emanate from the supply side (Chapter 9) while others come from the demand side (Chapters 10 and 11). Yet our picture of economic activity remains incomplete, for we have not yet brought in the financial system.

You will recall that the circular flow diagrams used in earlier chapters to explain equilibrium GNP had a "financial system" in their upper left-hand corners. Savings flowed into this system and investment flowed out. Something obviously goes on inside the financial system to channel the saving into investment, and it is time we learned just what this something is.

There is another, equally important, reason for studying the financial system. *Fiscal policy* is not the only lever the government has on the economy's aggregate demand curve: it also exercises significant control over aggregate demand by manipulating *monetary policy.* If we are to understand monetary policy (the subject of Chapters 13 and 14), we must first acquire some understanding of the financial system.

The present chapter has three major objectives. It first seeks to explain the nature of money: what it is, what purposes it serves, and how it is measured. Once this is done, we turn our attention to the banking system, explaining its historical origins, the nature of banking as a business, and why this industry is so heavily regulated. Finally, we learn how banks create money—a subject that is of great importance because it is simply impossible to understand monetary policy without knowing how money is created.

At the end of the chapter, we will see why government authorities must exercise control over the supply of money in a modern economy, and this leads naturally into the discussion in Chapter 13 of *central banking*, that is, the techniques used to implement monetary policy. Then, in Chapter 14 we integrate what we will by then have learned about money and monetary policy into our model of income determination, as the culmination of our study of macroeconomic theory.

Policy Issue: Why Regulate the Banks?

Banking is one of the most strictly regulated industries in America. Banks are told, to some degree, how much they may accept in deposits, how much interest they may pay on these deposits, what types of investments they may make, and so on. Yet banking is not heavily monopolized. While there are financial giants such as Bank of America (California) and Citibank (New York), the industry is populated by literally thousands of small banks located in cities and towns throughout the country. There are more than 14,000 commercial banks and over 5000 savings institutions nationwide. So why the extensive structure of government regulations?

A first reason is that the major "output" of the banking industry—the nation's supply of money—is of vital importance to the health of the economy. Bank managers presumably do what is best for their stockholders. That, at any rate, is their job. But as we shall see, what is best for bank stockholders may not be best for the whole economy. For this reason, the government does not allow bankers to determine the level of the nation's money supply by profit considerations alone.

A second reason for the extensive regulation of banks is concern for the safety of depositors. In a free-enterprise system, new businesses are born and die every day; and no one save those people immediately involved takes much notice of these goings-on. When a firm goes bankrupt, stockholders lose money and employees may lose their jobs. (The latter may not even happen if new management takes over the assets of the bankrupt firm.) But, except for the case of very large firms, that is about it.

But banking is different. If banks were treated like other firms, depositors would lose money whenever one went bankrupt. That is bad enough by itself, but the real danger comes in the case of **runs on a bank.** When depositors get jittery about the security of their money, they may all rush in at once to cash in their accounts. For reasons we will learn in this chapter, most banks could not survive a "run" like this and would be forced into insolvency. Worse yet, this disease is highly contagious. If Mrs. Smith hears that her neighbor has just lost her life savings because the Main Street National Bank went broke, she is quite likely to rush to her own bank to make a hefty withdrawal.

Without modern forms of bank regulation, therefore, one bank failure might lead to another; and indeed, bank failures were quite common throughout most of America's history (see Figure 12–1 on page 216). But the failure of a major bank nowadays is an event rare enough to be newsworthy. The reason is that government has taken steps to ensure that such an infectious disease, if it occurs, will not spread. It has done this in several ways that will be mentioned later in this chapter.

Barter Versus Monetary Exchange

Money is so much a part of our day-to-day existence that we are likely to take it for granted, failing to appreciate all that it accomplishes. But it is important to realize that money is very much a social contrivance. Like the wheel, it had to be invented. The most obvious way to trade commodities is not by using money, but by **barter**—a system in which people exchange one good directly for another. And the best way to appreciate what monetary exchange accomplishes is to imagine a world without it.

Under a system of direct barter, if Farmer Jones grows corn and has a craving for peanuts, he has to find a peanut farmer with a taste for corn. If he finds such a

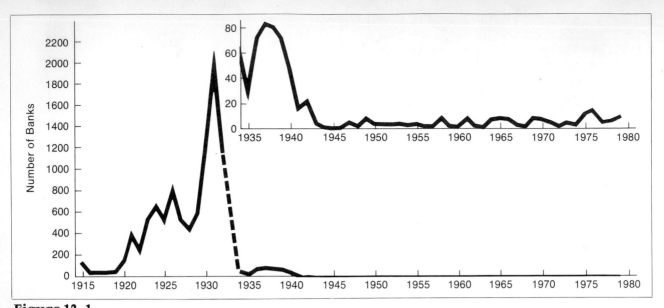

Figure 12–1

BANK FAILURES IN THE UNITED STATES, 1915–1979

This chart shows the number of commercial banks that failed each year from 1915 until 1979. Notice the sharp drop in the number of failures from 1932 (nearly 2200) to 1934 (about 60). Failures clearly are much less common in the postwar period than they were in earlier years.

SOURCE: Federal Deposit Insurance Corporation.

person (this was called the **double coincidence of wants** by the classical economists), they make the trade. If this sounds easy, try to imagine how busy Farmer Jones would be if he had to repeat the sequence for every commodity he consumed in a week. For the most part, the desired double coincidences of wants are more likely to turn out to be double wants of coincidence, where Jones gets no peanuts and the peanut farmer gets no corn. Worse yet, with so much time spent looking for trading partners, Jones would have far less time to grow corn.

Money greases the wheels of exchange, and thus makes the whole economy more productive.

Under a monetary system, the corn farmer gives up his corn for money. He does so not because he wants the money per se, but because of what that money can buy. Money makes Farmer Jones's shopping tasks much easier, for it allows him simply to locate a peanut farmer who wants money. And what peanut farmer does not?

For these reasons, monetary exchange replaced barter at a very early stage of human civilization, and only extreme circumstances, like massive wars and runaway inflations, have been able to bring barter (temporarily) back.

The Conceptual Definition of Money

Money is the standard object used in exchanging goods and services. In short, money is the **medium of exchange.**

Monetary exchange is the alternative to direct barter. In a system of monetary exchange, people trade **money** for goods when they purchase something and trade goods for money when they sell something, but they do not trade goods directly for other goods. This defines money's principal role as the **medium of exchange.** But once it has come into use as the medium of exchange, whatever object is serving as money is bound to take on other functions as well. For one, it will inevitably become the *unit of account,* that is, the standard unit for quoting prices. Thus, if inhabitants of an idyllic tropical island used coconuts as money, they would be foolish to quote prices in terms of sea shells.

Money may also come to be used as a **store of value.** If Farmer Jones temporarily produces and sells corn of more value than he wants to consume right away, he may find it convenient to store the difference in the form of money until he wants to use it. This is because he knows that money can be "sold" easily for goods and services at a later date, whereas land, gold, and other stores of value might not be. Of course, if money pays no interest and inflation is substantial, he may decide to forgo the convenience of money and store his wealth in some other form rather than see its purchasing power rapidly eroded. So this role of money is far from inevitable. Since money may not always serve as a store of value, and since there are many stores of value other than money, it is best not to include the store-of-value function as part of our conceptual definition of money. Instead, we simpy label as "money" whatever serves as the medium of exchange.

What Serves as Money?

Anthropologists and historians will testify that a bewildering variety of things have served as money in different times and places. Cattle, stones, wampum, cigarettes, woodpecker scalps, porpoise teeth, and candy bars are a few of the more colorful examples.

In primitive or less organized societies, the commodities that served as money generally had value in themselves. If not used as money, cattle could be slaughtered for food, cigarettes could be smoked, and so on. But such **commodity money** generally runs into several severe difficulties. To be useful as a medium of exchange the commodity must be divisible. This makes cattle a very poor choice. It must also be of uniform, or at least readily identifiable, quality so that inferior substitutes are easy to recognize. This may be why woodpecker scalps never achieved great popularity. The medium of exchange must also be storable and durable, which presents a serious problem for candy-bar money. Finally, because commodity moneys need to be carried and stored, it is helpful if the item is compact, that is, has high value per unit of volume and weight.

All of these traits make it natural that gold and silver have circulated as money in so many times and places. Since they have high value in nonmonetary uses, a lot of purchasing power can be carried without too much weight. Pieces of

gold are also storable, divisible (with a little trouble), and of identifiable quality (with a little more trouble).

The same characteristics suggest that paper would make an ideal money. Since we can print any number on it that we want, we can make paper money as divisible as we please and also make it possible to carry a large value in a lightweight and compact form. Paper is easy to store and, with a little cleverness, we can make counterfeiting very hard (though never impossible). Paper cannot, however, serve as a commodity money because its value per square inch in alternative uses is so small. A paper currency that is repudiated by its issuer can, perhaps, be used as wallpaper or to wrap fish, but these uses will surely represent only a small fraction of the paper's value as money. Contrary to the popular expression, such a currency literally *is* worth the paper it is printed on, which is to say that it is not worth very much.[1] Thus paper money is always **fiat money.**

Fiat money is money that is decreed as such by the government. It is of little value as a commodity, but it maintains its value as a medium of exchange because people have faith that the issuer will stand behind the pieces of printed paper and limit their production.

Money in the contemporary United States is almost entirely fiat money. Look at a dollar bill. Next to George Washington's picture it states: "This note is legal tender for all debts, public and private." Nowhere on the certificate is there a promise, stated or implied, that the U.S. government will exchange it for anything else. A dollar bill is convertible into 4 quarters, 10 dimes, 20 nickels, or any other similar combination, but not into gold, chocolate, or any other commodity.

Why do people hold these pieces of paper? Only because they know that others are willing to accept them for things of intrinsic value—food, rent, shoes, and so on. If this confidence ever evaporated, these dollar bills would cease serving as a medium of exchange and, given that they make ugly wallpaper, would become virtually worthless.

But don't panic. This is not likely to occur. Our current monetary system has evolved over hundreds of years during which *commodity money* was first replaced by *"full-bodied" paper money*—paper certificates that were backed by gold or silver of equal value held in the issuer's vaults. Then the full-bodied paper money was replaced by certificates that were only partially backed by gold and silver. Finally, we arrived at our present system, in which paper money has no "backing" whatsoever. Like a hesitant swimmer who first dips her toes, then her legs, then her whole body into a cold swimming pool, we have "tested the water" at each step of the way—and found it to our liking. It is unlikely that we will ever take a step back in the other direction.

How the Quantity of Money Is Measured

As we will learn in coming chapters, the amount of money circulating in the economy is of profound importance for the determination of national product and the price level. Thus it becomes important for the government to know how much money there is at any given time.

Our conceptual definition of money describes it as the medium of exchange. But this raises questions about just what items should be included and what items excluded when we count up the money supply. Some items are easy. All of our coins, the small change of our economic system, clearly should count as money. So should paper money, which accounts for a far greater volume of transactions. But we cannot stop here if we want to include the main vehicle for making payments in our society, because the lion's share of our nation's payments are

---

[1]The first paper money issued by the federal government, the Continental dollar, was essentially repudiated. (Actually, the new government of the United States redeemed the Continentals for 1 cent on the dollar in the 1790s.) This gave rise to the derisive expression, "It's not worth a Continental."

made neither in metal nor in paper money, but by check.

Checking deposits are actually no more than bookkeeping entries in bank ledgers. Many people think of checks simply as a convenient way to give coins or dollar bills to someone else. But, in fact, checks are something quite different, which is why the country can have more money in the form of checking deposits than it has in the form of currency. For example, if you pay the grocer $50 by check, no dollar bills or coins normally will change hands. Instead, that check will travel back to your bank, where $50 will be deducted from the bookkeeping entry that records your account and added to the bookkeeping entry for your grocer's account. (If you and the grocer hold accounts at different banks, more books get involved; but still no coins or bills are likely to be moved.) Since so many transactions are made by check, it seems imperative that checking deposits be included in any specific definition of the money supply.

At this point, many economists draw the line. They contend that these three things alone—coins, paper money, and checking account balances—constitute the nation's medium of exchange. This is our first measure of the amount of money in circulation—the narrowly defined money supply, or **M1.** The left-hand side of Figure 12–2 shows the composition of M1 as of December 1981. You can see that checking accounts in commercial banks predominate in M1.

We have stated that checkable deposits at banks and savings institutions should count in the money supply. But what about the non-checkable savings deposits that both these types of banks hold? In one respect, these accounts would seem quite different from checking accounts, since savings balances cannot immediately be used as a medium of exchange. But many economists feel this

> The narrowly defined money supply, usually abbreviated **M1,** is the sum of all coins and paper money in circulation, plus checkable deposit balances at banks and savings institutions.[2]

[2]This includes the so-called NOW (negotiable order of withdrawal) accounts, which are savings accounts on which depositors can write checks.

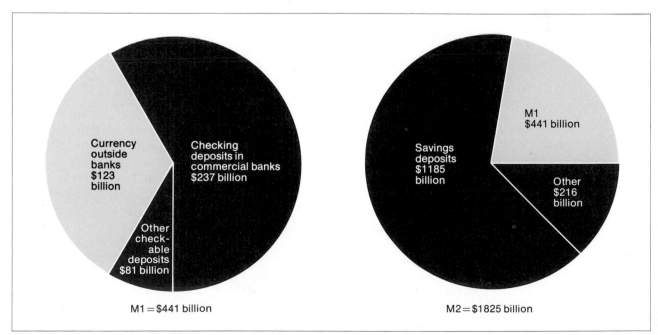

Figure 12–2
DEFINITIONS OF THE MONEY SUPPLY (December 1981)
SOURCE: Federal Reserve.

has become a false distinction. When a customer holds a checking *and* a savings account in the same bank, does it really matter where her money sits—especially if she can transfer funds from one account to the other simply by pushing a button on an automated teller? Because recent financial innovations have blurred the distinction between the two types of accounts (checking and savings), many economists now favor including most savings account balances as part of the money supply. This leads to our second, broader, definition of the money supply, called **M2.**

The broadly defined money supply, usually abbreviated **M2,** is the sum of all coins and paper money in circulation, plus all checking account balances, plus most forms of savings account balances, plus shares in money market mutual funds.

The last item in the definition of M2 needs some explanation. During 1974, when interest rates in the open market far exceeded the maximum interest rates that banks were permitted to pay, some enterprising men and women on Wall Street invented a new type of financial instrument that consumers found very attractive—money market mutual funds. These funds sell shares and use the proceeds to buy a variety of short-term securities. Since the securities that they buy often pay higher interest rates than banks, the funds can afford to pay higher interest rates to their customers than the banks do. This accounts for their popularity. But why should it make these funds candidates for inclusion in the money supply? The reason is that money market funds allow their customers to make withdrawals simply by writing a check, so depositors can use their holdings of fund shares just like checking balances. Because they can be used like checking accounts, balances held in money market funds are counted as part of M2. The composition of M2 as of December 1981 is shown on the right-hand side of Figure 12–2. You can see that savings accounts predominate, dwarfing everything that is included in M1.

Some economists do not want to stop counting at M2; they prefer still broader definitions of money (M3, and so on) which include more types of bank deposits and other closely related assets. The problem with this approach is that there is no clear-cut place to stop, no obvious line of demarcation between those assets that are "money" and those that are not. If we define an asset's **liquidity** as the ease with which it can be converted into cash, then there is a range of assets of varying degrees of liquidity. Everything in M1 is completely "liquid"; the money market fund shares and passbook savings accounts of M2 are a bit less so; and so on, until we encounter such things as short-term government bonds, which, while still quite liquid, would not normally be included in the money supply. Any number of different "M's" can be defined—and have been—by drawing the line in different places.

In this book, we adhere to the convention that only M1 is "money," because the items it includes—coins, paper money, and checks—are clearly used as the medium of exchange. Fortunately, no very important matters of principle hinge on the particular definition of money that is chosen.

Now that we have defined money and seen how it can be measured, we turn our attention to the creators of money—the banks.

How Banking Began

When Adam and Eve left the Garden of Eden, they did not encounter a branch of the Bank of America. Banking had to be invented, and some time passed before it came to be practiced as it is today. With a little imagination, we can see how the first banks must have begun.

When money was made of gold it was most inconvenient for consumers and merchants to carry it around and to have to weigh and assay it for purity every time a transaction was made. So it is not surprising that the practice developed of leaving one's gold in the care of a goldsmith, who had rather safe storage facilities, and carrying in its place a receipt from the goldsmith stating that John Doe did indeed own five ounces of gold of a certain purity. The goldsmiths, of course, charged a fee for this service. When people began trading goods and services for the goldsmiths' receipts, rather than for the gold itself, the receipts became an early form of paper money.

At this stage, paper money was fully backed by gold. But gradually the goldsmiths began to notice that the amount of gold they were actually required to pay out in a day was but a small fraction of the total gold they had stored in their warehouses. Then one day some enterprising goldsmith hit upon a momentous idea that must have made him fabulously wealthy.

His thinking probably ran something like this. "I have 2000 ounces of gold stored away in my vault, for which I collect storage fees from my customers. If I get much more, I'll need an expensive new vault. But in the last year, there has not been a single day on which I was called upon to pay out more than 100 ounces. What harm could it do if I lent out, say, half the gold I now have? I'll still have more than enough to pay off any depositors that come in for a withdrawal, so no one will ever know the difference. And I could earn 30 additional ounces of gold each year in interest on the loans I make (at 3 percent interest on 1000 ounces). With this profit, I could lower my service charges to depositors and so attract still more deposits. I think I'll do it."

With this resolution, the modern system of **fractional reserve banking** was born. This system has three important features—features that are crucially important to this chapter.

1. *Bank profitability.* By getting deposits at zero interest and lending some of them out at positive interest rates, goldsmiths made a profit. The history of banking as a profit-making industry was begun and has continued to this date. *Banks, like other enterprises, are in business to earn profits.*

2. *Bank discretion over the money supply.* When goldsmiths decided that they could get along by keeping only a fraction of their total deposits on reserve in their vaults and lending out the balance, they acquired the ability to *create money.* As long as they kept 100 percent reserves, each gold certificate represented exactly one ounce of gold. So whether people decided to carry their gold or leave it with their goldsmith did not affect the money supply, which was set by the volume of gold.

    With the advent of fractional reserve banking, however, new paper certificates were added whenever goldsmiths lent out some of the gold they held on deposit. The loans, in effect, created new money. In this way, the total amount of money came to depend on the amount of gold that each goldsmith felt compelled to maintain as reserves in his vault. For any given volume of gold on deposit, the lower the reserves the goldsmiths kept, the more loans would be made, and therefore the more money there would be. While we no longer use gold to back our money, this principle remains true today. *Bankers' business decisions influence the supply of money.*

3. *Exposure to runs.* A goldsmith who kept 100 percent reserves never had to worry about a run on his vault. Even if all his depositors showed up at the door at once, he always had enough gold to return their deposits. But as soon as the first goldsmith decided to get by with only fractional reserves, the possibility of a run on the vault became a real concern. If that first goldsmith

Fractional reserve banking is a system under which bankers keep in their vaults as reserves only a fraction of the funds they hold on deposit.

who lent out half his gold had found 51 percent of his customers at his door one unlucky day, he would have had a lot of explaining to do. Similar problems have worried bankers for centuries. *The danger of a run on the bank has induced bankers to keep prudent reserves and to lend out money carefully.*

Principles of Bank Management: Profits Versus Safety

Bankers have a reputation, probably deserved, for conservatism in politics, dress, and business affairs. From what has been said so far, the economic rationale for this conservatism should be clear. Checking deposits are pure fiat money. Years ago, these deposits were "backed" by nothing more than the bank's promise to convert them into currency on demand. If people lost trust in a bank, the bank was doomed. Thus, it has always been imperative for bankers to acquire a reputation for prudence. This they did (and continue to do) in two principal ways. First, they had to maintain a sufficiently generous level of reserves to minimize their vulnerability to runs. Second, they had to be somewhat cautious in making loans and investments, since any large losses on their loans could undermine the confidence of depositors.

It is important to realize that banking under a system of fractional reserves is an inherently risky business that is rendered relatively safe only by cautious and prudent management. America's history of bank failures bears sober testimony to the fact that many bankers were neither cautious nor prudent. Why? Because this is not a recipe for high profits. Bank profits are maximized by keeping reserves as low as possible, by making at least some risky investments, and by giving loans to borrowers of questionable credit standing (because these borrowers will pay the highest interest rates). The art of bank management is to strike the appropriate balance between the lure of profits and the need for safety. When a banker errs by being too stodgy, his bank will earn inadequate profits. When he errs by taking unwarranted risks, his bank may not survive at all.

Bank Regulation

The public authorities, however, apparently have decided that the balance struck by profit-minded bankers often would not be at the place where society would like it struck. So government has thrown up a web of regulations designed to insure the safety of depositors and to control the supply of money.

The principal innovation guaranteeing the safety of bank deposits is **deposit insurance.** Today most bank deposits are insured against loss by the **Federal Deposit Insurance Corporation (FDIC)** or by the **Federal Savings and Loan Insurance Corporation (FSLIC)**—two agencies of the United States government. If your bank belongs to the FDIC or the FSLIC (and most do), your checking account is insured for up to $100,000 regardless of what happens to the bank. Thus, while bank failures may spell disaster for the bank's stockholders, they do not give many depositors cause for concern. Deposit insurance eliminates the motive for customers to rush to their bank just because they hear some bad news about the bank's finances. Many observers give this innovation much of the credit for the pronounced decline in bank failures since 1933, the year in which the FDIC was established. (Refer back to Figure 12–1 on page 216.)

In addition to insuring depositors against loss, the government takes steps to see that banks do not get into financial trouble. For one thing, various regulatory authorities conduct periodic *bank examinations and audits* in order to keep tabs on the financial condition and business practices of the banks under their purview. For another, laws and regulations *limit the kinds and quantities of assets in which banks may invest.* For example, most banks are prohibited from purchasing common stock. Both these forms of regulation are clearly aimed at maintaining bank safety.

A final type of regulation also has some bearing on safety but is motivated primarily by the government's desire to control the money supply. We have seen that the amount of money any bank will issue depends on the amount of reserves it elects to keep. For this reason, most banks are subject by law to **minimum required reserves.** While banks may (and sometimes do) keep reserves in excess of these legal minimums, they may not keep less. It is this regulation that places an upper limit on the money supply. The rest of this chapter is concerned with the details of this mechanism.

How Bankers Keep Books

Before we can fully understand the mechanics of modern banking and the process by which money is "created," we must acquire at least a nodding acquaintance with the way in which bankers keep their books. The first thing to know is how to distinguish **assets** from **liabilities.**

There is an easy test to see whether some piece of paper or bookkeeping entry is a bank's asset or a liability. Ask yourself whether, if this paper were converted into cash, the bank would receive the cash (if so, it is an asset) or pay it out (if so, it is a liability). This test makes it clear that loans to customers are bank assets (when the loans are repaid, the bank collects), while customers' deposits are bank liabilities (when deposits are cashed in, the bank must pay up).

When accountants draw up a complete list of all the bank's assets and liabilities, the resulting document is called the bank's **balance sheet.** Typically, the value of all the bank's assets exceeds the value of all its liabilities. (On the rare occasions when this is not the case, the bank is in serious trouble.) In what sense, then, do balance sheets "balance"?

They balance because accountants have invented the concept of **net worth** to balance the books. Specifically, they have defined the net worth of a bank to be the difference between the value of all its assets and the value of all its liabilities. Thus, by definition, when accountants add net worth to liabilities, the sum they get must be the same as the value of the bank's assets. In short:

$$\text{Assets} = \text{Liabilities} + \text{Net Worth}.$$

Table 12–1 illustrates this with the balance sheet of a fictitious bank, Bank-a-mythica, whose finances are extremely simple. On December 31, 1981, it had only two kinds of assets (listed on the left-hand side of the balance sheet)— $1 million in cash, which it held as reserves in its vault, and $4,500,000 in outstanding loans to its customers, that is, in customers' IOUs. And it had only one type of liability (listed on the right-hand side)—$5 million in checking deposits. The difference between total assets ($5.5 million) and total liabilities ($5 million) was the bank's net worth ($500,000) and is shown on the right-hand side of the balance sheet.

An **asset** of a bank is something that the bank *owns.* This "thing" may be a physical object, such as the bank building, a typewriter, or a vault, or it may be just a piece of paper, such as an IOU of a customer to whom the bank has made a loan.

A **liability** of a bank is something that the bank *owes.* Most bank liabilities take the form of bookkeeping entries. For example, if you have a checking account in the Main Street Bank, your bank balance there is a liability of the bank. (It is, of course, an asset to you.)

Table 12–1
BALANCE SHEET OF BANK-A-MYTHICA
DECEMBER 31, 1981

ASSETS		LIABILITIES AND NET WORTH	
Assets		**Liabilities**	
Cash in vault	$1,000,000	Checking deposits	$5,000,000
Loans outstanding	4,500,000		
Total	$5,500,000		
Addendum: Bank Reserves		**Net Worth**	
Actual reserves	$1,000,000	Stockholders' equity	500,000
Required reserves	1,000,000		
Excess reserves	0	Total	$5,500,000

The Limits to Money Creation by a Single Bank

Let us now turn to the process of deposit creation. Many bankers will deny that they have any ability to "create" money. (The very phrase has a suspiciously hocus-pocus sound to it.) But they are not quite right. For although any individual bank's ability to create money is severely limited in a system with many banks, the banking system as a whole can achieve much more than the sum of its parts. Through the modern alchemy of **deposit creation,** it can turn one dollar into many dollars. But to understand this important process, we had better proceed in steps, beginning with the case of a single bank, our hypothetical Bank-a-mythica.

According to the balance sheet in Table 12–1, Bank-a-mythica is holding cash reserves in its vault that are equal to 20 percent of its deposits ($1 million in cash is equal to 20 percent of the $5 million in deposits). Let us assume that this is the minimum reserve ratio prescribed by law and that the bank strives to keep its reserves down to the legal minimum; that is, it strives to keep its **excess reserves** down to zero.

Excess reserves are any reserves held in excess of the legal minimum.

Now let us suppose that on January 2, 1982, an eccentric widower comes into Bank-a-mythica and deposits $100,000 in cash in his checking account. The bank now has acquired $100,000 more in cash reserves, and $100,000 more in checking

Table 12–2
CHANGES IN BANK-A-MYTHICA'S BALANCE SHEET, JANUARY 2, 1982

ASSETS		LIABILITIES	
Cash in vault	+ $100,000	Checking deposits	+ $100,000
Addendum: Changes in Reserves			
Actual reserves	+ $100,000		
Required reserves	+ 20,000		
Excess reserves	+ $ 80,000		

Bank-a-mythica receives a $100,000 cash deposit. It now holds excess reserves of $80,000, since required reserves rise by only $20,000 (20 percent of $100,000).

Table 12–3
CHANGES IN BANK-A-MYTHICA'S BALANCE SHEET, JANUARY 3–6, 1982

ASSETS		LIABILITIES	
Loans outstanding	+ $80,000		No change
Cash in vault	− 80,000		
Addendum: Changes in Reserves			
Actual reserves	− $80,000		
Required reserves	No change		
Excess reserves	− $80,000		

Bank-a-mythica gets rid of its excess reserves by making a loan of $80,000 to Hard-Pressed Construction Company.

deposits. But since deposit liabilities are up by $100,000, *required* reserves are up by only 20 percent of this amount, or $20,000, leaving $80,000 in *excess* reserves. Table 12–2 illustrates the effects of this transaction on Bank-a-mythica's balance sheet. It is tables such as this, which show *changes* in balance sheets rather than the balance sheets themselves, that will help us follow the money-creation process.

If Bank-a-mythica does not want to hold excess reserves, it will be unhappy with the situation illustrated in Table 12–2, for it is holding $80,000 in excess reserves on which it earns no interest. So as soon as possible—let us say by the end of the week—it will lend out the extra $80,000, leading to the balance sheet changes shown in Table 12–3.

By combining Tables 12–2 and 12–3, we arrive at Table 12–4, which summarizes all the bank's transactions for the week. We see that once the bank has had a chance to adjust to the inflow of deposits, it no longer holds excess reserves.

Looking at Table 12–4 and keeping in mind our specific definition of money, it appears at first that the chairman of Bank-a-mythica is right when he claims not to have engaged in the nefarious practice of "money creation." All that happened was that, in exchange for the $100,000 in cash it received, the bank issued the widower a checking balance of $100,000. This does not change M1; it merely converts one form of money into another.

Table 12–4
CHANGES IN BANK-A-MYTHICA'S BALANCE SHEET, WEEK OF JANUARY 2–6, 1982

ASSETS		LIABILITIES	
Cash in vault	+ $20,000	Checking deposits	+ $100,000
Loans outstanding	+ 80,000		
Addendum: Changes in Reserves			
Actual reserves	+ $20,000		
Required reserves	+ 20,000		
Excess reserves	No change		

When it receives $100,000 in cash deposits, Bank-a-mythica keeps only the required $20,000 in reserves and lends out the remaining $80,000 to Hard-Pressed Construction Company. Its excess reserves return to zero.

But wait. What happened to the $100,000 in cash? The table shows that $20,000 was retained by Bank-a-mythica in its vault. Since this currency is no longer in circulation, it no longer counts in the official money supply. (Notice that Figure 12–2 included only "currency outside banks.") But the other $80,000, which the bank lent out, is still in circulation and probably will be redeposited in some other bank. But even before the $80,000 is moved, the original $100,000 in cash has supported a rise in the money supply: there is now $100,000 in checking deposits and $80,000 in cash available for circulation, making a total of $180,000. The money-creation process has begun.

Multiple Money Creation by a Series of Banks

Let us now trace this $80,000 in cash and see how the process of money creation gathers momentum. Suppose that Bank-a-mythica's $80,000 loan goes (in cash) to the Hard-Pressed Construction Company, which banks across town at the First National Bank. Hard-Pressed presumably deposits these funds into its bank account; so First National's reserves increase by $80,000. But because deposits are up only $80,000, *required* reserves rise only 20 percent of this amount or $16,000. If the management of First National Bank behaves like that of Bank-a-mythica, the $64,000 of excess reserves will be lent out. Table 12–5 shows the effects of these events on First National Bank's balance sheet. (The preliminary steps corresponding to Tables 12–2 and 12–3 are not shown separately.) At this stage in the chain, the original $100,000 in cash has led to $180,000 in deposits—$100,000 at Bank-a-mythica and $80,000 at First National Bank—and $64,000 in cash, which is still in circulation (in the hands of the recipient of First National's loan—Al's Auto Shop). Thus, from the original $100,000, a total of $244,000 has been added to the money supply ($180,000 in checking deposits plus $64,000 in cash).

But, to coin a phrase, the bucks do not stop here. Al's Auto Shop will presumably deposit the proceeds from its loans into its own account at Second National Bank, leading eventually to the balance sheet adjustments shown in Table 12–6 when Second National makes an additional loan rather than hold on to excess reserves. You can see how the money-creation process continues.

Table 12–5
CHANGES IN FIRST NATIONAL BANK'S BALANCE SHEET

ASSETS		LIABILITIES	
Cash in vault	+ $16,000	Checking deposits	+ $80,000
Loans outstanding	+ 64,000		
Addendum: Changes in Reserves			
Actual reserves	+ $16,000		
Required reserves	+ 16,000		
Excess reserves	No change		

Hard-Pressed deposits its $80,000 in First National Bank, which sets aside the required $16,000 in reserves (20 percent of $80,000) and lends $64,000 to Al's Auto Shop.

Table 12–6
CHANGES IN SECOND NATIONAL BANK'S BALANCE SHEET

ASSETS		LIABILITIES	
Cash in vault	+ $12,800	Checking deposits	+ $64,000
Loans outstanding	+ 51,200		
Addendum: Changes in Reserves			
Actual reserves	+ $12,800		
Required reserves	+ 12,800		
Excess reserves	No change		

When Al deposits his $64,000 in Second National Bank, that bank retains $12,800 as required reserves (20 percent of $64,000) and lends out the remaining $51,200.

Table 12–7 adds up the balance-sheet changes of the first five banks in the chain (from Bank-a-mythica through the Fourth National Bank) on the assumptions that each bank holds exactly the 20 percent required reserves (no excess reserves), and that each loan recipient redeposits the proceeds in his own bank. At this stage, $336,160 in bank deposits have been created, and there is still $32,768 in cash circulating (the original $100,000 less $67,232 in cash in bank vaults), for a total increase in the money supply of $368,928.

But the chain does not end there. For the Main Street Movie Theater, which received the $32,768 loan from the Fourth National Bank, then deposits these funds into the Fifth National Bank. Fifth National has to keep only 20 percent of

---

Table 12–7
CHANGES IN THE COMBINED BALANCE SHEETS OF THE FIRST FIVE BANKS

ASSETS		LIABILITIES	
Cash in Vault		**Checking Deposits**	
Bank-a-mythica	+ $20,000	Bank-a-mythica	+ $100,000
First National Bank	+ 16,000	First National Bank	+ 80,000
Second National Bank	+ 12,800	Second National Bank	+ 64,000
Third National Bank	+ 10,240	Third National Bank	+ 51,200
Fourth National Bank	+ 8,192	Fourth National Bank	+ 40,960
Total	+ $67,232	Total	+ $336,160
Loans Outstanding			
Bank-a-mythica	+ $80,000		
First National Bank	+ 64,000		
Second National Bank	+ 51,200		
Third National Bank	+ 40,960		
Fourth National Bank	+ 32,768		
Total	+ $268,928		
Total change in assets	+ $336,160		

After five banks have participated, the chain of deposit creation looks like this. But there are still excess reserves in the system (held by Fifth National Bank), so the chain continues.

this deposit, or $6,553.60, on reserve and will lend out the balance. And so the chain continues.

What are the final effects on the money supply? If you look carefully at the three sections of Table 12–7, you will see that each column of numbers forms a *geometric progression*; specifically, each entry is equal to exactly 80 percent of the entry that preceded it. Recall that in the discussion of the multiplier in Chapter 10 we learned how to sum an infinite geometric progression, which is just what each of these chains eventually will be. In particular, if the common ratio is R, the sum of an infinite geometric progression is

$$1 + R + R^2 + R^3 + \ldots = \frac{1}{1 - R}.$$

By applying this formula to the chain of checking deposits on the right-hand side of Table 12–7, we get:

$$
\begin{aligned}
&\$100{,}000 + \$80{,}000 + \$64{,}000 + \$51{,}200 + \ldots \\
&= \$100{,}000 \times (1 + 0.8 + 0.64 + 0.512 + \ldots) \\
&= \$100{,}000 \times (1 + 0.8 + 0.8^2 + 0.8^3 + \ldots) \\
&= \$100{,}000 \times \frac{1}{1 - 0.8} = \frac{\$100{,}000}{0.2} = \$500{,}000.
\end{aligned}
$$

So eventually the original $100,000 in cash will support $500,000 in new checking deposits—a multiple expansion of $5 for every one original dollar. Table 12–8 shows the ultimate effect of the entire chain of deposit creation on the balance sheet of the banking system as a whole. The banks have converted $100,000 in cash into $500,000 in checking deposits.

Notice that 5 is the reciprocal of 20 percent (that is, $5 = 1/0.2$). This suggests the general formula for multiple deposit creation when the required reserve ratio is some number other than 20 percent:

OVERSIMPLIFIED FORMULA FOR MULTIPLE DEPOSIT CREATION
If the required reserve ratio is some fraction, R, an injection of $1 of reserves into the banking system can lead to the creation of $1/R$ in new deposits. That is:

$$\frac{\text{Change in deposits}}{\text{Change in reserves}} = \frac{1}{R}.$$

Table 12–8
CHANGES IN COMBINED BALANCE SHEET OF THE ENTIRE BANKING SYSTEM

ASSETS		LIABILITIES	
Cash in vault	+$100,000	Checking deposits	+$500,000
Loans outstanding	+ 400,000		
		Addendum: Change in Money Supply	
Addendum: Changes in Reserves		Demand deposits	+$500,000
Actual reserves	+$100,000	Currency outside banks	− 100,000
Required reserves	+ 100,000	Net change	+$400,000
Excess reserves	No change		

By the end of the chain of deposit creation, the entire $100,000 of cash has found its way into bank vaults, where it can support $500,000 in deposits. No excess reserves remain; and the money supply has expanded by $400,000.

While we have derived this result in a rather mechanical fashion, there is a simple piece of logic behind it. If banks want to hold only the legal minimum in cash reserves, then an injection of $1 in new reserves into the banking system must induce them to expand their loans until *required* reserves have risen by $1. Only then will all *excess* reserves have been eliminated.

But if each dollar of deposits requires only a fraction R ($\frac{1}{5}$ in our example) of a dollar in reserves, then deposits must expand by $1/R$ for each dollar of new reserves. This is the common sense behind the deposit-creation formula.

There is another way to state the same result that focuses attention more directly on the money supply. Notice in Table 12–8 that the *money supply* only grew by $400,000, not by $500,000. The reason is that the original $100,000 had been part of the money supply before it was deposited in Bank-a-mythica. While the checking deposit component of the money supply was growing by $500,000, the cash component of the money supply was shrinking by $100,000, leaving a net increase of $400,000.

The way to analyze this in terms of our deposit-creation formula is as follows. When the widower originally deposited $100,000 in cash into his checking account, he created *excess reserves* of $80,000—his $100,000 deposit less the $20,000 in reserves that Bank-a-mythica had to hold against it. This $80,000 in *excess* reserves led to an expansion of the *money supply* by $80,000 × 5 = $400,000. Thus, in our example, the banking system increased the money supply by $5 for each $1 in *excess* reserves it received. The general result when the required reserve ratio is R, rather than 20 percent, is:

OVERSIMPLIFIED FORMULA FOR MONEY CREATION
If the required reserve ratio is R, then an injection of $1 of *excess* reserves into the banking system leads to the creation of $1/R$ in new money. That is:

$$\frac{\text{Change in money supply}}{\text{Change in excess reserves}} = \frac{1}{R}.$$

Thus, to figure out what any event does to the money supply (rather than to deposits), we must ask two questions. First, what does it do to the banking system's *excess* reserves? Second, what is the deposit multiplier (the reciprocal of the required reserve ratio)? Multiplying the change in *excess* reserves by the reciprocal of the reserve ratio will give us our answer.

The Process in Reverse: Multiple Contractions of the Money Supply

Let us now briefly consider how this deposit-creation mechanism operates in reverse—as a system of deposit *destruction*. In particular, suppose that our eccentric widower came back to Bank-a-mythica to withdraw $100,000 from his checking account and return it to his mattress, where it rightfully belongs. Bank-a-mythica's *required* reserves would fall by $20,000 as a result of this transaction (20 percent of $100,000), but its *actual* reserves would fall by $100,000. The bank would be $80,000 short, as indicated in Table 12–9(a).

How does it react to this discrepancy? As some of its outstanding loans are routinely paid off, the bank will cease granting new ones until it has accumulated the necessary $80,000 in required reserves. The data for Bank-a-mythica's contraction are shown in Table 12–9(b), assuming that borrowers pay off their

Table 12-9
CHANGES IN THE BALANCE SHEET OF BANK-A-MYTHICA

(a)				(b)		
ASSETS		LIABILITIES		ASSETS		LIABILITIES
Cash in vault	−$100,000	Checking		Cash in vault	+$80,000	
		deposits −$100,000		Loans		
Addendum: Changes in Reserves				outstanding − 80,000		
Actual reserves	−$100,000			**Addendum: Changes in Reserves**		
Required reserves	− 20,000			Actual reserves	+$80,000	
Excess reserves	−$ 80,000			Required reserves	No change	
				Excess reserves	+$80,000	

When Bank-a-mythica loses a $100,000 deposit, it must reduce its loans by $80,000 to replenish its reserves.

loans in cash.[2] But where did the borrowers get this money? Probably by making withdrawals from other banks. In this case, let us assume it all came from First National Bank, which loses an $80,000 deposit and $80,000 in reserves. It finds itself short some $64,000 in reserves [see Table 12–10(a)] and therefore must reduce its loan commitments by $64,000 [see Table 12–10(b)]. This, of course, causes some other bank to suffer a loss of reserves and deposits of $64,000, and the whole process repeats just as it did in the case of deposit expansion. After five banks had become involved, the picture would be just as shown in Table 12–7, except that all the *plus* signs would be *minus* signs. And the final results are just the mirror image of Table 12–8. Deposits shrink by $500,000, loans fall by $400,000, bank reserves are reduced by $100,000, and the money supply falls by $400,000.

During the height of the radical student movement of the late 1960s, a circular appeared in Cambridge, Massachusetts, urging citizens to withdraw all funds from their checking accounts on a prescribed date, hold them in cash for

---

[2]In reality, they would probably pay with checks drawn on other banks. Bank-a-mythica would then cash these checks to acquire the reserves.

Table 12-10
CHANGES IN THE BALANCE SHEET OF FIRST NATIONAL BANK

(a)				(b)		
ASSETS		LIABILITIES		ASSETS		LIABILITIES
Cash in vault	−$80,000	Checking		Cash in vault	+$64,000	
		deposits −$80,000		Loans		
Addendum: Changes in Reserves				outstanding − 64,000		
Actual reserves	−$80,000			**Addendum: Changes in Reserves**		
Required reserves	− 16,000			Actual reserves	+$64,000	
Excess reserves	−$64,000			Required reserves	No change	
				Excess reserves	+$64,000	

First National Bank's loss of an $80,000 deposit forces it to cut back its loans by $64,000.

one week, and then redeposit them. This act, the circular argued, would surely wreak havoc upon the capitalist system. Obviously, some of these radicals were well-schooled in modern money mechanics, for the argument was basically correct. The tremendous multiple contraction of the banking system and consequent multiple expansion that a successful campaign of this sort could have caused might have disrupted the local financial system quite seriously. But history records that the appeal met with little success. Checking-account withdrawals are not the stuff of which revolutions are made.

Why the Money Creation Formula Is Oversimplified

So far, our discussion of the process of money creation has made it all seem rather mechanical. If all proceeds according to formula, each $1 in new reserves will lead to a $1/R increase in the money supply. But in reality things are not this simple. Just as we did in the case of the expenditure multiplier, we must stress that the oversimplified formula for money creation is accurate only under very particular circumstances. These circumstances require that:

1. Every recipient of a bank loan must redeposit the proceeds of that loan into another bank rather than hold it in cash.
2. Every bank must hold reserves no larger than the legal minimum.

Let us see what happens to the chain of deposit creation when either of these assumptions is violated.

Suppose first that the business firms and individuals who receive bank loans decide not to redeposit all of the proceeds into their bank accounts. For example, Hard-Pressed Construction Company and all the other borrowers might decide to hold half of their loan proceeds in cash and deposit only the remaining half. Then First National Bank would receive only a $40,000 deposit, and could, therefore, make only a $32,000 loan. Second National Bank would then receive only $16,000 (half of $32,000), and so on. The whole chain of deposit creation would be reduced drastically. Thus:

If individuals and business firms decide to hold more cash, the multiple expansion of the money supply will be curtailed because fewer dollars of cash will be available in bank vaults to be used as reserves to support new checking deposits. Consequently, the money supply will be smaller.

Normally, people's demands for cash fluctuate between narrow boundaries and are easily predictable. For instance, people always want more cash during the Christmas shopping season. But during the banking panics that occurred periodically in the days before universal deposit insurance, the public's propensity to hold cash would almost invariably rise dramatically. We now understand how this could cause a violent contraction of the money supply.

Next, suppose that Bank-a-mythica's management becomes very conservative, or that the outlook for loan repayments worsens because of a recession. The bank might then decide to keep more reserves than the legal requirement (say, $33\frac{1}{3}$ percent) and lend out less than the $80,000 assumed in Table 12–4 (say, $66,667). If this happens, then First National Bank will receive a smaller injection of cash reserves than that shown in Table 12–5. And if First National's management is as jittery as Bank-a-mythica's, it too will hold more in reserves and lend out less. Thus:

If banks wish to keep excess reserves, the multiple expansion of the money supply will be restricted. A given amount of cash will support a smaller supply of money than would be the case if banks held no excess reserves.

The Need for Monetary Control

If we pursue this point a bit further, we will see why government regulation of the money supply is so important for economic stability. We have just suggested that banks will wish to keep excess reserves when they do not foresee profitable and secure opportunities to make loans. This is likely to happen during the downswing and around the bottom of a business contraction. If it occurs, the propensity of banks to hold excess reserves will turn the money-creation process into one of money destruction.

During a recession, profit-oriented banks would be prone to reduce the money supply by increasing their excess reserves if the monetary authorities did not intervene. Since, as we will learn in subsequent chapters, the money supply is an important influence on aggregate demand, such a contraction of the money supply would exacerbate the severity of the recession.

On the other hand, banks will want to squeeze the maximum possible money supply out of any given amount of cash reserves by keeping their reserves at the bare minimum when the demand for bank loans is buoyant, profits are high, and many investments suddenly start to look profitable. This reduced incentive to hold excess reserves in prosperous times means that:

During an economic boom, the behavior of profit-oriented banks is likely to make the money supply expand, adding undesirable momentum to the booming economy and paving the way for a burst of inflation. The authorities must intervene to prevent this.

Regulation of the money supply, then, is necessary because bankers, in the pursuit of profit, might otherwise provide the economy with a wildly gyrating money supply that dances to the tune of the business cycle. Precisely how the authorities can keep the money supply under control is the subject of the next chapter.

Summary

1. It is much more efficient to exchange goods and services by using money as a medium of exchange than by bartering them directly.

2. In addition to being the medium of exchange, whatever serves as money is likely to become the standard unit of account and a popular store of value.

3. Throughout history, all sorts of things have served as money. Commodity moneys gave way to full-bodied paper money (certificates backed 100 percent by some commodity, like gold), which in turn gave way to partially backed paper money. Nowadays our paper money has no commodity backing whatsoever: that is, it is pure fiat money.

4. The most widely used definition of the U.S. money supply is M1, which includes coins, paper money, and checking deposits. However, many economists prefer to work with an M2 definition, which adds to M1 most savings deposits and several other items.

5. Under our modern system of fractional reserve banking, banks keep cash reserves equal to only a fraction of their total deposit liabilities. This is the key to their profitability, since their remaining funds can be loaned out at interest. But it also leaves them potentially vulnerable to runs.

6. Because of this vulnerability, bank managers are generally very conservative in their investment strategy, and they also like to keep a prudent level of reserves. Even so, the government keeps a watchful eye over banking practices.

7. Before 1933, bank failures were quite common; but they are rare events today. Many observers attribute this development to deposit insurance.

8. Because it holds only fractional reserves, even a single bank can create money. But its ability to do so is severely limited because the funds it lends out probably will be deposited in another bank.

9. As a whole, the banking system can create several dollars of deposits for each dollar of cash reserves it receives. Under certain assumptions, the ratio of new deposits to new reserves will be $1/R$, where R is the required reserve ratio.

10. The same process works in reverse, as a system of money destruction, when cash is withdrawn from the banking system.

11. Because banks and individuals may want to hold more cash when the economy is shaky, the money supply would probably contract under such circumstances if the monetary authorities did not intervene. Similarly, the money supply would probably expand rapidly in boom times if it were unregulated.

Concepts for Review

Run on a bank
Barter
Double coincidence of wants
Money
Medium of exchange
Store of value
Commodity money

Fiat money
M1 versus M2
Liquidity
Fractional reserve banking
Deposit insurance
Federal Deposit Insurance
 Corporation (FDIC)

Reserve requirements
Asset
Liability
Balance sheet
Deposit creation
Excess reserves

Questions for Discussion

1. If ours were a barter economy, how would you pay your tuition bill? What if your college did not want the goods or services you offered in payment?

2. How is "money" defined, both conceptually and in practice? Does the U.S. money supply consist of commodity money, full-bodied paper money, or fiat money?

3. What is fractional reserve banking, and why is it the key to bank profits? (*Hint:* What opportunities to make profits would banks have if reserve requirements were 100 percent?) Why does fractional reserve banking give bankers discretion over how large the money supply will be? Why does it make banks potentially vulnerable to runs?

4. Do you hold a checking account in a bank? If so, what will happen to your account if the bank goes bankrupt?

5. Suppose that no banks keep excess reserves and no individuals or firms hold on to cash. If someone suddenly discovers $1 million in buried treasure, explain what will happen to the money supply if the required reserve ratio is one-sixth (16.67 percent).

6. How would your answer to Question 5 differ if the reserve ratio were 25 percent? If the reserve ratio were 100 percent?

7. Each year during the Christmas shopping season, consumers and stores wish to increase their holdings of cash. Explain how this could lead to a multiple contraction of the money supply. (As a matter of fact, the authorities prevent this contraction from occurring by methods explained in the next chapter.)

8. Excess reserves make a bank less vulnerable to runs. Why, then, don't bankers like to hold excess reserves? What circumstances might persuade them that it would be advisable to hold excess reserves?

Central Banking and Monetary Policy

13

Victorians heard with grave attention that the Bank Rate had been raised. They did not know what it meant. But they knew that it was an act of extreme wisdom.

J.K. GALBRAITH

From what we learned in Chapter 12 about the normal practices of profit-oriented banks we might expect the money supply to expand rapidly during prosperous times and to grow sluggishly, or even to shrink, during recessions. Fortunately, the historical record for the postwar United States does not exhibit this pattern. Why not? One reason is that America's *central bank*, the *Federal Reserve System*, has prevented it from happening.

The "Fed," as it is often called, is a bank, but a very special kind of bank. Its customers are banks rather than individuals, and it performs some of the same services for them as your bank peforms for you. Though it turns out to be quite an effective profit maker, its actions are not guided by the profit motive. Instead, the Fed acts in what it perceives to be the national interest. While its actions are certainly not free from error, and while many people do not share its view of what constitutes the national interest, the Fed's actions have by and large caused the money supply to be a stabilizing influence on the U.S. economy. Just how the Fed regulates the money supply, and why its peformance has fallen short of perfection, are the main subjects of this chapter.

The Federal Reserve System: Origins and Structure

When the **Federal Reserve System** was established in 1914, the United States joined the company of most of the other advanced industrial nations. Up until then, the United States was almost the only modern economic power without a **central bank;** Britain's central bank, the Bank of England, for example, dates from 1694.

The impetus for the establishment of a central bank in the United States came not from the power of economic logic but from some painful experiences with economic reality. Four severe banking panics between 1873 and 1907 convinced legislators and bankers alike that a central bank that would regulate credit conditions was not a luxury but a necessity. After the 1907 crisis, the National Monetary Commission was established to find out just what was wrong with America's banking system. Its report in early 1912 led directly to the establishment of the Federal Reserve System.

Although the basic idea of central banking came from Europe, some changes

A **central bank** is a bank for banks. America's central bank is the **Federal Reserve System.**

were made when it was imported, making the Federal Reserve System a uniquely American institution. Owing to the vastness of our country, the extraordinarily large number of commercial banks, and our tradition of dual state–federal regulations, it was decided that the United States should have not one central bank but 12. The boundaries of the 12 Federal Reserve districts and the location of each of the 12 district banks are shown in Figure 13–1.

Technically, each of the Federal Reserve banks is a corporation; its stockholders are the banks that belong to it. But your bank, if it is a member of the System, does not enjoy the privileges normally accorded to stockholders: it receives only a token share of the Federal Reserve's immense profits (the bulk is donated to the U.S. Treasury), and it has no say in the decisions of the corporation. The private banks are more like customers of the Fed than like owners.

Who, then, controls the Fed? Most of the power resides in the seven-member Board of Governors of the Federal Reserve System, headquartered in Washington, and especially in its chairman, who is now Paul Volcker, an economist. Members of the board are appointed by the president of the United States, with the advice and consent of the Senate, for 14-year terms. The president also designates one of the members to serve a four-year term as chairman of the board, and thus to be the most powerful central banker in the world; for the United States differs from many other countries in that the Federal Reserve Board, once appointed by the president, is *independent* of the rest of the government. So long as it stays within the statutory authority delineated by Congress, it alone has responsibility for determining the nation's monetary policy. Closely allied with the Board of Governors is the powerful **Federal Open Market Committee (FOMC),** which meets periodically in Washington. For reasons to be explained in this chapter, the decisions of the FOMC largely determine the size of the U.S. money

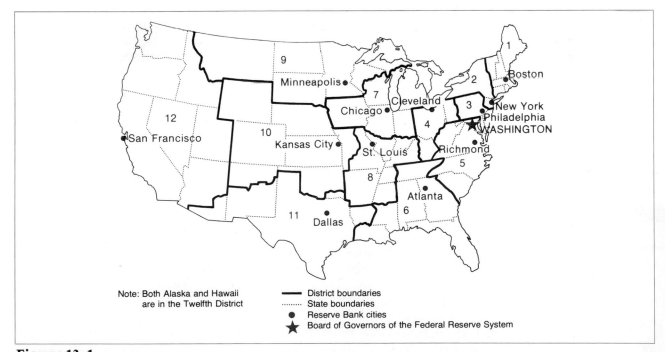

Figure 13–1
THE TWELVE FEDERAL RESERVE DISTRICTS
This map shows the boundaries of the 12 Federal Reserve districts and the locations of the 12 Federal Reserve banks. In which Federal Reserve district do you live?

supply. This 12-member committee consists of the seven governors of the Federal Reserve System and the presidents of five of the district banks.

The Independence of the Fed

The institutional independence of the Federal Reserve System is looked upon as a source of pride by some and as an antidemocratic embarrassment by others. The proponents of Federal Reserve independence argue that it enables monetary policy decisions to be made on objective, technical criteria and keeps monetary control out of the "political thicket." Without this independence, it is argued, there would be a tendency for politicians to force the Fed to expand the money supply too rapidly, thereby contributing to chronic inflation and undermining faith in America's financial system.

Opponents of this view counter that there is something profoundly undemocratic about having a group of unelected bankers and economists make decisions that affect the well-being of 225 million Americans. Monetary policy, they argue, ought to be formulated by the elected representatives of the people, just like fiscal policy. Those who argue for executive or congressional control over the Fed can point to historical instances in which monetary and fiscal policy have been at loggerheads—with the Fed undoing or even overwhelming the effects of fiscal policy decisions.

There is plenty of middle ground between the two extremes. One less drastic proposal, advocated by President Jimmy Carter while a candidate in 1976, would simply shift the term of the chairman of the Federal Reserve Board to make it coincide with that of the president. As things stand today, a newly elected president must retain the chairman that his predecessor appointed whether or not he agrees with his policies.

Another suggested reform would require the Fed to announce its ultimate targets for unemployment and inflation and explain how it expects its monetary policy actions to promote these goals. An extreme version of this proposal would require that the Fed adhere to the goals of the administration or of Congress. But a softer version simply would require that the Fed announce its own goals and subject them to public scrutiny. A small step in this direction was taken in 1975 when the Fed, in response to congressional wishes, began announcing "ranges of tolerance" for growth rates of the money supply (by several definitions!). That is, the chairman of the Federal Reserve Board now periodically tells Congress *in advance* what the maximum and minimum permissible growth rates for the money stock are in the coming months.

How people view these and other reform proposals that revolve around the issue of the Fed's independence depends on how they perceive the office. Are governors of the Federal Reserve System akin to judges, and therefore, at least in principle, best thought of as nonpartisan and independent technocrats? The 14-year terms of office certainly suggest an analogy to the judiciary, but the board's role is most assuredly one that involves policy making, not just "impartial" interpretation of the law. Or are the governors more like members of the Cabinet, that is, policy-making officials who should properly serve only at the pleasure of the president? Since neither analogy fits precisely, the issue is a vexing one.

Controlling the Money Supply: Reserve Requirements

Chapter 12 taught us one important way in which the monetary authorities influence and, with a little luck, control the nation's money supply: that is, by

Table 13–1

BALANCE SHEET OF MIDDLE AMERICAN BANK, October 25, 1982

ASSETS		LIABILITIES AND NET WORTH	
Reserves	$ 200,000	Checking deposits	$1,000,000
Loans outstanding	1,000,000	Net worth	200,000
Total assets	$1,200,000	Total liabilities plus net worth	$1,200,000

If the required reserve ratio is 20 percent, Middle American Bank holds exactly its required reserves on October 25, 1982—no more and no less. However, if the reserve ratio falls to 15 percent, its required reserves will fall to only $150,000 (15 percent of $1 million), and it will have $50,000 in excess reserves.

varying the minimum required reserve ratio. To see how this works, consider the balance sheet of a hypothetical bank shown in Table 13–1. If the minimum required reserve ratio is 20 percent, and the bank wishes to hold only the legal minimum in reserves, Middle American Bank is in equilibrium on October 25, 1982. Its $1 million in checking deposits mean that its required reserves amount to $200,000, which just matches its actual reserves. Excess reserves are zero.

Now suppose that the Federal Reserve Board decides that the money supply needs to be increased. One action it can take is to lower the required reserve ratio. As an exaggerated example, suppose it reduces reserve requirements to 15 percent of deposits. Middle American Bank's balance sheet is unaffected by this action, but the bank's managers are sure to react to it. For now required reserves are only $150,000 (15 percent of $1 million), so the bank is holding $50,000 in excess reserves—funds that are earning no interest for the bank. The effect is the same as if a new depositor had brought in cash: The bank now has more money to lend. Once it lends out this $50,000, its balance sheet will be as shown in Table 13–2; it now holds $50,000 less in reserves and $50,000 more in loans.

Although no new deposits are created by this transaction, we know from the previous chapter that the wheels of a multiple expansion of the banking system have been set in motion. For the recipient of the loan will deposit the proceeds in his own bank, giving that bank excess reserves and, therefore, the ability to grant more loans, and so on.

It is not hard for the Fed to estimate the extent to which the money supply will expand as a result of a change in the reserve ratio.[1] But *estimating* the ultimate monetary expansion is a far cry from *knowing it* with certainty. As we know from Chapter 12, the simple deposit-creation formula is predicated on the

[1] We know from the last chapter that each dollar of bank reserves can support $1/R$ dollars of checking deposits if the fraction R is the required reserve ratio. When R is lowered from 20 percent to 15 percent, this number rises from $1/0.20 = 5$ to $1/0.15 = 6.67$. So the demand–deposit component of the money supply should increase by about one-third (6.67 is one-third larger than 5).

Table 13–2

BALANCE SHEET OF MIDDLE AMERICAN BANK, October 26, 1982

ASSETS		LIABILITIES AND NET WORTH	
Reserves	$ 150,000	Checking deposits	$1,000,000
Loans outstanding	1,050,000	Net worth	200,000
Total assets	$1,200,000	Total liabilities plus net worth	$1,200,000

If Middle American Bank does not wish to hold excess reserves, its balance sheet will look like this after it loans out the extra $50,000 in excess reserves. At this point, it once again has no excess reserves.

assumptions that people will want to hold no more cash and that banks will want to hold no more excess reserves as the monetary expansion proceeds. In practice, these assumptions are unlikely to be literally true. So, if the Fed is to predict the eventual effect of its action on the money supply correctly, it must estimate both the amount that firms and individuals will want to add to their currency holdings and the amount that banks will want to add to their excess reserves. Neither of these can be estimated with great precision.

By lowering required reserve ratios, the central bank can increase the money supply. But, because of fluctuations in people's desires to hold cash and banks' desires to hold excess reserves, it cannot predict the consequences of these actions with perfect accuracy. Thus, over short periods, control over the money supply must of necessity be imperfect.

It does not take much imagination to see what the Fed must do to reserve requirements when it wants to engineer a *contraction* of the money supply. If banks are not holding excess reserves, an increase in the required reserve ratio will force them to contract their loans and deposits until their reserve deficiencies are corrected. Of course, if banks do have sufficient excess reserves, they can flout the Fed's wishes. But the Fed normally will be trying to rein in the money supply when the economy is booming, and these are precisely the times when banks will not want to hold more idle reserves than they have to.

In fact, the Fed does not rely much on the reserve ratio as a weapon of monetary control. Legislation passed in 1980 (but not fully effective until 1987) provides for a basic reserve ratio of 12 percent against checking deposits. This ratio is not expected to change frequently.

Controlling the Money Supply: Open Market Operations

Open market operations refer to the Fed's purchase or sale of government securities through transactions in the open market.

Partly for historical reasons, the Fed normally relies on what are called **open market operations** to manipulate the money supply. Whereas changes in reserve ratios leave the banks with either excess or deficient reserves by changing the legal requirements, open market operations have the effect of giving the banks more cash or taking cash away from them.

How does this work? Suppose the Federal Open Market Committee decides that the money supply is too low. It can issue instructions that the money supply be expanded through operations in the open market. Specifically, this means that the Federal Reserve System *purchases* U.S. government securities (generally short-term securities called "Treasury bills") from any individual or bank that wishes to sell, thus putting more reserves in the hands of the banks.[2] An example will illustrate the mechanics of open market operations. Suppose the order is to purchase $100 million worth of securities, and that commercial banks are the sellers. *The Fed makes payment by giving the banks $100 million in new reserves.* So, if they held only the required amount of reserves initially, the banks now have $100 million in excess reserves, as shown in Table 13–3. This will induce a multiple expansion of the banking system in the usual way.

Where does the Fed get the money that it gives to the banks in return for the securities? It could pay in cash, but normally does not. Instead, it manufactures

[2]In fact, the Fed almost always deals with one of a small group of dealers who "make a market" in government securities. However, this is an institutional detail that has no effect on the basic principles. The dealers are simply intermediaries, intervening between the ultimate buyer (the Fed) and the ultimate seller.

Table 13–3

EFFECTS OF AN OPEN MARKET PURCHASE OF SECURITIES
ON THE BALANCE SHEETS OF BANKS AND THE FED

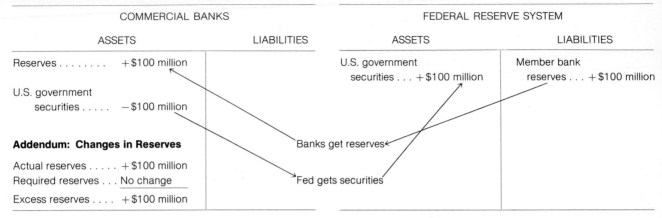

COMMERCIAL BANKS		FEDERAL RESERVE SYSTEM	
ASSETS	LIABILITIES	ASSETS	LIABILITIES
Reserves . . . . +$100 million		U.S. government securities . . . +$100 million	Member bank reserves . . . +$100 million
U.S. government securities . . . . . −$100 million			
Addendum: Changes in Reserves		Banks get reserves	
Actual reserves . . . . . +$100 million			
Required reserves . . . No change		Fed gets securities	
Excess reserves . . . . +$100 million			

When the Fed buys $100 million worth of securities from the banks, it adds this amount to the bookkeeping entries that represent the banks' accounts at the Fed (called "member bank reserves"). Since deposits have not increased at all, required reserves are unchanged by this transaction. But actual reserves are increased by $100 million, so there are $100 million in excess reserves. This will trigger a multiple expansion of the banking system.

the funds out of thin air, or, more literally, out of pen and ink. Specifically, the Fed pays the banks for the securities by adding the appropriate sums to the accounts that the banks maintain at the Fed. Balances held in these accounts constitute bank reserves, just like cash in bank vaults. While this process of creating bookkeeping entries at the Federal Reserve is commonly referred to as "printing money," the Fed does not literally run the printing presses. Instead, it simply exchanges its IOUs for an existing asset (a government security). But unlike your IOUs, the Fed's IOUs constitute legal bank reserves, and thus are the equivalent of cash in their ability to support a multiple expansion of the money supply. The banks, not the Fed, actually increase the money supply; but the Fed's actions give the banks the wherewithal to do it. To summarize briefly:

When the Federal Reserve System wants to increase the money supply, it purchases U.S. government securities in the open market. It pays for these securities by creating new bank reserves, and these additional reserves lead to a multiple expansion of the money supply.

The procedures followed when the FOMC wants to *contract* the money supply are just the opposite of those we have just explained. In brief, it orders a *sale* of government securities in the open market. This takes reserves *away* from banks, since banks pay for the securities by drawing down their deposits at the Fed. A multiple *contraction* of the banking system ensues. The principles are exactly the same as when the process operates in reverse.

In discussing reserve requirements, we emphasized that the Fed cannot know for sure how great an expansion of the money supply will be caused by a given change in legal reserve ratios. The same is true of changes in the Fed's holdings of government securities accomplished through operations in the open market—and for the same reasons. The Fed can control bank *reserves* very precisely through open market purchases and sales; but it can only rely on its past experience to *estimate* the ultimate effects of open market operations on the money supply. In normal times, these estimates are quite accurate (that, presumably, is the definition of "normal times"). But at other times banks may surprise the Fed by holding larger or smaller excess reserves than anticipated, or businesses and consumers may surprise it by holding more or less currency. In such cases, the Fed will not get the money supply it was shooting for, and will have to readjust its policies.

Controlling the Money Supply: Lending to Banks

When the Federal Reserve System was first established, its founders did not intend it to pursue an active monetary policy to stabilize the economy. Indeed, the basic ideas of economic stabilization policy were foreign at the time, dating only from Keynes's *General Theory of Employment, Interest, and Money* in 1936. Instead, the Fed's founders viewed it as a means of preventing the supplies of money and credit from drying up during economic contractions, as had happened so often in the pre-1914 period. One of the principal ways in which the Fed was to provide such insurance against financial panics was to act as a "lender of last resort." That is, when risky business prospects made commercial banks hesitant to extend new loans, the Fed would step in by lending money to the banks, thus inducing the banks to lend more money to their customers.

Loans from the Federal Reserve banks to individual commercial banks have existed from the very first days of the System. When the Fed extends borrowing privileges to a bank in need of reserves, that bank receives a credit in its deposit account at the Fed (see Table 13–4). This addition to bank reserves may lead to an expansion of the money supply; or it may eliminate a reserve deficiency, and thereby prevent a multiple contraction of the banking system. In either case, the Fed makes monetary conditions more expansive by making borrowing easier.

Federal Reserve officials regulate the volume of member bank borrowing in two ways. One is by setting the *rate of interest charged on these loans.* For historical reasons, this is called the "discount rate" in the United States. In most foreign countries, it is known as the "bank rate." If the Fed wants to give banks more reserves, it can reduce the interest rate that it charges, thereby tempting banks to borrow more. Alternatively, it can soak up reserves by raising its rate and persuading the banks to reduce their borrowings. While this type of *active*

Table 13–4
BALANCE SHEET CHANGES FOR BORROWING FROM THE FED

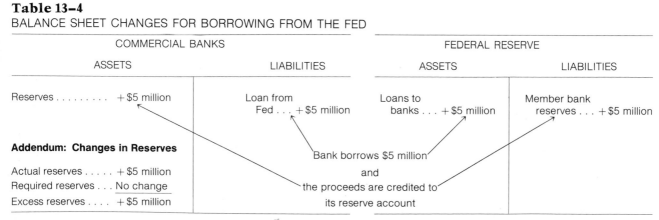

When the Fed lends $5 million to a bank, it simply adds this amount to the bookkeeping entry that represents that bank's account at the Fed. Once again, actual reserves increase while required reserves do not change (because commercial bank deposits have not changed). Hence this loan would be expected to initiate a multiple expansion of the banking system.

manipulation of the discount rate is practiced widely in foreign countries, where the bank rate is often the centerpiece of monetary policy, it is much less common in the United States, where the Fed usually relies on open market operations in conducting its monetary policy. More often the Fed adjusts its discount rate *passively* to keep it in line with market interest rates.

As in the case of changes in reserve requirements and open market operations, the Fed cannot know for sure how banks will react to changes in its lending rate. Sometimes they may respond vigorously to a cut in the rate, borrowing a great deal from the Fed and lending a correspondingly large amount to their customers. At other times they may essentially ignore the Fed's actions. The link between the lending rate and the money supply is, at times, a very loose one.

Often, though, the Fed tries to tighten this link by using its second way of controlling the volume of bank borrowing—**moral suasion.** This phrase refers to some not-so-subtle methods that the Fed has for letting banks know when it thinks they are borrowing too much. Since banks are anxious to maintain the good will of the Fed, they often respond to warnings that they have overused their borrowing privileges—especially when such warnings are accompanied by a veiled threat that these privileges might be suspended if the offending bank does not mend its ways. As the Fed often reminds the banks, borrowing is "a privilege, not a right."

Tightening Monetary Control: Some Suggested Reforms

The fact that each of the Federal Reserve's principal instruments of monetary control is somewhat imperfect has led to a number of suggested reforms designed to improve the System's ability to regulate the supply of money.

Because banks' discretion over the amount of reserves they hold (subject only to the legal minimums) makes the link between changes in Federal Reserve policy and changes in the money supply rather slippery, some economists would like to see a return to a system of 100 percent reserve requirements. Under such a rule, no bank could add to or subtract from its excess reserves because there would never be any excess reserves. Each dollar of bank reserves would support exactly one dollar of deposits, no more and no less; so there would be no such thing as a multiple expansion or contraction of the banking system. The Fed can now control bank reserves with great precision; and under a system of 100 percent reserve requirements its control over the money supply would be equally precise.

While such a change in banking regulations undoubtedly would make the Fed's job easier, it also would change the face of banking in dramatic and possibly unpredictable ways. It will be recalled from Chapter 12 that banking as we know it today evolved from that first goldsmith's momentous discovery that he could get along with only fractional reserves. This discovery has been the mainspring of bank profits ever since. Abolition of fractional reserve banking should therefore be viewed as a major overhaul of the financial system. This does not necessarily mean that it is a bad idea, only that it should be approached with some caution.

A less dramatic reform aimed at tightening the link between bank reserves and the money supply is to require all banks to keep the same required reserves as those banks that are members of the Federal Reserve System. After much discussion, this idea was enacted into law in 1980 and is currently being phased in over a period of years. Once fully effective, it will improve the Fed's ability to control the money supply because movements of deposits from one class of bank (members of the Fed) to another (nonmembers) will no longer change required (and hence excess) reserves.

Finally, some observers have suggested that lending to banks, far from aiding the Fed's monetary control, actually undermines it, and therefore the Fed should stop lending except in emergency cases. Their reasoning is as follows. When the Fed tries to force a contraction of the banking system, some banks may resist this desire by borrowing the reserves they need. Similarly, some banks may relinquish reserves to pay back loans just when the Fed wants the money supply to expand. No doubt this occasionally happens. But there are also occasions when Federal Reserve lending is a valuable supplement to open market policy. Since it is by no means clear that monetary control would be tighter if lending were abolished, the Fed is understandably reluctant to give up one of its major traditional weapons.

The Money Supply Mechanism: A Summary

This completes our discussion of the Fed's methods of controlling the money supply and the limitations of these methods. We can now begin to integrate what we have just learned about the financial system into the macroeconomic model presented in Chapters 8 through 11, and to study how money affects the national economy. For this purpose, the analyses of the last chapter and the present one can be summed up in the following statement:

As interest rates rise, banks normally find it more profitable to expand their volume of loans and deposits, thus increasing the supply of money. This poses the danger that the money supply might expand rapidly during a period of inflation and economic boom and advance slowly, or even contract, during a period of recession—just the opposite from what stabilization policy requires. However, the Fed can shift the relationship between the money supply and interest rates by employing any of its principal weapons of monetary control: open market operations, changes in reserve requirements, or changes in lending policy to banks.

These ideas are depicted graphically in Figure 13–2. Figure 13–2(a) shows a typical money supply schedule labeled MS, illustrating the fact that bank behavior makes the money stock rise as interest rates rise. Notice that the sensitivity of the money supply to interest rates is rather weak in the diagram—a large rise in the rate of interest (from 7 percent to 9 percent) induces only a small increase in the supply of money (from \$440 billion to \$450 billion). The drawing is deliberately constructed that way because that is what the statistical evidence shows.

The curve in Figure 13–2(a) shows the money supply schedule corresponding to some specific monetary policy. Figure 13–2(b) portrays how the money supply schedule responds to an *expansionary change in monetary policy*, such as an open market purchase of government bonds, a reduction in reserve requirements, or a drop in the Fed's lending rate. The money supply schedule shifts outward from M_0S_0 to M_1S_1, as indicated by the arrows. After banks have adjusted to the change, there is more money at any given interest rate. Figure 13–2(c) shows what happens in the reverse case—*contractionary monetary policy*, such as an open market sale of securities, an increase in reserve requirements, or a rise in the lending rate. The money supply schedule shifts inward from M_0S_0 to M_2S_2.

As we have stressed, the diagrams make things look rather more precise than they actually are. Since the Fed's control over the money supply schedule is imperfect in the short run, the actual MS schedule is obscured by a bit of fog. In

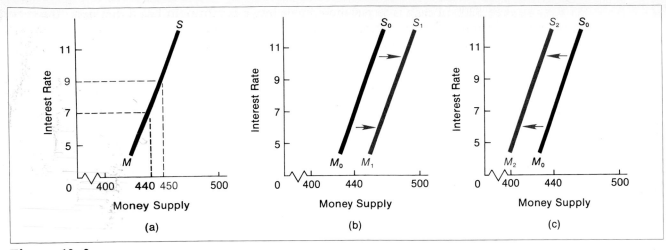

Figure 13–2

THE SUPPLY SCHEDULE FOR MONEY

Part (a) shows a typical supply schedule for money. It is rising as we move toward the right, meaning that banks will supply more money when interest rates are higher. Part (b) illustrates what happens to the money supply schedule when the Fed purchases securities in the open market, or lowers required reserves, or provides banks with more loans. The supply schedule shifts outward. Part (c) depicts the effect of using these same policy instruments in the opposite (contractionary) direction. The supply schedule shifts inward.

what follows, we portray all the graphs as clean straight lines only for pedagogical simplicity. The Fed wishes things were so simple in the real world!

The Demand for Money

Just as we must know something about both the supply of and the demand for wheat before we can predict how much will be sold and at what price, it is necessary to know something about the **demand for money** if we are to understand the amount of money actually in existence and the prevailing interest rate. The definition of money given in Chapter 12 suggests the most important reason why people hold money balances: the medium of exchange is needed to carry out purchases and sales of goods and services. Since the nominal gross national product (GNP) is considered to be the best measure of the total money value of all goods and services traded in the economy, it seems safe to say that the higher the nominal GNP, the higher will be the demand for money. And, indeed, an impressive amount of statistical evidence supports this supposition. Notice that nominal GNP, and hence the demand for money, rises if *either* real output *or* the price level rises—a fact that will assume some importance in the next chapter.

But income is not the only factor affecting the demand for money; interest rates matter, too. At first, that may seem surprising because many forms of money, such as currency and some checking deposits, pay no interest. Why, then, are interest rates relevant? They are relevant because money is only one of a variety of forms in which individuals can hold their wealth. Holders of money *give up* the opportunity to hold one of these other assets, such as government bonds, in order to gain the convenience of money. In so doing, they *give up* the interest that they could have earned on one of these alternative assets. This is another example of the concept of *opportunity cost*.[3] On the surface, it seems virtually costless to hold money. But, *compared with the next best alternative*, this action is not costless at all. For example, if the next best alternative to holding

[3]If you need to review this concept, see Chapter 3.

Velocity and the Quantity Theory of Money

We have now seen how money influences real output and the price level in the Keynesian model. But there is another way to look at these matters using a model that is much older and more traditional than the Keynesian model, and yet is at the heart of some very modern critiques of Keynesian economics. This model is known as the **quantity theory of money,** and it is easy to understand once we have introduced one new concept—*velocity*.

We learned in Chapter 12 that because barter is so cumbersome, virtually all economic transactions in advanced economies are conducted by the use of money. This means that if there are, say, $2500 billion worth of transactions in the economy during a particular year, and there is an average money stock of $500 billion during that year, then each dollar of money must get used an average of five times during the year (since 5 × $500 billion = $2500 billion). The number 5 in this example is called the **velocity of circulation,** or just **velocity** for short, because it indicates the speed at which money circulates. For example, a particular dollar bill might be paid by a firm to an employee in January; the employee might use it to buy a sweater in March; the storekeeper might then use it to pay his electric bill in May; the electric company could pay it out to a stockholder in October; and the stockholder might spend it on a Christmas present in December. This would mean that the dollar was used five times during the year. If it were used only four times during the year, its velocity would be only 4, and so on. Similarly, a $20 bill circulating with a velocity of 4 would be the monetary instrument used to finance $80 worth of transactions in that year.

Velocity indicates the number of times per year that an "average dollar" is spent on goods and services. It is the ratio of the nominal GNP to the number of dollars in the money stock. That is:

$$\text{Velocity} = \frac{\text{Nominal GNP}}{\text{Money stock}}.$$

As we noted in Chapter 13, the gross national product in current prices (nominal GNP) is the most widely used measure of the economy's total transactions (the number of dollars changing hands in a year). This measure leads to the specific definition of velocity found in the margin. Since nominal GNP is the product of real GNP times the price level, we can write this definition in symbols as:

$$V = \frac{P \times Y}{M}.$$

The **equation of exchange** states that the money value of GNP transactions must be equal to the product of the average stock of money times velocity. That is: $M \times V = P \times Y$.

By multiplying both sides of the equation by M, we arrive at an accounting identity called the **equation of exchange** that relates the money supply and nominal GNP:

$$\text{Money supply} \times \text{Velocity} = \text{Nominal GNP}.$$

Alternatively, stated in symbols, we have:

$$M \times V = P \times Y.$$

Here we have quite an obvious link between the stock of money, M, and the nominal value of the nation's output. But it is only a matter of arithmetic, not of economics. For example, it does not imply that the Fed can raise nominal GNP by increasing M. Why not? Because V might simultaneously fall by enough to prevent $M \times V$ from rising. That is, if there were more dollar bills in circulation than before, but each bill changed hands more slowly, total spending would not necessarily rise.

The *quantity theory of money* transforms the equation of exchange from an accounting identity into an economic model by assuming that changes in velocity are so minor that, for practical purposes, velocity can be taken to be a constant.

You can see that if V never changed, then it would be useful to turn the equation of exchange around to read,

$$P \times Y = V \times M$$

which would be a very simple economic model of income determination. It would say, for example, that if the Federal Reserve wanted to increase nominal GNP by 12.7 percent, it need only raise the money supply by 12.7 percent. In such a simple world, economists could use the equation of exchange to *predict* nominal GNP simply by predicting the quantity of money. And policymakers could *control* nominal GNP simply by controlling the money supply. In the real world things are not so simple, because velocity is not a fixed number. But this does not necessarily vitiate the usefulness of the quantity theory. We explained in Chapter 1 why all economic models make assumptions that are at least mildly unrealistic—without such assumptions they would not be models at all, just tedious descriptions of reality. The question is really whether the assumption of constant velocity is a useful abstraction from annoying detail or a gross distortion of facts.

Figure 14–5 sheds some light on this question by showing the behavior of velocity since 1929. You will undoubtedly notice a downward trend in the graph

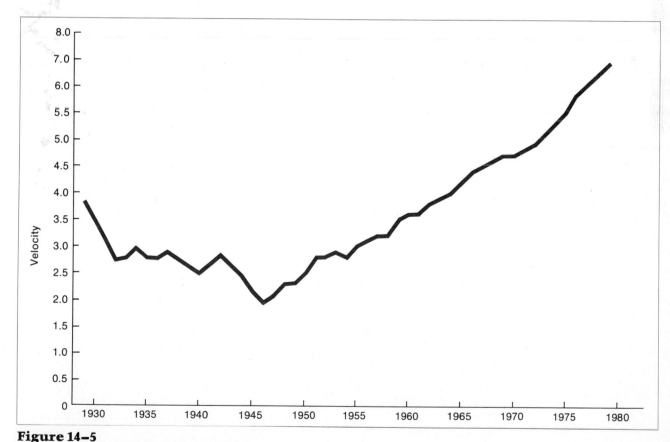

Figure 14–5
VELOCITY OF CIRCULATION, 1929–1980
During a period of American history of over 50 years, velocity fell from 3.5 in 1930 to about 2 in 1946, and since then has risen to over 6.5. Quite clearly velocity is not constant over long periods of time.
SOURCE: Constructed by the authors; data from Bureau of Economic Analysis and Federal Reserve Board.

from 1929 until 1946, and an upward trend thereafter. Quite clearly, *velocity is not constant over long periods of time.* Closer examination of monthly or quarterly data reveals some rather substantial fluctuations of velocity about its trend. Such fluctuations have led most economists to the conclusion that *velocity is not constant in the short run either.* Nor have predictions of nominal GNP based on the product of *V* times *M* fared very well. It seems, then, that the strict quantity theory of money is not an adequate model of aggregate demand.

The Determinants of Velocity

Since it is abundantly clear that velocity is a variable, not a constant, what, then, are the determinants of velocity? What factors decide whether *V* will be 4 or 5 or 6; that is, whether a dollar will be used to buy goods and services four or five or six times a year? Perhaps the principal factor is the *frequency with which paychecks are received.* This can best be explained through a numerical example. Consider a worker who earns $12,000 a year, paid to her in 12 monthly paychecks of $1000 each. Suppose that she spends the whole $1000 over the course of each month and maintains a minimum balance in her checking account of $500. Each payday her bank balance will shoot up to $1500 and then be gradually whittled down as she makes withdrawals to purchase goods and services. Finally, on the day before her next paycheck arrives, her checking balance will be just $500. Over the course of a typical month, then, her average checking account balance will be $1000 (halfway between $1500 and $500).

Now suppose her employer switches to a twice-a-month payroll. Her paychecks come twice as often, but are reduced to $500 each. There is no reason for her rate of spending to change, but her *cash balances* will change. For now her checking balance will rise only to $1000 on payday (the $500 minimum balance plus the $500 paycheck), and it will still be drawn down gradually to $500. Her average cash balance will therefore decline to $750 (halfway between $1000 and $500). Why is this so? Because, with the next paycheck coming sooner than before, it is not necessary to keep as much cash in the bank in order to carry out a given quantity of transactions. But what does this have to do with velocity? Notice that when she was on a monthly payroll, this worker's personal velocity was:

$$V = \frac{\text{Annual income}}{\text{Average cash balance}} = \frac{\$12,000}{\$1000} = 12 .$$

When she switched to a semimonthly payroll, velocity rose to:

$$V = \frac{\text{Annual income}}{\text{Average cash balance}} = \frac{\$12,000}{\$750} = 16 .$$

The general lesson to be learned is that:

More frequent wage payments mean that people can conduct their transactions with lower average cash balances. Since they will want to hold less cash, money will circulate faster. In other words, velocity will rise.

A second factor influencing velocity is the *efficiency of the payments mechanism,* including how quickly checks clear through banks, the use of credit cards, and other methods of transferring funds. It is easy to see how this works. The example in the previous paragraph assumed that our worker holds her entire paycheck in the form of money until she uses it to make a purchase. But, given that most money pays no interest, this method may not be the most rational behavior. If it is possible to convert interest-bearing assets into money on short notice and at low cost, a rational individual might use her paycheck to purchase such assets and then use credit cards for most purchases, making periodic transfers to her checking account as necessary. For the same amount of total transactions, then, she would require lower money balances. This means that money would circulate faster: velocity would rise.

The incentive to limit cash holdings depends on the ease and speed with which it is possible to exchange money for other assets. This is what we mean by the "efficiency of the payments mechanism." As computerization has speeded up the bookkeeping procedures of banks, as financial innovations have made it possible to transfer funds rapidly between checking accounts and other assets, and as credit cards have come to be used instead of cash, the need to hold money balances has declined. By definition, then, velocity has risen. Fortunately such basic changes in the payments mechanism usually take place only gradually, and thus often are easy to predict. But this is not always so. For example, a host of financial innovations since the 1970s have given analysts fits in predicting velocity.

A third determinant of velocity is the *rate of interest*. The basic motive for economizing on money holdings is that most money (at least M1) pays no interest, while many alternative stores of value do. The higher these alternative rates of interest, the greater the incentive to economize on holding money. Therefore, as interest rates rise, people want to hold less money. So the existing stock of money circulates faster, and velocity rises.

It is this factor that most directly undercuts the usefulness of the quantity theory of money as a guide for monetary policy. For in the last chapter we learned that expansionary monetary policy, which increases M, normally also decreases the interest rate. But if interest rates fall, other things equal, velocity (V) will also fall. Thus, *when the Fed raises the money supply (M), the product $M \times V$ may go up by a smaller percentage than does M itself.*

One component of the interest rate is worth singling out for special attention: *the expected rate of inflation*. We explained in Chapter 6 why an "inflation premium" equal to the expected inflation rate often gets built in to market interest rates.[2] Thus, in many instances, high inflation is the principal cause of high nominal interest rates. High rates of inflation, which erode the purchasing power of money, therefore lead both individuals and businesses to hold as little money as they can get by on—actions that increase velocity. To summarize this discussion of the determinants of velocity:

Velocity is not a strict constant but depends on such things as the frequency of payments, the efficiency of the financial system, the rate of interest, and the rate of inflation. Only by studying these determinants of velocity can we hope to predict the level of nominal GNP from knowledge of the money supply.

Monetarism: The Quantity Theory Modernized

The foregoing does not mean, however, that the equation of exchange cannot be a useful framework within which to organize macroeconomic analysis. It can be.

[2]If you need review, turn back to pages 100–101.

And during the past 25 years a group of economists called *monetarists* have convincingly demonstrated that this is so.

Monetarists recognize that velocity is not a constant. But they stress that it is fairly *predictable*—certainly in the long run and probably also in the short run. This leads them to the conclusion that the best way to study economic activity is to start with the *equation of exchange:* $M \times V = P \times Y$. From here, careful study of the determinants of M (which we provided in the previous two chapters) and of V (which we just completed) can be used to *predict* the behavior of nominal GNP. Similarly, given an understanding of movements in V, control over the money supply gives the Federal Reserve *control* over nominal GNP. These are the central tenets of **monetarism.** When something happens in the economy, monetarists ask:

Monetarism is a mode of analysis that uses the equation of exchange to organize macroeconomic data.

1. What does this event do to the stock of money?
2. What does this event do to velocity?

From the answers, they assert that they can predict the path of nominal GNP.

By comparing the monetarist approach with the Keynesian approach that we described earlier in this chapter, we can put both doctrines into perspective and gain an appreciation of the limitations of each. As we mentioned earlier, they differ more in style than in substance. Keynesians, as we learned in earlier chapters, divide economic knowledge into neat compartments—marked "C," "I," and "G"—and unite them all with the equilibrium condition that $C + I + G = Y$. In Keynesian analysis, money affects the economy by first affecting interest rates.

Monetarists, on the other hand, organize their knowledge into two alternative boxes—labeled "M" and "V"—and then use a simple accounting identity that says $M \times V = P \times Y$ to bring this knowledge to bear in predicting aggregate demand. The role of money in the national economy is not necessarily limited to working through interest rates in the monetarist model.

The bit of arithmetic that multiplies M and V to get $P \times Y$ is neither more nor less profound than the one that adds up C and I and G to get Y. And certainly both approaches are correct. The only substantive difference is that the monetarist equation leads to a prediction of *nominal* GNP, whereas the Keynesian equation leads to a prediction of *real* aggregate demand. Why, then, do we not simply mesh the two theories—using the monetarist approach to study nominal GNP and the Keynesian approach to study real GNP? It seems that by doing so we could use the separate analyses of real and nominal GNP to obtain a prediction of the future behavior of the price level, which, of course, is the source of any difference in behavior of real and nominal GNP.

The reason that this appealing procedure will not work helps point out the major limitation of each theory. Taken by itself, either theory is incomplete. It gives us a picture of the *demand* side of the economy without saying anything about the *supply* side. To try to predict both the price level and real output solely from these demand-oriented models would be like trying to predict the price of peanuts by studying only the behavior of consumers and ignoring that of farmers. It just will not work. In terms of our earlier aggregate supply and demand analysis:

Both the monetarist and Keynesian analyses are ways of studying the *aggregate demand curve.* In neither case is it possible to learn anything about both output and the price level without also studying the *aggregate supply curve.*

Economists thus are forced to choose between two alternative ways of predicting aggregate demand. If the monetarist route is chosen, the economist will use velocity and the money supply to study the demand for *nominal* GNP, that is, the demand for goods and services measured in money terms, and then turn to the supply side to estimate how any predicted change in nominal income gets apportioned between changes in production and changes in prices. On the other hand, an economist working with the Keynesian $C + I + G$ approach will start by predicting how monetary policy affects the demand for *real* GNP, that is, the demand for goods and services measured in dollars of constant purchasing power, and then turn to the aggregate supply curve to estimate the inflationary consequences of this real demand. It is therefore not surprising that some economists opt for one approach while others favor the alternative.

Reconciling the Keynesian and Monetarist Views

We have already come quite a long way toward reconciling the Keynesian and monetarist views of how the economy operates. Keynesian analysis, we have learned in earlier chapters, lends itself naturally to the study of fiscal policy, since G is a part of $C + I + G$. But we have seen in this chapter that Keynesian economics also provides a powerful and important role for monetary policy: an increase in the money supply reduces interest rates, which, in turn, stimulates the demand for investment. Monetarist analysis, we have just learned, provides an obvious and direct route by which monetary policy influences both output and prices. But can the monetarist approach also handle fiscal policy? It can, and the reason is that fiscal policy actions have important effects on the rate of interest.

It is not hard to understand why. Let's see what happens to real output and the price level following, say, a rise in government purchases of goods and services. We learned in Chapter 11 that both real GNP (Y) and the price level (P) rise. But Chapter 13's analysis of the demand for money taught us that rising Y and P pull up the demand for money. With greater demand for money, and no change in supply, the rate of interest must rise. So expansionary fiscal policy raises interest rates. If the government uses its spending and taxing weapons in the opposite direction, the same process operates in reverse. Falling output and (possibly) falling prices reduce the demand for money. With a given supply of money, equilibrium in the money market leads to a lower interest rate.

Thus, monetary policy is not the only type of policy that affects interest rates. Fiscal policy also affects interest rates. Specifically, increases in government spending or tax cuts normally push interest rates higher, whereas restrictive fiscal policies normally pull interest rates down.

The fact that fiscal policy affects interest rates gives it a role in the monetarist model despite the fact that the equation of exchange, $M \times V = P \times Y$, does not include either government spending or taxation among its variables. The way it works is that a rise in government spending, for example, pushes up the rate of interest. And rising interest rates push up velocity because people want to hold less money when the interest they can earn on alternative assets increases. So it is through the V term in $M \times V$ that fiscal policy does its work in the monetarist framework. Any of the government policies that a Keynesian would call expansionary—higher spending, lower taxes, and so on—forces interest rates higher, thus increasing V. The equation of exchange, $M \times V = P \times Y$, then implies that nominal GNP must rise when government spending increases, even if M is fixed. The given supply of money can finance more transactions when velocity is higher. Conversely, restrictive fiscal policies, like tax rises and expenditure cuts, reduce the demand for money and lower interest rates. The consequent drop in velocity lowers income through the equation of exchange, because the money supply circulates more slowly.

The translation, then, seems to be complete. The Keynesian story about how fiscal policy works can be phrased in the monetarist dialect. And the monetarist tale about monetary policy can be told with a Keynesian accent. Furthermore, both modes of analysis help only to explain the mysteries of aggregate *demand*, and must be supplemented by an analysis of aggregate *supply* to be complete. We must conclude, then, that:

The differences between Keynesians and monetarists have been grossly exaggerated by the news media. Indeed, when it comes to matters of basic economic theory, there are hardly any differences at all.

But this does not mean that Keynesians and monetarists must agree on everything any more than the fact that English prose can be translated into French implies that the English and the French always see eye to eye. There are important differences of emphasis and policy that we will take up in the following chapter.

The Crowding-Out Controversy

The seemingly mundane fact that expansionary fiscal policy pushes up interest rates has several important consequences. Recall, first, that higher interest rates deter private investment spending. This means that when the government raises the G component of $C + I + G$, one of the side effects of its action will be to reduce the I component (by raising interest rates). Consequently, the sum $C + I + G$ will not rise as much as simple multiplier analysis might suggest. In a word, the surge in government demand (G) discourages some private demand (I). This phenomenon provides another reason why the oversimplified multiplier formula, $1/(1 - \text{MPC})$, exaggerates the size of the multiplier:

Because any rise in G (or, for that matter, any autonomous rise in C or I) pushes interest rates higher, and hence deters some investment spending, the increase in the sum $C + I + G$ is smaller than what the oversimplified multiplier formula predicts.

There is another way of looking at this fact—a way that explains why it is often called the **crowding-out effect.** Consider what happens in financial markets when the government engages in deficit spending. When it spends more than it takes in through tax revenues, the government must borrow the balance from private citizens. It does this by issuing bonds, and these bonds compete with corporate bonds and other financial instruments for the available supply of funds. When some private savers are persuaded to buy government bonds, there must be a decline in the funds remaining to invest in private bonds. Thus some private borrowers will get "crowded out" of the financial markets as the government claims an increasing share of the economy's total pool of saving.

Some critics of fiscal policy who have taken this lesson to its illogical extreme argue that each $1 of deficit spending by government crowds out exactly $1 of private spending, so that fiscal policy has no net effect on total demand. In their view, when G rises, I falls by the same amount, so that $C + I + G$ is unchanged. Under normal circumstances, this would not be expected to occur. Why? First, moderate budget deficits will push up interest rates only moderately. Second, the sensitivity of private spending to interest rates is not that great. Even at the higher interest rates that government deficits cause, most corporations will continue to borrow to finance their investments.

Furthermore, there is a counterforce that might be called the **crowding-in effect.** Deficit spending in time of economic slack presumably quickens the pace of economic activity; that, at least, is its purpose. As the economy expands, businesses will find it both necessary and profitable to add to their capacity in order to meet the greater demands of consumers. Because of this *induced investment,* as we called it in earlier chapters, any increase in G tends to *increase* investment rather than *decrease* it as predicted by the crowding-out hypothesis. The strength of this crowding-in effect depends on how much additional real GNP is stimulated by the government spending (that is, on the size of the multiplier) and on how sensitive investment spending is to the improved profit opportunities that accompany rapid growth in real output. It is even conceivable that the crowding-in effect can dominate the crowding-out effect, so that investment will rise on balance.

But how can this be true in view of the crowding-out argument? Certainly, if government is borrowing more *and the total pool of saving is fixed*, then private industry must be borrowing less. While this little bit of arithmetic is correct, the fallacy in the strict crowding-out argument comes in supposing that the economy's pool of saving is really fixed. If government deficits succeed in their goal of raising production, there will be more income and therefore more saving. In that way *both* government *and* industry can borrow more.

Which effect dominates, crowding out or crowding in? The crowding-out hypothesis stems from the increases in interest rates that deficit spending causes; this is certainly bad for investment. But the crowding-in hypothesis stems from the increases in production and profitability, which are good for investment. Under different sets of circumstances, one or the other force may prove to be stronger. For example, a report issued by the Congressional Budget Office near the bottom of the Great Recession in June 1975 argued that "on balance . . . it appears likely that more investments would be 'crowded in' by a stimulative fiscal policy than would be 'crowded out,' given the present state of the economy."[3] The report explained that, with so much slack in the economy, a surge in G would very likely lead to a considerable increase in real output because the more buoyant demand would not cause much inflation and, consequently, the multiplier would be large. In terms of our graphical apparatus, the aggregate supply curve would be rather flat when the economy is in the range indicated by Region I in Figure 14–6 on the following page.

But the same report hastened to add, "The opposite conclusion might well be drawn if resources were more fully employed." This is because the economy would then be operating in the steep portion of Region III of the aggregate supply curve shown in Figure 14–6 so that demand stimulation would lead to only limited gains in real output.[4] If real GNP growth is minor, then so must be the amount of induced investment. The crowding-in effect therefore would be weak. Instead, government spending would push up the price level, raise the demand for cash balances, and crowd out private borrowers.

Let us summarize what we have learned about the crowding-out controversy.

SUMMARY

1. The basic argument of the crowding-out hypothesis is sound: *Unless there is enough additional saving,* more government borrowing will force out some

[3]Congressional Budget Office, *Inflation and Unemployment: A Report on the Economy* (Washington, D.C.: U.S. Government Printing Office, June 30,1975), page 58.

[4]EXERCISE: Show that any given horizontal shift in the aggregate demand curve has a smaller effect on real GNP in Region III than it does in Region I.

Figure 14–6
A TYPICAL AGGREGATE
SUPPLY CURVE
The aggregate supply curve depicted here has three regions. In Region I, output can increase with almost no change in prices, because there is a great deal of unused labor and spare industrial capacity; thus the supply curve is virtually horizontal. In Region III, resources are more-or-less fully employed, so even rather small increases in output necessitate substantial price increases; the supply curve is very steep. Region II is intermediate between these two extremes.

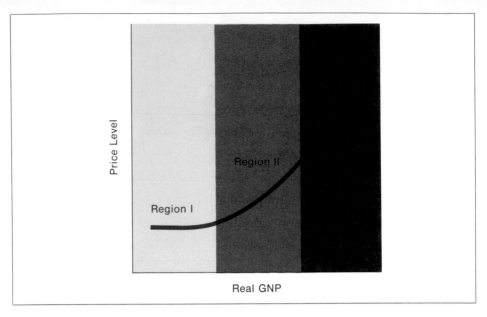

private borrowers who are discouraged by the high interest rates. This will reduce investment spending and cancel out some of the expansionary effects of higher government spending.
2. This force is very rarely strong enough to cancel out the *entire* expansionary thrust of government spending, however. Some net stimulus to the economy remains.
3. If the deficit spending induces substantial growth in GNP, then there will be more saving. There might even be so much more that private industry could borrow *more* than before, despite the increase in government borrowing.
4. The crowding-out effect is likely to dominate when the economy is operating near full employment. The crowding-in effect is likely to dominate when there is a great deal of slack.

Is the National Debt a Burden?*

Few subjects have been debated for so many years with so much heat and so little light as the national debt. Doomsayers have argued, year after year, that the next increase in debt would mark our downfall as a nation. Exactly how or why this was supposed to happen was always a bit mysterious, but the fact that it has never happened has not stopped the outcries against "ruinous" budget deficits. Shortly, we will review some of the bogus arguments that claim to show that the national debt is a "burden on future generations." We will see that our analysis of crowding-out and crowding-in helps us distinguish between bogus arguments and valid ones. But before doing so, it is worthwhile to get the facts straight. How large a public debt do we have? How did we get it? Who owns it? Is it really growing rapidly?

Some Facts About the National Debt

To begin with the simplest question, the public debt is enormous. At the end of 1981 it amounted to over $1000 billion, over $4400 for every man, woman, and

*In briefer courses, this topic may be omitted without loss of continuity.

child in America. But nearly 35 percent of this outstanding debt is owned by agencies of the U.S. government—in other words, one branch of the government owes it to another. If we deduct this portion, the net national debt is only about $675 billion, or around $3000 per person. Furthermore, when we compare the debt with the gross national product—the volume of goods and services our economy produces in a year—it does not seem so large after all. With a GNP of over $3000 billion in early 1982, the net debt was about one-fifth of the nation's yearly income. By contrast, many families who own homes owe *several years'* worth of income to the bank that granted them a mortgage. Many U.S. corporations also owe their bondholders much more than one-fifth of a year's sales.

But before these analogies make you feel too comfortable, we should point out that simple analogies between public and private debt are almost always misleading. A family with a large mortgage debt also owns a home with a value that presumably exceeds the mortgage. A solvent business firm has assets (factories, machinery, inventories, and so forth) that far exceed its outstanding bonds in value. Is the same thing true of the U.S. government? Nobody knows. How much is the White House worth? Or the national parks? And what about military bases, both here and abroad? Simply because these government assets are *not* sold on markets, no one can tell whether the federal government's assets exceed its debt or not. But, fortunately, the answer to this question is not momentous. For, while a family or a firm whose debts exceed its assets is in deep trouble, the same is not true of the U.S. government.

Figure 14–7 charts the irregular increase in the national debt from 1915 to 1980. You will notice that most of the debt was acquired either during wars,

Figure 14–7
THE U.S. NATIONAL DEBT, 1915–1980
This graph charts the behavior of the public debt in the United States, after subtracting out the portion of the debt that is held by government agencies. It is clear that just about all the increases can be accounted for by wars and by the recessions of the 1970s. Few people realize that the public debt was about the same in 1972 as it was in 1945.
SOURCE: Constructed by the authors from data in *Historical Statistics of the United States* and *Economic Report of the President*.

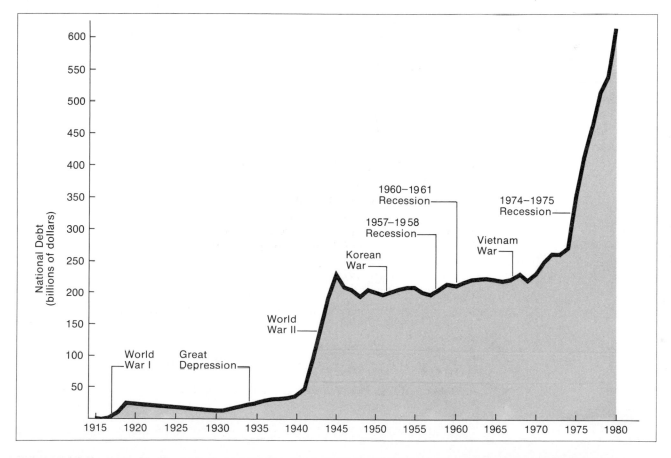

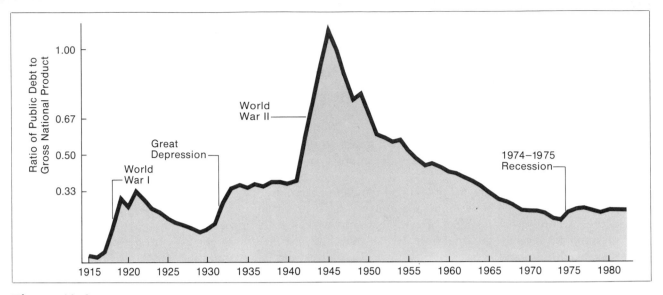

Figure 14–8
RATIO OF PUBLIC DEBT TO GROSS NATIONAL PRODUCT
This graph takes the data from Figure 14–7 and divides each year's debt by the gross national product of that year. We can see that the debt grew relative to GNP during the two world wars, during the Great Depression, and during the Great Recession. Other than that, the debt generally has fallen relative to GNP.

especially World War II, or during the last decade, which included two sharp recessions. When economic activity falls, tax receipts of the federal government fall because of the heavy reliance on income taxes. As we shall see later, the *cause* of the debt is quite germane to the question of whether or not the debt is a burden. So it is important to remember that except for recent years:

Most of the U.S. national debt stems from financing wars and from losses of tax revenues that accompany recessions.

The growth of the debt looks enormous in Figure 14–7. But we must remember that everything grows in a growing economy. Private debt and business debt have grown rapidly since 1915; it would be surprising indeed if the public debt had not grown also. Furthermore, the debt is measured in dollars and, in an inflationary environment, the amount of purchasing power that each dollar represents is declining each year. A good way to put the numbers into some perspective is to express each year's national debt as a fraction of that year's nominal GNP. This is done in Figure 14–8. Here, in contrast to Figure 14–7, we see an unmistakable downward trend since the dizzying heights of World War II, interrupted only by the huge deficits (the largest ever in peacetime) of the Great Recession of 1974–1975. In 1945, for example, the national debt was the equivalent of 13 months' national income. By 1974 this figure had been whittled down to two months. If we use this as a crude indicator of the nation's ability to "pay off" its debt, then the burden of the debt is certainly far smaller now than it was in 1945.

Bogus Arguments About the Burden of the Debt

Having gained some perspective on the facts, let us now turn to some of the arguments advanced by those who claim that by accumulating such a debt we have placed an intolerable burden on future generations.

Argument 1: Our children and grandchildren will be burdened by heavy interest payments. To meet these payments there will have to be higher taxes.

Answer: It is certainly true that a higher debt will necessitate higher interest payments and, other things being equal, this will lead to higher taxes paid by our children and grandchildren. But think who will receive the higher interest payments as income: our children and grandchildren! Thus one group of future Americans will, essentially, be making interest payments to another group of future Americans. We conclude that:

As long as the national debt is owned by domestic citizens, which the bulk of the U.S. debt is, the future interest payments merely shuffle money from one group of Americans to another, and this can hardly constitute a burden to the nation as a whole.

However, this argument *is* valid for the roughly 20 percent of our debt that is held by foreigners. To pay the interest on this portion of the debt will be a burden on future generations of Americans.

Argument 2: It will ruin the nation when we have to pay the enormous debt back.

Answer: A first answer to this merely rephrases the answer to the previous argument: Only the part owned by foreigners involves any burden; the rest is paid by one group of Americans to another. But there is a much more fundamental point. *Unlike a private family, the nation need never pay off its debt.* Instead, each time the principal is due, the U.S. Treasury can simply "roll it over" by floating more debt. Indeed, this is precisely what the Treasury does.

Is this a bit of chicanery? How can the U.S. government get away with making loans that it never intends to pay back? The answer is found by recognizing the fallacy of comparing the U.S. government to a family or individual. People cannot be extended credit in perpetuity because they will not live that long. Sensible lenders will not extend long-term credit to very old people because their heirs cannot be forced to pay up. But the U.S. government will never "die"; at least, we hope not! So this factor does not arise. In this respect, the government is in much the same position as a large corporation. The American Telephone and Telegraph Company never worries about paying off its debt. It too rolls it over by floating new debt all the time.

Argument 3: It will bankrupt the nation. Like any family or any business firm, a nation has a limited capacity to borrow. If it exceeds this limit, it is in danger of being unable to pay its creditors. It may go bankrupt with calamitous consequences for everyone.

Answer: This is another example of a false analogy. What is claimed about private debtors is certainly true. But the U.S. government need never fear defaulting on its debt. Why? First, because it has enormous power to raise revenues by taxation. If you had such power, you would never have to fear bankruptcy either. But there is a still more fundamental point—one that distinguishes the U.S. debt from that of many foreign nations. *The American national debt is an obligation to pay U.S. dollars:* each debt certificate obligates the Treasury to pay the holder so many U.S. dollars on a prescribed date. But the U.S. government is the source of these dollars; it prints them up! *No nation need ever fear defaulting on debts that call for repayment in its own currency.* At the very worst, it can always print whatever money it needs to pay off its creditors.

It does not follow, however, that acquiring debt through budget deficits is therefore always a good idea. Sometimes it is clearly a very bad idea. Printing money to pay the debt will expand aggregate demand and cause inflation, and this often will be undesirable. The point is not that budget deficits are either good or bad—we already know that they can be either under the appropriate circumstances. Rather, the point is that worrying about a possible default on the national debt is unnecessary and even foolish.

The True Burden of the National Debt

Having cleared the air of these fallacious arguments, we are now in a position to explore some real problems that may arise when the government spends more than it takes in through taxation.

The Inflationary Effects of Budget Deficits

One indictment of deficit spending that certainly *does* have validity under most circumstances is the charge that it is inflationary. Why? Because when government policy pushes up aggregate demand, firms may find themselves unwilling or unable to produce the higher quantities that are being demanded at the going prices. Prices will therefore have to rise.

Figure 14–9 is an aggregate supply and demand diagram that shows this analysis graphically. Initially, equilibrium is at point E_0—where demand curve D_0D_0 and supply curve SS intersect. Output is $1600 billion, and the price index is at 100. The diagram indicates that the economy is operating below full employment; there is a recessionary gap. If the government does nothing to reduce the resulting unemployment, we know from Chapter 9 that this recessionary gap will linger for a long time. The economy will suffer through a prolonged period of unemployment. Rather than permit such a long recession, we know that the government can raise its spending or cut its taxes enough to shift the aggregate demand schedule upward from D_0D_0 to D_1D_1. Such a policy can wipe out the recessionary gap and the associated unemployment—but not without an inflationary cost. The diagram shows that the new equilibrium price

Figure 14–9

THE INFLATIONARY
EFFECTS OF DEFICIT
SPENDING

In this diagram, expansionary fiscal policy pushes the aggregate demand curve out from D_0D_0 to D_1D_1, causing equilibrium to move from E_0 (where there is unemployment) to E_1 (where there is full employment). But because aggregate supply curve SS slopes upward, the price level is pushed up from 100 to 106; that is, there is a 6 percent inflation.

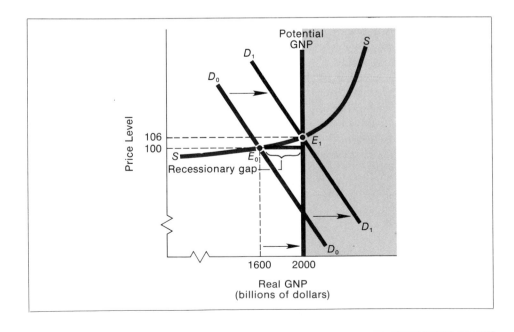

level is at 106—6 percent higher than before the government acted.

Thus the cries that budget deficits are "inflationary" have the ring of truth. How much truth, of course, depends on the slope of the aggregate supply curve. Deficit spending will not cause much inflation if the economy has lots of slack and the aggregate supply curve consequently is flat. But deficit spending will be highly inflationary in a fully employed economy with a steep aggregate supply curve.

The Valid Burden-of-the-Debt Argument

The fact that deficits are inflationary does not, of course, make them a "burden" on our children and grandchildren. The generation that ran the deficits will also suffer from the inflation. However, there is one sense in which the national debt truly does burden future generations:

Because of the large national debt, we may bequeath less physical capital to future generations. If they inherit less plant and equipment, these generations will be burdened by a lower productive capacity—a lower potential GNP.

The logic of this argument is simple and quite compelling, and follows immediately from our analysis of crowding out. When it runs a deficit and has to borrow funds, the U.S. Treasury drives up the rate of interest. But higher interest rates discourage investment. Future generations will therefore inherit less capital.

However, as we have already pointed out, there is also a "crowding-in" effect if there are unemployed resources. That is, the government spending or tax cuts that cause the deficit have multiplier effects on real GNP, and this GNP growth stimulates more investment spending and saving. Thus:

When government budget deficits take place in a high-employment economy, the crowding-out effect will probably dominate, so the deficits will exact a burden by leaving a smaller capital stock to future generations. However, deficits in a slack economy may well lead to more investment rather than less. In this case, where the crowding-in effect dominates, the debt is a blessing rather than a burden.

Let us now go back to the historical facts and recall how we have accumulated such a large national debt. The first cause was the financing of wars, especially World War II. This debt was contracted in a fully employed economy, and thus undoubtedly constituted a burden in the formal sense. It left future generations with less capital because some of our nation's resources were diverted from private investment into government production. The bombs, ships, and planes that it financed were used up in the war, not bequeathed as capital to future generations. Yet what were the alternatives? We could have tried to finance the entire war by taxation, and thus placed the burden on consumption rather than on investment. But that would truly have been ruinous, and probably even impossible, given the colossal wartime expenditures. Or we could have printed money, but that would have unleashed an inflation that nobody wanted. Or we could have just done much less government spending and perhaps not have won the war. So, in retrospect, the generations alive today and in the future may not feel unduly burdened by the decisions of the people in power in the 1940s. One need only imagine the sort of burden that would have been inherited had the United States not won the war.

The second major contributor to the national debt has been a series of recessions. But these are precisely the circumstances under which increasing the debt might prove to be a blessing rather than a burden. So, if we look for the classic type of deficits to which the valid burden-of-the-debt argument applies—deficits acquired in a fully employed peacetime economy—we do not find many in the U.S. record.

Let us now summarize our evaluation of the burden of the national debt, and thereby restate one of the 12 Ideas for Beyond the Final Exam introduced in Chapter 1. First, the arguments that a large national debt may lead the nation into bankruptcy, or unduly burden future generations who have to make onerous payments of interest and principal, are mostly bogus. Second, the national debt *will* be a burden if it is contracted in a fully employed peacetime economy, because in that case it will reduce the nation's capital stock. Third, there are circumstances in which budget deficits are quite appropriate for stabilization reasons. Fourth, and finally, the actual public debt of the United States government was mostly contracted as a result of wars and recessions—precisely the circumstances under which the valid burden-of-the-debt argument does not apply. We are thus led to the conclusion that the current national debt cannot reasonably be considered a serious burden.

Summary

1. Monetarist and Keynesian analyses are two different ways of studying the determination of aggregate demand. Neither is a complete theory of the behavior of the economy until aggregate supply is brought into the picture.

2. Investment spending (I), including business investment and investment in new homes, is sensitive to interest rates. Specifically, I is lower when r is higher.

3. This fact explains how monetary policy works in the Keynesian model. Raising M leads to lower r; the lower interest rates stimulate more investment spending; and this investment stimulus, via the multiplier, then raises aggregate demand.

4. However, prices are likely to rise as output rises. The amount of inflation caused by increasing the money supply depends on the levels of unemployment and of capacity utilization. There will be much inflation when the economy is near full employment, but little inflation when there is a great deal of slack.

5. The main reason why the aggregate demand curve slopes downward is that higher prices increase the demand to hold money in order to finance transactions. Given the money supply, this pushes interest rates up; and this, in turn, discourages investment.

6. Velocity (V) is the ratio of nominal GNP to the stock of money. It indicates how quickly money circulates, that is, how many times money changes hands in a year.

7. Among the determinants of velocity is the rate of interest (r). At higher interest rates, people find it less attractive to hold money because most money pays no interest. Thus, when r rises, money circulates faster, and V rises.

8. Monetarism is a type of analysis that focuses attention on velocity and the money supply (M). Though monetarists realize that V is not constant, they believe that it is predictable enough to make it a useful tool for policy analysis and forecasting.

9. Because it raises output and prices, and hence increases the demand for money, expansionary fiscal policy pushes interest rates higher. This is how a monetarist explains the effect of fiscal policy. Because higher r leads to higher velocity, it leads to a higher product $M \times V$ even if M is unchanged.

10. Since government deficit spending forces interest rates higher, it discourages private investment spending. This is called the *crowding-out* effect, and is another reason why the real-world multiplier is less than the oversimplified multiplier formula suggests.

11. But there is also a *crowding-in* effect from higher government spending (G): If expansionary fiscal policy succeeds in raising real output, there will be some induced investment caused by the higher Y.

12. Which effect is stronger, crowding out or crowding in, depends mainly on the state of the economy. When unemployment is high, crowding in probably dominates, so higher G does not cause lower I. But when the economy is near full employment, the proponents of the crowding-out hypothesis are probably right: high government spending just displaces private investment.

13. Arguments that the public debt will burden future generations because they will have to make huge payments of interest and principal are based on false analogies. In fact, most of these payments are simply transfers from some Americans to other Americans. Besides, the Treasury can, and normally does, "roll over" its debt rather than pay it off.

14. The bogus argument that a large national debt can bankrupt a country like the United States ignores the fact that our national debt consists of obligations to pay U.S. dollars—a currency the government can raise by taxation or create by printing money.

15. There is, however, one potentially real burden of the debt. Government borrowing pushes up interest rates and may crowd some private investors out of the financial markets. If so, the volume of private investment will be reduced and future generations will inherit less capital.

16. The validity of this argument depends on how and why the government ran these deficits in the first place. If deficits are contracted to fight recessions, it is possible that more investment is "crowded in" by the increases in income that these deficits make possible than is "crowded out" by the increases in interest rates. Deficits contracted to carry on wars certainly impair the future capital stock, though they may not be considered a burden for noneconomic reasons. Since these two cases account for most of America'a national debt, our debt cannot reasonably be considered a serious burden. This is one of the 12 Ideas for Beyond the Final Exam.

Concepts for Review

Why the aggregate demand curve slopes downward
Quantity theory of money
Velocity

Equation of exchange
Effect of interest rate on velocity
Monetarism
Effect of monetary policy on inflation

Effect of fiscal policy on interest rates
Crowding-out effect
Crowding-in effect
Burden of the national debt

Questions for Discussion

1. How much money (including cash and checking account balances) do you typically have at any particular moment? Divide this into your total income over the past 12 months to obtain your own personal velocity. Are you typical of the nation as a whole?

2. Just below you will find data on nominal gross national product and the money supply (M1 definition) for selected years. Compute velocity in each year. Can you see any trend?

YEAR	NOMINAL GNP (billions of dollars)	MONEY SUPPLY (M1) (billions of dollars) (end of year)
1960	507	142
1970	993	215
1980	2626	416

3. Use the concept of opportunity cost to explain why velocity is higher at higher interest rates.

4. How does monetarism differ from the quantity theory of money? How does it differ from Keynesian analysis?

5. Explain why both business investments and purchases of new homes are expected to decline when interest rates rise.

6. Explain what a $30 billion increase in the money supply will do to real GNP under the following assumptions:
   a. Each $10 billion increase in the money supply reduces the rate of interest by 1 percentage point.
   b. Each 1 percentage point decline in interest rates stimulates $25 billion of new investment spending.
   c. The expenditure multiplier is 2.
   d. There is so much unemployment that prices do not rise noticeably when demand increases.

7. Explain how your answer to Question 6 would differ if each of the assumptions were changed. Specifically, what sorts of changes in the assumptions would make monetary policy very weak?

8. Explain why the aggregate demand curve has a negative slope.

9. Comment on the following: "Deficit spending paves the road to ruination. If we keep it up, the whole nation will go bankrupt. Even if things do not go this far, what right have we to burden our children and grandchildren with these debts while we live high on the hog?"

10. Explain how the United States government has managed to accumulate a debt of more than $1000 billion. To whom does it owe this debt? Can this debt be considered a burden on future generations?

11. (More difficult) Consider an economy in which government purchases and taxes are both zero, the consumption function is:
$$C = 120 + 0.8\,Y,$$
and investment spending (I) depends on the rate of interest (r) in the following way:
$$I = 320 - 800\,r.$$
Find the equilibrium GNP if the Fed makes the rate of interest (a) 5 percent, (b) 10 percent, (c) zero.

The Keynesian–Monetarist Debate and Forecasting

15

Part Two of this text so far has been devoted to constructing a model of the economy that will enable us to understand how stabilization policy works; that is, how government spending, taxation, and the supply of money affect the amount of unemployment and the rate of inflation. Beginning with Chapter 7, and proceeding in steps through Chapter 14, we have developed a fairly comprehensive view of this process. Our discussion, however, has been almost entirely objective and technical. Because we have sought to understand *how* the national economy works and *how* government policies affect the economy, we have paid little attention to what the government *actually does* or to what it *should do.* We have, in a word, not considered the intense economic and political controversies that surround the conduct of stabilization policy. Chapters 15 through 17 are about precisely these issues. In this chapter, we will explore several of these controversies. The chapter title is derived from the fact that the opponents in these debates typically are groups of economists that the news media have dubbed *Keynesians* and *monetarists.*

We begin the chapter by considering whether it is best to rely on fiscal or monetary policy to stabilize the economy. While one would guess from reading the newspapers that this is the most important bone of contention between Keynesians and monetarists today, we shall see that in fact it is the *least* important. It is unimportant because debating it is futile—the job of stabilizing the economy is so difficult that it is foolish to argue over which of our hands we should tie behind our backs!

Instead, a much more important question will occupy our attention for most of the chapter: Should the government conduct any stabilization policy at all? Everything we have said in earlier chapters seems to indicate that it should. But, as we shall see, there are several important factors that point in the opposite direction—factors that we have not yet considered. These factors lead a number of economists, many of them monetarists, to conclude that it is unwise to try to stabilize the economy through monetary and fiscal policy. One reason for this conclusion is that economists' abilities to forecast the future are rather limited. So some time is spent at the end of the chapter considering the techniques and accuracy of economic forecasting.

Finally, we will examine a third major controversy between Keynesians and monetarists: When the authorities stimulate aggregate demand by fiscal or monetary policy, is the main result more likely to be a drop in unemployment or an acceleration of inflation? We shall see that Keynesians take the former position, monetarists take the latter, and that either can be right under the appropriate circumstances.

Keynesians Versus Monetarists: Fiscal Versus Monetary Policy

Let us start with the aspect of the Keynesian–monetarist debate over stabilization policy that has received the most attention in the news media: Should the government rely mainly on fiscal or on monetary policy? As we stressed in the last chapter, the Keynesian and monetarist approaches can be thought of as two different languages. And each language provides a role for *both* fiscal *and* monetary policy. Nonetheless, as is clear by comparing the English with the French, the language that people speak can influence their attitudes about many issues. This is illustrated nicely by a continuing dispute over terminology. If the government increases its budget deficit either by raising expenditures or by cutting taxes, it must either finance the deficit by issuing more government bonds or call upon the Federal Reserve to finance it by printing more money. When the second option is chosen, and an expansionary fiscal measure is financed by increasing the money supply, Keynesians like to call it *fiscal* policy while monetarists prefer to call it *monetary* policy. The argument, however, is only terminological. Both sides agree that such a combination of policies will exert a strong influence over aggregate demand.

A question of substance arises only when budget deficits are financed by issuing bonds rather than by printing money. The Keynesian language biases things subtly toward thinking that such pure fiscal actions are very important simply because they affect aggregate demand so directly; G is, after all, a part of $C + I + G$. Monetarists, on the other hand, are more taken by the "crowding-out" argument of the previous chapter. They are less convinced that fiscal expansion unaccompanied by monetary growth will have strong effects on output and prices. The roles are reversed in the analysis of monetary policy. To monetarists, the effect of the money supply (M) on aggregate demand is simple—it follows directly from velocity (V) through the equation of exchange: $M \times V = P \times Y$. While monetary policy also affects demand in the Keynesian model, the mechanisms are rather complex, and there is obviously room for a slip-up. Monetary expansion might not affect the interest rate very much, or a fall in the interest rate might not induce much additional investment. Thus Keynesians have their doubts when monetarists attribute great stabilizing powers to monetary policy. In sum:

While Keynesians and monetarists agree that both fiscal and monetary policy have significant effects on aggregate demand, Keynesians tend to look more toward fiscal policy while monetarists tend to rely more on monetary policy.

Lags in Fiscal and Monetary Policy

More important than the issue of which type of policy is more *powerful* is the related question: Which type of medicine—fiscal or monetary—cures the patient more *quickly*? In our discussions of fiscal and monetary policy so far, we have ignored such subtle questions of timing and proceeded as if the authorities instantly noticed the need for stabilization policy, decided upon a course of action, and administered the appropriate medicine. In reality, each of these steps is time consuming. First, delays in data collection and processing mean that the latest macroeconomic data pertain to the economy as it was a few months ago. Second, one of the prices of democracy is that the government often takes a good deal of time to decide what should be done, to muster the necessary political support, and to put its decisions into effect. Finally, our $3 trillion economy is a bit like a sleeping elephant—it reacts rather sluggishly to moderate fiscal and monetary prods. As it turns out, these **lags in stabilization policy,** as they are called, play a pivotal role in the choice between fiscal and monetary policy. It is not hard to see why.

The main policy tool for manipulating consumer spending (C) is the personal income tax, and Chapter 7 documented why the fiscal policy planner can feel fairly secure that each $1 of tax reduction will lead to about 90 to 95 cents of additional spending *eventually*. But not all of this will happen at once. First consumers must learn about the tax change. Then more time may elapse before many consumers are convinced that the change is permanent. Finally, there is the simple force of habit: households need time to adjust their spending habits when circumstances change. For all these reasons, consumers may increase their spending by only 30 to 50 cents for each $1 of additional income within the first few months after a tax cut. Only gradually, over a period of perhaps several years, will they raise their spending until they are finally consuming 90 to 95 cents of each additional dollar of income.

Lags are much longer for investment (I), which, while it also can be influenced by fiscal policy (tax incentives), provides the main vehicle by which monetary policy affects aggregate demand. Planning for capacity expansion in a large corporation is a long drawn-out process. Ideas must be submitted and approved. Plans must be drawn up, funding acquired, orders for machinery or contracts for new construction placed. And most of this occurs *before* any appreciable amount of money is spent. Economists have found that most of the response of investment to changes in interest rates or tax provisions is delayed for several years.

This last fact—that C responds more quickly than I—has important implications for the multiplier effects of alternative stabilization policies. The reason is that the most common varieties of fiscal policy affect aggregate demand either directly (G is a component of $C + I + G$) or work through consumption with a relatively short lag, while monetary policy has its major effects on investment. Therefore:

Conventional types of fiscal policy actions, such as changes in G or in personal taxes, probably affect aggregate demand much more promptly than do monetary policy actions.

Notice that the statement says nothing about which instrument is more *powerful*. It simply asserts that the fiscal weapon, whether it is stronger or weaker, acts more *quickly*. This important fact has been used to build a case that fiscal policy should bear the major burden of economic stabilization. But before you jump to such a conclusion, you should realize that the sorts of lags we have been discussing are not the only ones affecting the timing of stabilization policy.

Apart from these lags in expenditure, which are beyond the control of policymakers, there are futher lags that are due to the behavior of the policymakers themselves! We are referring here to the delays that occur while the policymakers are studying the state of the economy, contemplating what steps they should take, and putting their decisions into effect. And here most observers believe that monetary policy has an important edge; that is:

Policy lags are normally shorter for monetary policy than for fiscal policy.

The reasons for this are apparent. The Federal Open Market Committee (FOMC) meets frequently, so monetary policy decisions are made almost every month. And once the Fed decides on a course of action, it normally can be executed almost instantly by buying or selling bonds on the open market.

Contrast this with fiscal policy. Federal budgeting procedures operate on a one-year budget cycle. Except in rare circumstances, then, *major* fiscal policy initiatives that affect spending can only occur at the time of the annual budget. Tax laws can be changed at any time, but the wheels of Congress grind slowly and it may take many months before Congress acts on a presidential request to change taxes. In sum, one has to be very optimistic to suppose that important fiscal policy actions can be taken on short notice.

Where does the combined effect of expenditure lags and policy lags leave us? With nothing conclusive, we are afraid. As the late Arthur Okun put it, the debate over whether the nation should rely only on monetary policy or only on fiscal policy is a bit like arguing whether a safe car is one with good headlights or one with good brakes. It is not very wise to drive at night unless you have both.

Keynesians Versus Monetarists: Should the Government Intervene?

During the 1960s and early 1970s the choice between fiscal and monetary policy dominated the debate between the more partisan Keynesians and monetarists. Extreme monetarists claimed that fiscal policy was futile, while extreme Keynesians countered that monetary policy was useless. But during the 1970s, accumulating evidence made each extreme view seem less and less tenable. More and more monetarists had to admit that fiscal policy did affect output and prices, and at least *could* be put into action promptly. More and more Keynesians had to concede the same to monetary policy. By 1976, two economists surveying the debate could write that "the shift has been so great that we wonder whether anything more than machismo and habit propels the controversy today." While echoes of this battle are occasionally heard today, they sound more like quaint relics of the past than like live issues.

But the Keynesian–monetarist battles did not end there. As the proponents of the views that either fiscal policy or monetary policy did not matter gave up the fight, the two schools of thought regrouped along new, and more productive, battle lines. One major controversy that is still alive is over whether the government should conduct *any* stabilization policy at all, be it a monetary *or* a fiscal stabilization policy. This argument is not surprising given the political differences between these adversaries. As it happens, monetarists tend to be conservative politically and Keynesians tend to be liberal, which helps explain why the two schools differ markedly in the degree to which they think the government should try to manage the economy.

Monetarists point to the uncertainties that surround the operation of both fiscal and monetary policies—uncertainties that we have stressed repeatedly in earlier chapters. Will the Fed's actions have the desired effects on the money supply? What will these actions do to interest rates? How will they affect spending, and how long will it take before the effects appear? Can fiscal policy actions be taken promptly? Will consumers view tax changes as temporary or permanent? How large is the expenditure multiplier? The list could go on and on. Monetarists look at this formidable catalogue of difficulties, add a dash of skepticism about our ability to forecast the future state of the economy,[1] and conclude that stabilization policy is likely to do more harm than good. They advise both the fiscal and monetary authorities to pursue a passive policy rather than an active one—adhering to *fixed rules* that, while they will not iron out all the bumps in the economy's growth path, will at least keep it roughly on track in the long run.

Keynesians, though they admit that perfection is unattainable, are much *more optimistic* about the possibility of achieving a successful stabilization policy. And they are much *less optimistic* than the monetarists about how smoothly the economy would function in the absence of demand management. They therefore advocate discretionary increases in government spending (or decreases in taxes) and more rapid growth of the money supply when the economy has a recessionary gap. By this policy mix, they believe, government can keep the economy closer to its full-employment growth path.

Naturally, each side can point to evidence that buttresses its own view. Keynesians like to look back with pride at the tax cut of 1964 and the sustained period of economic growth that it helped usher in. They also point to the tax cut of 1975, which was enacted just about at the trough of our worst postwar recession. Monetarists remind us of the government's refusal to curb what was obviously a situation of runaway demand during the 1966–1968 Vietnam buildup, its overexpansion of the economy in 1972, and the monetary overkill that helped bring on the sharp recessions of 1974–1975 and 1980. The historical record of fiscal and monetary policy is far from glorious. It shows that while there were many instances in which appropriate stabilization policy could have been helpful, the authorities instead either took inappropriate steps or did nothing at all. The question of whether the government should adopt passive rules or attempt an activist stabilization policy therefore merits a closer look. As we shall see, the lags we have just been discussing play a pivotal role in the debate.

Lags and the Rules-Versus-Discretion Debate

The reason that lags lead to a fundamental difficulty for stabilization policy—a difficulty so formidable that it has led many economists to conclude that attempts to stabilize economic activity are likely to do more harm than good—can be explained best by reference to Figure 15–1. Here we chart the behavior of both actual and potential GNP over the course of a business cycle in a hypothetical economy in which no stabilization policy is attempted. At point *A*, the economy begins to slip into a recession and does not recover to full employment until point *D*. Then, between points *D* and *E*, it overshoots and is in an inflationary boom.

The case for stabilization policy runs like this. The recession is recognized to be a serious problem at point *B*, and appropriate actions are taken. These have their major effects around point *C* and thus curb both the depth and length of the recession.

But suppose the lags are really much longer than this. Suppose, for example, that policy lags delay policy actions until point *C* and that expenditure lags are so long that the major effects of stimulative policies are not felt until after point *D*. Then policy will be of little help during the recession, and will actually do harm by overstimulating the economy during the ensuing boom.

In the presence of long lags, attempts at stabilizing the economy can actually succeed in destabilizing it.

[1] Economic forecasting is discussed later in this chapter.

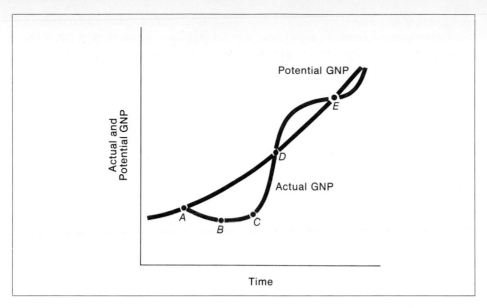

Figure 15–1
A TYPICAL BUSINESS
CYCLE
This is a stylized representation
of the relationship between actual and potential GNP during
a typical business cycle. The
imaginary economy slips into a
recession at point *A*, bottoms
out around point *B*, and is in a
recovery period until point *D*.
After point *D*, it enters an inflationary boom that lasts until
point *E*.

Because of this, some economists, like Milton Friedman, have argued that we are
better off letting the economy alone and relying on its natural self-corrective
forces to cure recessions and inflations. Instead of embarking on periodic
programs of monetary and fiscal stimulus or restraint, they advise policymakers to
stick to *fixed rules;* that is, to rigid formulas that ignore current economic
events.

The rule most emphasized by monetarists—that the Fed keep the money
supply growing at a constant rate—was discussed in Chapter 13. The corresponding rule for fiscal policy is to keep the high employment budget in balance. Notice
that, as we pointed out in Chapter 11 (page 204), this rule for fiscal policy allows
the actual budget to swing from surplus to deficit during a recession and from
deficit to surplus during an inflationary boom. The reason is that tax receipts
automatically rise when GNP rises and fall when GNP falls. Similarly, some items
of government expenditure, such as transfer payments, automatically increase
when unemployment rises and decrease when unemployment falls. So fiscal
policy automatically swings toward expansion when the economy sags and
toward contraction when the economy booms. This discussion actually illustrates a general class of mechanisms called **automatic stabilizers**—features
of the economy that reduce its sensitivity to shocks.

Examples of automatic stabilizers are not hard to find in the federal budget.
The personal income tax is the most obvious example. The ability of the income
tax to act as a shock absorber derives from the fact that it makes disposable
income, and thus consumer spending, less sensitive to fluctuations in GNP.
When GNP rises, disposable income (*DI*) rises also, but by less than the rise in
GNP because part of the income is siphoned off by the U.S. Treasury. This helps
limit the upward fluctuation in consumption spending. And when GNP falls, *DI*
falls less sharply because part of the loss is absorbed by the Treasury rather than by
consumers. So consumption does not drop as much as it otherwise might. Thus,
although everybody likes to grumble about it, the personal income tax—which
affected very few families in 1929, but affects almost everyone now—is one of the
many modern institutions that help ensure us against a repeat performance of the
Great Depression.

There are many other automatic stabilizers in our economy. For example, in
Chapter 6 we studied the U.S. system of unemployment insurance. This serves as

An **automatic stabilizer**
is any arrangement that automatically serves to support
aggregate demand when it
would otherwise sag and hold
down aggregate demand when
it would otherwise surge
ahead. In this way, an automatic stabilizer reduces the
sensitivity of the economy to
shifts in demand.

an automatic stabilizer in a similar way. When GNP begins to fall and people lose their jobs, unemployment benefits prevent the disposable incomes of the jobless from falling as much as their earnings. As a result, unemployed workers can maintain their spending, and consumption need not fluctuate as dramatically as employment. And the list could continue. The basic principle is the same: Each of these automatic stabilizers, in one way or another, serves as a shock absorber, and each does so without the need for any decisionmaker to take action. In a word, they work *automatically*.

Stabilization Policy: Discretionary Measures or Fixed Rules?

Believers in fixed rules assert that we should forget about discretionary policy and rely solely on automatic stabilizers and the economy's natural self-correcting mechanisms. Are they right? As usual, the answer depends on many factors.

How Fast Does the Economy's Self-Correcting Mechanism Work?

We stressed in Chapter 9 that the economy does have a self-correcting mechanism. If the economy can cure recessions and inflations very quickly by itself, then the case for intervention is weak. For if such problems typically last only a short time, then lags in discretionary stabilization policy mean that the medicine will often have its major effects only after the disease is over. (In terms of Figure 15–1, this would be a case where point D comes very close to point A.) While the more extreme advocates of rules argue that this is what indeed happens, most economists agree that the economy's self-correcting mechanism is slow and not terribly reliable, even when supplemented by the automatic stabilizers. On this count, then, a point is scored for discretionary policy.

How Long Are the Lags in Stabilization Policy?

As we explained, long lags before stabilization measures are adopted or can take effect make it unlikely that policy can do much good, while short lags point in the other direction. Thus, advocates of fixed rules emphasize the length of lags while proponents of discretion discount them. Who is really right depends on the circumstances. In the most optimistic scenario, fiscal policy actions are taken promptly, and the economy feels much of the stimulus from expansionary policy in less than a year after slipping into a recession. While far from an instant cure, these actions certainly are felt soon enough to do a lot of good. But, as we have seen, more pessimistic scenarios raise the possibility that policy may actually be destabilizing. History offers examples of both types of scenarios. No general conclusion can be drawn.

How Accurate Are Economic Forecasts?

One way to cut down the policy-making lag enormously is to have good economic forecasts. If we could see a recession coming a full year ahead of time (which we certainly *cannot* do), even a rather slow-acting policy response would still be timely. (In terms of Figure 15–1, this would be a case where the coming recession is predicted well before point A arrives.) Techniques of economic forecasting are considered later in this chapter. It is sufficient to say here that forecasts leave a lot of room for improvement. On balance, the record of economic forecasters probably shows a point scored for the advocates of fixed rules.

In trying to strike a balance among all these factors, one's basic view of the economy is very important. Some economists believe that the economy, if left unmanaged, would generate a series of ups and downs that are hard to predict, but that it would correct each of them by itself in a relatively short period of time. They conclude that, because of long lags and poor forecasts, our ability to anticipate whether the economy will be heading up or down by the time policy actions have their effects is quite limited. And so they are led to advocate fixed rules. Other economists liken the economy to a giant glacier with a great deal of inertia. This means that if we observe an inflationary or recessionary gap today, it is likely still to be there a year or two from now because the self-correcting mechanism is so slow. In such a world, accurate forecasting is not imperative, even if policy lags are long. If we base policy on a forecast of a $100 billion gap between actual and potential GNP a year from now, and the gap turns out to be only $50 billion, then we still will have done the right thing despite the horrible forecast. Holders of this view of the economy, then, are likely to advocate the use of discretionary policy.

While there is no consensus on this issue either among economists or among politicians, a prudent view might be that:

The case for active discretionary policy is strong when the economy has a serious deficiency or excess of aggregate demand. However, advocates of fixed rules are right that it is unwise to try to iron out every little wiggle in the growth path of GNP.

Other Dimensions of the Rules-Versus-Discretion Debate

While lags and forecasting play major roles in the debate between advocates of rules and advocates of discretionary policy, these are not the only battlegrounds. One bogus argument that is nonetheless quite often heard is that an activist fiscal policy must inevitably lead to a growing public sector. Since proponents of fixed rules tend also to be opponents of big government, they view this as undesirable. Of course, others think that a large public sector is just what society needs. This argument is, however, completely beside the point, as we pointed out first in the list of Ideas for Beyond the Final Exam in Chapter 1 and again in Chapter 11 (page 203).

One's opinion about the proper size of government should have nothing to do with one's view on stabilization policy. When recessions occur, advocates of big government can call for greater spending while advocates of small government can insist on tax cuts. Similarly, if there is a demand-induced inflation, we can make the public sector smaller by cutting expenditures or bigger by raising taxes. While such choices may be quite momentous from other points of view, they simply do not bear on the question of whether we should fight the recession or the inflation.

A particularly clear example of this point came in the early days of the Reagan administration. The new president advocated an extremely *activist* stabilization policy which was based on *shrinking* the size of the public sector through reductions in both taxes and government spending.

Advocates of rules are on stronger ground when they argue that frequent changes in tax laws, government spending programs, or monetary conditions will make it difficult for firms and consumers to formulate and carry out rational plans. They argue that by adhering to fixed rules, which are known to businesses and consumers, the authorities can provide a more stable environment for the private sector. While no one disputes that a stable environment is good for private planning, supporters of discretionary policy point out the difference between stability in the government budget (or in Federal Reserve operations) and stability in the economy. The goal of stabilization policy is to help *prevent* gyrations in the pace of economic activity by *causing* timely gyrations in the government budget (or in monetary policy). Which atmosphere is better for business, they ask, one in which fiscal and monetary rules keep things peaceful on Capitol Hill and at the Federal Reserve System while recessions and inflations rack the economy, or one in which policy instruments are changed abruptly on occasion but the economy grows more steadily? They think that the answer is self-evident.

A final argument used by advocates of rules is political rather than economic in nature. Fiscal policy, they note, is decided upon by elected politicians: the president and members of Congress. At least when elections are on the horizon (and for members of the House of Representatives they *always* are), these men and women are likely to be at least as concerned with keeping their offices as with doing what is right for the economy. This leaves fiscal policy subject to all sorts of "political manipulations," meaning that inappropriate actions may be taken to attain short-run political goals. In a system of purely automatic stabilization, its proponents argue, a rule of law would replace the rule of men, and this peril would be eliminated.

There is certainly a *possibility* that politicians could deliberately *cause* economic instability to help their own reelection—a possibility we will examine in the next chapter. And some observers of these "political business cycles" have claimed that several American presidents have taken full advantage of the opportunity. Furthermore, even if there is no insidious intent, politicians may take the wrong actions for perfectly honorable reasons. Decisions in the political arena are never clear-cut, and it certainly is easy to find examples of grievous errors in the history of U.S. fiscal policy. So, taken as a whole, the political argument against discretionary policy seems to have a great deal of merit. But what are we to do about it? It is foolhardy to believe that fiscal and monetary decisions could or should be made by a group of objective and nonpartisan technicians. Steering the economy is not like steering a rocket to the moon. Because policy actions that help on the employment front normally do harm on the inflation front, and vice versa, the "correct" policy action is almost always an inherently political matter. In a political democracy, if we take such decisions out of the hands of elected officials, in whose hands shall we put them?

This harsh fact may seem worrisome in view of the possibilities for political chicanery, but it should not bother us any more (or any less!) than similar maneuvering in other areas of policy making. After all, the same thing applies to international relations, issues of national defense, formulation and enforcement of the law, and so on. Politicians make all these decisions for us, subject only to sporadic accountability at election times. Is there really any reason why economic decisions should be different? To summarize:

The question of whether the government should take an active hand in managing the economy, which is one of the main bones of contention between Keynesians and monetarists today, is as much a matter of ideology as of economics. Liberals have always looked to government activism to solve social problems, while conservatives have consistently pointed out that many efforts of government fail despite the best of intentions.

Because of its political nature, we suspect that this disagreement will continue for some time, and that this is one area where consensus in the Keynesian–monetarist debate is a long way off.

Keynesians Versus Monetarists: The Aggregate Supply Curve

A third, and final, major battleground of the Keynesian–monetarist controversy today is over the shape of the economy's aggregate supply curve. We pointed out in the last chapter that either the Keynesian or the monetarist model must be supplemented by an aggregate supply curve if it is to tell us anything about output and prices. Most Keynesians tend to think of the aggregate supply curve as fairly flat in the short run, as in Figure 15–2(a), so that large increases in output can be achieved with rather little inflation. Monetarists, by contrast, picture the supply curve as quite steep, as in Figure 15–2(b), so that prices are very responsive to changes in output. The differences for public policy are substantial.

In the Keynesian view, expansionary fiscal or monetary policy that raises the aggregate demand schedule can buy large gains in real GNP at little cost in terms of inflation. This is shown in Figure 15–3(a). Here, stimulation of demand raises the aggregate demand curve from D_0D_0 to D_1D_1 and moves the economy's equilibrium from point E to point A. There is a substantial rise in output ($200 billion) with only a pinch of inflation (1 percent). Conversely, when the supply curve is so flat, a restrictive stabilization policy is not a very effective way to cure inflation; instead, it serves mainly to reduce real output, as Figure 15–3(b) shows. Here, a leftward shift of the aggregate demand curve moves equilibrium from point E to point B, lowering real GNP by $200 billion, but cutting the price level merely 1 percent.

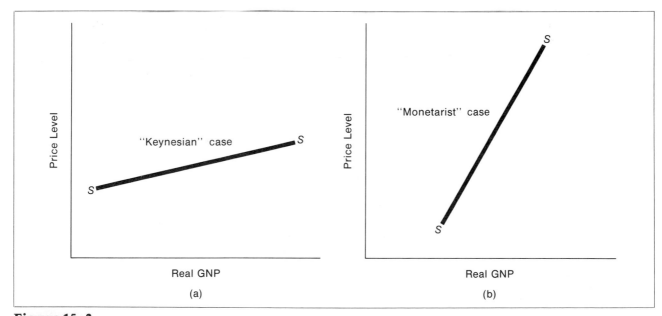

Figure 15–2
ALTERNATIVE VIEWS OF THE AGGREGATE SUPPLY CURVE
Keynesians tend to think of the economy's aggregate supply schedule as very flat, as in part (a), whereas monetarists tend to think of it as quite steep, as in part (b).

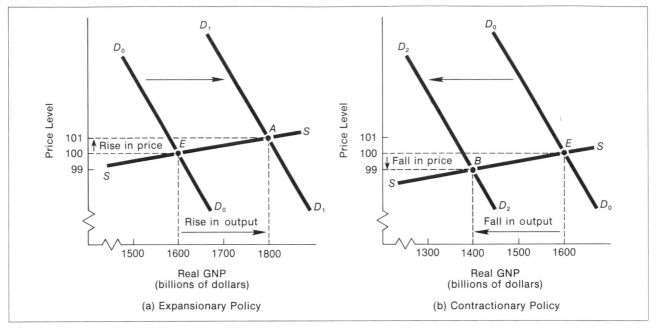

Figure 15–3

STABILIZATION POLICY WITH A FLAT AGGREGATE SUPPLY CURVE: THE KEYNESIAN CASE

These two diagrams show that stabilization policy is much more effective as an antirecession policy than as an anti-inflation policy when the aggregate supply curve is very flat. In part (a), monetary or fiscal policies push the aggregate demand curve outward from D_0D_0 to D_1D_1, causing equilibrium to shift from point E to point A. It can be seen that output rises substantially (from $1600 billion to $1800 billion), while prices rise only slightly (from 100 to 101, or 1 percent). So the policy is quite successful. In part (b), contractionary policies are used to combat inflation by pushing the aggregate demand curve inward from D_0D_0 to D_2D_2. Prices do fall slightly (from 100 to 99) as equilibrium shifts from point E to point B, but real output falls much more dramatically (from $1600 billion to $1400 billion); so the policy has had little success. Keynesians tend to believe in this case.

The monetarists see things differently. To them, the aggregate supply curve is so steep that expansionary fiscal or monetary policies are likely to cause a good deal of inflation without adding much to real GNP. [See Figure 15–4(a), where expansionary policies shift equilibrium from E to A.] Similarly, contractionary policies are effective ways of bringing down the price level without much sacrifice of real output, as shown by the shift from E to B in Figure 15–4(b).

The resolution of this debate is of fundamental importance for the proper conduct of stabilization policy. If the Keynesian view is right, stabilization policy is much more effective at combating recession than inflation. If the monetarist view is correct, the reverse is true. While the debate over aggregate supply is far less settled than that over aggregate demand, the dim outline of a consensus view seems to be emerging. This view stresses that the steepness of the aggregate supply schedule depends on the degree of slack in the economy.

If industry has a great deal of spare capacity, then increases in demand will not call forth large price increases. Similarly, when many workers are unemployed, employment can rise without causing much acceleration in the rate at which wages are growing. In a word, the aggregate supply curve is quite flat. On the other hand, when businesses are producing near capacity and unemployment is near the frictional level, greater demand for goods will induce firms to raise prices; and greater demand for labor will push wages up faster. In brief, the aggregate supply schedule will be steep.

Figure 15–5 shows a version of the aggregate supply curve that embodies these ideas. It has the same general shape as most of the supply curves that we have used in this book. At low levels of GNP, like Y_1, it is nearly horizontal; then

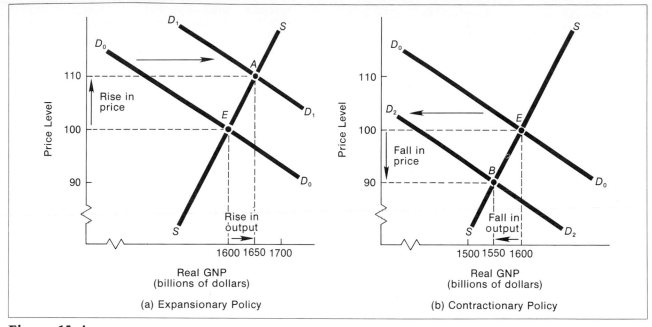

Figure 15–4
STABILIZATION POLICY WITH A STEEP AGGREGATE SUPPLY CURVE: THE MONETARIST CASE

These two diagrams show that stabilization policy is much more effective at fighting inflation than at fighting recession when the aggregate supply curve is very steep. In part (a), expansionary policies that push aggregate demand outward from D_0D_0 to D_1D_1 raise output by only $50 billion but push up prices by 10 percent, as equilibrium moves from point E to point A. So demand management is not a good way to end a recession. In part (b), contractionary policies that pull aggregate demand inward to D_2D_2 are successful in that they lower prices quite markedly (from 100 to 90, or about 10 percent) but reduce output only slightly (from $1600 billion to $1550 billion). Monetarists tend to believe in this case.

its slope starts to rise gradually until at very high levels of GNP, like Y_2, it becomes almost vertical. The implication is that any change in aggregate demand will have most of its effect on *output* when economic activity is slack (the Keynesian case) but on *prices* when the economy is operating near full employment (the monetarist case). In summary:

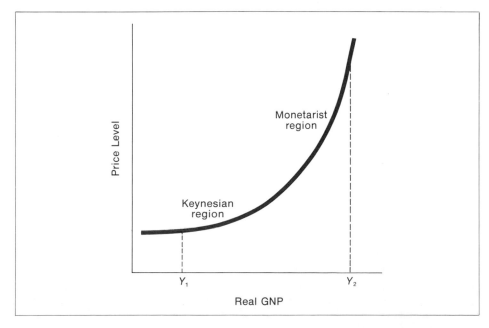

Figure 15–5
AN AGGREGATE SUPPLY CURVE WITH BOTH STEEP AND FLAT REGIONS

As this diagram suggests, either the Keynesians or the monetarists may be right under the appropriate circumstances. The Keynesian view of a flat supply curve is likely to be most accurate when there is much unemployment and unused capacity. The monetarist view of a steep supply curve is likely to be more accurate when there is full employment and high capacity utilization.

Keynesians believe that the aggregate supply curve is rather *flat* in many circumstances, especially when the economy is operating at low levels of resource utilization. They therefore stress the effects of demand management on output, and belittle the effects on prices. Monetarists believe that the aggregate supply curve is rather *steep* in many circumstances, especially when the economy has little slack. They therefore emphasize the effects of demand management on prices, and belittle the effects on real output. A middle-of-the-road view would hold that the Keynesian case is quite strong when there is a great deal of unemployment, while the monetarist case is stronger when the economy is near full employment. Not all economists accept this middle-of-the-road view, but many do.

Since the nature of the trade-off between output gains (which reduce unemployment) and inflation, as embodied in the slope of the aggregate supply schedule, plays such a fundamental role in the design of an appropriate stabilization policy, we devote the entire next chapter to an exploration of this trade-off.

Economic Forecasting: The Use of Econometric Models

We have seen in this chapter that the accuracy of economic forecasts plays a critical role in the Keynesian–monetarist debate over the advisability of trying to stabilize the economy through monetary and fiscal policy. It thus behooves us to take a look at the techniques that economists in universities, government agencies, and private businesses have developed over the years to assist them in predicting what the economy will do. There are a variety of techniques, none of them foolproof.

Among the most widely publicized forecasts are those generated by the use of an econometric model of the economy. Put simply, an **econometric model** is merely a mathematical version of the models of macroeconomic activity that we have been describing throughout Part Two. The difference is that the basic notions are cast in the form of mathematical equations rather than in diagrams. For example, our consumption function could have been expressed by the formula:

$$C = a + b\,DI,$$

where C is consumer spending and DI is disposable income, instead of by a graph.[2] The builder of an econometric model takes equations like these and uses actual data to estimate the sizes of a and b. For example, statistical analysis may lead a forecaster to the conclusion that the correct magnitude of a in the previous formula is approximately 120 and that the most reasonable value of b is 0.8. Then the consumption function formula is

$$C = 120 + 0.8\,DI.$$

This says that consumer spending is $120 (billion) plus 80 percent of disposable income. The economist can complete his model by adding a definition of disposable income as GNP minus tax receipts:

$$DI = Y - T,$$

[2] This is nothing but the formula for a straight line with a slope of b and an intercept of a.

and appending the fact that GNP is the sum of *C*, *I*, and *G*:

$$Y = C + I + G.$$

In this simple model, then, we have a total of three equations. If we hypothesize that government purchases, tax receipts, and investment are all unaffected by the relationships in the model, these three equations are just enough to determine the values of the three remaining variables: *C*, *DI*, and *Y*. These last three variables are called the model's *endogenous variables*, meaning that their values are determined *inside* the model. The remaining variables—*G*, *T*, and *I*—are called the model's *exogenous variables* because they must be provided from *outside* the model. With this nomenclature, it is easy to describe how the user of an econometric model forecasts the state of the economy:

An econometric forecaster uses a model to transform forecasts of the exogenous variables into corresponding forecasts of the endogenous variables.

Models actually used to forecast the behavior of the U.S. economy have hundreds of variables and equations. Because of their complexity, the only practical way to solve them for forecasts of all the endogenous variables is to use a high-speed computer. But you can understand what is going on inside these baffling machines if you can follow the illustrative example that is worked out in the boxed insert on page 288. The mechanics are that simple.

But making the forecast accurate is not simple because of the "garbage in, garbage out" problem: If you feed junk into the computer, that's exactly what will come out at the end. In the forecasting context, this "junk" can be either a bad set of predictions of the exogenous variables or an inaccurate set of equations. This is why model builders are constantly seeking to improve their equations. But they have yet to achieve anything like perfection. And, even if they did, their forecasts would still not be infallible because there is a certain amount of unavoidable randomness in macroeconomic behavior. After all, we are dealing with literally millions of individuals and business firms, and events essentially outside our control can sometimes exert a profound influence on our economy. (Example: Political turmoil in Iran in 1979 helped bring on the stagflation of 1979–1980.) So forecasts of the exogenous variables are bound to be wide of the mark at times.

Other Techniques of Economic Forecasting[3]

Leading Indicators

A second forecasting method, pioneered at the National Bureau of Economic Research, exploits observed historical timing relationships through the use of certain **leading indicators** that have in the past given advance warning of future economic events. For example, the stock market is often considered to be a leading indicator because stock market downturns normally begin several months before downturns in industrial production. *Why* is this happening? Does the decline in the stock market cause economic downturns by reducing consumer spending? Or are both the stock market and industrial production just reacting to some other influence, with the stock market's reaction coming sooner? Certainly these are fascinating questions. But the answers may not be crucial to a forecaster *if* the stock market continues to be as good a leading indicator for industrial production in the future as it has been in the past. In that event, we will be able to

A **leading indicator** is a variable that, experience has shown, normally turns down before recessions start and turns up before expansions get started.

[3]This section is adapted from Alan S. Blinder, *Fiscal Policy in Theory and Practice* (Morristown, N.J.: General Learning Press, 1973).

Forecasting with an Econometric Model

Modern econometric models of the whole economy are giants that defy description. But their basic logic is simple enough that we can illustrate their use through our example of a model with only three equations:

$$C = 120 + 0.8\, DI \qquad (1)$$
$$DI = Y - T \qquad (2)$$
$$Y = C + I + G. \qquad (3)$$

To obtain a forecast for the GNP, Y, we must first solve the equations for Y. It may seem at first that the last equation already gives us what we want. However, since the first two equations tell us that C also depends on Y, we actually have a situation in which Y appears on both sides of the equation. We therefore must collect terms to bring all the Ys together. If we substitute the first two equations into equation (3), we get:

$$
\begin{aligned}
Y = \quad & C && + \; I \; + \; G \\
= \; & 120 \; + \; 0.8 DI && + \; I \; + \; G \quad \text{[from equation (1)]} \\
= \; & 120 + 0.8(Y - T) && + \; I \; + \; G \quad \text{[from equation (2)]} \\
= \; & 120 + 0.8Y - 0.8T && + \; I \; + \; G.
\end{aligned}
$$

Subtracting $0.8Y$ from both sides gives:

$$0.2Y = 120 - 0.8T + I + G,$$

and dividing by 0.2 gives:

$$Y = \frac{120 + I + G - 0.8T}{0.2}.$$

The solution for Y can then be written as:

$$\boxed{Y = 600 + 5I + 5G - 4T.}$$

This last equation, which we have set off in a box, is our desired result. Given forecasts of I, G, and T, it enables us to forecast GNP. For example, if we expect I to be \$200 billion, G to be \$400 billion, and T to be \$500 billion, then our GNP forecast is:

$$
\begin{aligned}
Y &= 600 + (5 \times 200) + (5 \times 400) - (4 \times 500) \\
&= 600 + 1000 + 2000 - 2000 \\
&= \$1600 \text{ billion}.
\end{aligned}
$$

make use of the observed relationship between stock prices and industrial production for forecasting even if we do not entirely understand its origins.

As it turns out, however, excessive reliance on any single leading indicator produces a very unimpressive forecasting record. An obvious solution is to look at many indicators; but once we start to do this, we will often receive conflicting

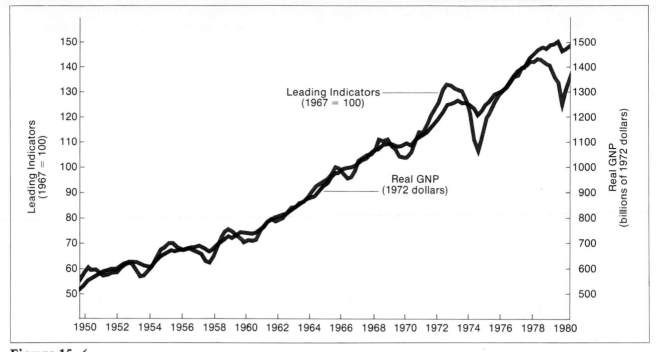

Figure 15-6
REAL GNP AND THE LEADING INDICATORS, 1950-1980
This diagram compares the path of the leading indicators (in blue) with that of real GNP (in black). The scales have been adjusted to make the two series comparable. It can be seen that the leading indicators sometimes give advance warning of a turning point in economic activity (for example, in 1973) but often give false signals of turning points that never occur (for example, 1956).
SOURCE: *Business Conditions Digest* and *Survey of Current Business*.

signals. If one indicator is rising rapidly while another is falling, what are we to do? One way to resolve this conflict is to form an average of several leading indicators. For example, the Commerce Department publishes a composite index that is a weighted average of 12 of their leading indicators. Figure 15-6 compares the behavior of this index with movements in real GNP. As you can see, the agreement is usually quite good. The leading indicators occasionally call for a recession that never comes (as in 1956), and occasionally they give clear early warning signals of a downturn (as in 1973 and 1979). But normally movements of the leading indicators are followed so closely by movements in real gross national product that the advance warning it provides comes too late to be of much use to policymakers.

Survey Data
A third source of information that is used by many forecasters is periodic surveys of the intentions of business and consumers. The Bureau of Economic Analysis of the Commerce Department and the Securities and Exchange Commission regularly ask firms how much money they plan to invest in factories and machinery over the next 3 to 12 months. These data are published in the financial press and are widely used by economists in industry, government, and academia. The Survey Research Center of the University of Michigan regularly conducts a survey of how consumers feel about both their personal finances and the general state of the economy. Some economists have found that this information on consumer sentiment helps improve forecasts of consumer spending.

Judgmental Forecasters

This term is used to describe those desperate (and probably prudent!) forecasters who refuse to rely on any one method, but look instead at every scrap of evidence they can get their hands on. They study the outputs of the econometric models; they watch the leading indicators; and they scrutinize the findings of surveys. At times, it seems, they even gaze at the stars! In any case, judgmental forecasters distill all this information in their heads and somehow arrive at a forecast of GNP and other key variables. How do they go about it? An outside observer can never really tell, since the very nature of judgmental forecasting precludes the existence of a formula that can be written down or described.

The Accuracy of Economic Forecasts

Which method wins the prize for the most accurate forecasts? First, no technique is clearly superior all the time. If it were, no one would do it any other way. Second, because econometric forecasters use surveys, lead-lag patterns, and judgment in forming their predictions of exogenous variables, and since judgmental forecasters watch the models, a clean comparison is impossible. In recent years, however, it seems that the most accurate forecasts have been derived by judgmental adjustment of forecasts from econometric models.

How accurate are economic forecasts? That depends both on the variable being forecast (consumption, for example, is usually easier than investment) and on the time period (for example, 1973–1975 were tough years for forecasters; 1976–1978 were much easier). To give a rough idea of magnitudes, forecasts of the annual inflation rate for 1973 and 1974 made late in the preceding year typically erred by 3 to 5 percentage points. This means that if forecasters predicted, say, a 10 percent inflation rate, the actual inflation rate might have been as low as 6 percent or as high as 14 percent. But these turbulent years were the worst for forecasters. In 1975–1977, by contrast, most inflation forecasts came within a single percentage point of being correct, and in recent years errors between 1 and 2 percent have been typical. Forecasts of real GNP for the coming year made during the 1970s and early 1980s typically erred by between $\frac{1}{2}$ and $1\frac{1}{2}$ percent.[4] Is this record good enough? That depends on what the forecasts are used for. It is certainly not good enough to support so-called "fine tuning," that is, attempts to keep the economy always within a hair's breadth of full employment. But it probably is good enough if our interest in using discretionary stabilization policy is to close persistent and sizable gaps between actual and potential GNP.

[4]Stephen K. McNees, "The Forecasting Record for the 1970s," *New England Economic Review*, September–October 1979, pages 33–53; and "The Recent Record of Thirteen Forecasters," *New England Economic Review*, September–October 1981, pages 5–21.

Summary

1. While Keynesian and monetarist theory both lead us to expect that fiscal *and* monetary policy can each affect aggregate demand, Keynesians tend to believe more in the effectiveness of fiscal policy while monetarists tend to believe more in the effectiveness of monetary policy.

2. Because fiscal policy actions affect aggregate demand either directly through G or indirectly through C, the expenditure lags between fiscal actions and their ef-

fects on aggregate demand are probably fairly short. By contrast, monetary policy operates mainly on investment, I, which responds very slowly to changes in interest rates.

3. However, the policy-making lag normally is much longer for fiscal policy than for monetary policy. Hence, when the two lags are combined, it is not clear which type of policy acts more quickly.

4. When there are long lags in the operation of fiscal and

monetary policy, it becomes possible that attempts to stabilize economic activity may actually succeed in destabilizing it.

5. Many monetarists believe that our imperfect knowledge of the channels through which stabilization policy works, and the long lags involved, make it unlikely that discretionary stabilization policy can succeed.

6. Keynesians recognize these difficulties but do not believe they are as serious as monetarists think. On the other hand, Keynesians place much less faith in the economy's ability to cure recessions and inflations on its own. They therefore think that discretionary policy is not only advisable, but essential.

7. The U.S. economy has a number of automatic stabilizers which make it less vulnerable to shocks than it would otherwise be. Among these are the personal income tax and unemployment benefits.

8. Keynesians believe that the aggregate supply curve is rather flat in the short run. This means that increases in aggregate demand will add much to the nation's real output and add little to the price level. Stabilization policy thus has much to recommend it as an anti-recession device, but it has little power to combat inflation.

9. Monetarists believe that the aggregate supply curve is very steep. This means that increases in aggregate demand increase real output rather little and succeed mostly in pushing up prices. Consequently, while stabilization policy can do much to fight inflation, it is not a very effective way to cure unemployment.

10. The Keynesian view probably is most applicable to an economy with much unemployment, while the monetarist view applies best to an economy producing near capacity levels.

11. Economic forecasts are made by econometric models, by exploiting leading indicators, and by judgment. Each method seems to play a role in arriving at good forecasts; but no method is foolproof, and economic forecasts are not as accurate as many people would like them to be.

Concepts for Review

Lags in stabilization policy
Automatic stabilizers
Rules versus discretionary policy

Shape of the aggregate supply curve
Econometric models

Leading indicators
Judgmental forecasts

Questions for Discussion

1. Distinguish between the expenditure lag and the policy lag in stabilization policy. Does monetary or fiscal policy have the shorter expenditure lag? What about the policy lag?

2. Explain why lags make it possible for policy actions intended to stabilize the economy actually to destabilize it instead.

3. Name some automatic stabilizers and explain how and what they "stabilize."

4. Which of the following events would strengthen the argument for the use of discretionary policy, and which would strengthen the argument for rules?
   a. Structural changes make the economy's self-correcting mechanism faster and more reliable than before.
   b. New statistical methods are found that improve the accuracy of economic forecasts.
   c. A Republican president is elected when there is an overwhelmingly Democratic Congress. The Congress and the president differ sharply on what should be done about the national economy.

5. Explain why their contrasting views on the shape of the aggregate supply curve lead Keynesians to argue much more strongly for stabilization policies to fight unemployment while monetarists argue much more strongly for stabilization policies to fight inflation.

6. (More difficult) Use the following hypothetical econometric model of the U.S. economy to obtain a forecast of the GNP in 1987:

$$C = 9 + 0.9\, DI$$
$$DI = Y - T$$
$$T = 10 + \tfrac{1}{3} Y$$
$$Y = C + I + G .$$

I and G are exogenous variables, and their forecasted values for 1987 are $I = 360, G = 600$.

7. Suppose the forecasts turn out to be correct. What will the actual budget surplus be in 1987? If high-employment for this economy corresponds to a GNP of 2700, what will be the high-employment surplus?

The Trade-Off Between Inflation and Unemployment

16

The rate of inflation, which was under 5 percent in 1976 (the year before President Jimmy Carter took office), exceeded 12 percent in 1980 (the final year of the Carter presidency). During the 1980 presidential campaign, the unemployment rate rose from below 6 percent to over $7\frac{1}{2}$ percent. Most observers believe that this poor performance of the economy helped Ronald Reagan hand Jimmy Carter one of the most lopsided electoral defeats in U.S. history.

Economic issues played a prominent role in the campaign. The challenger naturally placed the blame for the country's poor economic performance squarely on the lap of the incumbent. According to Mr. Reagan, Mr. Carter caused the acceleration of inflation by expansionary demand-management policies in 1977–1978 and caused the recession by contractionary policies in 1979–1980. The only way out, Reagan argued, was to adopt a series of "supply-side" tax reductions, which became the centerpiece of his economic policy. Carter disagreed both with the diagnosis and the proposed cure. He argued that the acceleration of inflation had been caused by a series of events beyond his control, especially the titanic increases in oil prices that occurred during 1979. A mild recession, he maintained, was necessary to wring the inflation out of the system. Notice the interesting juxtaposition of views here. According to Mr. Reagan, while the problems emanated from *demand-side* factors (like poorly conceived fiscal policy), the cure was to be found on the *supply side.* Mr. Carter, on the other hand, contended that although the problem had originated on the *supply side* (from such things as energy price increases), it could only be cured with *demand-side* medicine. The voters were given a clear choice between two economic theories, and apparently had little difficulty making up their minds in favor of Mr. Reagan's.

This chapter is, in a sense, about the things that voters would have found useful to know when they went to the polls in 1980. As we will see, there were elements of both truth and error in each candidate's position. Inflation can come from the demand side or from the supply side. And, regardless of the origins of inflation, government can seek a cure either through supply-side or demand-side initiatives. However, as we shall see, neither medicine kit holds any realistic promise of a quick and painless cure. There is no panacea.

You may recall from Chapter 1 that the existence of an agonizing trade-off between inflation and unemployment is one of the 12 Ideas for Beyond the Final Exam. The importance of this trade-off can hardly be overestimated. It is probably the one area of macroeconomics where confusion is most widespread. And because this confusion can have disastrous consequences for the conduct of stabilization policy, the trade-off merits the comprehensive examination that we give it in this chapter. Without a thorough understanding of the dimensions of this trade-off, it is impossible for a citizen to make an informed judgment about macroeconomic policy.

Demand-Side Inflation Versus Supply-Side Inflation: A Review

Let us begin our investigation of the trade-off by reviewing some of what we have learned about inflation in earlier chapters.

One major cause of inflation, though not the only one, is *excessive growth of aggregate demand.* What happens if, for some reason, either consumers or investors or the government decides to increase spending? We know, first of all, that such an autonomous increase in spending will have a multiplier effect on aggregate demand; that is, each additional $1 of C or I or G will lead to perhaps $2 to $2.50 of additional demand. Second, we know that such a stimulus to aggregate demand will normally pull up *both* real output *and* prices. The reason, to review our earlier findings, is that firms normally will find it profitable to supply the additional output only at higher prices.

Figure 16–1, which is familiar from earlier chapters, displays this conclusion. Initially, the economy is at point A, where aggregate demand curve D_0D_0 intersects aggregate supply curve SS. Then something happens to increase demand, and the aggregate demand curve shifts horizontally to D_1D_1. The new equilibrium is at point B, where both prices and output are higher than they were at A. The slope of the aggregate supply curve measures the amount of inflation

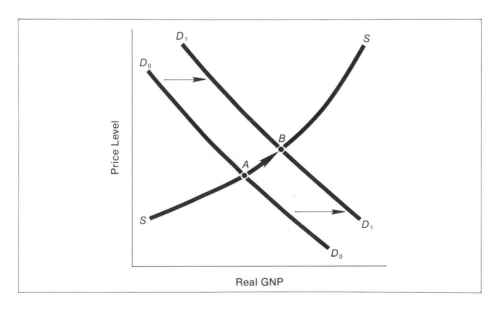

Figure 16–1
INFLATION FROM THE DEMAND SIDE
An increase in aggregate demand, whether it comes from consumers, investors, or the government, shifts the aggregate demand curve outward from D_0D_0 to D_1D_1. The economy's equilibrium moves from point A to point B. Since point B corresponds to a higher price level than does point A, there is *inflation* (that is, a rising price level) as the economy moves from A to B.

Figure 16–2
INFLATION FROM THE
SUPPLY SIDE

A decrease in aggregate supply—which can be caused by
such factors as an autonomous increase in wages, or by
an increase in the price of
foreign oil—can cause inflation. When the aggregate supply curve shifts to the left, from
S_0S_0 to S_1S_1, the equilibrium
point moves from A to B. Comparing B with A, we see that the
price level is higher, which
means there must have been
inflation (rising prices) in the interim. Notice also that adverse
supply shifts make real output
decline while prices are rising;
that is, they produce *stagflation*.

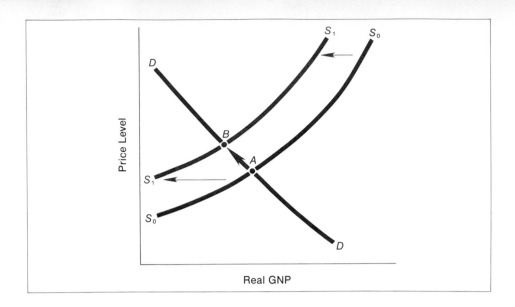

that accompanies any specified rise in output, and therefore embodies the most
important aspects of the trade-off between unemployment and inflation. We
concluded in the last chapter that this trade-off will be very favorable when the
economy is operating at low levels of capacity utilization and high levels of
unemployment. Under such circumstances, firms can expand their operations
substantially without running into higher costs. On the other hand, if demand
stimulus occurs in a fully employed economy, firms will find it quite difficult to
raise output, and so will respond mostly by raising prices. Thus, the trade-off is
very unfavorable when unemployment is low.

But we have learned in this book (especially in Chapter 9) that inflation need
not always emanate from the demand side. Restrictions in the growth of aggregate
supply—caused, for example, by an increase in the price of foreign oil—can shift
the economy's aggregate supply curve inward or upward. This is illustrated in
Figure 16–2, where the aggregate supply curve shifts from S_0S_0 to S_1S_1, and the
economy's equilibrium consequently moves from point A to point B. Prices rise
as output falls; we have *stagflation*. Thus, while inflation can be initiated from
either the demand side or the supply side of the economy, there is a crucial
difference. Demand-side inflation is normally accompanied by rising real GNP
(see Figure 16–1), while supply-side inflation may well be accompanied by falling
GNP (see Figure 16–2). This is an important distinction that will arise time and
again in this chapter.

Applying the Model to a Growing Economy

You may have noticed that our simple model of aggregate supply and aggregate
demand determines an equilibrium *price level* and an equilibrium *level of real
GNP*. But the real economy does not exhibit this type of equilibrium. Instead,
the price level and the level of real GNP are changing every year. This is
illustrated in Figure 16–3, which is a scatter diagram of the U.S. price level and the
level of GNP for every year from 1960 to 1981. The points are labeled for your
convenience, and it is quite clear that the general march of the economy through
time is upward and to the right—toward higher prices and higher levels of output.

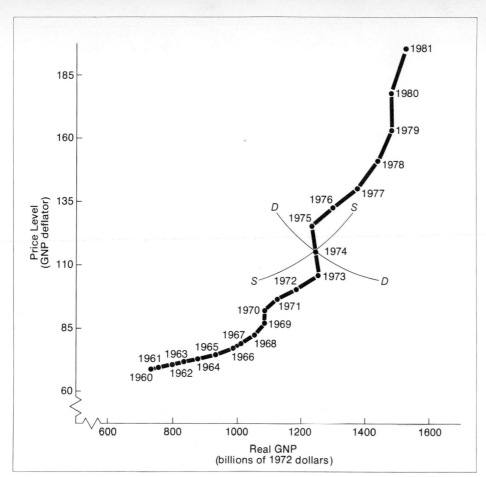

Figure 16–3
THE PRICE LEVEL AND
REAL OUTPUT IN THE
UNITED STATES,
1960–1981
This scatter diagram shows, for
each year from 1960 to 1981,
the price level (GNP deflator)
and real GNP for the United
States. Clearly the normal
state of affairs is for both vari-
ables to rise from one year to
the next.
SOURCE: U.S. Department of
Commerce, Bureau of Economic
Analysis

It is certainly no mystery why this occurs. The economy's aggregate supply and demand curves change each year. Aggregate supply normally grows because there are more workers, more machinery, and more factories each year, and because technology is improving. Aggregate demand normally grows because, with a growing population, there is more demand for both consumer and investment goods, and because the government increases its spending and the Federal Reserve increases the money supply. We can think of each point in Figure 16–3 as the intersection of an aggregate supply curve and an aggregate demand curve for that particular year. To help you visualize this, the curves for 1974 are sketched in the diagram.

One thing is clear from this diagram: if we want to apply our theoretical model to the real world, we must recognize that the normal state of affairs is for *both* the aggregate demand curve *and* the aggregate supply curve to shift to the right each year. Figure 16–4 illustrates this. The numbers are chosen so that curves D_0D_0 and S_0S_0 approximately represent the year 1977, and the curves D_1D_1 and S_1S_1 approximately represent 1978. Thus 1977's equilibrium was at point A, with real GNP of $1370 billion (in 1972 dollars) and a price level of 140, while 1978's equilibrium was at point B, with real GNP at $1440 billion and the price level at 150. The blue arrow in the diagram shows how equilibrium moved between 1977 and 1978. It points upward and to the right, meaning that both prices and output increased.

Figure 16–4

AGGREGATE SUPPLY AND DEMAND ANALYSIS OF A GROWING ECONOMY
This diagram illustrates how the aggregate supply and demand analysis of earlier chapters can be applied to a real-world economy, in which both the supply curve and the demand curve normally shift outward from one year to the next. In this example, demand curve D_0D_0 and supply curve S_0S_0 represent the U.S. economy in 1977. Equilibrium was at point A, with a price level of 140 and real GNP of $1370 billion. Demand curve D_1D_1 and supply curve S_1S_1 represent 1978. Between the two years, the price index rose by 10 points (about 7 percent) and output increased by $70 billion (about 6 percent).

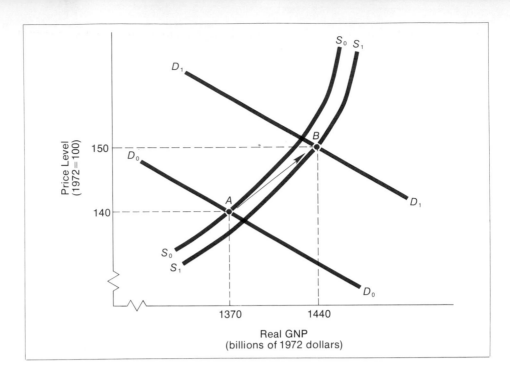

Demand-Side Inflation and the Phillips Curve

Let us now use our theoretical model to rerun history. Suppose that between 1977 and 1978 the aggregate demand curve grew either faster or slower than it actually did. What difference would this have made for the performance of the national economy?

The next two figures are intended to provide the answers. In Figure 16–5 we imagine that aggregate demand grew *faster* between 1977 and 1978 than it actually

Figure 16–5

THE EFFECTS OF FASTER GROWTH OF AGGREGATE DEMAND
In this hypothetical example, we imagine that, because either private citizens spent more or the government pursued expansionary policies, aggregate demand grew faster between 1977 and 1978 than it did in Figure 16–4. The consequence is that, in this diagram, the price level rises 17 points (or 12 percent) between 1977 and 1978, versus only 10 points (7 percent) in Figure 16–4. Growth of real output is also greater: $90 billion here versus only $70 billion in the previous figure.

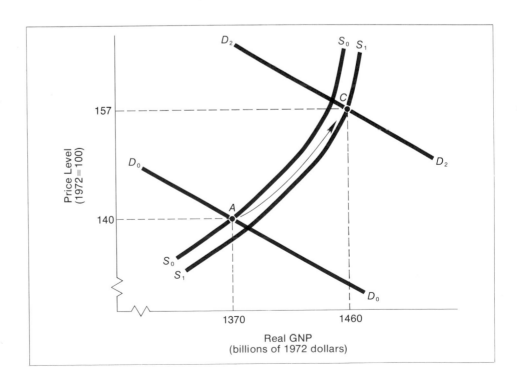

did. Thus, the demand curve D_0D_0 and both supply curves are exactly as they were in the previous diagram, but the demand curve D_2D_2 in Figure 16–5 is farther to the right than the demand curve D_1D_1 in Figure 16–4. Equilibrium is at point A in 1977 and point C in 1978. Comparing point C in Figure 16–5 with point B in Figure 16–4, we see that output would have increased more between 1977 and 1978 ($90 billion versus $70 billion) and prices would also have increased more (to 157 instead of to 150); that is, there would have been more inflation. This is generally what happens when the growth rate of aggregate demand speeds up.

For any given rate of growth of the aggregate supply curve, a faster rate of growth of the aggregate demand curve will lead to more inflation and faster growth of real output.

Figure 16–6 illustrates the opposite case. Here we imagine that the aggregate demand curve shifted out *less* than in Figure 16–4. That is, demand curve D_3D_3 in Figure 16–6 is to the left of demand curve D_1D_1 in Figure 16–4. The consequence, we see, is that the shift of the economy's equilibrium between 1977 (point A) and 1978 (point E) would have entailed *less inflation* and *slower growth of real output* than actually took place. This again is generally the case.

For any given rate of growth of the aggregate supply curve, a slower rate of growth of the aggregate demand curve will lead to less inflation and slower growth of real output.

If we put these two findings together, we have a very clear prediction from our theory:

If fluctuations in the economy's real growth rate from year to year are caused primarily by variations in the rate at which the aggregate demand curve shifts

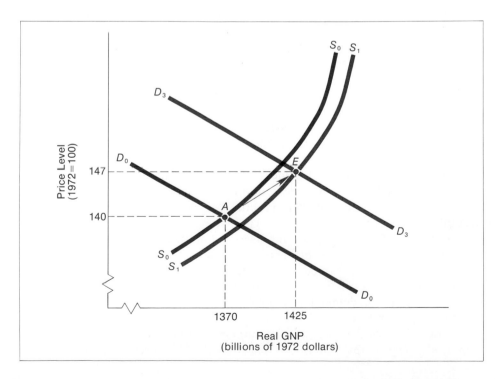

Figure 16–6
THE EFFECTS OF
SLOWER GROWTH OF
AGGREGATE DEMAND
Here, the aggregate demand
curve is assumed to shift outward less than it did in Figure
16–4. Consequently, the
movement from equilibrium
point A for 1977 to equilibrium
point E for 1978 entails a
smaller rise in the price level
and a smaller increase in real
output than actually occurred.

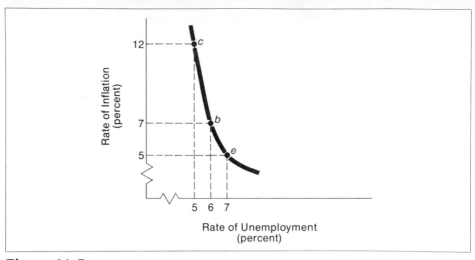

Figure 16–7

ORIGINS OF THE PHILLIPS CURVE

The three previous diagrams indicated three different rates of growth of real GNP between 1977 and 1978 and three different inflation rates. Since each different real growth rate corresponds to a different rate of unemployment, we can put the information contained in the three preceding diagrams together in a scatter diagram to show the relationship between inflation and unemployment. Points *b*, *c*, and *e* in this figure correspond to points *B*, *C*, and *E* in Figures 16–4, 16–5, and 16–6, respectively. The inflation numbers are read directly from the previous three graphs. The unemployment numbers are fabricated, but they represent the fact that faster growth (Figure 16–5) leads to lower unemployment (point *c*) while slower growth (Figure 16–6) leads to higher unemployment (point *e*). Scatter diagrams like this one are called "Phillips curves," after their inventor, A. W. Phillips.

outward, then the data should show that the most rapid inflation occurs during years when output expands most rapidly and the slowest inflation occurs during years when output expands more slowly.

Does the theory fit the facts? We will put it to the test in a moment, but first let us translate it into a prediction about the relationship between inflation and unemployment. Faster growth of real output naturally means faster growth in the number of jobs and, hence, *lower unemployment*. Conversely, slower growth of real output means slower growth in the number of jobs and, hence, *higher unemployment*. Thus, the unemployment rate and the growth rate of output should be inversely related—the faster the economy grows the lower the unemployment rate, and the slower the economy grows the higher the unemployment rate.

Figure 16–7 illustrates this idea. The actual unemployment rate in the United States in 1978 was 6 percent, and the inflation rate (based on the GNP deflator) was about 7 percent. This is point *b* in Figure 16–7, which corresponds to equilibrium point *B* in Figure 16–4. The faster growth rate of demand depicted by point *C* in Figure 16–5 would have led to higher inflation and lower unemployment. For the sake of a concrete example, we suppose that unemployment would have been 5 percent and inflation would have been 12 percent; this is point *c* in Figure 16–7. Point *E* in Figure 16–6 summarized the results of slower growth of aggregate demand: unemployment would have been higher and inflation lower. In Figure 16–7, this is represented by point *e*, with an unemployment rate of 7 percent and an inflation rate of 5 percent. This figure shows quite graphically the principal empirical implication of our theoretical model:

If fluctuations in economic activity are primarily caused by variations in the rate at which the aggregate demand curve shifts outward from year to year, then the data should show that low unemployment rates are associated with high inflation rates and high unemployment rates are associated with low inflation rates.

Now we are ready to look at real data. Do we actually observe such an inverse relationship between inflation and unemployment? About 25 years ago, economist A. W. Phillips plotted data on unemployment and the rate of change of *wages* (not prices) for several extended periods of British history on a series of scatter diagrams, one of which is reproduced as Figure 16–8. He then sketched in a curve that seemed to "fit" the data. This type of curve, which is now called a **Phillips curve,** shows that wage inflation normally is high when unemployment is low and is low when unemployment is high. So far, so good. Phillips curves have also been constructed for *price* inflation, and one of these for the postwar United States is shown in Figure 16–9. The curve appears to fit the data quite well, though not perfectly. As viewed through the eyes of our theory, these facts suggest that economic fluctuations in England between 1861 and 1913 and in the United States between 1948 and 1969 probably were accounted for primarily by changes in the growth of aggregate demand; that is, by changes in the spending habits of consumers, investors, and government. The simple model of demand-side inflation really does seem to describe what happened.

During the 1960s and early 1970s, economists often thought of the Phillips curve as a "menu" of the choices available to policymakers. In this view, policymakers could opt for low unemployment and high inflation—as was done in 1951 and 1969. Or they might prefer higher unemployment coupled with lower inflation—as, for example, in 1954 and 1961. The Phillips curve, it was thought, described the *quantitative* trade-off between inflation and unemployment. And, for a number of years, it worked rather well. Then something happened. The economy in the 1970s behaved far worse than expected in terms of the Phillips curve shown in Figure 16–9. In particular, given the unemployment rates in each of those years, inflation was astonishingly high by historical standards. This is shown in Figure 16–10, which simply adds to Figure 16–9 the points for 1970–1980. Clearly something had gone wrong with the old view of the Phillips curve as a menu for policy choices. As a result, a new view of the Phillips curve has emerged. We will discuss this "new view" next, and then return to the implications of the Phillips curve for the conduct of economic policy.

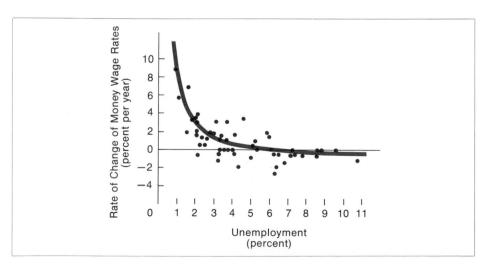

Figure 16–8
THE ORIGINAL PHILLIPS CURVE
This scatter diagram, reproduced from the original article by A. W. Phillips, shows the rate of change of money wages and the rate of unemployment in the United Kingdom between 1861 and 1913. Each year is represented by a point in the diagram.
SOURCE: A. W. Phillips, "The Relation Between Unemployment and the Rate of Change of Money Wages in the United Kingdom, 1861–1957," *Economica*, New Series, vol. 25, November 1958.

Figure 16–9
A PHILLIPS CURVE FOR
THE UNITED STATES
This Phillips curve relates *price*
inflation (rather than wage inflation) to the unemployment
rate in the United States for the
years 1948–1969. Though it
misses badly in a few instances
(for example, 1950), it generally ''fits'' the data quite well.

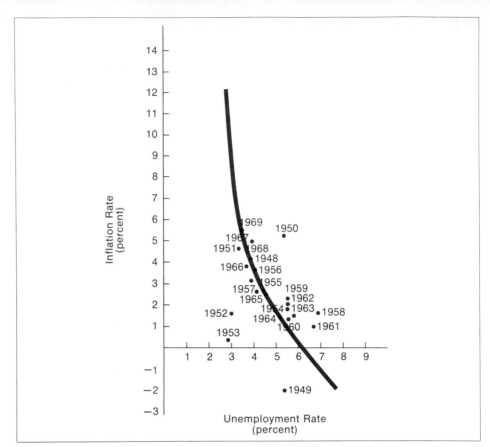

Figure 16–10
A PHILLIPS CURVE FOR
THE UNITED STATES?
This scatter diagram adds the
points for 1970–1980 to the
scatter diagram shown in Figure 16–9. It is clear that inflation in each of those years was
much higher than the Phillips
curve would have led us to
predict.

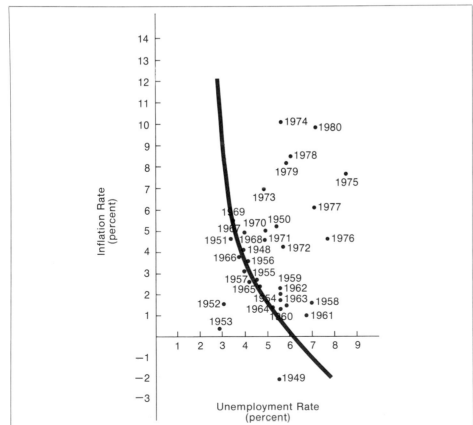

What the Phillips Curve Is Not

One view of what went wrong in the 1970s holds that policymakers misinterpreted the Phillips curve and tried to pick combinations of inflation and unemployment that were not in fact on the menu. Specifically, the Phillips curve is a *statistical relationship* between inflation and unemployment that we expect to emerge *if changes in the growth of aggregate demand are the predominant factor accounting for economic fluctuations.* But the curve was widely misinterpreted as depicting a number of *alternative equilibrium points* that the economy could achieve and from which policymakers could choose.

We can understand the flaw in this reasoning by quickly reviewing an earlier lesson. We know from Chapter 9 that the economy has a **self-correcting mechanism** that will cure both inflations and recessions *eventually* even if the government does nothing. Why is this relevant here? Because it tells us that many combinations of output and prices cannot be maintained indefinitely. Some will "self-destruct." Specifically, if the economy finds itself far away from the normal "full-employment" level of unemployment, forces will be set in motion that tend to erode the inflationary or recessionary gap.

For example, consider the case of an inflationary gap—that is, a situation in which equilibrium output exceeds potential GNP. With production exceeding normal capacity levels, firms will be prone to raise prices. And with employment exceeding "full employment," wages will be rising rapidly. The resulting inflation will destroy the inflationary gap by reducing aggregate demand. Specifically, higher prices will deter consumer spending by lowering the purchasing power of consumer wealth. And higher prices will deter investment spending by forcing up interest rates. The inflationary gap will destroy itself through a cumulative process of inflation. Figure 16–11 shows this conclusion diagrammatically. When the aggregate demand curve is DD and the aggregate supply curve is S_0S_0, the economy reaches a short-run equilibrium at point C, which is beyond full employment. There is an inflationary gap, measured by the distance EC, and both prices and wages begin to rise. The higher wages represent increases in production costs, which shift the aggregate supply curve upward toward higher prices. The process comes to an end only when the supply curve has reached the position

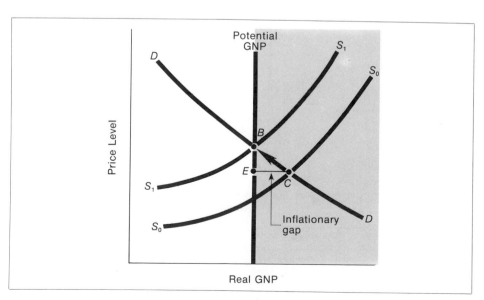

Figure 16–11

THE ELIMINATION OF AN INFLATIONARY GAP
When the aggregate supply curve is S_0S_0 and the aggregate demand curve is DD, the economy will reach equilibrium (point C) with an inflationary gap. The resulting inflation of wages will push the supply curve upward toward higher prices until it has shifted to the position indicated by curve S_1S_1. Here, with equilibrium at point B, the economy is at normal full employment. But, during the adjustment period from C to B, there will have been both inflation and falling output.

indicated by S_1S_1. Here, wages have risen enough to close the inflationary gap, the economy is at a full-employment equilibrium at point B, and the inflation ceases.[1]

So far this is all review. Now let us relate it to our discussion of the origins of the Phillips curve. Suppose the case depicted in Figure 16–4 corresponds to an economy that had been producing at potential GNP in 1978; that is, suppose potential GNP was $1440 billion. This means that the unemployment rate corresponding to point b in Figure 16–7 (6 percent) is the full-employment unemployment rate.

Now turn to the scenario of faster economic growth depicted in Figure 16–5. If potential GNP was $1440 billion in 1978, then point C in Figure 16–5 corresponds to an inflationary gap of the sort depicted in Figure 16–11. This means that point C cannot be sustained. It will self-destruct through a process of inflation and falling output similar to that depicted in Figure 16–11. Since point c on our Phillips curve diagram, which is repeated for convenience here as Figure 16–12, corresponds to point C in Figure 16–4, it follows that point c is not sustainable. Instead, as we have just argued, an economy that finds itself initially at point c will suffer rising inflation and rising unemployment (falling output) during the adjustment period. In the Phillips curve diagram (Figure 16–12), the movement will be northeasterly, as indicated by the blue arrow running from point c to point f, which is vertically above point b. Why vertically above? Because we have assumed in our example that 6 percent unemployment corresponds to "full employment." If the economy is to return to normal full-

[1]Inflation ceases, of course, only if the aggregate demand curve stays put. If it continues to shift outward, inflation can continue.

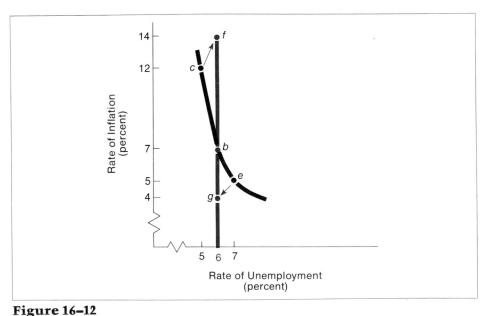

Figure 16–12
THE VERTICAL LONG-RUN PHILLIPS CURVE
In the long-run, points like c, where unemployment is lower than the normal "full-employment" unemployment rate, are unsustainable. The economy's natural self-correcting mechanism (which was described in Figure 16–11) will erode the inflationary gap by raising both inflation and unemployment. In the diagram, this will force the economy, which was initially propelled from point b to point c by a surge in aggregate demand, toward a point like f, which is vertically above b. The long-run choices, therefore, are among points like b and f, which constitute what is called the *vertical (long-run) Phillips curve*, not among points like b and c on the downward-sloping (short-run) Phillips curve.

employment rates of production, as it must, then point f must be vertically above point b.

Now we can see why the Phillips curve connecting points c, b, and e does not represent a menu of policy choices. While we can move from a point like b to a point like c by stimulating aggregate demand sufficiently, there is no way that we can stay at point c. Unemployment cannot be kept this low indefinitely. Instead, policymakers must choose from among points like b and f, all of which are vertically above one another. For rather obvious reasons, the line connecting these points has been dubbed the **vertical (long-run) Phillips curve.** It is this vertical Phillips curve (connecting points like b and f), not the downward-sloping Phillips curve (connecting points like b and c), that represents the true long-run "menu" of policy choices. Notice that every point on the vertical Phillips curve corresponds to the same rate of unemployment (6 percent in the example). Because the economy's natural self-correcting mechanism tends always to push the unemployment rate back to this critical rate, it has come to be called the **natural rate of unemployment.** The natural rate corresponds exactly to what we have so far been calling the "full-employment" unemployment rate.

SUMMARY

Our conclusions about the Phillips curve can be summarized in three statements:
1. To the extent that economic fluctuations emanate from the demand side, we expect to find an inverse relationship between unemployment and inflation— a downward-sloping Phillips curve.
2. In the short-run, it is possible to "ride up the Phillips curve" toward lower levels of unemployment by stimulating aggregate demand. Conversely, by restricting the growth of demand, it is possible to "ride down the Phillips curve" toward lower rates of inflation (see, for example, point e in Figure 16–12). There is, thus, a *trade-off between unemployment and inflation.* Stimulating demand will improve the unemployment picture but worsen inflation; restricting demand will lower inflation but aggravate the unemployment problem.
3. However, there is no such trade-off in the long run. The economy's self-correcting mechanism ensures that unemployment eventually will return to the "natural rate," no matter what happens to aggregate demand. In the long run, faster growth of demand leads only to higher inflation, not to lower unemployment; and slower growth of demand leads only to lower inflation, not to higher unemployment.

Fighting Inflation Through Fiscal and Monetary Policy

Let us now apply this analysis to a concrete policy problem, one that has vexed every American president from Lyndon Johnson to Ronald Reagan. How should the government's ability to manage aggregate demand through fiscal and monetary policy be used to fight inflation?

We have already spent many chapters discussing how the government's monetary and fiscal policy tools—tax rates, government spending, open market operations, and so on—can be used to increase or decrease aggregate demand. We have also discussed some of the practical problems that arise in using each of these weapons and some of the issues involved in choosing among them. Rather than repeat all this, let us just suppose that the government somehow controls aggregate demand, and wishes to use this ability to fight inflation. What has our discussion of the trade-off between inflation and unemployment taught us about this problem?

To stay with our concrete example, suppose that, like President Carter in 1978, we find ourselves at point *b* in Figure 16–12, with a 7 percent inflation rate and a 6 percent unemployment rate, and we want to move to a lower inflation rate. One option is to slow the growth of aggregate demand via contractionary fiscal and monetary policies, thereby opening up a recessionary gap. In a word—though no politician would ever use such blunt language—a decision is made to fight inflation by causing a recession.

This policy has, essentially, already been examined in Figures 16–4 and 16–6, where we compared two different aggregate demand curves for 1978, one below the other. Figure 16–13 collects the relevant information from these two earlier diagrams for your convenience. Curve S_1S_1 is the aggregate supply curve for 1978; curves D_1D_1 and D_3D_3 are two alternative aggregate demand curves; and points *B* and *E* are the two alternative equilibrium points. Full employment is assumed to occur when real GNP is $1440 billion. Notice that by comparison with point *B*, point *E* corresponds to less inflation. Prices between 1977 and 1978 would rise only 5 percent instead of about 7 percent. (Recall that the 1977 price level was 140.) In terms of the Phillips curve diagram in Figure 16–12, the restrictive policy pushes the economy down the Phillips curve from point *b* to point *e*.

But the anti-inflationary dividends of recession do not end there. At point *E* in Figure 16–13, or point *e* in Figure 16–12, there is a recessionary gap. Let us now recall from Chapter 9 how the economy's self-correcting mechanism works in such a situation. Unused industrial capacity and unsalable output act as restraints on firms that would like to raise prices. The availability of unemployed workers eager for jobs limits the rate at which labor can push up wages. Since the money wage is a principal determinant of the *height* of the aggregate supply curve, the recession will lead to lower aggregate supply curves *in 1979 and subsequent years.* But lower supply curves in future years mean lower prices in future years.

Figure 16–13
FIGHTING INFLATION BY CAUSING RECESSION
Instead of letting the aggregate demand curve move to the position D_1D_1 (which comes from Figure 16–4), the government—by raising taxes, cutting spending, or slowing down the growth of the money supply—can hold the aggregate demand curve to the position indicated by D_3D_3 (which comes from Figure 16–6). This would make the equilibrium for 1978 occur at point *E* instead of *B*, and open up a recessionary gap. Because of the economic slack, wages would increase more slowly during 1978 under this restrictive policy. So the aggregate supply curves *for 1979 and subsequent years* would be lower on account of the restrictive policy.

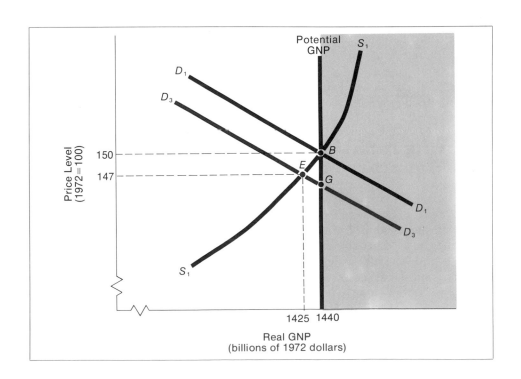

This is how a policy of recession works to limit inflation. In terms of the Phillips curve diagram in Figure 16–12, reductions in the rate of wage inflation push the economy downward (toward less price inflation and to the left toward less unemployment), from point *e* toward point *g*. Just as point *c* was not sustainable because unemployment was too *low*, point *e* is not sustainable because unemployment is too *high*. The economy's self-correcting mechanism works in both directions.

But let us recall another point made in Chapter 9. The self-correcting mechanism seems to work less well when it comes to eroding recessionary gaps. Because workers are reluctant to accept slowdowns in the rate of growth of wages, the inflation rate is somewhat resistant to the recessionary medicine. This means that the anti-inflation policy may not show very encouraging results at first. The movement from point *b* to point *e* in Figure 16–12 may be nearly horizontal, meaning that an alarming rise in unemployment is accompanied by rather little slackening of inflation. And then progress along the path from *e* to *g* may be agonizingly slow. Policymakers who embark on this course must be patient; the costs in terms of unemployment come early; the gains on the inflation front appear later.

Comparing point *g* with point *b* in Figure 16–12 shows that, in the end, there is less inflation and no more unemployment. In what sense, then, do policymakers have to face up to the trade-off between inflation and unemployment?

The cost of reducing inflation by restrictive fiscal and monetary policies is a *temporary* rise in unemployment.

Figure 16–14 and 16–15 are intended to give the flavor of what the real menu of choices looks like to a policymaker who is considering embarking on such a program. Figure 16–14 contrasts the behavior of the inflation rate over time under a "hands off policy" (which maintains the current growth rate of aggregate demand) with the behavior under a restrictive anti-inflationary policy (which deliberately slows the growth rate of aggregate demand). Inflation will continue at 7 percent per year if the government does not restrain the growth of demand.

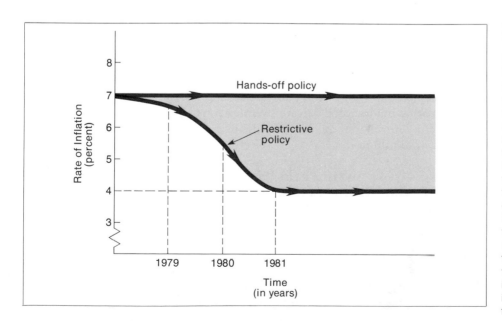

Figure 16–14
THE PAYOFF TO ANTI-INFLATION POLICY
If a recession is caused by restrictive fiscal and monetary policy, the inflation rate will not respond very much at first (this corresponds to the nearly horizontal movement from point *b* to point *e* in Figure 16–12). Gradually, however, inflation will yield to the slack caused by the restrictive policy. In this example, the inflation rate begins at 7 percent, falls only to 6¾ percent after one year, but is down to 5½ percent after two years, and 4 percent after three years. The shaded area indicates the gains that the policy has reaped on the inflation front.

Figure 16–15

THE COST OF ANTI-INFLATION POLICY
The inflation gains depicted in the preceding figure do not come to us without cost. The restrictive policy increases unemployment for a period; that is, it induces a recession. In this example, the unemployment rate takes about a year and a half to rise from 6 percent to 7 percent (the recession period), and then takes another year and a half to return to 6 percent (the recovery period). The shaded area indicates the extra unemployment that must be endured in order to get the inflation rate down from 7 percent to 4 percent.

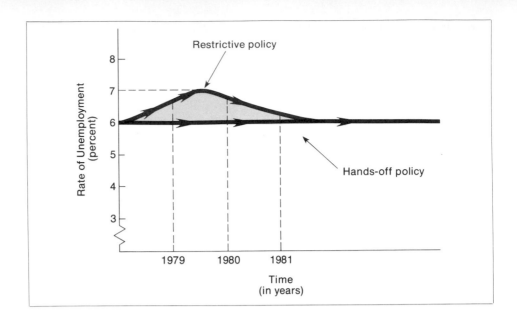

This is the "hands off policy" path shown in black in Figure 16–14. On the other hand, if a restrictive policy is followed and the growth of aggregate demand is restrained, inflation will begin to fall, slowly at first but then with increasing speed. In the example, we suppose that the inflation rate falls little in the first year, more in the second year, and is essentially down to 4 percent after three years. This is the "restrictive policy" path shown in blue in Figure 16–14. The shaded area in the figure summarizes the difference between these two paths, and therefore depicts the payoff to anti-inflation policy.

But there are also costs. Figure 16–15 gives a rough impression of how the unemployment rate might behave under the two alternative policies. The "hands off policy" keeps the unemployment rate at 6 percent, which is the natural rate. The restrictive policy results in a recession: unemployment rises gradually from 6 percent up to 7 percent, and then gradually falls back to the natural rate of 6 percent. The shaded area in Figure 16–15 shows what it costs to get the inflation rate down: for about three years unemployment is above the natural rate.

What Should Be Done?

Should the government pay the recessionary cost of fighting inflation? When the benefits depicted in Figure 16–14 are balanced against the costs shown in Figure 16–15, have we made a good bargain? While each of you will have to answer this question for yourself, our analysis has highlighted three critical issues on which your answer should rest.

The Costs of Inflation and Unemployment

We spent an entire chapter early in the book (Chapter 6) examining the social costs of inflation and unemployment. The costs of the extra unemployment depicted in Figure 16–15, we concluded, are easy to translate into dollars and cents; basically, we only need to estimate the real GNP that is lost each year. However, the costs of inflation are harder to put a price tag on, and hence the benefits from reducing inflation are harder to measure. Thus there is considerable controversy over the costs and benefits of using recession to fight inflation. Some economists and public figures believe that inflation is extremely costly, and so they look with favor on the trade-off that is embodied in Figures 16–14 and 16–15. Others have a lower estimate of the costs of inflation and find recession a terribly high price to pay.

The Position of the Economy

We have stated several times in this book that the shape of the economy's aggregate supply curve, and hence the shape of the short-run Phillips curve, depends very much on the degree of resource utilization. If resources are virtually fully employed, the aggregate supply curve (and thus the Phillips curve) will be rather steep, which means that the inflation gains will be substantial and the unemployment costs will be minimal. On the other hand, if there is a great deal of unemployed labor and unutilized industrial capacity, the aggregate supply curve (and hence the short-run Phillips curve) may be nearly horizontal. In that case, a great deal of unemployment will be needed to achieve even a slight reduction in inflation. Thus the trade-off depicted in our last two diagrams will look more favorable when the economy is in a boom and less favorable when there is already a good deal of unemployment.

The Efficiency of the Economy's Self-Correcting Mechanism

We have stressed that once government policy causes a recession, it is the economy's natural self-correcting mechanism that cures the recessionary gap. The obvious question here is: How long do we have to wait? If the self-correcting mechanism—which works through reductions in the rate of wage inflation—is slow and halting, the costs of fighting inflation will be enormous. On the other hand, if wage inflation responds promptly, the recession necessary to bring down inflation may not be very severe. This is another issue that is surrounded by controversy. One group of economists argues that the evidence points to very sluggish wage behavior. The rate of wage inflation, this group maintains, responds only slowly to economic slack. In terms of our Figure 16–12, this means that the economy will traverse the path from e to g at an agonizingly slow pace, so that a very long recession will be necessary if there is to be any appreciable effect on inflation.

But another group of economists finds this assessment far too pessimistic. This group argues that the costs of reducing inflation are not nearly so severe and that the key to a successful anti-inflation policy is its effects on people's *expectations*. But, to understand this argument, we must first examine why expectations are relevant to the Phillips-curve trade-off.

Inflationary Expectations and the Phillips Curve

The explanation starts with some more review. Recall from Chapter 9 that the main reason why the economy's aggregate supply curve slopes upward—that is, why output increases as the price level rises—is that businesses typically purchase labor and other inputs under long-term contracts that stipulate the cost of the input in *money* terms (for example, the nominal wage rate). If such contracts are in force when prices go up, then *real* wages will fall as prices rise. From businesses' point of view, labor is now cheaper in real terms, and firms will be induced to expand employment and output. Buying cheaply and selling dearly is, after all, the route to higher profits. Long-term contracts that set the nominal wage rate, then, explain why higher prices lead to more output; that is, why the aggregate supply curve slopes upward.

But now let us take note of something we ignored before. There is a sense in which labor is being "cheated" by this process. Workers agreed to sell their services for, say, $8 per hour when the price level was 100. If the price level now rises to 105 (a 5 percent inflation), the purchasing power of their wages will be reduced by 5 percent. However, if workers *expect inflation to occur*, they may insist on being compensated for it *in advance*. For example, they may demand a wage of $8.40 per hour (which is 5 percent more than $8 per hour) in anticipation of the rise in the price level. If workers actually behave this way, the money wages they will insist on will be systematically related to the prices they *expect* to prevail. Consider the following example of workers agreeing *today* on a money wage to prevail a year from now.

EXPECTED INFLATION RATE (percent)	EXPECTED PRICE LEVEL ONE YEAR FROM NOW	MONEY WAGE ONE YEAR FROM NOW (dollars per hour)	EXPECTED REAL WAGE ONE YEAR FROM NOW (dollars per hour)
0	100	8.00	8.00
5	105	8.40	8.00
10	110	8.80	8.00
20	120	9.60	8.00

Relative to the $8/hour wage they would settle for if they expected zero inflation, labor may demand 5 percent more ($8.40) if they expect 5 percent inflation; 10 percent more ($8.80) if they expect 10 percent inflation; and so on. Then, if expectations prove correct, prices and wages will go up together, leaving the real wage unchanged and the firms with no special incentive to produce more as prices rise. In a word, the aggregate supply curve would become *vertical*. In general:

If workers can see inflation coming, and if they demand compensation for it in advance so that inflation does not erode *real* wages, then the economy's aggregate supply curve will not slope upward. It will be a vertical line at the level of output corresponding to potential GNP.

Such a curve is shown in part (a) of Figure 16–16. Since we derived the Phillips curve from the aggregate supply curve earlier in the chapter, it follows that even the *short-run* Phillips curve will become vertical under these circumstances [see part (b) of Figure 16–16].

If this analysis is correct, it has profound implications for the trade-off and for the costs and benefits of inflation-fighting. This can be seen by referring back to Figure 16–12 on page 302, where we depicted the strategy of fighting inflation by causing a recession. We concluded there that in order to move from point *b* (representing 7 percent inflation) to point *g* (representing 4 percent inflation), the economy would have to take a detour through point *e*; that is, it would have to endure a recession. If, however, even the *short-run* Phillips curve were *vertical* rather than downward sloping, this detour would not be necessary. It would be possible for inflation to fall without unemployment rising. The economy could jump directly from point *b* to point *g*.

Is this analysis correct? Can we really slay the inflationary dragon so painlessly? As a piece of pure logic, the argument is impeccable. We must therefore ask ourselves whether the premises on which it rests seem realistic.

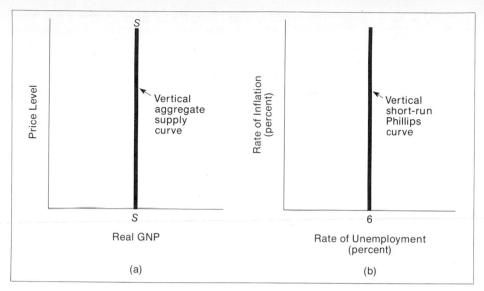

Figure 16–16
A VERTICAL AGGREGATE
SUPPLY CURVE AND THE
CORRESPONDING VERTICAL
PHILLIPS CURVE
If workers foresee inflation,
and if they also demand full
compensation for it in advance, then inflation will no
longer erode real wages. In
that case, firms will have no incentive to raise production as
prices rise, and the aggregate
supply curve will be vertical as
in part (a). Since we derived
the short-run Phillips curve
from the aggregate supply
curve, the short-run Phillips
curve will also become vertical
[part (b)].

There are several reasons why many economists think the expectations argument should not be applied uncritically to the modern economy.

Point 1.   The argument is predicated on the notion that inflation can be accurately foreseen. But many contracts for labor and other raw materials cover such long periods of time that the expectations that are held when the contracts are written may be very different from the current reality. If a restrictive policy reduces inflation below the rate firms and workers were expecting when they made their wage agreement, real wages will wind up higher than was intended, and hence firms will want to reduce employment and produce less.

Point 2.   Many people believe that inflationary expectations are quite sluggish, that they do not adapt quickly to changes in the economic environ- ment. If, for example, the government embarks on an anti-inflation policy, workers will continue to expect high inflation for quite a while. Thus they will continue to insist on high rates of increase in money wages. Then, if inflation actually slows down, real wages will wind up rising faster than anyone expected. Firms will therefore find labor "too expensive" relative to current selling prices, and unem- ployment will result. With lags in the reaction of expectations, then, the short-run Phillips curve retains its downward slope and inflation- fighting is costly.

The Theory of Rational Expectations

These two points, and others we have not mentioned, have persuaded most economists that the expectationist argument, while valid in part, should not be taken to extremes. Most economists nowadays accept the notion that the Phillips curve is downward sloping in the short run, and hence that a short-run trade-off does exist. But a vocal minority of economists disagrees. This group, believers in the doctrine of **rational expectations,** insists that the only type of inflation that leads to *increases* in output is *unexpected* inflation, because only unexpected inflation will reduce real wages. Similarly, they argue, the only type of reduction in inflation that leads to recession is an *unexpected* reduction.

And they take the argument further. Even though they recognize that inflation cannot always be accurately predicted, they claim that workers will not make *systematic* errors in forecasting inflation. Note that point 2 above suggests that inflationary expectations are typically *too low* when inflation is rising and *too high* when inflation is falling. Rational expectationists deny that this is possible. Workers, they argue, will always make the best possible forecast of inflation, using all the latest data and the best available economic models. Such forecasts will not err systematically in one direction or the other. Consequently, the difference between the *actual* rate of inflation and the *expected* rate of inflation (the forecasting error) will be a purely random number. Since employment is affected by inflation only to the extent that inflation differs from what was expected, it follows that the inflation rate can be reduced without the need for a period of high unemployment. Except for some random—and totally unpredictable—gyrations due to forecasting errors, the rational expectationists claim that unemployment will remain at the natural rate.

The implications of rational expectations for the conduct of economic policy are really quite revolutionary. According to this view, the government's ability to manipulate aggregate demand does not give it any control over real output and unemployment—not even in the short run. (To see why, experiment with moving an aggregate demand curve when the aggregate supply curve is vertical as in Figure 16–16.) Any *predictable* change in aggregate demand will lead to a change in the expected rate of inflation, and hence will leave real wages unaffected. The government influences output only if it makes *unexpected* changes in aggregate demand. But this is not easy to do when expectations are "rational." According to the rational expectationists, if the monetary and fiscal authorities typically react to high inflation by reducing aggregate demand, people will soon come to anticipate this reaction. And, as just mentioned, anticipated reductions in aggregate demand will not affect unemployment because they will not cause *unexpected* changes in inflation.

Since rational expectationists believe that inflation can be reduced without losses of output, they tend to be hawks in the war against inflation. Though the doctrine has attracted many adherents, rational expectationists remain in the minority. There are many reasons for this. For one, point 1 above remains valid even if expectations are rational. For another, many observers of the labor market continue to believe that inflationary expectations are quite sluggish; that is, they are not "rational." Finally, the facts have not been kind to the rational expectations point of view. The theory suggests that unemployment should hover around the natural rate most of the time, with random gyrations in one direction or the other. Yet this does not seem to be the case. The theory also denies that predictable monetary and fiscal policy actions will have effects on real output. Yet most observers think they can identify episodes in the past where such actions had significant effects on real GNP and unemployment. Pending convincing evidence to the contrary, most economists continue to believe that the Phillips curve is downward sloping, at least in the short run.

Fighting Recessions with Fiscal and Monetary Policy

We have covered a lot of ground in this chapter already, and introduced a number of new concepts. At this point it may be useful to pause and take stock of what we have learned. A good way to test your understanding is to run the analysis in reverse. Up to now we have been considering the use of monetary and fiscal policies to combat *inflation*. Let us now suppose instead that the crucial macroeconomic problem is *unemployment*.

We again turn to the Phillips curve diagram, Figure 16–12 on page 302, for a concrete example. Suppose that the economy somehow finds itself at a point like *e*, in a recession. And suppose that the president and Congress want to get the economy back to full employment. What should they do? We already know from our previous analysis what will happen if the current rate of growth of aggregate demand is simply maintained. Point *e* on the Phillips curve represents a recessionary gap, so the economy's self-correcting mechanism starts to work. High unemployment slows the rate of increase of money wages, which tends to push the aggregate supply curve downward (compared with where it would have been if full employment were maintained). This both puts a brake on inflation and encourages employment. The economy slowly travels down the path indicated by the blue arrow in Figure 16–12, from point *e* to point *g*. But, as we have noted before and repeat here for emphasis, the road from *e* to *g* may be slow and bumpy.

Is there a better way out of our economic problems? Perhaps. As we have learned, expansionary measures such as tax cuts, increases in government spending, or open market purchases of government securities can speed up the rate at which the aggregate demand curve moves to the right. (Compare Figure 16–5 and Figure 16–4.) Such a policy would enable the economy to "ride up" the short-run Phillips curve toward point *b*. Let us compare this active antirecession policy with the more passive "hands off" policy. Figures 16–17 and 16–18 will assist in the comparison. Under the "hands off" policy of relying on the economy's self-correcting mechanism, the unemployment rate gradually falls from the 7 percent that corresponds to point *e* on the Phillips curve to the 6 percent that corresponds to point *g*. But progress is agonizingly slow. The black "hands off policy" path in Figure 16–17 indicates that it takes three uncomfortable years to return to full employment. By contrast, if expansionary monetary and fiscal policy actions are taken, the return to full employment is much quicker. According to the blue "expansionary policy" path in Figure 16–17, we get there in about one and one-half years. The shaded area in the figure measures the payoff to antirecession policy; it shows how much unemployment we save during the three-year period.

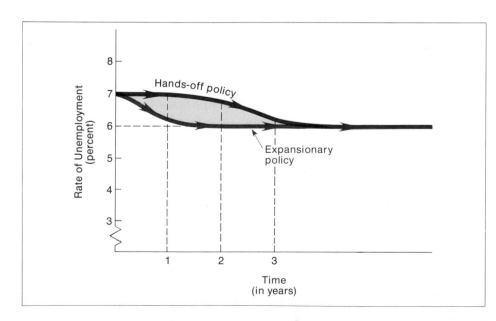

Figure 16–17
THE PAYOFF TO ANTI-
RECESSION POLICY
By stimulating aggregate demand through monetary and fiscal policy, the government can reduce unemployment more rapidly. If it relies exclusively on the economy's ability to right itself, unemployment will follow the black "hands off policy" path. If, instead, the government takes an active hand in fighting the recession, unemployment will follow the blue "expansionary policy" path. The shaded area measures the reduction in unemployment that the expansionary policy achieves.

Figure 16-18

THE COST OF ANTI-
RECESSION POLICY
The unemployment gains depicted in the previous figure
are not quite free. By stimulating the economy, the government policies cause a slight
acceleration in the inflation
rate—as shown by the blue
"expansionary policy" path.
If, instead, the government had
simply waited for the economy's natural self-correcting
mechanism to work, inflation
would have fallen slightly—see
the black "hands off policy"
path. The difference between
these two paths (the shaded
area) represents the inflationary cost of fighting the recession.

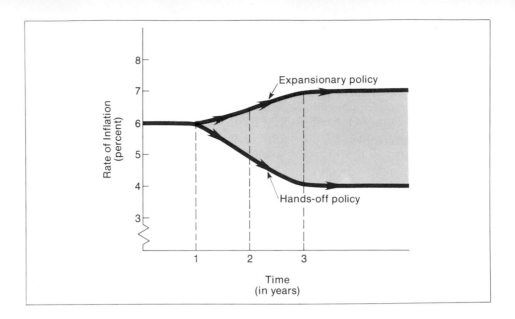

But, as we have by now come to expect, these gains are made at some cost. The black "hands off policy" path in Figure 16–18 shows the likely behavior of the inflation rate under the policy of waiting for the economy's self-corrective forces to work. Inflation falls gradually from the 6 percent rate that corresponds to point *e* on the Phillips curve to the 4 percent rate that corresponds to point *g*. But if the expansionary policy is pursued, inflation will not creep downward; instead it will creep upward, as indicated by the blue "expansionary policy" path in Figure 16–18. The shaded area in this figure shows the cost of fighting recession with monetary and fiscal policy: we wind up with more inflation.

In considering whether or not to fight a recession, policymakers face a trade-off between unemployment and inflation. If they take expansionary actions to reduce unemployment, they may wind up with a higher inflation rate at the end.

Are the inflationary costs depicted in Figure 16–18 worth the benefits of lower unemployment shown in Figure 16–17? This is not a question that can be answered with any assurance. The answer hinges on the same three issues we isolated before when considering anti-inflation policy:

1. ***The social costs of inflation and unemployment.*** Those who regard inflation as very costly will not want to pay the price of shortening the recession. Those who are more concerned with unemployment will find recession-fighting a good idea.

2. ***The position of the economy.*** As we have noted, the Phillips curve is likely to be flatter at higher rates of unemployment. As you can see by studying Figure 16–12, if the Phillips curve is rather flat, the extra inflation caused by fighting a recession will be minimal. On the other hand, if the short-run Phillips curve is steep, the inflationary price tag will be high. Thus the case for fighting deep recessions is stronger than the case for fighting shallow ones.

3. *The efficiency of the economy's self-correcting mechanism.* Naturally, if the economy's self-corrective forces worked rapidly, there would be little reason for the government to try to speed things up. On the other hand, if the mechanism is slow and unreliable or, worse yet, if it breaks down entirely, the case for government intervention is much stronger.

Why Economists (and Politicians) Disagree

These three factors help explain why economists sometimes differ so radically from one another in their recommendations as to the proper conduct of national economic policy. And they also help account for disagreements among politicians, such as those between presidents Carter and Reagan mentioned earlier. The question is: When a recession occurs, should the government take actions to bring it to a rapid end? You will say *yes* if you believe that (1) unemployment is more costly than inflation, (2) the short-run Phillips curve is rather flat, and (3) the economy's self-correcting mechanism—which works as unemployment slows the rate of growth of wages—is slow and unreliable. These views on the economy tend to be associated with economists of the Keynesian school, and with the (generally liberal) politicians who listen to them.

But you will say *no* if you believe that (1) inflation is more costly than unemployment, (2) the short-run Phillips curve is quite steep, and (3) the self-correcting mechanism works smoothly and quickly. These views are held by most monetarists, so it is not surprising that the (generally conservative) politicians who follow monetarist advice typically oppose strong measures to fight recessions.

The tables turn, however, when the question is whether or not to use policy to fight inflation. The Keynesian view of the world—that unemployment is costly, that the short-run Phillips curve is flat, and that the self-correcting mechanism is unreliable—leads to the conclusion that the costs of fighting inflation are high while the benefits are low. The monetarist positions on these three issues are just the reverse, and hence so are the policy conclusions.

Supply-Side Inflation and the Phillips Curve

Let us now return to the question posed early in the chapter: Why did the Phillips curve, which worked so beautifully in the 1950s and 1960s, seem to fall apart in the 1970s? (It may be useful to refer back to Figures 16–9 and 16–10 on page 300 to see the evidence.) We have already given one answer: economists and policymakers at that time mistakenly viewed the Phillips curve as a menu of *long-run* policy choices. Some, wanting to lower unemployment, adopted policies that pushed the economy up the Phillips curve. But, as we know, unemployment rates below the natural rate are not sustainable, and these policymakers got much more inflation than they had bargained for. (If you do not understand why, refer back to Figure 16–12 and read the caption carefully.)

But there is another answer, which claims that much of the inflation of the 1970s did not emanate from the demand side. Instead, the 1970s were full of adverse "supply shocks"—events like the crop failures of 1972–1973, and the oil price increases of 1974 and 1979—that pushed the economy's aggregate supply curve upward, or to the left. What kind of Phillips curve will be generated when economic fluctuations come from the supply side? To find out, let us take the events of 1979 and 1980 as an example. In Figure 16–19, aggregate demand curve D_0D_0 and aggregate supply curve S_0S_0 represent the economic situation in 1979.

Figure 16–19

STAGFLATION FROM A SUPPLY SHOCK

Instead of shifting outward as it normally does, the aggregate supply curve shifted inward—from S_0S_0 to S_1S_1—between 1979 and 1980. Coupled with fairly slow growth of the aggregate demand curve—from D_0D_0 in 1979 to D_1D_1 in 1980—equilibrium moved from point A to point B. There was virtually no growth of real output, and prices rose rapidly.

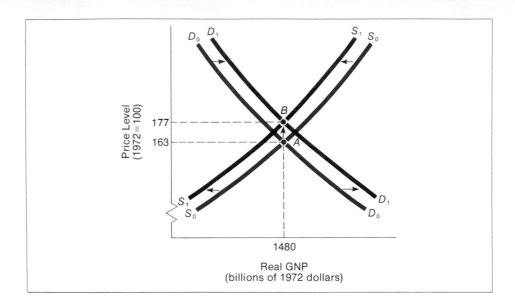

Equilibrium was at point A, with a price level of 163 and real output of $1480 billion. By 1980, the aggregate demand curve had shifted out to the position indicated by D_1D_1, and, under normal conditions, the aggregate supply curve would have shifted out as well. But 1979 was anything but normal. The Iranian revolution led to a shutdown of Iran's oilfields for months. The resulting worldwide scramble for oil led OPEC to double the price of its product during the year. Thus, instead of shifting to the *right* as it normally does from one year to the next, the aggregate supply curve shifted to the *left* during 1979, to S_1S_1. The equilibrium for 1980 (point B in the figure), therefore wound up almost vertically above the equilibrium point for 1979. Real output was essentially the same in both years, and prices—led by energy costs—rose rapidly.

Now, in a growing population with more people looking for jobs each year, a stagnant economy that is not generating new jobs will suffer a rise in the unemployment rate. This is precisely what happened in the United States; the unemployment rate averaged 5.8 percent in 1979 and 7.1 percent in 1980. Thus, the inflation rate and the unemployment rate increased at the same time: The Phillips curve was upward sloping! A general conclusion is that:

If fluctuations in economic activity emanate mainly from the supply side, higher rates of inflation will be associated with higher rates of unemployment, and lower rates of inflation will be associated with lower rates of unemployment.

The instances of major supply shocks during the 1970s stand out quite clearly in Figure 16–10. (Remember these are *real* data; they are not made up by some textbook writer.) Food prices boomed between 1972 and 1974 and again in 1978. Energy prices soared in 1973–1974 and again in 1979–1980. It is clear that the inflation and unemployment data generated by the U.S. economy between 1972 and 1974, and again between 1978 and 1980, are quite consistent with our theoretical model of supply-side inflation.

The Dilemma of Demand Management

We have just learned that when inflation comes from the supply side, inflation and unemployment will be positively associated: we will suffer from more of both or enjoy less of each. Does this mean that monetary and fiscal policymakers can escape the trade-off between inflation and unemployment? Certainly not.

Adverse shifts in the aggregate supply curve can cause both inflation and unemployment to rise together, and thus can destroy the Phillips curve relationship. Nevertheless, anything that monetary and fiscal policy can do will make unemployment and inflation move in opposite directions. The reason is that monetary and fiscal policy only give the government control over the aggregate demand curve, not the aggregate supply curve. If the government stimulates demand to cut down on unemployment, it will make inflation worse; if it restricts demand to fight inflation, it will increase unemployment.

Thus, no matter what the source of inflation, and no matter what happens to the Phillips curve, the makers of monetary and fiscal policy must still face up to the disagreeable trade-off between inflation and unemployment. This is a principle that many policymakers have failed to recognize, and one of the 12 Ideas that we hope you will remember well Beyond the Final Exam.

Naturally, the unpleasant nature of this trade-off has led to a vigorous search for a way out of the dilemma. Both economists and public officials have sought a policy that might offer improvements on both fronts simultaneously, or that might ease the pain of either unemployment or inflation. The next chapter will consider some of these ideas.

Conclusion: the Carter–Reagan Debate over Economic Policy

It is painfully clear that economics cannot provide politicians with a clear set of instructions about the "right" and "wrong" ways to deal with inflation and unemployment. Political leaders have many choices to make. They may seek to manage the economy in a way that promotes their own political fortunes (see the boxed insert on the following page), or they may courageously pursue what they view as the public interest regardless of the political consequences. But even in the latter case there are still many alternatives. It is in this light that we can best understand the 1980 debate over economic policy between presidents Reagan and Carter.

According to some observers, including Mr. Reagan, Mr. Carter allowed demand to grow too rapidly in 1978, thereby causing inflation to accelerate—as was suggested by Figure 16–5. But many other observers, and certainly Mr. Carter, disputed this claim. They insisted that the Carter strategy in 1978 was a steady-as-you-go policy, more like that shown in Figure 16–4. Regardless of who was right, it is clear that both sides recognized the trade-off between inflation and unemployment.

We know what actually happened next. Inflation did in fact accelerate— from 7.3 percent in 1978 to 8.5 percent in 1979 and to 9 percent in 1980. Does this mean that Reagan's diagnosis was correct, that Carter did overstimulate the economy? Not necessarily, because, as we have explained in this chapter, the U.S. economy was hit by a serious "supply shock" in 1979—a huge rise in the price of foreign oil that shifted the aggregate supply curve upward as in Figure 16–19. This adverse circumstance can explain why inflation would have accelerated even if Carter had followed a policy of restricting demand. It is this explanation that Carter's supporters favor.

As to the proper policy for the future, President Carter decided in 1979— without, of course, using the phrase—that we had to fight inflation by causing a

A Political Business Cycle?

Since the Phillips curve trade-off is reasonably favorable in the short-run (so that lower unemployment can be bought rather cheaply in terms of inflation), and since elected officials tend to have a hard time seeing past the next election, there is the possibility that politicians might deliberately cause business cycles in order to promote their own political ends.

Let us see how this might work with a hypothetical scenario. In January 1993, Les Scruples, a clever politician, takes office as president of the United States. The inflation rate is 8 percent and the unemployment rate is 6 percent (see the accompanying figure). President Scruples remembers from his college political science course that (a) voters tend to blame the president and Congress when economic conditions are bad and reward them when economic conditions are good, and (b) voters have very short memories when they go to the polls. In fact, President Scruples has seen studies that suggest that voters care

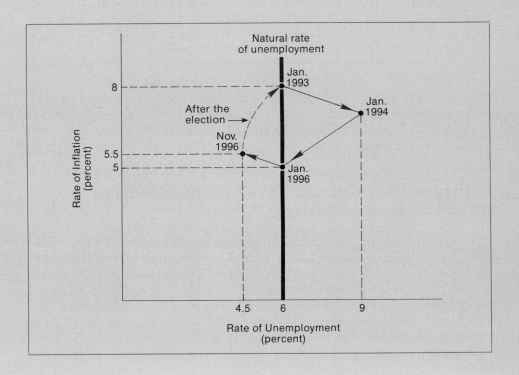

recession. As we have learned, this strategy is one realistic way to attack the inflation problem, though it is a costly one. Candidate Reagan decried this choice and—quite correctly—blamed the incumbent president for causing unemployment. As an alternative, Reagan offered a plan of "supply-side" tax cuts, which, as president, he subsequently put into effect. We shall see in the next chapter what this plan was intended to accomplish.

Summary

1. Inflation can be caused either by rapid growth of aggregate demand or by sluggish growth of aggregate supply.
2. When fluctuations in economic activity emanate from the demand side, prices will rise rapidly when real output grows rapidly. Since rapid growth means more jobs, unemployment and inflation will be inversely related.
3. This inverse relationship between unemployment and inflation is called the Phillips curve. It explains U.S. data for the 1950s and 1960s rather well, but fails miserably to account for the 1970s.

only about the economy's real growth rate in the *one year prior to election day*. (This, in fact, is what the studies do suggest.)

This gives Scruples an idea. "By wringing inflation out of the system with a recession early in my term, and then stimulating demand near the end of my term, I should be able to stand for reelection with the inflation rate well below 8 percent and the unemployment rate well below 6 percent. Sounds great. I wonder if I can do it?" The president consults his economic advisers who explain to him that while the long-run Phillips curve is vertical, the short-run Phillips curve is probably quite flat, so his plan should work. During his first year in office Scruples raises taxes and cuts government spending. A serious recession ensues: unemployment rises to 9 percent (again, see the accompanying figure). During the second and third years of the administration, the economy's natural self-correcting mechanism slowly and painfully erodes the recessionary gap, so that by January 1996—an election year—inflation is down to 5 percent and unemployment is back to 6 percent (see the figure). Now Les Scruples opens the sluice gates of federal spending and pushes a huge tax cut through Congress. The economy travels leftward along its short-run Phillips curve until, on election day 1996, the unemployment rate is down to $4\frac{1}{2}$ percent and inflation is only $5\frac{1}{2}$ percent. President Scruples runs "on his record" as the president who brought down both inflation and unemployment. He is reelected in a landslide. After the election, inflation accelerates and unemployment rises.

Sound fanciful? Perhaps it is. We certainly would not wish to exaggerate the ease with which such an operation can be pulled off. Successful orchestration of a political business cycle like the one just described requires both consummate skill and remarkable luck. But, of course, so does a successful campaign for the White House.

Has a political business cycle ever happened in the United States? Many observers feel that it has, and that the first Nixon administration is perhaps the best example. Upon assuming office in 1969 as the inheritor of President Johnson's Vietnam inflation, President Nixon took an appropriately hard line on government spending. With the Fed also clamping down on money and credit, the mild recession of 1969–1970 ensued, although the incipient gains on the inflation front were barely visible when wage and price controls were instituted in August 1971. These contractionary monetary and fiscal policies were abruptly reversed in the election year of 1972, as the federal pocketbook was proffered to all sorts of petitioners suddenly deemed "worthy." The result was predictable: 1972 was a boom year. Mr. Nixon's landslide reelection took place with income growing briskly, unemployment falling, and the inflation rate continuing to recede.

While this may have been the most extreme episode, the election year stimulation of the economy in 1972 was by no means unqiue. As one political scientist quipped, "It is apparent that the way to defeat the trade-off between inflation and unemployment is to hold a presidential election."* There is also evidence of politically induced business cycles in many foreign countries. But we would not like to leave the impression that deliberate political manipulation of the economy is the normal state of affairs. Both Presidents Ford and Carter running as incumbents in 1976 and 1980, respectively, refused to stimulate the economy even though unemployment was high and their political futures were at stake. Both paid dearly at the polls.

*Edward R. Tufte, *Political Control of the Economy* (Princeton: Princeton University Press, 1978), page 22.

---

4. One reason for this failure is that the Phillips curve was misinterpreted as a menu of *long-run* policy choices for the economy. But this view is incorrect because the economy's self-correcting mechanism guarantees that neither an inflationary gap nor a recessionary gap can last indefinitely.

5. Because of the self-correcting mechanism, the economy's true long-run choices lie along a *vertical* Phillips curve, which shows that the so-called "natural rate of unemployment" is the only unemployment rate that can persist indefinitely.

6. In the short-run, the economy can move up or down its short-run Phillips curve. *Temporary* reductions in unemployment can be achieved at the cost of higher inflation. Similarly, *temporary* increases in unemployment can be used to fight inflation.

7. Whether it is advisable to use unemployment to fight inflation depends on three principal factors: the relative social costs of inflation versus unemployment, the efficiency of the economy's self-correcting mechanism, and the current position of the economy (which influences the shape of the short-run trade-off between inflation and unemployment).

8. Since controversy surrounds each of these three factors, both economists and politicians often disagree on the proper conduct of stabilization policy.

9. If workers expect inflation to occur, and if they demand (and receive) compensation for inflation, output will be independent of the price level. Both the aggregate supply curve and the short-run Phillips curve are vertical in this case.

10. However, errors in predicting inflation will still change real wages, and hence will still change the quantity of output that firms wish to supply. Thus, *unpredicted* movements in the price level will lead to the normal sort of upward-sloping aggregate supply curve.

11. According to the doctrine of rational expectations, errors in predicting inflation will be purely random. This means that, except for some random (and uncontrollable) gyrations, the aggregate supply curve is vertical even in the short run.

12. Many economists reject the rational expectations view of the world. Some deny that expectations are "rational," and believe instead that people tend, for example, to underpredict inflation when it is rising. Others point out that contracts signed years ago cannot possibly embody expectations that are "rational" in terms of what we know today.

13. When fluctuations in economic activity are caused by shifts of the aggregate supply curve, output will grow slowly (causing unemployment to rise) when inflation speeds up. Hence, the rates of unemployment and inflation will be positively related.

14. Many observers feel that the adverse supply shifts during the 1970s help explain why the Phillips curve collapsed.

15. Even if inflation is initiated by supply-side problems, so that inflation and unemployment occur together, the monetary and fiscal authorities still face this trade-off: anything they do to improve unemployment is likely to worsen inflation, and anything they do to reduce inflation is likely to aggravate unemployment. The reason is that monetary and fiscal policy mainly influence the aggregate demand curve, not the aggregate supply curve. This is one of our 12 Ideas for Beyond the Final Exam.

Concepts for Review

Demand-side inflation
Supply-side inflation
Phillips curve
Self-correcting mechanism
Vertical (long-run) Phillips curve

Natural rate of unemployment
Trade-off between unemployment
    and inflation in the short-run
    and in the long-run
Inflationary expectations

Rational expectations
Stagflation caused by supply shocks

Questions for Discussion

1. Some observers during the 1970s claimed that policymakers no longer face a trade-off between inflation and unemployment. Why did they think this? Were they correct?

2. "There is no sense in trying to shorten recessions through fiscal and monetary policy because the effects of these policies on the unemployment rate are sure to be temporary." Comment on both the truth of this statement and its relevance for policy formulation.

3. Why is the economy's self-correcting mechanism more efficient at eliminating inflationary gaps than it is at eliminating recessionary gaps?

4. Why is it said that decisions on fiscal and monetary policy are, at least in part, political decisions that cannot be made on "objective" economic criteria?

5. Does the economy have a recessionary gap or an inflationary gap today? What should be done about this? What facts would you want to know in preparing an answer to this question?

6. What is a "Phillips curve"? Why did it seem to work so much better in the 1948–1969 period than it did in the 1970s?

7. Explain the dilemma that policymakers face when there is an episode of supply inflation. What do you think should have been done in 1979? What would you recommend if there were a severe bout with supply inflation today?

8. Explain why expectations about inflation affect the wages that result from labor–management bargaining.

9. What is meant by "rational" expectations? Why does the doctrine of rational expectations have such stunning implications for economic policy? Would believers in rational expectations want to shorten a recession by expanding aggregate demand? Would they want to fight inflation by reducing aggregate demand?

10. Based on what you now know, do you think Mr. Carter or Mr. Reagan had the better case in the economic debate of 1980? (Clearly there is room for disagreement on this question, and there is no single correct answer.)

Coping with Inflation

17

We must seek to reduce inflation at a lower
cost in lost output and employment.

JIMMY CARTER (January 1980)

This chapter is founded on the widely accepted assumption that inflation will be with us for some time to come. In the last chapter we learned that one way to fight inflation is to create economic slack by slowing the growth of aggregate demand; that is, to use recession to fight inflation. Though it is a genuine alternative, politicians react to it somewhat like children react to spinach. For in addition to its obvious economic costs, fighting inflation by causing unemployment is unpopular: it may well have cost both Gerald Ford and Jimmy Carter their jobs.

Consequently, a number of suggestions have been offered for improving the trade-off between inflation and unemployment or, better yet, for eliminating it entirely. Some of these plans have actually been tried; others are still untested ideas. They range from governmental exhortations to hold down inflation to outright prohibition of wage or price increases. They include efforts to improve the functioning of labor markets, plans to enlist the tax system in the battle against inflation, and institutional changes designed to rob inflation of its social costs. Although each of these ideas is worthy of consideration, we must emphasize in advance that none is a panacea. The war on inflation will last years, not months.

We begin the chapter by examining the plan upon which the Reagan administration has pinned its hopes—tax reductions designed to encourage aggregate supply. Then we turn to the interconnection between inflation and productivity growth in the long run. Next we examine some traditional methods by which governments have tried to "shift the Phillips curve" in a favorable direction. Fourth, we consider a variety of wage and price control programs aimed at influencing inflation directly. And, finally, we discuss *indexing* as a way of learning to live with inflation.

Supply-Side Tax Cuts in Theory

The basic idea of using supply-side tax cuts to fight inflation is quite simple, and was explained in Chapter 11.[1] If taxes can be cut in such a way that people's incentives to work are increased, *and if people actually respond to these incentives*, then the tax system can be used to increase the total amount of labor

[1] See, especially, pages 204–208.

that is available for employment. Similarly, if the tax system is changed in ways that encourage households to save more and businesses to invest more, *and if people respond to these changes in the way that policymakers hope*, then the total amount of capital that is available for use will begin to rise. Both sorts of tax policies, then, if successful, will increase aggregate supply. Figure 17–1 illustrates this conclusion on an aggregate supply and demand diagram. If policy measures can shift the economy's aggregate supply to position S_1S_1, then prices will be lower and output higher than if the aggregate supply curve were S_0S_0. They will have succeeded in reducing inflation and raising real output (lowering unemployment) at the same time. The trade-off between inflation and unemployment will have been defeated.

The supply-side argument is extremely attractive. It caught the imagination of candidate Ronald Reagan in 1980 and became the basis of his new economic policy in 1981. By enhancing individuals' incentives to work, save, invest, and innovate, Mr. Reagan argued, we can attack inflation and unemployment simultaneously. Shortly after taking office, the new president recommended that Congress enact an ambitious tax-cutting program similar to the one that Senator William Roth of Delaware and Congressman Jack Kemp of New York had proposed several years earlier. The Kemp-Roth proposal called for across-the-board reductions in personal income tax rates of 10 percent a year for three consecutive years. Thus, for example, a family initially in the 33 percent tax bracket would, under the Kemp-Roth plan, find itself in the 30 percent bracket in the next year, the 27 percent bracket in the following year, and the 24 percent bracket after three years. Such large cuts in tax rates, it was hoped, would strengthen incentives to work and save. To bolster incentives to invest, the Reagan administration offered businesses more generous tax write-offs for purchases of machinery and equipment. And to prevent aggregate demand from growing too quickly, the president recommended substantial cuts in federal government spending and urged the Federal Reserve to keep credit tight. This, in

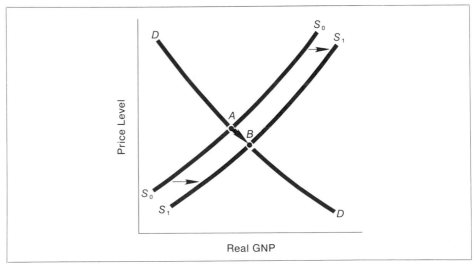

Figure 17–1
THE IDEA BEHIND SUPPLY-SIDE TAX CUTS
The basic idea of supply-side cuts is that if they achieve their desired objective, they will cause the economy's aggregate supply curve to shift outward to the right. For example, the aggregate supply curve might be S_1S_1 under a program of supply-side tax cuts, whereas it would only be S_0S_0 without such tax cuts. In this case, if aggregate demand is the same in either case, the tax cuts would lead to the equilibrium point B instead of the equilibrium point A. Comparing B with A, we see that the program leads to lower prices and higher output.

brief, was the Reagan economic program proposed early in 1981; and it emerged from Congress more or less as the president requested. The income-tax rate reductions were scaled back slightly (to 25 percent over three years, instead of 30 percent); but some other tax-reducing provisions were added. And the president's proposals for cuts in business taxes and expenditure programs were adopted virtually without change.

Some Flies in the Ointment

In view of all the attractive features of supply-side economics, why did President Carter and many private economists scoff at President Reagan's economic program, and even brand it *inflationary?* There were three basic reasons for their skepticism:

1. ***Demand-side effects.*** First, no one has yet figured out a way to cut taxes in a way that does not stimulate aggregate demand. If you cut personal taxes, individuals *may possibly* work more, but they *will certainly* spend more. If you reduce business taxes and thereby encourage expansion of industrial capacity, business firms will demand more investment goods. Look now at Figure 17–2, which repeats the two supply curves from Figure 17–1 but adds the fact that tax cuts, though aimed at aggregate supply, will also stimulate aggregate demand through the mechanisms we studied in earlier chapters. If, in the process of shifting the aggregate supply curve outward from S_0S_0 to S_1S_1, the tax cuts also shift the aggregate demand curve outward from D_0D_0 to D_1D_1, the anti-inflationary punch of the program may be dissipated. Indeed, if the demand shift is big enough, the program may turn out to be inflationary.

Two responses to this criticism have been made. Some of the more extreme proponents of supply-side economics have sought to deny the obvious, that is, to deny that supply-side tax cuts will stimulate aggregate demand. But

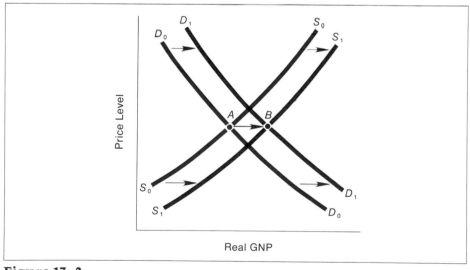

Figure 17–2
DEMAND-SIDE EFFECTS OF "SUPPLY-SIDE" TAX CUTS
Any reduction in taxes, even if specifically designed to increase incentives to supply labor and capital, will also stimulate demand. In this particular diagram, the tax cuts that shift the supply curve outward from S_0S_0 to S_1S_1 also shift the demand curve outward, from D_0D_0 to D_1D_1. As a consequence, equilibrium shifts from point A to point B. The downward push on prices that we saw in Figure 17–1 is entirely cancelled out. Naturally, if the demand shift is smaller than the one depicted here, some downward effect on prices will remain. However, if the demand shift is larger than depicted, the program will be inflationary on balance.

this is akin to thinking that simply by calling the tax cuts "supply-side cuts" they will magically lose their demand-side effects. This wishful thinking was, fortunately, not President Reagan's response. His plan was to link the tax cuts to reductions in government spending that would cancel out the demand-side effects. Let us review this reasoning briefly. We learned in earlier chapters that tax cuts push the aggregate demand curve to the right while reductions in government spending push it to the left. Thus, whatever demand stimulus is caused by the tax cuts, there is some expenditure reduction big enough to cancel its demand-side effects. By combining these two programs into a fiscal package, it may be possible to restore the situation to that depicted in Figure 17–1—a rise in aggregate supply with no accompanying rise in aggregate demand. The problem with this strategy is that if *large* tax cuts are made, then *large* spending cuts must accompany them. Many observers in 1981 worried that the expenditure cuts proposed by President Reagan, while substantial, were not nearly as large as the tax cuts.

2. ***The uncertainty of supply-side effects.*** The second problem is one we mentioned in Chapter 11. It is easy to design tax cuts that, for example, make working more *attractive* financially; that is, which raise take-home pay. This does not, however, guarantee that people will actually respond by working more. Instead, they may find themselves able to afford the goods and services they want with fewer hours of labor, and react by working less. Most of the statistical evidence suggests that it is unrealistic to expect tax reductions to lead to very substantial increases in either labor supply or household savings. In terms of the supply and demand diagram, then, the problem is that even very large cuts in taxes may lead to only small outward shifts in the aggregate supply curve, as in Figure 17–3. In that case, it does not take much of a demand shift to overwhelm the supply shift and make the program inflationary on balance. As one prominent economist critical of the supply-side approach put it, "Relying on huge supply-side responses to Kemp-Roth tax cuts would be tantamount to bolting the door against inflation with a boiled carrot."[2]

[2] Walter W. Heller, "Can We Afford the Costs of Kemp-Roth?", *The Wall Street Journal*, February 10, 1981, page 26.

Figure 17–3

A MORE PESSIMISTIC VIEW OF SUPPLY-SIDE TAX CUTS

If the effect of supply-side tax initiatives on the aggregate supply curve is actually much smaller than suggested by Figure 17–1, the anti-inflationary impact will be correspondingly smaller. As you can see in this diagram, it would not take a very large shift in the aggregate demand curve to overwhelm the favorable effects of the tax cuts on the price level.

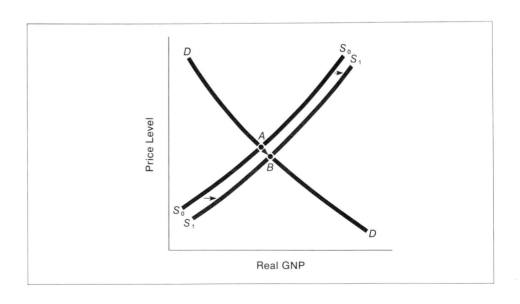

3. *Problems in timing.* The most promising types of supply-side tax cuts seek to encourage greater business investment by, for example, making depreciation allowances more generous or raising the investment tax credit. But investment does not create new industrial capacity overnight. It takes time to plan new investment projects, arrange the financing, get delivery on machinery, build factories, and then actually put these things into operation. The crucial point is that the *expenditures* on investment goods come before the *expansion of capacity.* That is, aggregate *demand* expands first and aggregate *supply* follows later. This means, of course, that the short-run impact of supply-side tax cuts is almost certainly inflationary.

On balance, most economists have reached the following conclusions about supply-side tax initiatives:

1. The likely effectiveness of supply-side tax cuts depends very much on what kinds of taxes are cut. Tax reductions aimed at stimulating business investment are likely to pack more punch than tax reductions aimed at getting people to work longer hours.
2. Such tax cuts probably *will* increase aggregate supply, but the increases in aggregate supply will come much more slowly than the increase in aggregate demand.
3. The demand-side effects are very likely to be larger than the supply-side effects. According to an estimate by the Council of Economic Advisers in January 1981, just before President Reagan took office, a supply-side tax cut that shifted the aggregate demand curve to the right by 1 percent would probably shift the aggregate supply curve to the right by only a fraction of a percent.

The conclusion, then, is that while the basic idea behind supply-side tax initiatives is sound, they have been drastically oversold by their more zealous proponents. While helpful, they cannot be expected to make more than a small dent in the inflation rate. And there is one further point. A one-time cut in a tax rate will, at best, have a once-and-for-all effect on the aggregate supply curve—pushing it rightward. The only way to increase the *growth rate* of aggregate supply by tax cuts is to cut taxes again and again, year after year. This, of course, may sound appealing since nobody likes to pay taxes; but it must be recognized that there is a limit to how far such a policy can be pursued. If the Reagan economic proposals of 1981 were repeated for, say, 10 years in a row, there would be very little government left to cut.

Productivity Growth and Inflation in the Long Run

The upshot of this last observation is that the only way in which supply-side initiatives can attack the problem of *long-run* inflation is by raising the rate at which **productivity** is growing. The arithmetic here is simple. Inflation depends on the difference between the rates at which the aggregate demand and aggregate supply curves are shifting outward over time. Aggregate supply is, as a matter of definition, the product of the amount of labor available times the amount of output produced by each hour of labor—the productivity of labor. There is little that can be done to affect the long-run growth rate of labor supply, which depends fundamentally on population growth. Thus, if supply-side policies are to increase the growth rate of aggregate supply, they must focus on productivity. Again, the arithmetic is straightforward. The productivity of labor

The **productivity** of labor is the amount of output produced per hour of labor input.

depends on the amount of machinery and other resources available to each worker and on the state of technical know-how, which determines how much output we get from any given combination of labor and capital inputs.

As we have just seen, many supply-side policies are in fact aimed at increasing investment, and thus at raising the growth rate of the amount of capital available. The other possibility is to try to speed up the pace of technological improvement through research and development (R and D) expenditures. This is also advocated by supply-siders, and quite properly so. The problem here is that no one is quite sure how to accomplish this goal. There is a connection between money spent on R and D and increases in productivity, but it is a loose one. While no one doubts that technological advances ultimately depend on the resources devoted to R and D, there have been many cases in which very small expenditures have led to fundamental advances in technology, and many others in which huge expenditures have borne little fruit. Thus, to *say* we should increase the rate of improvement of our industrial technology is one thing; to actually *do* it is quite another.

It is easy to see that a slowdown in productivity growth has contributed to the inflation problem. During the 1960s, the growth rate of productivity averaged 2.7 percent a year; during the 1970s it fell to only 1.4 percent a year. This slowdown in productivity growth reduced the annual growth rate of aggregate supply by about 1.3 percentage points, and hence added a similar amount to the rate of inflation. (See the accompanying boxed insert on the productivity slowdown.) It is also easy to see that raising the growth rate of productivity would help fight inflation. If, somehow, we could push productivity growth back to the rates we enjoyed during the 1960s, we could knock about 1.3 percentage points from the long-run inflation rate. However, the fact that the actual inflation rate averaged about 2.5 percent in the 1960s and about 6.5 percent in the 1970s, makes it clear that productivity is only a part of the problem. It is also clear that increases in productivity growth, if we can somehow achieve them, can only be part of the solution. Realistically, the major burden of fighting inflation must be shouldered by aggregate demand policy, and hence policymakers must face up to the trade-off between inflation and unemployment that was discussed at length in the preceding chapter.

Attempts to Shift the Phillips Curve

Increasing aggregate supply through selective tax cuts is a relatively novel idea, but the general idea of improving the trade-off between inflation and unemployment by working on the aggregate supply curve is an old one. If we cannot defeat the Phillips curve trade-off, we can at least try to nudge it a bit in a favorable direction. Since the long-run Phillips curve is believed to be approximately vertical, such policy initiatives in effect seek to reduce the "natural rate" of unemployment.

One class of policies that has this objective is vocational training and retraining programs. When successful, they help unemployed workers with obsolete skills acquire abilities that are currently in demand. In doing so they help alleviate upward pressures on wage rates in jobs where qualified workers are in short supply. For example, if an unemployed automobile worker is taught to assemble computers, then progress is made against both inflation *and* unemployment, since one former auto worker leaves the ranks of the unemployed while one new worker helps alleviate the shortage of skilled labor in the computer industry. Although the idea sounds appealing and has attracted many adherents,

The Productivity Slowdown and Inflation

A rising standard of living depends fundamentally on a rising level of productivity; in the long run, society as a whole can consume more only if it produces more. For this simple and compelling reason, contemporary observers of the U.S. economy are very concerned about the slowdown in productivity growth that has taken place over the last few decades.

The first column of Table A shows that there is indeed cause for concern. The growth rate of nonfarm productivity in the United States, which averaged 2.6 percent per year between 1948 and 1965, slipped to a mere 0.5 percent per year between 1973 and 1980. This rather abstract statistic means that the productivity of an average American worker rose only 3.3 percent *in total* over that seven-year period. The table also shows that since 1977 productivity growth has actually been *negative*; this means that output per worker in the United States actually was *lower* in 1980 than in 1977.

Since inflation depends on the relative growth rates of aggregate demand and aggregate supply, slower productivity growth—that is, slower growth in aggregate supply—contributes to inflation. The second column of Table A displays the facts. It is clear that inflation has risen steadily as productivity growth has slowed. However, the table makes it quite clear that the productivity slowdown

Table A
PRODUCTIVITY AND INFLATION
IN THE UNITED STATES

PERIOD	GROWTH RATE OF PRODUCTIVITY (percent per year)	RATE OF INFLATION (percent per year)
1948–1965	2.6	2.0
1965–1973	2.2	3.8
1973–1980	0.5	8.0
1973–1977	1.2	7.8
1977–1980	−0.5	8.4

SOURCE: U.S. Bureau of Labor Statistics. Data pertain to the nonfarm business sector.

Table B
THE PRODUCTIVITY SLOWDOWN
AROUND THE WORLD

COUNTRY	PRODUCTIVITY GROWTH RATES (percent per year)		
	1963–1973	1973–1980	CHANGE
United States	1.9	0.1	−1.8
Japan	8.7	3.4	−5.3
Germany	4.6	3.2	−1.4
United Kingdom	3.0	0.3	−2.7
Italy	5.4	1.6	−3.8

SOURCE: *Economic Report of the President, 1980.* Data pertain to GNP per employed worker.

cannot provide anything like a full explanation of the acceleration of inflation. Compare 1965–1973 with 1973–1980, for example. Productivity growth slowed by 1.7 percentage points, but inflation accelerated by 4.2 percentage points.

Why has productivity performance been so poor of late? No one really has a complete answer to this question. The tremendous increases in energy prices that have occurred since 1973 are perhaps the leading candidate. Others that have been suggested are government regulations, inadequate investment, and a diminution of entrepreneurial spirit. One thing is certain, however: explanations that focus on factors that are unique to the United States must be inadequate because the productivity slowdown has been a worldwide phenomenon.

Look at Table B. With the specific time periods and measure of productivity considered there, the United States suffered a 1.8 percentage point drop in productivity. But the Japanese suffered a 5.3 percentage point drop, and the Italians suffered a 3.8 percentage point drop. The productivity decline in the United States was, in fact, among the smallest of all the industrial nations. However, since the United States started from the lowest base, the decline that we did suffer virtually halted our productivity growth. There can be little doubt that raising the growth rate of productivity will be a major item on the national agenda throughout the 1980s.

successes achieved through training programs have, in practice, been rather limited. Too often, people are trained for jobs that do not exist by the time they finish their training—if indeed they ever existed. Even when successful, these programs are quite expensive, which restricts the number of workers that can be accommodated.

The United States Employment Service, and similar agencies at the state and local levels, also try to improve the match of workers to jobs, but not by retraining workers. Instead, they seek to funnel information from prospective employers to prospective employees. Firms are encouraged to list their job vacancies with the Employment Service and to inspect the Service's list of people looking for work. Unemployed workers, or people wanting to change jobs, are encouraged to register with the Employment Service and to study its list of openings. In this way, it is hoped, the simultaneous occurrence of unemployed workers with unfilled jobs will be reduced. Most observers agree that the idea is sound and that the U.S. Employment Service has been a constructive force. But, again, it has operated on a scale that is simply too small to make a serious dent in the natural rate of unemployment. Apparently, many workers and businesses do not know about the Employment Service or are reluctant to use it.

Over the last several years, many government regulations that serve to keep prices artificially high—ranging from agricultural price supports to control of airline passenger fares to requirements that trucks return empty after delivering their loads—have come under increasing public scrutiny. During the Ford administration, many of these government interferences with free-market processes came under vigorous verbal assault. And while President Carter was in office, real progress was made toward deregulation of the economy: government-imposed limitations on price reductions and other barriers to competition were reduced or removed entirely in the airline, trucking, railroad, and telecommunications industries. The fact that President Reagan chose Murray Weidenbaum, an economist whose opposition to costly and unproductive government regulations is well known, as his chief economic adviser suggests that deregulation will continue and even accelerate under the Reagan administration.[3] If so, that would be one influence serving to keep the 1980s less inflationary than the 1970s.[4]

Incomes Policy

Incomes policy is a generic term used to describe a wide variety of measures aimed at curbing inflation *without* reducing aggregate demand.

Yet another approach to the inflation problem, an approach that has been tried intermittently in the United States, is **incomes policy.** As practiced in this country during the last 20 years, incomes policy has run the gamut from verbal admonitions all the way to President Nixon's outright prohibition of wage and price increases in 1971. And in some foreign countries that rely upon incomes policy far more heavily than we do, a still more bewildering variety of alternative measures has emerged. Indeed, there may be only one common thread linking these disparate policies: No hard evidence exists that any of them has succeeded in *permanently* improving the trade-off between unemployment and inflation. Note that the emphasis here is on the word "permanently," for many attempts at incomes policy—including some in this country—have had temporary success.

Jawboning

The mildest form of incomes policy is commonly referred to as **jawboning.** The term is descriptive. It is meant to conjure up in your mind an image of the president of the United States calling some corporate executive on the carpet for announcing a price increase deemed to be contrary to the national interest. The objective is to persuade him to change his mind. And since corporate executives are likely to feel surrounded, and perhaps even threatened, under these circumstances, jawboning has occasionally enjoyed spectacular success.

[3]For a full discussion of regulation and deregulation, see Chapter 27.
[4]While these policies would have permanent effects only on the *price level*, not on the *rate of inflation*, their "temporary" effects on inflation might last several years.

Perhaps the best-known instance was President Kennedy's confrontation with the steel industry in 1962. All sorts of informal pressures were brought to bear on the big steel companies—ranging from a tongue-lashing by the president to a cancellation of steel orders by the Defense Department—until the industry caved in and rescinded a previously announced price increase. Years later, U.S. Steel's Roger M. Blough wrote that "never before in the nation's history have so many forces of the federal government been marshalled against a single American industry. . ."[5] Jawbones can have teeth. But, while this episode received the most notoriety, President Johnson probably jawboned more than anyone else, and it was President Nixon who first established an official agency to monitor price increases and "blow the whistle" on those that were unwarranted.

After a temporary hiatus under President Ford, this so-called "open mouth policy" was reinstated by President Carter in early 1978. Under his "deceleration strategy," the president urged both labor and business to increase their wages and prices at a slower rate in 1978 than they had in 1976 and 1977. But he relied on his Council on Wage and Price Stability to do most of the jawboning for him. President Reagan rejected this approach entirely; one of his first official acts was to abolish the Council on Wage and Price Stability.

The main argument in favor of jawboning is that it is a relatively painless way to try to improve the trade-off between inflation and unemployment. Large corporations, it is argued, have the market power to raise prices even when price rises are not justified by cost increases. But, since these corporate giants are also very conscious of their public-relations images, proponents of jawboning argue, why not use the prestige of the federal government to dissuade them from exercising their market power? Opponents of jawboning respond that market power, which undoubtedly exists, can explain *high* prices. But why, they ask, would a firm with market power wait until this month to raise prices when it could have done so last month, or the month before? They answer that large corporations raise prices only when changes in demand or cost considerations make it profitable to do so, not because they have a residue of unused market power. Furthermore, there is an inevitable element of inequity in jawboning. By its very nature it must be discriminatory, picking on some firms while letting others go scot-free.

On balance, a fair assessment of jawboning would probably conclude that it does little good and little harm.

Wage–Price Guideposts

The next step up from jawboning is the establishment of an official standard for "permissible" rates of increase in wages and prices. These so-called **wage–price guideposts** were initiated by the Kennedy administration in early 1962 but used most notably by the Johnson administration. Lacking an enforcement mechanism, they collapsed amid the inflationary pressures of 1967. Late in 1978, guideposts were resurrected by President Carter, who was by then convinced that jawboning was not enough. But inflation accelerated in 1979 and 1980 anyway, and President Reagan abandoned the guideposts immediately upon assuming office.

The logic behind guideposts is both simple and compelling. In an ideally functioning economy, if worker productivity rises by 2 percent a year, then wages can rise by 2 percent a year with no increase in costs or prices. Alternatively, wages can increase at a 4 percent annual rate while prices rise at 2 percent a year, and so on. In general, price inflation proceeds at a rate roughly 2 percentage points

[5]Roger M. Blough, *The Washington Embrace of Business* (New York: Columbia University Press, 1975), page 94.

below wage inflation. A set of wage–price guideposts is obtained by picking a target rate of inflation, say 6 percent a year, and adding 2 percent to get a consistent target for wage increases—8 percent in this example. The government then announces that (a) wage increases that exceed this standard will be deemed "inflationary," (b) firms enjoying productivity increases faster than the national average are expected to raise their prices more slowly than 6 percent a year while, (c) firms obtaining sub-par productivity improvements are allowed to have higher-than-average price increases so that, (d) the overall price level can increase at a rate of 6 percent a year.

As noted, guideposts are quite logical. The problem comes in deciding what to do if some union or corporation violates them. Experience shows that voluntarism goes only so far when economic self-interest is threatened. If the government responds by jawboning—as frequently happened in the 1960s—we are back to the first type of incomes policy, but with one important difference. The uniformity of the guideposts means that the firms or unions singled out for public scrutiny earned that status. Official guideposts remove much of the element of capriciousness from an *ad hoc* jawboning policy. An alternative approach is to give the guideposts the force of law, which brings us to the next variety of incomes policy.

Wage–Price Controls

Once the government is given the legal authority to *force* labor and industry to adhere to a set of guideposts, we have moved to a system of mandatory **wage–price controls.** While the United States used such a policy with great success during World War II and again during the Korean War, the Nixon administration's efforts to apply wage–price controls in peacetime is generally considered to have been a failure. This experience has soured many people on the idea of ever using them again.

Before considering some pros and cons of controls, let us stop for a moment to be clear about what economists mean when they say that the 1971–1974 price controls "failed." They surely do *not* mean that inflation was not reduced by controls; most studies of the period have found that in fact it *was* reduced. Instead, they mean that by 1975 the price level was no lower than it would have been without controls. The implication is that the *lower* inflation rates that prevailed while controls were in effect were counterbalanced by *higher* inflation rates during the year or so after controls were lifted. This is a fairly typical instance of an incomes policy that was effective in the short run but not in the long run. Instead of improving the trade-off, the controls managed to increase the variability of inflation—making it lower in 1972–1973 and higher in 1974 than it would otherwise have been. In Chapter 6 we pointed out that the *variability* of inflation often exacts more serious social costs than the *average level.* In this sense, then, the controls program was counterproductive, and this is why many economists say that it "failed."

A major justification for controls, to which spokesmen for the Nixon administration and others who supported controls appealed, is that inflation gathers a substantial momentum once workers, consumers, and business managers begin to expect that it will continue. **Inflationary expectations** encourage workers to demand higher wage increases. Firms, in turn, are willing to grant the workers' demands because they believe they will be able to pass the cost increases on to consumers in a general inflationary environment. Consumers contribute their part to the shell game by purchasing durable goods ahead of their needs in anticipation of higher prices in the future; an action that increases demand and helps fuel the inflation engine. Thus, to a great extent, *inflation occurs because people expect it to occur.* In terms of our aggregate supply and demand analysis, inflationary expectations shift the aggregate supply curve upward because workers insist on—and get—higher money wages to compensate them for the coming inflation. Phrased in terms of the Phillips curve, this means that inflationary expectations shift the Phillips curve upward, so that any given rate of unemployment corresponds to a higher rate of inflation.

This analysis provides the best intellectual case for controls. A tough and thorough program of wage and price controls, it is argued, can break the vicious cycle of inflationary expectations. By announcing a controls program, the government serves notice on workers that they do not need anticipatory wage increases to preserve their purchasing power. Firms are warned that they may not be able to pass on higher costs to consumers. And consumers may conclude that buying now to beat future price rises is a poor strategy. By breaking inflationary expectations, supporters argue, a controls program can shift the Phillips curve down and reduce the rate of inflation. And, under the right conditions, the argument may be correct. However, many economists question whether this line of reasoning is generally valid. For example, it may be that astute workers, business executives, and consumers realize that no controls program can remain in force forever—at least not in a free-market economy like ours. They may then view the temporary dip in the inflation rate caused by controls as an aberration soon to be corrected, and therefore not as a major event that warrants changing their long-term expectations.

Why cannot wage–price controls be a permanent feature of the U.S. economy? We learned the answer to this back in Chapter 4. When price ceilings are effective, they force the price below the equilibrium price, so that quantity demanded exceeds quantity supplied. This is shown in Figure 17–4, where the equilibrium price of hamburgers is assumed to be $1. If controls do not allow the price of hamburgers to rise above 75 cents, quantity demanded will exceed quantity supplied by one million hamburgers. With price no longer serving as the rationing device, some other method of rationing is necessary. One possibility is long lines of eager eaters waiting their turn for hamburgers. Scenes like this are quite typical in the Soviet Union, and were witnessed in this country at gas

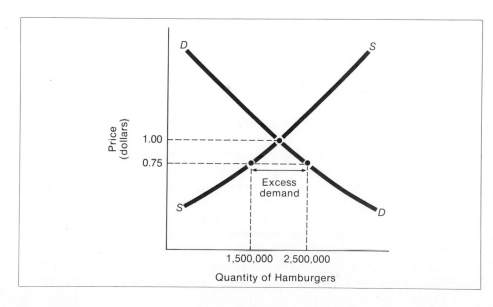

Figure 17–4

THE EFFECTS OF PRICE CONTROLS

This diagram portrays the market for hamburgers under an effective price control system. Since the equilibrium price is $1 per hamburger, a regulation that holds the price at 75 cents makes the quantity of hamburgers demanded (2,500,000 per year) exceed the quantity supplied (1,500,000 per year). There is a shortage of one million hamburgers per year, and some sort of rationing scheme probably will be necessary.

stations during 1979, when gasoline was in short supply. Another is government ration coupons, giving the owner the right to buy a hamburger—a device used successfully during World War II. Neither of these measures is likely to be popular with the electorate in peacetime. And both are likely to spawn a black market, which erodes respect for law and order at the same time that it abrogates the effects of controls. As critics of controls are fond of pointing out, controls give perfectly law-abiding citizens an incentive to become criminals by participating in illicit black-market activities.

Wage–Price Freezes

An extreme case of mandatory controls is a **wage–price freeze**—a statute making it illegal to increase wages or prices above their levels on some specified date. President Nixon ushered in his controls program with a three-month freeze beginning in mid-August 1971. And there was an even shorter freeze on prices (but not wages) in June–August 1973. Such an action cannot be considered a constructive incomes policy; it is meant to be a shock treatment—a dramatic action intended to break inflationary expectations. A wage–price freeze also gives an administration contemplating controls some breathing space to plan a rational program. Nothing could be worse than letting people know today that a controls program is on the way. Every firm in America would jack up prices violently. Even news reports that a controls program *may* begin can have this effect. According to former Secretary of the Treasury George P. Shultz, an epidemic of rumors of impending controls forced President Nixon's hand in 1971.

Tax-Based Incomes Policy

A relatively new type of incomes policy has been receiving increasing attention in recent years. Advocated originally by Professor Sidney Weintraub of the University of Pennsylvania, Governor Henry Wallich of the Federal Reserve System, and the late Arthur Okun of the Brookings Institution, **tax-based incomes policy (TIP)** seeks to use the tax system to fight inflation. The idea behind TIP is simple, though its implementation might be quite complex in practice. TIP would give employers and employees a financial stake in fighting inflation by lowering taxes for firms or workers who abided by national guideposts for wage–price behavior, or by raising taxes for those who violated them.

While there are many TIP plans, one particular example will bring out the flavor of all of them. Suppose the government wants to limit wage increases to 7 percent a year. It could pass legislation granting a 2 percent *decrease* in payroll taxes to all employees of firms in which average wages increased by no more than 7 percent. Then, for example, workers who settled for a (noninflationary) $6\frac{1}{2}$ percent raise would actually wind up with *more* after-tax income than those who settled for an (inflationary) 8 percent raise. They would get $6\frac{1}{2}$ percent more from their employers, plus 2 percent more from the government in the form of lower taxes, for a total gain of $8\frac{1}{2}$ percent. This incentive, it is hoped, would lead labor and management to settle for slower growth in wages; and these slower wage increases, in turn, would lead to slower price increases. Other TIP plans focus on corporation taxes rather than on payroll taxes, or utilize the "stick" rather than the "carrot" by penalizing the violaters of the wage–price guideposts rather than rewarding those who obey. But the basic goal is always the same: to make noninflationary behavior profitable for either firms or workers, or both.

Is TIP workable? We really have no way of knowing because it never has been tried. In 1978 President Carter asked Congress to enact a modified version of TIP, but Congress never gave the idea serious consideration. The Reagan administration has shown an equal lack of interest in TIP.

Indexing

A very different, and almost as untested, approach to the inflation–unemployment dilemma is **indexing.** The idea behind indexing is very different from the other proposals discussed in this chapter. Whereas these other proposals are all designed to lower the inflation rate, the primary purpose of indexing is to reduce the social costs of inflation.

The mechanics of indexing can be explained best through an example. In the United States the most common form of indexed contract is an *escalator clause* in a wage agreement. An escalator clause provides for an automatic increase in money wages—without the need for new contract negotiations—any time the price level rises by more than a specified amount. Suppose that with the Consumer Price Index (CPI) sitting at 280, a union and a firm agree on a three-year contract setting wages at $7 per hour this year, $8 next year, and $9 in the third year. They might then add an escalator clause stating that wages will be increased above these stipulated amounts by 5 cents per hour for each point by which the CPI exceeds 300 in any future year of the contract. Then, if the CPI in year three of the contract reaches 310, workers will receive an additional 50 cents per hour (5 cents for each of the 10 points by which 310 exceeds 300), for a total wage of $9.50 per hour. In this way, workers are partly protected from inflation. Nowadays, more than half of all workers employed by large unionized firms in the United States are covered by some sort of escalator clause. However, very few nonunion workers or employees of small firms enjoy such protection.

Interest payments on bonds or savings accounts can also be indexed, although this is not currently done in the United States.[6] The mechanics here are quite simple. If you had an indexed savings account, your bank might guarantee you a 1 percent *real interest rate* on your savings by automatically increasing your balance by the amount of inflation. For example, suppose you deposited $1000 on January 1 and withdrew it on December 31. An ordinary savings account, paying 6 percent interest, would pay you $1060 at the end of the year—your original $1000 plus 6 percent interest. But if this were an indexed bank account paying 1 percent, and prices rose by 10 percent during the year, your balance at year-end would be $1110—your original $1000 plus 1 percent real interest ($10) plus 10 percent ($100) to compensate you for your loss of purchasing power. The *nominal interest rate* would thus be 11 percent.[7] In general, the nominal rate would be 1 percent *plus* the rate of inflation. Thus if inflation turned out to be less than 5 percent that year, you would receive less than $1060.

Indexing is not designed to keep interest rates *high*, but to make real interest payments independent of inflation—to cut down the chances that the purchasing power of savings will be eroded by inflation.

With a conventional 6 percent savings account you get a real interest rate of 6 percent if there is zero inflation, 2 percent if there is 4 percent inflation, −2 percent if there is 8 percent inflation, and so on. With an imaginary 1 percent

Indexing refers to provisions in a law or a contract whereby monetary payments are *automatically* adjusted whenever a specified price index changes. Wage rates, pensions, interest payments on bonds, income taxes, and many other things can be indexed in this way, and have been. Sometimes such contractual provisions are called *escalator clauses*.

---

[6] Some other countries, with much higher inflation than ours, do extensive indexing of interest rates. Brazil and Israel are notable examples.

[7] The distinction between real and nominal interest rates, one of our 12 Ideas for Beyond the Final Exam, was discussed in detail in Chapter 6.

indexed account, you would receive 1 percent real interest no matter what the inflation rate. Indexing thus enables the saver to avoid gambling on inflation. For this reason, many economists have advocated that the U.S. government issue an indexed savings bond that small savers could use to protect themselves against inflation.

Indexing and the Social Costs of Inflation

The most extensive indexing to be found in the United States today is in government transfer payments. Social security benefits, for instance, are fully indexed so that retirees are not victimized by inflation. A variety of government income maintenance and social insurance programs also pay benefits that are tied directly to prices. Some economists believe that the United States should follow the example of several foreign countries and adopt a much more widespread system of indexing. Why? Because, they argue, it would take most of the sting out of inflation. To see how indexing would accomplish this, let us review some of the social costs of inflation that we enumerated in Chapter 6.

One important cost is the capricious redistribution of income caused by unexpected inflation or deflation. We saw that borrowers and lenders normally incorporate an *inflation premium* equal to the *expected rate of inflation* into the nominal interest rate. Then, if inflation turns out to be higher than expected, the borrower has to pay to the lender only the agreed-upon nominal interest rate, including the premium for expected inflation; he does not have to compensate the lender for the (higher) actual inflation. Thus the borrower enjoys a windfall gain and the lender loses out. The opposite happens if inflation turns out to be lower than was expected. Again the borrower pays the lender the agreed-upon nominal interest rate, but now his rate includes an inflation premium that overcompensates the lender for the actual inflation. But if interest rates on loans were indexed, none of this would occur. Borrowers and lenders would agree on a fixed *real* rate of interest, and then the borrower would compensate the lender for whatever *actual inflation* occurred. No one would have to guess what the inflation rate would be.

A second social cost we mentioned in Chapter 6 stems from the fact that certain legal restrictions and regulations on interest and profit rates that may or may not be sensible in a noninflationary world can have incredibly perverse effects in an inflationary environment. For example, we cited the case of usury ceilings on home mortgages, which, while intended to protect home buyers, have in the past made it almost impossible to build a home when inflation rates are high. If these regulations were stated in terms of *real* interest and profit rates, many of these strange—and unintended—distortions would not arise.

A final problem noted in Chapter 6 is that uncertainty over future price levels makes it difficult to enter into long-term contracts—rental agreements, construction agreements, and so on. One way out of this problem is to write indexed contracts, which specify all future payments in real terms.

In the face of all these benefits, and others we have not mentioned here, why do many economists oppose indexing? Probably the major reason is the fear that indexing will lead to an acceleration of inflation. With the costs of inflation reduced so markedly, they argue, what will persuade governments to pay the price of fighting inflation? What will stop them from inflating more and more? They fear that the answer to these questions is, Nothing. Voters who stand to lose nothing from inflation are unlikely to pressure their legislators into stopping it. Opponents of indexing worry that a mild inflationary disease could turn into a ravaging epidemic in a highly indexed economy.

Summary

1. Supply-side tax cuts aim to push the economy's aggregate supply curve outward to the right. If successful, they can raise employment and reduce prices at the same time. That is, they can fight inflation and unemployment simultaneously.

2. Critics point out three problems with supply-side tax cuts: they also stimulate aggregate demand; the beneficial supply-side effects may be quite small; and the demand-side effects are certain to occur before the supply-side effects. For these reasons, critics claim, supply-side tax cuts are likely to be inflationary.

3. The long-run inflation rate depends on the difference between the growth rates of the aggregate demand and aggregate supply curves. Government policy can affect the long-run growth rate of aggregate supply only if it affects the growth rate of productivity.

4. While speeding up productivity growth is highly desirable for many reasons, including its anti-inflationary effects, it is very hard to achieve. For this reason, aggregate demand policy must bear the brunt of inflation fighting.

5. Policies that improve the functioning of the labor market—including retraining programs and various types of employment services—can improve the trade-off between inflation and unemployment by lowering the natural rate of unemployment. To date, however, the U.S. government has had only modest success with these measures.

6. Some small amount of progress against inflation may also be made by eliminating some of the government regulations that keep prices high. Indeed, some of this has already been done.

7. Many varieties of incomes policies have been used in this and other countries in an effort to improve the trade-off between inflation and unemployment. While some have led to notable temporary improvements, their lasting effects have been minimal.

8. The weakest varieties of incomes policies simply set up standards for permissible wage and price increases (wage–price guideposts) and apply verbal admonitions against violators (jawboning). Stronger variants may actually set legal limits on wage and price increases or even ban them outright (a wage–price freeze).

9. One argument in favor of short-term wage–price controls is that they can reduce inflationary expectations and thereby rob inflation of some of its momentum.

10. A new and different approach to incomes policy would use tax incentives to encourage more moderate wage and price increases. This so-called "tax-based incomes policy" has yet to be tried.

11. Indexing is another way to approach the trade-off problem. Instead of trying to improve the trade-off, it concentrates on reducing the social costs of inflation—perhaps eliminating them altogether. Opponents of indexing worry, however, that the economy's resistance to inflation may be lowered by indexing.

Concepts for Review

Supply-side tax cuts	Wage–price guideposts	Tax-based incomes policy (TIP)
Productivity	Wage–price controls	Indexing (escalator clauses)
Incomes policy	Inflationary expectations	Real versus nominal interest rates
Jawboning	Wage–price freezes	

Questions for Discussion

1. Explain the basic argument in favor of supply-side tax reductions. What assumptions must be fulfilled in order to make this policy work?

2. The Council of Economic Advisers of the outgoing Carter administration evaluated the Kemp-Roth proposal in January 1981 and concluded that "even under the most optimistic circumstances, a 10 percent reduction in (personal income) tax rates would not induce enough additional work, saving, or investment to offset more than a fraction of the 2 percent increase in aggregate demand that would accompany the tax cut."

   a. The proposed tax cut amounted to roughly 1 percent of GNP. Why did the Council estimate that it would raise aggregate demand by 2 percent?

   b. What do you suppose might be some of the "optimistic circumstances" referred to by the Council?

   c. Why do you suppose the Council judged these circumstances unlikely to occur?

3. Which of the following changes is likely to raise the productivity of labor, and why?

   a. Tax cuts are offered to firms that modernize their factories.

   b. Workers are offered a 2 percent reduction in payroll taxes if they lower the rate of wage inflation to 6 percent.

   c. A clever plant manager discovers a new way to organize the assembly line so that the same amounts of labor and capital can produce more output.

d. Computer engineers continue to discover new ways to improve the speed of computers.

e. A brilliant physicist invents a perpetual-motion machine.

f. Labor unions that were blocking the introduction of new labor-saving devices mend their ways and allow these machines to be used.

4. Which of the above is likely to raise the *growth rate* of productivity? Why?

5. Do you think it is proper for the president of the United States to "jawbone" some corporations into reducing their price increases?

6. Explain some of the differences between wage–price guideposts and wage–price controls.

7. Suppose that a program of wage–price controls is under consideration by the government. What are the possible benefits to the nation from such a program? What are the possible costs? How would you go about balancing the benefits against the costs?

8. Explain the basic idea behind "TIP" (tax-based incomes policy). Try to devise a TIP plan of your own. Can you foresee some practical difficulties with your plan?

9. Ordinary savings accounts now pay approximately $5\frac{1}{2}$ percent *nominal* interest. Would you prefer to trade yours in for an indexed bank account that paid a zero *real* rate of interest? What if the real interest rate offered were 1 percent? What if it were −1 percent? What do your answers to these questions reveal about your personal attitudes toward inflation?

The Price
System
and the
Invisible Hand

III

The Common Sense of Consumer Choice

18

Everything is worth
what its purchaser
will pay for it.

PUBLILIUS SYRUS (1st century B.C.)

I
t is clear from our initial look at supply and demand in Chapter 4 that if we are to understand how markets function and how they react to changes in the economic environment, we will have to delve more deeply into the nature of both demand and supply. What influences determine the shapes and positions of the demand and supply curves? How do the curves shift in response to various events? The purpose of Part Three is to answer questions like these and thereby to provide the analytical tools we will need to pursue the central theme of the microeconomic portions of this book: the virtues and shortcomings of the market mechanism.

We begin on the demand side of the market. In this chapter we emphasize that the demand curves of Chapter 4 depend on choices made by consumers, and we then explore the logic underlying these choices. Since a demand curve tells us how much of a good consumers want to purchase at each possible price, its origins must in some sense rest in consumer psychology. But since economists claim no qualifications for making deep pronouncements about consumer psychology, our exploration will not go very far below the surface. It will, however, describe some powerful tools used in the analysis of consumer choice and cast some light on a number of important issues, including the negative slope of the demand curve.

In Chapter 19 we take up some further aspects of demand curves that are essential for understanding the workings of the market mechanism and expand our analysis from demand curves for single consumers to demand curves for a total market. Then, in Chapters 20 through 22, we turn our attention to the supply side of the market.

A Puzzle:
Should Water Be Worth More than Diamonds?

When Adam Smith was lecturing at the University of Glasgow in the 1760s, he introduced the study of demand by posing a puzzle. Common sense, he said, suggests that the price of a commodity must somehow depend on what that good is worth to consumers—on the amount of *utility* that commodity offers. Yet, Smith pointed out, there are cases in which a good's utility apparently has little influence on its price. Two examples he gave were diamonds and water. He noted that water, which is essential to life and therefore undoubtedly of enormous value to most consumers, generally sells at a very low price, while diamonds, on the other hand, cost thousands of dollars even though their uses are quite limited. A century later, this puzzle, called the **diamond-water paradox,** helped stimulate the invention of what is perhaps the most powerful set of tools in the economist's toolkit—*marginal analysis.* Fortunately, we need only wait a few pages, not a century, to learn how marginal analysis—a general method for making optimal decisions—helps to resolve the paradox.

Total and Marginal Utility

The focus of this chapter is the relationship between the utility that a commodity offers to a consumer and the consumer's decision as to how much of that commodity to buy. We must first, therefore, define what we mean by utility and then consider how it is related to the individual's decisions. Economists are concerned with two types of utility—total and marginal. The **total utility** to a consumer of some bundle of goods, say, six pounds of bananas, is a number meant to indicate how much pleasure, usefulness, or benefit the consumer obtains from the bananas. The trouble is that no one has yet invented a reliable sensory detector to tell us directly how much utility a bundle of goods provides. To get around the problem, we can measure the total utility of a particular good to a particular consumer by asking what is the largest sum of money that person will voluntarily give up in exchange for it. Suppose, for example, an individual is considering purchasing six pounds of bananas. She has determined that she will not buy them if they cost more than $2.22, but she will buy them if they cost $2.22 or less. Thus, the total utility of six pounds of bananas to her is $2.22—the maximum amount she is willing to spend to have them.

> The **total utility** of a quantity of goods to a consumer (measured in money terms) is the maximum amount of money he or she is willing to give in exchange for it.

Total utility, as you can see, is a way to measure the benefit a consumer derives from any purchase. The higher the total utility she obtains, the better off she is. By definition, then, the consumer's *optimal* purchase decisions are those that make her total utility as large as possible. It is total utility that really matters to the consumer. But to understand which decisions most effectively promote *total* utility we must consider the related concept of **marginal utility.** This term refers to the *additional* utility that an individual derives by consuming *one more unit* of any good. Table 18–1 helps clarify the distinction between marginal and total utility and shows how the two are related. The first two columns show how much *total* utility (measured in money terms) a consumer derives from various quantities of bananas ranging from zero up to eight. For example, a single pound is worth (no more than) 60 cents to her, two pounds are worth $1.16, and

> The **marginal utility** of a commodity to a consumer (measured in money terms) is the maximum amount of money he or she is willing to pay *for one more unit* of it.

Table 18–1

TOTAL AND MARGINAL UTILITY OF BANANAS (MEASURED IN MONEY TERMS)

NUMBER OF POUNDS	TOTAL UTILITY (in dollars)	MARGINAL UTILITY (in dollars)
0	0	
1	.60	.60
2	1.16	.56
3	1.60	.44
4	1.96	.36
5	2.14	.18
6	2.22	.08
7	2.26	.04
8	2.26	0

so on. The *marginal* utility is the *difference* between any two successive total utility figures. For example, if the consumer already has three pounds (worth $1.60 to her), an *additional* pound brings her total utility up to $1.96. Her marginal utility is thus the difference between the two, or 36 cents.

The "Law" of Diminishing Marginal Utility

So far we have been dealing primarily with definitions—not even with the "superficial" human psychology we had promised. But with our definitions we can now propose a simple hypothesis about consumer tastes: The more of a good a consumer has, the less *marginal* utility an additional unit will bring. In general, this is a plausible proposition. The idea is based on the assertion that every person has a hierarchy of uses to which he or she will put a particular commodity. All of these uses are valuable, but some are more valuable than others. Let's consider bananas again. Our consumer may use them to give to her family to eat, to feed a pet monkey, to make banana cream pie (which is a bit rich for her tastes), or to give to a brother-in-law, for whom she has no deep affection. If she has only one pound, it will be used solely for the family to eat. The second, third, and fourth pounds may be used to feed the monkey; and a fifth may go into the banana cream pie. But the only use she has for a sixth pound, alas, is to give it to her brother-in-law.

The **"law" of diminish-ing marginal utility** as-serts that additional units of a commodity yield successively smaller contributions to a con-sumer's well-being. As the in-dividual's consumption in-creases, the marginal utility of each additional unit declines.

The point is obvious. Each pound of bananas contributes something to the satisfaction of the consumer's needs for the product; but each additional pound contributes less than its predecessor because the use to which it can be put has a lower priority. This, in essence, is the logic behind the **"law" of diminishing marginal utility.** The last column of Table 18–1 illustrates this concept. The marginal utility (abbreviated MU) of the first pound of bananas is 60 cents; that is, the consumer is willing to pay *up to* 60 cents for the first pound. The second pound offers a marginal utility of 56 cents, a third pound only 44 cents, and so on until, after the fifth pound, the consumer is willing to pay only 8 cents for an additional pound (the MU of a sixth pound is 8 cents).

The assumption upon which this "law" is based is plausible for most consumers and for most commodities. But, like most laws, there are exceptions. For some people, the more they have of a particular good, the more they want. Consider the needs of addicts and collectors, for example. The stamp collector who has a few stamps may consider the acquisition of one more to be mildly amusing. The person who has a large and valuable collection may be prepared to go to the ends of the earth for another stamp. Similarly, the alcoholic who finds a dry martini quite pleasant when he first starts drinking may find one more to be absolutely irresistible once he has already consumed four or five. Economists, however, generally treat such cases of *increasing marginal utility* as abnormali-ties. For most goods and most people, marginal utility probably declines as consumption increases.

The Rule for Optimal Purchases

Now let us put the concept of marginal utility to work. Given a limited budget, how can a consumer interested in maximizing *total utility* decide how much of each commodity to buy? The answer leads us to the following rule:

It always pays the consumer to buy more of any commodity whose marginal utility (measured in money) exceeds its price, and less of any commodity whose marginal utility is less than its price. When possible, the consumer should buy the quantity at which price (P) and marginal utility (MU) are exactly equal; that is, at which

$$P = \text{MU},$$

because only this quantity will maximize the *total utility* he or she gains from the purchase.

Notice that while our concern is with *total* utility, the rule is framed in terms of *marginal* utility. Marginal utility is not important for its own sake, but rather as an instrument used to calculate the level of purchases that maximizes total utility.

To see why this rule works, refer back to the table of marginal utilities of bananas (Table 18–1). Suppose the supermarket is selling bananas for 23 cents a pound and our consumer considers buying only two pounds. We see that this is not a wise decision, because the marginal utility of a third pound of bananas (44 cents) is greater than its 23-cent price. If the consumer were to increase her purchase to three pounds, the additional pound would cost 23 cents but yield 44 cents in marginal utility; thus the additional purchase would bring her a clear net gain of 21 cents. Obviously, at the 23-cent price she is better off with three pounds of bananas than with two.

Similarly, at this price, five pounds is *not* an optimal purchase because the 18-cent marginal utility of the fifth pound is less than its 23-cent price. Our consumer would be better off with only four pounds, since that would save her 23 cents with only an 18-cent loss in utility—a net gain of five cents from the decision to buy one pound less. Our rule for optimal purchases tells us that our consumer should buy four pounds, since any purchase above this amount yields a marginal utility that is less than price, and any purchase below this amount leaves MU greater than P.

From Marginal Utility to the Demand Curve

We can use the optimal purchase rule to show that the "law" of diminishing marginal utility implies that demand curves typically slope downward to the right, that is, they have negative slopes.[1] For example, it is possible to use the list of marginal utilities in Table 18–1 to determine precisely how many bananas a consumer would buy at any price. Table 18–2 gives several alternative prices, and the optimal purchase quantity corresponding to each. (To make sure you understand the logic behind the optimal purchase rule, verify that the entries in the right-hand column of Table 18–2 are in fact correct.) This *demand schedule,*

[1] If you need review, turn back to page 55 in Chapter 4.

Table 18–2
LIST OF OPTIMAL QUANTITY TO PURCHASE AT ALTERNATIVE PRICES

PRICE (in dollars)	QUANTITY TO PURCHASE
.02	7
.06	6
.14	5
.22	4
.40	3
.50	2
.58	1

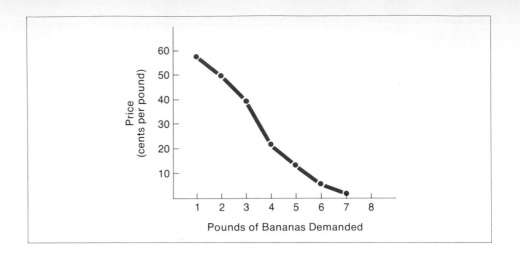

Figure 18–1

A TYPICAL
DEMAND CURVE

This demand curve is derived
from the consumer's table of
marginal utilities by following
the optimal purchase rule. The
points in the graph correspond
to the numbers in Table 18–2.

which relates quantity demanded to price, may be translated into the consumer's *demand curve* shown in Figure 18–1. You can see that it has the characteristic negative slope commonly associated with demand curves.

Let us examine the logic underlying the negatively sloped demand curve a bit more carefully. If the consumer is purchasing the optimal number of bananas, and then the price falls, she will find that her marginal utility of bananas is now above the suddenly reduced price. For example, Table 18–1 tells us that at a price of 40 cents per pound it is optimal to buy three pounds, because the marginal utility (MU) of the fourth pound is 36 cents. But, if price is reduced to 30 cents, it then pays to purchase the fourth pound because its MU exceeds its price. This additional pound of bananas will lower the marginal utility of the next pound of bananas (to 18 cents in the example) and thereby bring it back into balance with price, as prescribed in the optimal purchase rule. Note the critical role of the "law" of diminishing marginal utility. If P falls, a consumer who wishes to maximize total utility will see to it that MU falls. According to the "law" of diminishing marginal utility, the only way to do this is to increase the quantity purchased.

While this explanation is a bit abstract and mechanical, it can easily be rephrased in practical terms. We have seen that the various uses to which an individual puts a commodity have different priorities. For our consumer, giving bananas to her family has a higher priority than using them to make pie, which in turn is of higher priority than giving them to her brother-in-law. If the price of bananas is high, it will pay the consumer to buy only enough for the high-priority uses—those that offer a high marginal utility. When price declines, however, it pays to purchase more of the good—enough for some lower-priority uses. This is the essence of the analysis. It tells us that the same assumption about consumer psychology underlies both the "law" of diminishing marginal utility and the negative slope of the demand curve. They are really two different ways of describing the assumed attitudes of consumers.

The Diamond–Water Paradox: The Puzzle Resolved

We can use marginal utility analysis to remove the mystery from Adam Smith's diamond–water paradox—his observation that the price of diamonds is much higher than the price of water even though water seems to offer far more utility.

The resolution of the diamond—water paradox is based on the distinction between marginal and total utility.

The *total* utility of water—its life-giving benefit—is indeed much higher than that of diamonds, just as Smith observed. But price, as we have seen, is not related directly to total utility. Rather, the optimal purchase rule tells us that price will tend to be equal to *marginal* utility. And there is every reason to expect the marginal utility of water to be very low while the marginal utility of diamonds is very high. Water is extremely plentiful in many parts of the world. If consumers use correspondingly large quantities of water, by the principle of diminishing marginal utility, its marginal utility to a typical household will be pushed down to a very low level. On the other hand, diamonds are very scarce. As a result, the quantity of diamonds is not large enough to drive the MU of diamonds down very far. The scarcer the commodity, the higher its *marginal* utility, and, consequently, the higher its market price, regardless of the size of its *total* utility.

Thus, like many paradoxes, the diamond—water puzzle has a straightforward explanation. In this case, all one has to remember is that:

Scarcity raises *marginal* utility but not necessarily *total* utility; it is marginal not total utility that is related to price.

Income and Demand: Inferior Goods

So far our analysis of marginal utility has led us to consider only one determinant of quantity demanded: the price of the product. But quantity demanded is also affected by other variables, such as advertising, prices of other goods, and consumer incomes. We will have much more to say about these influences in the following chapter. Here let us briefly consider the effects of only one of these—the income of consumers.

Normally, we expect a simple relationship between income and quantity demanded: the more money consumers have to spend, the more they are able to buy, and so the more we expect them to buy. For most goods, this is true; but there are exceptions. Economists have given the rather descriptive name **inferior goods** to the class of commodities for which quantity demanded moves in the opposite direction from what we normally expect when income rises. The reason is rather straightforward. As people become wealthier they generally reduce their purchases of such items as reconditioned automobile tires, poor-quality clothing, and bus tickets. These are inferior goods because in each instance a more desirable alternative is available. The upshot is that we cannot draw definite conclusions about the effects of a rise in consumer incomes on quantity demanded. For *most* commodities, if incomes rise and prices do not change, there will be an increase in quantity demanded. But for the inferior goods there will be a decrease in quantity demanded.

An **inferior good** is a commodity whose quantity demanded falls when the purchaser's income rises, all other things remaining equal.

Income and Substitution Effects of a Price Change*

A fall in the price of a commodity leads to a rise in the consumer's *real* income—the amount that her wages will purchase. But anything that increases or decreases real income will have an effect on quantity demanded, as we just

*This section contains rather more difficult material, which, in shorter courses, may be omitted without loss of continuity.

The **income effect** is a *portion* of the change in quantity of a good demanded when its price changes. A rise in price cuts the consumer's purchasing power (real income), which leads to a change in the quantity demanded of that commodity. That change is the income effect.

The **substitution effect** is the change in quantity demanded of a good resulting from a change in its relative price, exclusive of whatever change in quantity demanded may be attributable to the associated change in real income.

learned. The effects of the increase in purchasing power caused by a fall in a commodity's price are much the same as if the consumer's wages had risen: she will buy more of any commodity that is not an inferior good. This process, producing the **income effect,** has three stages: (1) the price of the good falls causing (2) an increase in the consumer's real income, which leads to (3) a change in quantity demanded. Of course, if the price of a good rises, it will produce the same effect in reverse. The consumer's real income will decline, leading to the opposite change in quantity demanded.

A change in the price of a commodity produces another effect on quantity demanded that is rather different from the income effect. This is the **substitution effect,** which is the effect on quantity demanded attributable to the fact that the new price is now higher or lower than before *relative to the prices of other goods.* The substitution effect of a price change is the portion of the change in quantity demanded that can be attributed *exclusively* to the resulting change in relative prices rather than to the associated change in real income. If the relative price of some good falls, its quantity demanded will rise, even if the attendant gain in purchasing power were somehow taken away. Thus, if we consider the substitution effect *alone,* a decline in price always increases quantity demanded and a rise in price always reduces quantity demanded.

These two concepts, the income effect and the substitution effect, which many beginning economics students think were invented to torture them, are really quite useful. Let us consider an example of how economists use them. Suppose, for example, that the price of hamburgers declines while the price of cheese remains unchanged. The *substitution effect* clearly induces the consumer to buy more hamburgers in place of grilled cheese sandwiches, because hamburgers are now comparatively cheaper. What of the *income effect?* Unless hamburger is an inferior good, it leads to the same decision. The fall in price makes consumers richer, which induces them to increase their purchases of all but inferior goods. This example alerts us to two general points:

If a good is not inferior, it must have a downward-sloping demand curve, since income and substitution effects reinforce each other. However, an inferior good may violate this pattern of demand behavior because the income effect of a decline in price leads consumers to buy less.

Do *all* inferior goods, then, have upward-sloping demand curves? Certainly not, for we have the substitution effect to reckon with; and the substitution effect always favors a downward-sloping demand curve. Thus we have a kind of tug-of-war in the case of an inferior good. If the income effect predominates, the demand curve will slope upward; if the substitution effect prevails, the demand curve will slope downward. Economists have concluded that the substitution effect generally wins out; so while there are many examples of inferior goods, there are few examples of upward-sloping demand curves. When might the income effect prevail over the substitution effect? Certainly not when the good in question (say, margarine) is a very small fraction of the consumer's budget, for then a fall in price makes the consumer only slightly "richer," and therefore creates a very small income effect. But the demand curve could slope upward if an inferior good constitutes a substantial portion of the consumer's budget.

We conclude this discussion of income and substitution effects with a warning against an error that is frequently made. Many students mistakenly close their books thinking that price changes cause substitution effects while income changes cause income effects. This is incorrect. As the foregoing example of hamburgers made clear:

The Theory of Consumer Choice and White Rats

Recently, a team of economists and psychologists has been studying whether the theory of consumer choice that we have just outlined—including the different income and substitution effects of a price change—applies to animal species other than *homo sapiens.* According to their research, it does.*

In one experiment, standard laboratory rats were placed in experimental chambers equipped with two levers; pressing one lever rewarded them with a prescribed amount of commodity A (say, water) while pressing the other rewarded them with a prescribed amount of commodity B (say, food). The rats were given a limited "budget" because they could only press the levers a fixed number of times per day. Once they had exhausted their "income" by pressing the levers, say, 250 times, the lights above the levers would go out, signaling the rats that their presses would no longer result in rewards. Apparently, the little creatures learned the meaning of the lights quite quickly.

In this controlled environment, *income effects* could be observed by varying the permitted number of lever presses per day. The results showed clearly that when more lever presses were allowed, rats chose to consume more of both goods. Apparently, none of the goods such as food, water, root beer, and Tom Collins mix, are inferior goods from the point of view of rats.

Measuring *substitution effects* was a bit trickier since, as we have stressed, a price change sets in motion *both* an income effect *and* a substitution effect. In the experiment, the "price" of each commodity was controlled by the amount of food or liquid produced by each lever press. Substitution effects were measured, for example, by raising the "price" of food (i.e., reducing the amount of food yielded by each press), while at the same time allowing the rat enough additional lever presses to compensate him for his loss of purchasing power. As the analysis of this chapter has suggested, the rats responded to this change in their environment by "buying" less food.

Putting the two effects together, then, a higher price of food led to less consumption of food via the income effect and also to less consumption of food via the substitution effect. The demand curves of these rats were indeed negatively sloped.

*John H. Kagel, Raymond C. Battalio, Howard Rachlin, and Leonard Green, "Demand Curves for Animal Consumers," *Quarterly Journal of Economics*, vol. XCVI, February, 1981 pages 1–16.

Any change in price sets in motion both a substitution effect and an income effect, both of which affect quantity demanded.

This completes our discussion of the logic behind consumer choice. In the next chapter we will use this analysis as a base upon which to build a theory of demand, thereby taking our first major step toward understanding how the market system operates.

Summary

1. Economists distinguish between total and marginal utility. Total utility, or the benefit a consumer derives from a purchase, is measured by the maximum amount of money he or she would give up in order to have the good in question. Rational consumers seek to maximize total utility.

2. Marginal utility is the maximum amount of money a consumer is willing to pay for an additional unit of a particular commodity. Marginal utility is useful in calculating what set of purchases maximizes total utility.

3. The "law" of diminishing marginal utility is a psychological hypothesis stating that as a consumer acquires more and more of a commodity, the marginal utility of additional units of the commodity will decrease.

4. To maximize the total utility obtained by spending money on a commodity, the consumer must purchase a quantity such that the price is equal to the commodity's marginal utility (in money terms).

5. If the consumer acts to maximize utility, and if his marginal utility of some good declines when larger quantities are purchased, then his demand curve for

the good will have a negative slope. A reduction in price will induce the purchase of more units, leading to a lower marginal utility.

6. Abundant goods tend to have a low marginal utility regardless of whether their total utility is high or low. That is why water can have a low price despite its high total utility.

7. An inferior good, such as second-hand clothing, is a commodity consumers buy less of when they get richer, all other things held equal.

8. A rise in the price of a commodity has two effects on quantity demanded: (a) a substitution effect, which makes the good less attractive because it has become more expensive than it was previously, and (b) an income effect, which decreases the consumer's total utility because higher prices cut his purchasing power.

9. Any increase in the price of a good always has a *negative* substitution effect; that is, considering only the substitution effect, a rise in price must reduce the quantity demanded.

10. The income effect of a rise in price may, however, push quantity demanded up or down. For normal goods, the income effect of a higher price (which makes consumers poorer) reduces quantity demanded; for inferior goods, the income effect of higher prices actually increases quantity demanded.

Concepts for Review

Diamond–water paradox
Marginal analysis
Total utility
Marginal utility

The "law" of diminishing marginal utility
Optimal purchase rule ($P = MU$)

Scarcity and marginal utility
Inferior goods
Income effect
Substitution effect

Questions for Discussion

1. Describe some of the different things you do with water. Which would you give up if the price of water rose a little? If it rose by a fairly large amount? If it rose by a very large amount?

2. Which is greater: your *total* utility from 10 gallons of water per day or from 20 gallons per day? Why?

3. Which is greater: your *marginal* utility at 10 gallons per day or your marginal utility at 20 gallons per day? Why?

4. Some people who do not understand the optimal purchase rule argue that if a consumer buys so much of a good that its price equals its marginal utility, he could not possibly be behaving optimally. Rather, they say, he would be better off quitting when ahead, that is, buying a quantity such that marginal utility is much greater than price. What is wrong with this argument? (*Hint:* What opportunity does the consumer then miss? Is it maximization of marginal or total utility that serves the consumer's interests?)

5. What inferior goods do you purchase? Why do you buy them? Do you think you will continue to buy them when your income is higher?

6. Suppose that gasoline and safety pins each rise in price by 10 percent. Which will have the larger income effect upon the purchases of a typical consumer? Why?

7. Around 1850, Sir Robert Giffen observed that Irish peasants actually consumed more potatoes as the price of potatoes increased. Use the concepts of income and substitution effects to explain this phenomenon.

Appendix
Indifference Curve Analysis

The analysis of consumer demand presented in this chapter, while correct as far as it goes, has one analytical shortcoming: By treating the consumer's decision about the purchase of each commodity as an isolated event, it conceals the necessity of choice imposed on the consumer by his limited budget. It does not indicate explicitly the hard choice behind every purchase decision—the sacrifice of some goods to obtain others. If you spend more money on rent, you have less to spend on entertainment. If you buy more clothing, you have less money for food. To represent the consumer's choice problem explicitly, economists have invented two geometric devices, the *budget line* and the *indifference curve*, which this appendix describes.

Geometry of the Available Choices: The Budget Line

Suppose, for simplicity, that there were only two commodities produced in the world, cheese and records. The decision problem of any household then would be to determine the allocation of its income between these two goods. Clearly, the more it spends on one the less it can have of the other. But just what is the trade-off? A numerical example will answer this question, and also introduce the graphical device that economists use to portray the trade-off.

Suppose that cheese costs $2 per pound, records sell at $3 each, and our consumer has $12 at his disposal. He obviously has a variety of choices—as displayed in Table 18–3. For example, if he buys no records, he can go home with six pounds of cheese,

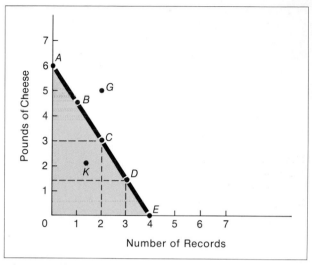

Figure 18–2
A BUDGET LINE
This budget line shows the different combinations of cheese and records the consumer can buy with $12 if cheese costs $2 per pound and records cost $3 each. At point *A* the consumer buys six pounds of cheese and has nothing left over for records. At point *E* he spends the entire budget on records. At intermediate points (such as *C*) on the budget line, the consumer buys some of both goods (two records and three pounds of cheese).

and so on. Each of the combinations of cheese and records that the consumer can afford can be shown in a diagram in which the axes measure the quantities of each commodity that is purchased. In Figure 18–2, pounds of cheese are measured along the vertical axis, number of records is measured along the horizontal axis, and each of the combinations enumerated in Table 18–3 is represented by a labeled point. For example, point *A* corresponds to spending everything

Table 18–3
ALTERNATIVE PURCHASE COMBINATIONS FOR A $12 BUDGET

NUMBER OF RECORDS (at $3 each)	EXPENDITURE ON RECORDS (in dollars)	REMAINING FUNDS (in dollars)	NUMBER OF POUNDS OF CHEESE (at $2 each)
0	0	12	6
1	3	9	$4\frac{1}{2}$
2	6	6	3
3	9	3	$1\frac{1}{2}$
4	12	0	0

on cheese, point E corresponds to spending everything on records, and point C corresponds to buying two records and three pounds of cheese.

If we connect points A through E by a straight line, the blue line in the diagram, we can trace out all the possible ways to divide the $12 between the two goods. For example, point D tells us that if the consumer buys three records there will be only enough money left over to purchase one and one-half pounds of cheese. This is readily seen to be correct from Table 18–3. Line AE is therefore called the **budget line.**

The **budget line** for a household represents graphically all the possible combinations of two commodities that it can purchase, given the prices of the commodities and some fixed amount of money at its disposal.

Properties of the Budget Line

Let us now use r to represent the number of records purchased by our consumer and c to indicate the amount of cheese he acquires. Thus, at $2 per pound, he spends on cheese a total of $2 \times$ (number of pounds of cheese bought) $= 2c$ dollars. Similarly, he spends $3r$ dollars on records, making a total of $2c + 3r = \$12$, if the entire $12 is spent on the two commodities. This is the equation of the budget line. It is also the equation of the straight line drawn in the diagram.[2]

We note also that the budget line represents the *maximal* amounts of the commodities that the consumer can afford. Thus, for any given purchase of records, it tells us the greatest amount of cheese his money can buy. If our consumer wants to be thrifty, he can choose to end up at a point below the budget line, such as K. Clearly, then, the choices he has available include not only those points on the budget line AE, but also any point in the shaded triangle formed by the budget line AE and the two axes. By contrast, points above the budget line, such as G, are not available to the consumer given his limited budget. A bundle consisting of five pounds of cheese and two records would cost $16, which is more than he has to spend.

[2]The reader may have noticed one problem that arises in this formulation. If every point on the budget line AE is a possible way for the consumer to spend his money, there must be some manner in which he can buy fractional records. Perhaps the purchase of one and one-half records can be interpreted to include a down payment of $1.50 on a record on his next shopping trip! Throughout this book it is convenient to assume that commodities are available in fractional quantities when drawing diagrams. This makes the graphs clearer and does not really affect the analysis.

The position of the budget line is determined by two types of data: the prices of the commodities purchased and the income at the buyer's disposal. We can complete our discussion of the graphics of the budget line by examining briefly how a change in either of these magnitudes affects its location.

Obviously, any increase in the income of the household increases the range of options available to it. Specifically, *increases in income produce parallel shifts in the budget line*, as shown in Figure 18–3. The reason is simply that a, say, 50 percent increase in available income, if entirely spent on the two goods in question, would permit the family to purchase exactly 50 percent more of *either* commodity. Point A in Figure 18–2 would shift upward by 50 percent of its distance from the origin, while point E would move to the right by 50 percent.[3] Figure 18–3 shows three such budget lines corresponding to incomes of $9, $12, and $18, respectively.

[3]An algebraic proof is simple. Let M (which is initially $12) be the amount of money available to our household. The equation of the budget line can be solved for c, obtaining

$$c = -(3/2)r + M/2 .$$

This is the equation of a straight line with a slope of $-3/2$ and with a vertical intercept of $M/2$. A change in M, the quantity of money available, will not change the *slope* of the budget line; it will lead only to parallel shifts in that line.

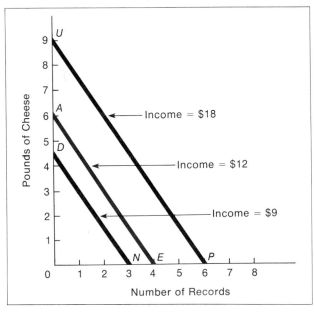

Figure 18–3
THE EFFECT OF INCOME CHANGES ON THE BUDGET LINE
A change in the amount of money in the consumer's budget causes a parallel shift in the budget line. A rise in the budget from $12 to $18 raises the budget line from AE to UP. A fall from $12 to $9 lowers the budget line from AE to DN.

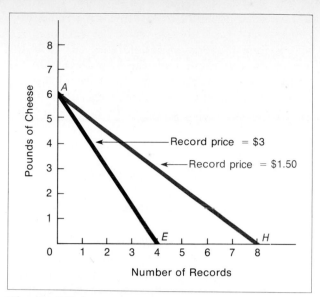

Figure 18–4
THE EFFECT OF PRICE CHANGES
ON THE BUDGET LINE
A fall in the price of records causes the end of the budget line on the records axis to swing away from the origin. A fall in record price from $3 to $1.50 swings the price line from *AE* to blue line *AH*. This happens because at the higher price, $12 buys only four records, but at the lower price it can buy eight records.

Finally, we can ask what happens to the budget line when there is a change in the price of some commodity. In Figure 18–4, we see that when the price of records *decreases*, the budget line moves outward, but the move is no longer parallel because the point on the cheese axis remains fixed. Once again, the reason is fairly straightforward. A 50 percent reduction in the price of records permits the family's $12 to buy twice as many records as before: point *E* is moved rightward to point *H*, at which eight records are shown to be obtainable. However, since the price of cheese has not changed, point *A*, the amount of cheese that can be bought for $12, is unaffected. Thus we have the general result that a reduction in the price of one of the two commodities swings the budget line outward along the axis representing the quantity of that item while leaving the location of the other end of the line unchanged.

What the Consumer Prefers: The Indifference Curve

The budget line tells us what choices are *available* to the consumer. We next must examine the consumer's *preferences* in order to determine which of these possibilities he will want to choose.

After much investigation, economists have determined what they believe to be the minimum amount of information they need about a purchaser in order to analyze his or her choices. This information consists of the consumer's *ranking* of the alternative bundles of commodities that are available. Suppose, for instance, the consumer is offered a choice between two bundles of goods, bundle *W*, which contains three records and one pound of cheese, and bundle *T*, which contains two records and three pounds of cheese. The economist wants to know for this purpose only whether the consumer prefers *W* to *T*, *T* to *W*, or whether he is *indifferent* about which one he gets. Note that the analysis requires no information about *degree* of preference— whether the consumer is wildly more enthusiastic about one of the bundles or just prefers it slightly.

Graphically, the preference information is provided by a group of curves called **indifference curves** (Figure 18–5).

An **indifference curve** is a line connecting all combinations of the commodities in question that are equally desirable to the consumer.

But before we examine these curves, let us see how such a curve is interpreted. A single point on an

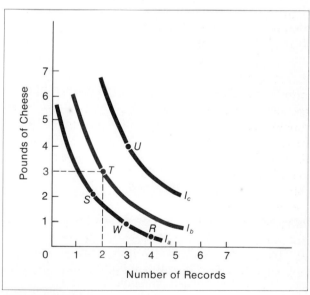

Figure 18–5
THREE INDIFFERENCE CURVES
FOR CHEESE AND RECORDS
Any point in the diagram represents a combination of cheese and records (for example, *T* represents two records and three pounds of cheese). Any two points on the same indifference curve (for example, *S* and *W*) represent two combinations of the goods that the consumer likes equally well. If two points, such as *T* and *W*, lie on different indifference curves, the one on the higher indifference curve is preferred by the consumer.

indifference curve tells us nothing about preferences. For example, point R on curve I_a simply represents the bundle of goods composed of four records and one-half pound of cheese. It does *not* suggest that the consumer is indifferent between one-half pound of cheese and four records. For the curve to tell us anything, we must consider at least two of its points, for example, points S and W. Since they represent two different combinations that are on the same indifference curve, they are equally desirable to our consumer.

Properties of the Indifference Curve

We do not know yet which bundle our consumer prefers; we know only that a choice between certain bundles will lead to indifference. So before we can use an indifference curve to analyze the consumer's choice, we must examine a few of its properties. Most important for us is the fact that:

As long as the consumer desires *more* of each of the goods in question, *every* point on a higher indifference curve will be preferred to *any* point on a lower indifference curve.

In other words, among indifference curves, higher is better. The reason is obvious. Given two indifference curves, say I_b and I_c in Figure 18–5, the higher curve will contain points lying above and to the right of some points on the lower curve. Thus, point U on curve I_c lies above and to the right of point T on curve I_b. This means that at U the consumer gets more records *and* more cheese than at T. Assuming that he desires both commodities, our consumer must prefer U to T. Since every point on curve I_c is, by definition, equal in preference to point U, and the same relation holds for point T and all other points along curve I_b, *every* point on curve I_c will be preferred to *any* point on curve I_b.

Another property that characterizes the indifference curve is its *negative slope*. Again, this holds only if the consumer wants more of both commodities. Consider two points, such as S and R, on the same indifference curve. If the consumer is indifferent between them, one cannot contain more of *both* commodities than the other. Since point S contains more cheese than R, R must offer more records than S, or the consumer could not be indifferent about which he gets. This means that if, say, we move toward the one with the larger number of records, the quantity of cheese must decrease. The curve will

always slope downhill toward the right, a negative slope.

A final property of indifference curves is the nature of their curvature—the way they round toward the axes. As drawn, they are "bowed in"—they flatten out (their slopes decrease in absolute value) as they extend from left to right. To understand why this is so we must first examine the economic interpretation of the slope of an indifference curve.

The Slopes of an Indifference Curve and of a Budget Line

In Figure 18–6 the average slope of the indifference curve between points M and N is represented by RM/RN. RM is the quantity of cheese the consumer gives up in moving from M to N. Similarly, RN is the increased number of records acquired in this move. Since the consumer is indifferent between bundles M and N, the gain of RN records must just suffice to compensate him for the loss of RM pounds of cheese. Thus the ratio RM/RN represents the terms on which the consumer is just willing—*according to his*

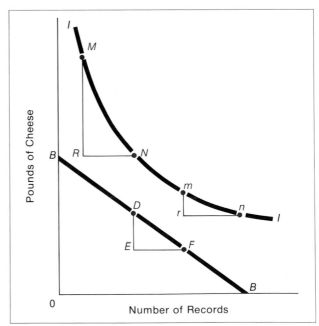

Figure 18–6
SLOPES OF A BUDGET LINE
AND AN INDIFFERENCE CURVE
The slope of the budget line shows how many pounds of cheese, *ED*, can be exchanged for *EF* records. The slope of the indifference curve shows how many pounds of cheese, *RM*, the consumer is just willing to exchange for *RN* records. When the consumer has more records and less cheese (point *m* as compared with *M*), the slope of the indifference curve decreases, meaning that the consumer is only willing to give up *rm* pounds of cheese for *rn* records.

own preferences—to trade one good for the other. If RM/RN equals two, the consumer is willing to give up (no more than) two pounds of cheese for one additional record.

The *slope of an indifference curve,* referred to as the **marginal rate of substitution** between the commodities involved, represents the maximum amount of one commodity the consumer is willing to give up in exchange for one more unit of another commodity.

The slope of budget line *BB* in Figure 18–6 is also a rate of exchange between cheese and records. But it no longer reflects the consumer's subjective willingness to trade. Rather, the slope represents the rate of exchange *the market* offers to the consumer when he gives up money in exchange for cheese and records. Recall that the budget line represents all commodity combinations a consumer can get by spending a fixed amount of money. The budget line is thus a curve of constant expenditure. At current prices, if the consumer reduces his purchase of cheese by amount *DE* in Figure 18–6, he will save just enough money to buy an additional amount, *EF*, of records, since at points *D* and *F* he is spending the same total number of dollars.

The *slope of the budget line* is the amount of one commodity the market requires an individual to give up in order to obtain one additional unit of another commodity without any change in the amount of money spent.

The slopes of the two types of curves, then, are perfectly analogous in their meaning. The slope of the indifference curve tells us the terms on which the *consumer* is willing to trade one commodity for another, while the slope of the budget line reports the *market* terms on which the consumer can trade one good for another.

It is useful to carry our interpretation of the slope of the budget line one step further. Common sense tells us that the market's rate of exchange between cheese and records would be related to their prices, p_c and p_r, and it is easy to show that this is so. Specifically, the slope of the budget line is equal to the ratio of the prices of the two commodities. The reason is straightforward. If the consumer gives up one record, he has p_r more dollars to spend on cheese. Since the price of cheese is p_c per pound, these additional funds permit him to buy p_r/p_c more pounds of cheese. Thus the slope of the budget line is p_r/p_c.

Before returning to our main subject, the study of consumer choice, we pause briefly and use our interpretation of the slope of the indifference curve to discuss the third of the properties of the indifference curve—its characteristic curvature—which we left unexplained earlier. With indifference curves being the shape shown, the slope decreases as we move from left to right. We can see in Figure 18–6 that at point *m*, toward the right of the diagram, the consumer is willing to give up far less cheese for one more record (quantity *rm*) than he is willing to trade at point *M*, toward the left. This is because at *M* he initially has a large quantity of cheese and few records, while at *m* his initial stock of cheese is low and he has many records. In general terms, the curvature premise on which indifference curves are usually drawn asserts that consumers are relatively eager to trade away a commodity of which they have a large amount but are more reluctant to trade goods of which they hold small quantities. This psychological premise, which reflects the "law" of diminishing marginal utility, is what is implied in the curvature of the indifference curve.

The Consumer's Choice

We can now use our indifference curve apparatus to analyze how the consumer chooses among the combinations he can afford to buy; that is, the combinations of records and cheese shown by the budget line. Figure 18–7 brings together in the same diagram the budget line from Figure 18–2 and the indifference curves from Figure 18–5.

Since according to the first of the properties of indifference curves the consumer prefers higher to lower curves, he will go to the point on the budget line that lies on the highest indifference curve attainable. This will be point *T* on indifference curve I_b. He can afford no other point that he likes as well. For example, neither point *K* below the budget line nor point *W* on the budget line gets him on as high an indifference curve, and any point on an indifference curve above I_b, such as point *U*, is out of the question because it lies beyond his financial means. We end up with a simple rule of consumer choice:

Consumers will select the most desired combination of goods obtainable for their money. The choice will be that point on the budget line at which the budget line is tangent to an indifference curve.

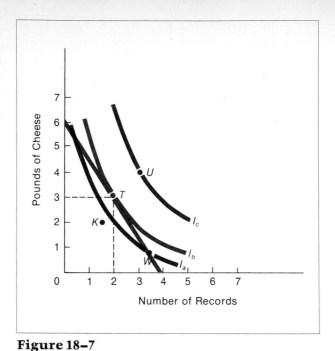

Figure 18–7
OPTIMAL CONSUMER CHOICE
Point *T* is the combination of records and cheese that gives the consumer the greatest benefit for his money. I_b is the highest indifference curve that can be reached from the budget line. *T* is the point of tangency between the budget line and I_b.

We can see why no point except the point of tangency, *T* (two records and three pounds of cheese), will give the consumer the largest utility that his money can buy. Suppose the consumer were instead to consider buying three records and one pound of cheese. This would put him at point *W* on the budget line and on indifference curve I_a. But then, by buying fewer records and more cheese (a move to the left on the budget line), he could get to an indifference curve that was higher and hence more desirable. It clearly does not pay to end up at *W*. Only at the point of tangency, *T*, is there no room for improvement.

At a point of tangency where the consumer's benefits from purchasing cheese and records are maximized, the slope of the budget line equals the slope of the indifference curve. This is true by the definition of a point of tangency. We have just seen that the slope of the indifference curve is the marginal rate of substitution between cheese and records, and that the slope of the budget line is the ratio of the prices of records and cheese. We can therefore restate the requirement for the optimal division of the consumer's money between the two commodities in slightly more technical language:

Consumers will get the most benefit from their money by choosing a combination of commodities whose marginal rate of substitution is equal to the ratio of their prices.

It is worth reviewing the logic behind this conclusion. Why is it not advisable for the consumer to stop at a point like *W*, where the marginal rate of substitution (slope of the indifference curve) is less than the price ratio (slope of the budget line)? Because by moving upward and to the left along his budget line, he can take advantage of market opportunities to obtain a commodity bundle that he likes better. And this will always be the case if the rate at which the consumer is *personally* willing to exchange cheese for records (his marginal rate of substitution) differs from the rate of exchange offered *on the market* (the slope of the budget line).

Consequences of Income Changes: Inferior Goods

Next, consider what happens to the consumer's purchases when there is a rise in income. We know that a rise in income produces a parallel outward shift in the budget line, such as the shift from *BB* to *CC* in Figure 18–8. This moves the consumer's equilibrium

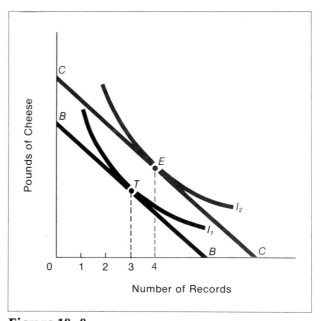

Figure 18–8
EFFECTS OF A RISE IN INCOME
WHEN NEITHER GOOD IS INFERIOR
The rise in income causes a parallel shift in the budget line from *BB* to *CC*. The quantity of records demanded rises from three to four, and the quantity demanded of cheese also increases.

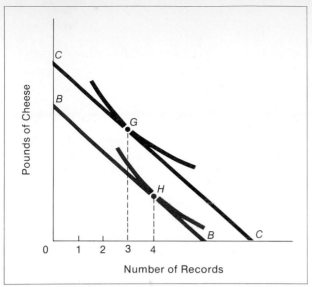

Figure 18–9
EFFECTS OF A RISE IN INCOME
WHEN RECORDS ARE AN INFERIOR GOOD
The upward shift in the budget line from *BB* to *CC* causes the quantity of records demanded to fall from four (point *H*) to three (point *G*).

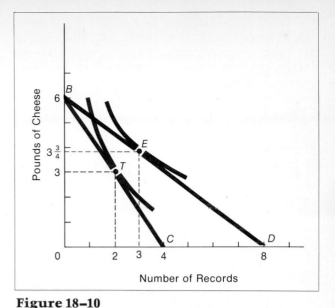

Figure 18–10
CONSEQUENCES OF PRICE CHANGES
A fall in record price swings the budget line outward from line *BC* to *BD*. The consumer's equilibrium point (the point of tangency between the budget line and an indifference curve) moves from *T* to *E*. The desired purchase of records increases from two to three, and the desired purchase of cheese increases from three pounds to three and three-fourths pounds.

from tangency point *T* to tangency point *E* on a higher indifference curve.

A rise in income may or may not increase the demand for a commodity. In the case shown in Figure 18–8, the rise in income does lead the consumer to buy more cheese *and* more records. But his indifference curves need not always be positioned in a way that yields this sort of result. In Figure 18–9 we see that as the consumer's budget line rises from *BB* to *CC*, the tangency point moves leftward from *H* to *G*, so that when his income rises he actually buys *fewer* records. In this case we infer that records are an *inferior* good.

Consequences of Price Changes: Deriving the Demand Curve

Finally, we come to the main question underlying demand curves: How does our consumer's choice change if the price of one good changes? We learned earlier that a reduction in the price of a record causes the budget line to swing outward along the horizontal axis while leaving its vertical intercept unchanged. In Figure 18–10, we depict the effect a decline in the price of records has on the quantity of records demanded. As the price of records falls, the budget line

swings from *BC* to *BD*. The tangency points, *T* and *E* also move in a corresponding direction, causing the quantity demanded to rise from two to three. The price of records has fallen, and the quantity demanded has risen: the demand curve for records is negatively sloped.

The demand curve for records can be constructed directly from Figure 18–10. Point *T* tells us that two records will be bought when the price of a record is $3. Point *E* tells us that when the price of a record falls to $1.50, quantity demanded rises to three records.[4] These two pieces of information are shown in Figure 18–11 as points *t* and *e* on the demand curve for records. By examining the effects of other possible prices for records (other budget lines emanating from point *B* in Figure 18–10), we can find all the other points on the demand curve in exactly the same way.

The indifference curve diagram also brings out an important point that the demand curve does not show. A change in the *price of records* also has consequences for the *quantity of cheese demanded*

[4]How do we know that the price of records corresponding to budget line *BD* is $1.50? Since the $12 total budget will purchase at most eight records (point *D*), the price per record must be $12 ÷ 8 = $1.50.

because it affects the amount of money left over for cheese purchases. In the example illustrated in Figure 18–10, the decrease in the price of records increases the demand for cheese from three to three and three-fourths pounds.

Figure 18–11

DERIVING THE DEMAND CURVE FOR RECORDS
The demand curve is derived from the indifference curve diagram by varying the price of the commodity in question. Specifically, when the price is $3 per record, we know from Figure 18–10 that the optimal purchase is two records (point *T*). This information is recorded here as point *t*. Similarly, the optimal purchase is three records when the price of records is $1.50 (point *E* in Figure 18–10). This is shown here as point *e*.

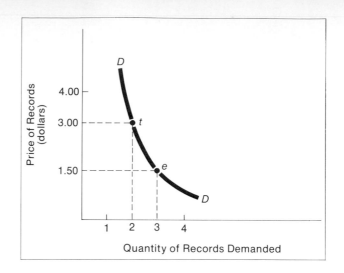

Summary

1. Indifference-curve analysis permits us to study the interrelationships of the demands for two (or more) commodities.
2. The basic tools of indifference-curve analysis are the consumer's budget line and indifference curves.
3. A budget line shows all combinations of two commodities that the consumer can afford, given the prices of the commodities and the amount of money the consumer has available to spend.
4. The budget line is a straight line whose slope equals the ratio of the prices of the commodities. A change in price changes the slope of the budget line. A change in the consumer's income causes a parallel shift in the budget line.
5. Two points on an indifference curve represent two combinations of commodities such that the consumer does not prefer one of the combinations over the other.

6. Indifference curves normally have negative slopes and are "bowed in" toward the origin. The slope of an indifference curve indicates how much of one commodity the consumer is willing to give up in order to get an additional unit of the other commodity.
7. The consumer will choose the point on his budget line that gets him to the highest attainable indifference curve. Normally this will occur at the point of tangency between the two curves. This choice indicates the combination of commodities that gives him the greatest benefits for the amount of money he has available to spend.
8. The consumer's demand curve can be derived from his indifference curve.

Concepts for Review

Budget line
Indifference curves

Marginal rate of substitution
Slope of an indifference curve

Slope of a budget line

Questions for Discussion

1. John Q. Public spends all his income on gasoline and hot dogs. Draw his budget line when:
   a. his income is $60 and the cost of one gallon of gasoline and one hot dog is $1.20 each.
   b. his income is $90 and the two prices are as in part a.
   c. his income is $60 and hot dogs cost $1.20 each and gasoline costs $2 per gallon.
2. Draw some hypothetical indifference curves for John Q. Public on a diagram identical to the one you constructed for part a. of Question 1.

   a. Approximately how much gasoline and records will Public buy?
   b. How will these choices change if his income increases to $90, as in part b. of Question 1? Is either good an inferior good?
   c. How will these choices change if, instead, gasoline prices rise to $2 per gallon, as in part c. of Question 1?
3. Explain what information the *slope* of an indifference curve conveys about a consumer's preferences. Use this to explain the typical U-shaped curvature of indifference curves.

The Nature of Consumer Demand

19

Economists who work for business firms are frequently assigned the task of studying consumer demand for the products their companies produce. Business managers count the results of such studies among the most important of all the information they get—but they also know it is among the most difficult to obtain. Government agencies, too, are very interested in demand information, which they use for estimating such widely diverse variables as general business conditions and receipts from sales taxes.

The quantity demanded in any market depends on many things: the incomes of consumers, the price of the good, the prices of other goods, the volume and effectiveness of advertising, and so on. Demand analysis deals with all these influences, but it has traditionally focused on the price of the good in question. The reason is that price plays the crucial role of bringing quantity supplied into balance with quantity demanded. This role of price was studied in Chapter 4, and we will return to it time and again throughout the book.

We begin this chapter by showing how the market demand curve for a product is derived from the individual demand curves of each consumer. Next we turn to the "law" of demand, which tells us that quantity demanded decreases as price increases. Third, the important concept of elasticity is introduced as a way to measure the responsiveness of quantity demanded to price. Fourth, we turn to the variables other than price that influence quantity demanded. And, finally, we explain the importance of the time period to which a demand curve applies, and how this can create problems in obtaining demand information from statistical data.

An Application:
Did the Advertising Program Work?

One of the nation's largest producers of packaged foods conducted a statistical study to determine the effectiveness of its advertising expenditures, which amounted to nearly $100 million a year. A company statistician collected year-by-year figures on company sales and advertising outlays, and discovered, to his delight, that they showed a remarkably close relationship to one another. The trouble was that the relationship seemed just too perfect. In economics, data about demand and any one of the elements that influence it almost never make such a neat pattern. Human tastes and other pertinent influences are just too variable to permit such regularity.

Suspicious company executives asked an economist not connected with the firm to examine the analysis. The economist was able to explain the too-neat relationship between observed sales and advertising outlays quite easily. More important, he was able to show that the statistical relationship was *not* what the company's management was looking for and that it was in fact potentially misleading. No deep, dark methods of economic analysis were needed to reach this conclusion. By the end of this chapter, you will understand how the economist reached his conclusions and be able to avoid similar pitfalls yourself.

Individual Demand Curves and Market Demand Curves

In the last chapter we studied how *individual demand curves* are derived from the logic of consumer choice. Each consumer seeks to attain the highest total utility permitted by his limited budget, and in the process will typically react to a higher price by reducing his quantity demanded. But to understand how the market system works we must derive the relationship between price and quantity demanded *in the market as a whole*—the **market demand curve.**

A **market demand curve** shows how the total quantity demanded of some product during a specified period of time changes as the price of that product changes, holding other things constant.

If each individual pays no attention to other people's purchase decisions when making his own, it is straightforward to derive the market demand curve from the customers' individual demand curves. We simply *add* the negatively sloping individual demand curves *horizontally* as shown in Figure 19–1. There we see the individual demand curves *DD* and *SS* for two people, Daniel and Sabrina, and the total (market) demand curve *MM*. Specifically, this market demand curve is constructed as follows: *Step 1:* Pick any relevant price, say $10. *Step 2:* At that price, determine Daniel's quantity demanded (9 units) from Daniel's demand curve in part (a) and Sabrina's quantity demanded (6 units) from Sabrina's demand curve in part (b). Note that these quantities are indicated by line segment *AA* for Daniel and line segment *BB* for Sabrina. *Step 3:* Add

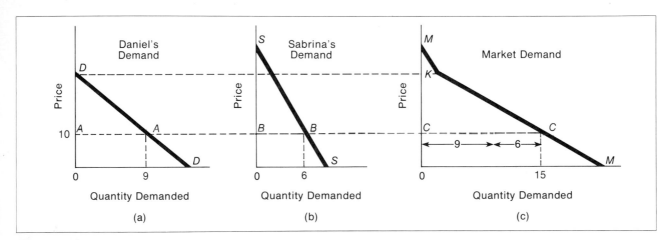

Figure 19–1
THE RELATIONSHIP BETWEEN TOTAL MARKET DEMAND
AND THE DEMANDS OF INDIVIDUAL CONSUMERS WITHIN THAT MARKET
If Daniel and Sabrina are the customers for a product, and at a price of $10 Daniel demands 9 units [line *AA* in part (a)] and Sabrina demands 6 units [line *BB* in part (b)], then total quantity demanded by the market at that price is 9 + 6 = 15 [line *CC* in part (c)]. In other words, we obtain the market demand curve by adding horizontally all points on each consumer's demand curve at each given price. Thus, at a $10 price we have length *CC* on the market demand curve, which is equal to *AA* + *BB* on the individual demand curves. (The sharp angle at point *K* on the market curve occurs because it corresponds to the price at which Daniel first enters the market. At any higher price, only Sabrina is willing to buy anything.)

Sabrina's and Daniel's quantities demanded at the $10 price (segment AA + segment $BB = 9 + 6 = 15$) to yield the total quantity demanded by the market at that price [line segment CC, with total quantity demanded equal to 15 units, in part (c)]. Now repeat the process for all alternative prices to obtain other points on the market demand curve until the shape of the entire curve MM is indicated. That is all there is to the adding-up process.

The "Law" of Demand

A formal definition of the demand curve for an entire market was given in Chapter 4 and again on the opposite page. We shall pay much attention in this chapter to the "other things" referred to in this definition. But for now, let us focus on price, and note that quantity demanded normally moves in the opposite direction from price. Economists call this relationship the **"law" of demand.** Notice that we have put the word *law* in quotation marks. By now you will have observed that economic laws are not always obeyed, and we shall see in a moment that the "law" of demand is not without its exceptions. But first let us see why the "law" usually holds.

In Chapter 18 we learned that individual demand curves are usually downward sloping because of the "law" of diminishing marginal utility. If individual demand curves slope downward, then we see from the preceding discussion of the adding-up process that the market demand curve must also slope downward. This is just common sense: If every consumer in the market buys fewer bananas when the price of bananas rises, then the total quantity demanded in the market must surely fall.

But market demand curves may slope downward even when individual demand curves do not, because not all consumers are alike. For example, if a bookstore reduces the price of a popular novel, it may draw many new customers, but few customers will be induced to buy two copies. Similarly, people differ in their fondness for bananas. True devotees may maintain their purchases of bananas even at exorbitant prices, while others will not eat a banana even if it is offered free of charge. As the price of bananas rises, the less enthusiastic banana eaters drop out of the market entirely, leaving the expensive fruit to the more devoted consumers. Thus the quantity demanded declines as price rises simply because higher prices induce more people to kick the banana habit. Indeed, for many commodities, it is the appearance of new customers in the *market* when prices are lower, rather than the negative slope of *individual* demand curves, that accounts for the law of demand.

We conclude, therefore, that the law of demand stands on fairly solid ground. If individual demand curves are downward sloping, then the market demand curve surely will be, too. And the market demand curve may slope downward even when individual demand curves do not. Nevertheless, exceptions to the law of demand have been noted. One common exception occurs when quality is judged on the basis of price—the more expensive the better. For example, some people buy vegetables labeled "organic" even though they are more expensive than other vegetables. Even if the two kinds of vegetables are identical to a biologist, some consumers may assume that the "organic" vegetables are superior simply because they are more expensive. Should organic vegetables then become cheaper, consumers might assume that they are no longer superior, and actually reduce their purchases.

Another possible cause of an upward-sloping demand curve is snob appeal. If part of the reason for purchasing a Rolls Royce is to advertise one's wealth, a decrease in the car's price may actually reduce sales, even if the quality of the car

The **"law" of demand** states that a lower price generally increases the amount of a commodity that people in a market are willing to buy. So, for most goods, demand curves have a negative slope.

is unchanged. Other types of exceptions have also been noted by economists; but, for most commodities, it seems quite reasonable to assume that demand curves have a negative slope, an assumption that is supported by the data.

Responsiveness to Price Changes: Elasticity of Demand

For many purposes, it is useful to have a numerical measure of just how quickly quantity demanded rises as price falls or falls as price rises. To fill this need, economists have invented the concept of the **price elasticity of demand,** or simply, the **elasticity of demand.**

Calculating Elasticity

As usual, the concept is best explained by an example. Suppose the price of milk in a certain city rises from 50 cents to 75 cents per quart and, as a result, the quantity of milk demanded falls from 100,000 to 80,000 quarts per week. The decline in quantity demanded is 20 percent (from 100,000 to 80,000) and the rise in price is 50 percent (from 50 cents to 75 cents). Hence, according to the formula, the elasticity of demand is:

$$\text{Elasticity of demand} = \frac{20\%}{50\%} = 0.4 \; .$$

Notice that in this calculation we neglect the fact that the change in quantity demanded is *negative* (a decrease) while the change in price is *positive* (an increase). This is to avoid confusion. Because demand curves normally have negative slopes, the changes in price and quantity demanded generally go in opposite directions so that, strictly speaking, the calculated elasticity number should be negative. To be able to use positive numbers to describe elasticity, economists typically drop the negative sign.[1] Notice also that there is an ambiguity in the elasticity calculation. Suppose we made the preceding calculation of the elasticity of demand for milk in the opposite direction. We would conclude that when price decreases by $33\frac{1}{3}$ percent (from 75 cents to 50 cents), quantity demanded increases by 25 percent (from 80,000 to 100,000). Hence, according to the formula:

$$\text{Elasticity} = \frac{\%\text{ change in quantity demanded}}{\%\text{ change in price}} = \frac{25\%}{33.33\%} = 0.75 \; .$$

This is a different answer from the one we obtained before. To avoid this ambiguity, many economists prefer to calculate percentage changes by using the *average* quantity and the *average* price. In this example, the average quantity is 90,000, so the percentage change in quantity is 20,000/90,000 = 22.22 percent. Similarly, the average price is 62.5 cents, so the percentage change in price is 25 cents/62.5 cents = 40 percent. By this definition, then, elasticity is:

$$\text{Elasticity} = \frac{\%\text{ change in quantity demanded}}{\%\text{ change in price}} = \frac{22.22\%}{40\%} = 0.56 \; .$$

The **(price) elasticity of demand** is the ratio of the percentage change in quantity demanded to the percentage change in price that brings about the change in quantity demanded; that is,

Price elasticity of demand

$$= \frac{\%\text{ change}}{\text{in quantity demanded}}{\%\text{ change in price}} \; .$$

---

[1]If we did not do this, we would be put in the awkward (and mathematically incorrect) position of saying that an elasticity of −2 is *bigger* than an elasticity of −1.

Your instructor will tell you which of the calculation procedures he or she prefers.[2]

Elasticity and Units of Measurement

These calculation procedures are far less important than understanding the basic idea behind the elasticity concept. Why is it that we use *percentage* changes to measure elasticity? Why do we not measure elasticity as, for example,

$$\frac{\text{Change in quantity demanded}}{\text{Change in price}} = \frac{100{,}000 - 80{,}000 \text{ quarts}}{75 - 50 \text{ cents}} = \frac{20{,}000}{25} = 800 \text{ ?}$$

The answer is that in economics we have no standardized units of measurement. We could, for example, just as well measure milk in gallons as in quarts. But, if we did this, our last calculated figure would obviously change. With quantity demanded falling from 25,000 to 20,000 gallons, and price rising from $2 per gallon to $3, our number would become:

$$\frac{\text{Change in quantity demanded}}{\text{Change in price}} = \frac{25{,}000 - 20{,}000 \text{ gallons}}{\$3 - \$2} = \frac{5000}{1} = 5000 \text{ .}$$

Here the facts have not changed; yet our responsiveness figure would have changed just because we switched from quarts to gallons in measuring milk. This is a very undesirable state of affairs, particularly if we want to use such a number to compare the price responsiveness of different products.

If such comparisons are to be made, we must have a measure of responsiveness that does not depend on units of measurement. Percentage changes are the natural choice. If the quantity of milk demanded declines by 5 percent when the price of milk rises by 10 percent, and if the quantity of beef demanded declines by 8 percent in response to a 10-percent rise in the price of beef, then we can say that the demand for beef is *more responsive* to price changes than is the demand for milk. Note that price changes are also measured in percentage terms because, even though the dollar is a standardized unit for all commodities, the economic significance of a dollar is not. A $1 change in the price of a ball-point pen presumably has a much greater significance for the consumer's purchase decision than does a $1 change in the price of a new car. Once again, the percentage change seems to capture the variation in which we are interested.

Elasticity and the Shape of Demand Curves

Figure 19–2 indicates how elasticity of demand is related to the shape of the demand curve. We begin with two extreme but important cases. Part (a) depicts a demand curve that is simply a vertical line. This curve is called *perfectly inelastic* throughout because its elasticity is zero. That is, since quantity demanded remains at 90 units no matter what the price, the percentage change in quantity is always zero, and hence the elasticity is zero. Such a demand curve is quite unusual. It may perhaps be expected when the price range being considered already involves very low prices from the point of view of the consumer. (Will anyone use more salt if its price is lowered?) It may also occur when the item (such as medicine) is considered absolutely essential by the consumer, although

---

[2]When we deal with small changes, all three calculation methods yield approximately the same answer. You can verify this for yourself by supposing that a rise in price to 51 cents per quart would reduce quantity demanded to 99,000 quarts.

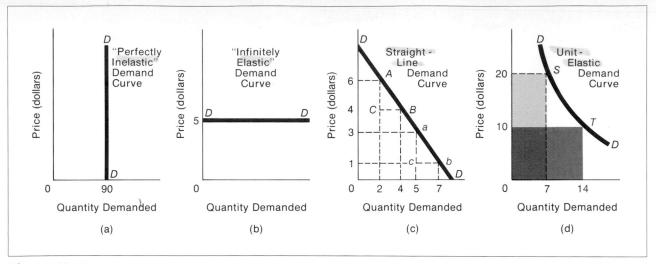

Figure 19–2

DEMAND CURVES WITH DIFFERENT ELASTICITIES

The vertical demand curve in part (a) is *perfectly inelastic* (elasticity = 0)—quantity demanded remains the same regardless of price. The horizontal demand curve in part (b) is *perfectly elastic*—at any price above $5, quantity demanded falls to zero. Part (c) shows a *straight-line demand curve*. Its *slope* is constant, but its *elasticity* is not. Part (d) depicts a demand curve with a constant elasticity of 1.0 throughout (a *unit-elastic* demand curve). A change in price pushes quantity demanded in the opposite direction, but does not affect total expenditure. When price equals $20, total expenditure is price times quantity, or $20 × 7 = $140; and when price equals $10, expenditure equals $10 × 14 = $140.

even here the demand curve will remain vertical only so long as price does not exceed what the consumer can afford.

Part (b) of Figure 19–2 shows the opposite extreme: a horizontal demand curve. It is said to be *perfectly elastic* (or "infinitely elastic"). If there is the slightest rise in price, quantity demanded will drop to zero; that is, the percentage change in quantity demanded would be infinitely large. This may be expected to occur where a rival product that is just as good in the consumer's view is available at the going price ($5 in our diagram). In cases where no one will pay more than the going price, the seller will lose all his customers if he raises his price even one penny.

Part (c) depicts a case between these two extremes; a *straight-line* demand curve, which is neither vertical nor horizontal. Though the *slope* of a straight-line demand curve is constant throughout its length, its *elasticity* is not. The numbers on the axes illustrate this point. For example, when we move from point A to point B, the price decrease is the same as when we move from point a to point b ($2 in each case). But in the former case the *percentage* price decrease is smaller since we start from a higher initial price. The price is $6 at A but only $3 at a, so the percentage price decline is 33⅓ percent between A and B, but 66⅔ percent between a and b. Similarly, the percentage quantity increase from A to B is much greater than that from a to b. Thus, between A and B the elasticity of the demand curve in Figure 19–2(c) is different from that between a and b (it is, in fact, higher).[3]

If a straight-line demand curve has a variable elasticity, what is the appearance of a demand curve with the same elasticity throughout its length? For reasons given in the next section, it looks like the curve in Figure 19–2(d), which is a curve with elasticity equal to one throughout (a *unit-elastic* demand curve).

[3]EXERCISE: Use the numbers in Figure 19–2(c) to calculate the slope of the demand curve between points A and B and between points a and b. Show that they are equal. Then calculate the elasticities between points A and B and between points a and b, and show that they are not equal.

Elasticity and Total Expenditure

It is conventional to speak of a curve whose elasticity is greater than one as an *elastic* demand curve, and of one whose elasticity is less than one as an *inelastic* curve. When elasticity is exactly one, we say the curve is *unit elastic*. This terminology is convenient for discussing the last important property of the elasticity measure.

The elasticity of demand conveys useful information about the effect of a price change on the buyer's *total expenditure*. In particular, it can be shown that:

If demand is elastic, a rise in price will decrease total expenditure. If demand is unit elastic, a change in price will leave total expenditure unaffected. If demand is inelastic, a rise in price will raise total expenditure.

These relationships hold because total expenditure equals price times quantity demanded, $P \times Q$, and a rise in price has two opposing effects on $P \times Q$. It increases P and, if the demand curve is negatively sloped, it decreases Q. The net outcome depends on the elasticity. If price goes up 10 percent and quantity demanded declines 10 percent (a case of *unit elasticity*), the two will cancel out: $P \times Q$ will remain constant. On the other hand, if price goes up 10 percent and quantity demanded declines 15 percent (a case of *elastic* demand), $P \times Q$ will decrease. Finally, if a 10-percent price rise leads to a 5-percent decline in quantity demanded (an inelastic case), $P \times Q$ will rise.

The connection between elasticity and total expenditure is easily seen in a graph. For example, Figure 19–3 shows an elastic portion of a demand curve, *DD*. At a price of $6 per unit, the quantity sold is four units, so total expenditure is $4 \times \$6 = \$24$. This is represented by the gray shaded rectangle because the formula for the area of a rectangle is area = height × base, which in this case is equal to $4 \times \$6 = \$24$. When price falls to $5 per unit, 12 units are bought in this example. Consequently, the new expenditure ($\$60 = \$5 \times 12$), now measured by the blue rectangle, will be larger than the old. In contrast Figure 19–2(d), the unit-elastic demand curve, shows a case in which expenditure remains constant even though selling price changes. Total spending is $140 whether the price is $20 and seven units are sold (point *S*) or the price is $10 and 14 units are sold (point *T*).

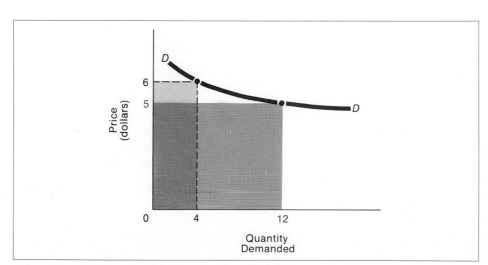

Figure 19–3
AN ELASTIC DEMAND CURVE
When price falls, quantity demanded rises by a greater percentage, increasing the total expenditure. Thus, when price falls from $6 to $5, quantity demanded rises from 4 to 12, and total expenditure rises from $6 × 4 = $24 to $5 × 12 = $60.

The preceding result warns us that a rise in price may not always increase the total amount consumers will spend on a company's product. A price increase will raise total spending only if demand is *inelastic*. Similarly, a price cut will increase the amount of money a firm gets from its customers only if demand is *elastic*.

Quantity Demanded Depends on Many Variables

It is clear from what we have just said that a firm will be very interested in the elasticity of its demand curve. But this is not where its interest in demand ends, for, as we have noted, quantity demanded depends on other things besides price. While it is impossible to list all the determinants of quantity demanded, it is worth mentioning some of the more important ones.

Consumer Tastes

In Chapter 18 we learned how individual demand curves, and hence the market demand curve, depend on consumer preferences (tastes). While changes in tastes are difficult to predict and even to explain, it is clear that if fashions shift from French to Chinese restaurants, or from yo-yos to frisbees, this can have a substantial effect on the quantities demanded of these products.

Advertising Expenditures

Cognizant of this, many large firms try to influence consumer tastes by advertising. Although there is much disagreement over the degree to which this is successful, it is clear that if a firm is to decide rationally on the size of its advertising budget, it must have an estimate of the effect of advertising on quantity demanded. As we shall see at the end of the chapter, such information may be difficult to obtain.

Consumer Incomes

As we pointed out in the last chapter, an increase in consumer incomes raises the quantity demanded of most goods. Thus the state of the overall economy is highly relevant to the position of the demand curve of most products.

Prices of Related Goods: Substitutes and Complements

There are many products whose quantities demanded depend on the quantities and prices of other products. Certain goods make one another more desirable. For example, cream and sugar can increase the desirability of coffee, and vice versa. The same is true of mustard or ketchup and hamburgers. In some extreme cases, neither of two products ordinarily has any use without the other—an automobile and tires, a pair of shoes and shoelaces, and so on. Such goods, each of which makes the other more valuable, are called **complements.**

The demand curves of complements are interrelated, meaning that a rise in the price of coffee is likely to affect the quantity of sugar demanded. Why? When coffee prices rise, less coffee will be drunk and therefore less sugar will be demanded. The opposite will be true of a fall in coffee prices. A similar relationship holds for other complementary goods.

At the other extreme, there are goods that make one another *less* valuable. These are called **substitutes.** Ownership of a motorcycle, for example, may decrease the desire for a bicycle. If your pantry is stocked with cans of tuna fish, you are less likely to rush out and buy cans of salmon. As you might expect, demand curves for substitutes are also interrelated, but in the opposite direction.

Two goods are called **complements** if an increase in the price of one reduces the quantity demanded of the other, all other things remaining constant.

Two goods are called **substitutes** if an increase in the price of one raises the quantity demanded of the other, all other things remaining constant.

When the price of a new house rises, people demand fewer new houses, so the quantity of old houses demanded goes up. When the price of coffee goes up, people drink less coffee; instead, they consume more tea or tomato juice.

A measure that is useful for determining whether two products are substitutes or complements is their **cross elasticity of demand.** This measure is defined much like the ordinary price elasticity of demand, only instead of measuring the responsiveness of the quantity demanded of, say, coffee to a change in the price of coffee, cross elasticity of demand measures the responsiveness of the quantity demanded of coffee to a change in the price of, say, sugar. For example, if a 20-percent rise in the price of sugar reduces the quantity of coffee demanded by 5 percent (a change of *minus* 5 percent in quantity demanded), then the cross elasticity of demand will be

$$\frac{\text{\% change in quantity of coffee demanded}}{\text{\% change in sugar price}} = \frac{-5\%}{20\%} = -.25 \ .$$

The **cross elasticity of demand** for product X to a change in the price of another product, Y, is the ratio of the percentage change in quantity demanded of product X to the percentage change in the price of product Y that brings about the change in quantity demanded.

Using the cross elasticity of demand measure, we come to the following rule about complements and substitutes:

If two goods are substitutes, their cross elasticity of demand will normally be positive. If two goods are complements, their cross elasticities will normally be negative.[4]

This result is really a matter of common sense. If the price of a good goes up and there is a substitute available, people will tend to switch to the substitute. If the price of Coke goes up (and the price of Pepsi does not), at least some people will switch to Pepsi. Thus, a *rise* in the price of Coke causes a *rise* in the quantity of Pepsi demanded. Both percentage changes are positive numbers and so their ratio, the cross elasticity of demand, is also positive.

On the other hand, if two goods are complements, a rise in the price of one will discourage its own use and will also discourage use of the complementary good. Automobiles and car radios are obviously complements. A large increase in the price of cars will depress the sale of cars, and this will in turn reduce the sale of car radios. Thus, a positive percentage change in the price of cars leads to a negative percentage change in the quantity of car radios demanded. The ratio of these numbers, the cross elasticity of demand for cars and radios, is therefore negative.

In addition to these rather general determinants of the quantity demanded of almost every good, there are always other variables that are pertinent to specific goods. For example, rainfall affects the quantity of umbrellas demanded; temperature affects the demand curves for air conditioners and for fuel; the amount of soot in the atmosphere affects the quantity of soap demanded; and so forth. You can easily think of more examples.

Shifts in Demand Curves

Demand is obviously a complex phenomenon. We have studied in detail the dependence of quantity demanded on price, and we have just seen that quantity demanded depends on other variables such as incomes, advertising, and tastes. Because of these "other variables," demand curves often do not sit still; they shift

---

[4]Because cross elasticities can be positive or negative, it is *not* customary to drop minus signs as we do when calculating ordinary price elasticity of demand.

Cross Elasticity in Practice: The Supreme Court's Decision in the DuPont Antitrust Case

In 1956 the Supreme Court decided a historic antitrust case. The Department of Justice had sued DuPont, charging that it "monopolized trade in cellophane." DuPont sold about 75 percent of the cellophane used in the United States, so it was clear that it produced most of the product. But the Supreme Court also considered whether substitute products provided enough competition to prevent DuPont from acting like a monopolist. It used cross elasticity of demand as an important piece of evidence on the matter and concluded that DuPont was not guilty—that it did not "monopolize." Here is an excerpt from the Court's decision:

Sec. 2-B DuPont & Co. (Cellophane) 247

An element for consideration as to cross elasticity of demand between products is the responsiveness of the sales of one product to price changes of the other. If a slight decrease in the price of cellophane causes a considerable number of customers of other flexible wrappings to switch to cellophane, it would be an indication that a high cross elasticity of demand exists between them; that the products compete in the same market. The court below held that the "[g]reat sensitivity of customers in the flexible packaging markets to price or quality changes" prevented DuPont from possessing monopoly control over price. The record sustains these findings. . . .

SOURCE: *U.S. Reports*, vol. 351 (Washington, D.C., 1956), page 400.

around. And, as we learned in Chapter 4, shifts in demand curves have predictable consequences for both quantity and price. But in public or business discussions one often hears vague references to a "change in demand." By itself, this expression does not really mean anything. Remember from our discussion in Chapter 4 that it is vital to distinguish between a response to a price change (*which is a movement along the demand curve*) and a change in the relationship between price and quantity demanded (*which is a shift in the demand curve*).

When price falls, quantity demanded generally responds by rising. This is a movement *along* the demand curve. On the other hand, an effective advertising campaign may mean that more goods will be bought at *any given price*. This would be a rightward *shift* in the demand curve. In fact, such a shift can be caused by a change in the value of any of the variables affecting quantity demanded other than price. While the distinction between a shift in a demand curve and a movement along it may at first seem trivial, it is a significant difference in practice and can cause confusion if it is ignored. So let us pause for a moment to consider how changes in some of these other variables shift the demand curve.

As an example, consider the effect of a change in consumer income on the demand curve relating the price of jeans to the quantity of jeans demanded. In Figure 19–4(a), the black curve D_0D_0 is the original demand curve for jeans. Now suppose that parents start sending more money to their needy sons and daughters in college. If the price of jeans were to stay the same, we would expect students to use some of their increased income to buy more jeans. For example, if the price

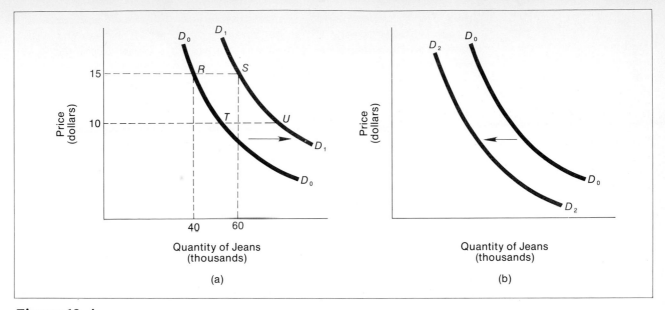

Figure 19–4

SHIFTS IN A DEMAND CURVE

A rise in consumer income or an increase in advertising or a rise in the price of a competing product can all produce a rightward (outward) shift of the demand curve for a product, as depicted by the shift from the black curve D_0D_0 to the blue curve D_1D_1 in part (a). This means that at any fixed price (say $15), the quantity of the product demanded will rise. (In the figure, it rises from 40,000 to 60,000 units.) Similarly, a fall in any of the variables, such as consumer income, will produce a leftward (inward) shift in the demand curve, as in part (b) of the figure.

were to remain at $15, quantity demanded might rise from 40,000 (point R) to 60,000 (point S). Similarly, if price had instead been $10, and had remained at that level, there might be a corresponding change from T to U. In other words, the rise in income would be expected to *shift* the entire demand curve to the right from D_0D_0 to D_1D_1. In exactly the same way, a fall in consumer income can be expected to lead to a leftward shift in the demand curve for jeans, as shown in Figure 19–4(b).

Other variables that affect quantity demanded can be analyzed in the same way. For example, a rise in TV advertising for jeans might lead to a rightward (outward) shift in the demand curve for jeans like the one depicted in Figure 19–4(a). The same thing might occur if there were an increase in the price of a substitute product, such as skirts or corduroy trousers, because that would put jeans at a competitive advantage. Conversely, if a product that is complementary to jeans (perhaps a certain type of belt) becomes more expensive, we would expect the demand curve for jeans to shift to the left, as in Figure 19–4(b). In summary:

A demand curve is expected to shift to the right (outward) if consumer incomes rise, if tastes change in favor of the product, if substitute goods become more expensive, or if complementary goods become cheaper. A demand curve is expected to shift to the left (inward) if any of these factors goes in the opposite direction.

The Time Dimension of the Demand Curve and Decision Making

There is one more feature of a demand curve that does not show up on a graph but that is very important nevertheless. A demand curve indicates, at each possible price, the quantity of the good that is demanded *during a particular period of time.* That is, all the alternative prices considered in a demand curve must refer to *the same* time period. We do not compare a price of $10 for January with a price of $8 for September. This feature imparts a peculiar character to the demand curve and makes statistical estimates more difficult than might be supposed. Why, then, do economists adopt this apparently peculiar approach? The answer is that the time dimension of the demand curve is dictated inescapably by the logic of decision making.

When management undertakes to find the best price for one of its products for, say, the next six months, it must consider the range of alternative prices available to it for that six-month period and the consequences of each possible choice. For example, if management is reasonably certain that the best price lies somewhere between $3.50 and $5.00, it should perhaps consider each of the four possibilities, $3.50, $4.00, $4.50, and $5.00, and estimate how much it can expect to sell at each of these potential prices during the six-month period in question. The result of these estimates may appear in a format similar to that shown in the table below.

Potential price	$3.50	$4.00	$4.50	$5.00
Expected quantity demanded	75,000	73,000	70,000	60,000

This table, which supplies management what it needs to know to make a pricing decision, also contains precisely the information an economist uses to draw a demand curve.

The demand curve describes a set of hypothetical responses to a set of potential prices, only one of which can actually be charged. All of the points on the demand curve refer to alternative possibilities for the *same* period of time—the period for which the decision is to be made.

Thus the demand curve as just described is no abstract notion that is useful primarily in academic discussion. Rather it offers precisely the information that businesses need for rational decision making.

Statistical Analysis of Demand Relationships*

The peculiar time dimension of the demand curve, in conjunction with the fact that many variables other than price can influence quantity demanded, makes it surprisingly hard to discover the shape of the demand curve from statistical data. It can be done, but the task is full of booby traps and can usually be carried out successfully only by using advanced statistical methods. Let us see why these two characteristics of demand curves cause problems.

The most obvious way to go about estimating a demand curve statistically is to collect a set of figures on prices and quantities sold in different periods, like those given in Table 19–1. These points can then be plotted on a diagram with price and quantity on the axes, as shown in Figure 19–5. One can then proceed to draw in a line (the dotted line *TT*) that connects these points reasonably well and that appears to be the demand curve. Unfortunately, line *TT*, which summarizes the historical data, may bear no relationship to the demand curve we are after.

*This section contains more difficult material and, in shorter courses, may be omitted without loss of continuity.

Table 19–1
HISTORICAL DATA ON PRICE AND QUANTITY

	JANUARY	FEBRUARY	MARCH	APRIL	MAY
Price	$7.20	$8.00	$7.70	$8.00	$8.20
Quantity sold	95,000	91,500	95,000	90,000	91,000

You may notice at once that the prices and quantities represented by the historical points in Figure 19–5 refer to different periods of time, and that they all have been *actual*, not *hypothetical*, prices and quantities at some time. The distinction is not insignificant. Over the period covered by the historical data the true demand curve, which is what we really want, may well have shifted because some of the other variables affecting quantity demanded changed.

What actually happened may be as shown in Figure 19–6. Here we see that in January the demand curve was given by *JJ*, but by February the curve had shifted to *FF*, by March to *MM*, and so on. That is, there was a separate and distinct demand curve for each of the relevant months, and none of them need have any resemblance to the plot of historical data, *TT*. In fact, the slope of the historical plot curve, *TT*, can be very different from the slopes of the true underlying demand curves, as is the case in Figure 19–6. This means that the decision maker can be seriously misled if he selects his price on the basis of the historical data. He may, for example, think that demand is quite insensitive to changes in price (as line *TT* in the diagram seems to indicate), and so he may reject the possibility of a price reduction when in fact the true demand curves show that a price reduction will increase quantity demanded substantially. For example, if in February he were to charge a price of $7.80 rather than $8, the historical plot would suggest to him a rise in quantity demanded of only 1000 units. (Compare point *R*, with sales of 91,500 units, and point *S*, with sales of 92,500 units, in Figure 19–5.) However, as can be seen in Figure 19–6, the true demand curve for February (line *FF* in Figure 19–6) promises him an increment in sales of 2500 units (from point *R*, with sales of 91,500, to point *W*, with sales of 94,000) if he reduces February's price from $8 to $7.80. A manager who based his decision on the historical plot, rather than on the true demand curve, might be led into serious error.

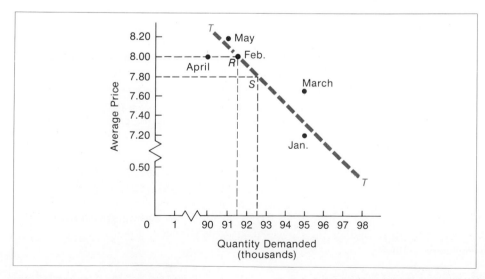

Figure 19–5
PLOT OF HISTORICAL DATA ON PRICE AND QUANTITY
The dots labeled Jan., Feb., and so on, represent actual prices and quantities sold in the months indicated. The blue line *TT* is drawn to approximate the dots as closely as possible.

Figure 19–6

PLOT OF HISTORICAL DATA AND TRUE DEMAND CURVES FOR JANUARY, FEBRUARY, AND MARCH

An analytical demand curve shows how quantity demanded in a particular month is affected by the different prices considered during that month. In the case shown, the true demand curves are much flatter (more elastic) than is the line plotting historical data. This means that a cut in price will induce a far greater increase in quantity demanded than the historical data suggest.

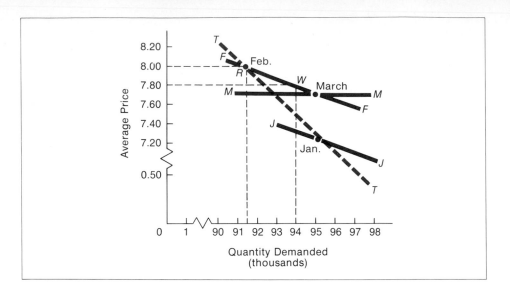

In light of this discussion it is astonishing how often in practice one encounters demand studies that use apparently sophisticated techniques to arrive at no more than a graph of historical data. One must not allow oneself to be misled by the apparent complexity of the procedures employed to fit a curve to historical data. If these merely plot historical quantities against historical prices, the true underlying demand curve is unlikely to be found.

Our Real Illustration: The Advertising–Demand Relationship

A disregard for the principles just presented explains the suspiciously close statistical relationship between sales and advertising expenditure described at the beginning of this chapter—a relationship the company had hoped to use in determining its advertising outlays. The investigator had in fact constructed a graph of historical data on sales and advertising expenditure. The statistician was quite pleased to find that the data exhibited a regular pattern showing a close and stable relationship between advertising expenditure and sales, which suggested to him that every increase in advertising expenditure brought with it a proportionate increase in sales.

However, a little deliberation showed that matters were not what they seemed. The stability of the relationship arose from the fact that, in the past, the company had based its advertising outlays on its sales, automatically allocating a fixed percentage of its sales revenues to advertising. The historical advertising–demand relationship described only the company's budgeting practices. If management had used this curve in planning its advertising campaigns, it might have made some regrettable decisions.

Summary

1. A market demand curve for a product can be obtained by summing horizontally the demand curves of each individual in the market; that is, by adding up at each price the quantities demanded by each consumer.

2. The "law" of demand says that demand curves normally have a negative slope, meaning that a rise in price reduces quantity demanded.

3. To measure the responsiveness of quantity demanded to price we use the elasticity of demand, which is defined as the percentage change in quantity demanded divided by the percentage change in price.
4. If demand is elastic (elasticity greater than one), a rise in price will reduce total expenditure. If demand is unit elastic (elasticity equal to one), a rise in price will not change total expenditure. If demand is inelastic (elasticity less than one), a rise in price will increase total expenditure.
5. Demand is not a fixed number. Rather, it is a relationship showing how quantity demanded is affected by price and other pertinent influences. If one or more of these other variables change, the demand curve will shift.
6. Goods that make each other more desirable (hot dogs and mustard, wrist watches and watch straps) are called *complements*. Goods such that if we have more of one we usually want less of another (steaks and hamburgers, Coke and Pepsi) are called *substitutes*.
7. Cross elasticity of demand is defined as the percentage change in the quantity demanded of one good divided by the percentage change in the price of the other good. Two substitute products normally have a positive cross elasticity of demand. Two complementary products normally have a negative cross elasticity of demand.
8. All points on a demand curve refer to the *same* time period—the time during which the price will be in effect.
9. Simply comparing statistics of sales with prices over a period of time does not give us the demand curve, since demand curves are likely to shift from period to period.

Concepts for Review

Market demand curve
"Law" of demand
(Price) elasticity of demand

Elastic, inelastic, and unit elastic demand curves
Complements

Substitutes
Cross elasticity of demand
Shift in a demand curve

Questions for Discussion

1. What variables besides price and advertising are likely to affect the quantity of a product that is demanded?
2. Describe the probable shifts in the demand curves for
   a. railroad trips when there is an improvement in the trains' on-time performance
   b. automobiles when railroad fares rise
   c. automobiles when gasoline prices rise
   d. electricity when average temperature in the U.S. rises during a particular year. (Note: The demand curve for electricity in Maine and the demand curve for electricity in Florida should respond in different ways. Why?)
3. Which of the following goods may conceivably have positively sloping demand curves? Why?
   a. diamonds
   b. steel
   c. aspirin
   d. glue
4. A rise in price of a certain commodity from $10 to $20 reduces quantity demanded from 60,000 to 40,000 units. Calculate the price elasticity of demand.
5. Which of the following product pairs would you expect to be substitutes and which would you expect to be complements?
   a. trousers and belts
   b. gasoline and big cars
   c. bread and crackers
   d. butter and margarine
6. For each of the previous product pairs, what would you guess about their cross elasticity of demand?
   a. Do you expect it to be positive or negative?
   b. Do you expect it to be a large or small number? Why?
7. (More difficult) Explain why the following statement is true. "A firm with an inelastic demand curve can always increase its profits by raising its price and selling less." (Hint: Refer back to the discussion of elasticity and total expenditure on page 359.)

The Common Sense of Business Decisions: Inputs and Costs

20

The last two chapters dealt with consumer decisions and the nature of demand. We now turn our attention to business decisions and the supply side of the market. In this chapter we analyze the firm's choices among the various inputs such as labor, fuel, and raw materials, and we investigate how to determine the least costly way firms can produce whatever quantity of product they choose to supply. We will see that this cheapest method of production typically will change when the amount of output produced changes. For example, if a firm produces only 1000 automobiles a year, the cheapest way to do so may be to rely on the work of individual craftsmen and to be relatively sparing in the use of large, costly machinery. But for a firm that produces three million cars a year, the reverse is undoubtedly true. We will see in this chapter just how such decisions on input proportions can be reached. In doing so, we will also see how input prices and the available technology determine the cost of producing 1000 or three million or any other number of products a year. This information makes up what we call the firm's **cost curves**—graphical representations of the relationship between a firm's costs and the quantity of product it produces. These cost curves, together with the demand curves discussed in the preceding chapters, will then be used in the next chapter to examine how the firm decides how much to produce and what price to charge for its product.

Illustrative Issue: Do Large Firms Produce at Lower Cost?

Economies of large-scale production are thought to be a pervasive feature of modern industrial society. Automation, assembly lines, and sophisticated machinery are widely believed to reduce production costs dramatically. But if this equipment has enormous capacity and requires a very large investment, small companies will not be able to benefit much from these products of modern technology. In this case, only large-scale production can offer the associated savings in costs. Where such *economies of scale*, as economists call them, exist, production costs per unit will decline as output expands. But this favorable relationship between low costs and large size does not characterize every industry. When a court is called upon to decide whether a giant firm should be broken up into smaller units, officials need to know whether the industry has significant economies of scale. Those who support breaking up large firms argue that industrial giants concentrate economic power, which is something these

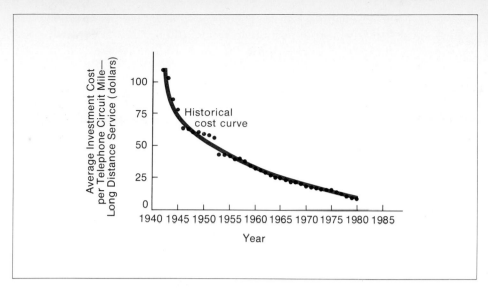

Figure 20–1
HISTORICAL COSTS FOR LONG-DISTANCE TELE-PHONE TRANSMISSION
By 1980, the dollar cost per circuit mile had fallen to about 10 percent of what it was in 1942. Because prices had more than tripled in that period, the decline in *real* cost was even more sensational. In constant dollars, in 1980 the investment cost per circuit mile was about 2 percent of its 1942 level. Yet this diagram of historical costs is not legitimate evidence *one way or the other* about scale economies in tele-communications.
SOURCE: AT&T.

individuals wish to avoid. Those who oppose such breakups point out that if significant economies of scale are present, large firms will be much more efficient producers than will a number of small firms. It is crucial, therefore, to be able to decide whether economies of scale are present. What kind of evidence will speak to this issue?

Sometimes data like those shown in Figure 20–1 are offered to the courts when they consider such cases. These figures, provided by AT&T, indicate that since 1942, as the volume of messages rose, the capital cost of long-distance communication by telephone dropped enormously. Yet economists maintain that while this graph may be valid evidence of efficiency, innovation, and perhaps other virtues of the telecommunications industry, it does *not* constitute legitimate evidence, one way or another, about the presence of economies of scale. Specifically, though this information shows that costs fell as the telephone company's volume of business grew, it does *not* show that a large firm is more efficient than a small one. At the end of this chapter we will see precisely what is wrong with such evidence and what sort of evidence really is required.

Substitutability: The Choice of Input Combination

The central theme of this chapter is how a firm selects the least costly input combination to produce its output. But casual observation of industrial processes deludes many people into thinking that management really has very little discretion in choosing its inputs. Technological considerations alone, it would appear, dictate such choices. A particular type of furniture-cutting machine may require two operators working for an hour on a certain amount of wood to make five desks, no more and no less. But this is an overly narrow view of the matter; whoever first declared that there are many ways to skin a cat saw things more clearly.

The furniture manufacturer may have several alternative production processes capable of making desks. For example, there may be simpler and cheaper machines that can change the same pile of wood into five desks using more than two hours of labor. Or still more workers could eventually do the job with simple hand tools, using no machinery at all. The firm will seek the *least costly* method of production. In advanced industrial societies, where labor is expensive and machinery is cheap, it may pay to use the most automated process; in more primitive societies, where machinery is scarce and labor abundant, making desks by hand may be the most economical solution.

In other words, one input can generally be *substituted* for another. A firm can produce the same number of desks with less labor, *if* it is prepared to sink more money into machinery. But whether it *pays* to make such a substitution depends on the relative costs of labor and machinery. Several general conclusions follow from this discussion.

1. Normally, there are different options available to a firm wanting to produce a particular volume of output. Input proportions are rarely fixed immutably by technological considerations.
2. Given a target level of production, if a firm cuts down on the use of one input (say, labor), it will normally have to increase its use of another input (say, machinery). This is what we mean when we speak of *substituting* one input for another.
3. Which combination of inputs represents the least costly way to produce the desired level of output depends on the relative prices of the various inputs.

A method of analysis that a business firm can use to select the least costly production process is described in this chapter. But you should know at the outset that the analysis is applicable well beyond the confines of business enterprises. Nonprofit organizations, like your own college, are interested in finding the least costly ways to accomplish a variety of tasks (for example, maintaining the grounds and buildings); government agencies are concerned with meeting their objectives at minimum costs. Even in the household, there are many "cats" that can be "skinned" in different ways. Thus our present analysis of cost minimization is of very wide applicability.

We start the analysis of efficient production decisions with the simplest case—a firm deciding how much of a single input to use. Once the logic of this decision is understood, it will be relatively simple to extend the analysis to choices among two or more inputs.

Total Product and Marginal Physical Product

Consider, as an example of a firm, farmer Phil Pfister, who grows corn by himself on a 40-acre plot of land. Ultimately, he can vary all his input quantities: he can hire many or few farmhands, buy more land, or sell some of the land he owns. But suppose that for the moment his only choice is how much fertilizer to apply to his land. Farmer Pfister has studied the relationship between his input of fertilizer and his output of corn, and concluded that, at least up to a point, more fertilizer leads to more output. The relevant data are displayed in Table 20–1. We can see that 1000 bushels of corn will grow on the 40 acres even with no fertilizer at all, but that use of some fertilizer yields additional output; for instance, with four tons of fertilizer, output is 2200 bushels. Eventually, however, a saturation point is reached beyond which additional fertilizer actually reduces the corn crop (any amount beyond eight tons). These data are portrayed graphically in what we call a **total product curve** in Figure 20–2.

Table 20–1
FARMER PFISTER'S TOTAL PRODUCT SCHEDULE

CORRESPONDING LABEL IN FIGURE 20-2	FERTILIZER INPUT (tons)	CORN OUTPUT (bushels)
A	0	1000
B	1	1250
C	2	1550
D	3	1900
E	4	2200
F	5	2450
G	6	2600
H	7	2650
I	8	2650
J	9	2600

Our question is, How much fertilizer should Farmer Pfister use? We shall approach this question in stages. We begin by introducing a new concept, which is analogous to the concept of marginal utility that we found so useful in Chapter 18.

If Farmer Pfister is to decide how much fertilizer to use, he must know how much *additional* corn output he can expect from each *additional* ton of fertilizer. The concept that answers such questions is called **marginal physical product.** Thus, the marginal physical product of, for example, the fourth ton of fertilizer is the total output of corn when four tons of fertilizer are used *minus* the total output when three tons are used. The marginal physical product schedule of fertilizer on Farmer Pfister's land is given in the third column of Table 20–2, in which the total product schedule is repeated for convenience. For example, since three tons of fertilizer yield 1900 bushels of corn and four tons yield 2200 bushels,

The **marginal physical product** (abbreviated, **MPP**) of an input is the increase in total output that results from a one-unit increase in the input, holding the amounts of all other inputs constant.

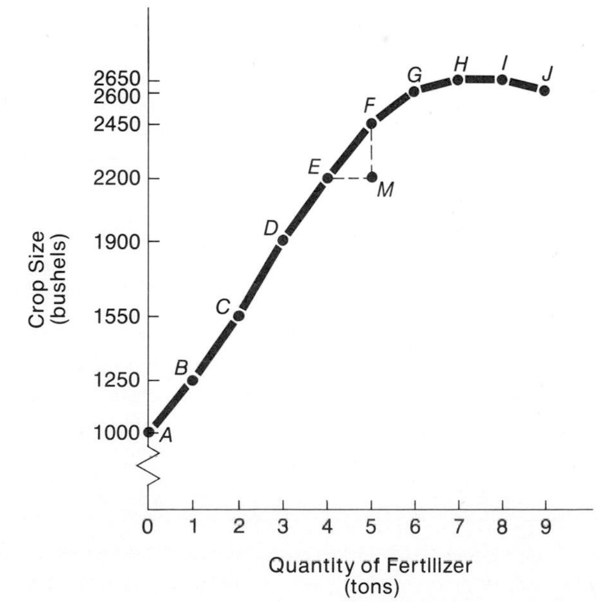

Figure 20–2
TOTAL PRODUCT WITH DIFFERENT QUANTITIES OF FERTILIZER
This graph shows how Farmer Pfister's corn crop varies as he uses more and more fertilizer on his fixed plot of land. (Other inputs, such as labor, are also held constant in this graph.)

Table 20-2
FARMER PFISTER'S TOTAL AND MARGINAL PHYSICAL PRODUCT SCHEDULES

FERTILIZER INPUT (tons)	TOTAL PRODUCT (corn output in bushels)	MARGINAL PHYSICAL PRODUCT (in bushels)
0	1000	—
1	1250	250
2	1550	300
3	1900	350
4	2200	300
5	2450	250
6	2600	150
7	2650	50
8	2650	0
9	2600	−50

the marginal physical product (MPP) of the fourth ton is $2200 - 1900 = 300$ bushels. The other entries in Table 20–2 are calculated from the total product data in the same way. Figure 20–3 displays these numbers graphically. For obvious reasons, it is called a **marginal physical product curve.**

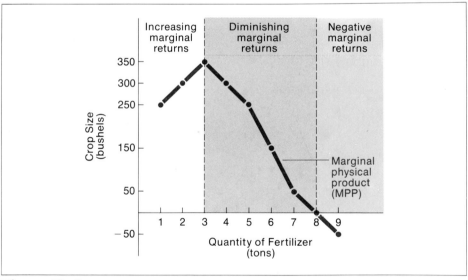

Figure 20–3
FARMER PFISTER'S MARGINAL PHYSICAL PRODUCT (MPP) CURVE
This graph of marginal physical product (MPP) shows how much *additional* corn Farmer Pfister gets from each application of an additional ton of fertilizer. The relation between the MPP curve and the total product curve in Figure 20–2 is simple and direct: the MPP curve at each level of input shows the *slope* of the corresponding total product curve. To see why, suppose we want to know what happens when Farmer Pfister increases fertilizer usage from four tons to five tons; that is, we want to determine the MPP of the fifth ton. In Figure 20–2 this brings us from point *E* to point *F* on the total product curve, so that output increases from 2200 bushels to 2450 bushels. The difference, 250 bushels, is the marginal physical product of the fifth ton of fertilizer. It is measured by the slope of the total product curve between points *E* and *F* because it corresponds to the rise in the curve (distance *MF*) resulting from a move to the right by one unit (distance *EM*)—which is precisely the definition of slope.

The "Law" of Diminishing Marginal Returns

We notice something interesting in the marginal physical product graph that was not quite so apparent in the total product graph shown earlier. Up until three tons of fertilizer are used, the marginal physical product of fertilizer is *increasing*; between three tons and eight tons it is *decreasing*, but still *positive*; and beyond eight tons the MPP of fertilizer actually becomes *negative*. The graph has been divided into three zones to highlight these three cases. The leftmost zone is called the region of **increasing marginal returns,** the middle zone (shaded gray) is called the region of **diminishing marginal returns,** while the rightmost zone (shaded blue) is the zone of **negative marginal returns.** In this graph, the marginal returns to fertilizer increase at first and then diminish. This is a typical pattern.

The **"law" of diminishing marginal returns,** which has played a key role in economics for two centuries,[1] asserts that when we increase the amount of any one input, *holding the amounts of all others constant*, the marginal returns to the expanding input ultimately begin to diminish. The so-called "law" is no more than an empirical regularity based on some observation of the facts; it is not a theorem deduced analytically.

The reason why returns to a single input are usually diminishing is straightforward. As we increase the quantity of one input while holding all others constant, the input whose quantity we are increasing gradually becomes more and more abundant compared with the others. As the farmer uses more and more fertilizer with his fixed plot of land, the soil gradually becomes so well fertilized that adding yet more fertilizer does little good. Eventually the plants are absorbing so much fertilizer that any further increase in fertilizer will actually harm them. At this point the marginal physical product of fertilizer becomes *negative*.

Diminishing Returns
and the Optimal Quantity of an Input

We will see in later chapters that the phenomenon of diminishing marginal returns is relevant to issues as seemingly diverse as the population problem and the distribution of income. But our interest in it here is more mundane. Let us see how it helps Farmer Pfister decide how much fertilizer to use.

The first two columns of Table 20–3 repeat the marginal physical product schedule from Table 20–2. (The third column will be explained presently.) Suppose fertilizer costs $350 per ton, that the farmer's product is worth $2 per bushel, and he is using three tons of fertilizer. Is this optimal for him? The answer is no, because the marginal physical product of the fourth ton is 300 bushels (fourth entry in the marginal physical product column of Table 20–3). This means that although a fourth ton of fertilizer would cost him $350, it would yield him an additional 300 bushels, which at the price of $2 would add $600 to his revenue. Thus he comes out $600 − $350 = $250 ahead if he adds a fourth ton.

It is convenient to have a specific name for the additional revenue that accrues to a firm when it increases the quantity of some input by one unit; we call it **marginal revenue product.** So if Farmer Pfister's crop sells at a fixed price

> The **marginal revenue product (MRP)** of an input is the additional revenue the producer is able to earn as a result of increased sales when he uses an additional unit of the input.

---

[1] The "law" is generally credited to Anne Robert Jacques Turgot (1727–1781), one of the great Comptrollers-General of France before the Revolution, whose liberal policies, it is said, represented the old regime's last chance to save itself. But, with characteristic foresight, the king fired him.

Table 20-3
MARGINAL PHYSICAL PRODUCTS AND MARGINAL REVENUE PRODUCTS
OF FARMER PFISTER'S FERTILIZER

TONS OF FERTILIZER	MARGINAL PHYSICAL PRODUCT (bushels)	MARGINAL REVENUE PRODUCT (dollars)
1	250	500
2	300	600
3	350	700
4	300	600
5	250	500
6	150	300
7	50	100
8	0	0
9	−50	−100

(say, $2 per bushel), the marginal revenue product of the input equals its marginal physical product multiplied by the price of the product:

$$\text{MRP} = \text{MPP} \times \text{Price of output} .$$

For example, we have just seen that the marginal revenue product (MRP) of the fourth ton of fertilizer to Farmer Pfister is $600, which we obtained by multiplying the MPP of 300 bushels by the price of $2 per bushel. The other entries in Table 20–3 are obtained in precisely the same way. The concept of MRP enables us to formulate a simple **rule for the optimal use of any input.** Specifically:

When the marginal revenue product of an input exceeds its price, it pays the producer to expand his use of that input. Similarly, when the marginal revenue product of the input is less than its price, it pays the producer to use less of that input.

Let us test this rule out for Farmer Pfister. We have observed that three tons of fertilizer cannot be enough because the marginal revenue product (MRP) of the fourth ton ($600) exceeds its price ($350). What about the fifth ton? Table 20–3 tells us that the MRP of the fifth ton ($500) also exceeds its price, and hence stopping at four tons cannot be optimal. The same cannot be said of the sixth ton, however. A sixth ton is not a good idea, since its MRP is only $300, which is less than its $350 cost.

Notice the crucial role of diminishing returns in this analysis. Because the "law" of diminishing marginal returns holds true for Pfister's farm, the marginal *physical* product (MPP) of fertilizer eventually begins to decline. Therefore the marginal *revenue* product also begins to decline. At the point where MRP falls below the price of fertilizer, it is appropriate for Pfister to stop increasing his purchases. In sum, it always pays the producer to expand his input use until diminishing returns set in and reduce the marginal revenue product to the price of the input.

A common expression suggests that it does not pay to continue doing something "beyond the point of diminishing returns." As we see from this analysis, quite to the contrary, it normally does pay to do so! Only when the marginal revenue product of an input has been reduced (by diminishing returns) to the level of the input's price has the proper amount of the input been employed. In a word, the optimal quantity of an input is that at which the marginal revenue product is equal to its price (P). In symbols,

$$\text{MRP} = P \text{ of input}.$$

Choice of Input Proportions: The Production Function

So far we have dealt with the choice of each input quantity as if it could be decided separately from the others by setting the MRP of each input equal to its price. This is somewhat misleading, for the choices of how much fertilizer, labor, and land to employ must and do depend upon one another. For example, the amount of fertilizer it pays Farmer Pfister to use depends on the number of acres he farms, because the marginal physical product of fertilizer depends on the amount of land that is used, and vice versa. Decisions about how much of each different input to employ are therefore interdependent.

To help select the combination of inputs that can produce the desired output most cheaply, economists have invented a concept they call the **production function.** The production function summarizes the technical and engineering information about the relationship between inputs and output in a given firm, taking *all* the firm's inputs into account. It indicates, for example, just how much output Farmer Pfister can produce if he has a given amount of land, labor, fertilizer, and so on. When there are only two inputs—which are enough to indicate the basic principles involved—a production function can be represented graphically (which we do in the appendix to this chapter) or by a simple table. Table 20–4 indicates Farmer Pfister's production function for the use of labor and fertilizer to produce corn on his farm. To make the table easier to read, most of the numbers that normally would be entered (but that are irrelevant for our purposes) have been omitted and replaced by dashes.

The table is read like a mileage chart. Thus, if we want to see how much can be produced with three months of labor and two tons of fertilizer, we locate the 2 in the column of numbers on the left, which indicates the quantity of fertilizer, and the 3 in the row of numbers across the top, which represents the months of

The **production function** indicates the *maximum* amount of product that can be obtained from any specified *combination* of inputs, given the current state of knowledge. That is, it shows the *largest* quantity of goods that any particular collection of inputs is capable of producing.

Table 20-4
A PRODUCTION FUNCTION

			QUANTITY OF LABOR (months)				
		0	1	2	3	4	5
QUANTITY OF FERTILIZER (tons)	0	0	1000	—	—	—	2600
	1	0	1250	1900	2400	2600	—
	2	0	1550	2250	2600	2800	—
	3	0	1900	2450	2750	—	—
	4	0	2200	2600	—	—	—
	5	0	2450	3000	—	—	—
	6	0	2600	—	—	4900	—
	7	0	2650	—	—	—	—
	8	0	2650	3700	4600	5400	6000
	9	0	2600	—	—	—	—

labor. Then, in the spot horizontally to the right of the 2 and vertically below the 3 we find the number 2600, meaning that this input combination can produce 2600 bushels of output per month. Similarly, you should be able to verify that with eight tons of fertilizer and three months of labor, 4600 bushels per month can be produced.

The zero entries in the first column of Table 20–4 tell us that Farmer Pfister can produce nothing with no labor. The second column, which corresponds to alternative amounts of fertilizer used in combination with *one* month of labor, is familiar to us already—it is just the total product schedule that we have been using for Farmer Pfister working alone with various amounts of fertilizer. The other columns represent alternative production arrangements in which Pfister hires one or more farmhands to help him.

How much labor and fertilizer should Farmer Pfister use if he wants to grow 2600 bushels of corn? The production function table shows us that there are a variety of alternatives available to him. He can, for example, work alone and use six tons of fertilizer. Or he can hire a second worker and use only four tons. Or, at the other extreme, he can grow 2600 bushels without fertilizer by using five workers. The blue entries in Table 20–4 indicate all the different ways in which Farmer Pfister can conceivably meet his 2600 bushel production target.

Which will he choose? Naturally, the one that costs him the least. Table 20–5 shows Farmer Pfister's cost calculations. It is assumed here that fertilizer costs $350 per ton, that farm labor costs $500 per month, and that Pfister's fixed costs for such items as land and machinery amount to $1700 per month. Thus, for example, the first line tells us that Pfister can produce 2600 bushels using only his own labor (which costs $500),[2] six tons of fertilizer (which cost $2100), and land and machinery that cost $1700 per month, for a total cost of $500 + $2100 + $1700 = $4300. The other lines in Table 20–5 can be read in the same way. So we see that the cheapest way to produce 2600 bushels of corn is by using three workers and two tons of fertilizer, for a total cost of $3900, which is less than any of the other alternatives.

Notice that two types of information are relevant to Farmer Pfister's decision. The *technological information* embodied in the production function tells Pfister all the possible ways that 2600 bushels can be produced; that is, it tells him

[2]*Question:* Why does Farmer Pfister "charge himself" $500 for his own labor time?

Answer: Because he must include, as part of his true costs, the opportunity cost of his labor; that is, what he could be earning if he worked for someone else. If you need to review the concept of opportunity cost, see pages 38–39.

Table 20-5
PRODUCTION COSTS UNDER ALTERNATIVE INPUT COMBINATIONS
CAPABLE OF PRODUCING 2600 BUSHELS

QUANTITY OF LABOR (months)	COST OF LABOR (at $500 per month)	QUANTITY OF FERTILIZER (tons)	COST OF FERTILIZER (at $350 per ton)	FIXED COSTS (for land, machinery, etc.)	TOTAL COST
1	$500	6	$2100	$1700	$4300
2	1000	4	1400	1700	4100
3	1500	2	700	1700	3900
4	2000	1	350	1700	4050
5	2500	0	0	1700	4200

about the possibilities for factor substitution. Then *financial information*—the prices of the two inputs—is needed to tell him which of these alternatives is the least costly. If either of these sets of data changes, Farmer Pfister's decision on input combinations is likely to change as well. For example, if fertilizer gets much more expensive, he might switch to an alternative that uses more labor and less fertilizer.

Does the "marginal revenue product equals price" rule continue to hold when there are two or more inputs? Let us see by testing whether the rule is satisfied when Pfister uses three months of labor and two tons of fertilizer. (Table 20–5 has just shown us that this input combination is the least costly way to produce 2600 bushels.) We know from Table 20–4 that when three months of labor are used, the marginal *physical* product (MPP) of the second ton of fertilizer is 200 bushels (2600 bushels minus 2400 bushels). Since the price of a bushel of corn is $2, the marginal *revenue* product (MRP) of the second ton of fertilizer is $400, which exceeds its price ($350). Therefore, Farmer Pfister should purchase the second ton. But should he purchase the third? Its MPP is 150 bushels (2750 minus 2600), so its MRP is $2 × 150 = $300. This is less than what the third ton would cost, so Pfister should stop at two tons.

What about months of labor? Reading across the row corresponding to two tons of fertilizer, we see that the marginal physical product of the third month of labor is 350 bushels (2600 − 2250) while the MPP of the fourth month of labor is only 200 bushels. At a $2 price for corn, the corresponding MRPs are $700 for the third month of labor and only $400 for the fourth month. Since labor costs $500 per month, it is optimal to stop at three months.

Because we have not considered fractional amounts in our production function table, we have not been able to satisfy the MRP = *P* rule exactly. But we can see that Farmer Pfister has indeed followed the basic logic of the rule and has come as close as possible to setting:

$$\text{MRP of fertilizer} = P \text{ of fertilizer}$$
$$\text{MRP of labor} = P \text{ of labor} .$$

If we remember that the MRP of each input is its marginal *physical* product (MPP) times the price of corn, we can see that these rules are just a formalization of common sense. They say, for example, that if one input costs twice as much as another, then optimal input use requires that the first input be twice as productive (on the margin) as the second.[3]

---

[3] A little algebra is helpful in restating this rule. Letting P_F, P_L, and P_C represent the prices of fertilizer, labor, and corn, respectively, and letting MRP_F and MPP_F represent the marginal revenue product and the marginal physical product of fertilizer, respectively, with similar notation for labor, our two rules for optimal input use become

$$P_F = \text{MRP}_F = P_C \times \text{MPP}_F \quad \text{and} \quad P_L = \text{MRP}_L = P_C \times \text{MPP}_L .$$

Then if we divide the first optimality rule by the second, we obtain

$$\frac{P_F}{P_L} = \frac{\text{MRP}_F}{\text{MRP}_L} = \frac{\text{MPP}_F \times P_C}{\text{MPP}_L \times P_C} .$$

Since P_C can be divided out of both numerator and denominator, the general rule for optimal input combinations is

$$\frac{P_F}{P_L} = \frac{\text{MPP}_F}{\text{MPP}_L} .$$

In words, variable inputs should always be combined in such a way that their prices are proportional to their marginal physical products.

This common-sense reasoning leads to an important conclusion. Suppose the price of fertilizer rises while the price of labor remains the same. The rule

$$P \text{ of fertilizer} = \text{MRP of fertilizer} = \text{MPP of fertilizer} \times \text{price of corn}$$

tells us that optimal use of fertilizer now requires that the MPP of fertilizer must be higher than before. (The price of corn has not changed.) By the "law" of diminishing returns, the MPP of fertilizer is *higher* only when *less* fertilizer is used. Thus a rise in the price of fertilizer leads the farmer to use *less* fertilizer and, if he still wants to produce 2600 bushels of output, to use *more* labor. In general:

As any one input becomes more costly relative to other competing units, the firm is likely to substitute one input for another; that is, to reduce its use of the input that has become more expensive and to increase its use of competing inputs.[4]

This general principle of input substitution applies in industry just as it does on Farmer Pfister's farm. For one important application of the analysis, see the boxed insert on the opposite page.

The Firm's Cost Curves

The **total cost curve** shows the smallest sum of money a firm can spend to produce each alternative quantity of output it may consider producing.

Business firms are, of course, interested in more than simply minimizing the cost of producing some fixed amount of output. They presumably want to make a profit as well. To do so, they must compare alternative production levels and choose among them—using techniques we will explain in the next chapter. In the present example, an output of 2600 bushels is not likely to be the only possible production level that Farmer Pfister is considering. He might wonder, for example, about the least costly way to produce 2100 bushels or 3100 bushels.

By exactly the same procedures outlined in Table 20–5 (page 376), Farmer Pfister can compute the minimum cost of producing *any* particular quantity of output. Let us suppose he has done this and come up with the minimum total costs for alternative production levels displayed in Table 20–6. Here we have the numbers Pfister needs to plot five different points on his **total cost curve** (columns 1 and 2 of the table), which is the curve shown in Figure 20–4. Point A shows the $2880 total cost of 1600 bushels of output, point B shows the $3360 total cost of 2100 bushels, and so on. By dividing the total cost (TC) for each output by

[4]*EXERCISE:* Suppose that fertilizer rises in price to $600 per ton. Construct a new version of Table 20–5 (page 376) and use it to show that it will be optimal to reduce fertilizer use from two tons to zero and to increase the use of labor from three months to five months.

Table 20–6
DATA FOR FARMER PFISTER'S COST CURVES

(1) OUTPUT LEVEL (bushels)	(2) TOTAL COST (TC) (dollars)	(3) AVERAGE COST (AC) (dollars per bushel)
1600	2880	1.80
2100	3360	1.60
2600	3900	1.50
3100	4805	1.55
3600	5940	1.65

Do Public Utilities Use Too Much Capital?

In the United States, electric companies and other public utilities are regulated by government agencies, which, among other things, set ceilings on the profits that these companies are permitted to earn. Though few people argue against the desirability of some sort of restriction on the profits of the largest of the regulated firms, regulatory restrictions sometimes have unintended, undesirable side effects. For example, it has been argued before regulatory agencies that a ceiling on profits provides an incentive to the regulated firm to use too much machinery relative to labor.

The connection between a regulatory ceiling on company profits and the firm's decision on its input combination may seem remote, but it is not. The reason is that regulators usually do not set a limit on *total* profits but instead determine what they call "a fair rate of return" on the company's investment. The utility may be permitted to earn, say, 10 percent *on its investment* but no more. Thus a large electric company will be permitted to earn 10 percent on its multibillion-dollar investment while a smaller firm is permitted to earn the same 10 percent on its much smaller investment. This provides a suitable ceiling on earnings, but, as we will see, such regulations can also affect input choice. How?

A firm's equipment and plants are, by definition, part of its investment. So if a company meets an upward shift in its demand curve by investing $25 million in a new plant, it is permitted to earn more dollars in profit; specifically, it is allowed to add 10 percent of $25 million to its profits. But if, instead, it chooses to meet the higher demand by adding more labor, its *investment* has not increased (because money spent on labor is not considered an investment) and the firm is not permitted to earn any more profit on the higher level of sales.

In sum, because spending more on machinery adds to the firm's allowable profit whereas spending more on labor does not, the process of profit regulation may give the utility an incentive to purchase equipment instead of labor. It is as if the use of capital by the firm were given a subsidy that lowers its price relative to the price of labor. As we have learned, a fall in the price of capital relative to labor will induce the firm to use more capital and less labor. That is precisely what happens here. And it explains why regulation of profits may have unintended side effects on the firm's input decisions, which would not have occurred if matters had been left to the market.

---

the quantity (Q) of the output, we obtain the corresponding **average cost (AC);** that is, the cost per unit of output. For example, when output is 2600 bushels, total cost is $3900; so average cost is $3900/2600 = $1.50. The general

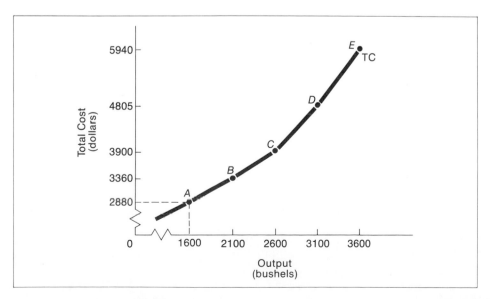

Figure 20–4
TOTAL COST CURVE, FROM THE COST AND OUTPUT DATA IN TABLE 20–6
Point A shows that to produce 1600 bushels per month, a total of $2880 in cost must be incurred, just as Table 20–6 indicates.

Figure 20–5

AVERAGE COST CURVE FOR THE FIRM FROM DATA IN TABLE 20–6
The points *a*, *b*, *c*, *d*, and *e* correspond to points *A*, *B*, *C*, *D*, and *E*, respectively, in Figure 20–4. For example, point *A* in Figure 20–4 and point *a* in Figure 20–5 both correspond to an output of 1600 bushels. And since point *A* in Figure 20–4 indicates that the total cost of this output is $2880, its average cost is $2880/1600 = $1.80, as shown by point *a*.

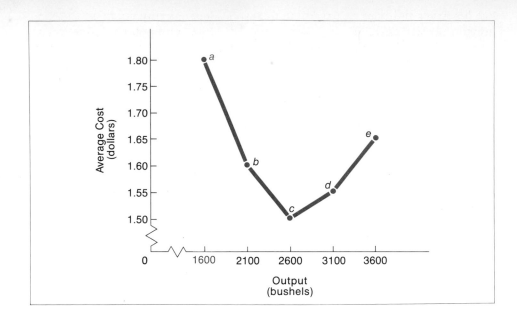

relationship between any total cost figure and its corresponding average cost is quite straightforward. By definition:

$$\text{Average cost} = \frac{\text{Total cost}}{\text{Quantity of output}},$$

or in symbols:

$$AC = \frac{TC}{Q}.$$

The **average cost curve** shows the smallest average cost, or cost per unit, at which it is possible to produce each alternative level of output. The average cost curve is obtained from the total cost curve by the relationship: $AC = TC/Q$.

Using this formula, the table gives us four other AC figures that can be used to plot the **average cost curve** shown in Figure 20–5. For example, point *c* in Figure 20–5 corresponds to point *C* in Figure 20–4. It shows that the average cost of producing 2600 bushels is $1.50 per bushel.

We can learn a good deal about the behavior of both total and average cost curves simply by remembering how they were derived: by finding the input combinations that produce any given output at minimum cost. This immediately tells us that the principal determinants of the shapes and positions of the TC and AC curves are, first, the firm's technology, as embodied in its production function, and, second, the prices of the inputs that the firm buys. Thus a decline in the price of any input, or a technological improvement that allows the same output to be produced with smaller input quantities, will shift *both* the TC and the AC curves *downward.* Conversely, rising input prices or a deterioration in technology (for example, if an efficient production process is banned because it violates environmental regulations) will shift both the TC and the AC curves *upward.* The two curves always move together.

Short Run Versus Long Run

We have studied the firm's ability to *substitute* one input for another, and have seen how the process of cost minimization leads to total and average cost curves.

But the firm's ability to vary its input quantities depends very much on the time horizon under consideration. The reason is that, at any point in time, many input choices will be *precommitted* by past decisions. If, for example, the firm purchased machinery a year ago, it is committed to that decision for the remainder of the machine's economic life, unless the company is willing to take the loss involved in getting rid of it sooner.

An input to which the firm is committed for a short period of time, however, is not a fixed commitment when a longer planning horizon is considered. For example, a two-year-old machine with a nine-year economic life is a fixed commitment for the next seven years; but it is not a fixed commitment in plans that extend beyond the seven years. Economists summarize this notion by speaking of different "runs" for decision making—the **short run,** the **intermediate run,** and the **long run.** These terms will recur time and again in this book. They interest us now because of their relationship to the issue of substitutability. In the short run, there is relatively little opportunity for input substitution because the firm's input quantities have been largely predetermined by its past decisions. Over the long run, however, input substitution becomes a crucial issue for the decision maker.

Think of Farmer Pfister, for example. Once the crop is planted, he has little discretion over how much of the various inputs to use. Over a somewhat longer planning horizon, he can decide how much labor to employ and how much seed to use. Over a still longer period, he can acquire new equipment and increase or decrease the size of his farm. Much the same is true of big industrial firms. In the short run, management has little control over the production technique. But with some advance planning, different types of machines using different amounts of labor and energy can be acquired, factories can be redesigned, and other choices can be made. Indeed, over the longest run, no inputs remain committed; all of them can be varied both in quantity and design.

It should be noted that short, intermediate, and long runs do not refer to the same period of time for all firms; rather, they vary in length depending on the nature of the firm's commitments. If, for example, the firm can change its work force every week, its machines every two years, and its factory every 20 years, then a week will be the short run, 20 years will be the long run, and any period between a week and 20 years will constitute an intermediate run.

The Average Cost Curve in the Short and Long Runs

The firm's average cost curve is the outcome of **cost minimization**—a process that involves making optimal use of all inputs whose quantities are *variable*. But as we just observed, which inputs can be varied and which are precommitted depends on the time horizon under consideration. It follows that:

The average (and total) cost curve depends on the firm's planning horizon. The average (and total) cost curve pertinent to the long run differs from that for the short run because more inputs become variable.

We can, in fact, be much more specific about the relationships between short-run and long-run average cost (AC) curves. Consider, as an example, the publisher of a small newspaper. In the short run, the firm can choose only the number of typesetters, printers, paper, and ink it uses; but in the long run, it can also choose between two different sizes of printing press. If the firm purchases the smaller press, the AC curve looks like curve *SL* in Figure 20–6. That means that if the paper is pleasantly surprised and its circulation grows to 50,000 copies per day, its

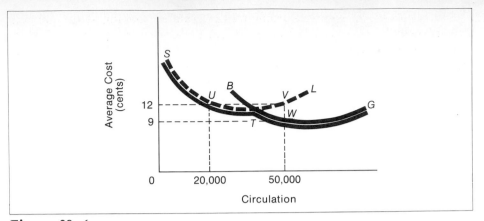

Figure 20–6

SHORT- AND LONG-RUN AVERAGE COST CURVES FOR A NEWSPAPER

The publisher has a choice of two printing plants, a small one with AC curve *SL*, and a big one with AC curve *BG*. These are the short-run curves that apply as long as the newspaper is stuck with its chosen plant. But in the long run, when it has its choice of plant size, it can pick any point on the colored lower boundary of these curves. This lower boundary, *STG*, is the long-run average cost curve.

cost will be 12 cents per copy (point *V*). It may then wish it had purchased the bigger press (whose AC curve is shown as *BG*), which would have enabled the firm to cut unit cost to 9 cents (point *W*). However, in the short run nothing can be done about this decision; the AC curve remains *SL*. Similarly, had it bought the larger press, its short-run AC curve would have been *BG* and it would have been committed to this cost curve even if business were to decline sharply.

In the long run, however, the machine must be replaced, and management has its choice once again. If it expects a circulation of 50,000 copies, it will purchase the larger press and its cost will be 9 cents per copy. Similarly, if it expects sales of only 20,000 copies, it will arrange for the smaller press and for average costs of 12 cents (point *U*). In sum, in the long run, the firm will select the plant size (that is, the short-run AC curve) that is most economical for the output level it expects to produce. The long-run average cost curve then consists of all the *lower* segments of the short-run AC curves. In Figure 20–6, this composite curve is the blue curve *STG*.

The Long-Run Average Cost Curve and Economies of Scale

Production is said to involve **economies of scale,** also referred to as **increasing returns to scale,** if, when all input quantities are doubled, the quantity of output is more than doubled.

We are now beginning to put together the apparatus we need to address the question posed at the start of this chapter: How can we tell if a firm has substantial **economies of scale?** As an example of economies of scale, turn back to the production function for Farmer Pfister in Table 20–4 on page 375 and assume that labor and fertilizer are the only two inputs.[5] Notice that with two months of labor and four tons of fertilizer, output is 2600 bushels. What happens if we double both inputs—to four months of labor and eight tons of fertilizer? The table shows us that output rises to 5400—that is, it more than doubles. So Farmer Pfister's production function, at least in this range, displays **increasing returns to scale** (economies of scale).

[5]This is necessary because the definition requires that *all* inputs be doubled simultaneously. So, to be true to the definition, labor, fertilizer, *land, and machinery* would all have to double.

It is possible to recognize economies of scale by looking at the *long-run average cost curve* instead of at the production function. Notice that the definition requires a doubling of *every input*. If twice as large a quantity of each input is purchased, then total cost must double. If output *more* than doubles, as would be the case if there are economies of scale, then cost per unit (average cost) must decline. In other words:

Production functions with economies of scale lead to long-run average cost curves that decline as output expands.

An example will clarify the arithmetic behind this rule. We saw earlier (Table 20–5) that it costs $4100 to produce 2600 bushels with two months of labor and four tons of fertilizer. The average cost was thus $4100/2600, or approximately $1.58 per bushel. If, as the production function states, doubling all inputs (and thus doubling costs to $8200) leads to production of 5400 bushels, then cost per unit will become $8200/5400, or approximately $1.52. Economies of scale in the production function thus lead to *decreasing* average cost as output expands; in this case, average cost decreased by 6 cents—from $1.58 to $1.52.

A decreasing average cost curve is depicted in Figure 20–7(a). But this is only one of three possible shapes the long-run average cost curve can take. A second possibility is shown in part (b) of the figure. In this case we have an example of **constant returns to scale,** where both total cost (TC) and quantity of output (Q) double, so average cost (AC = TC/Q) remains constant. Finally, it is possible that output less than doubles when all inputs double. This would be a case of **decreasing returns to scale,** which leads to a rising long-run average cost curve like the one depicted in part (c) of Figure 20–7.

It should be pointed out that the same production function can display increasing returns to scale in some ranges, constant returns to scale in others, and decreasing returns to scale in yet others. Farmer Pfister's production function in Table 20–4 provides an illustration of this. We have already seen that it displays increasing returns to scale when inputs are doubled from two months of labor and four tons of fertilizer to four months of labor and eight tons of fertilizer. But,

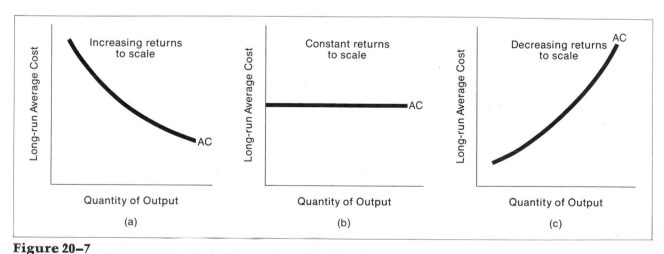

Figure 20–7
THREE POSSIBLE SHAPES FOR THE LONG-RUN AVERAGE COST CURVE
In part (a), long-run average costs are decreasing as output expands because the firm has significant economies of scale (increasing returns to scale). In part (b), constant returns to scale lead to a long-run AC curve that is flat; costs per unit are the same for any level of output. In part (c), which pertains to a firm with decreasing returns to scale, long-run average costs rise as output expands.

looking back at Table 20–4 (page 375), we can see that there are constant returns to scale when inputs double from two months of labor and three tons of fertilizer (2450 bushels of output) to four months of labor and six tons of fertilizer (4900 bushels). We can also find a region of decreasing returns to scale. Notice that with two months of labor and one ton of fertilizer the yield is 1900 bushels, while with double those inputs—four months of labor and two tons of fertilizer—the yield is only 2800 bushels.

There seem to be many cases in which a firm can benefit from increasing returns to scale as output expands from low and moderate levels (perhaps because it can put bigger and more efficient machinery into service) but then runs into decreasing returns to scale when it grows very large (perhaps because of the difficulties of coordinating a giant enterprise). In this case, the long-run average cost curve would have the U-shape depicted earlier, in Figures 20–5 and 20–6, with AC falling at first and then rising. In much of what follows, we shall assume that an average cost curve of this general shape is typical.

Diminishing Returns and Returns to Scale

Earlier in this chapter we discussed the "law" of diminishing marginal returns. Is there any relationship between economies of scale and the phenomenon of diminishing returns? It may seem at first that the two are contradictory. After all, if a producer gets diminishing returns from his inputs as he uses more of each of them, doesn't it follow that by using more of *every* input he cannot obtain economies of scale? The answer is that there is no contradiction, for the two principles deal with fundamentally different issues.

1. ***Returns to a single input.*** Here we must ask the question, How much can output expand if we increase the quantity of just *one* input, *holding all other input quantities unchanged?*

2. ***Returns to scale.*** Here the question is, How much can output expand if *all* inputs are increased *simultaneously* by the same percentage?

The "law" of diminishing returns provides an answer to the first question while economies of scale pertains to the second.

Table 20–4 shows us that Farmer Pfister's production function satisfies the "law" of diminishing returns to a single input. To see this, we must hold the quantity of one input constant while letting the other vary. The row corresponding to eight tons of fertilizer will serve as an example, since an entry is provided for every quantity of labor. Reading across the row, we see from the second entry that the use of one month of labor and eight tons of fertilizer yields 2650 bushels of corn. The next entry shows that the same eight tons of fertilizer plus one additional month of labor produces a marginal product of 1050 bushels (that is, the total of 3700 bushels produced by the two months of labor minus the 2650 bushels obtained from the first month's labor). In the third column we find that another month of labor (still holding fertilizer use at eight tons) brings in a smaller marginal product of 900 (4600 total bushels minus 3700 bushels from the first two months). The "law" of diminishing returns is clearly satisfied.

Returns to scale, on the other hand, describe the production response to a proportionate increase in *all* inputs. We have already seen that this production function displays increasing returns to scale in some ranges, constant returns to scale in others, and decreasing returns to scale in yet others. Thus the "law" of diminishing returns (to a single input) is compatible with *any* sort of returns to scale. In summary:

Returns to scale and returns to a single input (holding all other input quantities constant) refer to two distinct aspects of a firm's technology. A production function that displays diminishing returns to *a single input* may show diminishing, constant, or increasing returns when *all input quantities are increased proportionately.*

Historical Costs
Versus Analytical Cost Curves

In the previous chapter, we made much of the fact that all points on a demand curve pertain to the *same* period of time, and that a plot of historical data on prices and quantities is normally *not* the demand curve that the decision maker needs. A similar point relating to cost curves will resolve the problem posed at the beginning of the chapter as to whether declining historical costs are evidence of economies of scale.

All points on any of the cost curves used in economic analysis refer to the same period of time.

One point on the cost curve of an auto manufacturer tells us, for example, how much it would cost it to produce 2.5 million cars during 1983. Another point on the curve tells us what happens to the firm's costs if, *instead*, it produces, say, 3 million cars in 1983. Such a curve is called an **analytical cost curve** or, when there is no possibility of confusion, simply a cost curve. This curve must be distinguished from a diagram of **historical costs,** which shows how costs have changed from year to year.

The different points on an analytical cost curve represent *alternative possibilities,* all for the same time period. In 1983, the car manufacturer will produce either 2.5 or 3 million cars (or some other amount), but certainly not both. Thus, at most, only one point on this cost curve will ever be observed. The company may, indeed, produce 2.5 million in 1983 and 3 million in 1984; but the latter is not relevant to the 1983 cost curve. By the time 1984 comes around, the cost curve may well have shifted, so the 1983 cost figure will not apply to the 1984 cost curve. We can, of course, draw a different sort of graph that indicates, year by year, how costs and outputs have varied. Such a graph, which gathers together the statistics for a number of different periods, is not, however, a *cost curve* as that term is used by economists. An example of such a diagram of historical costs was given at the beginning of the chapter in Figure 20–1.

But why do economists rarely use historical cost diagrams and instead deal primarily with analytical cost curves, which are much more difficult to explain and to obtain statistically? The answer is that analysis of real policy problems—such as the desirability of having a single supplier of telephone services—leaves no choice in the matter. Rational decisions require analytical cost curves. Let us see why.

Resolving the Economies of Scale Puzzle

Since the 1940s there has been great technical progress in the telephone industry. From ordinary open wire, the industry has gone to microwave systems, to telecommunications satellites and coaxial cables of enormous capacity, and new techniques using laser beams are on the way. Innovations in switching techniques and in the use of computers to send messages along uncrowded routes are equally impressive. All of this means that the *entire* analytical cost curve of telecommunications must have shifted downward quite dramatically from year

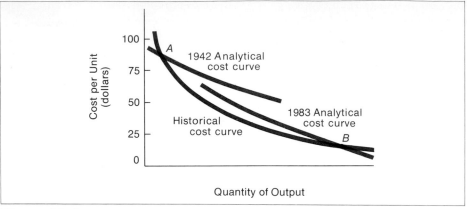

Figure 20–8

DECLINING HISTORICAL COST CURVE WITH THE
ANALYTICAL AVERAGE COST CURVE ALSO DECLINING IN EACH YEAR
The two analytical cost curves shown indicate how the corresponding points (*A* and *B*) on the historical cost diagram are generated by that year's analytical curve. Because the analytical cost curves are declining, we know that there are economies of scale in the production activity whose costs are shown.

to year. Innovation must have reduced not only the cost of large-scale operation *but also the cost of smaller-scale operations.*

Now if we are to determine whether in 1983 a single supplier can provide telephone service more cheaply than can a number of smaller firms, we must compare the costs of *both* large- and small-scale production *in 1983.* It does no good to compare the cost of a large supplier in 1983 with its own costs as a smaller firm back in 1942, because that cannot possibly give us the information we need. The cost situation in 1942 is irrelevant for today's decision between large and small suppliers because no small firm today would use the obsolete techniques of 1942. Until we compare the costs of the large and small supplier *today* we cannot make a rational choice between single- and multifirm production. It is the analytical cost curve, all of whose points refer to the same period, that, by definition, supplies this information.

Figures 20–8 and 20–9 show two extreme hypothetical cases, one in which economies of scale are present and one in which they are not. Yet both of them are based on the same historical cost data (in black) with its very sharply declining costs. (This curve is reproduced from Figure 20–1.) They also show (in blue) two possible average cost curves, one for 1942 and one for 1983. In Figure 20–8 the analytical AC curve (in blue) has shifted downward very sharply from 1942 to 1983, as technological change reduced all costs. Moreover, both of the AC curves slope downward to the right, meaning that, in either year, the larger the firm the lower its average costs. Thus, the situation shown in Figure 20–8 really does represent a case in which there are economies of large-scale production so that one firm can produce at lower cost than many.

But now look at Figure 20–9, which shows exactly the same historical costs as Figure 20–8. Here, both analytical AC curves are U-shaped. In particular, we note that the 1983 average cost curve has its minimum point at an output level, *A*, that is less than one-half the current output, *B*, of the large supplier. This means that in the situation shown in Figure 20–9, despite the sharp downward trend of historical costs, a smaller company can produce more cheaply than a large one can. In this case, one cannot justify domination of the market by a single large firm on the grounds that its costs are lower. In sum, the behavior of historical

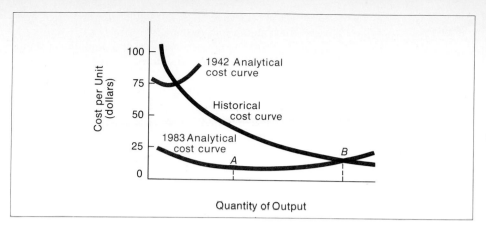

Figure 20–9
DECLINING HISTORICAL
COST CURVE WITH
U-SHAPED ANALYTICAL
COST CURVES IN EACH
YEAR
Here the shape of the average
cost curve does not show
economies of scale.

costs tells us nothing about the cost advantages or disadvantages of a single large firm. More generally:

Because a diagram of historical costs does not compare the costs of large and small firms at the same point in time, it cannot be used to determine whether there are economies of large-scale production. Only the analytical cost curve can supply this information.

Cost Minimization in Theory and Practice

Lest you be tempted to run out and open a business, confident that you now understand how to minimize costs, we should point out that decision making in business is a good deal harder than we have indicated here. Rare is the business executive who knows for sure what his production function looks like, or the exact shapes of his marginal revenue product schedules, or the precise nature of his cost curves. No one can provide a cookbook for instant success in business. What we have presented here is a set of principles that constitutes a guide to good decision making.

Business management has been described as the art of making critical decisions on the basis of inadequate information, and in our complex and ever-changing world there is often no alternative to an educated guess. Actual business decisions will at best approximate the cost-minimizing ideal outlined in this chapter. Certainly, there will be mistakes. But when management does its job well and the market system functions smoothly, the approximation may prove amazingly good. While no system is perfect, inducing firms to produce at the lowest possible cost is undoubtedly one of the jobs the market system does best.

Summary

1. It is normally possible to produce the same quantity of output in a variety of ways by substituting more of one input for less of another. Firms normally seek the least costly way to produce any output.
2. The marginal physical product of an input is the increase in total output resulting from a one-unit increase in the use of that input, holding the quantities of all other inputs constant.
3. The "law" of diminishing marginal returns states that if we increase the amount of one input (holding all

other input quantities constant), the marginal physical product of the expanding input will eventually begin to decline.
4. The marginal revenue product of an input is the additional revenue the firm earns from the increased sales resulting from the use of one more unit of the input.
5. A firm that wants to minimize costs will use each input up to the point where its marginal revenue product (MRP) is equal to its price (P).

6. The production function shows the relationship between inputs and output. It indicates the maximum quantity of output obtainable from any given combination of inputs.
7. A firm's total cost curve shows the lowest possible cost for producing any given level of output. It is derived by applying the rule for optimal input combinations to the production function.
8. A firm's average cost curve shows the lowest cost per unit at which it is possible to produce any given level of output. It is derived from the total curve by simple arithmetic: $AC = TC/Q$.
9. If a doubling of all the firm's inputs *just* permits it to double its output, the firm is said to have constant returns to scale. If with doubled inputs it can *more than* double its output, it has increasing returns to scale (or, economies of scale). If a doubling of inputs produces *less than* double the output, the firm has decreasing returns to scale.
10. With increasing returns to scale, the firm's long-run average costs are decreasing; constant returns to scale are associated with constant long-run average costs; and decreasing returns to scale are associated with increasing long-run average costs.
11. We cannot tell if there are economies of scale (increasing returns to scale) simply by inspecting a diagram of historical cost data. Only the underlying analytical cost curve can supply this information.

Concepts for Review

Substitutability of inputs
Total product curve
Marginal physical product (MPP)
"Law" of diminishing marginal returns
Marginal revenue product (MRP)

Rule for optimal input use
 ($MRP = P$ of input)
Production function
Total cost curve
Average cost curve
Short, intermediate, and long runs

Cost minimization
Economies of scale (increasing returns to scale)
Constant returns to scale
Decreasing returns to scale
Historical versus analytical cost relationships

Questions for Discussion

1. If the marginal revenue product of a kilowatt hour of electric power is 8 cents and the cost of a kilowatt hour is 12 cents, what can the firm do to increase its profits?
2. A firm hires two workers and rents 15 acres of land for a season. It produces 100,000 bushels of crop. If it had doubled its land and labor, production would have been 300,000 bushels. Does it have constant, diminishing, or increasing returns to scale?
3. Suppose wages are $10,000 per season and land rent per acre is $3000. Calculate the average cost of 100,000 bushels and the average cost of 300,000 bushels, using the figures in Question 2 above. (Note that average costs diminish when output increases.) What connection do these figures have with the firm's returns to scale?
4. Farmer Pfister has bought a great deal of fertilizer. Suppose he now buys more *land*, but not more fertilizer, and spreads the fertilizer evenly over all his land. What may happen to the marginal physical product of fertil-

izer? What, therefore, is the role of input proportions in the determination of marginal physical product?
5. Labor costs $10 per hour. Nine workers produce $180 of product per hour. Ten workers produce $196 of product; 11 workers produce $208; and 12 workers produce $215. Draw up a table of the marginal revenue products of 9, 10, 11, and 12 workers. What is the optimal amount of labor for the firm to hire?
6. (More difficult) A firm finds there is a sudden increase in the demand for its product. In the short run, it must operate longer hours and pay higher overtime wage rates. In the long run, however, it will pay the firm to install more machines and not operate them for longer hours. Which do you think will be lower, the short-run or the long-run average cost of the increased output? How is your answer affected by the fact that the long-run average cost includes the new machines the firm buys, while the short-run average cost includes no machine purchases?

Appendix:
Production Indifference Curves

To describe a production function—that is, the relationship between input combinations and size of total output—we can use a graphic device called the **production indifference curve** instead of the sort of numerical information described in Table 20–4 in the chapter.

A **production indifference curve** (sometimes called an *isoquant*) is a curve in a graph showing quantities of *inputs* on its axes. Each indifference curve indicates *all* combinations of input quantities capable of producing *a given* quantity of output; thus, there must be a separate indifference curve for each quantity of output.

If you have read the appendix on indifference curves in Chapter 18 (on consumer choice), you will recognize a close analogy in logic (and in geometric shape) between consumers' and producers' indifference curves. Figure 20–10 represents different quantities of labor and capital capable of producing given amounts of wheat. The indifference curve labeled

220,000 indicates that an output of 220,000 bushels of wheat can be obtained with the aid of *any one* of the combinations of inputs represented by points on that curve. For example, it can be produced by 10 years of labor and 200 acres of land (point *A*) or, instead, it can be produced by the labor–capital combination shown by point *B* on the same curve. Because it lies considerably below and to the right of point *B*, point *A* represents a productive process that uses more labor and less land than shown at point *B*.

Points *A* and *B* can be considered *technologically* indifferent because each represents a bundle of inputs capable of yielding the same quantity of finished goods. However, "indifference" in this sense does not mean that the producer will be unable to make up his mind between input combinations *A* and *B*. Input prices will permit him to arrive at that decision, because the two input choices are not *economically* indifferent.

The production indifference curves in a diagram, such as Figure 20–10, constitute a complete description of the production function. For each combination of inputs, they show how much output can be produced. Since it is drawn in two dimensions, the diagram can deal only with two inputs at a time. In more realistic situations, there may be more than two inputs, and an algebraic analysis must be used. But all the principles we need to analyze such a situation can be derived from the two-variable case.

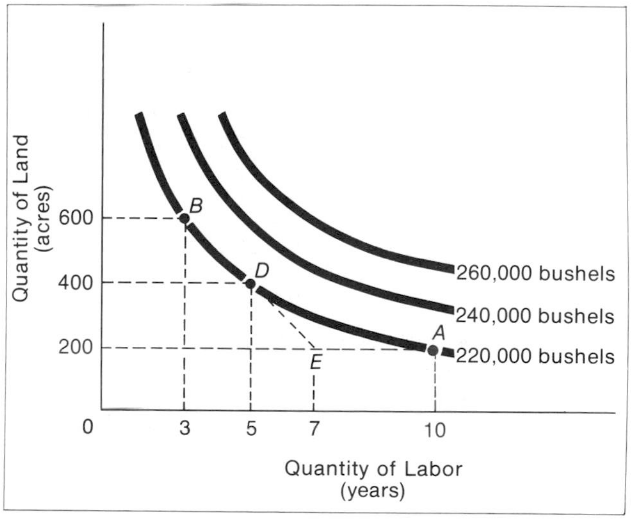

Characteristics of the Production Indifference Curves

Before discussing input pricing and quantity decisions, we first examine what is known about the shapes of production indifference curves. The main characteristics are straightforward and entirely analogous to the properties of consumer indifference curves discussed in the appendix to Chapter 18.

Characteristic 1: Higher curves correspond to larger outputs. Points on a higher indifference curve represent larger quantities of *both* inputs than the corresponding points on a lower curve. Thus, the higher the curve, the larger the output it represents.

Figure 20–10
A PRODUCTION INDIFFERENCE MAP
The figure shows three indifference curves, one for the production of 220,000 bushels of wheat, one for 240,000 bushels, and one for 260,000 bushels. For example, the lowest curve shows all combinations of land and labor capable of producing 220,000 bushels of wheat. Point *A* on that curve shows that 10 years of labor and 200 acres of land are enough to do the job.

Characteristic 2: The indifference curve will generally have a negative slope— it goes downhill as we move toward the right. This means that if we reduce the quantity of one input used, and we do not want to cut production, we must use more of another input. For example, if we want to use less labor to produce 220,000 bushels of wheat, we will have to farm more land to make up for the reduced labor input.

Characteristic 3: The curves are typically assumed to curve inward toward the origin near their "middle." This is a reflection of the "law" of diminishing returns to a single input. For example, in Figure 20–10, points B, D, and A represent three different input combinations capable of producing the same quantity of output. At point B a large amount of land and relatively little labor is used, while the opposite is true at point A. Point D is intermediate between the two. Indeed, point D is chosen so that its use of land is exactly halfway between the amounts of land used at A and at B.

Now consider the choice among these input combinations. As the farmer considers first the input combination at B, then the one at D, and finally the one at A, he is considering the use of less and less land, making up for it by the use of more and more labor so that he can continue to produce the same output. But the trade-off does not proceed at a constant rate because of diminishing returns in the substitution of labor for land.

When the farmer considers moving from point B to point D, he gives up 200 acres of land and instead hires two additional years of labor. Similarly, the move from D to A involves giving up another 200 acres of land. But this time, hiring an additional two years of labor does not make up for the reduced use of land. Diminishing returns to labor as he hires more and more workers to replace more and more land means that now a much larger quantity of additional labor, five years rather than two, is needed to make up for the reduction in the use of land. If there had been no such diminishing returns, the indifference curve would have been a straight line, DE. The curvature of the indifference curve through points D and A reflects diminishing returns to substitution of inputs.

The Choice of Input Combinations

A production indifference curve only describes what input combinations *can* produce a given output; it indicates the technological possibilities. A business cannot decide which of the available options suits its purposes best without the corresponding cost information: that is, the relative prices of the inputs.

Just as we did for the consumer in the appendix to Chapter 18, we can construct a **budget line**—a representation of equally costly input combinations—for the firm. For example, if farmhands are paid $9000 a year and land rents for $1000 per acre a year, then a farmer who spends $360,000 can hire 40 farmhands but rent no land (point K in Figure 20–11), or he can rent 360 acres but have no money left for farmhands (point J). But it is undoubtedly more sensible for him to pick some intermediate point on his budget line, JK, at which he divides the $360,000 between the two inputs.

There is an important difference, however, in how this budget line is used. The consumer had a fixed budget and sought the highest indifference curve attainable with these limited funds. The firm's problem in minimizing costs is just the reverse. Its budget is not fixed. Instead, it wants to produce a given quantity of output (say, 240,000 bushels) with the *smallest possible budget*.

A way to find the minimum budget capable of producing 240,000 bushels of wheat is illustrated in Figure 20–12, which combines the indifference curve for 240,000 bushels from Figure 20–10 with a variety of budget lines similar to JK in Figure 20–11. The firm's problem is to find the lowest budget line that will allow it to reach the 240,000 bushel indifference

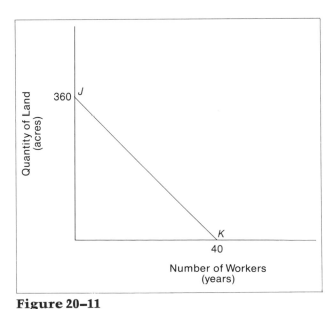

Figure 20–11
A BUDGET LINE
The firm's budget line, JK, shows all the combinations of inputs it can purchase with a fixed amount of money—in this case $360,000.

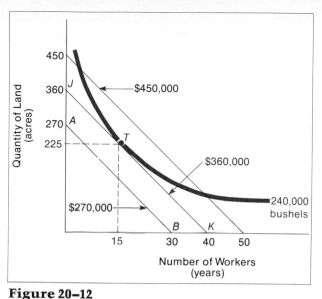

Figure 20–12

COST MINIMIZATION

The least costly way to produce 240,000 bushels of wheat is shown by point *T*, where the production indifference curve is tangent to budget line *JK*. Here the farmer is employing 15 workers and using 225 acres of land. It is not possible to produce 240,000 bushels on a smaller budget, and any larger budget would be wasteful.

curve. Clearly, an expenditure of $270,000 is too little; there is no point on budget line *AB* that permits production of 240,000 bushels. Similarly, an expenditure of $450,000 is too much, because the firm can produce its target level of output more cheaply. The solution is at point *T*, meaning that 15 workers and 225 acres of land are used to produce the 240,000 bushels of wheat. In general:

The least costly way to produce any given level of output is indicated by the point of tangency between a budget line and the production indifference curve corresponding to that level of output.

Effects of Changes in Input Prices

Suppose now that the cost of renting land increases and the wage rate of labor decreases. This means that the budget lines will differ from those depicted in Figure 20–12. Specifically, with land now more expensive, any given sum of money will rent fewer acres, so the intercept of each budget line on the vertical (land) axis will shift *downward*. Conversely, with labor cheaper, any given sum of money will buy more labor, so the intercept of the budget line on the horizontal (labor) axis will shift to the *right*. A series of budget lines corresponding to a $1500 per acre rental rate for land and a $6000 annual wage for labor is depicted in Figure 20–13. We see that these budget lines are less steep than those shown in Figure 20–12, and that the least costly way to produce 240,000 bushels of wheat is now given by point *E*.

To assist you in seeing how things change, Figure 20–14 combines in a single graph budget line *JK* and tangency point *T* from Figure 20–12 and budget line *WV* and tangency point *E* from Figure 20–13. Notice that point *E* lies below and to the right of *T*, meaning that as wages decrease and rents increase the firm will hire more labor and rent less land. As common sense suggests, when the price of one input rises in comparison with that of others, it will pay the firm to hire less

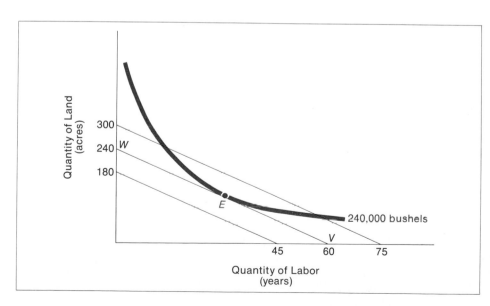

Figure 20–13

OPTIMAL INPUT CHOICE AT A DIFFERENT SET OF INPUT PRICES

If input prices change, the combination of inputs that minimizes costs will normally change, too. In this diagram, land rents for $1500 per acre (more than in Figure 20–12) while labor costs $6000 per year (less than in Figure 20–12). As a result, the least costly way to produce 240,000 bushels of wheat shifts from point *T* in Figure 20–12 to point *E* here.

of this input and more of other inputs to make up for its reduced use of the more expensive input.

In addition to this substitution of one input for another, a change in the price of an input may induce the firm to alter the level of output that it decides to produce. But this is the subject of the next chapter.

Figure 20–14
HOW CHANGES IN INPUT PRICES AFFECT INPUT PROPORTIONS
When land becomes more expensive and labor becomes cheaper, the budget lines (such as *JK*) become less steep than they were previously (see *WV*). As a result, the least costly way to produce 240,000 bushels shifts from point *T* to point *E*. The firm uses more labor and less land.

Summary

1. A production function can be fully described by a family of production indifference curves, each of which shows all the input combinations capable of producing a specified amount of output.

2. As long as each input has a positive marginal physical product, production indifference curves will have a negative slope and the higher curves will represent larger amounts of output than the lower curves. Because of diminishing returns, these curves characteris-

   tically bend toward the origin near their middle.

3. The optimal input combination for any given level of output is indicated by the point of tangency between a budget line and the appropriate production indifference curve.

4. When input prices change, firms will normally use more of the input that becomes relatively less expensive and less of the input that becomes relatively more expensive.

Concepts for Review

Production indifference curve
Budget line
Point of tangency between the budget
    line and the corresponding
    production indifference curve

Questions for Discussion

1. Typical Manufacturing Corporation (TMC) produces gadgets with the aid of two inputs: labor and glue. If labor costs $5 per hour and glue costs $5 per gallon, draw TMC's budget line for a total expenditure of $100,000.

   In this same diagram, sketch in a production indifference curve indicating that TMC can produce no

   more than 1000 gadgets with this expenditure.

2. Now suppose that wages rise to $10 per hour and glue prices rise to $6 per gallon. How are TMC's optimal input proportions likely to change? (Use a diagram to explain your answer.)

The Common Sense of Business Decisions: Outputs and Prices

Annual income twenty pounds, annual expenditure nineteen six, result happiness. Annual income twenty pounds, annual expenditure twenty pounds ought and six, result misery.

CHARLES DICKENS

W hen Chrysler Corporation introduced a new line of cars in 1980, it had to decide on the prices at which each model would be offered and the number of each to produce. These were clearly among the most crucial decisions the firm ever made. They had a vital influence on Chrysler's labor requirements, on the reception given the product by consumers, and, indeed, on the very survival of the company.

This chapter describes the tools that firms like Chrysler can use to make decisions on outputs and prices—tools that are equally useful to government agencies and nonprofit organizations in making analogous decisions. We begin the chapter by examining the relationship between the firm's price decisions and the quantity of product it sells. We then discuss the assumption of profit maximization before turning to the techniques firms can use to achieve the largest possible profit. We will explore, in words, with numerical examples, and with graphs, several methods of finding the level of output that maximizes profits. Each of these methods teaches us something else about the nature of the firm's decision-making process and provides some general lessons about the use of marginal analysis. A number of new terms, which will be used heavily in the following chapters, are introduced here for the first time; chief among these are *marginal revenue* and *marginal cost*. The chapter will explain why what are commonly called "overhead" expenses may not affect a firm's pricing or production decisions, and it will also show how it may be possible for a firm to make a profit by selling below cost.

Two Illustrative Cases[1]

Price and output decisions can perplex even the most experienced business people, as the following real-life illustrations show.

CASE 1: PRICING A SIX-PACK
The managers of one of America's largest manufacturers of soft drinks became concerned when a rival company introduced a cheaper substitute for one of their leading products. As a result, some of the firm's managers advocated a reduction

[1] The figures in these examples are doctored to help preserve the confidentiality of the information and to simplify the calculations. The cases, however, are real.

in the price of a six-pack from $1.50 to $1.35. This stimulated a heated debate. It was agreed that the price should be cut if it was not likely to reduce the company's profits. Although some of the managers maintained that the cut made sense because of the demand it would stimulate, others held that the price cut would hurt the company by cutting profit per unit of output. The company had reliable information about costs, but knew rather little about consumer responsiveness to price changes. At this point a group of consultants was called in to offer their suggestions. Their recommendation and the tools of analysis they used are described later in this chapter.

CASE 2: SAVING THE COMPANY BY SELLING BELOW COSTS
A supplier of a canned meat product was selling 10 million units per year at a wholesale price of $11 per unit. It found that rising wages and raw material prices had increased its costs to $13 per unit, which was clearly a losing proposition. Yet the availability of competing canned meats convinced the firm's managers that they could not get away with a price increase. At this point a purchasing agent for a foreign government approached the firm and offered to buy an additional 10 million units, but at a price of only $7 per unit. At first, management considered the offer ludicrous, since the $7 price came nowhere near covering the unit cost of $13. But after some analysis, management was able to show that the firm could actually clear up its financial problem by agreeing to the proposed sale even though it was "below cost." At the end of the chapter we will explain just how this was possible.

Price and Quantity: One Decision, Not Two

This chapter is about how firms, like those in the preceding cases, select a *price* and a *quantity* that best serve their financial interests. While it would seem that firms must choose two numbers, in fact they can pick only one. Once they have selected the *price*, the *quantity* they will sell is up to consumers. Alternatively, firms may decide *how much* they want to sell, but then they must leave it to the market to determine the *price* at which this quantity can be sold.

Management gets its two numbers by making only one decision because the firm's demand curve tells it, for any quantity it may decide to market, the highest possible price its product can fetch. For purposes of illustration, consider a hypothetical firm, Computron, Inc., which produces giant computers. Computron's demand curve, *DD* in Figure 21–1, shows that if the company decides to charge the relatively high price of $15 million per computer (point *a* on the curve), then it can sell only one unit per year. On the other hand, if it wants to sell as many as six computers per year, it can do so only by offering its product at the low price of $8 million (point *f*). In summary:

Each point on the demand curve represents a price–quantity pair. The firm can pick any such pair. But it can never pick the price corresponding to one point on the demand curve and the quantity corresponding to another point, since such an output would never be sold at the selected price.

Throughout this chapter, then, we will not discuss price and output decisions separately, for they are merely two different aspects of the same decision. To analyze this decision, we will make a strong assumption about the behavior of business firms, which, while not literally correct, seems to be a useful simplification of a much more complex reality—the assumption that firms strive for the largest possible total profit.

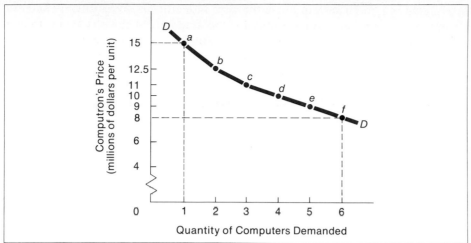

Figure 21–1
COMPUTRON'S
DEMAND CURVE
This graph shows the quantity
of product demanded at each
price. For example, the curve
shows that at a price of $8 mil-
lion (point *f*), six units will be
demanded.

Computron's Price
(millions of dollars per unit)

Quantity of Computers Demanded

Do Firms Really Maximize Profits?

Naturally, many people have questioned whether firms really try to maximize
profits. Business people are like other human beings: their motives are varied and
complex. Given the choice, many executives might prefer to control the largest
firm rather than the most profitable one. Some may be influenced by envy, others
by a desire to "do good." Different managers within the same firm may not
always agree with one another. Thus, any attempt to summarize the objectives of
management in terms of a single number (profit) is bound to be an oversimplification.

In addition, the exacting requirements for maximizing profits are more easily
stated than adhered to. In practice, they are met infrequently. In deciding on
how much to invest, on what price to set for a product, or on how much to allocate
to the advertising budget, the range of available alternatives is enormous. And
information about each alternative is often expensive and difficult to acquire. As
a result, when a firm's management decides on an $18 million construction
budget it rarely compares the consequences of that decision in any detail with the
consequences of the possible alternatives—such as budgets of $17 million or $19
million. Rather, management normally studies with care only the likely effects of
the proposed decision itself: What sort of plant will it obtain for the money? How
costly will it be to operate the plant? How much revenue is it likely to obtain from
the sale of the plant's output?

Management's concern is with *whether the decision will produce results
that satisfy the firm's standards of acceptability*—whether its risks will not be
unacceptably great, whether its profits will not be unacceptably low, and so on.
Such analysis does not necessarily lead to the maximum possible profit, because,
though the decision may be good, some of the alternatives that have *not* been
investigated may be better. Decision making that seeks only acceptable solutions
has been called **satisficing** to contrast with optimizing. Some analysts, such as
Carnegie-Mellon University's Nobel Prize winner Herbert Simon, have concluded
that decision making in industry and government is often of the satisficing
variety.

But even if this is true, it does not necessarily make profit maximization a bad
assumption. Recall our discussion of abstraction and model-building in Chapter
1. A map of Los Angeles that omits thousands of roads is no doubt "wrong" if

interpreted as a literal description of the city. Nonetheless, by capturing the most important elements of reality, it may help us understand the city better than a map that is cluttered with too much detail. Similarly, we can learn much about the behavior of business firms by assuming that they try to maximize profits, even though we know that *all* of them do not act this way *all* of the time.

Total Profit: The Important Difference

A firm's **total profit** is, by definition, the difference between what it earns in the form of sales revenue and what it pays out in the form of costs:

$$\text{Total profit} = \text{Total revenue} - \text{Total costs} .$$

As suggested in the opening quotation of this chapter, it matters quite a lot to the firm whether this difference turns out to be positive (a profit) or negative (a loss). Mindful of the preceding discussion, we shall assume throughout the chapter that the firm seeks to maximize its total profit.

We know from preceding chapters that both **total revenue** (TR) and **total cost** (TC) depend on the output–price combination the firm selects. Total revenue can be calculated directly from the demand curve, since it is the product of price times quantity:

$$\text{TR} = P \times Q .$$

Table 21–1 shows how the total revenue schedule is derived from the demand schedule for our illustrative firm, Computron. The first two columns simply express the demand curve of Figure 21–1 in tabular form. The third column gives, for each quantity, the product of price times quantity. For example, if Computron markets three computers per year at a price of $11 million per computer, its annual sales revenue will be $3 \times \$11$ million $= \$33$ million.

Figure 21–2 displays Computron's total revenue schedule in graphical form as the black TR curve. This graph shows precisely the same information as the demand curve in Figure 21–1, but in a somewhat different form. For example, point *d* on the demand curve in Figure 21–1, which shows a price–quantity combination of $P = \$10$ million and $Q = 4$ computers, appears as point *D* in Figure 21–2 as a total revenue of $40 million ($10 million price per unit times 4

Table 21–1
DEMAND SCHEDULE AND TOTAL REVENUE SCHEDULE FOR COMPUTRON, INC.
(Data corresponding to Figure 21–1)

NUMBER OF COMPUTERS (per year)	PRICE (millions of dollars per computer)	TOTAL REVENUE (millions of dollars per year)
0	—	0
1	15	15
2	12.5	25
3	11	33
4	10	40
5	9	45
6	8	48

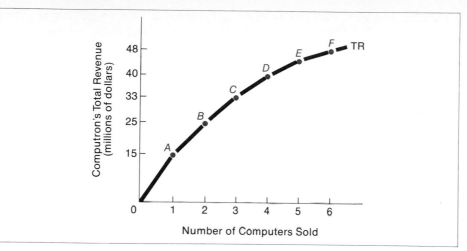

Figure 21–2
COMPUTRON'S TOTAL
REVENUE CURVE
The total revenue curve for
Computron, Inc., is derived directly from the demand curve,
since total revenue is the product of price times quantity.
Points *A, B, C, D, E,* and *F*
in this diagram correspond
to points *a, b, c, d, e,* and *f,*
respectively, in Figure 21–1.

units) corresponding to a quantity of four computers. Similarly, each point on
the TR curve in Figure 21–2 corresponds to the similarly labeled point in Figure
21–1.

The relationship between the demand curve and the TR curve can be
rephrased in a slightly different way. Since the price of the product is the revenue
per unit that the firm receives, we can view the demand curve as the curve of
average revenue. Average revenue (AR) and total revenue (TR) are related
to one another in the same way as average cost and total cost.[2] Specifically, since

Average revenue (AR) is
total revenue (TR) divided by
quantity.

$$AR = \frac{TR}{Q} = \frac{P \times Q}{Q} = P,$$

average revenue and price are two names for the same thing.

The revenue side is, of course, only one-half the profit picture. We must turn
to the cost side for the other half. The last chapter explained how the total cost
(TC) and average cost (AC) schedules are determined by the firm's production
techniques and the prices of the inputs it buys. Rather than repeat this analysis,
we simply list the total and average cost schedules for Computron in Table 21–2.
Figure 21–3 depicts the total cost curve as the blue TC curve.

[2]See the appendix to this chapter for a general discussion of the relationship between totals and
averages.

Table 21–2
TOTAL AND AVERAGE COSTS FOR COMPUTRON, INC.

NUMBER OF UNITS (per year)	TOTAL COST (millions of dollars)	AVERAGE COST (millions of dollars per unit)
0	2	—
1	9	9
2	14	7
3	21	7
4	32	8
5	45	9
6	60	10

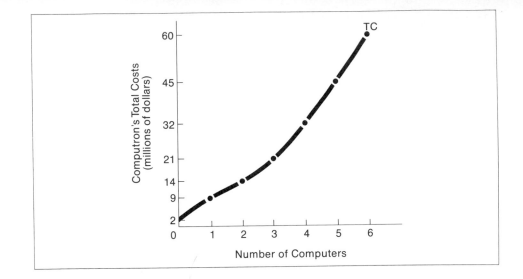

Figure 21–3

COMPUTRON'S TOTAL COST CURVE

The graph shows, for each possible level of output, Computron's total costs. Because Computron has some fixed costs, the level of total cost at zero output is $2 million, not zero.

Fixed costs are costs that do not depend on the volume of output that is produced.

Variable costs are costs that vary with the quantity of output.

Notice that total costs at zero output are not zero. Computron incurs **fixed costs** of $2 million per year even if it produces nothing. For example, Computron will have to pay the rent for its factory and the salary of its president whether it produces one computer, five computers, or ten. These are *fixed costs*. On the other hand, the amount of labor Computron hires and the number of integrated circuits it buys depend on how many computers it manufactures. These are examples of **variable costs,** which naturally increase as output increases. The distinction between fixed and variable costs will assume great importance later in the chapter.

To study how total profit depends on output, we bring together in Table 21–3 the total revenue and total cost schedules. The last column in Table 21–3, total profit, is just the difference between total revenue and total cost for each level of output. Remembering that Computron's assumed objective is to maximize its profits, it is a simple matter to determine the level of production it will choose. By producing and selling three computers per year, Computron achieves the highest level of profits it is capable of achieving—some $12 million per year. Any higher or lower rate of production would lead to lower profits. For example, profits would drop to $8 million if output were expanded to four units.

Table 21–3

TOTAL REVENUES, COSTS, AND PROFIT FOR COMPUTRON, INC.

NUMBER OF UNITS (per year)	TOTAL REVENUE	TOTAL COST	TOTAL PROFIT
		(millions of dollars per year)	
0	0	2	−2
1	15	9	6
2	25	14	11
3	33	21	12
4	40	32	8
5	45	45	0
6	48	60	−12

Profit Maximization: A Graphical Interpretation

Precisely the same analysis can be presented graphically. In the upper portion of Figure 21–4 we bring together into a single diagram the total revenue curve from Figure 21–2 and the total cost curve from Figure 21–3. Total profit, which is the difference between total revenue and total cost, appears in the diagram as the *vertical* distance between the TR and TC curves. For example, when output is four units, total revenue is $40 million (point *A*), total cost is $32 million (point *B*), and total profit is the distance between points *A* and *B*, or $8 million.

In this graphical view of the problem, Computron wants to maximize total profit, which is the vertical distance between the TR and TC curves. The curve of total profit is drawn in the lower portion of Figure 21–4. We see that it reaches its maximum value, $12 million, at an output level of three units per year. This is, naturally, the same conclusion we reached with the aid of Table 21–3.

The total profit curve in Figure 21–4 is shaped like a hill. Though such a shape is not inevitable, we expect a hill shape to be typical for the following reason. If a firm produces nothing, it certainly earns no profit, and it will probably incur a loss if it has an idle factory on its hands and must spend money to guard it and keep it from deteriorating. At the other extreme, a firm can produce so much output that it swamps the market, forcing price down so low that it again loses money. Only at intermediate levels of output—something between zero and the

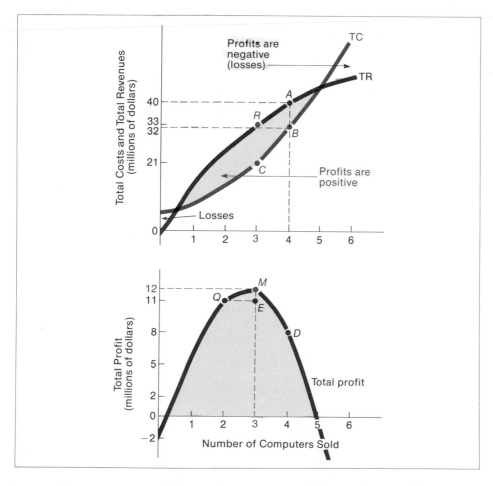

Figure 21–4
PROFIT MAXIMIZATION: A GRAPHICAL INTERPRETATION
Computron's profits are maximized when the vertical distance between its total revenue curve, TR, and its total cost curve, TC, is at its maximum. In the diagram, this occurs at an output of three units per year; total profits are CR, or $12 million. The total profit curve is also shown in the figure. Naturally, it reaches its maximum value ($12 million) at three units (point *M*).

amount that floods the market—will the company earn a positive profit. Consequently, the total profit curve will rise from zero (or negative) levels at a very small output, to positive levels in between; and, finally, it will fall to negative levels when output gets too large. Thus, the total profit curve will normally be a hill like the one shown in Figure 21–4.

Marginal Analysis and Profit Maximization

If management really knew the exact shape of its profit hill, choosing the optimal level of output would be a simple task indeed. It would only have to locate a point like M in Figure 21–4, the top of its profit hill. However, management rarely if ever has so much information, so a different technique for finding the optimum is required. That technique is **marginal analysis**—the same set of tools that the consumer used to maximize utility in Chapter 18 and that the firm used to minimize costs in Chapter 20.

Marginal profit is the addition to total profit that results when the firm adds one unit to its total output.

To see how marginal analysis helps solve Computron's problem, we introduce a new concept: **marginal profit.** Referring back to Table 21–3, for example, we see that an increase in Computron's annual output from two to three computers would raise total profit from $11 million to $12 million. That is, it would generate $1 million in *additional* profits, which we call the *marginal profit* resulting from the addition of the third unit. Similarly, marginal profit from the fourth unit would be:

$$\frac{\text{Total profit}}{\text{from 4 units}} - \frac{\text{Total profit}}{\text{from 3 units}} = \$8 \text{ million} - \$12 \text{ million} = -\$4 \text{ million} .$$

The marginal rule for finding the optimal level of output is easy to understand:

If the marginal profit from increasing output by one unit is positive, then output should be increased. If the marginal profit from increasing output by one unit is negative, then output should be decreased.

In the Computron example, the marginal profit from the third unit is $+\$1$ million, so it pays to produce the third unit. But marginal profit from the fourth unit is $-\$4$ million, so the firm should not produce the fourth. Since Computron is dealing in whole numbers (for example, it cannot produce 3.12 computers) it cannot achieve a marginal profit of exactly zero. But by producing three units per year it comes quite close.

The profit hill in Figure 21–4 gives us a graphical interpretation of the "marginal profit equals zero" condition. Marginal profit is defined as the additional profit that accrues to the firm when output rises by one unit. So, when output is increased, say, from two units to three units (the distance QE in Figure 21–4), total profit rises by $1 million (the distance EM) and marginal profit is therefore EM/QE. This is precisely the definition of the *slope* of the total profit curve between points Q and M. In general:

Marginal profit is the slope of the total profit curve.

With this geometric interpretation in hand, we can easily understand the logic of the marginal profit rule. At a point such as Q, where the total profit curve is rising, marginal profit (= slope) is positive. Profits cannot be maximal at such a point, because we can increase profits by moving farther to the right. A firm that decided to stick to point Q would be wasting the opportunity to increase profits by increasing output. Similarly, the firm cannot be maximizing profits at a point like *D*, where the slope of the curve is negative, because there marginal profit (= slope) is negative. If it finds itself at a point like *D*, the firm can raise its profit by decreasing its output. Only at a point such as *M*, where the total profit curve is neither rising nor falling, can the firm possibly be at the top of the profit hill rather than on one of the sides of the hill. And point *M* is precisely where the slope of the curve—and hence the marginal profit—is zero. *An output decision cannot be optimal unless the corresponding marginal profit is zero.*

The firm is not interested in marginal profit for its own sake, but rather for what it implies about *total* profit. Marginal profit is like the needle on the pressure gauge of a boiler: the needle itself is of no concern to anyone, but if one fails to watch it the consequences may be quite dramatic.

One common misunderstanding that arises in discussions of the marginal criterion of optimality is the idea that it seems foolish to go to a point where marginal profit is zero. "Isn't it better to earn a positive marginal profit?" This notion springs from a confusion between the quantity one is seeking to maximize (*total* profit) and the gauge that indicates whether such a maximum has in fact been attained (*marginal* profit). Of course it is better to have a positive *total* profit than zero total profit. But a zero value on the *marginal* profit gauge merely indicates that all is apparently well, that *total* profit may be at its maximum.

Marginal Revenue and Marginal Cost: Guides to an Optimum

If, as we suggested before, the firm really does not know what its total profit curve looks like, how can it determine whether marginal profit is positive, negative, or zero? To answer this, refer back to Figure 21–4, where the profit hill was constructed from the total revenue (TR) and total cost (TC) curves. Observe that there is another way of finding the profit-maximizing solution. We want to maximize the vertical distance between the TR and TC curves. This distance, we see, is not maximal at an output level such as two units, because there the two curves are growing farther apart. If we move farther to the right, the vertical distance between them (which is total profit) will increase. Conversely, we have not maximized the vertical distance between TR and TC at an output level such as four units, because there the two curves are coming closer together. We can add to profits by moving farther to the left (reducing output).

TP = TR−TC

The conclusion from the graph, then, is that total profit (the vertical distance between TR and TC) is maximized only when the two curves are neither growing farther apart nor coming closer together; that is, when their *slopes* are equal. While this conclusion is rather mechanical, we can breathe some life into it by interpreting the slopes of the two curves as **marginal revenue** and **marginal cost,** two terms that are defined in the margin. These terms permit us to restate the geometric conclusion we have just reached in an economically significant way:

Profit can be maximized only at an output level at which marginal revenue is (approximately) equal to marginal cost. In symbols:

$$MR = MC.$$

Table 21–4 illustrates the construction of marginal revenue and marginal cost figures from the corresponding data on total revenue and total cost. The process is by now familiar. The table also shows, as must be the case, that the MR = MC rule leads us to the same conclusion as the marginal profit equals zero

Marginal revenue, often abbreviated MR, is the *addition* to total revenue resulting from the addition of one unit to total output. Geometrically, marginal revenue is the *slope* of the total revenue curve.

Marginal cost, often abbreviated MC, is the *addition* to total cost resulting from the addition of one unit to total output. Geometrically, marginal cost is the *slope* of the total cost curve.

Table 21–4

MARGINAL REVENUE AND MARGINAL COST FOR COMPUTRON, INC.

NUMBER OF UNITS	TOTAL REVENUE	MARGINAL REVENUE	TOTAL COST	MARGINAL COST	MP
0	0	—	2	—	
1	15	15	9	7	8
2	25	10	14	5	5
3	33	8	21	7	1
4	40	7	32	11	−4
5	45	5	45	13	
6	48	3	60	15	

rule:[3] Computron should produce and sell three computers per year. The marginal revenue of the third computer is $8 million ($33 million from selling three computers less $25 million from selling two) while the marginal cost is only $7 million ($21 million minus $14 million). So the firm should produce the third unit. But the fourth computer brings in only $7 million in marginal revenue while its marginal cost is $11 million—clearly a losing proposition.

Because graphs will prove so useful in the following chapters, Figure 21–5 shows the MR = MC condition for profit maximization graphically. The black curve labeled MR in the figure is the marginal revenue schedule from Table 21–4. The blue curve labeled MC is the marginal cost schedule. They intersect at point E, which is, therefore, the point where marginal revenue and marginal cost are equal. The optimal output for Computron is three units.[4]

[3]You may have surmised by now that just as total profit = total revenue − total cost, it must be true that marginal profit = marginal revenue − marginal cost. This is in fact correct. It also shows that when marginal profit = 0 we must have MR = MC.

[4]One important qualification must be entered. Sometimes marginal revenue and marginal cost curves do not have the nice shapes depicted in Figure 21–5, and they may intersect more than once. In such cases, while it remains true that MC = MR at the output level that maximizes profits, there may be other output levels at which MC is also equal to MR but at which profits are not maximized.

Figure 21–5

PROFIT MAXIMIZATION: ANOTHER GRAPHICAL INTERPRETATION

Profits are maximized where marginal revenue (MR) is (approximately) equal to marginal cost (MC), for only at such a point will *marginal profit* be zero. This diagram shows the MR = MC condition for profit maximization graphically as point E, where output is close to three computers. Since Computron does not produce fractions of computers, the best it can do is to produce three of them.

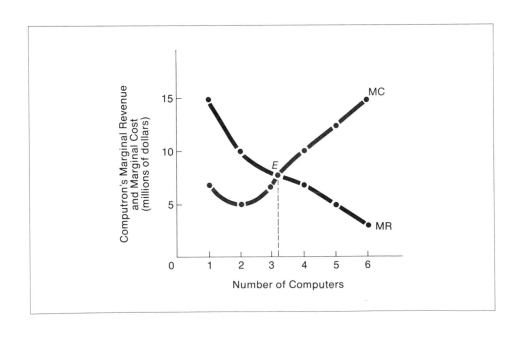

Fixed and Marginal Costs

The pivotal role of marginal cost in the determination of the optimal level of output explains why our earlier distinction between *fixed* costs and *variable* costs is so important. The reason is that *marginal fixed cost is always zero.* This fact follows directly from the definition of marginal fixed cost as the *additional* fixed cost attributable to increasing output by one unit.[5] Since fixed costs do not change when output is increased, marginal fixed cost must be zero. This seemingly trivial piece of arithmetic is important because it tells us that changes in a firm's fixed costs do not affect marginal fixed cost (which is always zero), and hence do not affect the marginal cost (MC) curve. As a consequence:

∴ MC = MVC.

Since changes in fixed costs do not affect the marginal cost (MC) curve, they cannot affect the firm's choice of a profit-maximizing output level.

Thus, for example, if Computron's fixed costs were to rise to $4 million or fall to zero, the marginal cost curve that we drew in Figure 21–5 would be unaffected, and it would still be optimal to produce three computers and charge a price of $11 million, just as before.

This startling finding often confuses both students and business managers. You may be asking yourself, Can this be true? Does the firm really not care about substantial changes in its fixed costs? The answer is that the firm certainly *does* care very much. It is not indifferent to changes in fixed costs, and will do everything in its power to keep them as low as possible (to "cut down on overhead"). A rise in fixed costs can cause stockholders to lose money and may cost the managers their jobs. The point, however, is that:

Changes in fixed costs will change the amount of profit that the firm earns, and might even turn profits into losses. But they do not give the firm any reason to change its price–output decision.

To convince yourself of the validity of this conclusion, go back to Computron's cost data in Table 21–2 and suppose that fixed costs increased from $2 million per year to $14 million per year—a rise of $12 million. Computron's cost picture would now be as shown in Table 21–5, where we now distinguish between fixed

[5] For a general discussion of the relationships among totals, averages, and marginals, see the appendix to this chapter.

Table 21–5
COST DATA FOR COMPUTRON, INC. AFTER A RISE IN FIXED COST

(1)	(2)	(3)	(4)	(5)	(6)	(7)
	TOTAL	TOTAL			AVERAGE	
NUMBER OF	FIXED	VARIABLE	TOTAL	AVERAGE	VARIABLE	MARGINAL
UNITS SUPPLIED	COST	COST	COST	COST	COST	COST = MVC.
0	14	0	14	—	—	—
1	14	7	21	21	7	7
2	14	12	26	13	6	5
3	14	19	33	11	6.33	7
4	14	30	44	11	7.50	11
5	14	43	57	11.40	8.60	13
6	14	58	72	12	9.67	15

and variable costs. Total fixed cost is $14 million for any level of output (column 2). Total variable cost in column 3 is the same as it was previously. (You can verify that each entry in column 3 of Table 21–5 is exactly $2 million less than the total cost figures we used in previous tables.) Total cost, the sum of total fixed cost plus total variable cost, is given in column 4, and average cost is calculated in column 5. Column 6 lists a new concept that we have not encountered before: **average variable cost.** Its definition is fairly obvious.

The most important information in Table 21–5 is in column 7, which lists Computron's marginal costs after the rise in fixed cost. We observe that the huge increase in fixed cost has had no effect on the marginal cost schedule, just as was claimed. A change in fixed cost, therefore, can have no effect on optimal output. It will, however, have a very dramatic effect on the profitability of Computron, Inc. As you can verify by comparing the total cost figures in Table 21–5 with the total revenue figures in Table 21–4, it is now impossible for Computron to make a profit. The best it can do is break even (total cost = total revenue), which it achieves by producing the same three units it was producing before.[6]

Fixed costs, it would appear, are totally irrelevant to optimal decision making. This conclusion, however, is subject to one important qualification. If fixed costs become too high, the firm will be better off in the long run if it closes its doors and saves the fixed costs. In the example just considered, $14 million is the highest value of fixed costs under which Computron will continue to operate. Should fixed costs rise to $15 million, even the optimal level of production would give Computron a $1 million loss. In this case, Computron would be better off going out of business.

Marginal Analysis in Real Decision Problems

We can now put the analysis of profit maximization to work to unravel the puzzles with which we began this chapter.

CASE 1: THE SODA-PRICING PROBLEM
Our first problem dealt with a firm's choice between keeping the price of a brand of soda at $1.50 per six-pack or reducing it to $1.35 when a competitor entered the market. The trouble was that to know what to do, the firm needed to know its demand curve (and hence its marginal revenue curve). However, the firm did not have enough data to determine the shape of its demand curve. How, then, could a rational decision be made?

As we indicated, the debate among the firm's managers finally reached agreement on one point: The price should be cut if, as a result, profits were not likely to decline; that is, if *marginal profit* were not negative. Fortunately, the data needed to determine whether marginal profit was positive were obtainable. Initial annual sales were 10 million units, and the firm's engineers maintained emphatically that marginal costs were very close to constant at $1.20 per six-pack over the output range in question. Instead of trying to determine the *actual* increase in sales that would result from the price cut, the team of consultants decided to try to determine the *minimum necessary* increase in quantity demanded required to avoid a decrease in profits.

It was clear that the firm needed additional revenue at least as great as the

---

[6]EXERCISE: Use the new total cost data from Table 21–5 and the old total revenue data from Table 21–3 to construct a new total profit hill. Compare it with the bottom portion of Figure 21–4, and show that both reach a maximum at the same level of output.

Average variable cost is the variable cost per unit of output. It is calculated by dividing total variable cost by the level of output.

additional cost of supplying the added volume, if profits were not to decline. The consultants knew that sales at the initial price of $1.50 per six-pack were $15 million ($1.50 per unit times 10 million units). Letting Q represent the (unknown) quantity of six-packs that would be sold at the proposed new price of $1.35, the economists compared the added revenue with the added cost of providing the Q new units. Since MC was constant at $1.20 per unit, the added cost amounted to:

$$\text{Added cost} = \$1.20 \times (Q - 10 \text{ million}).$$

This was to be compared with the added revenue:

$$\text{Added revenue} = \text{New revenue} - \text{Old revenue}$$
$$= \$1.35Q - \$15 \text{ million}.$$

No loss would result from the price change if the added revenue was greater than or equal to the added cost. The minimum Q necessary to avoid a loss therefore was that at which added revenue equaled added cost, or

$$1.35Q - 15 \text{ million} = 1.2Q - 12 \text{ million},$$

or

$$0.15Q = 3 \text{ million}.$$

This would be true if, and only if, Q, the quantity sold at the lower price, would be

$$Q = 20 \text{ million units}.$$

In other words, this calculation showed that the firm could break even from the 15-cent price reduction only if the quantity of its product demanded rose at least 100 percent (from 10 to 20 million units). Since past experience indicated that such a rise in quantity demanded was hardly possible, the price reduction proposal was quickly abandoned. Thus the concept of marginal profit, plus a little ingenuity, enabled the consultants to deal with a problem that at first seemed baffling.

CASE 2: THE UNPROFITABLE CANNED MEAT PRODUCER
Our second case study concerned a firm that was losing money (because the price of its canned meat product was less than its average cost) and that was then offered the questionable opportunity to sell more of its product to a foreign buyer at a price that was lower still. The relevant information is summarized in Table 21–6. Obviously, this firm was in a bad way financially. Its average cost was $13, and yet the price it was charging for its product was only $11 per unit; so it was losing money on this product. Indeed, we see that it lost $20 million on the 10 million units of output it sold.

Table 21–6
INITIAL COSTS AND REVENUES OF THE CANNED MEAT PRODUCER

UNITS SOLD (millions)	TOTAL COST (millions of dollars)	AVERAGE COST	MARGINAL COST	PRICE (dollars)	TOTAL REVENUE	TOTAL COST	PROFIT OR LOSS
		(dollars)			(millions of dollars)		
10	130	13	3	11	110	130	−20

Table 21–7

COST AND REVENUES OF THE SUPPLIER OF CANNED MEAT AFTER SALES "BELOW COST"

UNITS SOLD (millions)	TOTAL COST (millions of dollars)	AVERAGE COST	MARGINAL COST	TOTAL REVENUE	TOTAL COST	PROFIT OR LOSS
			(dollars)		(millions of dollars)	
20	160	8	3	180	160	+20

Management might well have reasoned this way: It would be desirable to expand our volume, but we can't afford to do so. Instead, we must raise our price above our $13 average cost, even if it cuts down our sales. While the managers were pondering their dilemma, a foreign purchasing group offered to buy an additional 10 million units of the company's canned meat product if the company would supply the units at a discount price of $7. On an average cost calculation this arrangement seemed disastrous. After all, AC was $13 and the company was already losing money at a price of $11. How could it possibly afford to sell at an even lower price?

But was the proposition so ludicrous? With its marginal costs approximately constant at $3, by accepting the offer the company could change its situation from that shown in Table 21–6 to that shown in Table 21–7. We see that the total number of units sold will have doubled, from 10 to 20 million. Total costs will have risen from $130 million to $160 million. That is, they will have gone up $30 million (the MC of $3 on each of the 10 million additional units). The arithmetic shows that, as a consequence, AC *must* have fallen from $13 = $130/10 to $8 = $160/20. The last three columns report the resulting "miracle." The apparently ridiculous proposition that 10 million additional units of canned meat be sold at a price below either the old or the new average cost in fact succeeded in eliminating the deficit and actually put the company into the black, to the tune of $20 million in net profits. Just how was this "miracle" accomplished? The answer becomes clear when we apply the rules we have learned in this chapter. In Table 21–6, it can be seen that AC was indeed $13; but the corresponding MC figure was only $3. Therefore, every *additional* unit sold to the foreign buyer at a price of $7 brought in a marginal profit of $7 − $3 = $4. On such terms the more one sells the better off one is.

This case illustrates a point that is encountered frequently. The canned meat supplier was offered an opportunity to deal with a new class of customers at a price that appeared not to cover costs but really did. The same sort of issue frequently faces a firm considering the introduction of a new product or the opening of a new branch office. In many such cases the new operation may not cover *average* costs as measured by standard accounting methods. Yet to follow the apparent implications of those cost figures would amount to throwing away a valuable opportunity to add to the net earnings of the firm and, perhaps, to contribute to the welfare of the economy. Only *marginal* analysis can reveal whether the contemplated action is really worthwhile.

Conclusion: The Fundamental Role of Marginal Analysis

One of the most important conclusions that can be drawn from the last four chapters, a conclusion brought out vividly by the two examples we have just discussed, is that:

In any decision about whether to expand an activity, it is always the *marginal* cost and *marginal* revenue that are the relevant factors. A calculation based on *average* figures is likely to lead the decision maker to miss all sorts of opportunities, some of them critical.

More generally, if one wants to make *optimal* decisions, *marginal analysis* should be used in the planning calculations. This is true whether the decision applies to a business firm seeking to maximize profit or minimize cost, to a consumer trying to maximize utility, or to a less developed country striving to maximize per capita output. It applies as much to decisions on input proportions and advertising as to decisions about output levels and prices. Indeed, this is such a general principle of economics that it is one of the 12 Ideas for Beyond the Final Exam.

A real-life example far removed from profit maximization will illustrate the way in which marginal criteria are useful in decision making. For some years before women were admitted to Princeton University (and to several other colleges), the cost of the proposed change was frequently cited as a major obstacle. It had been decided in advance that any woman coming to the university would constitute a net addition to the student body because, for a variety of reasons involving relations with alumni and other groups, a reduction in the number of male students was not feasible. Presumably on the basis of a calculation of average cost, some critics spoke of figures as high as $80 million.

To economists it was clear, however, that the relevant figure was the *marginal* cost, the addition to total cost that would result from the introduction of the additional students. The women students would, of course, bring to Princeton additional tuition fees (marginal revenues). If these fees were just sufficient to cover the amount they would add to costs, the admission of the women would leave the university's financial picture unaffected.

A careful calculation showed that the admission of women would add far less to the university's financial problems than the *average cost* figures indicated. One reason was that women's course preferences are characteristically different from men's and hence women frequently elect courses that are undersubscribed in exclusively male institutions. Therefore, the admission of one thousand women to a formerly all-male institution may require fewer additional courses than if one thousand more men had been admitted.[7] More important, it was found that a number of classroom buildings were underutilized. The cost of operating these buildings was nearly fixed—their total utilization cost would be changed only slightly by the influx of women. The corresponding marginal cost was therefore almost zero and certainly well below the average cost (cost per student).

For all these reasons, it turned out that the relevant marginal cost figure was much smaller than the figures that had been bandied about earlier. Indeed, this cost was something like a third of the earlier estimates. There is little doubt that this careful marginal calculation played a critical role in the admission of women to Princeton and to some other institutions that made use of the calculations in the Princeton analysis. Subsequent data, incidentally, confirmed that the marginal calculations were amply justified.

[7]See Gardner Patterson, "The Education of Women at Princeton," *Princeton Alumni Weekly*, Vol. LXIX, September 24, 1968.

A Look Back and a Look Forward

We have now completed four chapters describing how consumers and business managers can make optimal decisions. Can you go to Wall Street or Main Street and find executives calculating marginal cost and marginal revenue in order to decide how much to produce? Hardly. Not any more than you can find consumers in stores computing their marginal utilities in order to decide what to buy. Like consumers, successful business people often rely heavily on intuition and "hunches" that cannot be described by any set of rules.

However, we have not sought a literal *description* of consumer and business behavior, but rather a *model* to help us analyze and predict this behavior. Just as astronomers construct models of the behavior of objects that do not think at all, economists construct models of consumers and business people who do think, but whose thought processes may be rather different from those of economists. In the chapters that follow we will use these models to serve the purposes for which they were designed: to analyze the functioning of a market economy, and to see what things it does well and what things it does poorly.

Summary

1. A firm can choose the quantity of its product it wants to sell or the price it wants to charge. But it cannot choose both because price affects the quantity demanded.

2. In economic theory, it is usually assumed that firms seek to maximize profits. This should not be taken literally, but rather interpreted as a useful simplification of reality.

3. If the firm wants to choose the output combination that maximizes its *total* profit, it must find an output at which *marginal* profit equals zero.

4. Geometrically, the profit-maximizing output level occurs at the highest point of the total profit curve. There the slope of the total profit curve is zero, meaning that marginal profit is zero.

5. Marginal revenue is the additional revenue earned by increasing sales by one unit. Marginal cost is the additional cost incurred by increasing production by one unit.

6. The requirement for maximum profit can be restated as choosing the level of output at which marginal revenue is equal to marginal cost.

7. A fixed cost is defined as a cost that does not change when the firm increases its output. Marginal fixed cost is therefore always zero.

8. Fixed costs never affect the optimal output decision in the short run. Fixed costs influence only the long-run decision of whether to produce any output at all.

9. It may pay a firm to expand its output if it is selling at a price greater than marginal cost, even if that price happens to be below average cost.

10. Optimal decisions must be made on the basis of marginal cost and marginal revenue figures, not average cost and average revenue figures. This is one of the 12 Ideas for Beyond the Final Exam.

Concepts for Review

Profit maximization
Satisficing
Total profit
Total revenue and cost

Average revenue and cost
Fixed costs
Variable costs
Marginal analysis

Marginal profit
Marginal revenue and cost
Average variable cost

Questions for Discussion

1. "It may be rational for a firm not to try to maximize profits." Discuss the circumstances under which this statement may be true.

2. Suppose the firm's demand curve indicates that at a price of $5 per unit, customers will demand two million units of its product. Suppose management decides to pick *both* price and output, produces three million units of its product, and prices it at $7. What will happen?

3. Suppose a firm's management would be pleased to increase its share of the market, but if it expands its production the price of its product will fall and so its profits will decline somewhat. What choices are available to this firm? What would you do if you were president of this company?

4. Why does it make sense for a firm to seek to maximize *total* profit, rather than to maximize *marginal* profit?

5. A firm's marginal revenue is $17 and its marginal cost is $9. What amount of profit does the firm fail to pick up by refusing to increase output by one unit?

6. A firm has fixed costs of $200. Construct a table showing its total, average, and marginal fixed costs for outputs up to and including four units. Draw the graphs of these three costs.

7. A firm's total cost is $150 if it produces one unit, $250 if it produces two units, and $300 if it produces three

units of output. Draw up a table of total, average, and marginal costs for this firm.

8. Draw an average and marginal cost curve for the firm in Question 7. Describe the relationship between the two curves.

9. A firm with no fixed costs has the demand and total cost schedules given in the table below. If it wants to maximize profits, how much output should it produce?

QUANTITY	PRICE (dollars)	TOTAL COST (dollars)
1	5	1
2	4	2
3	3	4
4	2	7
5	1	11

Appendix
The Relationships Among Total, Average, and Marginal Data

You may have surmised that there is a close connection between the average revenue and average cost curves and the corresponding marginal revenue and marginal cost curves. After all, we deduced our total revenue figures from the average revenue and then calculated our marginal revenue figures from the total revenues; and a similar chain of deduction applied to costs. In fact:

Marginal, average, and total figures are inextricably bound together. From any one of the three, the other two can be calculated. Total, average, and marginal figures bear relationships to one another that hold for *any* variable—such as revenue, cost, or profit—that is affected by the number of units in question.

To illustrate and emphasize the wide applicability of marginal analysis, we switch our example from profits, revenues, and costs to a noneconomic variable, human body weights. We do so because calculation of weights is more familiar to most people than calculation of profits, revenues, or costs, and we can use this example to illustrate several fundamental relationships between average and marginal figures. The necessary data are in Table 21–8.[8] We begin with an empty room (total weight of occupants is

[8]Note that in this illustration, "persons in room" is analogous to units of output, "total weight" to total revenue or cost, and so on.

equal to zero). A person weighing 100 pounds enters; marginal and average weight are both 100 pounds. If the person is followed by a person weighing 140 pounds (marginal weight equals 140 pounds), the average weight rises to 120 pounds (240 ÷ 2), and so on.

The way to calculate average weight from total weight is quite clear. When, for example, there are four persons in the room with a total weight of 500 pounds, the average weight must be 500 ÷ 4 = 125 pounds, as shown in the corresponding entry of the third column. In general, the rule for converting totals to averages, and vice versa, is:

Table 21–8
WEIGHTS OF PERSONS IN A ROOM

NUMBER OF PERSONS IN ROOM	TOTAL WEIGHT	AVERAGE WEIGHT (pounds)	MARGINAL WEIGHT
0	0	—	—
1	100	100	100
2	240	120	140
3	375	125	135
4	500	125	125
5	600	120	100
6	660	110	60

Rule 1a. Average weight equals total weight divided by number of persons.

Rule 1b. Total weight equals average weight times number of persons.

And this rule naturally applies equally well to cost, revenue, profit, or any other variable of interest.

Calculation of *marginal* weight from *total* weight follows the *subtraction* process we have already encountered in the calculation of marginal utility, marginal cost, and marginal revenue. Specifically:

Rule 2a. The marginal weight of, say, the third person equals the total weight of three people minus the total weight of two people.

For example, when the fourth person enters the room, *total* weight rises from 375 to 500 pounds, and hence the corresponding marginal weight is 500 − 375 = 125 pounds, as is shown in the last column of Table 21–8. We can also go in the opposite direction—from marginal to total—by the reverse, *addition*, process.

Rule 2b. The total weight of, say, three people equals the marginal weight of the first person plus the marginal weight of the second person plus the marginal weight of the third person.

Rule 2b can be checked by referring to Table 21–8. There it can be seen that the total weight of three persons, 375 pounds, is indeed equal to 100 + 140 + 135 pounds, the sum of the preceding marginal weights. A similar relation holds for any other total weight figure in the table, as the reader should verify.[9]

In addition to these familiar arithmetic relationships, there are two other useful relationships. The first of these may be stated as:

Rule 3. In the absence of fixed weight (costs), the marginal, average, and total figures for the first person must all be equal.

This rule holds because when there is only one person in the room, whose weight is X pounds, the average weight will obviously be X, the total weight must be X, and the marginal weight must also be X (since the total must have risen from 0 to X pounds). Put another way, when the marginal person is alone,

he or she is obviously also the average person, and also represents the totality of all relevant persons.

Now for the final and very important relationship:

Rule 4. If marginal weight is lower than average weight, then average weight must fall when the number of persons increases. If marginal weight exceeds average weight, average weight must rise when the number of persons increases; and if marginal and average weight are equal, the average weight must remain constant when the number of persons increases.

These three possibilities are all illustrated in Table 21–8. Notice, for example, that when the third person enters the room, the average weight rises from 120 to 125 pounds. That is because this person's (marginal) weight is 135 pounds, which is above the average, as Rule 4 requires. Similarly, when the sixth person—who is a 60-pound child—enters the room, the average falls from 120 to 110 pounds because marginal weight, 60 pounds, is below average weight.

The reason Rule 4 works is easily explained with the aid of our example. When the third person enters, we see that the average rises. At once we know that this person must be above average weight, for otherwise his arrival would not have pulled up the average. Similarly, the average will be pulled down by the arrival of a person whose weight is below the average (marginal weight is less than average weight). And the arrival of a person of average weight (marginal equals average weight) will leave the old average figure unchanged. That is all there is to the matter.

It is essential to avoid a common misunderstanding of this rule: it does *not* state, for example, that if the average figure is rising, the marginal figure must be rising. When the average rises, the marginal figure may rise, fall, or remain unchanged. The arrival of two persons both well above average will push the average up in two successive steps even if the second new arrival is lighter than the first. We see such a case in Table 21–8, where the arithmetic shows that while average weight rises successively from 100 to 120 to 125, the marginal weight falls from 140 to 135 to 125.

Graphic Representation of Marginal and Average Curves

We have shown how, from a curve of total profit (or total cost or total anything else), one can determine the corresponding marginal figure. We noted several

---

[9]There is an exception in the case of costs. Summing up marginal cost figures as in Rule 2b leads to total *variable* cost. If there are *fixed* costs, these must be added in to arrive at total (variable plus fixed) costs.

times in the chapter that the marginal value at any particular point is equal to the *slope* of the corresponding total curve at that point. But for some purposes it is convenient to use a graph that records marginal and average values directly rather than deriving them from the curve of totals.

We can obtain such a graph by plotting the data contained in a table of marginal figures, such as Table 21–8. The result looks like the graph shown in Figure 21–6. Here we have indicated the number of persons in the room on the horizontal axis and the corresponding average and marginal figures on the vertical axis. The solid dots represent average weights; the small circles represent marginal weights. Thus, for example, point *A* shows that when two persons are in the room, their average weight is 120 pounds, as was reported on the third line of Table 21–8. Similarly, point *B* on the graph represents information provided in the next column of the table; that is, that the marginal weight of the third person who enters the room is 135 pounds. For visual convenience these points have been connected into a marginal curve and an average curve, represented respectively by the solid and the broken curves in the diagram. This is the representation of marginal and average values that economists most frequently use.

Figure 21–6 illustrates two of our rules. Rule 3 says that, for the first unit, the marginal and average values will be the same. And that is precisely why the two curves start out together at point *C*. When there is only one person in the room, marginal and average weight *must* be the same. The graph also obeys Rule 4: between points *C* and *E*, where the average curve is *rising*, the marginal curve lies *above* the average.

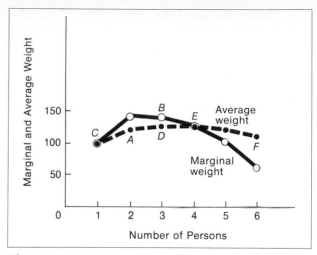

Figure 21–6

THE RELATIONSHIP BETWEEN MARGINAL AND AVERAGE CURVES

If the marginal curve is above the average curve, the average curve will be pulled upward. Thus, wherever the marginal is above the average the average must be going upward (blue segment of curves). The opposite is true where the marginal curve is below the average curve.

(Notice, however, that over part of this range the marginal curve *falls* even though the average curve is rising—Rule 4 says nothing about the rise or fall of the marginal curve.) We see also that over range *EF*, where the average curve is falling, the marginal curve is below the average curve, again in accord with Rule 4. Finally, at point *E*, where the average curve is neither rising nor falling, the marginal curve meets the average curve: average and marginal weights are equal at that point.

Questions for Discussion

1. Suppose the following is your record of exam grades in Principles of Economics:

EXAM DATE	GRADE	COMMENT
September 30	65	You got off to a slow start.
October 28	85	A big improvement.
November 26	90	Happy Thanksgiving!
December 13	84	Slipped a little.
January 24	96	Well done.

Use these data to make up a table of total, average, and marginal grades for the five exams.

2. From the data in your table, illustrate each of the rules mentioned in this appendix. Be sure to point out an instance where marginal grade falls but average grade rises.

The Firm in the Marketplace: Perfect Competition

Competition . . . brings about the only . . . arrangement of social production which is possible. . . . [Otherwise] what guarantee [do] we have that the necessary quantity and not more of each product will be produced, that we shall not go hungry in regard to corn and meat while we are choked in beet sugar and drowned in potato spirit, that we shall not lack trousers to cover our nakedness while buttons flood us in millions.

FRIEDRICH ENGELS

In Chapter 20 we analyzed how a firm's input decisions determine its cost curves and in Chapter 21 we saw that cost and demand curves together lead to a decision about how much to produce. It may seem, therefore, that we have completed the analysis of the supply side of the market. This is not so, however, because firms do not operate in a vacuum. A single firm is but one component of a market, and what one firm does may affect the others. Thus our discussion of supply is not complete until we have analyzed how *all* the firms in an industry interact in the marketplace.

Industries differ dramatically in how populated they are and in the size of a typical firm. Some industries, like fishing, have a great many very small firms; others, like autos, are composed of a few industrial giants. This chapter deals with a very particular type of market structure—called *perfect competition*—in which firms are numerous and small. The chapter begins by comparing alternative market forms and defining perfect competition precisely. We then use the tools acquired in Chapter 21 to analyze the behavior of the perfectly competitive firm and derive its supply curve. Next, we consider the supply curve of *all* the firms in an industry—the industry supply curve—and we investigate how developments at the industry level reverberate back on individual firms. As an application of the analysis, we consider why gasohol could be a boon to farmers.

A Puzzle: Can Good Weather Be Bad for Farmers?

If you do your own gardening, you no doubt hope for the best possible weather—a nice mixture of sunshine and rain to help the plants grow. Drought and frost are your mortal enemies. For farmers, however, ideal weather sometimes spells disaster. After a bumper crop comes in, farmers often trek to Washington to picket the White House complaining about the low prices that result. Legislators are urged to "protect" the farmer from these low prices, which is to say, to protect them from the consequences of good weather. On the other hand, adverse weather often leaves farmers *as a whole* rather well off. Even though it ruins some particular farmers, picket lines typically do not appear after droughts, floods, and premature frosts. What accounts for this strange behavior? The tools we are about to describe—the analysis of competitive supply—will permit us to answer this question at the end of the chapter.

Varieties of Market Structure: A Sneak Preview

It will be helpful to open our discussion by explaining clearly what is meant by the word *market.* Economists do not reserve the term to denote only an organized exchange operating in a well-defined physical location. The more general and abstract notion of a market refers to a set of sellers and buyers whose activities affect the price at which a *particular commodity* is sold. For example, two separate sales of General Motors stock at different ends of the country may be considered as taking place on the same market, while the sale of bread and carrots in neighboring stalls of a market square may, in our sense, occur on totally different markets.

Economists distinguish among different markets according to (1) how many firms there are, (2) whether the products of the different firms are identical or somewhat different, and (3) how easy it is for new firms to enter the market. Table 22–1 summarizes the main features of the four market structures we will study in this and subsequent chapters. It is provided here as a kind of road map of where we are going. *Perfect competition* is obviously at one extreme (many small firms selling an identical product) while *pure monopoly* (a single firm) is at the other. In between there are hybrid forms—called *monopolistic competition* and *oligopoly*—that share some of the characteristics of perfect competition and some of the characteristics of monopoly. Perfect competition is far from the typical market form in the U.S. economy. Indeed, it is quite rare. Many farming and fishing industries approximate perfect competition, as do many financial markets (such as the New York Stock Exchange). Pure monopoly—literally *one* firm—is also infrequently encountered. Most of the products you buy are no doubt supplied by oligopolies or monopolistic competitors—terms we will be defining precisely in Chapter 26.

Table 22–1
VARIETIES OF MARKET STRUCTURE

| TYPE OF MARKET STRUCTURE | DEFINITION | | | WHERE TO FIND IT | |
	NUMBER OF SELLERS	NATURE OF THE PRODUCT	BARRIERS TO ENTRY	IN THE U.S. ECONOMY	IN THIS TEXTBOOK
Perfect competition	Many	All firms produce identical products (example: wheat)	None	Some agricultural markets and parts of retailing come close	Chapter 22
Monopolistic competition	Many	Different firms produce somewhat different products (example: restaurant meals)	Few, if any	Most of the retailing sector, textiles, and restaurants	Chapter 26
Oligopoly	Few	Firms may produce identical or differentiated products (example: brands of toothpaste)	May be considerable	Much of the manufacturing sector, especially autos, steel, and cigarettes	Chapter 26
Pure monopoly	One	Unique product	May be considerable	Public utilities	Chapter 25

Perfect Competition Defined

You can appreciate just how special perfect competition is once we provide a comprehensive definition. A market is said to operate under **perfect competition** when the following four conditions are satisfied:

1. *Numerous participants.* Each seller and purchaser constitutes so small a portion of the market that their decisions have no effect on the price. This requirement rules out trade associations or other collusive arrangements strong enough to affect price.

2. *Homogeneity of product.* The product offered by any seller is identical to that supplied by any other seller. As a result, consumers do not care from whom they buy.

3. *Freedom of entry and exit.* New firms desiring to enter the market face no special impediments that the existing firms can avoid. Similarly, if production and sale of the good proves unprofitable, there are no barriers preventing firms from leaving the market.

4. *Perfect information.* Each firm and each customer is well informed about the available products and their prices.

These are obviously exacting requirements that are met infrequently in practice. One example might be a market for common stock: there are literally millions of buyers and sellers of AT&T stock; all of the shares are exactly alike; anyone who wishes can enter the market easily; and most of the relevant information is readily available in the daily newspaper. But other examples are hard to find. Our interest in perfect competition is surely not for its descriptive realism.

Why, then, do we spend time studying perfect competition? The answer takes us back to the central theme of the microeconomic portions of this book. It is under perfect competition that the market mechanism performs best. So, if we want to learn what markets do well, we can put the market's best foot forward by beginning with perfect competition. As Adam Smith suggested some two centuries ago, perfectly competitive firms use society's scarce resources with maximum efficiency. And as Friedrich Engels suggested in the opening quotation of this chapter, perfectly competitive firms serve consumers' tastes effectively. So by studying perfect competition, we can learn just how much an *ideally functioning* market system might accomplish. This is the topic of the present chapter and the next one. Then, in Part Four, we will consider other market forms and see how they deviate from the perfectly competitive ideal. Still later chapters (especially in Parts Five and Six) will examine many important tasks that the market does not perform at all well, even under perfect competition. These chapters combined should provide a balanced assessment of the virtues and vices of the market mechanism.

The Competitive Firm and Its Demand Curve

To discover what happens in a market in which perfect competition prevails, we must deal separately with the behavior of the *firm* and the behavior of the *industry.* One basic difference between the firm and the industry under competition relates to *pricing.* Under perfect competition, the firm has no control over the price it charges. This follows from the definition of perfect competition. The presence of a vast number of competitors, each offering identical products, forces

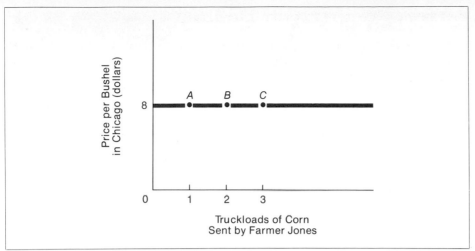

Figure 22–1

DEMAND CURVE FOR A
FIRM UNDER PERFECT
COMPETITION
Under perfect competition the
size of the output of a firm is so
small a portion of the total industry output that it cannot
affect the market price of the
product. Even if the firm's output increases many times,
market price remains $8.

each firm to meet but not exceed the price charged by the others. Like a
stockholder with 100 shares of General Electric, the firm simply finds out the
prevailing price on the market and either accepts that price or refuses to sell. But
while the individual firm has no influence over price under perfect competition,
the industry does. This influence is not conscious or planned—it happens
spontaneously through the impersonal forces of supply and demand, as we
observed in Chapter 4.

With two important exceptions, the analysis of the behavior of the firm
under perfect competition is exactly the same as that pertaining to any other firm,
so the tools developed in Chapters 20 and 21 can be applied directly. The two
exceptions are the special shape of the competitive firm's demand curve and the
effects on the firm's profits of freedom of entry and exit. We will consider them in
turn, beginning with the demand curve.

In Chapter 21, we always assumed that the firm's demand curve sloped
downward; if a firm wished to sell more (without increasing its advertising or
changing its product specifications), it had to reduce the price of its product. The
competitive firm is an exception to this general principle.

A perfectly competitive firm has a **horizontal demand curve.** This
means it can double or triple its sales without any reduction in the price of its
product.

How is this possible? The answer is that the competitive firm is so insignificant
relative to the market as a whole that it has absolutely no influence over price.
The farmer who sells his corn through an exchange in Chicago must accept the
current quotation his broker reports to him. Because there are thousands of
farmers, the Chicago price per bushel will not budge because Farmer Jones decides
he doesn't like the price and holds back a truckload for storage. Thus, the
demand curve for Farmer Jones's corn is as shown in Figure 22–1; the price he is
paid in Chicago will be $8 per bushel whether he sells one truckload (point *A*) or
two (point *B*) or three (point *C*).

Short-Run Equilibrium
of the Competitive Firm

We now have sufficient background to analyze how the competitive firm decides
how much to produce. To begin, recall from Chapter 21 that profit maximization

requires the firm to pick an output level that makes its *marginal cost equal to its marginal revenue*: MC = MR. The only feature that distinguishes the profit-maximizing equilibrium of the competitive firm from that of any other type of firm is its horizontal demand curve. Because the demand curve is horizontal, the competitive firm's marginal revenue curve is a horizontal straight line that coincides with its demand curve; hence, MR = price (*P*). It is easy to see why this is so. If the price does not depend on how much the firm sells (which is what a horizontal demand curve means), then each *additional* unit sold brings in an amount of revenue (the *marginal* revenue) exactly equal to the market price. So marginal revenue always equals price under perfect competition; the demand curve and the MR curve coincide.

Once we know the shape and position of a firm's marginal revenue curve, we can use this information and the marginal cost curve to determine its optimal output and profit, as shown in Figure 22–2. As usual, the profit-maximizing output is that at which MC = MR (point *B*). This competitive firm produces 50,000 bushels per year—the output level at which MC and MR are equal to the market price, $8. Thus:

The *short-run equilibrium* of a profit-maximizing firm in a perfectly competitive market comes at the output level at which marginal cost is equal to price, or in symbols:

$$MC = P.$$

Is the firm making a profit or incurring a loss? To answer this question; the graph also contains the firm's *average cost* (AC) curve, which was explained in Chapter 20. We see in the example that average cost at 50,000 bushels per year is only $6 per bushel (point *A*). Since the price is $8 per bushel (point *B*), the firm is making a profit of $2 per bushel, which appears in the graph as the vertical distance between points *A* and *B*. Notice that in addition to showing the profit *per unit*, the graph can be used to show the firm's *total profit*. Since total profit is the profit per unit ($2 in this example) times the number of units (50,000 per year), total profit appears as the *area* of the shaded rectangle whose height is the profit per unit ($2) and whose width is the number of units (50,000).[1] Thus, profits are $100,000 per year in this case.

[1]Recall that the formula for the area of a rectangle is area = height × width.

Figure 22–2
SHORT-RUN
EQUILIBRIUM OF THE
COMPETITIVE FIRM
The profit-maximizing firm will select the output (50,000 bushels per year) at which marginal cost equals marginal revenue (point *B*). The demand curve, *D*, is horizontal because the firm's output is too small to affect market price; thus it is also the marginal revenue curve. In the short run, demand may be either high or low in relation to cost. Therefore each unit it sells may return a profit (*AB*) or a loss.

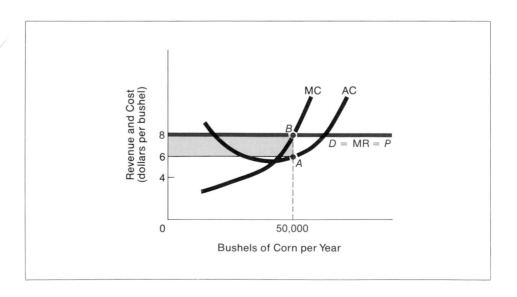

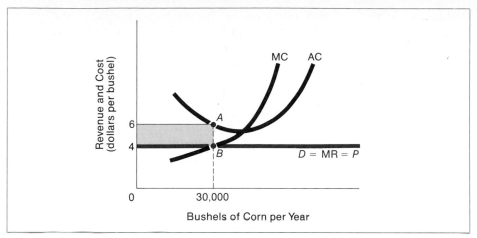

Figure 22–3
SHORT-RUN
EQUILIBRIUM OF THE
COMPETITIVE FIRM WITH
A LOWER PRICE
In this diagram, the cost curves
are the same as in Figure 22–
2, but the demand curve (*D*)
has shifted down to a market
price of $4 per bushel. The
firm still does the best it can by
setting MC = *P* (point *B*). But
since its average cost at
30,000 bushels per year is $6
per bushel, it runs a loss (shown
by the shaded rectangle).

The market is obviously treating this farmer rather nicely. But what if the market were not so generous in its rewards? What if, for example, the market price were only $4 per bushel instead of $8? Figure 22–3 shows the equilibrium of the firm under these circumstances. The firm still maximizes profits by producing the level of output at which price is equal to marginal cost—point *B* in the diagram. But this time "maximizing" profits really means keeping the loss as small as possible. At the optimal level of output (30,000 bushels per year) average cost is $6 per bushel (point *A*), which exceeds the $4 per bushel price (point *B*). The firm is therefore running a loss of $2 per bushel times 30,000 bushels, or $60,000 per year. This loss, which is represented by the shaded rectangle in Figure 22–3, is the best the firm can do. If it selected any other output level, its loss would be even greater.

The firm will always equate MC and *P*, but in the short run it may wind up with either a profit or a loss.

There is, however, a limit on how much the firm would ever have to lose. If the output level dictated by setting MC = *P* produced a tremendous loss, the firm would be better off shutting down, producing nothing, and losing an amount equal to its fixed costs. The *lowest* price that keeps the firm from shutting down can be shown in the graph by introducing one more curve: the **average variable cost** (AVC) curve mentioned in the last chapter. Why is this curve relevant? Because the choice between shutting down entirely and producing at the point where MC = *P* comes down to this: If the firm produces nothing, **total variable costs** (TVC) will be zero and so will total revenue (TR). Its loss will simply be its fixed costs, say $80,000, no more and no less. If, instead, it produces and sells some output, it will take in some revenue and incur some variable costs. The decision to produce will lower the operating loss below $80,000 only if the revenue taken in (TR) *exceeds* the additional costs incurred (TVC). Thus:

It pays the firm to produce something only if, when MC is set equal to *P*, total revenue (TR) exceeds total variable cost (TVC). Since, if we divide both TR and TVC by quantity (Q) we get TR/Q = *P* and TVC/Q = AVC, this condition may be stated equivalently as the requirement that price exceed AVC.

The conclusion, then, is that the firm will produce nothing unless price lies above the minimum point on the AVC curve. Figure 22–4 illustrates this principle by showing an MC curve, an AVC curve, and several alternative demand

Figure 22–4

SHUTDOWN ANALYSIS
At a price as low as P_1, the firm cannot even cover its average variable costs; it is better off shutting down entirely. At a price as high as P_3, the firm selects point A, but operates at a loss (because P_3 is below AC). However, it is more than covering its average variable costs (since P_3 exceeds AVC), so it pays to keep producing. Price P_2 is the borderline case. With this price, the firm selects point B and is indifferent between shutting down and staying open.

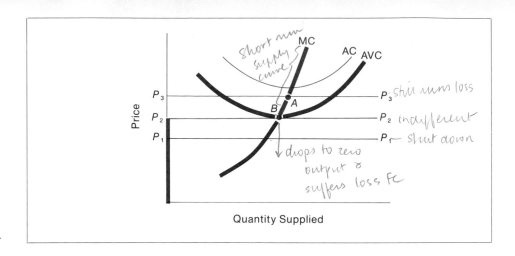

curves corresponding to different possible prices. Price P_1 is below the minimum average variable cost. With this price, the firm cannot even cover its variable costs and is better off shutting down (producing zero output). Price P_3 is higher. While the firm still runs a loss if it sets $MC = P$ at point A (because AC exceeds P_3), it is at least covering its *variable* costs, and so it pays to keep operating in the short run. Price P_2 is the borderline case. If the price is P_2, the firm is indifferent between shutting down and staying in business and producing at a level where $MC = P$ (point B). P_2 is thus the *lowest* price at which the firm will produce anything. As we see from the graph, P_2 corresponds to the minimum point on the AVC curve.

The Supply Curve of the Competitive Firm

Without realizing it, we have now derived the **supply curve of the competitive firm** in the short run. Why? Recall that a supply curve summarizes the answers to such questions as, If the price is so and so, how much will the firm produce? We have now discovered that there are two possibilities, as indicated by the thick blue line in Figure 22–4.

1. If the price exceeds the minimum AVC, in the short run it pays a competitive firm to produce the level of output that equates MC and P. Thus, for any price above point B, we can read the corresponding quantity supplied from the firm's MC curve.
2. If the price falls below the minimum AVC, then it pays the firm to produce nothing. Quantity supplied falls to zero.

Putting these two observations together, we conclude that:

The short-run supply curve of the perfectly competitive firm is its marginal cost curve above the point where it intersects the average variable cost curve; that is, above the minimum level of AVC. If price falls below this level, the firm's quantity supplied drops to zero.

The firm's long-run supply curve differs only slightly. Remember that the long run for a firm is defined as a period of time long enough so that *every* input becomes variable. This means that *all* costs become *variable* costs, so the distinction between average cost (AC) and average variable cost (AVC) disappears. As a consequence:

The long-run supply curve of the competitive firm is its MC curve above the point where it intersects its long-run AC (= AVC) curve.[2]

The Short-Run Supply Curve of the Competitive Industry

Having completed the analysis of the competitive firm's supply decision, we turn our attention next to the competitive *industry*. Again we need to distinguish between the short run and the long run, but the distinction is different here. The short run for the *industry* is defined as a period of time too brief for new firms to enter the industry or for old firms to leave, so the number of firms is fixed. By contrast, the long run for the industry is a period of time long enough for any firm that so desires to enter (or leave). We begin our analysis of industry equilibrium in the short run.

With the number of firms fixed, it is a simple matter to derive the **supply curve of the competitive industry** from those of the individual firms. At any given price, we simply *add up* the quantities supplied by each of the firms to arrive at the industry-wide quantity supplied. For example, if each of 1000 identical firms in the corn industry supplies 45,000 bushels when the price is $6 per bushel, then the quantity supplied by the industry at a $6 price will be 45,000 bushels per firm × 1000 firms = 45 million bushels. This process of deriving the *market* supply curve from the *individual* supply curves of firms is perfectly analogous to the way we derived the *market* demand curve from the *individual* demand curves of consumers in Chapter 19. Graphically, what we are doing is *summing the individual supply curves horizontally*, as illustrated in Figure 22–5. At a price of $6, each firm supplies 45,000 bushels [point *c* in part (a)], so the industry supplies 45 million bushels [point *C* in part (b)]. At a price of $8, each firm supplies 50,000 bushels [point *e* in part (a)], and so the industry supplies 50 million bushels [point *E* in part (b)]. Similar calculations can be done for any other price.

[2]The relationship between short-run and long-run average cost curves was discussed in Chapter 20, pages 380–382.

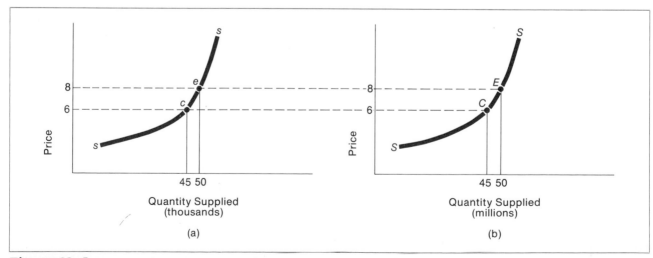

Figure 22–5
DERIVATION OF THE INDUSTRY SUPPLY CURVE FROM THE SUPPLY CURVES OF THE INDIVIDUAL FIRMS
In this hypothetical industry of 1000 identical firms, each individual firm has the supply curve *ss* in part (a). For example, quantity supplied is 45,000 bushels when the price is $6 per unit (point *c*). By *adding up* the quantities supplied by each firm at each possible price, we arrive at the industry supply curve *SS* in part (b). For example, at a unit price of $6, total quantity supplied by the industry is 45 million units (point *C*).

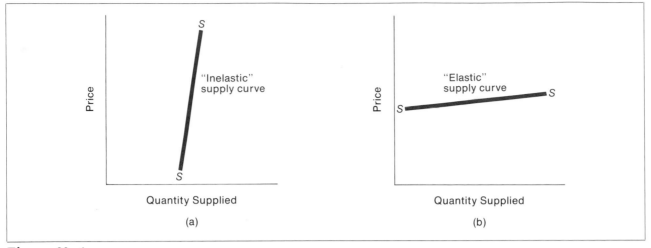

Figure 22–6

ELASTICITY OF SUPPLY

The steep supply curve in part (a) has a low elasticity of supply: quantity supplied does not increase very much when price rises. The flat supply curve in part (b) has a much higher elasticity; that is, it exhibits a much greater quantity response to any change in price. (The scales of the two diagrams are the same.)

The supply curve of the competitive industry in the short run is derived by *summing* the supply curves of all the firms in the industry *horizontally*.

Notice that if the supply curves of individual firms are upward sloping, then the supply curve of the competitive industry will be upward sloping, too. We have seen that the firm's supply curve is its marginal cost curve (above the level of minimum average variable cost), so it follows that rising marginal costs lead to an upward sloping *industry* supply curve.

Elasticity of Supply

The **elasticity of supply** is the ratio of the percentage change in quantity supplied to the percentage change in price that elicits the supply response.

Chapter 19 introduced a concept called *elasticity of demand* as a numerical measure of the responsiveness of quantity demanded to price.[3] The parallel measure for the supply curve is called **elasticity of supply.** For example, according to the supply curve in Figure 22–5(b), a 25-percent reduction in price (from $8 to $6) leads to a decrease in quantity supplied of 10 percent (from 50 million to 45 million). Applying the definition in the margin, we see that:

$$\text{Elasticity of supply} = \frac{\text{Percentage change in quantity supplied}}{\text{Percentage change in price}} = \frac{-10}{-25} = 0.4 \,.$$

By direct analogy with our discussion of elasticity of demand, we can see that rather steep supply curves, like that in Figure 22–6(a), correspond to cases of *inelastic* supply, while rather flat supply curves, like that in Figure 22–6(b), indicate *elastic* supply. Similarly, a vertical supply curve would be called *perfectly inelastic,* while a horizontal supply curve would be called *infinitely elastic.* This terminology is familiar from the discussion of demand curves.

Industry Equilibrium in the Short Run

Now that we have derived the industry supply curve, we need only add a market demand curve to determine the price and quantity that will emerge. This is done for our illustrative corn industry in Figure 22–7, where the industry supply curve

[3]If you need review, see pages 356–358.

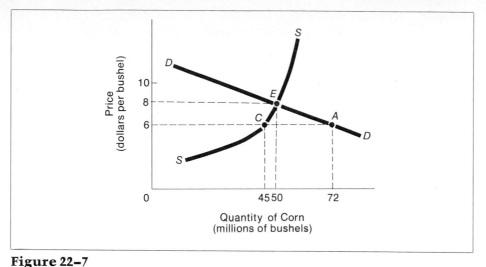

Figure 22–7

SUPPLY–DEMAND EQUILIBRIUM OF A COMPETITIVE INDUSTRY

The only equilibrium combination of price and quantity is a price of $8 and a quantity of 50 million bushels, at which the supply curve SS and the demand curve DD intersect (point E). At a lower price, such as $6, quantity demanded (72 million bushels as shown by point A on the demand curve) will be higher than the 45 million bushel quantity supplied (point C). Thus the price will be driven back up toward the $8 equilibrium. The opposite will happen at a price such as $10, which is above equilibrium.

[carried over from Figure 22–5(b)] is SS and the demand curve is DD. Point E is the equilibrium point for the competitive industry, because only at that combination of price, $8, and quantity, 50 million bushels, are neither purchasers nor sellers motivated to upset matters. At a price of $8, sellers are willing to offer exactly the amount consumers want to purchase.

Should we expect price actually to reach, or at least to approximate, this equilibrium level? The answer is yes. To see why, we must consider what happens when price is not at its equilibrium level. Suppose it takes a lower value, such as $6. Our diagram tells us that at that price, quantity supplied (45 million bushels) is lower than quantity demanded (72 million bushels). Thus, unsatisfied buyers will probably offer to pay higher prices, which will force price *upward* in the direction of its equilibrium value, $8. Similarly, if we begin with a price higher than the equilibrium price, we may readily verify that quantity supplied will exceed quantity demanded. Under these circumstances, frustrated sellers are likely to reduce their prices, so price will be forced downward. In the circumstances depicted in Figure 22–7, then, there is in effect a magnet at the equilibrium price of $8 that will pull the actual price in its direction if for some reason the actual price starts out at some other level.

In practice, there are few cases in which competitive markets, over a long period of time, seem not to have moved toward equilibrium prices. Matters eventually seem to work out as depicted in Figure 22–7. Of course, numerous transitory influences can jolt any real-world market away from its equilibrium point—a strike that cuts production, a sudden change in consumer tastes, and so on. And there also have been periods, sometimes of distressingly long duration, when the "bottom has dropped out" of some nearly competitive markets, such as stock exchanges. During such market "crashes," it certainly did not seem that prices were moving toward equilibrium. Yet, as we have just seen, there are powerful forces that do push prices back toward equilibrium—toward the level at which the supply and demand curves intersect. These forces are of fundamental importance for economic analysis, for if there were no such forces, prices in the real world would bear little resemblance to equilibrium prices, and there would be little reason to study supply–demand analysis. Fortunately, the required equilibrating forces do exist.

Industry Equilibrium in the Long Run

The equilibrium of a competitive industry in the long run may differ from the short-run equilibrium that we have just studied. The reason is that in the long run, the number of firms in the industry (1000 in our example) is not fixed. What will lure new firms into the industry or repel old ones? Profits. Remember that when a firm selects its optimal level of output by setting $MC = P$, it may wind up with either a profit or a loss. Such profits or losses must be *temporary* for a competitive firm, because the freedom of new firms to enter the industry or of old firms to leave it will, in the long run, eliminate them.

Suppose very high profits accrue to firms in the industry. Then new companies will find it attractive to enter the business, and expanded production will force the market price to fall from its initial level. Why? Recall that the industry supply curve is the horizontal sum of the supply curves of individual firms. Under perfect competition, new firms can enter the industry *on the same terms as existing firms.* This means that new entrants will have the *same* individual supply curves as old firms. If the market price did not fall, entry of new firms would lead to an increased number of firms with no change in output *per firm.* Consequently, the total quantity supplied on the market would be higher, and would exceed quantity demanded. But, of course, this means that in a free market entry of new firms *must* push the price down.

Figure 22–8 shows how the entry process works. In this diagram, the demand curve DD and the original (short-run) supply curve S_0S_0 are carried over from Figure 22–7. The entry of new firms seeking high profits *shifts the short-run supply curve outward to the right,* to S_1S_1. The new market equilibrium is at point A (rather than at point E), where price is $6 per bushel and 72 million bushels are produced and consumed. Entry of new firms reduces price and raises total output. (Had the price not fallen, quantity supplied after entry would have been 80 million bushels—point F.)

Figure 22–8

A SHIFT IN THE INDUSTRY SUPPLY CURVE CAUSED BY THE ENTRY OF NEW FIRMS

This diagram shows what happens to the industry equilibrium when new firms enter the industry. Quantity supplied at any given price increases; that is, the supply curve shifts to the right, from S_0S_0 to S_1S_1 in the figure. As a result, the market price falls (from $8 to $6) and the quantity increases (from 50 million bushels to 72 million bushels).

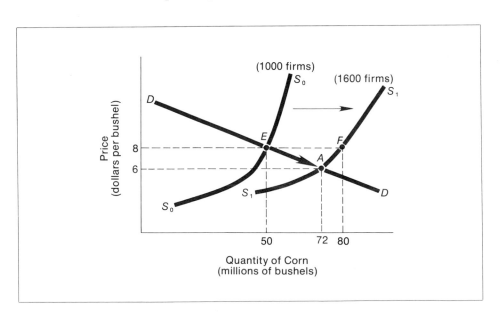

To see where the entry process stops, we must consider how the entry of new firms affects the behavior of old firms. At first, this may seem to contradict the notion of perfect competition; perfectly competitive firms are not supposed to care what their competitors are doing. Indeed, these corn farmers do not care. But they *do* care very much about the market price of corn, and, as we have just seen, the entry of new firms into the corn-farming industry lowers the price of corn.

In Figure 22–9 we have juxtaposed the diagram of the equilibrium of the competitive firm (Figure 22–2 on page 416) and the diagram of the equilibrium of the competitive industry (Figure 22–8). Before entry, the market price was $8 [point E in Figure 22–9(b)] and each of the 1000 firms was producing 50,000 bushels—the point where marginal cost and price were equal [point e in Figure 22–9(a)]. The demand curve facing each firm was the horizontal line D_0 in Figure 22–9(a). There were profits because average costs (AC) at 50,000 bushels per firm were less than price. Now suppose 600 new firms are attracted by these high profits and enter the industry. Each has the cost structure indicated by the AC and MC curves in Figure 22–9(a). As we have noted, the industry supply curve in Figure 22–9(b) shifts to the right, and price falls to $6 per bushel. Firms in the industry cannot fail to notice this lower price. As we see in Figure 22–9(a), each firm reduces its output to 45,000 bushels in reaction to the lower price (point a). But now there are 1600 firms, so total industry output is $45,000 \times 1600 = 72$ million bushels [point A in Figure 22–9(b)].

At point a in Figure 22–9(a), there are still profits to be made because the $6 price exceeds average cost. Thus the entry process is not yet complete. Where will it end? Only when all profits have been competed away. Only when entry shifts the industry supply curve so far to the right [S_2S_2 in Figure 22–10(b)] that the demand curve facing individual firms falls to the level of minimum average cost [point m in Figure 22–10(a)] will all profits be eradicated and entry cease.

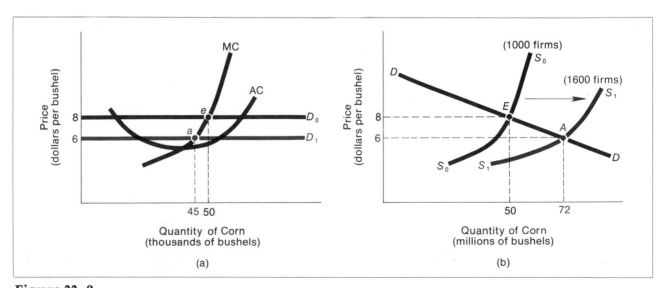

Figure 22–9
THE COMPETITIVE FIRM AND THE COMPETITIVE INDUSTRY
Here we show the interaction between developments at the industry level [in part (b)] and developments at the firm level [in part (a)]. An outward shift in the industry supply curve from S_0S_0 to S_1S_1 in part (b) lowers the market price from $8 to $6. In part (a), we see that a profit-maximizing competitive firm reacts to this decline in price by curtailing output. When the demand curve of the firm is D_0 ($8), it produces 50,000 bushels (point e). When the firm's demand curve falls to D_1 ($6), its output declines to 45,000 bushels (point a). However, there are now 1600 firms rather than 1000, so total industry output has expanded from 50 million bushels to 72 million bushels [part (b)]. Entry has reduced profits. But since P still exceeds AC at an output of 45,000 bushels per firm in part (a), some profits remain.

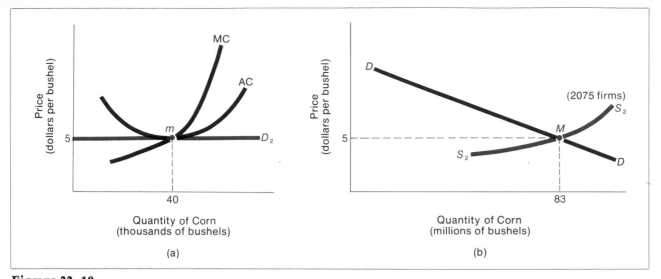

Figure 22–10

LONG-RUN EQUILIBRIUM OF THE COMPETITIVE FIRM AND INDUSTRY

By the time 2075 firms have entered the industry, the industry supply curve is S_2S_2 and the market price is $5 per bushel. At this price, the horizontal demand curve facing each firm is D_2 in part (a), so the profit-maximizing level of output is 40,000 bushels (point m). Here, since average cost and price are equal, there is no economic profit.

The two panels of Figure 22–10 show the competitive firm and the competitive industry in long-run equilibrium.[4] Notice that at the equilibrium point [m in part (a)], profit maximization has forced MC to be equal to P and free entry has forced AC to be equal to P. Thus:

When a perfectly competitive industry is in long-run equilibrium, firms maximize profits so that $P = MC$ and entry forces the price down until it is tangent to the average cost curve ($P = AC$). Thus:

$$P = MC = AC.$$

Zero Economic Profit: The Opportunity Cost of Capital

At this point, something may be troubling you. Why would there be any firms in the industry *at all* if there were no profits to be made? What sense does it make to call a position of zero profit a "long-run equilibrium?" The answer is that the zero profit concept used in economics does not mean the same thing that it does in ordinary usage. When economists measure average cost, they include the cost of *all* the firm's inputs, *including the cost of the capital provided by the firm's owners.* Since the firm may not make explicit payments to those who provide it with capital, this element of cost may not be picked up by the firm's accountants. So what economists call *zero economic profit* may correspond to some positive amount of profit as measured by conventional accounting techniques. Yet the cost of capital is every bit as real as the cost of labor or raw materials, because investors who provide funds to the company *give up* the opportunity to invest

[4]If the original short-run equilibrium had involved losses instead of profits, firms would have exited from the industry, shifting the industry supply curve inward, until all losses were eradicated and we would end up in a position exactly like Figure 22–10. To test your understanding, draw the version of Figure 22–9 that corresponds to this case.

these funds elsewhere. They therefore incur an **opportunity cost** of capital.[5] For example, if investors can earn 15 percent by lending their funds elsewhere, then the firm must earn a 15-percent rate of return to cover its opportunity cost of capital.

Economists consider this 15-percent opportunity cost to be the *cost of the firm's capital*, and they include it in the AC curve because it represents the amount the firm's investors could have earned if they had invested their money elsewhere. If the firm cannot earn at least 15 percent on its capital, funds will not be made available to it. And this holds true even if the firm's owners provide the capital, because their funds also have a 15-percent opportunity cost. Economists therefore assign an opportunity cost figure to the capital supplied by the owners. So, in the economist's language, in order to break even—earn zero **economic profit**—a firm must earn enough not only to cover the cost of labor, fuel, and raw materials, but also the cost of its funds, including the opportunity cost of any funds supplied by the owners of the firm.

To illustrate the difference between economic profits and accounting profits, suppose U.S. government bonds pay 15 percent, and the owner of a small shop earns 10 percent on her business investment. The shopkeeper might say she is making a 10-percent profit, but an economist would say she is *losing* 5 percent on every dollar she has invested in her business. The reason is that by keeping her money tied up in the firm, she gives up the chance to buy government bonds and receive a 15-percent return. With this explanation of the meaning of economic profit we can now understand the logic behind the zero-profit condition for the long-run industry equilibrium.

Zero profit in the economic sense simply means that firms are earning the normal economy-wide rate of profit in the accounting sense. This condition is guaranteed by freedom of entry and exit.

Freedom of entry guarantees that those who invest in a competitive industry will receive a rate of return on their capital *no greater than* the return that capital could earn elsewhere in the economy. If economic profits were being earned in some industry, capital would be attracted. The new capital would shift the industry supply curve to the right, which would drive down prices and profits. This process would continue until the return on capital in this industry was reduced to the return that capital could earn elsewhere—its opportunity cost.

Similarly, freedom of exit of capital guarantees that in the long run, once capital has had a chance to move, no industry will provide a rate of return *lower than* the opportunity cost of capital. For if returns in one industry were particularly low, resources would flow out of it. Plant and equipment would not be replaced as it wore out. As a result, the industry supply curve would shift to the left, and prices and profits would rise toward their opportunity cost level.

Perfect Competition and Economic Efficiency

Economists have long admired perfect competition as a thing of beauty, like a jewel in a glass case (and just as rare!). Adam Smith's invisible hand produces results that are considered *efficient* in a variety of senses that we will examine carefully in the next chapter. But one aspect of the great efficiency of perfect competition follows immediately from the analysis we have just completed.

The **opportunity cost** of a given investment is the highest return that money can earn in any other market. It is the potential earnings that investors forfeit by tying up their money in the industry in which they invest.

Economic profit equals net earnings, in the accountant's sense, minus the firm's opportunity cost of capital.

[5] The fundamental concept of opportunity cost—one of our 12 Ideas for Beyond the Final Exam—was introduced in Chapter 3.

In long-run competitive equilibrium, every firm produces at the minimum point on its average cost curve. Thus the outputs of competitive industries are produced at the lowest possible cost to society.

That this kind of cost efficiency characterizes perfect competition in the long run can be seen in Figures 22–9 and 22–10. Before full long-run equilibrium is reached (Figure 22–9), firms may not be producing in the least costly way. For example, the 50 million bushels being produced by 1000 firms at points e and E in Figures 22–9(a) and (b) could be produced more cheaply by more firms, each producing a smaller volume, because the point of minimum average cost lies to the left of point e in Figure 22–9(a). This problem is rectified, however, in the long run by entry of new firms seeking profit. We see in Figure 22–10 that after the entry process is complete, every firm is producing at its most efficient (lowest AC) level—40,000 bushels. As Adam Smith might have put it, even though each farmer cares only about his own profits, the corn-farming industry as a whole is guided *by an invisible hand* to produce the amount of corn that society wants at the lowest possible cost.

Application: Why Corn Farmers Liked President Carter's Energy Program (For a While)

To test our understanding of the operation of perfectly competitive markets, it is useful to put the apparatus we have just constructed through its paces by studying what happens when the demand for the product of a competitive industry increases. We take as our example a real case (though the numbers are totally fabricated).

As part of his comprehensive energy program introduced in early 1980, President Carter included a program to encourage the production and use of gasohol—a mixture of gasoline and alcohol manufactured from corn that allegedly saves energy by improving mileage and economizing on the use of crude oil.[6]

The gasohol program shifted the demand curve for corn, which we may assume is produced by an industry that is approximately perfectly competitive, by providing an additional use for the product. In Figure 22–11(b) we show the initial effect of the program as a rightward shift of the demand curve for corn from D_0D_0 to D_1D_1. Initially, both the price and quantity of corn rise as equilibrium moves from point E to point A. Figure 22–11(a) indicates what all this means to individual corn farmers. Before the gasohol program was announced, we assume they were in long-run equilibrium, at point e. MC, AC, and P were all equal (at $5) and economic profits were zero. Because the gasohol program shifts the market demand curve to the *right* in Figure 22–11(b), it shifts each firm's horizontal demand curve *upward* from D_0 to D_1 in Figure 22–11(a). Consequently, each firm is induced to increase its output from 40,000 bushels (point e) to 50,000 bushels (point a).

At points a and A in the two diagrams, however, excess profits are being made. These profits are shown by the shaded rectangle in Figure 22–11(a), whose height is the vertical distance from g to a and whose base is 50,000 units of output. In the long run, the lure of high profits attracts more capital into corn farming, eventually pushing the industry supply curve outward from S_0S_0 all the way to S_1S_1. At point B in Figure 22–11(b), long-run equilibrium is reestablished at a

---

[6]The facts of this matter are in some dispute. Many critics contend that the alleged savings from gasohol disappear once the energy required to produce the gasohol is included in the calculation. For more on the energy problem, see Chapter 36.

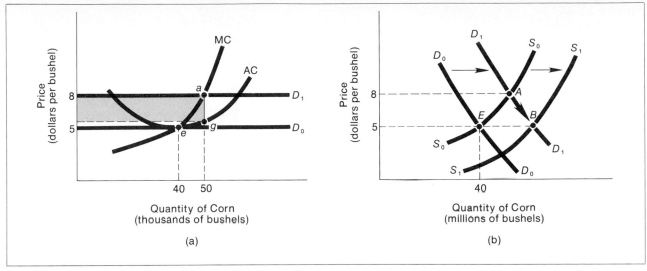

Figure 22–11

THE EFFECTS OF THE GASOHOL PROGRAM ON THE CORN FARMING INDUSTRY

In the short run, the rise in the demand for corn for purposes of manufacturing gasohol [from D_0D_0 to D_1D_1 in part (b)] increases the equilibrium price of corn from \$5 to \$8 per bushel. Individual farmers in part (a) respond by raising production from 40,000 bushels (point *e*) to 50,000 bushels (point *a*), and are temporarily earning excess profits—as indicated by the shaded rectangle in part (a). In the long run, however, new firms are attracted into the industry, pushing the supply curve outward to S_1S_1. The market price returns to \$5 per bushel and excess profits disappear.

price of \$5 per bushel, every individual firm returns to 40,000 bushels of output, and no excess profits are being earned. The one lasting change is that more resources are attracted into the corn-farming business.

Why Good Weather Can Be Bad for Farmers

The interactions between the competitive firm and the competitive industry that we have just studied permit us to resolve the puzzle with which we began the chapter: Why is it that farm incomes often decline when the harvest is good and increase when the harvest is bad?

First, we should clarify the point. The statement is not that *every* farmer benefits from a drought or a flood. Obviously, these calamities can ruin the particular farmers who are Mother Nature's victims. The claim is that farmers who are not severely affected by bad weather come out ahead, and the reason is not hard to understand. Once crops are planted, the supply curve of the farming industry is very nearly vertical. The harvest will be almost the same whether the price is high or low. A bumper crop means that the supply curve is far to the right, like S_1S_1 in Figure 22–12, instead of in its "normal" position (which is indicated by S_0S_0 in the figure). Consequently, a bumper crop leads to low prices—equilibrium will be at price P_1 instead of price P_0. As the graph indicates, the drop in price is often quite severe because the demand curves for most farm products are rather *inelastic*. Each farmer's quantity produced may be increased by the good weather. But because the market price falls *by an even greater percentage*, the farmer's total income declines.[7] As noted at the outset of this chapter, this often sends farmers scurrying off to Washington crying "Foul!"

---

[7]This is a consequence of the inelasticity of the demand curve. Recall that in Chapter 19 (page 359) we showed that a reduction in price *lowers* the firm's total revenue if the demand curve is inelastic. This is the result we are using here.

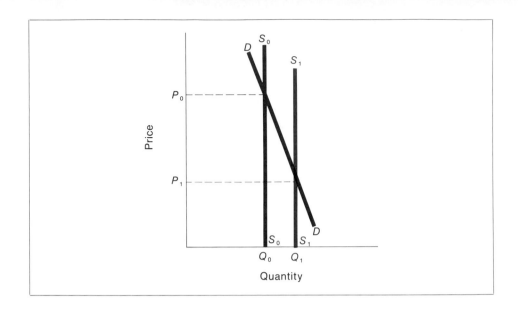

Figure 22–12

THE PROBLEM WITH FARM INCOMES
The demand curve for most farm products is quite inelastic. Thus if good weather conditions lead to a bumper crop (the supply curve shifts outward from $S_0 S_0$ to $S_1 S_1$), the market price typically falls so much that farm income (the product of price times quantity sold) actually declines. Conversely, farm income often rises when the weather is bad and farm prices are high.

On the other hand, suppose bad weather damages the crop but that Farmer Jones escapes relatively unscathed. Because of the inelastic market demand curve, the market price shoots up. (To see this, just use Figure 22–12 in reverse: Suppose $S_1 S_1$ is the supply curve under normal weather conditions and $S_0 S_0$ is the supply curve when the weather is bad.) Farmer Jones's harvest falls slightly, but the price he gets for each unit rises smartly, and Jones comes out ahead of the game. Nothing is quite so good for a farmer as a drought *in some other state!*

Summary

1. Markets are classified into several types depending on the number of firms in the industry, the degree of similarity of their products, and the possibility of impediments to entry.

2. The four main market structures are monopoly (single-firm production), oligopoly (production by a few firms), monopolistic competition (production by many firms with somewhat different products), and perfect competition (production by many firms with identical products and free entry and exit).

3. Few industries satisfy the conditions of perfect competition exactly, although some come close. Perfect competition is studied because it is easy to analyze and because it is useful as a yardstick to measure the performance of other market forms.

4. The demand curve of the perfectly competitive firm is horizontal because its output is so small a share of the industry's production that it cannot affect price. With a horizontal demand curve, price, average revenue, and marginal revenue are all equal.

5. The short-run equilibrium of the perfectly competitive firm is at the level of output that maximizes profits; that is, where marginal cost equals price. This equilibrium may involve either a profit or a loss.

6. The short-run supply curve of the perfectly competitive firm is the portion of its marginal cost curve that lies above its average variable cost curve.

7. The industry's short-run supply curve under perfect competition is the horizontal sum of the supply curves of all its firms.

8. Elasticity of supply is a measure of the responsiveness of quantity supplied to price. It is defined, analogously to elasticity of demand, as the ratio of the percentage change in quantity supplied to the percentage change in price that elicits the supply response.

9. In the long run, freedom of entry forces the perfectly competitive firm to earn zero economic profit; that is, no more than the firm's capital could earn elsewhere (the opportunity cost of the capital).

10. Industry equilibrium under perfect competition is at the point of intersection of the industry supply and demand curves.

11. In long-run equilibrium under perfect competition, the firm's output is chosen so that average cost, marginal cost, and price are all equal. Output is at the point of minimum average cost, and the firm's demand curve is tangent to its average cost curve at its minimum point.

Concepts for Review

Perfect competition
Pure monopoly
Monopolistic competition
Oligopoly
Horizontal demand curve

Short-run equilibrium
Average variable cost
Total variable cost
Supply curve of the firm
Supply curve of the industry

Elasticity of supply
Long-run equilibrium
Opportunity cost
Economic profit

Questions for Discussion

1. Explain why a perfectly competitive firm does not expand its sales without limit if its horizontal demand curve means that it can sell as much as it wants to at the current market price.

2. Explain why a demand curve is also a curve of average revenue. Recalling that when an average revenue curve is neither rising nor falling, marginal revenue must equal average revenue, explain why it is always true that $P = MR = AR$ for the perfectly competitive firm.

3. Explain why in the short-run equilibrium of the perfectly competitive firm $P = MC$, while in long-run equilibrium $P = MC = AC$.

4. Which of the four attributes of perfect competition (many small firms, freedom of entry, standardized product, perfect information) are primarily responsible for the fact that the demand curve of a perfectly competitive firm is horizontal.

5. Which of the four attributes of perfect competition is primarily responsible for the firm's zero economic profits in long-run equilibrium?

6. It is indicated in the text (page 418) that the MC curve cuts the AVC curve at the *miminum* point of the latter. Explain why this must be so. (*Hint:* Since marginal costs are, by definition, all variable costs, the MC curve can be considered the curve of *marginal variable costs.* Apply the general relationships between marginals and averages explained in the appendix to Chapter 21.)

7. Explain why it is not sensible to close a business firm if it earns zero economic profits.

8. If a 12 percent rise in price leads to a 6 percent rise in quantity supplied, what is the elasticity of supply?

9. If the firm's lowest average cost is $7 and the corresponding average variable cost is $4, what does it pay a perfectly competitive firm to do if
   a. the market price is $8?
   b. the price is $6?
   c. the price is $3?

10. If the market price in a competitive industry is above its equilibrium level, what would you expect to happen?

The Price System and the Case for Laissez Faire

23

If there existed the universal mind that . . . would register simultaneously all the processes of nature and of society, that could forecast the results of their inter-reactions, such a mind . . . could . . . draw up a faultless and an exhaustive economic plan. . . . In truth, the bureaucracy often conceives that just such a mind is at its disposal; that is why it so easily frees itself from the control of the market.

LEON TROTSKY (a leader of the Russian Revolution, who was later assassinated).

Early in the book, we posed a question that provides an organizing framework for our study of microeconomics: What does the market do well, and what does it do poorly? Given what we have learned about demand in Chapters 18 and 19 and about supply in Chapters 20 through 22, we are now in a position to offer a fairly comprehensive answer to the first part of this question: What does the market do well? We begin by returning to two important themes raised in Chapters 3 and 4: First, that because all resources are scarce, it is critical to utilize them efficiently; second, that an economy must have some way to coordinate the actions of many individual consumers and producers. Specifically, we emphasize that society must somehow choose *how much* of each good to produce, *what input quantities* to use in the production process, and *how to distribute* the resulting outputs among consumers.

As the opening quotation suggests, these tasks are exceedingly difficult for central planners to accomplish effectively. But they are rather simple for a market system, which is why observers with philosophies as diverse as those of Adam Smith and Leon Trotsky have been admirers of the market. But the chapter should not be misinterpreted as a piece of salesmanship, for that is not its purpose. The version of the price system we shall study here is an idealized one in which every good is produced under the exacting conditions of perfect competition. Our real economy is as different from this idealized world as the physical world is from a frictionless vacuum tube. But just as the physicist uses the vacuum tube to illustrate the laws of gravity with a clarity that is otherwise unattainable, the economist uses the theoretical concept of a perfectly competitive economy to illustrate the virtues of the market. There will be plenty of time in later chapters to study its vices.

Efficient Resource Allocation: The Concept

The fundamental fact of scarcity limits the volume of goods and services that any economic system can produce. In Chapter 3 we illustrated the concept of scarcity with a graphical device called a *production possibilities frontier,* which we repeat here for convenience as Figure 23–1. The frontier, curve *BC,* depicts all combinations of missiles and milkshakes that this society can produce given the limited resources at its disposal. For example, if it decides to produce 300 missiles, it will have enough resources left over to produce *no more than* 500 million milkshakes (point *D*). Of course, it is always possible to produce fewer than 500 million milkshakes—at a point, such as *G,* below the production possibilities frontier. But if society does this, it is wasting some of its productive potential; that is, it is not operating *efficiently.*

In Chapter 3 we defined efficiency rather loosely as the absence of waste. Since the main subject of this chapter is how a competitive market economy allocates resources efficiently, we now need a more precise definition. It is easiest to define an **efficient allocation of resources** by saying what it is *not.* Suppose it were possible to rearrange things so that some people would have more of the things they want and no one would have to give up anything. Then failure to change the allocation of resources to take advantage of this opportunity would surely be wasteful—that is, *inefficient.* When there are no such possibilities of reallocating resources to make some people better off without making anyone else worse off, we say that the allocation of resources is *efficient.* Figure 23–1 illustrates the idea. Points below the frontier, like *G,* are inefficient because, if we start at *G,* we can make *both* milkshake lovers *and* missile lovers better off by moving to a point *on* the frontier, like *E.* Thus *no point below the frontier* can represent an efficient allocation of resources. By contrast, *every point on the frontier* is efficient because, no matter where on the frontier we start, it is impossible to get more of one good without giving up some of the other.

This example brings out two important features of the concept of efficiency. First, it is strictly a technical concept; there are no value judgments stated or implied, and tastes are not questioned. An economy is judged efficient if it is good

An **efficient allocation of resources** is one that takes advantage of every opportunity to make some individuals better off in their own estimation while not worsening the lot of anyone else.

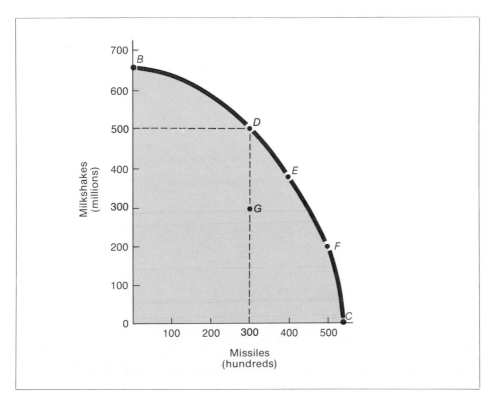

Figure 23–1
THE PRODUCTION POSSIBILITIES FRONTIER AND EFFICIENCY
Every point on the production possibilities frontier, *BC,* represents an efficient allocation of resources, because it is impossible to get more of one item without giving up some of the other. Points below the frontier, like *G,* are inefficient, since it is possible to obtain more of both goods.

at producing *whatever* people want. Thus the economy in the example is just as efficient when it produces only missiles at point *C* as when it produces only milkshakes at point *B*. Second, there are normally *many* efficient allocations of resources; in the example, *every* point on frontier *BC* is efficient. As a rule, the concept of efficiency does not permit us to tell which allocation is "best" for society. In fact, the most amazing thing about the concept of efficiency is that it gets us anywhere at all. At first blush, the criterion seems vacuous. It asserts, in effect, that anything agreed to unanimously is desirable. If some people are made better off *in their own estimation*, and none are harmed, then society is certainly better off by anyone's definition. Yet, as we shall see in this chapter, the concept of efficiency can be used to formulate surprisingly detailed rules to steer us away from situations in which resources are being wasted.

Scarcity and the Need to Coordinate Economic Decisions

An economy may be thought of as a complex machine with literally millions of component parts. If this machine is to function efficiently, some way must be found to make the parts work in harmony. A consumer in Peoria may decide to purchase two dozen eggs, and on the same day similar decisions are made by thousands of shoppers throughout the country. None of these purchasers knows or cares about the decisions of the others. Yet, scarcity requires that these demands must somehow all be coordinated with the production process so that the total quantity of eggs demanded does not exceed the total quantity supplied. The supermarkets, wholesalers, shippers, and chicken farmers must somehow arrive at consistent decisions, for otherwise the economic process will deteriorate into chaos. And there are many other such decisions that must be coordinated. One cannot run machines that are completed except for a few parts that have not been delivered. Refrigerators and cars cannot be used unless there is an adequate supply of fuel.

In an economy that is planned and centrally directed, it is easy to imagine how such coordination takes place—though the implementation turns out to be far more difficult than the idea. Central planners set production targets for firms, and may even tell firms how to meet these targets. In extreme cases, consumers may even be told, rather than asked, what they want to consume.

In a market system, prices are used to coordinate economic activity instead. High prices discourage consumption of the resources that are most scarce while low prices encourage consumption of the resources that are comparatively abundant. For example, if supplies of oil begin to run out while enormous reserves of coal remain, the price of oil can be expected to rise in comparison with the price of coal. As the price of oil rises, only those for whom oil offers the greatest benefits will continue to buy it. Firms or individuals that can get along almost equally well with coal or gas will switch to these more economical fuels. Some business firms will transform their equipment, and new homes will be built with heating systems that use gas. Only those who find alternative fuels a poor or unacceptable substitute for oil will continue to use oil despite its higher price. In this way, prices are the instrument used by Adam Smith's invisible hand to organize the economy's production.

The invisible hand has an astonishing capacity to handle a coordination problem of truly enormous proportions—one that will remain beyond the capabilities of electronic computers at least for the foreseeable future. It is true that like any mechanism this one has its imperfections, some of them rather serious. But without understanding the nature of the overall task performed by the market system, it is all too easy to lose sight of the tremendously demanding task that it constantly accomplishes—unnoticed, undirected, and at least in some respects, amazingly well. Let us, then, examine in more detail just what this coordination problem is like.

Three Coordination Tasks in the Economy

Any economic system, whether planned or unplanned, must find answers to three basic questions of resource allocation:

1. How much of each commodity should be produced (output selection)?
2. What quantities of each of the available inputs should be used to produce each good (production planning)?
3. How should the resulting products be divided among the consumers (distribution)?

Let us look at how each of these questions is answered by a system of free and unfettered markets, the method of economic organization that the eighteenth-century French economists named **laissez faire.** Under laissez faire, the government would prevent crime, enforce contracts, and build roads and other types of public works; but it would not set prices and would interfere as little as possible with the operation of free markets. How does such an unmanaged economy solve the three coordination problems?

Laissez faire refers to a program of minimal interference with the workings of the market system. The term means that people should be left alone in carrying out their economic affairs.

Output Selection

In a free-market system, it is the price mechanism that decides what to produce. It does so by what we have called the "law" of supply and demand. Where there is a shortage—that is, where quantity demanded exceeds quantity supplied—the market mechanism pushes the price up, thereby encouraging more production and less consumption of the commodity in short supply. Where there is a surplus—that is, where quantity supplied exceeds quantity demanded—the same mechanism works in reverse: the price falls, which discourages production and stimulates consumption.

We can make these abstract ideas more concrete by looking at a particular example. Suppose millions of people wake up one morning with a craving for omelettes. For the moment, the quantity of eggs demanded exceeds the quantity supplied. But within days the market mechanism swings into action to meet this sudden change in demand. The price of eggs rises, which stimulates the production of eggs. In the first instance, farmers simply bring more eggs to market by taking them out of storage. Over a somewhat longer period of time, chickens that otherwise would have been sold for meat are kept in the chicken coops laying eggs. Finally, if the high price of eggs persists, farmers begin to increase their flocks, build more cages, and so on. Thus, a shift in consumer demand leads to a shift in society's resources; more eggs are wanted, and so the market mechanism sees to it that more of society's resources are devoted to the production of eggs.

The same sort of result follows if a technological breakthrough reduces the input quantities needed to produce some item. Electronic calculators are a marvelous example. Only a decade ago, calculators were so expensive that they could be found only in business firms and scientific laboratories. Then advances in science and engineering reduced their cost dramatically, and the market went to work. With costs sharply reduced, prices fell dramatically and the quantity demanded skyrocketed. Electronics firms flocked into the industry to meet this demand, which is to say that more of society's resources were devoted to producing the calculators that were suddenly in such great demand. These examples lead us to conclude that:

Under laissez faire, the allocation of society's resources among different products depends on two basic influences: consumer preferences and the relative difficulty of producing the goods, that is, their production costs.

Notice that no bureaucrat or central planner arranges the allocation of resources. Instead, allocation is guided by an unseen force—the lure of profits, which is the invisible hand that guides chicken farmers to increase their flocks and electronics firms to build new factories.

Production Planning

Once the composition of output has been decided, the next coordination task is to determine just how those goods are going to be produced. As a matter of fact, these two decisions cannot be made separately. The method chosen for production determines what combinations of, say, coffee and bananas can be obtained, though it is simpler to think of these decisions as if they occurred one at a time. The production-planning problem includes, among other things, the assignment of inputs to enterprises—that is, which farm or factory will get how much of which materials. These decisions can be crucial. If a factory runs short of an essential input, the entire production process may grind to a halt.

Once again, under laissez faire it is the price system that apportions fuels and other raw materials among the different industries in accord with those industries' requirements. The firm that needs a piece of equipment most urgently will be the last to drop out of the market for that product when prices rise. If more grain is demanded by millers than is currently available, the price will rise and bring quantity demanded back into line with quantity supplied, always giving priority to those users who are willing to pay the most for grain. Thus:

In a free market, inputs are assigned to the firms that can make the most productive (most profitable) use of them.

This task, which sounds so simple, is actually almost unimaginably complex. It is also one on which many centrally planned systems have floundered. We will return to it shortly, as an illustration of how difficult it is to replace the market by a central planning bureau. But first let us consider the third of our three coordination problems—the distribution of goods among consumers.

Distribution of Products Among Consumers

The third task of any economy is the critical decision as to which consumer gets each of the goods that have been produced. The objective is to distribute the available supplies so as to match the differing preferences of consumers as well as possible. Coffee lovers must not be flooded with tea while tea drinkers are showered with coffee.

The price mechanism solves this problem by assigning the highest prices to the goods in greatest demand and then letting individual consumers pursue their own self-interests. Consider our example of the rising price of eggs. We focussed earlier on the effects of price increases on the supply side of the market. But analogous forces operate on the demand side. As the price of eggs rises, those whose craving for omelettes is not terribly strong will begin to buy fewer eggs. In effect, the price acts as a rationing device, which apportions the available eggs among the consumers who are willing to pay the most for them. But the price mechanism has one important advantage over other rationing devices: it is able to pay attention to consumer preferences. If eggs are rationed by the most obvious and usual means (say, two to a person), everyone ends up with the same quantity—whether he thinks eggs the more unpleasant component of his breakfast or the ingredients of his evening's souffle, for which he pangs all day long. The price system, on the other hand, permits each consumer to set his own priorities. If you just barely tolerate eggs, a rise in their price quickly induces you to get your protein from some other source. But the egg lover is not induced to switch so readily. Thus:

The price system carries out the distribution process by rationing goods on the basis of preferences *and relative incomes.*

Notice the last three words. This rationing process *does* favor the rich, and this is a problem that market economies must confront. However, we may still want to think twice before declaring ourselves opposed to the price system. If equality is our goal, might not a more reasonable solution be to use the tax system to equalize incomes, and *then* let the market mechanism distribute goods in accord with preferences?

We have just seen, in broad outline, how a laissez faire economy addresses the three basic issues of resource allocation: what to produce, how to produce it, and how to distribute the resulting products. Since it performs these tasks quietly, without central direction, and with no apparent concern for the public interest, many radical critics have predicted that such an unplanned system must degenerate into chaos. Yet that does not seem to be the way things work out. Unplanned the market may be, but its results are far from chaotic. In fact, quite ironically, it is the centrally planned economies that often find themselves in economic chaos. Perhaps the best way to appreciate the accomplishments of the market is to consider how a centrally planned system copes with the coordination problems we have just outlined. For this purpose, we will concentrate on just one of the problems: production planning.

In this cartoon from a Soviet humor magazine, one construction worker comments to another, "A slight mistake in the plans, perhaps."

Input–Output Analysis: The Near Impossibility of Perfect Central Planning

Of the three coordination tasks of any economy, production planning—that is, the assignment of inputs to specific industries and firms—has claimed the most attention of central planners. The reason is that, because the production processes of the various industries are *interdependent*, the whole economy can grind to a halt if the production-planning problem is not solved satisfactorily. Let's take a simple example. Gasoline is used not only by consumers to run cars, but also by the trucking industry. Unless the planners allocate enough gasoline to the truckers, products will not get to market; and unless they allocate enough trucks to haul the gasoline to gas stations, consumers will not be able to get to the market to buy the products.

Clearly, these problems must be dealt with together, not separately. Because the output required for any industry depends on the output desired from every other industry, planners cannot be sure that the production of the various outputs will be sufficient to meet both consumer and industrial demands unless they take explicit account of the interdependencies among industries. If they change the output target for one industry, every other industry's output target also must be adjusted. For instance, if planners decide to provide consumers with more electricity, then more steel will have to be produced for more electric generators. But the increase in steel output will require more coal to be mined. More mining in turn means that still more electricity is needed to light the mines, to run the elevators, and perhaps even to run some of the trains that carry the coal, and so on and on. Any single change in production, like the illustrative rise in electricity output, sets off a chain of adjustments throughout the economy that require still further adjustments.

To decide how much of each output an economy must produce, the planner must use statistics to form a set of equations, one equation for each product, and then solve those equations *simultaneously*. The technique used to solve these complicated equations—**input–output analysis**—was invented by economist Wassily Leontief, and it won him the Nobel Prize in 1973. The equations of input–output analysis, which are illustrated in the accompanying boxed insert, take account of the interdependence among industries by describing precisely how each industry's target output depends on every other industry's target. Only by solving these equations *simultaneously* for the required outputs of electricity, steel, coal, and so on, can one be sure of a consistent solution that produces the required amounts of these products.

The example of input–output analysis that appears in the box is not provided so that you can learn how to apply the technique yourself. Its real purpose is to illustrate the *very complicated* nature of the problem that faces a central planner. For the problem faced by a real planner, while analogous to the one in the box, is enormously more complex. In any real economy, the number of commodities is far greater than the three outputs in the example. In the United States, some large manufacturing companies individually deal in hundreds of thousands of items, and the armed forces keep several *million* different items in inventory. In planning, it is ultimately necessary to make calculations for each such item. It is not enough to plan the right number of bolts *in total*; we must make sure that the required number *of each size* is produced. (Try to put five million large bolts into five million small nuts.) So, to be sure our plans will really work, we need a separate equation for every size of bolt and one for every size and type of nut. But then, to replicate the analysis described in the boxed insert, we will have to solve simultaneously several *million* equations! Unfortunately, there is as yet no

Input–Output Equations: An Example

For simplicity, think of an economy with only three outputs: electricity, steel, and coal; and let E, S, and C represent the dollar value of their respective outputs. Suppose that for every dollar's worth of steel, \$0.20 worth of electricity is used up, so that the total electricity demand of steel manufacturers is $0.2S$. Similarly, assume the coal manufacturers use up \$0.30 of electricity in producing \$1 worth of coal, or a total of $0.3C$ units of electricity. Since E dollars of electricity are produced in total, the amount left over for consumers, after subtraction of industrial demands for fuel, will be

$$E \quad - \quad 0.2S \quad - \quad 0.3C$$

(available   (use in steel   (use in coal
electricity)   production)   production) .

Suppose further that the central planners have decided to supply \$15 million worth of electricity to consumers. We end up with the electricity output equation

$$E - 0.2S - 0.3C = 15 .$$

The planner will also need such an equation for each of the two other industries, specifying for each of them the net amounts intended to be left for consumers after the industrial uses of these products. The full set of equations might then be:

$$
\begin{aligned}
E - 0.2S - 0.3C &= 15 \\
S - 0.1E - 0.06C &= 7 \\
C - 0.15E - 0.4S &= 10 .
\end{aligned}
$$

These are typical equations in an input–output analysis. Only, in practice, a typical analysis has dozens and sometimes hundreds of equations with similar numbers of unknowns. This, then, is the logic of input–output analysis.

---

electronic computer capable of doing this. Worse still is the data problem. Each of our three equations requires *three* pieces of statistical information, making 3×3, or 9, numbers in total. This is because the equation for electricity must indicate on the basis of statistical information how much electricity is needed in steel production, how much in coal production, and how much is demanded by consumers. Therefore, in a five-industry analysis, 5×5, or 25, pieces of data are needed, a 100-industry analysis requires 100^2, or 10,000 numbers, and a million-item input–output study might need one *trillion* pieces of information. The data-gathering problems are therefore no easy task, to put it mildly. While there are other, somewhat more technical, complications that need not be gone into here, we have seen enough to conclude that:

A full, rigorous central-planning solution to the production problem is a tremendous task, requiring an overwhelming quantity of information and some incredibly difficult calculations. Yet this very difficult job is carried out automatically and unobtrusively by the price mechanism in a free-market economy.

Efficient Output Selection: What to Produce

We have now seen how the market mechanism solves the three basic coordination problems of any economy—what to produce, how to produce, and how to distribute the goods to consumers. And we have suggested that these same tasks pose almost insurmountable difficulties for central planners. One critical question remains. Is the allocation of resources that the market mechanism selects *efficient*, according to the definition of efficiency presented earlier in this chapter? The answer is that, under the idealized circumstances of perfect competition, it is. Since a detailed proof of this assertion for all three coordination tasks would be long and time-consuming, we will present the proof only for the first of the three tasks—output selection. The corresponding analyses for the production planning and distribution problems are quite similar, and are reserved for the appendix.

Our specific question, then, is this: Given the bill of goods selected by the market mechanism, is it possible to improve matters by producing more of one good and less of another? Might it be "better," for example, if society produced more beef and less lamb? We shall answer this question in the negative by first developing a criterion for efficient output selection, and then establishing that a perfectly competitive economy *automatically* meets this criterion. We first state the rule for efficient output selection:

Efficiency in the choice of output quantities requires that, for each of the economy's outputs, the marginal cost (MC) of the last unit produced be equal to the marginal utility (MU) of the last unit consumed. In symbols:

$$MC = MU.$$

Let us use an example to see why this rule *must* be satisfied for the allocation of resources to be efficient. Suppose the marginal utility of an additional pound of beef to consumers is $8, while its marginal cost of production is only $5. Then the value of the resources that would have to be used up to produce one more pound of beef (its MC) would be $3 less than the value of that additional pound to consumers (its MU).[1] In a sense, society could get more out of the economic machine (the MU) than it was putting in (the MC) by increasing the output of beef by one pound. Thus an increase in output must be an improvement for society, so the initial output cannot be optimal. The opposite is true if the MC of beef exceeds the MU of beef. In that case, the last pound of beef must have used up more value (MC) than it produced (MU). It would therefore be better to have less beef and more of something else.

What we have shown, then, is that if there is *any* product for which MU is not equal to MC, the economy must be wasting an opportunity to produce a net improvement in consumers' welfare. This is exactly what we mean by using resources *inefficiently*. Just as was true at point G in Figure 23–1, if MC $\neq$ MU for any commodity, it is possible to rearrange things so as to make some people better off while harming no one. It follows that efficiency in the choice of outputs is achieved only when MC = MU for *every* good.

The next step in the argument is to show that under perfect competition the price system *automatically* leads buyers and sellers to behave in a way that makes MU and MC equal. To see this, recall from the last chapter that under perfect competition it is most profitable for each beef-producing firm to produce the quantity of beef at which the marginal cost of the beef is equal to the price of beef:

$$MC = P.$$

This must be so because, if the marginal cost of beef were less than the price, the farmer could add to his profits by increasing the size of his herd (or the amount of grain that he feeds his animals); and the reverse would be true if the marginal cost of beef were greater than its price. Thus, under perfect competition, the lure of profits leads each producer of beef (and of every other product) to supply the quantity that makes MC = P.

We also learned, in Chapter 18, that it is in the interest of each consumer to

[1] Remember that we are measuring marginal utility in terms of money. See Chapter 18.

purchase the quantity of beef at which the marginal utility of beef is equal to the price of beef:

$$MU = P.$$

If he did not do this, we saw, either an increase or a decrease in his purchase of beef would leave him better off. Putting these last two equations together, we see that the invisible hand enforces the following string of equalities:

$$MC = P = MU.$$

But if both the MC of beef and the MU of beef are equal to the same price, P, then they must surely be equal to each other. That is, it must be true that the quantity of beef produced and consumed in a perfectly competitive market satisfies the equation:

$$MC = MU,$$

which is precisely our rule for efficient output selection. Since the same must be true of every other product supplied by a competitive industry:

Under perfect competition, the uncoordinated decisions of producers and consumers can be expected *automatically* to produce a quantity of each good that satisfies the MC = MU rule for efficiency in deciding what to produce. That is, under the idealized conditions of perfect competition, the market mechanism, *without any government intervention*, is capable of allocating society's scarce resources efficiently.

This is truly a remarkable result. How can the price mechanism automatically satisfy all the exacting requirements for efficiency—requirements that no central planner can hope to handle because of the masses of statistics and the enormous calculations they require? The conclusion seems analogous to the rabbit suddenly pulled from the magician's hat. But, as always, rabbits come out of hats only if they were hidden there in the first place. What really is the machinery by which our act of magic works?

The secret is that the price system lets consumers and producers pursue their own best interests—something they are probably very good at doing. Prices are the dollar costs of commodities to consumers. So, in pursuing their own best interests, consumers will buy the commodities that give them the most satisfaction *per dollar.* As we learned in Chapter 18, this means that each consumer will continue to buy beef until the marginal utility of beef is equal to the market price. And since every consumer pays the same price in a perfectly competitive market, the market mechanism ensures that *every* consumer's MU will be equal to this common price.

Turning next to the producers, we know from Chapter 22 that competition equates prices with marginal costs. And, once again, since every producer faces the same market price, the forces of competition will bring the MC of *every* producer into equality with this common price. Since MC measures the resource cost (in every firm) of producing one more unit of the good and MU measures the value (to every consumer) of consuming one more unit, then when MC = MU *the cost of the good to society is exactly equal to the value that consumers place on it.* Therefore:

When all prices are set equal to marginal costs, the price system is giving the correct cost signals to consumers. It has set prices at levels that induce consumers to use the resources of society with the same care they devote to watching their own money.

This is the magic of the invisible hand. Unlike central planners, consumers need not know how difficult it is to manufacture a certain product, nor how scarce are the inputs required by the production process. Everything the consumer needs to know to make his or her decision is embodied in the market price, which, under perfect competition, accurately reflects marginal costs.

Can Price Increases Ever Serve the Public Interest?

This last discussion raises a point that people untrained in economics always find difficult to accept: *low prices may not always be in the public interest.* The reason is clear enough. If prices are set "too low," that is, below marginal cost, then consumers will receive the "wrong" signals and be encouraged to consume too much, thereby squandering society's precious resources. A historic illustration is perhaps the most striking way to bring out the point. In 1834, some ten years before the great potato famine brought so many people from Ireland to the United States, a professor of economics named Mountifort Longfield lectured at the University of Dublin about the price system. And he offered the following remarkable illustration of his point:

Suppose the crop of potatoes in Ireland was to fall short in some year one-sixth of the usual consumption. If [there were no] increase of price, the whole . . . supply of the year would be exhausted in ten months, and for the remaining two months a scene of misery and famine beyond description would ensue. . . . But when prices [increase] the sufferers [often believe] that it is not caused by scarcity. . . . They suppose that there are provisions enough, but that the distress is caused by the insatiable rapacity of the possessors . . . [and] they have generally succeeded in obtaining laws against [the price increases] . . . which alone can prevent the provisions from being entirely consumed long before a new supply can be obtained.[2]

Longfield's reasoning can be phrased in modern terminology. If the crop fails, potatoes become scarcer; the marginal cost (MC) of a potato rises. If society is to use its resources efficiently, the marginal utility (MU) of potatoes must rise to match the higher MC. But a higher MU is achieved only by cutting back on the consumption of potatoes—which is just what rising prices would do *automatically* if the market mechanism were left to its own devices. However, if the price is held artificially below marginal cost, then consumers setting $MU = P$ will inadvertently be setting MU below MC, which is to say they will be using society's resources inefficiently. In this case, the inefficiency shows up in the form of famine and suffering when the year's crop is consumed before the next crop arrives.

It is not easy to accept the notion that higher prices can serve the public interest better than lower ones. Politicians who voice this view are put in the position of the proverbial father who, before spanking his child, announces, "This is going to hurt me much more than it hurts you!" Since advocacy of higher prices courts political disaster, the political system often rejects the market solution when resources suddenly become more scarce. The pricing of oil in the

[2]Mountifort Longfield, *Lectures on Political Economy*, (Dublin: 1834), pages 53–56.

United States provides an excellent contemporary example. For years after OPEC drastically increased the price of oil in 1973, legislation in the United States held domestic oil prices below free-market levels. The consequence, as economists were quick to point out, was that American consumers faced a market price for oil that was below the true marginal cost of oil to society. Consumers were therefore encouraged to use too much oil, and our dependence on imported oil increased. Suggestions to end the price controls, first by President Ford and later by President Carter, were rebuffed by lawmakers who feared the political consequences. Only in 1979 did President Carter begin the decontrol process, a process that was completed by President Reagan in 1981—more than seven years after OPEC's actions had caused a scarcity of oil.

Prevention of a rise in prices where a rise is appropriate can have serious consequences indeed. We have seen from Longfield's example that it can contribute to famine. We know that it caused nationwide chaos in gasoline distribution after the sudden fall in Iranian oil exports in 1979. It has contributed to the surrender of cities under military siege when effective price ceilings discouraged the efforts of those who were taking the risk of smuggling food supplies through enemy lines. And it has discouraged the construction of housing in cities, when rent controls made building a losing proposition.

Recall from Chapter 4 that one of the 12 Ideas for Beyond the Final Exam states that interfering with free markets by preventing price increases can sometimes serve the public very badly. In extreme cases it can even produce havoc—undermining production and causing extreme shortages of vitally needed products. The reason is that prohibiting price increases in situations of true scarcity prevents the market mechanism from allocating resources efficiently. The invisible hand is not permitted to do its work.

Of course there are cases in which it is appropriate to resist price increases— where unrestrained monopoly would otherwise succeed in gouging the public; where taxes are imposed on products capriciously and inappropriately; and where rising prices fall so heavily on the disadvantaged that rationing becomes the more acceptable option. But it is important to recognize that artificial restrictions on prices can produce serious and even tragic consequences—consequences that should be taken into account before a decision is made to tamper with the market mechanism.

Other Roles of Prices: Income Distribution and Fairness

So far we have stressed the role of prices most emphasized by economists: prices guide the allocation of resources. But a different role of prices often commands the spotlight in public discussions: prices influence the distribution of income between buyers and sellers. For example, high rents often make tenants poorer and landlords richer. This rather obvious role of prices draws the most attention from the public, politicians, and regulators, and is one we should not lose sight of.[3] Markets only serve demands that are backed up by consumers' desire *and ability* to pay. Though the market system may do well in serving a poor family, giving that family more food and clothing than a less efficient economy would provide, it offers far more to the family of a millionaire. Many observers object that such an arrangement represents a great injustice, however efficient it may be.

[3]Income distribution is the subject of Part Six.

Often, recommendations made by economists for improving the economy's efficiency are opposed on the grounds that they are unfair. For example, economists frequently advocate higher prices for transportation facilities at the time of day when they are most crowded. They propose a pricing arrangement called *peak, off-peak pricing* under which prices for public transportation are higher during rush hours than during other hours. The rationale for this proposal is quite clear from our discussion of efficiency. A seat on a train is a much scarcer resource during rush hours than during other times of the day when the trains run fairly empty. Thus, according to the principles of efficiency outlined in this chapter, seats should be assigned higher prices during rush hours to discourage those consumers who have a choice about when they travel from using the trains during peak periods. The same notion applies to other services. Charges for nighttime long-distance telephone calls are lower than those in the daytime and, in some places, electricity is sold more cheaply at night, when demand does not strain the supplier's generating capacity.

Yet the proposal that higher fares should be charged for public transportation during peak hours—say, from 8:00 A.M. to 9:30 A.M., and from 4:30 P.M. to 6 P.M.—has often run into stiff opposition on the grounds that most of the burden will fall on lower-income working people who have no choice about the timing of their trips. For example, a survey in Great Britain of members of Parliament and of economists found that while high peak-period fares were favored by 88 percent of the economists, only 35 percent of the Conservative Party M.P.'s and just 19 percent of the Labor Party M.P.'s approved of this arrangement (see Table 23–1). We may surmise that the M.P.'s reflected the views of the public more accurately than did the economists. In this case, people simply find the efficient solution unfair, and so refuse to adopt it.

A Case Study: Pricing of Bridges Near San Francisco

Our entire discussion of pricing and resource allocation can be illustrated very well by a real-life example—the prices (tolls) that are charged to use the bridges in

Table 23–1
REPLIES TO A QUESTIONNAIRE

QUESTION: In order to make the most efficient use of a city's resources, how should subway and bus fares vary during the day?	Economists (percent)	Conservative Party M.P.'s (percent)	Labor Party M.P.'s (percent)
a. They should be relatively low during rush hour to transport as many people as possible at lower costs.	1	—	40
b. They should be the same at all times to avoid making travelers alter their schedules because of price differences.	4	60	39
c. They should be relatively high during rush hour to minimize the amount of equipment needed to transport the daily travelers.	88	35	19
d. Impossible to answer on the data and alternatives given.	7	5	2

SOURCE: Adapted from Samuel Brittan, *Is There an Economic Consensus?* (London: Macmillan, 1973), page 93.

the San Francisco Bay area. We will see that although proper pricing of these scarce resources (the bridges) can enhance efficiency, people nonetheless have often resisted the efficient solution.

Figure 23–2 shows a map of the San Francisco Bay area, featuring the five bridges that serve the bulk of the traffic in and around the bay. A traveler going from north of Berkeley (point *A*) to Palo Alto (point *B*) has a choice of at least three routes:

1. Over the Richmond–San Rafael Bridge, across the Golden Gate Bridge, through San Francisco, and on southward.
2. Cross the bay on the San Francisco–Oakland Bay Bridge, and continue on southward as before.
3. Come down the eastern side of the bay, cross on the San Mateo–Hayward Bridge or the Dumbarton Bridge, and then head on to Palo Alto.

Let's consider which of these three choices utilizes society's resources most efficiently. The most crowded of the five bridges is the Golden Gate, followed closely by the San Francisco–Oakland Bay Bridge. The first carries nearly 16,000 cars per lane per day, and the second nearly 10,000. During rush hours, delays are frequent and traffic barely crawls across these bridges. In other words, space is

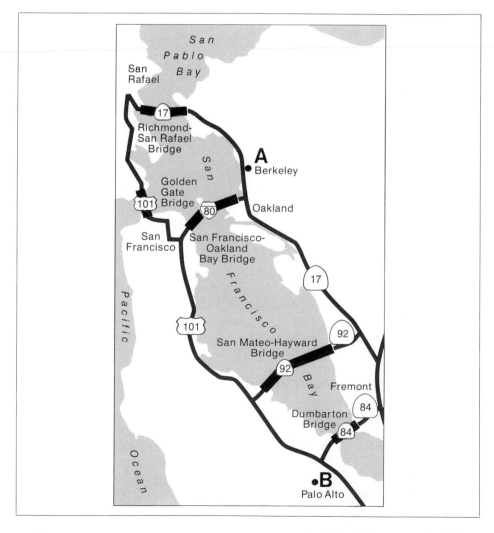

Figure 23–2
TOLL BRIDGES OF THE SAN FRANCISCO BAY AREA

scarce, and every car that uses these bridges makes it that much harder for others to get across. On the other hand, the San Mateo and Dumbarton bridges carry approximately 3000 and 4000 cars per lane per day, respectively. From the efficiency point of view, it is best if any driver who has a choice of routes takes the one using the least crowded bridges. This will help reduce the amount of time wasted by the population as a whole in getting where they are going. Specifically, in our illustration, Route 1, using the Golden Gate Bridge, is not a socially desirable way for our driver to get to Palo Alto. Route 2, with its use of the San Francisco–Oakland Bay Bridge, is almost as bad because of the added delays it contributes to everyone else. Route 3 is the best choice from the viewpoint of the public interest. The pattern of prices that would promote the most efficient utilization of bridges would involve a higher price (very likely a substantially higher price) for the use of the most crowded bridges, on which space is such a scarce resource, balanced by lower prices on the uncrowded bridges. Such a pricing system would induce more drivers to use the uncrowded bridges. This is just the same reasoning that leads economists to advocate low prices for abundant minerals and high prices for scarce ones, and to advocate low prices on trains during hours when space is abundant and higher prices during rush hours when space is scarce.

Since these principles seem so clear and rational, the reader may be interested to see at what levels the actual bridge tolls were set when this book was written. Travel on the crowded Golden Gate Bridge required a $1.25 toll for a round trip. But the San Francisco–Oakland Bay, Dumbarton, and San Mateo–Hayward bridges each carried a 75-cent toll even though the Bay Bridge was far more crowded than the others. Even stranger, the Richmond–San Rafael Bridge, which was about as sparsely used as any, charged a $1 toll.

From the point of view of efficiency, this pattern of tolls obviously seems quite irrational. Some of the least crowded bridges were assigned the highest tolls! Yet some widely held notions of "fairness" explain why the authorities placed rather low tolls on some highly congested bridges. Many people feel that it is fair for those who travel on a bridge to pay for its costs. In this view, it would be unjust for those who use the crowded San Francisco–Oakland Bay Bridge to pay for the less-crowded Richmond–San Rafael Bridge. Naturally, a bridge that is traveled heavily more quickly takes in the revenue necessary to recoup the cost of building, maintaining, and running it. That is why fairness is believed to dictate low tolls on crowded bridges. On the other hand, the relatively few users of a less-crowded bridge must pay higher tolls in order to make a fair contribution toward its costs. Of course, such a pattern of tolls slows traffic and lures even more drivers to the already overcrowded bridges.

Prices that offer a bonus for the use of overcrowded facilities almost certainly impose losses of time and other costs upon many people, and thereby contribute to inefficiency. But one cannot legitimately conclude that advocates of such prices are "stupid." Whether the pattern of prices illustrated by the tolls in the San Francisco Bay area is or is not desirable must be decided, ultimately, on the basis of the public's sense of what constitutes fairness and justice in pricing and the amount it is willing to pay in terms of delays, inconvenience, and other inefficiencies in order to avoid apparent injustices. Economics alone cannot decide the appropriate trade-off between fairness and efficiency. It cannot even pretend to judge which pricing arrangements are fair and which are unfair. But it can and should indicate whether a particular pricing decision, proposed because it is considered fair, will impose heavy inefficiency costs upon the community. Economic analysis also can and should indicate how to evaluate these costs, so that the issues can be decided on the basis of an understanding of the facts.

Toward Assessment of the Price Mechanism

Our analysis of the case for laissez faire is not meant to imply that the free-enterprise system is an ideal of perfection, without flaw or room for improvement. In fact, it has a number of serious shortcomings that we will explore in subsequent chapters. But recognition of these imperfections should not conceal the enormous accomplishments of the price mechanism. We have shown that, given the proper circumstances, it is capable of meeting the most exacting requirements of allocative efficiency, requirements that go well beyond the capacity of any central planning bureau. The market mechanism has provided an abundance of goods unprecedented in human history. Even centrally planned economies use the price mechanism to carry out considerable portions of the task of allocation, most notably the distribution of goods among consumers. No one has invented an instrument for directing the economy that can replace the price mechanism, which no one ever designed or planned for, but that simply grew by itself, a child of the processes of history.

Summary

1. An allocation of resources is considered *inefficient* if it wastes opportunities to change the use of the economy's resources in any way that makes consumers better off. Resource allocation is called *efficient* if there are no such wasted opportunities.

2. Resource allocation involves three basic coordination tasks: (a) How much of each good to produce, (b) What quantities of the available inputs to use in producing the different goods, and (c) How to distribute the goods among different consumers.

3. Under perfect competition, the free-market mechanism adjusts prices so that the resulting resource allocation is efficient. It induces firms to buy and use inputs in ways that yield the most valuable outputs per unit of input; it distributes products among consumers in ways that match individual preferences; and it produces commodities whose value to consumers exceeds the cost of producing them.

4. Efficient decisions about what goods to produce require that the marginal cost (MC) of producing each good be equated to its marginal utility (MU) to consumers. If the MC of any good differs from its MU, then society can improve resource allocation by changing the level of production.

5. Because the market system induces firms to set MC equal to price, and induces consumers to set MU equal to price, it automatically guarantees that the MC = MU condition is satisfied.

6. Sometimes improvements in efficiency require some prices to increase in order to stimulate supply or to prevent waste in consumption. This is why price increases can sometimes be beneficial to consumers.

7. In addition to allocating resources, prices also influence the distribution of income between buyers and sellers.

8. The workings of the price mechanism can be criticized on the grounds that it is unfair because of the preferential treatment it accords wealthy consumers.

Concepts for Review

Efficient allocation of resources

Coordination tasks: output selection, production planning, distribution of goods

Laissez faire
Input–output analysis
MC = MU condition

Questions for Discussion

1. What are the possible social advantages of price rises in each of the two following cases?
   a. Charging higher prices for electrical power on very hot days when many people use air conditioners.
   b. Raising water prices in drought-stricken areas.

2. Discuss the fairness of the two preceding proposals.

3. Discuss the nature of the inefficiency in each of the following cases:
   a. An arrangement whereby relatively little coffee and much tea is made available to people who prefer coffee and that accomplishes the reverse for tea lovers.

b. An arrangement in which watchmakers are assigned to ditch digging and unskilled laborers to repairing watches.

c. An arrangement that produces a large quantity of trucks and few cars, assuming both cost about the same to produce and to run but that most people in the community prefer cars to trucks.

4. In reality, which of the following circumstances might give rise to each of the preceding problem situations?
   a. Regulation of output quantities by a government.

b. Rationing of commodities.

c. Assignment of soldiers to different jobs in an army.

5. In a free market, how will the price mechanism deal with each of the inefficiencies described in Question 3?

6. Suppose a given set of resources can be used to make either one handbag or two wallets, and the MC of a handbag is $14 while the MC of a wallet is $7. If the MU of a wallet is $7 and the MU of a handbag is $18, what can be done to improve resource allocation? What can you say about the gain to consumers?

Appendix

The Invisible Hand in the Distribution of Goods and in Production Planning

On pages 437–440 of this chapter we offered a glimpse of the way economists analyze the workings of the invisible hand by showing how the market handles the problem of efficiency in one of the three tasks of resource allocation: the selection of outputs. We explained the MC = MU rule that must be followed for a set of outputs to be efficient, and showed how a free market can induce people to act in a way that satisfies that rule. In this appendix we complete the story, examining how the price mechanism handles the two other tasks of resource allocation: the distribution of goods among consumers and the planning of production.

Efficient Distribution of Commodities: Who Gets What?

While decisions about distribution among consumers depend critically on value judgments, a surprising amount can be said purely on grounds of efficiency. For example, consumers' desires are not being served efficiently if large quantities of milk are given to someone whose preference is for apple cider, while gallons of cider are assigned to a milk lover. Deciding how much of which commodity goes to whom is a matter that requires delicate calculation. It causes great difficulties during wartime when planners must ration goods. They generally end up utilizing a crude egalitarianism: the same amount of

butter to everyone, the same amount of coffee to everyone, and so on. This may be justified, to paraphrase the statement of a high official in another country, by an "unwillingness to pander to acquired tastes," but it is easy to see that such fixed rations are unlikely to produce an efficient result.

The analysis of the efficient distribution of the economy's different products among its many consumers turns out to be quite similar to our previous analysis of efficient output selection. Suppose there are two individuals, Mr. Steaker and Ms. Chop, and that Steaker wants lots of beef and little lamb, while the opposite is true of Chop. Suppose each is getting one pound of lamb and one pound of beef per week. It is then possible to make *both* people better off without increasing their total consumption of two pounds of beef and two pounds of lamb if Mr. Steaker trades some of his lamb to Ms. Chop in return for some beef. The initial distribution of goods was not efficient because it left room for trades that yield *mutual* gains.

It is easy enough to think of allocations of commodities among consumers that are *inefficient*—simply assign to each person only what he does not like. But how does one define an allocation that *is* efficient? After all, there are many of us whose preferences have much in common. If two individuals both like beef and lamb, how shall the available amounts of the two commodities be divided between them? We will now show that, as in the analysis of efficient output selection, there is a simple rule that must be satisfied by *any* efficient distribution of products among consumers. Consider any two commodities in the economy, such as beef and lamb, and any two consumers, like Steaker and Chop, each of whom likes to eat some of each type of meat. Then:

The basic rules for the efficient distribution of beef and lamb between Steaker and Chop are that

$$\text{Steaker's MU of beef} = \text{Chop's MU of beef}$$

and

$$\text{Steaker's MU of lamb} = \text{Chop's MU of lamb} .$$

Analogous equations must be satisfied for every other pair of individuals, and for every other pair of products.

Why are these equalities required for efficiency? Recall that a distribution of commodities among consumers can be efficient only if it has taken advantage of every potential gain from trade. That is, if two people can trade in a way that makes them *both* better off, then the distribution cannot be efficient. We can show that if *either* of the previous equations is not satisfied, then such trades are possible. Suppose, for example, that the following are the relevant marginal utilities:

$$\text{Steaker's MU of beef} = \$4$$
$$\text{Chop's MU of beef} = \$2$$

$$\text{Steaker's MU of lamb} = \$1$$
$$\text{Chop's MU of lamb} = \$1$$

In such a case a mutually beneficial exchange of beef and lamb can be arranged. For example, if Steaker gives Chop three pounds of lamb in return for one pound of beef, they will both be better off. Steaker loses three pounds of lamb, which are worth \$3 to him, and gets a pound of beef, which is worth \$4 to him. So he winds up \$1 ahead. Similarly, Chop gives up one pound of beef, which is worth \$2 to her, and gets in return three pounds of lamb, worth \$3 to her. So she also gains \$1. Such a mutually beneficial exchange is possible here because the two consumers have different marginal utilities for beef. Each can benefit by giving up what he or she considers less valuable in exchange for something valued more highly. The initial position in which the two equations were not both satisfied was therefore not efficient because *without any increase in the total amounts of beef and lamb available to them, both could be made better off.* The lesson of this example is quite general:

Any time that two persons have unequal MU's for any commodity, the welfare of both parties can be increased by an exchange of commodities. Efficiency requires that any two individuals have the same MU's for any pair of goods.

The great virtue of the price system is that it induces people to carry out *voluntarily* all opportunities for mutually beneficial swaps. Without the price system, Steaker and Chop might not make the trade because they do not know each other. But, as we will see, the price system enables them to trade with each other by trading with the market. Remember from our discussion of consumer choice in Chapter 18 that it pays any consumer to buy any commodity up to the point where the good's money marginal utility is just equal to its price. In other words, in equilibrium:

$$\text{Mr. Steaker's MU of beef} = \text{Price of beef}$$
$$= \text{Ms. Chop's MU of beef} .$$

This is so because, if, say, Mr. Steaker's MU of beef were greater than the price of beef, he could improve his lot by exchanging more of his money for beef. And the reverse could be true if Steaker's MU of beef fell short of the price of beef. For the same reason, since the price of lamb is the same to both individuals, each will choose voluntarily to buy quantities of lamb at which:

$$\text{Mr. Steaker's MU of lamb} = \text{Price of lamb}$$
$$= \text{Ms. Chop's MU of lamb} .$$

Thus, we see that as long as both consumers face the same prices for lamb and beef, their independent decisions *must* satisfy our criterion for efficient distribution of beef and lamb between them:

$$\text{Steaker's MU of beef} = \text{Chop's MU of beef}$$
$$\text{Steaker's MU of lamb} = \text{Chop's MU of lamb} .$$

Given any prices for two commodities, each consumer, acting only in accord with his or her preferences and with no necessary consideration of the effects on the other person, will automatically carry out the purchase behavior that efficiently serves the mutual interests of both purchasers.

This time, where have we sneaked the rabbit into our price system argument? The answer is that the market acts as a middleman between any pair of consumers. Given the prices offered by the market, each consumer will use his or her dollars in a way that exhausts all opportunities for gains from trade *with the market*. Mr. Steaker and Ms. Chop each take advantage of every such opportunity to gain by trading with the market, and in the process they automatically take advantage of every opportunity for advantageous trades between themselves.

Efficient Production Planning: Allocation of Inputs

Finally, we note briefly that a similar analysis shows how the price system leads to an efficient allocation of inputs among the different production processes— the third of our allocative issues. For precisely the same reasons as in the case of the distribution of products among consumers:

Efficient use of two inputs (say, labor and fertilizer) in the production of two goods (say, wheat and corn) requires that

$$\begin{array}{ll} \text{Marginal revenue product} & \text{MRP of fertilizer} \\ \text{(MRP) of fertilizer} = & \text{in corn} \\ \text{in wheat production} & \text{production} \end{array}$$

$$\frac{\text{MRP of labor}}{\text{in wheat production}} = \frac{\text{MRP of labor in}}{\text{corn production}}.$$

By the same logic as before, it can be shown that if these equations do not hold, it is possible to produce more corn and more wheat using no more labor and fertilizer than before but merely by redistributing the quantities of the two inputs between the two crops.[4]

Similarly, since we learned in Chapter 20 that maximum profits require each farmer to hire each input until the input's marginal revenue product equals its price, and since the price of a ton of fertilizer is the same for both wheat farmers and corn growers, it follows that we must have:

$$\begin{array}{l} \text{MRP of fertilizer in wheat production} \\ = \text{Price of fertilizer} \\ = \text{MRP of fertilizer in corn production}. \end{array}$$

The same relationship must be true for labor inputs:

$$\begin{array}{l} \text{MRP of labor in wheat production} \\ = \text{Price of labor} \\ = \text{MRP of labor in corn production}. \end{array}$$

Thus, we conclude that by making the independent choices that maximize their own profits, and without necessarily considering the effects on anyone else, each farmer (firm) will *automatically* act in a way that satisfies the efficiency condition for the allocation of inputs among different products.

[4]See Discussion Question 2 at the end of this appendix.

Summary

1. The condition for efficient distribution of commodities among consumers is that every consumer have the same marginal utility (MU) for every product. If this condition is not met, then two consumers can arrange a swap that makes both of them better off.
2. In a free market, all consumers pay the same prices. So, if they pursue their own self-interest by setting $MU = P$, they automatically satisfy the condition for efficient distribution of commodities.

3. The condition for efficient allocation of inputs to the various production processess is that the marginal revenue product (MRP) of any input be the same in every industry.
4. Since all producers pay the same prices for inputs under perfect competition, if each firm pursues its own self-interest by setting its MRP of any input equal to that input's market price, the condition for efficient production planning will be satisfied automatically.

Questions for Discussion

1. Show that commodities are not being distributed efficiently if Mr. Olson's marginal utilities of a pound of tomatoes and a pound of potatoes are, respectively, 40 cents and 20 cents while Mr. Johnson's are, respectively, 30 cents and 50 cents.
2. Suppose the marginal revenue product of a gallon of

petroleum in the trucking industry is $1.95 while the marginal revenue product of petroleum in the auto-racing industry is $1.10. Show that petroleum inputs are being allocated inefficiently. Why would a market system tend to prevent this situation from occurring?

Big
Business
and Market IV
Power

Firms in Reality: The Corporation and the Stock Market

24

The action of the stock market must necessarily be puzzling at times since otherwise everyone who studies it only a little bit would be able to make money in it.

B. GRAHAM, D. L. DODD, AND S. COTTLE

The last two chapters dealt with the idealized world of perfect competition, where the performance of the market mechanism is at its very best. In this part of the book we come closer to reality and learn why the performance of the market, like everything else, falls short of perfection. In our economy, firms are sometimes big, sometimes small, sometimes weak, sometimes powerful; and while the market system often serves consumer interests well, it does not do so perfectly. To understand how market imperfections arise, and to evaluate their significance, we will need to develop a bit more theory. But first, in this chapter, we describe firms as they are in the real world. We will encounter small firms operated by their individual owners, partnerships, and corporations of all sizes. We will also learn something about the ways in which firms acquire the resources they need for investment. In particular, we will take a look at the markets where stocks and bonds are sold and to which many individuals bring their money, hoping to make that money grow.

The stock market is really something of an enigma. No other economic activity is reported in such detail in so many newspapers and followed with such concern by so many people; yet no activity seems to have been so successful in eluding those who devote themselves to predicting its future. There is no shortage of "experts" who are prepared to evaluate the future of one stock versus that of another. And usually they are paid well for their efforts. But there are real questions about what these experts deliver. For example, Burton G. Malkiel of Yale University reported the following results from a study of leading analysts' predictions of company earnings, on which they based their price forecasts for the companies:

We wrote to nineteen major Wall Street firms . . . among the most respected names in the investment business.

We requested—and received— past earnings predictions on how these firms felt earnings for specific companies would behave over both a one-year and a five-year period. These estimates . . . were . . . compared with actual results to see how well the analysts forecast short-run and long-run earnings changes.

Bluntly stated, the careful estimates of security analysts (based on industry studies, plant visits, etc.) do little, if any, better than those that would be obtained by simple extrapolation of past trends.

For example . . . the analysts' estimates were compared [with] the assumption that every company in the economy would enjoy a growth in earnings of about 4 percent over the next year (approximately the long-run rate of growth of the national income). It turned out that . . . this naïve forecasting model . . . would make smaller errors in forecasting long-run earnings growth than . . . [did] the forecasts of the analysts.

When confronted with the poor record of their five-year growth estimates, the security analysts honestly, if sheepishly, admitted that five years ahead is really too far in advance to make reliable projections. They protested that while long-term projections are admittedly important, they really ought to be judged on their ability to project earnings changes one year ahead.

Believe it or not, it turned out that their one-year forecasts were even worse than their five-year projections.[1]

Later in this chapter we will be in a position to give the explanation many economists offer for this poor performance record.

Firms in the United States

It is customary to divide firms into three groups: *corporations, partnerships,* and *individual proprietorships* (businesses having a single owner). To understand how important corporations are in the economy, consider that annual sales of corporations amount to more than 70 percent of GNP in the United States. Almost all large American firms are corporations. The Exxon Corporation by itself sold over $100 billion in 1980, and Mobil, General Motors, and Texaco each sold over $50 billion. The sales of these four firms alone amount to more than the GNP of Austria, Belgium, the Netherlands, Sweden, Switzerland, and many, many more countries.

But while economic power resides in the corporations, this form of business organization actually constitutes a *minority* of American business firms, measured in terms of the total number of enterprises. The reason is that most firms are small. Even a large proportion of the corporations are quite small—more than half of them have total assets (cash and physical property) worth less than $100,000. But by far the greatest number of firms (counting all firms large and small, and including the corner grocery store and shoe repair shop) are proprietorships. For example, about 90 percent of family farms are proprietorships. Of the more than 15 million (!) business firms in the United States, over 11 million are proprietorships, somewhat more than 2 million are corporations, and somewhat more than a million are partnerships. Thus, just as is true of the income of individuals:

A very small proportion of American firms accounts for a very large share of U.S. business—obviously, business is not distributed equally among firms.

This result is brought out strikingly by *Fortune* magazine's annual listing of the largest American firms, their assets, and their volume of business. Taken together, in 1980 the 500 largest industrial corporations—that is, a negligible proportion of America's almost 15 million firms—had over one and one-half trillion dollars in sales amounting to nearly 60 percent of the nation's GNP in that year. Most industries in which these giant firms are found are *oligopolies*, a market form we will analyze in Chapter 26. A few are *monopolies*, the market

[1] Burton G. Malkiel, *A Random Walk Down Wall Street* (New York: W.W. Norton & Company, Inc., 1973), pages 140–41.

form discussed in the following chapter.

At the other end of the spectrum, the nation's small business firms have a disproportionately small share of U.S. business. These small firms have earnings that are not only relatively low but also very risky; risky in the sense that the average new firm does not last very long—its average life is reported to be less than 7 years. When making economic decisions it is not only the buyer who has to beware!

Just what are the three basic forms of organization of business firms, and what induces organizers of a firm to choose one of these forms rather than another?

Proprietorships

A **proprietorship** is a business firm owned by a single person.

The **proprietorship** is the form of business organization involving the fewest legal complications. Most small retail firms, farms, and many small factories are run as proprietorships. To start a proprietorship, an individual simply decides to go into business and opens up a new firm or takes over an existing firm. Aside from special regulations, such as health requirements for a restaurant or zoning restrictions that limit business activity to particular geographical areas, the individual does not need anyone's permission to go into business. This is one of the main advantages of the proprietorship form of organization. But probably its main attraction is the fact that the owner can be his or her own boss and the firm's sole decision maker. No partners or stockholders have to be consulted when the proprietor wants to expand or change the company's product line or modify the firm's advertising policy. A proprietorship also has tax advantages, particularly compared with the corporation. The proprietor's income is only taxed once. If the firm were to incorporate, its income would be taxed twice—once as income of the firm (corporate income tax) and again as personal income of the owner.

Unlimited liability is a legal obligation of a firm's owner(s) to pay back company debts with whatever resources he or she owns.

There are, on the other hand, two basic disadvantages of a proprietorship, difficulties that make it almost impossible to organize large-scale enterprises as proprietorships. First, the owner has **unlimited liability** for the debts of the firm. If the company goes out of business leaving unpaid bills, the former owner can be forced to pay them out of personal savings. The owner can be made to sell the family home, private collections of stamps or paintings, or any other personal assets, no matter how unrelated to the business, so that the proceeds can be used to pay off the company's obligations. Often proprietors guard themselves against this danger by signing away all their property to other members of their families or to others whom they feel they can trust. But such transfers are subject to federal and state gift taxes. In any event, there are many tales of tragedy that begin with the signing away of all of one's possessions—King Lear's betrayal by his daughters might well serve as the classic warning to those proprietors who are apt to be too trusting.

A second and equally basic shortcoming of the proprietorship is that it inhibits expansion of the firm by making it difficult to raise money. People outside the company are reluctant to put money into a firm over which they exercise no control. This means that the proprietorship's capital is usually no greater than the amount its owner is willing and able to put into it, plus the amount that banks or other commercial lenders are willing to provide.

SUMMARY
The three main advantages of the individual proprietorship are:

1. It leaves full control in the hands of the owner.
2. It involves little legal complication.

3. It generally subjects its owner to lower taxes.

Its two main disadvantages are:

1. The unlimited liability of the owner for the obligations of the company.
2. The difficulty of increasing the amount of funds that can be raised for the firm.

Partnerships

Measured in terms of the amount of their capital, **partnerships** tend to be larger than proprietorships but smaller than corporations. However, the largest partnerships greatly exceed the smallest corporations in terms of both their financing and their influence. For example, some of the most prestigious law firms and investment banks are partnerships. When you call a law firm and are greeted by "Smith, Jones, Brown, and Pfafufnik, Good Morning," you are almost certainly being treated to a listing of the company's senior partners (the partners who own the largest share of the firm or who founded the firm).

A **partnership** is a firm whose ownership is shared by a fixed number of proprietors.

The advantage of the partnership over the proprietorship is that it brings together the funds and expertise of a number of people and permits them to be combined to form a company larger than any one of the owners could have financed or managed alone. If one cannot hope to run a particular type of firm with an inventory of less than $2 million, a person who is not rich may be unable to get into the business without the aid of a partner. A partnership may also bring together a variety of specialists, as often happens in a medical practice. The partnership also offers the advantage of freedom from double taxation, a benefit it shares with the proprietorship.

But the partnership has disadvantages, some of them substantial. Decision making in a partnership may be harder than in any other type of firm. The sole proprietor need consult no one before acting; and the corporation appoints officers who are authorized to decide things for the company. But in a partnership it may be necessary for every partner to agree before any steps are taken by the firm, and this is the primary bane of this form of enterprise. A partnership has been compared to two people in a horse costume, each supplying two of the legs, each prepared to go off in a different direction, and each unable to move without the other. Furthermore, in a partnership, as in a proprietorship, the individual partners have unlimited liability, meaning that they can conceivably be in danger of losing their personal possessions to pay off company debts. Finally, the partnership suffers from unique legal complications. A partnership agreement is like a marriage contract entered into solely for the financial advantage of the participants, and so there is likely to be considerable haggling about the terms. And under the law, if a partner dies, or decides to leave the firm, or the others decide to buy that person's share in the enterprise, the partnership may have to be dissolved and haggling about the contract may start all over again.

SUMMARY
The benefits of the partnership to the owners of the firm are:

1. Access to larger quantities of capital.
2. Protection from double taxation.

Its disadvantages are:

1. The need to obtain the agreement of many if not all partners to all major decisions.

2. Unlimited liability of the partners for the obligations of the company.
3. The legal complications, including automatic dissolution of the partnership, when there is *any* change in ownership.

Corporations

A **corporation** is a firm that has the legal status of a fictional individual. This fictional individual is owned by a number of persons, called its stockholders, and is run by a set of elected officers (usually headed by a president) and a board of directors, whose chairman is often also in a powerful position to influence the affairs of the firm.

Limited liability is a legal obligation of a firm's owners to pay back company debts only with the money they have already invested in the firm.

Most big firms are **corporations,** a form of business organization that has quite a different legal status from a proprietorship or a partnership. Because a corporation is an individual in the eyes of the law, its earnings, like those of other individuals, are taxed. This leads to double taxation of the stockholders, who also pay tax on any dividends they receive from the firm. But this disadvantage is counterbalanced by an important advantage: Any debt of the corporation is regarded as an obligation of that fictitious individual, and not as a liability of any stockholder. This means that the stockholders benefit from the protection of **limited liability**—they can lose no more than the money they have put into the firm. Creditors cannot force them to sell their personal possessions to help repay any outstanding debts incurred by the firm.

Limited liability is the main secret of the success of the corporate form of organization. Thanks to that provision, individuals from every part of the world are willing to put money into firms whose operations they do not understand and whose managements they do not know. A giant firm may produce computers, locomotives, and electrical generators; it may have, as subsidiaries, publishing houses and shoe factories. Few of its stockholders will know or care about all the firm's activities. Yet each investor knows that by providing money to the firm in return for a share of its ownership, no more is risked than the amount of money provided. This has permitted corporations to obtain financing from literally millions of shareholders, each of whom receives in return a claim on the firm's profits, and, at least in principle, a portion of the company's ownership.

As indicated, the profits of a corporation are subject to taxation. Smaller corporations get a tax break, but the larger firms, whose total profits are high, pay a federal tax rate of 46 percent on all *net* earnings over $100,000. In addition, most states levy corporate taxes of their own, pushing the total tax rate above 50 percent. This means that corporate investors whose personal income tax also falls into the 50 percent bracket will be left with less than 25 cents of each dollar of earnings that the firm pays to them in dividends. Compare this with investors in a partnership or a proprietorship who are in the same income bracket; they will get to keep twice as high a share of company earnings.

SUMMARY
The main advantage of the corporate form of organization is *limited liability*, which enables such a firm to raise vast amounts of money from many stockholders. Its main disadvantage is the tax that must be paid on its profits.

It is worth digressing briefly to consider the economic effects of the double taxation of corporate earnings. Does an investor end up earning less by putting money in a corporation than by putting it in a company that is about equally risky but not subject to double taxation? Paradoxically, the answer is that investors, on the average, will *not* lose anything by choosing the corporation. The tax will not and cannot put those who make one type of investment at a disadvantage in comparison with those who choose any other.

How is this possible? How does the effect of the additional tax on corporate stocks disappear before it reaches the stockholder? There are two processes that achieve this act of magic. First, corporations are forced to avoid some investment opportunities that partnerships and proprietorships can afford to take on. Suppose that in 1983 the market rate of return to people who provide money to firms is 9 percent, and a new product is invented that is expected to bring a 12 percent return to a firm that manufactures it. An individual proprietor can afford to produce the new item—borrowing the necessary funds at 9 percent and keeping the 3 percent additional return on the new item for herself. But a large corporation *cannot* afford to produce the new item. For in order to compete for funds, it must also pay investors 9 percent, which means that it will have to earn at least 18 percent on its investments since more than half of that money will be siphoned off into taxes. Thus, double taxation keeps corporate business out of various economic activities that offer a real, but limited, earnings potential. This effect may be unfortunate from the viewpoint of the efficiency of the economy, because it means that many firms are induced to stay out of activities in which it might be useful for them to take part. For instance, corporations may find it too costly to open retail outlets in slum areas or to run trains to isolated rural areas—activities that might be profitable in the absence of the tax.

Second, there is another fail-safe mechanism that protects new investors in corporate stocks from earning a lower return on the average than they would on other securities of equal risk. Suppose two otherwise identical securities, A and B, each offer a return of $60 per year but A is subject to a 50 percent tax while B is not. *Question:* If the market price of security B is $1000, what will be the market price of A? *Answer:* The price of A will be only $500, exactly half the price of security B. Why? Because since it will bring in only $30 per year after taxes, exactly half of what security A returns, investors will be willing to pay only half as much for it as they are willing to pay for the untaxed security.

Double taxation of corporate earnings tends to restrict the activities of corporate firms, keeping them out of relatively low-profit operations. However, double taxation does not mean that the individual investor earns less by putting money into a corporation than by putting it into other businesses.

Financing Corporate Activity

Our discussion of the earnings of an investor in corporate securities introduces a subject of interest to millions of Americans—*stocks* and *bonds*, the financial instruments that provide funds to the corporate sector of the economy. When a corporation needs money, it can get it by printing new stocks and new bonds and selling them to people who are looking for something in which to invest their money. What enables the firm to get money in exchange for printed paper? Doesn't the process seem a bit like counterfeiting? If done improperly, there are grounds for the suspicion. But, carried out appropriately, it is a perfectly rational economic process.

As long as the funds derived from a new issue of stocks and bonds are used effectively to increase the firm's capacity to produce and earn a profit, then these funds will automatically yield the means for any required repayment and for the payment of appropriate amounts of interest and dividends to the purchasers of the new bonds and stocks. But there have been times when this did not happen. It is alleged that one of the favorite practices of the more notorious nineteenth century manipulators of the market was "watering" of company stocks—the issue of stocks with little or nothing to back them up. The term is derived from the practice of some cattle dealers who would force their animals to drink large quantities of water just before bringing them to be weighed for sale.

Another major source of funds is **plowback.** For example, if a company

Plowback is the portion of a corporation's profits that management decides to keep and invest back into the firm's operations rather than to pay out directly to stockholders in the form of dividends.

earns $30 million after taxes and decides to pay out only $10 million in dividends and invest the remaining $20 million back into the firm, that $20 million is called plowback.

When business is profitable so that management has the funds to reinvest in the company, it will often prefer plowback to other sources of funding. One reason for this preference is that it is less risky to management. This source of funds does not require prior approval by the Securities and Exchange Commission (SEC), as do other sources.[2] Moreover, plowback does not depend on the availability of eager customers for new company stocks and bonds, for an issue of such new securities turns into a disappointment if there is little demand for them when they are offered to the public. Above all, a plowback decision generally does not lead anyone to reexamine the efficiency of management's operation in the way that a new stock issue invariably does. In these instances, the SEC, potential buyers of the stock, and their professional advisers all scrutinize the company carefully. A second reason for the attractiveness of plowback is that issuing new stocks and bonds is usually an expensive and lengthy process. The company is required by the SEC to gather masses of data in its prospectus—a document describing the financial condition of the company—before the new issue is approved. Not only is this costly, but the many months of delay that are involved require the firm to wait for the funds when it needs them quickly, and also to subject the firm to the risk of a change in stock market conditions (during the period of delay a brisk demand for new stocks and bonds may conceivably dwindle or even evaporate).

Finally, plowback can offer a tax advantage to stockholders. If profits are paid out in the form of dividends, many stockholders will simply reinvest the money in this company or some other. But in the process, they will pay income taxes on their dividends. Plowback automatically reinvests part of the stockholders' money in the original firm, and does so without a round of income taxes. Of course, stockholders gain from plowback of their funds only if the reinvestment is profitable—that is, only if the new investment permits a corresponding increase in company earnings. And in that case, stockholders will ultimately have to pay taxes on those gains. But the tax will be assessed at the lower tax paid on **capital gains.** Capital gains occur when an asset appreciates in value over time. For example, if you buy some stock for $100, and two years later happily sell it for $5000, you have realized a capital gain of $4900. While dividends may be taxed at rates as high as 50 percent, capital gains are taxed at less than half of normal income tax rates up to a maximum of 20 percent.

This tax advantage has often been decried as a *loophole*—a provision that permits the wealthy to escape their share of taxes. However, at least three reasons have been offered to justify this relatively low tax rate on capital gains. First, the tax applies to **nominal** not to **real capital gains.** This means that during an inflationary period one is required to pay capital gains taxes even on property whose value has not kept up with the price level—that is, on investments that have actually lost some purchasing power. Second, capital gains are sometimes earned over many years, so that even if the *total* increase in value over the lifetime of the investment is high, it will represent a much lower *annual* yield. If the real value of a house doubles over 25 years, the rate of return amounts to only about 3 percent a year—a rate of return that many think is low enough so that it should not be taxed very heavily. But under our system of progressive taxation, the percentage of income taxed away is higher for larger incomes. If such a

A **capital gain** is an increase in the market value of a piece of property, such as a security or a house, that occurs during the period between when it is bought and when it is sold.

A **real capital gain** is any increase in the price of a piece of property beyond the rate of increase in the average level of prices in the economy that has occurred since it was purchased. If the price of a house increases 30 percent during a period when the economy's price level has been inflated 20 percent, the real capital gain is 10 percent. The overall 30 percent rise in dollar price is called the **nominal capital gain.**

[2]The Securities and Exchange Commission, established in 1934, protects the interests of people who buy securities. It requires firms that issue stocks and other securities to provide information about their financial condition, and it regulates the issue and trading of securities.

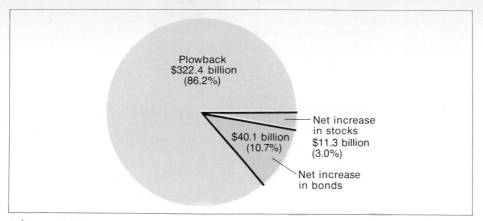

Figure 24–1

SOURCES OF NEW FUNDS, U.S. CORPORATIONS, 1979

Corporations in the United States get about 86 percent of their investment funds from plowback. A little over one-third of this consists of money earned by the firms as profits but not paid out to stockholders. The remaining two-thirds of plowback consists of depreciation—funds accumulated for replacement of plant, equipment, and so on, as it wears out or becomes obsolete. New stocks account for only 3 percent of the total new funding of corporations.

Source: *Federal Reserve Bulletin*, January 1981.

long-term capital gain were taxed as ordinary income in the year the house was sold, it would therefore be taxed at a very high rate because it would add a great deal to the taxpayer's income during that year. If this is unfair, as many observers believe, then it is another argument supporting special lower rates on capital gains. Finally, it is often argued that our economy can only function effectively if people can be induced to risk their savings in new investments; and capital gains are the rewards that induce people to take those risks.

A final way for a company to obtain money is by borrowing it from banks, insurance companies, or other private firms with money to lend out. It may also sometimes borrow from a U.S. government agency either directly or with the agency's help (the agency serves as guarantor in this instance, promising to make sure the loan is repaid). For example, loans may be arranged with the help of the national defense agencies if they want a private firm to undertake the design and production of an expensive new weapons system. Small business firms, too, are eligible for various forms of assistance in borrowing.

Figure 24–1 (a pie diagram) shows the relative importance of each of the different sources of funds to U.S. corporations. It indicates that plowback is by far the most important source of corporate financing, constituting some 86 percent of the total financing to the corporate sector of the economy in 1979. This is followed by issues of new bonds, which supply 11 percent of the total, while new stocks supply only 3 percent.

The Financing of Corporate Activity: Stocks and Bonds

We return now to the other major sources of corporate financing besides plowback and direct borrowing—the corporate securities, like **common stocks** and **bonds.** Stocks represent ownership of part of the corporation. For example, if a company issues 100,000 shares, then a person who owns 1000 shares actually owns 1 percent of the company and is entitled to 1 percent of the

A **common stock** of a corporation is a piece of paper that gives the holder of the stock a share of the ownership of the company.

A **bond** is simply an IOU by a corporation that promises to pay the holder of the piece of paper a fixed sum of money at the specified *maturity* date, and some other fixed amount of money (the *coupon* or the *interest payment*) every year up to the date of maturity.

company's *dividends*, which are the corporation's annual payments to stockholders. The shareholder's vote counts for 1 percent of the total votes in an election of corporate officers or in a referendum on corporate policy, and he or she is entitled to 1 percent of the total number of opportunities to participate in running the corporation.

Bonds differ from stocks in several ways. First, whereas the purchaser of a corporation's stock *buys* a share of its ownership and receives some control over its affairs, the purchaser of a bond simply *lends* money to the firm. Second, whereas stockholders have no idea how much they will receive for their stocks when they sell them, or how much they will receive in dividends each year while they own them, bondholders know with a high degree of certainty how much money they will be paid if they hold on to their bonds to maturity. For instance, a bond with a face value of $1000, with an $80 coupon that matures in 1990, will provide to its owner $80 per year every year until 1990, and in addition it will repay the $1000 to the bondholder in 1990. Unless the company goes bankrupt, there is no doubt about this repayment schedule. Third, bondholders have a *legally prior claim* on company earnings, which means that nothing can be paid by the company to its stockholders until interest payments to the company's bondholders have been met. For all these reasons, bonds are considered less risky than stocks.

In reality, however, some of the differences between stocks and bonds are not as clear-cut as have just been described. Two such misconceptions are particularly worth noting. First, the ownership of the company represented by the holding of a few shares of its stock may be more apparent than real. A holder of 0.002 percent of the stocks of General Motors—which is a *very large* investment—exercises no real control over GM's operations. In fact, many economists believe that the ownership of large corporations is so diffuse that no stockholder or stockholder group has *any* effective control over management. In this view, the management of a corporation is a largely independent decision-making body; as long as it keeps enough cash flowing to stockholders to prevent discontent and rebellion, management can do anything it wants within the law. Looked at in another way, this last conclusion really says that stockholders are merely another class of persons who provide loans to the company. The only real difference between stockholders and bondholders, according to this interpretation, is that stockholders' loans are riskier and therefore entitled to higher payments.

Second, bonds *can* be quite risky to the bondholder. Persons who try to sell their bonds before maturity may find that the market price for bonds happens to be low, so that if they need to raise cash in a hurry, they may have to sell at a substantial loss. Also, bondholders may be exposed to losses from inflation. Whether the $1000 promised the bondholder at the 1990 maturity date represents substantial purchasing power or only a little depends on what happens to the general price level in the meantime. And no one can predict the price level this far in advance with any accuracy.

Bond Prices and Interest Rates

Why is investment in bonds risky? That is, what makes their price go up and down? The main element in the answer is that changes in interest rates cause bond prices to change. There is a straightforward relationship between bond prices and interest rates. Whenever one goes up, the other must go down. For example, suppose that Sears Roebuck had issued some 15-year bonds when interest rates were comparatively low, so that the company had to offer to pay only 6 percent to find buyers for these bonds. People who invested $1000 in new

Sears bonds received in return a contract that promised them $60 per year for 15 years plus the return of their $1000 at the end of that period. Suppose further that two years later interest rates in the economy rise so that new 15-year bonds of companies of similar quality pay 12 percent. Now for $1000 one can buy a contract that offers $120 per year. Obviously, no one will any longer pay as much as $1000 for a bond that promises only $60 per year. Consequently, the market price of the two-year-old Sears bonds must fall. There are many bonds in existence now that were issued years ago at interest rates of 6 percent and even less. In today's markets, with interest rates well above 10 percent, such bonds sell for a price well below their original value.

When interest rates in the economy rise, there must be a fall in the prices of previously issued bonds with their lower interest earnings. For the same reason, when interest rates in the economy fall, the prices of previously issued bonds must rise.

It follows that as interest rates in the economy change because of changes in monetary policy or for other reasons, bond prices will also fluctuate. That is one reason why investment in bonds can be risky.

Types of Stocks and Bonds

Stocks and bonds come in many varieties, and the potential investor should be acquainted with the range of available choices. For example, we have described common stocks, but some companies also issue a type of security called a **preferred stock,** which is a sort of hybrid between a stock and a bond. Preferred stocks are considered less risky than common stocks because they have a stated rate of dividend payments. However, they are riskier than bonds, because even the holders of preferred stock can be paid only *after* bondholders have received their interest payments. In recent years, preferred stocks have become less popular and fewer firms offer them for sale. One primary reason for this decline is that they have a disadvantageous tax status compared with bonds. An interest payment to a bondholder is considered an *expense* to the corporation, and so is not subject to the corporate income tax. On the other hand, dividend payments to holders of preferred stocks are considered to be part of company *profit* and are therefore taxed at the full corporate income tax rate.

Bonds, too, come in different varieties. There are, for example, **short-term bonds** and **long-term bonds.** A bond is considered to be of short or long term depending on its maturity date. A bond that will be paid off in 20 years in the future is a long-term bond, while a bond due to be paid off in three years is considered a fairly short-term bond.[3] The prices of long- and short-term bonds tend to go up and down together, but they will not always do so. When people expect interest rates to be higher in a few years than they are now, long-term bonds will generally fall in price compared with short-term bonds, and the reverse will often be true when the future is expected to bring a sharp reduction in interest rates. The reason is straightforward. Suppose you have $5000 to invest for 10 years and are offered your choice of a 5-year or a 10-year bond, each of which offers an interest rate of 6 percent a year until maturity. If you expect the interest rate to rise to 8 percent five years from now, you would pick the short-term bond, so that when you get your money back in five years you can reinvest it in another 5-year bond, which at that time offers the higher 8 percent

Payments to holders of **preferred stocks** are not guaranteed as are payments to bondholders. However, it is stipulated that a specified payment to preferred stockholders must be made before anything can be paid to holders of common stocks. In addition, holders of preferred stocks generally are not entitled to vote for company officers.

[3] There are even shorter-term securities like bonds that are issued for periods as brief as 90 days. When issued by the U.S. Treasury, these are called *Treasury bills.*

rate. But if, instead, you expect the interest rate to fall to 4 percent five years from now, you would buy the long-term bond and nail down the 6 percent interest rate it promises over its lifetime. These differences in demand will produce corresponding adjustments in the prices of the two types of bonds. So, in the first case, the short-term bond will rise in price in comparison with the longer-term bond. And, in the second case, the reverse must be true.

While the interest on most bonds is taxable, some bonds are tax-exempt. **Tax-exempt bonds** are what their name suggests: bonds on whose interest earnings one pays no federal income tax, and, if the owner lives in the state in which the bonds are issued, no state income tax either. Tax-exempt bonds sound like a good deal—they pay interest that is not taxed. But there is a catch: tax exempts usually pay much lower interest rates than do taxable bonds. When taxable bonds may be paying 17 percent, tax exempts are likely to return something in the neighborhood of 14 percent. Thus, if your income falls in a low tax bracket, tax exempts are not for you. They appeal only to high-income earners who make up in tax saving all that they lose in lower interest rates—and more.

Tax exemption is primarily a way for the federal government to subsidize borrowing by state and local governments. For example, if a state wants to attract private industry, it may authorize the issue of tax-exempt bonds (called *industrial development bonds*) to help raise the capital. Because they are tax exempt, the money can be raised at a low interest cost, which makes them attractive to corporations. The companies and the state both reap gains. It is the federal government that loses out in terms of unpaid tax. Because only rich people can invest profitably in tax-exempt bonds, many reformers and economists have attacked tax exemption as an inequitable way to subsidize state and local government borrowing. It is also believed to be an inefficient way to provide such subsidies. Estimates suggest that the federal government's losses of income tax revenues *exceed* the interest saved by the states and localities.

Buying Stocks and Bonds and Following Their Performance

Although stocks and bonds can be purchased through any brokerage firm, not all brokers charge the same fees. Until recent years the charges to small investors were fixed by collusive agreement and did not vary from broker to broker. But in 1975, the SEC ruled this fixed price to be illegal. Since then, bargain brokerage houses have appeared and proliferated. They usually advertise in the financial pages of newspapers, offering investors very little service—no advice, no research, no other frills—other than merely buying or selling what the customer wants them to, at lower fees than those charged by higher-service brokerage firms.

Many investors are not aware of the various ways in which stocks can be purchased (or sold). The following are some of the possibilities: (a) *Round lot* purchases: Purchases of 100 shares or 200 shares or any number of shares in multiples of 100. (b) *Odd lot* purchases: The purchase of some number of shares that is not a multiple of 100. The brokerage fee per dollar of investment is normally higher on an odd lot than on a round lot. (c) A *market order* purchase simply tells the broker to buy a specified quantity of stock (either a round lot or an odd lot) at the best price the market currently offers. (d) A *limit order* is an agreement to buy a given amount of a stock when its price falls to a specified level. If the investor offers to buy at $18, then shares will be purchased by the broker if and when the market price falls to $18 per share or less.

There are many investment information services that supply subscribers with a variety of information on performance of stocks, bonds, and other securities. These firms offer analyses of particular companies, forecasts, and

52 Weeks High	Low	Stock	Div.	Yld %	P-E Ratio	Sales 100s	High	low	Close	Net Chg.
			– R–R–R –							
11⅞	6¾	RBInd	.28	3.5	20	21	8	7⅞	8	.....
33	21	RCA	1.80	8.5	8	637	21½	21	21⅛	– ⅛
73½	47	RCA pf	4	8.2	..	1	49	49	49	+1
25⅞	19	RCA pf	2.12	11.	..	66	19⅛	19	19	.....
31⅝	25	RCA pf	3.65	15.	..	38	25	d24⅞	25	.....
18	11¼	RLC	.64	4.8	11	112	13¼	13⅛	13¼	+ ¼
10¼	6¾	RTE	.40	4.5	18	51	8⅞	8¾	8⅞	+ ⅛
14⅝	9¼	RalsPur	.72	6.0	7	1096	12⅛	11⅞	12	.....
11⅞	6⅜	Ramad	.12e	1.5	12	864	8¼	8	8⅛	+ ⅛
25⅜	17⅞	Rampc	1.80e	7.8	16	62	23½	23	23	– ⅝
16¼	11¼	Ranco	.84	7.6	31	82	11½	d10⅞	11	– ½
31½	16⅞	Raybt	.60	3.4	583	7	17¾	17½	17½	.....
36	16⅞	Raymdl	1	4.4	11	992	23⅜	22½	22½	– ¼
55⅝	39¾	Rayth	s 1.20	2.9	12	1388	42½	41½	42	.....
59¾	27⅞	ReadBt	.80	2.2	9	465	38⅝	35¼	36	– 1⅞
54	27	RdBat	pf2.13	6.7	..	18	34¼	31¾	31¾	– 1⅝
12	8	RltRef	1.09e	13.	8	10	8½	8⅜	8½	+ ⅛
21	8	RecnEq		..	22	89	10⅞	10⅝	10¾	+ ⅛
14¼	7½	Redmn	.30	2.6	11	123	12	11⅜	11⅜	– ⅝
10⅜	7½	Reece	.60	7.0	13	11	8¾	8⅝	8⅝	.....
41½	29½	ReevsB	2.20	5.8	5	37	38¼	37¾	38¼	+ ½
16	11	ReichCh	.48	3.5	5	63	13⅞	13⅝	13⅝	– ¼
100¼	63½	RelGp	3	3.5	7	105	87⅞	86¾	86¾	– ¾
23½	17⅞	RelG pf	2.60	14.	..	5	18½	18	18	– ½
23⅞	19⅞	RelIn	pf2.68	13.	..	16	20⅜	20⅜	20⅜	.....
11⅝	5¼	RepAir	.10	1.4	..	942	7⅞	7¼	7¼	– ⅝
35¾	20⅞	RepCp	.60	2.0	8	13	30¼	30⅛	30⅛	– ⅛
30	16¾	RepFnS	1.20	4.9	8	5	24½	24¼	24¼	.....
4	2½	RepMtg		..	11	25	3⅛	3	3	.....
41½	26	RepNY	1.20	3.2	6	25	38¼	38	38	.....
20⅞	15	RNY pf	2.12	13.	..	4	16½	16½	16½	+ ¼
23¾	20	RNY	pfA3.13	15.	..	16	21⅝	21⅜	21⅜	– ¼
32⅛	20⅝	RepStl	2	7.4	7	104	27¾	27⅛	27⅛	– ½
45¾	26⅝	RepTex	1.40	3.4	7	99	41	40⅜	40⅝	– ⅜
21⅛	12¾	RshCot	.32	2.5	8	75	13¼	12⅞	13	.....
40¾	27½	RevcoD	1	2.9	11	157	35⅝	34⅞	35	– ¼
25⅜	13⅝	Revere	10e	.5	6	193	22⅜	21½	21¾	– ¼
53⅞	39½	Revlon	1.84	4.6	8	467	40	39¾	39⅞	+ ¼
29	23¾	Revln pf		..	..	1	26⅛	26⅛	26⅛	+ ½

Figure 24–2
EXCERPT FROM A STOCK MARKET PAGE
This table from *The Wall Street Journal* gives the highest and lowest price in the current year, the current dividend rate, the dividend yield, the ratio of stock price to company earnings (P/E ratio), the number of shares sold, the highest, lowest, and final price on the previous day, and the change in price from the day before.
Source: Reprinted by permission of *The Wall Street Journal*, © Dow Jones & Company, Inc. 1981.

advice. In addition, newspapers carry daily information on stock and bond prices. Figure 24–2 is an excerpt from a *Wall Street Journal* stock market report. In the first two columns, before the company name, the report gives the stock's highest and lowest price in the last year. In the highlighted example, the price of RCA stock is reported to have ranged between \$33 and \$21. Next, after the name of the stock, there appears the annual dividend per share (\$1.80). Following that is the yield, or the dividend as a percent of the closing price. The next column reports the *price earnings* (P/E) ratio (8.8 for RCA). This latter figure is the price per share divided by the company's net earnings per share in the previous year, and is usually taken as a basic measure indicating whether the current price of the stock overvalues or undervalues the company. However, no simple rule enables us to interpret the P/E figures—for example, a very risky firm or a slowly growing firm with a low P/E may be considered overvalued, while a safe, rapidly growing firm with a high P/E may still be a bargain. The next column indicates the number of shares that were traded on the previous day (63,700), an indication of whether that stock is actively traded. Finally, the last four figures indicate yesterday's highest price ($\$21\frac{1}{2}$), its lowest price (\$21), the price at which the last transaction of the day took place ($\$21\frac{1}{8}$), and the change in that price from the previous day (down $\frac{1}{8}$).

Figure 24–3, also from *The Wall Street Journal*, gives similar information about bonds. The first thing to notice here is that a given company may have several different bonds—differing in maturity date and coupon (annual interest payment). For example, Shell Oil offers four different bonds. The one that is highlighted is labeled Shell Oil $7\frac{1}{4}$ 02, meaning that these are bonds that pay an annual interest of $7\frac{1}{4}$ percent on their face value (this is called their "coupon"), and that their maturity (redemption) date is 2002. Next, the current yield is reported as 13 percent. This is simply the coupon divided by the price. Since that yield, 13 percent, is higher than the coupon, it means that the bond must be selling at a price below its face value, so that the return per dollar is correspond-

Figure 24–3
EXCERPT FROM A BOND PRICE TABLE
This report from *The Wall Street Journal* shows annual payment, the year in which the bond will be redeemed (that is, the year in which the company will repay that debt), the yield (that is, the annual payment per dollar of current market price), and the previous day's highest, lowest, and closing price of the bond, as well as the change in price from the day before that.
Source: Reprinted by permission of *The Wall Street Journal,* © Dow Jones & Company, 1981.

Bonds	Cur Yld	Vol	High	Low	Close	Net Chg.
Sears 7⅞07	14.	20	56½	56½	56½	+ ½
SearA 8⅜86	11.	57	74½	74	74	+ ¾
SecP 9¾06	cv	30	104	103½	103½	.....
SLR 10¾03	15.	15	72	71	72	+ 1½
SLR 15¼90	16.	29	97	96½	96½	– ½
ShellO 8½00	14.	4	62⅛	62⅛	62⅛	– ⅝
ShellO 7¼02	13.	3	53⅞	53⅞	53⅞	+ ¼
ShellO 8s07	14.	5	56⅛	56⅛	56⅛	– 2⅜
ShellO 13⅞91	15.	20	95	95	95	.....
ShWi 5.45s92	12.	3	46	46	46	.....
Singer 8s99	15.	10	55	54	54	– 1¾
sohioB 9¾99	14.	5	69¼	69¼	69¼	– ¼
SohioB 8⅝83	9.6	15	89¾	89¾	89¾	.....
SoAtT 6¾82f	..	5	92	92	92	+ 11-16
SoCBl 8¼04	14.	10	58¾	58¾	58¾	+ ⅜
SoCBl 7⅜07	14.	16	53	52½	52½	– 2⅛
SoCBl 8¼13	14.	5	57¼	57¼	57¼	.....
SoCBl 9.2s10	14.	10	64½	64	64½	– ½
SoCBl 8¼17	14.	8	58¼	58¼	58¼	- 1¾
SoCBl 8¼15	14.	3	57¾	57¾	57¾	+ ¼
SoCBl 9⅞18	15.	25	67	65¾	66½	.....
SoestB 10s83	11.	5	89⅛	89⅛	89⅛	.....
SoBIT 2¾85	3.9	1	71	71	71	+ ½
SoBIT 7⅜10	14.	20	53⅝	53½	53⅝	+ ⅝
SoBIT 7⅝13	14.	5	53	53	53	.....
SoBIT 8s14	14.	38	56½	55½	55½	– 1¼
SoBIT 8¼16	14.	44	57⅜	57⅛	57¼	– ¾
SoBIT 10.9s19	14.	12	76¼	76¼	76¼	– ½
SoCG 8.85s95	14.	28	65½	63⅞	65½	+ 1⅞
SCouG 9½95	14.	6	69½	69¼	69½	+ ¾
SoNG 7.7s91	11.	5	72	72	72	.....
SNET 8⅛08	14.	5	56⅞	56⅞	56⅞	+ 1½
SNET 9⅝10	15.	3	63	63	63	– 2

ingly high. The remaining information in the table means the same as that reported for stock prices.

Stock Exchanges and Their Functions

The *New York Stock Exchange*—the "Big Board"—is the most prestigious of the stock markets. Located just at the beginning of Wall Street in New York City, it is "*the* establishment" of the securities industry. Only the best known and most heavily traded of securities are dealt with by the New York Stock Exchange, which handles over 2000 stocks altogether. The leading brokerage firms hold "seats" on the Stock Exchange, which enable them to trade directly on the floor of the Exchange. Altogether, the Exchange has about 570 member organizations. Seats are traded on the open market, and today a seat can be purchased for approximately $270,000. Some years ago a seat on the New York Stock Exchange was worth more than $500,000, but various regulatory actions that increased competition among brokers have since reduced their profits, and so depressed the value of a seat.

Someone who wants to buy a stock on the New York Stock Exchange must use a broker who will deal with a firm that has a seat on the Exchange. Suppose you live in Ohio and want to buy 200 shares of General Motors. The broker you approach may be employed by a firm that holds a seat on the Exchange, or she may work through another firm that holds one. The broker who is to fill your order contacts a person called a "specialist," who works on the floor of the Exchange and who handles GM stock. The specialist will usually own some GM stock of his own that he will offer for sale to you if no other sellers are available at the moment. Usually, in addition, a number of investors will previously have given to the specialist limit orders offering to sell specified quantities of GM stock at specified prices. There may, for example, be one offer to sell 5000 shares at any price above $55 and another offer to sell 1200 shares at any price above $60. Similarly, the specialist is likely to have in his hands a number of limit orders to buy at various specified prices. Your order is brought by the floor broker to the specialist who determines a price that, in his judgment, more or less balances supply and demand as indicated by his recent sales and purchases and the limit orders in his possession. At this price the specialist will fill your order either from one of the limit orders to sell (he must do so whenever that is possible) or he will fill it from his personal inventory of General Motors stock. The price determination process that has just been described is sometimes called "the auction market" process.

The New York Stock Exchange is not the only exchange on which stocks are traded. While 80 percent of stock market transactions (in dollars) are handled by the Big Board, the *American Stock Exchange*, located a few blocks away, trades many stocks that are heavily demanded but that are not exchanged in quite as large a volume as those handled by the Big Board. Nearly 11 percent of the dollar volume of stock trades occurs on the American Stock Exchange. There are also *regional exchanges*—such as the Midwest, Cincinnati, Pacific Coast, Philadelphia, and Boston exchanges—which deal in many of the same stocks that are handled on the New York Stock Exchange. A good portion of the business of regional exchanges is serving large "institutional" customers, such as banks, insurance companies, and mutual funds. Their volume amounts to about 10 percent of the total stock traded.

In addition to the trading on these organized exchanges, stocks are traded on the so-called *third market*. The third market is not a public market at all. It is not a place where many buyers and sellers meet to make their exchanges simultaneously. Rather, the third market is run by a number of firms, each operating more or less independently of the others. When a buyer brings an order to such a firm, the broker will simply shop around by telephone, seeking to find someone to match the purchase demand with a corresponding supply offer, or the broker may buy or sell for his own account the stocks supplied or demanded by the order. Thus, in dealing on the third market, each broker does the job that is done by a specialist on one of the exchanges. Obviously, trading on the third market is a much less structured and less organized affair than it is on the exchanges.

With the advent of computers and improved electronic means of communication, there is now talk of arranging what is, in effect, a single national market. It would consist of an electronic network through which every buy or sell order would be announced from coast to coast, as would the price and quantity of every completed transaction. In this way, the market would, indeed, have the opportunity to match all supplies and demands and to produce an equilibrium reflecting the demands of every market participant. There are those who predict that such a national market will be in operation within a few years, and that it will increase the efficiency with which the stock market serves the economy.

Stock Exchanges and Corporate Capital Needs

While corporations often raise the funds they need by selling stocks, they do not normally do so through any of the stock exchanges. When new stocks are offered by a company, the new issue is usually handled by a special type of bank called an *investment bank*. In contrast, the stock markets trade almost exclusively in "secondhand securities"—stocks in the hands of individuals and others who had bought them earlier and who now wish to sell them.

Thus the stock market does not provide funds to corporations that need the financing to expand their productive activities. The markets only provide money to persons who already hold stocks previously issued by the corporations.

Yet stock exchanges have two functions that are of critical importance for the financing of corporations. First, by providing a secondhand market for stocks, they make it much less risky for an individual to invest in a company. Investors know that their money is not locked in—if they need the money, they can always sell their stocks to other investors or to the "specialist" at the price the market currently offers. This reduction in risk makes it far easier for corporations to issue new stocks. Second, the stock market determines the current price of the company's stocks. That, in turn, determines whether it will be hard or easy for a corporation to raise money by selling new stocks. For example, suppose a company initially has one million shares and wants to raise $10 million. If the price is $40 per share, an issue of 250,000 shares can bring in the required funds, leaving the original stockholders with four-fifths of the company's ownership. But if the price of the stock is only $20, then 500,000 new shares will have to be issued, cutting the original stockholders back to two-thirds of the ownership of the company. This is a less attractive proposition.

Some people believe that the price of a company's stock is closely tied to the efficiency with which its productive activities are conducted, the effectiveness with which it matches its product to consumer demands, and the diligence with which it goes after profitable innovation. In this view, those firms that can make effective use of funds because of their efficiency are precisely the corporations whose stock prices will usually be comparatively high. In this way the stock market tends to channel the economy's investment funds to those firms that can make best use of the money. In sum:

If a firm has a promising future, its stock will tend to command a high price on the stock exchanges. The high price of its stock will make it easier for it to raise capital by permitting it to amass a large amount of money through the sale of a comparatively small number of new stocks. Thus, *the stock market helps to allocate the economy's resources to those firms that can make the best use of those resources.*

The Issue of Speculation

Individuals who engage in **speculation** deliberately invest in risky assets, hoping to obtain a profit from the expected changes in the prices of these assets.

Dealings in securities are often viewed with hostility and suspicion because it is felt that they are an instrument of **speculation.** When something goes wrong in the market, say, when there is a sudden fall in prices, *speculators* are often blamed. The word speculators is used by editorial writers as a term of strong disapproval, implying that those who engage in the activity are parasites who produce no benefits for society and often do it considerable harm.

Economists disagree vehemently with this judgment. They say that speculators perform two vital economic functions: (a) They sell *protection from risk* to other people, much as a fire insurance policy sells protection from risk to the owner of a home. (b) They help to smooth out price fluctuations by purchasing items when they are abundant (and cheap) and holding them and reselling them when they are scarce (and expensive). In that way, they play a vital economic role in helping to alleviate and even prevent shortages.

Some examples from outside the securities markets will make the role of speculators clear. A ticket broker attends a preview of a new musical comedy and suspects that it is likely to be a hit. He decides to speculate by buying a large block of tickets for future performances. In that way he takes over some of the producer's risk, for the producer now has some hard cash and has reduced his inventory of risky tickets. If the show opens and is a flop, the broker will be stuck with the tickets. If it is a hit, he can sell them at a premium, if the law allows (and be denounced as a speculator or a "scalper"). Similarly, speculators enable farmers or producers of metals and other commodities whose future price is uncertain to get rid of their risk. A farmer who has planted a large crop but who fears its price may fall before harvest time can protect himself by signing a *contract for future delivery* at an agreed upon price at which the speculator will purchase the crop when it comes in. In that case, if the price happens to fall, it is the speculator and not the farmer who will suffer the loss. Of course, if the price happens to rise, the speculator will reap the gain—that is the nature of risk bearing. The speculator who has agreed to buy the crop at the preset price, regardless of market conditions at the time the sale takes place, has, in effect, sold an insurance policy to the farmer. Surely this is a useful function.

The second role of the speculator is perhaps even more important; in effect, it is arranging for the accumulation and storage of goods in periods of abundance and making them available in periods of scarcity. Suppose the speculator has reason to suspect that next year's crop of a storable commodity will not be nearly as abundant as this year's. He will buy up some now, when it is cheap, for resale when it becomes scarce and expensive. In the process, he will smooth out the swing in prices by adding his purchases to the total market demand in the period of low prices (which tends to bring the price up), and bringing in his supplies during the period of high prices (which tends to push the price down).[4]

Thus, the successful speculator will help to relieve matters during periods of extreme shortage. There are cases in which he literally helps to relieve famine by releasing the supplies he has deliberately hoarded for such an occasion. Of course, he is cursed for the high prices he charges on such occasions. But those who curse him do not understand that prices might have been even higher if the speculator's foresight and avid pursuit of profit had not provided for the emergency. On the securities market, famine and severe shortages are not an issue, but the fact remains that successful speculators tend to reduce price fluctuations by increasing demand for stocks when prices are low and contributing to supply when prices are high. Far from aggravating instability and fluctuations, speculators work as hard as they can to iron out fluctuations, for that is how they make their profits.

The role of speculation is one of the 12 Ideas for Beyond the Final Exam in our study of economics. Even among government officials, journalists, and other thoughtful individuals, it is widely believed that speculators perform no real service for the economy; that their activity generally aggravates high prices and increases scarcity in times of shortages; and that they add to the instability of the economy in other ways. These impressions are virtually the reverse of the truth. Whether or not speculators are personally virtuous is not the point. The fact is that in earning their profits they make several vital contributions to the workings of the economy: (a) They take over risks from individuals seeking protection from risk; (b) They tend to add to supplies in periods of shortages; and (c) They work to depress prices when they are unusually high and to raise prices when they are unusually low—*for that is how they earn profits*—*by buying things when they are cheap in anticipation of their resale when they become expensive.*

Stock Prices as Random Walks

The beginning of this chapter cited evidence indicating that the best professional securities analysts have a forecasting record so miserable that investors may do as

[4]For a diagrammatic analysis of this function, see Discussion Question 7 at the end of the chapter.

well predicting earnings by hunch, superstition, or any purely random process as they would by following the advice of the professional. Similarly, it has been said that an investor is well advised to pick stocks by throwing darts at the stock market page—since it is far cheaper to buy a set of darts than to obtain the apparently useless advice of a professional analyst. Indeed, there have been at least two experiments, one by a U.S. senator and one by *Forbes* magazine, in which stocks picked by dart throwing actually outperformed the mutual funds, whose stocks are selected by the experts. Does this mean that the analysts are incompetent people who do not know what they are doing? Not at all. Rather, there is overwhelming evidence that their poor forecasting performance is attributable to the fact that the task they have undertaken is basically impossible.

How can this be so? The answer is that to make a good forecast of any variable—GNP, population, or fuel usage—there must be something in the past whose behavior is closely related to the future behavior of the variable whose path it is desired to predict. If a 10 percent rise in this year's consumption always produces a 5 percent rise in next year's GNP, this fact provides us with an obvious procedure that can help us predict future GNP on the basis of current observations. But if we want to forecast the future of a variable whose behavior is completely unrelated to the behavior of *any* current variable, then there is no objective evidence that can help us make that forecast. Throwing darts or gazing into a crystal ball is no less effective than the analysts' calculations.

There is by now a mass of statistical evidence that the behavior of stock prices is in fact unpredictable. In other words, the behavior of stock prices is essentially random; the paths they follow are what statisticians call **random walks.** A random walk is like the path followed by a drunk. All we know about his position after his next step is that it will be given by his current position plus whatever random direction his next haphazard step will carry him. The relevant feature of randomness, for our purposes, is that it is by nature unpredictable, which is just what the word *random* means.

If the evidence that stock prices follow a random walk stands up to research in the future as it has so far, it is easy enough to understand why the stock market predictions are as poor as they are. The analysts are trying to forecast behavior that is basically random; in effect, they are trying to predict the unpredictable.

Two questions remain. First, does the evidence that stock prices follow a random walk mean that investment in stocks is a pure gamble and never worthwhile? And, second, how does one explain the random behavior of stock prices?

To answer the first question, it is false to conclude that investment in stocks is generally not worthwhile. The statistical evidence is that, taken over the long run, stock prices *as a whole* have had a marked upward trend, perhaps reflecting the long-term growth of the economy. The evidence of the past *does* indicate that stock prices are likely to rise if one waits long enough for them to do so. Thus the random walk does not proceed in just any direction—rather, it represents a set of erratic movements *around the basic trend in stock prices.* Moreover, it is not in the *overall* level of stock prices that the most pertinent random walk occurs, but in the performance of one company's stock compared with another's. For this reason professional advice may be able to predict that investment in the stock market is likely to be a good thing over the long haul. But, if the random walk evidence is valid, there is no way professionals can tell us *which* of the available stocks is most likely to go up—that is, which combination of stocks is best for the investor to buy.

The time path of a variable, such as the price of a stock, is said to constitute a **random walk** if its magnitude in one period (say, May 2, 1983) is equal to its value in the preceding period (May 1, 1983) plus a completely random number. That is:

> Price on May 2, 1983 = Price on May 1, 1983 + Random number

where the random number (positive or negative) might be obtained by a roll of dice or some such procedure.

The only appropriate answer to the second question is that no one is sure of the explanation. There are two widely offered hypotheses—each virtually the opposite of the other. The first asserts that stock prices are random because clever professional speculators are able to foresee almost perfectly every influence that is *not* random. For example, suppose a change occurs that makes the probable earnings of some company higher than had previously been expected. Then, according to this view, the professionals will instantly become aware of this change and immediately drive up the price of the company's stock accordingly. Then, the only thing for that stock price to do between this year and next is wander randomly, because the professionals cannot predict random movements, and hence cannot force current stock prices to anticipate them.

The other explanation of random behavior of stock prices is at the opposite pole from the view that all nonrandom movements are wiped out by supersmart professionals. And that view is that people who buy and sell stocks have learned that they cannot predict the future of stock prices. As a result they latch on to any signal they can get, however irrational and irrelevant it appears. If the president catches cold, stock prices fall. If an astronaut's venture is successful, prices go up. For, according to this view, investors are, in the last analysis, trying to predict, not the prospects of the economy or of the company whose shares they buy, but the supply and demand behavior of other investors, which will ultimately determine the course of stock prices. Since all investors are equally in the dark, their groping can only result in the randomness that we observe. The classic statement of this view of stock market behavior was provided by Lord Keynes, a successful professional speculator himself:

Professional investment may be likened to those newspaper competitions in which the competitors have to pick out the six prettiest faces from a hundred photographs, the prize being awarded to the competitor whose choice most nearly corresponds to the average preferences of the competitors as a whole; so that each competitor has to pick not those faces which he himself finds prettiest, but those which he thinks likeliest to catch the fancy of the other competitors, all of whom are looking at the problem from the same point of view. It is not a case of choosing those which, to the best of one's judgment, are really the prettiest, nor even those which average opinion genuinely thinks the prettiest. We have reached the third degree where we devote our intelligences to anticipating what average opinion expects the average opinion to be. And there are some, I believe, who practice the fourth, fifth and higher degrees.[5]

Conclusion

In this chapter we have looked briefly at the types of firms that populate the markets in our economy. We have encountered large firms and small ones, individual proprietorships, partnerships, and corporations, and we have studied some of the institutions that are involved in the financing of the corporations. But in a sense, this is merely background to the analysis of our basic theme, the virtues and shortcomings of the market mechanism. We have found in this chapter that many firms are quite different from those we encountered in the model of perfect competition. In the next two chapters we return to our theoretical analysis of firms and industries. But we will no longer assume that industries are perfectly competitive, and we will investigate how that fact affects the efficiency of the market mechanism.

[5]John Maynard Keynes, *The General Theory of Employment, Interest, and Money* (New York: Harcourt Brace Jovanovich, 1936), page 156.

Summary

1. The three basic types of firms are corporations, partnerships, and individual proprietorships. Most U.S. firms are individual proprietorships, but most U.S. manufactured goods are produced by corporations.

2. Individual proprietorships and partnerships have tax advantages over corporations. But corporate investors have greater protection from risk because they have *limited liability*—they cannot be asked to pay more than they have invested in the firm.

3. Higher taxation of corporate earnings tends to limit the things in which corporations can invest and may lead to inefficiency in resource allocation.

4. Corporations finance their activities mostly by plowback (that is, by retaining part of their earnings and putting it back into the company) or by the sale of stocks and bonds.

5. A stock is a share in the ownership of the company. A bond is an IOU by a company for money lent to it by the bondholder. Many observers argue that the purchase of a stock also really amounts to a loan to the company—a loan that is riskier than the purchase of a bond.

6. If interest rates rise, bond prices will fall. In other words, if some bond amounts to a contract to pay 8 percent and the market interest rate goes up to 10 percent, people will no longer be willing to pay the old price for that bond.

7. If stock prices correctly reflect the future prospects of different companies, promising firms are helped to raise money because they are able to sell each stock they issue at favorable prices.

8. Speculation affects stock market prices, but (contrary to what is widely assumed) there is reason to believe that speculation actually *reduces* the frequency and size of price fluctuations.

9. Speculators are also useful to the economy because they undertake risks that others wish to avoid, thereby, in effect, providing others with insurance against risk. This is one of the 12 Ideas for Beyond the Final Exam.

10. Statistical evidence indicates that individual stock prices behave randomly.

Concepts for Review

Proprietorship
Unlimited liability
Partnership
Corporation
Limited liability

Plowback
Capital gain
Common stock
Bond
Preferred stock

Short- and long-term bonds
Tax-exempt bond
Stock exchanges
Speculation
Random walk

Questions for Discussion

1. Why would it be difficult to run General Motors as a partnership or an individual proprietorship?

2. Do you think it is fair to tax a corporation more than a partnership doing the same amount of business? Why or why not?

3. If you hold shares in a corporation and management decides to plow back the company's earnings some year instead of paying dividends, what are the advantages and disadvantages to you?

4. Suppose interest rates are 6 percent in the economy and a safe bond promises to pay $6 a year in interest forever. What do think the price of the bond will be? Why?

5. Suppose in the economy in the previous example, interest rates suddenly double, rising to 12 percent. What will happen to the price of the bond that pays $6 per year?

6. If you want to buy a stock, when might it be to your advantage to buy it using a market order? When will it pay to use a limit order?

7. Show in diagrams that if a speculator were to buy when price is high and sell when price is low he would increase price fluctuations. Why would it be in his best interest *not* to do so? (*Hint:* Draw two supply–demand diagrams, one for the high-price period and one for the low-price period. How would the speculator's activities affect these diagrams?)

8. If stock prices really are a random walk, can you nevertheless think of good reasons for getting professional advice before investing?

Pure Monopoly and the Market Mechanism

25

The price of monopoly is upon every occasion the highest which can be got.

ADAM SMITH*

I n Chapters 22 and 23 we described an idealized market system in which all industries are perfectly competitive, and we extolled the beauty of that system. In this chapter, we turn to one of the blemishes—the possibility that some industries may be monopolized, and the consequences of such monopolization.

We begin by defining *monopoly* precisely and investigating some of the reasons for its existence. Then, using the tools of Chapter 21, we consider the monopolist's choice of an optimal price–output combination. As we shall see, while it is possible to analyze how much a monopolist will choose to produce, a monopolist has no "supply curve" in the usual sense. This fact requires certain modifications in our supply–demand analysis of the market mechanism, modifications that lead us to the central message of this chapter: that monopolized markets do not match the ideal performance of perfectly competitive ones. In particular, we will see that in the presence of monopoly the market mechanism no longer allocates society's resources efficiently. This observation opens up the possibility that government actions to curb the abuses of monopoly might actually improve the workings of the market—a possibility we will study in detail in Chapters 27 and 28.

Application:
Monopoly and Pollution Charges

We begin, as usual, by examining a real-life problem. Chapter 1 noted that most economists favor controlling pollution by charging the polluter heavily, making him pay increasing amounts to the pollution-control agency the more pollution he emits. Making it sufficiently expensive for firms to pollute, it is said, will induce them to find ways to reduce their emissions.[1] A common objection to this proposal is that it simply will not work when the polluter is a monopolist: "The monopolist can just raise the price of his product, pass the pollution charge on to his customers, and go on polluting as before, with total impunity." After all, if a firm is a monopoly, what is to stop it from raising its price when it is hit by a pollution charge? Yet observation of the behavior of firms faced with the prospect of pollution charges suggests that there is something wrong with this objection. If the polluter could escape the penalty completely, we would expect him to

*But Adam Smith's statement is incorrect! See Discussion Question 5 at the end of the chapter.
[1]Details on this method of pollution control are provided in Chapter 31.

acquiesce or to put up only token opposition. Yet wherever it has been proposed to levy a charge on the emission of pollutants (or any other financial incentive against environmental damage), the outcries of the potentially affected firms have been enormous, even among firms with no important rivals. Lobbyists are dispatched at once to do their best to stop the legislation. In fact, rather than agree to being charged for their emissions, firms usually indicate a preference for direct controls that *force* them to adopt specific processes that are less polluting than the ones they are now using. For some reason, even firms in a monopoly position act as if they cannot make their customers pay the pollution charges. The tools of this chapter will enable us to understand whether the monopolist is justified in his apparent fear that such fees cannot be passed on.

Monopoly Defined

A **pure monopoly** is an industry in which there is only one supplier of a product for which there are no close substitutes, and in which it is very hard or impossible for another firm to coexist.

Pure monopoly was defined back in Table 22–1 on page 413; the definition is quite stringent. First, there must be only one firm in the industry—the monopolist must be "the only supplier in town." Second, there must be no close substitute for the monopolist's product. Thus, even the sole provider of natural gas in a city would not be considered a pure monopoly, since other firms offer close substitutes like heating oil and coal. Third, there must be some reason why survival of a potential competitor is extremely unlikely, for otherwise monopoly could not persist.

These rigid requirements make pure monopoly a rarity in the real world. The telephone company and the post office are good examples of one-firm industries that face little or no effective competition. But most firms face competition from substitute products. Even if only one railroad serves a particular town, it must compete with bus lines, trucking companies, and airlines. Similarly, the producer of a particular brand of beer may be the only supplier of that specific product but is not a monopolist by our definition. Since many other beers are close substitutes for its product, the company will lose much of its business if it tries to raise its price much above the prices of other brands. And there is one further reason why the unrestrained pure monopoly of economic theory is rarely encountered in practice. We will learn in this chapter that pure monopoly has several undesirable features. As a consequence, in markets where pure monopoly might otherwise prevail, the government has intervened to prevent monopolization or to limit the discretion of the monopolist to set its price.

If we do not study pure monopoly for its descriptive realism, why do we study it? Because, like perfect competition, pure monopoly is an idealized market form that is easier to analyze than the more realistic market structures that we will consider in the next chapter. Thus, pure monopoly is a stepping stone toward models of greater reality. Also, the "evils of monopoly" stand out most clearly when we consider monopoly in its purest form, and this greater clarity will help us understand why governments have rarely allowed unfettered monopoly to exist.

Causes of Monopoly: Barriers to Entry and Cost Advantages

The key element in preserving a monopoly is keeping potential rivals out of the market. One possibility is that some specific impediment prevents the establishment of a new firm in the industry. Economists call such impediments **barriers to entry.** Some examples are:

1. **Legal restrictions.** The U.S. Postal Service has a monopoly position because Congress has given it one. Private companies that might want to compete with the postal service are prohibited from doing so by law. Local monopolies of various kinds are sometimes established either because government grants some special privilege to a single firm (for example, the right to operate a food concession in a municipal stadium) or prevents other firms from entering the industry (for instance, by licensing only a single local radio station).

2. **Patents.** A special, but very important, class of legal impediments to entry are **patents.** To encourage inventiveness, the government gives exclusive production rights for a period of time to the inventor of certain products. As long as the patent is in effect, the firm has a protected position and is a monopoly. For example, Xerox had for many years (but no longer has) a monopoly in plain paper copying.

3. **Control of a scarce resource or input.** If a certain commodity can be produced only by using a rare input, a company that gains control of the source of that input can establish a monopoly position for itself. For example, the DeBeers syndicate in South Africa owns almost the only land on earth on which diamonds can be mined.

   Obviously, such barriers can keep rivals out and ensure that an industry is monopolized, but monopoly can also occur in the absence of explicit barriers to entry if a single firm has important cost advantages over its potential rivals. One example of this is:

4. **Technical superiority.** A firm whose technological expertise vastly exceeds that of potential competitors can, for a period of time, maintain a monopoly position. For example, IBM for many years had very little competition in the computer business mainly because of its technological virtuosity. Eventually, however, competitors caught up.

Natural Monopoly

A second way that cost advantages can lead to monopoly is important enough to merit special attention. In some industries, economies of large-scale production or economies from simultaneous production of a large number of items (for example, car motors and bodies, truck parts, and so on) are so extreme that the industry's output can be produced at far lower cost by a single firm than by a number of smaller firms. In such cases, we say there is a **natural monopoly,** because once a firm gets large enough relative to the size of the market for its product, its natural cost advantage will enable it to drive the competition out of business. A natural monopoly need not be a large firm if the market is small enough. *What matters is the size of a single firm relative to the total market demand for the product.* Thus a small bank in a rural town or a gasoline station at a lightly traveled intersection may both be natural monopolies even though they are very small firms.

Figure 25–1 shows the sort of average cost (AC) curve that leads to natural monopoly. Suppose that any firm producing widgets would have this AC curve, and that, initially, there are two firms in the industry. Suppose also that the large firm is producing two million widgets at an average cost of $2.50, and the small firm is producing one million widgets at an average cost of $3. Clearly, the large firm can drive the small firm out of business by offering its output for sale at a

A **natural monopoly** is an industry in which advantages of large-scale production make it possible for a single firm to produce the entire output of the market at lower average cost than a number of firms each producing a smaller quantity.

Figure 25–1

NATURAL MONOPOLY

When the average cost curve of a firm is declining, as depicted here, natural monopoly may result. A firm producing two million widgets will have average costs of $2.50, which are well below those of a smaller competitor producing one million widgets (average cost = $3). It can cut its price to a level (lower than $3) that its competitor cannot match, and thereby drive the competitor out of business.

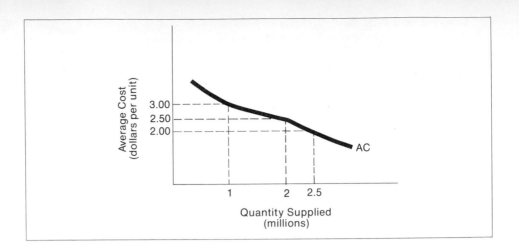

price below $3 (so the small firm can match the price only by running a loss) but above $2.50 (so it can still make a profit). The managers of the large firm will no doubt be smart enough to realize this possibility, and hence a monopoly will arise "naturally" even in the absence of barriers to entry. Once the monopoly is established (producing, say, 2.5 million widgets) the economies of scale act as a very effective deterrent to entry because no new entrant can hope to match the low average cost ($2) of the existing monopoly firm.

Many public utilities are permitted to operate as monopoly suppliers for exactly this reason. It is believed that the technology of producing or distributing their output enables them to achieve substantial cost reductions when they produce large quantities. It is therefore often considered desirable to permit these firms to obtain the lower costs they achieve by having the entire market to themselves, and to subject them to regulatory supervision rather than break them up into a number of competing firms. The issue of regulating natural monopolies will be examined in detail in Chapter 27. To summarize this discussion:

There are two basic reasons why a monopoly may exist: barriers to entry, such as legal restrictions and patents, and cost advantages of large-scale operation, such as those that lead to natural monopoly.

For the rest of this chapter we will assume that the monopoly is not a natural monopoly but has arisen for one of the other four reasons listed earlier. We will analyze how such a monopoly may be expected to behave if its freedom of action is not limited by the government.

The Monopolist's Supply Decision

A monopolist does not have a "supply curve," as we usually define the term. He does not say to himself: "The price of my product is $6. How much should I produce?" For, unlike the case of a perfect competitor, a monopolist is not at the mercy of the market; he does not have to take the market price as given and react to it. Instead, the monopolist has the power to set the price, or rather to select the price–quantity combination on his demand curve that he prefers. For any price that the monopolist might choose, the demand curve for his product tells him how much consumers will buy. If we make the usual assumption that the monopolist wants to maximize his profits, the methods of Chapter 21 can be used to determine which price the monopolist will prefer.

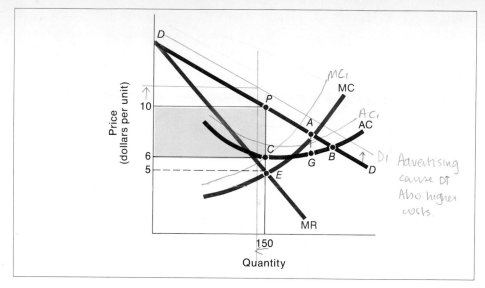

Figure 25–2
PROFIT-MAXIMIZING
EQUILIBRIUM FOR A
MONOPOLIST
This monopolist has the cost
structure indicated by the
black average cost (AC) curve
and the blue marginal cost
(MC) curve. His demand
curve is the black line labeled
DD, and his marginal revenue
curve is the blue line labeled
MR. He maximizes profits by
producing 150 units, because
at this level of production
MC = MR (point *E*). The price
he charges is $10 per unit (as
given by point *P* on the demand curve). Since his average cost per unit ($6) is given
by point *C* on the AC curve, his
total profit is indicated by the
shaded rectangle.

For this purpose, a marginal cost (MC) curve and a marginal revenue (MR) curve for a typical monopolist are drawn in Figure 25–2, which also contains the monopolist's demand curve (*DD*). Notice that the marginal revenue curve is always *below* the demand curve. This is an important fact, and is easy to explain. A monopolist normally must charge the same price to all his customers. If he wants to raise his sales by one unit, he must lower his price somewhat; that is the meaning of a downward-sloping demand curve. But when he cuts his price, all his previous customers benefit from the price reduction. Thus the *additional* revenue that he takes in when he increases sales by one unit (which is the definition of *marginal revenue*) is the price he collects from his new customer *minus* the revenue he loses by cutting the price paid by all his old customers. This means that MR is necessarily *less than* price; graphically, it implies that the MR curve is *below* the demand curve, as in Figure 25–2.

Figure 25–3 illustrates the relationship between price and marginal revenue in a specific example. Suppose a monopolist is initially selling 15 units at a price of $2.10 per unit (point *A*), and wishes to increase sales by one unit. The demand curve tells him that in order to sell the 16th unit, he will have to reduce his price to $2 (point *B*). How much revenue will he gain from this increase in sales; that is, how large is his marginal revenue? As we know, *total revenue* at point *A* is the area of the rectangle whose upper right-hand corner is point *A*, or $2.10 × 15 = $31.50. Similarly, total revenue at point *B* is the area of the rectangle whose upper right-hand corner is point *B*, or $2 × 16 = $32. The *marginal revenue* of the 16th unit is, by definition, total revenue when 16 units are sold minus total revenue when 15 units are sold, or $32 − $31.50 = $0.50. In Figure 25–3, marginal revenue appears as the area of the tall blue rectangle ($2) *minus* the area of the flat gray rectangle ($1.50). We can see that MR is less than price by observing that the price is shown in the diagram by the area of the blue rectangle.[2] Clearly, the price (area of the blue rectangle) must exceed the marginal revenue (area of the blue rectangle *minus* area of the gray rectangle), as was claimed.[3]

[2]Because the width of this rectangle is one unit, its area is height × width = ($2 per unit) × (1 unit) = $2.

[3]There is another way to arrive at this conclusion. Recall that the demand curve is the curve of *average revenue*. Since the average revenue is declining as we move to the right, it follows from one of the rules relating marginals and averages (see the appendix to Chapter 21) that the marginal revenue curve must always be below the average.

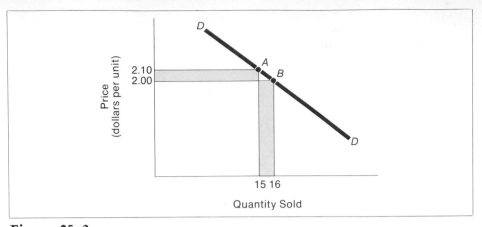

Figure 25–3

THE RELATIONSHIP BETWEEN MARGINAL REVENUE AND PRICE

Line *DD* is the demand curve of a monopolist. In order to raise his sales from 15 to 16 units, he must cut his price from $2.10 (point *A*) to $2 (point *B*). If he does this, his revenues *go up* by the $2 price he charges the buyer of the 16th unit (the area of the tall blue rectangle), but *go down* by the 10-cent price reduction he offers to his previous customers (the area of the flat gray rectangle). His marginal revenue, therefore, is the difference between these two areas. Since the price is the area of the blue rectangle, it follows that marginal revenue is less than price for a monopolist.

We return now to the supply decision of the monopolist depicted in Figure 25–2. Like any other firm, the monopoly maximizes its profits by setting marginal revenue (MR) equal to marginal cost (MC). It selects point *E* in the diagram, where output is 150 units. But point *E* does not tell us the monopoly price because, as we have just seen, price exceeds MR for a monopolist. To learn what price the monopolist charges, we must use the demand curve to find the price at which consumers are willing to purchase 150 units. The answer, we see, is given by point *P*. The monopoly price is $10 per unit, which naturally exceeds both MR and MC (which are equal at $5). The monopolist depicted in Figure 25–2 is earning a tidy profit. This profit is shown in the graph by the shaded rectangle whose height is the difference between price (point *P*) and average cost (point *C*) and whose width is the quantity produced (150 units). In the example, profits are $4 per unit, or $600.

Comparison of Monopoly and Perfect Competition

This completes our analysis of the monopolist's price–output decision. At this point it is natural to wonder whether there is anything distinctive about monopoly, and whether its consequences are desirable or undesirable. For the purpose of finding out, we need a standard of comparison. Perfect competition provides this standard because, as we learned in Chapters 22 and 23, it is a benchmark of ideal performance against which other market structures can be judged. By comparing the results of monopoly with those of perfect competition, we will see why economists since Adam Smith have condemned monopoly as inefficient.

The first difference between competition and monopoly is a direct consequence of the absence of barriers to entry in the former. Profits such as those shown in Figure 25–2 would be competed away by free entry in a competitive market. But they can persist under monopoly because entry is virtually impossible. The fates are kind to a monopolist who is allowed to set his price as he sees fit; he is able to grow wealthy at the expense of the consumer. Because people find such accumulations of wealth objectionable, monopoly is widely condemned and, when monopolies are regulated by government, limitations are almost always placed on the profits monopolists can earn.

Excess monopoly profits may be a problem, but the second difference between competition and monopoly is even more worrisome in the opinion of economists:

As compared with the perfectly competitive ideal, the monopolist restricts his output and charges a higher price.

To see that this is so, let us conduct the following thought experiment. Imagine that a court order breaks up the monopoly firm depicted in Figure 25–2 into a large number of competitive firms. Suppose further that the industry demand curve is unchanged by this event, and that the MC curve in Figure 25–2 is also the (horizontal) sum of the MC curves of all the newly created competitive firms. Under these assumptions, we can easily compare the output–price combinations that would emerge in the short run under monopoly and perfect competition.

Since the short-run supply curve of the competitive industry is the sum of the MC curves of all the individual firms (above minimum average variable costs), the MC curve in Figure 25–2 would constitute the supply curve of the competitive industry. Equilibrium under perfect competition would occur at point A, where quantity demanded (which we read from the demand curve) and quantity supplied (which we read from the MC = supply curve) are equal. By comparing point A with the monopolist's equilibrium (point E), we can see that the monopolist produces fewer units of output than would a competitive industry with the same demand and cost conditions. Since the demand curve slopes downward, producing less output is equivalent to charging a higher price. The monopolist's price, indicated by point P, exceeds the price that would result from perfect competition, point A. This is the essence of the truth behind the popular view that monopolists "gouge the public."

In fact, the reduction in output and increase in price may be even greater than we have indicated. Our analysis so far is correct, but only for the short run. In the short run, monopoly output is determined by MC = MR (point E) while competitive output is determined by MC = P (point A). But in the long run, as we learned in Chapter 22, the lure of profits will attract more firms into a perfectly competitive industry. In Figure 25–2, we can see that there *are* profits to be made. When the industry produces at point A, the market price (point A) clearly exceeds the average cost of production (point G). Each competitive firm will then be earning profits in excess of the opportunity cost of capital. But, as we know, such a situation cannot persist if there is free entry. New firms will enter the industry, thereby pushing the supply (= MC) curve outward to the right. (The AC curve will also shift rightward as total industry capacity expands.) Long-run competitive equilibrium will eventually be established at a point similar to B, where price and average cost are equal (and hence economic profits are zero). Comparing point B with point A, we see that competitive output is *even higher* and competitive price is *even lower* than we indicated at first.

We conclude, then, that a monopoly will charge a higher price and produce a smaller output than will a competitive industry with the same demand and cost conditions. Why do economists find this situation so objectionable? Because, as you will recall from Chapter 23, a competitive industry devotes "just the right amount" of society's scarce resources to the production of its particular commodity. Therefore, if a monopolist produces less than a competitive industry, it must be producing too little. Remember from Chapter 23 that efficiency in resource allocation requires that the marginal utility (MU) of each commodity be equal to its marginal cost, and that perfect competition guarantees that:

$$MU = P \text{ and } MC = P, \text{ so } MU = MC.$$

Under monopoly, consumers continue to maximize their own welfare by setting MU equal to P. But the monopoly producer, we have just learned, sets MC equal to MR. Since MR is *below* the market price, P, we conclude that in a monopolized industry:

$$MU = P \text{ and } MC = MR < P, \text{ so } MU > MC.$$

Because MU exceeds MC, too few of society's resources are being used to produce the monopolized commodity. Adam Smith's invisible hand is sending out the wrong signals. Consumers are willing to pay an amount for an additional unit of the good (its MU) that exceeds what it costs to produce that unit (its MC). But the monopolist refuses to increase his production, for if he raises output by one unit, the revenue he will collect (the MR) will be less than the price the consumer will pay for the additional unit (P). So the monopolist does not increase his production and resources are allocated inefficiently. To summarize this discussion of the consequences of monopoly:

Because it is protected from entry, a monopoly firm earns profits in excess of the opportunity cost of capital. At the same time, monopoly breeds inefficiency in resource allocation by producing too little output and charging too high a price. For these reasons, some of the virtues of laissez faire evaporate if an industry becomes monopolized.

Can Anything Good Be Said About Monopoly?

Except for the case of natural monopoly—where a single firm offers important cost advantages—it is not easy to find arguments in favor of monopoly. But the comparison between monopoly and perfect competition in the real world is not quite as clean as it is in our example. For one thing, we have assumed that the market demand curve is the same whether the industry is competitive or monopolized. But is this necessarily so? The demand curve will be the same if the monopolist does nothing about his demand, but that hardly seems likely.

Under perfect competiton, purchasers consider the products of all suppliers in an industry to be identical, and so no supplier has any reason to advertise. A farmer who sells wheat through one of the major markets has absolutely no motivation to spend money on advertising because he can sell all the wheat he wants to at the going price. When the monopolist takes over, however, it may very well pay him to advertise. If he believes that the touch of Madison Avenue can make consumers' hearts beat faster as they rush to the market to purchase the wheat whose virtues have been extolled on television, the monopolist will allocate a substantial sum of money to accomplish this feat. This should shift his demand curve outward; after all, that is the purpose of these expenditures. The monopolist's demand curve and that of the competitive industry will then no longer be the same. The higher demand curve for the monopolist's product will perhaps induce him to expand his volume of production and to reduce the difference between the competitive and the monopolistic output levels indicated in Figure 25–2. It will also, however, induce him to charge even higher prices.

Similarly, the advent of a monopoly may produce shifts in the average and marginal cost curves. One reason for higher costs is the advertising we have just been discussing. Another is that the sheer size of the monopolist's organization may lead to bureaucratic inefficiencies, coordination problems, and the like. On the other hand, the monopolist may be able to eliminate certain types of duplication that are unavoidable for a number of small independent firms: one purchasing agent may do the job where many buyers were needed before; and a few large machines may replace many small items of equipment in the hands of the competitive firms. In addition, the large scale of his input purchases may permit the monopolist to avail himself of quantity discounts not available to small competitive firms. If the unification achieved by monopoly does succeed in producing a downward shift in the marginal cost curve, monopoly output will thereby tend to move up closer to the competitive level, and the monopoly price will tend to move down closer to the competitive price.

In addition to this, some economists, most notably the late Joseph Schumpeter, have argued that it is potentially misleading to compare the cost curves of a monopoly and a competitive industry *at a single point in time*. Because it is protected from rivals, and therefore sure to capture the benefits from any cost savings it can devise, a monopoly has a particularly strong motivation to invest in research, they argue. If this research bears fruit, then the monopolist's costs will be lower than those of a competitive industry in the long run, even if they are higher in the short run. Monopoly, according to this view, may be the handmaiden of innovation. While the argument is an old one, it remains controversial. The statistical evidence is decidedly mixed.

Finally, we must remember that the monopoly depicted in Figure 25–2 is not a natural monopoly. But some of the monopolies you find in the real world are. Where the monopoly is natural, costs of production would be much higher if the single large firm were broken up into many smaller firms. (Refer back to Figure 25–1 on page 472.) In such cases, it may be in society's best interest to allow the monopoly to exist so that consumers can benefit from the economies of large-scale production. But then it may be appropriate to place legal limitations on the monopolist's ability to set a price; that is, to *regulate* the monopoly. Regulation of business is an issue that will occupy our attention in Chapter 27.

Monopoly and the Shifting of Pollution Charges

We conclude our discussion of monopoly by returning to the illustrative application that began this chapter—the effectiveness of pollution charges as a means to reduce emissions. Recall that the question is whether a monopoly can raise its price enough to cover any pollution fees, thus shifting these charges entirely to its customers and evading them altogether. The answer is that any firm or industry can, usually, shift *part* of the pollution charge to its customers. Economists argue that this shifting is a proper part of a pollution-control program since it induces consumers to redirect their purchases from goods that are highly polluting to goods that are not. For example, a significant increase in taxes on leaded gasoline with, perhaps, a simultaneous decrease in the tax on unleaded gasoline will send more motorists to the unleaded-gas pumps, and that will reduce dangerous lead emissions into the atmosphere.

But more important for our discussion here is the other side of the matter. While some part of a pollution charge is usually paid by the consumer, *the seller will usually be stuck with some part of the charge, even if he is a monopolist.* Why? Because of the negative slope of his demand curve. If he raises his price he will lose customers, and that will eat into his profits. He will then always be better off if he absorbs *some* of the charge himself rather than try to pass all of it on to his customers.

This is illustrated in Figure 25–4. In part (a) we show the monopolist's demand, marginal revenue, and marginal cost curves. As in Figure 25–2, equilibrium output is again 150 units—the point at which marginal revenue (MR) equals marginal cost (MC). And price is again $10—the point on the demand curve corresponding to 150 units of output (point A). Now, let a charge of $5 per unit be put on the firm's polluting output, shifting the marginal cost curve up uniformly to the curve labeled "MC plus fee" in Figure 25–4(b). Then the profit-maximizing output falls to 100 units (point F), for here MR = MC + pollution fee. The new output, 100 units, is lower than the precharge output, 150 units. Thus, the charge leads the monopolist to restrict his polluting output. The price of his product rises to $12 (point B), the point on the demand curve corresponding to 100 units of output. But the rise in price from $10 to $12 is less than half the $5 pollution charge per unit. Thus:

The pollution charge *does* hurt the polluter even if he is a profit-maximizing monopolist, and it *does* force him to cut his polluting outputs.

No wonder the polluter's lobbyists fight it so vehemently! Polluters realize that they often will be far better off with direct controls that impose a financial penalty *only* if they are caught in a violation, prosecuted, and convicted—and even then the fines are often negligible, as we will see in Chapter 31.

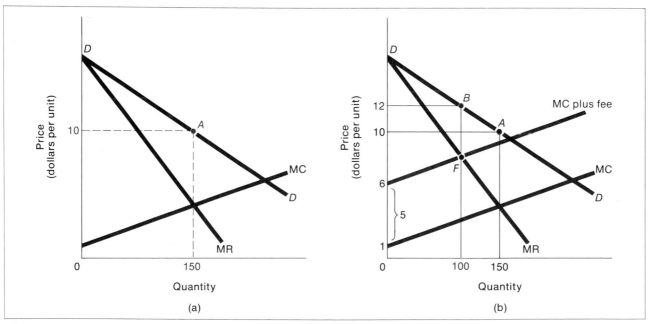

Figure 25–4
MONOPOLY PRICE AND OUTPUT WITH AND WITHOUT A POLLUTION CHARGE
Part (a) shows the monopoly equilibrium without a pollution charge, with price equal to $10 and quantity equal to 150. In part (b) a $5 fee is levied on each unit of polluting output. This raises the marginal cost curve by the amount of the fee, from the black to the blue line. As a result, the output at which MC = MR falls from 150 to 100. Price rises from $10 to $12. Note that this $2 price rise is less than the $5 pollution fee, so the monopolist will be stuck with the remaining $3 of the charge.

Summary

1. A pure monopoly is a one-firm industry producing a product for which there are no close substitutes.
2. Monopoly can persist only if there are important cost advantages to single-firm operation or barriers to free entry. These barriers may be legal impediments (patents, licensing) or some unique advantage the monopolist acquires for himself (control of a scarce resource).
3. One important case of cost advantages is natural monopoly: instances where only one firm can survive because of important economies of large-scale production.
4. A monopoly has no supply curve. It maximizes its profit by producing an output at which its marginal revenue equals its marginal cost. Its price is given by the point on its demand curve corresponding to that output.
5. In a monopolistic industry, if demand and cost curves are the same as those of a competitive industry, and if the demand curve has a negative slope and the supply curve a positive slope, output will be lower and monopoly price will be higher than those of the competitive industry.
6. Advertising may enable the monopolist to shift his demand curve above that of a comparable competitive industry's, and through economies such as large-scale input purchases, he may be able to shift his cost curves below those of a competitive industry.
7. If a pollution charge is imposed on the product of a profit-maximizing monopoly, that monopoly will raise its price, but normally not by the full amount of the charge. That is, the monopolist will end up paying part of the pollution fee.

Concepts for Review

Pure monopoly
Barriers to entry
Patents

Natural monopoly
Monopoly profits

Inefficiency of monopoly
Shifting of pollution charges

Questions for Discussions

1. Which of the following industries are pure monopolies?
   a. the only supplier of water in an isolated desert town
   b. the only supplier of Exxon gas in town
   c. the only supplier of fuel oil in town
   Explain your answers.
2. Suppose a monopoly industry produces less output than a similar competitive industry. Discuss why this may be considered "socially undesirable."
3. The following are the demand and *total* cost schedules for Company Town Water Company, a local monopoly.

OUTPUT (gallons)	PRICE (dollars per gallon)	TOTAL COST (dollars)
50,000	.10	3,000
100,000	.09	6,500
150,000	.08	11,000
200,000	.07	16,000
250,000	.06	23,000
300,000	.04	32,000

How much output will Company Town produce, and what price will it charge? Will it earn a profit? How much? (*Hint:* You will first have to compute its MR and MC schedules.)

4. Suppose a tax of $5 is levied on each item sold by a monopolist, and as a result he decides to raise his price by exactly $5. Why may this decision be against his own best interest?
5. Use Figure 25–2 to show that Adam Smith was wrong when he claimed that a monopoly would always charge "the highest price which can be got."

Between Competition and Monopoly

26

Most productive activity in the United States, as in any advanced industrial society, can be found between the two theoretical poles considered so far: perfect competition and pure monopoly. Thus, if we want to understand the workings of the market mechanism in a real, modern economy, we must look between competition and monopoly, at the hybrid market structures first mentioned in Chapter 22: *monopolistic competition* and *oligopoly.*

This chapter begins with a precise definition of monopolistic competition, a market structure characterized by many small firms selling somewhat different products. Monopolistic competition is quite prevalent in the retail sector of our economy; shoe stores, restaurants, and gasoline stations are some good examples. We will use the theory of the firm described in Chapter 21 to analyze the price–output decision of a monopolistically competitive firm, and then consider industrywide adjustments, as we did in Chapter 22. Then we turn to oligopoly, a market structure in which a few large firms dominate the market. Industries like steel, automobiles, and tobacco are good examples of oligopoly in our economy. The critical feature distinguishing an oligopolist from either a monopolist or a perfect competitor is that the oligopolist cares very much about what other firms in his industry will do. And the resulting interdependence of decisions, we will see, makes oligopoly very hard to analyze. Consequently, economic theory contains not one but many models of oligopoly (some of which will be reviewed in this chapter), and it is often hard to know which model to apply in any particular situation.

At several points in this chapter we will raise the following critical question: How good is the market mechanism at allocating resources when a commodity is produced under monopolistic competition or under oligopoly? A definitive answer is not usually possible, but we shall see that the case for laissez faire is seriously compromised by the existence of either monopolistic competition or oligopoly.

Some Puzzling Observations

It is easy to see that we need to study the hybrid market structures considered in this chapter, for many things we observe in the real world defy understanding within the framework of either perfect competition or pure monopoly. Here are some examples:

1. **Advertising.** While some advertising is primarily informative (for example, help-wanted ads), much of the advertising that bombards us on TV and in magazines is part of a competitive struggle for our business. Many big companies use advertising as the principal weapon in their battle for customers, and advertising budgets can constitute a very large share of their expenditures. Yet oligopolistic industries containing a few giant firms are often accused of being "uncompetitive" while farming is considered as close to perfect competition as any industry in our economy. But most individual farmers spend nothing at all on advertising,[1] while oligopolistic firms spend enormous amounts—an advertising budget of $100 million per year for a single firm is not unknown. Why do the allegedly "uncompetitive" oligopolists make such heavy use of advertising while very competitive farmers do not?

2. **Oversupply.** You have all seen intersections with three or four gasoline stations in close proximity. Often, two or three of them may have no cars waiting to be served and the attendants are unoccupied. There seem to be more gas stations than the available amount of traffic warrants, with a corresponding waste of labor time, equipment, and other resources. Why do they all stay in business?

3. **Sticky Prices.** Many prices in the economy change from minute to minute. Every day the latest prices of such items as soybeans, cocoa, and copper are published. But if you want to buy one of these at 11:45 A.M. some day, you cannot use yesterday's price because it has probably changed since then. Yet prices of other products, such as cars and refrigerators, generally change at most several times a year, even when inflation is proceeding at a double-digit pace. The firms that sell cars and refrigerators know that market conditions change all the time. Why don't they adjust their prices more often?

This chapter will offer explanations of each of these three phenomena.

Monopolistic Competition

For years, economic theorists had only two workable models of the behavior of firms: the monopoly model and the perfectly competitive model. This gap was partially filled, and the realism of economic theory was thereby greatly increased, by the work of the late Edward Chamberlin of Harvard University and Joan Robinson of Cambridge University during the 1930s. The market structure they first analyzed is called **monopolistic competition.** This is a market form that we encounter frequently in our economy. It is particularly characteristic of retailing, where the small shopkeeper still plays a significant role, and of many of the economy's services, such as medical and legal, which are provided under similar conditions. Gas stations and restaurants are other good examples.

Notice that monopolistic competition differs from perfect competition in only one respect (item 2 in the definition). While all products are identical under perfect competition, under monopolistic competition products differ from seller to seller—in quality, in packaging, or in supplementary services offered (for example, length of the guarantee, car window washing by a gas station, and so on). The factors that serve to differentiate products need not be "real" in any objective or scientific sense. For example, differences in packaging or in associated services can and do distinguish products that are otherwise identical. On the other hand, two products may perform quite differently in quality tests, but if consumers know nothing about this difference, it is irrelevant.

A market is said to operate under conditions of **monopolistic competition** if it satisfies four conditions, three of which are the same as under perfect competition: (1) *Numerous participants*—that is, many buyers and sellers, all of whom are small; (2) *Heterogeneity of products*—as far as the buyer is concerned, each seller's product is at least somewhat different from every other's; (3) *Freedom of exit and entry*; and (4) *Perfect information.*

[1] But farmers' *associations*, like Sunkist and various dairy groups, do spend money on advertising.

Since the defining characteristic of monopolistic competition is that competing products are not identical, there is no reason to expect them to sell at the same price, nor any reason to expect the price of any firm's product to remain unchanged when the quantity supplied varies. Each seller, in effect, deals in a market slightly separated from the others and caters to a set of customers who vary in their "loyalty" to his product. If he raises his price somewhat, he may expect to drive some but not all of his customers into the arms of his competitors. If he lowers his price, he may expect to attract some trade from his rivals. But since his product is not a perfect substitute for theirs, if he undercuts them slightly he will not attract away *all* their business as he would in the perfectly competitive case. Thus his demand curve is negatively sloped, like that of a monopolist, rather than horizontal, like that of a perfect competitor.

Since his product is distinguished from all others, a monopolistic competitor has something akin to a small monopoly. Can we therefore expect him to earn more profit than a perfect competitor? In the short run, perhaps he will. But in the long run, high economic profits will attract new entrants into a monopolistically competitive market—not entrants with products *identical* to an existing firm's, but with products sufficiently similar to hurt. If one ice-cream parlor's location enables it to do a thriving business, it can confidently expect another, selling a *different* brand, to open nearby. When one seller adopts a new, attractive package, he can be sure that his rivals will soon follow suit, with a slightly different design and color of their own. In this way freedom of entry ensures that the monopolistically competitive firm earns no more on its capital in the long run than it could earn elsewhere. Just as under perfect competition, price will be driven to the level of average cost, including the opportunity cost of capital.

Price and Output Determination Under Monopolistic Competition

The short-run equilibrium of the firm under monopolistic competiton differs little from the case of monopoly. Since the firm faces a downward-sloping demand curve (labeled D in Figure 26–1), its marginal revenue (MR) curve will lie below its demand curve. Profits are maximized at the output level at which marginal revenue and marginal cost (MC) are equal. In Figure 26–1, the profit-maximizing output for a hypothetical gasoline station is 12,000 gallons per week, and it sells this output at a price of $1.50 per gallon (point P on the demand curve). This diagram, you will note, looks much like Figure 25–2 (page 473) for a monopoly. The only difference is that the demand curve of a monopolistic competitor is likely to be much more elastic (flatter) than the pure monopolist's because there are many close substitutes for the monopolistic competitor's product. If our gas station raises its price to $1.65 per gallon, most of its customers will go across the street. If it lowers its price to $1.20, it will have long lines at its pumps.

The gas station depicted in Figure 26–1 is making economic profits. Since average cost at 12,000 gallons per week is only $1.35 per gallon (point C), the station is making a profit on gasoline sales of 15 cents per gallon, or $1800 per week in total (the shaded rectangle). Under monopoly, such profits can persist. But under monopolistic competition they cannot, because new firms will be attracted into the market. While the new stations will not offer the identical product, they will offer products that are close enough to take away some business from our firm (for example, they may sell Mobil or Shell gasoline instead of Exxon). When more firms share the market, the demand curve facing any individual firm must fall.

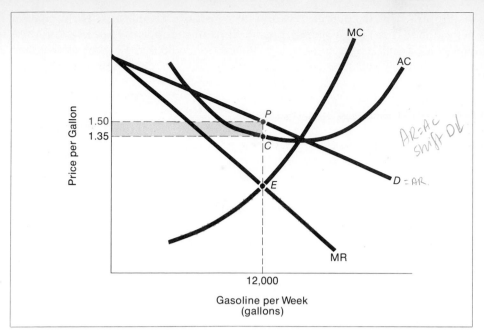

Figure 26–1
SHORT-RUN EQUILIBRIUM OF THE FIRM UNDER MONOPOLISTIC COMPETITION
Like any firm, a monopolistic competitor maximizes profits by equating marginal cost (MC) and marginal revenue (MR). In this example, the profit-maximizing output level is 12,000 gallons per week and the profit-maximizing price is $1.50 per gallon. The firm is making a profit of 15 cents per gallon, which is depicted by the vertical distance from C to P.

But how far? The answer is basically the same as it was under perfect competition: until the best that can be done by maximizing profits is to achieve zero economic profits, for only then will entry cease.

Figure 26–2 depicts the same monopolistically competitive firm as in Figure 26–1 *after* the adjustment to the long run is complete. The demand curve has been pushed down so far that when the firm equates MC and MR in order to maximize profits (point E) it simultaneously equates price (P) and average cost (AC) so that profits are zero (point P). As compared with the short-run

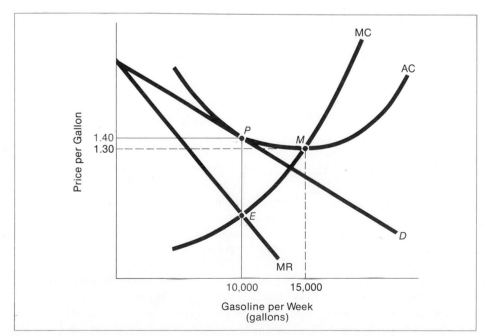

Figure 26–2
LONG-RUN EQUILIBRIUM OF THE FIRM UNDER MONOPOLISTIC COMPETITION
In this diagram the cost curves are identical to those of Figure 26–1, but the demand curve (and hence also the MR curve) has been depressed by the entry of new competitors. When the firm maximizes profits by equating marginal revenue and marginal cost (point E), its average cost is equal to its price ($1.40), so economic profits are zero. For this reason, the diagram depicts a *long-run* equilibrium position.

equilibrium depicted in Figure 26–1, price in long-run equilibrium is *lower* ($1.40 per gallon versus $1.50), there are *more firms* in the industry, and each firm is producing a *smaller* output (10,000 gallons versus 12,000) at a *higher* average cost per gallon ($1.40 versus $1.35).[2] In general:

Long-run equilibrium under monopolistic competition requires that the firm's demand curve be tangent to its average cost curve.

Why? Because if the two curves intersected, there would be output levels at which price exceeded average cost, which means that economic profits could be earned and there would be an influx of new substitute products. Similarly, if the average cost curve failed to touch the demand curve altogether, the firm would be unable to obtain returns equal to those that its capital can get elsewhere, and firms would leave the industry. This analysis of entry is quite similar to the perfectly competitive case. Moreover, the notion that firms under monopolistic competition earn exactly zero economic profits seems to correspond fairly well to what we see in the real world. Filling station operators, whose market has the characteristics of monopolistic competition, do not earn notably higher profits than do small farmers, who operate under conditions closer to perfect competition.

The Excess Capacity Theorem and Resource Allocation

But there is one important difference between perfect and monopolistic competition. Look at Figure 26–2 again. The tangency point between the average cost and demand curves, point *P*, occurs along the *negatively sloping portion* of the average cost curve, since only there does the AC curve have the same (negative) slope as the demand curve. If the AC curve is U-shaped, the tangency point must therefore lie above and to the left of the *minimum point* on the average cost curve, point *M*. By contrast, under perfect competition the firm's demand curve is horizontal, so tangency must take place at the minimum point on the average cost curve, as is easily confirmed by referring back to Figure 22–10(a) on page 424. This observation leads to the following important conclusion:

Under monopolistic competition, the firm in the long run will tend to produce an output lower than that which minimizes its unit costs, and hence unit costs of the monopolistic competitor will be higher than is necessary. Since the level of output corresponding to minimum average cost is naturally considered to be the firm's optimal capacity, this result has been called the **excess capacity theorem of monopolistic competition.**

It follows that if every firm under monopolistic competition were to expand its output, cost per unit of output would be reduced. But we must be careful about jumping to policy conclusions from that observation. It does *not* follow that *every* monopolistically competitive firm should produce more. After all, such an overall increase in industry output means that a smaller portion of the economy's resources will be available for other uses; and from the information at hand we have no way of knowing whether that leaves us ahead or behind in terms of social benefits. Yet the situation represented in Figure 26–2 can still be interpreted to represent a substantial *inefficiency*. While it is not clear that society would gain if *every* firm were to achieve lower costs by expanding its production, society *can*

---

[2]*Exercise:* Show that if the demand curve fell still further, the firm would incur a loss. What would then happen in the long run?

save resources if firms combine into a smaller number of larger companies that produce the same total output. For example, suppose that in the situation shown in Figure 26–2 there are 15 monopolistically competitive firms each selling 10,000 gallons of gas per week. The total cost of this output, according to the figures given in the diagram, would be

$$\text{(Number of firms)} \times \text{(Output per firm)} \times \text{(Cost per unit)}$$
$$= 15 \times 10,000 \times \$1.40 = \$210,000 .$$

If, instead, the number of stations were cut to 10, and each sold 15,000 gallons, total production would be unchanged. But total costs would fall to $10 \times 15,000 \times \$1.30 = \$195,000$, a net saving of \$15,000 *for the same total output*. This result is not dependent on the particular numbers used in our illustration. It follows directly from the observation that lowering the cost per unit must always reduce the total cost of producing any given output. The excess capacity theorem explains one of the puzzles mentioned at the start of this chapter. The intersection with four filling stations, where two could serve the available customers with little increase in delays and at lower costs, is a practical example of excess capacity.

The excess capacity theorem seems to imply that there are too many sellers in monopolistically competitive markets and that society would benefit from a reduction in their numbers. However, such a conclusion would be a bit hasty. Even if a smaller number of larger firms could reduce costs, society may not benefit from the change because it would leave consumers a smaller range of choice. Since all products are at least slightly different under monopolistic competition, a reduction in the number of firms means that the number of different products falls as well. We achieve greater efficiency at the cost of greater standardization. In some cases consumers may agree that this trade-off represents a net gain, particularly where the variety of products available was initially so great that it only served to confuse them. But for other products, most consumers would probably agree that the diversity of choice is worth the extra cost involved.

Oligopoly

In terms of the dollar value of all manufactured goods produced in our economy, there seems little doubt that first place must be assigned to our final market form—**oligopoly.** In highly developed economies, it is not monopoly, but oligopoly, that is virtually synonymous with "big business." Any oligopolistic industry includes a group of giant firms, each of which keeps a watchful eye on the actions of the others.[3] It is under oligopoly that rivalry among firms takes its most direct and active form. Here one encounters such actions and reactions as the frequent introduction of new products, free samples, and aggressive—if not downright nasty—advertising campaigns. One firm's price decision is likely to elicit a cry of pain from its rivals, and firms are engaged in a continuing battle in which strategies are planned day by day and each major decision can be expected to induce a direct response.

The manager of a large oligopolistic firm who has occasion to study economics is somewhat taken aback by the notion of perfect competition, because it is devoid of all harsh competitive activity as he knows it. Remember that under perfect competition the managers of firms make no price decisions—they simply

An **oligopoly** is a market dominated by a few sellers, at least several of which are large enough relative to the total market to be able to influence the market price.

[3]Notice that nothing is said in the definition about the degree of product differentiation. Some oligopolies sell products that are essentially identical (such as steel plate from steelmakers) while others sell products that are quite different in the eyes of consumers (for example, Chevrolets, Fords, and Plymouths).

accept the price dictated by market forces and adjust their output accordingly. As we observed at the beginning of the chapter, a competitive firm does not advertise; it adopts no sales gimmicks; it does not even know who most of its competitors are. But since oligopolists are not as dependent on market forces, they do not enjoy such luxuries. They must worry about prices, spend fortunes on advertising, and try to understand their rivals' behavior patterns.

The reasons for such divergent behavior should be clear. First, a perfectly competitive firm can sell all it wants at the current market price. So why should it waste money on advertising? By contrast, Ford and Chrysler cannot sell all the cars they want at the current price. Since their demand curves are negatively sloped, if they want to sell more they must either reduce prices or advertise more (to shift their demand curve outward). Second, since the public believes that the products supplied by firms in a perfectly competitive industry are identical, if seller A advertises his product, the advertisement is just as likely to bring customers to seller B. Under oligopoly, however, products are usually not identical. Ford advertises to try to convince consumers that its automobiles are better than GM's or Toyota's. And if the advertising campaign succeeds, GM and Toyota will be hurt and probably will respond by advertising on their own. Thus, it is the firm in an oligopoly with differentiated products that is forced to compete via advertising, while the perfectly competitive firm gains little or nothing by doing so.

Why Oligopolistic Behavior Is So Hard to Analyze

The relative freedom of choice in pricing of at least the largest firms in an oligopolistic industry, and the necessity for them to take direct account of their rivals' responses, are potentially troublesome. Producers that are able to influence the market price may find it expedient to adjust their outputs so as to secure more favorable prices. Just as in the case of monopoly, such actions are likely to be at the expense of the consumer and detrimental to the economy's efficient use of resources.

It is not easy to reach definite conclusions about resource allocation under oligopoly, however. The reason is that oligopoly is much more difficult to analyze than the other forms of economic organization. The difficulty arises from the interdependent nature of oligopolistic decisions. For example, Ford's management knows that its actions will probably lead to reactions by General Motors, which in turn may require a readjustment in Ford's plans, thereby producing a modification in GM's response, and so on. Where such a sequence of moves and countermoves may lead is difficult enough to ascertain. But the fact that Ford executives know all this in advance, and may try to take it into account in making their initial decision, makes even that first step difficult, if not impossible, to analyze and predict.

The truth is that almost anything can happen under oligopoly, and sometimes does. The early railroad kings went so far as to employ gangs of hoodlums who engaged in pitched battles to try to prevent the operation of a rival line. At the other extreme, overt or more subtle forms of collusion have been employed to avoid rivalry altogether—to transform an oligopolistic industry, at least temporarily, into a monopolistic one. Arrangements designed to make it possible for the firms to live and let live have also been utilized: price leadership (see below) is one example; an agreement allocating geographic areas among the different firms is another. Because of this rich variety of behavior patterns it is not surprising that economists have been unable to agree on a single, widely accepted model of oligopoly behavior. Nor should they. Since oligopolies in the real world are so diverse, oligopoly models in the theoretical world should also come in various shapes and sizes. The theory of oligopoly contains some really remarkable pieces of economic analysis, some of which we will review in the following sections.

A Shopping List

An introductory course cannot hope to explain all the different models of oligopoly; nor would that serve any purpose but to confuse you. Since economists differ in their opinions about which approaches to oligopoly theory are the most interesting and promising, we offer in this section a quick catalogue of some of the major models of oligopoly behavior. Then, in the remainder of the chapter, we will describe in detail a few of the models in our catalogue.

Ignore Interdependence

One simple approach to the problem of oligopolistic interdependence is to assume that the oligopolists themselves ignore it; that they behave as if their actions will not elicit reactions from their rivals. It *is* possible that an oligopolist, finding the "if he thinks that I think that he thinks . . ." chain of reasoning just too complex, will decide to ignore his rivals' behavior. He may then just maximize profits on the assumption that his decisions will not affect those of his rivals. In this case, the analysis of oligopoly is identical to the analysis of monopoly in the previous chapter.

Another argument for the view that the oligopolist sometimes ignores interdependence emphasizes the fact that oligopoly firms are managed by hired executives rather than by the firms' owners. Since managers may be more interested in pure *size* than in profits, it has been suggested that some giant oligopoly firms may try to *maximize sales revenue* rather than profits. This model is discussed further below.

While it is possible that *some* oligopolies ignore interdependence *some* of the time, it is very unlikely that such models offer a general explanation for the behavior of *most* oligopoly behavior *most* of the time. The reason is quite simple. Because they operate in the same market, the price and output decisions of the makers of Brand X and Brand Y soap suds *really are* interdependent. Suppose, for example, that the management of Brand X, Inc., decides to cut its price to $1.05 (in order to raise either sales or profits) on the assumption that Brand Y, Inc., will continue to charge $1.12 per box, to manufacture five million boxes per year, and to spend $1 million per year on advertising. It may find itself surprised when Brand Y, Inc., cuts its price to $1 per box, raises production to eight million boxes per year, and sponsors the Super Bowl. If so, Brand X's profits will suffer, and the company will wish it had not cut its price. Most important for our purposes, it will learn not to ignore interdependence in the future. Thus it seems imperative to consider models that deal explicitly with oligopolistic interdependence.

Cartels

The opposite end of the spectrum from ignoring interdependence is for all the firms in an oligopoly to collude overtly with one another, thereby tranforming the industry into a giant monopoly—a **cartel.** A notable example of the formation of a cartel is the Organization of Petroleum Exporting Countries (OPEC), which first began to make decisions in unison in 1973. OPEC is one of the most spectacularly successful cartels in history. By restricting output, the member nations managed to quadruple the price of oil in 1973–1974. Then, unlike most cartels, which come apart in internal bickering or for other reasons, OPEC held

A **cartel** is a group of sellers of a product who have joined together to control its production, sale, and price in the hope of obtaining the advantages of monopoly.

together through two worldwide recessions and a variety of unsettling political events, and struck again with huge price increases in 1979–1980.

But the story of OPEC is not the norm. Cartels are difficult to organize and even more difficult to preserve. Firms do not find it easy to agree on such things as the amount by which each will reduce its output in order to help push up the price. Once price is driven up and profitability is increased, it becomes very tempting for each participant to offer secret discounts in order to lure some very profitable customers away from others in the cartel. When this happens, or is even suspected by cartel members, it is often the beginning of the end of the collusive arrangement.

Many economists consider cartels to be one of the least desirable forms of market organization. If a cartel is successful, it may end up charging the monopoly price and obtaining monopoly profits. But because the firms do not actually combine their operations but continue to produce separately, the cartel offers the public no offsetting benefits in the form of economies of large-scale production. For these and other reasons, open collusion among firms is illegal in the United States, as we will see in Chapter 28, and outright cartel arrangements are rarely found. (However, in many other countries cartels are common.)

Price Leadership

Though overt collusion is quite rare, some observers think that *tacit collusion* is quite common among oligopolists in our economy. Oligopolists who do not want to rock what amounts to a very profitable boat may seek to develop some indirect way of communicating with one another and signaling their intentions. One common example of tacit collusion is **price leadership,** an arrangement in which one firm in the industry is, in effect, assigned the task of making pricing decisions for the entire group. It is expected that other firms will adopt the prices set by the price leader, even though there is no explicit agreement, only tacit consent. Typically, the price leader will be the dominant firm in the industry. But in some price-leadership arrangements the role of leader may rotate from one firm to another. For example, it has been suggested that the steel industry for many years conformed to the price leadership model with U.S. Steel and Bethlehem Steel assuming the role of leader at different times.

Price leadership *does* overcome the problem of oligopolistic interdependence, though it is not the only possible way of doing so. If Brand X, Inc., is the price leader for the soap suds industry, it can predict how Brand Y, Inc., will react to any price increases it announces. (Brand Y will match the increases.) Similarly, Brand Z executives will be able to predict Brand Y's behavior as long as the price-leadership arrangement holds up. But one problem besetting price leadership is that, while the oligopolists as a group may benefit by avoiding a damaging price war, one of them may benefit more than the others. The firm that is the price leader is clearly in a better position to maximize its own profits than are any of the rival firms, which must simply fall in line. It is thus the responsibility of the price leader to take into account its rival's welfare when making its price decision—or else it may find itself dethroned! For this reason, a price-leadership arrangement, if effective, can lead to the same sort of price and production decisions as would a cartel. Alternatively, leadership can break down entirely.

To help preserve its privileged position, a price leader may change price rather infrequently, and only when there is a clear signal that a price change is warranted (for example, when all the industry's firms sign a new union contract calling for higher wages). Many students of oligopoly have, in fact, maintained that price changes in oligopolistic markets tend to occur far less frequently than in competitive markets.[4] A well-developed theoretical model—the so-called *kinked*

---

[4]It should be noted that other students of the subject dispute this claim.

demand curve model—has been devised to explain this phenomenon, and we will outline this model a bit later in the chapter.

The Game-Theory Approach

The most direct, but also the most difficult, approach to the problem of interdependence is to tackle it head on—to try to study and understand the basic logic of decision making in such an environment. The same sort of problem that arises in oligopoly also arises in international relations, military strategy, and simple parlor games. A branch of mathematics called *game theory* has been devised to analyze exactly this type of problem—decision making when you are dealing with a rival or rivals whose interests conflict with your own—and we will explain the rudiments of game theory later in the chapter.

Having outlined the varieties of behavior displayed by oligopolistic markets and indicated the types of analysis relevant to each, we devote the remainder of this chapter to more detailed descriptions of three oligopoly models: sales maximization, the kinked demand curve model, and the game-theory approach.*

Sales Maximization

Early in our analysis of the theory of the firm, we discussed the hypothesis that firms try to maximize profits and noted that other objectives are possible (see pages 395–396). Among these alternative goals, the one that has achieved the most attention is **sales maximization.** As mentioned above, modern industrial firms are managed and owned by entirely different groups of people. The managers are paid executives who work for the company on a full-time basis and may grow to identify their own welfare with that of the company. The owners may be a large and diffuse group of stockholders, most of whom own only a tiny fraction of the outstanding stock, take little interest in the operations of the company, and do not feel that the company is "theirs" in any real sense. In such a situation, it is not entirely implausible that the company's decisions will be influenced more heavily by management's goals than by the goal of the owners (which is, presumably, to maximize profit). It has been suggested, for example, that management's salary and prestige may be tied more directly to the company's *size,* as measured by its sales volume, rather than to its *profits.* Therefore, the firm's managers may select a price–output combination that maximizes sales rather than profits. But does sales maximization lead to different decisions than does profit maximization? We shall see now that the answer is yes.

Figure 26–3 is a diagram that should be familiar by now. It shows the marginal cost (MC) and average cost (AC) curves for a firm—in this case Brand X, Inc.,—along with its demand and marginal revenue (MR) curves. We have used such diagrams before and know that if the company wants to maximize profits, it will select point *A*, where MC = MR. This means that it will produce 2.5 million boxes of soap suds per year and sell them at a price of $1 each. Since average cost at this level of output is only 80 cents per box, profit per unit is 20 cents. Total profits are therefore $.20 × 2,500,000 = $500,000 per year. This is the highest attainable profit level for Brand X, Inc.

Now what if Brand X wants to maximize sales revenue instead? In this case, it will want to keep producing until marginal revenue (MR) is depressed to *zero;* that is, it will select point *B.* Why? By definition, MR is the *additional* revenue obtained by raising output by one unit. If the firm wishes to maximize revenue,

---

*The three sections that follow may be read in any combination, and in any order, without loss of continuity.

Figure 26–3

SALES-MAXIMIZATION
EQUILIBRIUM
A firm that wishes to maximize
sales revenue will expand output until marginal revenue
(MR) is zero—point B in the
diagram, where output is 3.75
million boxes per year. This is
a greater output level than it
would choose if it were interested in maximizing profits. In
that case, it would select point
A, where MC = MR, and produce only 2.5 million boxes.
Since the demand curve is
downward sloping, the price
corresponding to point B (75
cents) must be less than the
price corresponding to point
A ($1).

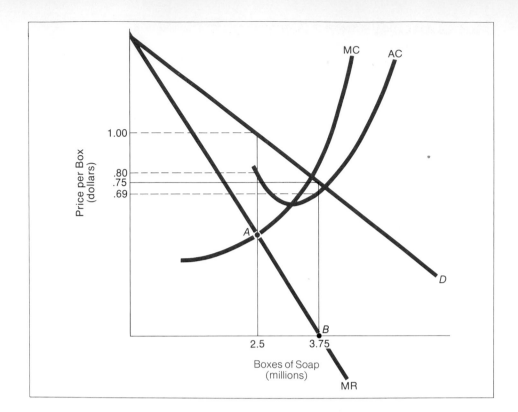

then any time it finds that MR is positive it will want to increase output further, and any time it finds that MR is negative it will want to decrease output. Only when MR = 0 can the maximum sales revenue have possibly been achieved.[5] Thus if Brand X, Inc., is a sales maximizer it will produce 3.75 million boxes of soap suds per year, and charge 75 cents per box. Since average costs at this level of production are only 69 cents per box, profit per unit is 6 cents and, with 3.75 million units sold, total profit is $225,000. Naturally, this level of profit is less than what the firm can achieve if it reduces output to the profit-maximizing level. But this is not the firm's goal. Its sales revenue at point B is 75 cents per unit times 3.75 million units, or $2,812,500, whereas at point A it was only $2,500,000 (2.5 million units at $1 each). What we conclude, then, is that:

If a firm is maximizing sales revenue, it will produce more output and charge a lower price than it would if it were maximizing profits.

We see clearly in Figure 26–3 that this result holds for Brand X, Inc. But does it always hold? The answer is yes. Look again at Figure 26–3, but ignore the numbers on the axes. At point A, where MR = MC, marginal revenue must be positive because it is equal to marginal cost (which, we may assume, is *always* positive). At point B, MR is equal to zero. Since the marginal revenue curve is negatively sloped, the point where it reaches zero (point B) must necessarily correspond to a higher level of output than the point where it cuts the marginal cost curve (point A). Thus, sales-maximizing firms always produce more than profit-maximizing firms and, to sell this greater volume of output, they must charge a lower price.

[5]The logic here is exactly the same as the logic that led to the conclusion that a firm maximized *profits* by setting *marginal profit* equal to zero. If you need review, consult Chapter 21, especially pages 400–401.

The Game-Theory Approach

Game theory, contributed in 1944 by mathematician John von Neumann (1903–1957) and economist Oskar Morgenstern (1902–1977), adopts a more imaginative approach than any other analysis of oligopoly. It attacks the issue of interdependence directly by assuming that each firm's managers proceed on the assumption *that their rivals are extremely ingenious decision makers.* In this model, each oligopolist is seen as a competing player in a game of strategy. Since managers believe their opponents will always adopt the most profitable counter-move to any move they make, they seek the optimal defensive strategy.

Two fundamental concepts of game theory are the *strategy* and the *payoff matrix.* A strategy represents an operational plan for one of the participants. In its simplest form it may refer to just one of a participant's possible decisions. For example, "I will add to my product line a car with a TV set that the driver can also watch," or "I will cut the price of my car to $5500." Since much of the game-theory analysis of oligopoly has focused on an oligopoly of two firms—a *duopoly*—we illustrate the payoff matrix for a two-person game in Table 26–1. This matrix is a table of numbers reporting the payoffs that our firm will receive for each possible pair of its own and its rival's strategies. It is read like a mileage chart. For example, if our firm selects strategy B (cut price to $5500) and its rival chooses W (offer diesel engine), we see that our company will end up with 70 percent of the market (third column, second row). The special case of pure rivalry, in which every gain for our firm means an *exactly* equal loss for its competitor, and vice versa, is referred to as a **zero-sum game.** In the zero-sum case, the payoff matrix has the convenient property of telling us all we need to know about our competitor's payoff matrix as well as our own. Given the market share of one firm, we can immediately deduce the other firm's market share by subtraction. For example, if the matrix tells us that our firm's market share will be 70 percent, we know that the rival's market share must be 30 percent.

We can now begin to discuss optimal strategy choices for the two firms. Since our firm is in direct conflict with the other firm, we know that our rival will try to keep our market share as low as possible, and vice versa. Thus, in evaluating its strategies, the management of our firm may reason as follows: "If I select strategy A, the worst that can happen to me is that my adversary will select counterstrategy W, which would cut my market share to its minimum level, 30 percent (the blue number in the first row of the payoff matrix). Similarly, if I utilize strategy B, the

---

Table 26-1

A PAYOFF MATRIX

		Rival's Strategy	
	U: Set Price at $6000	V: Set Price at $5000	W: Offer Diesel Engine
A: Install TV set	80	35	30
B: Cut price to $5500	28	45	70
C: Offer three-year loan	60	50	90

(Our Strategy)

The entries represent the share of market our firm will receive under any combination of strategies offered by itself and its competitor.

Ronald Reagan, Game Theorist

There was plenty of political jockeying in 1981 as President Reagan tried to push his new economic program through Congress. In selecting his strategy, the president proved to be an astute game theorist, as the following newspaper article suggests:

President Reagan's decision to order his staff to repudiate a report that he was willing to compromise on the tax-cut portion of his economic plan probably demonstrates that he is a natural and gifted game theorist, better than the three sub-Cabinet officers who had led Representative James R. Jones, chairman of the House Budget Committee, to believe that the President would accept a one-year, rather than a three-year, tax cut.

For Mr. Reagan has sensed that the Republicans have what game theorists call a "dominant strategy"—one that makes a player better off than his opponent, no matter what strategy his opponent chooses.

The basic Republican strategic choice . . . is between (A) to support the President's program completely and (B) to compromise with the Democrats. The Democrats also have two basic strategies: (I) mainly support Mr. Reagan's economic program or (II) attack it.

The dominant strategy for the Republicans is (A). As the accompanying matrix shows, if the Republicans completely support the President, they will score higher than the Democrats whether the Democrats go along with or attack the President's program.

Actually, if the Democrats attack and the Republicans stick with the President down the line, a stalemate might result. But that outcome would be unstable because the Democrats would be better off to support the President rather than attack him and incur their worst result, suffering public condemnation and the likelihood of still heavier losses in the 1982 Congressional elections.

The only stable outcome of the political game, as set forth here, would thus be the (2, 4) payoff in the upper left

		REPUBLICANS	
		Support Reagan Completely (A)	Compromise (B)
DEMOCRATS	Mainly Support Reagan (I)	Republicans triumph; Democrats avoid blame (2,4)	Republicans win but vex Reagan; Democrats share credit (3,3)
	Attack Reagan (II)	Republican program blocked in House, Democrats incur blame (1,2)	Republicans lose much of program; Democrats look fiscally responsible (4,1)

Key: 4 = best; 3 = next best; 2 = next worst; 1 = worst
(First number in pair is outcome for Democrats, second is outcome for Republicans.)

corner, with the Republicans winning a complete victory and the Democrats cutting their losses by supporting the popular President.

Last Friday, four days before an agitated Mr. Reagan told his three top White House aides . . . to reject the compromise strategy, two astute game theorists . . . said in interviews that the correct game-theoretic solution was for the Republicans to hold to their dominant strategy (A).

SOURCE: Leonard Silk, "Game Theory: Reagan's Move," *The New York Times*, April 15, 1981, page D2. © 1981 by The New York Times Company. Reprinted by permission.

outcome we must be prepared for is 28 percent, which is the (blue) minimum payoff to that strategy. Finally, if I use strategy C, my rival can damage me most by using strategy V, which gives me 50 percent." What, if anything, can the management of our firm do to maximize its chances for success? Game theory suggests that it should select the strategy whose minimum payoff is higher than the minimum payoff for any other strategy. This is called the **maximin criterion**—one seeks the *maximum* of the *minimum* payoffs to the various strategies, the highest of the blue entries. In this case, the maximin payoff is 50 percent and leads to the choice of strategy C by our firm (and V by its adversary).

There is, of course, a great deal more to game theory than we have been able to suggest in a few paragraphs. We have only sought to suggest a little of its flavor. Game theory provides, for example, an illuminating analysis of coalitions, indicating, for cases involving more than two firms, which firms would do well to align themselves together against which others. The theory of games has also been used to analyze a variety of complicated problems outside the realm of oligopoly theory. It has been employed in management training programs and by a number of government agencies. It is used in political science (see the boxed insert, opposite) and in formulating military strategy. It has been presented here to offer the reader a glimpse of the type of work that is taking place on the frontiers of economic analysis and to suggest how economists think about complex analytical problems.

The Kinked Demand Curve Model[6]

As our final example of oligopoly analysis, we describe a model designed to account for the alleged stickiness in oligopolistic pricing, meaning that prices in oligopolistic markets change far less frequently than do prices in competitive markets. It will be recalled that this is one of the puzzling phenomena with which we began this chapter. The prices of corn, soybeans, cocoa, and silver, all of which are sold in markets with large numbers of buyers and sellers, change minute by minute. But prices of such items as cars, TV sets, and dishwashers, all of which are supplied by oligopolists, may change only every few months. These prices seem to resist frequent change even in periods of inflation.

The model that is designed to help explain this phenomenon makes use of two different demand curves representing two different but relevant conditions. One curve represents the quantities a given oligopolistic firm can sell at different prices *if competitors match its price moves*, and the other demand curve represents what happens when competitors stubbornly *stick to their initial price levels*. Point A in Figure 26–4 represents the initial price and output of our firm: 1000 units at $10 each. Through that point pass two demand curves: *DD*, which represents our company's demand if competitors keep their prices fixed, and *dd*, the curve indicating what happens when competitors match our firm's price changes. The *DD* curve is the more elastic (flatter) of the two, and a moment's

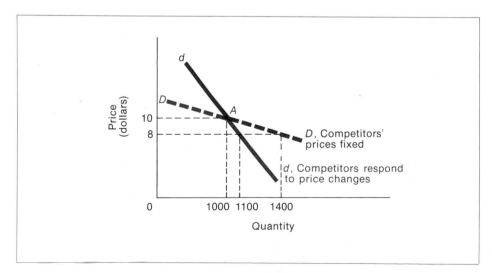

Figure 26–4
THE KINKED DEMAND CURVE

It has been suggested that oligopolists are deterred from changing prices frequently because they fear the reactions of their rivals. If they raise prices, they will lose many customers to competitors because the competitors will not match the price increase. (Elastic demand curve *DD* therefore applies to price increases.) But if they cut prices, competitors will be forced to match the price cut, so that price cut will not bring many new customers. (The inelastic demand curve *dd* applies to price cuts.) Thus, the demand curve facing the firm is the kinked, blue curve *DAd*.

[6]Variants of this model were constructed by Hall and Hitch in England and by Sweezy in the United States. See R. L. Hall and C. J. Hitch, "Price Theory and Business Behavior," *Oxford Economic Papers*, No. 2, May 1939, and P. M. Sweezy, "Demand Under Conditions of Oligopoly," *Journal of Political Economy*, vol. 47, August 1939.

thought indicates why this should be so. If our firm cuts its price from its initial level of $10 to, say, $8, and if competitors do not match this cut, we would expect our firm to get a large number of customers away from its rivals (its quantity demanded will jump to 1400) than it would if its competitors responded by also reducing their prices (its quantity demanded will rise to only 1100). Conversely, when it raises its price, our firm may expect a larger loss of sales if its rivals fail to match its increase, which the reader may readily verify by observing the relative steepness (inelasticity) of the curve *dd* in Figure 26–4.

How does this relate to sticky oligopolistic prices? Here our firm's fears and expectations must be brought into the matter. The hypothesis of those who designed this model was that a typical oligopolistic firm has good reason to fear the worst. If it lowers its prices and its rivals do not, its sales will seriously cut into its competitor's volume, and so the rivals will *have* to match the price cut in order to protect themselves. The inelastic demand curve, *dd*, will therefore apply if our firm decides on a price reduction (points below and to the right of point *A*). On the other hand, if our company chooses to *increase* its price, management will fear that its rivals will continue to sit at their old price levels, calmly collecting the customers that have been driven to them. Thus, the relevant demand curve for price increases will be *DD*. In sum, our firm will figure that it will face a segment of the elastic demand curve *DD* if it raises its price and a segment of the inelastic demand curve *dd* if it decreases its price. Its true demand curve will then be given by the heavy blue line. For obvious reasons, this is called a **kinked demand curve.**

In these circumstances, it will pay management to vary its price only under extreme provocation, that is, only if there is an enormous change in costs. For the kinked demand curve represents a "heads you lose, tails you lose" proposition in terms of any potential price change. If it raises its price, the firm will lose many customers (demand is elastic); if it lowers its price, the increase in volume will be comparatively small (demand is inelastic).

Figure 26–5 illustrates this conclusion graphically. The two demand curves, *dd* and *DD*, are carried over precisely from the previous diagram. The dashed

Figure 26–5
THE KINKED DEMAND CURVE AND STICKY PRICES

The kinked demand curve *DAd* that we derived in the previous diagram leads to a marginal revenue curve that follows MR down to point *B*, then drops directly down to point *C*, and finally follows mr thereafter. Consequently, marginal cost curves a little higher or a little lower than the MC curve shown in the diagram will lead to the same price–output decision. Oligopoly prices are "sticky," then, in the sense that they do not respond to minor changes in costs. Only cost changes large enough to push the MC curve out of the range *BC* will lead to a change in price.

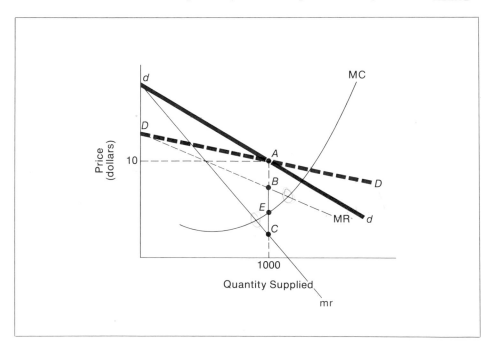

marginal revenue curve, labeled MR, is the marginal curve associated with DD, while the solid marginal revenue curve, labeled mr, is the marginal revenue curve associated with dd. Since the marginal revenue curve relevant to the firm's decision making is MR for any output level *below* 1000 units (that is, any price above $10) but mr for any output level *above* 1000 units (that is, any price below $10), the composite marginal revenue curve facing the firm is shown by the thin blue line. The marginal cost curve drawn in the diagram cuts this composite marginal revenue curve at point E, which indicates the profit-maximizing combination of output and price for this oligopolist. Specifically, the quantity supplied at point E is 1000 units, and the price is $10, which we read from curve DAd. The unique aspect of this diagram is that the kinked demand curve leads to a marginal revenue curve that takes a sharp plunge between points B and C. Consequently, moderate upward or downward shifts of the MC curve will still leave it intersecting the marginal revenue curve somewhere between B and C, and thus will *not* lead the firm to change its price–output decision. (Try this for yourself in Figure 26–5.) This is the sense in which the kinked demand curve makes prices "sticky."

If this is in fact the way oligopolists feel about their competitors' behavior, it is easy to see why they may be reluctant to make frequent price changes. We can also understand why a system of price leadership might arise. The price leader can, in times of inflation for instance, raise prices when he thinks it appropriate, confident that he will not be left out on a limb (a kink?) by others' unwillingness to follow.

Summary

1. Under monopolistic competition, there are numerous small buyers and sellers; each firm's product is at least somewhat different from every other firm's product— that is, each firm has a partial "monopoly" of some product characteristics, and thus a downward-sloping demand curve; there is freedom of entry and exit; and perfect information.

2. In long-run equilibrium under monopolistic competition, free entry eliminates economic profits by forcing the firm's demand curve into a position of tangency with its average cost curve. Therefore, output will be below the point at which average cost is lowest. This is why monopolistic competitors are said to have "excess capacity."

3. An oligopolistic industry is composed of a few large firms selling similar products in the same market.

4. Under oligopoly, each firm carefully watches the major decisions of its rivals and will often plan counter-strategies. As a result, rivalry is often vigorous and direct, and the outcome is difficult to predict.

5. One model of oligopoly behavior assumes that the oligopolists ignore interdependence and simply maximize profits or sales. Another assumes that they join together to form a cartel, and thus act like a monopoly. A third possibility is price leadership, where one firm sets prices and the others follow suit. A fourth is that each firm might assume that its rivals will adopt the optimal countermove to any move it makes.

6. A firm that maximizes sales will continue producing up to the point where marginal revenue is driven down to zero. Consequently, a sales maximizer will produce more than a profit maximizer, and will charge a lower price.

7. Game theory provides new tools for analyzing business strategies under conditions of oligopoly.

8. If a firm thinks that its rivals will match any price cut but fail to match any price increase, its demand curve becomes "kinked" and its price will be sticky—that is, it will be adjusted less frequently than would be the case under either perfect competition or pure monopoly.

Concepts for Review

Monopolistic competition
Excess capacity theorem
Oligopoly
Oligopolistic interdependence

Cartel
Price leadership
Sales maximization
Game theory

Zero-sum game
Maximin criterion
Kinked demand curve
Sticky price

Questions for Discussion

1. How many real industries can you name that are oligopolies? How many that operate under monopolistic competition? Perfect competition? Which of these is hardest to find in reality? Why do you think this is so?

2. Consider some of the products that are widely advertised on TV. By what kind of firm is each produced—a perfectly competitive firm, an oligopolistic firm, or what? How many major products can you think of that are *not* advertised on TV?

3. In what ways may the small retail sellers of the following products differentiate their goods from those of their rivals to make themselves monopolistic competitors: hamburgers, gasoline, aspirin, facial tissues?

4. Pricing of securities on the stock market is said to be done under conditions in many respects similar to perfect competition. The auto industry is an oligopoly. How often do you think the price of a share of Ford Motor Company's common stock changes? How about the price of a Ford Pinto? How would you explain the difference?

5. Suppose Chrysler hires a popular singer to advertise its compact automobiles. The campaign is very successful and the company increases its share of the compact-car market substantially. What is Ford likely to do?

6. Using game theory, set up a payoff matrix similar to one Chrysler's management might employ in the above problem.

7. Discussion Question 3 at the end of Chapter 25 presented cost and demand data for a monopolist, and asked you to find the profit-maximizing solution. Use these same data to find the sales-maximizing solution. Are the answers different? Explain.

Limiting Market Power: Regulation of Industry

27

Because the market system may not function ideally in monopolistic or oligopolistic industries, governments have frequently intervened in these areas. In the United States, such intervention has followed two basic patterns. Antitrust laws, which will be studied in detail in the next chapter, have sought to prohibit the acquisition of monopoly power and to ban certain monopolistic practices. Alternatively, some firms have been subjected to regulatory supervision, which seeks to influence their pricing policies and other decisions. In this chapter, we will describe the functioning of some of the principal regulatory agencies. We will then offer a more detailed account of the reasons for regulation, discuss the evidence on the effects and the effectiveness of regulation, consider the reasons why regulatory agencies have devoted a great deal of attention to limitation of price cuts, and examine both some of the criticisms of the regulatory process and some of the suggestions that have been made to improve it. We will also discuss some recent moves toward deregulation; that is, toward reducing the number of regulations and the powers of the regulatory agencies. This deregulation process is still underway and it is too soon to say just how it will all end up. Finally, we will conclude the chapter with a few comments on nationalization of industries.

Monopoly, Regulation, and Nationalization

Throughout the Western economies a number of industries are traditionally run as monopolies. These include postal services, telephone services, and electricity generation; transportation and gas supply also are frequently accorded monopoly status. Since there are no competitive pressures to protect the interests of consumers from monopolistic exploitation in these cases, it is generally agreed that some substitute form of protection from excessive prices and restricted outputs should be found. Most of Western Europe has adopted **nationalization** as its solution, which means that the state owns and operates certain monopolistic industries. In the United States, we are more reluctant to have government involved in the running of businesses. Yet even here it has happened to some degree. Most cities now run their own public transport systems; the post office and much of the passenger railroad system in the United States are run by public corporations; and the Tennessee Valley Authority is one of this country's major experiments in electricity supply by a public agency.

In the United States, however, the main instrument of control of public utility industries has been the regulatory agency. Both the federal and the state governments have created a large number of agencies that regulate prices, standards of service, provisions for safety, and a variety of other aspects of the operations of telephone companies, radio and television stations, electric utilities, airlines, trucking companies, and firms in many other industries. Many of these industries are not pure monopolies, but include firms that nevertheless possess so much market power that their regulation is considered to be in the public interest.

Practical Problem: Price Floors Versus Price Ceilings

In a famous passage in *The Wealth of Nations*, Adam Smith tells us:

It always is and must be the interest of the great body of the people to buy whatever they want of those who sell it cheapest. The proposition is so very manifest, that is seems ridiculous to take any pains to prove it; nor could it ever have been called into question had not the interested sophistry of merchants and manufacturers confounded the common sense of mankind.[1]

Since regulation of industry has presumably been instituted to protect "the interest of the great body of the people," it is quite natural to surmise that the bulk of the work of the regulatory agencies would have been devoted to the imposition of price reductions. Thus, one would think that the typical case before a regulatory agency would be based on the complaint that a firm with monopoly power was charging prices that were excessively high, and that a typical decision of the regulatory agency would require such prices to be reduced.

In fact, this seems to be virtually the reverse of what has happened. Although in some cases, notably in the supply of natural gas, regulation *has* kept prices below the levels they might have reached in a free market, the bulk of cases devoted to price regulation have dealt with complaints that prices charged by the regulated firm are *too low!* Often the outcome in such cases has been a requirement on the part of regulators that the firms raise their prices higher than they wanted to. Where buyers have had a choice among several suppliers—for example, shippers of freight who have had a choice among trucks, railroads, and barges—the regulatory agency has effectively prevented the consumer from purchasing from "those who sell cheapest." Because the cost of additional shipments via railroad is sometimes lower than the cost of shipping via barges, regulators have required the low-priced suppliers (railroads) to raise their fees to match the prices charged by their high-cost competitors (barges).

How did regulation get itself into this curious pattern? What just reason is there for a regulatory agency to devote itself primarily to the imposition of *price floors* rather than *price ceilings?* Later in this chapter, through our analysis of the regulatory process, we will be able to indicate just how and why this has happened.

Who Is Regulated by Which Agencies?

The regulatory agencies in the United States can be divided, roughly, into two classes: those devoted to limiting the market power of regulated firms and those

---

[1] Adam Smith, *The Wealth of Nations* (New York: Modern Library, Random House, Inc., 1937), page 461.

devoted to consumer and worker protection and safety. A primary example of an agency working toward the latter goal is the Food and Drug Administration (FDA), which is assigned the task of protecting the public from the sale of harmful, impure, infected, or adulterated foods, drugs, and cosmetics. It also has the task of preventing the mislabeling or bad packaging of any of these products. Similarly, the U.S. Department of Agriculture supervises the packing and grading of meats and poultry going into interstate commerce—tasks it has had since 1906.

The federal government also has become involved in regulating the safety of automobiles and mines and the use of such poisonous substances as dangerous pesticides. This last job is performed by the Environmental Protection Agency (EPA), whose tasks include the protection of the health and welfare of the general public. An enormous proportion of the nation's economic activity is affected by these sorts of regulations. For instance, the drug industry, agriculture, auto manufacturing, and the chemical and power industries are just some of the businesses affected in one way or another by regulations designed to protect public health and safety; and virtually every manufacturing industry is affected by environmental regulations.

Equally pervasive are regulations designed to limit market power. At the federal level alone the number of agencies charged with this sort of task is substantial. Table 27–1 lists the largest industries in the United States whose prices are subject to regulation, and it also indicates their share of total GNP. The figures indicate that these industries together provide well over 10 percent of the GNP of the United States. Note that this table does not include those industries regulated just for the safety of their products or for protection of the environment.

Regulation of industry in the United States first began when indignation over abuse of market power by the nation's railroads led to the establishment of the Interstate Commerce Commission (ICC) in 1887. In particular, there was a public

Table 27–1

SHARE IN GNP OF SOME PRINCIPAL REGULATED U.S. INDUSTRIES

INDUSTRY		PERCENT OF 1980 GNP
Transportation and public utilities		8.9
Transportation	3.7	
Scheduled air carriers*	1.3	
Class I railroads*	1.1	
Large freight motor carriers*	.59	
Other transportation	.76	
Communication	2.6	
Telephone	2.2	
Other communication	.47	
Electric, gas and sanitary services	2.6	
Finance and insurance		3.8
Total		12.7

*Partially deregulated or being deregulated altogether.

This table shows that more than 10 percent of GNP in the United States is produced by regulated industries. Our economy is far from being controlled entirely by the free market!

SOURCE: U.S. Bureau of Economic Analysis, *The National Income and Product Accounts of the U.S. 1929–74* and *Survey of Current Business*, July, September 1981.

outcry over the support the railroads gave John D. Rockefeller, Sr., in the battle of his Standard Oil Company against its rivals. This, along with other abuses by the railroads, invited government intervention. But for several decades afterward there was little attempt to expand regulation to other industries. Then the Federal Power Commission (FPC) was established in 1920 and the Federal Communications Commission (FCC) in 1934; a substantial proportion of the remaining regulatory agencies were also formed during the 1930s as part of Roosevelt's New Deal.

Today, the principal regulatory agencies of the federal government that control prices include the ICC, which regulates railroads, barges, pipelines, and some categories of trucking; the FCC, which regulates broadcasting and telecommunications; the Federal Energy Regulatory Commission (FERC), which regulates interstate transmission of electric power and sales of natural gas; the Civil Aeronautics Board (CAB), which supervises the operation of the airlines; the Securities and Exchange Commission (SEC), which regulates the sale of securities (stocks); and several agencies led by the Federal Reserve System, which control banking operations. The work of these agencies is complemented by a variety of state agencies, which regulate activities that do not enter into interstate commerce.

Economists have long questioned the effectiveness of regulation and the desirability of some of its consequences, but not until the mid-1970s did such questions begin to be raised seriously outside of academic discussions. Recently, several bills have gone before Congress limiting the powers of the regulatory agencies. Several industries, notably domestic passenger aviation and trucking, have been "deregulated"—that is, most of the powers of the regulatory agencies over these activities are now being eliminated. (See the boxed insert, opposite.)

Why Regulation?

As we learned in Chapter 25, one main reason for regulation of industry is the phenomenon of *natural monopoly.* In some industries it is apparently far cheaper to have production carried out by one firm rather than by a number of different firms. One reason why this may occur is because of economies of large-scale production. An example of such **economies of scale** might be a milk-processing plant to which individual farmers send their product daily to be pasteurized by giant machinery rather than perform that crucial process at home. Use of the more elaborate equipment, which only becomes economical when it is employed by many farmers, reduces significantly the cost per gallon of pasteurization. Here is a case in which savings are made possible by expanding the volume of an activity—a case of economies of scale.

Economies of scale are savings that are acquired through increases in quantities produced.

Another reason why a single large firm may have a cost advantage over a group of small firms is that it is sometimes cheaper to produce *a number of different commodities together* rather than turn them out separately, each by a different firm. The saving made possible by simultaneous production of many different products is called **economies of scope.** An example of economies of scope is the manufacture of both cars and trucks by the same producer. The techniques employed in producing both commodities are sufficiently similar to make specialized production by different firms impractical.

Economies of scope are savings that are acquired through simultaneous production of many different products.

In industries where there are great economies of scale *and* scope, society will obviously incur a significant cost penalty if it insists on maintaining competition. Supply by a number of smaller competing firms will be far more costly and use up far larger quantities of the community's resources in the production process than it would if the good were supplied by a monopoly. Moreover, in the presence of

What's New in Regulation? Deregulation!

Presidents Ford, Carter, and Reagan all have believed that economic activity was overregulated and that these regulations caused unnecessary costs to consumers. Deregulation began in earnest during the Carter Administration—with airlines, trucks, and railroads the first targets.

Air Travel. Under the chairmanship of economist Alfred E. Kahn, the Civil Aeronautics Board (CAB) began a process unprecedented in U.S. history—a regulatory agency voluntarily giving up use of its powers. Regulatory suicide became unnecessary in 1978 when Congress passed the Airline Deregulation Act, under which the CAB is scheduled to go out of existence by 1984. Meanwhile, there were gradual reductions in the use of its power to limit fare reductions, to prevent an airline from initiating service along a new route, or to prevent an airline from discontinuing service along any other route. Initially, deregulation brought sharp reductions in fares, big increases in air traffic, and high profits for airlines. Everybody was happy. Then the recession of 1979–1980 cut into the volume of air travel while rising fuel prices cut into profits and curtailed fare reductions. Still, there is statistical evidence strongly suggesting that without deregulation fares would have risen even higher and airline profits would have fallen even further.

Trucking. The Motor Carrier Act of 1980 reduced the powers of the Interstate Commerce Commission over interstate trucking in a way similar to the Airline Deregulation Act's reduction of the CAB's power. Rates, entry, and exit all have been made substantially freer, and proponents of deregulation suggest this may save the public as much as $8 billion a year. Surprisingly, the Reagan administration in its early days took steps to slow the deregulation of trucking.

Railroads. The Staggers Rail Deregulation Act also was passed in 1980. However, because entry into railroading is not as easy as entry into trucking, and because railroads face little competition along certain routes and in the shipment of certain items (such as loads too wide to be transported along highways), deregulation of this industry cannot be as complete as it is in the airline and trucking industries. For example, the law still sets upper limits on the ratio of prices to costs. But the railroads are freer than before to adjust rates, to abandon unprofitable routes, and to enter into long-term contracts. It is hoped that these new areas of freedom will restore efficiency and profitability to the railroads.

Question: Why did many airline and trucking companies oppose the deregulation acts despite the freedoms they offered?*

*The answer surely involves a variety of influences. But one factor that undoubtedly played a role was fear of new competition. With regulatory impediments to the entry of new competitors reduced or eliminated, there were certain to be new entrants whose presence existing firms felt would reduce profits and make their life harder generally.

---

strong economies of scale and economies of scope, society *will not be able to preserve free competition, even if it wants to*. The large, multiproduct firm will have so great an advantage over its rivals that the small firms simply will be unable to survive. We say in such a case that free competition is *not sustainable*.

Where monopoly production is cheapest, and where free competition is not sustainable, the industry is a natural monopoly. Because monopoly is cheaper, society many not want to have competition; and if free competition is not sustainable, it will not even have a choice in the matter.

But even if society reconciles itself to monopoly, it will generally not want to let the monopoly firm do whatever it wants to with its market power. Therefore, it will consider either regulation or nationalization of these firms.

A second reason for regulation is the desire for "universal service," that is, the availability of service at "reasonable prices" even to small communities where the small scale of operation makes costs extremely high. In such cases, regulators have sometimes encouraged a public utility to supply services to some consumers at a financial loss. But a loss on some sales is financially feasible only when the firm is permitted to make up for it by obtaining higher profits on its other sales. This "averaging" of gains and losses is possible only if the firm is protected from price competition and free entry of new competitors in its more profitable markets. If no such protection is provided by a regulatory agency, potential competitors will sniff out the profit opportunities in the markets where service is supplied at a price well above cost. Many new firms will enter the business and cause prices to be driven down in those markets. This practice is referred to as "cream skimming." The entrants choose to enter only into the profitable markets and skim away the cream of the profits for themselves, leaving the unprofitable markets (the skimmed milk) to the supplier who had attempted to provide universal service. This phenomenon is one reason why regulatory rules, until recently, made it very difficult or impossible for new firms to enter when and where they saw fit.

Airlines and telecommunications are two industries in which these issues have arisen. In both cases, fears have been expressed that without regulation of entry and rates, or the granting of special subsidies, less populous communities would effectively be isolated, losing their airline services and obtaining telephone service only at cripplingly high rates. Many economists question the validity of this argument for regulation, which, they say, calls for hidden subsidy of rural consumers by all other consumers. The airline deregulation act provided for government subsidies to help small communities attract airline service. In fact, what has happened is that this market has been taken over to a considerable extent by specialized "commuter" airlines flying much smaller aircraft than the major airlines, which have withdrawn from many such routes.

A third reason for regulation is to help prevent **self-destructive competition,** which, for example, economies of scale make possible. In an industry such as railroading, equipment—including roadbeds, tracks, switching facilities, locomotives, and cars—is extremely expensive. Suppose that two railroads, having been built and equipped, are competing for some limited business that happens to be insufficient to use their total facilities to anything near capacity. That is, to meet this level of consumer demand, each railroad may only have to run 40 percent as many trains over the track as can conveniently be scheduled over that route. The management of each road will feel that, with its unused capacity, any business will be worthwhile, provided that it covers more than its short-run marginal costs—fuel, labor, and expenses other than plant and equipment. If the short-run marginal cost of shipping an additional ton of, say, coal is $5, then either railroad will be happy to lure coal-shipping customers away from the other at a price of, say, $7 per ton, even though that price may not cover the entire cost of track and equipment.

Each ton of business that pays $7 when marginal cost is $5 will put the railroad $2 ahead of where it would have been without the business. The new business does not add to the cost of the tracks or locomotives or other equipment, which must be paid for whether that business is acquired or not. Thus, even if the new business only pays for its own marginal cost and a little more, it seems financially desirable. But the temptation to accept business on such terms will drive both firms' prices down toward their marginal costs, and, in the process, both railroads are likely to go broke. If no customer pays for the track, the roadbed, and the equipment, the railroad simply will be unable to go on. Thus there are those who believe that regulation of rates can be sensible, even in industries subject to competitive pressures, simply to protect the industries from themselves. Without this regulation, self-destructive competition could end up sinking those industries financially, and the public would thereby be deprived of vital services.

A fourth reason often given for public regulation is that some industries base their operations on a public resource of limited capacity, so that a public agency must intervene to ration out that resource "fairly." The most notable example of the need for this type of rationing is radio and television broadcasting. The frequency spectrum that is available for broadcasting is rather limited, and so it must be divided up among the users. If it were not divided up, and entry were not limited, the airwaves might become crowded and interference of broadcasters with one another's transmissions would undermine the quality of reception and perhaps even make the airwaves totally useless.

Many economists have argued that government has no business allocating scarce resources like the radio and TV spectrum among commerical users who employ such public resources for a profit. These economists argue that government rationing of the airwaves is a giveaway of public resources to favored individuals who then grow rich at the public's expense—even though the FCC, in return, does retain some right to regulate the content of broadcasts. Rather, it is proposed that firms be required to bid against one another for licenses to run radio and TV stations. In that way the licenses would go to those who can make the best use of them—an ability that would be determined by their bids. The profits would then go into the public treasury rather than private pockets, and they could be used to finance nonprofit public-interest activities, such as public broadcasting.

A final reason for regulation is the danger that consumers will be misinformed, cheated, or subjected to health hazards by unscrupulous sellers or even conscientious sellers forced to keep up with the questionable practices of less scrupulous rivals. This sort of protection is the province of the second type of regulatory agency described earlier, and because economists have less to say about this category of regulation than about regulation of rates, the subject will not be discussed further in this chapter.

SUMMARY

There are five basic reasons for the activities of the regulatory agencies:

1. Prevention of excess profits and other undesirable practices in an industry that is considered to be a natural monopoly.
2. The desire for universal service—that is, the desire to provide service at relatively low rates to customers whom it is particularly expensive to serve, and to do so without government subsidy.
3. The desire to prevent self-destructive price competition in multifirm industries with large capital costs and low marginal costs.
4. The desire to allocate fairly public facilities of limited capacity.
5. The desire to protect customers from being cheated or endangered by unscrupulous suppliers.

Has Rate Regulation Made a Difference?

An obvious question is whether rate regulation has worked. In particular, has it made any difference in the rates paid by consumers? Would, for example, unregulated public utilities end up charging prices significantly higher than they are permitted to charge under regulation? The answer is by no means obvious. As a matter of fact, some analysts suggest that regulation may indeed make little or no difference in prices. In one careful study comparing rates charged for electric power by regulated and unregulated utility firms over the period 1912 to 1937, a period when there were a substantial number of firms in both categories, the authors concluded that there was no significant difference between the average rates charged in the two categories.[2] The interpretation of the figures found in the study has been disputed, and the factual issue is by no means settled. But if further research should support the conclusion that regulation has not had any significant effects on *average* prices, it would severely undercut the case of those who advocate the regulatory approach.

Several explanations are possible for a conclusion that regulation has not reduced average prices. The first is that the regulatory procedure is simply a sloppy process that is inherently incapable of making much difference, one way or another. A second explanation that is often proposed is that the regulatory agencies are simply captives of the firms they are intended to regulate. Owing to the great political clout of these big firms (so the argument goes), and because of the skillful lawyers and consultants they are able to afford, the regulated firm can overwhelm the regulatory agency, which has only a small staff and a limited budget. In this way the firm can get virtually anything it wants out of the agency. But the evidence against this conclusion is substantial. One need only look at the frequency with which regulated firms lose crucial cases before the regulatory agencies to see the weakness of this argument. The railroads time and again have lost vital chunks of business when the ICC ruled against the price arrangements under which some new business was obtained. And AT&T is faced with more and more competition, plus the requirement by the FCC that it permit customers to attach equipment produced by firms other than Bell System suppliers to their telephone lines. Many other such examples can easily be cited. A third explanation for the conjecture that regulation does not significantly affect *average* prices is the fact that regulators, for reasons we will discuss just below, often impose on the regulated firms prices *higher* than they would like to charge. That is precisely what the ICC did in the railroad regulation cases just mentioned. If regulators sometimes impose price increases, and sometimes impose price decreases, it is at least conceivable that *on the average* regulation will not affect the price level very much. In fact, two more recent studies of the effects on prices resulting from the activities of the CAB[3] and the ICC[4] have concluded that these agencies *did* make a substantial difference and that they both raised prices significantly.

Whatever the overall effect of regulation on average prices, there is no doubt that in many individual cases it has significant effects on *particular* prices charged by regulated firms. One of the most widely publicized examples was the difference in airplane fares between San Francisco and Los Angeles and those between Washington, D.C., and New York City before the airlines were deregulated. The former fare was never regulated by the CAB (since the flight is entirely within the state of California), whereas the CAB did control the interstate flight between New York and Washington, D.C. The distance of the California trip is nearly twice as great as the East Coast trip, and neither is sparsely traveled nor beset by any other noteworthy features that would make for substantial differences in cost per passenger mile. Yet at the time of deregulation, fares were a little over $40 for the long California trip and a little over $50 for the short Washington to New York trip.

[2]See George Stigler and Clair Friedland, "What Can Regulation Regulate?—The Case of Electricity." *Journal of Law and Economics*, October 1962, pages 1–16.

[3]W.A. Jordan, "Producer Protection, Prior Market Structure and the Effects of Government Regulation," *Journal of Law and Economics*, Vol. II, April 1972, pages 151–76.

[4]G. Kolko, *Railroads and Regulation, 1877–1976* (Princeton: Princeton University Press, 1965), page 50*ff*.

Why Regulators Sometimes Raise Prices

Why should regulators ever push for higher prices? The answer is that typically they do so when they want to introduce or preserve competition in an industry. We saw earlier that where there are strong economies of scale and scope it simply may be impossible for a number of firms to survive. The largest of the firms in the industry will have such cost advantages over their competitors that it will be able to drive them out of the market while still operating at prices that are profitable. Most observers applaud low prices and price cuts that reflect such cost advantages. However, a firm that wants the market for itself may conceivably engage in price cutting even when such cuts are not justifiable in terms of cost. Low prices then are merely temporary bargains that, once they succeed in driving out the competition, will promptly be withdrawn. This sort of practice, sometimes referred to as **predatory pricing,** is considered undesirable by most persons who have analyzed regulatory issues.

But regulation sometimes goes beyond the prevention of predatory pricing. Firms that feel they are hurt by competitive pressures will complain to regulatory commissions that the prices charged by their rivals are unfairly low. The commission, afraid that unrestrained pricing will reduce the number of firms in the industry, then attempts to "equalize" matters by imposing price floors that permit all the firms in the industry to operate profitably. The ICC once described itself as a "giant handicapper" whose task was presumably to make sure that no firm within its jurisdiction got too far ahead of the others. It did not seem to show a similar concern with whether consumers were winning or losing. This attitude has produced many strange patterns of resource utilization. For example, there is evidence that for distances of more than, say, 200 miles, railroads have a clear-cut cost advantage over trucks. Yet ICC influence over railroad rates has forced those rates upward sufficiently to make it possible for trucks to "compete" from coast to coast. The resulting waste of resources is probably enormous.

Many economists maintain that this approach to pricing is a perversion of the idea of competition. The virtue of competition is that, where it occurs, firms force one another to supply consumers with products of high quality at *low* prices. If competition does not do this, it loses its purpose because to the economist it is a means to an end, not an end in itself. An arrangement under which firms are enabled to coexist only by *preventing* them from competing with one another preserves the appearance of competition but destroys its substance.

Marginal Versus Full-Cost Rate Floors

The issue of price floors has raged over hundreds of thousands of pages of records of regulatory hearings and has involved literally hundreds of millions of dollars of expenditures in fees for lawyers, expert witnesses, and research in preparation of the cases. The question has been not whether all floors on the prices of regulated utilities are improper, for virtually everyone agrees that some sort of lower boundary on prices is required in order to prevent predatory pricing practices, but rather what constitutes the proper *nature* of the rate floors.

The use of prices as a means to induce an efficient allocation of resources, the function of prices that usually concerns the economist most (see Chapter 23), is not the main concern of the regulatory hearings. Rather, the two primary concerns of price regulation are: (1) Whether the prices under dispute are in some sense *unfair to competitors;* and (2) Whether the prices are *unfair to customers of other products* produced by the same firm. In other words, is that supplier overcharging for products for which he has little competition in order to be able to undercut his rivals in the supply of products for which competition is substantial? The issues are questions of equity and justice rather than efficiency in the use of resources. Two alternative criteria have been proposed to determine appropriate floors for prices.

Criterion 1. The price of a commodity should never be less than its *long-run marginal cost*.

Criterion 2. The price should not be less than that commodity's *fully distributed cost*—that is, its "fair share" of the firm's total cost as determined by some accounting calculation.

To calculate the **fully distributed costs** of the various products of the firm, one simply takes the firm's total costs and divides them up in some way among its various products. First, one allocates to each product the costs for which it is obviously directly responsible. For example, a railroad allocates to coal transportation the cost of hauling all cars that were devoted exclusively to carrying coal, plus the cost of operating locomotives on runs in which they carried only coal cars, and so on. Then, one takes all costs that are incurred *in common* for several or all of the outputs of the company (such as the cost of constructing the roadbed and tracks) and divides them on the basis of some rule of thumb (generally conceded to be arbitrary) among the firm's various products. Usually, the basis of this allocation is some measure of the relative use of the common facilities by the different products. But even "relative use" is an ambiguous term. How does one divide up the cost of the track of a railroad among its shipments of lead, lumber, and gold? If relative use is defined by the weight of the shipments, then the accountants will assign a high proportion of the cost to lead shipments. If prices are then required to exceed full cost, under this definition of "relative use" the railroad will be placed at a disadvantage in competing for lead traffic. If, instead, relative use is defined in terms of bulk, the railroad's lumber business will be harmed; if relative use is defined in terms of market value, it will lose out in competing for gold shipments.

The **long-run marginal cost** of an output is the *addition* to the supplier's total cost resulting from the supply of that ouput *including whatever additional plant and equipment* is needed in the long run to provide that output. The inclusion of this marginal capital cost (the cost of the necessary additions to plant and equipment) is the crucial feature that distinguishes *long-run* marginal cost from *short-run* marginal cost.

Those who advocate the use of *marginal cost* rather than fully distributed cost as the appropriate basis for any floor on prices argue that **long-run marginal cost** is the relevant measure of the cost that any shipment actually incurs. For, by definition, marginal cost is the difference that an additional shipment makes to the firm's total cost—it is the difference between the cost to the firm if that shipment takes place and the cost to the firm if the shipment is carried by some other means of transportation. The advocates of marginal cost criteria argue that customers of *every* product of the supplier may benefit if the company is permitted to charge a price based on long-run marginal cost, particularly if, as is usual under regulation, there is a legal ceiling on the firm's total profits.

Suppose that a railroad considers taking on some new business whose marginal cost is $7 and whose fully distributed cost is figured at $12. Suppose also that at any price over $10 the railroad will lose the business to truckers. If the railroad charges $10 and gets the business, the price does not cover the fully distributed cost, but it still adds $3 to the company's net earnings for every unit it sells to the new customers. If it was already earning as much profit as the law allows, the company would normally have to reduce its prices on other products. Thus every group of customers can gain—the new customers because they get the product more cheaply than it can be supplied by competitors, and the old customers because the prices on their products must be cut in order to satisfy the

Marginal Versus Fully Distributed Cost in Rate Regulation

In the following dissenting opinion, Commissioner Benjamin Hooks of the FCC (who now heads the National Association for the Advancement of Colored People—the NAACP) argues that a fully distributed cost floor is illogical. He says that a marginal cost test may cause more work for the regulator, but points out that it is the public interest, not an easy job for regulators, that is important. The rest of the commission disagreed, and voted for a fully distributed cost criterion.

The Commission here, over all dictates of common sense, views of Congressional experts, the practices of other regulatory agencies, and the protestations of state regulatory agencies, has adopted a Fully Distributed Cost accounting method that is all but unyielding and defies every proven rule of economic logic. Virtually every economist-observer cited in this proceeding concedes that incremental costs methods are the closest approximation to a free market environment and the courts have ratified the use of marginal cost pricing in the utility field.

I concede that there are imperfections inherent in monitoring marginal costing structures in terms of regulatory administration not present with a simplistic, Fully Distributed Cost basis. However, governmental decisions should not be predicated disproportionately on convenience to the government, but on the broader public interest. What was clearly called for out of this Docket was a system which allows flexibility. . . . Instead we have ordered *rigor mortis*.*

*FCC Docket 18128, October 1, 1976, *FCC Reports*, second series.

---

firm's profit ceiling. Everyone gains except the company's competitors, who will, of course, complain that the price is unfair because it does not cover fully distributed cost. (For an example of an opinion by a regulator defending the use of marginal cost analysis against fully distributed cost, see boxed insert, above.)

A Problem with Marginal Cost Pricing

Setting price equal to marginal cost is a solution generally favored by most economists, *where it is feasible.* However, a serious problem prevents the use of the principle of marginal cost pricing in many regulated industries and marginal cost pricing in regulated industries is, consequently, not very common in practice. The problem is easily stated:

 In many regulated industries, if prices were set equal to marginal cost, the firms would go bankrupt.

This seems a startling conclusion, but its explanation is really quite simple. The conclusion follows inescapably from three simple facts:

Fact 1: In many regulated industries, there are significant economies of large-scale production.   As we pointed out earlier, economies of scale are one of the main reasons why certain industries were regulated in the first place.

Fact 2: In an industry with economies of scale, the long-run average cost curve is downward sloping.   This means that long-run average cost falls as the quantity produced rises, as illustrated by the AC curve in Figure 27–1. Fact 2 is something we learned back in Chapter 20 (see pages 382–384).

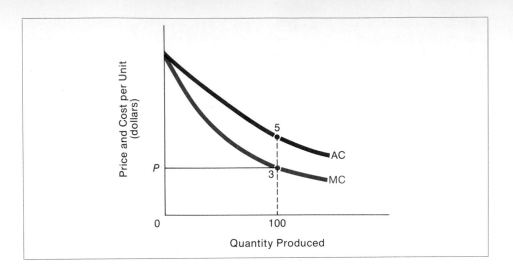

Figure 27–1

MARGINAL COST PRICING UNDER ECONOMIES OF SCALE
Economies of scale imply that the average cost (AC) curve is declining, and therefore that the marginal cost (MC) curve is below the average cost curve. If, for example, the regulator forces the firm to produce 100 units and charge a price equal to its marginal cost ($3 per unit), then the firm will take in $300 in revenues. But, since its average cost at 100 units is $5 per unit, its total cost will be $500, and the firm will lose money.

The reason, to review briefly, is that total costs must double if all input quantities are doubled. But, where there are economies of scale, output will *more* than double if all input quantities are doubled. Since average cost (AC) is simply total cost (TC) divided by quantity (Q), AC = TC/Q must decline when all input quantities are doubled.

Fact 3: If average cost is declining, then marginal cost must be below average cost. This fact follows directly from one of the general rules relating marginal and average data that were explained in the appendix to Chapter 21. Once again, the logic is simple enough to review briefly. If, for example, your average quiz score is 90 percent but the next quiz pulls your average down to 87 percent, the grade on this most recent test (the marginal grade) must be below both the old and the new average quiz scores. That is, it takes a marginal grade (or cost) that is below the average to pull the average down.

Putting these three facts together, we conclude that in many regulated industries marginal cost (MC) will be below average cost, as depicted in Figure 27–1. Now suppose regulators set the price at the level of marginal cost. Since P = MC, P must be below AC. But P < AC (price per unit less than cost per unit) means that the firm must be losing money, which is the conclusion we set out to demonstrate.

In industries where there are economies of scale, therefore, a regulation that requires P = MC is simply not an acceptable option. What, then, should be done? One possibility is to nationalize the industry, set price equal to marginal cost, and make up for the deficit out of public funds. Nationalization, however, is not very popular in the United States. (More is said about nationalization at the very end of the chapter.) A second option, which is quite popular among regulators, is to (try to) set price equal to *average cost.* In practice, this principle leads to pricing at *fully distributed cost.* But, as explained in the previous section, this method of pricing is neither desirable nor possible to carry out except on the basis of arbitrary decisions. The problem is that almost no firm produces only a single commodity. Almost every company produces a number of different varieties and qualities of some product, and often they produce thousands of different products, each with its own price. Even General Motors, a fairly specialized firm, produces many makes and sizes of cars and trucks in addition to refrigerators, washing machines, and quite a few other things. In a multiproduct firm we cannot even define AC = TC/Q, since to calculate Q (total output) we would have to add up all the apples and oranges (and all the other different items) the firm produces. But we know that one cannot add up apples and oranges. So, since we cannot calculate AC for a multiproduct firm, it is hardly possible for the regulator to require P = AC for each of the firm's products, though regulators sometimes *think* they can do so.

The Ramsey Pricing Rule

In recent years economists have been attracted to a very imaginative third approach to the problem of pricing in regulated industries that produce a multiplicity of products. This approach derives its name from its discoverer, Frank Ramsey, a brilliant English mathematician who died in 1930 at the age of 26 after making several enduring contributions to both mathematics and economics. The basic idea of Ramsey's pricing principle can be explained in a fairly straightforward manner. We know that prices must be set *above* marginal costs if a firm with increasing returns to scale is to break even. But how much above? In effect, Ramsey argued as follows: The reason we do not like prices to be above marginal costs is that such high prices distort the choices made by consumers, leading them to buy "too little" of the goods whose prices are set way above MC. Yet, it is necessary to set prices somewhat above marginal costs to allow the firm to survive. Therefore it makes sense to raise prices *most* above marginal cost where consumers will respond the *least* to such price increases; that is, where the *elasticity of demand* is the lowest so that price rises will create the least distortion of demand. This line of argument led Ramsey to formulate the following rule:

Ramsey Pricing Rule: Where prices must exceed marginal cost in order to permit the regulated firm to break even, the ratios of P to MC should be largest for those products whose elasticities of demand are the smallest.

Many economists accept this pricing rule as the correct conclusion on theoretical grounds. It has even been proposed for postal and telephone pricing, and is now under consideration for railroads. However, its use in actual rate-setting cases has so far been quite limited.

Regulation and Efficiency of Operation

Many opponents of regulation maintain that it seriously impairs the efficiency of American industry. Government regulation, these critics argue, interferes with the operation of Adam Smith's invisible hand. One source of inefficiency—the seemingly endless paperwork and complex legal proceedings that impede the firm's ability to respond quickly to changing market conditions—is obvious enough. (Though what to do about this administrative problem is far from obvious.)

But there is another source of inefficiency that may be even more important. It stems from the problem regulators have of trying to prevent the regulated firm from earning excessive profits, while at the same time (a) offering it financial incentives for maximum efficiency of operation, and (b) allowing it enough profit to attract the capital it needs when growing markets justify expansion. From this point of view, it would be ideal if the regulator would just permit the firm to take in that amount of revenue that covers its costs, including the cost of its capital. That is, the firm should earn exactly enough to pay for its ordinary costs plus the normal profit that potential investors could get elsewhere for the same money. Thus, if the prevailing rate of return is 10 percent, the regulated firm should recover its expenditures plus 10 percent on its investment and not a penny more or less. The trouble with such an arrangement is that it removes all incentive for efficiency, responsiveness to consumer demand, and innovation. For under such an arrangement the firm is in effect *guaranteed* just *one standard rate* of profit, no more and no less. This is so whether its management is totally incompetent or extremely talented and hard working.

Competitive markets do *not* work in this way. While under perfect competition the *average* firm generally will earn just the opportunity cost of capital, a firm with a specially ingenious and efficient management will do better, and a firm with an incompetent management is likely to go broke. It is the possibility of great rewards and harsh punishments that gives the market mechanism its power to cause firms to strive for high efficiency.

We have strong evidence that where firms are guaranteed a fixed return, no matter how well or poorly they perform, gross inefficiencies are likely to result. For example, many contracts for purchases of military equipment have offered prices calculated on a *cost-plus* basis, meaning that the supplier was guaranteed that his costs would be covered and that, in addition, he would receive some prespecified amount as a contribution to profit. Studies of the resulting performance of cost-plus arrangements have confirmed that the suppliers' inefficiencies have been enormous.

A regulatory arrangement that in effect guarantees a firm its cost plus a "fair rate of return" on its investment is virtually the same as a cost-plus contract. Fortunately, under regulation, matters do not work out in exactly the same way. For one thing, when a regulated industry is in financial trouble, as is true of the railroads, there is nothing the regulator can do to guarantee a "fair rate of return." If the current return on capital is 10 percent, but market demand for railroading is only sufficient to give it 3 percent at most, the regulatory agency cannot help matters by any act of magic. Even if it grants higher prices to the railroad (or forces the railroad to raise its prices) the result will be to drive even more business away and therefore cause the firm to earn still lower profits.

There is a second reason why profit regulation does not work in the same way as does a cost-plus arrangement. Curiously, this is a result of the much-criticized delays that characterize many regulatory procedures. In a number of regulated industries, a proposed change in rates is likely to take a minimum of several months before it gets through the regulatory machinery. Where it is bitterly contested, the resulting hearings before the regulatory commission, the appeals to the courts, and so on, are likely to last for years. Rate cases lasting ten years are not unknown. This was true, for example, in the case before the FCC referred to in the boxed insert on page 507. This phenomenon, known as **regulatory lag,** is perhaps the main reason that profit regulation has not eliminated all rewards for efficiency and all penalties for inefficiency.

Suppose, for example, the regulatory commission approves a set of prices calculated to yield exactly the "fair rate of return" to the company, say 10 percent. If management then invests successfully in new processes, which reduce its costs sharply, the rate of return under the old prices may rise to, say, 12 percent. If it takes two years for the regulators to review the prices they previously approved, and adjust them to the new cost levels, the company will earn a 2 percent bonus reward for its efficiency during the two years of regulatory lag. Similarly, if management makes a series of bad decisions, which reduces the company's return to 7 percent, the firm may well apply to the regulator for some adjustments in prices to permit it to recoup its losses. If the regulator takes 18 months to act, the firm suffers a penalty for its inefficiency. It may be added that where mismanagement is *clearly* the cause of losses, regulators will be reluctant to permit the regulated firm to make up for such losses by rate adjustments. But in most cases it is difficult to pinpoint responsibility for a firm's losses.

All in all, those who have studied regulated industries have come away deeply concerned about the effects of regulation upon economic efficiency. Although some regulated firms seem to operate very efficiently, others seem to behave in quite the opposite way.

While regulatory lag does permit some penalty for inefficiency and some reward for superior performance by the regulated firm, the arrangement only works in a rough and ready manner. It still leaves the provision of incentives for efficiency as one of the fundamental problems of regulation. How can one prevent regulated firms from earning excessive profits, but also permit them to earn enough to attract the capital they need while still allowing rewards for superior performance and penalties for poor performance?

Modifications in Regulatory Arrangements to Preserve Efficiency

The problems of regulation just mentioned, along with some other criticisms, have in recent years produced a number of proposals for changes in the regulatory process. Three such proposals are discussed below.

Deregulation Plus Increased Competition

One of the most widely advocated proposals is for regulators to get out of the business of regulating, leaving much more (if not all) of the task of looking after consumer interests to the natural forces of competition. This approach appears to be promising in areas of the economy in which competition can be expected to survive without government intervention—for example, in freight transportation, airlines, and pipelines. As a consequence, a number of economists representing a broad range of political views have been advocating at least some deregulation in these fields. And, as we have seen, deregulation of air travel and freight transportation by truck and rail has already begun. Of course, deregulation will not work in industries where competitors can survive only if government protects them from real competition.

Performance Criteria for Permitted Rate of Return

The argument for deregulation addresses itself to all of the problems discussed in the previous section, but there are other proposals that are concerned with only one or another of these problems. We turn now to proposals designed to prevent profit controls from discouraging efficiency.

Some observers have advocated that the legally permitted rate of return not be set at a fixed number, say 10 percent, but that it be varied from firm to firm depending on the firm's record of efficiency and performance. That is, if some measure of quality of performance can be agreed upon (a measure that should take account of cost efficiency as well as product and service quality), then the better the performance score of the regulated firm the more it would be permitted to earn. A firm that performed well in a given year might be permitted 12 percent profits for that year, whereas a firm that did badly might be allowed only 8 percent, and a firm that performed abominably might be permitted only 4 percent.

Such incentives sometimes can be successfully built into the rules that control the operations of the firm. For example, in 1974 such a program was designed for Amtrak, the public corporation that, in effect, rents passenger transportation service from U.S. railroads. Under this program the amount Amtrak pays them depends upon such features as promptness of arrival of trains, infrequency of breakdowns of locomotives, and so on. Thus, the more frequently its trains are on time, the more Amtrak pays to that railroad. The results were dramatic. While over the period 1973 to 1975 the percentage of trains arriving on time increased for railroads as a whole by about 17.5 percentage points from its miserable 60 percent figure in 1973, the railroads that signed incentive contracts increased their on-time arrivals by about 29.5 percentage points from their initial (1973) average of 61 percent.

However, financial incentives cannot easily be built into rate of return formulas that contain no good objective criteria of performance (such as number of minutes behind schedule for a railroad train). Moreover, it is difficult to balance incentives for different aspects of performance. For example, if the formula assigns too high a weight to product quality and too low a weight to economy, the firm will be encouraged to incur costs that are unjustifiably high from the point of view of public welfare in order to turn out products whose slightly higher quality is not worth their extra cost. And of course the reverse will be true if it is economy rather than efficiency that is assigned too much weight.

Institutionalized Regulatory Lag

It has been proposed that instead of regulatory lag working haphazardly as it does now, regulation should consciously take advantage of the incentive for efficiency made possible by the lag. Under such a program, the regulator would assign product prices to the firms they oversee, decreeing that, *aside from automatic adjustments for inflation*, these prices are unchangeable until the next regulatory review, to occur *at a time selected by the agency.* The regulated firm would be told that the next review will occur, say, sometime between two and six years in the future, depending on what events occur in the economy. But in the meantime, any firm that can manage cost savings by economy or innovation, or that can attract more customers by improving its product without increasing its costs, will be permitted to keep the higher profits that this superior performance elicits. Of course, for the regulated firm there is a catch. If the firm proves able to reduce costs by, say, 30 percent during a period between regulatory reviews, it can, at the next review, expect to have its prices reduced correspondingly. Thus, in order to earn profits, management would constantly be forced to look for ever more economical ways of doing things.

This approach, too, has its problems. For one thing, in a period of inflation, when costs go up no matter how efficient management is, it is not clear how regulated prices should be adjusted to make up for inflation *between* review periods.

Some Final Comments on the Regulatory Process

The problems we have described here and the proposals that have been made to deal with them are by no means all of the criticisms that have been raised or all of the proposals that have been offered. We have attempted only to provide some feeling for the complexity of the regulatory process and to show the difficulty of finding workable alternatives. It is too easy simply to seek villains and lay blame on them for all that has gone wrong—as many observers of regulation tend to do.

For instance, it is often argued that what is wrong with the regulatory process is that the commissions have become captives of the firms they are supposed to regulate, doing whatever those companies want them to do. And perhaps there are some cases where the charge has some validity. But most of the time, matters are much more complicated. The regulated firms are often just as convinced that the regulators are "out to get them" and that the best they can hope for from a set of hearings is to delay a decision for as long as possible.

In truth, under the current process of regulation, virtually everyone may be dissatisfied by the decisions that are likely to emerge. The tendency of regulatory agencies to emphasize the prevention of low rather than high prices may in part be the source of this general dissatisfaction. The regulator does not enjoy the role of defender of high prices; the regulated firm that is prevented from charging proposed lower prices feels deprived of vital business; and customers certainly are not pleased by having to pay prices higher than the company wants to offer. On all these counts it is clear that the regulation of prices is not working as one might wish. But the solutions to these problems must be worked out by thoughtful deliberation; they will not disappear simply by wishing them away.

A Word on Nationalization

As we indicated at the beginning of the chapter, in industries in which monopoly or near monopoly offers clear advantages to society over competition, there is an alternative to regulation. This alternative is government ownership and operation of the firms in that industry, or *nationalization*. In the United States, tradition does not favor such government operation, but the exceptions are growing in number. For example, we have government supply of electricity by the TVA; the U.S. Postal Service; and, more recently, the operation of railroads by the publically owned agencies Amtrak and Conrail, which may be regarded as an intermediate step in the direction of nationalization. A number of cities operate their own public transport facilities, collect their own garbage, and offer other services that elsewhere are provided by private enterprise.

It is almost an instinctive reaction by people in the United States to consider such public enterprises as being prone to extreme mismanagement and waste. And the near-legendary problems of the Post Office do seem to support this supposition. However, here too, one should be careful not to jump to conclusions. In recent decades, when railroading was entirely in private hands, that industry had difficulties no less serious than those of the Post Office. It is true that visitors find the nationalized French telephone system a model of chaos and mismanagement. But at the same time, the Swedish telephone system, which is also nationalized, is smooth-working and efficient. And the French government-supplied electricity system has set world standards in its use of the most modern analytic techniques of economics and engineering, and has adopted innovative pricing policies that promote efficiency.

Despite these accomplishments, no one has yet found a systematic incentive mechanism for efficiency that can do for nationalized industries what the profit motive does for private enterprise. Where the market is unsparing in its rewards for accomplishments and in its penalties for poor performance, one can be quite sure that a firm's inefficiency will not readily be tolerated. But nationalized industries have no such automatic mechanism handing out rewards and penalties dependably and impartially. We have seen, however, that there are analogous problems under regulation; where profits are controlled by the regulator, the rewards for efficiency are also far from automatic. (The boxed insert on the next page offers further evidence in support of these conclusions.)

Evidence of Efficiency in Public Enterprise

A study conducted by European producers and distributors of electricity yielded the following average figures for *annual rate of growth in productivity.*

A. Countries in which electricity is supplied largely by government-owned firms:

England and Wales	2.4%
France	4.5
Ireland	4.5
Netherlands	8.5
Spain	3.5
Sweden	7.5
Average	5.2%

B. Countries in which electricity is supplied largely by private firms:

Germany	2.1%
Switzerland	3.5
Average	2.8%

SOURCE: The Group of Experts on Overall Productivity, "The Overall Productivity of the Electricity Supply Industry." The Hague Congress, Tariffs Study Committee, Aug. 27–31, 1973.

Evidence of Inefficiency in Public Enterprise

Since residential garbage collection is a relatively homogeneous task and is carried out both by government and private firms, this service is particularly well suited to comparing the costs of competition, private monopoly, and government monopoly. A study of the relative costs of private and public collection of garbage in about 300 municipalities in the United States found that collection costs were about the same whether the job was done by government or by a group of competing firms.* Competition was expensive because each firm served only scattered customers, and there was much duplication of routes. On the other hand, the costs of both government collection and competitive private collection were some 34 percent higher than the costs of service by a private monopoly collector working under contract to the municipal government. The government services typically had significantly larger crews, higher rates of employee absenteeism, smaller trucks, and less frequent use of incentive systems than did the private collectors.

*E.S. Savas, "Evaluating the Organization of Service Delivery: Solid Waste Collection and Disposal; A Summary." Center for Government Studies, Graduate School of Business, Columbia University, April 1976.

Summary

1. Regulation has two primary purposes: to put brakes on the decisions of industries with monopoly power and to contribute to public health and safety.
2. Railroads, trucks, telecommunications, and gas and electricity supply are among the industries that are regulated in the United States. In Europe the firms that provide these services are usually owned by the government (they are nationalized).
3. In recent years there has been a major push toward reduction of regulation. So far, air, truck, and rail transportation have been deregulated in whole or in part.
4. Among the major reasons given for regulation are (a) economies of scale and scope, which make industries into natural monopolies; (b) the danger of self-destructive competition in industries with low (short-run) marginal costs; (c) the desire to provide service to isolated areas where supply is expensive and unprofitable; (d) the desire for fair allocation of scarce resources (such as radio and television air space); and (e) the protection of consumers from unscrupulous suppliers.
5. Some economists believe that regulation has had very little effect on regulated industries, but this conclusion is not accepted by everyone.
6. Regulators often reject proposals by regulated firms to cut their prices, and sometimes the regulators even force firms to raise their prices. The purpose of such action is to prevent "unfair competition," and to protect customers of some of the firm's products from being forced to subsidize customers of other products. Many economists disagree with such actions and argue that the result is usually to stifle competition and make all customers pay more than they otherwise would.
7. Economists generally argue that a firm should be permitted to cut its price as long as it covers its long-run marginal cost. However, others (usually noneconomists) argue that fully distributed cost is a better criterion. A fully distributed cost criterion, in this sense, usually means that price will be higher than it will be if marginal cost is used as the standard.

8. Regulation is often criticized for providing little or no incentive for efficiency, for tending to push prices upward, and for forcing the regulated parties to engage in an expensive and time-consuming adversary process.

9. Nationalized (government-run) industries are frequently suspected of being wasteful and inefficient, but the evidence is not uniform and there are exceptions.

Concepts for Review

Nationalization
Price floor
Price ceiling
Natural monopoly
Economies of scale

Economies of scope
Self-destructive competition
Predatory pricing
Fully distributed cost

Short- and long-run marginal cost
Marginal-cost pricing
Ramsey Pricing Rule
Regulatory lag

Questions for Discussion

1. Why is an electric company in a city usually considered to be a natural monopoly? What would happen if two competing electric companies were established? How about telephone companies?

2. Suppose a 20 percent cut in the price of freight transportation brings in so much new business that it permits a railroad to cut its passenger fares by 2 percent. In your opinion, is this equitable? Is it a good idea or a bad one?

3. In some regulated industries, prices are prevented from falling by the regulatory agency and as a result many firms open up business in that industry. In your opinion, is this competitive or anticompetitive? Is it a good idea or a bad one?

4. What industries in the United States can be considered nationalized or partly nationalized? What do you think of the quality of their services? Why might this criterion be inadequate as evidence on which to base a judgment of the idea of nationalization?

5. List some industries with regulated rates whose services you have bought. What do you think of the quality of their service?

6. In which if any of the regulated industries mentioned in your previous answer is there competitive rivalry? Why is regulation appropriate in these cases? (Or is it inappropriate in your opinion, and if so, why?)

7. Regulators are much concerned about the prevention of "predatory pricing"—pricing policies designed to destroy competition. The U.S. Court of Appeals has, however, noted that "the term probably does not have a well-defined meaning, but it certainly bears a sinister connotation." How might one go about distinguishing "predatory" from "nonpredatory" pricing? What would you do about it? (Note that no one has yet come up with a final answer to this problem.)

8. A regulated industry is prohibited from earning profits higher than it now is getting. It begins to sell a new product at a price above its long-run marginal cost. Explain why the prices of other company products will, very likely, have to be reduced.

Limiting Market Power: Antitrust Policy

28

The preceding chapter described the process of regulation, one of the two main instruments used by the U.S. government to offset the undesirable effects that unrestrained monopoly and oligopoly would have on the market mechanism. This chapter analyzes the second of these instruments, *antitrust policy*. **Antitrust policy** is the term used to describe programs designed to control the growth of monopoly and to prevent powerful firms from engaging in practices that are considered "undesirable." Such "undesirable practices" are vaguely defined by a number of federal laws and by a large number of court decisions. Firms accused of violating these antitrust laws are likely to be sued in court by the federal government, seeking a ruling that both prevents the practice from recurring and punishes the offender by fines or even a prison term.

Antitrust suits are likely to be well-publicized affairs, because the accused firms are often the giants of industry. The more spectacular cases in the history of antitrust policy involve such names as Standard Oil, U.S. Steel, the Aluminum Company of America (Alcoa), and General Electric. More recently, International Business Machines (IBM) and American Telephone and Telegraph (AT&T) have been sued by the Department of Justice for alleged violations of antitrust laws. (See the boxed insert on next page.) The magnitude of an antitrust suit is difficult to envision. After the charges have been filed, it is not unusual for more than five years to elapse before the case even comes up for trial. The parties spend this period preparing their cases: assembling witnesses, gathering evidence, and drawing up numerous documents. With the permission of the courts, the parties may undertake massive searches of one another's files. Dozens of lawyers, scores of witnesses, and hundreds of researchers are likely to participate in the process of preparation. The trial itself is likely to run for years, with each day's proceedings producing a fat volume of transcript. A major case can literally pour forth several thousand volumes of material, and the total cost to the defendant can easily run to *several hundred million* dollars.

What all this means is that when the Department of Justice or the Federal Trade Commission decides to bring suit against a company, it automatically imposes a huge financial penalty upon that company *whether or not* that firm is subsequently found to have violated the law—or even if the case is thrown out of court before it ever comes to trial. That is an awesome power and a great responsibility. What justifies the investment of so much power in a government

Antitrust: Current Prospects

Even though there is little difference between Democratic and Republican administrations in terms of the vigor of antitrust policy, the election of Ronald Reagan inevitably brought with it uncertainties about the future of this program. Mr. Reagan appointed William F. Baxter as assistant attorney general in charge of antitrust policy. Baxter, a professor at Stanford University whose knowledge of economic analysis is unusual, has indicated that his top priority is to protect the interests of consumers and not necessarily those of small firms. Economic efficiency is the main criterion. Thus, where giant enterprises serve consumers more cheaply and more efficiently, he believes they should not be interfered with.

Nevertheless, even though the Secretary of Defense urged the Department of Justice to settle its case against AT&T promptly, Baxter vowed to "litigate it to the eyeballs." His objective, he implied, was to separate many of the firm's activities from the parent company. There are also moves underway in Congress to settle the future of AT&T by legislation.

All this leaves the direction of antitrust policy under the Reagan administration quite unclear. The administration inherited a number of major cases from its predecessors. Besides the AT&T case, two others of note are:

The IBM case. This twelve-year-old suit brought against IBM by the Department of Justice involves a charge that the company monopolized part of its operations. Consequently, the department is trying to break up the company. As the Reagan administration came into office, this case seemed to be completely bogged down. It is noteworthy that IBM has also been sued on similar grounds by twenty-four other firms, and each of these cases was either settled, dismissed, or won by IBM (though most of the verdicts are still being appealed).

The Cereals case. The Federal Trade Commission sued Kelloggs, General Mills, and General Foods, charging that they had together effectively achieved a "shared" monopoly that earned excessive profits and that discouraged new firms from entering the cereals market. The FTC proposed that Kelloggs be broken up into several smaller firms, and that it be required to permit anyone who so desired to produce any Kelloggs' products (with some exceptions). Under this proposal, Kelloggs would have received no payments from these imitators of its products. But the Reagan administration apparently had little sympathy for the Cereals case and dropped it in January 1982. It may seek to curtail the antitrust activities of the FTC generally.

---

agency? What are the purposes of the antitrust laws; and how well has the program succeeded? These questions are the main concerns of this chapter. Starting with a little history, we describe how the antitrust program has fared over the nine decades since its inception. We outline the activities that are currently prohibited by law, and then examine the role of monopoly in the economy and the pros and cons of the antitrust program from the viewpoint of economic analysis.

The Public Image of Business at the Time the Antitrust Laws Were Born

The Sherman Antitrust Act, the forerunner of all modern antitrust legislation, was passed in 1890. To understand what brought Congress to attempt to interfere with freedom of business enterprise, we must glance briefly at the character of the most publicized business practices in the United States during the half century following the Civil War. There were, no doubt, many businessmen at that time whose mode of operation was beyond reproach. But these were not the businessmen who made the headlines and who amassed the most spectacular fortunes. The adventures of the more daring breed of entrepreneurs, those who have been described as "the robber barons," compete in lurid detail with the tales of their contemporaries in the Wild West.

One of the most widely publicized cases was that of John D. Rockefeller, Sr., and his Standard Oil Company. About five years after starting in the oil refining business with an investment of $4000, Rockefeller and his partners formed the Standard Oil Company in 1870. Its headquarters were in Cleveland, and its original capital was $1 million. The rapid progress of the company relative to its competitors led to an early investigation, which revealed that Standard was receiving secret rebates (price discounts) from the railroads—rebates that were not being given to Rockefeller's competitors. But soon, competition among railroads forced the lines to give rebates to other refiners as well, and the high profits that Standard Oil and others were earning attracted new investors into the oil refining business. Refining capacity grew to about twice the level of demand, oil prices dropped sharply, and the profitability of refineries was threatened.

At this point a number of refineries and other shippers formed a cooperative powerful enough to force the railroads not only to provide rebates to them alone, but even to give the group "drawbacks"—that is, payments on every shipment of oil refined by a rival firm. In 1872 the organization controlled only about 10 percent of the country's refining capacity. Yet only seven years later, in 1879, Standard Oil and its associated companies were producing some 90 percent of the nation's refined oil and had control of all its pipeline capacity. Then, in 1882, lacking confidence in the trustworthiness of the alliance, and because of legal obstacles to its interstate operations, the group formed the Standard Oil Trust (from which the word "antitrust" was derived). This involved the appointment of a group of nine trustees into whose hands the forty associated firms placed enough of their stock to give irrevocable control to the trustees. The trust closed down "excessive" and inefficient refinery operations, involving more than half its plants, in an effort to limit output and keep prices at levels that yielded monopoly profits.

While the oil trust was the first to be established in the United States, others soon followed. Successful trusts were formed in sugar, whiskey, lead, cottonseed oil, and linseed oil. In 1892 the Supreme Court of Ohio ordered the dissolution of the Standard Oil Trust, which nevertheless managed to survive as a cooperating set of firms by arranging for the directors of the major refining companies to serve on one another's boards. Finally, when the State of New Jersey liberalized its rules on corporate activity, control of what had been the trust was given to the Standard Oil Company of New Jersey. Thus, by flexibility and ingenuity, this organization retained control over an industry composed, at least initially, of a considerable number of firms.

Other, more lurid tales of business practices in this period are easy to find: how J. P. Morgan hired an army of toughs to engage literally in pitched battle for a contested section of railroad outside Binghamton, New York; how Philip Armour and his confederates obtained control of meat processing by an understanding with their rivals that each day a different one of them would offer a low bid for the morning shipment of cattle and no one else would ever enter a higher bid. It is easy to go on and on with such stories. But the point is clear:

There was good reason in 1890 for popular distrust of free-swinging business activity: business practices in the preceding decades had been ridden by scandal.

Business leaders repeatedly indicated their contempt for the public interest. J. P. Morgan announced, "I owe the public nothing," and people long remembered W. H. Vanderbilt's phrase "the public be damned." The population was warned by advocates of control measures that it faced a country "in which the citizen was born to drink the milk furnished by the milk trust, eat the beef of the beef trust, illuminate his home by grace of the oil trust and die and be carried off by the coffin trust."[1] The circumstances were clearly propitious for some legislative action.

The Antitrust Laws

There are five acts of Congress that constitute the basis of the federal government's antitrust policy. Major provisions of these acts are summarized in Table 28–1. The **Sherman Act** is brief and very general, containing two main provisions: a prohibition of all contracts, combinations, and conspiracies in restraint of trade (Section 1), and a prohibition of any acts of, or attempts at, monopolization of trade (Section 2). However, the Sherman Act provided for no special agency to oversee its enforcement, and thirteen years elapsed after its passage before the antitrust division of the Department of Justice was established under the energetic antitrust proclivities of Theodore Roosevelt.

It was felt by many during Woodrow Wilson's administration that the Sherman Act did not provide adequate protection to the public against restrictive business practices. Consequently, in 1914 Congress passed two supplemental laws, the Clayton Act and the Federal Trade Commission Act.

The **Clayton Act** deals with certain specific practices thought to be conducive to encroachment of monopoly. It took two steps toward protecting smaller firms from what was considered unfair competition by larger rivals. First, it prohibited **price discrimination,** which is the act, by a seller, of charging different prices to different buyers of the same product. This provision would, for example, have prohibited the railroad rebates that Rockefeller had used to squeeze out his rivals. Second, the Clayton Act prohibited *tying contracts*—arrangements under which a customer who wants to buy some product from a given seller is

[1]Matthew Josephson, *The Robber Barons, The Great American Capitalists 1861–1901,* (New York: Harcourt Brace Jovanovich, 1934), page 358.

Table 28–1
BASIC ANTITRUST LAWS

NAME	DATE	MAJOR PROVISIONS
Sherman Act	1890	Prohibits "all contracts, combinations and conspiracies in restraint of trade" (Section 1), and monopolization in interstate and foreign trade (Section 2).
Clayton Act	1914	Prohibits price discrimination, contracts in which the seller prevents buyers from purchasing goods from the seller's competitors (tying contracts), and acquisition by one corporation of another's shares if these acts are likely to reduce competition or tend to create monopoly; also prohibits directors of one company from sitting on the board of a competitor's company.
Federal Trade Commission Act	1914	Establishes the FTC as an independent agency with authority to prosecute unfair competition and to prevent false and misleading advertising.
Robinson-Patman Act	1936	Prohibits special discounts and other discriminatory concessions to large purchasers unless based on differences in cost or "offered in good faith to meet an equally low price of a competitor."
Celler-Kefauver Antimerger Act	1950	Prohibits any corporation from acquiring the assets of another where the effect is to reduce competition substantially or to tend to create a monopoly.

required as part of the price to agree to buy some other product or products exclusively from that same seller. In addition, the Clayton Act prohibited one firm from purchasing the stock of another if that acquisition tended to reduce competition. While this provision was intended to prevent a firm from buying out its rivals, business found it possible to circumvent the intent of the law by buying a rival's stocks and then merging assets. When this practice was recognized, a new law—the **Celler-Kefauver Antimerger Act** of 1950—was enacted to prohibit it. Finally, the Clayton Act prohibited *interlocking directorates* between competitors, arrangements under which two companies have in common some of the members of their boards of directors.

The **Federal Trade Commission Act** created a commission to investigate "unfair" and "predatory" competitive practices and declared illegal all "unfair methods of competition in commerce." But since no definition of "unfairness" was provided by the law, and since, in any event, the Commission's powers were substantially restricted by the courts, the FTC was a rather ineffective agency for the first quarter century of its existence. In 1938, however, it was given the task of preventing false and deceptive advertising, a task to which it has subsequently devoted a substantial portion of its energies.

In 1936, Congress passed the **Robinson-Patman Act,** which was designed to protect independent sellers—both wholesalers and retailers (primarily in groceries and drugs)—from the "unfair competition" of chain stores and mass distributors. The Robinson-Patman Act was not a natural step in the succession of antitrust laws, since it sought to *restrain* competition by protecting small firms from the competition of larger ones. It was felt that large firms were powerful enough to wrest special financial terms from their suppliers, which gave them an unfair competitive edge over their rivals. Accordingly, the Act prohibited several types of discriminatory arrangements, such as:

1. Special concessions, like promotional allowances by sellers to any favored set of buyers; any such allowances being legal only if available to all buyers on essentially equal terms.
2. Special discounts to favored buyers who purchase the same goods in the same quantities as other buyers who do not get the discount.
3. Lower prices in one geographic area than in another, or prices that are "unreasonably low," if the objective is to eliminate competition.
4. Payment of brokerage fees to a buyer who does not actually use a middleman broker.
5. Discounts for larger purchases, or any other form of discrimination that tends to *reduce* competition or encourage monopoly. This was perhaps the most important provision of the Act, although it did continue to permit price discrimination if it could be justified either by differences in costs or by the necessity of meeting the price charged by a competitor.

The Courts and the Sherman Act

From the earliest days of the Sherman Act, the courts have been rather consistent in their use of Section 1—the part of the Act that prohibits all contracts, combinations, and conspiracies in restraint of trade. Section 1 has been invoked primarily against price-fixing agreements—that is, agreements under which several ostensibly competing firms undertake to coordinate their pricing decisions. The courts have held that such agreements are illegal *per se;* that is, they have held that no excuses or exonerating circumstances can render a price-fixing agreement acceptable to the law. In the Addyston Pipe case of 1899, six manufacturers of cast-iron pipe argued that the prices they had agreed upon were reasonable and that, had there been no agreement, prices would have been driven to ruinous levels. But Justice William Howard Taft rejected the argument, affirming that *any* price-setting agreement was illegal. This doctrine has been confirmed many times, most notably in the G.E.-Westinghouse case, which was decided in 1961. General Electric, Westinghouse, and several dozen other producers of electrical equipment had gotten together to divide the market up among themselves and to agree on prices. The firms were found guilty of a conspiracy to fix prices, and were fined several million dollars. Even more remarkable was that officers of the major companies were sentenced to (brief) prison terms.

Cases in which there are no *explicit* price agreements, but in which there are grounds for suspicion that more subtle means have been used to attain the same goals, have proven more difficult for the courts in dealing with Section 1 of the Sherman Act. For example, a large firm may publish a price list so that all its competitors know in advance what prices it is going to charge. If it also announces in advance that it will reduce its price to equal that of any competitor who attempts to undercut it, this may effectively force rivals to match the published prices. A variety of such types of behavior patterns have been held to facilitate coordination of prices; and some, though not all, of them have been held to be illegal.

Section 2 of the Sherman Act deals with persons "who shall monopolize or attempt to monopolize . . . any part of the trade or commerce among the several states, or with foreign nations." At first the courts proceeded very timidly in dealing with industrial cases under Section 2. For example, in the E. C. Knight case of 1895, the court held that a monopoly of sugar manufacturing was legal on the grounds that manufacturing was not commerce! But the Supreme Court's position toughened markedly in 1911, when it decided to require both the American Tobacco Company and the Standard Oil Company to give up substantial shares of their holdings in other firms. Many of today's leading gasoline suppliers—including Standard Oil of California, Exxon, and Sohio—are offsprings of the original Standard Oil Company, spawned by the Court's decision.

At the same time, however, the Court also formulated the troublesome **rule of reason,** which held that trade restraints are not *necessarily* illegal per se. According to this rule, a restraint is against the law only if it is "unreasonable." On that basis, U.S. Steel was exonerated in 1920 even though, when it was formed, it controlled 80 to 95 percent of U.S. output of some steel products. The Court held that mere size does not constitute an offense—that a firm must commit objectionable overt acts before it can be found guilty of violating Section 2 of the Sherman Act. Eastman Kodak and International Harvester, each with very large market shares, were found not guilty on similar grounds. Thus, while the courts held that there were *no* excusable cases of price fixing under Section 1, they ruled that there *were* excusable monopolies under Section 2.

However, a profound departure from this doctrine was enunciated in the decision on the Department of Justice's case against Alcoa. Launched in 1937, the case was settled only eight years later. The Court ruled that Alcoa was guilty *because it controlled some 90 percent of the market*, even though it had not used means to gain this control that would previously have been declared "unreasonable." Thus, the Court's decision took the position that a firm's monopoly power, if sufficiently great, was illegal when *consciously maintained*, even if the firm had done nothing illegal to acquire that power. In other words, the Court decided that the legality of the organization of an industry could be determined at least in part from its observable **structure** (for example, from the market share of the largest firm) as well as from the **conduct** of any firm in that industry. This feature of the Alcoa decision has so far not been used widely as a precedent for other cases, and some commentators claim it was just an aberration. Others, though, feel that the conclusion about the illegality of monopoly, however acquired, heralds a new phase in the history of antitrust policy.

A final landmark decision of the postwar period was the Brown Shoe Company case of 1962, in which the Brown Shoe Company, by no means the nation's largest manufacturer of shoes, was ordered to divest itself of the Kinney retail firm with which it had merged several years earlier. The decision was based on the Court's finding that the merger established both *vertical* and *horizontal relationships* between the two firms. Since Brown was a producer of shoes and Kinney was a shoe retailer, their union was a **vertical merger.** On the other hand, since Brown itself had retail outlets, the acquisition also involved a **horizontal merger.** The Supreme Court objected to both these elements of the merger on the grounds that they involved the likelihood of substantial reduction in competition. Consequently, Brown was ordered to divest itself of Kinney. This decision set the precedent that while merger per se is not illegal, it does violate the law if the result may be *a significant reduction in competition.* For a long time after this decision, virtually no horizontal mergers brought before the courts have been approved. Under the Reagan administration, a new policy of permissiveness toward mergers was launched and a mass of merger activity followed quickly.

A **vertical merger** is the union of two companies, one of which supplies products that the other uses as inputs. For example, an automobile manufacturer who acquires a tire producer, or a filmmaker who acquires a chain of movie houses, is engaged in a vertical merger. A **horizontal merger** is the union of two companies that carry out the same or similar competing economic activities.

Issues in Concentration of Industry

Having reviewed the antitrust laws and their interpretation by the courts, the next logical question is: Do they work? One very rough way to measure the success of antitrust legislation is to look at what has happened to the share of American business in the hands of the largest firms. First, we can compare the degree of domination by large firms in the U.S. economy with that in other countries. American programs designed to limit monopoly power go back further and involve more powerful government machinery than do comparable programs in virtually any other major free-market economy. Indeed, in some European countries, monopoly is not really discouraged. Thus, one way to evaluate the effectiveness of an antitrust program is to compare the status of the larger firms in the United States with that of their counterparts abroad.

A second method of evaluation involves observations of firms over a long period of time. Some observers, particularly the Marxists, have predicted that one of the basic tendencies of capitalism is **concentration of industry,** because small firms are increasingly driven out of business, especially during economic crises, and large firms consequently acquire ever-larger shares of the market. One can therefore investigate whether such a tendency has been observed in the United States. If, in fact, concentration has *not* increased, someone who holds these views might be led to surmise that the antitrust program has had a hand in preventing the growth of monopoly. But first we should consider what might have been expected to happen to concentration in the United States in the absence of any countermeasures by government. Is there good reason to expect an inexorable trend toward bigness, as the Marxists suggest?

There are two basic reasons why the larger firms in an industry may triumph over the small. First, larger firms may obtain monopoly power, which they can use to their advantage. They can force sellers of equipment, raw materials, and other inputs to give them better terms than are available to small competitors; and they can also force retailers to give preferences to their products. These are, of course, the sorts of advantages to bigness that the antitrust laws were designed to eliminate.

The second reason why an industry's output may tend to be divided among fewer and larger firms with the passage of time has to do with technology. In some industries, fairly small firms can produce as cheaply or more cheaply than large ones, while in other industries only rather large firms can achieve maximal economy. By and large, the difference in number of firms from one industry to another has tended to correspond to the size of firm that is least costly. Automobile, steel, and airplane manufacturing are all industries in which tiny companies cannot hope to produce economically and, indeed, these are all industries made up of a relatively few large firms. In clothing production and farming, matters go quite the other way.

Frequently, innovation seems to have increased the plant size that minimizes costs. Such examples as automated processes or assembly lines suggest that new techniques always call for gigantic equipment; but this is not always true. For example, the invention of the internal combustion engine and the consequent rise of trucking gave much of the freight-shipping market to smaller firms, taking it away from the giant railroads. Technological change also seems to have favored the establishment of small electronics firms. Similarly, the continued development of cheaper and smaller computers is likely to provide a competitive advantage to smaller firms in many other industries. Furthermore:

If innovation provides increased cost advantages to larger firms, the growth of firms will be stimulated. But a fall in the number of firms in the industry need not inevitably result. If demand for the industry's output grows faster than the optimal size of firm, we may end up with a larger number of firms, each of them bigger than before, but each having a smaller share of an expanded market.

For example, suppose in some industry a new process is invented that requires a far larger scale of operation than currently is typical. Specifically, suppose that the most efficient (that is, least costly) plant size becomes twice as large. If demand for the industry's product increases only a little, we can expect a decrease in the number of firms. But if demand for the industry's product happens to triple at the same time, then the optimal number of firms will in fact increase to one and a half times the original number—each firm will be twice as big as before, so that together they serve three times the volume. In such a case, each firm's share of industry output will in fact have declined.

In the twentieth century, technological developments do, for the most part, seem to call for larger firms, which are best adapted to take advantage of the resulting economies. Probably this has somewhat outstripped even the rate of growth in output—that is, the growth of GNP. Thus, we should expect some fall in the number of firms in a typical industry, somewhat as many Marxists expect. However, not all technological change has worked in this direction. For example, many firms in the electronics industry are relatively small, and there are observers who argue that new techniques will permit firms to supply some telecommunications services without incurring high costs. We must turn to the evidence to judge whether or not American industry has grown more concentrated.

Evidence of Concentration in Industry

A **concentration ratio** is the percentage of an industry's output produced by its *four* largest firms. It is intended to measure the degree to which the industry is dominated by large firms, that is, how closely it approximates a monopoly.

There have been many statistical studies of concentration in American industry. One common way of measuring concentration is to calculate the share of the four largest firms in an industry, the so-called **concentration ratio.** Of course, there is no reason why the three or five or ten largest firms could not be used for the purpose, but conventionally four firms are used as the standard.

Table 28–2 shows concentration ratios in a number of industries in the United States. We see that concentration varies greatly from industry to industry: automobiles, cigarettes, and photocopying equipment are produced by highly concentrated industries, while the book publishing, clothing, and soft drink industries show very little concentration. But only comparisons over time and by geographic area can reveal the most significant implications of these figures. Here, the available evidence suggests that (perhaps simply because the American market is larger) concentration in U.S. industry is somewhat lower than it is in most other industrialized countries. But the differences are not substantial; and, because of other differences that make comparison difficult, the significance of these differences has been questioned.

In the United States there seems to have been little trend in the concentration ratio, at least since the beginning of this century. The evidence is that, on the average during this period, concentration ratios remained remarkably constant. It has been estimated that at the turn of the century 32.9 percent of manufactured goods were produced by larger-enterprise industries in which the concentration ratio was 50 percent or more (meaning that at least 50 percent of industry output was produced by the four largest firms). By 1963 the figure had risen only to 33.1 percent. And by 1970 it actually fell to 26.3 percent, though it has risen slightly since then. These figures and those for other years are shown in Table 28–3. In a frequently quoted statement, M. A. Adelman, a noted authority on the subject, concluded, "Any tendency either way, if it does exist, must be at the pace of a glacial drift."[2] Or, as a more recent report puts it, "Almost all observers of the industrial scene . . . agree that . . . the evidence fails to support a claim that competition has declined. While concentration has increased in some areas, decreases have occurred elsewhere, leaving the overall structure unaffected."[3]

[2]M. A. Adelman, "The Measurement of Industrial Concentration," *Review of Economics and Statistics*, Vol. 33 (Nov. 1951), pages 295–96.
[3]P. W. McCracken and T. G. Moore, "Competition and Market Concentration in the American Economy," Subcommittee on Antitrust and Monopoly, U.S. Senate, March 29, 1973.

Table 28–2
1977 CONCENTRATION RATIOS FOR REPRESENTATIVE INDUSTRIES

INDUSTRY	4-FIRM RATIO	INDUSTRY	4-FIRM RATIO
Razor blades and razors, except electric	99	Farm machinery and equipment	46
		Industrial trucks and tractors	46
Motor vehicles and car bodies	94	Radio and TV receiving sets	44
Coin-operated amusement machines	92	Motors and generators	39
Cigarettes	88	Gasoline	30
Photocopying equipment	87	Pharmaceutical preparations	25
Household refrigerators and freezers	82	Men's and boys' suits and coats	20
		Fluid milk	17
Household detergents	80	Book publishing	16
Primary aluminum	76	Bottled and canned soft drinks	14
Tires and inner tubes	71	Women's and misses' dresses	7
Aircraft	61	Miscellaneous plastic products	7
Electronic computers	49		

SOURCE: "Concentration Ratios in Manufacturing," Bureau of the Census MC77(SR)-9, issued May 1981.

Table 28–3

THE TREND IN CONCENTRATION IN MANUFACTURING INDUSTRIES (SELECTED YEARS)

	AROUND 1901	1947	1954	1958	1963	1966	1970	1972
Percent of value added in industries with 4-firm concentration ratios over 50 percent	32.9	24.4	29.9	30.2	33.1	28.6	26.3	29.0

SOURCES: P. W. McCracken and T. G. Moore, "Competition and Market Concentration in the American Economy," Subcommittee on Antitrust and Monopoly, U.S. Senate, March 29, 1973, and F. M. Scherer, *Industrial Market Structure and Economic Performance*, Houghton Mifflin, Boston, 1980, page 68.

Concentration in the United States seems to be somewhat lower than it is in most other industrialized economies. Over the course of the twentieth century, *concentration in individual U.S. industries has shown no tendency to increase.*

Since concentration is intended as a measure of the "bigness" of the firms in an industry, from such information one can perhaps surmise that the antitrust program has been effective to some degree in inhibiting whatever trend toward bigness may in fact exist. But even this very cautious conclusion has been questioned by some observers. In fact, some economists and other observers have expressed the view that these laws have made virtually no difference in the size and the behavior of American business. Whether it is desirable for the antitrust program or for some other program to inhibit concentration is an issue we turn to next.

The Pros and Cons of Bigness

Why has antitrust become so accepted a part of government policy? Are the effects of bigness or monopoly always undesirable? We *do* know that monopoly power can be abused; the history of the Rockefellers, the Armours, and the Morgans described at the beginning of this chapter confirms that adequately. But even when the giants of business are not so swashbuckling in their operations, unrestrained monopoly and bigness give rise to a number of problems:

1. *Distribution of income.* The flow of wealth to firms with market power—and thus to those who are able to influence prices in their favor—is widely considered to be unfair and socially unacceptable.

2. *Restriction of output.* We learned in Chapter 25 that if an unrestrained monopoly is to maximize its profits, it must restrict its output to below the amount that would be provided by an equivalent competitive industry. This means that unregulated monopolized industries are likely to produce smaller outputs than the quantities that serve the interests of the community.

3. *Lack of inducement for innovation.* It is sometimes argued that firms in industries in which competitors are few, or in which competition is altogether absent, may be under less pressure to introduce new production methods and new products than are firms in industries in which each is constantly trying to beat out the others. Without competition, the management of a firm may choose the quiet life, taking no chances on risky

investments in research and development. But a firm that operates in constant fear that its rivals will come up with a better idea, and come up with it first, can afford no such luxury.

So far we have presented only one side of the picture. In fact, bigness in industry need not be advantageous only to the firm. It can also, at least *sometimes*, work to the advantage of the general public. Again, there are several reasons:

1. *Economies of large size.* Probably the most important advantage of bigness is to be found in those industries in which technology dictates that small-scale operation is inefficient. One can hardly imagine the costs if automobiles were produced in little workshops rather than giant factories. The notion of a small firm operating a long-distance railroad does not even make sense, and a multiplicity of firms replicating the same railroad service would clearly be incredibly wasteful. On these grounds, most policymakers have never even considered an attempt to eliminate bigness. Their objective, rather, is to curb its potential abuses and to try at the same time to help the public benefit from its advantages. Of course, it does not follow that every industry in which firms happen to be big is one in which big firms are best. There are observers who argue that many firms in fact exceed the size required for cost minimization.

2. *Required scale for innovation.* Some economists have argued that only large firms have the resources and the motivation for really significant innovation. While many inventions are still contributed by individuals, to put a new invention into commercial production is often an expensive, complex venture that can only be carried out on a large scale. And only large firms can afford the funds and bear the risks that such an effort demands. In addition, according to this view, only the large firm has the motivation to lay out the funds required for the innovation process, because it is the large firm that will get to keep a considerable share of the benefits. A small company, on the other hand, will find that its innovative idea is soon likely to be followed by close imitations, which enable competitors to profit from its research outlays. There have been many studies of the relationship between firm size, competitiveness of the industry, and the level of expenditure on research and development (R and D). While the evidence is far from conclusive, it does indicate that highly competitive industries comprising very small firms tend not to produce significant innovation. Up to a point, R and D outlays and innovation seem to increase with size of firm and concentration of industry. However, with some exceptions, after some point, greater concentration appears to provide no further stimulus to innovation and, in some cases, may even act as a deterrent. By and large, the evidence suggests that firms of intermediate size and intermediate levels of concentration are most innovative.

Other Government Programs Related to Bigness

Because the issues raised by bigness and concentration are complex, they would appear to call for a variety of policy measures. Certainly, antitrust programs alone cannot do everything that the public interest requires. For example, in cases where large firms are far more efficient than small ones, it does not seem reasonable to break up industrial giants. In fact, it is sometimes even considered most desirable, on grounds of economy, to permit a market to be served by only a single firm—such as a supplier of electricity, local transportation, or telecommunications services.

Where one firm offers considerable savings in comparison to a multiplicity of suppliers—that is, where the industry is a *natural monopoly*—it is usually agreed that it would not serve the social interest to subdivide the supplying firm into a number of rival companies. Instead, one of two policies is usually adopted. Either (as is often done in Europe) the monopoly firm is nationalized and run as a government enterprise (telephone service in England and electricity generation in France are publicly owned and operated). Or, as is typical in the United States, the natural monopoly is left as a private firm but its operations are regulated in one of the ways described in the previous chapter.

The possibility of inhibition of innovation by competition is another important issue, which, as we have seen, affects policy toward bigness and concentration. The main instrument government has employed in this area is the **patent system,** which rewards the innovator in even a small firm in a highly competitive industry by the grant of a temporary monopoly. The patent restricts imitation and is designed to offer small-firm innovators the same advantages from their research activities as are enjoyed by innovators in industries that contain no competitors ready to erode profits by imitation. Thus, somewhat ironically, while government prohibits monopolies, it also guarantees monopoly power to protect small firms in competitive industries. Of course, sometimes the protected firms themselves grow big with the help of the protection. Once-small firms like Polaroid and Xerox grew into industrial giants with the help of government protection through the patent laws.

Questions have been raised about the effectiveness of patents in inducing expenditure on R and D, and the evidence certainly does not provide overwhelming support for the view that patents constitute a strong stimulus for innovation. Questions have also been raised about the desirability of granting an innovator an unrestricted monopoly for seventeen years, as the patent program now does in the United States. Similar issues have been raised about copyright laws, which restrict reproduction of written works.

Finally, government has provided special help to small business in a variety of ways. For example, there are programs designed to make it easier for small firms to raise capital; and special government agencies, such as the Small Business Administration, have been set up for the purpose. There is also some degree of *progressivity* in business taxation, meaning that smaller firms are subject to taxes lower than those paid by larger firms. And special legislation, such as the "fair trade" laws—which, though since repealed, permitted manufacturers to designate and enforce "fair" retail prices for products—are intended, in part, to protect small retailers from the competition of larger rivals.

Issues in Antitrust Policy

In recent years there has been a searching reexamination of government policy toward business. For example, there have been calls for a decrease in the overall power of the regulatory agencies; and the antitrust program is unlikely to be ignored in such a review. Some voices call for abolition of the antitrust laws altogether, while others advocate their strengthening and expansion. But even if one grants the desirability of an antitrust program with "teeth" in it, there still remain questions about whom or what to "bite."

A major issue is the relative weights that should be assigned to *structure* and *conduct* in deciding which firms it is in the social interest to prosecute. Most people accept the basic notion that socially damaging conduct, such as price fixing or threats of physical violence, should be discouraged; though there is not always complete agreement on what types of conduct are undesirable. But many more questions are raised about the use of structural criteria in antitrust policy. Is bigness always undesirable per se? What if the large firm is more efficient and has engaged in no practices that can reasonably be considered to constitute predatory competition? Many economists have reservations about the prosecution of such a firm, fearing that it will only serve to grant protection to inefficient competitors and do so at the expense of consumers. They also point out the danger that successful firms will be singled out for attention under the antitrust laws simply because their success makes them noticeable and their efficiency enables them to outstrip their competitors. The fear is that such an orientation will discourage efficiency and entrepreneurship.

It is now widely recognized that policy in this area can in fact prove anticompetitive and inhibit efficiency, despite its contrary intentions. For example, the "fair trade" laws were repealed because it was finally recognized that they effectively prevented price competition by drug, appliance, and liquor retailers, among many others. The primary victims of the "fair trade" laws were consumers, who were forced by law to pay higher prices, while the primary beneficiaries were the least-efficient retailers who, without the protection of those laws, would have been forced out of business.

Another example of the lack of agreement between economists and law-makers about the sorts of conduct that the law should proscribe concerns the is-sue of *price discrimination*, which, we learned earlier in the chapter, is the sale of the same item to two different customers at different prices. To economists, this legal definition is misleading. Suppose, for instance, that one person lives on a mountaintop far from the place where a good is produced, and another customer is located in an area that enjoys easy access to the good in question. Economists would say that it is not discriminatory to charge each a different price. *On the contrary, economists hold that in such cases it is discriminatory to charge both customers the same price, because it does not account for the substantial difference in the two delivery costs.*

Even more important than this definitional argument, though, is the issue of the desirability or undesirability of discrimination. The word *discrimination* is what has been called a "persuasive term"—in this case, a word that automatically implies gross misconduct. *But, in fact, price discrimination can sometimes be beneficial to all parties to a transaction.* Suppose, for instance, a commodity is available to the poor only if it is sold at a relatively low price, though one that still more than covers the good's marginal cost (the cost incurred in expanding into the lower-income market). In this case, the contribution from the lower-income market may permit *some* reduction in price to the rich, since the firm might not be able to cover its total cost if it were to charge the rich the *same* low price necessary for entry into the low-income market. The result is that everyone—the poor, the wealthy, and the selling firm—will benefit from this discriminatory pricing. Another example is that of pricing by doctors, who often charge higher fees to their wealthy patients than to their poor ones. If the reduced fees permit more poor patients to visit them, the doctors may be able to earn an even better income than they could by charging a uniformly high fee to everyone. Even the fee to the rich may go down in the process because of the doctors' increased earnings from their enlarged pool of poor patients. Again, all parties are better off—the wealthy patients, the poor ones, and the doctors.

Regulated firms, whose overall earnings are restrained by a regulatory profit ceiling, have often argued that lower fees to some classes of buyers can bring in profits from markets that would not otherwise be served. In such cases, it is asserted, the regulatory profit ceiling forces the firm to charge lower fees than it would have otherwise—to all its customers. Are such acts of discrimination really so unjust?

Summary

1. Antitrust policy refers to programs designed to control the growth of monopoly and to prevent big business from engaging in "undesirable" practices.
2. The Sherman Act is the oldest U.S. antitrust law. It prohibits contracts, combinations, and conspiracies in restraint of trade and also prohibits monopolization.
3. The Clayton Act prohibits price discrimination that tends to reduce competition or create monopoly; it also prohibits competing firms from sharing directors.
4. There are several other important antitrust laws, including the Federal Trade Commission Act, which set the commission up as an independent antitrust agency, and the Robinson-Patman Act, which generally prohibits discriminatory price discounts.
5. In their early cases, the courts generally held that a large share of market by a single firm was only illegal if the firm had acquired its relatively large share by illegal means; but in the early postwar period the courts seemed to take the view that bigness per se was presumed to be illegal unless such bigness was "thrust upon

the firm" by economies of scale, unusual efficiency, or other similar influences.
6. The evidence indicates that there has been no significant increase in the concentration of individual American industries into larger firms during the twentieth century. Evidence as to whether antitrust laws have been effective in preventing monopoly is inconclusive, and observers disagree on the subject.
7. The arguments *against* unregulated monopoly are that it is likely to distribute income unfairly, produce undesirably small quantities of output, and provide inadequate motivation for innovation.
8. Defenders of big business argue that only large firms have funds sufficient for effective research, development, and innovation, and that where economies of scale are available, large firms can serve customers more cheaply than can small ones.
9. Contrary to popular thinking, price discrimination is not necessarily undesirable per se. Discriminatory pricing in some instances can be beneficial to all parties to a transaction.

Concepts for Review

Antitrust policy	Federal Trade Commission Act	Horizontal merger
Sherman Act	Robinson-Patman Act	Concentration of industry
Clayton Act	Rule of reason	Concentration ratio
Price discrimination	Structure versus conduct	Patent system
Celler-Kefauver Antimerger Act	Vertical merger	

Questions for Discussion

1. Suppose Sam lives in the central city while Fran's home is far away, so that it requires much more gas to deliver newspapers to Fran than to Sam. Yet the newspaper charges them exactly the same amount. Would the courts consider this to be price discrimination? Would an economist? Would you? Why?
2. A shopkeeper sells his store and signs a contract that restrains him from opening another store in competition with the new owner. The courts have decided that this contract is a *reasonable* restraint of trade. Can you think of any other types of restraint of trade that seem reasonable? Any that seem unreasonable?
3. Which of the following industries do you expect to

have high concentration ratios? Cigarettes, production of farm machinery, production of women's clothing, production of automobiles, production of TV sets. Compare your answers with Table 28–2.
4. Why do you think the industries you selected in Question 3 are highly concentrated?
5. Do you think structure or conduct is the more reasonable basis for antitrust regulation? Give reasons for your answer.
6. Do you think it is in the public interest to launch an antitrust suit that costs a billion dollars (as may well be true of the IBM and the AT&T cases)? What leads you to your conclusion?

Market Failure and Resource Allocation V

Shortcomings of the Market Mechanism and Government Attempts to Remedy Them

29

When she was good
She was very, very good,
But when she was bad she was horrid.
HENRY WADSWORTH LONGFELLOW

What does the market do well, and what does it do poorly? These questions constitute the central theme of our study of microeconomics, and we are by now well on our way toward getting some answers. We began in Part Three by explaining and extolling the workings of Adam Smith's invisible hand—the mechanism by which a perfectly competitive economy allocates resources efficiently without any guidance from government. While the theoretical model studied there was an idealized one, observation of the real world confirms the accomplishments of the market mechanism. Free-market economies have achieved levels of output, productive efficiency, variety in available consumer goods, and general prosperity that are unprecedented in history.

Yet the market mechanism also displays some glaring weaknesses. One of these—the fact that large and powerful business firms can interfere with the invisible hand and lead both to concentrations of wealth and to misallocation of resources—was the subject of Part Four. Now, in Part Five, we take a more comprehensive view of the failures of the market and some of the things that can be done to remedy these failures. That the market cannot do everything we would like it to do is quite apparent. Amid the outpouring of goods and services, we find areas of depressing poverty, cities choked with traffic and pollution, and educational institutions and artistic organizations in serious financial trouble. Our economy, although capable of yielding an overwhelming abundance of material wealth, seems far less capable of eradicating social ills and controlling environmental damage. In this chapter, we will examine the reasons for the market's failings in these areas and indicate specifically why the price system *by itself* may be incapable of dealing with them.

What's Wrong with the Market?

While it is probably impossible to come up with an exhaustive list of the shortcomings of the market mechanism, we can identify seven major areas in which the market has been accused of failing. We list them now in the form of indictments:

1. Market economies suffer from severe business fluctuations.
2. The market distributes income quite unequally.

3. Where markets are monopolized, they allocate resources inefficiently.
4. The market cannot deal properly with the incidental side effects of many economic activities.
5. The market cannot provide public goods, such as national defense.
6. The market mechanism makes public and personal services increasingly expensive.
7. The market does a poor job of allocating resources between the present and the future.

Let us now examine each of these charges in turn.

Business Fluctuations

To appreciate the significance of the problem of business fluctuations, we remind the reader that almost a third of this book is devoted to this topic. With the market economy's propensity, from time to time, to breed inflation, recession, and unemployment, one need hardly be reminded how serious this problem can be, both in terms of its devastating effects upon the individuals most heavily affected and the resulting losses in output and well-being to the community as a whole. This problem was examined in depth in Part Two. The point to be emphasized here is that while many people believe that the market mechanism can take care of business fluctuations by itself in the *long run*, it certainly is not able to do so in the *short run*. While recessions have rarely lasted longer than a few years, even when governments have done nothing about them, the free market has been unable to avoid these periods of widespread misery on its own.

Income Inequality

A second thing the free market has not done is to close the gap between the rich and the poor. In fact, by providing plentiful rewards to those who are successful and offering little to those who are not, it actually *contributes* to differences in wealth. Moreover, the market responds to the desires of the wealthy more effectively than it does to the demands of the poor, because the wealthy have more money with which to back up their desires. Unlike the political system, where the rule is "one person, one vote," a free-market economy runs on the principle of "one dollar, one vote." For this reason, those who have a strong desire for equality in wealth, income, and the enjoyment of goods and services, find the workings of the market system in these areas less than ideal. This is such an important problem that we devote three entire chapters to it later (Part Six).

Monopoly

When we compared the price and output of a monopoly with that of a perfectly competitive industry in Chapter 25, we concluded, with some reservations, that there is a tendency for monopolies to produce less output and to charge higher prices than competitive industries do. This is, of course, consistent with the widely held view that monopolies, if not regulated by government, tend to restrict output in order to force buyers to pay higher prices for their products. It also implies that unregulated monopolies have a tendency to misallocate resources. Specifically, if there is some tendency for perfect competition to yield the outputs required for efficient resource allocation, then monopoly must produce less than the efficient amounts. Thus, we suspect that an undesirably small proportion of society's resources will end up being used in the production of the goods sold by monopolists and, consequently, too large a share of those resources will go to the rest of the economy. This suspicion is one reason why many economists advocate government intervention in the market where monopoly exists; and Chapters 27 and 28 described some of the ways in which this intervention is accomplished.

The remaining four items on our list constitute the subject matter of the rest of this chapter. Each of these, like monopoly, is an instance in which the efficiency of the market mechanism is compromised. Therefore, to help us analyze these problems, we offer next a brief review of the concept of efficient resource allocation, which was discussed in detail in Chapter 23.

Efficient Resource Allocation: A Review

The basic problem of resource allocation is deciding how much of each commodity the economy should produce. At first glance, it may seem that the solution is simple: the more the better; so we should produce as much of each good as we can. But careful thinking tells us that this is not necessarily the right decision. Outputs are not created out of thin air. They are produced from the available supplies of labor, fuel, raw materials, and machinery. And if we use these resources to produce, say, more handkerchiefs, we must take them away from some other products, such as linens. So, to decide whether increasing the production of handkerchiefs is a good idea, we must compare the utility of that increase with the loss of utility caused by having to produce, for instance, less hospital linen. The increased output will be a good thing only if society considers the additional handkerchiefs more valuable than the forgone hospital linen.

Here it is worth remembering the concept of *opportunity cost*, one of our 12 Ideas for Beyond the Final Exam. The opportunity cost of an increase in the output of some product is the value of the other goods and services that must be forgone when inputs (resources) are taken away from their production in order to increase the output of the product in question. In our example, the opportunity cost of the increased handkerchief output is the decrease in output of hospital linen that results when resources are reallocated from the latter to the former. The general principle is that an increase in some output represents a *misallocation* of resources if the utility of that increased output is less than its opportunity cost.

To illustrate this idea, we repeat a graph encountered several times in earlier chapters—a *production possibilities frontier*—but we put it to a somewhat different use. Curve *ABC* in Figure 29–1 is a production possibilities frontier showing the alternative combinations of handkerchiefs and hospital linens the economy can produce by reallocating its resources between the production of the two goods. For example, point *A* amounts to allocation of all the resources to handkerchief production, so that 100 million of these items and no hospital linens are produced. Point *C* represents the reverse situation, with all resources allocated to hospital linens and none to handkerchiefs. Point *B* represents an intermediate allocation, resulting in the production of eight million yards of linen and 60 million handkerchiefs.

Suppose now that point *B* represents the *optimal* resource allocation—that combination of attainable outputs that best satisfies the wants of society. Two questions are pertinent to our discussion of the price system:

1. What prices will get the economy to select point *B*; that is, what prices will yield an *efficient* allocation of resources?
2. How can the wrong set of prices lead to a misallocation of resources?

The first question was discussed extensively in Chapter 23. There we saw that:

An efficient allocation of resources requires each product's price to equal its marginal cost; that is:

$$P = MC.$$

The reasoning, in brief, is as follows. In a free market, the price of any good reflects the value to consumers of an additional unit; that is, its *marginal utility* (MU). Similarly, if the market mechanism is working well, the *marginal cost* (MC) measures the value (the opportunity cost) of the resources needed to produce an additional unit of the good. Hence, if prices are set equal to marginal costs, then consumers, by using *their own money* in the most effective way to maximize their own satisfaction, will automatically be using *society's resources* in the most effective way. That is, as long as it sets prices equal to marginal costs, the market mechanism automatically satisfies the MC = MU rule for efficient resource allocation that we studied in Chapter 23.[1] In terms of Figure 29–1, this means that if P = MC for both goods, the economy will automatically gravitate to point B, which we assumed to be the optimal point.

This chapter is devoted mainly to the second question: How can the "wrong" prices cause a misallocation of resources? The answer to this question is not too difficult, and we can use the case of monopoly as an illustration. The "law" of demand tells us that a rise in the price of a commodity normally will reduce the quantity demanded. Suppose, now, that the linen industry is a monopoly, so the price of linens exceeds their marginal cost.[2] This will decrease the demand for linens below the eight million yards that we have assumed to be socially optimal (point B in Figure 29–1). So the economy will move from point B to a point like K, where too few linens and too many handkerchiefs are being produced for maximal consumer satisfaction. By setting the "wrong" prices, then, the market fails to achieve the most efficient use of the economy's resources.

[1] If you need review, consult pages 437–440.
[2] To review why price under monopoly may be expected to exceed marginal cost, you may want to reread pages 472–474.

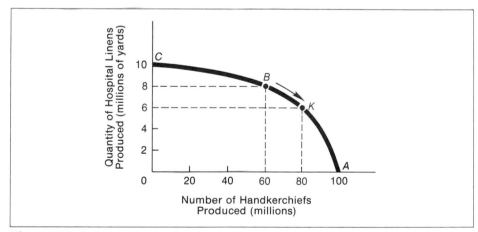

Figure 29–1
THE ECONOMY'S PRODUCTION POSSIBILITIES FRONTIER FOR THE PRODUCTION OF TWO GOODS
This graph shows all combinations of outputs of the two goods that the resources available to the economy enable it to produce. If B is the most desired output combination among those that are possible, it will correspond to a market equilibrium in which each good's price is equal to its marginal cost. If the price of linen is above its marginal cost, or the price of a handkerchief is below its marginal cost, then linen output will be inefficiently small and handkerchief output inefficiently large (point K).

In sum, if the price of a commodity is above its marginal cost, the economy will tend to produce less of that item than maximizes consumer benefits. The opposite will occur if an item's price is below its marginal cost.

In the remainder of this chapter, we will encounter several other instances in which the market mechanism may set the "wrong" prices.

Externalities

We come now to the fourth item on our list of market failures—one of the least obvious yet one of the most consequential of the imperfections of the price system. Many economic activities provide incidental benefits to others for whom they are not specifically intended. For example, a homeowner who plants a beautiful garden in front of her house, incidentally and unintentionally provides pleasure to her neighbors and to those who pass by—people from whom she receives no payment. We say then that her activity generates a **beneficial externality.** Similarly, there are activities that indiscriminately impose costs on others. For example, the operator of a motorcycle repair shop, from which all sorts of noise besieges the neighborhood and for which he pays no compensation to others, is said to produce a **detrimental externality.** Pollution constitutes the classic illustration of a detrimental externality.

An activity is said to generate a **beneficial** or **detrimental externality** if that activity causes incidental benefits or damages to others, and no corresponding compensation is provided to or paid by those who generate the externality.

To see why the presence of externalities causes the price system to misallocate resources, we need only recall that the system achieves efficiency by rewarding producers who serve consumers well—that is, at as low a cost as possible. This argument breaks down, however, as soon as some of the costs and benefits of economic activities are left out of the profit calculation. When a firm pollutes a river, it uses up some of society's resources just as surely as when it burns coal. However, if it pays for coal but not for the use of water, it is natural for management to be economical in its use of coal and wasteful in its use of water. Similarly, a firm that provides benefits to others for which it receives no payment is unlikely to be generous in allocating resources to the activity, no matter how socially desirable it may be.

In an important sense, the source of the difficulty is to be found in the definition of "property rights." Coal mines are *private property;* their owners will not let anyone take coal without paying for it. Thus, coal is costly and so is not used wastefully. But waterways are not private property. Since they belong to everyone in general, they belong to no one in particular. They therefore can be used free of charge as dumping grounds for wastes by anyone who chooses to do so. Because no one pays for the use of the oxygen in a public waterway, that oxygen will be used wastefully. That is the problem to which detrimental externalities lead.

Externalities and Inefficiency

Using these concepts, we can see precisely why an externality has undesirable effects on the allocation of resources. In discussing externalities, it is crucial to distinguish between *social* and *private* marginal cost. We define **marginal social cost** (MSC) as the sum of two components: (1) **marginal private cost** (MPC), which is the share of marginal cost caused by an activity that is paid for by the persons who carry out the activity; and (2) *incidental cost*, which is the share borne by others.

If increased output by a firm increases the smoke it emits, then, in addition to its direct private costs as recorded in the company accounts, expansion of its production imposes incidental costs on others in the form of increased laundry bills, medical expenditures, outlays for air conditioning and electricity, as well as the unpleasantness of living in a cloud of noxious fumes. These are all part of the activity's marginal *social* cost.

Where the firm's activities generate detrimental externalities, its marginal social cost will be greater than its marginal private cost. In symbols, MSC > MPC. Since, in equilibrium, that firm will choose an output for which its marginal benefits (MB) are equal to its marginal private cost (MB = MPC), it follows that marginal benefits are *smaller* than marginal social costs. Society would then necessarily benefit if output of that product were *reduced*. It would lose the marginal benefit, but save the marginal social cost; and since MSC > MB, society would come out ahead. We conclude that:

Where the firm's activity causes detrimental externalities, free markets will leave us in a situation where marginal benefits are less than marginal social costs. Smaller outputs than those that maximize profits will be socially desirable.

We have already indicated why this is so. Private enterprise has no motivation to take into account costs that it causes to others but for which it does not have to pay. So goods that cause such externalities will be produced in undesirably large amounts by private firms. For precisely analogous reasons:

Where the firm's activity generates beneficial externalities, free markets will produce too little output. Society would be better off with larger output levels.

These principles can be illustrated with the aid of Figure 29–2. This diagram repeats the two basic curves needed for the analysis of the equilibrium of the firm: a marginal revenue curve and a marginal cost curve (see Chapter 21). These represent the *private* costs and revenues accruing to a particular firm (in this case, a paper mill). The mill's maximum profit is attained with 100,000 tons of output corresponding to the intersection between the marginal cost and marginal revenue curves (point *A*). Now suppose that the factory's wastes pollute a nearby waterway, so that its production creates a detrimental externality whose cost the owner does not himself pay. Then marginal social cost must be higher than marginal private cost, as shown in the diagram.

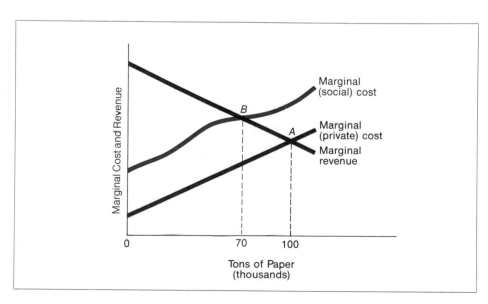

Figure 29–2
EQUILIBRIUM OF A FIRM WHOSE OUTPUT PRODUCES DETRIMENTAL EXTERNALITIES (POLLUTION)
The firm's profit-maximizing output, at which its marginal private cost and its marginal private revenue are equal, is 100,000 tons. But if the firm paid all the social costs of its output instead of shifting some of them to others, its marginal cost curve would be the curve labeled "marginal (social) cost." Then it would pay the firm to reduce its output to 70,000 tons, thereby reducing the pollution it causes.

Notice that if instead of being able to impose the external costs on others the mill's owner were forced to pay them himself, his own private marginal cost curve would correspond to the higher of the two curves shown. His output of the polluting commodity would then fall to 70,000 tons, corresponding to point B, the intersection between the marginal revenue curve and the marginal *social* cost curve. But because the firm does not in fact pay for the pollution damage its output causes, it produces an output (100,000 tons) that is larger than the output it would produce if the cost imposed on the community were instead borne by the firm (70,000 tons). The same sort of diagram can be used to show that the opposite relationship will hold when the firm's activity produces beneficial externalities. The firm will produce less of its beneficial output than it would if it were rewarded fully for the benefits that its activities yield.

But these results can perhaps be seen more clearly with the help of a production possibilities frontier diagram similar to that in Figure 29–1. In Figure 29–3 we see the frontier for two industries: electricity generation, which causes air pollution (a detrimental externality), and tulip growing, which makes an area more attractive (a beneficial externality). We have just seen that detrimental externalities make marginal social cost greater than marginal private cost. Hence, if the electric company charges a price equal to its own marginal (private) cost, that price will be less than the true marginal (social) cost. Similarly, in tulip growing, a price equal to marginal private cost will be above the true marginal cost to society.

We saw earlier in the chapter that an industry that charges a price above marginal cost will reduce quantity demanded through this high price, and so it will produce an output too small for an efficient allocation of resources. The opposite will be true for an industry whose price is below marginal social cost. In terms of Figure 29–3, suppose point B again represents the efficient allocation of resources, involving the production of E kilowatt hours of electricity and T dozen tulips. Because the polluting electric company charges a price below marginal social cost, it will produce more than E kilowatt hours of electricity. Similarly, because tulip growers generate external benefits, and so charge a price above marginal social cost, they will produce less than T dozen tulips. The economy will end up with the resource allocation represented by point K rather than that represented by point B. There will be too much smoky electricity production and too little attractive tulip growing. More generally:

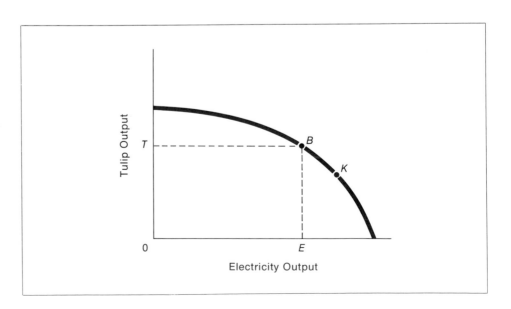

An industry that generates detrimental externalities will have a marginal social cost higher than its marginal private cost. If its price is equal to its own marginal private cost, it will therefore be below the true marginal cost to society. The market mechanism thereby tends to encourage inefficiently large outputs of products that cause detrimental externalities. The opposite is true of products that cause beneficial externalities—private industry will provide inefficiently small quantities of these products.

The Universality of Externalities

Externalities occur throughout the economy. Many are beneficial. A factory that hires unskilled or semiskilled laborers gives them on-the-job training and provides the external benefit of better workers to future employers. Benefits to others are also generated when firms produce useful but unpatentable products, or even patentable products that can be imitated by others to some degree. Detrimental externalities are also widespread. The emission of air and water pollutants by factories, cars, and airplanes is the source of some of our most pressing environmental problems. The abandonment of buildings causes the quality of a neighborhood to deteriorate, and is the source of serious externalities for the city.

Externalities lie at the heart of some of society's most pressing problems: the problems of the cities, the environment, research policy, and a variety of other critical issues. For this reason, the concept of externalities is one of our 12 Ideas for Beyond the Final Exam. It is a subject that will recur again and again in this book as we discuss some of these problems in greater detail.

Government Policy and Externalities

Because of the market's inability to cope with externalities, governments have found it appropriate to support activities that are felt to generate external benefits. Education is subsidized not only because it helps promote equal opportunity for all citizens but also because it is believed to generate beneficial externalities. For example, educated people normally commit fewer crimes than uneducated people, so the more we educate people, the less we will need to spend on crime prevention. Also, academic research that has been provided partly as a byproduct of the educational system often benefits the entire population. We have consequently come to believe that if education were offered only by profit-making insititutions, the output of these beneficial services would be provided at less than the optimal level.

Similarly, governments have recently begun to impose fines on companies that contribute heavily to air and water pollution. This approach to policy is in fact suggested by the economists' standard analysis of the effects of externalities upon resource allocation. The basic problem, as we have seen, is that in the presence of externalities, the price system fails to allocate resources efficiently. Resources are used for which no price is charged, and benefits are offered without financial compensation. As a result, with detrimental externalities, for example, the price does not cover the entire marginal social cost. Consequently:

One effective way to deal with externalities may be through the use of taxes and subsidies.

For example, firms that generate beneficial externalities should be given a subsidy per unit of their output equal to the difference between their marginal social costs and their marginal private costs. Similarly, those that generate detrimental externalities should be taxed on analogous terms, so that the firm that creates such externalities will have to pay the entire marginal cost it imposes on society. In terms of Figure 29–2, after paying the tax, the firm's marginal private cost curve will be shifted up until it coincides with its marginal social cost curve, and price can once again be set in a manner consistent with an efficient resource allocation.

While there is much to be said for this approach in principle, it often is not easy to implement in practice. Social costs are rarely easy to estimate, partly because they are so widely diffused throughout the community (everyone in the city is affected by pollution) and partly because many of the costs and benefits (effects on health, unpleasantness of living in smog) are not readily assessed in monetary terms. The pros and cons of this approach and the alternative policies available for the control of externalities will be discussed in greater detail in Chapter 31 on environmental problems.

Public Goods

A **public good** is a commodity or service whose benefits are *not depleted* by an additional user and for which it is generally difficult or *impossible to exclude* people from its benefits, even if they are unwilling to pay for it. In contrast, a **private good** is characterized by both excludability and depletability.

Another area in which the market may fail to perform adequately is in the provision of **public goods.** It is easiest to explain what is meant by public goods by contrasting them with the sort of commodities called **private goods,** which are at the opposite end of the spectrum.

Private goods are characterized by two important attributes. One is called **excludability,** meaning that anyone who does not pay for the good can be excluded from enjoying its benefits. If you do not buy a ticket, you are excluded from the ball game. If you do not pay for an electric guitar, the storekeeper will not give it to you. But some goods or services are such that, if they are provided to anyone, they automatically become available to many other persons whom it is difficult, if not impossible, to exclude from the benefits. If a street is cleared of snow, everyone who uses the street benefits, regardless of who paid for the snowplow. If a country provides a strong military establishment, everyone receives its protection, even persons who do not happen to want it.

The other property that characterizes private goods but not public goods is **depletability.** If you eat a steak or use up a gallon of gasoline, there is that much less beef or fuel in the world available for others to use. Your consumption depletes the supply available for other people, either temporarily or permanently. But a pure public good is like the legendary widow's jar of oil, which always remained full no matter how many people used it. Once the snow has been removed from a street, the improved driving conditions are available to every driver who uses that street, whether 10 or 1000 cars pass that way. One passing car does not make the road less snow-free for another. The same is true of the spraying of swamps near a town to kill disease-bearing mosquitoes. The cost of the spraying is the same whether the town contains 10,000 or 20,000 persons. A resident of the town who benefits from this service does not deplete its advantages to others.

A public good is defined as a good that lacks both of these attributes— excludability and depletability. Notice two important implications of this definition. First, since nonpaying users cannot be excluded from enjoying a public good, suppliers of such goods will find it *difficult or impossible to collect fees* for the benefits they provide. This is the so-called "free rider" problem. How many people, for example, will *voluntarily* cough up $3000 a year to support our national defense establishment? Yet this is roughly what it costs, per American family. Services like national defense and public health, where excludability is simply impossible, *cannot* be provided by private enterprise because no one will pay for what he can get free. Since private firms are not in the business of giving services away, the supply of nonexcludable public goods must be left to government authorities and nonprofit institutions.

The second thing we notice is that, since the supply of a public good is not depleted by an additional user, *the marginal cost of serving an additional user is zero.* With zero marginal cost, the basic principle of optimal resource allocation calls for provision of public goods and services to anyone who wants them *at no charge.* In a word, not only is it often *impossible* to charge a market price for a public good, it is often *undesirable* as well. Any nonzero price would discourage some users from enjoying the public good; but this would be inefficient, since one more person's enjoyment of the good costs society nothing. To summarize:

It is usually *not possible* to charge a price for a pure public good because people cannot be excluded from enjoying its benefits. It may also be *undesirable* to charge a price for it because that would discourage some people from using it even though using it does not deplete its supply. For both these reasons we find government supplying many public goods. Without government intervention, public goods simply would not be provided.

Referring back to our example in Figure 29–1, if hospital linens were a public good and their production were left to private enterprise, the economy would end up at point *A* on the graph, with zero production of hospital linens and far more output of handkerchiefs than is called for by efficient allocation (point *B*). Usually, communities have not been content to let that happen; and today a quite substantial proportion of government expenditure, indeed the bulk of municipal budgets, is devoted to the financing of public goods or to services believed to generate substantial external benefits. National defense, public health, police and fire protection, and research are among the services provided by governments because they offer beneficial externalities or because they are public goods.

The Cost Disease of the Service Sector

Our next problem may or may not be considered a failure of the market mechanism. While private standards of living have increased and material possessions have grown, the community has simultaneously been forced to cope with deterioration in a variety of services, both public and private. Throughout the world, streets and subways have grown increasingly dirty. Public safety has declined as crimes of violence have become more commonplace in almost every major city. Bus and train service has been reduced. In the middle of the nineteenth century in suburban London, there were twelve mail deliveries per day on weekdays and one on Sundays. We all know what has happened to postal services since then.

There have been parallel cutbacks in the quality of private services. Doctors have become increasingly reluctant to visit patients at home; in many areas, the house call, which fifty years ago was a commonplace event, has now become something that occurs only in a life and death emergency, if even then. Another example, though undoubtedly a matter for less general concern, is what has happened to restaurants. Although they are reluctant to publicize the fact, a great number of restaurants, including some of the most elegant and expensive, serve preprepared, frozen, and reheated meals. They charge high prices for what amounts to little more than TV dinners.

There is no single explanation for all these matters. It would be naïve to offer any cut-and-dried hypothesis purporting to account for phenomena as diverse as the rise in crime and violence throughout Western society and the deterioration in postal services. Yet at least one common influence underlies all these problems of deterioration in service quality—an influence that is economic in character and that may be expected to grow more serious with the passage of time. The issue has been called the **cost disease of the personal services.**

Consider these facts. During the inflationary 1970s, virtually all costs in the economy rose; but the costs of services rose even faster than most. During earlier periods, when the nation's price level was nearly constant, service costs nevertheless rose at a significant rate. One typical example will illustrate the point. Between 1945 and 1965, the cost of public education per pupil day rose, on the average, 4 percent a year *more rapidly* than the general price level. This means that every year—even when other prices in the economy were not increasing—the cost of education was rising. These cost differentials were cumulative and compounded so that over the two decades as a whole the cost of education per pupil rose more than 200 percent relative to the cost of manufactured goods. By the end of the period, the cost of an education was therefore equivalent to twice as many cars or refrigerators as it was at the beginning. A similar pattern has been followed by the costs of other services, such as health care, libraries, doctor's fees, and theater tickets.

One serious consequence of this phenomenon is that a terrible financial burden has been placed on municipal budgets by the soaring costs of education, health care, and police and fire protection. But what accounts for these ever-increasing costs? Are they attributable to inefficiencies in government management or to political corruption? Perhaps, in part, to both. But there is another reason—one that could not be avoided by any municipal administration no matter what its integrity and efficiency—and one that affects private industry just as severely as it does the public sector. The problem stems from the basic nature of services. Most services require direct contact between those who consume the service and those who provide it. Doctors, teachers, and librarians are all engaged in activities that require direct person-to-person contact. Moreover, the quality of the service deteriorates if less time is provided by doctors, teachers, and librarians to each user of their services.

In contrast, the buyer of an automobile usually has no idea who worked on it, and could not care less how much labor time went into its production. A labor-saving innovation in auto production need not imply a reduction in product quality. As a result, it has proved far easier for technological change to save labor in manufacturing than in providing services. While output per hour of labor in manufacturing and agriculture went up between 1948 and 1978 at an average rate of something like 3 percent a year, the number of teacher hours per pupil actually *increased* because classes became smaller. These disparate performances in productivity have grave consequences for prices. When wages in manufacturing rise 3 percent, the cost of manufactured products is not affected because increased productivity makes up for the rise in wages. But the nature of services makes it very difficult to introduce labor-saving devices in the service sector. So a 3-percent rise in the wages of teachers or police officers is not offset by higher productivity, and must lead to an equivalent rise in municipal budgets. Similarly, a 3-percent rise in the wages of hairdressers must lead beauty salons to raise their prices.

 In the long run, wages and salaries throughout the economy tend to go up and down together, for otherwise the activity whose wage rate falls seriously behind will tend to lose its labor force. Auto workers and police officers will see their wages rise at roughly the same rate in the long run. But if productivity on the assembly line advances while productivity in the patrol car does not, then police protection must grow ever more expensive as time goes on.

This phenomenon is another of our 12 Ideas for Beyond the Final Exam. Because productivity improvements are very difficult for most services, their cost can be expected to rise faster, year in, year out, than the cost of manufactured goods. Over a period of several decades, this difference in the growth rate in costs of the two sectors can add up, making services enormously more expensive compared with manufactured goods. This is the *cost disease of the service sector* and it helps explain the chronic financial problems of governments.

If services continue to grow ever more expensive in comparison to goods, the implications for life in the future are profound indeed. This analysis portends a world in which the typical home contains luxuries and furnishings that we can hardly imagine; but it is a home surrounded by garbage and perhaps by violence. It portends a future in which the services of doctors, teachers, and police officers are increasingly mass-produced and impersonal, and in which the arts and crafts are increasingly supplied only by amateurs because the cost of professional work in these fields is too high. If this is the shape of the economy a hundred years from now, it will be significantly different from our own, and some persons will undoubtedly question whether the quality of life has increased commensurately with the increased material prosperity. Some may even ask whether it has increased at all.

Is this future inevitable? Is there anything that can be done to escape it? The answer is that it is by no means inevitable. To see why, we must first recognize that the source of the problem, paradoxically, is the growth in productivity of our economy—or rather, the *unevenness* of that growth. Trash removal costs go up not because garbage collectors become less efficient but because labor in car manufacturing becomes *more* efficient, thus enhancing the sanitation worker's value as a potential employee on the automotive assembly line. His wages must go up to keep him at his job of garbage removal. But increasing productivity can never make a nation poorer. It can never make it unable to afford things it was able to afford in the past. Increasing productivity means that we can afford more of *all* things—medical care and education as well as TV sets and electric toothbrushes.

The role of services in our future depends on how we order our priorities. If we value services sufficiently, we can have more and better services—at *some* sacrifice in the rate of growth of manufactured goods. Whether that is a good choice for the community is not for economists to say. But it is important for the community to recognize that it *does* have a choice, and that if it fails to exercise it, matters are very likely to proceed relentlessly in the direction they are now headed—toward a society in which there is an enormous abundance of material goods and a great scarcity of many of the things that most people now consider primary requisites for a high quality of life.

Allocation of Resources Between Present and Future

In principle, the market mechanism should be as efficient in allocating resources between present and future uses as it is in allocating resources among different outputs at any one time. If future demands for a particular commodity, say computers for the home, are expected to be higher than they are today, it will pay manufacturers to plan now to build the necessary plant and equipment so they will be ready to turn out the computers when the expanded market materializes. More resources are thereby allocated to future consumption.

The allocation of resources between present and future can be analyzed with the aid of an opportunity cost diagram just like Figure 29–1. Suppose the issue is how much labor and capital to devote to producing consumer goods and how much to devote to construction of factories to produce output in the future. Then, instead of handkerchiefs and linens, the graph will show consumer goods and number of factories on its axes, but otherwise it will be exactly the same as Figure 29–1. Such a graph appears here as Figure 29–4.

The profit motive directs the flow of resources between one time period and another just as it handles resource allocation among different industries in a given period. The profit motive directs resources to those products *and those time periods* in which high prices promise to make output most profitable. But one feature of the process of allocation of resources among different time periods distinguishes it from the process of allocation among industries. This is the special role that the *interest rate* plays in allocation among the periods. If the receipt of a given amount of money is delayed until some time in the future, the recipient suffers an *opportunity cost*—the interest that the money could have earned if it had been received earlier and invested. For example, if the rate of interest is 9 percent and you can persuade someone who owes you money to make a $100 payment one year earlier than originally planned, you come out $9 ahead. Put the other way, if the rate of interest is 9 percent and the payment of $100 is postponed one year, you lose the opportunity to earn $9. Thus, the rate of interest determines the size of the opportunity cost to a recipient who gets money at some date in the future instead of now. For this reason, as we saw in Chapter 8:

Low interest rates will persuade people to invest more now, since investments yield many of their benefits in the future. Thus, more resources will be devoted to the future if interest rates are low. Similarly, high interest rates make investment, with its benefits in the future, less attractive. And so high interest rates will tend to increase the use of resources for current output at the expense of reduced future outputs.

Figure 29–4
PRODUCTION POSSIBILI-
TIES FRONTIER BETWEEN
PRESENT AND FUTURE
With a given quantity of resources, the economy can produce one million cars for immediate use and build no factories for the future (point *A*). Alternatively, at the opposite extreme (point *B*), it can build 10 factories where products will become available in the future, while no cars are produced for current consumption. At points in between on the frontier, such as *C*, the economy will produce a combination of some cars for present consumption and some factories for future use.

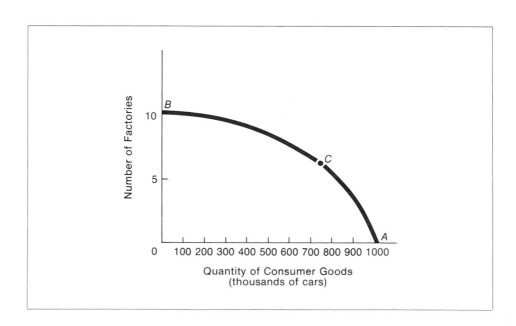

On the surface, it seems that the price system can allocate resources among different time periods in the way consumers prefer. For the supply of and demand for loans, which determine the interest rate, reflects the public's preferences between present and future. Suppose, for example, that the public suddenly became more interested in future consumption (say, people wanted to save more for their old age). The supply of funds available for borrowing would increase and interest rates would tend to fall. This would stimulate investment and add to the future output of goods at the expense of current consumption.

But several questions have been raised about the effectiveness, in practice, with which the market mechanism allocates resources among different time periods. One thing that makes economists uneasy is that the rate of interest, which is the price that controls allocation over time, is also used for a variety of other purposes. As we saw in Chapter 14, the interest rate can be used to deal with business fluctuations. And in Chapter 38 we shall see that it plays an analogous role in international monetary relations. As a result, governments frequently manipulate interest rates deliberately. In so doing, policymakers seem to give little thought to the effects on the allocation of resources between present and future, and so one may well worry whether the resulting interest rates are the most appropriate ones.

Second, it has been suggested that even in the absence of government manipulation of the interest rate, the market may devote too many resources to immediate consumption. One British economist, the late A. C. Pigou, argued simply that people suffer from "a defective telescopic faculty"—that they are too short-sighted to give adequate weight to the future. A "bird in hand" point of view leads people to care so much about the present that they sacrifice the legitimate interests of the future. As a result, too much goes into today's consumption and too little into investment for tomorrow.

A third reason why the free market may not invest enough for the future is that investment projects, like the construction of a new factory, are much greater risks to the investor than to the community. Even if a factory falls into someone else's hands through bankruptcy, it will probably go on turning out goods. But the profits will not go to the investor or his heirs. Therefore, the loss to the individual investor will be far greater than the loss to society. On such grounds, it is asserted, one may expect individual investment for the future to fall short of the amounts that are socially optimal; investments too risky to be worthwhile to any group of private individuals may nevertheless be advantageous to society as a whole.

Fourth, our economy shortchanges the future when it despoils irreplaceable natural resources, exterminates whole species of plants and animals, floods canyons, "develops" attractive areas into acres of potential slums, and so on. Worst of all, industry, the military, and individuals bequeath a ticking time bomb to the future when they leave behind lethal and slow-acting residues, such as nuclear wastes, which may remain dangerous for hundreds or even thousands of years and whose disposal containers are likely to fall apart long before their contents lose their lethal qualities. Such actions are essentially **irreversible.** If a factory is not built this year, the deficiency in facilities provided for the future can be remedied by building it next year. But a canyon, once destroyed, can never be replaced. For this reason:

Many economists believe that *irreversible decisions* have a very special significance and must *not* be left entirely in the hands of private firms and individuals.

Recently, however, several writers have questioned the general conclusion that the free market will not tend to invest enough for the future. They have pointed out that the prosperity of our economy has grown fairly steadily from one decade to the next, and that there is every reason to expect future generations to have real incomes and an abundance of consumer goods far greater than our own. Pressures to increase investment for the future then may be like taking from the poor to give to the rich—a sort of backward Robin Hood redistribution of income.

Some Other Sources of Market Failure

We have now completed our survey of the most important imperfections of the market mechanism. But that list is not complete, and it can never be. In this imperfect world nothing ever works out ideally, and by examining anything with a sufficiently powerful microscope one can always detect some more blemishes. However, some of the items we have omitted from our list may not be of minor importance. Let us therefore conclude with a brief mention of two of them.

Imperfect Information
The analysis of the virtues of the market mechanism in Chapter 23 assumed that consumers and producers have all the information they need for their decision making. But in reality things are very different. Consumers in particular suffer from lack of information. When buying a house or a second-hand car, or when selecting a doctor, consumers are vividly reminded of how little they know about what they are purchasing. "Let the buyer beware" is the old motto describing the hazards to which consumers are exposed. Obviously, if participants in the market are ill-informed, they will not always make the optimal decisions described in our theoretical models.

Yet, not all economists agree that imperfect information is really a failure of the market mechanism. They point out that information, too, is a commodity that costs money to produce. Neither firms nor consumers have complete information because it would be irrational for them to spend the enormous amounts needed to get it. As always, the optimum is a compromise. One should, ideally, stop buying information at the point where the marginal benefit of further information is no greater than its cost. With this amount of information, the business executive or the consumer is able to make what have been referred to as "optimally imperfect" decisions.

Moral Hazard
Another problem besetting the market mechanism that has received a good deal of attention is associated with the availability of insurance. Insurance—the provision of protection against risk—is viewed by economists as a commodity like shoes or the provision of information. And like most commodities it can benefit both sellers and buyers. But it also creates a problem by encouraging the very risks against which it provides protection. For example, if an individual has jewelry which is fully insured against theft, she has little motivation to take steps to protect it against burglars. She may, for example, fail to lock it up in a safe-deposit box, and this failure makes burglary a more attractive and lucrative profession. This problem—the tendency of insurance to encourage the source of risk—is called **moral hazard,** and it makes a free market in insurance hard to operate.

On the Role of Government

This chapter has pointed out some of the most noteworthy failures of the invisible hand. We seem forced to the conclusion that a market economy, if left entirely to itself, is likely to produce results which are, at least in some respects, far from

The Politics of Economic Policy

In 1978, Alfred Kahn, an economist in the Carter administration, advocated reducing pollution by raising the tax on leaded gasoline and lowering the tax on unleaded gasoline. *The Washington Post*, in an editorial excerpted below, agreed that Kahn's idea was a sound one, but worried about what might emerge from Congress:

GROPPER, William. *The Senate.* (1935)

If the administration adopts the Kahn plan, recent history offers a pretty clear view of the rest of the story.

Mr. Kahn will draft a one-page bill to raise the tax on the one kind of gas and lower it on the other. But the White House political staff will immediately point out that his draft fails to address profound questions of social equity. What about the poor, who buy unleaded gas because it's cheaper? What about young people driving old cars? What about the inhabitants of lower Louisiana, who need their outboard motors to get around the swamps and bayous? There will have to be a rebate formula. It will take into account each family's income, the number and ages of its various automobiles and the distance from its front doorstep to the bus stop. The legislative draftsmen at the Energy Department have had a lot of experience with that kind of formula, and eventually the 53-page bill will be sent to Congress. . . .

The real fun will start when it arrives at the Senate Finance Committee. First the committee will add tuition tax credits for families with children in private schools. Then, warming to its work, it will vote import quotas on straw hats from Hong Kong, beef from Argentina and automobiles from Japan. At that point Chairman Russell Long (D-La.) will complain publicly that the committee is running out of control. As if to prove the accusation, it will then add several obscure but pregnant provisions that seem to refer to the tax treatment of certain oil wells in the Gulf states. When the 268-page bill comes to the Senate floor, the administration will narrowly manage to defeat an amendment to improve business confidence by repealing the capital-gains tax and returning to the gold standard.

When the bill gets back to the House, liberal Democrats will denounce it as an outrage and declare all-out war. They will succeed in getting all references to gasoline taxes and the environment stricken—but not, unfortunately, the import quotas or the obscure tax changes for the oil wells. By the time the staff of the Joint Committee on Taxation has straightened out a few technical difficulties, the bill will run to 417 pages and Ralph Nader will be calling on President Carter to veto it. But the feeling at the White House will be that Congress has worked so long and hard on the bill that he has no choice but to sign it. By the time the bill is finally enacted, late in the autumn of 1980, Mr. Kahn might well wish he had chosen some other instrument of policy.

SOURCE: *The Washington Post*, December 26,1978. Copyright *The Washington Post*.

---

ideal. In our discussion we have noted either directly or by implication some of the things government can do to correct these deficiencies. But the fact that government often *can* intervene in the operation of the economy in a constructive way does not always mean that it actually *will* succeed in doing so. The fact is that governments cannot be relied upon to behave ideally any more than business firms can be expected to do so.

It is apparently hard to make this point in a way that is suitably balanced. Commentators too often stake out one extreme position or the other. Those who think the market mechanism is inherently unfair and biased by the greed of those who run its enterprises seem to think of government as the savior that can cure all economic ills. Those who deplore government intervention are prone to consider the public sector as the home of every sort of inefficiency, graft, and bureaucratic stultification. The truth, as usual, lies in between. Governments are inherently imperfect, like the humans who compose them. The political process leads to compromises which sometimes bear little resemblance to rational decisions. For example, legislators' versions of the policies suggested by economic analysis are sometimes mere caricatures of the economists' ideas. (For a satirical editorial illustrating this point, see the box at the top of this page.) Yet, often the problems engendered by an unfettered economy are too serious to be left to the free market. The problems of dealing with inflation, environmental decay, and the provision of public goods are cases in point. In such instances, government intervention is likely to yield substantial benefits to the general public. But in other areas the market mechanism as described in previous chapters is likely to work reasonably well, and what small imperfections there are do not constitute adequate justification for intervention. In any event, *even where government intervention is appropriate, it is essential to consider marketlike instruments as the means to correct the deficiencies in the workings of the market mechanism.* The tax incentives described in our discussion of externalities are an outstanding example of what we have in mind.

Evaluative Comments

This chapter, like Chapter 23, has offered a rather unbalanced assessment of the market mechanism. We spent Chapter 23 extolling the market's virtues and spent this chapter cataloguing its vices. We come out, as in the nursery rhyme, concluding that the market is either very, very good or it is horrid. There seems to be nothing moderate about its performance. As a means of achieving efficiency in the production of ordinary consumer goods and of responding to changes in consumer preferences, it is unparalleled. It is, in fact, difficult to overstate the accomplishments of the price system in these areas. On the other hand, it has proven itself unable to cope with business fluctuations, income inequality, or the consequences of monopoly. It has proved to be a very poor allocator of resources among outputs that generate external costs and external benefits, and it has shown itself completely incapable of arranging for the provision of public goods. Some of the most urgent problems that plague our society—the deterioration of services in the cities, the despoliation of our atmosphere, the social unrest attributable to poverty—can be ascribed in part to one or another of these shortcomings of the market system.

Most economists conclude from these observations that while the market mechanism is virtually irreplaceable, the public interest nevertheless requires considerable modifications in the way it works. Proposals designed to deal directly with the problems of poverty, monopoly, and resource allocation over time abound in the economic literature. All of them call for the government to intervene in the economy, either by supplying directly those goods and services that, it is believed, private enterprise does not supply in adequate amounts, or by seeking to influence the workings of the economy more indirectly through regulation. Many of these programs have been discussed in earlier chapters; others will be encountered in chapters yet to come.

Summary

1. There are at least seven major imperfections in the workings of the market mechanism: inequality of income distribution, fluctuations in economic activity (inflation and unemployment), monopolistic output restrictions, beneficial and detrimental externalities, inadequate provision of public goods, deteriorating quality and rising costs of services, and finally, misallocation of resources between present and future.

2. Efficient resource allocation is basically a matter of balancing the benefits of producing more of one good against the benefits of devoting the required inputs to the production of some other good.

3. A detrimental externality occurs when an economic activity incidentally does harm to others; a beneficial externality occurs when an economic activity incidentally creates benefits for others.

4. When an activity causes a detrimental externality, the marginal social cost of the activity (including the harm it does to others) must be greater than the

marginal private cost to those who carry on the activity. The opposite will be true when a beneficial externality occurs.

5. If manufacture of a product causes detrimental externalities, its price will generally not include all the marginal social cost it causes, since part of the cost will be borne by others. The opposite is true for beneficial externalities.

6. The market will therefore tend to overallocate resources to the production of goods that cause detrimental externalities and underallocate resources to the production of goods that create beneficial externalities. This is one of the 12 Ideas for Beyond the Final Exam.

7. A public good is defined by economists as a commodity that (like clean air) is not depleted by additional users and from whose use it is difficult to exclude anyone, even those who refuse to pay for it. A private good, in contrast, is characterized by both excludability and depletability.

8. Free-enterprise firms generally will not produce a public good even if it is extremely useful to the community, because they cannot charge money for the use of the good.

9. Because personal services—such as education, medical care and police protection—are not amenable to labor-saving innovations, they suffer from a cost disease whose symptom is that their costs tend to rise considerably faster than costs in the economy as a whole. This cost disease of the service sector is another of our 12 Ideas for Beyond the Final Exam.

10. Many observers feel that the market often shortchanges the future, particularly when it makes irreversible decisions that destroy natural resources.

Concepts for Review

Opportunity cost
Resource misallocation
Production possibilities frontier
Price above or below marginal cost
Externalities (detrimental and beneficial)

Marginal social cost and marginal private cost
Public goods
Private goods
Excludability

Depletability
Cost disease of the personal services
Irreversible decisions
Moral hazard

Questions for Discussion

1. Specifically, what is the opportunity cost to society of a pair of shoes? Why may not the price of those shoes adequately represent that opportunity cost?

2. Suppose that because of a new disease that attacks coffee plants, far more labor and other inputs are required to raise a pound of coffee than before. How might that affect the efficient allocation of resources between tea and coffee? Why? How would the prices of coffee and tea react in a free market?

3. Give some examples of goods whose production causes detrimental externalities and some examples of goods that create beneficial externalities.

4. Compare cleaning an office building with cleaning the atmosphere of a city. Which is a public good and which is a private good? Why?

5. Give some other examples of public goods, and discuss in each case why additional users do not deplete them and why it is difficult to exclude people from using them.

6. Think about the goods and services that your local government provides. Which of these are "public goods" as economists use the term?

7. In recent decades, college tuition costs have risen faster than the general price level even though the wages of college professors have failed to keep pace with the price level. Can you explain why?

Taxation, Government Spending, and Resource Allocation

30

The taxing power of the government must be used to provide revenues for legitimate government purposes. It must not be used to regulate the economy or bring about social change.

RONALD REAGAN (1981)

The last chapter examined several reasons why the government might want to interfere with the workings of the market mechanism. Some of these interferences involve levying taxes; for example, we noted that taxes may be useful in correcting misallocations of resources caused by externalities. Other interferences involve direct spending by government—provision of national defense is a good example—and this spending, in turn, requires that taxes be levied to raise the necessary revenue. These, then, are the two main reasons for taxes: to improve resource allocation and to raise revenue for what President Reagan termed "legitimate government purposes." Of the two, it is clear that the revenue-raising function is by far the more important in practice. So this chapter opens with a brief look at the things governments in the United States spend money on; or, the reasons why government needs revenue. We then turn to the types of taxes that are used to raise this revenue, the effects these taxes have on the allocation of resources and the distribution of income, and the principles that distinguish "good" from "bad" taxes.

Government Spending: An Overview

During the 1982 fiscal year, the federal government spent about $700 billion. This sum is literally beyond comprehension; perhaps the best way to understand it is to note that federal spending amounted to over $3000 for every man, woman, and child in America. Figure 30–1 shows where the money went. More than one-third went for so-called *income security* programs, which include both social insurance programs, like social security and unemployment compensation, and programs designed to assist the poor. Over one-quarter went for *national defense*. If we add interest on the national debt, these three functions alone accounted for almost 75 percent of federal spending. The rest went for health and education (about 14 percent of the budget), and for support of such activities as science, agriculture, housing, and transportation. Government spending at the state and local levels was about two-thirds as large as federal spending. Education claimed the lion's share of state and local government budgets (39 percent), with health and public welfare programs in second place (25 percent).

It is interesting to relate these spending programs to last chapter's discussion of the reasons for government intervention in the marketplace. Income security

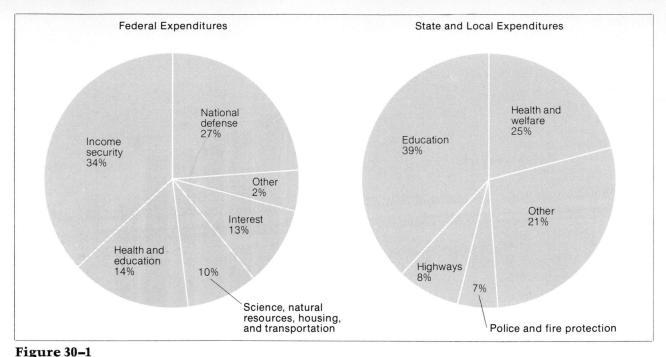

Figure 30–1
THE ALLOCATION OF GOVERNMENT EXPENDITURES
These graphs show how the government dollar is spent. The federal government spends most of its money on national defense (27 percent) and on transfer payments to retirees, the poor, the unemployed, and veterans (34 percent). Most of state and local government spending goes for education (39 percent), with health and welfare expenditures (25 percent) in second place.

and welfare programs are designed to *redistribute income:* from the young to the old (social security), from the nonpoor to the poor (welfare programs), from the employed to the unemployed (unemployment insurance), and so on. National defense is the classic example of a *public good.* Some of the other spending programs can be rationalized on the grounds that they provide *beneficial externalities* (education, support of research), though critics of "big government" question how strong these externalities really are. A variety of other public services (the post office, various transportation programs, and so on) are difficult to rationalize on any of the grounds enumerated in Chapter 29; but, for one reason or another, governments have not left provision of these services to the free market. We should not lose sight of the fact that political, not economic, considerations often dictate what services the government will provide.

Taxes in America

To finance this array of goods and services, taxes are required. Sometimes it seems that the tax collector is everywhere. We have income and payroll taxes withheld from our paychecks, sales taxes added to our purchases, property taxes levied on our homes; we pay gasoline taxes, liquor taxes, and so on and on. According to the old saying, nothing is certain but death and taxes. And, if there is one thing that all Americans seem to agree on it is that there are too many taxes and that they are too high.

Yet by international standards, Americans are among the most lightly taxed people in the industrialized world. Figure 30–2 compares the fraction of income paid in taxes in the United States with that paid by residents of other industrialized nations. The tax collector clearly is much gentler here than in Sweden and

Figure 30–2
THE BURDEN OF TAXA-
TION IN SELECTED
COUNTRIES, 1978
Americans are not heavily
taxed in comparison with the
citizens of other advanced
industrial countries. The
Swedes and the Dutch, for
example, pay far higher taxes
than we do. The Japanese,
however, pay much lower
taxes.
SOURCE: *National Accounts of
OECD Countries.* 1961–1978,
Volume II.

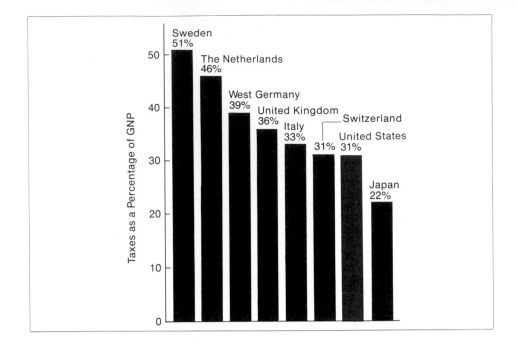

the Netherlands, although Americans do pay substantially more taxes than do the Japanese.

Another way to put the burden of taxation into perspective is to study how it has changed over time. Figure 30–3 helps you to do this by charting the behavior of both federal and state and local taxes *as a percentage of GNP* since 1929. The figure shows that the share of federal taxes in GNP has been rather steady for about 35 years. It climbed from less than 4 percent in 1929 to 20 percent during

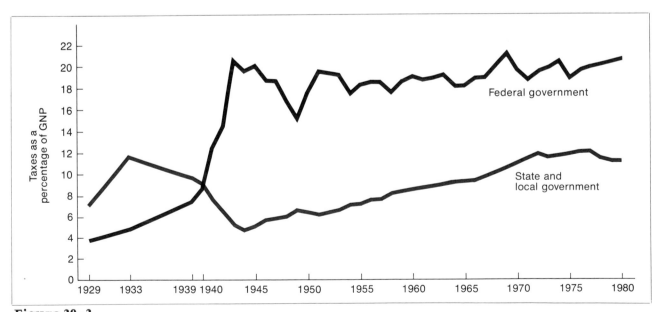

Figure 30–3
TAXES AS A PERCENTAGE OF GROSS NATIONAL PRODUCT
Federal taxes have accounted for a fairly constant fraction of GNP since the 1940s. State and local taxes, however, absorbed an ever-increasing portion from the 1940s until the 1970s.
SOURCE: Economic Report of the President, 1981.

World War II, fell back to 15 percent in the postwar period, and has fluctuated in the 18 to 20 percent range ever since. It simply is not true that the federal government has been thrusting its hand deeper and deeper into our pockets each year. But the same cannot be said of state and local governments.

The share of GNP taken in taxes by the federal government has not increased since World War II. There was, however, an unmistakable upward trend in the fraction of GNP taken in state and local taxes until the late 1970s.

This fraction climbed from 6.6 percent in 1950 to 8.6 percent in 1960, and to 11.2 percent in both 1970 and 1980. This trend worries many tax reformers who, for reasons to be explained in this chapter, view the federal tax system as far superior to that of the states and localities.

The main reason for the faster growth of state and local taxes than of federal taxes seems to be the differing expenditure patterns of the various levels of government. Apart from national defense, the federal government spends very little on purchases of goods and services; but direct provision of public services accounts for the preponderant share of state and local budgets. It seems that citizens demand more and better schools, hospitals, parks, and other public services as the economy gets richer. And—for reasons explained in the last chapter—these services become more and more expensive each year. The resulting strain on state and local budgets has forced these units of government into tax increases that the federal government has, by and large, managed to avoid.

Progressive, Proportional, and Regressive Taxes

Economists like to classify taxes according to whether they are *progressive*, *proportional*, or *regressive*. Under a **progressive tax,** the fraction of income paid in taxes *rises* as a person's income increases. Under a **proportional tax,** this fraction is constant. And under a **regressive tax,** the fraction of income paid to the tax collector *declines* as income rises. Since the fraction of income paid in taxes is called the **average tax rate,** these definitions can be formulated as they are in the margin. Often, however, the *average* tax rate is less interesting than the **marginal tax rate,** which is the fraction of each *additional* dollar that must be paid to the tax collector. The reason, as we will see, is that the marginal tax rate, not the average tax rate, most directly affects economic incentives.

A **progressive tax** is one in which the average tax rate paid by an individual rises as his income rises. A **proportional tax** is one in which the average tax rate is the same at all income levels. A **regressive tax** is one in which the average tax rate falls as income rises.

Direct Versus Indirect Taxes

Another way to classify taxes is to divide them into two broad categories: **direct taxes** and **indirect taxes.** Direct taxes are levied directly on *people*. Primary examples are *income taxes* and *inheritance taxes*, though the notoriously regressive *head tax*—which charges every person the same amount—is also a direct tax. In contrast, indirect taxes are levied on goods and services, such as buying gasoline, using the telephone, owning a home, and so on. *Sales taxes* and *property taxes* are the most important indirect taxes in the United States, although many other countries rely heavily on the *value-added tax,* a tax that has never been adopted in the United States.[1] In fact, as a broad generalization, the U.S. government relies more heavily on direct taxation than do the governments of most other countries. It is only a slight distortion of the facts to say that the federal government raises revenues by direct taxes, while the states and localities raise funds via indirect taxes. Just what are these direct and indirect taxes?

[1]The concept of value added was defined and explained in an appendix to Chapter 7. The value-added tax simply taxes each firm on the basis of its value added.

The Federal Tax System

The **personal income tax** is the biggest single source of revenue to the federal government. Most people do not realize that the **payroll tax**—a tax levied on wages and salaries up to a certain limit—is the next biggest source. Furthermore, payroll taxes are growing much more rapidly than income taxes. In 1958, payroll tax collections were only one-third as large as personal income tax collections; by 1969, this fraction had reached one-half; and by 1980, payroll taxes amounted to about two-thirds of personal income tax collections. Recent legislation will push this ratio still higher. The rest of the federal government's revenues come mostly from the *corporate income tax* and from various excise (sales) taxes. Figure 30–4 shows the breakdown of federal revenues anticipated for the fiscal year 1982 budget. Let us look at these taxes in more detail.

The Federal Personal Income Tax

The tax on individual incomes began with the Sixteenth Amendment to the Constitution in 1913, but was inconsequential until the beginning of World War II. Then, the tax was raised substantially to finance the war and has been the major source of federal revenue ever since. The personal income tax has been much in the news of late because President Reagan made reductions in personal tax rates the cornerstone of his new economic policy in 1981.[2]

It is well known that the personal income tax is progressive. Table 30–1 is an abbreviated version of the tax table that applied to U.S. taxpayers during 1982. The progressivity is shown quite clearly by the way average tax rates rise as income rises. However, notice that average tax rates are well below marginal tax rates.

In fact, the federal personal income tax is not nearly as progressive as Table 30–1 suggests. The major reason for this gap between appearance and reality is the existence of a bewildering variety of **tax loopholes,** some of which will be discussed in Chapter 34. These loopholes enable large amounts of income to escape taxation, and, since they are beneficial mainly to high-income taxpayers, they erode the progressivity of the tax quite seriously.

[2]For a detailed discussion of the Reagan tax cuts, see Chapters 9, 11, and 17.

Figure 30–4
SOURCES OF FEDERAL GOVERNMENT REVENUE, FISCAL YEAR 1982 (PROJECTION)
This pie diagram gives the projected shares of each of the major sources of federal revenues for fiscal year 1982 (October 1981 through September 1982). Personal income taxes and payroll taxes clearly account for the majority of federal revenues.
SOURCE: Congressional Budget Office.

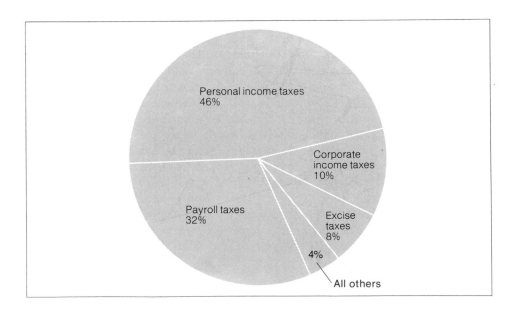

Table 30–1
FEDERAL PERSONAL INCOME TAX RATES IN 1982*

TAXABLE INCOME	TAX	AVERAGE TAX RATE (percent)	MARGINAL TAX RATE (percent)
$ 3,000	$ 0	—	—
5,000	192	3.8	12
10,000	930	9.3	16
15,000	1823	12.2	19
25,000	4153	16.6	29
50,000	13,305	26.6	44
100,000	37,449	37.4	50
250,000	112,449	45.0	50
1,000,000	487,449	48.7	50

*For a married couple filing jointly.

Many taxpayers actually have very little tax to pay when the annual April 15th day of reckoning comes around, because income taxes are *withheld* from payrolls by employers and forwarded to the U.S. Treasury. In fact, many taxpayers are "overwithheld" during the year and receive a refund check from Uncle Sam in the spring.

The Payroll Tax

The second most important tax in the United States is the payroll tax, whose proceeds are earmarked to be paid into various "trust funds." These funds, in turn, are used to pay social security benefits, unemployment compensation, and other social insurance dividends.

The payroll tax is levied at a fixed percentage rate (now about 14 percent) that is divided between employees and employers, each paying roughly half the amount. This means that a firm paying an employee a gross monthly wage of, say, $1000 will deduct $70 (7 percent of $1000) from that worker's check, add an additional $70 of its own funds, and send the $140 to the government. On the face of it, this seems like a *proportional* tax, but it is actually highly *regressive* for two reasons. First, only wages and salaries are subject to the tax. People whose incomes come from interest and dividends do not pay. Second, because there are upper limits on social security benefits, earnings above a certain level (which changes each year) are exempted from the tax. In 1982, this level was $32,400 per year. Above this limit, the *marginal tax rate* on earnings is zero.

The Corporate Income Tax

The tax on corporate profits is also considered to be a "direct" tax, because corporations are considered to be fictitious "people" in the eyes of the law.[3] The basic marginal tax rate is now 46 percent, and this rate is paid by all large corporations (firms with smaller profits pay a lower rate). Since the tax applies to *profits*, not to income, all wages, rents, and interest paid by the corporation are deducted before the tax is applied.

Excise Taxes

An excise tax is what is more commonly called a sales tax—a tax on the purchase of some goods or services. While sales taxation is traditionally the preserve of the

[3]For a full discussion of corporations and other forms of business organization, see Chapter 24.

state and local governments in the United States, the federal government does levy excise taxes on a hodgepodge of miscellaneous goods and services, including cigarettes, gasoline, and tires. These taxes constitute a minor source of federal government revenue, but raising revenue is not their only goal. Some of these taxes are designed to discourage consumption of a good by raising its price.

The Payroll Tax and the Social Security System

In government statistical documents, the payroll tax is euphemistically referred to as "contributions for social insurance," though these "contributions" are far from voluntary. The term signifies the fact that, unlike other taxes, the proceeds from this particular tax are set aside in "trust funds" for use in paying benefits to social security recipients and others.

But the standard notion of a trust fund really does not apply in this case. A private pension plan *is* a trust fund: You pay in money while you are working, it accumulates at compound interest, and then you withdraw it bit by bit in your retirement years. But the social security system does not operate in this way. Since its early years, the system simply has taken the payroll tax payments of the current working generations and handed them over to the current retired generation. The benefit checks that your grandparents receive each month are not, in any real sense, the dividends on the investments they made while they were working. Instead they are the payroll taxes that you and your parents pay each month.

So far this "pay as you go" system has managed to give every retired generation more in benefits than it contributed in payroll taxes. Social security "contributions" have indeed been a good investment! How has this miracle been achieved? It has relied very heavily on growth: both population growth and economic growth. As long as there is continued population growth, there are always more and more young people to tax in order to pay the retirement benefits of senior citizens. Similarly, as long as wages keep increasing, the same payroll tax *rates* will permit the government to pay benefits to each generation that exceed that generation's contributions, without endangering the solvency of the system. Ten percent of today's average wage is clearly a lot more money than 10 percent of the wage your grandfather earned 50 years ago.

Yet the social security trust fund almost ran out of money in the early 1980s. There were two principal reasons why benefits had been exceeding payroll tax receipts, and at least one of them is likely to be with us for some time.

The first was, perhaps, transitory; but it lasted long enough to become quite worrisome. Steady growth in real wages, one of the cornerstones of the solvency of the pay-as-you-go system, ceased in the 1970s. Real wages at the end of 1980 were about what they were in 1968. But during this time social security benefits continued to grow rapidly and in 1975 became fully protected from inflation by *indexing*, whereas wages are not.[4]

The second reason poses a much longer-run problem: population growth has slowed significantly in the United States. Birthrates in this country were very high from the close of World War II until about 1958 (the "postwar baby boom") and have generally been falling since then. As a result, the fraction of the U.S. population that is over 65 has climbed from only 7.5 percent in 1945 to 11.4 percent in 1980, and is certain to go much higher. Projections clearly show that by the time the people born between 1945 and 1958 reach retirement age, it will be impossible to have a social security system as generous as we have now if the

[4]For a full discussion of indexing, see Chapter 17.

current method of financing is maintained, and perhaps impossible under any method of financing. Long before that time, the projections show, something will have to be done either to increase the inflow of money into the social security trust fund or to decrease the outflow. Thus far Congress has relied exclusively on the first remedy, and current legislation makes provisions for continued increases in payroll taxes right through to the year 2011.

Nobody seems very eager to try the second remedy—cutting social security benefits. For example, a proposal by President Reagan to trim benefits was resoundingly rejected by the Senate in 1981. Consequently, many economists have suggested that we change the method of financing. One suggested reform would simply have the system drop the "trust fund" idea and rely instead on the great revenue-raising powers of the federal government to guarantee benefits to senior citizens. If social security benefits were financed out of general tax revenues—which, aside from payroll taxes, come mainly from income taxes—there would no longer be any danger of insolvency for the trust fund. When higher benefits need to be paid, Congress would simply raise income taxes. Of course, the resulting tax burdens might become quite high during the first half of the twenty-first century, when the ratio of retired people to working people is sure to be much higher than it is today.

It seems a reasonable prediction that by the year 2020, say, either the retirement age will be pushed back beyond 65, or retirement benefits will be lower relative to wages than they are today, or both. And it seems certain that the debate over social security will continue over the next several years.

The State and Local Tax System

Indirect taxes are the backbone of state and local government revenues, though income taxes are becoming increasingly popular. Sales taxes are the principal source of revenue to the states, while cities and towns rely heavily on property taxes. Figure 30–5 shows the breakdown of state and local government receipts for fiscal year 1978–1979.

Sales and Excise Taxes

These days, the majority of states and large cities levy a broad-based sales tax on the purchase of most goods and services, with certain specific exemptions. For

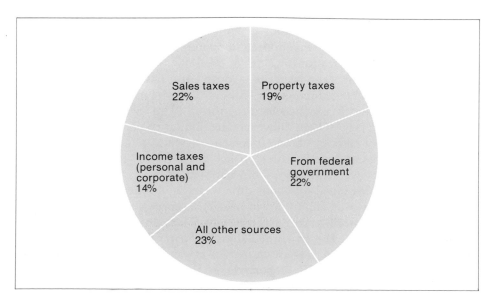

Figure 30–5
SOURCES OF STATE AND LOCAL REVENUE, FISCAL YEAR 1978–1979
As this pie diagram shows, sales taxes, property taxes, and grants-in-aid from the federal government are about equally important as sources of revenue to state and local governments. Income taxes are less important, though they are growing rapidly.
SOURCE: Economic Report of the President, 1981.

example, food is exempted from sales tax in many states. Overall sales tax rates are typically in the 5 to 7 percent range. In addition, there are special excise taxes in most states on such things as tobacco products, liquor, gasoline, and luxury items.

Property Taxes

Municipalities raise revenue by taxing the values of properties, such as houses and office buildings, again with certain exemptions (educational institutions, church property, and so on). The procedure is generally to assign to each taxable property an *assessed value*, which is an estimate of its market value, and then to place a tax rate on the community's total assessed value that yields enough revenue to cover expenditures on local services. Because properties are *reassessed* much less frequently than market values change, certain inequities arise. For example, one person's house may be assessed at almost 100 percent of its true market value while another's may be assessed at little more than 50 percent of its value. Property taxes generally run about 2 to 4 percent of true market value, though some communities deviate markedly from this norm. For example, property tax rates in cities tend to be much higher than they are in the suburbs.

At present, the property tax is perhaps the most controversial in the entire U.S. tax system. Some economists view it as a tax on one particular type of wealth—real estate. In this view, since families with higher incomes generally own much more real estate than do families with low incomes, the property tax is *progressive* relative to income; that is, the ratio of property tax to income rises as we move up the income scale. However, other economists view the property tax as an excise tax on rents; and since expenditures on rent generally account for a larger fraction of the incomes of the poor than of the rich, this makes it seem *regressive* relative to income.

There is also intense political controversy over the property tax. Because local property tax revenues have been the traditional source of financing for public schools, wealthy communities with a lot of expensive real estate have been able to afford higher-quality schools than have poor communities. The reason is made clear with a simple arithmetical example. Suppose that real estate holdings in a wealthy school district average $100,000 per family, while in a poor district real estate holdings average only $40,000 per family. If both districts levy a 2 percent property tax to pay for their schools, the wealthy community will generate $2000 per family in tax receipts, while the poor one will generate only $800. In the 1970s, glaring inequalities like this led the supreme courts of many states to declare unconstitutional the financing of public schools by local property tax revenues because it deprives children in poorer districts of an equal opportunity to receive a good education.

The property tax has also been the favorite target of the "taxpayer's revolt." The most publicized tax-reduction measures in recent years—California's Proposition 13 in 1978 and Massachusetts' Proposition $2\frac{1}{2}$ in 1980—both drastically reduced property taxes. There, however, the similarity ends. Proposition 13, which cut property taxes by about 60 percent, was precipitated by California's rapidly rising real estate values, which pushed tax *payments* up even though tax *rates* in California were roughly at the national average. The effects of the proposition were cushioned for about three years by a multibillion dollar state budget surplus. However, conditions in Massachusetts when Proposition $2\frac{1}{2}$ cut property taxes dramatically were quite different. Massachusetts had some of the highest property tax rates in the United States, property values were not soaring, and there was no surplus in the state treasury to cushion the blow. Proposition $2\frac{1}{2}$ (so named because it reduced property taxes to $2\frac{1}{2}$ percent of market value) initiated cutbacks in public services and precipitated a fiscal crisis whose repercussions are still being felt.

State and Local Income Taxes

Although some states and localities have been taxing individual and corporate incomes for many years, only recently have taxes on individual incomes begun to account for a substantial share of state and local revenue. Between 1938 and 1960, only one state enacted a personal income tax. Since 1961, however, nine additional states have joined the club, with New Jersey being the latest (in 1976). It seems safe to predict that personal income taxes will be an increasingly important source of state and local revenues in years to come. Experts in public finance generally applaud this trend because, for reasons we will explain at the end of this chapter, they view the personal income tax as perhaps the best way to raise revenue.

Fiscal Federalism

Figure 30–5 pointed out that grants from the federal government are a major source of revenue to state and local governments. In addition, grants from the states are vital to local governments. This system of transfers from one level of government to the next is referred to as **fiscal federalism,** and has a long history.

Aid from this source has come traditionally in the form of *restricted grants*, that is, money given from one level of government to the next on the condition that it be spent for a specific purpose. For example, the U.S. government may grant funds to a state *if* that state will use it to build highways. Or a state government may give money to a school district for expenditure on a specified program or facility. Since the 1970s there has been a trend toward **revenue sharing** by the federal government, which now gives state and local governments substantial sums of money in the form of *unrestricted grants*, to be spent as the states and localities see fit. The shift from restricted to unrestricted grants was accelerated by the Reagan administration, which argued that giving the states and localities more freedom to spend as they please would promote efficiency in government.

The Concept of Equity in Taxation

Taxes are judged on two criteria: *equity* (Is the tax fair?) and *efficiency* (Does the tax interfere unduly with the workings of the market economy?). It is curious that economists have been mostly concerned with the latter, while public discussions about tax proposals almost always focus on the former. Let us, therefore, begin our discussion by investigating the concept of equitable taxation.

Horizontal Equity

There are three distinct concepts of tax equity. The first is **horizontal equity,** which simply asserts that equally situated individuals should be taxed equally. Stated in this way, there are few who would quarrel with the principle. But it is often quite difficult to apply in practice, and violations of horizontal equity can be found throughout the tax code.

Horizontal equity is the notion that equally situated individuals should be taxed equally.

Consider, for example, the personal income tax. Horizontal equity calls for two families with the same income to pay the same tax. But what if one family has eight children and the other has one? Well, you answer, we must define "equally situated" to include equal family sizes, so only families with the same number of children can be compared on grounds of horizontal equity. But what if one family has unusually high medical expenses, while the other has none? Are they still "equally situated"? By now the point should be clear: Determining when two families are "equally situated" is no simple task. In fact, the U.S. tax code lists hundreds of requirements that must be met before two families are construed to be "equal."

Vertical Equity

The second concept of fair taxation seems to flow naturally from the first. If equals are to be treated equally, it appears that unequals should be treated unequally. This precept is known as **vertical equity.** Just saying this, of course, does not get us very far. For the most part, vertical equity has been translated into the **ability-to-pay-principle,** according to which those most able to pay should pay the highest taxes. But this still leaves a definitional problem similar to the problem of defining "equally situated": How do we measure ability to pay? The nature of each tax often provides a straightforward answer. In income taxation, we measure ability to pay by income; in property taxation, we measure it by property value; and so on.

A thornier problem arises when we try to translate the notion into concrete terms. Consider the three alternative income-tax plans listed in Table 30–2. Under all three plans, families with higher incomes pay higher income taxes. So all three plans could be said to operate on the ability-to-pay concept of vertical equity. Yet the three are quite different in their distributive consequences. Plan 1 is a progressive tax, something like the individual income tax in the United States: the average tax rate is higher for richer families. Plan 2 is a proportional tax: every family pays 10 percent of its income. Plan 3 is quite regressive: since tax payments rise more slowly than income, the tax rate for richer families is lower than that for poorer families.

Which plan comes closest to the ideal notion of vertical equity? Many people find that Plan 3 offends their sense of "fairness," but there is much less agreement over the relative merits of Plan 1 (progressive taxation) and Plan 2 (proportional taxation). Very often, in fact, the notion of vertical equity is taken to be synonymous with progressivity. Other things being equal, progressive taxes are seen as "good" taxes in some ethical sense while regressive taxes are seen as "bad." On these grounds, advocates of greater equality of incomes support progressive income taxes and oppose sales taxes.

The Benefits Principle

Whereas the principles of horizontal and vertical equity, for all their ambiguities and practical problems, at least do not conflict with one another, the third principle of fair taxation may often violate commonly accepted notions of vertical

Vertical equity refers to the notion that differently situated individuals should be taxed differently in a way that society deems to be fair.

The **ability-to-pay principle** refers to the idea that people with greater ability to pay taxes should pay higher taxes.

Table 30–2
THREE ALTERNATIVE INCOME-TAX PLANS

	TAX PAYMENTS			AVERAGE TAX RATES (percent)		
INCOME	PLAN 1	PLAN 2	PLAN 3	PLAN 1	PLAN 2	PLAN 3
$ 1,000	$ 100	$ 100	$ 100	10	10	10
10,000	2,000	1,000	500	20	10	5
100,000	40,000	10,000	2,500	40	10	$2\frac{1}{2}$

equity. According to the **benefits principle of taxation** those who reap the benefits from government services should pay the taxes. One clear example is gasoline taxes. Receipts from gasoline taxes typically are earmarked for maintenance and construction of roads. Thus, those who use the roads pay the tax roughly in proportion to the amount they use them. Most people seem to find this system fair.

The Concept of Efficiency in Taxation

The concept of economic *efficiency* is the central notion of Parts Three through Five of this text. The economy is said to be *efficient* if it has used every available opportunity to make someone better off without making someone else worse off. In this sense, taxes almost always introduce *inefficiencies*. That is, if the tax were removed, some people could be made better off without anyone being harmed. However, a comparison of a world with taxes to a world without taxes is not terribly pertinent. The government does, after all, need to raise revenues to pay for the goods and services it provides. For this reason, when economists discuss notions of "efficient" taxation, they are usually looking for the taxes that cause the *least* amount of inefficiency.

To explain the concept of efficient taxation, we need to introduce one new term. Economists define the **burden of a tax** as the amount of money the taxpayer would have to be given to make him just as well off in the presence of the tax as he is in its absence. An example will clarify this notion and also make clear why *the burden of a tax normally exceeds the revenues raised by the tax.* Suppose the government, in the interest of energy conservation, levies a high tax on the biggest gas-guzzling cars, with progressively lower taxes on smaller cars.[5] For example, a simple tax schedule might be the following:

CAR TYPE	TAX
Cadillac	$1000
Dodge	500
Pinto	0

Harry has a taste for big cars, and has always bought Cadillacs. (Harry is clearly no pauper.) Once the new tax takes effect, he has three options. He can still buy a Cadillac and pay $1000 in tax, he can switch to a Dodge and avoid half the tax, or he can switch to a Pinto and avoid the entire tax.

If Harry chooses the first option, we have a case in which the burden of the tax is exactly equal to the amount of tax the person pays. Why? Because if Harry's rich uncle gives him $1000, Harry winds up in exactly the same position that he was before the tax was enacted. Hence, he must be just as happy as before. In general:

When a tax induces no change in economic behavior, the burden of the tax can be measured accurately by the revenue collected.

However, this is not what we normally expect to happen. And it is certainly not what the government intends by levying a tax on big cars. Normally, we expect taxes to induce some people to alter their behavior in ways that reduce or avoid tax payments. So let us look into Harry's other two options.

[5]President Carter actually proposed such a tax in 1977 as part of his energy program.

The **benefits principle of taxation,** which is often applied when the proceeds from certain taxes are earmarked for specific public services, holds that people who derive the benefits from the service should pay the taxes that finance it.

The **burden of a tax** to an individual is the amount of money he would have to be given to make him just as well off with the tax as he was without it.

Excess Burden and Mr. Figg

Humorist Russell Baker discussed the problem of excess burden in the newpaper column reproduced below. It seems that every time his mythical Mr. Figg took a step to avoid paying taxes and to satisfy the tax man, he became less and less happy.

American Way of Tax
By Russell Baker

New York—The tax man was very cross about Figg. Figg's way of life did not conform to the way of life several governments wanted Figg to pursue. Nothing inflamed the tax man more than insolent and capricious disdain for governmental desires. He summoned Figg to the temple of taxation.

"What's the idea of living in a rental apartment over a delicatessen in the city, Figg?" he inquired. Figg explained that he liked urban life. In that case, said the tax man, he was raising Figg's city sales and income taxes. "If you want them cut, you'll have to move out to the suburbs," he said.

To satisfy his local government, Figg gave up the city and rented a suburban house. The tax man summoned him back to the temple.

"Figg" he said, "you have made me sore wroth with your way of life. Therefore, I am going to soak you for more federal income taxes." And he squeezed Figg until beads of blood popped out along the seams of Figg's wallet.

"Mercy, good tax man" Figg gasped. "Tell me how to live so that I may please my government, and I shall obey."

The tax man told Figg to quit renting and buy a house. The government wanted everyone to accept large mortgage loans from bankers. If Figg complied, it would cut his taxes.

Figg bought a house, which he did not want, in a suburb where he did not want to live, and he invited his friends and relatives to attend a party celebrating his surrender to a way of life that pleased his government.

The **excess burden** of a tax to an individual is the amount by which the burden of the tax exceeds the tax that is paid.

If he decides to purchase a Dodge, Harry pays only $500 in tax. But this is an inadequate measure of the burden of the new tax because Harry is greatly chagrined by the fact that he no longer drives a Cadillac. How much money would it take to make Harry just as well off as he was before the tax? Only Harry knows for sure. But we do know that it is more than the $500 tax that he pays. Why? Because, even if someone were to give Harry the $500 needed to pay his tax bill, he would still be less happy than he was before the tax was introduced, owing to his switch from a Cadillac to a Dodge. Whatever the (unknown) burden of the tax is, the amount by which it exceeds the $500 tax bill is called the **excess burden** of the tax.

Harry's final option makes the importance of understanding excess burden even more clear. If he switches to buying a Pinto, Harry will pay no tax. Are we therefore to say he has suffered no burden? Clearly not, for he longs for the Cadillac that he no longer has. The general principle is:

Whenever a tax induces people to change their behavior—that is, whenever it "distorts" their choices—the tax has an excess burden. This means that the revenue collected by the tax systematically understates the true burden of the tax.

The excess burdens that arise from tax-induced changes in economic behavior are precisely the inefficiencies we referred to at the outset of this discusssion. And the basic precept of efficient taxation is to try to devise a tax system that minimizes these inefficiences. In particular:

In comparing two taxes that raise the same total revenue, the one that produces less excess burden is the more efficient.

The tax man was so furious that he showed up at the party with blood-shot eyes. "I have had enough of this, Figg" he declared, "Your government doesn't want you entertaining friends and relatives. This will cost you plenty."

Figg immediately threw out all his friends and relatives, then asked the tax man what sort of people his government wished him to entertain. "Business associates," said the tax man. "Entertain plenty of business associates, and I shall cut your taxes."

To make the tax man and his government happy, Figg began entertaining people he didn't like in the house he didn't want in the suburb where he didn't want to live.

Then was the tax man enraged indeed. "Figg," he thundered, "I will not cut your taxes for entertaining straw bosses, truck drivers and pothole fillers."

"Why not?" said Figg. "These are the people I associate with in my business."

"Which is what?" asked the tax man.

"Earning my pay by the sweat of my brow," said Figg.

"Your government is not going to bribe you for performing salaried labor," said the tax man. "Don't you know, you imbecile, that tax rates on salaried income are higher than on any other kind?"

And he taxed the sweat of Figg's brow at a rate that drew exquisite shrieks of agony from Figg and little cries of joy from Washington, which already had more sweated brows than it needed to sustain the federally approved way of life.

"Get into business, or minerals, or international oil," warned the tax man, "or I shall make your taxes as the taxes of 10."

Figg went into business, which he hated, and entertained people he didn't like in the house he didn't want in the suburb where he did not want to live.

At length the tax man summoned Figg for an angry lecture. He demanded to know why Figg had not bought a new plastic factory to replace his old metal and wooden plant. "I hate plastic," said Figg. "Your government is sick and tired of metal, wood and everything else that smacks of the real stuff, Figg," roared the tax man, seizing Figg's purse. "Your depreciation is all used up."

There was nothing for Figg to do but go to plastic, and the tax man rewarded him with a brand new depreciation schedule plus an investment credit deduction from the bottom line.

SOURCE: *International Herald Tribune*, April 13, 1977, page 14. ©1977 by The New York Times Company. Reprinted by permission.

Notice the proviso that the two taxes being compared must yield the *same* revenue. We are really interested in the *total* burden of each tax. Since:

$$\text{Total burden} = \text{Tax collections} + \text{Excess burden},$$

only when tax collections are equal can we unambiguously state that the tax with less excess burden is more efficient. Since excess burdens arise when consumers and firms alter their behavior on account of taxation, this precept of sound tax policy can be restated in a way that sounds consistent with President Reagan's statement at the beginning of this chapter:

In devising a tax system to raise revenue, try to raise any given amount of revenue through taxes that induce the smallest changes in behavior.[6]

Shifting the Burden of Taxation: Tax Incidence

When economists speak of the **incidence of a tax,** they are referring to who actually bears the burden of the tax. In discussing the tax on gas-guzzling autos, we have adhered so far to what has been called the **flypaper theory of tax incidence:** that the burden of any tax sticks where the government puts it. In this case, the theory holds that the burden stays on Harry. But often things do not

[6]Sometimes, in contrast to President Reagan's statement, a tax is levied not primarily as a revenue-raiser, but as a way of inducing individuals or firms to alter their behavior. This possibility will be discussed in a later section.

work out this way. Consider, for example, what will happen if thousands of Harrys all over America decide to stop buying luxury cars like Cadillacs. The demand schedule for luxury cars will shift downward sharply, as depicted in Figure 30–6 by the movement from D_0D_0 to D_1D_1. Assuming that the supply schedule of luxury cars is unchanged, we see that the price falls from $15,000 to $14,500 in the example—a drop of $500. This means that those consumers who continue to buy luxury cars will now be paying $14,500 to the dealer plus $1000 to the U.S. Treasury for a total of $15,500. This is only $500 more than what they were paying before the tax, so the burden that they bear is only $500—just half the tax that they pay!

Does this mean that the tax imposes a *negative* excess burden? Certainly not. What it means is that consumers who refrain from buying the taxed commodity have managed to *shift* much of the burden of the tax away from consumers as a whole, including those who continue to buy luxury cars. To whom has the tax been shifted? In our example, there are two main candidates. First are the automakers, or, more precisely, their stockholders. Stockholders bear the burden to the extent that the tax, by reducing auto sales, cuts into their profits. The other principal candidates are auto workers. To the extent that reduced production leads to layoffs, or to lower wages, the automobile workers bear part of the burden of the tax.

People who have never studied economics almost always believe in the flypaper theory of incidence, which holds that sales taxes are borne by consumers, property taxes are borne by homeowners, and taxes on corporations are borne by stockholders. Perhaps the most important lesson of this chapter is that:

The flypaper theory of incidence is often wrong.

Failure to grasp this basic point has led to all sorts of misguided tax legislation in which Congress, or state legislatures, *thinking* they were placing a tax burden on one group of people inadvertently placed it squarely on another. Of course, there are cases where the flypaper theory of incidence comes very close to being correct. So let us consider some specific examples of tax incidence.

Tax shifting occurs when the economic reactions to a tax cause prices and outputs in the economy to change, thereby shifting part of the burden of the tax onto others.

Figure 30–6

THE INCIDENCE OF AN EXCISE TAX

When the government imposes a $1000 tax on luxury cars, the demand curve relating quantity demanded to price *exclusive of tax* shifts downward from D_0D_0 to D_1D_1. The equilibrium price in this example falls from $15,000 to $14,500, so the burden of the tax is shared equally between car sellers (who receive $500 less) and car buyers (who pay $500 more, including the tax). In general, how the burden is shared depends on the elasticities of demand and supply.

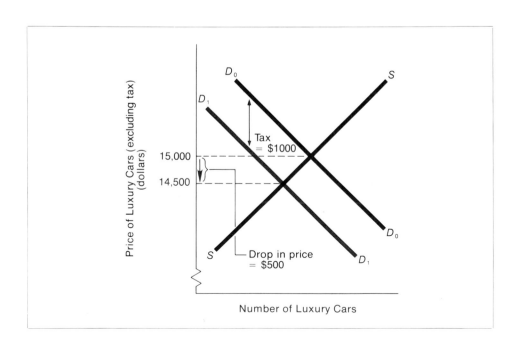

The Incidence of Excise Taxes

Excise taxes have already been covered by our automobile example, because Figure 30–6 could represent any commodity that is taxed. The basic finding is that *part* of the burden will fall on consumers of the taxed commodity (including those who stop buying it because of the tax), and part will be shifted to the firms and the workers who produce the commodity.

The amount that is shifted depends on the sensitivity of the demand curve to the tax and on the slope of the supply curve. We can see intuitively how this works. If consumers are very loyal to the taxed commodity so that they will continue to buy almost the same quantity no matter what the price, then it is clear that they will be stuck with most of the tax bill because they have left themselves vulnerable to it. Thus we would expect that the more inelastic the demand for the product is, the larger the share of the tax consumers will pay. Similarly, if suppliers are determined to supply the same amount of the product no matter how low the price (that is, if supply is very inelastic), then more of the tax will be borne by suppliers.

One extreme case arises when no one stops buying luxury cars when their prices rise. The demand curve becomes vertical, like the demand curve *DD* in Figure 30–7, and does not move at all when the tax is enacted. Then there can be no tax shifting. The price of a luxury car (exclusive of tax) remains at $15,000. So consumers bear the entire burden.

The other extreme case arises when the supply curve is vertical as in Figure 30–8. Since the number of luxury cars supplied is the same at any price, the automakers must bear the full burden of any tax that is placed on their product. Figure 30–8 shows that the before-tax price falls by the full amount of the tax, which, of course, means that the after-tax price (the price that buyers pay) cannot be changed by the tax.

Demand and supply schedules for most goods and services are not as extreme as those depicted in Figures 30–7 and 30–8, so the burden is shared. Precisely how it is shared depends on the elasticities of supply and demand curves.

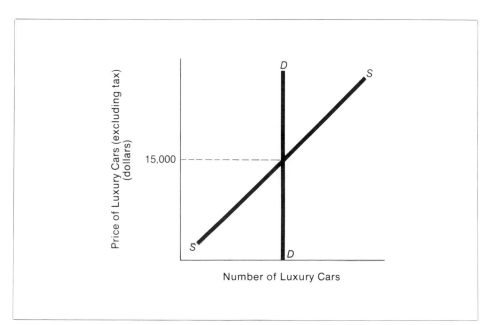

Figure 30–7
AN EXTREME CASE OF TAX INCIDENCE
If the quantity demanded is totally insensitive to price (completely *inelastic*), then the demand curve will be vertical and it will not shift when a tax is imposed. As the diagram shows, the price *exclusive of tax* remains at $15,000 so suppliers bear none of the burden. Since price *inclusive of tax* rises to $16,000, the entire burden falls on the buyers.

Figure 30–8

ANOTHER EXTREME
CASE OF TAX INCIDENCE
If the quantity supplied is totally
insensitive to price, then the
supply curve *SS* will be vertical. When the demand curve
shifts vertically downward from
D_0D_0 to D_1D_1 on account of an
excise tax, the seller will bear
the entire burden, because the
price that he receives
($14,000) will fall by the full
amount of the tax.

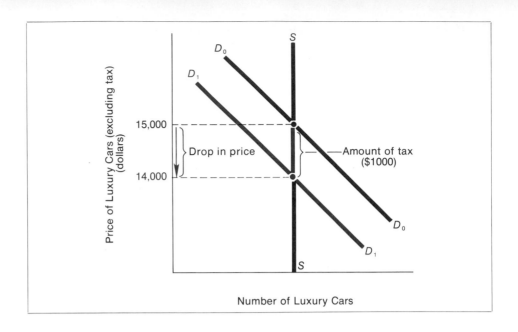

When demand for a commodity or service is very inelastic, consumers will bear much of the burden of any tax that is placed on it. On the other hand, market forces will shift most of the burden away from consumers and onto firms when supply is quite inelastic.

The Incidence of the Payroll Tax

The payroll tax may be thought of as an excise tax on the employment of labor. As we mentioned earlier, the U.S. payroll tax comes in two parts: half is levied on the employees (payroll deductions) and half on employers. A fundamental point, which people who have never studied economics often fail to grasp, is that:

The incidence of a payroll tax is the same whether it is levied on employers or employees.

A simple numerical example can illustrate how this works. Consider an employee earning $100 a day with a 14 percent payroll tax that is "shared" equally between the employer and the employee, as under our present law. How much does it cost the firm to hire this worker? It costs $100 in wages paid to the worker plus $7 in taxes paid to the government, for a total of $107 a day. How much does the worker receive? He gets $100 in wages paid by the employer less $7 deducted and sent to the government, or $93 a day. The difference between wages paid and wages received is $107 − $93 = $14.

Now suppose Congress tries to "shift" the burden of the tax entirely onto firms, by raising the employer's tax to 14 percent while lowering the employee's tax to zero. Firms would still demand the same amount of labor at a cost of $107 a day, and workers would still supply the same amount at $93 a day. The necessary $14 difference between the wage that the firm pays and the wage that the worker receives can be restored by lowering the stated wage to $93 a day. Since firms still pay $107, and workers still receive $93, nothing real has changed. Nor would things be any different if the worker were forced to "pay" the full 14 percent payroll tax. If the firms paid the workers $107 a day, workers would still earn $93 after tax.

This is one of those cases where Congress, misled by the flypaper theory of incidence, thinks it is "taxing firms" when it raises the employer's share and that it is "taxing workers" when it raises the employee's share. In truth, who is really paying depends on the incidence of the tax. But no difference results from a change in the employee's and the employer's shares. To think that there can be a difference is like thinking that the tax on cigarettes would have a different incidence if the government made the buyers, rather than the sellers, collect the revenues. Apart from the dubious enforceability of the tax if the buyers had to collect it, the two situations are identical.

Who, then, really bears the burden of the payroll tax? Like an excise tax, the incidence of the payroll tax depends on the elasticities of the supply and demand schedules. In the case of labor supply, there is a large body of empirical evidence pointing to the conclusion that the quantity of labor supplied is not very responsive to price for most population groups. The supply curve is almost vertical, like that shown in Figure 30–8. The result is that workers as a group are able to shift very little of the burden of the payroll tax.

But employers *can* shift it in most cases. Firms view their share of the payroll tax as an additional cost of using labor. So when payroll taxes go up, firms try to substitute cheaper factors of production (capital) for labor wherever they can. This reduces the demand for labor, lowering the wage received by workers (see Figure 30–8). And this is how market forces shift part of the tax burden from firms to workers.

To the extent that the supply curve of labor has some positive slope, the quantity of labor supplied will fall when the wage goes down, and in this way workers can shift some of the burden back onto firms. But the firms, in turn, can shift that burden onto consumers by raising their prices. As we know from Part Three, prices in competitive markets generally rise when costs (like labor costs) increase. It is doubtful, therefore, that firms bear any of the burden of the payroll tax. Here, the flypaper theory of incidence could not be further from the truth. Even though the tax is collected by the firm, it is really borne by workers and consumers.

When Taxation Can Improve Efficiency

We have spent much of this chapter discussing the kinds of inefficiencies and excess burdens that arise from taxation. But, before we finish this discussion, two things must be pointed out.

First, economic efficiency is not society's only goal. For example, the hypothetical tax on gas-guzzling cars causes inefficiencies if it changes people's behavior patterns. But this, presumably, was exactly what the government sought to accomplish. The government wanted to reduce the number of big cars on the road to conserve energy, and it was willing to tolerate some economic inefficiency to accomplish this end. We can, of course, argue whether this was a good idea—whether the conservation achieved was worth the efficiency loss. But the general point is that:

Some taxes are a good idea because even when they introduce economic inefficiencies, they help achieve some other goal.

A second, and more fundamental, point is that:

Some taxes that change economic behavior may lead to efficiency *gains*, rather than to efficiency *losses*.

As you might guess, this can only happen when there is an inefficiency in the system prior to the tax. Then an appropriate tax may help set things right. A very clear-cut example of this will occupy much of the next chapter. There we will see that because firms and individuals who despoil clean air and clean water often do so without paying any price, these precious resources are used inefficiently. A corrective tax on pollution can remedy this problem.

Equity, Efficiency, and the Optimal Tax

In a perfect world, the ideal tax would reflect society's views on equity in taxation, and it would induce no changes in economic behavior and so would have no excess burden. Unfortunately, there is no such tax.

Sometimes, in fact, the taxes with the smallest excess burdens are the most regressive. For instance, a head tax, which charges every person the same number of dollars, is very regressive. But it is also quite efficient. Since there is no change in economic behavior that will enable anyone to avoid it, there is no reason for anyone to change his or her behavior. As we have noted, the regressive payroll tax also seems to have small excess burdens.

Fortunately, however, there is a tax that, while not ideal, still scores very high on both the equity and efficiency criteria: the personal income tax. While it is true that income taxes can be avoided by earning less income, we have already observed that in reality the supply of labor is changed little by taxation. So income from work responds very little. Investing in relatively safe assets (like government bonds) rather than risky ones (like common stocks) is another possible reaction that would reduce tax bills, since less risky assets pay lower rates of return. But it is not clear that the income tax actually induces such behavior because, while it takes away some of the profits when investments turn out well, it also offers a tax deduction when investments turn sour. Because the tax reduces the return on saving, many economists have worried that it would discourage saving, and thus retard economic growth. But the empirical evidence does not suggest that this has happened to any great extent. On balance then, while there are still unresolved questions and research is continuing:

Most of the studies that have been conducted to date suggest that the personal income tax induces few of the behavioral reactions that would reduce consumer well-being, and thus has a rather small excess burden.

On the equity criterion, we know that personal income taxes can be made as progressive as society deems desirable, though if marginal tax rates on rich people get extremely high, some of the potential efficiency losses might get more serious than they now seem to be. On both grounds, then, many economists—including both liberals and conservatives—view the personal income tax as the best way for a government to raise revenue. And this is why most tax reformers view the federal tax system, with its heavy reliance on the personal income tax, as superior to the state and local tax system.

Summary

1. Spending patterns differ greatly at the various levels of government. The federal government spends money mostly on national defense and income security programs. States and localities spend more on education, health, and public welfare.

2. Taxes in the United States are generally lower than they are in most other industrial countries. While federal taxes as a percentage of gross national product have been quite constant, state and local taxes have been increasing.

3. The federal government raises most of its revenue by direct taxes, such as the personal and corporate income taxes and the payroll tax. Of these, the payroll tax is increasing the most rapidly.

4. While the personal income tax is not as progressive as it might be because of its many loopholes, it undoubtedly is a progressive tax. The payroll tax, by contrast, is a regressive tax.

5. Keeping the social security system solvent has been a serious problem since the 1970s, and is likely to remain a serious problem because of the decrease in population growth. Changes in the method of financing, or reductions in retirement benefits, may be necessary to keep the system afloat.

6. State and local governments raise most of their tax revenues by indirect taxes. States rely mainly on sales taxes, while localities are dependent upon property taxes.

7. There is controversy over whether the property tax is progressive or regressive, and even more controversy over whether local property taxes are an equitable way to finance public education.

8. In our multilevel system of government, the federal government makes various sorts of grants to state and local governments, and states in turn make grants to municipalities and school districts. This system of intergovernmental transfers is called fiscal federalism.

9. There are three concepts of fair, or "equitable," taxation that occasionally conflict. Horizontal equity simply calls for equals to be treated equally. Vertical equity, which calls for unequals to be treated unequally, has often been translated into the ability-to-pay principle—that people who are more able to pay taxes should be taxed more heavily. The benefits principle of tax equity ignores ability to pay and seeks to tax people according to the benefits they receive.

10. The burden of a tax is the amount of money an individual would have to be given to make her as well off with the tax as she was without it. This burden normally exceeds the taxes that are paid; and the difference between the two is called the excess burden of the tax.

11. Excess burden arises when a tax induces some people or firms to change their behavior. Excess burdens represent economic inefficiencies, so the basic principle of efficient taxation is to utilize taxes that have small excess burdens.

12. When people change their behavior on account of a tax, they often shift the burden of the tax onto someone else. This is why the "flypaper theory of incidence"—the belief that the burden of any tax always stays where Congress puts it—is often incorrect.

13. The burden of a sales or excise tax normally is shared between the suppliers and the demanders. The manner in which it is shared depends on the elasticities of supply and demand.

14. The payroll tax is like an excise tax on labor services. Since the supply of labor is much less elastic than the demand for labor, workers bear most of the burden of the payroll tax. This includes both the employer's and the employee's share of the tax.

15. Sometimes, "inefficient" taxes—that is, taxes that cause a good deal of excess burden—are nonetheless desirable because the changes in behavior they induce further some other social goal.

16. When there are inefficiencies in the system for reasons other than the tax system (for example, externalities), taxation can conceivably improve efficiency.

17. When both equity and efficiency are considered, most economists feel that the personal income tax is the best way to raise revenue.

Concepts for Review

Progressive, proportional, and regressive taxes
Direct and indirect taxes
Personal income tax
Payroll tax
Average and marginal tax rates
Tax loopholes

Social security system
Property tax
Fiscal federalism
Revenue sharing
Horizontal and vertical equity
Ability-to-pay principle

Benefits principle of taxation
Burden of a tax
Excess burden
Incidence of a tax
Flypaper theory of incidence
Tax shifting

Questions for Discussion

1. "If the federal government continues to raise taxes as it has been doing, it will ruin the country." Comment.

2. Why have state and local taxes been increasing so much faster than federal taxes? Is this trend likely to continue?

3. Using the adjacent hypothetical income tax table, compute the marginal and average rates of tax. Is the tax progressive, proportional, or regressive?

INCOME	TAX
$100	$10
200	12
300	15
400	16

4. Which concept of tax equity, if any, seems to be served by each of the following:
   a. the progressive income tax
   b. the federal tax on gasoline
   c. the property tax
5. Use the example of Mr. Figg (see the boxed insert on pages 562–563) to explain the concepts of efficient taxes and excess burden.
6. Think of some tax that you personally pay. What steps have you taken or could you take to reduce your tax payments? Is there an excess burden on you? Why or why not?
7. Suppose the supply and demand schedules for cigarettes are as follows:

PRICE PER CARTON (dollars)	QUANTITY DEMANDED (millions of cartons per year)	QUANTITY SUPPLIED (millions of cartons per year)
3.00	240	120
3.25	230	140
3.50	220	160
3.75	210	180
4.00	200	200
4.25	190	220
4.50	180	240
4.75	170	260
5.00	160	280

Now the government levies a 75-cent per carton excise tax on cigarettes.
   a. What is the equilibrium price paid by consumers before and after the tax?
   b. What is the equilibrium price received by producers before and after the tax?
   c. Explain why it makes no difference whether Congress levies the 75-cent tax on the consumer or the producer. (Relate your answer to the discussion of the payroll tax on pages 566–567 of the text.)
   d. Suppose the tax is levied on the producers. How much of the tax are producers able to shift onto consumers? Explain how they manage to do this.
   e. Will there be any excess burden from this tax? Why? Who bears this excess burden?
   f. By how much has cigarette consumption declined on account of the tax? Why might the government be happy about this outcome, despite the excess burden?
8. The country of Taxmania produces only two commodities: bread and mink coats. The poor spend all their income on bread, while the rich purchase both goods. Both demand for and supply of bread are quite inelastic. In the mink coat market, both supply and demand are quite elastic. Which good would be heavily taxed if Taxmanians cared mostly about efficiency? What if they cared mostly about vertical equity?
9. Discuss President Reagan's statement on taxes quoted at the beginning of the chapter. Do you agree with the president?

The Economics of Environmental Protection

31

> Everything's a trade-off. If you want a high standard of living, you have to settle for a low quality of life.
>
> Overheard conversation reported at a meeting of the American Philosophical Society

We learned in Chapter 29 that *externalities* (or, the incidental benefits or damages imposed upon people not directly involved in an economic activity) can cause the market mechanism to malfunction. This chapter takes up a particularly important application of the analysis of externalities—the problem of environmental deterioration.

Environmental problems are by no means new. What *is* new and different is the amount of attention the community is now prepared to give them. Perhaps much of this increased interest can be attributed to rising incomes, which have freed people from the more urgent concerns about food, clothing, and shelter, and thus have allowed them the luxury of concentrating on the next level of needs—the *quality* of their lives.

Economic thought on the environment preceded the outburst of public concern with the subject by nearly half a century. Just after the first decade of the twentieth century, a noted British economist, A. C. Pigou, wrote a remarkable book called *The Economics of Welfare*, which offered the explanation of the market economy's poor environmental performance that is still generally accepted by economists today. What is more, that same book outlined an approach to environmental policy that is still favored by most economists and that is beginning to attract the attention of lawmakers and bureaucrats as well. Pigou's analysis of how the tax system can be used to protect the environment will be explained here in some detail. In particular, we will learn that a system of charges on emissions may be an effective and efficient means of controlling pollution. In this way, the price mechanism can remedy one of its own shortcomings!

The Delaware: How *Not* to Clean Up a River

Some of the measures that have been taken to clean up the Delaware River illustrate well the nature of the standard government approach to environmental policy and some of the ways that economists believe it can be improved.[1]

A major rehabilitation program was planned for this river, which flows through four states and past a number of industrial cities. The authorities decided that the best way to improve the quality of the river was to require

---

[1]The following discussion is based primarily on Bruce A. Ackerman, Susan Rose Ackerman, James W. Sawyer, Jr., and Dale W. Henderson, *The Uncertain Search for Environmental Quality* (New York: The Free Press, 1974).

everyone who had been discharging wastes into it to reduce the amount of discharge (measured in terms of its expected oxygen use) by approximately the same percentage—a reduction of between 85 and 90 percent. While this approach may seem both fair and effective, it turned out to have neither of these virtues. In fact, when a team of economists assessed the cost of achieving the stated goals in this way, they estimated that the proposed technique would be between 100 and 150 percent more expensive than the use of pollution charges.[2] In addition, after the haggling and negotiations had been completed, it turned out that the required reductions in emissions were far from uniform. For example, petroleum refineries of rather similar output capacity were assigned quotas for reductions in emissions of wastes between 2900 and 14,400 pounds per day.

The analysis presented in this chapter will enable us to see why assignment of equal percentage reductions, the method often favored by environmental authorities, is, in general, both inefficient and grossly inequitable.

The Environment in Perspective: Is Everything Getting Steadily Worse?

Much of the discussion of environmental problems in the popular press leaves the reader with the impression that matters have been growing steadily worse, and that pollution is largely a product of the profit system and modern industrialization. Neither of these conclusions is correct. Medieval cities were pestholes—the streets and rivers were littered with garbage and the air stank of rotting wastes. At the beginning of the eighteenth century, a German traveler reported that to get a view of London from the tower of St. Paul's, one had to get there very early in the morning "before the air was full of coal smoke." And early in the twentieth century the automobile was hailed as a source of major improvement in the cleanliness of city streets, which until then had fought a losing battle against the proliferation of horse dung.

Since World War II there has been marked progress in solving a number of pollution problems, much of it the result of concerted efforts to protect the environment. Progress in cleaning up New York City's dirty air has been remarkable. In Manhattan, the concentration of pollutant particles has dropped 66 percent from its level right after World War II; and in Brooklyn, the corresponding fall is more than 80 percent. Data from 25 major U.S. metropolitan areas show that the number of "unhealthful" days declined by 15 percent and the number of "very unhealthful" days declined by 32 percent between 1974 and 1977. The improvements were due mainly to decreases in automotive pollution.[3] The famous, or rather infamous, "fogs" of London are almost a thing of the past because of the improvement in air quality since 1950. The cleaner air in Britain's capital city has resulted in an astounding 50 percent increase in the number of hours of winter sunshine. In short, pollution problems are not new, nor is every part of the environment deteriorating relentlessly.

Environmental problems do not occur exclusively in capitalist economies. The Soviet Union has all sorts of serious environmental troubles, to which it has given substantial publicity in its own newspapers and magazines.[4] For example,

---

[2]For details see A. Kneese, S. Rolfe, and J. Harned, editors, *Managing the Environment: International Economic Cooperation for Pollution Control* (New York: Praeger Publishers, 1971), Appendix C, pages 225–274.

[3]*Environmental Quality, the Tenth Annual Report of the Council on Environmental Quality* (Washington, D.C.: U.S. Government Printing Office, 1979), page 17. It should, however, be noted that the air in New York City and Los Angeles in 1977 still registered in the "unhealthful" range on more than two-thirds of the days of the year.

[4]For an excellent nontechnical discussion see Marshall Goldman, *The Spoils of Progress* (Cambridge, Mass.: M.I.T. Press, 1972).

because of smoke in the air, the number of clear daylight hours is 40 percent lower in Leningrad than in Pavlovsk—a town only 20 miles away. The Iset and the Volga rivers are so filled with chemicals that they have actually caught fire! The number of dams, canals, and reservoirs along the waterways leading into the Aral and Caspian seas have caused so much evaporation that both seas have fallen rapidly. In fact, some claim that by the end of the century, the Aral Sea may have deteriorated into a salt marsh.

The preceding discussion is not meant to suggest that all is well with our environment, nor that there is nothing more to do. Along with the improvements that have been described, our world has been subject to a number of new pollutants, some of which are more dangerous than those we have reduced, even though they are less visible and less malodorous. A variety of highly toxic substances—PCBs (polychlorinated biphenyls), chlorinated hydrocarbons, fluoro-carbons, and radioactive materials—are dumped carelessly, left to cause cancer and threaten life and health in other ways. Other substances break down so slowly that they are likely to constitute a threat for many thousands of years. The accumulation of these and other byproducts of recent technology may well cause damage that is all but irreversible.

While environmental problems are neither new nor confined only to capitalist, industrialized economies, these facts are not legitimate grounds for complacency. The potential damage that we may be inflicting on ourselves, as well as on our surroundings, is very real and very substantial.

The Law of Conservation of Matter and Energy

It is impossible to describe completely all the ways in which we damage our environment. Our very existence creates pollution problems. We exhale "used" air and excrete food wastes; we cut down trees for housing and clear fields to plant crops; the examples can go on and on. Nevertheless, three major sources of environmental damage have continued to play a major role in these difficulties. They are: (1) the law of conservation of matter and energy, which tells us that all produced goods that are not recycled must ultimately constitute disposal prob-lems; (2) the "edifice complex," which is the notion that anything that can be done by the bulldozer and the crane necessarily constitutes progress—and the bigger the project the better; and (3) the problem of externalities, the fact that under current economic arrangements the harm done by the polluter predomi-nantly affects people other than himself, so that he has no economic motivation to bring under control the damage he does to the environment. We will discuss each of these issues in turn.

The physical law of conservation of matter and energy tells us there is no way that objects can be made to disappear—at most they can be changed into something else. Oil, for instance, can be transformed into heat (and smoke) or into plastic—but it will never vanish. This means that after a raw material has been used, either it must be used again (recycled) or it becomes a waste product that must somehow be disposed of.

If it is not recycled, any input used in the production process *must* ultimately become a waste product. It may end up on the garbage heap of some municipal dump. It may literally go up in smoke, contributing its bit to the pollution of the atmosphere. Or it may even be transformed into heat, warming up adjacent waterways and killing aquatic life in the process. The laws of physics tell us there is nothing we can do to make used inputs disappear altogether from the earth.

Environmental Causes of Disease

Insidious health hazards have been introduced by people into their environment for centuries. The superbly engineered aqueducts of Rome brought the populace not only water but poisonous lead, which leaked from the lead pipes into the drinking supply. Documented cases of sterility and permanent mental impairment have been traced to lead poisoning; some historians even believe that lead poisoning may have contributed to the fall of the Empire. Similarly, coal-fired smog hanging above the sunless, Dickensian factory towns and big city slums of the nineteenth century has been linked to a hormone deficiency among children. Insufficient exposure to the sun's ultraviolet radiation, which activates the formation of the vitamin D essential to healthy growth, is thought to have caused a widespread incidence of crippling rickets. The "mad hatters" of the nineteenth century suffered from neurological disorders caused by inhalation of mercury used in treating furs and felts.

Thus disease caused by or associated with chemicals introduced into the environment is nothing new. In our own day, various lung diseases such as emphysema have been linked with air pollution. Oxygen transport by the blood can be impaired by nitrite—sometimes found in well water or used as a preservative in many meat products—and it can also be impaired by carbon monoxide. Chemicals are

believed to affect the incidence of heart disease (carbon monoxide), cause permanent nerve disorders (mercury), and induce bone abnormalities (vinyl chloride). A disconcerting, growing body of evidence indicates that subtle, man-made hazards are supplanting famine and infectious disease as significant determinants of life expectancy in twentieth century developed nations.

Discovering links between chemicals and health problems is a slow process, usually succeeding only after a relatively long history of use or exposure. In the meantime, however, chemical development proceeds at a rapid pace. About 2 million chemical compounds are known, and each year thousands more are discovered by the U.S. chemical industry and hundreds are introduced commercially. We know very little about the possible health consequences of these new compounds.

SOURCE: *Environmental Quality, The Sixth Annual Report of the Council on Environmental Quality* (Washington, D.C.: U.S. Government Printing Office, December, 1975, pages 11–12).

In fact, only a small proportion of the economy's inputs are made up of recycled materials, and recycling activities have in many cases been declining despite the large amount of volunteer effort and publicity that has been devoted to them in recent years. The recycling of waste paper declined relative to the use of raw-material paper during the 1960s. And during recessions some voluntary collection centers have been forced to close their doors because they simply could find no takers for the products that had previously enabled them to meet their expenses. In 1977 the U.S. converted only 8 percent of its municipal solid waste into usable products. As Figure 31–1 shows, even optimistic projections predict that the amount of waste recycled will rise only to 10 percent of the total waste generated by the late 1980s.[5]

The upshot is that in an economy whose output is growing and whose input use is consequently increasing, waste disposal or pollution or both is virtually certain to be a growing problem. There are only three ways to ameliorate these difficulties: (1) increased recycling, (2) increased durability or reuse of the products (that is, the use of returnable bottles instead of throwaway containers), and (3) increased efficiency in the use of raw materials so that smaller quantities

[5] *Environmental Quality, The Tenth Annual Report of the Council on Environmental Quality*, pages 256–261.

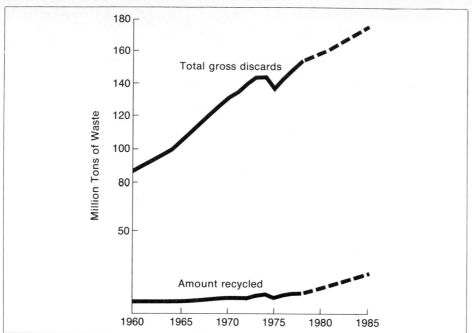

Figure 31–1
ESTIMATED U.S.
MUNICIPAL SOLID
WASTE GENERATED
AND RECYCLED,
1960–1985[a]
SOURCE: *Environmental Quality,
the Tenth Annual Report of the
Council on Environmental Quality,*
1979, page 257, which cites as its
source: Analysis by Franklin Asso-
ciates, Ltd. for U.S. Environmental
Protection Agency, Office of Solid
Waste.

[a]Projections assume no major new
federal policies to reduce waste
generation.

are utilized in a given quantity of output. In fact, this last remedy has already
been used to some extent in our economy, in which nearly two-thirds of our
output growth has been achieved without an increased use of raw materials.

The Edifice Complex

Many think of industry as the primary villain in environmental damage. But:

While private firms have done their share in harming the environment, private
individuals and government have also been prime contributors.

In the United Kingdom the open fireplace in the private home may well have
been the largest single source of air pollution, and the emissions of private
passenger cars play an important role in the air pollution problems of most major
cities. Wastes from flush toilets and residential washing machines also cause
significant harm. Governments, too, add to the problem. The wastes of municipal treatment plants are a major source of water pollution. Military aircraft leave
a long trail of exhaust and make a lot of noise. Obsolete atomic materials and
byproducts associated with chemical and nuclear weapons are among the most
dangerous of all wastes, and the problem of their disposal is far from solved.

There is at least one type of environmental damage that, in particular, has
been closely associated with government activity. Government agencies, presumably in an attempt to maximize their influence, have undertaken the
construction of giant dams and reservoirs that flood farmlands and destroy
canyons, that render other soil unusable because of seepage of salts into the earth,
and that change the water table (the level of water under the ground) by
evaporation and seepage. Often, the drainage of swamps has subsequently altered
local ecology irrevocably; the building of canals has diverted the flow of rivers;
and the construction of dams has flooded and destroyed irreplaceable areas of
natural beauty. The U.S. Army Corps of Engineers, in particular, has been

accused of acting on the basis of this "edifice complex," although it seems recently to have modified its behavior.

But the edifice complex has reached its greatest heights in the communist states. Perhaps the leading advocate of giant earth-moving projects was Stalin, and his pride in enormous hydroelectric installations and huge canals was well publicized in the Soviet press.

Environmental Damage as an Externality

We have already indicated that our very existence means that some environmental damage is inevitable. Products of the earth must be used up, and wastes must be generated in the process of creating the means of subsistence.

There is no question of reducing environmental damage to zero. As long as the human race survives, complete elimination of such damage is literally impossible. *It is not even desirable to get as close as possible to zero damage.* Some pollutants in small quantities are quickly dispersed and rendered harmless by natural processes, and it is not worth the opportunity cost to eliminate others whose damage is slight. Use of a large quantity of resources for this purpose may so limit their supply that there will not be materials available for the construction of hospitals, schools, and other things more important to society than the elimination of some pollutants.

The real issue then is not whether pollution should exist at all, but whether environmental damage in an unregulated market economy tends to be more serious and widespread than the public interest can tolerate. This issue immediately raises three key questions. First, why do economists believe that environmental damage is unacceptably severe *in terms of the public interest?* And how do they measure "the public interest"? Second, why does the market mechanism, which is so good at providing about the right number of toasters and trucks, generate too much pollution? What goes wrong with the system? And, third, what can we do about it? We will consider these questions in order.

Economists do not claim any special ability to judge what is good for the public interest. They normally prefer to accept the wishes of the members of the public as adequate indicators of "the public interest." When the economy reflects these wishes as closely as it can, given the resources and technology available, economists conclude that it is working effectively. When it operates in a way that frustrates the desires of the people, they conclude that the economy is functioning improperly. Why, then, do economists believe that the market mechanism generates "too much" pollution?

To answer this, we must deal with the fundamental 1911 analysis of A. C. Pigou that we referred to at the beginning of this chapter. In Chapter 29 we discussed some of the failures of the market mechanism and singled out externalities as a primary cause of market failure. An *externality*, it will be recalled, is an incidental consequence of some economic activity that can be either beneficial or detrimental to someone who neither controls the activity nor is intentionally served by it. The emission of pollutants constitutes one of the most clear-cut and standard examples of a detrimental externality. The smoke from a chemical plant affects persons other than the management of the plant or its customers. Because the damage done by the smoke to parties incidentally involved does not enter the financial accounts of the firm whose plant produces the emissions, the owners of the firm have no financial incentive to restrain those emissions, particularly since emission control costs money. Instead, they will find it profitable to produce their chemical product and to emit their smoke as though it caused no external damage to the community.

One way to look at the matter is as a failure of the pricing system. Through the smoke externality, the business firm is able to use up some of the community's clean air without paying for the privilege. Just as the firm would undoubtedly use oil and electricity wastefully if they were obtainable at no charge, the firm will also use the community's air wastefully, despoiling it with smoke far beyond the level that the public interest can justify. Rather than being at the (low) socially desirable level, the quantity of smoke will be at whatever (usually high) level is necessary to save as much money as possible for the firm that emits it, because the external damage caused by the smoke costs the firm nothing.

Externalities play a crucial role affecting the quality of life. They show why the market mechanism, which is so efficient in supplying consumers' goods, has a much poorer record in terms of its effects on the environment. The problem of pollution illustrates the importance of externalities for public policy and indicates why their analysis is one of our 12 Ideas for Beyond the Final Exam.

Supply–Demand Analysis of Environmental Problems

Basic supply–demand analysis can be used to explain both how externalities lead to environmental problems and how these problems can be cured. As an illustration, let us deal with the problem of solid wastes—and the damage that the massive generation of garbage is doing to our environment.

In Figure 31–2 we see a demand curve, DE, for garbage removal. As usual, this curve has a negative slope, meaning that if the price of garbage removal is set sufficiently high, people will become more sparing in the amount of garbage

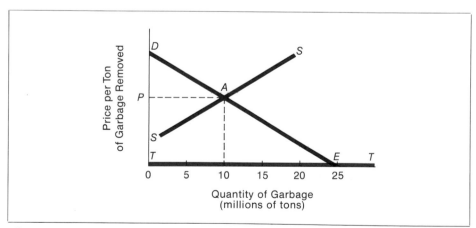

Figure 31–2
FREE DUMPING OF POLLUTANTS AS AN INDUCEMENT TO ENVIRONMENTAL DAMAGE
Whether wastes are solid, liquid, or gaseous, they impose costs upon the community. If the emitter is not charged for the damage, it is as though the resulting wastes were removed with zero charges to the polluter (blue removal supply curve TT). The polluter is then induced to pollute a great deal (25 million tons in the figure). If the charges to him reflected the true cost to the community (supply curve SS of waste removal), it would pay to emit a much smaller amount (10 million tons in the figure).

removal they order. They may more often bring papers, bottles, and cans to recycling centers and public dumps; they may repair broken items rather than throwing them out; and so on. In short, a higher price of garbage removal can be expected to reduce the quantity demanded of garbage removal services.

The graph also shows the supply curve, SS, which we can expect to prevail in an ideal market for garbage removal. Garbage disposal is expensive to society—it requires people and trucks to haul it away; garbage dumps occupy valuable land; and the use of fire or other means to get rid of the garbage creates pollution which, as we have seen, has a high real cost to the community. As we saw in our analysis of competitive industries (Chapter 22), the position of the market's supply curve depends on the marginal cost of garbage removal. If suppliers had to pay the full costs of garbage removal, the supply curve would be comparably high (as drawn in the graph) and have a positive slope, meaning that the marginal cost of garbage disposal rises as the quantity rises. We see that, for the community depicted in the graph, the price of garbage removal will be P dollars per ton, and at that price 10 million tons will be generated (point A).

But what if the community's government decides to remove garbage "free"? Of course, that means the government is really charging the consumer for the service in the form of taxes, but not in a way that makes each consumer pay an amount that reflects the quantity of garbage that he produces. The result is that the supply curve is no longer SS; rather, it becomes the blue line TT, which lies along the horizontal axis. What this says is that any one household can increase the garbage it throws away as much as it wishes and still pay a zero price for the additional amount. Now the intersection of the supply and demand curve is no longer point A. Rather it is point E, at which the price is zero and the quantity of garbage generated is 25 million tons—an amount substantially greater than would be produced if those who made the garbage had to pay the cost of getting rid of it.

Similar problems occur if the community offers the oxygen of its waterways and the purity of its atmosphere at a zero price to all who choose to utilize them, however wastefully and however great the quantities they decide to use up. The amount that will be wasted and otherwise used up is likely to be enormously greater than it would be if users had to pay for the cost of their actions to society. And that, in the view of economists, is one major reason for the severity of our environmental problems. Several conclusions follow:

1. The magnitude of our pollution problem is attributable in large part to the fact that the community lets individuals, firms, and government agencies deplete such resources as oxygen in the water and pure air without financial charge.
2. One way of dealing with pollution problems is to charge those who emit pollution, and who despoil the environment in other ways, a price commensurate with the costs they impose on the community.
3. This is another instance in which higher prices—on environmentally damaging activities—can be beneficial to the community.

Basic Approaches to Environmental Policy

In broad terms, three general methods have been proposed for the control of activities that damage the environment.

1. **Voluntary programs,** such as nonmandatory investment in pollution control equipment by firms that decide to act in a manner that meets their social responsibilities, or voluntary separation of solid wastes by consumers who deliver them to collection centers for recycling.

2. **Direct controls,** which either (a) impose legal ceilings on the amount any polluter is permitted to emit (as in the Delaware River program); or (b) specify how particular activities must be carried on—for example, they may prohibit backyard incinerators, or the use of high-sulfur coal, or require smokestack "scrubbers" to capture emissions of electric-generating installations.

3. **Taxes on emissions,** or the use of other monetary incentives or penalties to make it unattractive financially for emitters of pollutants to continue to pollute as usual.

Each of these methods has its place. If used appropriately, together they can constitute an effective and efficient environmental program. Let us consider each of them in turn.

Voluntarism

We can deal very briefly with voluntary programs. Voluntary control of pollution has usually proved to be weak and unreliable. Voluntary programs for the collection and separation of garbage into different and easily recyclable materials have rarely managed to reroute more than a small fraction of a community's wastes from the garbage dump to the recycling plants. Some business people with strong consciences have manifested good intentions and made sincere attempts to improve the practices of their companies. Yet competition has usually prevented them from spending more than token amounts for this purpose. No business, whatever its virtues, can long afford to have the prices of its products undercut by rival suppliers. As a result, voluntary business programs have often been more helpful to the companies' public relations activities than to the environment, and those with a real interest in environmental protection have called for legislation that *requires* all firms, including competitors, to undertake the same measures, thereby subjecting all firms in the industry to similar handicaps. Even then, competitive pressures and weak consciences may lead to behavior that is more than a bit questionable, as exemplified by the spurt of dumping of toxic wastes just before new regulations went into effect in November 1980 (see the boxed insert on the next page).

Yet voluntary measures do have their place. They are appropriate where alternative measures are not readily available. Where surveillance and, consequently, enforcement is impractical, as in the prevention of littering by campers in isolated areas, there is no choice but an appeal to people's consciences. And in brief but serious emergencies, in which there is no time to plan and enact a systematic program, there may also be no good substitute for voluntary compliance. Several major cities have, for example, experienced episodes in which there were temporary but dangerous concentrations of pollutants and the authorities were forced to appeal to the public to avoid activities that would have aggravated the problem. One can easily cite cases in which experience shows that public response to appeals requiring cooperation for short periods has been enthusiastic and gratifying. To summarize:

Voluntary programs are not dependable ways to protect the environment. However, in brief, unexpected emergencies or where effective surveillance is impossible, the policymaker may have no other choice. Sometimes in these cases voluntary programs even work.

Direct Controls

Direct controls have been the chief instrument of environmental policy in the United States. The federal government, through the Environmental Protection

Toxic Wastes Hurriedly Dumped Before New Law Goes into Effect

BOSTON, Nov. 15—Thousands of tons of hazardous and toxic wastes are being hurriedly dumped into city sewer systems, spilled from moving trucks onto busy interstate highways and abandoned in shopping center parking lots around the country in a last-minute rush to dispose of the chemicals before a Federal "cradle-to-grave" waste monitoring system begins next week. . . .

Hugh Kaufman, the Environmental Protection Agency's chief hazardous waste investigator, said, "The pressure is on the companies that make and use these chemicals to get the stuff off their site and onto somebody else's court before Nov. 19, when they have to accept responsibility for them."

"Nobody wants to have a paper trail back to them so that they can be sued some day, not if they can help it," he added. . . .

Techniques used to dispose of wastes illegally have included shipments of chemicals by railroad car to fictitious addresses hundreds of miles away, the renting of warehouses by disposal companies that later disappear and cannot be traced after leaving hundreds of barrels of chemicals behind, and "midnight dumping."

The latter practice is usually discovered when residents report tank trucks, their headlights out and their license plates obscured, roaring down country roads late at night. Investigation often finds that the trucks have dumped dangerous chemicals, some of them cancer-causing, into streams, swamps, fields and landfill areas, chemicals that later work their way into ground-water supplies.

SOURCE: Michael Knight, "Toxic Wastes Hurriedly Dumped Before New Law Goes Into Effect." *The New York Times*, November 16, 1980. © The New York Times Company. Reprinted by permission.

Agency, formulates standards for air and water quality and requires state and local governments to adopt rules that will assure achievement of those goals. Probably the best known of these are the standards for automobile emissions. Since 1968, new automobiles have been required to pass tests showing that their emissions of a number of pollutants do not exceed specified amounts. In addition, several states have required that used cars also adhere to certain limits on emissions. As another example, localities may prohibit the use of particularly "dirty" fuels by industry or may require the adoption of certain processes to "cleanse" those fuels or their emissions. Typical of these programs are local ordinances regulating the type and sulfur content of the fuels used by power plants, factories, and other stationary sources of sulfur dioxide pollution. Relocation of such pollution sources outside populated areas, and the required installation of smokestack emissions controls, have also contributed to better air quality.

Taxes on Emissions

Most economists agree that a nearly exclusive reliance on direct controls is a mistake and that, in most cases, financial penalties on polluters can do the same job more dependably, more effectively, and more economically. The most common suggestion is that firms be permitted to pollute all they want but be forced to pay a tax for the privilege to make them *want* to pollute less. A tax on emissions simply requires the polluter to install a meter that records his emissions in the same way his electric meter records his use of electricity. At the end of the month the government automatically sends him a bill charging him a stipulated amount for each gallon of wastes (the amount must also vary with the quality of the wastes—a higher tax rate being imposed on wastes that are more dangerous or unpleasant). Thus, the more damage the polluter does the more he must pay. This tax is deliberately designed to *encourage* the use of its glaring loophole—the polluter *can* reduce the tax he pays by decreasing the amount he emits. In terms of Figure 31–2, if the tax is used to increase the payment for waste emissions from zero (blue supply line *TT*) and instead forces the polluter to pay its true cost to society, emissions will automatically be reduced from 25 down to 10 million tons.

People do respond to such taxes. The most widely publicized example is the Ruhr River basin in West Germany, where emissions taxes have been used for more than three decades. Though the Ruhr is one of the world's most concentrated industrial centers, those of its rivers that are protected by taxes are sufficiently clean to be usable for fishing and other recreational purposes. Firms have also found it profitable to avoid the taxes by extracting pollutants from their liquid discharges and recycling them. For example, almost 40 percent of the industrial acids used in the Ruhr have been recovered in this way.

Emissions Taxes Versus Direct Controls

It is important to see why taxes on emissions may prove more effective and reliable than direct controls. Direct controls essentially rely on the enforcement mechanism of the criminal justice system. Rules are set up that the polluter must obey. If the polluter violates those rules, he must first be caught. Then the regulatory agency must decide whether it has enough evidence to prosecute. Next, it must win its case before the courts. And, finally, the courts must impose a penalty that is more than just a token gesture. If any one of these steps does not occur, then the polluter gets away with his damaging activities.

Enforcing Direct Controls

The enforcement of direct controls requires vigilance and enthusiasm by the regulatory agency, which must assign the resources and persons needed to carry out the task of enforcement. Yet experience indicates that regulatory vigor is far from universal and often evaporates as time passes and public concern recedes. In many cases the resources devoted to enforcement are pitifully small. Under the Reagan administration environmental outlays have, indeed, been cut severely.

The effectiveness of direct controls also depends upon the speed and rigor of the courts. Yet the courts are often slow and lenient. An example is the notorious case of the Reserve Mining Company. Several Minnesota communities, environmentalists, federal agencies, and officials from three states attempted to stop this company from pouring its wastes (which contain certain asbestos-like fibers believed to cause cancer) into Lake Superior, which is the source of the communities' drinking water. Only after 12 years of litigation and 16 judicial decisions did the courts manage to force Reserve to curb this discharge in March 1980.

Finally, direct controls can work only if the legislation imposes sizable penalties for violators. But the following is not atypical: "During three years of intense environmental regulation in Connecticut (1971–1974), only 16 of 1469 air pollution violations were referred to the State Attorney General for possible prosecution. . . . Of the 16 cases . . . by 1975, the state [environmental] agency had obtained three injunctions and no fines or penalties of any type."[6] One can cite many cases in which large firms have been convicted of polluting and fined less than $5000—an amount beneath the notice of even a relatively small corporation. The following newspaper excerpts illustrate the sorts of fines to which polluters may be subjected:

[6]William Drayton, "Economic Law Enforcement," *Harvard Environmental Law Review* 4, No. 1 (1980), page 2, fn. 3.

Ten Philadelphia firms were fined a total of $2900 Friday in the seventh week of the City's accelerated drive for violation of the air-pollution code.[7]

Seven companies, six from the Chicago area, have been charged with pollution of area rivers and waterways . . . the corporations could be fined up to $2500 on each count if convicted.[8]

A New Jersey company was fined $2125 for illegal discharge of hydrofluoric acid into a parking lot from which it could seep into the ground water.[9]

[New York City] has collected $800,000 in fines against [all] air and noise polluters over the last three years. . . .[10]

Where more drastic penalties are available, their very magnitude may make the authorities reluctant to impose them. In an extreme case, in which the only legal remedy is to force the closing of an offending plant, the government agency is likely to back down under local pressure to preserve the community's source of jobs and income.

Enforcing Taxes

In contrast, pollution taxes are automatic and certain. No one need be caught, prosecuted, convicted, and punished. The tax bills are just sent out automatically by the untiring tax collector. The only sure way for the polluter to work his way out of paying pollution charges is to cut down his emissions.

A second difference between direct controls and taxes is worth noting. Suppose there is a ruling under a program of direct controls that Filth, Inc., must cut its emissions by 50 percent. Then that firm has absolutely no motivation to go one drop further. Why should it cut its emissions by 55 or even 52 percent when the law offers it neither reward nor encouragement for going beyond the selected quota? Under a system of emission taxes, however, the more the firm cuts back on its pollution, the more it saves in tax payments.

A third important difference between direct controls and taxes on emissions is the greater efficiency of the latter in the use of resources. It is claimed that the tax approach can do the job far more cheaply, saving labor, fuel, and raw materials, which can instead be used to build schools, hospitals, and housing for low-income groups. Statistical estimates for several pollution control programs suggest that the cost of doing the job through direct controls can easily be twice as high as under the tax alternative.

Why should there be such a difference? The answer is that under direct controls the job of cutting back emissions is apportioned among the various polluters on some principle (usually intended to approximate some standard of fairness) that is selected by the regulators. This rarely assigns the task in accord with ability to carry it out cheaply and efficiently. Suppose it costs firm A only 3 cents a gallon to reduce emissions while firm B must spend 20 cents a gallon to do the same job. If both firms spew out 2000 gallons of pollution a day, a 50 percent reduction in pollution can be achieved by ordering both firms to limit emissions

[7]Joseph H. Trachtman, "10 Firms Fined a Total of $2,900 in Phila.'s Pollution Crackdown." Reprinted by permission of *The Philadelphia Inquirer*, October 30, 1970.

[8]Robert Davis, "7 Firms Charged with Water Pollution." *Chicago Tribune*, September 21, 1971, page 8, Section 1A. Reprinted courtesy of the *Chicago Tribune*.

[9]"DEP Fines Firm in Dumping," *Newark StarLedger*, October 2, 1980.

[10]"Pollution Fines $800,000 in 3 Years." *The New York Times*, June 25, 1974, page 37. ©1974 by The New York Times Company. Reprinted by permission.

to 1000 gallons a day. This may or may not be fair, but it is certainly not efficient. The social cost will be 1000 times 3 cents, or $30, to firm A and 1000 times 20 cents, or $200, to firm B, a total of $230.

If, instead, a tax of 10 cents a gallon had been imposed, all the work would have been done by firm A—which can do it more cheaply. Firm A would have cut its emissions out altogether, paying the 3 cents a gallon this requires, to avoid the 10 cents a gallon tax. Firm B would go on polluting as before, because it is cheaper to pay the tax than the 20 cents a gallon it costs to control its pollution. In this way, under the tax, *total daily emissions will still be cut by 2000 gallons a day.* But the entire job will be done by the polluter who can do it more cheaply, and the total daily cost of the program will therefore be $60 (3 cents × 2000 gallons) instead of the $230 it would cost under direct controls.

The secret of the efficiency induced by a tax on pollution is straightforward. Only polluters who can reduce emissions cheaply and efficiently can afford to take advantage of the built-in loophole—the opportunity to save on taxes by reducing emissions. The tax approach simply assigns the job to those who can do it most effectively.

Advantages and Disadvantages
Given all these advantages of the tax approach, why would anyone want to use direct controls?

There are three general and important situations in which direct controls have a clear advantage:

1. *Where an emission is so dangerous that it is decided to prohibit it altogether.* Here there is obviously nothing to be gained by installing complicated procedures for the collection of taxes that will never be paid because there will be no emissions for which payment is required.

2. *Where a sudden change in circumstances—for example, a dangerous air quality crisis—calls for prompt and substantial changes in conduct, such as temporary reductions in use of cars or incinerators.* It is difficult and clumsy to change tax rules, and direct controls will usually do a better job here. The mayor of the threatened city can, for example, forbid the use of private passenger cars until the crisis passes.

3. *Where effective and dependable metering devices have not been invented or are prohibitively costly to install and operate.* In such cases there is no way to operate an effective tax program because the amount of wastes the polluter has emitted cannot be determined and so his tax bill cannot be calculated. In that case the only effective option may be to *require* him to use "clean" fuel, or install emissions-purification equipment.

In reality there is often no device analogous to a gas or water meter that can be used to measure pollution emissions cheaply and effectively. For example, to evaluate emissions in waterways, the standard procedure is to take samples, bring them to a laboratory, and subject them to a series of complicated tests that often take weeks to carry out, to determine the chemical contents of the emissions. For a polluter whose emissions are very large, this may be worth doing. But for the emitter who only spews out a few gallons of pollutants a day, the cost of such a complex process is likely to exceed the benefits. Whatever their other inefficiencies, direct controls are still likely to do the job of controlling such sources of pollution more cheaply. On the other side of the argument, however, the widespread adoption of emissions charges and the resulting rise in demand for metering devices may lead to research and development that produces cheaper and more effective meters.

Other Financial Devices to Protect the Environment

The basic idea underlying the emissions-tax approach to environmental protection is that it provides financial incentives that induce the polluter to reduce the damage he does to the environment. But emissions taxes are not the only form of financial inducement that have been proposed. There are at least two others that deserve consideration: *subsidies for reduced emissions* and the requirement of *emissions permits* for polluters, each permit authorizing the emission of a specified quantity of pollutant. Such permits would be offered for sale in limited quantities fixed by the authorities at prices set by demand and supply.

Subsidies

Subsidies are already in use. Their advocates say that financial inducements can be just as effective when they take the form of a reward for good behavior as when they are composed of penalties (taxes) on behavior that is considered harmful. A donkey can be induced to move forward just as surely (and with much less unpleasantness) by dangling a carrot in front of his nose as by applying a stick to his rump. Environmental subsidies usually take one of two forms:

1. Partial payment of the cost of installation of some sort of pollution control equipment.
2. The offer of a fixed reward for every reduction in emissions from some base level, usually some amount that the polluter used to emit in the past.

A subsidy to help defray the cost of control equipment can be effective when the purchaser of the equipment was considering doing it anyhow but did not because of the high cost. This may be the case for a municipality that wants to treat its wastes more thoroughly but has not found a way to afford the cost. It may also be the case in private industry, where collection of the wastes that would otherwise be emitted can yield products that are valuable and reusable but where the equipment required for the process is too costly. But where the polluter gains nothing from such control, a partial subsidy for the purchase of control equipment is not likely to be very effective. It simply reduces the cost of something he does not want to do in any event.

The second type of subsidy—a reward based on quantity of reduced emissions—does indeed have the same sort of incentive effects as a tax for the *individual* polluter. In both cases the more he emits, the worse off he is financially, either because he receives a smaller subsidy payment or because his tax bill is higher. But as far as the *industry* is concerned, there is a world of difference between the effect of a tax and the effect of a subsidy. *A tax discourages the output of commodities whose production causes pollution, whereas a subsidy encourages such output to expand.* Consider the difference between the tax and subsidy approaches in the case of automotive emissions. A tax will increase the cost of operating cars, thereby encouraging the use of public transportation (which produces far lower quantities of emissions than does the automobile per passenger-mile traveled). On the other hand, a subsidy for the installation of emissions-control devices will tend to encourage the use of autos at the expense of public transportation by keeping down the price of cars.

It is a paradox that a subsidy intended to induce an industry to reduce its emissions can actually *increase* the size of the industry's output and consequently *increase* its total emissions.

This paradox is readily illustrated with the help of a standard supply–demand diagram for a competitive industry. We see in Figure 31–3 that a tax on polluting output will raise the costs of the industry and hence raise the price of whatever quantity it supplies. Thus, the supply curve will be shifted upward by a tax to the curve labeled "supply after tax." Similarly, the subsidy will reduce dollar costs to the industry and so will shift the supply curve downward to the curve labeled "supply after subsidy." So, under a tax on emissions, the equilibrium point will move from point E to point T, reducing the output of the polluting product from e to t. But the subsidy, which moves the supply–demand equilibrium point from E to S, will actually increase the output of the polluting industry from e to s! How does this happen? While the pollution-reduction subsidy will induce firms to decrease their emissions somewhat, it will attract new polluting firms into the industry, and as the graph shows, the net result may be that the subsidy will backfire, and instead of reducing pollution, as it is intended to do, it will actually increase it.

The main advantage of subsidies over taxes as a financial inducement to decrease pollution is that subsidies attract less opposition and are therefore more easily adopted through the political process. Obviously, industry always prefers a subsidy to a tax. But the rest of the community may well be worse off if a subsidy is selected instead of an emissions tax.

Emissions Permits

A third type of financial inducement strongly advocated by some economists, but so far not adopted directly by any government, is the sale of *emissions permits.*

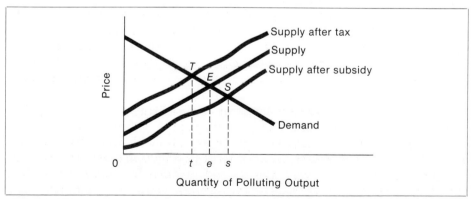

Figure 31–3
SUPPLY–DEMAND EQUILIBRIUM IN A POLLUTING COMPETITIVE INDUSTRY
A tax on pollution raises costs and so shifts the supply curve upward; that is, a higher price is needed to elicit a given quantity supplied. This causes equilibrium output to fall from e to t and succeeds in its purpose—reducing pollution. But a subsidy to those who decrease their polluting output reduces costs and shifts the supply curve downward. By reducing costs, it attracts more firms into the industry. Paradoxically, output of the polluting product actually must increase from e to s.

Under this arrangement, the environmental agency decides what quantity of emissions per unit of time (say, per month) is tolerable and then issues a batch of permits authorizing (altogether) just that amount of pollution. The permits are offered for sale to the highest bidders. Their price is therefore determined by demand and supply. It will be high if the number of permits offered for sale is small and there is a large amount of industrial activity that must use the permits. Similarly, the price of a permit will be low if many permits are issued but the quantity of pollution for which they are demanded is small.

The emissions permit in many ways works like a tax—it simply makes it too expensive for the polluter to continue emitting as much as he would have without it. In addition, the permit offers two clear advantages over the tax approach. First, it reduces uncertainty about the quantity that will be emitted into the community. Under a tax we cannot be sure about this in advance, since that depends on the extent to which polluters respond to the tax rate that is selected. In the case of permits, the ceiling on emissions is decided in advance by the environmental authorities, who enforce the ceiling simply by issuing permits authorizing a specific total quantity of emissions.

Second, a given tax on emissions can be made ineffective by inflation. For example, a tax of X dollars may become insignificant as inflation erodes the value of the dollar, even though it may have been effective when it was first enacted and the price level was much lower. However, as long as there is no change in quantity of emissions authorized by license, inflation will obviously have no effect on the amount of pollution. It will simply raise the price of a license along with the prices of other commodities.

A shortcoming of the pollution license idea is its apparent political unattractiveness. Many people react indignantly to the notion of "licenses to pollute." Yet the EPA has recently introduced some compromise measures which can be regarded as approximations to a market in emissions permits (see the boxed insert on the next page). It is too soon to judge the effectiveness of these new programs, but they do illustrate how much can be achieved by intelligent compromise in policy making.

On the Equity and Cost of Some Current Programs

This chapter began with a discussion of some shortcomings in the plans for the protection of the Delaware River. We are now in a position to identify the sources of those shortcomings and to note why the same difficulties are likely to be encountered in other environmental programs. It will be recalled that the two issues that were raised were the unnecessarily high costs of the plans for the Delaware and the inequities that appear to beset the emissions quotas assigned under the program.

The source of the inefficiencies should be clear from the discussion of the last section. The Delaware program is one of direct controls, and consequently it does not have any procedures to apportion the task of emissions reduction in accord with the relative efficiency with which different emitters can carry it out. Because much of the job is assigned to those for whom the cost of controlling discharges is high, the entire program becomes unnecessarily costly. This is just a particular example of the cost of using direct controls rather than a tax on emissions, a cost to which, economists believe, policymakers have given inadequate attention.

Under direct controls the authorities usually aim at an *equitable* assignment of emissions quotas. For example, they may require all polluters to reduce their

What's New in Environmental Protection?

As indicated in the text, one remedy for pollution favored by economists as an alternative to direct controls is the issuance of a limited set of pollution permits which would be sold on a free market. Recently, the Environmental Protection Agency (EPA) has begun to experiment with two programs, the "bubble concept" and the emissions offset program, both of which work very much like a market in emissions permits.

THE EMISSIONS OFFSET PROGRAM.
In several rulings issued in the late 1970s, the EPA introduced a new program designed to facilitate economic growth while holding the line on air pollution. This policy allows new factories or other new sources of air pollution to be constructed so long as their emissions are more than offset by reductions in pollution from sources that are already in operation. Firm A can open for business if it can induce firm B (via direct payments or in some other way) to adopt pollution controls which cut down B's emissions by an amount at least equal to A's proposed emissions. This program opens up the possibility that what amounts to a market in pollution permits might spring up, in which current polluters sell some of their permitted emissions levels to potential polluters. The sale price would constitute a tax on emissions which should be effective in discouraging them. So far few of the offsets transactions have worked out quite this way. Instead, firms have obtained permits to build new plants either by offsetting reductions in other plants they own (for example, the U.S. Steel Corporation's factory in Birmingham, Alabama, was required by the local pollution board to cut back its emissions before adding new facilities) or by offsetting reductions in emissions by some government agency (in Pennsylvania state officials worked out a trade-off involving a switch to nonpolluting road-paving materials on the state's highways to offset the pollution from a new Volkswagen auto assembly plant in New Stanton). But interest in the program seems to be rising and there is reason to believe that it may lead to an effective market, levying a charge on emissions, like that advocated by economists.

THE BUBBLE CONCEPT.
This program, begun in 1979, deals with firms already in operation rather than newly established plants or firms, as the offset program does. In other respects, however, the programs are similar. Under the bubble program a firm is permitted to satisfy its mandatory air pollution ceiling in any way it finds most economical. With the old direct controls, each pollution discharge point in a factory or plant was regulated. But under the bubble concept, rather than requiring a firm to reduce emissions from one discharge point by 10 tons, emissions from another discharge point by 10 tons, and emissions from a third discharge point by 20 tons, the firm can divide its required 40-ton reduction among its discharge points in any way it wants (subject to a number of conditions). The entire set of operations by the firm is thus considered to be encased in an imaginary bubble with a single discharge point. The EPA does not care what goes on inside the bubble, that is, whether emissions come from one point or another, as long as emissions from the entire bubble stay within the required limits.

More recently, firms whose total emissions fall below the required limits are permitted to sell the unused emission rights to other firms whose "bubbles" are not performing so well. One recent and rather careful study indicates that the program can reduce a chemical firm's cost of meeting its pollution requirements by more than 80 percent, so that interest in the program by business firms may well grow substantially.

discharges by the same percentage. How, then, did it happen that one large firm was assigned a quota five times as large as another, similar enterprise? The answer is that equal percentage reductions turn out to be far less equitable than they sound at first. As a result, any attempt to put them into practice almost always results in complaints, political pressures, renegotiation of quotas, and a consequent set of assignments that seem to have been designed with the aid of a roulette wheel rather than a deliberate decision-making process.

Why are equal percentage reductions in emissions not generally equitable? We have already seen one reason: Costs of reduction are not the same for all industries or all plants in an industry. For example, the cost for a typical beet sugar plant to reduce its emissions (as measured in terms of the oxygen these wastes use up) is only about one-sixth as large as an equivalent reduction for a petroleum refinery. A modern paper plant can usually decrease its discharges at much less cost than can an antiquated plant in the same industry. Is it really *fair* to require all these firms to cut back their emissions by the same amounts when, through no fault of their own, the resulting financial burden is so different?

There are even clearer examples of the potential inequity in equal percentage reductions. Consider two companies, one run by a conscientious environmentalist who has voluntarily installed substantial amounts of equipment to cleanse and reduce his emissions, and the other run by an irresponsible management, which has continued to allow as much garbage to pour into public waterways as maximum profitability requires. Is it really fair for both these firms to be told to cut back equally?

Once such problems and others like them are recognized, and an attempt made to reassign emissions quotas accordingly, it will become clear that each emitter is a special case requiring special treatment. The regulator is almost forced to proceed case by case, and the resulting quotas end up following complex patterns that are at best difficult to defend in terms of equity or efficiency.

Two Cheers for the Market

The lesson of this chapter is a very general one. The focus of Parts Three through Five has been to learn which tasks the market mechanism performs well and which it performs poorly. We have seen in this chapter that protecting the environment is one task that cannot be left to the free market: because of the important externalities involved, the market will systematically allocate too few resources to the job. However, this market failure does not imply that the price mechanism must be discarded. On the contrary, we have seen that a market solution—based on pollution charges—may well be the best way to protect the environment. At least in this case, the power of the market mechanism can be harnessed to correct its own failings.

Summary

1. Pollution is as old as human history; and contrary to some popular notions, some forms of pollution were actually decreasing even before recent programs were initiated to protect the environment.

2. Both planned and market economies suffer from substantial environmental problems.

3. The production of commodities *must* cause waste disposal problems unless everything is recycled, but even recycling processes cause pollution (and use up energy).

4. Industrial activity causes environmental damage, but so does the activity of private individuals (as when they drive cars that emit pollutants). Government agencies also damage the environment (as when military airplanes emit noise and exhaust, or a hydroelectric project floods large areas).

5. Pollution is an externality—when a factory emits smoke, it dirties laundry and may damage the health of persons who neither work for the smoking factory nor buy its products. Hence, pollution control cannot be left to the free market. This is another of our 12 Ideas for Beyond the Final Exam.

6. Pollution can be controlled by voluntary programs, direct controls, taxes on emissions, or other monetary incentives for the reduction of emissions.

7. Most economists believe that the tax approach is the most efficient and effective way to control detrimental externalities.

8. Subsidies for reduced pollution by the individual firm may actually backfire by making it profitable for more polluting firms to go into business.

Concepts for Review

Externality	Pollution charges (taxes on emissions)	Emissions permits
Direct controls	Subsidies for reduced emissions	

Questions for Discussion

1. What sorts of pollution problems would you expect in a small African village? In a city in India? In communist China? In New York City?
2. Economists maintain that while *some reduction* in pollution is usually desirable, it is not desirable to reduce most pollutants to zero. Why may this be a reasonable view?
3. Suppose you are assigned the task of drafting a law to impose a tax on the emission of smoke. What provisions would you put into the law?
   a. How would you decide the size of the tax?
   b. What would you do about smoke emitted by a municipal electricity plant?
   c. Would you use the same tax rate on densely and sparsely settled areas?

   What information will you need to collect before determining what you would do about each of the preceding provisions?
4. Production of commodity X creates 10 pounds of emissions for every unit of X produced. The demand and supply curves for X are described by the following table:

Price (dollars)	10	9	8	7	6	5
Quantity demanded	80	85	90	95	100	105
Quantity supplied	100	95	90	85	80	75

   What is the equilibrium price and quantity, and how much pollution will be emitted?
5. If the price of X to consumers is $9, and the government imposes a tax of $2 per unit, show that because suppliers get only $7 they will produce only 85 units of output, not the 95 units of output they would produce if they received the full $9 per unit.
6. Show that, with this tax, the equilibrium price is $9 and the equilibrium quantity demanded is 85. How much pollution will now be emitted?
7. Compare your answers to Questions 4 and 6 and show how large a reduction in pollution emissions occurs because of the $2 tax on the polluting output.

The
Distribution
of Income VI

Pricing the Factors of Production: Interest, Rent, and Profits

32

> The most common and durable source of factions has been the various and unequal distribution of property.
>
> JAMES MADISON

arts Three, Four, and Five have been devoted to examining the things the free-market system does well and the things it does poorly. We have noted, especially in Chapter 29, that the market mechanism cannot be counted on to distribute income in accord with ethical notions of "fairness" or "justice," and we have listed this failing as one of the market's shortcomings. But there is much more to be said about how income is distributed in a market economy and about how governments interfere with and alter this distribution process. These are the subjects of Part Six.

The broad outlines of how the market mechanism distributes income are familiar to all of us. Each person owns some **factors of production**—the inputs used in the production process. Many of us have only our own labor; but some of us also have funds that we can lend, land that we can rent, or natural resources that we can sell. These factors are sold on markets at prices determined by supply and demand. So the distribution of income in a market economy is determined by the distribution of the factors of production and by their prices.

For purposes of discussion, the factors of production may be grouped into five broad categories: land, labor, capital, exhaustible natural resources, and a rather mysterious input called **entrepreneurship.** In this chapter, we will study the payments made for the use of three of these factors: the interest paid to capital, the rent of land, and the profits earned by entrepreneurs. Exhaustible natural resources are treated in Chapter 36. There is so much to be said about the labor market and wages that Chapter 33 will be devoted entirely to that important subject. Then, in Chapter 34, we will turn our attention to how and why the government influences the distribution of income.

Entrepreneurship is the act of starting new firms, introducing new products and technological innovations, and, in general, taking the risks that are necessary in seeking out business opportunities.

As James Madison realized (see the quotation at the beginning of the chapter), the distribution of income is perhaps the one area in economics in which any one individual's interests almost inevitably conflict with someone else's. By definition, if a larger share of the total income is distributed to me, a smaller share will be left for you. It is also a topic about which emotions run high and the facts or the logic of the issues are often ignored. In this chapter we will encounter several examples of serious misunderstandings about the facts: misapprehensions about the true magnitudes of interest rates and profits, people's unwillingness to face up to the consequences of rent controls, and so forth.

The Principle of Marginal Productivity

By now it will not surprise you to learn that factor prices are analyzed in terms of supply and demand. The supply sides of the markets for the various factors differ enormously from one another, which is why each factor market must be considered separately. But one basic principle, **the principle of marginal productivity,** has been used to explain the demand for every input. Before restating the principle, it will be useful to recall two concepts that were introduced in Chapter 20: **marginal physical product** (MPP) and **marginal revenue product** (MRP).

Table 32–1, which repeats Table 20–3 (page 374), helps us review these two concepts by recalling the example of Farmer Pfister who had to decide how much fertilizer to apply to his fixed plot of land. The marginal *physical* product (MPP) column tells us how many additional bushels of corn each additional ton of fertilizer yields. For example, according to the table, the fourth ton increases the crop by 300 bushels. The marginal *revenue* product (MRP) column tells us how many dollars this marginal physical product is worth. In the example in the table, corn is assumed always to sell at $2 per bushel, so the marginal revenue product of the fourth ton of fertilizer is $2 per bushel times 300 bushels, or $600. We can now state the marginal productivity principle formally:

The marginal productivity principle states that when factor markets are competitive it always pays a profit-maximizing firm to hire that quantity of any input at which the marginal revenue product is equal to the price of the input.

The basic logic behind the principle is both simple and powerful. If the input's marginal revenue product is, for example, greater than its price, it will pay the firm to hire more and more of it until diminishing returns reduce the marginal revenue product (MRP) to the level of the input's price. Conversely, if MRP is less than price, the firm is using too much of the input. Let us use Table 32–1 to demonstrate how the marginal productivity principle works.

Suppose the firm were using four tons of fertilizer at a cost of $350 per ton. Since the table tells us that a fifth ton has a marginal revenue product of $500, the firm could obviously add $150 to its profit by buying a fifth ton. Only when the firm has used so much fertilizer that (because of diminishing returns) the MRP of still another ton is less than $350 does it pay to stop expanding the use of fertilizer.

> The **marginal physical product** (MPP) of an input is the increase in output that results from a one-unit increase in the use of the input, holding the amounts of all other inputs constant.
>
> The **marginal revenue product** (MRP) of an input is the additional sales revenue the firm takes in by selling the marginal physical product of that input.

Table 32–1

MARGINAL PHYSICAL PRODUCTS AND MARGINAL REVENUE
PRODUCTS OF FARMER PFISTER'S FERTILIZER

TONS OF FERTILIZER	MARGINAL PHYSICAL PRODUCT (bushels)	MARGINAL REVENUE PRODUCT (dollars)
1	250	500
2	300	600
3	350	700
4	300	600
5	250	500
6	150	300
7	50	100
8	0	0
9	−50	−100

In this example, five tons is the optimal amount to use.

One corollary of the principle of marginal productivity is obvious: the quantity of the input demanded depends on its price. The lower the price of fertilizer, the more it pays a firm to hire. In the example of the previous paragraph, it pays the firm to use five tons when the price of fertilizer is $350 per ton. But if fertilizer were more expensive, say $550 per ton, that price would exceed the value of the marginal product of the fifth ton. It would, therefore, pay the firm to stop after the fourth ton. Thus, *marginal productivity analysis shows that the quantity demanded of an input normally will decline as the price of the input rises.* The "law" of demand applies to inputs just as it applies to consumer goods.

The Derived Demand Curve for an Input

We can, in fact, be much more specific than this, for the marginal productivity principle tells us precisely how the demand curve for any input is derived from its marginal revenue product (MRP) curve.

Figure 32–1 presents graphically the MRP schedule from Table 32–1. Recall that, according to the marginal productivity principle, the quantity demanded of the input is determined by setting MRP equal to the input's price. Figure 32–1 considers three different possible prices for a ton of fertilizer: $600, $500, and $300. At a price of $600 per ton, we see that the quantity demanded is four tons (point *A*). If the price of fertilizer drops to $500 per ton, quantity demanded rises to five tons (point *B*). Finally, should the price fall all the way to $300 per ton, the quantity demanded would be six tons (point *C*). Points *A*, *B*, and *C* are therefore three points on the demand curve for fertilizer. Thus:

The demand curve for any input is the downward-sloping portion of its marginal revenue product curve.

Note that we restrict ourselves to the *downward-sloping* portion of the MRP curve. The logic of the marginal productivity principle dictates this. For example, if the price of fertilizer is $500 per ton, there are two input quantities for which MRP is $500: one ton (point *D*) and five tons (point *B*). But point *D* cannot be the optimal stopping point because the MRP of a second ton ($600) is greater than the cost of the second ton ($500). The marginal productivity principle applies only in the range where returns are diminishing.

Figure 32–1

A MARGINAL REVENUE PRODUCT SCHEDULE
This diagram depicts the data in Table 32–1, which show how the marginal revenue product (MRP) of fertilizer first rises and then declines as more and more fertilizer is used. Since the optimal purchase rule is to keep applying fertilizer until MRP is reduced to the price of fertilizer, the *downward- sloping portion* of the MRP curve is Farmer Pfister's demand curve for fertilizer.

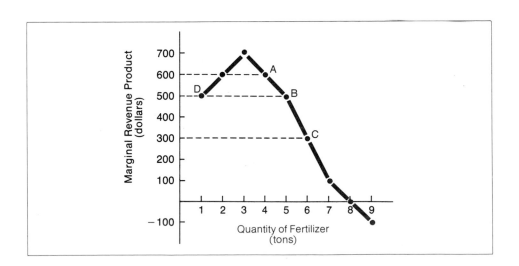

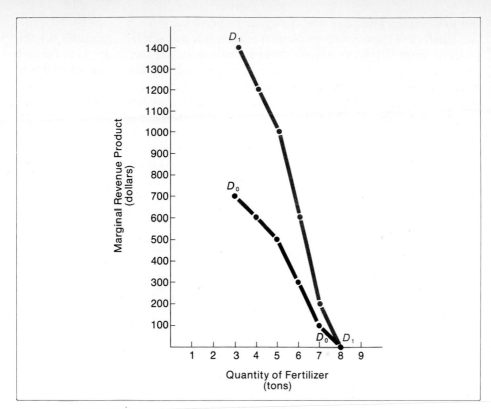

Figure 32–2
A SHIFT IN THE DEMAND
CURVE FOR FERTILIZER
If the price of corn goes up, the
marginal *revenue* product
curve shifts upward—from
D_0D_0 to D_1D_1 in the diagram—
even though the marginal
physical product curve has not
changed. In this sense, a
greater demand for corn leads
to a greater *derived* demand
for fertilizer.

The demand for fertilizer (or for any other input) is called a **derived demand** because it is derived from the underlying demand for the final product (corn in this case). For example, suppose that a surge in demand drove the price of corn to $4 per bushel. Then, at each level of fertilizer usage, the marginal revenue product would be twice as large as when corn fetched $2 per bushel. This is shown in Figure 32–2 as an *upward shift* of the (derived) demand curve for fertilizer, from D_0D_0 to D_1D_1.[1] We conclude that, in general:

An outward shift in the demand curve for any commodity causes an outward shift of the derived demand curve for all factors utilized in the production of that commodity.

Conversely, an inward shift in the demand curve for a commodity leads to inward shifts in the demand curves for factors used in producing that commodity.

This completes our discussion of the marginal productivity principle as a general explanation of the *demand* for any and all inputs. Now we will deal with the main factors of production individually, and see how their earnings are determined by the interaction of demand *and* supply. We begin with *interest payments*, the return to money capital.

The Issue of Usury Laws: Are Interest Rates Too High?

The rate of interest is the price at which money can be rented (borrowed). And, like other factor prices, the rate of interest is determined by supply and demand.

---

[1]To make the diagram easier to read, the (irrelevant) upward-sloping portions of each curve have been omitted.

However, this is one area in which many people have been dissatisfied with the outcome of the market process. Fears that interest rates, if left unregulated, would climb to exorbitant levels have made usury laws quite popular in many times and places. In recent U.S. history, for example, usury laws have set maximum rates on consumer loans, home mortgages, and the like. However, usury laws, when they are effective, interfere with the operation of supply and demand and are often harmful to economic efficiency.[2]

Whether a usury ceiling will or will not be effective depends on what the equilibrium rate of interest would have been in a free market. For example, a ceiling of 18 percent annual interest on consumer loans is quite irrelevant if the free-market equilibrium is 15 percent, but it can have important effects if the free-market rate is 25 percent. To see why this is so, we turn to the market determination of interest rates through the forces of supply and demand.

Investment, Capital, and Interest

There are many ways in which funds are rented: home mortgages, corporation or government bonds, consumer credit, and so on. On the demand side of these credit markets are *borrowers*—people or institutions that, for one reason or another, wish to spend more money than they currently have. The marginal productivity principle governs the demand for funds just as it governs the demand for fertilizer:

Firms will demand borrowed funds up to the point where the marginal revenue product of the investment financed by the money is reduced to the cost of borrowing.

Investment is the *flow* of resources into the production of new capital. It is the labor, steel, and other inputs devoted to the *construction* of factories, warehouses, railroads, and other pieces of capital during some period of time.

To make the relationships clear, consider the example of a business loan. To the business executive who "rents" (borrows) money in order to finance an **investment** and pays interest in return, the money really represents an intermediate step toward the acquisition of the machines, buildings, inventories, and other forms of physical **capital** that the firm will purchase with the funds. Though the words "investment" and "capital" are often used interchangeably in everyday parlance, it is important to keep the distinction in mind. The relation between investment and capital has an analogy in the filling of a bathtub: the accumulated water in the tub is analogous to the stock of capital, while the flow of water from the tap (which adds to the tub's water) is like the investment. Just as the tap must be turned on in order for more water to accumulate, the capital stock increases only when there is investment. If investment ceases, the capital stock stops growing. Notice that when investment is *zero*, the capital stock *remains constant;* it does not fall to zero any more than a bathtub suddenly becomes empty when you shut the tap.

Capital refers to an inventory (*a stock*) of plant, equipment and other productive resources held by a business firm, an individual, or some other organization.

The process of building up capital by investing, and then using this capital in production can be divided into five steps, which are listed below and summed up in Figure 32–3.

Step 1. The firm decides to enlarge its stock of capital.
Step 2. It raises the funds with which to finance its expansion.
Step 3. It uses these funds to hire the inputs, which are put to work building factories, warehouses, and the like. This step is the act of *investment*.
Step 4. After the investment is completed, the firm ends up with a larger stock of *capital*.

[2]For example, we learned in Chapter 6 that they used to cause particularly severe problems for housing during periods of rapid inflation.

Step 5. The capital is used (along with other inputs) either to expand production or to reduce costs. At this point the firm starts earning *returns* on its investment.

Notice that what the investor puts into the investment process is *money*, either his own or money that he has borrowed from others. The money is then transformed, in a series of steps, into a physical input suitable for use in production. If the money was borrowed, the investor will someday return it to the lender with some payment for its use. This payment is called **interest,** and it is calculated as a percentage per year of the amount borrowed. For example, if the *interest rate* is 12 percent per year and $1000 is borrowed, the annual interest payment is $120.

There is one noteworthy feature of capital that distinguishes it from other inputs, like coal, for example. The coal employed to make steel is used once and then it is gone; but the blast furnace, which is part of the firm's capital, normally lasts many years. The furnace is a *durable* good; and because it is durable it contributes not only to today's production, but also to future production. This fact makes calculating the marginal revenue product more complex for a capital good than for other inputs.

To determine whether the MRP of a capital good is greater than the cost of financing it (that is, to decide whether an investment is profitable), we need a way to compare money values received at different times. To make such comparisons, economists and business people use a calculation procedure called **discounting.** Discounting is explained in detail in Appendix A to this chapter, but it is not important that you master this technique in an introductory course. There are really only two important points to learn:

1. A sum of money received at a future date is worth less than a sum of money received today.
2. This difference in values between money today and money in the future is greater when the rate of interest is higher.

It is not difficult to understand why this is so. Consider what you could do with a dollar that you received today rather than a year from today. If the annual rate of interest were 10 percent, you could lend it out (for example, by putting it in a bank account), and receive $1.10 in a year's time—your original $1 plus 10 cents interest. For this reason, money received today is worth more than the same

> **Interest** is the payment for the use of funds employed in the production of capital; it is measured as a percent per year of the value of the funds tied up in the capital.

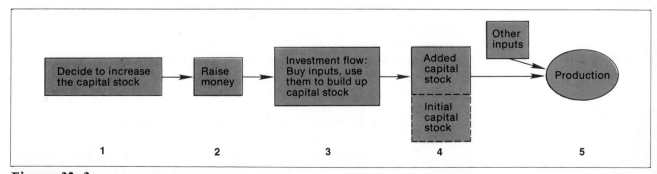

Figure 32–3
THE INVESTMENT-PRODUCTION PROCESS
The investor (1) decides to increase the capital stock; (2) raises money; (3) uses the money to buy inputs that produce capital stock (this step is called *investment*); (4) now holds more capital than before; and (5) uses this capital and other inputs to produce goods and services.

number of dollars received later. Specifically, at a rate of interest of 10 percent per year, $1.10 to be received a year from today is equivalent to $1 of today's money. This illustrates the first of our two points.

Now suppose the annual rate of interest was 15 percent instead. In this case $1 invested today would grow to $1.15 (rather than $1.10) in a year's time, which means that $1.15 (not $1.10) received a year from today would be equivalent to $1 received today. This illustrates the second point.

The Market Determination of Interest Rates

The Downward-Sloping Demand Curve for Funds

These two points are all we need to explain why the quantity of funds demanded declines when the interest rate rises, or, why the demand curve for funds has a negative slope. Remember that the demand for borrowed funds is a *derived demand*, derived from the desire to invest in capital goods. But part, and perhaps all, of the marginal revenue product of a machine or a factory is received in the future. Hence, the value of this MRP *in terms of today's money* shrinks as the rate of interest rises. The consequence of this shrinkage is that a machine that appears to be a good investment when the rate of interest is 10 percent may look like a terrible investment when the rate of interest is 15 percent.

Here is a simple example that is easy to work out. Suppose a particular machine costs $1000 and its MRP is $1140, all of which is received one year from today. Should the machine be bought? If the rate of interest is 10 percent, $1000 in today's money is worth the same as $1100 in money a year from today. Since the machine will return $1140, the machine is worth more than its $1000 price. It is therefore a good investment. But what if the rate of interest were 15 percent instead? Then the $1000 that it takes to buy the machine would grow to $1150 after a year. Since this sum ($1150) is more than the machine will yield ($1140), it would be unwise for the firm to purchase the machine. While this example is quite contrived, the basic principle is valid:

As the rate of interest on borrowing rises, more and more investments that previously looked profitable start to look unprofitable. The demand for borrowing for investment purposes, therefore, is lower at higher rates of interest.

An example of a derived demand schedule for borrowing is given in Figure 32–4. Its negative slope illustrates the conclusion we have just stated—the higher the interest rate, the less money people and firms will want to borrow to finance their investments.

The Supply of Funds

Similar principles apply on the supply side of the market for funds—where the *lenders* are consumers, banks, and other types of business firms. Money lent out is usually returned to the owner (with interest) only over a period of time. Loans will look better to lenders when they bear higher interest rates, so it is natural to think of the supply schedule for loans as being upward sloping—at higher rates of interest, lenders supply more funds. Such a supply schedule is shown by the curve SS in Figure 32–5, where we also reproduce the demand curve, DD, from Figure 32–4.

It is interesting to note, incidentally, that some lenders may have supply curves that do not slope uphill to the right like curve SS. Suppose, for example, that Jones is saving to buy a $10,000 boat in three years, and that if he lends money out at interest in the interim, at current interest rates he must save $3000 a year to

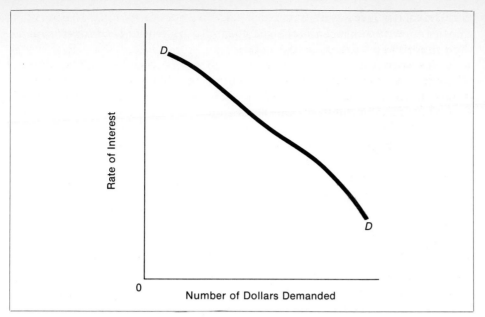

Figure 32–4
THE DERIVED DEMAND
CURVE FOR LOANS
The rate of interest is the cost
of a loan to the borrower. The
lower the rate of interest, the
more it will pay a business firm
to borrow in order to finance
new plant and equipment.
That is why this demand curve
has a negative slope.

reach his goal. If interest rates were higher, he could save less than $3000 each
year and still reach his $10,000 goal. (The higher interest payments would, of
course, contribute the difference.) So his saving (and lending) might decline. But
this argument applies only to savers, like Jones, with a fixed accumulation goal.
Generally, we do expect that the supply of loans will rise when the interest reward
rises, so the supply curve will have a positive slope, like SS in Figure 32–5. The
equilibrium rate of interest is, as always, at point E, where quantity supplied and
quantity demanded are equal. If we suppose that the example refers to loans made
by banks to consumers, then we conclude that the equilibrium interest rate on
consumer loans is 17 percent.

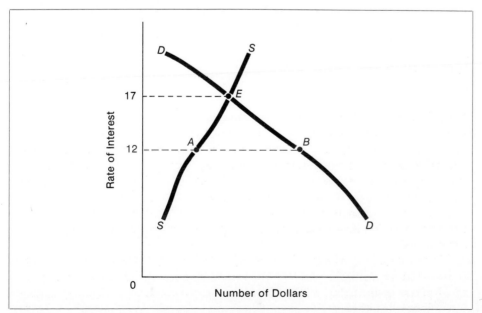

Figure 32–5
EQUILIBRIUM IN THE
MARKET FOR LOANS
Here the free-market interest
rate is 17 percent. At this interest rate, the quantity of loans
supplied is equal to the quantity demanded. However, if an
interest-rate ceiling is imposed,
say, at 12 percent, the quantity
of funds supplied (point A) will
be smaller than the quantity
demanded (point B).

Ceilings on Interest Rates

Consider now what happens if there is a usury law that prohibits interest of more than 12 percent per annum on consumer loans. At this interest rate, the quantity supplied (point *A* in Figure 32–5) falls short of the quantity demanded (point *B*). This means that many applicants for consumer loans are being turned down even though the banks consider them to be credit worthy.

Who generally gains and who loses from this usury law? The gainers are easiest to identify: those lucky consumers who are able to get loans at 12 percent even though they would have been willing to pay 17 percent. The law represents a windfall gain for them. The losers come on both the supply side and the demand side. First, there are the consumers who would have been willing and able to get credit at 17 percent but who are not lucky enough to get it at 12 percent. Then there are the banks (or, more accurately, bank stockholders) who could have made profitable loans at rates of up to 17 percent if there were no interest-rate ceiling.

This analysis helps explain the political popularity of usury laws. Few people sympathize with bank stockholders; indeed, it is the feeling that banks are "gouging" their borrowers that provides much of the impetus for usury laws. The consumers who get loans at lower rates will, naturally, be quite pleased with the result of the law. The others, who would like to borrow at 12 percent but cannot because quantity supplied is less than quantity demanded, are quite likely to blame the bank for refusing to lend, rather than blaming the government for outlawing mutually beneficial transactions.

This analysis has little good to say about usury ceilings, and economists generally oppose them. However, as is the case for minimum wage laws (see the next chapter), interest-rate ceilings can play a constructive role when there is a monopoly over credit. If there is a monopoly lender, the analysis of Chapter 25 leads us to expect him to restrict his "output" (the volume of loans) by raising his "price" (the interest rate). Under such circumstances, an interest-rate ceiling may conceivably make sense.[3] But *may* is not *will*. Most economists believe that, except for isolated instances, the credit market is far closer to the competitive model than it is to the monopoly model.

The Determination of Rent: Simple Version

In dealing with interest, the special feature is that both the demand curve and the supply curve depend on the evaluation of flows of money received at different dates. When we turn our attention to the market for land—the second main factor of production—the special feature occurs on the supply side: land is one factor of production whose quantity supplied is the same at every possible price. Indeed, the classical economists used this notion as the working definition of land. And the definition seems to fit, at least approximately. Although people may clear land, drain its swamps, fertilize it, build on it, or convert it from one use (a farm) to another (a housing development), it is very difficult to change the total supply of land by human effort.

What does this fact tell us about the determination of land rents? Figure 32–6 helps to provide an answer. The vertical supply curve *SS* represents the fact that no matter what the level of rents there are still 1000 acres of land in a small hamlet called Littletown. The demand curve *DD* is a typical marginal revenue product curve, predicated on the notion that the use of land, like everything else, is subject to diminishing returns. The free-market price is determined, as usual, by the

---

[3]As we will see in the appendix to the next chapter, in such a case a usury ceiling might actually increase the volume of loans.

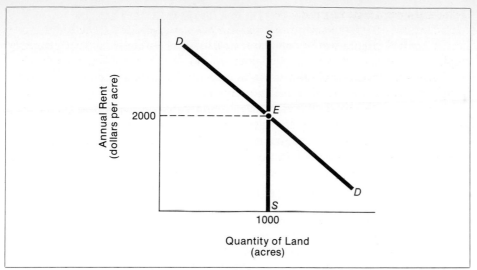

Figure 32–6
DETERMINATION OF
LAND RENT
IN LITTLETOWN
The supply curve of land, *SS*, is
vertical, meaning that 1000
acres are available in Littletown regardless of the level of
rent. The demand curve for
land slopes downward for the
usual reasons. Equilibrium is
established at point *E*, where
the annual rental rate is $2000
per acre.

intersection of the supply and demand curves. In this example, each acre of land in Littletown rents for $2000 per year. The interesting feature of this diagram is that, because quantity supplied is rigidly fixed at 1000 acres whatever the price:

The market level of rent is entirely determined by the demand side of the market.

If, for example, the relocation of a major university in Littletown attracts more people who want to live there, the *DD* curve will shift outward, as depicted in Figure 32–7. Equilibrium in the market will shift from point *E* to point *A*; there will still be only 1000 acres of land, but now each acre will command a rent of $2500 per acre. The landlords will collect more rent, though they themselves have done nothing productive.

The same process also works in reverse, however. Should the university shut its doors and the demand for land decline as a result, the landlords will suffer even though they in no way have contributed to the decline in the demand for land. (To see this, simply reverse the logic of Figure 32–7. The demand curve begins at D_1D_1 and shifts to D_0D_0.)

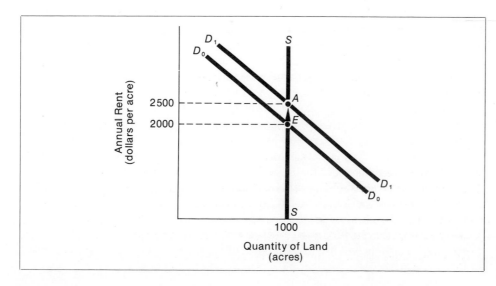

Figure 32–7
A SHIFT IN DEMAND WITH
A VERTICAL SUPPLY
CURVE
Now imagine that something
happens to increase the demand for land—that is, to shift
the demand curve from D_0D_0 to
D_1D_1. Quantity supplied cannot change, but the rental rate
can, and does. In this example, the annual rental for an
acre of land increases from
$2000 to $2500.

The Rent of Land: Some Complications

If every parcel of land were of identical quality, this would be all there is to the theory of land rent. But, of course, plots of land do differ—in quality of soil, in topography, in access to sun and water, in proximity to marketplaces, and in other ways. The classical economists realized this, of course, and took it into account in their analysis of rent determination—a remarkable piece of economic logic formulated late in the eighteenth century and still considered valid today.

The basic notion is that capital invested on any piece of land must yield the same return as capital invested on any other piece that is actually used. Why? If it were not so, capitalists would bid against one another for the more profitable pieces of land until the rents of these parcels were driven up to a point where their advantages over other parcels had been eliminated. Suppose that on one piece of land a given crop is produced for $160,000 per year in labor, fertilizer, fuel, and other nonland costs, while the same crop is produced for $120,000 on a second piece of land. The rent on the second parcel must be *exactly* $40,000 per year higher than the rent on the first, because otherwise production on one plot would be cheaper than on the other. If, for example, the rent difference were only $30,000 per year, it would be $10,000 cheaper to produce on the second plot of land. No one would want to rent the first plot and every grower would instead bid for the second plot. Obviously, rent on the first plot would be forced down by a lack of customers, and rent on the second would be driven up by eager bidders. These pressures would come to an end only when the rent difference reached $40,000, so that both plots became equally profitable.

At any given time, there are some pieces of land of such low quality that it does not pay to use them at all—remote deserts are a prime example. Any land that is exactly on the borderline of being used is called **marginal land.** By definition, marginal land earns no rent because if any rent were charged for it, there would be no takers.

We now combine these two observations—that the difference between the costs of producing on any two pieces of land must equal the difference between their rents, and that zero rent is charged on marginal land—to conclude that:

Rent on any piece of land will equal the difference between the cost of producing the output on that land and the cost of producing it on marginal land.

That is, competition for the superior plots of land will permit the landlords to charge prices that capture the full advantages of their superior parcels.

A useful feature of this analysis is that it helps us to understand more completely the effects of an outward shift in the demand curve for land. Suppose there is an increase in the demand for land because of a rise in population. Naturally, rents will rise. But we can be more specific than this. In response to an upward shift in the demand curve, two things will happen:

1. *It will now pay to employ some land whose use was formerly unprofitable.* The land that was previously on the zero-rent margin will no longer be on the borderline, and some land that is so poor that it was formerly not even worth considering will now just reach the borderline of profitability. The settling of the American West illustrates this process quite forcefully. Land that once could not be given away is now quite valuable.

2. *People will begin more intensive use of the land that was already in use.* Farmers will use more labor and fertilizer to squeeze larger crops out

of their acreage, as has happened in recent decades. Urban real estate on which two-story buildings previously made most sense will now be used for high-rise buildings, as can be seen in sunbelt cities like Dallas and Houston.

Rents will be increased in a predictable way by these two developments. Since the land that is marginal *after* the change must be inferior to the land that was marginal previously, rents must rise by the difference in yields between the old and new marginal lands. Table 32–2 illustrates this point. We deal with three pieces of land: A, a very productive piece; B, a piece that was initially marginal; and C, a piece that is inferior to B but nevertheless becomes marginal when the upward shift in the demand curve for land occurs. The crop costs $80,000 more when produced on B than on A, and $12,000 more when produced on C than on B. Suppose, initially, that demand for the crop is so low that C is unused and B is just on the margin between being used and left idle. Since B is marginal, it will yield no rent. We know that the rent on A will be equal to the $80,000 cost advantage of A over B. Now suppose demand for the crop increases enough so that plot C is just brought into use. Plot C is now marginal land, and B acquires a rent of $12,000, the cost advantage of B over C.

But there is a second factor pushing up land rents—the increased intensity of use of land that was already in cultivation. As farmers apply more fertilizer and labor to their land, the marginal productivity of land increases just as factory workers become more productive when they are given better equipment. Once again, the landowner is able to capture this increase in productivity in the form of higher rents. (If you do not understand why, refer back to Figure 32–7 and remember that the demand curves are marginal revenue product curves.) Thus, we can summarize the classical theory of rent as follows:

As the use of land increases, landlords receive higher payments from two sources:
1. Increased demand leads the community to employ land previously not good enough to use; the advantage of previously used land over the new marginal land increases, and rents go up correspondingly.
2. Land is used more intensively; the marginal revenue product of land rises, thus increasing the ability of the producer who uses the land to pay rent.

As late as the end of the nineteenth century, this analysis still exerted a powerful influence beyond technical economic writings. An American journalist, Henry George, was nearly elected mayor of New York in 1886, running on the platform that all government should be financed by "a single tax"—a tax on

---

Table 32–2
NONRENT COSTS AND RENT ON THREE PIECES OF LAND

TYPE OF LAND	NONLAND COST OF PRODUCING A GIVEN CROP	TOTAL RENT	
		Before	After
A. A tract that was better than marginal before and after	$120,000	$80,000	$92,000
B. A tract that was marginal before but is not anymore	200,000	0	12,000
C. A tract that was previously not worth using but is now marginal	212,000	0	0

landlords who, he said, are the only ones who earn incomes while contributing nothing to the productive process and who reap the fruits of economic growth without contributing to economic progress.

Generalization: What Determines Johnny Carson's Salary?

Land is not the only scarce input whose supply is fixed, at least in the short run. Toward the beginning of this century some economists realized that the economic analysis of rent can be applied to inputs other than land. As we will see, this extension yielded some noteworthy insights.

Consider as an example the earnings of television star Johnny Carson. Such TV personalities seem to have little in common with plots of land on New York's Fifth Avenue. Yet, to an economist, the same analysis—the theory of rent—explains the incomes of these two factors of production. To understand why, we first note that there is only one Johnny Carson (or so he would like his employer to believe). That is, he is a scarce input whose supply is fixed just like the supply of land. Because he is in fixed supply, the price of his services must be determined in a way that is similar to the determination of land rents. Hence, economists have arrived at a more general definition of **economic rent** as *any payment made to a factor that is not necessary to keep that factor on the market.*

Economic rent is said to be earned whenever a factor of production receives a reward that exceeds the minimum amount necessary to keep the factor in its present employment.

A moment's thought shows how this general notion of rent applies both to land and to Johnny Carson. The total quantity of land available for use is the same whether rent is high, low, or zero; no payments to landlords are necessary to induce land to be supplied to the market. So, by definition, the payments to landholders for their land are entirely economic rent—payments that are not necessary to induce the provision of the land to the economy. Johnny Carson is (almost) similar to land in this respect. He is a factor of production that is completely unique and cannot be reproduced. What determines the income of such a factor? Since the quantity supplied of such a unique, nonreproducible factor is absolutely fixed, and therefore unresponsive to price, the analysis of rent determination summarized in Figure 32–6 applies. *The position of the demand curve determines the price.*

Figure 32–8 summarizes the "Johnny Carson market." Vertical supply curve *SS* represents the fact that no matter what wage he is paid there is only one Johnny Carson. Demand curve *DD* is a marginal productivity curve of sorts, but not quite the kind we encountered earlier in the chapter. Since the question, "What would be the value of a second unit of Johnny Carson?" is nonsensical, the demand curve is constructed by considering only the *portion* of his time demanded at various wage levels. The curve indicates that at an annual salary of $6 million, no employer can afford even a little bit of Johnny Carson. At a lower salary of, say, $4 million per year, however, there are enough profitable uses to absorb two-thirds of his time. At $3 million per year, Carson's full time is demanded; and at lower wage rates, the demand for Carson's time exceeds the amount of it that is for sale.[4]

Equilibrium is at point *E* in the diagram, where the supply of and demand for his time are equal. His annual salary here is $3 million. Now we can ask: How much of Johnny Carson's salary is economic rent? According to the economic definition of rent, his entire $3 million salary is rent. Since, according to the vertical supply schedule, Carson's financial reward is unnecessary to get him to supply his services, every penny he earns is rent.

[4]These numbers are not entirely hypothetical. According to newspaper reports, Carson is paid nearly $3 million per year by NBC for working three to four nights a week.

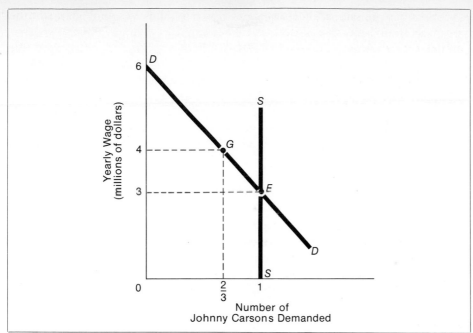

Figure 32–8
HYPOTHETICAL MARKET FOR JOHNNY CARSON'S SERVICES
At an annual wage of $6 million or more, no one is willing to bid for his time. At a somewhat lower wage, $4 million, two-thirds of his time will be demanded (point *G*). Only at an annual wage no higher than $3 million will all of Carson's available time be demanded (point *E*).

This is why we said that personalities like Carson are *almost* good examples of pure rent. For, in fact, if his salary were low enough, Carson would probably prefer to stay home much of the time and watch someone else perform on TV. Suppose, for example, that $50,000 per year is the lowest salary at which Carson will offer even one minute of his services, and that his labor supply then increases with his wage up to an annual salary of $300,000, at which point he is willing to work full time. Then, while his equilibrium salary will still be $3 million per year, not all of it will be rent, because some of it, at least $50,000, is required to get him to supply any services at all.

This same analysis applies to any factor of production whose supply curve is not horizontal, that is, whose *elasticity of supply* is less than infinite. Any such factor earns some rent—or gets paid more than the minimum amount that would induce it to work. Almost all employees earn some rent. What sorts of factors earn no rent? Those that can be exactly reproduced by a number of producers at constant cost. No supplier of ball bearings will ever receive any rent on a ball bearing, at least in the long run, because any desired number of them can be produced at (roughly) constant costs. If one supplier tried to charge a price that included rent, someone else would undercut him and take his customers away.

Rent Controls: The Misplaced Analogy

Why is the analysis of economic rent important? Because only economic rent can be taxed away without reducing the quantity of the input supplied. And here common English gets in the way of sound reasoning. Many people feel that the *rent* that they pay to their landlord is economic rent. After all, their apartments will still be there if they pay $500 per month, or $300, or $100. This view, while true in the short run, is quite myopic.

Like the ball-bearing producer, the owner of a building cannot expect to earn *economic* rent because there are too many other potential owners whose costs of construction are roughly the same as his own. If he tried to charge a price that included some economic rent—that is, a price that exceeded his production costs plus the opportunity cost of his capital—other builders would undercut him. Thus, far from being in perfectly *inelastic* (vertical) supply, like raw land, buildings come rather close to being in perfectly *elastic* (horizontal) supply, like ball bearings. As we have learned from the theory of rent, this means that builders and owners of buildings cannot collect economic rent in the long run. Since apartment owners collect very little economic rent, the payments that tenants make in a free market must be just enough to keep those apartments on the market. (This is the definition of zero economic rent.) If rent controls push these prices down, the apartments will start disappearing from the market.[5]

Issue: Are Profits Too High or Too Low?

This completes our analysis of rent. We turn next to business profits, a subject whose discussion seems to elicit more passion than logic. With the exception of some economists, almost no one thinks that the rate of profit is at about the right level. Critics on the left point accusingly at the billion-dollar profits of some giant corporations and argue that they are unconscionably high. They call for much stiffer profits taxes. On the other hand, the Chambers of Commerce, National Association of Manufacturers, and other business groups complain that regulations and "ruinous" competition keep profits too low, and they are constantly petitioning Congress for tax relief.

The public has many misconceptions about the nature of the U.S. economy, but probably none is more severe than the popular view of the amount of profit that American corporations earn. We suggest to you the following experiment. Ask five of your friends who have never had an economics course what fraction of the nation's income they imagine is accounted for by profits. While the correct answer varies from year to year, the data given in Table 7–5 on page 133 show that in 1981 only 11 percent of GNP (before-tax) was business profits. This says that 12 percent of the prices you pay represent before-tax profit. Most people think this figure is much, much higher. (See the boxed insert at top of the next page).

As you have no doubt noticed by now, economists are reluctant to brand factor prices as "too low" or "too high" in some moral or ethical sense. Rather, they are likely to ask, first, What is the market equilibrium price? And then they will ask whether there are any good reasons to interfere with the market solution. This, however, is not so easy to do for profits, since it is hard to apply supply and demand analysis when you do not know what factor of production earns profit.

In both a bookkeeping and an economic sense, *profits are the residual:* they are what remains from the selling price after all other factors have been paid.

But what factor of production receives this reward? What factor's marginal productivity constitutes the profit rate?

What Accounts for Profits?

Economic profit, it will be recalled from Chapter 22, is the amount a firm earns *over and above* the payments for all other inputs, including the interest payments for the capital it uses and the opportunity cost of any capital provided by the

[5]None of this is meant to imply that temporary rent controls in certain locations cannot have salutory effects in the short run. In the short run, the supply of apartments and houses really is fixed, and large shifts in demand would hand windfall gains to landlords—gains that are true economic rents. Controls that eliminate such windfalls should not cause serious dislocations. But knowing when the "short run" fades into the "long run" can be a tricky matter. "Temporary" rent control laws, as we learned in Chapter 4, have a way of becoming rather permanent.

Public Opinion on Profits

Most Americans think corporate profits are much higher than they actually are. A public opinion poll in 1979, for example, found that the average citizen thought that corporate profits *after tax* amounted to 32 percent of sales for the typical manufacturing company. The actual profit rate at the time was only 5.2 percent! Interestingly, when these same people were asked how much profit they thought was "reasonable," they answered 26 cents on every dollar of sales—roughly five times as large as profits actually were.

SOURCE: "Public Attitudes Toward Corporate Profits," Opinion Research Corporation *Public Opinion Index*, Princeton, N.J., October 1979.

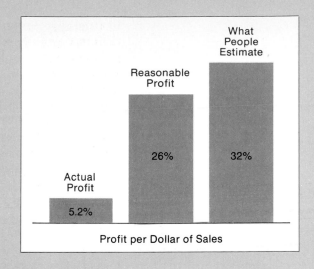

Profit per Dollar of Sales

owners of the firm. The profit rate and the interest rate are closely related. In an imaginary (and uninteresting) world in which everything was certain and unchanging, capitalists who invested money in firms would simply earn the market rate of interest on their funds. Profits beyond this level would be competed away. Profits below this level could not persist, because capitalists would withdraw their funds from the firms and deposit them in banks. Capitalists in such a world would be mere moneylenders.

But the real world is not at all like this. Some capitalists are much more than moneylenders and the amounts they earn often exceed the interest rate by a considerable margin. Those activist capitalists who seek out or even create earnings opportunities are called **entrepreneurs.** They are the ones who are responsible for the constant change that characterizes business firms and who prevent the operations of the firms from stagnating. Since they are always trying to do something new, it is difficult to provide a general description of their activities. However, we can list three primary ways in which entrepreneurs are able to drive profits above the level of interest rates.

Exercise of Monopoly Power. If the entrepreneur can establish a monopoly over some or all of his products, even for a short while, he can use the monopoly power of his firm to earn monopoly profits. The nature of these monopoly earnings was analyzed in Chapter 25.

Risk Bearing. The entrepreneur may engage in risky activities. For example, when a firm prospects for oil it will drill an exploratory shaft hoping to find a pool of petroleum at the bottom. But a high proportion of such attempts produce only dry holes, and the cost of the operation is wasted. Of course, if the investor is lucky and does find oil, he may be rewarded handsomely. The income he obtains is a payment for bearing risk.

Obviously, a few lucky individuals make out well in this process, while most suffer heavy losses. How well can we expect risk takers to do on the average? If, on the average, one exploratory drilling out of ten pays off, do we expect its return to be exactly ten times as high as the interest rate, so that the *average* firm will earn exactly the normal rate of interest? The answer is that the payoff will be *more* than ten times the interest rate if investors dislike gambling; that is, if they prefer to avoid risk. Why? Because investors who dislike risk will be unwilling to put their money into a business in which nine firms out of ten lose out unless there is some compensation for the financial peril to which they expose themselves.

In reality, however, there is no certainty that things always work out this way. Some people love to gamble, and these people tend to be overoptimistic about their chances of coming out ahead. They may plunge into projects to a degree unjustified by the odds. If there are enough such gamblers, the average payoff to risky undertakings may end up below the interest rate. The successful investor will still make a good profit, just like the lucky winner in Las Vegas. But the average participant will have to pay for the privilege of bearing risk.

Returns to Innovation.   The third major source of profits is perhaps the most important of all from the point of view of social welfare. The entrepreneur who is first to market a desirable new product, or to employ a new cost-saving machine, or to innovate in some other way will receive a special profit as his reward. **Innovation** is different from **invention.** Invention is the act of generating a new idea; innovation is the next step, the act of putting the new idea into practical use. Business people are rarely inventors, but they are often innovators.

When an entrepreneur innovates, even if his new product or his new process is not protected by patents, he will be one step ahead of his competitors. He will be able to capture much of the market either by offering customers a better product or by supplying the product more cheaply. In either case he will temporarily find himself with some monopoly power left by the weakening of his competitors, and monopoly profit will be the reward for his initiative.

However, this monopoly profit, the reward for innovation, will only be temporary. As soon as the success of the idea has demonstrated itself to the world, other firms will find ways of imitating it. Even if they cannot turn out precisely the same product or use precisely the same process, they will have to find ways to supply close substitutes if they are to survive. In this way, new ideas are spread through the economy. And in the process the special profits of the innovator are brought to an end. The innovator can only resume earning special profits by finding still another promising idea.

Entrepreneurs are forced to keep searching for new ideas, to keep instituting innovations, and to keep imitating those that they have not been the first to put into operation. This process is at the heart of the growth of the capitalist system. It is one of the secrets of its extraordinary dynamism.

The Issue of Profits Taxation

So profits in excess of the market rate of interest can be considered as the return on entrepreneurial talent. But this is not really very helpful, since no one can accurately say what entrepreneurial talent is. Certainly we cannot measure it; nor can we teach it in a college course (though business schools try!). Therefore, we do not know how the observed profit rate relates to the minimum reward necessary to attract entrepreneurial talent into the market—a relationship which is crucial for the contentious issue of profits taxation.

Consider the windfall profits tax on oil companies as an example. If oil company profit rates are well above this minimum, they contain a large element of economic rent. In that case, we could tax away these excess profits (rents) without fear of reducing oil production. On the other hand, if the profits being earned by oil companies do not contain much economic rent, then the windfall profits tax might seriously curtail exploration and production of oil.

This example illustrates the general problem of deciding how heavily profits should be taxed. Critics of big business who call for high, if not confiscatory, profits taxes believe that profits are mostly economic rent. But if they are wrong, if most of the observed profits are necessary to attract people into entrepreneurial roles, then a high profits tax can be dangerous. It can threaten the very lifeblood of the capitalist system. Business lobbying groups are quite sure that this is the case. We will do best by ignoring both groups of polemicists. The jury is still out on this important matter.

Critiques of Marginal Productivity Theory

The theory of factor pricing described in this chapter is another example of supply–demand analysis. Its special feature is its heavy reliance on the principle of marginal productivity to derive the shape and position of the demand curve. For this reason, the analysis is often rather misleadingly called *the marginal productivity theory of distribution.*

Over the years this analysis has been subject to attack on many grounds. One frequent accusation, which is largely (but not entirely) groundless, is the assertion that marginal productivity theory is merely an attempt to justify the distribution of income which the capitalist system yields—that it is a piece of pro-capitalist propaganda. According to this argument, when marginal productivity theory claims that each factor is paid exactly its marginal revenue product, this is only a sneaky way of asserting that each factor is paid exactly what it deserves. These critics claim that the theory legitimizes the gross inequities of the system—the poverty of many and the great wealth of the few.

The argument is straightforward but wrong. Payments are made not to *factors of production* but to the people who happen to own them. If an acre of land earns $2000 because that is its marginal revenue product, this does not mean the payment is *deserved* by the landlord, who may even have acquired it by fraud.

Second, an input's marginal revenue product (MRP) does not depend only on "how hard it works" but also on how much of it happens to be employed—for, according to the "law" of diminishing returns, the more that is employed the lower its MRP. Thus, that factor's MRP is not (and cannot legitimately be interpreted as) a measure of the intensity of its "productive effort." In any event, what an input deserves may be taken to depend on more than what it does in the factory. A worker may be held to deserve funds because he is sick, because he has many children, and for many reasons other than his productivity. On these and other grounds, no economist today claims that marginal productivity analysis shows that distribution under capitalism is either just or unjust. It is simply wrong to claim that marginal productivity theory is pro-capitalist propaganda.[6] The marginal productivity principle is just as relevant to organizing production in a socialist society as it is in a capitalist one.

Others have attacked marginal productivity theory for using rather complicated reasoning to tell us very little about the really urgent problems of income distribution. In this view, it is all very well to say that everything depends on supply and demand and to express this in terms of many complicated equations (as is done in more advanced books and articles). But these equations do not tell us what to do about such serious distribution problems as malnutrition among Indians in Latin America or poverty among minority groups in the United States.

Though it does exaggerate somewhat, there is certainly truth to this criticism. We have seen in this chapter that the theory does provide some insights on

[6]For more on this criticism of marginal productivity theory, see Chapter 42, especially pages 818–819.

real policy matters, though perhaps not as many as the obsolete Ricardian model described in Appendix B to this chapter, and certainly not as many as we would like. In Chapters 34 and 39 we will see that economists do have things to say about the problems of poverty and underdevelopment. But much of this does not flow from marginal productivity analysis.

Perhaps, in the end, what should be said for marginal productivity theory is that it is the best model we have at the moment, that is offers us *some* valuable insights into the way the economy works, and that until a more powerful model is found we are better off hanging on to what we have.

Income Shares in Practice

Since this chapter has focused on the *theories* of interest, rents, and profits, it may be useful to conclude with a brief look at how much these factors earn *in reality*. According to U.S. data for 1980, interest payments accounted for about $8\frac{1}{2}$ percent of national income, land rents for a mere $1\frac{1}{2}$ percent, corporate profits for about $8\frac{1}{4}$ percent, and other profits for about 6 percent. In total, the returns to all the factors of production dealt with in this chapter amounted to about one-quarter of national income. Where did the rest of it go? The answer is that three-quarters of national income was composed of employee compensation—wages and salaries. The huge share of labor in national income is one of the reasons why the next chapter is devoted entirely to this subject.

Summary

1. A profit-maximizing firm purchases the quantity of any input at which the price of the input equals its marginal revenue product.
2. Interest rates are determined by the supply of and demand for funds. The demand for funds is a derived demand, since these funds are used to finance business investment. Thus the demand for funds depends on the marginal productivity of capital.
3. A dollar obtainable sooner is worth more than a dollar obtainable later because of the interest that can be earned in the interim.
4. Increased demand for a good that needs land to produce it will drive up the prices of land either because inferior land will be brought into use or because land will be used more intensively.
5. Rent controls do not significantly affect the supply of land, but they do tend to reduce the supply of buildings.
6. Economic rent is any payment to the supplier of a factor of production that is greater than the minimum amount needed to induce the desired quantity of the factor to be supplied.
7. Factors of production that are unique in quality and difficult or impossible to reproduce will tend to be paid relatively high economic rents because of their scarcity.
8. Factors of production that are easy to produce at a constant cost and that are provided by many suppliers will earn little or no economic rent.
9. Economic profits over and above the cost of capital are earned (a) by exercise of monopoly power, (b) as a payment for bearing risk, and (c) as the earnings of successful innovation.
10. The desirability of increased taxation of profits depends on its effects on the supply of entrepreneurial talent. If most profits are economic rents, then higher profits taxes will have few deleterious effects. But if most profits are necessary to attract entrepreneurs into the market, then higher profit taxes can threaten the capitalist system.

Concepts for Review

Factors of production
Entrepreneurship
Marginal productivity principle
Marginal physical product
Marginal revenue product
Derived demand

Usury law
Investment
Capital
Interest
Discounting

Marginal land
Economic rent
Entrepreneurs
Risk bearing
Invention versus innovation

Questions for Discussion

1. Which of the following inputs do you think include a relatively large economic rent in their earnings? (a) nails, (b) coal, (c) a champion racehorse. Use supply–demand analysis to explain your answer.

2. Three machines are employed in an isolated area. They each produce 1000 units of output per month, the first requiring $17,000 in raw materials, the second $21,000, and the third $23,000. What would you expect to be the monthly charge for the first and second machines if the services of the third machine can be hired at a price of $9000 a month? What part of the charges for the first two machines is economic rent?

3. Distinguish between *investment* and *capital*.

4. Illustrate the difference between an invention and an innovation. Give an example of each.

5. "Marginal productivity does not determine how much a worker will earn—it only determines how many workers will be hired at a given wage. Therefore, marginal productivity analysis is a theory of demand for labor, not a theory of distribution." What, then, do you think determines wages? Does marginal productivity affect their level? If so, how?

Appendix A:
Discounting and Present Value

Frequently, in business and economic problems, it is necessary to compare sums of money received (or paid) at different dates. Consider, for example, the purchase of a machine that costs $11,000 and will yield a marginal revenue product of $14,520 two years from today. If the machine can be financed by a three-year loan bearing 10 percent interest, it will cost the firm $1100 in interest for each of the three years, plus $11,000 in principal repayment in the third year (see the table below). Is the machine a good investment?

COSTS AND BENEFITS OF INVESTING IN A MACHINE

	Year 1	Year 2	Year 3
Benefits			
Marginal revenue product of the machine	0	0	$14,520
Costs			
Interest and principal on loan	$1100	$1100	$12,100

The total costs of owning the machine over the three-year period ($1100 + $1100 + $12,100 = $14,300) are less than the total benefits ($14,520). But this is clearly an invalid comparison, because the $14,520 in future benefits are not worth $14,520 in terms of today's money. Adding up dollars received (or paid) at different dates is a bit like adding apples and oranges. The process that has been invented for making these magnitudes comparable is called **discounting, or computing the present value** of a future sum of money.

To illustrate the concept of present value, let us ask how much $1 received a year from today is worth *in terms of today's money.* If the rate of interest is 10 percent, the answer is about 91 cents. Why? Because if we invest 91 cents today at 10 percent interest, it will grow to 91 cents plus 9.1 cents in interest = 100.1 cents in a year. Similar considerations apply to any rate of interest. In general:

If the rate of interest is i, the present value of $1 to be received in a year is: $\dfrac{\$1}{(1 + i)}$.

This is so, because in a year $\dfrac{\$1}{(1 + i)}$ will grow into

$\dfrac{\$1}{(1 + i)} (1 + i) = \$1$.

What about money to be received two years from today? Using the same reasoning, $1 invested today will grow to $1 × (1.1) = $1.10 after one year and to $1 × (1.1) × (1.1) = $1 × (1.1)² = $1.21 after two years. Consequently, the present value of $1 to be received two years from today is:

$$\frac{\$1}{(1.1)^2} = \frac{\$1}{1.21} = 82.64 \text{ cents} .$$

A similar analysis applies to money received three years from today, four years from today, and so on.

The general formula for the present value of $1 to be received N years from today when the rate of interest is i is: $\dfrac{\$1}{(1 + i)^N}$

The present value formula highlights the two variables that determine the present value of any future flow of money: the rate of interest (i) and how long you have to wait before you get it (N).

Let us now apply this analysis to our example. The present value of the revenue is easy to calculate since it all comes two years from today. Since the rate of interest is assumed to be 10 percent ($i = 0.1$) we have:

$$\text{Present value of revenues} = \frac{\$14,520}{(1.1)^2}$$

$$= \frac{\$14,520}{1.21}$$

$$= \$12,000 .$$

The present value of the costs is a bit trickier in this example since costs occur at three different dates. The present value (in year 1 money) of the $1100 interest payment in year 1 is, of course, just $1100. The present value of the next interest payment is $1100/(1 + i) = $1100/1.1 = $1000. And the present value of the final payment of interest plus principal is:

$$\frac{\$12,100}{(1 + i)^2} = \frac{\$12,100}{(1.1)^2} = \frac{\$12,100}{1.21} = \$10,000 .$$

Now that we have expressed each sum in terms of its present value, it is permissible to add them up. So the present value of all costs is:

Present value of costs
    2nd yr's value ↓
    $= \$1100 + \$1000 + \$10,000 = \$12,100$.

Comparing this to the $12,000 present value of the revenues clearly shows that the machine is a poor investment after all. This same calculation procedure is applicable to all investment decisions.

Cost > Revenue.

Summary

To determine whether a loss or a gain will result from a decision whose costs and returns will come at several different periods of time, the figures represented by these gains and losses must all be discounted to obtain their present value. For this, one uses the present value formula for X dollars receivable N years from now:

$$\text{Present value} = \frac{X}{(1 + i)^N} .$$

One then adds together the present values of all the returns and all the costs. If the sum of the present values of the returns is greater than the sum of the present values of the costs, then the decision to invest will promise a net gain.

Concepts for Review

Discounting
Present value

Questions for Discussion

1. Compute the present value of $1000 to be received in four years if the rate of interest is 15 percent.
2. A government bond pays $100 in interest each year for three years and also returns the principal of $1000 in the third year. How much is it worth in terms of today's money if the rate of interest is 10 percent? If the rate of interest is 15 percent?

Appendix B:
David Ricardo's Theory of Income Distribution

Theories of the supply and demand for each factor of production enable us to determine both the price and employment of each factor, and thus that factor's income. Once this sort of analysis is applied to all factors of production, we have a complete *theory of income distribution*, because the entire national income is accounted for. That is, we are in a position to analyze the share of an economy's output that goes to workers, to capitalists, and to landlords.

The first such complete theory of income distribution was worked out in the early part of the nineteenth century by the British stockbroker-turned-economist David Ricardo. Though much of Ricardo's work has been rendered obsolete by the passage of almost 200 years, it is in many ways still a model of what an economic theory of income distribution should be. It shows clearly the role of landholders, capitalists, and workers, and seeks to bring out explicitly the extent to which their interests conflict or are held in common. It also attempts to account directly for the relative wealth or poverty of the different economic classes. And it relates directly to issues of policy, suggesting measures that can be used to increase equality, stimulate economic growth, and so forth. Ricardo's analysis rests on five major premises:

1. That land rents are determined in the way described in this chapter (see pages 602–604).
2. That, after landlords are paid, the remainder of the product is divided between labor and capital, with the wage of labor determined by the law of supply and demand.
3. That an increase in wages above what constitutes the normal standard of living for workers in the economy ("the subsistence level of wages") simply enables workers to expand their families, thus leading to expansion of the population (the Malthusian population model).
4. That an increased population working with a fixed quantity of land will run into diminishing returns to increased quantities of labor input.
5. That the basic objective of capitalists is to accumulate wealth, and that they reinvest whatever profits they do not consume in order to expand their earning power.

These five assumptions lead to a simple scenario. Capitalists accumulate and invest their money. The resulting expansion of business activity increases the demand for labor and raises wages. Workers respond by increasing the size of their families. Ultimately, the rise in population affects distribution in three ways:

1. It lowers wages back toward subsistence as the supply of labor expands.
2. It increases the use of land and raises rents in the way described in this chapter.
3. It ultimately must reduce profits because wages cannot be pushed below subsistence, because rents are increasing, and because (as a result of diminishing returns) production does not keep up with population size.

This last and crucial conclusion follows as a matter of simple arithmetic. Subsistence wage payments must increase in proportion to the labor force, but diminishing returns cause production to expand less rapidly than the labor force. With landlords increasing their share of the pie, less must be left over for profits.

Figure 32–9 summarizes the story. As we move from left to right in the diagram, we see what happens as the population and the size of the labor force increase. The top curve represents total production of the economy. Because of diminishing returns it flattens out as the size of the labor force increases. The lower curve shows what remains of production after rent is deducted from it. Since rents increase as population grows, this curve must flatten out even faster than the total product curve. However, since the subsistence wage is a fixed amount per worker, total subsistence wages must increase *proportionately* with the size of the labor force. That is why *total* subsistence wages are represented by an upward-sloping straight line.

At a particular size of labor force, L, total wage

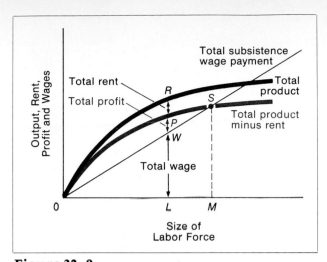

Figure 32–9

THE RICARDIAN DISTRIBUTION MODEL

This diagram illustrates the division of total product into wages, profit, and rent. Rent is determined by differences in quality of the lands that are in use and by diminishing returns to other inputs. If wages approximate subsistence, then profit is what is left over. As population increases, profits are squeezed by diminishing returns to labor and rising rents. When the labor force reaches M, profit vanishes (point S), and accumulation of capital ceases.

payments are represented by LW, the distance to the subsistence wage line. Total profit is represented by WP, the distance between the subsistence wage line and the curve of total product minus rent. Total rent is therefore shown by PR, the amount of total product that has gone neither to wages nor to profits.

We see that as population increases—that is, as we move to the right in the graph—both rent and total wage payments increase, but total profits are squeezed lower and lower. That is, there is less and less distance between the subsistence wage line and the curve of production minus rent. The two finally meet at point S when population reaches M, and there profits are eliminated altogether. The classical economists called this point *the stationary state* in which all growth ceases and stagnation is the normal state of affairs.

It would seem that only capitalists are hurt by this process. But, in fact, the workers suffer too. For, as we saw, it is only capital accumulation that raises wages above subsistence. Once profits are eliminated, there is no further motive to save and invest,

so wages are permanently limited to the subsistence level. This is in marked contrast with a period of growth and high profits when rapid accumulation will generally make the forces of supply and demand work more favorably for labor. Ricardo drew several main conclusions from his analysis.

1. Only landlords benefit from population growth. Capitalists are hurt by it directly, and workers suffer indirectly because it reduces the reward for investment, which decreases the demand for labor and drives wages toward subsistence.

2. Unrestricted trade with foreign countries, by indirectly increasing the supply of land used by the economy, retards the speed with which diminishing returns set in and therefore makes the whole process less painful.

3. There are two ways in which workers' standards of living can be raised. First, incentives for capital accumulation increase the demand for labor and lead wages to be bid up by the forces of supply and demand. Second, by getting workers to insist on higher living standards before they are ready to have children, the rate of population growth can be retarded and therefore the downward pressure on wages can be reduced. If people were unwilling to marry and have children until their earnings were high enough to support their families in a "decent" style of living, that, in Ricardo's judgment, would be the best thing that could happen from the point of view of workers' welfare. For that is the way to hold back the growth of population that subjects the labor market to oversupply and the economy to diminishing returns.

Nowadays, when workers' wages are bargained for by powerful unions, when continued innovations have held off the workings of diminishing returns for two centuries, and when population growth in the industrialized Western world has declined in some places almost to zero, the Ricardian model of income distribution seems more than a little out of date. But its relevance to the agricultural economies of its day was more immediate, as was its impact on policy. And, as we will see in Chapter 39, there are many places in the Third World today where its message is still all too relevant.

The Labor
Market
and Wages

33

Masters are always and every where in a sort of
tacit, but constant and uniform combination,
not to raise the wages of labour . . .

ADAM SMITH

Labor is by far the most important factor of production. As we learned in the previous chapter, the earnings of labor amount to about 75 percent of national income. Wages and employment are important because they represent the primary source of income to the vast majority of Americans and because they are related to a variety of important social and political issues.

The chapter is divided into two main parts. In the first part we deal with the determination of wages and employment in *competitive labor markets;* that is, labor markets in which there are many buyers and many sellers, none of whom is large enough to have any appreciable influence on wages. We consider why some types of workers are paid far more than others and explore a number of important issues, including the effects of education on wages and of minimum wage legislation. In the second part of the chapter we consider labor markets that are monopolized on the selling side by trade unions. First, the development of the labor movement in America is summarized. Then we consider alternative goals for a union and how these goals might be pursued. Finally, we turn to situations in which a single seller of labor (a union) confronts a single buyer of labor (a monopsony firm), and examine some of the analytical and practical difficulties that arise under collective bargaining.

Issue: The Minimum Wage and Unemployment

Unemployment among teen-agers is always higher than it is in the labor force as a whole, and among black teen-agers it is significantly higher still. Figure 33–1 shows the record. It indicates that whenever unemployment rates went down in the economy as a whole, they almost always decreased for both black and white teen-agers. However, young workers and especially young black workers, have always suffered more from unemployment than the average worker. When things are generally bad, things are much, much worse for them. Despite social and legislative pressures against race discrimination, efforts to improve the quality of education available to children in the ghettos, and many related programs, there has been no improvement in the relative standing of young blacks in recent years.

Many economists feel less surprised than other concerned persons about the intractability of the problem. They maintain that despite all the legislation that has been adopted to improve the position of black people, there is a law on the

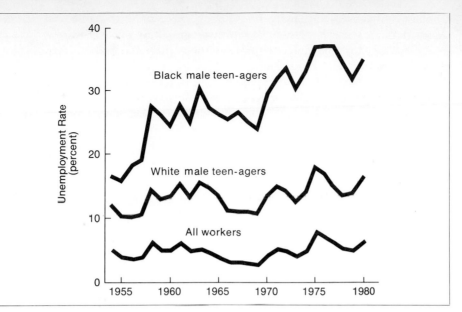

Figure 33–1
THE TEEN-AGE UNEM-
PLOYMENT PROBLEM
Teen-age unemployment rates
have consistently been much
higher than the overall unemployment rate, and black teen-
agers have fared worse than
white teen-agers. For the most
part, the three employment
rates have moved up and down
together, as can be seen in this
chart.
SOURCE: U.S. Department of
Labor, Bureau of Labor Statistics.

books, which, though apparently designed to protect low-skilled workers, is actually an impediment to any attempt to improve job opportunities for blacks. As long as this law remains effective, the young, the inexperienced, and those with educational disadvantages will continue to find themselves handicapped on the job market, and attempts to eliminate their more serious unemployment problems will stand little chance of success.

What is the law? None other than the **minimum wage law.** Later in this chapter we will explain why this law may have such pernicious—and presumably unintended—effects.

Competitive Labor Markets

The minimum wage law interferes with the operation of a free labor market. But to understand how, we must first understand how the labor market would operate in its absence. We approach this in three steps. First we consider the determi-nants of the supply of labor, then the determinants of demand, and finally the market equilibrium, in which both wages and employment levels are established.

The Supply of Labor

The economic analysis of labor supply is based on the following simple observa-tion: Given the fixed amount of time in a week, a person's decision to *supply labor* to firms is simultaneously a decision to *demand leisure* time for oneself. Assuming that after necessary time for eating and sleeping is deducted a worker has 90 usable hours in a week, a decision to spend 40 of those hours working is simultaneously a decision to demand 50 of them for other purposes.

This suggests that we can analyze the *supply* of this particular input— labor—with the same tools we used in Chapter 18 to analyze the *demand* for commodities. In this case, the commodity is leisure. A consumer "buys" her own leisure time, just as she buys bananas, or back scratchers, or pizzas. In

Chapter 18 we observed that any price change has two distinct effects on quantity demanded: an income effect and a substitution effect. Let us review these two effects and see how they operate in the context of the demand for leisure (that is, the supply of labor).

1. ***Income effect.*** Higher wages make consumers richer. We expect this increased wealth to increase their demand for most goods, leisure included.

The income effect of higher wages probably leads most workers to want to work less.

2. ***Substitution effect.*** Consumers "purchase" their own leisure time by giving up their hourly wage, so the wage rate is the "price" of leisure. When the wage rate rises, leisure becomes more expensive relative to other commodities that consumers might buy. Thus, we expect a wage increase to induce them to buy *less* leisure time and *more* goods.

The substitution effect of higher wages probably leads most workers to want to work more.

Putting these two effects together, we are forced to conclude that some workers may react to an increase in their wage rate by working more, while others may react by working less. Still others will have little or no discretion over their hours of work. In terms of the market as a whole, therefore, higher wages could lead to either a larger or smaller quantity of labor supplied. Statistical studies of this issue in the United States have reached the conclusions that (a) the response of labor supply to wage changes is not very strong for most workers; (b) for low-wage workers the substitution effect seems clearly dominant, so they work more when wages rise; and (c) for high-wage workers the income effect just about offsets the substitution effect, so they do not work more when wages rise. Figure 33–2 depicts these approximate "facts." It shows labor supply rising (slightly) as wages rise up to point *A*. Thereafter, labor supply is roughly constant as wages rise.

Does the theory of labor supply apply to college students? A 1975 study of the

Figure 33–2
A TYPICAL LABOR
SUPPLY SCHEDULE
The labor supply schedule depicted here has a positive slope up to point *A*, as substitution effects outweigh income effects. At higher wages, however, income effects become just as important as substitution effects, and the curve becomes roughly vertical.

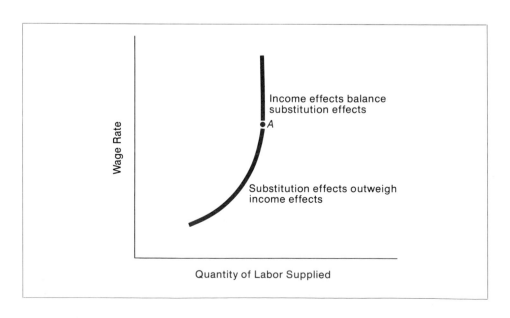

hours of work performed by students at Princeton University found that it does.[1] Estimated substitution effects of higher wages on the labor supply of Princeton students were positive and income effects were negative, just as the theory predicts. Apparently, substitution effects outweighed income effects by a slim margin, so that higher wages attracted a somewhat greater supply of labor. Specifically, a 10-percent rise in wages was estimated to increase the hours of work of the Princeton student body by about 3 percent.

An Application: The Labor Supply Paradox

Labor supply analysis helps explain the following puzzling observation. Throughout the twentieth century, wages have generally been rising, both in number of dollars paid per hour and in the quantity of goods those dollars can buy, as is clearly shown by the data depicted in Figure 33–3. Yet labor has asked for and received *reductions* in the length of the workday and workweek. At the beginning of the century, a workweek of $5\frac{1}{2}$ days and a workday of 10 or more hours was standard, making a workweek of 50 to 60 hours. Since then, labor hours have generally declined. Today the standard workweek is down to 35 to 40 hours. Where has the common-sense view of the matter gone wrong? Why, as hourly wages have risen, have workers not sold more of the hours they have available instead of pressing for a shorter and shorter workweek?

Part of the answer becomes clear when one recalls that any wage increase sets in motion *both* a substitution effect *and* an income effect. If only the substitution

[1]Mary P. Hurley, "An Investigation of Employment among Princeton Undergraduates During the Academic Year," Senior thesis submitted to the Department of Economics, May 1975.

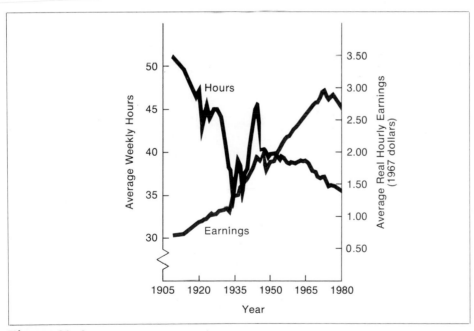

Figure 33–3
TRENDS IN REAL WAGES AND HOURS WORKED
This graph shows how real wages (measured in dollars of 1967 purchasing power) have been rising throughout the twentieth century in the United States, while hours worked per week have been declining, despite the higher rewards for each hour of work. The sharp drop in hours during the 1930s reflects the high unemployment of the Great Depression, and the sharp rise in hours in the 1940s reflects the unusual circumstances of World War II.
SOURCE: Compiled by the authors from data in *Historical Statistics of the United States* and *Economic Report of the President.* Data on both weekly hours and hourly earnings pertain to the entire economy for the 1947–1980 period, but only to the manufacturing sector for earlier years because of the unavailability of economywide data.

effect operated, then rising wages would indeed cause people to work longer hours because the high price of leisure makes leisure less attractive. But this reasoning leaves out the income effect. As higher wages make workers richer, they will want to buy more of most commodities, including vacations and other leisure-time activities. Thus the income effect of increasing wages induces workers to work fewer hours. It is the strong income effect of rising wages that may account for the fact that labor supply has responded in the "wrong" direction, with workers working ever-shorter hours despite their rising real wages.

The Demand for Labor and the Determination of Wages

There is not much to be said about the demand for labor that has not already been said about the demand for other inputs. Like any factor of production, labor has a marginal revenue product curve from which a downward-sloping demand curve for labor can be derived. This demand curve is shown in Figure 33–4 as curve *DD*. The figure also includes a supply curve, labeled *SS*, much like the one depicted in Figure 33–2.

If there are no interferences with the operation of a free market in labor (such as minimum wages or unions—which we will consider later), equilibrium will be at point *E*, where the supply and demand curves intersect. In this example, 500,000 workers will be employed at a wage of $300 per week.

Why Wages Differ

But, of course, there is not one labor market but many—each with its own supply and demand curves and its own equilibrium wage. We all know that certain groups in our society (the young, the black, the uneducated) earn relatively low wages, and that some of our most severe social ills (poverty, crime, drug addiction) are related to this fact. But why are some wages so low while others are so high?

Supply-and-demand analysis at once tells us everything and nothing about this question. It implies that wages are relatively high in markets where demand is great and supply is small [see Figure 33–5(a)], while wages are comparatively low in markets where demand is weak and supply is high [see Figure 33–5(b)].

Figure 33–4
EQUILIBRIUM IN A COMPETITIVE LABOR MARKET
In a competitive labor market, equilibrium will be established at the wage that equates the quantity supplied with the quantity demanded. In this example, equilibrium is at point *E*, where demand curve *DD* crosses supply curve *SS*. The equilibrium wage is $300 per week and equilibrium employment is 500,000 workers.

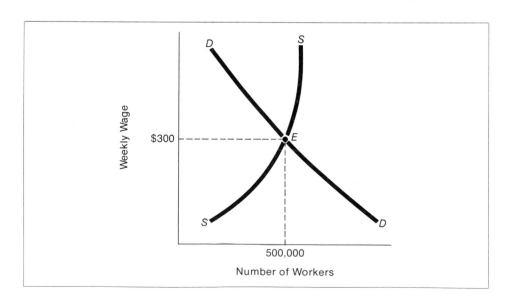

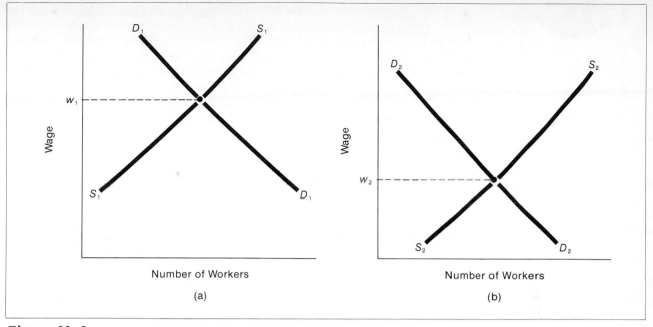

Figure 33–5
WAGE DIFFERENTIALS
(a) The market depicted here has a high equilibrium wage, w_1, because demand is high relative to supply. This can occur if qualified workers are scarce, or if productivity on the job is high, or if the demand for the product is great. (b) By contrast, the equilibrium wage, w_2, is low here, where supply is high relative to demand. This can result from an abundant supply of qualified workers, or low productivity, or weak demand for the product.

This can hardly be considered startling news. But to make the analysis useful, we need to breathe some life into the supply and demand curves.

We begin our discussion on the demand side. Why is the demand for labor greater in some markets than in others? The marginal productivity principle teaches us that there are two types of influences to be considered. Since a worker's marginal revenue product depends both on his *marginal physical product* and on the *price of the product* that he produces, variables that influence either of these will influence his wage.

The determinants of the prices of commodities were discussed at some length in earlier chapters, and there is no need to repeat the analysis here. It is sufficient to remember that because the demand for labor is a *derived demand*, anything that raises or lowers the demand for a particular product will tend to raise or lower the wages of the workers that produce that product.

A worker's marginal physical product depends on several things, including, of course, his own *abilities* and *degree of effort* on the job. But sometimes these characteristics are less important than the *other factors of production* that he has to work with. Workers in American industry are more productive than workers in many other countries because they have generous supplies of machinery, natural resources, and technical know-how to work with. As a consequence, they earn high wages.

Turning next to the supply of labor, it is clear that the *size of the available working population* relative to the magnitude of industrial activity in a given area is of major importance. This helps explain why wages rose so high in sparsely populated Alaska when the Alaska pipeline created many new jobs, and why wages have been and remain so low in Appalachia, where industry is dormant.

Second, it is clear that the *nonmonetary attractiveness* of any job will also influence the supply of workers to it. (The monetary attractiveness is the wage itself, which governs movements *along* the supply curve.) Jobs that people find pleasant and satisfying—such as teaching—will attract a large supply of labor, and will consequently pay a low wage. In contrast, a premium will have to be paid to attract workers to jobs that are onerous, disagreeable, or dangerous—such as washing the windows of skyscrapers.

Finally, the amount of ability and training needed to enter a particular job or profession is relevant to its supply of labor. Brain surgeons and professional football quarterbacks earn generous incomes because there are few people as highly skilled as they, and because it is time consuming and expensive to acquire these skills even for those who have the ability.

Ability and Earnings

In considering the effects of ability on earnings, it is useful to distinguish between skills that can be duplicated easily and skills that cannot. If Jones has an ability that Smith cannot acquire, even if he undergoes extensive training, then the wages that Jones earns will contain an element of *economic rent*, just as in the case of Johnny Carson.[2] The salaries of professional athletes provide particularly clear examples of how economic rents can lead to huge wage differentials. Virtually anyone with moderate athletic ability can be taught to hit a baseball. But in most cases, no amount of training will teach the player to hit a baseball like Reggie Jackson. Jackson's high salary is a reward for his unique ability.

But many of the abilities that the market rewards generously—such as the skills of doctors and lawyers—clearly are duplicable. Here the theory of rent does not apply, and we need a different explanation of the high wages that these skilled professionals earn. Once again, however, part of our analysis from Chapter 32 finds an immediate application because the acquisition of skills, through formal education and other forms of training, has much in common with business investment decisions. Why? Because the decision to undertake more education in the hope of increasing future earnings involves a sacrifice of *current* income for the sake of *future* gain—precisely the hallmark of an investment decision.

Investment in Human Capital

That education is an investment is a concept familiar to most college students. You made a conscious decision to go to college rather than to enter the labor market, and you are probably acutely aware that this decision is now costing you money—lots of money. Your tuition payments may be only a minor part of the total cost of going to college. Think of a high school friend who chose not to go to college and is now working. The salary that he or she is earning could, perhaps, have been yours. You are deliberately giving up this possible income in order to acquire more education.

In this sense, your education can be thought of as an *investment* in yourself—a *human investment*. Like a firm that devotes some of its money to building a plant that will yield profits at some future date, you are investing in your own future, hoping that your college education will help you earn more than your high-school-educated friend or enable you to find a more pleasant or prestigious job when you graduate. Economists call activities like going to college **investments in human capital** because such activities give the human being many of the attributes of a capital investment.

Doctors and lawyers earn such high salaries partly because of their many years of training. That is, part of their wages can be construed as a *return on their*

---

[2]See the previous chapter, pages 604–605.

(*educational*) *investments*, rather than as economic rent. Unlike the case of Reggie Jackson, there are a number of people who conceivably *could* become surgeons if they found the job sufficiently attractive to endure the long years of training that are required. Few, however, are willing to make such a large investment of their own time, money, and energy. Consequently, the few who do become surgeons earn very generous incomes.

Economists have devoted quite a bit of attention to the acquisition of skills through human investment. There is an entire branch of economic theory— called **human capital theory**—which analyzes an individual's decisions about education, training, and so on in exactly the same way as we analyzed a firm's decision to buy a machine or build a factory in the previous chapter. Though educational decisions can be influenced by love of learning, desire for prestige, and a variety of other preferences and emotions, human capital theorists find it useful to analyze a schooling decision as if it were made purely as a business plan. The optimal length of education, from this point of view, is to stay in school until the marginal revenue (in the form of increased future income) of an additional year of schooling is exactly equal to the marginal cost.

One implication of human capital theory is that college graduates should earn enough more than high school graduates to compensate them for their extra investments in schooling. Do they? Will your college investment pay off? Many generations of college students have supposed that it would, and for years studies of the incomes earned by college students indicated that they were right. These studies showed that the income differentials earned by college graduates provided a good "return" on the tuition payments and sacrificed earnings that they "invested" while in school. But college investments turned a bit sour in the 1970s. The reason was the obvious one: relative to high school graduates, the supply of college graduates expanded much more rapidly than the demand.[3]

This, of course, does not mean that only fools go to college. What it does mean is that the financial incentive *alone* is not what it used to be. If you simply enjoy the experience, or want to acquire knowledge for its own sake rather than for the money it may subsequently help you earn, attending college can still be a perfectly rational decision. It does not, however, offer quite the financial bonanza it once did.

Human capital theory stresses that jobs that require more education *must* pay higher wages if they are to attract enough workers, because people insist on a financial return on their human investments. But the theory does not address the other side of the question: What is it about more-educated people that makes firms willing to pay them higher wages? The theory explains that the quantity *supplied* of educated people is limited because some people will not make the investments needed to become educated. But the theory does not explain why the quantity *demanded* of such people is substantial even at high wages.

Most human capital theorists complete their analyses by assuming that students in high schools and colleges are acquiring particular skills that are productive in the marketplace. In this view, educational institutions are factories that take less-productive workers as their raw materials, apply doses of training, and produce more-productive workers as outputs. It is a view of what happens in schools that makes educators happy and accords well with common sense. However, a number of social scientists dispute this notion of how schooling raises earning power.

Education and Earnings: Dissenting Views
Just why is it that jobs with stiffer educational requirements typically offer higher

[3]Richard B. Freeman, *The Over-educated American* (New York: Academic Press, 1976).

wages? The common-sense view that educating people makes them more productive is not universally accepted.

Education as a Sorting Mechanism   One alternative view denies that the educational process teaches students anything directly relevant to their subsequent performance on jobs. On this view, people differ in ability when they enter the school system and differ in more or less the same way when they leave. What the educational system does, according to this theory, is to *sort* individuals by ability. Skills like intelligence and self-discipline that lead to success in schools, it is argued, are closely related to the skills that lead to success in jobs. As a result, more able individuals stay in school longer and perform better. Prospective employers know this, and consequently seek to hire those whom the school system has suggested will be the most productive workers.

The Radical View of Education[4]   Radical economists question whether the educational system really sorts people according to ability. The rich, they note, are better situated to buy the best education and to keep their children in school regardless of ability. Thus, education may be one of the instruments by which a more privileged family passes its economic position on to its heirs while making it appear that there is a legitimate reason for firms to give them higher earnings. As radicals see it, education sorts people according to their social class, not according to their ability.

Radicals also hold a different idea about what happens inside schools to make workers more "productive." Instead of the conventional stress on acquiring knowledge and learning how to think, radicals suggest that what schools really do is teach people discipline—how to show up five days a week at 9 A.M., how to speak in turn and respectfully, and so on. These characteristics, radicals claim, are what business firms prefer and what causes them to seek more-educated workers.

The Dual Labor Market Theory   A third view of the linkages among education, ability, and earnings is part of a much broader theory of how the labor market operates—the theory of **dual labor markets.** Proponents of this theory suggest that there are two very different types of labor markets, with relatively little mobility between them.

The "primary labor market" is where most of the economy's "good jobs" are—jobs like computer programming, business management, and skilled crafts that are interesting and offer considerable possibilities for career advancement. The educational system helps decide which individuals get assigned to the primary labor market and, for those who make it, greater educational achievement does indeed offer financial rewards. The privileged workers who wind up in the primary labor market are offered opportunities for additional training on the job; they augment their skills by experience, and by learning from their fellow workers; and they progress in successive steps to more responsible, better paying positions. Where jobs in the primary labor market are concerned, dual labor market theorists agree with human capital theorists that education really is productive. But they agree with the radicals that admission to the primary labor market depends in part on social position, and that firms probably care more about steady work habits and punctuality than about reading, writing, and arithmetic.

Everything is quite different in the "secondary labor market"—where we find all the "bad jobs." Jobs like domestic service and fast-food service, which are often the only ones ghetto residents can find, offer low rates of pay, few fringe

[4]Radical economics is considered in greater depth in Chapter 42, especially pages 815–821.

benefits, and virtually no training to improve the workers' skills. They are dead-end jobs with little or no hope for promotion or advancement. As a result, lateness, absenteeism, and thievery are expected as a matter of course, so that workers in the secondary labor market tend to develop the bad work habits that confirm the prejudices of those who assigned them to inferior jobs in the first place. In the secondary labor market, increased education leads neither to higher wages nor to increased protection from unemployment—benefits that increased schooling generally offers elsewhere in the labor market. For this reason, workers in the secondary market have little incentive to invest in education.

In sum, we have a well-established fact—that people with more education generally earn higher wages—but very little agreement on the theory that accounts for this fact.

The Effects of Minimum Wage Legislation

As we have observed, the "labor market" is really composed of many sub-markets for labor of different types, each with its own supply and demand curves. To understand the effects of minimum wage legislation, it suffices to consider two such markets, which we call for convenience "skilled" and "unskilled" labor and portray in the two parts of Figure 33–6. As drawn, the demand curve for skilled workers is higher than that for unskilled workers. The reason is obvious: skilled workers have higher productivity. Conversely, we have drawn the supply curve of skilled workers farther to the left than the supply curve of unskilled workers to reflect the greater scarcity of skilled workers. The consequence, as we can see in Figure 33–6, is that the equilibrium wage is much higher for skilled workers. In the example, the equilibrium wages are $8 per hour for skilled workers and $2.50 per hour for unskilled workers.

Now suppose the government, seeking to protect unskilled workers, imposes

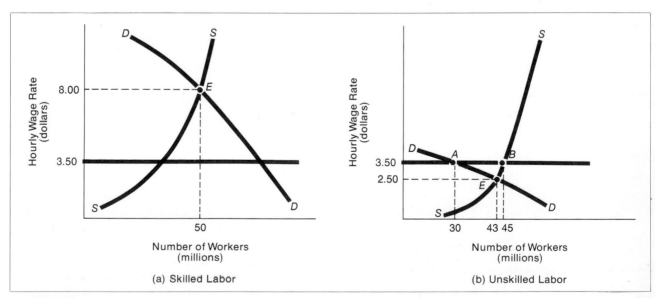

Figure 33–6
THE EFFECTS OF MINIMUM WAGE LEGISLATION
(a) Imposing a minimum wage of $3.50 per hour does not affect the market for skilled labor because the equilibrium wage there ($8 per hour) is well above the legal minimum. (b) However, the minimum-wage legislation does have important effects in the market for unskilled labor. There the equilibrium wage ($2.50 per hour) is below the minimum, so the minimum wage makes the quantity supplied (45 million workers) exceed the quantity demanded (30 million workers). The result is unemployment of unskilled labor.

Minimum Wages in Illinois and in Zimbabwe

Minimum wage laws have proven to be politically popular in many countries. The following two news items suggest that their effects are quite similar in the United States and in Africa.

Rise in Minimum Wage Spurs Some Firms to Cut Work Hours and Hiring of Youths

LOMBARD, Ill.—Last summer Janet Straka started work at the Steak n Shake restaurant here in this Chicago suburb at 9 A.M. to get ready for the 10 o'clock opening.

But in January the federal minimum wage rose to $2.65 an hour from $2.30. Steak n Shake, seeking to blunt the impact, decided to open an hour later, since there were few early customers anyway. Steak n Shake also cut the opening waitress's preparation time to 30 minutes. So Miss Straka, a schoolteacher who works summers part-time at the hamburger chain, now starts work at 10:30 A.M., and her weekly earnings are down to about $36 from $40 last summer.

Her shortened workday shows one way in which the higher minimum wage is affecting employment in the U.S. There haven't been wholesale layoffs of low-wage workers, but some workers are putting in fewer hours on the job.

Another effect is that teen-agers, especially blacks, are having more trouble finding work as companies like Steak n Shake look for older, more qualified workers likely to stay at a job longer. . . .

SOURCE: *The Wall Street Journal*, August 15, 1978. Reprinted by permission of *The Wall Street Journal*, © Dow Jones & Company, Inc., 1978. All rights reserved.

Zimbabwe Minimum Wage Spurs Many Dismissals

SALISBURY, Zimbabwe, July 6 (Reuters)—A Government decision to set a minimum wage for workers has backfired for thousands with dismissals reported throughout the country.

Officials of the ruling party of Prime Minister Robert Mugabe said today that in the Salisbury area alone more than 5,000 workers were dismissed before the minimum wage bill went into effect last Tuesday.

Worst hit, according to the officials, were domestic servants and farm workers for whom the minimum has been set at $45 a month. Employees in the commercial and industrial sectors, where the minimum has been fixed at $105 a month have also been dismissed. The officials said that every party office in the country was dealing with hundreds of workers each day complaining of unfair dismissal.

SOURCE: *The New York Times*, July 7, 1980. Copyright ©1980 by The New York Times Company. Reprinted by permission.

---

a legal minimum wage of $3.50 per hour (the heavy blue line in both parts of Figure 33–6). Turning first to part (a), we see that the minimum wage has no effect in the markets for skilled workers like carpenters and electricians. Since their wages are well above $3.50 per hour, a law prohibiting the payment of wage rates below $3.50 cannot possibly matter.

But the effects of the minimum wage are quite pronounced in the markets for unskilled labor—and presumably quite different from those that Congress intended. Figure 33–6(b) indicates that at the $3.50 minimum wage, firms want to employ only 30 million unskilled workers (point A) whereas employment of unskilled workers would have been 43 million (point E) in a free market. Although the 30 million unskilled workers lucky enough to retain their jobs do indeed earn a higher wage ($3.50 instead of $2.50 per hour), 13 million of their compatriots earn no wage at all because they have been laid off. The job-losers will clearly be those workers with the lowest productivity, since the minimum wage effectively bans the employment of workers whose marginal revenue product is less than $3.50 per hour. (See the boxed insert above.)

Although the minimum wage does lead to higher wages for those unskilled workers who retain their jobs, it also restricts employment opportunities for unskilled workers.

In addition, minimum wages may have particularly pernicious effects on those who are the victims of discrimination. Because of the minimum wage, as Figure 33–6(b) shows, employers of unskilled labor have more applicants than job openings. Consequently, they will be able to pick and choose among the available applicants, and may, for example, discriminate against blacks. For these reasons, most economists feel that the teen-age unemployment problem, and especially the black teen-age unemployment problem, will be very difficult to solve as long as the minimum wage remains effective.

Unions and Collective Bargaining

Our analysis of competitive labor markets has ignored one rather important fact: The supply of labor is not at all competitive in many labor markets; instead it is controlled by a labor monopoly, a **union.**

While important, unions in America are not nearly so important as is popularly supposed. For example, most people who are not acquainted with the data are astonished to learn that only about 20 percent of American workers belong to unions. This fraction is much higher than it was before the New Deal, when unions were quite unimportant in this country, but lower than it was in the heyday of unionism in the mid-1950s—just over 25 percent (see Figure 33–7).

Unions seem much more prevalent than this to the public because they are such large, and therefore newsworthy, institutions. The giant Teamster's union, for example, has almost 2 million members; the United Auto Workers (UAW) and the United Steelworkers (USA) each have nearly 1½ million; and the largest labor federation, the American Federation of Labor and Congress of Industrial Organizations (AFL-CIO), has more than 17 million members. Because of their

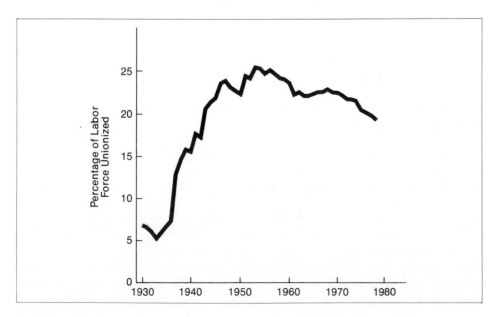

Figure 33–7
UNIONIZATION IN THE UNITED STATES, 1930–1978
In 1930, unions had enrolled just under 7 percent of the U.S. labor force; and by 1933 this figure had slipped to barely above 5 percent. Unionization took off with the New Deal, reaching almost 16 percent of the labor force by 1939. It then drifted irregularly upward, to a peak of about 25 to 26 percent of all workers in the mid-1950s, and has since trailed off to less than 20 percent.
SOURCE: U.S. Department of Labor, Bureau of Labor Statistics.

The Way It Was

The calamitous Triangle Shirtwaist Factory fire of 1911, in which 146 women and girls lost their lives, was a landmark in American labor history. It galvanized public opinion behind the movement to improve conditions, hours, and wages in the sweatshops. Pauline Newman went to work in the Triangle Shirtwaist Factory at the age of eight, shortly after coming to the Lower East Side. Many of her friends lost their lives in the fire. She went on to become an organizer and later an executive of the newly formed International Ladies Garment Workers' Union, of which she is now, at the age of 86, educational director.*

By Pauline Newman

We started work at seven-thirty in the morning, and during the busy season we worked until nine in the evening. They didn't pay you any overtime and they didn't give you anything for supper money. Sometimes they'd give you a little apple pie if you had to work very late. That was all. Very generous. . . .

We had a corner on the floor that resembled a kindergarten—we were given little scissors to cut the threads off. It wasn't heavy work, but it was monotonous.

Well, of course, there were laws on the books, but no one bothered to enforce them. The employers were always tipped off if there was going to be an inspection. "Quick," they'd say, "into the boxes!" And we children would climb into the big boxes the finished shirts were stored in. Then some shirts were piled on top of us, and when the inspector came—no children. The factory always got an okay from the inspector, and I suppose someone at City Hall got a little something, too.

The employers didn't recognize anyone working for them as a human being. You were not allowed to sing. . . . We weren't allowed to talk to each other. . . . If you went to the toilet and you were there longer than the floor lady thought you should be, you would be laid off for half a day and sent home. And, of course, that meant no pay. You were not allowed to have your lunch on the fire escape in the summertime. The door was locked to keep us in. That's why so many people were trapped when the fire broke out. . . .

The employers had a sign in the elevator that said: "If you don't come in on Sunday, don't come in on Monday." You were expected to work every day if they needed you and the pay was the same whether you worked extra or not.

Conditions were dreadful in those days. We didn't have anything. . . . There was no welfare, no pension, no unemployment insurance. There was nothing. . . . There was so much feeling against unions then. The judges, when one of our girls came before him, said to her: "You're not striking against your employer, you know, young lady. You're striking against God," and sentenced her to two weeks.

I wasn't at the Triangle Shirtwaist Factory when the fire broke out, but a lot of my friends were. . . . The thing that bothered me was the employers got a lawyer. How anyone could have *defended* them!—because I'm quite sure that the fire was planned for insurance purposes. And no one is going to convince me otherwise. And when they testified that the door to the fire escape was open, it was a lie! It was never open. Locked all the time. One hundred and forty-six people sacrificed, and the judge fined Blank and Harris seventy-five dollars!

*This introduction and the following narrative are excerpted from the book *American Mosaic: The Immigrant Experience in the Words of Those Who Lived It*, by Joan Morrison and Charlotte Fox Zabusky.

SOURCE: *The New York Times*, September 1, 1980. Copyright © 1980 by The New York Times Company. Reprinted by permission.

---

size, the actions of these unions are reported daily in the media. By contrast, unless you are a student of labor statistics, you will hardly ever hear anything about the more than 80 million workers in America who do not belong to unions.

Unionization is also much less prevalent in America than it is in most other industrialized countries. For example, about 50 percent of British workers and about 80 percent of Swedish workers belong to unions. The differences are quite striking and doubtless have something to do with our tradition of "rugged individualism."

The Development of Unionism in America

While its roots can be traced back earlier, serious unionism in America is only about 100 years old. Large-scale unions in this country began with the Knights of Labor—a very politically motivated workers' organization that was quite different from the unions of today. Toward the end of the nineteenth century, membership in the Knights of Labor approached 750,000 workers; but it failed to achieve higher wages or better working conditions for its members, and the organization declined rapidly. Today American unions are noteworthy for their basically nonpolitical stance, in contrast to the highly politicized unions of many European countries.

The American labor movement as we know it today began to take shape in 1881 with the founding of the American Federation of Labor by Samuel Gompers, who headed the AFL for nearly 50 years and did more to shape the American labor movement than any other person. At that time, working conditions were incredibly bad by today's standards (see box, opposite). Gompers believed strongly that unions should be nonpolitical organizations seeking to get *more* for their members: more pay, better working conditions, longer vacations, and so on. He also believed that unions should be organized along craft lines—carpenters in one union, plumbers in another—rather than trying to include all types of workers in a given industry. Finally, he was a staunch advocate of free collective bargaining without government interference.

Before 1914 unions were subject to attack as monopolies under the Sherman Antitrust Act, but the Clayton Act exempted labor from such prosecution. The AFL grew rather steadily from about 1900 until the 1920s, but then went into decline during the Roaring Twenties, when capitalism was booming and every worker, it seemed, dreamed of getting rich in the stock market.

The favorable attitudes and legislation of the Roosevelt administration provided a great stimulus to unionism in this country in the 1930s. The Norris-La Guardia Act of 1932 sharply limited the power of the federal courts to interfere in labor disputes. In 1938 the Fair Labor Standards Act abolished child labor, imposed a minimum wage on most activities whose products entered into interstate commerce, and wrote extra pay for overtime work into law. Even more important, the National Labor Relations Act (Wagner Act) in 1935 guaranteed workers the right to form unions and to choose the union that would represent them in collective bargaining. It also set up the National Labor Relations Board (NLRB) to protect labor from "unfair labor practices" by employers. Today the NLRB oversees elections in business firms to determine which union will represent the workers. It can also force employers to take back workers whom it considers to have been fired unjustly.

By no coincidence, in the year of the Wagner Act, John L. Lewis founded the Congress of Industrial Organizations (CIO), a federation of many **industrial unions** that at first rivaled the AFL for leadership of the U.S. labor movement. It was felt by those who advocated industrial unions that many specialized **craft unions** (which often quarreled among themselves) were not likely to be very powerful in their dealings with large employers. Despite their differences, the AFL, with its craft unions, and the CIO, with its industrial unions, eventually merged in 1955.

The favorable public attitude toward unions soured somewhat after World War II, perhaps because of the rash of strikes that took place in 1946 (see Figure 33–11 on page 635). One result of these strikes was the **Taft-Hartley Act** of 1947, which specified and outlawed certain "unfair labor practices" by unions. Specifically, the act:

An **industrial union** represents all types of workers in a single industry, such as auto manufacturing or coal mining.

A **craft union** represents a particular type of skilled worker, such as newspaper typographers or electricians, regardless of what industry they work in.

A **closed shop** is an arrangement that permits only union members to be hired.

A **union shop** is an arrangement under which nonunion workers may be hired, but then must join the union within a specified period of time.

1. Severely limited the extent of the **closed shop.**
2. Permitted state governments, at their discretion, to ban the **union shop.** These so-called right-to-work laws have been adopted by several states.
3. Provided for court injunctions to delay strikes that threaten the national interest for an 80-day "cooling-off" period.

Today, the character of American unionism is still somewhat unsettled. Unions are struggling very hard to make inroads into labor markets that by tradition have not been unionized—such as the agricultural and white-collar office markets. Notable successes have been achieved in organizing teachers and many government employees. But at the same time union membership as a percent of the labor force is on the decline, largely because the manufacturing sector—the traditional home of unions—is becoming a smaller fraction of the whole economy. Whether unions are too strong or too weak remains a controversial issue.

Unions as a Labor Monopoly

Unions require that we alter our economic analysis of the labor market in much the same way that monopolies required us to alter our analysis of the goods market (see Chapter 25). You will recall that in a monopolized product market the firm selects the point on its demand curve that maximizes its profits. Much the same idea applies to unions, which are, after all, monopoly sellers of labor. They too face a demand curve—derived this time from the marginal productivity schedules of firms—and can choose the point on it that suits them best.

The problem for the economist trying to analyze union behavior—and perhaps also for the union leader trying to select a course of action—is how to decide which point on the demand curve is "best." There is no obvious goal analogous to profit maximization that clearly delineates what the union should do. Instead there are a number of *alternative* goals that sound plausible.

Alternative Union Goals

These goals can be illustrated with the aid of Figure 33–8, which depicts a demand curve for labor, labeled *DD*. The union leadership must decide which point on the curve is best. One possibility is to treat the size of the union as fixed and force employers to pay the highest wage they will pay and still employ all the union members. If, for example, the union has 4000 members, this would be point *A*, with a wage of $12 per hour. But this is a high-risk strategy for a union. Firms forced to pay such high wages will be at a competitive disadvantage compared with firms that have nonunion labor, and may even be forced to shut down.

Alternatively, union leaders may be interested in increasing the size of their unions. As an extreme case of this, they might try to make employment as large as possible without pushing the wage below the competitive level. If the competitive wage were $6 per hour in the absence of the union, this strategy would correspond to selecting point *C*, with employment for 8000 workers. In this case the existence of the union has no effect on wages or on employment.

An intermediate strategy that has often been suggested is that the union maximize the total income of all workers. This would dictate choosing point *B*, with a wage of $9 per hour and jobs for 6000 workers. Other possible strategies can also be imagined, but these suffice to make the basic point clear.

Unions, as monopoly sellers of labor, have the power to push wages above the competitive levels. However, since the demand curve for labor is downward

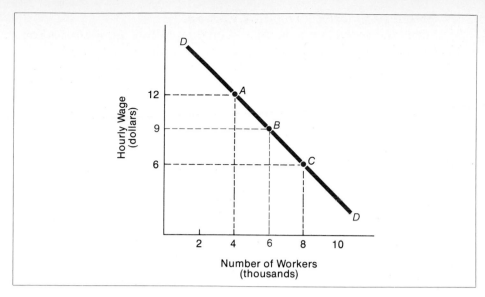

Figure 33–8
ALTERNATIVE GOALS
FOR A UNION
Line *DD* is the demand curve
for labor in a market that becomes unionized. Point *C* is
the equilibrium point before the
union, when wages were $6
per hour. If the union wants to
push wages higher, it normally
will have to sacrifice some
jobs. Points *A* and *B* show two
of its many alternatives.

sloping, such increases in wages normally can be achieved only by reducing the number of jobs. Just as the monopolist must limit his output to push up his price, so the union must restrict employment to push up the wage.

This can be seen clearly by comparing points *B* and *A* with point *C* (the competitive solution). If it selects point *B*, the union raises wages by $3 per hour, but at the cost of 2000 jobs. If it goes all the way to point *A*, wages are raised to twice the competitive level, but employment is cut in half.

What do unions actually try to do? There are probably as many different choices as there are unions. Some seem to pursue a maximum-employment goal much like point *C*, raising wages very little. Others seem to push for the highest possible wages, much like point *A*. Most probably select an intermediate route. This implies, of course, that the effects of unionization on wage rates and employment will differ markedly among industries.

Alternative Union Strategies

How would a union that has decided to push wages above the competitive level accomplish this task? Two principal ways are illustrated in Figure 33–9, where we suppose that point *U* on demand curve *DD* is the union's choice, and point *C* is the competitive equilibrium.

In Figure 33–9(a), we suppose that the union pursues its goal by *restricting supply*. By keeping out some workers who would like to enter the industry or occupation, it shifts the supply curve of labor inward from S_0S_0 to S_1S_1. This sort of behavior is often encountered in craft unions, which may require a long period of apprenticeship. Such unions sometimes offer only a small number of new memberships each year, largely to replace members who have died or retired. Membership in such a union is very valuable and is sometimes offered primarily to children of current members.

In Figure 33–9(b), instead of restricting supply, the union simply *sets a high wage rate*, *W* in the example. In this case, it is the employers who will restrict entry into the job, because with wages so high they will not want to employ many workers. This second strategy is more typically employed by industrial unions like the United Automobile Workers or the United Mine Workers. As the figure makes clear, the two wage-raising strategies achieve the same result (point *U* in

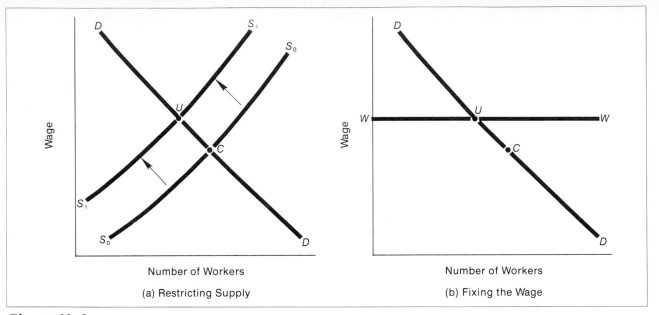

Figure 33-9

TWO UNION STRATEGIES

The two parts indicate two alternative ways for the union to move from point C to point U. In part (a), it keeps some workers out of the industry, thereby moving the supply curve to the left from S_0S_0 to S_1S_1. As a consequence, wages rise. In part (b), it fixes a high wage (W), and provides labor only at this wage. As a consequence, firms reduce employment. The effects are the same under both strategies.

either case) by what turns out to be the same means. Wages are raised only by reducing employment in either case.

In some exceptional cases, however, a union may be able to achieve wage gains without sacrificing employment. To do this, the union must be able to exercise effective control over the demand curve for labor. Figure 33–10 illustrates such a possibility. Union actions push the demand curve outward from D_0D_0 to D_1D_1, simultaneously raising both wages and employment. Typically, this is difficult to do. One way to do it is by *featherbedding*—forcing management to employ more workers than they really need.[5] Quite the opposite technique is to institute a campaign to raise worker productivity, which some unions seem to have been able to do. Alternatively, the union can try to raise the demand for the company's product either by flexing its political muscle (for example, by obtaining legislation to reduce foreign competition) or by appealing to the public to buy union products.

Have Unions Really Raised Wages?

The theory of unions as monopoly sellers of labor certainly suggests that unions have some ability to raise wages, but it also shows that they may be hesitant to use this ability for fear of reducing employment. To what extent do union members actually earn higher wages than nonmembers? The consensus that has emerged from economic research on this question would probably surprise most people. It seems that most union members earn wages 10 to 20 percent above those of nonmembers who are otherwise identical (in skill, geographical location, and so on). While certainly not negligible, this can hardly be considered a huge differential.

[5]The best-known example of featherbedding involved the railroad unions, which for years forced management to keep "firemen" in the cabs of diesel engines, in which there were no burning fires. Similarly, the musicians' union in New York City forces producers of Broadway musicals to employ a minimum number of musicians—whether or not they actually play music.

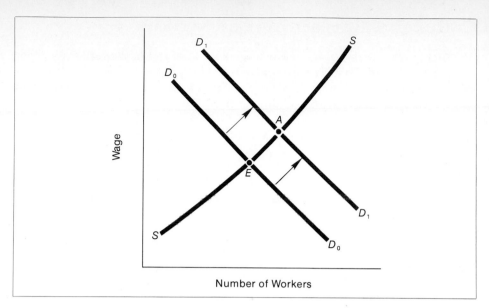

Figure 33–10
UNION CONTROL OVER
THE DEMAND CURVE
This diagram indicates yet a
third way in which unions may
affect the labor market—a
pleasant alternative for workers in that wages can be raised
while adding to employment.
Strong unions may succeed in
raising the demand curve from
D_0D_0 to D_1D_1 by (a) featherbedding, (b) raising worker
productivity, or (c) using their
influence to increase demand
for the product. Equilibrium
then shifts from point E to
point A.

Monopsony and Bilateral Monopoly

While the analysis we have just presented has its applications, it oversimplifies matters in several important respects. For one thing, it envisions a market situation in which one powerful union is dealing with many powerless employers. The labor market is assumed to be monopolized on the selling side but competitive on the buying side. There are industries that more or less fit this model. The giant Teamsters' union negotiates with a trucking industry that comprises thousands of firms, most of them quite small and powerless. Similarly, most of the unions within the construction industry are much larger than the firms with which they bargain.

But there are many cases that simply do not fit the model. The "Big Four" automakers do not stand idly by while the UAW picks its favorite point on the demand curve for auto workers. Nor does the Steelworkers' union sit across the bargaining table from representatives of a perfectly competitive industry. In these and other industries, while the union certainly has a good deal of monopoly power over labor supply, the firms also have some **monopsony** power over labor demand. Just as a monopoly union on the selling side of the labor market does not passively sell labor at the going wage, a monopsony firm on the buying side does not passively purchase labor at the going wage, nor at the wage suggested by the labor union. Analysts find it very difficult to predict the wage and employment decisions that will emerge when both the buying and selling side of a market are monopolized—a situation called **bilateral monopoly.**

The difficulties here are quite similar to those we encountered in considering the behavior of oligopolistic industries in Chapter 26. Just as one oligopolist, in planning his strategy, is acutely aware that his rivals are likely to react to anything he does, a union dealing with a monopsony employer knows that any move it makes will elicit a countermove by the firm. And this knowledge makes the first decision that much more complicated. In practice, the outcome of bilateral monopoly will depend partly on economic logic, partly on the relative power of the union and management, partly on the skill and preparation of the negotiators, and partly on luck.

Monopsony refers to a market situation in which there is only one buyer.

Bilateral monopoly is a market situation in which there is both a monopoly on the selling side and a monopsony on the buying side.

Collective Bargaining and Strikes

The process by which unions and management settle upon the terms of a labor contract is called **collective bargaining.** Unfortunately, there is nothing as straightforward as a supply–demand diagram to tell us what wage level will emerge from a collective bargaining session. Furthermore, actual collective bargaining sessions range over many more issues than wages. For example, fringe benefits—such as pensions, health and life insurance, paid holidays, and the like—may be just as important as wages to both labor and management. Wage premiums for overtime work and seniority privileges will also be negotiated. Work conditions, such as the speed with which the assembly line should move, are often crucial issues. Many labor contracts specify in great detail the rights of labor and management to set work conditions—and also provide elaborate procedures for resolving grievances and disputes. This list could go on and on. The final contract that emerges from collective bargaining may well run to many pages of fine print.

With the issues so varied and complex, and with the stakes so high, it is no wonder that both labor and management employ skilled professionals who specialize in preparing for and carrying out these negotiations, and that each side enters a collective bargaining session armed with reams of evidence supporting its positions. The bargaining in these sessions is often heated, with outcomes riding as much on personalities and the skills of the negotiators as on cool-headed logic and economic facts. Negotiations may last well into the night, with each side seeming to try to wear the other out. Each side may threaten the other with grave consequences if it does not accept its own terms. Unions, for their part, generally threaten to strike or to carry out a work slow-down. Firms counter with the threat that they would rather face a strike than give in, or may even close the plant without a strike. (This is called a "lock-out.")

Mediation and Arbitration

Where the public interest is seriously affected, or when the union and firm reach an impasse, government agencies may well send in a **mediator,** whose job is to try to speed up the negotiation process. This impartial observer will sit down with both sides separately to discuss their problems, and will try to persuade each side to yield a bit to the other. At some stage, when an agreement looks possible, he may call them back together for another bargaining session in his presence.

A mediator, however, has no power to force a settlement. His success hinges on his ability to smooth ruffled feathers and to find common ground for agreement. Sometimes, in cases where unions and firms simply cannot agree, and where neither wants a strike, differences are finally settled by **arbitration**—the appointment of an impartial individual empowered to settle the issues that negotiation could not resolve. In fact, in some vital sectors where a strike is too injurious to the public interest, the labor contract or the law may stipulate that there must be *compulsory arbitration* if the two parties cannot agree. However, both labor and management are normally reluctant to accept this procedure.

Strikes

Most collective bargaining situations do not lead to strikes. But the right to strike, and to take a strike, remain fundamentally important for the bargaining process. Imagine, for example, a firm bargaining with a union that was prohibited from striking. It seems likely that the union's bargaining position would be quite weak. On the other hand, a firm that always capitulated rather than suffer a strike would be virtually at the mercy of the union. So strikes, or more precisely, the possibility of strikes, serve an important economic purpose.

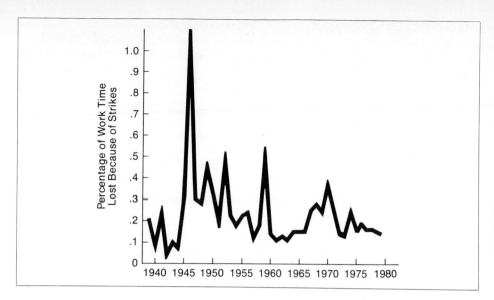

Figure 33–11
TIME LOST BECAUSE OF
STRIKES, 1939–1979
The fraction of total work time
lost to work stoppages varies
greatly from year to year, but is
never very large. In most
years, it is between one-tenth
and one-quarter of 1 percent.
The worst year for strikes was
1946, and it is probably no co-
incidence that the Taft-Hartley
Law was enacted in the follow-
ing year.
SOURCE: U.S. Department of
Labor, Bureau of Labor Statistics,
Handbook of Labor Statistics,
December 1980.

Fortunately, however, the incidence of strikes is not nearly so common as many people believe. Figure 33–11 reports the percentage of worker-days of labor lost as a result of strikes in the United States from 1939 to 1979. Despite the headline-grabbing nature of major national strikes, the total amount of work time lost to strikes is truly trivial—far less, for example, than the time lost to coffee breaks! Compared with other nations, America suffers more from strikes than, say Germany or Japan, but has many fewer strikes than such countries as Italy and Canada (see Figure 33–12).

Collective Bargaining in the Public Sector

We have argued that strikes serve an important function in private-sector bargaining, as a way of dividing the fruits of economic activity between big labor and big business. But does the same rationale for strikes apply to the public sector, where strikes or work stoppages seem increasingly common among mail carriers,

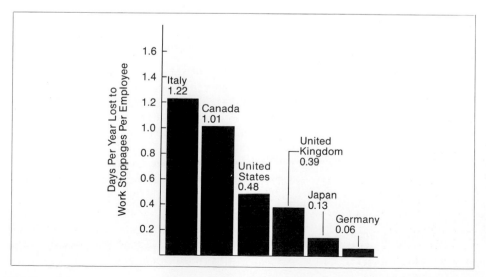

Figure 33–12
THE INCIDENCE OF
STRIKES IN INDUSTRIAL
COUNTRIES
Contrary to popular impres-
sions, the United States loses
more work time to strikes than
does the United Kingdom. And
although strikes here are much
less common than they are in
Italy or Canada, they are much
more common here than in
Japan or Germany. (*Note:*
Data are averages for the five-
year period 1974–1978.)
SOURCE: U.S. Department of
Labor, *Handbook of Labor Statis-
tics,* December 1980.

police, fire fighters, air-traffic controllers, and so on?

It is not clear that it does. In most private-sector strikes, labor and management are inflicting harm upon one another in a kind of battle of "survival of the fittest." Consumers normally suffer only mild inconveniences. When General Motors is on strike, many potential car buyers will be disappointed, but they can turn to Ford, Chrysler, and American Motors, not to mention imports. Similarly, when other private products disappear from the shelves because of strikes, the consumer can easily replace them with close substitutes. Thus, in many cases we can think of consumers as being relatively innocent and unharmed spectators when large unions and large private firms slug it out.

But public-sector bargaining is different. Here, management does not represent the interests of capital against those of labor; rather, it represents the public. And there is no pool of profits to be divided between the union and the stockholders. Instead, what management agrees to give to the union comes out of the pockets of the taxpayers. Finally, it is quite clear that the public is not just a spectator in such strikes, but is the primary victim. When police or fire-protection services are reduced, when mail delivery ceases, when public schools or airports shut down, consumers cannot find substitutes for these services. In a very real sense, then, strikes in the public sector are strikes against citizens, not strikes against management. They pit representatives of a particular group of workers against representatives of taxpayers as a whole.

For these reasons, the right of public employees to strike has traditionally been much more severely limited than the corresponding right of private-sector workers. In some states, public-sector strikes are simply outlawed, although this ban has proved hard to enforce. This system seemed logical and worked tolerably well when unionization in the public sector was rather rare. The public was protected, but the public-sector workers were not. As more and more government employees became organized, however, America's system of labor relations for public employees started showing signs of strain. Illegal strikes or "job actions," for example, have become increasingly common. Lawyers, economists, politicians, and specialists in labor relations today are struggling to hammer out some more viable system of public collective bargaining that will protect the rights of both public-sector workers and citizens as a whole. Their task, however, was never easy under the best of circumstances, and was made even more difficult by the stringent government budgets of the late 1970s and early 1980s.

Summary

1. The supply of labor is determined by free choices made by individuals. Because of conflicting income and substitution effects, the quantity of labor supplied may rise or fall as a result of an increase in wages.

2. Historical data show that hours of work per week have fallen as wages have risen, suggesting that income effects may be dominant.

3. The demand curve for labor, like the demand curve for any factor of production, is derived from the marginal revenue product curve. It slopes downward because of the "law" of diminishing marginal returns.

4. In a free market, the wage rate and the level of employment are determined by the interaction of supply and demand. Workers in great demand or short supply will command high wages and, conversely, low wages will be assigned to workers in abundant supply or with skills that are not in great demand.

5. Some valuable skills are virtually impossible to duplicate. People who possess such skills will earn economic rents as part of their wages.

6. But most skills can be acquired by "investments in human capital," such as education. The financial rate of return on college education, while still positive, is not as high as it was in the 1960s.

7. Human capital theory assumes that people make educational decisions in much the same way as businesses make investment decisions, and tacitly assumes that people learn things in schools that increase their productivity on jobs.

8. Other theories of the effects of education on earnings deny that schooling actually raises productivity. One view is that the educational system primarily sorts people according to their abilities. Another view holds

that schools sort people according to their social class, and teach them mainly discipline and obedience.

9. According to the theory of dual labor markets, there are two distinct types of labor markets with very little mobility between them. The primary labor market contains the "good" jobs, where wages are high, prospects for advancement are good, and higher education pays off. The secondary labor market contains the "bad" jobs, with low wages, little opportunity for promotion, and little return to education.

10. One reason that teen-agers, and especially black teen-agers, suffer from such high unemployment rates is that minimum wage laws prevent the employment of low-productivity workers.

11. About 20 percent of all American workers belong to unions, which can be thought of as monopoly sellers of labor. Compared with many other industrialized countries, the union movement in America is younger, less widespread, and less political.

12. Analysis of union behavior is complicated by the fact that a union can have many goals. For the most part, unions probably force wages to be higher and employment to be lower than they would be in a competitive labor market. However, there are exceptions.

13. Collective bargaining agreements between labor and management are complex documents covering much more than employment and wage rates.

14. Strikes play an important role in collective bargaining as a way of dividing the fruits of economic activity between big business and big labor. Fortunately, strikes are not nearly so common as is often supposed.

15. Strikes in the public sector, however, take on a different character because the adversaries are no longer "labor" versus "capital" but rather "labor" versus the "public interest." For this reason, the rights of public employees to strike have been curtailed.

Concepts for Review

Minimum wage law	Union	Bilateral monopoly
Income and substitution effects	Industrial and craft unions	Collective bargaining
Economic rent	Taft-Hartley Act (1947)	Mediation
Investments in human capital	Closed shop	Arbitration
Human capital theory	Union shop	Public-sector bargaining
Dual labor markets	Monopsony	

Questions for Discussion

1. Colleges are known to pay rather low wages for student labor. Can this be explained by the operation of supply and demand in the local labor market? Is the concept of monopsony of any use? How might things differ if students formed a union?

2. College professors are highly skilled (or at least highly educated!) labor. Yet their wages are not very high. Is this a refutation of the marginal productivity theory?

3. The following table shows the number of pizzas that can be produced by a large pizza parlor employing various numbers of pizza chefs.

NUMBER OF CHEFS	NUMBER OF PIZZAS PER DAY
1	80
2	150
3	205
4	240
5	250
6	230

   a. Find the marginal physical product schedule of chefs.
   b. Assuming a price of $3 per pizza, find the marginal revenue product schedule.
   c. If chefs are paid $30 per day, how many will this pizza parlor employ? How would your answer change if chefs' wages rose to $40 per day?

   d. Suppose the price of pizza rises from $3 to $4. Show what happens to the derived demand curve for chefs.

4. Discuss the concept of the financial rate of return to a college education. If this return is less than the return on a bank account, does that mean you should quit college? Why might you wish to stay in school anyway? Are there circumstances under which it might be rational not to go to college, even when the financial returns to college are very high?

5. It seems to be a well-established fact that workers with more years of education typically receive higher wages. What are some possible reasons for this?

6. Explain why many economists blame the minimum wage law for much of the employment problems of youth.

7. Approximately what fraction of the American labor force belongs to unions? (Try asking this question of a person who has never studied economics.) Why do you think this fraction is so low?

8. What are some reasonable goals for a union? Use the tools of supply and demand to explain how a union might pursue its goals, whatever they are. Consider a union that has been in the news recently. What was it trying to accomplish?

9. "Strikes are simply intolerable and should be outlawed." Comment.

10. "Public employees should have the same right to strike as private employees." Comment.

Appendix:
The Effects of Unions and Minimum Wages Under Monopsony

We have argued in this chapter that if a union or a minimum wage law raises wages, it must necessarily reduce employment. In this appendix we examine a possible exception to this rule.

When there is a monopsony on the buying side of the labor market, a union or a minimum wage law might succeed in raising wages without reducing employment. It might even be able to increase employment.

The Hiring Decisions of a Monopsonist

To establish these results, we begin by considering the hiring decision of a single firm operating in a labor market that is competitive on the supply side. (Later we will bring unions into the picture.) In such a market structure, there is a competitive *supply* curve for labor as usual, but there is a rather different sort of *demand* curve. In Figure 33–13, the supply curve is labeled *SS* and the firm's marginal revenue product (MRP) schedule is labeled *RR*. In this context, however, the MRP schedule is *not* the demand curve. The diagram has one additional curve, which will be explained presently.

How many workers will the monopsonist wish to hire? Table 33–1 helps us answer this question by displaying the monopsonist's cost and revenue calculations. What does he gain by hiring an additional worker? He gains that worker's marginal revenue product which is given in column 5 of the table. What does he lose? Not just the wage he pays to the new worker. Because he is the only employer, and because the labor supply schedule is upward sloping, he can attract an additional worker only by *raising the wage rate*. And this higher wage must be paid to *all his employees*, not just the new one. For this reason, the cost of hiring an additional worker—what we call **marginal labor costs**—exceeds the wage rate. By how much? Table 33–1 provides the answer. The first two columns are just the labor supply schedule, curve *SS* of Figure 33–13. By multiplying the wage rate by the number of workers, we can compute the *total labor cost*, which is shown in column 3. For example, the total labor cost of hiring

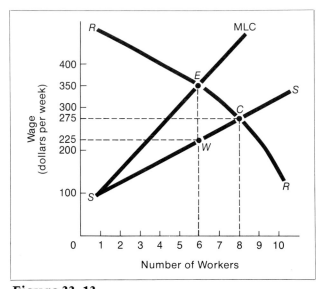

Figure 33–13

LABOR MARKET EQUILIBRIUM UNDER MONOPSONY
Under monopsony, labor market equilibrium occurs at the employment level that equates marginal labor cost (curve MLC in the diagram) to the marginal revenue product (curve *RR*). In this case, equilibrium is at point *E*, where six workers are employed. The corresponding wage is $225 per week. By contrast, if this were a competitive market, equilibrium would be at point *C*, with a wage of $275 and employment of eight workers.

five workers is five times the weekly wage of $200, or $1000. From these data, *marginal labor costs* are computed in the usual way—as the changes in successive total labor costs—and the results are displayed in column 4. This is the information the monopsonist wants, for it tells him that the first worker costs him $100, the next $150, and so on. The numbers in column 4 are displayed on the graph by the blue curve labeled MLC (marginal labor cost).

What employment level maximizes the monopsonist's profits? The usual marginal analysis applies. As he hires more workers, his profits rise if the marginal revenue product exceeds the marginal labor cost. For example, when he expands from one worker to two, he receives $450 more in revenue and pays out only an additional $150 to labor; so profits rise by $300. This continues up to the point where marginal

Table 33–1

LABOR COSTS AND MARGINAL REVENUE PRODUCT OF A MONOPSONIST

(1) NUMBER OF WORKERS	(2) WAGE RATE	(3) TOTAL LABOR COST	(4) MARGINAL LABOR COST	(5) MARGINAL REVENUE PRODUCT
1	$100	$ 100	$100	$475
2	125	250	150	450
3	150	450	200	425
4	175	700	250	400
5	200	1000	300	375
6	225	1350	350	350
7	250	1750	400	325
8	275	2200	450	275
9	300	2700	500	225
10	325	3250	550	150

labor costs and the marginal revenue product are equal—at six workers in the example. Pushing beyond this point would reduce profits. For example, hiring the seventh worker would cost $400 and bring in only $325 in increased revenues—clearly a losing proposition. We therefore conclude:

A monopsonist maximizes profits by hiring workers up to the point where marginal labor costs are equal to the marginal revenue product.

In the example, it is optimal for the firm to hire six workers, and it does this by offering a wage of $225 per week. This solution is shown in Figure 33–13 by points E and W. Point E is the equilibrium of the firm, where marginal labor costs and marginal revenue product are equal. To find the corresponding wage rate, we move vertically downward from E until we reach the supply curve at point W.

Let us compare this result with what would have emerged in a competitive labor market. As we know, equilibrium would be established where the supply curve of labor intersects the marginal revenue product curve because the marginal revenue product curve *is* the demand curve of a competitive industry. Figure 33–13 shows that this competitive equilibrium (point C) would have been at a wage of $275 and employment of eight workers.[6] In contrast, the monopsonist hires fewer workers (only six) and pays each a lower wage (only $225 per week). This finding is quite a general result:

[6]This conclusion can also be seen in Table 33–1 where, in a competitive market, columns 1 and 2 give the supply curve, while columns 1 and 5 give the demand curve. Quantity supplied equals quantity demanded when the wage is $275.

As long as the supply curve of labor is upward sloping and the marginal revenue product schedule is downward sloping, a monopsonist will hire fewer workers and pay lower wages than would a competitive industry.

Unions Under Monopsony

Where monopsony firms exist, their workers are very likely to be unionized. Let us therefore consider what would happen if the workers organized into a union and demanded a wage of no less than $250 per week. This action would change the supply curve, and hence the MLC curve, that the monopsonist faces in a straightforward way. No labor could be hired at wages below $250 per week. At that wage, the monopsonist could attract up to seven workers (see column 2 of Table 33–1). At higher wages, he could attract still more labor according to the supply curve. Thus, his new effective supply curve would be *horizontal* at the wage of $250 up to the employment level of seven workers, and then would follow the old supply curve. This is given numerically in column 2 of Table 33–2 and is shown graphically by the kinked supply curve SWS in Figure 33–14.

From this information, we can compute the revised marginal labor cost (MLC) schedule just as we did before. Column 3 in Table 33–2 gives us total labor costs at each employment level, and column 4 shows the corresponding marginal cost. The heavy blue curve labeled MLC in Figure 33–14 depicts this information graphically. Notice that the marginal labor cost schedule has become *horizontal* up to the point where seven workers are hired. This is a result of the union's behavior, which tells the monopsonist

Table 33–2
LABOR COSTS AND MARGINAL REVENUE PRODUCT OF A MONOPSONIST FACING A UNION

(1) NUMBER OF WORKERS	(2) WAGE RATE	(3) TOTAL LABOR COST	(4) MARGINAL LABOR COST	(5) MARGINAL REVENUE PRODUCT
1	$250	$ 250	$250	$475
2	250	500	250	450
3	250	750	250	425
4	250	1000	250	400
5	250	1250	250	375
6	250	1500	250	350
7	250	1750	250	325
8	275	2200	450	275
9	300	2700	500	225
10	325	3250	550	150

that he must pay the *same* wage per worker whether he hires one or seven employees. Beyond seven workers, the schedule returns to its previous level since the union minimum is irrelevant.

The condition for profit maximization is unchanged, so the monopsonist seeks the employment level at which marginal labor costs and marginal

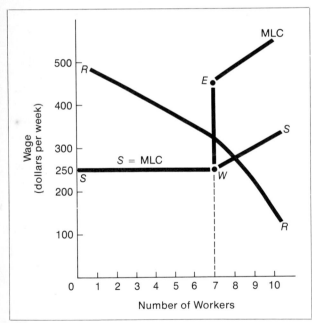

Figure 33–14
THE EFFECTS OF A UNION UNDER MONOPSONY
A union can change the character of the MLC schedule facing a monopsonist. In this example, MLC is horizontal up to seven workers, and then jumps as indicated by the heavy blue line. Consequently, equilibrium employment is determined by point *E*, where seven workers are employed at a wage of $250. Comparing this with Figure 33–13, we see that the union can raise both wages and employment.

revenue product are equal. Since MLC jumps abruptly from $250 for the seventh worker to $450 for the eighth, this cannot be achieved exactly. But Table 33–2 makes it quite clear that it is now profitable to employ the seventh worker (marginal labor cost equals $250, marginal revenue product equals $325), but unprofitable to employ the eighth (marginal labor cost equals $450, marginal revenue product equals $275). Points *E* and *W* in Figure 33–14 show, once again, the monopsonist's equilibrium point and the wage he must pay.

Comparing Figures 33–13 and 33–14 (or Tables 33–1 and 33–2), we see that the union has raised wages from $225 to $250 per week, and at the same time has *increased* employment from six to seven workers. As was claimed, the union can raise both wages and employment in the presence of monopsony.

Minimum Wage Laws Under Monopsony

Virtually the same kind of result as the one just discussed *can* be achieved by a minimum wage law under monopsony. That is, *if* the government selects the right minimum wage, it might succeed in raising both wages and employment.

Refer back to Figure 33–13, in which we depicted the equilibrium wage ($225 per week) and employment level (six workers) in a monopsonized labor market with no minimum wage. Just like a union, a minimum wage law creates a horizontal supply curve at the minimum wage. The effects will be just the same as the effects of the union. In both cases, the differences between wages and marginal labor costs are eliminated. As an exercise, use Figure 33–13 to convince yourself that a minimum wage can succeed in raising *both* wages *and* employment by imposing a horizontal supply curve of labor at a wage between $225 and $350 per week. (*Hint:* What will be the monopsonist's MLC under the minimum wage?)

We caution you against reading strong policy conclusions into this finding, however. Examples of actual monopsony (one buyer) in labor markets are quite hard to find. Certainly the types of service establishments that tend to hire the lowest-paid workers—restaurants and snack bars, amusement parks, car washes, and so on—have no monopsony power whatever. While minimum wage laws *can* conceivably raise employment, few economists believe that they actually have this pleasant effect except in some exceptional cases.

Summary

1. A profit-maximizing monopsonist hires labor up to the point where the marginal revenue product equals the marginal labor cost.
2. Because marginal labor cost exceeds the wage rate, this results in less employment and lower wages than would emerge from a competitive labor market.
3. By eliminating the difference between marginal labor costs and wages, it is possible that a union could raise both wages and employment under monopsony.
4. For the same reason, a minimum wage law can conceivably raise wages without sacrificing jobs if the employer is a monopsonist.

Concept for Review

Marginal labor costs

Questions for Discussion

1. Consider the pizza chef example of Question 3 on page 637 and suppose that pizzas sell for $3 each. Let the supply curve of chefs be as follows:

NUMBER OF CHEFS	WAGE PER DAY
1	$10
2	15
3	20
4	25
5	30
6	40

a. How many chefs will be employed, and at what wage, if the market is competitive?
b. How many chefs will be employed, and at what wage, if the market has a monopsony pizza parlor? (*Hint:* First figure out the schedule of marginal labor cost.)
c. Compare your answers to a. and b. What do you conclude?
d. Now suppose that a union is organized to fight the monopsonist. If it insists on a wage of $30 per day, what will the monopsonist do?
2. Given what you have learned about minimum wage laws in the chapter and in the appendix, do you think they are a good or a bad idea?

Poverty, Inequality, and Discrimination

34

> Today for the first time in all the history of the human race, a great nation is able to make and is willing to make a commitment to eradicate poverty among its people.
>
> LYNDON B. JOHNSON (1964)

The last two chapters analyzed the principles by which factor prices—wages, rentals, and interest rates—are determined in a market economy. One reason for concern with this issue is that these factor payments determine the *incomes* of the people to whom the factors belong. The study of factor pricing is, therefore, an indirect way to learn about the *distribution of income* among individuals. In this chapter we turn to the problem of income distribution more directly. Specifically, we seek answers to the following questions: How much income inequality is there in the United States, and why? How can society decide rationally on how much equality it wants? And, once this decision is made, what policies are available to pursue this goal? In trying to answer these questions, we must necessarily consider the related problems of poverty and discrimination, and so these issues, too, receive attention in this chapter.

We will also offer a full explanation of one of the 12 Ideas for Beyond the Final Exam: *the fundamental trade-off between economic equality and economic efficiency.* Taking it for granted that equality and efficiency are both important social goals, we shall learn why policies that promote greater income equality (or less poverty or less discrimination) often threaten to interfere with economic efficiency. In this chapter we explain *why* this is so and *what* can be done about it.

The Politics and Economics of Inequality

It is apparent that the trade-off between equality and efficiency is not widely understood. Social reformers often argue that society should adopt even the most outlandish programs to reduce discrimination or increase income equality or eradicate poverty, regardless of the potential side effects these policies might have. Defenders of the status quo, for their part, often seem so obsessed with these undesirable side effects—whether imagined or actual—that they ignore the benefits of redistribution or of antidiscrimination programs.

The continuing debate over supply-side economics is a good illustration.[1] Many of the tax incentives advocated by supply siders, such as reducing or

---

[1]Other aspects of this debate are considered elsewhere in this book, see especially Chapter 11, pages 204–208, and Chapter 17, pages 319–323.

eliminating taxes on interest, dividends, and capital gains, clearly would be of greatest benefit to the wealthy. The poor, after all, do not own much corporate stock. On the other hand, these measures are designed to increase the incentives to save and invest; and, if they are successful, the whole nation will benefit from the resulting increase in productivity. The more zealous advocates of supply-side initiatives trumpet the hoped-for gains in productivity and show little appreciation of the harmful effects on income equality. Some of their opponents vocally decry the widening of income differentials and show little concern for increasing the nation's productivity. Each side claims to have virtue in its corner.

Economists try not to paint these issues in black and white. They prefer to phrase things in terms of trade-offs—to reap gains on one front, you often must make sacrifices on another. A policy is not necessarily ill conceived simply because it has some undesirable side effects, *if* it makes an important enough contribution to one of society's basic goals. But, on the other hand, some policies have such severe side effects that they deserve to be rejected, even if they serve a laudable goal. Admitting that there is a trade-off between equality and efficiency—that while supply-side tax cuts may help solve the productivity problem, they may also increase inequality—may not be the best way to win votes; but it does face the facts. And in that way it helps us make the inherently political decisions about what should be done. If we are to understand these complex issues, a good place to start is, as always, with the facts.

The Facts: Poverty

In 1962, Michael Harrington published a little book called *The Other America*, which was to have a profound effect on American society. The "other Americans" of whom Harrington wrote were the poor who lived in the land of plenty. Ill clothed in the richest country on earth, inadequately nourished in a nation where obesity was a problem, infirm in a country with some of the world's highest health standards, these people lived an almost unknown existence in their dilapidated hovels, according to Harrington. And, to make matters worse, their inadequate nutrition, lack of education, and generally demoralized state often condemned the children of the "other Americans" to repeat the lives of their parents. There was, Harrington argued, a "cycle of poverty"—a cycle that could be broken only by government action.

The work of Harrington and others touched the hearts of many Americans who, it seemed, really had no idea of the abominable living conditions of some of their countrymen. Within a few years, the growing outrage over the plight of the poor had crystallized into a "War on Poverty," which was declared by President Lyndon Johnson in 1964. An official definition of poverty was adopted: The poor were those families with an income below $3000 in 1964. This dividing line between the poor and nonpoor was called the **poverty line,** and a goal was established: to get all Americans above the poverty line by the nation's bicentennial in 1976. The definition of the poverty line was subsequently modified to account for differences in family size and other considerations, and it is now also adjusted each year to reflect changes in the cost of living. In 1980, the poverty line for a typical family of four was about $8400, and about 10 percent of American families remained in poverty by official definitions. Who are these people? Relative to their proportions in the overall population, they are more likely to be black than white, to have less education and inferior health, and, in many cases, to live in households headed by a woman.

Substantial progress toward eliminating poverty was made in the decade from 1964 to 1974 (see Figure 34–1). And, after a setback during the Great

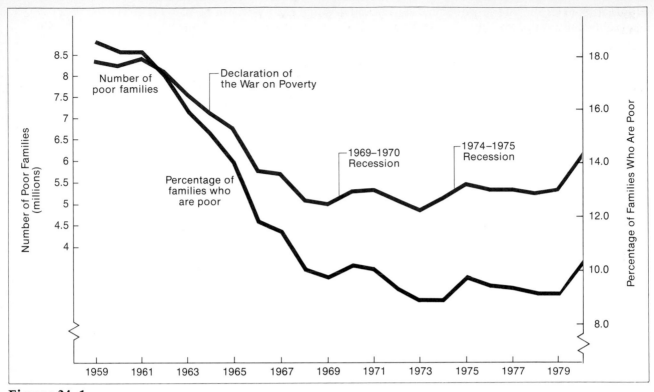

Figure 34–1
PROGRESS IN THE WAR ON POVERTY, 1959–1980
This figure charts the declines in the number and percentage of American families classified as "poor" by official definitions. While substantial progress has been made in the War on Poverty, about 9 percent of American families remain below the poverty line.
SOURCE: U.S. Bureau of the Census.

Recession of 1974–1975, the fraction of poor families fell again until 1980. By the beginning of the 1980s, although, by official definitions, Johnson's goal still had not been achieved, some journalists and economists were claiming that poverty could be considered a thing of the past if the official definition (based on cash income) were amended to include the many goods that the poor were being given in kind: public education, public housing, health care, food, and the like.

The downward drift in the poverty count vividly raises a fundamental question of definition: Just how do we define "the poor"? Continuing economic growth will eventually pull almost everyone above an arbitrarily established poverty line. Does this event mark the end of poverty? Some would say, "Yes." But others would insist that the biblical injunction is right: "The poor ye have always with you."

There are two ways to define poverty. The more optimistic definition uses an *absolute concept of poverty:* If you fall short of a certain minimum standard of living, you are poor; once you pass this standard, you are no longer poor. The second definition is based on a *relative concept of poverty:* The poor are those who fall too far behind the average income.

Each definition has its pros and cons. The basic problem with the absolute poverty concept is that it is arbitrary. Who sets the line? Most of the people of Bangladesh would be delighted to live a bit below the U.S. poverty line; they

Life in a Slum and in a Castle

There can be little doubt that the unfortunate souls who inhabit America's worst urban slums are "poor" by any reasonable definition. Yet there are striking parallels between the standard of living of these people and that of the powerful but vermin-covered barons of the Middle Ages, as the following two passages show. Together these passages graphically point out the need for a relative concept of poverty.

A Twentieth Century Slum

We were living in deplorable conditions. We would cook a pot of oatmeal in the morning, then reheat it up on the radiator in the afternoon. . . . Whenever the sewer would back up, all that filth would come up under our floor and run around all over the floor . . . One time this went on for four days. My wife had to keep the kids up on the bed. All that stuff floating around through the apartment until they got the Roto-Rooter man there.

In the wintertime . . . we go to bed with all our clothes on. . . .

When it's real cold, we close off the two bedrooms completely and burn the oven and then we all sleep in here together. . . .

One of my babies has been in the hospital twice for lead poisoning. She'd pick plaster and paint and stuff off the walls. . . .*

*Herb Goro, *The Block* (New York: Random House, 1970), pages 82–86.

A Medieval Castle

The knight's castle was extremely simple and must have been most uncomfortable. There were usually two rooms: the hall and the chamber. In the hall the knight did his business. . . . The chamber was the private room of the lord and his family. There he entertained guests of high rank. At night the lord, his lady, and their children slept in beds, while their personal servants slept on the chamber floor. . . . The castles were cold and drafty. The windows were covered by boards, or open. If the castle was of wood—as most were before the thirteenth century—the knight could not have a fire. In a stone castle one could have fire, but as chimneys did not appear until the late twelfth century, the smoke must have been almost unbearable. It seems likely that if one of us were offered the choice between spending a winter night with the lord or his serf, he would choose the comparatively tight mud hut with the nice warm pigs on the floor.‡

‡Sydney Painter, *A History of the Middle Ages 284–1500* (New York: Alfred A. Knopf, 1953), page 122.

---

would consider themselves quite prosperous. Similarly, the standard of living that we now call "poor" would probably not have been considered so in America in 1780, and certainly not in Europe during the Middle Ages. (See the boxed insert above.) Different times and different places apparently call for different poverty lines.

The fact that the concept of poverty is culturally, not physiologically, determined suggests that it must be a relative concept. But relative concepts can also run into trouble. For example, suppose we call the 20 percent of the population with the lowest incomes "the poor"—a definition that has been suggested by many. Then the War on Poverty becomes unwinnable, because the poverty population, *by definition*, grows at the same rate as the total population. In fact, once we start moving away from an absolute concept of poverty toward a relative concept, the sharp distinction between the poor and the nonpoor starts to evaporate. Instead, we begin to think of a parade of people from the poorest soul to the richest millionaire. The "poverty problem," then, seems to be that the disparities in income are "too large" in some sense. The poor are so poor because the rich are so rich. If we follow this line of thought far enough, we are led away from the narrow problem of *poverty* toward the broader problem of *inequality of income.*

The Facts: Inequality

There is nothing in the market mechanism that works to prevent large differences in incomes. On the contrary, it tends to breed inequality, for the basic source of the great efficiency of the market mechanism is its system of rewards and penalties. The market is generous to those who are successful in operating efficient enterprises that are responsive to consumer demands, and it is ruthless in penalizing those who are unable or unwilling to satisfy consumer demands efficiently. Its financial punishment of those who try and fail can be particularly severe. At times it even brings down the great and powerful. Robert Morris, once perhaps the wealthiest resident of the American colonies, ended up in debtors' prison. A few years ago one of the heirs to the Du Pont fortune went bankrupt and his creditors agreed to let him pay off his debt over a 10-year period at 20 cents to the dollar.[2]

Most people have a pretty good idea that the income distribution is quite spread out—that the gulf between the rich and the poor is a wide one. But few have any concept of where they stand in the distribution. In the next paragraph, you will find some statistics on the 1980 income distribution in the United States. But before looking at these, try the following experiment. First, write down what you think your family's income before tax was in 1980. (If you do not know, take a guess.) Next, try to guess what percentage of American families had incomes *lower* than this. Finally, if we divide America into three broad income classes—rich, middle class, and poor—to which group do you think your family belongs?

Now that you have written down answers to these three questions, look at the income distribution data for 1980 in Table 34–1. If you are like most college

[2]*The New York Times*, July 4, 1976, page 20.

Table 34–1

DISTRIBUTION OF FAMILY INCOME IN THE UNITED STATES IN 1980

INCOME RANGE (dollars)	PERCENTAGE OF ALL FAMILIES IN THIS RANGE	PERCENTAGE OF FAMILIES IN THIS AND LOWER RANGES
Under 2500	2.1	2.1
2500 to 4999	4.1	6.2
5000 to 6999	6.2	12.4
7000 to 9999	6.5	18.9
10,000 to 12,499	7.3	26.2
12,500 to 14,999	6.9	33.1
15,000 to 19,999	14.0	47.1
20,000 to 24,999	13.7	60.8
25,000 to 49,999	32.5	93.3
50,000 and over	6.7	100.0

SOURCE: U.S. Bureau of the Census.

If your family's income falls close to one of the end points of the ranges indicated here, you can approximate the fraction of families with income *lower* than yours just by looking at the last column.

If your family's income falls within one of the ranges, you can interpolate the answer. *Example:* Your family's income was $35,000. This is two-fifths of the way from $25,000 to $50,000 so your family was richer than roughly (2/5) × 32.5 percent = 13 percent of the families in this class. Adding this to the percentage of families in lower classes (60.8 percent in this case) gives the answer—about 73.8 percent of all families earned less than yours.

Table 34-2

INCOME SHARES IN SELECTED YEARS

INCOME GROUP	1980	1970	1960	1950
Lowest fifth	5.1	5.5	4.9	4.5
Second fifth	11.6	12.0	12.0	12.0
Middle fifth	17.5	17.4	17.6	17.4
Fourth fifth	24.3	23.5	23.6	23.5
Highest fifth	41.6	41.6	42.0	43.6

SOURCE: U.S. Bureau of the Census.

students, these figures will contain a few surprises for you. First, if we adopt the tentative definitions that the lowest 20 percent are the "poor," the highest 20 percent are the "rich," and the middle 60 percent are the "middle class," many fewer of you belong to the celebrated "middle class," than thought so. In fact, the cut-off point that defined membership in the "rich" class in 1980 was only about $35,000 before taxes, an income level exceeded by the parents of many college students. (Your parents may be shocked to learn that they are rich!) Next, use Table 34-1 to estimate the fraction of U.S. families that have incomes lower than your family's. (The caption to Table 34-1 has instructions to help you do this.) Most students who come from households of moderate prosperity have an instinctive feeling that they stand somewhere near the middle of the income distribution; so they estimate about half, or perhaps a little more. In fact, if your parents earn about $55,000 a year, more than 95 percent of American families are poorer than yours!

This exercise has perhaps brought us down to earth. America is not nearly so rich as Madison Avenue would like us to believe. Let us now look past the average level of income and see how the pie is divided. Table 34-2 shows the shares of income accruing to each fifth of the population in 1980 and several earlier years. In a perfectly equal society, all the numbers in this table would be "20 percent" since each fifth of the population would receive one-fifth of the income. In fact, as the table shows, this is certainly not the case. In 1980, for example, the poorest fifth of all families had just above 5 percent of the total income, while the richest fifth had more than 41 percent—eight times as much.

Depicting Income Distributions: The Lorenz Curve

Statisticians and economists use a convenient tool to portray data like these graphically. The device, called a **Lorenz curve,** is shown in Figure 34-2. To construct a Lorenz curve, we first draw a square whose vertical and horizontal dimensions both represent 100 percent. Then we record the percentage of families (or persons) on the horizontal axis and the percentage of income that these families (or persons) receive on the vertical axis, using all the data that we have. For example, point B in Figure 34-2 depicts the fact (known from Table 34-2) that the bottom 40 percent (the two lowest fifths) of American families in 1980 received 16.7 percent of the total income. Similarly, points A, C, and D represent the other information contained in Table 34-2. We can list four important properties of a Lorenz curve.

Figure 34-2

A LORENZ CURVE FOR THE UNITED STATES

This Lorenz curve for the United States is based on the 1980 distribution of income given in Table 34–2. The percentage of families is measured along the horizontal axis, and the percentage of income that these families receive is measured along the vertical axis. Thus, for example, point *C* indicates that the bottom 60 percent of American families received 34.2 percent of the total income in 1980.

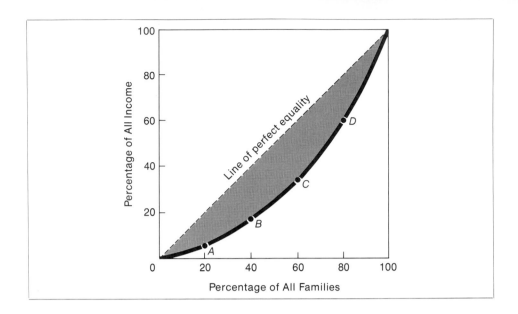

1. It begins at the origin, where zero families of course have zero income.
2. It always ends at the upper-right corner of the square, since 100 percent of the nation's families must necessarily receive all the nation's income.
3. If income were distributed equally, the Lorenz curve would be a straight line connecting these two points (the dashed line in Figure 34–2). This is because, with everybody equal, the bottom 20 percent of the families would receive 20 percent of the income, the bottom 40 percent would receive 40 percent, and so on.
4. In a real economy, with significant income differences, the Lorenz curve will "sag" downward from this line of perfect equality. It is easy to see why this is so. If there is any inequality at all, the poorest 20 percent of families must get less than 20 percent of all the income. This corresponds to a point below the equality line, such as point *A*. Similarly, the bottom 40 percent of families must receive less than 40 percent of the income (point *B*), and so on.

In fact, the size of the area between the line of perfect equality and the Lorenz curve (the shaded area in Figure 34–2) is often used as a handy measure of inequality. The larger this area, the more unequal is the income distribution. For U.S. family incomes, this so-called area of inequality usually fills up about 40 percent of the total area underneath the equality line.

Standing by itself, the Lorenz curve tells us rather little. To interpret it, we must know what it looked like in earlier years or what it looks like in other countries. The historical data in Table 34–2 show that *the U.S. Lorenz curve has not moved much in the last 30 years.* To some, this remarkable stability in the income distribution is deplorable. To others, it suggests some immutable law of the capitalist system. In fact, neither view is correct. The apparent stability in the income distribution is the result of a standoff between certain demographic forces that were pushing the Lorenz curve outward, such as more young and old people and more families headed by women, and other forces that were pulling it inward, such as government antipoverty programs.

Comparing the United States with other countries is much harder, since no two countries use precisely the same definition of income distribution. In 1976, the Organization for Economic Cooperation and Development (OECD) made a heroic effort to standardize the income distribution data of its member countries so they could be compared.[3] In this analysis, Japan stood out as the industrialized country with the most equal income distribution, with Australia, West Germany, the Netherlands, and Sweden bunched rather closely in second place. France and the United States seemed to have the most inequality. Before extrapolating from these findings, it should be pointed out that only 12 industrial countries were compared. Israel, which is often thought to have the most equal income distribution in the noncommunist world, is not in the OECD. Nor are any of the less developed countries, which are generally found to have much more inequality than the developed ones. The conclusion seems to be that:

The United States has rather more income inequality than most other developed countries.

Some Reasons for Unequal Incomes

Let us now begin to formulate a list of the causes of income inequality. Here are some that come to mind.

1. *Differences in ability.* Everyone knows that people have different capabilities. Some can run faster, ski better, do calculations more quickly, type more accurately, and so on. Hence it should not be surprising that some people are more adept at earning income. Precisely what sort of ability is relevant to earning income is a matter of intense debate among economists, sociologists, and psychologists. The kind of talents that make for success in school seem to have some effect, but hardly an overwhelming one. The same is true of innate intelligence ("IQ"). It is clear that some types of inventiveness are richly rewarded by the market, and the same is true of that elusive characteristic called "entrepreneurial ability."

2. *Differences in intensity of work.* Some people work longer hours than others, or labor more intensely when they are on the job. This results in certain income differences that are largely voluntary.

3. *Risk taking.* Most people who have acquired large sums of money have done so by taking risks—by investing their money in some uncertain venture. Those who gamble and succeed become wealthy. Those who try and fail go broke. Most others prefer not to take such chances and wind up somewhere in between. This is another way in which income differences arise voluntarily.

4. *Compensating wage differentials.* Some jobs are more arduous than others, or more dangerous, or more unpleasant for other reasons. To induce people to take these jobs, some sort of financial incentive normally must be offered. For example, factory workers who work the night shift normally receive higher wages than those who work during the day.

5. *Schooling and other types of training.* In Chapter 33 we spoke of schooling and other types of training as "investments in human capital." We meant by this that workers can sacrifice *current* income in order to improve their skills so that their *future* incomes will be higher. When this is done, income differentials naturally rise. Consider a high school friend who did not go on to college. Even if you are working at a part-time job, your earnings are probably much below his or hers. Once you graduate from college, however, the statistics suggest that your earnings will rise and soon overtake your

[3]Malcolm Sawyer, "Income Distribution in OECD Countries," *OECD Occasional Studies*, July 1976, pages 3–36.

friend's earnings. It is generally agreed that differences in schooling are an important cause of income differentials. But this particular cause has both voluntary and involuntary aspects. Young men or young women who *choose* not to go to college have made voluntary decisions that affect their incomes. But many never get the choice: their parents simply cannot afford to send them. For them, the resulting income differential is not voluntary.

6. ***Inherited wealth.*** Not all income is derived from work. Some is the return on invested wealth, and part of this wealth is inherited. While this cause of inequality does not apply to very many people, a great number of America's super-rich got that way through inheritance. And financial wealth is not the only type of capital that can be inherited; so can human capital. In part this happens naturally through genetics: parents of high ability tend to have children of high ability, although the link is an imperfect one. But it also happens partly for economic reasons: well-to-do parents send their children to the best schools, thereby transforming their own *financial* wealth into *human* wealth for their children. This type of inheritance may be much more important than the financial type.

7. ***Luck.*** No observer of our society can fail to notice the role of chance. Some of the rich and some of the poor got there largely by good or bad fortune. A farmer digging for water discovers oil instead. An investor strikes it rich on the stock market. A student trains herself for a high-paying occupation only to find that the opportunity has disappeared while she was in college. A construction worker is unemployed for a whole year because of a recession that he had no part in creating. The list could go on and on. Many of the large income differentials among people arise purely by chance.

The Facts: Discrimination

Some of the factors we have just listed lead to income differentials that are widely accepted as "just." For example, few quarrel with the idea that it is "fair" for people who work longer hours to receive higher incomes. Other factors on our list ignite heated debates. For example, some people view income differentials that arise purely by chance as perfectly acceptable. Others find these same differentials intolerable. However, almost no one is willing to condone income inequalities that arise strictly because of discrimination.

The facts about discrimination are not easy to come by. The definition of **economic discrimination** given in the margin is hard to apply in practice because we cannot always tell when two factors of production are "equivalent." Probably no one would call it "discrimination" if a woman with only a high school diploma receives a lower salary than a man with a college degree (though one might legitimately ask whether discrimination helps to explain the difference in their educational attainments). Even if they have the same education, the man may have 10 more years of work experience than the woman. If they receive different wages for this reason, are we to call that "discrimination"? Ideally, we would compare men and women whose *productivities* are equal. In this case, if women receive lower wages than men, we would clearly call it discrimination. But, very often, discrimination takes much more subtle forms than paying unequal wages for equal work. For instance, employers can simply keep women relegated to inferior jobs, thus justifying the lower salaries they pay them.

One clearly *incorrect* way to measure discrimination is to compare the typical incomes of different groups. Table 34–3 displays such data for white men, white women, black men, and black women in 1980. Virtually everyone agrees

Economic discrimination occurs when equivalent factors of production receive different payments for equal contributions to output.

Table 34–3

MEDIAN INCOMES IN 1980

POPULATION GROUP*	MEDIAN INCOME	PERCENTAGE OF WHITE MALE INCOME
White males	$13,328	100
Black males	8009	60
White females	4947	37
Black females	4580	34

*Persons 15 years old and over

SOURCE: U.S. Bureau of the Census.

that the amount of discrimination is less than these differentials suggest, but far greater than zero. Precisely how much is a topic of continuing economic research. One study several years ago concluded that about 40 percent of the observed wage differential between black and white men, and about two-thirds of the differential between white women and white men, was caused by discrimination in the labor market (though more might have been due to discrimination in education, and so on). Other studies have reached somewhat different conclusions. While no one denies the existence of discrimination, its quantitative importance is a matter of ongoing controversy and research.

The Economic Theory of Discrimination*

Let us see what economic theory tells us about discrimination. In particular, consider the following two questions:

1. Must the existence of *prejudice*, which we define as arising when one group dislikes associating with another group, always lead to *discrimination* (unequal pay for equal work)?
2. Are there "natural" economic forces that tend either to erode or to exacerbate discrimination over time?

As we shall see now, the analysis we have provided in previous chapters sheds light on both these issues.

Discrimination by Employers

Most attention seems to focus on discrimination by employers, so let us start there. What happens if, for instance, some firms refuse to hire blacks? Figure 34–3 will help us find the answer. Part (a) pertains to firms that discriminate; part (b) pertains to firms that do not. There are supply and demand curves for labor in each part based on the analysis of Chapter 33. We suppose the two demand curves to be identical. However, the supply curve in part (b) must be farther to the right than the supply curve in part (a) because whites *and* blacks can work in part (b) whereas *only* whites can work in part (a). The result is that wages will be lower in part (b) than in part (a). Since all the blacks are forced into part (b), we therefore conclude that there is discrimination against blacks.

But now consider the situation from the point of view of the employers. Firms in part (a) in Figure 34–3 are paying more for labor; they are paying for the

*This section may be omitted in shorter courses.

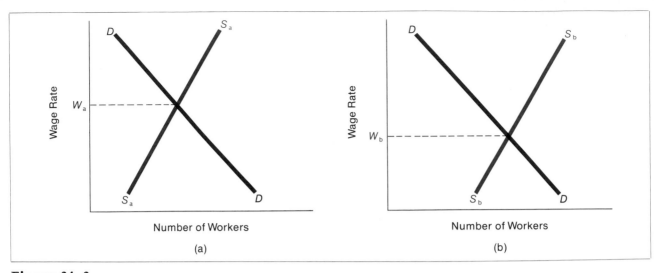

Figure 34–3
WAGE DISCRIMINATION
Part (a) depicts supply and demand curves for labor among discriminatory firms; part (b) shows the same for nondiscriminatory firms. Since only whites can work in part (a), while both races can work in part (b), the supply curve in part (b) is farther to the right than the supply curve in part (a). Consequently, the wage rate in part (b), W_b, winds up below the wage rate in part (a), W_a. Workers in part (b) are discriminated against.

privilege of discriminating against blacks. The nondiscriminatory firms in part (b) have a cost advantage. As we learned in earlier chapters, if there is effective competition, these nondiscriminatory firms will tend to capture more and more of the market. The discriminators will gradually be driven out of business. If, on the other hand, many of the firms in part (a) have protected monopolies, they will be able to remain in business. But they will pay for the privilege of discriminating by earning lower monopoly profits than they otherwise could (because they pay higher wages than they have to).

Discrimination by Fellow Workers
We have just seen that if employers are the source of discrimination, then competitive forces will tend to reduce discrimination over time. Such optimistic conclusions cannot necessarily be reached, however, if it is workers who are prejudiced. Consider what happens if, for example, men do not like to have women as their supervisors. If men do not give their full cooperation, female supervisors will be less effective than male supervisors, and hence will earn lower wages. Here prejudice does lead to discrimination, even in the long run. However, there is a possible way out: nondiscriminatory employers may start firms which hire *only* women. If women are in fact just as productive as men, the all-female firms will be just as efficient as the all-male firms and female workers will earn just as much as male workers. In this case, prejudice by workers may lead to *segregation* in the workplace without discrimination in wages.

Statistical Discrimination
A final type of discrimination, called **statistical discrimination,** may be the most stubborn of all, and may survive even in the absence of prejudice. Here is an important example. It is, of course, a fact that only women can have babies. It is also a fact that many, though certainly not all, working women who have babies quit their jobs (at least for a while) to care for their newborns. Employers

know this. What they cannot know, however, is *which* women of child-bearing age are likely to drop out of the labor force for this reason. Suppose three candidates apply for a job that requires a long-term commitment. Susan plans to quit after a few years to raise a family. Jane does not plan to have any children. Jack is a man. If he knew all the facts, the employer would prefer either Jane or Jack to Susan, but would be indifferent between Jane and Jack. But the employer cannot tell Susan and Jane apart. He therefore presumes that both Jane and Susan, being young women, are more likely to quit to raise a family than Jack is; so he hires Jack, even though Jane is just as good a prospect. Jane is discriminated against.[4]

In terms of the two questions with which we began this section, we conclude that different types of discrimination lead to different answers. Some types of prejudice lead to economic discrimination, but other types lead to segregation instead. And discrimination may occur even in the absence of prejudice. Finally, the forces of competition will tend to erode some, but not all, of the inequities caused by discrimination. Most observers feel that much more must be done to combat the effects of discrimination; the market will not do the job by itself.

The Optimal Amount of Inequality

We have seen that substantial income inequality exists in America and have noted some reasons for it. Let us now ask a question that is loaded with value judgments, but to which economic analysis has something to contribute none-theless: *How much inequality is the ideal amount?* We shall not, of course, be able to give a definitive answer to this question. Nobody can do that. Our objective is rather to see the type of analysis that is relevant to answering the question. We begin our analysis in a simple setting in which the answer is easily obtained. Then we shall see how the real world differs from this simple model.

Consider a world in which there are two people, Smith and Jones, and suppose that we want to divide $100 between them. Suppose further that Smith and Jones are alike in their ability to enjoy money, and we wish to divide the $100 in a way that yields the most *total utility*. Technically, we say that their *marginal utility* schedules are identical.[5] This identical marginal utility schedule is depicted in Figure 34–4 on the next page. We can prove the following result: *The optimal distribution of income is to give $50 to Smith and $50 to Jones*, which is point E in Figure 34–4.

To prove it, we show that if the income distribution is unequal, we can improve things by moving closer to equality. So suppose that Smith has $75 (point S in the figure) and Jones has $25 (point J). Then, as we can see, because of the law of diminishing marginal utility, Smith's *marginal* utility (which is s) must be *less* than Jones's (which is j). If we take $1 away from Smith, Smith *loses* the low marginal utility, s, of a dollar to him. Then, when we give it to Jones, Jones *gains* the high marginal utility, j, that a dollar gives him. On balance, then, society's total utility must rise by $j - s$ because Jones's gain exceeds Smith's loss. Therefore, a distribution with Smith getting only $74 is better than one in which he gets $75. Since the same argument can be used to show that a $73-$27 distribution is better than $74-$26, and so on, we have established our result that a $50-$50 distribution—point E—is best. Now in this argument there is nothing

---

[4]Lest it be thought that this example justifies discrimination against women, it should be pointed out that women generally have less absenteeism and job turnover for nonpregnancy health reasons than men do.

[5]If you need to refresh your memory about marginal utility, see Chapter 18, especially pages 337–338.

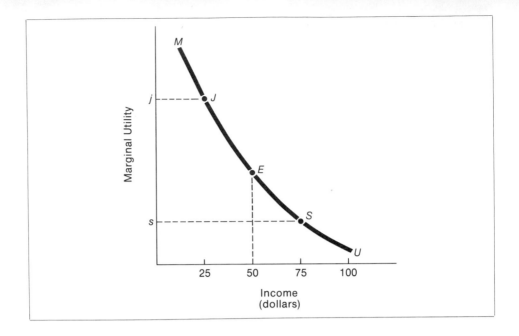

Figure 34–4

THE OPTIMAL DISTRIBUTION OF INCOME
If Smith and Jones have the identical marginal utility schedule (the curve *MU*) then the optimal way to distribute $100 between them is to give $50 to each (point *E*). If income is not distributed this way, then their marginal utilities will be unequal, so that a redistribution of income can make society better off. This is illustrated by points *J* and *S*, representing an income distribution in which Jones gets $25 (and hence has marginal utility *j*), while Smith gets $75 (and hence has marginal utility *s*).

special about the fact that we assumed only two people or that exactly $100 was available. Any number of people and dollars would do as well. What really *is* crucial is our assumption that the same amount of money would be available no matter how we chose to distribute it. Thus we have proved the following general result:

To maximize total utility, the best way to distribute any fixed amount of money among people with identical marginal utility schedules is to divide it equally.

The Trade-Off Between Equality and Efficiency

If we seek to apply this analysis to the real world, two major difficulties arise. First, people are different and have different marginal utility schedules. Thus *some* inequality can probably be justified.[6] The second problem is much more formidable.

The total amount of income in society is *not* independent of how we try to distribute it.

To see this in an extreme form, ask yourself the following question: What would happen if we tried to achieve perfect equality by putting a 100 percent income tax on all workers and then dividing the tax receipts equally among the population? No one would have any incentive to work, to invest, to take risks, or to do anything else to earn money, because the rewards for all such activities would disappear. The gross national product (GNP) would fall drastically, perhaps even vanish. While the example is extreme, the same principle applies to more moderate policies to equalize incomes: any such policy lessens the rewards for income-producing activities. It reduces the rewards of high-income earners while

[6]It can be shown that if we know that people differ, but cannot tell who has the higher marginal utility schedule, then the best way to distribute income is still in equal shares.

raising the rewards of low-income earners, and hence reduces the incentive to earn high income.

This gives rise to a trade-off that is one of the most fundamental in all of economics, and one of our 12 Ideas for Beyond the Final Exam.

THE TRADE-OFF BETWEEN
EQUALITY AND EFFICIENCY

Measures taken to increase the amount of economic equality will often reduce economic efficiency—that is, lower the gross national product. In trying to divide the pie more equally, we may inadvertently reduce its size.

Because of this trade-off, the result that equal incomes are always optimal cannot be applied to the real world. Instead:

The optimal distribution of income will always involve *some* inequality.

But this does not mean that attempts to reduce inequality are always misguided. What we should learn from this analysis are two things:

Lesson 1. There are better and worse ways to promote equality. In pursuing further income equality (or fighting poverty), we should seek policies that do the least possible harm to the nation's productivity.

Lesson 2. Equality is bought at a price. Thus, like any commodity, we must decide rationally how much to purchase. We will probably want to spend some of our potential income on equality, but not all of it.

Figure 34–5 illustrates both these lessons. The curve *abcde* represents possible combinations of GNP and income equality that are obtainable under the present system of taxes and transfers. If, for example, point *c* is the current position of the economy, raising taxes on the rich to finance more transfers to the poor might move us downward to the right, toward point *d*. Equality increases, but GNP falls. Similarly, reducing both taxes and social welfare programs might move us upward to the left, toward point *b*. The curve *ABCDE* represents possible combinations of GNP and equality under some new, more efficient, redistributive policy. The first lesson is that we should stick to the higher of the two curves. Any point chosen on curve *abcde* can be improved upon by moving to the corresponding point on curve *ABCDE*. By picking the more efficient redistributive policy, we can have more equality *and* more GNP. (In the rest of this chapter we discuss alternative policies and try to indicate which ones are more efficient.) The second lesson is that neither point *B* nor point *E* would normally be society's optimal choice. At point *B* we are seeking the highest possible GNP with utter disregard for whatever inequality might accompany it. At point *E* we are forcing complete equality, even if a minuscule GNP is the result.

It is astonishing how much confusion is caused by a failure to understand these two lessons. Proponents of measures that further economic equality often feel obligated to deny that their programs will have any harmful effects on economic efficiency. At times these vehement denials are so obviously unrealistic that they undermine the very case that the egalitarians are trying to defend.

Figure 34–5
THE TRADE-OFF
BETWEEN EQUALITY
AND EFFICIENCY

This diagram represents the fundamental trade-off between equality and efficiency. If the economy is initially at point *c*, then movements toward greater equality (to the right) normally can be achieved only by reducing economic efficiency, and thus reducing the gross national product. The movements from points *C* and *c* toward points *D* and *d* represent two alternative policies for equalizing the income distribution. The policy that leads to *D* is preferred since it is more efficient.

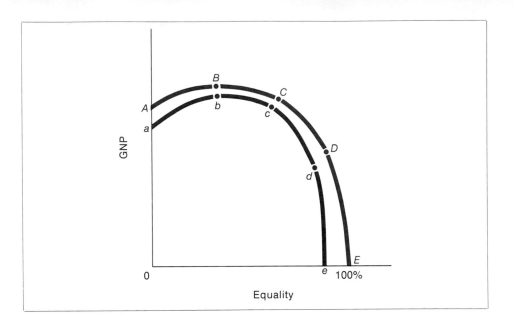

Conservatives who oppose these policies also undercut the strength of their case by making outlandish claims about the efficiency losses that are likely to arise from greater equality. Neither side, it seems, is willing or able to acknowledge the basic trade-off between equality and efficiency depicted in Figure 34–5. And hence the debate generates more heat than light. Since these debates are sure to continue for the next 10 or 20 years, and probably for the rest of your lives, we hope that some understanding of this trade-off stays with you well beyond the final exam.

But just understanding the terms of the trade-off will not tell you what the right answer is. By looking at Figure 34–5, we know that the optimal amount of equality lies between points *B* and *E*, but we do not know what it actually is. Is it something like point *D*, with more equality and less GNP than we now have? Or is it a movement back toward point *B*? Everyone will have a different answer to this question, because it is basically one of value judgment. Just how much is more equality worth to you? The late Arthur Okun, a former chairman of the Council of Economic Advisers, put the issue graphically. Imagine that money is liquid, and that you have a bucket that you can use to transport some money from the rich to the poor. The problem, however, is that the bucket is leaky. As you move the money, some gets lost. Will you use the bucket if only 1 cent is lost for each $1 you move? Probably everyone would say yes. But what if each $1 taken from the rich results in only 10 cents for the poor? Only the most extreme egalitarians will still say yes. Now try the hard questions. What if 20 to 40 cents is lost for each $1 that you move? If you can answer questions like these, you can decide how far down the hill from point *B* you think society should travel, for you will have expressed your value judgments in quantitative terms.

Policies to Combat Poverty

Let us take it for granted that the nation has a commitment to reduce the amount of poverty. What are some policies that can promote this goal? Which of these is most efficient? The traditional approach to poverty fighting in the United States has utilized a variety of programs collectively known as *public assistance*. The best known, and most controversial, of these is **Aid to Families with Dependent Children (AFDC).** This program provides money to families in which there are children but no breadwinner, perhaps because there is no father and the children are too young to permit the mother to work. In 1982, about 22 million people received benefits from AFDC, and the average grant was about $500 per person. In total, some $11 billion was spent.

AFDC has been attacked as a classic example of an inefficient redistribution program. Why? One reason is that it provides little incentive for the mother to earn income; welfare payments are reduced by 67 cents for each $1 that the family earns as wages. Thus, if a member of the family gets a job, the family is subjected to a 67 percent tax rate. It is little wonder that many welfare recipients do not look very hard for work. A second criticism is that AFDC provides an incentive for families to break up. As originally conceived, welfare was not to be paid to a family with a father who could work, even if he was unemployed. So if this father earned very little, or if he had no job, the children would get more income if he left them. Some fathers did. About half the states have now started a special AFDC-UF program (the "UF" stands for unemployed father) so that benefits can be paid to families with an unemployed father. A third problem is geographical disparities in benefits. It is widely thought (though not conclusively proven) that many black families migrated from the South to northern cities because of the more generous welfare benefits available there. This placed an enormous financial burden on these cities. Finally, the tedious case-by-case approach of AFDC, with its cumbersome bureaucracy and mountains of detailed regulations, seems to frustrate all parties concerned.

Another welfare program that has burgeoned in recent years is **food stamps,** under which poor families are sold stamps, which they can exchange for food. The dollar amount of the stamps they receive, and how much they pay for them, depends on the family's income. The more income the family earns, the more it must pay for the stamps. About 20 million people now receive food stamps.

In addition, many of the poor are provided with a number of important goods and services, either at no charge or at prices that are well below market levels. Medical care under the Medicaid (as opposed to Medicare) program,[7] and subsidized public housing are two notable examples. These programs significantly enhance the living standards of the poor. However, most of them offer benefits that decline as family income rises. Taken as a whole, all the antipoverty programs may actually put a poor family in a position where it is *worse* off if its earnings *rise*—an effective tax rate of more than 100 percent. When this occurs, there is a powerful incentive not to work.

The Negative Income Tax

These problems, and others like them, have contributed to the "welfare mess," and have led to frequent calls to scrap the whole system and replace it with a simple structure designed to get income into the hands of the poor without providing such adverse incentives. The solution suggested most frequently, at least by economists, is the so-called **negative income tax (NIT).**

The name "negative income tax" derives from its similarity to the regular (positive) income tax. Let us illustrate how NIT would work. To describe a particular NIT plan we require two numbers: a minimum income level below

---

[7]The *Medicaid* program pays for the health care of low-income people, whereas *Medicare* is available to all elderly people, regardless of income.

which no family is allowed to fall (the "guarantee") and a rate at which benefits are "taxed away" as income rises. Consider a plan with a $4000 guaranteed income (for a family of four) and a 50 percent tax rate. A family with no earnings would then receive a $4000 payment (a "negative tax") from the government. A family earning $1000 would have the basic benefit reduced by 50 percent of its earnings. Thus, since half its earnings is $500, it would receive $3500 from the government plus the $1000 earned income for a total income of $4500 (see Table 34–4).

Notice in Table 34–4 that the increase in total income as earnings rise is always half of the increase in earnings. With a 50 percent tax rate, there is always *some* incentive to work under an NIT system. Notice also that there is a "break-even" level of income at which benefits cease. In this case, the break-even level is $8000. This is not another number that policymakers can arbitrarily select in the way they select the guarantee level and the tax rate. Rather, it is dictated by the choice of the guarantee level and the tax rate. This is easy to explain. In our example, since $4000 is the maximum possible benefit, and since benefits are reduced by 50 cents for each $1 of earnings, then benefits must cease when 50 percent of the earnings (the benefit reduction) is equal to $4000 (the maximum benefit). This occurs when earnings are $8000.

Other NIT plans can be devised that are either more or less generous than this. But the fact that the break-even level is completely determined by the guarantee and the tax rate creates an annoying problem. The general relation is:

$$\text{Guarantee} = \text{Tax rate} \times \text{Break-even level.}$$

If we are truly to make a dent in the poverty population through an NIT system, the guarantee will have to come fairly close to the poverty line. But then, if we are to keep the tax rate moderate, the break-even level will have to be much above the poverty line. This means that families who are not considered "poor" (though they are certainly not very rich) will also receive benefits. For example, a low tax rate of $33\frac{1}{3}$ percent means that some benefits are paid to families whose income is as high as three times the guarantee level.

This problem can be avoided only by raising the tax rate (which brings the guarantee and the break-even level closer together). But as the tax rate rises, the incentive to work shrinks, and with it the principal rationale for the NIT in the first place. So the NIT is no magic cure-all. Difficult choices must be made. As

Table 34–4
ILLUSTRATION OF A NEGATIVE INCOME TAX PLAN

EARNINGS	BENEFITS PAID	TOTAL INCOME
$ 0	$4000	$4000
1000	3500	4500
2000	3000	5000
3000	2500	5500
4000	2000	6000
5000	1500	6500
6000	1000	7000
7000	500	7500
8000	0	8000
Above 8000	0	Same as earnings

summarized by the preceding formula, we must be willing to sacrifice one of the following three objectives (or some combination of them):

1. **Preserving strong incentives to work**, which we get by keeping the tax rate low.
2. **Keeping people out of poverty**, which we accomplish through a generous guarantee.
3. **Concentrating benefits on the poverty population**, which requires that the break-even level be kept low.

The Negative Income Tax and Work Incentives

For people now covered by AFDC and other welfare programs, the NIT would substantially increase the incentive to work. However, we have just seen that it is virtually inevitable that a number of families who are now too well-off to collect welfare benefits would become eligible for NIT payments. For these people, the NIT imposes obvious work disincentives, both because it provides them with more income and because it subjects them to the relatively high NIT tax rate, which reduces their after-tax wage rate.[8]

These possible disincentive effects have worried both social reformers and legislators, so in the late 1960s the government initiated a series of social experiments to estimate the effect of the NIT on the supply curve of labor. Families from a number of American cities were selected to participate in the experiment. Each was offered negative income tax payments in return for filling out questionnaires that enabled social scientists to monitor their behavior. A matched set of "control" families, who were not given NIT payments, were also observed. The idea was to measure how the behavior of the families receiving NIT payments differed from that of the families that did not receive them. The experiments lasted about a decade, and analysis of the data is still going on. But enough has been learned to indicate that the net effects of the NIT on labor supply were quite small. Apparently, the fears of those who claimed that NIT payments would induce people to stop working were unfounded.

Economists have been advocating the NIT for years, at least since Milton Friedman's influential book *Capitalism and Freedom* (1962). And in 1970, after it was known that the initial results from the negative income tax experiment looked quite favorable, the United States almost got a negative income tax. Proposed by President Nixon under the title "Family Assistance Plan" as a major welfare reform, this program was greeted enthusiastically in some quarters. Unfortunately, it was killed in the Senate by an alliance of liberals who thought its benefit levels were insultingly low and conservatives who opposed the NIT on principle. In the 1972 presidential campaign, Democratic candidate George McGovern strongly endorsed a rather generous NIT, but the idea was packaged in a politically unattractive form that probably cost him more votes than it won. After that the idea remained politically dormant for a while until President Ford approved a small-scale version of it as an "earned income credit" in 1975. Then, as part of his multifaceted welfare reform proposal in 1977, President Carter proposed (without using the name) an NIT plan that looked very much like the one illustrated in Table 34–4. The proposal, however, got nowhere.

In terms of Figure 34–5, economists believe that it is more efficient to redistribute income through an NIT system than through the existing welfare

---

[8]For a review of income and substitution effects in labor supply analysis, refer to Chapter 33, pages 617–620.

system. The NIT is curve *ABCDE*, while the present system is curve *abcde*. If this view is correct, then by replacing the current welfare system with NIT, we can have more equality *and* more efficiency at the same time. But this does not mean that equalization would become costless. The curve *ABCDE* still slopes downward—by increasing equality, we still diminish the GNP.

The Personal Income Tax

If we take the broader view that society's objective is not just to eliminate poverty, but to reduce income disparities, then the fact that many nonpoor families would receive benefits from the NIT is perhaps not a serious drawback. After all, unless the plan is outlandishly generous, these families will still be well below the average income. Still, in popular discussions the NIT is largely thought of as an antipoverty program, not as a tool for general income equalization.

By contrast, the federal personal income tax *is* thought to be a means of promoting equality. Indeed, it is probably given more credit for this than it actually deserves. The reason is that the income tax is widely known to be *progressive*.[9] The fact that the tax is progressive means that incomes *after* tax are distributed more equally than incomes *before* tax because the rich turn over a larger share of their incomes to the tax collector. This is illustrated by the two Lorenz curves in Figure 34–6. These curves, however, are not drawn accurately to scale. If they were, they would lie almost on top of each other because the degree of equalization that can be attributed to the tax is rather modest.

Why such modest equalizing effects from a tax whose marginal tax rates escalate upward from zero to a maximum of 50 percent? One principal reason for the modest equalizing effect of the progressive income tax is that firms and individuals, acting in their own best interests, often take steps that frustrate the equalizing intent of the tax. An example from each end of the income distribution will illustrate how this might work. Looking first at the rich, it is clear that a steeply progressive tax tries to place a heavy tax burden on a corporate executive. In order to preserve his incentive to work, his company may react by raising his before-tax salary, or by giving him fringe benefits (such as a company car, use of a

[9]For definitions of progressive, proportional, and regressive taxes, see Chapter 30, page 553.

Figure 34–6
THE EFFECT OF PROGRESSIVE INCOME TAXATION ON THE LORENZ CURVE
Since a progressive income tax takes proportionately more income from the rich than from the poor, it reduces income inequality. Graphically, this means that society's Lorenz curve shifts in the manner shown here. The magnitude of the shift, however, is exaggerated to make the graph more readable. In reality, the income tax has only a very small effect on the Lorenz curve.

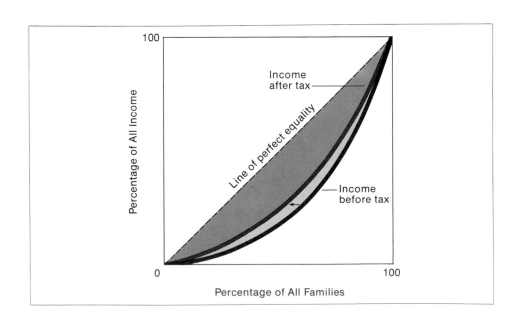

yacht, expense accounts, and so on) which often escape taxation. At the other end of the income scale, welfare programs that give payments to the poor may lead the beneficiaries to "spend" some of their newly found income on "leisure," that is, to work less, and therefore to earn less.

Thus, a redistributive tax system might induce the *before-tax* incomes of the rich to rise, and those of the poor to fall. Ironically, efforts to *equalize* the *after-tax* distribution of income may lead to more *inequality* in the *before-tax* distribution. In terms of Figure 34–6 this means that even the small distance between the two Lorenz curves *overstates* the equalizing effects of the income tax. The income distribution that we would have *if there were no income tax* is probably somewhere in between these two curves.

Some Tax Loopholes

The other principal reason why the personal income tax does not redistribute income as much as many people think is that the wealthy have learned, with the aid of expensive legal and financial advisers, about a variety of **tax loopholes,** and have managed to pare their tax payments significantly. There is nothing sinister about this tax avoidance; it is all perfectly legal and aboveboard. The simple truth is that Congress has provided so many loopholes that the tax system has been compared to a sieve. Let us see what some of them are.

Lenient taxation of capital gains.   Our laws tax a **capital gain** at less than half the rates at which other sources of income are taxed. Since such gains accrue almost exclusively to upper-income groups, this loophole is the reserve of the rich. Why did Congress do such a thing? One reason is to encourage people to save and invest. Another is that extremely high taxes would be paid on large capital gains if they were treated like ordinary income. For example, Jane Doe earns $70,000 a year and owns $100,000 worth of stock that she bought 10 years ago for $20,000. If she sells her stock this year, she will enjoy an $80,000 capital gain, which will push her income for the year up to $150,000. The tax bill on such an income is quite substantial. In particular, because of progressive rates, it is much larger than the tax she would have paid if the $80,000 capital gain had been earned evenly at the rate of $8000 a year over 10 years. To reduce this burden, Congress decided to exempt 60 percent of all capital gains, so that Jane's taxable income is only 70,000 + $32,000 = $102,000. But, tax reformers point out, there are many other ways to ease the tax burden on such gains. The simplest way perhaps is to charge individuals the tax they would have paid if the gain really had occurred gradually; that is, to tax Jane Doe as if her income had been $70,000 + $8000 = $78,000 a year for 10 years.

A **capital gain** is the profit made from the sale of an asset at a higher price than was paid for it.

Tax exempt status of municipal bonds.   As a way of helping state and local governments and certain public authorities raise funds, Congress has made their bonds exempt from federal income tax. Whether or not this was the intent of Congress, this provision has turned out to be one of the biggest loopholes for the very rich, who invest much of their wealth in municipal bonds. In fact, this tax exemption is the principal reason why many millionaires pay no income tax at all.

Tax benefits for homeowners.   Among the sacred cows of our income tax system is the deductibility of payments that homeowners make for mortgage interest and property taxes. These deductions substantially reduce the taxes homeowners pay and give them preferential treatment compared with renters. Since, on the average, homeowners are richer than renters, this too erodes the progressivity of the income tax. But why do we call this a "loophole" when other

Table 34–5
OWNING VERSUS RENTING A HOME

ITEM	MUTT (owner)	JEFF (renter)
Income	$20,000	$20,000
Mortgage interest	4,000	—
Property tax	2,000	—
Rent	—	6,000
Taxable income	$14,000	$20,000

interest expenses and taxes (such as those paid by shopkeepers, for example) are considered to be legitimate deductions? The answer is that it is a loophole because—unlike shopkeepers—homeowners do *not* have to declare the income they earn by incurring these expenses. This is because the "income" from owning a home accrues not in cash, but in the form of living without paying rent.

Once again, an example will make things clear. Mutt and Jeff are neighbors. Each earns $20,000 a year and lives in a $60,000 house. The difference is that Mutt owns his home while Jeff rents. Most observers would agree that Mutt and Jeff *should* pay the same income tax. Ignoring other deductions and exemptions, let us compare the taxable income of the two men. Mutt has a $50,000 mortgage at an 8 percent interest rate, so he pays about $4000 a year in interest. Suppose he pays an additional $2000 a year in local property taxes. Since both these payments are tax deductible, he pays income tax on only $20,000 − $4000 − $2000 = $14,000 (see Table 34–5). Now consider Jeff, who, we may assume, pays $6000 in annual rent. (This just covers the bills that his landlord has to pay.) He pays tax on his entire $20,000 income and thus pays far more tax than Mutt. How could this situation be rectified? One way is to allow renters to deduct their rent bills. Another way would be to disallow the interest and tax deductions of homeowners. Still a third alternative would be to force homeowners to add their "imputed rent" ($6000 a year in this example) to their income. All of these would give Mutt and Jeff the same taxable income.

We could go on and on listing more tax loopholes, but enough has been said to illustrate the point:

Since most loopholes are mainly beneficial to rich people, they erode the progressivity of the income tax.

Death Duties and Other Taxes

Taxes on inheritances and estates levied both by the state and federal governments are another equalizing feature of our tax system. And in this case they seem clearly aimed at limiting the incomes of the rich, or at least at limiting their ability to transfer this largesse from one generation to the next. But the amount of money involved is too small to make much difference to the overall distribution of income. In 1980, for example, total receipts from estate and gift taxes by all levels of government were only about $8 billion—under 1 percent of total tax revenues, and a phased cut in federal estate taxes will lower this yet further during the 1980s.

There are many other taxes in the U.S. system, and most experts agree that the remaining taxes as a group—including sales taxes, payroll taxes, and property taxes—are decidedly regressive. On balance, the evidence seems to suggest that:

The tax system as a whole is only slightly progressive.

Policies to Combat Discrimination

The policies that we have considered so far for combating poverty or reducing income inequality are all based on taxes and transfer payments—on moving dollar bills from one set of hands to another. This has not been the approach used to fight discrimination. Instead, governments have decided to make it *illegal* to discriminate. Perhaps the major milestone in the war against discrimination was the Civil Rights Act of 1964, which outlawed many forms of discrimination and established the **Equal Employment Opportunities Commission (EEOC).** When you read a want ad in which a company asserts it is "an equal opportunity employer," the firm is proclaiming its compliance with this and related legislation.

Originally, it was thought that the problem could best be attacked by outlawing discrimination in rates of pay and in hiring standards—and by devoting resources to enforcement of these provisions. While progress toward the elimination of discrimination according to race and sex undoubtedly was made between 1964 and the early 1970s, some people felt the pace was too slow. One reason was that discrimination in the labor market proved to be more subtle than was first thought. Officials rarely could find proof that unequal pay was being given for equal work because determining when work was "equal" turned out to be a formidable task. And, as noted early in this chapter, discrimination often takes the form of paying the *same* wages to blacks and whites (or men and women) who perform the same job, but segregating the less privileged groups into inferior jobs.

So, in the early 1970s, a new wrinkle was added. Firms and other organizations with suspiciously small representation of blacks or women in their work forces were required not just to end discriminatory practices, but also to demonstrate that they were taking **affirmative action** to remedy this imbalance. That is, they had to *prove* that they were making efforts to locate members of minority groups and females and to hire them if they proved to be qualified. This new approach to fighting discrimination was highly controversial and remains so to this day. (See the boxed insert on the next page.) Critics claim that affirmative action really means hiring quotas and compulsory hiring of unqualified workers simply because they are black or female. Proponents counter that without affirmative action discriminatory employers would simply claim they could not find qualified minority or female employees. The difficulty revolves around the impossibility of deciding on *purely objective criteria* who is "qualified" and who is not. What one person sees as government coercion to hire an unqualified applicant to fill a quota, another sees as a discriminatory employer being forced to mend his ways. Nothing in this book—or anywhere else—will teach you which view is correct in any particular instance.

This controversy provides yet another example of the trade-off between equality and efficiency. Without a doubt, giving more high-paying jobs to members of minority groups and to women would move society's Lorenz curve in the direction of greater equality. Supporters of affirmative action seek this result. But if it is done by disrupting industry and requiring firms to replace "qualified" white males by other "less qualified" workers, economic efficiency may suffer.

The Supreme Court on Affirmative Action

The legal issues surrounding affirmative action programs are many and complex. Among the charges raised by opponents to such programs is that the "reverse discrimination" inherent in school admissions or hiring programs that favor disadvantaged groups constitutes a form of discrimination against white males. And this, they argue, violates the Fourteenth Amendment to the Constitution and the Civil Rights Act of 1964. In two landmark cases, which will be discussed and interpreted for years to come, the U.S. Supreme Court rejected this claim.

Affirmative Action in the Schools: The Bakke Decision

Allan Bakke, then a 32-year-old white engineer from Los Altos, California, sought admission to the medical school of the University of California at Davis in 1973 and again in 1974. Both times he was rejected, while minority applicants with substantially inferior grades and test scores were accepted under the school's affirmative action admissions program—a program that reserved 16 out of 100 places in each entering class for minority students. Bakke filed suit, charging that the medical school had violated both the Civil Rights Act and the Fourteenth Amendment by denying him admission solely because of his race. He won in the lower courts, and after four years of litigation, the case reached the U.S. Supreme Court.

The Court's decision, handed down in July 1978, was a momentous one for affirmative action, and for civil rights in general, because the California courts had ruled that race could not be considered a factor in making admissions decisions. The U.S. Supreme Court rejected this view. Justice Lewis F. Powell, Jr., writing for the majority, ruled that admissions programs that use race as one among many criteria, but that do not attempt to enforce rigid quotas, are legal and valid. However, Allan Bakke was ordered admitted to the Davis medical school on the grounds that the rigid quota system used there was indeed illegal and did deprive him of his civil rights. Thus, both detractors and supporters of affirmative action could find solace in the Bakke decision, and the case raised as many questions as it answered.

Affirmative Action in the Workplace: The Weber Decision

A year later, the Court handed down a more definitive decision in the case of the *United Steelworkers of America v. Weber*. In 1974, Kaiser Steel and the Steelworkers Union reached an affirmative action agreement under which half the places in a special training program were reserved for blacks, who at that time held very few skilled jobs. Brian Weber, then a 28-year-old worker at Kaiser's Gramercy, La., plant, sued on the grounds that the quota system discriminated against white workers like himself. Again, the lower courts ruled in his favor. But in June 1979 the U.S. Supreme Court delivered a resounding verdict in support of affirmative action.

Justice William J. Brennan, Jr., writing for the majority, rejected the idea that Congress intended to bar reverse discrimination through the Civil Rights Act of 1964, claiming that such an interpretation would undermine the very purposes of the Act. While the Weber decision did not give a blanket endorsement to *any* conceivable affirmative action plan, it certainly made it plain that the Court would not invalidate reasonable plans, even if they were based on numerical quotas.

Opponents of affirmative action are greatly troubled by these potential losses. How far should affirmative action be pushed? A good question, but one without a good answer.

Postscript on the Distribution of Income

Having completed our analysis of the distribution of income, it may be useful to see how it all relates to our central theme. We have learned that a market economy uses the marginal productivity principle to assign an income to each individual. In so doing, the market attaches high prices to scarce factors and low prices to abundant ones, and therefore guides firms to make *efficient* use of society's resources. This is certainly desirable. However, by attaching high prices to some factors and low prices to others, the market mechanism often creates a distribution of income that is quite unequal; some people wind up fabulously rich while others wind up miserably poor. For this reason, the market has been widely criticized for centuries for doing a rather poor job of distributing income in accord with commonly held notions of *fairness* and *equity*. The criticism seems justified: the market certainly has both virtues and vices. On balance, most observers feel that the market mechanism is extraordinarily good at promoting efficiency but rather inadequate at promoting equality.

Summary

1. The War on Poverty was declared in 1964; by 1981 it had still not been won, though the fraction of families considered poor by official definitions had dropped substantially.

2. The difficulty in agreeing on a sharp dividing line between the poor and the nonpoor leads one to broaden the problem of poverty into the problem of inequality in incomes.

3. In the United States today, the richest 20 percent of families receive over 41 percent of the income, while the poorest 20 percent of families receive just above 5 percent. These numbers have changed little over the past 30 years and represent somewhat more inequality here than in many other advanced industrial nations.

4. Individual incomes differ for many reasons. Discrimination, differences in native ability, in the desire to work hard and to take risks, in schooling, and in inherited wealth also account for income disparities. All of these factors, however, explain only part of the inequality that we observe. A portion of the rest is due simply to good or bad luck, and the balance is unexplained.

5. Prejudice against a minority group may lead to discrimination in rates of pay, or to segregation in the workplace, or to both. However, discrimination may also arise even when there is no prejudice (this is called statistical discrimination).

6. There is a trade-off between the goals of reducing inequality and enhancing economic efficiency: policies that help on the equality front normally harm efficiency, and vice versa. This is one of the 12 Ideas for Beyond the Final Exam.

7. Because of this trade-off, there is an optimal degree of inequality for any society. Society finds this optimum in the same way that a consumer decides how much to buy of different commodities: the trade-off tells us how costly it is to "purchase" more equality, and preferences then determine how much should be "bought." However, since people differ in their value judgments about the importance of equality, there will inevitably be disagreement over the ideal amount of equality.

8. There may, however, be some hope of reaching agreement over the policies to use in pursuit of whatever goal for equality is selected. This is because the more efficient redistributive policies let us buy any amount of equality at a lower price in terms of lost output. Economists claim, for example, that a negative income tax is preferable to our current welfare system on these grounds.

9. Even the negative income tax, though, is no magical cure. Its primary virtue lies in the way it preserves incentives to work. But if this is done by keeping the tax rate low, then either the minimum guaranteed level of income will have to be very low or many relatively nonpoor families will become eligible to receive benefits.

10. The goal of income equality is also pursued through the tax system, especially through the progressive federal income tax. However, the equalization achieved by this tax is much less than is commonly believed because of tax loopholes and because people who are heavily burdened by the tax often can take steps to relieve themselves of these burdens. In addition, taxes other than income taxes are typically regressive, so that the tax system as a whole is only slightly progressive.

11. The problem of economic discrimination has been attacked by making it illegal, not through the tax and transfer system. But simply declaring discrimination to be illegal is much easier than actually ending discrimination. The trade-off between equality and efficiency applies once again: strict enforcement of affirmative action will certainly reduce discrimination and increase income equality, but it may do so at a serious cost in terms of economic efficiency.

Concepts for Review

Poverty line
Absolute and relative concepts of
    poverty
Lorenz curve
Economic discrimination
Statistical discrimination

Optimal amount of inequality
Trade-off between equality and
    efficiency
Aid to Families with Dependent
    Children (AFDC)
Food stamps

Negative income tax (NIT)
Tax loopholes
Capital gains
Equal Employment Opportunities
    Commission (EEOC)
Affirmative action

Questions for Discussion

1. Discuss the "leaky bucket" analogy (page 656) with your classmates. What maximum amount of income would you personally allow to leak from the bucket in transferring money from the rich to the poor? Explain why people differ in their answers to this question.
2. Continuing the leaky bucket example, explain why economists believe that replacing the present welfare system with a negative income tax would help reduce the leak.
3. Suppose you were to design a negative income tax system for the United States. Pick a guaranteed income level and a tax rate that seem reasonable to you. What break-even level of income is implied by these choices? For the plan you have just devised, construct a corresponding version of Table 34–4 (page 658).
4. Following is a complete list of the distribution of income in Disneyland. From these data, construct a Lorenz curve for Disneyland.

NAME	INCOME
Donald Duck	$ 50,000
Mickey Mouse	100,000
Minnie Mouse	25,000
Pluto	10,000
Ticket taker	15,000

How different is this from the Lorenz curve for the United States (Figure 34–2 on page 648)?

5. Suppose the War on Poverty were starting anew and you were part of a presidential commission assigned the task of defining the poor. Would you choose an absolute or relative concept of poverty? Why? What would be your specific definition of poverty?
6. Discuss the concept of the "optimal amount of inequality." What are some of the practical problems in determining how much inequality really is optimal?

Economic Growth and the World Economy

VII

Economic Growth: Causes, Virtues, and Vices

35

The development of capitalist production makes it constantly necessary to keep increasing the amount of capital laid out. . . . It compels [the individual capitalist] to keep constantly extending his capital . . . by means of progressive accumulation. . . . Fanatically bent on making value expand itself, he ruthlessly forces the human race to produce for production's sake; he thus forces the development of the productive powers of society, and creates those material conditions, which alone can form the real basis of a higher form of society.

KARL MARX

I n this chapter we discuss the factors that determine the rate at which an economy grows and examine the desirability of rapid growth. While our primary focus is the free-market economy, like the one in which we live, much of the discussion is applicable to any growing economy. We begin by considering how growth can be measured and go on to examine the effects of population growth on prospects for rising incomes per capita. Next, we examine the views of those who have argued that economic growth is a mixed blessing that may do more harm than good; and finally, we describe several of the conditions necessary for achieving more growth.

Some Issues in the Analysis of Growth

Capital accumulation and economic expansion have been subjects of controversy ever since economics became a specialized discipline. One of the main topics for discussion has been the effect of saving on economic growth. It seems more than a little curious that some eminent economists have emphasized the vital role saving plays in the process of economic growth, arguing that economic expansion without saving is all but impossible, while other, equally prominent, economists have warned that saving tends to undermine the growth process and, in practice, is often the most dangerous enemy of growth. Even more curious, as we will see, is that *both* viewpoints are essentially right. If you object that two contradictory positions *cannot* be right, we can assure you that you are also right!

The resolution of this important controversy hinges on the fact that the two positions are each correct *in different circumstances*, and each is of considerable importance for issues in economic policy. Later in this chapter we will see how a more comprehensive view of this matter enables economists to assign proper places to the two positions in the accumulation process. We will find that each interpretation of the role of saving has valid and important implications for policy issues. One of them will help us to understand the requisites for growth in an underdeveloped area or in a nation seeking to expand its output rapidly. The other will make clearer the source of the problem of an economy whose expansion is threatened by recession and unemployment. In short, the explanation of the enigma that saving is an absolute requirement of growth, and yet its most dangerous enemy, will help us analyze some of the most significant of the world's economic issues.

There are, however, other controversies surrounding the subject of growth. For instance, there is a heated debate over the desirability of growth itself. Here again, knowledgeable people hold positions that are almost diametrically opposed. Some see in growth the only possible cure to many of the world's more serious economic ills. Others see growth as a major *cause* of such problems. In this dispute, while it is not quite possible to conclude that both positions are right, there is a considerable and important element of truth in each of them. The trick, from the point of view of the welfare of humanity, will be to use growth in a way that extracts its benefits and yet avoids, or at least minimizes, its dangers. Though this may seem easier to suggest than to carry out, we will find that the problem is by no means beyond us—economics offers methods that appear able to deal effectively with these issues.

How to Measure Growth: Total Output or Output per Capita?

Preoccupation with economic growth and with the ability of an economy to produce an outpouring of goods and services goes back at least to Adam Smith, who in 1776 published the book that was to become the root of modern economics. One of the primary messages of Smith's book was that the free-market economy is an efficient instrument for the production of an abundance of outputs, as long as it is unhampered by artificial monopoly or arbitrary government restrictions. The abbreviated title of the book, *The Wealth of Nations*, indicates clearly Smith's main concern in the volume—the material prosperity of the society.

Not only did Smith, like many of his successors, take it for granted that expansion of productive capacity is inherently desirable, he also took it for granted, apparently without examining the matter very closely, that growth in the size of population is to be wished for. He spoke of "the sober and industrious poor who generally bring up the most numerous families, and who principally supply the demand for useful labor."[1]

Thus, the reason for Smith's approval of population growth seems to have been that a larger population provides a larger work force, and a larger work force makes possible a larger national output.

Few economists since Smith's time have argued in this way. Nowadays we usually measure a nation's prosperity not in terms of its total output but in terms of its output *per person*. India has a GNP more than twice as large as Sweden's. But with a population more than 80 times as large as Sweden's, India remains a poor country while Sweden is highly prosperous. The point is that:

If the objective of growth is the material welfare *of the individuals* who make up a country, then the proper measure of the success of a program of economic

---

[1]Adam Smith, *The Wealth of Nations*, Edwin Cannan, ed. (New York: Modern Library, Random House), page 823.

development is how much it adds to output per person. The relevant index is not total output. It is total output *divided by total population;* that is, *output per capita.*

From this point of view, the appropriate objective of growth is not, as the old cliché puts it, "the greatest good for the *greatest number"* — it is the greatest good *per person* in the economy. Per capita figures tell this story well. To make the appropriate comparison of well-being in Sweden and India, we note that per capita GNP in Sweden is almost $12,000 a year, whereas in India, even after a generous adjustment to correct for lower prices in that country, the figure is under $200 a year.

Only where the objective of the government is grandeur or military strength may the number of inhabitants alone seem an appropriate part of its goal. A small country like Finland, for instance, cannot hope to overwhelm a giant neighbor like the Soviet Union, even if Finland has a much high per capita GNP than the Soviet Union.[2] But where the goal of the government is not national power but the elimination of poverty, illiteracy, and inadequate medical care, sheer increase in population becomes a questionable pursuit.

On Growth in Population: Is Less Really More?

Just before the beginning of the nineteenth century, in 1798, the Reverend Thomas R. Malthus (who was to become England's first professor of political economy) published *An Essay on the Principle of Population.* This book was to have a profound effect on people's attitudes toward population growth. Malthus argued that sexual drives and other influences induce people to reproduce themselves as rapidly as their means permit. Unfortunately, he said, when the number of humans increases, the production of food and other consumption goods generally cannot keep up. As the earth becomes more crowded, people are forced to farm land more intensively, using more labor, fertilizer, and equipment to extract larger outputs from the same acreage. Besides working each farmed piece of land much more intensively than before, people will also have to look for new lands to farm. But neither of these ways to increase the product will help enough to meet the increased need. There are limits to what a given piece of land can produce. Moreover, as people put soil under cultivation, they will naturally tend to pick the best lots first. Thus, as they extend the area that is cultivated, people will be forced to make use of increasingly inferior farmland.

Together, these two phenomena lead to the noted *law of diminishing returns* to additional labor used with a fixed supply of land, a relationship we encountered before (in Chapter 20). This hypothesis states if we use more and more labor to cultivate a fixed stock of land, ultimately we will reach a point at which each additional laborer will contribute less additional output than the previous laborer. Ultimately, as the labor force increases, output per worker will decline.

Based on these observations, Malthus and his followers concluded that the tendency of humankind to reproduce itself must constantly also be exerting pressure on the economy to keep living standards from rising. There will be a tendency for wages to approximate some minimal subsistence level—the lowest income on which people are willing to marry and raise a family. If wages are above subsistence level, the population can and will grow. But, as we have seen,

---

[2]Even where military power is the primary objective, a large but impoverished population may not be a very effective means to that end. China has long had an enormous population, but in the modern era its military presence is certainly quite recent.

rising population without any rise in available land must reduce output per worker because of the law of diminishing returns. Thus, a wage that is above subsistence will set forces into motion that will force the wage level down toward subsistence.

Sometimes, according to Malthus, the population will grow beyond the capability of the economy to support it. Then the number of people will be brought back into line by means that are far more unpleasant than a decrease in wages—it can happen by starvation and disease or by wars that produce the required number of casualties.

Later in the nineteenth century and during the first half of the twentieth century, the gloomy Malthusian vision seemed to lose credibility. New technology and improved agricultural practices generally enabled the output of food and other agricultural products to increase faster than the population (at least in the wealthier industrialized nations). In addition, it turned out that as living standards rose, people became less anxious to reproduce, and so the expansion of population slowed substantially. Figures 35–1(a) and 35–1(b) illustrate this trend in Germany over a 130-year period. All in all, it began to look as though

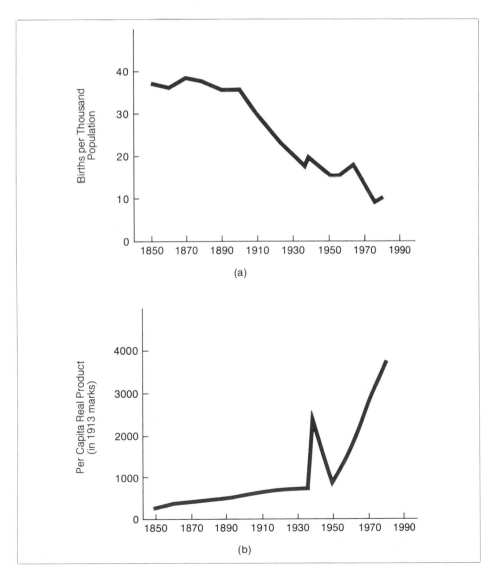

Figure 35–1
GERMAN BIRTHRATES AND REAL NET PRODUCT PER CAPITA, 1850–1980
(a) German birthrate (births per thousand population); (b) German product per capita (net real social product, in marks of 1913 purchasing power per capita). Note the steady fall in birthrate and the rise in product per capita.
SOURCE: Statistisches Bundesamt, *Statistisches Jahrbuch* (Weisbaden, Germany).

A Population Crisis in Africa

This report shows that the Malthusian spectre still haunts part of the globe:

Population pressure on the fragile desert ecosystem has been steadily gathering force in the African countries that border the Sahara. On the southern fringe in the Sahelian zone, a prolonged drought beginning in the late sixties and continuing into the seventies brought the deteriorating situation into painfully sharp focus. . . .

There is no record of how many lives were claimed as food systems collapsed all across Africa. In an appearance before a Congressional committee

after a tour of the Sahelian zone, Michael Latham, Professor of International Nutrition at Cornell University and a Member of the Committee on International Nutrition Programs of the National Academy of Sciences, testified that the number of lives lost was probably somewhere between 100,000 and a quarter of a million; no one will ever know for sure, he said.

SOURCE: Lester R. Brown, *World Population Trends: Signs of Hope, Signs of Stress*, Worldwatch Paper 8, October 1976, pages 23–24.

population growth constituted no significant threat—it was something with which human technological skills and ingenuity could cope.

More recently, however, there has been a renewed concern over the population problem. With improvements in medicine—notably improved hygiene in hospitals, the use of such public health measures as swamp drainage, and the discovery of antibiotics—death rates have plunged in the developing countries, especially for infants. At the same time, birth control programs in most of these countries have, at least until quite recently, not been very successful. As a result, the populations of developing countries have continued to expand dramatically, eating up a good proportion of any output increases obtained through their governments' economic development programs.

Currently, the populations of North America and Europe are growing so slowly that if present rates continue it will take a century or more for them to double. But in Africa populations double about every 25 years, and in Asia every 39 years.

From these observations, it has been widely concluded that significant improvement in living standards in the developing areas is impossible without a substantial reduction in the population growth rates of those areas. But the neo-Malthusians, as one dedicated group is sometimes called, go further than this, arguing that a rapid approach to birthrates so low that populations cease expanding—that is, to *zero population growth*—is virtually a matter of life and death even for the most prosperous nations. It is illuminating to consider the logic of their argument.

The Crowded Planet: Exponential Population Growth

In advocating his position, Malthus adopted a line of argument that has caught the imagination of students of Malthusian theory ever since.

Population, when unchecked, increases in a geometrical ratio. Subsistence increases only in an arithmetical ratio. A slight acquaintance with numbers will shew the immensity of the first power in comparison of the second.[3]

[3]Malthus, *An Essay on the Principle of Population* (London, 1798), page 20.

Population growth in what Malthus called a "geometric ratio" has a simple structure. In modern discussions, such a growth pattern is referred to as **exponential growth,** or "compounded growth" or "snowballing."

Exponential growth is growth at a constant *percentage* rate. For example, at a 10 percent growth rate, a population of 100 persons will increase by 10 persons a year; but a population of a million persons will increase by 100,000 persons a year. Thus, although the *rate* of growth is the same for large and small populations, the *numbers* are dramatically different. The bigger the population, the more it will add annually. And each year's growth implies still faster growth in the following year. It is like a snowball rolling downhill, accumulating more snow the bigger it gets and so expanding faster and faster all the time.

If the population doubles (grows 100 percent) in 35 years, it will quadruple (grow another 100 percent) in 70 years, increase 8-fold in 105 years, 16-fold in 140 years, and so on indefinitely. The doubling sequence 2, 4, 8, 16, 32, 64, and so on, is the basic pattern of exponential growth. Figure 35–2 shows how astronomical such a growth sequence can be. By projecting the world's population 175 years into the future on the assumption that population will grow exponentially at about its current rate, it shows that by the year 2155 the population will have grown to about 128 billion, with more than 30 times as many inhabitants on the earth as there are today.

It turns out that in his assumptions about exponential growth, Malthus was being conservative. He did not begin to spell out the wonders and the horrors that his premise implied. Consider some calculations by one leading authority on population (who has derived his conclusions simply by carrying through the arithmetic of exponential growth rates):

- *If population were to grow at today's rates for another 600–700 years, every square foot of the surface of the earth would contain a human being;*

- *If it were to expand at the same rate for 1200 years, the combined weight of the human population would exceed that of the earth itself;*

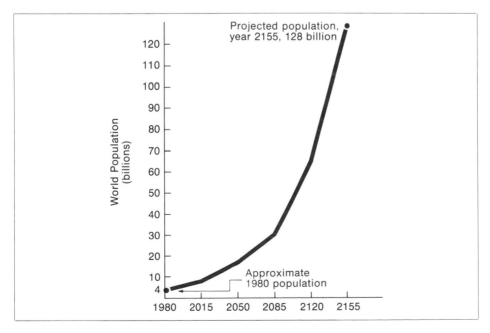

Figure 35–2
PROJECTED GROWTH OF THE WORLD'S POPULATION IN 175 YEARS AT A CONSTANT 2 PERCENT RATE OF GROWTH
This figure shows the sensational acceleration of population growth *if* population expands exponentially.

Figure 35–3

ANNUAL PERCENTAGE
GROWTH RATE OF THE
U.S. POPULATION
Note how rapidly the rate has
fallen in recent years. It has
just about returned to the low
level it was at during the Great
Depression.
SOURCE: U.S. Bureau of the
Census, *Current Population Re-
ports.* Series P-25.

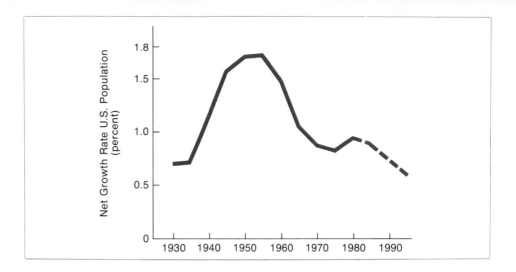

- *If that growth rate were to go on for 6000 years (a very short period of time in terms of biological history), the globe would constitute a sphere whose diameter was growing with the speed of light.*[4]

And none of this is conjecture. It is *sure* to come about *if* the present (exponential) rate of growth of the earth's population (about 2 percent a year) continues unabated.

Of course, none of this can really happen. Our finite earth just does not have room for that sort of expansion. The fate of humanity is not determined by the rules of arithmetic—it depends on the course of nature and on the behavior of the human race. It is true that if the number of humans continues to swell until it presses upon the earth's capacity, the process will ultimately be brought to a halt in a Malthusian apocalypse. Disease, famine, and war must finally put a stop to the expansion process. But there is a better alternative. People can choose to stop raising large families. There is no inevitability about the family of six or ten children. As we have just noted, there has in fact been a decline in the rate of expansion in the wealthier societies—so much so that in the United States in the last few years the rate of reproduction has reached what can ultimately give us zero population growth (see Figure 35–3). Even in the developing nations, as we will see in Chapter 39, the birthrate has recently been decelerating.

A more balanced view of the matter recognizes the serious difficulties that rapid population growth can lead to, and suggests that its encouragement will not serve the interests of society. Yet, it does *not* imply that a great catastrophe is at hand or that the appropriate reaction is panic.

Is More Growth Really Better?

A number of writers have raised questions about the desirability of faster economic growth as an end in itself. Yet faster growth means more wealth, and to most people the desirability of wealth is beyond question. "I've been rich and I've been poor—and I can tell you, rich is better," a noted stage personality is said to have told an interviewer, and most people seem to have the same attitude about the economy as a whole. To those who hold this belief, a healthy economy is one that is capable of turning out vast quantities of shoes, food, cars, and TV sets. An

[4]Ansley J. Coale, "Man and His Environment," *Science*, vol. 179 (October 9, 1970), pages 132–36. Copyright 1970 by the American Association for the Advancement of Science.

economy whose capacity to provide all these things is not expanding is said to have succumbed to the disease of *stagnation*.

Economists from Adam Smith to Karl Marx saw great virtue in economic growth. Marx argued that capitalism, at least in its earlier historical stages, was a vital form of economic organization by which society got out of the rut in which the medieval stage of history had trapped it. As we saw in the opening quotation of this chapter, Marx believed that "the development of the productive powers of society . . . alone can form the real basis of a higher form of society. . . . " Marx went on to tell us that only where such great productive powers have been unleashed can one have "a society in which the full and free development of every individual forms the ruling principle."[5] In other words, only a wealthy economy can afford to give all individuals the opportunity for full personal satisfaction through the use of their special abilities in their jobs and through increased leisure activities.

Yet the desirability of economic growth has been questioned on grounds that undoubtedly have a good deal of validity. It is pointed out that the sheer increase in quantity of products has imposed an enormous cost on society in the form of pollution, crowding, proliferation of wastes that need disposal, and debilitating psychological and social effects. It is said that industry has transformed the satisfying and creative tasks of the artisan into the mechanical and dehumanizing routine of the assembly line. It has dotted our roadsides with junkyards, filled our air with smoke, and poisoned our food with dangerous chemicals. The question is whether the outpouring of frozen foods, talking dolls, CB radios, and headache remedies is worth its high cost to society. As one well-known economist put it:

The continued pursuit of economic growth by Western Societies is more likely on balance to reduce rather than increase social welfare. . . . Technological innovations may offer to add to men's material opportunities. But by increasing the risks of their obsolescence it adds also to their anxiety. Swifter means of communications have the paradoxical effect of isolating people; increased mobility has led to more hours commuting; increased automobilization to increased separation; more television to less communication. In consequence, people know less of their neighbors than ever before in history.[6]

Virtually every economist agrees that these concerns are valid, though many question whether economic growth is their major cause. Nevertheless, they all emphasize that pollution of air and water, noise and congestion, and the mechanization of the work process are very real and very serious problems. There is every reason for society to undertake programs that grapple with these problems. Chapter 31, which dealt with problems of the environment, examined these issues more closely and described some policies to deal with them.

Economists agree also that growth in human well-being is measured very poorly by statistics such as GNP, which indicates only the growth rate of the production of *material* goods and services and takes no account of the effects of growth on the quality of life. Two economists at Yale University, William Nordhaus and James Tobin, have attempted to calculate a better set of figures for the purpose. Their index, the *measure of economic welfare* (MEW), attempts to take into account such items as pollution and congestion as well as the more tangible products of the economy.[7] Thus, for example, if the output of goods and

---

[5] Marx, *Capital*, vol. I (Chicago: Charles H. Kerr Publishing Co., 1906), page 649.

[6] E. J. Mishan, *The Costs of Economic Growth* (New York: Frederick A. Praeger Publishers, 1967), pages 171, 175.

[7] W. Nordhaus and J. Tobin, "Is Growth Obsolete?" *Fiftieth Anniversary Colloquium*, V, National Bureau of Economic Research (New York: Columbia University Press, 1972).

services were to go up slightly some year but there was also a huge increase in pollution, the statistics would report that GNP had risen but that MEW, or the quality of life, had decreased. In fact, the calculations show that throughout most of the post-World War II period, both GNP per capita and MEW per capita have been growing but that growth in the latter has been considerably slower.

Despite the costs of growth in terms of human and environmental damage, there is strong evidence that if the economy's total output were kept at its present level, the community would pay a high price over and above the loss of additional goods and services.

First, it is not easy to carry out a decision to prevent further economic growth. Mandatory controls are abhorrent to most Americans. We cannot *order* people to stop inventing means to expand productivity. Nor does it make any sense to order every firm and industry to freeze its output level, since changing tastes and needs require some industries to expand their outputs at the same time that others are contracting. But who is to decide which should grow and which should contract, and how shall such decisions be made? *The achievement of zero economic growth may very well require government intervention on a scale that becomes expensive and even repressive.*

Second, zero economic growth may seriously hamper efforts to eliminate poverty both within our economy and throughout the world. Much of the earth's population today lives in a state of extreme want. And though wealthier nations have been reluctant to provide more than token amounts of help to the underdeveloped countries, less wealth means there would be even less to share. So perhaps the only hope for improved living standards in the impoverished countries of Africa, Asia, and Latin America lies in continued increases in output.

Finally, without continued growth, it will be no easy matter to finance effective programs of environmental protection. To improve the purity of our air and water and to clean up urban neighborhoods, tens of billions of dollars must be made available every year. Continued growth would enable the required resources to be provided without any reduction in the availability of consumer goods. But without such growth, we may actually be forced to cut back on our programs to protect the environment. Society could thus end up with fewer goods and a worse environment.

Requirements for Increased Growth

Assuming that we do want to increase the growth rate of the economy—as most countries do—the next question is, What can be done about it? Unfortunately, no one has a handy list of recipes for the stimulation of economic growth. If there were such a list, much of the world's hunger and disease could be eliminated.

Growth can only be attributed to a number of factors that no one knows how to explain: (1) *inventiveness*, which produces the new technology and other innovations that have contributed so much to economic expansion; (2) *entrepreneurship*, the leadership that recognizes no obstacles and undertakes the daring industrial ventures needed to move the economy ahead; and (3) *the work ethic* that leads a work force to high levels of productivity. No one really knows what features of economic organization and social psychology actually lead a community to adopt these goals, as Great Britain is said to have done at the beginning of the nineteenth century, as the United States is reputed to have done in the first half of the twentieth century, and as Japan is apparently doing today. We do know, however, that:

Growth requires two things that people can influence directly:

1. A large expenditure on *capital equipment:* factories, machinery, transportation, and telecommunications equipment.
2. The devotion of considerable effort to research and development from which innovations are derived.

Both these types of expenditures help to increase the economy's ability to *supply* goods. But additional supplies will not be produced unless the *demand* is there to provide a market for these outputs.

This observation brings us back to the analysis of Part Two of this book, where it was stressed that the level (and, consequently, the growth) of national income is determined by the interaction of aggregate supply and aggregate demand. Much attention was devoted to the monetary and fiscal techniques by which aggregate demand can be managed and to the consequences of a failure to perform this task skillfully. There we paid less attention to the determinants of supply and its rate of growth.

The need for capital equipment in any growth process provides a vital link between aggregate demand and aggregate supply. How does an economy acquire a larger capital stock? By investing. Recall that aggregate demand is the sum of consumption, investment, and government spending, $Y = C + I + G$. But I is the only part of Y that creates more capital for the future.

The *composition* of aggregate demand is a major determinant of the rate of economic growth. If a larger fraction of total spending goes toward investment rather than toward consumption or government purchases, the capital stock will grow faster and the aggregate supply schedule will shift more quickly to the right.

Accumulating Capital by Sacrificing Consumption: The Case of Soviet Russia

The importance of the *composition* of demand stands out in sharp relief if we turn away from the United States and consider a *centrally planned* economy, such as the Soviet Union.

When the Soviet Union undertook to expand its industrial output very rapidly, it was clear from the earliest stage of planning that a tremendous amount of capital equipment would be required to carry out the expansion. Not only did the Russians have to build modern factories and acquire sophisticated machinery, they also needed a **social infrastructure**—a transportation network to bring raw materials to the factories and take finished products to the markets, an efficient telecommunications system, and schools in which to train the population sufficiently to be an effective labor force. All this and much more was needed, and all of it required raw material and fuel for its construction.

Obviously, such a use of resources has its *opportunity cost.* Fuel and steel that are employed to build a train become unavailable for the production of refrigerators and washing machines. The real price of accumulating plant, equipment, and infrastructure is paid in the form of consumer goods that must be given up in order to build that capital equipment. In other words:

Through saving, the public gives up some consumption, which is the price it must pay for the accumulation of plant, equipment, and infrastructure. Without this sacrifice, growth generally cannot occur.

This is the hard lesson that the inhabitants of the Soviet Union have been living with for over half a century. Ever since the Russian Revolution in 1917, the

Soviet leadership has been determined to promote rapid economic growth and has imposed on the general public whatever sacrifices of current consumption were deemed necessary for the purpose. Only in the most recent decades has an increase in the supply of consumer goods been assigned any priority. Yet, even now, investment in the U.S.S.R. is still 25 percent of GNP, while in the United States the figure is about half that amount. As a result, Soviet living standards have been rising very slowly, particularly because the demands of the military forces have joined those of the growth planners in competing for the resources that might otherwise go into consumption.

The reason for this harsh trade-off is clear enough. If the economy is producing at its full potential—and the Russian economy generally has been—then real output Y cannot be increased further. Since $Y = C + I + G$, a decision to devote more resources to the production of heavy machinery (which is in I) or armaments (which are in G) is simultaneously a decision to forgo some consumption. Where resources are already fully employed, it is simply not possible to have both more guns and more butter.

This is precisely the sense in which saving is an absolute prerequisite for growth. If the economy is to grow, consumers must be coaxed, cajoled, or forced into saving. Every planner who adopts growth as his goal must decide just how he is going to generate the necessary saving.

The Payoff to Growth: Higher Consumption in the Future

We may seem to be painting a rather grim picture of growth, and indeed, the process has often been harsh in the U.S.S.R. and in other nations that have enforced a high rate of economic growth. But it is also true that if the growth process is successful, the sacrifice of consumption that it requires is only a temporary loss. Consumers give up goods and services now in order to make possible the construction of a productive capacity that will permit them to consume even more goods and services at a later date. After all, from the consumers' point of view, that is what growth is all about. It is not an end in itself, but a means to an end—a standard of living higher than they could have attained without the process of economic expansion.

At least in a consumer-oriented economy, the decision to save in order to promote economic growth is simply an *exchange between present and future consumption.* Consumers sacrifice consumption now in order to be able to increase consumption in the future by more than they gave up in the past.

Of course, the payoff may never come if something goes wrong. An earthquake may destroy factories and roads, or a government with military ambitions may divert the increased productive capacity into the manufacture of armaments. So there is a risk in the decision to give up consumption now for increased consumption later. The growth process is a gamble—it means trading in a relatively sure thing (present consumption) for a risky future return (increased future consumption).

But betting on the future is not necessarily foolhardy. Economies would remain stagnant if people were unwilling to take chances. And some of the risk of investment plans can be reduced if decision makers understand fully the terms of the trade-off.

Growth Without Sacrificing Consumption: Something for Nothing?

Of course, some growth can be achieved without much sacrifice of present consumption. For at least one of the main engines of growth can be powered with relatively small increases in the nation's stock of factories, equipment, and infrastructure. Research and development can teach society new and more efficient ways of using the nation's productive resources. Thus, *innovation*—the process of putting inventions into operation—can permit an economy to get more output from the same inputs rather than by *expansion* of capital stock.

Everyone knows that this has in fact occurred. From the invention of the steam engine to that of the modern computer, our economy has benefited from a stream of inventions, some sensational, some more routine, which together have increased enormously the productivity of the nation's resources. Estimates of the relative contributions of innovation and accumulation to the growth process differ. A number of analysts attribute considerably more than half of the economic growth of the United States to research and invention. But whatever the correct figure, it is certainly large.

Another way of describing this conclusion is to say that while a substantial proportion of growth is *embodied* in increased quantities of plant, equipment, and infrastructure, a very large proportion of the economy's growth is *disembodied.* That is, it is attributable to better ideas—to improved methods of finding and using the same quantities of resources.

Typically, though, growth involves a combination of the two: the new ideas and the commitment of capital to put them into effect. The widespread use of computers could not have happened without the electronic gear from which they are composed and the flow of electricity by which they are operated. Computers are worthwhile because they reduce the quantities of resources necessary to do a given job, but originally some accumulation of resources was required in order to make possible the resulting savings.

For the long run, society has a considerable stake in the relative role of embodied and disembodied growth. Embodied growth has two serious costs that disembodied growth avoids. First, embodied growth necessarily speeds up the use of society's depletable resources: its iron ore, its petroleum supplies, and its stocks of other minerals and fuels. This means that smaller quantities of those resources will be available to future generations.

The second cost of embodied growth is of comparable importance. The resources that are used up in a process of embodied growth must ultimately end up on society's garbage heap. The physical laws of conservation of matter and energy tell us that no raw material can ever disappear. It can be transformed into smoke or solid waste, but unless it is recycled *entirely* (something that is both beyond the capability of our technology and impractical for other reasons), the greater the quantity of resources used in the productive process, the greater the quantity of wastes that must ultimately result.

Economist Kenneth Boulding has likened our planet to a spaceship hurtling through the solar system but constrained by terrestrial littering laws to keep its garbage on board. In spaceship Earth, we can transform waste materials into other forms—as by melting old bottles for reuse or converting them into energy, or by burning combustible garbage for heat—but we cannot simply toss them overboard.

Both of these environmental concerns—resource depletion and waste disposal—lead us to favor disembodied over embodied growth. To the extent that we can succeed in increasing the productivity of our resources, we can reduce both the rate at which they are depleted and the severity of the community's waste-disposal problems.

So far, we have enjoyed substantial success in our efforts to achieve growth in output without commensurate increases in our use of resources. One statistical analysis, for example, has provided evidence that attributes only about half of the growth in the United States during the period 1929–1969 to increased use of physical inputs. The remainder must be ascribed to improvements in technology as well as to increased education and skill of the labor force.[8]

One final remark on disembodied growth is in order. Economists are fond of pointing out that there is no such thing as a free lunch. Except in rare instances, improvements in technology are not "manna from heaven." They result, instead, from the work of scientists and technicians in government and industrial laboratories, from the labor of inventors in their basements or garages, and from the effort of management specialists studying the organization of factories and assembly lines. This means that labor (along with other resources) is diverted from other activities into the production of knowledge. *In a fully employed economy, the opportunity costs of investing in the discovery of new knowledge are the consumption of and physical investment in goods that would otherwise have been produced.* So even here, we cannot get something for nothing.

Saving as the Enemy of Growth: The Paradox of Thrift

[If] the capitalists themselves, together with the landlords and other rich persons . . . have . . . agreed . . . by depriving themselves of their usual conveniences and luxuries to save from their revenue and add to their capital . . . how is it possible to suppose that [an] increased quantity of commodities . . . should find purchasers [?][9]

We have now explained how saving works as the handmaiden of growth. But at the start of this chapter we mentioned an alternative view: that saving can be an impediment to growth. How can this be?

We can find the answer by worrying less about the consequences of saving for the *supply* of goods and more about its effect on *demand.* As we learned in Part Two, an unplanned economy—where saving and investing are typically done by different people—often has trouble keeping aggregate demand in line with aggregate supply. Keynesian national income analysis shows how *an effort to save more can actually result in everyone saving less.*

This so-called **paradox of thrift** is a phenomenon we have encountered earlier (in Chapter 10). Let us recall the analysis used there. With no government, aggregate demand is the sum $C + I$. Figure 35–4 is a typical 45° line diagram: curve C is the consumption function and curve $C + I$ is the total expenditure schedule, that is, the sum of consumption and investment demand. National income, as we know, is determined by the intersection of the $C + I$ curve with the 45° line (point A in the figure). The GNP is $1200 billion, of which $1000 billion is consumed and $200 billion is invested. Since saving is the

---

[8]Edward F. Denison, *Accounting for United States Economic Growth 1929–1969* (Washington: The Brookings Institution, 1974). More recently, however, there has been a decline in the rate of growth in output relative to input quantities used. See E. F. Denison, *Accounting for Slower Economic Growth* (Washington, D.C., The Brookings Institution, 1979), page 62.

[9]T. R. Malthus, quoted by Piero Sraffa in *The Works and Correspondence of David Ricardo,* vol. 2 (Cambridge: Cambridge University Press, 1951), pages 302–303.

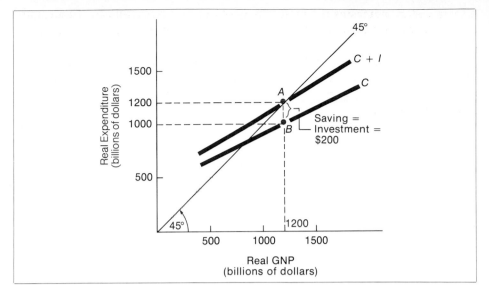

Figure 35-4
DETERMINATION OF
NATIONAL INCOME IN
KEYNESIAN ANALYSIS
This figure reviews the Keynesian national income analysis
that was first introduced in
Chapter 8. The equilibrium
level of GNP is determined by
the intersection of the $C + I$
schedule and the 45° line—
point A in the diagram. At this
level of income, both saving
and investment are $200 billion, as indicated by the distance AB.

gap between income ($1200 billion) and consumption ($1000 billion), it is shown by the vertical distance AB from the 45° line to the consumption schedule.

Now suppose that after a government campaign to reduce consumption, people agree to save a higher proportion of their incomes. The result, of course, is a drop in the consumption function. Figure 35–5, which repeats the C and $C + I$ curves from Figure 35–4 (in black), shows the new consumption function as the blue line C' and the new aggregate demand schedule as the blue line $C' + I$. National income will spiral down to point D, where GNP is only $900 billion, because aggregate demand is insufficient to support the previous production level. *Because saving depends on income*, saving—which is now the distance DE between the 45° line and the C' consumption function—drops to $175 billion. Thus the *attempt* to save more (the fall in the consumption function) is frustrated by the drop in GNP.

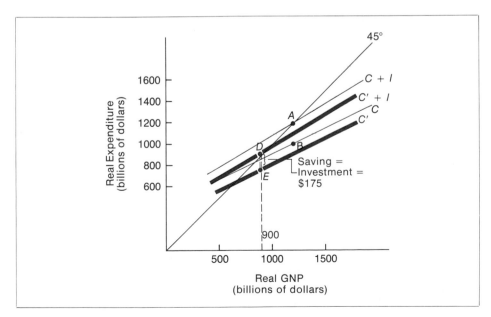

Figure 35–5
THE PARADOX OF THRIFT
This diagram indicates how a
successful campaign to persuade consumers to save
more might actually result in
less total saving—the so-called
paradox of thrift. The increased desire to save shifts
the $C + I$ schedule downward
to the position indicated by
schedule $C' + I$, because saving more out of any given income means spending less.
Equilibrium drops from point A
to point D—from a GNP of
$1200 billion to one of only
$900 billion. In this example,
total saving at this lower equilibrium point—distance DE—is
only $175 billion, whereas it
was formerly $200 billion.

The explanation of the paradox of thrift is quite straightforward. If people are set on saving a large proportion of their income, then only a low quantity of output will find a market. Output will have to be low because there will be no demand for larger quantities of production. But because the public's income will consequently be low, it will not be able to save very much—it simply will not be able to afford to put large quantities of resources into saving. In this way, a strong desire to save may actually *reduce* the amount the community can ultimately manage to save, and that is the paradox of thrift.

More important for our purposes, this mechanism shows how a strong desire to save can spell trouble for growth. Every increase in desired saving constitutes, other things being equal, an identical *reduction* in the demand to purchase goods for consumption. For saving, by definition, implies abstinence from consumption. And as we know, lack of demand for goods naturally leads the nation's businesses to reduce their production levels.

To engineer a successful acceleration in the rate of economic growth, any increase in the propensity to save must be matched by an increase in the willingness of firms to invest. That is, business firms must compensate for the reduction in consumers' demand for goods, which is a consequence of their increased saving, by increasing their (firms') demand for output, that is, by increasing their investment.

Resolution of the Saving Enigma

Now that we have examined the arguments on both sides, we are in a position to resolve the enigma with which this chapter began: How can saving be both a blessing and a curse for economic growth?

The answer, of course, is that increased saving cannot be both desirable and undesirable at the same place and time. It is beneficial under certain circumstances and detrimental under others. And it is not difficult, in principle, to indicate which is which. In essence, economic growth can be impeded either by demand-side difficulties or by supply-side problems. If there is insufficient *demand* to permit firms to increase their outputs profitably, then we have a case of **demand-constrained growth.** On the other hand, in an economy with a plentiful group of potential buyers, but which lacks the equipment, resources, and skills to meet their desire for more output, growth is clearly impeded by the inability to *supply* the output. We call this condition **supply-constrained growth.**

Now, increased saving is likely to make matters worse if demand is the roadblock that prevents growth; but increased saving can help matters if supply problems are the impediment. The reason is clear. If consumers decide to save more it means, automatically, that they plan to buy less. Thus, a decision to save more will aggravate any deficiency in demand. On the other hand, because saving supplies the resources that can be used to build plant, equipment, and other means of production, increased saving can ease a supply-side problem for growth.

Which type of growth problem prevails in the real world? Both—at different places and at different times.

We have already considered the case of a centrally planned economy as an example of supply-constrained growth. Since the managers of the Russian economy set aggregate demand wherever they please, they need never worry about insufficient demand. They do, however, have to cajole or coerce Russian consumers into abstaining from consumption so that more factories can be built.

The growth problem is rather similar in most of the developing nations of the world. While these poor countries desperately need to build the factories, machinery, and infrastructure necessary to support a modern economy, their inhabitants barely have enough income to survive. Such poor people can be expected to consume almost entirely what little income they have, so they will be unable to provide the saving that can be used to build roads and factories. In such an economy, saving and accumulation will represent a very great sacrifice. Policymakers in this situation rarely, if ever, will have to deal with the problem of what to do with an embarrassing surplus of savings. Their task will be to know just how far they can go in inducing accumulation without causing unbearable hardships for the population.

A final example of a supply-constrained growth process is provided by a *developed economy operating at or near capacity levels.* When aggregate demand is sufficient to employ all the available capital and labor, the only way to speed up growth (apart from accelerating the pace of innovation) is to divert resources away from consumption or government spending and toward investment. As we learned in Part Two, one way to do this is to pursue a national economic policy predicated on a combination of "easy money" to hold interest rates down (to stimulate investment) and government budget surpluses either through high taxes (to hold consumption down) or low government spending.

However, as we stressed in Part Two, the situation in the rich, industrialized capitalist economies—especially the United States—is sometimes one of inadequate aggregate demand, so that economic expansion becomes demand-constrained. Under these circumstances, a kind of "free lunch" becomes possible, since *both* consumption *and* investment can be increased through an increase in aggregate demand. Here, more saving can only make a bad situation worse.

Summary

1. If growth is evaluated in terms of its effect upon the well-being of individuals, a country's economic growth should be measured in terms of *per capita* income, not in terms of GNP or some other index of total output of the economy.

2. A rapidly rising population poses a threat to growth of per capita incomes.

3. On our finite planet, exponential growth (growth at a constant percentage rate) is, in general, impossible except for relatively brief periods.

4. Many observers argue that even if continued growth does not lead to catastrophes in terms of rapid depletion of resources, famine, and so forth (as some have predicted), its desirability is nevertheless questionable because it produces pollution, overcrowding, and many other undesirable consequences.

5. Those who favor growth argue that without it there is no chance of ridding the world of poverty.

6. Increases in growth depend heavily on entrepreneur-

ship, accumulation of capital equipment, and research and development.

7. Saving is necessary for the accumulation of resources with which to produce factories, machinery, and other capital equipment. Thus, saving is a critical requisite for growth, particularly in less developed countries.

8. In some circumstances, particularly in industrialized countries, substantial saving by consumers can impede growth by reducing consumption demand and therefore cutting down the amount it pays business firms to produce.

9. A strong desire to save may actually reduce the economy's saving by cutting consumer demand and thereby reducing income, which is the source of saving. This is called the paradox of thrift.

10. Saving and investment involve a sacrifice of current consumption in exchange for more output in the future. It is a trade-off between current and future consumption.

Concepts for Review

Questions for Discussion

1. Which do you think has the higher total GNP, Pakistan or Luxembourg? Which has the higher per capita GNP? In which do you think people are better off economically?

2. Suppose population grows at a constant exponential rate and doubles every 10 years. How many times will it have grown in 30 years? How many years does it require to expand to 16 times its initial level?

3. Can you think of any innovations that permit growth without proportionate increases in use of inputs?

4. Name as many undesirable consequences of growth as you can think of.

5. Are the undesirable consequences of growth more likely to be considered serious in a less developed country or in an industrialized country? Why?

6. During a period of peak aggregate demand, is increased saving likely to be a stimulus or a hindrance to growth? Explain.

The Economics of Energy and Natural Resources

36

Since Fuel is become so expensive, and will of course grow scarcer and dearer; any new Proposal for saving the [fuel] . . . may at least be thought worth Consideration.

BENJAMIN FRANKLIN (1744)

The decade of the 1970s witnessed a marked dampening of the buoyant optimism which previously was widely held to characterize American attitudes. The energy situation probably contributed significantly to this change. The old attitude that unlimited stocks of resources promise unlimited growth was proven wrong in a very rude way. In the 1970s and early 1980s we suddenly found ourselves facing shortages of a great variety of commodities— coffee, paper products and, above all, energy. People were led to wonder, as one headline in a leading magazine put it, "Are we running out of everything?"

This chapter will try to put matters into perspective. It will show that neither the earlier optimism nor the more recent panic is quite justified by the facts. Natural resources have always been scarce, and one may argue with good reason that they have been used wastefully. On the other hand, we are *not* about to run out of most vital resources; there is reason to be optimistic about the availability of substitutes; and many of the shortages of the 1970s can with some justice be ascribed as much to the folly of government programs and misunderstanding by the general public as to any signs of imminent exhaustion of petroleum and other natural resources.

This chapter begins by reviewing the facts and allegations about the available stocks of natural resources. It then describes what economic theory tells us will happen in a free market to the prices and usage of finite resources as time passes and the available quantities decline. Then the history of the energy crisis will be examined. Finally, several important policy issues—such as energy independence, rationing, and protection of the environment—will be discussed.

A Puzzle: Those Resilient Resource Supplies

It is a plain fact that nature provided mankind with only finite quantities of such vital resources as oil, copper, lead, coal, and many others. This fact has fascinated pessimists through the years. In 1972 extreme pessimism assumed its most scientific guise in a publication by the Club of Rome of a volume called *The Limits to Growth.* Using computers to project the world of the future, the authors concluded "with some confidence" that if there is "no major change in the present system . . . industrial growth will certainly stop within the next century, at the latest." As they describe the process, "The behavior mode of the system is one of overshoot and collapse. . . . Growth . . . depletes a large

Table 36–1

SOME WORLD RESERVE/DEMAND RATIOS (Number of years' demand that can be met from available reserves), 1976.

ZINC	OIL	LEAD	TIN	COPPER
19.2	26	26.4	36	38

fraction of the resource reserves available . . . the industrial base collapses, taking with it the services and agricultural systems . . . [and] population finally decreases when the death rate is driven upward by lack of food and health services."[1]

Table 36–1 shows the sort of data that are frequently used to support such doomsday forecasts. Roughly speaking, it shows for five minerals the number of years of consumption (at current rates of use) that could be met by known supplies of the resources as of 1976. Reading this table without knowing what lies behind it can indeed be frightening. It seems to say we will run out of all five resources in less than 40 years. For example, according to this table, by 1982 we should have only 32 years of copper reserves, 30 years of tin reserves, 20 years of lead and oil reserves, and only 13 years of zinc reserves remaining. What happens after that?

But now look at Table 36–2, which compares the 1976 figures with similar data for a quarter-century earlier. Surely, something mysterious is going on! We see that in 1950 only about a 19-year supply of zinc was apparently left to mankind. Yet 26 years later, despite all the zinc that had been used in the meantime, the reserves of zinc were still enough to last 19 years! And each of the other resources now actually had *larger* reserves relative to consumption rates, even though rates of consumption had themselves risen in the interim. This does indeed seem like a funny way to keep score.

In part, this puzzle is ascribable to the misleading nature of figures on "known reserves," though these are the sorts of statistics commonly cited by pessimists on resource depletion. But economic principles also help a great deal in clearing up the mystery, as we will see at the end of the chapter.

The Free Market and Pricing of Depletable Resources

If figures on known reserves behave as peculiarly as those we have just seen, one begins to doubt their ability to indicate whether we are really coming uncomfortably close to running out of certain resources. Is there some other indicator of growing scarcity that seems more reliable? Most economists agree that there

[1]Donella H. Meadows, *et al., The Limits to Growth* (New York: Universe Books, 1972), pages 125–126.

Table 36–2

SOME WORLD RESERVE/DEMAND RATIOS, 1950 and 1976.

	ZINC	OIL	LEAD	TIN	COPPER
1950	18.8	13.8	9.8	14.4	27.9
1976	19.2	26	26.4	36	38

SOURCE: *Mineral Commodity Summaries*, 1978, Washington, D.C., Bureau of Mines, U.S. Department of the Interior.

Note: We had more years' supply of each of the depletable resources in 1976 than in 1950, despite 26 years of consumption!

is—that the *price of the resource* serves this function well.

As a resource becomes scarcer, we expect its price to rise for several reasons. One is that for most resources the process of depletion is not simply a matter of gradually using up the supply of a homogeneous product, every unit of which is equally available. Rather, the most accessible and highest quality of the resource is generally used up first, then industry turns to less accessible sources containing resources of lower purity or quality and then, in turn, to deposits which are still harder or more costly to get at or of still poorer quality. Oil is a clear example of this. First, Americans relied primarily on the most easily found domestic oil wells. Then they turned to imports from the Middle East with their higher transport costs. At that point it was not yet profitable to embark on the dangerous and extremely costly process of bringing up oil from the floor of the North Sea. (See the box on the following page for an illustration of what sort of investment it takes to extract oil from deep sea beds.) We know that the United States still possesses tremendous stocks of petroleum embedded in shale (rock), but so far this has been too difficult and, therefore, too costly to get at.

Increasing scarcity of a resource such as oil is not usually a matter of imminent and total disappearance. Rather, it takes the form of exhaustion of the most accessible and cheapest sources so that new supplies become more costly.

A second reason for rising resource prices is hidden in the operation of the supply–demand mechanism. To see how it works let us consider the simpler (if less realistic) case in which extraction of a resource does not grow increasingly difficult as its reserves dwindle. That is, we envision the earth's supply of a mythical mineral, Zipthon, all of identical quality, which can be extracted and delivered to market with negligible transportation cost. How quickly will the reserves of Zipthon be used up, and what will happen to its price with the passage of time?

If the market for Zipthon is perfectly competitive, we can provide a remarkably concrete answer about the behavior of prices. The answer, which was discovered by the American economist Harold Hotelling, tells us that as long as the supply of Zipthon lasts, its price must rise at a rate equal to the rate of interest. That is, if in 1982 the price of Zipthon is $100 per ounce and the rate of interest is 10 percent, then its price in 1983 must be $110.

Under perfect competition the price of a depletable resource whose cost of extraction is not changing must rise at the rate of interest. If the rate of interest is 10 percent, the price of the resource must rise 10 percent every year.

Why is this so? The answer is simple. People who have money tied up in inventories of Zipthon must earn exactly as much per dollar of investment as they would by putting their money into, say, a government bond. For suppose instead that $100 invested in bonds would next year rise in value to $112, while $100 in Zipthon would grow only to $110, and suppose the two were equally risky. What would happen? People who owned Zipthon would obviously find it profitable to sell the Zipthon and put their money into bonds instead. But as more Zipthon was dumped on the market it would become increasingly abundant today and increasingly scarce tomorrow. So its expected *future* price would rise while its actual *current* price would fall. This and other associated changes in Zipthon prices and bond prices would continue until there was no further advantage in the one investment as against the other—that is, until both offered the same rate of return per dollar of investment.

The Search at Sea*

Imagine a tower nearly as tall as the Empire State Building set on the ocean bottom in 455 feet of water 120 miles from shore—a tower that weighs 715,000 tons, whose platform covers six acres, houses 200 workers, and generates enough electricity for a city of 33,000.

Science fiction? Hardly. That giant structure, larger even than the rocket that helped land Americans on the moon, is the Mobil-operated Statfjord A drilling and production platform. Constructed at a cost of $1.3 billion, Statfjord A will eventually produce 300,000 barrels of oil a day from the turbulent North Sea, where winds can howl at 120 miles per hour and waves reach a height of 100 feet. The tower's enormous size and cost reflect the increasingly huge projects required to get oil out of almost inaccessible pockets of the earth. . . . According to a recent estimate by the U.S. Geological Survey, North America's outer continental shelf alone may contain as much as 38 billion barrels of oil and 139 trillion cubic feet of gas—enough to heat all the homes in the United States for 60 years.

The problem—and the challenge—is how to get at this undersea resource. Most offshore drilling takes place in waters less than 600 feet deep. In depths greater than 1000 feet, costs and technological problems multiply. In fact, even a Statfjord-type tower is unsuited for such deep water. For this reason, engineers have had to devise other solutions.

One such solution, still in the planning stage, is a Mobil-pioneered, deep-sea production system that would eliminate the conventional platform altogether. Wellhead, terminal, and pipelines would be placed on the seabed by remote-controlled mechanisms, making it possible to produce in depths of up to 2500 feet—far deeper than divers can work. . . .

*SOURCE: From a Mobil Oil Corporation Advertisement, *New York Times*, August 14, 1980, page A 23. Copyright ©1981 by Mobil Corporation.

The same process, working in reverse, would apply if Zipthon prices were rising faster than the rate of interest. Investors would switch from bonds to Zipthon, and with more Zipthon held for investment rather than released for current consumption, current prices of Zipthon would rise. At the same time the abundance of future stocks would be increased and thus expected future prices would fall.

Following this fundamental principle about the pricing of a scarce resource with fixed extraction costs, let us see what will happen to the price of $100 worth of Zipthon over the course of, say, four years. We have the following pattern of Zipthon prices:

INITIAL DATE	ONE YEAR LATER	TWO YEARS LATER	THREE YEARS LATER	FOUR YEARS LATER
$100	$110	$121	$133.10	$146.41

These prices follow from the fact that $110 is 10 percent higher than $100, $121 is 10 percent higher than $110, and so on. What is to be noted is that because of the compounding effect, the dollar quantity of the price increase is greater and greater each year. Zipthon rises in value by $10 in the first year, $11 in the second year, $12.10 in the third, $13.31 in the fourth, and so on indefinitely. Thus we conclude:

The basic law of pricing of a depletable resource tells us that as its stocks are used up its price in a perfectly competitive market will rise every year by greater and greater dollar amounts.

Notice that we have been able to make these predictions about the price of Zipthon without any knowledge about the supply of Zipthon or consumer demand for it. This is really remarkable. But if we want to go on to determine what will happen to the consumption of Zipthon—the rate at which its inventory will be used up—we do need to know something about supply and demand.

In Figure 36–1(a) there is a demand curve for Zipthon, *DD*, which shows the amount people want to use up *per year* at various price levels. On the vertical axis we show how the price must rise from year to year in the pattern we have just calculated—from $100 per ton in the initial year to $110 in the next year, and so on. Because of the negative slope of the demand curve it follows that each year consumption of Zipthon will fall. That is, *if there is no shift in the demand curve*, consumption will fall from 100,000 tons initially, to 95,000 tons in the next year, and so on.

But in reality such demand curves rarely do stay still. As the economy grows and population and per-capita incomes increase, demand curves can be expected to shift outward. And there is every reason to believe that this has been true of the demands for most scarce resources. Shifts in the demand curve will naturally tend to increase consumption, thereby offsetting at least part of the reduction in quantity demanded that results from rising prices. Nevertheless, it remains true

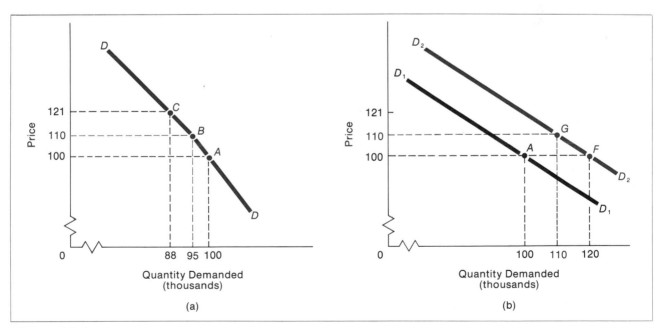

Figure 36–1
CONSUMPTION OVER TIME OF A DEPLETABLE RESOURCE
The price of the resource must rise, year after year (from $100 to $110 to $121, and so on). If the demand curve does not shift [part (a)], quantity demanded will be reduced every year. Even if the demand curve does shift outward [as in part (b)], the increasing price will keep any rise in quantity demanded lower than it would otherwise have been.

that rising prices do help to cut back consumption growth relative to what it would have been if price had remained constant. In Figure 36–1(b) we depict an outward shift in demand from curve D_1D_1 in the initial period to curve D_2D_2 a year later. If price had remained constant at the initial value, $100 per ton, quantity consumed per year would have risen from 100,000 tons to 120,000 tons. But since, in accord with the basic principle, price must rise to $110, quantity demanded will only increase to 110,000 tons—which is smaller than 120,000 tons. Thus, whether or not the demand curve shifts, we conclude:

The ever-rising prices that accompany increasing scarcity of a depletable resource discourage consumption (encourage conservation). Even if quantity demanded is growing, it will grow less rapidly than if prices were not rising.

Resource Prices in the Twentieth Century

How do the facts match up with this theoretical analysis? As we will see now, their correspondence is very poor indeed. Figure 36–2 shows the behavior of the prices of three of the metals in our previous tables: lead, zinc, and tin, since the beginning of the twentieth century. These figures are all expressed in real terms; that is, they have all been recalculated in terms of dollars of constant purchasing power to eliminate the effects of inflation or deflation.

What we find is that instead of rising steadily, as the theory might have led us to expect, two of them actually remained amazingly constant. Between 1900 and 1940 lead and zinc prices actually rose more slowly than the general price level while tin prices just about kept pace with general inflation between 1900 and 1945. More recently the price of tin has gone up substantially faster than other prices—in 1979 its relative price was nearly twice as high as it was in 1970. But even during the 1970s zinc and lead prices rose only slightly faster than prices in general.

Figure 36–3 shows similar figures for the relative price of crude oil in the United States since 1947. It gives price at the wellhead, that is, at the point of production, with no transportation cost included. The data show that in 1973 the price of oil was actually about 8 percent lower, relative to other prices, than it was in 1948. Only since 1973 has it been rising faster than prices in general. There are even more peculiar cases. From 1923 (the earliest date for which figures are available) to 1980, the price of magnesium actually fell relative to other prices by nearly 84 percent.

How does one explain this strange behavior of the prices of finite resources, which surely are being used up, even if only gradually? Have the laws of supply and demand somehow broken down? Actually, what these figures indicate is that reality is much more complicated than our simple analytic model, and that sometimes the complications grow so extreme that prices behave very differently from what the simple theory predicts. While many things can interfere with the price patterns that the theory led us to expect, we will mention only four:

1. *Unexpected discoveries of reserves whose existence was previously not suspected.* If we were to stumble upon a huge and easily accessible reserve of Ziphton, which came as a complete surprise to the market, the price of Ziphton would obviously fall. This is illustrated in Figure 36–4, where we see that people originally believed the available supply curve to be that represented by curve S_1S_1. The discovery of the new Ziphton reserves leads them to recognize that the supply is much larger than they had thought

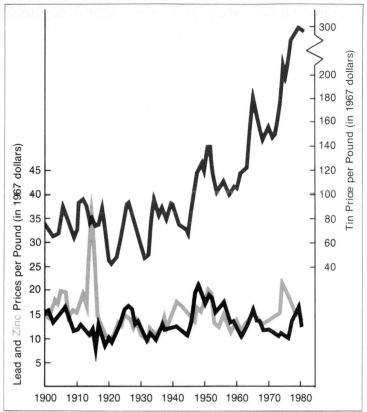

Figure 36–2
PRICES OF LEAD, TIN, AND ZINC 1900–1980, IN 1967 DOLLARS[1]
Note that these prices have not been rising steadily even though all three minerals are gradually being used up.
SOURCE: *Historical Statistics of the U.S.* and *Metal Statistics*, 1981, American Metal Market, Fairchild Publications.
[1] As deflated by the wholesale commodity price index (all commodities).

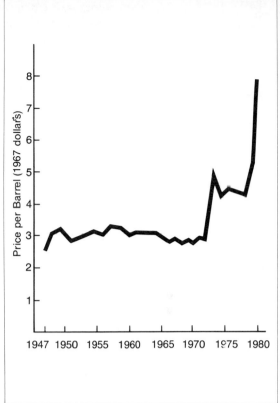

Figure 36–3
PRICE OF OIL AT THE WELLHEAD 1947–1980, IN 1967 DOLLARS
Note the long period of near constancy in real oil prices.
SOURCE: *Historical Statistics of the U.S.*, *Monthly Energy Review* and *Minerals Year Book*.
[1] As deflated by the wholesale commodity price index (all commodities).

(curve S_2S_2). Like any outward shift in a supply curve, this can be expected to cause a fall in price. A clear historical example was the discovery of gold and silver in Central and South America by the Spaniards in the sixteenth century. This led to sharp and substantial drops in the prices of these precious metals in Europe, and was a source of major economic problems for the Tudor monarchs.

2. ***The invention of new methods of mining or refining may significantly reduce extraction costs.*** This, too, can lead to a rightward shift in the supply curve as it becomes profitable for suppliers to deliver a larger quantity at any given price. The situation is therefore again represented by a diagram like Figure 36–4. Only it is now a reduction in cost, not a new discovery of reserves, that shifts the supply curve to the right.

3. ***A government subsidy.*** From the point of view of the supplier, a government subsidy is exactly the same as a reduction in mining or processing costs—either technological improvement or a handout from the government will decrease his cost per ton of supplying the resource. Thus the supply curve will shift to the right (from S_1S_1 to S_2S_2 in Figure 36–4) and the price will fall.

Figure 36–4

PRICE EFFECTS OF A DISCOVERY OF ADDITIONAL RESERVES
A discovery causes a rightward shift in the supply curve of the resource. That is so because the cost to suppliers of any given quantity of the resource is reduced by the discovery, so it will pay them to supply a larger quantity at any given price. This must lead to a price fall (from P_1 to P_2).

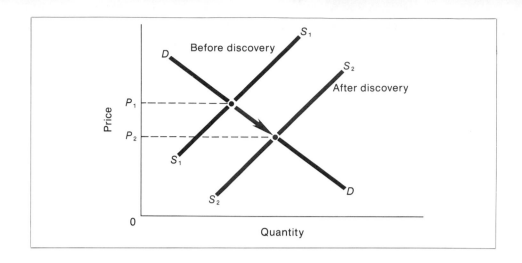

4. *Price controls can also hold prices down or can actually decrease them.* A legislature can pass a law prohibiting the sale of the resource at a price higher than P^* (see Figure 36–5). Sometimes this works, though not always, for in many cases an illegal black market emerges, where very high prices are charged more or less secretly. But even where it does work it causes problems. Since the objective is to make the legal ceiling price, P^*, lower than the market equilibrium price, P, at price P^* quantity demanded (five million tons in the figure) will be higher than the free-market level (four million tons). Similarly, we may expect that now quantity supplied (two million tons in the figure) will be less than its free-market level. Thus, as always happens in these cases, the quantity supplied is insufficient to match the quantity demanded—a shortage emerges.

Many economists believe that this is exactly what happened after 1971 when President Nixon decided to experiment with price controls. It was just at this time that the economy experienced a sudden plague of shortages and we seemed to be "running out of nearly everything." But the shortages apparently were attributable to the controls, not to anything happening to resource supplies or the productive process. And after price controls ended in 1974, most of the "shortages" disappeared.

Figure 36–5

CONTROLS ON THE PRICE OF A RESOURCE
By law, price is kept to P^* which is below the equilibrium price, P. This reduces quantity supplied from four to two million tons and raises quantity demanded from four to five million tons. A shortage measured by length AB, or three million tons, is the result.

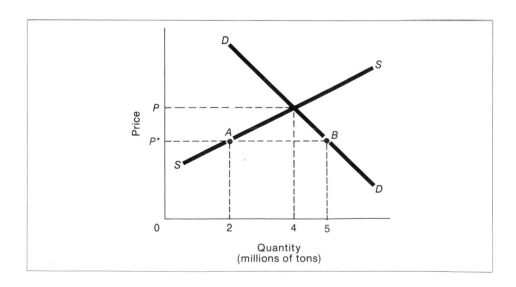

Each of the examples of minerals whose prices did not rise can be explained by one or more of these factors. For example, both zinc and magnesium have benefited from technological changes that lowered extraction costs. In the case of the latter, the process that turns the mineral into ingots has grown far more efficient than it was in the 1920s. The case of lead is quite different. There, some new mines in Missouri turned out to hold abundant quantities of ore that was much easier to extract and much cheaper to refine than what had been available before. This was apparently enough to keep the price of lead from rising very fast. Obviously, events in reality are more complex than a naïve reading of theoretical models might lead us to believe.

Yet, despite these influences, which have postponed the price rises in depletable resources predicted by the theory, both logic and evidence indicate that in the long run supply and demand must win out. As a resource really becomes scarce and costly to obtain, its free-market price must ultimately rise, and so must its actual price, unless government interferes.

The Messy Story of Oil Prices

The case of oil must be singled out both because of its critical importance for our economy and because it illustrates how different the real world can be from the pure supply–demand model of perfect competition. Yet we will see that even with almost constant government interference and control by a powerful cartel (that is, a monopolistic association of suppliers), the forces of supply and demand continue to play a crucial role. Indeed, we will see that the cartel succeeded not *in spite of* the supply–demand mechanism, but *because* it was able to use that mechanism. The big price rises occurred when the supply curve was shifted either by accident or by deliberate acts.

The great gasoline shortage of 1973 began a seemingly endless spiral of price increases that awakened Americans to the fact that a cheap and abundant supply of energy was no longer a fact of life. What had been a buyers' market suddenly became a sellers' market when the oil-producing nations learned how to gain control of the incredibly valuable hydrocarbon resources that lay below their land.

Traditionally, the oil industry had been virtually controlled by seven large companies, which made price and production decisions, negotiated terms separately with each of the oil-producing countries, and extracted the oil from the ground. Their power was great, not only because of their technological capabilities but because of their control over the markets. In 1951 when Mohammed Mossadegh, Prime Minister of Iran, tried to seize the assets of British Petroleum, the "seven sisters," acting together, simply increased production in more docile areas, refused to buy Iranian oil, and waited for his government to be overthrown.

Throughout the 1950s, a period of tremendous industrial development, the world market price of oil remained low, enabling oil to drive out many competing energy sources. Both the world's output and energy consumption tripled during this decade, and oil became very nearly the unchallenged source of power. During the 1960s it apparently became increasingly difficult for production to keep up with the burgeoning demand, a sure sign that prices were being kept artificially low.

The oil-producing countries sought to overcome the oil companies' domination. After some earlier abortive attempts, Iran, Iraq, Kuwait, Saudi Arabia, and Venezuela formed the Organization of Petroleum Exporting Countries (OPEC) in Baghdad on September 14, 1960. Little notice was taken, but a pattern of negotiation between the oil companies and OPEC rather than with the individual countries emerged. In 1968 OPEC adopted a "Declaratory Statement of Petroleum Policy in Member Countries" which, though almost ignored at the time, sought to relegate the companies to a technical role, and assumed the right to set prices. A very important precedent was set in 1970 when Muammar al-Qaddafi, President of Libya, bypassed the process of negotiation and opened an offensive to gain control of oil resources in his country. He applied pressure by the use of production cutbacks and threatened shutdowns against individual companies, beginning with the weaker independents. Working in Libya's favor were the growing costs of finding and extracting non-Middle East oil, particularly of the low-sulfur variety found in Libya, and the growing aversion on the part of the governments of oil-producing countries to political interference. Unlike the Mossadegh incident, no British cruiser appeared in the Persian Gulf. Qaddafi achieved a price rise of 30 cents a barrel, and increased the tax rate from 50 percent to 55 percent. The other oil-producing countries, having remained on the sidelines throughout the confrontation, demanded and won similar concessions under the Teheran Agreement of February 13, 1971.

By 1973, partly through extensive expropriation by the OPEC countries, the role of the oil companies had been reduced to that of technical contractors. The OPEC countries now imposed massive price increases. The price of crude oil rose 12 percent in June 1973, 66 percent in October 1973, and doubled in January 1974.

The immediate cause of these price increases was the attempt by eleven oil-producing countries to punish the United States and Holland for their support of Israel in October 1973. The Arab countries announced a production cutback of 5 percent, and an embargo of sales to those countries, thus causing an inward shift of the supply curve and a sharp price rise. The public, waiting in mile-long gas lines, had time to ruminate on the new look of world energy: its rising cost and the fact that a high proportion of the supply to the industrialized world was controlled by powers that did not necessarily wish them well.

For a while thereafter, OPEC price increases became more moderate, roughly keeping pace with world inflation. Then suddenly, in January 1979, the government of the Shah of Iran toppled and was replaced by the Islamic Republic. Oil exports dropped sharply, again shifting the supply curve inward. Predictably, the price of oil shot up, rising from $12 a barrel in the beginning of 1979 to more than $25 at the end of that year. But even in the presence of the cartel, forces of supply and demand beyond its control played a part. In 1980 and 1981 widespread recession in the industrialized world together with measures to induce conservation led to cutbacks in demand for imported oil and the world price actually dropped. By mid-1981 oil consumption outside the Communist countries had fallen to 46 million barrels per day from 49.5 million a year earlier.

This, then, is the story of the *world* oil market in the postwar period. Inside the United States, meanwhile, domestic policy affected the oil market in a variety of ways. For a while the price of crude oil was kept artifically *high*. The competition of foreign crude might have driven down the price of domestic oil had not Congress in 1959 passed the Mandatory Oil Import Program, which kept the level of crude oil imports to 12.2 percent of domestic production in order to protect domestic industry and, presumably, to decrease U.S. dependence on foreign oil. Beginning about 1968 the major oil companies found themselves challenged by independent refiners in a series of "price wars" while the independents introduced new marketing ideas such as self-service gas stations. In consequence, the domestic profits of the major oil companies fell and this may have contributed to a lag in construction of new refinery capacity in the United States—which later increased the severity of our fuel problems.

Although the price of crude oil in the United States had already been influenced by government policy for a considerable period, in 1973 Congress adopted the Emergency Petroleum Allocation Act which imposed a three-tiered program of price controls. "Old oil" (about 35 percent of 1979 U.S. production), that is, oil from sources in production before 1971, was permitted a price no higher than about $5.25 per barrel. "New oil" (also about 35 percent of U.S. output in 1979) was permitted a price of about $13 per barrel at the wellhead. The remainder, called "uncontrolled oil," came from Alaska, from the Naval Petroleum Reserve, and from wells producing fewer than 10 barrels per day. It was priced at the free-market level, which in 1979 amounted to about $18.50 per barrel. On the average, these rules kept the U.S. price about 30 percent below the world price.

Obviously, as in Figure 36–5, this artificially low price stimulated U.S. consumption and depressed U.S. production. It did not, however, automatically create a shortage because the difference could be made up by imports—which rose from 3.5 million barrels per day in 1970 to about 8.3 million in 1979. While this increase was not all attributable to the price controls, that program seemed clearly to be deepening our dependence on imports. Accordingly, in 1979 President Carter undertook the gradual elimination of these controls, which were completely eliminated by 1981. Decontrol, which is expected to cut imports by about 600,000 barrels per day by 1985 (5 percent of anticipated imports), was accompanied by a complex Windfall Profits Tax, intended to gather up some of the profits that the oil producers would otherwise have reaped.

In sum, we have not had anything like a free market in oil, though with decontrol something like a free market has recently been restored. Let us consider next what such a free market is likely to do.

The Free Market and Resource Depletion

Popular views of the process of depletion of a vital resource envision a scenario in which consumption grows year after year and stocks of the item dwindle as a result until, one day, quantity supplied can no longer keep up with quantity demanded. From then on, the nation faces a history of steady shortfalls, with rationing or chaos the inevitable result. Economists pay little attention to such scenarios. Though it seems implausible to anyone who has not studied economics, it is nevertheless true that:

In a free market, quantity demanded can never exceed quantity supplied, even if a finite resource is undergoing rapid depletion. The reason is simple: In any free market, quantity demanded must always equal quantity supplied, for price will automatically adjust to eliminate any difference between them.

In fact, there have been cases of real shortages in the past. For example, twice during the 1970s the quantities of gasoline supplied were, in many parts of the United States, lower than the quantities demanded, and chaos did indeed result. There were long lines of cars at those gas stations that remained open, and huge amounts of petroleum and time were wasted in the process as the cars inched forward (sometimes for hours) toward the gas pumps. During World War II, meat, sugar, and other commodities were in short supply, and there was a period in the 1970s when supplies of paper, copper, and other commodities were inadequate to meet demand. But in every such case there were regulations or laws which prohibited full adjustment of prices. In a sense, then, it was these price regulations, and not any disappearance of resources, that were responsible for the shortages.

In theory, any shortage—any excess of quantity demanded over quantity supplied—must be artifical; that is, it must be ascribed to a decision to prevent the price mechanism from doing its job.

To say that the cause is artifical, of course, does not settle the basic issue—whether freedom of price adjustments is desirable when resource depletion is underway, or whether interference with the pricing process is justified. We will see that there are, in fact, valid grounds on which to question the desirability of completely unrestricted freedom of pricing in such circumstances. However, there are many economists who believe that this is another of those cases in which the disease—shortages and the resulting dislocations in the economy—is far worse than the cure—deregulation of prices. They hold that the general public is misguided in its clamor against the rising prices that must ultimately accompany depletion of a resource, and that people are mistaken in regarding these price rises as the problem, when in fact they are part of the cure.

It is, of course, easy to understand why no consumer loves a price rise. And it is also easy to understand why many consumers ascribe any such price rise to a plot—to a conspiracy by greedy suppliers who somehow deliberately arrange shortages in order to force prices upward. Sometimes, this view is even correct. For example, the members of OPEC have openly and frankly undertaken to influence the flow of oil in order to increase the price they receive for it. But it is important to recognize from the principles of supply and demand that when a resource grows scarce its price will tend to rise automatically, even without any conspiracies or plots.

Let us first see how economists can possibly say that rising prices for scarce resources are good for the economy. Then we will turn to some valid reservations about the desirability of an unfettered market solution.

On the Virtues of Rising Prices

Rising prices help control the process of resource depletion in three basic ways:

1. They discourage consumption and waste and provide an inducement for conservation.
2. They stimulate more efficient use of the resource by industry, providing incentives for the employment of processes that are more sparing in their use of the resource or that use substitute resources.
3. They encourage innovation—the discovery of other, more abundant resources that can do the job and of new techniques that permit these other resources to be used economically.

Let us examine each of these a bit more carefully.

It used to be said that consumer demand for oil was highly *inelastic*—that prices would never make a significant dent in consumption of petroleum. Recent events seem to have proved otherwise. With rising fuel prices people have begun to insulate their homes, to keep home temperatures lower, to take fewer shopping trips, and to buy smaller automobiles. All of this has had striking results. From 1973 to 1978 oil imports increased over 33 percent, but in 1980 imports actually fell more than 10 percent below those of 1979, and by 1981 there was even talk of an oil glut. In part, the reduced demand was undoubtedly attributable to recession in the United States; but observers have concluded that reactions to rising prices also played a substantial role. As a matter of fact, energy consumption as a percent of real GNP has fallen steadily since 1973, by about 1.5 percent per year. Moreover, in the long run, we can expect even more demand adjust-ment—that is, the long-run demand curve for oil is probably more elastic than the short-run curve. As the nation's fleet of cars wears out they will all gradually be replaced by vehicles that economize on fuel. New homes will be built more snugly to save on heat, and they will be located closer to the workplace to save on fuel in transportation. Another piece of evidence indicating how much differ-ence price can make is fuel consumption in Europe. There, fuel taxes have long habituated the public to gasoline prices of $1.50 to $3 per gallon, and fuel consumption per capita is over 45 percent less than it is in the United States, even in countries like Sweden with its harsh climate and its great driving distances.[2]

The second way in which a price increase helps to conserve a scarce resource is through its effect on industrial usage. Like a final consumer, a business firm can economize on its use of a resource. It can use more fuel-efficient means of transportation and more insulation. It can locate its new plants in ways that reduce the need for transportation. And it can substitute labor and other inputs for scarce resources. The use of a pick and shovel involves the employment of more labor to save the fuel that might have been used by a bulldozer. Farmers who gather manure save the fuel necessary to produce chemical fertilizers. There is evidence that such substitutions are already occurring. Warehouses that used to have open loading bays have installed doors to keep in heat, hiring people to open and close them. Because of rising gas prices, ranchers in the southwest reportedly are hiring additional cowhands to drive cattle on foot instead of carrying them on trucks. The examples can be multiplied indefinitely.

Finally, rising prices help to slow the disappearance of a resource by stimulating the production of substitutes and even by inducing more production of the resource itself. The last statement is paradoxical—If a resource is finite how can more be produced? Certainly it can be extracted and sold faster, but that only hastens the process of depletion. How can we get *more* of a *finite* resource? Of course, we cannot. But rising prices will make it feasible to use repositories of the resource that otherwise would have been considered too inaccessible and simply not worth the effort. It has recently proved profitable, for example, to reopen old oil wells using expensive procedures to force out substantial amounts of petro-leum which had been abandoned because they did not flow out unaided. Producers are now considering extraction of natural gas from "tight sands"—rocklike formations from which it was formerly too expensive to remove the gas. Similarly, the extraction of oil from shale has long been talked about, but only higher prices will make it feasible.

And higher prices of the vanishing resource also stimulate research and development which lead to the emergence of substitute products. It is high oil prices that will transform solar energy, wind energy, and biomass energy from romantic notions, which cynics can deride as impractical, into effective sources of fuel which may some day make substantial contributions to the economy's energy flows. At the oil prices in effect during the 1960s these sources simply could not compete. Those who favor the use of solar, wind, and other similar sources for other reasons are likely to argue that when the nation faces a major crisis mere unprofitability should not be permitted to stand in the way of their use. But we will see later in the chapter that more than "mere money" is at issue—for unprofitability is an indication that it may not yet be the time to introduce such innovative processes.

A final word on the price mechanism and resource conservation is in order. One often hears about the rape of our natural resources by greedy owners who

[2] J. Darmstadler, J. Dunkerley, and J. Alterman, *How Industrial Societies Use Energy*, Resources for the Future, Washington, 1977, page 5.

rush to exchange them for profits without any thought for the needs of the future. But the price mechanism has built-in incentives to prevent this from happening. We have seen how a resource's price can be expected to rise automatically as its stocks dwindle. Obviously, when the price rise is sufficiently rapid it becomes more profitable to leave more of it underground for future extraction rather than to sell it now at today's lower prices. That, indeed, is one of the things some of the OPEC countries may now be doing and one of the reasons oil prices have risen so rapidly. One may legitimately object to this for many reasons, but surely *not* on the grounds that oil supplies are being squandered by excessive and irresponsible rates of extraction.

Freedom of pricing of a dwindling resource induces conservation by consumers and by industry; it encourages the introduction of substitute products; and it induces moderation in rates of extraction by the owners of their sources.

As we have seen, virtually any absolute shortage—a case in which consumers simply cannot lay their hands on the quantities of resources they want and are willing to pay for—must be attributable to interference with the price mechanism. Such interference does not result from the whims of politicians and bureaucrats. Rising resource prices that accompany depletion are extremely likely to bring demands for price controls. And politicians are extremely likely to accede to these demands. Those who believe the price mechanism can do no wrong will interpret this as a misguided attempt to undermine the market's painful cure, and point out that government interferences are likely to worsen the disease. The question is whether there is anything rational to be said on the other side; and the answer is that there certainly is.

Valid Objections to Price Increases for Disappearing Resources

Part of the problem with the scenario that we have just outlined is that it idealizes the economy. As we have seen, the marketplace in which the prices of resources are determined is not the free and perfectly competitive one of pure theory. Its suppliers are often large and sometimes have monopoly power, as the story of OPEC illustrates dramatically. Taxes and other government measures affect prices directly and indirectly.

Though the price mechanism does encourage suppliers to save resources for the future, it is by no means clear that the welfare of future generations is given adequate weight. There are those who believe that the price mechanism does not induce sufficient conservation for the future, arguing that risks and inadequate foresight by resource owners induce them to dump unjustifiably large amounts on the market in an effort to take advantage of the bird in hand. Others argue that the very opposite is true—that too much is held back from current use in an effort to extract monopoly profits, and that innovation can be relied upon to protect the interests of future generations, who are in any case likely to be far better off than we are. Whichever conclusion seems the more plausible—that the market tends to hold back too much for the future, or too little—it is clear that one can have little confidence that free markets in the real world will induce exactly the optimal rate of conservation.

These objections to leaving resource conservation entirely to the price mechanism may perhaps seem a little abstract and theoretical, but there are two other objections which are much more concrete.

First, many object to the way in which large price increases redistribute incomes. It is widely believed, for example, that increases in the price of energy resources inevitably favor rich consumers relative to poor ones. Both are clearly hurt by higher prices, but the poor cannot readily afford to switch to smaller, more fuel-efficient cars or to insulate their homes or to move closer to work, while the rich can do all these things more easily. Hence, it is argued, the poor are hit harder by a rise in oil prices. As usual, in reality matters are not so straightforward. Who is hurt most depends, for example, on whether the poor, the middle class, or the rich spend the largest share of their incomes on fuel. If Ellen spends 20 percent of her income on fuel while Sabrina spends only 10 percent, a doubling of fuel prices will hurt Ellen much more than Sabrina. Evidence on this point suggests that a fuel price rise may hurt the middle class more than it does the poor, though the issue is far from settled.

What is clear, however, is that a rise in resource prices adds enormously to the incomes of those who own the wells and the mines and to the companies who distribute and sell the resources. Between 1981 and 1985, decontrol of oil has been estimated to promise something on the order of $12 billion a year in additional revenues to domestic oil producers alone.[3] The desirability of such a dramatic change in the distribution of incomes is a very real question, to say the least. It was partly this concern that in 1980 led to President Carter's badly misnamed "Windfall Profits Tax." This tax, which is basically a rather complicated excise tax on oil, is intended to take away at least part of the profits that would otherwise accrue to U.S. oil companies as a result of the elimination of controls on domestic oil prices.

A second very real concern about rising resource prices is that such price rises can have serious effects on overall inflation. Particularly when the economy is already having inflationary problems, rising costs of resources can inflame expectations of future price rises, leading everyone to push harder for price and wage increases in a desperate effort to stay ahead of the game. At the same time, such price increases may inhibit production and depress the economy. We are referring here to the phenomenon of *stagflation* caused by restrictions in aggregate supply—a subject that has been discussed in earlier chapters. Figure 36–6 reproduces Figure 9–7 and shows how the rising costs of energy caused an

[3]"Decontrol of Domestic Oil Prices: An Overview," Congressional Budget Office, 1979, page 28.

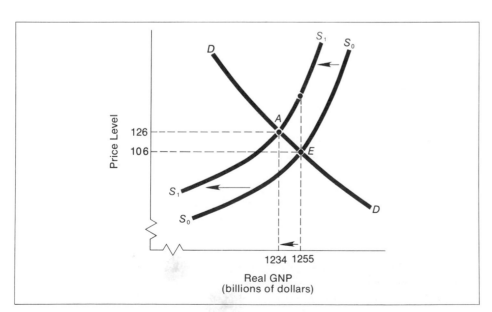

Figure 36–6
STAGFLATION FROM A SUPPLY SHOCK
If the aggregate supply curve shifts inward from S_0S_0 to S_1S_1 and the aggregate demand curve, DD, does not shift, equilibrium will move from point E to point A. Output will fall while prices rise.

inward shift in the aggregate supply curve from S_0S_0 (black curve) in 1973 to S_1S_1 (blue curve) in 1975, leading simultaneously to a rise in the price level (from 106 to 126) and to a fall in real GNP (from $1255 billion to $1234 billion). Between 1982 and 1984, decontrol of oil prices in the United States has been estimated to be likely to contribute between 0.1 and 0.3 percent per year to the rate of inflation, to reduce the rate of growth of real output perhaps as much as 0.2 percent, and to contribute as much as 0.2 percentage points to the unemployment rate.[4] While these figures are not catastrophic, they certainly do not lead us to view uninhibited price increases with equanimity.

Price increases can be particularly damaging when they are sharp and sudden rather than slow and gradual. Much of the damage to our economy caused by the fourfold increase in the price of oil in 1973–1974 and the doubling in 1979 is undoubtedly attributable to their abruptness. Oil prices, as we have seen, were held down for over 20 years and then, in several great bounds, caught up with and then ran ahead of the general rate of inflation. Why is a given rise in price likely to be worse if it occurs suddenly in two months rather than gradually over 20 years? Partly, because it is a much greater psychological shock, but mainly because it catches consumers and firms by surprise. Unlike a gradual price rise, a sudden jump in the price of oil provides no warning to decision makers and gives them no chance to make appropriate adjustments in their plans. People who did not know oil prices were about to jump precipitately may, just before the price rise, have bought a home far from work, bought a gas-guzzling car, or started to build a factory far from its market. This could all have been avoided by a gradual price change, which would have made the situation clear to everyone in advance.

The Special Problem of Oil

Those economists who believe the price system can do a good job of allocating depletable resources generally take the view that government intervention in resource markets is only likely to make things worse. However, even some economists who hold this opinion are ready to concede that the case of oil is different, and that some government measures are appropriate in this case. Several things do, indeed, make the case of petroleum very special:

1. The OPEC nations seem determined to use this resource as a political weapon, seeking to dictate foreign policy to the United States and other industrialized countries.
2. The suppliers of oil do not constitute a competitive industry; rather, they have formed a cartel that has proved very effective in manipulating the price of their commodity and making unorganized consumers vulnerable to exploitation.
3. The oil-exporting countries have experienced tremendous export surpluses, often earning far more from their exports than they spend on their imports. In 1974 alone, OPEC acquired a surplus of investable funds amounting to some $71 billion dollars. This surplus then declined for a while as the relative value of OPEC imports rose, but by 1980 it had risen again to more than $100 billion. Outflows of funds from the United States and other countries to OPEC continue to rise. In 1979 the United States alone paid some $60 billion for its oil purchases. Such enormous sums seeking outlets for investment have caused significant fluctuations in financial markets. That is, the rising price of oil has posed a serious threat to international money and investment markets simply because of the sheer magnitude of the amounts involved. If, for

[4]"Decontrol of Domestic Oil Prices, An Overview," Congressional Budget Office, 1979, page 45.

example, OPEC investors were suddenly to pull their money out of the United States and to pour it into Japan instead (or vice versa), the resulting financial disturbances in both countries could be monumental.

These three problems—the threat of political blackmail, the presence of a cartel with monopoly power, and the threat of disruption of the world's financial system by OPEC's huge surpluses—all mean that the oil issue is no ordinary problem of resource depletion, and that extraordinary measures are at least worth considering.

Is Energy Independence a Rational Goal?

One early reaction to the threat of political blackmail—the threat of interruption of oil flows to the United States if its foreign policy were to displease the oil suppliers seriously, as it did in 1973—led to a proposal by U.S. politicians that we embark on a policy of "energy independence." If this means total elimination of reliance on imports, it seems to be a hopeless undertaking. The Congressional Budget Office has projected that by 1985 U.S. oil demand will reach 19.5 million barrels per day, and that only 8 million of these can be supplied from domestic sources. By 1990 these figures are expected to become worse, with the demand figure approaching 20 million and the domestic supply figure falling to 7.5 million. There is virtually no chance of a reduction in demand or an increase in domestic supply sufficient to close this tremendous gap. Complete decontrol of oil prices is expected only to reduce demand by 200,000 barrels per day and to increase domestic production by 400,000 barrels per day in 1985, together closing only 5 percent of the projected 11.5 million barrel gap.[5]

Obviously, reductions in oil consumption in the United States will help to decrease the pressures that accompany huge oil imports. We have already seen how rising prices can contribute to achievement of this goal, and later we will discuss other measures that may help to curb consumption. It may seem on first thought that an increase in domestic oil production would also help matters, but here things are not exactly what they seem.

Every increase in the flow of oil from domestic sources into the U.S. market helps to use up U.S. oil reserves. It therefore increases the nation's vulnerability to future exploitation by the cartel, to political blackmail, and, in particular, to the threat of interruption of foreign supplies.

Thus, there is a dangerous fallacy in the argument that the United States will be helped by incentives to increase domestic oil production. It is an argument which, naturally, has been espoused vociferously by the oil companies and, as we will see later, it is not *altogether* fallacious. Of course, it will help the U.S. position if effort is devoted to the *discovery* of more domestic reserves—but only if that effort is successful and if those reserves are not quickly used up. But the perils of increased consumption of oil from U.S. sources are not generally recognized by the public, the newspapers, or our political leaders. This shows, incidentally, that if the Windfall Profits Tax does discourage increased oil output from domestic sources, as the oil companies claim, that may not be quite as bad as it sounds.

However, this discussion does suggest one other measure that may be appropriate. This is the accumulation of a *strategic reserve*, an inventory of oil stored by the U.S. government that would be available if imports were interrupted. Such a program has, in fact, been adopted, though it has not been carried

[5]"The World Oil Market in the 1980s," Congressional Budget Office, 1980, pages 11, 14, and 25.

out very vigorously. In 1977 Congress enacted legislation authorizing the storage of oil, and an inventory goal of one billion barrels by 1985 was subsequently adopted. In fact, by 1980 the actual reserve had grown only to 226 million barrels. Part of the reason for the lag was foreign pressure. Saudi Arabia in particular expressed its displeasure at the oil reserve plan, and offered to keep its rate of production high as an inducement for the United States not to pursue the program vigorously. Moreover, as long as quantity demanded was increasing and oil prices were rising rapidly, the government was understandably reluctant to withdraw large quantities from the market to put into inventories. In addition, the cost of holding oil inventories is high. The construction of storage facilities alone is a very substantial undertaking. While the costs are clear, the benefits are hard to measure. The question is whether the costs are justified by the degree of insurance the program can provide against the threat of cutoff of foreign supplies and against vulnerability to pressures by foreign governments. And the answer is not obvious.

Other Government Programs

What other government measures have been suggested? There are many, but three in particular merit discussion: (1) A tariff on imported oil, (2) fuel rationing, and (3) subsidies to such innovative energy sources as oil shale conversion, wind energy, and nuclear fusion.

Tariffs. Most economists who believe the price mechanism is the best instrument for the job favor the tariff approach. A tariff, as will be discussed in the next chapter, is simply a tax on imports of some commodity, in this case on oil purchased from outside the United States. If adopted, it would raise energy prices even higher than they would go in a completely free market, thereby even further encouraging both conservation and the search for new energy sources. It has yet another advantage. Unlike an ordinary rise in market price, the potentially huge revenues from an oil tariff will flow into the U.S. Treasury rather than into the pockets of OPEC suppliers. Of course, a tariff may add to inflationary pressures, and will increase the profits of domestic oil producers, who do not pay it. These problems and the political unpopularity of any price rise led Congress to prevent President Carter in 1980 from imposing even a very moderate tariff on imports— one amounting to about 10 cents per gallon of gasoline. Economists believe that the appropriate tariff is probably many times this amount, but the political prospects for such a program do not seem promising. Yet a fairly comparable measure, a heavy tax on consumption, does seem to work in Europe where in most countries gasoline is taxed far more than a dollar per gallon.

Rationing. We turn next to fuel rationing, an arrangement under which consumers are simply prevented from consuming more than certain amounts determined by law or by regulatory agencies. For example, it may simply be decreed that each driver can get a maximum of 10 gallons of gasoline per week. If fuel prices are not permitted to rise to their free-market levels, there may indeed turn out to be no alternative to rationing. For, as we have already noted, if price is below its free-market level there must normally be an excess of quantity demanded over quantity supplied—a shortage. To prevent total chaos and unfairness in distributing the available supplies among the consumers who clamor for it, some sort of rationing arrangement must be adopted.

Where a resource is scarce there are only three methods known for its allocation among consumers: (1) free-market pricing, which makes quantity demanded equal to quantity supplied, (2) rationing, and (3) total chaos.

Ordinary rationing arrangements, which normally have been used only during wartime, have a history that offers little encourgement for their use today. Elaborate bureaucracies were set up to determine what exceptions should be made. At first, doctors and farmers were given extra gas, then taxi drivers and delivery people and so forth, until, finally, almost everyone became an exception. Black markets arose on which people bought extra supplies illegally at tremendous prices. The entire system grew rigid, cumbersome, and almost unworkable.

Economists who support a rationing approach have therefore proposed a variant of the rationing process which they feel will work better. They want everyone to get the same number of ration coupons, with every coupon worth, say one gallon of fuel. Then a legal market (a "white market") in fuel coupons would be established. If Sabrina has more coupons than she needs, she can then sell them on this market; and Ellen, who needs additional coupons, can then buy them. None of the exceptions that bedevil ordinary rationing schemes will have to be made. Moreover, unlike a rise in price, which may turn out to be a burden upon the poor, a rationing program with a white market may actually help them, since if they are careful in their use of fuel they can actually make money by selling their surplus ration coupons.

For the moment, the political prospects for a rationing program to cut down U.S. fuel consumption are very poor. Only with great difficulty was President Carter in 1980 able to get Congress to approve standby authority to inaugurate a rationing program, and then only if a very serious shortage were to develop.

Subsidies for Alternative Energy Sources. Since the politicians are unwilling to support either a tariff or rationing, they have been attracted by a third possibility: a program of massive subsidies for the development of innovative energy sources. It is proposed to pour tens of billions of dollars into the encouragement of shale oil production, nuclear fusion, solar energy, and other unconventional energy sources. This is an attractive approach but it, too, has its drawbacks. A new energy source uses up energy directly and indirectly in the research and manufacturing processes necessary to produce it. For example, it is reported that at just one of the experimental sites studying the fusion process, more electricity is used every day than is used by a city of 250,000 people. It takes tremendous amounts of energy to make the solar cells that are used in many solar energy devices, and to make the steel that is used in the machinery that will extract oil from shale. Unfortunately, then, there is a very real possibility that a new process will actually use up more energy than it produces! Some economists have gone so far as to suggest that any process that needs a subsidy in order to be viable economically should be suspected of using more energy directly and indirectly than it provides. The basis for this concern is rather technical and cannot be described here, but it certainly suggests that a program of subsidies to new energy sources must be handled with care, lest it do more harm than good. The laws of physics are unrelenting; there just are no easy solutions to the energy problem.

Environmental Considerations

The energy issue is also complicated by the environmental problems with which it is associated. Virtually every major energy source causes some environmental damage. The dangers of nuclear power have been publicized widely by its opponents, as has the damage done by strip mining (that is, the mining of coal from the surface rather than from underground). Even a form of energy like wind harnessed by turbines and windmills, which is widely favored by those who oppose nuclear sources, generates some damage. If used extensively, it would be a source of significant noise pollution and a serious threat to birds.

Attempts to deal with such environmental problems have contributed to the rise in the cost of energy. By requiring the installation of devices that limit the emissions of electricity-generating stations, automobiles, and other major sources of pollution, fuel efficiency has been decreased. Many (but by no means all) observers believe that the additional usage of fuel is well worth it, but it is important to recognize that there is a cost and that it is real and substantial. For example, it has been estimated by the U.S. Council on Environmental Quality that pollution controls can raise the cost of generating a given quantity of electricity from coal by about 25 percent.[6]

Environmental issues also have other implications for fuel policy. For example, they inhibit the substitution of coal for oil in electricity generation. The United States has enormous reserves of coal, at least enough to meet domestic fuel demands for 1000 years at current rates of consumption. But coal is also a treacherous energy source. Its extraction regularly kills many miners and seriously damages the health of others. Its use releases sulfur dioxide and particulate pollution into the atmosphere, both of which endanger the health of the population and, generally, make for dirtier communities whose buildings deteriorate more rapidly. And strip mining leaves behind it scars that turn beautiful countryside into unsightly ditches.

We have not yet mentioned what is potentially the most serious environmental problem of all: The burning of any fossil fuel—coal, oil, or wood—creates concentrations of carbon dioxide in the earth's atmosphere that have a remarkable durability. About half of the CO_2 ever generated by industry is still in the atmosphere. Many observers believe that within a few decades this will cause the atmosphere to begin to act like a greenhouse and lead to a significant increase in the temperature of the globe with potentially disastrous effects on crops, melting of the polar icecaps (causing massive flooding), and other calamitous consequences. Some analysts who are usually fairly calm and conservative believe that by the end of the century very radical steps will have to be taken to curb the use of fuels that contribute to this potentially catastrophic problem.

Growing Reserves of Exhaustible Resources: Our Puzzle Revisited

We began this chapter with a brief discussion of some of the more pessimistic views about future resource supplies, including the allegation that by 1982 we may have only 20 years worth of oil reserves, 30 years of tin, and 32 years of copper left; implying that before another half-century has passed we will have exhausted all these resources. Yet in Table 36–2 (page 686) we saw, paradoxically, that in the quarter-century since 1950 the reserves of all of the finite resources actually increased!

In fact, the paradox has a straightforward economic explanation: rising reserves are a tribute to the success of exploration activity that took place in the meantime. Minerals are not discovered by accident. They are discovered by difficult and costly work requiring the services of geologists and engineers and the use of extremely expensive machinery. Exploration requires an enormous expenditure which industry does not find worth making when reserves are already high and when mineral prices are low.

Consequently, over the course of the twentieth century proven reserves have not changed very much. Every time some mineral's known reserves fell, particularly if its price therefore tended to rise, exploration increased until the decline was offset. The law of supply and demand worked. Falling reserves or rising

[6]Council on Environmental Quality, *Environmental Quality*, 1966, page 160, and 1979, page 439.

prices of a mineral caused an upsurge in exploration, just as we expect from supply–demand analysis. In the 1970s, for example, the rising price of oil led to very substantial increases in oil exploration, which helped to build up reserves. In this respect, oil companies have a valid point when they complain that the Windfall Profits Tax will discourage U.S. supplies. While, to protect ourselves from OPEC, it may not be wise for us to *consume* more oil from American sources, it certainly does seem prudent for us to increase our reserves through exploration. Increased profitability of exploration is perhaps the most effective way to get that done.

A Few Words on Future Prospects

We close this chapter with a few words about the future. Despite the 1981 oil glut, there seems to be good reason to fear that for the next decade or two fuel problems will continue to be serious. OPEC is not the only cause of the problems by any means. Easily accessible sources of oil *are* growing scarcer, and this means that the cost of oil must rise. Construction of electricity-generation facilities has lagged, both because of the opposition of those who fear their environmental effects and because suppliers have not been permitted to raise their prices enough to make up for inflation. These and other such problems spell trouble both in terms of prices and in terms of the likely effects on real GNP in the industrialized countries. It will probably have even more serious effects upon less developed countries with meager fuel supplies.

But for the longer run, if the problem of the greenhouse effect and its threat to the earth's temperature is somehow avoided, there is reason for optimism. Past history and research already underway suggest that new techniques will become available as higher prices encourage the development of alternative energy sources. Already solar heating has become economically viable in certain cases (especially for private homes in the Sun Belt states) and can be expected to spread. Scientists are studying the use of geothermal energy, and, probably most important, nuclear fusion promises a virtually unlimited supply of energy if we can learn to harness it.

In all these ways, then, higher prices will lead to a lower quantity demanded and a greater quantity supplied of energy, thus helping to avert an "energy crisis." Calculations that show when current demand will exhaust the current supply are simply beside the point.

Yet we do not want to paint too rosy a picture. Adjustment to higher relative prices can be painful, as owners of gas-guzzling cars and fuel-inefficient homes have already found out. In peering into the crystal ball, we can see that goods and services that rely either directly or indirectly on fossil fuels are likely to remain relatively expensive. This can hardly be considered good news. But the point to emphasize is that we *can* see an end to this process. And this end is not a cataclysmic one where we run out of energy, industrial activity ceases, and we all freeze. Instead, it is one where new technology based on nondepletable energy resources like the sun and the atom takes over the business of powering vehicles, heating homes, and turning the wheels of industry. Energy then will probably be more expensive than it is today, but it *will* be available.

Summary

1. The quantity demanded of a scarce resource can exceed the quantity supplied only if something prevents the market mechanism from operating freely.

2. As a resource grows scarce on a free market, its price will rise, inducing increased conservation by consumers, increased exploration for new reserves, and increased substitution of other items that can serve the same purpose.

3. In fact, in the twentieth century the relative prices of many resources have remained roughly constant, largely because of the discovery of new reserves and because of cost-saving innovations.
4. The price mechanism and rationing are the only known alternatives to chaos in the allocation of scarce resources.
5. In the 1970s, OPEC succeeded in raising the relative price of petroleum, but the rise in price led to a substantial decline in world demand as well as to an increase in production in countries outside OPEC.
6. Increased consumption of domestic oil depletes U.S. reserves and may increase our economy's vulnerability to the OPEC cartel.
7. Paradoxically, subsidies to new sources of energy such as gasohol and shale oil may actually reduce U.S. reserves if their production processes use up more fuel as inputs than they produce as outputs. In many cases this is a very real possibility.
8. Many programs for the reduction of oil consumption have undesirable environmental consequences.
9. Known reserves for depletable scarce resources have not tended to fall with the passage of time because as the price of the resource rises with increasing scarcity, increased exploration for new reserves becomes profitable.

Concepts for Review

Known reserves
OPEC
Windfall Profits Tax
Artificial shortage

Strategic reserve
Tariff on imported oil
Rationing

Subsidies for alternative energy sources
Paradox of growing reserves of finite resources

Questions for Discussion

1. Discuss some valid and some invalid objections against letting rising prices eliminate shortages of supplies of scarce resources.
2. Describe what must be done by a government agency that is given the job of rationing a scarce resource.
3. Some observers believe that a program of rationing may work fairly satisfactorily for a few months or for one or two years, particularly during an emergency period when patriotic spirit is strong. However, they believe that over longer periods and when there is no upsurge of patriotism it is likely to prove far less satisfactory. Do you agree or disagree? Why?
4. Try to describe the various ways that fuel is used up in the production of gasohol, including that used up making the required equipment, that used up in transporting the fuel inputs, and so on.
5. Why may a rise in the price of fuel lead to more conservation after several years have passed than it does in the months following the price increase? What does your answer imply about the relative size of the long-run elasticity of demand for fuel and its short-run elasticity?

International Trade and Comparative Advantage

37

While the United States can satisfy its own requirements for such goods as coal and sugar, it is almost *entirely* dependent on the rest of the world for other products, such as rubber and coffee. For these and many other vital inputs—like oil and copper—the United States must depend on trade with other countries. Still, in numerical terms, imports and exports are not nearly as important for the United States as they are for smaller nations, such as Great Britain, Israel, and the Netherlands. For instance, in 1979 exports constituted only 9 percent of the GNP in the United States, whereas corresponding figures for the Israelis and the Dutch were 41 and 52 percent, respectively.

In this chapter, we will examine the purposes of foreign trade and the ways in which governments have sought to influence or limit it. First, we will examine why countries engage in trade. Second, we will see why the populations of both the exporting and the importing countries may benefit from an exchange even though they are, in effect, merely "swapping goods." Third, we will study the crucial *law of comparative advantage*, which determines what commodities a country finds advantageous to export and what commodities it finds advantageous to import. Fourth, we will see how the prices of goods traded between countries are determined by supply and demand. And, finally, we will examine the pros and cons of tariffs and other devices designed to protect a country's industries from foreign competition.

Issue: The Competition of "Cheap Foreign Labor"

When analyzing the issues of international trade, common sense can be extremely valuable; indeed, there is no substitute for it. Yet sometimes conclusions based on common sense without factual confirmation and careful analysis can be very misleading.

One example of a foreign trade issue that has been misunderstood for lack of factual analysis is the argument that buying products made by cheap foreign labor is unfair and destructive to domestic interests. Some U.S. business people and union leaders argue that such purchases take bread out of the mouths of American workers and depress standards of living in this country. According to this view, cheap imports cause job losses and put pressure on U.S. businesses to lower wages. Moreover, they encourage the continued exploitation of workers in the countries from which we obtain our imports by providing rewards to sweatshop proprietors abroad and by making clear to them that low prices and, consequently, low wages are the only basis on which they can compete.

Yet the facts do not seem entirely consistent with this scenario. First, wages have risen spectacularly among the industrialized suppliers of products bought by Americans, where earning rates were indeed relatively low 10 to 20 years ago. As Table 37–1 shows, a dramatic change occurred during the decade of the 1970s. Note that in 1970, hourly wages in manufacturing in seven countries of Western Europe and in Japan averaged about 45 percent of those in the United States. Yet by mid-1980, the average hourly compensation in these countries had surpassed the U.S. level by about 3 percent. Specifically, four of the countries had well exceeded the U.S. level, and one other had almost equaled it. International comparisons like those in the table do run into some problems because of the different currencies. American workers are paid in dollars and Japanese workers are paid in yen, and during the period in question the value of the yen increased substantially relative to the dollar. Yet the basic pattern that emerges from the table correctly indicates the underlying reality: American imports of Volkswagens from Germany, Volvos from Sweden, and Datsuns from Japan have continued, despite the fact that wages have risen in those countries.

More important, the rise in these foreign wages, compared with those in the United States, has not brought with them an increasing strength in the American position in the international marketplace. In the 1950s, when European and Japanese wages were far below those in the United States, we had no trouble marketing our products abroad. It was far easier then than now to sell the amount of exports needed to pay for the amount of goods that were imported. In fact, the main problem then was to bring imports up to the level at which they roughly balanced our exports. Then, in the 1960s and 1970s, as wages in Europe and Japan began to rise closer to those in the United States, America ran into serious trouble in its ability to sell goods abroad. We were, and still are, often unable to export enough to pay for our imports. Clearly, cheap foreign labor does not always serve as a crucial obstacle to U.S. sales abroad as a "common sense" view of the matter suggests. In this chapter we will see what is wrong with that view.

Table 37–1
HOURLY COMPENSATION RATES
IN NINE INDUSTRIALIZED COUNTRIES

| | MIDYEAR | |
	1970	1980
Belgium	$2.08	$13.39
Britain	1.48	7.06
France	1.74	9.63
Germany	2.35	12.19
Italy	1.76	9.07
Japan	0.99	5.71
Netherlands	2.14	12.34
Sweden	2.93	12.46
United States	4.17	9.89

Data are compensation estimates per hour worked and relate essentially to all employees in the manufacturing sector.
SOURCES: U.S. Bureau of Labor Statistics unpublished estimates.

Why Trade?

The main reason that countries trade with one another rather than try to run completely independent economies is that the earth's resources are not equally distributed across its surface. The United States has an abundant supply of coal, an energy source that is quite scarce in most of the rest of the world. Saudi Arabia has very little land that is suitable for farming, but it sits atop a huge pool of oil. By contrast, Israel, despite its proximity to the world's richest petroleum deposits, has virtually no oil of its own. Because of this seemingly whimsical distribution of vital resources, every nation must trade with others to acquire what it lacks. In general, the more varied the endowment of a particular country, the less it will have to depend on others to make up for its deficiencies.

Even if countries had all the resources they would like to use, other differences in natural endowments—differences in climate, terrain, and so on—would lead them to engage in trade. Americans *could*, with great difficulty, grow their own banana trees and coffee shrubs in hothouses; but these items are much more efficiently grown in such places as Honduras and Brazil, where the climate is appropriate. On the other hand, wheat grows in the United States with little difficulty, while mountainous Switzerland is not good at growing either bananas or wheat.

The skills of a country's labor force also play a role. If Argentina has a large group of efficient farmers and few workers with industrial experience while the opposite is true in Great Britain, it will generally pay Argentina to specialize in agriculture and let Great Britain concentrate on manufacturing.

This last point suggests one other important reason why countries trade—the advantage of **specialization.** If one country were to try to produce everything, it would end up with a number of industries whose scale of operation was too small to permit the use of mass-production techniques, specialized training facilities, and the other arrangements that can give a cost advantage to large-volume operations. Even now, despite the considerable volume of trade in the world economy, this problem seems to arise for some countries whose operation of their own international airlines or their own steel mills, for example, seems explainable only in political rather than economic terms. Inevitably, nations with small markets for goods produced by industries that are economical only when their scale of operation is large find that these enterprises can survive only with the aid of large government subsidies.

To summarize: International trade is essential for the prosperity of the trading nations for at least three reasons: (1) every country lacks some vital resources that it can get only by trading with others; (2) each country's climate, labor force, and other endowments make it a relatively efficient producer of some goods and an inefficient producer of other goods; and (3) specialization permits larger outputs and can therefore offer economies of large-scale production.

> **Specialization** means that a country devotes its productive activities only to a small proportion of the total set of goods it uses. This allows the economy to benefit from special skills, resources, or scale economies, thereby giving the country an advantage in the production of those goods, which are then traded to other nations in exchange for items it does not itself produce.

Mutual Gains from Trade

In some of the very early writings on international trade, it was implied that one nation could gain from an exchange only at the expense of another. It was argued (fallaciously) that since nothing is produced in the act of trading, the total collection of goods in the hands of the two parties at the end of the exchange could not be greater than it was before the exchange took place. Therefore, if one country gets more out of a swap than it put in, the other country must necessarily end up with less than it started with.

One of the consequences of this view was the policy prescription calling for each country, in the interests of its citizens, to do its very best to act to the disadvantage of its trading partners—in Adam Smith's terms, to "beggar its neighbors." The idea that one nation's gain must be another's loss means that a country can promote its own welfare only by harming others.

Yet, as Adam Smith and others after him emphasized, in any *voluntary exchange*, unless there is misunderstanding of the facts, both parties *must* gain (or at least expect to gain) something from the transaction. Otherwise why would both parties agree to the exchange?

But how can mere exchange, in which no net production takes place, actually leave both parties better off? The answer is that while there can of course be no gain in the physical quantity of the products exchanged, the holdings of both parties can end up much better suited to the needs of each. Suppose individual A has four sandwiches and nothing to drink, while B has four bottles of Coke and nothing to eat. A trade of two sandwiches for two bottles of Coke does not increase the total supply of either food or beverages, but it clearly produces a net increase in the welfare of both parties.

Any *voluntary exchange* must promise to make *both* parties better off. Trade can bring about mutual gains by redistributing products in such a way that both participants end up holding a combination of goods that is better adapted to their preferences than the goods they held before.

And this, as we shall see, is precisely what trade among nations accomplishes.

International Versus Intranational Trade: Mobility of Inputs

Trading takes place not only among countries but also among regions of a country. Florida and California "export" oranges to states in the East and Middle West, which in turn produce automobiles and grain for other regions of the country. The logic of such domestic exchange is essentially no different from that underlying trade among different countries; the basic reasons for international trade are equally applicable to trade *within* countries.

If one can learn about trade from strictly domestic exchanges why study international trade as a special subject? There are at least three basic reasons: (1) domestic trade takes place under a single government, while foreign trade must involve at least two governments; (2) domestic trade involves only one currency, while foreign trade must involve the monies of different countries; and (3) in domestic trading it is usually easier for labor and capital to move to the jobs where they are most needed, whereas in international trading labor and capital must move from one country to another—a much more difficult task. Let us look a bit more closely at these differences between domestic and international trade.

Political Factors in International Trade

At least in theory, the government of a nation is concerned with the welfare of all its citizens. But governments are usually much less deeply concerned with the welfare of the countries with which they trade. In this spirit, the Constitution of the United States prohibits overt tariffs and other impediments to domestic trade, barriers which would seek to increase the gains from trade of one group of its inhabitants at the expense of another. But the Constitution does not prohibit the U.S. from imposing tariffs on imports from abroad. A major issue in the economic analysis of international trade is the use and misuse of impediments to free international trade. Later in the chapter such trade barriers will be discussed in some detail.

The Many Currencies Involved in International Trade

All trade within the borders of the United States is carried out in dollars. But the trade of American grain for British woolens involves two different monetary units—dollars and pounds. Rates of exchange between different currencies can and do change. Thirty years ago the pound was worth more than $4; since then it has been as low in value as $1.55. This variability in exchange rates brings with it a host of complications and policy problems that are discussed in the next chapter.

Impediments to Mobility of Labor and Capital

If there are jobs in California but none in Michigan, workers can move freely to follow the job opportunities. Of course, there are personal costs—not only the dollar cost of moving, but also the psychological cost of giving up friends and familiar surroundings. But such moves are not inhibited by immigration quotas, by laws restricting the employment of foreigners, or by the need to learn a new language, as are moves from one country to another.

There are also greater impediments to the transfer of capital from one country to another than to its movement within a country. The shipment of plant and equipment between countries can be expensive, and the international shipment of capital in the form of money to be invested in foreign firms is likely to encounter many restrictions (for example, in many countries there are rules limiting the share of foreign ownership in a company). Such investment abroad is also subject to special risks, such as the danger of outright expropriation if, say, after a political revolution the new government decides to take over all foreign properties without compensation. But even if nothing so extreme occurs, capital invested abroad faces risks from possible variations in exchange rates. An investment yielding a million pounds a year will be worth $3 million to American investors if the pound is worth $3 but only $2 million if the pound should fall to $2.

While labor, capital, and other factors of production do move from country to country when offered an opportunity to increase their earnings abroad, they are less likely to do so than to move from one region of a country to another to gain similar increases.

Comparative Advantage: The Fundamental Principle of Specialization

We have seen that trade can be beneficial to both parties. Some of the reasons are obvious. But now we turn to an important source of mutual benefit which is far from obvious.

We know that coffee can be produced in Colombia using less labor and smaller quantities of other inputs than would be needed to grow it in the United States. And we know that the United States can produce large passenger aircraft at a lower resource cost than can Colombia. We say then that Colombia has an **absolute advantage** over the United States in coffee production, and the United States has an absolute advantage over Colombia in aircraft production.

Obviously, if the United States wants coffee and Colombia wants airplanes, both can save resources by trading—each exporting to the other the good in which it has an absolute advantage.

One country is said to have an **absolute advantage** over another in the production of a particular good if it can produce that good using smaller quantities of resources than can the other country.

Suppose, however, that one country is more efficient than another in producing *every* item. Can they still gain by trading? The surprising answer is *definitely yes.*

How is this possible? A simple parable will help make the reason clear: The work of a highly paid business consultant frequently requires computer analysis. The consultant herself began her career as a computer operator, doing her own key punching and programming and had been extremely good at it. Consequently, in her current position she grows impatient with the slow, sloppy work of some of the low-paid key punchers who work for her, and at times is tempted to do all the work herself. Good judgment, however, tells her that though she is better *both* at giving business advice *and* at key punching than are her employees, it is foolish to devote any of her valuable time to the low-skilled key-punching job.

One country is said to have a **comparative advantage** over another in the production of a particular good relative to other goods it can produce if it produces that good least inefficiently as compared with the other country.

Here is an example of **comparative advantage** at work. The consultant specializes in business advice despite her absolute advantage in key punching because she has a *still greater* absolute advantage in her role as a business consultant. Every hour she decides not to devote to key punching causes her some direct loss because it puts the work into hands less competent than hers. But that loss is more than compensated for by the earnings she makes selling her services to clients during that hour.

This example brings out the fundamental principle that underlies the bulk of economic analysis of patterns of specialization and exchange among different nations, and that is one of our 12 Ideas for Beyond the Final Exam. The principle, called the *law of comparative advantage*, was discovered by David Ricardo, one of the giants in the history of economic analysis.

Even if one country is at an absolute *dis*advantage relative to another country in the production of *every* good, it is said to have a *comparative advantage* in making the good in whose production it is *least inefficient* in comparison with the other country.

Ricardo's basic finding was that even if one country is more efficient than another in the production of every commodity (that is, it has an absolute advantage in every commodity), both countries can still gain by trading.

Let's see precisely how this works using numbers based on Ricardo's own example. Suppose labor is the only input and it takes less labor in Portugal than in England to produce either a yard of cloth or a barrel of wine, so that Portugal has an absolute advantage in both cloth and wine production. If Portugal's advantage in wine production is proportionately greater than its advantage in cloth production, for the reasons specified in our consultant–keypuncher example, it may nevertheless pay Portugal to specialize in the production of wine and to get cloth from England. In summary, Ricardo found that:

In determining the most efficient patterns of production, what matters is *comparative* advantage not *absolute* advantage. Thus it will often pay country X to import a certain good from country Y even if that good can be produced at home more efficiently than it can in country Y. Such imports will be profitable if country X produces *even more* efficiently the goods that it exports in exchange.

The Arithmetic of Comparative Advantage

A numerical illustration should help you grasp more clearly the logic behind the principle of comparative advantage. Table 37–2 gives some hypothetical figures

Table 37–2

HYPOTHETICAL LABOR REQUIREMENTS
TO ILLUSTRATE COMPARATIVE ADVANTAGE

	IN ENGLAND (hours)	IN PORTUGAL (hours)
One yard of cloth	2	1
One barrel of wine	40	10

indicating how much labor is required to produce a yard of cloth and a barrel of wine in England and Portugal. We see from the figures that Portugal produces cloth twice as efficiently as England, taking only one hour of labor to produce a yard of cloth, while two hours are required for the purpose in England. However, Portugal is *four* times as efficient as England in wine production, taking only 10 hours to England's 40 to supply a barrel of wine.

Before we can calculate the gains from trade that are made possible by comparative advantage, we must first discuss a bit further the implications of these numbers. In either country it is possible to increase cloth production at the expense of wine production (or vice versa) by shifting part of the labor force from one industry to the other. The table enables us to calculate the ratio in which the two products can be traded for each other domestically. For example, we see that in England it takes twenty times as long to make a barrel of wine as to make a yard of cloth. It is possible to give up one barrel of wine, switch the released 40 hours of labor into cloth production, and thereby produce 20 yards of cloth. Similarly, in Portugal it takes 10 hours of labor to make a barrel of wine, and one hour to make a yard of cloth. Therefore, each one-barrel decrease in wine production releases 10 hours of labor and therefore permits Portugal a 10-yard increase in cloth production. So Portugal's domestic cloth–wine trade-off is 10 yards to one barrel, and England's cloth–wine trade-off is 20 yards to one barrel.

With this information we can now see quickly what free trade can do for the two countries. In the absence of trade, each country would produce all its requirements of each good. Suppose now that trade opens and Portugal decides to specialize more in the production of wine, at which it is comparatively more efficient. Suppose Portugal increases its wine output by 5 million barrels, while England reduces its wine output by 4 million barrels. Total world wine output would rise by 1 million barrels. But what then happens to the two countries' production of cloth? The trade-off figures give us the answer. Portugal's cloth–wine trade-off, 10 to one, tells us that for every additional barrel of wine it must give up 10 yards of cloth. Therefore, the 5-million barrel increase in wine output must reduce cloth output by $5 \times 10 = 50$ million yards. But England's cloth–wine trade-off is 20 to one. Therefore, in England the decrease in wine output of 4 million barrels permits an increase in cloth output of $4 \times 20 = 80$ million yards. Thus we end up with the following output changes:

	ENGLAND	PORTUGAL	TOTAL
Wine	− 4	+ 5	+ 1
Cloth	+ 80	− 50	+ 30

In sum, without any change in total labor time, the two countries together have come out ahead by one million barrels of wine and 30 million yards of cloth.

Biographical Note: David Ricardo (1772–1823)

David Ricardo was born four years before publication of Adam Smith's *Wealth of Nations*. Descended from a family of well-to-do stockbrokers of the Jewish faith who migrated to London from Amsterdam and were, in turn, descended from Portuguese Jews, he had about twenty brothers and sisters. At a school in Amsterdam, Ricardo's formal education ended at the age of 13, and so he was largely self-educated. He began his career by working in his father's brokerage firm. At age 21, Ricardo married a Quaker woman and decided to become a Unitarian, a sect then considered "little better than atheist." By Jewish custom, Ricardo's father broke with him, though apparently they remained friendly. Ricardo then decided to go into the brokerage business on his own and was enormously successful. During the Napoleonic Wars he regularly scored business coups over leading British and foreign financiers, including the Rothschilds. After gaining a huge profit on government securities that he had bought just before the Battle of Waterloo, Ricardo decided to retire from

---

Surely a nice outcome, but there seems to be some sleight of hand here. All that has taken place is an exchange; yet, in the process, Portugal and England each gain both cloth and wine. How can such gains in physical output be possible for both parties?

The explanation is that the trade process we have just described involves more than just a swap of a fixed bundle of commodities. It is also a change in the *production* arrangements, with some of England's wine production taken over by the more efficient producers of Portuguese wine, and with some of Portugal's cloth production taken over by English weavers who are *less in*efficient at producing cloth than English vintners are at producing wine.

When every country does what it can do best, all countries can benefit because more of every commodity can be produced without increasing the given quantity of labor.

Just how much each country actually will gain in the process depends on the price that will be set for wine and cloth. The process by which that price is determined by supply and demand will be described in a later section. For now we need merely note that the higher the price of wine (Portugal's export), the greater the share of the gain that will go to Portugal; and the higher the price of cloth, the greater the share that will go to England.

The Graphics of Comparative Advantage

We can also use a graph to show how comparative advantage works. Figure 37–1 depicts the two countries' production possibilities frontiers corresponding to the numbers in Table 37–2 and a given quantity of labor.[1] Given, say, 80 million hours of labor, the line *EF* tells us what combinations of wine and cloth England

[1]To review the concept of the production possibilities frontier, see Chapter 3, pages 40–43.

business when he was just over 40 years old.

He purchased a country estate, Gatcomb (now owned by the royal family), where a brilliant group of intellectuals met regularly. Particularly remarkable for the period was the number of women included in the circle, among them Maria Edgeworth, the novelist (who wrote extravagant praise of Ricardo's mind), and Jane Marcet, an author of textbooks, one of which was probably the first text in economics. Ricardo's close friends included the economists T. R. Malthus and James Mill, father of John Stuart Mill the noted philosopher—economist. Malthus remained a close friend of Ricardo even though they disagreed on many subjects and continued their arguments in personal correspondence and in their published works.

James Mill persuaded Ricardo to go into Parliament. As was then customary, Ricardo purchased his seat by buying a piece of land that entitled its owner to a seat in Parliament. There he proved to be a noteworthy liberal, strongly supporting many causes that were against his personal interests.

James Mill also helped persuade Ricardo to write his masterpiece, *The Principles of Political Economy and Taxation*, which may have been the first book of pure economic theory. It was noteworthy that Ricardo, the most practical of practical men, had little patience with empirical economics and preferred instead to rest his analysis explicitly and exclusively on theory.

His book made considerable contributions to the analysis of pricing, wage determination, and the effects of various types of taxes, among many other subjects. It also gave us the law of comparative advantage. In addition, the book described what has come to be called the Ricardian rent theory—even though Ricardo did not discover the analysis and explicitly denied having done so.

Ricardo died in 1823 at the age of 51. He seems to have been a wholly admirable person—honest, charming, witty, conscientious, brilliant—altogether too good to be true.

can produce. For example, since it takes England 40 labor hours to produce one barrel, if it used those 80 million hours to produce only wine, it would end up at point E, with 2 million barrels of wine and zero cloth. Similarly, if it devoted all 80

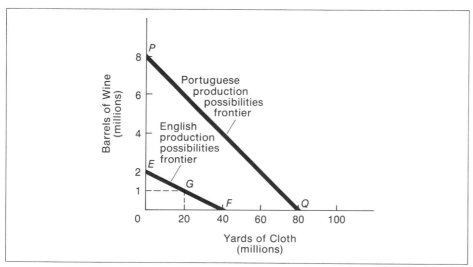

Figure 37–1
ABSOLUTE AND COMPARATIVE ADVANTAGE SHOWN BY TWO COUNTRIES' PRODUCTION POSSIBILITIES FRONTIERS
Portugal's absolute advantage is shown by its ability to produce more of every commodity using the same quantity of labor as does England. Therefore, Portugal's production possibilities frontier, PQ, is higher than England's, EF. But England has a comparative advantage in cloth production in which it is only half as productive as Portugal (it can produce 40 million yards, point F, compared with Portugal's 80 million, point Q.) On the other hand, England is one-quarter as productive in wine production (point E) as is Portugal (point P). Thus, England is least inefficient in producing cloth, where it consequently has a comparative advantage.

million hours to cloth production at two hours per yard, it would obtain 40 million yards of cloth and no wine (point *F*). Or it could devote some labor to wine and some labor to cloth. For example, with a 50/50 division of its labor between the two outputs, it is easy to see that it would obtain 1 million barrels of wine and 20 million yards of cloth (point *G*). In short, line *EF* shows all the options in terms of wine and cloth output that its 80 million labor hours make available to England.

Using precisely the same reasoning, we deduce that line *PQ* shows all the wine and cloth output options available to Portugal if it had exactly the same amount of labor time available as England does—80 million hours. For example, point *P* is obtained because if Portugal produces nothing but wine, at 10 labor hours per barrel, it will be able to produce 8 million barrels and no cloth.

Note that Portugal's production possibilities frontier lies above England's throughout the diagram. That is because Portugal is the more efficient producer of both commodities. With the same amount of labor, it can obtain more wine and more cloth than England. Thus, the higher position of Portugal's frontier is the graph's way of showing Portugal's *absolute* advantage.

Portugal's comparative advantage in wine production and England's comparative advantage in cloth production are shown in a different way—by the relative slopes of the two production possibilities frontiers. Portugal's frontier is not only higher than England's, it is also steeper. What does this mean economically? One way of looking at the difference is to remember that while Portugal can produce four times as much wine as England (compare points *P* and *E*), it can produce only twice as much cloth as England (points *Q* and *F*). England is, relatively speaking, only half as bad at cloth production as at wine production. That is what is meant when we say it has a *comparative* advantage in the former.

We may express this difference more directly in terms of the slopes of the two lines. The slope of Portugal's production possibilities frontier is $OP/OQ = \frac{8}{80} = \frac{1}{10}$. This means that if Portugal switches from pure wine production (point *P*) to pure cloth production (point *Q*), it must give up one barrel of wine for every 10 yards of cloth it obtains. That is, the *opportunity cost* of cloth to Portugal is $\frac{1}{10}$ of a barrel of wine for each yard of cloth it produces.

In the case of England, the slope of the production possibilities frontier is $OE/OF = \frac{2}{40} = \frac{1}{20}$. That is, to get an additional yard of cloth, it must give up only half as much wine production as is required in Portugal. Why? Because, in the example, English workers are such bad wine producers that by transferring them out of such work, the resulting loss in wine production is so much smaller than Portugal's.

A country's absolute advantage in production over another country is shown by its having a higher production possibilities frontier. The difference in the comparative advantages of the two countries is shown by the difference in the slopes of their frontiers.

Comparative Advantage and Competition of "Cheap Foreign Labor"

The principle of comparative advantage takes us a good part of the way toward an explanation of the fallacy in the "cheap foreign labor" argument described earlier in the chapter. Given the assumed productive efficiency of Portuguese labor and the inefficiency of British labor in Ricardo's example, we would expect wages to be much higher in Portugal than in England. Indeed, if workers receive all of the nation's output, and wine and cloth are produced in the same proportions in both countries, then this *must* be so, because output per person in Portugal is so much higher.

In these circumstances, one can expect some Portuguese workers to be apprehensive about an agreement to permit trade between the countries—"How can we hope to meet the unfair competition of those underpaid British workers?" And British laborers are also likely to be concerned—"How can we hope to meet the competition of those Portuguese, who are so efficient in producing everything?"

The principle of comparative advantage shows us that both fears are unjustified. As we have just seen, when trade is opened up between Portugal and England *workers in both countries will be able to earn higher real wages than before* because of the increased productivity that comes about through specialization.

The numerical example shows this fact quite directly. We have seen from our illustration that, with trade, England can end up with more wine and more cloth than it had before, and so the living standards of its workers can rise even though they have been left vulnerable to the competition of the superefficient Portuguese. Portugal also can end up with more wine and with more cloth, so the living standards of its workers can rise even though they have been exposed to the competition of cheap British labor.

The lesson to be learned here is that nothing helps raise standards of living more than does a greater abundance of goods.

Supply–Demand Equilibrium and Pricing in Foreign Trade

In our discussion of comparative advantage we obtained an initial idea of how countries determine the prices at which they will trade their goods. In this section we will go further in analyzing price determination. As is true elsewhere, prices in international trade are affected by a variety of influences acting through many different mechanisms. The Organization of Petroleum Exporting Countries (OPEC) tries to set prices of oil unilaterally, by decision of its members. Grain deals have been arranged between Soviet and American exporters based on terms arrived at in secret negotiations. But though such acts of pricing partially circumvent the normal market process and are greatly influenced by political considerations, they are also heavily affected by supply and demand. OPEC's deliberations are influenced by new oil discoveries and by estimates of the response of future world demand to their pricing decisions. While negotiated prices of wheat deviate from the prices found in the competitive marketplace, prices on the free market clearly set limits on the price range open to the negotiators. In short, in international exchange, as elsewhere in the economy, supply and demand are at the center of the price-determination mechanism.

In the context of international trade, the supply–demand model runs into several complications we have not encountered before. First, it involves at least two demand curves: that of the exporting country and that of the importing country. Second, it may also involve two supply curves, since the importing country may produce some part of the amount it uses. The third and final complication is that equilibrium does not take place at the intersection point of *either* pair of supply–demand curves. Why? Because if there is any trade, the exporting country's quantity supplied must be *greater* than its quantity demanded, while the quantity supplied by the importing country must be *less* than the quantity demanded by its inhabitants at the equilibrium price.

These complications are illustrated in Figure 37–2, where we show the supply and demand curves of a country that exports wine, (a), and the supply and

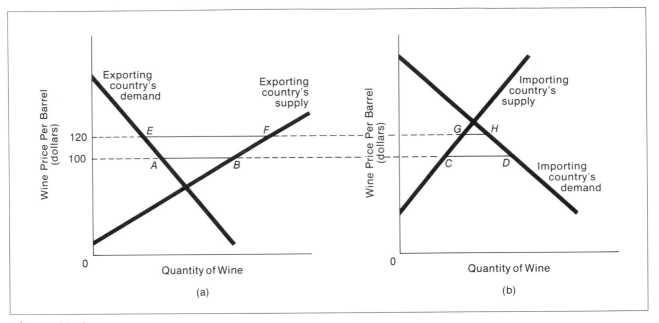

Figure 37–2

SUPPLY–DEMAND EQUILIBRIUM IN THE INTERNATIONAL WINE TRADE

Equilibrium requires that the net export supply, *AB* (which is the exporting nation's quantity supplied, *B*, minus the exporter's quantity demanded, *A*), exactly balances *net* demand, *CD*, by the importing country. At $100 per barrel of wine, there is equilibrium. But at a higher price, say $120, there is disequilibrium because net export supply, *EF*, exceeds net import demand, *GH*.

demand curves of a country that imports wine, (b). For simplicity, we assume that these countries do not deal in wine with anyone else. The equilibrium price of wine is shown as $100 per barrel. At that price, the horizontal distance *AB* between the exporting country's supply and demand curves shows the difference between what the country produces (point *B*) and what residents of the exporting country want to consume themselves (point *A*). Similarly, the distance *CD* is the gap between the quantity demanded by residents of the importing country (point *D*) and the quantity supplied by its own producers (point *C*). Where these two horizontal distances are equal, the amount the exporting country has available to sell abroad is exactly equal to the amount the importer wants to buy, and matters are in balance. In the example, the distance *AB* is equal to distance *CD*, so $100 per barrel is the market price.

At a price higher than $100, we can expect producers in both countries to want to sell more and consumers in both countries to want to buy less. For example, if the price rises to $120 per barrel, the exporter's quantity supplied will rise from *B* to *F*, and the exporter's quantity demanded will fall from *A* to *E*, as shown in Figure 37–2(a). As a result, there will be a rise in the amount available for export, from *AB* to *EF*. For exactly the same reason, the price rise will cause higher production and lower sales in the importing country, leading to a shrinkage in the amount the importing country wants to import—from *CD* to *GH* in part (b). This means that the new price, $120 per barrel, cannot be sustained if the international market is free and competitive. With export supply *EF* far greater than import demand *GH*, there must be downward pressure on price and a move back toward the $100 equilibrium price. Similar reasoning shows that prices below $100 also cannot be sustained.

We can now see the straightforward role of supply–demand equilibrium in international trade:

In international trade, the equilibrium price must be at a level at which the excess of the exporter's quantity supplied over its domestic quantity demanded is exactly equal to the excess of the importer's quantity demanded over its quantity supplied. Equilibrium will occur at a price at which the horizontal distance AB in Figure 37–2(a) (the excess of the exporter's quantity supplied over its quantity demanded) is equal to the horizontal distance CD in Figure 37–2(b) (the excess of the importer's quantity demanded over its quantity supplied). At this price, the *world's* quantity demanded is equal to the *world's* quantity supplied.

Tariffs, Quotas, and Other Interferences with Trade

Despite the mutual gains obtained, international trade has historically been subjected to unrelenting pressure for government interference. Such interference has come in the form of three main devices that modern governments use to control trade: **tariffs, import quotas,** and **export subsidies.**

Until the rise of a free-trade movement in England at the end of the eighteenth and the beginning of the nineteenth centuries (with such economists as Adam Smith and David Ricardo at its vanguard), it was taken for granted that one of the essential tasks of government was the imposition and administration of regulations to impede trade, presumably in the national interest.

There were many who argued then (and some who still argue today) that a nation's wealth consists of the amount of gold or other monies at its command. Consequently, the proper aim of government policy is to do everything it can to promote exports (in order to increase the amount foreigners owe to it) and to discourage imports (in order to decrease the amount the country owes to foreigners).

Obviously, there are limits to which this policy can be carried out. A country *must* import vital foodstuffs or critical raw materials that it cannot supply for itself; for if it does not, it must suffer a severe fall in living standards as well as a deterioration in its military strength. Morever, it is mathematically impossible for *every* country to sell more than it buys—one country's exports *must* be some other country's imports. If everyone competes in this game and cuts imports to the bone, then obviously exports must go the same way. The result must be that everyone is deprived of most of the mutual gains that trade can provide.

In more recent times, notably in the United States during the first three decades of the twentieth century, there was a return to an active policy designed to reduce the competition of foreign imports. Since then, the United States has gradually assumed a leading role in attempts to promote freedom of trade, and barriers have gradually been reduced; though, very recently, there have been pressures to move back the other way.

The most recent round of major international negotiations to promote freedom of trade ended in 1979, after achieving some modest degree of success. Like other such negotiations, it was conducted under the sponsorship of GATT, the General Agreement on Tariffs and Trade, which is an international agency specially created for this purpose. The most recent round is credited with the following three main accomplishments.

1. It achieved some reductions in tariff levels. The participating countries agreed to mutual reductions in the tax rates that each levied upon imports of one another's products. These reductions presented a continuation of the 30-year process which has, since World War II, made significant contributions to freedom of trade.

A **tariff** is a tax on imports. An importer of wine, for example, may be charged 10 cents per dollar of wine bought or $2 per barrel.

A **quota** specifies the maximum amount of a good that is permitted into the country from abroad per unit of time; for example, no more than 2 million barrels of wine per year.

An **export subsidy** is a payment by the government to exporters to permit them to reduce the selling price of their goods so they can compete more effectively in foreign markets. For example, they may be given 5 cents per dollar of wine or $1 per barrel of wine they export.

2. For the first time, agreement was reached on workable definitions of "subsidization" and "dumping," and on procedures to be used to prevent these practices. These terms refer to the sale by country A of products to customers in country B at prices which do not cover A's costs of supplying them (subsidization) or at prices lower than the same goods are offered for sale inside country A (dumping). Such sales are generally considered by the producers of country B to constitute unfair competition.

3. Preliminary steps were taken toward reduction of a major trade barrier which had previously resisted such attempts: that is, the practice of governments, when making purchases for their own use, to favor goods supplied by their own producers, even when foreign suppliers offered better and cheaper substitutes. "Buy American" rules for U.S. government agencies are mild compared with those of a number of foreign governments that impose similar regulations upon their nationalized industries, including telecommunications, railroads, and so on. While no specific rules for the elimination or restriction of such practices were adopted, steps toward the formulation of such rules were agreed upon for the first time. International negotiations are rarely quick and easy.

How Tariffs and Quotas Work

Both tariffs and quotas will restrict supplies coming from abroad into the country that imposes them, and they will also drive up prices. The tariff works by raising prices and hence cutting down the demand for imports, while the sequence associated with a quota goes the other way—restriction in supply forces prices up.

Let us use our international trade diagrams (Figure 37–2) to see what a quota does. The supply and demand curves in Figure 37–3 are like those of Figure 37–2. In Figure 37–3 we see that, with no quota, free trade in wine yields an equilibrium price of $100 per barrel (in both countries), with the exporting country exporting 5 million barrels to the importing country. The exports are shown in Figure 37–3(a) as the difference between quantity supplied (10 million, point B) and quantity demanded (5 million, point A), and the corresponding imports are shown in Figure 37–3(b) as the difference between quantity demanded (8 million, point D) and quantity supplied (3 million, point C).

Now suppose the government of the importing nation imposes an import quota of (no more than) 3 million barrels. The free-trade equilibrium is no longer possible. Instead, the importing country must reduce its imports to the distance QT (3 million) in Figure 37–3(b). As the figure indicates, this pushes up the price of wine in the importing nation to $110 per barrel, because only at this price will quantity demanded exceed quantity supplied by 3 million barrels. At the same time, the quota limits the exporting nation's exports to the same 3 million barrels—the distance RS in Figure 37–3(a). We see that, in order for quantity supplied to exceed quantity demanded by 3 million barrels in the exporting country, the domestic price of wine must fall from $100 to $95 per barrel. In summary:

An import quota on a product normally will reduce the volume of that product traded, raise the price in the importing country, and reduce the price in the exporting country.

The same restriction of trade can be accomplished through a tariff. In the example we have just completed, a quota of 3 million barrels resulted in a price that was $15 higher in the importing country than in the exporting country

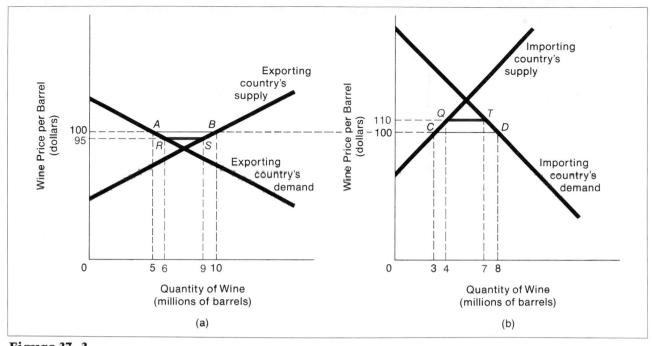

Figure 37–3

QUOTAS AND TARIFFS IN INTERNATIONAL TRADE

Under free trade, the equilibrium price of wine is $100 per barrel. The exporting country, in part (a), sends *AB,* or 5 million barrels, to the importing country (distance *CD*). If a quota of 3 million barrels is imposed by the importing country, these two distances must shrink to 3 million barrels. The solution is shown by distance *RS* for exports and distance *QT* for imports. Exports and imports are equal, as must be the case, but the quota forces prices to be unequal in the two countries. Wine sells for $110 per barrel in the importing country but only $95 per barrel in the exporting country. A tariff achieves the same result differently. It *requires* that the prices in the two countries be $15 apart. And this, as the graph shows, dictates that exports (= imports) will be equal at 3 million barrels.

($110–$95). Suppose, then, that instead of a quota the importing nation posts a $15 per barrel tariff. International trade equilibrium then must satisfy the following two requirements:

1. The price that consumers in the importing country pay for wine must exceed the price that suppliers in the exporting country receive by $15 (the amount of the tariff).
2. The quantity of wine exported (the excess of the exporting country's quantity supplied over its quantity demanded) must equal the quantity of wine imported (the excess of the importing country's quantity demanded over its quantity supplied).

By consulting the graphs in Figure 37–3, you can see exactly where these two requirements are satisfied. If the exporter produces at *S* and consumes at *R,* while the importer produces at *Q* and consumes at *T,* the exports and imports are equal (at 3 million barrels) and the two domestic prices differ by exactly $15. (They are $110 and $95.)

What we have just discovered is a very general result of international trade theory:

Any restriction of international trade (exports and imports) that is accomplished by a quota normally can also be accomplished by a tariff.

In this case, the tariff corresponding to an import quota of 3 million barrels is $15 per barrel.

But while tariffs and quotas can accomplish the same reduction in international trade and lead to the same domestic prices in the two countries, there *are* some important differences between the two types of restrictions. First, profits from the price increases in the importing country produced by a quota usually go into the pockets of the foreign and domestic sellers of the product. Because supplies are limited by quotas, customers in the importing country must pay more for the product. So the suppliers, be they foreign or domestic, receive more for every unit they sell. On the other hand, when trade is restricted by a tariff, the profits go as tax revenues to the *government* of the importing country that enacts it. In effect, the government increases its tax revenues partly at the expense of its citizens and partly at the expense of foreign exporters, who must accept a reduced price because of the resulting decrease in quantity demanded in the importing country. (Domestic producers again benefit, because they are exempt from the tariff.) In this respect, a tariff is certainly a better proposition than a quota from the viewpoint of the country that enacts it.

Another important distinction between the two measures is the difference in their implications for productive efficiency and long-run prices. A tariff handicaps all exporters equally. It still awards sales to the importers who are most efficient and can therefore supply the goods most cheaply.

A quota, on the other hand, necessarily awards its import licenses more or less capriciously—perhaps on a first-come, first-served basis or in proportion to past sales or by some other arbitrary standard or even on some political criteria. There is not the slightest reason to expect the most efficient and least costly suppliers to get the import permits. In the long run, the population of the importing country is likely to end up with significantly higher prices, poorer products, or both.

We conclude that if a country must inhibit imports, there are two important reasons for it to give preference to tariffs over quotas: (1) some of the resulting financial gains from tariffs go to the government of the importing country rather than to foreign and domestic producers; and (2) unlike quotas, tariffs offer no special benefits to inefficient exporters.

Why Inhibit Trade?

To state that tariffs are a better way to inhibit international trade than quotas leaves open a far more basic question: Why limit trade in the first place? There are two primary reasons for the adoption of measures that restrict trade: First, they may help the importing country get more advantageous prices for its goods, and second, they protect particular industries from foreign competition.

How can a tariff make prices more advantageous for the importing country if it raises consumer prices there? The answer is that it forces foreign exporters to sell more cheaply. Because their market is restricted by the tariff, they will be left with unsold goods unless they cut their prices. Suppose, as in Figure 37–3(b), that a $15 tariff on wine raises the price of wine in the importing country from $100 to $110 per barrel. This rise in price, in turn, will drive down the quantity demanded for imports, from an amount represented by the length of the solid black line *CD* to the smaller amount represented by the solid blue line *QT*. And to the exporting country, this must mean an equal reduction in quantity demanded for its exports [see the change from *AB* to *RS* in Figure 37–3(a)].

What this means is that the price at which the exporting country can sell its wine will be driven down (from \$100 to \$95 in the example), while at the same time, producers in the importing country—being exempt from the tariff—can charge \$110 per barrel.

In effect, such a tariff amounts to government intervention to rig import prices in favor of domestic producers and to exploit foreign sellers by forcing them to sell more cheaply than they otherwise would. However, this technique works only as long as foreigners accept tariff exploitation passively. And they rarely do. Instead, they retaliate, usually by imposing tariffs of their own on their imports from the country that first began the tariff game. This can easily lead to a tariff war in which no one gains in terms of more favorable prices and everyone loses in terms of the resulting reductions in overall trade. Something like this happened to the world economy in the 1930s and helped prolong the worldwide depression.

Tariffs can benefit a country that is able to impose them without fear of retaliation. But when every country uses them, everyone is likely to lose in the long run.

Restricting Trade to Protect Particular Industries

The second and probably more frequent reason why countries undertake programs to restrict trade is to protect particular industries that are vulnerable to foreign competition. If foreigners can produce steel or watches or shoes more cheaply, domestic businesses and unions in these industries are quick to demand protection; and their government is often reluctant to deny it to them. It is here that the cheap foreign labor argument is most likely to be invoked.

But the fact is that in a free market, the industries that are unable to compete will be those whose relative inefficiency does not permit them to beat foreign exporters at their own game. Protective tariffs and quotas are designed to undercut the harsh competition that gives consumers the benefits of international specialization. In Ricardo's example of comparative advantage, one can well imagine the complaints from Portuguese cloth makers as the opening of trade with England led to increased Portuguese importation of cloth. At the same time, the English grape growers would, very likely, have expressed equal concern over the flood of imported wine from Portugal.

Usually, when an industry feels itself threatened by foreign competition it will be argued that some form of protection against imports is needed to prevent loss of jobs. Now we know from the macroeconomics discussion in Chapters 8 through 14 that there are other (and better) ways to stimulate employment. Yet it must be admitted that any method that prevents the competition of foreigners can, in the short run, preserve jobs in the protected industry. It will work, but often at a very considerable cost to consumers in the form of higher prices and to the economy in the form of inefficient use of resources. For example, a recent (1980) study by the Federal Trade Commission[2] calculated that a tariff on imports of CB radios would cost U.S. consumers \$80,000 for every job it preserved! And this was by no means the worst example among the various industries it examined.

Nevertheless, union complaints over proposals to reduce a tariff are well justified unless something is done to ease the cost to the individual workers of

[2] Morris E. Morkre and David G. Tarr, *Staff Report on Effects of Restrictions on United States Imports: Five Case Studies and Theory* (Washington, D.C.: Bureau of Economics, Federal Trade Commission, June 1980), page. 74.

Trade Adjustmentment Assistance— A Case of Overkill?

Just about everyone agrees that when a tariff is removed or trade is freed in some other way the workers whose jobs are threatened as a result should be aided by society in readjusting to the new conditions. Congress in fact enacted such a program, called the Trade Adjustment Assistance Program. Under its provisions, workers in domestic industries adversely affected by imports were offered supplementary unemployment benefits and assistance in retraining. The Reagan administration trimmed the program considerably. But, previously, workers who qualified received 70 percent of their normal wages *tax free* for as long as one year, with a maximum payment of $269 a week.

Since they paid no taxes on this income, the unemployed workers may have ended up receiving just as much income as they obtained by working. It is no wonder that many of the half-million people who received such support, as reports indicated, preferred to remain unemployed. Moreover, according to the General Accounting Office, only 4 percent of them enrolled in the retraining programs offered by the government.

switching to those lines of production that trade has now made profitable. The rationale for free trade between countries cannot be considered airtight if there is no adequate program to assist the minority of citizens in each country who will be harmed whenever patterns of production change drastically, as would happen, for example, if tariff and quota barriers were suddenly brought down. Owners of wineries in Britain and of textile mills in Portugal may see heavy investments suddenly rendered unprofitable as would workers in these vineyards and factories whose investments in acquiring special skills and training are no longer marketable. Nor are the costs to displaced workers only monetary. Often they will have to move to new locations as well as to new industries, uprooting their families, losing old friends and neighbors, and so on. That the *majority* of citizens undoubtedly will gain from free trade will be no consolation to those who are its victims.

To help alleviate this problem, the United States (and other countries) has set up programs to assist workers who have lost jobs because of the changing patterns of world trade. In the United States such "adjustment assistance" is supplied to firms or workers who, as a result of a government agreement to ease international trade, suffer idle facilities, unprofitability, and unemployment because of sharp increases in imports. Firms may be eligible for technical assistance designed to improve their efficiency, financial assistance in the form of government loans or government guarantees of private loans, and tax assistance in the form of permission to delay tax payments. Workers are eligible for retraining programs, lengthened periods of eligibility for unemployment compensation, and allowances to help pay for the cost of moving to other jobs. In sum, the United States and other countries recognize how important it is to help those who suffer when trade barriers come down.

Two other protectionist arguments warrant mention: the national defense argument and the infant-industry argument. Each has some merit in special circumstances.

National Defense and Other Noneconomic Considerations

There are times when a tariff or some other measure to interfere with trade may be justified on noneconomic grounds. If a country considers itself vulnerable to military attack, it may be perfectly rational to keep alive industries whose outputs can be obtained more cheaply abroad but whose supplies may dry up during an emergency. For example, airplane production by small countries makes sense only in such circumstances. The danger is that every industry, even those with the most peripheral defense relationship, is likely to invoke this argument on its behalf. For instance, the U.S. watch-making industry claimed protection for itself for many years on the grounds that it trained skilled workers whose crafts-manship would be invaluable in wartime. Perhaps so, but a technicians' training program probably could have done the job more cheaply and even more effectively by teaching exactly the skills needed for military purposes.

Noneconomic reasons also explain quotas on importation of whaling prod-ucts and total prohibition of imports of alligator skins and the furs of other endangered species. These quotas may be a competitive boon to the domestic leather and fur industries, but protection of endangered species rather than protection of industries is their justification.

The Infant-Industry Argument

It is often suggested that temporary protection of a newly established industry can serve the national interest. Until that industry can expand to a point at which it is able to compete unaided with established foreign firms, it may be essential to prevent its strangulation by foreign competition.

The argument, while valid in certain instances, is less defensible than it may at first appear. It makes sense only if the industry's prospective future gains are sufficient to pay the social losses incurred by protection during its establishment. But if it really is likely to be so profitable in the future, why doesn't private capital rush in to take advantage of the prospective net profits? The annals of business are full of cases in which a new product or a new firm lost money at first but profited handsomely later. Only where funds are not available to a particular industry for some reason, despite its glowing profit prospects, does the infant-industry ar-gument for protection stand up fully.

It is hard to think of examples, but even if such a case were found one would have to be careful that the industry not remain in diapers forever. There are too many cases in which new industries were awarded protection when they were being established and, somehow, the time to withdraw that protection never arrived. One must beware of infant industries that never grow up.

What Import Price Levels Benefit a Country?

One of the most curious features of the protectionist position is the fear of low prices charged by foreign sellers. Earlier we mentioned export subsidies, a practice that always elicits great indignation, for countries that make such payments are accused of "dumping"—of getting rid of their goods at unconscionably low prices. For example, in the last few years the member countries of the European Economic Community (EEC) have frequently been accused of dumping various goods on the United States market because these EEC governments exempt ex-ports from taxes that are levied on goods sold within their borders.

A moment's thought should indicate why this fear must be considered curi-ous. As a nation of consumers, we should be indignant when the prices of our imports are very *high*, not when they are *low*. That is the common-sense rule that guides every consumer, and the consumers of imported commodities should be no exception. Only from the topsy-turvy viewpoint of an industry seeking pro-tection from competition are high prices seen as being in the public interest.

Unfair Foreign Competition

Satire and ridicule are often more persuasive than logic and statistics. Exasperated by the spread of protectionism to so many industries under the prevailing Mercantilist philosophy, French economist Frédéric Bastiat decided to take the protectionist argument to its illogical conclusion. The fictitious petition of the French candlemakers to the Chamber of Deputies, written in 1845 and excerpted below, has become a classic in the battle for free trade.

We are subject to the intolerable competition of a foreign rival, who enjoys, it would seem, such superior facilities for the production of light, that he is enabled to *inundate* our *national market* at so exceedingly reduced a price, that, the moment he makes his appearence, he draws off all custom for us; and thus an important branch of French industry, with all its innumerable ramifications, is suddenly reduced to a state of complete stagnation. This rival is no other than the sun.

Our petition is, that it would please your honorable body to pass a law whereby shall be directed the shutting up of all windows, dormers, skylights, shutters, curtains, in a word, all openings, holes, chinks, and fissures through which the light of the sun is used to penetrate our dwellings, to the prejudice of the profitable manufactures which we flatter ourselves we have been enabled to bestow upon the country . . .

We foresee your objections, gentlemen; but there is not one that you can oppose to us . . . which is not equally opposed to your own practice and the principle which guides your policy. . . .

Labor and nature concur in different proportions, according to country and climate, in every article of production . . . If a Lisbon orange can be sold at half the price of a Parisian one, it is because a natural and gratuitous heat does for the one what the other only obtains from an artificial and consequently expensive one . . .

Does it not argue the greatest inconsistency to check as you do the importation of coal, iron, cheese, and goods of foreign manufacture, merely because and even in proportion as their price approaches *zero*, while at the same time you freely admit, and without limitation, the light of the sun, whose price is during the whole day at *zero?*

SOURCE: F. Bastiat, *Economic Sophisms* (New York: G. P. Putnam's Sons, 1922).

Ultimately, it is always in the interest of a country to get its imports as cheaply as possible. It would be ideal for the United States if the rest of the world were willing to provide its exports to us free or virtually so. We could then live in luxury at the expense of the rest of the world.

The notion that low import prices are bad for a country is a fitting companion to the idea—so often heard—that it is good for the country to export much more than it imports. True, this means that foreigners will end up owing us a good deal of money. But it also means that we will have given them large quantities of our products and have gotten relatively little value in foreign products in exchange. That surely is not an ideal way for a country to benefit from its foreign transactions!

Our gains from trade do not consist of accumulations of gold or of heavy debts owed us by foreigners. Rather, our gains are composed of the goods and services that others provide minus the goods and services we must provide them in return.

Conclusion: A Last Look at the "Cheap Foreign Labor" Argument

The preceding discussion should indicate the fundamental fallacy in the argument that American workers have to fear cheap foreign labor. If workers in other countries are willing to supply their products to us with little compensation, this must ultimately *raise* the standard of living of the average American worker. As long as the government's monetary and fiscal policies succeed in maintaining high levels of employment at home, how can we possibly lose out by getting the products of the world at little cost to ourselves?

It must be admitted that there are two dangers to this prognosis. First, our employment policy may not be effective. If workers who are displaced by foreign competition cannot find jobs in other industries, then American workers will indeed suffer from international trade. But that is a shortcoming of the government's employment program, not of its international trade policies.

Second, we have noted that an abrupt stiffening of foreign competition resulting from a major innovation in another country, or from a discovery of a new and better source of raw materials, or from a sharp increase in export subsidies by a foreign country, *can* hurt U.S. workers by not giving them an adequate chance to adapt gradually to the new conditions. The more rapid the change, the more painful it will be. If it occurs fairly gradually, workers can retrain and move on to those industries that now require their services. If the change is even more gradual, no one may have to move. People who retire or leave the threatened industry for other reasons simply need not be replaced. But competition that inflicts its damage overnight is certain to impose very real costs upon the affected workers, costs that are no less painful for being temporary.

But these are, after all, minor qualifications to an overwhelming argument. They call for intelligent monetary and fiscal policies and for transitional assistance to unemployed workers, not for abandonment of free trade.

In the long run, labor will be "cheap" only where it is not very productive. Wages will tend to be highest in those countries in which high labor productivity keeps costs down and permits exporters to compete effectively despite high wages. It is thus misleading to say that the United States has held its own in the international marketplace over the years despite the high wages of its workers. Rather it is much more illuminating to point out that the high wages of American workers were a result of high worker productivity, which gave the United States a heavy competitive edge in the international marketplace.

We note that in this matter it is absolute advantage, not comparative advantage, that counts. The country that is most efficient in every output can pay its workers more in every industry.

Summary

1. Countries trade because differences in their natural resources and other inputs create discrepancies in the efficiency with which they can produce different goods, and because specialization may offer them greater economies of large-scale production.

2. Voluntary trade will generally be advantageous to both parties in an exchange.

3. Both countries will gain from trade with one another if each exports goods in whose production it has a comparative advantage. That is, even a country that is generally inefficient will benefit by exporting the goods in whose production it is least inefficient. This is one of the 12 Ideas for Beyond the Final Exam.

4. The "cheap foreign labor" argument ignores the principle of comparative advantage, which shows that real wages can rise in both the importing and exporting countries as a result of specialization and, thus, increased productivity.

5. The prices of goods traded between countries are determined by supply and demand, but one must consider explicitly the demand curve and the supply curve of *each* country involved. Thus, in international trade, the equilibrium price must be where the excess of the exporter's quantity supplied over its domestic quantity demanded is equal to the excess of the importer's quantity demanded over its quantity supplied.

6. Tariffs and quotas are designed to protect a country's industries from foreign competition. Such protection may sometimes be advantageous to that country, but not if foreign countries adopt tariffs and quotas of their own as a means of retaliation.

Concepts for Review

Imports	Absolute advantage	Quota
Exports	Comparative advantage	Export subsidy
Specialization	"Cheap foreign labor" argument	Infant-industry argument
Mutual gains from trade	Tariff	

Questions for Discussion

1. You have a dozen eggs worth 80 cents and your neighbor has a pound of bacon worth about the same. You decide to swap six eggs for a half pound of bacon. In financial terms, neither of you gains anything. Explain why you are nevertheless both likely to be better off.

2. In the eighteenth century, some writers argued that one person in a trade could be made better off only by gaining at the expense of the other. Explain the fallacy in the argument.

3. A brilliant chemist is also a master glass blower. In what circumstances does it pay him to hire a glass blower for his lab? When does it make sense for him to do some glass blowing for himself?

4. Country A has lots of hydroelectric power, a cold climate, and a highly skilled labor force. What sorts of products do you think it is likely to produce? What are the characteristics of the countries with which you would exect it to trade?

5. Upon removal of a tariff on watches, a U.S. watch-making firm goes bankrupt. Discuss the pros and cons of the tariff removal in the short and long runs.

6. Country A's government believes that it is best always to export more (in money terms) than the value of its imports. As a consequence, it exports more to country B every year than it imports from country B. After 100 years of this arrangement, both countries are destroyed in an earthquake. What were the advantages and disadvantages of the surplus to country A? To country B?

The International Monetary System: Order or Disorder?

38

In the last chapter, we discussed the reasons for international trade and the benefits that accrue to all nations when countries specialize in producing those goods in which they have a comparative advantage. But the movement of goods across national borders generally requires the movement of money in the opposite direction. For example, when the United States buys coffee from Brazil, we must send money to the Brazilians. When Japan purchases petroleum from Saudi Arabia, it must send money to the Saudis, and so on. This chapter takes a look at the system that has been set up to handle these international movements of money—the **international monetary system.**

In the first parts of this chapter, we investigate two polar forms of the international monetary system. The first is a system in which rates of exchange among national currencies are determined in free markets by the laws of supply and demand. Here the key concept to be studied is the *exchange rate:* what it is and what determines its value. The other polar system is one in which exchange rates are rigidly fixed by government authority. Here the key concept is the *balance of payments*, and, as we shall see, even the simple question "What is it?" turns out to be quite difficult to answer.

These two systems are studied to illustrate the important principles, *not* to describe the actual international monetary system as it is now or as it was at any time in the past. Therefore, in the remainder of the chapter we turn to more realistic intermediate systems that have elements of both pure forms, including the old *gold standard*, the so-called *gold-exchange system* that prevailed from 1944 until 1971, and the current *mixed* system—a system that defies any short description because each country, it seems, handles its international monetary relations somewhat differently.

What Are Exchange Rates?

The 50 states of the United States may be the most eloquent testimony to the power of comparative advantage and free trade. Florida specializes in growing oranges, Iowa in growing corn, Pennsylvania makes steel, and Michigan builds cars. All these states trade freely with one another and enjoy great material prosperity. Try to imagine how much lower living standards would be if your

Table 38–1
EXCHANGE RATES WITH THE U.S. DOLLAR, JANUARY 1982
(dollars per unit of foreign currency)

COUNTRY	CURRENCY UNIT	SYMBOL	COST IN DOLLARS
Australia	dollar	$	$1.11
Canada	dollar	$	0.84
France	franc	FF	0.17
Germany	mark	DM	0.43
Italy	lira	L	0.0008
Japan	yen	¥	0.0044
Mexico	peso	$	0.038
Sweden	krona	Kr	0.18
Switzerland	franc	S. Fr.	0.54
United Kingdom	pound	£	1.87

SOURCE: *The Wall Street Journal.*

own state had to make all of these goods, plus the thousands of other things you consume each year.

But the states of the United States have an important advantage that facilitates trade: there are no national borders to be crossed when, say, California lettuce is shipped to Massachusetts. The consumer in Boston pays with *dollars*, just the currency that the farmer in Salinas wants. But if that same farmer ships his lettuce to Japan, consumers there will have only Japanese *yen* with which to pay, rather than the dollars the farmer in California wants. Thus if international trade is to take place, there must be a way to transform one currency (yen) into another (dollars). The rates at which such transformations are made are called **exchange rates.**

The **exchange rate** states the price, in terms of one currency, at which another currency can be bought. Thus there is an exchange rate between every pair of currencies.

For example, $1 is currently the equivalent of almost 6 French francs. The exchange rate between the franc and the dollar, then, may be expressed as "6 francs to the dollar" (meaning that it costs 6 francs to buy a dollar) or about "17 cents to the franc" (meaning that it costs 17 cents to buy a franc). Similarly, there is an exchange rate between the U.S. dollar and every other currency. Although these rates change all the time, Table 38–1 gives an indication of exchange rates prevailing in January 1982, showing how many dollars or cents it cost at that time to buy each unit of foreign currency.

A nation's currency is said to **appreciate** when exchange rates change so that a unit of its own currency can buy more units of foreign currency. The currency is said to **depreciate** when exchange rates change so that a unit of its currency can buy fewer units of foreign currency.

Under our present system, currency rates change frequently. When other currencies get more expensive in terms of dollars, we say that they have **appreciated** relative to the dollar. Alternatively, we can look at this same event in terms of the dollar buying less foreign currency, meaning that the dollar has **depreciated** relative to another currency. Notice that *what is a depreciation to one country must be an appreciation to the other*. For example, if the dollar cost of a German mark rises from 40 cents to 50 cents, the cost of a U.S. dollar in terms of marks simultaneously falls from $2\frac{1}{2}$ marks to 2 marks. The Germans have had a currency *appreciation* while we have had a currency *depreciation*.

Notice also that, when many currencies are changing in value, the dollar may be appreciating with respect to one currency but depreciating with respect to another. Consider, for example, this set of actual recent exchange rates:

ACTUAL EXCHANGE RATES		
	January 1979	**January 1981**
British pound	1 pound = $2.03	1 pound = $2.41
German mark	1 mark = $0.55	1 mark = $0.50

Between January 1979 and January 1981 the dollar *depreciated* relative to the pound but *appreciated* relative to the mark.

While this is the terminology used to describe movements of exchange rates in free markets, another set of terms—**devaluation** and **revaluation**—is used to describe decreases and increases in currency values when these values are set by government decree.

Exchange Rate Determination in a Free Market

Why is it that a German mark costs 40 cents and not 30 cents or 50 cents? If exchange rates were **floating** freely, with no government interferences, the answer would be fairly straightforward. In such a world, exchange rates would be determined by the forces of supply and demand, just like the prices of apples, or typewriters, or haircuts.

In a leap of abstraction, imagine that the United States and West Germany were the only countries on earth, so there was only one exchange rate to be determined. Figure 38–1 depicts the determination of this exchange rate at the point (denoted *E* in the figure) where demand curve *DD* crosses supply curve *SS*. At this price (40 cents per mark), we know that the number of marks demanded is equal to the number of marks supplied.

In a free market, exchange rates are determined by the law of supply and demand. If the rate were below the equilibrium level, the quantity of marks demanded would exceed the quantity of marks supplied, and the price of a mark would be bid up. If the rate were above the equilibrium level, quantity supplied

When an officially set exchange rate is altered so that a unit of a nation's currency can buy *fewer* units of foreign currency, we say there has been a **devaluation** of that currency. When the exchange rate is altered so that the currency can buy *more* units of foreign currency, we say there has been a **revaluation.**

Floating exchange rates are rates determined in free markets by the law of supply and demand.

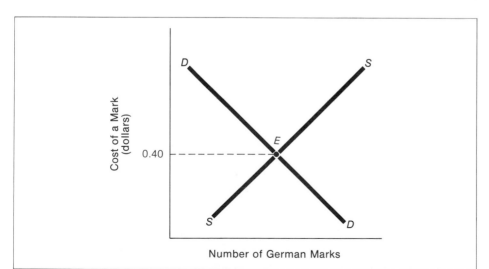

Figure 38–1
DETERMINATION OF EXCHANGE RATES IN A FREE MARKET
Like any price, an exchange rate will be determined by the intersection of the demand and supply curves in a free market. Point *E* depicts this point for the exchange rate between the U.S. dollar and the German mark, which settles at 40 cents per mark in this example.

would exceed quantity demanded, and the price of a mark would fall. Only at the equilibrium exchange rate is there no tendency for the rate to change.

As usual, supply and demand determine price. What we must ask in this case is: Where do the supply and demand come from? Why does anyone demand a German mark?

1. **International trade in goods and services.** This was the subject of the last chapter. If, for example, Jane Doe, an American, wants to buy a German automobile, she will first have to buy marks with which to pay the dealer in Munich.[1] So Jane's demand for a German *car* leads to a demand for German *marks*. In general, *demand for a country's export goods and services leads to a demand for its currency.*

2. **International trading in financial instruments like stocks and bonds.** For example, if American investors want to purchase German stocks, they will first have to acquire the marks that the sellers will insist on. In this way, demand for German financial assets leads to demand for German marks. Thus, *demand for a country's financial assets leads to a demand for its currency.*

3. **Purchases of physical assets like factories and machinery overseas.** If IBM wants to buy out a small German computer manufacturer, the owners will no doubt want to receive marks. So IBM will first have to acquire German currency. In general, *direct foreign investment leads to a demand for a country's currency.*

Now, where does the supply come from? To answer this, we need only turn all of these transactions around. Germans wanting to buy U.S. goods and services, or to invest in U.S. financial markets, or to make direct investments in America will have to offer their marks for sale in the foreign-exchange market (which is similar to the stock market) to acquire the needed dollars. To summarize:

The *demand* for a country's currency is derived from the demands of foreigners for its export goods and services and for its assets, including financial assets, factories, and machinery. The *supply* of a country's foreign currency arises from its imports, and from foreign investment by its own citizens.

To appreciate the usefulness of even this simple supply and demand analysis, let us consider how the exchange rate between the dollar and the mark would change if there were an economic boom in the United States. One important effect of such a boom would be to stimulate American demand for German products, such as automobiles, cameras, and wines. In terms of the supply–demand diagram shown in Figure 38–2, the increased desires of Americans for German products would shift the demand curve for German marks out from D_1D_1 (the black line in the figure) to D_2D_2 (the blue line). Equilibrium would shift from point E to point A, and the exchange rate would rise from 40 cents per mark to 45 cents per mark. In a word, the increased demand for marks by U.S. citizens causes the mark to appreciate relative to the dollar.

EXERCISE
Test your understanding of the supply and demand analysis of exchange rates by

[1]Actually she will not do this because banks generally handle foreign exchange transactions for consumers. An American bank probably will buy the marks for her. But the effect is exactly the same as if Jane had done it herself.

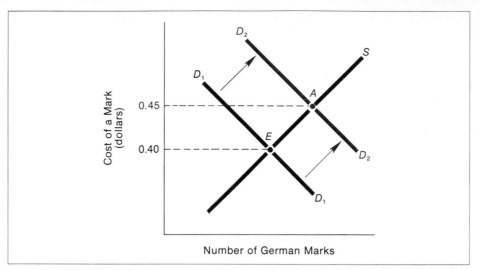

Figure 38–2
THE EFFECT OF AN
ECONOMIC BOOM ON
THE EXCHANGE RATE
If the U.S. economy suddenly
booms, Americans will spend
more on Imports from Ger-
many. Thus the demand curve
for German marks will rise from
D_1D_1 to D_2D_2 as Americans
seek to acquire the marks they
need. The diagram shows that
this will cause the mark to appreciate, from 40 cents to 45
cents, as equilibrium shifts
from point E to point A. Looked
at from the U.S. perspective,
the dollar will depreciate.

showing why each of the following events also would lead to an appreciation of
the mark (depreciation of the dollar) in a free market:

1. A recession in Germany cuts German purchases of American goods.
2. American investors are attracted by prospects for profit in the German stock
   market.
3. Interest rates on government bonds fall in the United States but are stable in
   Germany. (*Hint:* Which country's citizens will be attracted by high interest
   rates in the other country?)

To say that supply and demand determine exchange rates in a free market is
at once to say everything and to say nothing. If we are to acquire some
understanding of the reasons why some currencies appreciate while others
depreciate, we must look into the factors that move the supply and demand
curves. Economists believe that the principal determinants of exchange rate
movements are rather different in the long, medium, and short runs. So we turn
in the next three sections to the analysis of exchange rate movements over these
three "runs." We begin with the long run.

The Purchasing-Power Parity Theory:
The Long Run

As long as there is free trade across national borders, exchange rates eventually
will adjust so that the same product costs the same number of dollars (or the same
amount of any other currency) in every country, except for differences attributable to transportation costs and the like. This simple statement forms the basis of
the major theory of exchange rate determination in the long run.

The **purchasing-power parity theory of exchange rate determination** holds that the exchange rate between any two national currencies
adjusts to reflect differences in the price levels in the two countries.

An example will bring out the basic truth in this theory and also suggest some
of its limitations. Suppose that Swedish and American steel are identical and that
these two nations are the only producers of steel for the world market. Suppose
further that steel is the only tradable good that either country produces.

Question: If American steel costs $75 per ton and Swedish steel costs 300 kronor per ton, what must be the exchange rate between the dollar and the krona?

Answer: Since 300 kronor must be the equivalent of $75, each krona must be worth 25 cents. Why? Because if a krona cost 30 cents, then Swedish steel would cost $90 per ton (300 kronor at 30 cents each) while American steel would cost $75 per ton, and all foreign customers would shop for their steel in the United States. The exchange rate of 30 cents per krona would be too high.

EXERCISE
Show why an exchange rate of 20 cents per krona is too low.

The purchasing-power parity theory is used to make long-run predictions about the effects of inflation on exchange rates. To continue our example, suppose that over a five-year period, prices in the United States rise by one-third while prices in Sweden rise by two-thirds. The purchasing-power parity theory predicts that the krona would depreciate relative to the dollar. It also predicts the amount of the currency depreciation. Say that after the inflation, American steel costs $100 per ton (one-third more than $75) while Swedish steel costs 500 kronor per ton (two-thirds more than 300 kronor). For these two prices to be equivalent, 500 kronor must be worth $100, or one krona must be worth 20 cents. The krona, therefore, must have fallen from 25 cents to 20 cents.

According to the purchasing-power parity theory, differences in domestic inflation rates are a major cause of adjustments in exchange rates. For instance, if one country has a faster rate of inflation than another, then its exchange rate must be depreciating.

In a broad sense, this implication of the theory is certainly borne out. Consider as an example the exchange rate between the dollar and the German mark during the 1974–1979 period. Inflation in the United States averaged about 8 percent per year while inflation in Germany averaged only 4 percent. The theory predicts that the mark should have appreciated relative to the dollar, and this is just what happened. However, when we consider its precise numerical predictions, the theory does not look quite as good. Since the U.S. inflation rate exceeded the German rate by 4 percentage points (8 percent versus 4 percent), the theory suggests that the average annual rate of appreciation of the mark should have been 4 percent. In fact, however, it was 6 percent. Clearly, the theory is missing something. There are a number of complications which the purchasing-power theory ignores.

First, changes in any of the interferences with free trade, such as tariffs and quotas, can upset simple calculations based on purchasing-power parity. For example, if Swedish prices rise faster than American prices but, at the same time, foreign countries erect tariff barriers to keep American (but not Swedish) steel out, then the krona might not have to depreciate.

Second, some goods and services cannot be traded across national frontiers. Land and buildings are only the most obvious examples; most services can be traded only to a limited extent (as when tourists from one country have their hair cut in another). Inflation rates for goods and services that are *not tradable* have little bearing on exchange rates.

Third, few of the goods that different nations produce and trade are as uniform as the Swedish and American steel in our example. A Volvo and a Buick, for example, are not identical products. So the price of a Volvo *in U.S. dollars* can rise faster than the price of a Buick without driving Volvos out of the market entirely. On balance:

Most economists believe that other factors are much more important than relative price levels for exchange rate determination in the short run. But in the long run, purchasing-power parity plays a decisive role.

Economic Activity and Exchange Rates: The Medium Run

Since consumer spending increases quite regularly when income expands, and decreases when income contracts, the same is likely to happen to spending on imported goods. For this reason:

A country's imports will rise quickly when its economy is booming and slowly when its economy is stagnating.

We have already illustrated this point with Figure 38–2. There we saw that a boom in the United States would shift the demand curve for marks outward and therefore lead to a depreciation of the dollar (appreciation of the mark) as American imports from Germany surge. However, if Germany were booming at the same time, German citizens would be buying more American exports, which would shift the supply curve of marks outward. On balance, the value of the dollar might or might not fall. What matters is whether exports are growing faster than imports. The general lesson is that:

Holding other things equal, a country that grows faster than the rest of the world normally finds its currency depreciating because its imports grow faster than its exports, so that its demand curve for foreign currency shifts outward more rapidly than its supply curve.

The exchange rate between the dollar and the mark is again a case in point. During the recovery from the worldwide recession of 1974–1976, the U.S. economy expanded quite a bit more rapidly than the German economy. This is one reason why the dollar depreciated and the mark rose in value from about 42 cents in late 1976 to about 53 cents in late 1978.

Interest Rates and Exchange Rates: The Short Run

While economic activity is very important for exchange rate determination in the medium run, "other things" often are not equal in the very short run. Specifically, one factor that often seems to call the tune in determining exchange rates in the short run is *interest rate differentials*. There is an enormous fund of so-called "hot money"—owned by banks, multinational corporations, and wealthy individuals of all nations, and amounting to perhaps $100 to $200 billion—that travels around the globe in search of the highest interest rates.

Thus suppose that U.S. government bonds are paying a 10 percent rate of interest when yields on equally safe British government securities rise to 15 percent. American investors will be attracted by the high interest rates in the United Kingdom and will offer dollars for sale in order to buy pounds, planning to use those pounds to buy British securities. At the same time, British investors will

Figure 38–3

THE EFFECT OF A RISE IN BRITISH INTEREST RATES
When Britain raises its interest rates, more Americans will want to buy British bonds, and so the demand curve for pounds will shift upward from D_1D_1 to D_2D_2. At the same time, fewer Britons will seek to buy American bonds, so the supply curve of pounds will shift inward from S_1S_1 to S_2S_2. The combined effect of these two shifts is to move the market equilibrium from point E_1 to point E_2. The British pound appreciates, and the dollar depreciates.

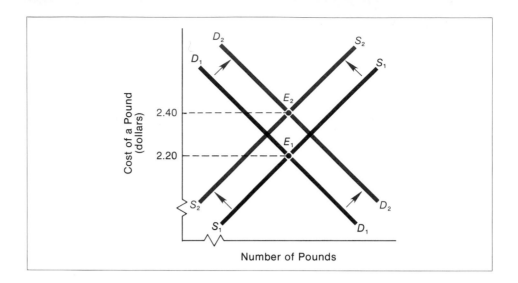

no longer find investing in the United States attractive, so fewer pounds will be supplied to this country.

When the demand schedule rises and the supply curve falls, the effect on price is quite predictable: the pound will appreciate, as Figure 38–3 shows. In the figure, the demand curve for pounds rises from D_1D_1 to D_2D_2 when American investors seek to acquire the pounds needed to purchase British securities. At the same time, British investors offer fewer pounds for sale because they no longer wish to invest in American securities. Thus the supply curve shifts inward from S_1S_1 to S_2S_2. The result, in our example, is an appreciation of the pound from $2.20 to $2.40. In general:

Holding other things equal, countries with high interest rates are able to attract more capital than are countries with low interest rates. Thus a rise in interest rates often will lead to an appreciation of the currency, and a drop in interest rates will lead to a depreciation.

The U.S. dollar in early 1981 provided a vivid example of the power of this phenomenon when high U.S. interest rates caused a sharp appreciation of the dollar. Most experts in international finance agree that international money is so volatile that interest rate movements are the chief determinant of exchange rate fluctuations in the short run. So, when a country finds its currency depreciating, a typical reaction is to attempt to jack up its interest rates. Chapter 13 described how this can be done by using any of the tools of central banking.

Market Determination of Exchange Rates: Summary

We can summarize this discussion of exchange rate determination in free markets as follows:

1. Currencies generally will be *appreciating* in countries whose inflation rates are lower than the rest of the world, for otherwise it would be increasingly difficult for the other countries to market their goods.
2. Exchange rates would also be expected to rise in countries whose levels of

economic activity are lower than average, because these countries will be importing rather little.

3. We expect to find appreciating currencies in countries whose interest rates are high because these countries will attract capital from all over the world.

Reversing each of these, we expect that currencies will be *depreciating* in countries with relatively high inflation rates, or high levels of economic activity, or low interest rates.

Fixed Exchange Rates and the Definition of the Balance of Payments

History records rather few instances of truly free exchange rates, determined by supply and demand without government interference. Much more typical are cases where governments have stubbornly resisted market forces and kept their exchange rates either above or below the equilibrium price for long periods of time. For this reason, we turn our attention next to the opposite of free (or floating) exchange rates, a system of **fixed exchange rates,** or rates that are set by governments. Naturally, under such a system the exchange rate (being fixed) is not closely watched. Instead, international financial specialists focus on a country's **balance of payments**—a term we are now ready to define.

To understand what the balance of payments is, look at Figure 38–4, which depicts a situation that might represent, say, Great Britain before its major devaluation in 1967—an *overvalued* currency. While the supply and demand curves for British pounds indicate an equilibrium exchange rate of $2.40 to the pound (point *E*) the British government is keeping the rate at $2.80. Notice that at $2.80 more people are supplying pounds than are demanding them. In the example, suppliers are selling £22 billion per year, but demanders are purchasing only £20 billion.

This gap between the £22 billion that some people sell and the £20 billion that other people buy is what we mean by Britain's **balance of payments deficit**—£2 billion per year in this case. It is shown by the horizontal distance between points *A* and *B* in Figure 38–4.

The **balance of payments deficit** is the amount by which the quantity supplied of a country's currency (per year) exceeds the quantity demanded. Balance of payments deficits arise whenever the exchange rate is pegged at an artificially high level.

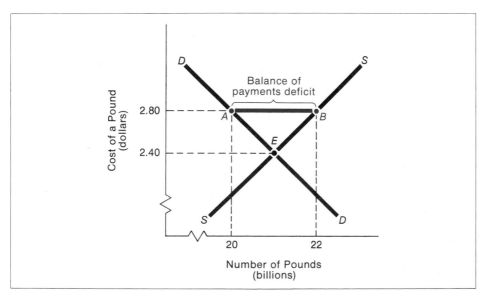

Figure 38–4
A BALANCE OF PAY-
MENTS DEFICIT
At a fixed exchange rate of
$2.80 per pound, which is well
above the equilibrium level of
$2.40 per pound, England's
currency is overvalued in this
example. As a consequence,
more pounds will be supplied
(point *B*) than are demanded
(point *A*). The difference—distance *AB*, or £2 billion per
year—represents Britain's
balance of payments deficit.

How can market forces be flouted in this way? Since sales and purchases on any market must be equal, as a simple piece of arithmetic, the excess of quantity supplied over quantity demanded for currency (£2 billion per year in this example) must be bought by the Bank of England, Britain's central bank. In buying these pounds, it must give up some of the gold and foreign currencies that it keeps as *reserves*. Thus the Bank of England would be losing £2 billion in reserves per year as the cost of keeping the pound at $2.80.

Naturally, this cannot go on forever; the reserves eventually will run out. And this is the fatal flaw in the system of fixed exchange rates. Once speculators become convinced that the exchange rate can be held only a short while longer, they will sell pounds in massive amounts rather than hold on to a currency whose value they soon expect to fall sharply. The supply curve of pounds will shift outward drastically, as shown in Figure 38–5, causing an astronomical rise in the balance of payments deficit (from £2 billion to £4 billion in the example). This is called a "run" on the currency. Lacking sufficient reserves, the central bank will have to permit the exchange rate to fall to its equilibrium level, and this might amount to an even larger devaluation than would have been required before the speculative run on the pound began.

For an example of the reverse case, a severely *undervalued* currency, let us consider Germany in 1973. Figure 38–6 depicts a demand and supply curve for marks that intersect at an equilibrium price of 40 cents per mark (point E in the diagram). Yet, in the example, we suppose that the German authorities are holding the rate at 35 cents. At this rate, the quantity of marks demanded (50 billion) greatly exceeds the quantity supplied (40 billion). The difference is Germany's **balance of payments surplus,** and is shown by the horizontal distance *AB*.

The **balance of payments surplus** is the amount by which the quantity demanded of a country's currency (per year) exceeds the quantity supplied. Balance of payments surpluses arise whenever the exchange rate is pegged at an artificially low level.

Germany can keep the rate at 35 cents only by providing the marks that foreigners want to buy: 10 billion marks per year in this example. In return, it receives U.S. dollars, British pounds, French francs, gold, and so on. All of this serves to increase Germany's reserves of foreign currencies. But notice the important difference between this case and Britain's overvalued pound.

The accumulation of reserves rarely will *force* a central bank to revalue in the way that depletion of reserves can force a devaluation.

Figure 38–5

A SPECULATIVE RUN ON THE POUND

When speculators become convinced that a devaluation of the pound is in the offing, they will rush to sell all their pounds. Their actions shift the supply curve outward from S_1S_1 to S_2S_2 and, in the process, widen England's balance of payments deficit from *AB* to *AC*.

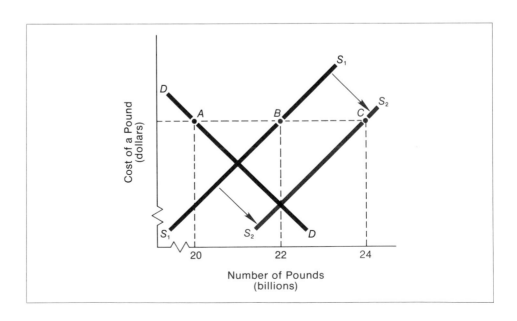

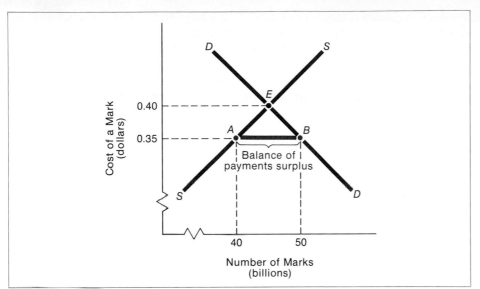

Figure 38–6
A BALANCE OF PAY-
MENTS SURPLUS
In this example, Germany's
currency is undervalued at 35
cents per mark, since the equilibrium exchange rate is 40
cents per mark. Consequently,
more marks are being de-
manded (point B) than are
being supplied (point A). The
gap between quantity de-
manded and quantity sup-
plied—distance AB, or 10 billion marks per year—measures
Germany's balance of pay-
ments surplus.

This was another weakness of the old system of fixed exchange rates. In principle, imbalances in exchange rates could be cured either by a devaluation by the country with a balance of payments deficit or by an upward revaluation by the country with a balance of payments surplus. In practice, though, it was almost always the deficit countries that were forced to act.

Why did the surplus countries refuse to revalue? One reason was a simple misunderstanding of basic economics. They viewed the disequilibrium as the problem of the deficit countries and believed that the deficit countries, therefore, should take the corrective steps. This, of course, is nonsense. Some currencies are overvalued *because* some other currencies are undervalued. In fact, the two statements mean exactly the same thing.

The other reason is that exporters in Germany, Japan, and other surplus countries resisted upward revaluations because they knew that such actions would make their products more expensive to foreigners and thus cut into their sales. And these exporters had the political clout to make that view stick. Meanwhile, since the values of the mark and the yen on world markets were artificially held down, German and Japanese consumers were put in the unenvi- able position of having to pay more for imported goods than they need have paid. Rather than buy these excessively expensive foreign goods, they watched domes- tically produced goods go overseas in return for pieces of paper (dollars, francs, pounds, and so on).

Defining the Balance of Payments in Practice

From the preceding discussion it may seem that measuring a nation's balance of payments position is a simple task: we simply count up the private demand for and supply of its currency and subtract quantity supplied from quantity de- manded. Conceptually, this is all there is to it. But in practice, the difficulties are great because we never have statistics on the number of dollars demanded and supplied. There is no way to observe these directly.

If we look at actual market transactions, we will see that the number of U.S. dollars actually *purchased* and the number of U.S. dollars actually *sold* are identical. Unless someone has made a bookkeeping error, this must always be so.

How, then, can we recognize a balance of payments surplus or deficit? Easy, you say. Just look at the transactions of the central bank, whose purchases or sales must make up the difference between private demand and private supply. If the Federal Reserve is buying dollars, its purchases measure our balance of payments deficit. If it is selling, its sales represent our balance of payments surplus.

Thus the suggestion is to measure the balance of payments by *excluding official transactions among governments*. This is roughly how the balance of payments surplus or deficit is defined today, though, for a variety of complicated reasons, the U.S. government decided in the mid-1970s to stop publishing any official statistic called "the balance of payments deficit." Instead, all foreign transactions are listed and readers are invited to define the balance of payments in any way they wish. Let us now see just what data are published in these official accounts.

The U.S. Balance of Payments Accounts

Using 1980 as an example, Table 38–2 shows the official U.S. balance of payments accounts. There is nothing that purports to measure America's overall balance of payments surplus or deficit. The top section of the table summarizes America's trade in currently produced goods and services—the so-called *current account*. The positive or negative sign attached to each entry indicates whether the transaction represented a *gain* (+) or a *loss* (−) of foreign currency. Looking first at the top of the table, we see that in merchandise transactions Americans

Table 38–2

U.S. BALANCE OF PAYMENTS ACCOUNTS, 1980 (billions of dollars)

Current Account		
(1) Balance of trade		− $25.3
(2) Merchandise exports	+ 224.0	
(3) Merchandise imports	− 249.3	
(4) Net military transactions		− 2.5
(5) Travel and transportation (net)		− 0.8
(6) Net income from investments and other services		+ 39.4
(7) Balance on goods and services (Lines 1 plus 4 plus 5 plus 6)		+ 10.8
(8) Unilateral transfers		− 7.1
(9) Private	− 1.1	
(10) U.S. government (nonmilitary)	− 6.0	
(11) Balance on current account (Lines 7 plus 8)		+ 3.7
Capital Account		
(12) Net private capital flows		− 36.7
(13) Change in U.S. assets abroad	− 71.5	
(14) Change in foreign assets in the U.S.	+ 34.8	
(15) Net governmental capital flows		+ 3.3
(16) Change in U.S. government assets	− 12.2	
(17) Change in foreign official assets in the U.S.	+ 15.5	
(18) Balance on capital account (Lines 12 plus 15)		− 33.4
Addendum		
(19) Sum of lines (11) and (18)		− 29.7
(20) Statistical discrepancy		− 29.7

SOURCE: *Survey of Current Business*, June 1981. Organization of table changed by authors.

imported about $25 billion more than they exported, leading to a whopping deficit in what is called the *balance of trade* (see lines 1–3).

The entry in line 4 indicates the net effect of a large number of dollars spent by U.S. military installations abroad (transactions that cost us foreign currency), and a large amount of foreign currency earned by selling armaments. On balance, these cost the United States about $2.5 billion in foreign currency. Line 5 shows that in 1980 American tourists and shippers spent about $0.8 billion more on foreign services than foreign tourists and shippers spent here. Line 6 displays our major source of foreign currency earnings in the services category: We earned about $39 billion more on our investments overseas (and on some other miscellaneous services) than foreign investors earned here.

Line 7 gives the net result of all trading in goods and services—the balance on goods and services. The entry in line 7 means that the United States received almost $11 billion more than it spent during 1980. Lines 8–10 indicate the so-called "unilateral transfers," including both private gifts to foreigners and official foreign aid. Together these cost us just over $7 billion in foreign currency. When these unilateral transfers are subtracted from the surplus on goods and services, we find (in line 11) a surplus of $3.7 billion in America's *current account*.

But this hardly represents our "balance of payments," as it leaves out all purchases and sales of assets. This group of transactions is shown in the *capital account* (lines 12–18). Line 12 shows that, on balance, American individuals and businesses bought almost $37 billion more in assets abroad than private foreign investors bought here. The net entry is *minus* $36.7 billion because $71.5 billion dollars flowed *out of* the United States to buy foreign assets (line 13), while only $34.8 billion in foreign money flowed *into* the United States to buy American assets (line 14).

This large deficit in private capital flows, coupled with a small surplus in the current account, left the United States with a yawning balance of payments deficit. How are such deficits financed? Normally, by government capital flows in the opposite direction (such as when foreign governments buy U.S. government bonds). But line 15 tells us that such was not the case in 1980. While foreign governments bought $15.5 billion worth of U.S. assets (line 17), our government bought $12.2 billion in foreign assets (line 16), leaving a scant surplus on governmental capital flows of only $3.3 billion (line 15). You may notice that the accounts do not balance. When we add up the current account (line 11) plus the overall (private plus government) capital account (line 18), we get a $29.7 billion deficit (line 19). But, of course, this is impossible. Since it is a simple matter of arithmetic that the two accounts together must balance (dollars purchased = dollars sold), the difference is considered a *statistical discrepancy* (line 20). While part of this huge discrepancy simply comes from errors in data collection and computation, the lion's share reflects the U.S government's inability to monitor all the flows of money, goods, and services across its borders. In particular, it is suspected (but not known for sure) that much of the discrepancy comes from unrecorded capital inflows into the United States—items that should appear in line 14, and would appear if they went through normal banking channels.

A Bit of History: The Gold Standard

Just as in the case of pure floating rates, it is hard to find examples of strictly fixed exchange rates in the historical record. About the only time that exchange rates were truly fixed was under the old **gold standard,** at least when it was practiced in its ideal form.[2]

Under the gold standard, fixed exchange rates were maintained by an automatic equilibrating mechanism that went something like this: All currencies were defined in terms of gold; indeed, some were actually made of gold. When a nation had a deficit in its balance of payments, this meant, essentially, that more gold was flowing *out* than was flowing *in*. Since the domestic money supply was based on gold, losing gold to foreigners meant that the quantity of money automatically fell. Thus, "monetary policy" *automatically* turned restrictive, and interest rates rose, attracting foreign capital. At the same time, the restrictive monetary policy pulled down national output and prices, thus discouraging imports and encouraging exports. The balance of payments problem quickly rectified itself. This means, however, that:

Under the gold standard, no nation had control of its domestic monetary policy, and therefore no country could control its domestic economy very well.

At least in principle, the effects on surplus countries were perfectly symmetrical under the gold standard. A balance of payments surplus led, via gold inflows, to an increase in the domestic money supply whether the surplus country liked the idea or not. This raised prices and output, thereby increasing imports and decreasing exports. And it also lowered interest rates, thereby encouraging outflows of capital. Because of these automatic adjustments, nations rarely reached the point at which devaluations or revaluations were necessary. Exchange rates were fixed as long as countries abided by the rules of the gold standard game.

In addition to the complete loss of control over domestic monetary conditions, the gold standard posed one other serious difficulty.

A fundamental problem with the gold standard was that the world's commerce was at the mercy of gold discoveries.

Discoveries of gold meant higher prices in the long run and higher real economic activity in the short run, through the standard monetary-policy mechanisms that we studied in Part Two. And when the supply of gold did not keep pace with growth of the world economy, prices had to fall in the long run and employment had to fall in the short run.

The Bretton Woods System and the International Monetary Fund

The gold standard, which had faltered many times before, finally collapsed amid the financial chaos of the Great Depression of the 1930s. Without it, the world struggled through nearly 15 years of almost complete breakdown in international trade.

Then, as World War II drew to a close, with much of Europe in ruins and with the United States holding the lion's share of the free world's reserves, officials of the industrial nations met at Bretton Woods, New Hampshire, in 1944 to try to establish a new international economic order. Their goal was to provide a stable monetary environment that would facilitate world trade. And since the

---

[2] As a matter of fact, while the gold standard lasted (on and off) for hundreds of years, it was rarely practiced in its ideal form. Except for a brief period of fixed exchange rates in the late nineteenth and early twentieth centuries, there were periodic adjustments of exchange rates even under the gold standard.

dollar was almost the only "strong" currency at that time, it was natural that the nations of the world would turn to the dollar as the basis of the new international monetary system.

That is just what they did. The Bretton Woods agreements reestablished a system of fixed exchange rates based not on the old gold standard but on the free convertibility of the U.S. dollar into gold. The United States agreed to buy or sell gold to maintain the $35 per ounce price that had been established by President Franklin Roosevelt in 1933. And the other signatory nations, which had almost no gold in any case, agreed to buy and sell dollars to maintain their exchange rates at agreed-upon levels. Thus all currencies were indirectly on a modified "gold standard." A holder of French francs, for example, could exchange these for dollars at (roughly) 5 francs per dollar and then exchange these into gold at $35 per ounce. In this way, the value of the franc was fixed at 175 francs per ounce of gold (5 francs per dollar times 35 dollars per ounce). The new system was dubbed the **gold-exchange system,** and often referred to as the **Bretton Woods system.**

The **International Monetary Fund (IMF)** was set up to police and manage this new system. Using funds that had been contributed by member countries, the IMF was empowered to make loans to countries that were running low on reserves. Only in the case of a "fundamental disequilibrium" in a nation's balance of payments was a change in exchange rates to be permitted. For it was believed that only relatively fixed exchange rates could provide the stable climate needed to restore world trade.

Of course, the Bretton Woods conferees did not define clearly what a "fundamental disequilibrium" was, nor could they have. As the system evolved, it came to mean a chronic deficit in the balance of payments of sizable proportions. Such nations would then *devalue* relative to the dollar; that is, they would reduce the value of their currencies in terms of dollars. So the system was not really one of fixed exchange rates but rather one where rates were "fixed until further notice."

Several flaws in the Bretton Woods system have already been mentioned in our discussion of the pure system of fixed exchange rates. First, since devaluations were permitted only after a long run of balance of payments deficits, these devaluations (a) could be clearly foreseen, and (b) normally had to be quite large. Speculators then saw opportunities for profit and would "attack" weak currencies with a wave of selling. This led many economists to question whether the system of fixed exchange rates was really providing the stable climate for world trade that had been intended. Was a system where rates were constant for long periods and then altered by very large amounts really more conducive to international trade than one where overvalued currencies would gradually depreciate, as they would under a system of floating rates?

The second problem arose from the custom that deficit nations were expected to devalue when forced to, while surplus nations (mainly Germany and Japan) could resist upward revaluations. Since the U.S. dollar defined the monetary value of gold (at $35 per ounce), America was the one nation in the world that had no way to devalue its currency relative to gold, no matter how "fundamental" the disequilibrium became. The only way exchange rates between the dollar and foreign currencies could change was if the surplus nations revalued their currencies upward relative to the dollar. They did not do this frequently enough, so the United States, with its chronically overvalued currency, ran persistent balance of payments deficits. Between 1957 and 1968, for example, this country had to sell more than half its gold stock in an effort to keep the dollar pegged at the artificially high rate of $35 per ounce of gold.

Adjustment Mechanisms
Under the Bretton Woods System

Under the Bretton Woods system, devaluation was viewed as a last resort, to be used only after other methods of adjusting to payments imbalances had failed. What were these other methods?

We have already encountered most of them in our discussion of exchange rate determination in free markets (see pages 731–737). Any factor that increases the demand for, say, British pounds or that reduces the supply will push the exchange rate upward if it is free to adjust. If, however, the exchange rate is pegged, it is the balance of payments deficit rather than the exchange rate that will adjust when supply of or demand for a nation's money changes. Specifically, the British balance of payments deficit will shrink if either the demand for pounds increases or the supply decreases.

The two panels of Figure 38–7 illustrate this adjustment. In each case, the United Kingdom has a payments deficit, since the official exchange rate ($2.80) exceeds the equilibrium rate ($2.40). The deficit starts at AB in each diagram. Then either the demand curve moves outward as in part (a), or the supply curve moves inward as in part (b). With the exchange rate held at $2.80, the balance of payments deficit shrinks—to CB in part (a) or AC in part (b).

Referring back to our earlier discussions of the factors that underlie the demand and supply curves, then, we see that one way a deficit nation can improve its balance of payments is to reduce its *aggregate demand*, thus discouraging imports and cutting down its demand for foreign currency. Another is to *slow its rate of inflation*, thus encouraging exports and discouraging imports. Finally, it can *raise its interest rates* in order to attract more foreign capital. In a word, deficit nations were expected to follow restrictive monetary and fiscal policies *voluntarily* just as they would *automatically* have done under the old gold standard. However, just as under the gold standard, this medicine was often

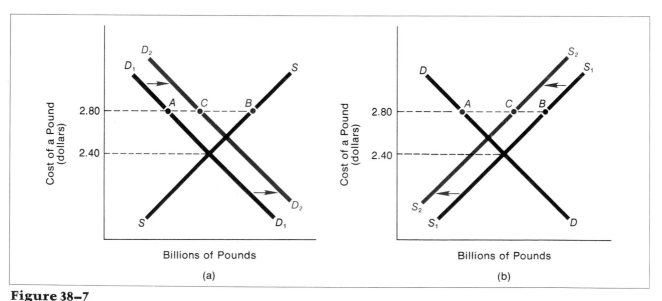

Figure 38–7
ADJUSTING TO BALANCE OF PAYMENTS DEFICITS
The two parts of this diagram illustrate alternative ways to cut England's balance of payments deficit while maintaining the exchange rate at $2.80 per pound. Part (a) might represent a reduction in British inflation, which would increase world demand for her export products. Or it could represent a rise in British interest rates, which would attract foreign capital. Part (b) might represent a reduction in British incomes, which would diminish English appetites for foreign goods. In either case, whether demand rises or supply falls, the balance of payments deficit is reduced: from AB to CB in part (a) and from AB to AC in part (b).

unpalatable, so deficit nations frequently resorted to a bewildering variety of **exchange controls**—laws and regulations that made it very difficult for its nationals to sell their own currency to get foreign exchange. Many countries still have such controls.

Surplus nations could, of course, have taken the opposite measures: pursuing expansive monetary and fiscal policies to increase economic growth and lower interest rates. But they often did not relish the inflation that would come with such actions, and, once again, left the burden of adjustment to the deficit nations. The general point about fixed exchange rates is that:

Under a system of fixed exchange rates, the government of a country loses some control over its domestic economy. There may be times when balance of payments considerations force it to contract its economy in order to cut down its demand for foreign currency, even though domestic needs are calling for expansion. Conversely, there may be times when the domestic economy needs to be reined in, but balance of payments considerations suggest expansion.

For these and other reasons, the gold-exchange standard that prevailed from 1944 to 1971 was not really one of fixed exchange rates but of rates that were fixed until they were changed.

The system worked fairly well for a number of years, but it finally broke down over its inability to "devalue" the U.S. dollar. In August 1971, the rapid depletion of America's reserves and the accumulation of foreign debts resulting from America's chronic balance of payment deficits forced President Richard M. Nixon to end fixed exchange rates. He unilaterally abolished the Bretton Woods system by announcing that the United States would no longer peg the value of the dollar by buying and selling gold. The industrial nations attempted to restore fixed rates at a meeting held at the Smithsonian Institution in late 1971, but their success was short-lived. In early 1973, the United States was forced to devalue once again, and this ended the Bretton Woods system for good.

Most observers today agree that the gold-exchange system could not have survived the incredible events of the 1970s in any case. The worldwide inflationary boom of 1972, the poor food harvests in 1972–1974, the huge increases in the price of oil in 1973–1974 and again in 1979, and the great worldwide recession of 1974–1976 all helped create a world in which the major countries were experiencing dramatically different inflation rates. For example, between 1972 and 1979 inflation averaged 5 percent per year in Germany, 8 percent in the United States, and 15 percent in Italy. As the purchasing-power theory reminds us, large differences in inflation rates call for *major* changes in currency values. And the Bretton Woods system was ill-suited to handle such major changes.

Why Try to Fix Exchange Rates?

In view of these and other severe problems with the Bretton Woods system, why did the international financial community work so hard to maintain fixed rates for so many years? The answer is that floating exchange rates, determined in free markets by supply and demand, also pose problems.

Chief among these was the worry that freely floating rates would be highly variable rates, which would add an unwanted element of riskiness to foreign trade. For example, if the exchange rate is 20 cents to the French franc, then a 1000-franc Parisian dress will cost $200. But should the franc appreciate to 25 cents, this same dress would cost $250. An American department store thinking of buying this dress may need to place its order far in advance and will want to know the cost *in dollars*. It may be worried about the possibility that the value of

"Then it's agreed. Until the dollar firms up, we let the clamshell float."

Drawing by Ed Fisher
© 1971, The New Yorker Magazine, Inc.

the franc will rise, so that the dress will cost more than $200. And such worries might inhibit trade.

There were two answers to this worry. First, we could hope that freely floating rates would prove not to be very volatile. Prices of many domestic consumer goods, for example, are determined by supply and demand in free markets and yet do not fluctuate unduly. Second, speculators might relieve business firms of exchange rate risks—for a fee, of course. Consider the department store example. If French francs cost 20 cents today, the department store manager can assure herself of paying exactly $200 for the dress several months from now by arranging for a speculator to deliver francs to her at 20 cents on the day she needs them. If the franc appreciates in the interim, it is the speculator, not the department store, that will take the financial beating. (And, of course, if the franc depreciates, the speculator will pocket the profits.)

This role of speculation, which is one of our 12 Ideas for Beyond the Final Exam, has been described earlier in the text—first in Chapter 1 and later in our discussion of the stock market in Chapter 24. The widespread fears that speculative activity in free markets will lead to wild gyrations in prices, while occasionally valid, are more often unfounded. The reason is quite simple. International currency speculators, if they are to make profits, must buy a currency when its value is low (thus helping to support the currency by pushing up its demand curve) and sell it when its value is high (thus holding down the price by adding to the supply curve).

This means that, if they are successful, speculators will be coming into the market as *buyers* just when demand is weak (or when supply is strong), and coming in as *sellers* just when demand is strong (or supply is scant). In doing so, they will help limit price fluctuations. Looked at the other way around, speculators can destabilize prices only if they are systematically willing to lose money.

Notice the stark contrast to the system of fixed exchange rates in which speculation often led to wild "runs" on currencies that were on the verge of devaluation. Speculative activity, which may very well be destabilizing under fixed rates, is likely to be stabilizing under floating rates.

We do not mean to imply here that there are no difficulties at all under floating exchange rates. Indeed, it may prove impossible to eliminate all exchange rate risks through speculation. And at the very least, speculators will demand a fee for their services—a fee that adds to the costs of trading across national borders. We only suggest that life is liable to be more placid than is commonly supposed.

The experience under floating rates since 1973 seems to have delivered clear verdicts on these two issues. First, exchange rates have in fact proven to be quite volatile—more volatile than many of the advocates of floating rates anticipated. Second, however, international trade has flourished despite this volatility. Speculators, we may surmise, are doing their job.

The Current Mixed System

Our current international financial system—where some currencies are still pegged in the old Bretton Woods manner, others are floating freely, and many more are floating subject to government interferences—has evolved gradually since President Nixon severed the dollar's link to gold. Though it continues to change and adapt, at least three features are quite evident.

The first is the decline in the notion that exchange rates should be fixed for relatively long periods of time. The demand by many countries in the early 1970s that the world quickly return to fixed exchange rates had largely subsided by the mid-1970s. Even where rates are still pegged to the dollar, devaluations and revaluations are now much more frequent—and smaller—than they were in the 1944–1971 period. Most free-world currency rates change very slightly on a day-to-day basis, and market forces generally determine the basic trends, up or down.

Second, however, it is clear that central banks do not hesitate to intervene to moderate exchange movements whenever they feel that such actions are appropriate. Typically, these interventions are aimed at ironing out transitory fluctuations. But there have been many instances in which central banks have, for a time, opposed basic trends in exchange rates. Deficit nations have bought their own currencies to prevent them from depreciating. Surplus nations have sold their own currencies to prevent them from appreciating. While we certainly no longer have many fixed exchange rates, few if any of the major currencies can really be said to be freely floating. The terms "dirty float" or "managed float" have been coined to describe this mongrel system.

The third unmistakable feature of the present international monetary system is the declining role of gold. The trend away from gold actually began before President Nixon's dramatic announcement in 1971, and by now it is only a minor exaggeration that gold plays no role in the world's financial system.

The decline of gold in international monetary affairs began much as it did in the history of domestic monies—with the introduction of a paper substitute. In 1970, the IMF began to issue bookkeeping entries called **Special Drawing Rights (SDRs).** SDRs serve as a form of international reserves, supplanting gold to some extent, because member nations can exchange SDRs for currency among themselves. They were quickly dubbed "paper gold" by the news media. The advantage of SDRs over gold, of course, is that they can be created whenever the world's commerce seems to need them, rather than when South African gold mines are in high gear. Just as central banking gave nations control over their money supplies, SDRs have given the world control over its supply of reserves.

The next stage in the decline of gold came when the link between the dollar and gold was severed in August 1971. The overvalued dollar immediately depreciated relative to many other currencies, and the price of gold skyrocketed. The drift away from gold picked up steam in 1975 and 1976 through a series of important events. First, the U.S. Treasury auctioned off a small part of its gold stock in 1975 and indicated that it was prepared to sell more in an effort to "demonetize" gold. Then, the IMF abolished the official price of gold in 1975, and subsequently followed the lead of the U.S. Treasury by initiating a program of periodic gold sales that continues to this day.

Nowadays there is a *free market*, which enables those who wish to invest in gold—dentists, jewelers, industrial users, speculators, and ordinary citizens who think of gold as a good store of value—to buy or sell as they wish. The price of gold, determined each day by the law of supply and demand, has proved to be quite volatile. Fortunes have been made and lost by investors in gold.

Developments in International Financial Markets Since 1973

Oil Prices and "Petrodollars"

The system of "dirty floating" is generally dated from early 1973. It received its first test in late 1973 and early 1974, when the Organization of Petroleum

Exporting Countries (OPEC) quadrupled the price of oil. This naturally led to huge surpluses in the balance of payments of the OPEC nations: Their combined current account surplus in 1974, for example, was a colossal $70 billion. Because the sum of the current-account balances of all nations must necessarily be zero (since one country's exports are another's imports), this meant that the rest of the world had a combined deficit of $70 billion. And this $70 billion total deficit was distributed quite unevenly across the nations of the world. The United States, with its large supplies of domestic energy resources, suffered a deficit in the current account of only about $3.5 billion in 1974, while the much smaller economy of the United Kingdom (which did not yet have oil from the North Sea) had a deficit of about $8.5 billion. It is hard to imagine fixed exchange rates being maintained under such circumstances.

The fact that OPEC's oil exports exceeded its imports by such large amounts led to a financial problem that journalists dubbed "recycling petrodollars." The OPEC nations could not or would not spend all of their enormous receipts from oil sales. Instead, they invested their unspendable revenues in the securities of several of the advanced industrial nations. While America, Switzerland, and other industrial nations were paying much more for oil, Arab funds were flowing back into New York, Zurich, and other financial centers. Thus the balance of payments problems were manageable for these countries. But virtually none of this capital flowed to the less developed countries that did not export oil. This left these poor countries in an almost impossible position: They needed foreign exchange to pay for oil, but they did not receive any through capital flows.

To deal with this problem, the IMF set up a *recycling facility* through which the foreign capital flowing into some developed countries could be funneled to the countries most in need of foreign exchange. This facility, which lasted only until 1976, helped alleviate the short-run crisis in some nations. But as it turned out, much of the financial assistance went from the advanced nations who were in good shape to the advanced nations who were in distress. This left the developing nations to solve their foreign currency problems by borrowing in the private market, and several years of this practice left them heavily in debt.

Well before they could begin to pay off these debts, OPEC struck again. The price of oil more than doubled during 1979, and the combined current account surplus of the OPEC nations (the rest of the world's deficit) skyrocketed from "only" $47 billion in 1978 to $158 billion in 1980. As in 1974, the currencies of the developed countries withstood the shock fairly well; they once again financed their oil deficits through capital inflows. And the nonoil developing nations again turned to borrowing on the private market. No one yet knows how they will deal with the long-run problem of earning enough foreign currency to pay their oil bills and redeem their IOUs.

The European Monetary System

As already noted, floating exchange rates are no magical cure-all. One particular problem beset the members of the European Economic Community (EEC). These Common Market countries seek a unified market like the United States and have a long-range goal of establishing a single currency for all member countries. Floating rates would make this goal impossible. So in 1973 some of the member countries entered into an agreement whereby exchange rates among their currencies would remain relatively *fixed* while Common Market currencies as a group would rise or fall *relative to the rest of the world*. International financial institutions seem always to acquire colorful nicknames, and this one was dubbed "the snake."

Within a short time, however, both Britain and Italy found themselves unable to maintain parity with the strong currencies of Germany and the Netherlands. Britain was the first to break the snake and let the pound float. But soon Italy and France also had to devalue relative to the mark. Several countries subsequently dropped in and out of the snake, and by early 1978, only Belgium, Denmark, Germany, the Netherlands, and Norway remained members.

In 1979 the snake was strengthened and formalized into the *European Monetary System* (EMS), and broadened to include France and, with special arrangements, Italy and the United Kingdom. The EMS includes detailed provisions for coping with exchange rates which threaten to get out of line with the others, and it is widely regarded as the first step, albeit a small one, toward a unified European currency.

Concluding Remark: Where Do We Go from Here?

The 1970s saw drastic changes in the international monetary system, and no one can be sure that the changes during the 1980s will not be equally dramatic. Just where is the international monetary system headed? No one really knows. The system is still in a state of flux, as each nation decides to what extent it wants to influence its exchange rate, and how.

In such an environment, predictions are no doubt foolhardy. Yet it seems unlikely that the world will move back to a system of fixed exchange rates as under the Bretton Woods agreements. For better or for worse, floating rates are here to stay—at least in some form. And most economists feel that the change has been for the better.

Summary

1. Exchange rates state the value of one currency in terms of another, and thus influence the patterns of world trade in important ways.

2. If governments do not interfere, exchange rates will be determined in free markets by the usual laws of supply and demand. Such a system is called floating exchange rates.

3. Demand for a nation's currency is derived from foreigners' desires to purchase that country's goods and services or to invest in its assets. Any change that increases the demand for a nation's currency will cause its exchange rate to appreciate under floating rates.

4. Supply of a nation's currency is derived from the desire of that country's citizens to purchase foreign goods and services or to invest in foreign assets. Any change that increases the supply of a nation's currency will cause its exchange rate to depreciate under floating rates.

5. In the long run, purchasing-power parity plays a major role in exchange rate movements. The purchasing-power parity theory states that relative price levels in any two countries determine the exchange rate between their currencies. Therefore, countries with relatively low inflation rates normally will have appreciating currencies.

6. Over shorter periods, the pace of economic activity and the level of interest rates exert a greater influence on the exchange rate.

7. Exchange rates can be fixed at nonequilibrium levels by governments that are willing and able to mop up any excess of quantity supplied over quantity demanded, or provide any excess of quantity demanded over quantity supplied. In the first case, the country is suffering from a balance of payments deficit because of its overvalued currency. In the second, an undervalued currency has given it a balance of payments surplus.

8. This conceptual definition of the balance of payments is often hard to apply in practice, so the actual U.S. balance of payments statistics are rather complicated and are sometimes difficult to interpret.

9. In the early part of this century, the world was on a particular system of fixed exchange rates called the gold standard, in which the value of every nation's currency was fixed in terms of gold. But this created problems because nations could not control their own money supplies and because the world could not control its total supply of gold.

10. After World War II, the gold standard was replaced by

the gold-exchange (or Bretton Woods) system where rates were again fixed, or rather, fixed until further notice. In this system, the U.S. dollar was the basis of international currency values.

11. The gold-exchange system served the world well and helped restore world trade, but it got into trouble when the dollar became chronically overvalued since the system provided no way to remedy this situation.

12. Since 1971, the world has gradually been moving toward a system of relatively free exchange rates, though there are plenty of exceptions. We now have a thoroughly mixed system of "dirty" or "managed" floating which continues to evolve and adapt.

13. Floating rates are not without their problems; importers and exporters justifiably worry about fluctuations in exchange rates. But these problems seem manageable, if not completely solvable, and few people think that a return to fixed exchange rates is likely.

Concepts for Review

International monetary system	Fixed exchange rates	Gold-exchange system (Bretton
Exchange rate	Balance of payments deficit	Woods system)
Appreciation	and surplus	International Monetary Fund (IMF)
Depreciation	Current account	Exchange controls
Devaluation	Capital account	"Dirty" or "managed" floating
Revaluation	Balance of trade	Special Drawing Rights (SDRs)
Floating exchange rates	Gold standard	The European Monetary System
Purchasing-power parity theory		

Questions for Discussion

1. What items do you own, or routinely consume, that are produced abroad? What countries do these come from? How have your purchases affected the exchange rates between the dollar and these currencies?

2. If the dollar appreciates relative to the Japanese yen, will the Sony stereo you have longed for become more or less expensive? What effect do you imagine this will have on American demands for Sonys? Does the American demand curve for yen, therefore, slope upward or downward? Explain.

3. Inflation in West Germany has been steadily below that in the United States. What, then, does the purchasing-power parity theory predict should be happening to the exchange rate between the mark and the dollar? Ask your instructor what actually has happened.

4. Use supply and demand diagrams to analyze the effect on the exchange rate between the dollar and the British pound if:
   a. Britain's flow of North Sea oil becomes so large that England starts exporting oil to America.
   b. British dockworkers refuse to unload ships that arrive with cargo from America but continue to load ships that sail from Britain.
   c. The Federal Reserve raises interest rates in America.
   d. The U.S. government, to help settle the problems of the Middle East, gives huge amounts of foreign aid to Israel and her Arab neighbors.

5. How are the problems of a country faced with a balance of payments deficit similar to those posed by a government regulation that holds the price of peanuts above the equilibrium level? (*Hint:* Think of each in terms of a supply–demand diagram.)

6. Look at the U.S. balance of payments accounts table in the text (Table 38–2 on page 740). Figure out where each of the following actions you could have taken in 1980 would have been recorded in these accounts:
   a. You spent the summer traveling in Europe.
   b. You sent $25 to your uncle in Canada as a birthday present.
   c. You bought a new Volkswagen.
   d. You sold stock on the Japanese stock market.
   e. You drove over the Canadian border carrying American records in your trunk and sold them to a friend in Canada. (*Hint:* Would your sale have been recorded anywhere?)

7. Under the old gold standard, what do you think happened to world prices when there was a huge gold strike in California in 1849? What do you think happened when the world went without any important new gold strikes for 20 years or so?

8. Explain why the members of the Bretton Woods conference in 1944 wanted to establish a system of fixed exchange rates. What was the flaw that led to the ultimate breakdown of the system in 1971?

9. Suppose you want to reserve hotel rooms in London for the coming summer but are worried that the value of the pound may rise between now and then, making the rooms too expensive for your budget. Explain how a speculator could relieve you of this worry. (Don't actually try it. Speculators deal only in very large sums!)

Problems of the Less Developed Countries

I n this chapter we will describe some of the special problems of the **less developed countries (LDCs)** and look at the measures that have been proposed to increase their rate of growth. We will show that although in recent years standards of living in the LDCs have begun to rise significantly, their rapid population growth and their vulnerability to such external shocks as the rise in oil prices and other similar perils mean that many problems still threaten their economies. Next, we will examine the problems that impede growth in the LDCs, including scarcity of capital, poor natural resources, lack of education, and unemployment. Then we consider what the LDCs can do to help themselves and what the rest of the world can do to help them. Finally, we describe some specific forms of aid advanced countries can and do provide to the developing nations.

Living in the LDCs

Just about two-thirds of the world's population lives in countries whose per capita GNP is less than $500 per year, evaluated (as well as it is possible to do) in terms of today's prices in the United States. Table 39–1 shows that there are a number of countries in which annual per capita income is under $200. Even after adjustment for differences in measurement of GNP in the United States and the poorer countries, this probably comes to an annual income figure under $600. To us, residents of an economy that offers an average income more than 10 times as high, such a figure is not only likely to seem incredible, it is all but incomprehensible. Few of us can *really* imagine what life would be like if our family income were reduced to, say, $2000 per year. It is even hard to envision survival on such amounts. It must be emphasized that these figures do *not* represent the living standards of a small group of outcasts from their own societies. Rather, they are *typical* of perhaps a majority of those who live in Asia, Africa, and Latin America.

What can life be like in such circumstances? No brief description can really bridge the gulf between our range of experience and theirs. Yet it can offer us a glimpse into a way of life that few of us will want to share.

Inhabitants of many of the less developed countries live with their large families in one-room shanties or apartments, their water supplies are scanty, polluted, and often miles from home, their only source of energy is that of man

Table 39–1
PER CAPITA GNP IN DEVELOPED
AND LESS DEVELOPED
COUNTRIES, 1979

	(measured in U.S. dollars)
Developed Countries	
United States	$10,820
West Germany	11,730
Sweden	11,920
Less Developed Countries	
Bolivia	$550
Burma	160
Egypt	460
Ethiopia	130
Haiti	260
India	190

SOURCE: Population Reference Bureau.

Table 39–2
INFANT MORTALITY AND LIFE EXPECTANCY
IN DEVELOPED AND LESS DEVELOPED
COUNTRIES, 1978 or 1979

	INFANT MORTALITY (deaths per 1000 births)	LIFE EXPECTANCY AT BIRTH (years)
Developed Countries		
United States	13	74
West Germany	15	72
Sweden	7	75
Less Developed Countries		
Bolivia	168	51
Burma	140	53
Egypt	90	55
Ethiopia	178	39
Haiti	130	51
India	134	52

SOURCE: Population Reference Bureau.

and beast, and their sparse harvests are wrung from miserable soil in good years, with starvation threatened perhaps every five years when the rains do not come and the crops fail.[1] With no surplus in production, no food can be put into reserves, and the old, the infirm, and the very young are likely to perish.

The life of a man in an LDC is hard enough, with its low nutritional level, its lack of equipment to help him in his work, and its frequency of debilitating diseases. But his life is luxurious compared with that of his wife. She is usually married by the age of 14, bears 8 or 10 children, and by 35 is often a toothless old crone. If (as is true of some 80 percent of the population) she inhabits a rural area, she may have to trudge miles every day to fetch water for the family. She sews all the family's clothes by hand and cooks its meals. There is not enough money for preground flour, so part of the woman's daily work is to pound the grain by hand for food for the family—perhaps an additional two hours of hard labor. She also tends the gardens that produce food for the family, although, except in Moslem countries where women are sequestered, she is also expected to put in a full day in the fields during the six months of the agricultural season.

Another duty of the woman in an LDC is to bring produce, wood, or whatever she has to trade to market a couple of times a week, and she must often walk as many as 10 miles each way with bundles as heavy as she can carry on her back or on her head. She has no respite in the raising of her children, since they are likely not to have a school to attend when they are well or a hospital to go to when they are sick. It is no wonder that she ages so much faster than a woman in our society.

Table 39–2 gives the percentage of infant deaths for each 1000 live births and

[1]It has been estimated that in some famine years in the 1970s, half a million people died as a result in Bangladesh; 200,000 in Ethiopia; 100,000–250,000 in the Sahelian zone of Africa; and more than 800,000 in just three of the states of India (*The New York Times*, October 27, 1976).

the average life expectancy of a newborn child in some countries ranging from the most underdeveloped to the most affluent. The contrasts are dramatic. In Bolivia, 168 babies die of every 1000 that are born, while the comparable figure in Sweden is only seven. In many countries people survive only until their late 40s, while in Scandinavia they live to be 75. There is little question about the quality of life in less developed lands.

Most of the inhabitants of many LDCs are shockingly poor. Malnutrition and disease are widespread. The sheer process of living and surviving taxes the people to the utmost and makes them old before their time.

Recent Trends

Do recent trends offer hope of improvement? Here there is both good news and bad. The good news is perhaps the most remarkable. In the last decade, real GNP in the LDCs has been estimated to have grown, on average, at 5.6 percent a year (see Table 39–3). Even more important, income per capita has been growing at an annual rate greater than $2\frac{1}{2}$ percent. This means that:

Despite population increases, some LDCs have succeeded in breaking out of the stagnation trap. If growth continues as it has recently, an average family in an underdeveloped area can look forward to a doubling of its living standards in less than 30 years. Or put another way, standards of living will be increasing faster than they did in the United States in the nineteenth century!

Clearly, for the first time there is hope for a major reduction in absolute poverty in the LDCs.

Thus, the good news is very good indeed. The bad news is not so straight-forward, and its seriousness is partially a matter of interpretation. There are several developments that can be considered either as merely unfortunate or as thoroughly ominous.

First, while the percentage rates of growth of per capita incomes in the LDCs have been very impressive, the industrialized countries, with their initially high incomes, have not exactly been standing still. Indeed, largely because their population growth has been slower, the percentage growth rate in per capita incomes has been higher in the developed countries. But even if the *percentage* increases in their per capita incomes had been very similar, *absolute* incomes would have continued to rise more quickly in the richer lands. Where per capita income is $100 a year, a $2\frac{1}{2}$ percent growth rate translates into a $2.50 annual improvement; however, where per capita income is $5000 a year, the same $2\frac{1}{2}$ percent rate of growth adds $125 a year to the income of the average person. As a result:

The purchasing power of the average family in an LDC is falling further behind that of a typical family in a wealthy economy. That is, relative poverty (the difference between the purchasing power of families in the two types of economies) continues to grow worse, despite the noteworthy postwar improvement in the LDCs.

Second, many critics, notably those on the left, believe that the $2\frac{1}{2}$ percent growth rate has been accompanied by a worsening distribution of income in the LDCs. The rise in population has worsened the living standards of people on marginal lands with inadequate rain (about 40 percent of Indian farmers and a

Table 39–3
AVERAGE ANNUAL GROWTH RATES OF REAL
GROSS DOMESTIC PRODUCT IN DEVELOPED
AND LESS DEVELOPED COUNTRIES,
APPROXIMATELY 1965–1978

	APPROXIMATELY 1965–1970 (percent)	APPROXIMATELY 1973–1978 (percent)
Developed Countries		
United States	3.2	2.8
West Germany	4.5	2.0
Sweden	3.9	0.9
Less Developed Countries		
Colombia	6.9	5.5
Haiti	1.2	4.5
Iraq	4.2	9.4
Pakistan	4.8	4.9
Panama	7.8	1.6
Tanzania	5.3	5.6
Zambia	1.8	1.5

SOURCE: United Nations.

Table 39–4
BIRTHRATE MINUS DEATH RATE
IN DEVELOPED AND LESS
DEVELOPED COUNTRIES, 1975–1980
(ESTIMATED)

	(births minus deaths per 1000 population)
Developed Countries	
United States	7
West Germany	−2
Sweden	1
Less Developed Countries	
Bolivia	25
Burma	24
Egypt	30
Ethiopia	25
Haiti	26
India	21

SOURCE: Population Reference Bureau.

large proportion of Africans). Add the massive explosion of urban unemployment, and one gets several hundred million people who are no better off and possibly worse off.

Third, a continuing problem within the LDCs is the relatively high growth rate of their populations.

While in the United States and some countries of Western Europe, net population growth has fallen almost to zero, the population explosion continues in many of the LDCs.

Table 39–4 tells the story. For the sample of LDCs shown, the annual growth rate of population continues perhaps ten times as high as it is in the industrialized countries. Clearly, the more closely the growth in population approximates the growth in national income, the more slowly standards of living will rise, since there will be that many more persons among whom the additional product must be divided. If population growth is exactly equal to the growth rate of national income, obviously the average standard of living must be at an absolute standstill. A recent estimate indicates that the rise in population in LDCs is in fact consuming nearly half the increase in their GNP.

Fourth, the relatively high growth rate in per capita incomes has not been uniform throughout the LDCs. In some countries, such as Sri Lanka, Malaysia, and Cuba, growth rates have been extremely low.

Finally, the LDCs have shown themselves highly vulnerable to such shocks as the oil crisis in 1979. Much as the fall in Iranian exports and rise in oil prices affected the industrialized economies, it undoubtedly damaged the LDCs even more, leading to enormous deficits and foreign debts for the countries least able to afford them. In other words, the new growth trends in the LDCs may be quite fragile, and their continuation cannot simply be taken for granted.

Before leaving the issue of recent growth in the LDCs, it may be helpful to offer a little perspective on the entire matter. First, it should be recognized that sustained growth is a very recent invention, dating from the Industrial Revolution—the beginning of the eighteenth century. It has been estimated that per capita income in England in 1800 was no higher than in third-century Rome. Before the Industrial Revolution, real wages in England may have reached their peak in the fifteenth century—the end of the Middle Ages—from which they fell to their lowest level ever reached after the Middle Ages in the reign of Queen Elizabeth, more than a century later.

On the other hand, growth in the LDCs is not an innovation of recent decades. In the three decades before World War I, exports from the tropical countries grew faster than national income in the wealthier countries, and, no doubt, in these LDCs output per capita was also growing. Since income data for that period are not available, we do not know by how much, but we do know that the earlier growth was vulnerable to disruption—World War I, the Great Depression, and other catastrophic events all but ended growth in the LDCs for nearly 40 years. Thus, today's high growth rates cannot just be taken for granted and extrapolated into the future.

Impediments to Prosperity in the LDCs

No one has produced a definitive list of causes of the poverty of the LDCs, just as no one can pretend to have produced a foolproof prescription for its cure. Yet there is a general agreement on the main conditions contributing to the economic problems of LDCs. These include lack of physical capital, scarcity of valuable natural resources, rapid growth of populations, lack of education, unemployment, and social and political impediments to business activity. Let us examine each of these in turn.

Scarcity of Physical Capital

The LDCs are obviously handicapped by their lack of modern factories and machinery. In addition, they lack infrastructure—good roads, railroads, port facilities, and so on. But capital is not easy to acquire. If it is to be provided by the populations of the LDCs themselves, they must save the required resources—that is, as we saw in Chapter 35, they must give up consumption in order to free the resources needed to build plants, equipment, and roads. That is fairly easy in a rich community, where substantial saving still leaves the public well off in terms of current consumption. But in an LDC, where malnutrition is a constant threat, the bulk of the inhabitants cannot save except at enormous sacrifice to their families. Moreover, in many of the LDCs, tradition imputes little virtue to investment in business, so that even the wealthy are not terribly anxious to put their savings into productive equipment. Thus:

Because of poverty, which makes saving difficult, if not impossible, and because of traditions that do not encourage investment, the LDCs' growth rates of domestically financed capital are lower than those in the developed countries. In an industrialized country, 15 percent or more of its GNP typically goes into capital formation, while for the LDCs the figure is closer to 10 percent.

One way to help matters is to obtain the funds for investment from abroad. There is a long tradition of foreign investment in developing countries. For example, throughout the first half of the nineteenth century the United States almost constantly drew capital from abroad, though the amounts involved were only a small proportion of U.S. GNP. In recent decades a considerable share of the resources going to the LDCs from abroad has come from foreign governments as part of their aid programs. While some of the resources provided in this way have been used wastefully, informed observers generally agree that the waste incurred under these programs has not been spectacularly great, and they conclude that these capital transfers from the rich countries to the poor have at least worked in the right direction.

Capital can also be transferred to an LDC when a private firm chooses to invest money in such a country to build a factory or to explore for oil in order to increase its own profits. This too seems to have been helpful to the LDCs. In earlier days, it sometimes gave an unacceptable degree of political influence to the foreign firms, particularly when the LDC was a colony of an industrial country. In recent years this difficulty may have become rarer. Nowadays, it is more often the outside firm that is afraid of the government of the LDC rather than vice versa, with foreign proprietors frequently fearful of rigid control by the government of the LDC in which it invests. Sometimes it even fears outright expropriation—that the government will simply take over its property in the LDC with, or even without, compensation because of the hostile attitudes that residents of many LDCs hold toward large foreign companies.

It is difficult for a resident of an industrialized country like the United States to realize how much hatred and resentment is felt in less developed countries toward the "northern imperialist powers." This resentment is focused in particular on *multinational corporations*—companies like IBM, Royal Dutch Shell, Volkswagen, and Unilever—which have their headquarters in an industrialized country and their operations in a variety of less developed countries. Multinationals may first process their own raw materials in one country, ship them to another to make them into parts, and assemble them in still a third. Some of these corporations, among them the oil companies, specialize in the extraction and/or marketing of raw materials, while others, like IBM and Volkswagen, specialize in manufacturing. Many LDCs regard these and other giant foreign corporations as instruments of imperialist exploitation, not as firms which happen to carry on their activities wherever the dictates of efficiency require, contributing benefits to each of the countries in which they operate.

It is true that foreign firms hope to make more money out of an LDC than they put into it, but that is only natural, since otherwise their investment would not have been expected to be profitable, and the funds would therefore not have been invested in the first place. But there are usually *mutual* gains from trade. Investment will be useful to the LDCs if in the process of earning these profits foreign firms build factories, infrastructure, and provide jobs that leave the community wealthier than it would otherwise have been. The evidence is that this is in fact what foreign private investment has typically accomplished in recent decades.

A problem with foreign business investment that is more serious is the danger that foreign firms will fail to train native personnel in the skills necessary to run the factories built by those companies. Often the foreigner will bring with him his own managers, engineers, and technicians, and the work force from the LDCs is kept in menial jobs in which on-the-job training is minimal. In recent years the LDCs have begun to deal with this problem by restricting immigration of foreign personnel, giving them work permits only for limited periods and requiring at least some minimum employment of native personnel in key positions.

Another danger posed by foreign investment is that it may prevent future financial independence. Profits are a major source of the funds used for investment. If foreign investment takes over the LDCs' most profitable industries, then newly formed capital—new plants and equipment—will also be owned predominantly by foreigners.

Scarcity of Valuable Natural Resources

Many of the LDCs suffer from poor natural resources—shortages of minerals, large desert areas, and climates that are not conducive to productivity because they are too dry or too hot. Obviously, a country in which natural resources are poor in quality suffers a serious handicap. Of those LDCs whose incomes have grown most rapidly in the postwar period, a high proportion have been rich in mineral products, which they were able to export—copper, iron ore, bauxite, and especially oil.

Yet abundant natural resources are not absolutely essential for economic growth. Nearly half the LDCs whose national incomes have grown more than 5 percent a year in recent decades have *not* been major exporters of raw materials. And several industrial countries, notably Switzerland and Japan, have achieved high and rapidly rising living standards despite their very limited endowments of natural resources.

The importance of a country's raw material endowment depends very heavily on the cost of transportation. When transport is expensive and risky, the economy that must get its raw materials from abroad suffers a serious handicap. But as the cost of transportation declines, this problem is correspondingly diminished. The invention of railroads and of steamships with metal hulls has made a tremendous difference in the cost of transportation of bulky inputs from abroad, as has the substitution of oil and electricity for coal—a fuel that is extremely bulky and costly to transport. Improved methods of iron and steel processing, which have sharply reduced the amount of coal needed per ton of metal, have also helped a good deal.

Thus, while natural resources are important for economic development, they are less critical than they once were, and they have never been an absolute precondition for economic growth. In any event, the scarcity or abundance of raw materials is not a promising instrument for development policy, since a country can do little about the quality of natural resources with which it is endowed (though it *can* influence the rate of exploration for them and the rate at which they are depleted).

Population Growth

Population growth is often described as the primary villain in the LDCs. We have already noted that, on the average, their populations grow far more rapidly than those in the wealthier countries. And though the growth rate has recently been declining in many of the less developed countries, overall the population of the LDCs is expanding at a rate that will double in less than 30 years, requiring a doubling of housing, schools, hospitals, and so on—a heavy real cost for an LDC.

The growth in population has perhaps been stimulated by improvements in medical care, which have reduced death rates spectacularly. Today, in some areas, death rates (ratio of deaths to population) are only one-quarter or one-fifth as high as birthrates. While formerly it was not unusual for half a nation's children to die before the age of 20, today in many countries this is true of only some 4 percent of those populations. This dramatic decline can be attributed primarily to inexpensive public health measures—reduction in stomach diseases through purer water supplies, reduction in the incidence of malaria by the draining of swamps, insecticide spraying of the breeding grounds of infectious mosquitoes, eradication of smallpox by vaccination, and so forth. The more expensive treatment of illness, using modern medical techniques and miracle drugs, seems to have contributed far less to population growth than have public health measures.

But not all LDCs suffer from serious population problems. India, Indonesia, and Egypt are frequently cited examples of population pressures. On the other hand, many African countries and parts of Latin America still have populations so small that they are denied economies of larger scale communication and transportation. The economy of a sparsely settled country whose electric power and telecommunication lines must traverse great unpopulated areas is under a costly handicap.

Even most countries with rapidly growing populations have somehow been able to increase their per capita outputs. New technology, particularly in agriculture, has played a critical role. The *green revolution*—breeding new species of grain whose yields per acre are spectacularly greater than their predecessors'—has contributed enormously. Of course, no one can guess how long food production can stay ahead of population growth in this vital race.

Experience has shown also that there is no iron law of population growth such as that envisioned by Malthus. Higher incomes do not inevitably lead to a corresponding rise in population. On the contrary, as countries have grown wealthier, more urbanized, and their people better educated, population growth has often declined significantly, perhaps because consumers had other things to occupy them, or perhaps because they needed to depend less on a large family for security in old age or for a labor force on the family farm.

There is also evidence that campaigns for family planning can significantly decrease birthrates in LDCs if these programs are adequately organized, planned, and financed. In sum: Population growth is a crucial problem for economic growth in the LDCs, whose governments have begun to realize what a large capital drain it represents. Yet not all LDCs suffer from overpopulation; and while there have been some failures, birth control programs appear to be promising.

Educational and Technical Training

Everyone knows that educational levels in the LDCs are much lower than they are in the wealthier countries. There are fewer graduates of elementary schools, far fewer graduates of high schools, and enormously fewer college graduates. The percentage of the population that is literate is much lower than in industrialized nations. The issue is how much of a handicap this constitutes for economic growth.

If, by "education," we refer to general learning rather than technical (trade) schooling, the evidence is that it makes considerably less difference for economic growth than is often believed. For example, the number of jobs that clearly require secondary (high school) education rarely seems to exceed 10 percent of the labor force. Various studies that have investigated whether there is a statistical relationship between the economic growth of an economy and its typical educational level have so far failed to turn up any significant correlation between the two. Other suggestive evidence can easily be cited. For example, in 1840 when Great Britain ruled the markets of the world, only 59 percent of the British adult population was literate, while in the United States, Scandinavia, and Germany, then all relatively undeveloped countries, the figure was about 80 percent.

All of this is not meant to imply that education is worthless. On the contrary, it obviously offers many benefits in and of itself, which need not be discussed here. But it does suggest that if a government invests in education *purely as a means to stimulate economic growth*, only a very limited outlay is justifiable on these grounds.

Matters are quite different when we turn to technical training. There is clearly a high payoff to the training of electricians, machinists, draftsmen, construction workers, and the like. While the number of persons involved need not be very high in proportion to the population, the role played by such specialists is crucial. However, the LDCs would find it a very heavy drain upon their scarce foreign currency to send young people abroad to learn these skills in the numbers called for by the needs of the economy. One of the main inhibitions to adequate training in these areas is that in many countries such skills are held in low esteem and considered inferior to training in the liberal arts. Consequently, technical education is often handicapped by low budgets, low teacher salaries— which discourage good people from entering the field—and the prejudice of potential students against such fields.

Training in improved farming methods also has a great deal to contribute. In many of the LDCs, agricultural methods produce yields far lower than the best of the known techniques can offer. As one leading observer, Nobel Prize-winner Sir W. Arthur Lewis, has remarked:

If this gap could be closed, the economies of these countries would be unrecognizable. Indeed . . . no impact can be made on mass living standards without revolutionizing agricultural performance.[2]

There seem to be no easy ways to provide the necessary education to the farmers who cannot spare the time to attend schools; and training their children also involves a number of critical obstacles. Religious beliefs often lead parents to object to schooling of their children, particularly of girls; in areas where literacy is low (where the problem is generally most serious), truly literate and knowledgeable teachers are almost impossible to find in any substantial numbers; and children who do complete schooling have a tendency to leave the farms and move to the cities. Programs to provide help to the peasants on their own farms have had only limited success. Indeed, lack of training is only part of the problem. Many other things are needed to make modern farming methods possible—farms larger than the five acres that are typical in a number of countries are required to permit the use of modern machinery where it is appropriate. Roads and storage facilities must be built. Credit must be made available to farmers. Financial arrangements must be changed so the farmer need no longer give up half his crop to landlords and tax collectors whom he can surely regard as little more than parasites and who undermine his incentives for improved productivity.

Unemployment

One of the most noteworthy features of the growth of the LDCs has been an increase in unemployment as population shifted out of agriculture into the cities. Increased schooling has stimulated the migration out of the rural areas, as has

[2]W. A. Lewis, *Development Economics, An Outline* (Morristown, N.J.: General Learning Press, 1974), page 25.

unionization, which has often produced a huge gap between urban and rural wages. Government investment policies have also favored construction of schools, hospitals, and other facilities in the cities, and as a result, large numbers of migrants have entered the cities to swell the ranks of the unemployed. The unemployment rate among young urban workers has been particularly high; indeed, rates as high as 50 percent are not unheard of.

These figures are compounded by the phenomenon of **disguised unemployment.** For example, ten persons may do a job for which only six are needed. The statistics would show no unemployment among the ten workers, even though four of them really contribute nothing to output. Some observers believe that this is such a widespread problem in rural areas that even a substantial reverse migration of the urban unemployed back to the farms would add very little to production, at least in some of the LDCs.

An important consequence of all this is that in many LDCs unemployment may not be accompanied by any substantial reduction in output, in contrast to the situation in industrialized economies. But this does not mean that unemployment in the LDCs is not a serious problem. What it does mean is that it may sometimes be desirable for those economies to avoid the use of labor-saving equipment, partly because it will result in better use of an abundant resource, and partly because it will contribute to the solution of a serious social problem. Thus, increased output is desirable perhaps primarily because it helps to sop up unemployed labor. This is in contrast to the usual situation in the developed countries in which increased employment is desirable perhaps primarily because it increases income and output.

Social Impediments to Entrepreneurship

One of the magic ingredients of economic growth is **entrepreneurship.** As discussed in Chapter 32, entrepreneurship is a combination of attributes: imagination, daring, willingness to take risks, a sense of timing, and an ability to recognize profitable opportunities, all driven by a love of money, power, or some other such goal, which together combine to make up the quality of business leadership. There are many persons who believe that the main source of the decline of the British economy is the disappearance of entrepreneurship, and others suggest that in the United States the drive for achievement, which is needed to produce effective entrepreneurs, is not what it once was. Countries with remarkable growth records, such as Japan, are said to be today's centers of entrepreneurial drive.

Whatever the truth of these diagnoses, it is clear that the LDCs need entrepreneurs if their economies are to grow rapidly. But in many of these economies, there are serious inhibitions to entrepreneurship. Traditional social values often accord relatively low status to business activity. Indeed, those traditional values even prevent businesses from seeking ways to attract and please their customers and their work force. In addition, high positions in business in many LDCs are often determined by family connections and inheritance, not by ability.

In the LDCs growth will be inhibited until customs can be modified to increase the social status of economic activity, to make it respectable for private business people and managers of public enterprises to do their best to attract business and increase productivity, and to assign responsibility on the basis of ability rather than family connections.

Government Inhibition of Business Activity

In addition to social impediments to business, the political situation in the LDCs often is detrimental to business success. Business is not helped by unstable governments or by the uncertainty that accompanies such an environment, especially if there is a high likelihood of revolution. Foreign investment will be discouraged where there is fear of expropriation or of unstable currencies that may fall in value and wipe out hard-earned profits. And native business people may live in fear of nationalization or even imprisonment—possibilities that are not likely to encourage investment.

In addition, in the normal course of events, governments in the LDCs are often inclined to interfere with business activity in a variety of ways that seem relatively innocuous—but whose effects can be deadly. Price controls are often imposed at levels that make the controlled activity totally unprofitable and cause it to wither. Licenses and other direct controls are frequently administered by incompetent bureaucrats, who tie up business activity in red tape. As a matter of prestige of the currency, exchange rates are often set so high that exports from the LDC cannot compete on the world market. The governments sometimes expropriate and seek to operate foreign firms before they have trained native personnel to run them. In short:

Poorly conceived economic policies can impede business activity and hence economic growth in the LDCs. But, then, it must be admitted that the LDCs have no monopoly on foolish economic policies!

What LDCs Can Do to Help Themselves

This completes our list of some of the main problems that limit growth in the LDCs. Of course, no such list can really be complete, but it can indicate the sorts of issues that have occupied the attention of development economists.

The list also indicates directly some of the things that governments in the LDCs may do to stimulate the development of their economies. Since population growth is such an overwhelmingly important problem, it seems logical to begin there.

Control of Population Growth

As we have noted, rapid population growth is a major problem for a number of LDCs, and governments have been struggling to find a workable solution. Programs set up to distribute contraceptives and propaganda against large families have achieved modest success; but in some countries with particularly severe population problems the governments have been dissatisfied with the results of these voluntary efforts. In India a program making use of compulsory sterilization aroused the anger of the public and finally led to the downfall of the government. Ironically enough, it was communist China which, along with Singapore, decided to employ strong financial incentives for the purpose. In China, government support is provided for a first child. For a second, the support is withdrawn and some financial penalties imposed; and for a third child, the penalties are really prohibitive for most people. Because this program has been launched only very recently it is impossible to provide clear evidence of its success or failure. However, observers come away impressed with its initial impact. Everywhere in China one meets people who say they are determined to have only one child. If this proves to be reasonably accurate, it may produce one of the most dramatic decreases in birthrates the world has ever seen.

Paradoxically, the hidden disadvantages of a large and sharp reduction in the birthrate may be greater than the obvious advantages. One of the immediate advantages of a diminution in births is a decreased burden of child dependency, which begins as soon as the birth-control measures take effect. But keep in mind that until very recently the birthrate in China has been high; about 50 percent of the population is under 20. And this population group will be 20 to 40 years old in the year 2000. Thus, if the official target of zero growth for the year 2000 is met, the birthrate will have to be very low indeed, considering the huge number of persons of child-bearing age. If the target is attained, the burden of dependent children in the year 2000 will be small; the number of the aged (born before 1940) will also be moderate relative to the size of the economically active population. But a generation later, the very small number of persons born at the turn of the century will have reached the prime working ages, and the bumper birth crop of 1955 to 1975 will be over 60 years old. There will in fact be more persons aged 60 to 70 than in any other age decade, and these people will be dependent, and an enormous burden, on the small labor force that must support them. It will be a high price to pay for the rapid cessation of population growth.

Structural Economic Reform

Let's deal briefly now with a number of changes in the economic structure of the LDCs that many experts believe would help the process of development enormously, and which it seems within the power of these governments to achieve (at least in part.)

1. The government of an LDC should go as far as possible to eliminate red tape in the administration of any regulations that control business activity.
2. Any price controls, if they cannot be avoided altogether, must establish levels of prices that do not destroy the economic activities to which they apply.
3. Exchange rates must not be set so high as to discourage exports of the products of the LDC. Foreign trade is of critical importance to the developing countries, and it is essential that the country's monetary and exchange rate policies not prevent its exports from competing on the world market.
4. The government should do what it can to encourage mobility of people and resources to where they are needed most. It must do what it can to remove impediments to innovation and entrepreneurial initiative. One type of measure that can help in this respect is a change in agricultural ownership arrangements, which now effectively subjugate small farmers, keep them in poverty, and discourage or prevent the use of modern agricultural techniques. Another important step is the encouragement of equal opportunity by vigorous opposition to discrimination by race or creed, which has all too frequently repressed entrepreneurial activity by unpopular minority groups in the LDCs.
5. Priority must be given to the training of skilled artisans and technicians, as well as to the preparation of persons for administrative positions in government and business.
6. Investment and saving must be provided. The experience of the Soviet Union has confirmed how important it is for rapid economic growth to encourage the nation to save until it hurts. Of course in the LDCs a good part of the new capital will have to come from abroad in the form of grants and loans, but they will not be able to rely exclusively on foreign resources.

These last two requirements are by perhaps the most critical.

How the Industrialized Economies
Can Help the LDCs

We have just seen that the two primary needs of the LDCs are technical skills and capital resources. Happily, these are precisely the things that the more prosperous nations are in a position to offer. Educational facilities in the industrial world have grown to a magnitude unprecedented in human history. Never before has such a high proportion of the population of developed countries received a college education. This means that we now have the trained teachers, classrooms, laboratories, and equipment necessary to provide an education of the highest quality to students from the LDCs. Thus, one of the main things that the United States and other advanced countries can offer is encouragement and financing to students from less developed lands, particularly to graduate students receiving professional training.

However, there are several dangers here. One that has received a great deal of attention is the so-called *brain drain*—the temptation for students from LDCs to try to stay in the countries where they have studied and enjoy the higher living standard they offer, rather than returning home where their abilities are needed so badly. There are several ways to deal with this issue. For example, one can use arrangements requiring students to return to their homelands for at least some given number of years after completion of the educational program, or offer higher wages for trained persons in the LDCs to make returning more attractive. Yet the problem is there, and the large number of doctors, teachers, and other skilled personnel from LDCs who are seeking jobs in the developed countries suggests that the issue is not negligible.

Another danger in the training offered by the wealthier countries stems from the fact that, as in the LDCs, the developed countries have tended to give higher prestige to training in the liberal arts than to technical training. This may well be the right choice from our own point of view. In our abundant economies, emphasis on the contribution of education to production is less urgent than it is in a country whose people live on the edge of survival. But the tendency to accord higher prestige to nontechnical training may also discourage students from abroad from entering those fields in which trained personnel are needed most urgently in their homelands.

A second major contribution that the wealthier countries can make to the LDCs is to offer them trained technicians and technical advice from their own populations. Such counseling and personnel can be very helpful as a temporary measure, but in the long run they can prove detrimental if provision for the training of local personnel for the ultimate replacement of the foreign technicians and advisers is not built into the program.

A third, and very important, type of assistance from the developed to the less developed countries takes the form of money or physical resources provided either as loans made on favorable terms or as outright grants (gifts). In a moment we will consider some of the contributions that the industrial world has recently made in this area.

Fourth, the world can help the LDCs through research. One of the hardest problems for the developing world is what to do in the rural areas that suffer from inadequate rainfall, where several hundred million people live in both Asia and Africa. These people are badly in need of new dry-farming techniques. Until some are discovered, their poverty will increase as their numbers grow. An international research organization devoted to food production in problem areas in the LDCs would have much to contribute.

Finally, and perhaps most important, the developed countries can help by encouraging freedom of trade and investment. This will help those LDCs whose exports are readily expanded but that are now being held back by barriers to trade. Exports of sugar, meat, cotton, and other agricultural products are inhibited by tariffs and other restrictions. There are many discriminatory duties against processed, as distinct from crude, materials. A significant number of LDCs would also benefit substantially from a lifting of quotas and other restrictions upon the export of manufactured goods. Increased freedom of trade will also help those LDCs whose economies offer business prospects sufficiently bright to attract significant quantities of private capital from abroad. All in all, increased freedom of trade is a matter of highest priority for the LDCs.[3]

Loans and Grants by the United States and Others

In the post-World War II period a number of countries have provided capital resources to the LDCs. Indeed, soon after World War II an international organization was set up with aid to LDCs as one of its major tasks. This organization, the International Bank for Reconstruction and Development, commonly referred to as the **World Bank,** has 135 member countries. Each member provides an amount of capital to the bank that is related to the member country's wealth; for instance, the United States has contributed approximately one-third of the total. The Bank makes loans that are financed by bonds that it issues and sells, and has acted as guarantor of repayment to encourage some private lending. The World Bank has established two affiliated agencies, the International Development Association and the International Finance Corporation, that have played major roles in providing funds to the LDCs.

The Bank has loaned more than $40 billion to LDCs and to countries that can be considered on the borderline. It has tended to emphasize loans for infrastructure, dams, communications and transportation, and, in addition, has provided technical assistance and planning advice. Some economists have criticized the Bank's conservatism in its lending policies and its unwillingness to take risks. Recently, however, it and its affiliates have become more adventuresome in their lending practices.

The United States itself has been a major source of funds to the LDCs. Indeed, its loans and grants have exceeded the total given by all other countries and international agencies. U.S. interest rates and its allowed length of time for repayment of loans have generally been far more generous than the terms offered by other governments. However, the bulk of the assistance provided by the United States has gone to a small number of countries, such as India, Pakistan, South Korea, and Turkey.

During the 1960s, our expenditures on aid ran to more than $3 billion per year, with about half this amount consisting of loans and the remainder made up of grants. In the past few years, expenditures on foreign aid have become less

---

[3]However, not everyone agrees with this conclusion. There are those who have argued that participation of LDCs in international trade is bad for them because it weakens their capacity to develop as self-reliant, mature economies. It is held that new manufacturing industries in the LDCs will not take off without protection from foreign competition. Development of primary product exports creates a rich and politically powerful vested interest that inhibits measures that would favor manufacturing. The exent to which foreign trade and production of exports are in foreign hands inhibits domestic saving and the development of local entrepreneurship.

In this view, LDCs are therefore held back by international trade and they would do better to integrate regionally and develop their own home markets without foreigners, who also bring unsuitable habits, unsuitable tastes, and unsuitable technology, and impart a crippling inferiority complex to the natives.

popular politically, and the amounts provided consequently have gone down sharply and steadily from about half a percent of U.S. GNP in 1965 to well under 0.2 percent of GNP in 1980. This is bad enough. But, curiously, the industrialized nations also seem to be blamed for the huge deficits imposed on the less developed countries by the rise in oil prices which has caused their expenditures on oil imports to rise from $7 billion in 1973 to nearly ten times that amount in 1980. The OPEC countries seem to be subject to little if any of the anger to which this has given rise.

In addition to the United States, aid has come from other industrialized countries, notably France, Great Britain, and West Germany. The Soviet Union has also become a major source of assistance to the LDCs, now providing, along with its associated countries, about $1 billion a year. While the Soviet funds have obviously been distributed in a way intended to maximize its political advantage, it can hardly be claimed that the U.S. foreign aid program has been entirely free of political considerations.

Many economists have advocated greater generosity in our assistance to LDCs and have deplored the recent cuts in our aid programs. Aside from any moral responsibility to help the impoverished countries, it is argued that an effective aid program that really helps the growth of LDCs will also serve our own interests. By making those countries more stable economically and politically, we can contribute to our own economic tranquility. By increasing the LDCs' power to buy and sell, we are in effect contributing to the prosperity of the entire world.

The "North–South" Controversy and Commodity Stabilization

The conflict of interests between the LDCs and the industrialized countries has recently begun to be called, somewhat inaccurately, the "North–South confrontation" with the "North" referring to the wealthy nations and the "South" standing for the poor countries. The international trade arrangements, which the North considers to constitute a free market for the unhampered exchange of goods for the mutual benefit of all participants, are widely viewed in the South as a thinly disguised instrument of old-fashioned imperialism to be used to exploit the poorer economies.

A major cause of this discontent is the prices of the commodities, such as cocoa and sugar, which the South considers to be unfairly low and distressingly unstable. There has been considerable pressure for international agreements that will take steps to reduce the upswings and downswings of these prices. It has been proposed that a stabilization fund be organized and used to buy such commodities when their prices are falling and to sell them when their prices are rising. That is, by shifting demand outward when prices are relatively low, the fund would raise these prices; and by shifting demand downward when prices are comparatively high, it would force these prices downward. But negotiations have stalled over at least two issues. First, the industrialized countries want much of the money for the stabilization fund to be supplied by the less developed countries themselves, while the latter want most of the fund to be financed by the industrialized countries who buy these products. So far, a tentative agreement has been reached for the creation of a modest fund with both North and South contributing to it. But the second issue is perhaps more serious. The North intends the stabilization fund to do only what its name implies: to iron out fluctuations in commodity prices, not to raise or lower those prices on the average. But to many southern countries "stabilization" actually is a diplomatic way of referring to their desire to *raise* commodity prices, something the North is predictably reluctant to do.

Can LDCs Break Away from Poverty?

It is easy to jump to the conclusion that the economic problems of the LDCs are staggering and that the prospects of their ever catching up with the industrialized countries are negligible. Yet a number of LDCs and former LDCs have made enormous progress. The African countries Kenya, Cameroon, and the Ivory Coast have been increasing their GNPs at a rate of about 5 to 6 percent a year, which is considerably faster than their population growth. In the Americas, Mexico's performance has been comparable. Even more striking is the expansion of output in a number of places in the Far East—particularly Hong Kong, Taiwan, South Korea, and Singapore, where prosperity is unprecedented and economic activity is expanding at an astonishing rate. Here per capita GNPs have been growing at a rate of about 6.5 percent a year.

But the most impressive case is that of Japan. Many of your professors will remember clearly when U.S. business feared the flood of goods produced by Japanese cheap labor, and when the label "made in Japan" suggested inexpensive and shoddy merchandise. From one of the world's impoverished countries, Japan has risen to one of the world's richest. Its goods are now feared by American manufacturers not because they are produced and sold so cheaply, but because their quality is so high. Japanese cars and sophisticated electronic equipment find a ready market in the United States. And as a result, per capita income in Japan has surpassed that in Great Britain. A less developed country need not lag behind forever.

Summary

1. Standards of living in many LDCs are extremely low; per capita incomes that are equivalent to $600 a year are not uncommon. Life expectancy is low and daily living is very difficult, particularly for women.

2. GNP and per capita incomes in the LDCs have grown considerably in recent years.

3. Nevertheless, the gap between family incomes in the less developed and the industrialized countries has continued to widen.

4. In many LDCs population continues to grow much faster than that in the industrialized countries.

5. Growth in the LDCs is impeded by shortages of capital caused by poverty, traditions that do not encourage investment, poor natural resources, rapid population growth, poor education, unemployment, lack of entrepreneurship, and government impediments to business.

6. The LDCs can encourage their own growth by cutting government red tape, by minimizing those interferences with prices and exchange rates that discourage economic activity, by encouraging mobility of people and resources to where they are needed, by encouraging technical training and education, and by encouraging saving and investment.

7. Industrialized countries can help the LDCs by providing capital through loans and grants, by offering training and education to people from those lands, and by encouraging freedom of trade with the LDCs.

8. In the post-World War II period many countries, including the United States and the Soviet Union, have provided large amounts of money to the LDCs in the form of loans and grants. At its peak, the United States provided about $3 billion per year, and the Soviet Union and its allies have been providing about $1 billion annually.

9. Several international organizations, most notably the World Bank, have been organized to provide economic assistance to the LDCs.

Concepts for Review

Less developed countries (LDCs)	Multinational corporations	Brain drain
Growth rate in GNP	Disguised unemployment	World Bank
Growth rate in per capita income	Entrepreneurship	"North–South controversy"

Questions for Discussion

1. To many families living in less developed countries, an income equivalent to $2000 per year is considered a high standard of living. Can you make up a budget for a U.S. family of four earning $2000 a year?

2. Explain how it is possible for the per capita income of an LDC to grow at a faster rate than that in the United States and yet for the difference between the incomes of average families in both countries to increase. Can you give a numerical example showing how this happens?

3. Discuss the advantages and disadvantages to an LDC of a U.S. manufacturing company investing in that country.

4. If you were economic adviser to the president of an LDC, what might you suggest that he or she do to encourage increases in saving and investment?

5. No one knows what encourages or discourages the supply of entrepreneurs. Do you have any ideas about policies that may be capable of stimulating entrepreneurship?

6. Name some countries in which entrepreneurship seems to be abundant these days; some countries in which it seems to be scarce. What is your impression about what is happening to the supply of entrepreneurs in the United States?

Marxian Economics

40

What is certain is that I am not a Marxist.

Karl Marx to his son-in-law.[1]

For more than a century radical and reformist groups throughout the world have drawn inspiration from the writings of Karl Marx. Nations with governments claiming to be run on Marxist principles include the Soviet Union, the People's Republic of China, Cuba, and at least a dozen other countries in Eastern Europe, Asia, Africa, and Latin America, containing among them more than one-third of the world's population.

In this chapter we summarize the major ideas in Marx's economic theories. And one of the main conclusions we draw is that his work contains very little that is helpful to a communist economy. This judgment is made not because the Marxian analysis is poor in quality or short of ideas. On the contrary, even some very conservative economists have acknowledged the originality and importance of at least some of Marx's analyses. Rather, we find that his ideas are not particularly helpful to a central planner because Marx chose to devote almost all his attention to the *capitalist* economy, seeking to explain the principles of its evolution, its strengths, and its weaknesses. Hence, he left wide open the questions about how a communist economy should be run.

It is a mistake to think that Marx despised every feature of capitalism. It is true that he believed its accomplishments exacted a very high cost in human misery and exploitation. And he believed also that it was rapidly outliving its usefulness and its historical role. But he was a profound admirer of its early vigor and enormous accomplishments, which, in his phrase, rescued humanity from the "universal mediocrity" that feudalism had imposed upon the economy.

Except for Marx's use of the word *bourgeoisie*, the following passage from the *Communist Manifesto* (1848) might have been penned by a publicist for the Chamber of Commerce:

---

[1]Quoted in a letter from Friedrich Engels to Eduard Bernstein in November 1882. Much of the material in this chapter conflicts very strongly with popular (mis)conceptions about what Marx really said. It is, perhaps, important to emphasize that this chapter's contents are based on years of research and study of Marx's published and (until recently) unpublished writings, his letters, and many, many other documents. In Marx's lifetime, the process of misinterpreting what he had plainly written, by people who had not read him carefully, had already begun. Marx's son-in-law was a "Marxist" of this sort—which is what led Marx to make the statement quoted here.

The bourgeoisie . . . has accomplished wonders far surpassing Egyptian pyramids, Roman aqueducts, and Gothic cathedrals. . . . The bourgeoisie cannot exist without constantly revolutionizing the instruments of production. . . . The bourgeoisie, during its rule of scarce one hundred years, has created more massive and more colossal productive forces than have all preceding generations together."[2]

The Marxian Framework: Historical Materialism

To Marx, a historical perspective was essential to understand the capitalist system, or any other form of economic organization. All economic systems evolve from others that are very different, and they can each be expected to be replaced by some other form of economic organization. Thus, to understand how a particular economy works we must keep in mind the predecessor from which it evolved and the process by which it grew. Marx frequently criticized the classical economists for their nonhistorical viewpoint, their treatment of all other economic forms as more or less mini-capitalist systems, and their tacit assumption that capitalism will prevail throughout all time. He said, with some scorn, that to these economists "there has been history, but there is no longer any."

What determines the evolutionary direction of a society? According to Marx the primary influence is economic—the current state of technology and the method of organizing production. At each stage of history, these factors determine which group will be in charge of the economy and which groups will be subjugated. In the feudal economy, for instance, the manor lords were in control of the economy while the serfs were under their domination. Under the free-enterprise economy, the medieval lord has been replaced by the modern capitalist and the serf by the free laborer—in reality a propertyless proletarian who "has nothing to sell but his hands." But the relationship between the serf and his lord was, of course, very different from that between the free laborer and the capitalist. Technology, which is primarily responsible for this difference, affected the productivity of the two economies, which in turn changed the course of the economy's growth and the character of the struggle between the dominant and dominated groups.

By saying that economic conditions determine the direction of the evolutionary process, Marx did *not* mean that people care only about their financial well-being. Unlike a number of later historians and modern (non-Marxist) economists who have analyzed everything in human activity—from crime and marriage to the provisions of the U.S. Constitution—in terms of the narrow economic interests of those involved, Marxian analysts have always recognized that history is affected by altruism, passion, prejudice, social pressures, and a wide variety of other *non*economic influences. Nevertheless, these Marxists are quick to point out that such influences are themselves strongly affected by the nature of the economic system. This analysis of social evolution is the basis of Marx's theory of **historical materialism.**

To underline the distinction between the Marxian view of the process of change and the view that people are motivated only by their own economic interests, one need only look at the fact that revolutionary fervor among lower income groups often accelerates rather than wanes when their economic conditions improve. The reason, according to some Marxian economists, is that

Marx's **historical materialism** asserts that we cannot understand any economy without recognizing its place in history. It asserts also that while historical events are influenced primarily (though not exclusively) by economic conditions, the form of this influence is often very indirect and subtle—filtering through current social customs, political organizations, and so forth. Historical materialism does *not* assert that people follow only their monetary self-interest.

---

[2]Karl Marx, *Communist Manifesto, Collected Works,* vol. 6 (New York: International Publishers, 1976), pages 487–89.

Biographical Note: Karl Marx (1818–1883)

Karl Marx was born in Trier, Germany, the son of a successful Jewish lawyer who later converted to Christianity. Marx's acquaintances considered him brilliant, but he was also stubborn and quarrelsome.

Throughout his life he broke with one associate after another, with the only exception being Friedrich Engels, his lifelong friend, collaborator, and benefactor.

Marx studied at the universities of Bonn and Berlin, hoping first to become a poet. After a resounding failure at poetry, he entered a circle of young philosophers in Berlin, all devoted followers of Hegel, whose ideas about the crucial role of history in understanding current events, art, and science had recently swept German universities. The young Hegelians, however, were radical in their opposition to Hegel's religious views, and this attitude may have influenced Marx's later attacks against religion. Marx received his doctorate of philosophy at the age of 23, meanwhile having married ("above his station") Jenny von Westphalen, the daughter of his father's closest friend. Jenny's family opposed the marriage, and, as it turned out, their reasons were justified, since Marx was never able to support her. Much of their lives was spent in great poverty, and

increased income and leisure finally afford the poorest members of the economy the time to think about their miserable condition and the material strength and means to do something about it. Thus, economic conditions are indeed an important determinant of the timing of revolutionary unrest, but unrest does not necessarily peak at the moment in history when the lowest classes have the most to gain from it.

On the Nature of Communist Society

Among the many thousands of pages Marx wrote and published, and among those published by others after his death, there are scarcely a dozen dealing with the nature of the economy under socialism (which Marx never distinguished clearly from communism). Marx did tell us that socialism must come, and that it must begin with "the dictatorship of the proletariat," though this concept, too, is left somewhat fuzzy. There is no doubt, however, about his ideology. He clearly and repeatedly stated that this "higher form of society" will be dedicated to "the full and free development of every individual," with work transformed into a stimulating and pleasant activity and the deadening effects of extreme specialization brought to an end.

Perhaps Marx's most famous passage on the nature of socialism appears in one of his last economic writings, in which he envisions the post-capitalist society passing through two stages. In the first, there is already "common ownership of production." But this early socialist society is "still stamped with the birth marks of the old society from whose womb it emerges." In this stage, the income of the individual is exactly equivalent to the amount of labor he contributes.

He receives a certificate from society that he has furnished such and such an amount of labour . . . and with this certificate he draws from the social stock of means of consumption as much as costs the same amount of labour. The same the deaths of three of their six children were probably the result of privation.

After a brief stint as a newspaper editor, Marx's troubles with the authorities propelled him first out of Germany and then Paris and Belgium. It was in Paris that Marx first met Engels, and in Brussels they together wrote the *Communist Manifesto*, a revolutionary pamphlet that was the only writing of Marx's to achieve wide circulation during his lifetime. After the demise of the revolutions that shook all of Europe in 1848, but in which Marx played little part, he fled finally to London where he spent the rest of his life. There Marx helped form revolutionary groups, and otherwise spent most of his time cloistered in the British Museum studying the history of economic thought and writing *Das Kapital*. Aside from some meager earnings as correspondent for *The New York Tribune*, a job he held for about ten years, Marx lived entirely on money given to him by Engels (who, although an anticapitalist, nevertheless owned factories in Manchester and Germany) and by other admirers.

Marx was never very successful in organizing revolutionary groups, and he finally engineered the breakup of The First International, the revolutionary organization that he had helped found and develop but which seemed about to fall into the hands of opponent radicals. Marx finished writing volume I of *Capital* and saw it published in 1867. He had previously written most of volumes II and III, but never completed them in the 15 years that remained to him. It was left to Engels to edit and publish these volumes after Marx's death. Marx died in 1883, two years after the death of his wife, Jenny, and only several months after the unexpected death of his eldest daughter, Jenny Longuet.

Throughout his life Marx attracted and fascinated many people by his brilliance and through the force of his personality and ideas. And though most of his associates eventually became estranged from Marx the man, almost all retained their allegiance to his ideas.

amount of labour which he has given to society in one form he receives back in another. [However,] . . . in a higher phase of communist society, after the enslaving subordination of the individual to the division of labour, and with it also the antithesis between mental and physical labour, has vanished; after labour has become not only a means of life but itself life's prime want; after the productive forces have also increased with the all-round development of the individual, and all the springs of co-operative wealth flow more abundantly—only then can the narrow horizon of bourgeois right be crossed in its entirety and society inscribe on its banners: From each according to his ability, to each according to his needs![3]

About the only other concrete attribute of a communist society described in Marx's writings is the abolition of the division of labor, which, claimed Marx, transforms workers from creative, satisfied humans into discontented, alienated near-machines. According to Marx and Engels:

In communist society, where nobody has one exclusive sphere of activity but each can become accomplished in any branch he wishes, society regulates the general production and thus makes it possible for me to do one thing today and another tomorrow, to hunt in the morning, fish in the afternoon, rear cattle in the evening, criticise after dinner, just as I have a mind, without ever becoming hunter, fisherman, cowboy or critic.[4]

Certainly these are fascinating notions, but they tell us nothing about the coordination of production, the planning of new plant and equipment, the

[3] Karl Marx, *Critique of the Gotha Programme* (Moscow: Progress Publishers, 1971), pages 17–18.
[4] K. Marx and F. Engels, *The German Ideology, Collected Works*, vol. 5 (New York: International Publishers, 1976), page 47.

arrangements for industrial research, the devising of a monetary policy (if money is to be used), and the many other issues that must be settled in designing any (even a communist) economy.

It seems clear that Marx did not intend to provide detailed guidance to the leaders of communist societies. Rather, his work was devoted to a meticulous analysis and critique of capitalism.

Commodities, Productive Labor, and Capital

One of the reasons it is hard to understand Marx is that he often employed words to mean things other than what they mean in ordinary usage. (Marx was, after all, an economist!) Since Marx considered it so important to distinguish capitalism from all other economic systems, he defined his basic economic terms and concepts in a way intended to emphasize their role in a free-enterprise economy.

A *commodity* for Marx is therefore not simply any good or service that consumers consider useful—which is how modern economists would define the term. Thus, when a primitive stoneworker trades some of his handiwork (say, arrowheads) for the meat that has been brought in by a hunter, neither the meat nor the arrowheads are "commodities" in Marxian terminology. Meat and arrowheads become commodities only when they are processed or produced by commercial firms. And not because they are any more useful than the meat and arrowheads traded by the stoneworker and the hunter, but because they are produced as means to earn *profits*.

Commodity production is therefore just another element serving the one central purpose of the capitalist system—the accumulation of wealth, which in turn is the engine for the continuing expansion of the economy.

Analogously, Marx called labor under capitalism "productive" only when it turns out commodities, that is, when its outputs are offered for sale as part of the normal process of profit making and accumulation. Two pieces of work may appear perfectly identical, yet one can be productive and the other unproductive in Marx's view. Thus, a baker on the staff of the White House who makes a cake for a diplomatic dinner is engaged in "unproductive activity" (as are the diplomats!). The cake has no part in the capitalistic economy and does not differ in any way from the work of a baker in the court of a medieval prince. But another baker who makes an identical cake for a commercial bakery is "productive" because, to his employer, he is producing not cake but profit.

Capital also was defined by Marx in a way that differs from the modern economists' use of the term, who employ it to mean plant, equipment, and other produced means of production. To Marx, capital meant a social process rather than a set of physical objects. The term can include the hiring of labor power, the construction of machinery, the production of commodities, the exchange of products for money, and the reinvestment of that money into another round of the profit-generating process. *Capitalism* is the all-embracing term that includes every one of the steps of this mechanism. With such a broad definition, it is no wonder that Marx chose the word "capital" as the title of his most important book.

Marx's Value Theory: Surplus as the Source of Accumulation

Perhaps the single most confusing thing about Marx's book *Capital* is its use of the term *exchange value*. To classical economists, this term was a synonym for *price*, and much of their work was intended to explain how market prices are determined—why a particular pair of shoes sells for a price twice as high as a certain hat, for example. But to Marx, the revolutionary, this was not an important issue. Rather, his central purpose, as we shall see, was to explain the accumulation process. And for this it was convenient to use a totally different concept of value.

Central to Marx's value analysis is something he regarded as a puzzle of fundamental importance—one whose solution had escaped his predecessors. Accumulation, the engine of economic growth, is financed out of profits, and profits appear to come from the sale of commodities. But how, he asked, can that possibly be? If two people exchange two goods of equal value, they may both be better off, for each may prefer the goods he gets to the goods he gives up. But in such a process neither party can gain *financially* since each has given as much value as he has received. It is true that one party in the exchange can profit at the expense of the other if he delivers less value than he receives, but the other party must then lose as much as the first one gains. The mystery, then, is this: How can the economy as a whole pour forth the profits needed for accumulation if the exchange process on which accumulation is based is fundamentally incapable of yielding net gains to the group of parties involved?

Marx's proposed solution starts off with a definition: The *value* of a commodity is precisely equal to the labor time necessary for its production. Note that Marx clearly stated that this is a *definition*, not a deduction: "[A good] which is not the product of labour cannot have a value; in other words, it cannot be *defined* . . . as the social expression of a certain quantity of labour."[5]

Ricardo and other predecessors of Marx had already proposed something that *sounded* very similar but really was not. They had argued that, in certain circumstances, pure competition tends to drive relative market prices of different goods very close to the relative amounts of labor needed to produce them. Notice that this can be *deduced* from economic theory if most production costs are labor costs, since under perfect competition, as we saw in Chapter 22, price tends to equal marginal cost. But Marx spurned this theory and criticized Ricardo severely for it, saying that in fact prices usually differ substantially from each good's labor content. Though Ricardo considered such deviations to be exceptions to a generally accurate rule, Marx said they happen so often that Ricardo's "rule becomes the exception and the exception the rule."

By divorcing the concepts of price and value, Marx freed himself to play with the word *value*. He could now define value and labor time to be the same thing, even though he believed that prices differ systematically from the labor time required in the production process.

Why did he adopt this apparently curious definition? Because, in his view, it helps to explain where profits really come from and, concurrently, how wealth is accumulated. For this purpose he formulated one more concept, the value of labor power, about which he wrote:

The value of labour-power is determined, as in the case of every other commodity, by the labour-time necessary for the production, and consequently also the reproduction, of this special article. . . . The value of labour-power is the value of the means of subsistence necessary for the maintenance of the labourer.[6]

[5] Karl Marx, *Theories of Surplus Value*, vol. III (Moscow: Progress Publishers, 1963), page 520. Italics added.
[6] Karl Marx, *Capital*, vol. I (Chicago: Charles H. Kerr Publishing Company, 1906), pages 189–96.

In defining the *value of labor power* as a *minimum* subsistence level for the worker, Marx did not mean that *wages* are in fact always set at that subsistence level. Just as the price of a commodity is not generally equal to its (Marxian) value, the wage for an hour of labor need not be equal to the value of that much labor power. In fact, Marx argued vigorously that the level of wages is determined by the outcome of a constant struggle between workers and capitalists, and that one of the main purposes of union activity is to force wages above bare subsistence.

The value analysis gave Marx his solution to his puzzle about the origin of profits. Suppose that the average worker needs to labor for five hours to produce a day's subsistence but that the standard workday is eight hours. Then, in one workday, labor power, which has a value of five hours, is transformed into a product that carries a value of eight hours. The difference, which Marx called **surplus value,** is the portion of output that does not have to be consumed by the worker for his survival and that instead can be accumulated and used by the capitalist to expand his property and to make the economy grow.

According to Marx, profits and accumulation are possible only because the value of labor power—the amount of labor needed to produce a worker's daily subsistence—is no more than a fraction of a workday. The remainder of the worker's day goes into the production of surplus value, which can be accumulated by the capitalist.

The Ethics of Surplus Value

Over the years, many people have concluded that Marx's aim was to establish that capitalism is immoral and that profits amount to robbery of the worker who really deserves the surplus he earns. Marx explicitly and repeatedly denied that this was his opinion; in fact, his anger was aroused by others who did hold such views. Marx made clear, right at the point in *Capital* where he defined the value of labor power, that:

> *It is a very cheap sort of sentimentality which declares this method of determining the value of labour-power, a method prescribed by the very nature of the case, to be a brutal method.*[7]

But if it was not Marx's goal to show that surplus value is robbery, then what was the purpose of the value theory? Engels stated that the purpose of Marx's analysis, the very analysis on which he based his revolutionary demands, was to demonstrate "the inevitable collapse of the capitalist mode of production." Later in this chapter we will see how the value theory could, in Marx's view, help explain the "laws of motion of capitalism." It was these laws that he interpreted as calling for precisely the sort of revolutionary change he was advocating—the replacement of capitalism by a communist society.

There is also a second issue that the theory of surplus value was intended to deal with. In providing himself the answer to the question of how profits can be produced by an exchange economy, Marx believed he had also shown that profits (as well as rents and interest payments) are *produced by workers*. Put the other way, Marx believed he had shown that profit is *not* produced by the capitalist, that interest is *not* produced by the moneylender, and that rent is *not* produced by the landlord.

In saying this, Marx never denied that land and produced means of pro-

[7] Karl Marx, *Capital*, vol. I (Chicago: Charles H. Kerr Publishing Company, 1906), page 192.

duction contribute to the output of the economy. Nor did he ever argue that labor is the only useful means of production:

> [*When he does his work, the laborer*] *is constantly helped by natural forces. We see, then, that labour is not the only source of material wealth, of use-values produced by labour. . . . labour is its father and the earth its mother.*[8]

But while *land* (or natural resources generally) contributes to production, it does not necessarily follow that the *landlord*, the person who happens to own the land, contributes anything. A given output can be produced just as well if the land is publicly owned and there is no landlord to collect income from the production process. It was Marx's contention, therefore, that labor is the only *human* (he called it "social") input that contributes to production. True, a capitalist may sometimes help in the production process by organizing and planning it, but then, according to Marx, he is merely serving as a (part-time) laborer. In sum:

Marx emphasized that labor is not the only useful factor of production. However, he did argue that it is the only useful factor of production contributed by *human society*. In this sense he considered it necessary to define all value and, therefore, all surplus value (profit, interest, and rent) as something that is produced by labor.

The Marxian Analysis of Pricing and Profit

If in Marxian economics, price and value are generally *unequal*, then how are prices determined? The answer is that they are determined in exactly the same way as proposed by the classical economists, such as Adam Smith and David Ricardo. Marx repeatedly stated that he had no new analysis of pricing to offer. But he did maintain that he had an important new insight into the relationship between price and value, which underlies the relationship between surplus values and profits.

Having asserted that only labor is capable of producing surplus value, Marx concluded that the surplus value produced by any industry will be roughly proportional to the amount of labor time it uses. This means that such service industries as restaurants and theaters—whose inputs contain a very high proportion of labor—can be expected to yield a great deal of surplus value while other sorts of industries, such as public utilities—which use enormous amounts of equipment but relatively little labor—will end up producing comparatively small amounts of surplus value. If each industry kept all the surplus value it generated, it would follow that a theater would be far more profitable than an electric utility company. But the competitive mechanism permits no such imbalance in the *profitability* of different industries.

Where differences in profitability do occur, investors rush to withdraw their funds from the less profitable businesses and transfer them to those industries whose earnings are high. This means that the industries that are initially more profitable expand, and that their increased production then forces down their prices and hence their profits. At the same time, the industries that are initially *less* profitable will have to reduce production levels as their capital exits, which will then raise the prices of their products and hence their profit rates. Competition will always tend to eliminate differences in profit rates among industries in this way. For as long as one industry is significantly more profitable than another, funds will flow into the more profitable industry and out of the industry in which

---

[8] Marx, *Capital*, vol. I, page 50.

profits are low. This mechanism, which had already been described in detail by Smith and Ricardo, was adopted by Marx without reservation.

Thus, regardless of how much surplus value is produced by any one industry, competition will force prices and outputs to adjust in ways that redistribute the goods and services that make up this surplus value and every capitalist will end up with an equal share of the wealth. He called this type of sharing "capitalist communism."

According to Marx, then, prices under capitalism are set so as to redistribute the *surplus value* produced by the entire economy. All capitalists end up receiving an equal rate of return on their investments. And in order for this to happen, the price of each commodity must be equal to its cost of production, including the opportunity cost of capital (the standard rate of profit on each capitalist's investment). Price must cover the wages of labor, the cost of raw materials, and the opportunity cost of capital.

As we learned in Chapter 22, this analysis of the way prices will be set under perfect competition is precisely the view taken by modern economists. It is also exactly the same as the one Adam Smith outlined nearly a century before Marx. Marx knew this very well, and said so repeatedly:

> *The price of production includes the average profit. . . . It is, as a matter of fact, the same thing which Adam Smith calls* natural price, *Ricardo* price of production, *or* cost of production.[9]

In Marxian theory, commodity prices are equal to long-run average costs of production, including a competitive return to capital. This is the pricing rule that appears both in classical and modern competitive analyses. Marx recognized that there was nothing new in this pricing result.

The Purpose of the Marxian Price–Value Analysis

If Marx knew that his pricing analysis got him to exactly the same point at which the classical economists had all arrived much earlier, why did he make so much of his discussion of price? Why did he get back to Smith's pricing principle in such a roundabout manner, that is, by starting with the *unequal production* of surplus value by different industries and its *redistribution* through the price mechanism? Marx explains that prices and the resulting distribution of profits are merely an "outward disguise," that they show simply how the economy *appears* to work, whereas through his value analysis, "the actual state of things is here revealed for the first time."

The fact that profits are paid to capitalists in proportion to the amount they invest, and that landlords are paid rent in proportion to the amount of land they provide, makes it *appear* as though two inanimate things, money and land, had actually produced the surplus value received by owners.

> *It is an enchanted, perverted, topsy-turvey world, in which Mister Capital and Mistress Land carry on their goblin tricks as social characters and at the same time as mere things. . . . these are the forms of the illusion . . . proclaiming the natural necessity and eternal justification of [the ruling classes'] sources of revenue.*[10]

---

[9] Marx, *Capital*, vol. III (Chicago: Charles H. Kerr Publishing Company, 1909), page 233.
[10] Marx, *Capital*, vol. III, pages 66–67.

Marx said that value analysis taught us that labor time, not inanimate land and equipment, produces surplus value. Land and equipment do, of course, play a role in the production of goods, but labor is the only factor that human society contributes to the production of surplus value. And it is surplus value that constitutes the resources that enable both the economy's production and the capitalists' wealth to grow.

While Marx's value analysis does *not* claim to give us any new model of price determination, it does claim to give us a new insight into the source of surplus value by stripping away "the forms of illusion" created by the manner in which prices redistribute labor's products.

Alienation

From the time Marx began to write about economics in 1843 until about 1858 (roughly a decade before *Capital* was published), he devoted a significant portion of his writing to a phenomenon he called **alienation.** Yet hardly a word on the subject was published during his lifetime. Thus we do not know whether Marx really considered it important and would have included it in the portions of *Capital* published after his death, or whether he purposely did not publish it because he changed his mind and decided it was a false direction.

It was not until the middle of the twentieth century, when the Soviet Union began to publish some of Marx's accumulated notes and manuscripts, that the materials on alienation became available to the public. But once the idea was made public, it attracted a great deal of attention among Marxist scholars, particularly among those who specialized in political science and sociology. And while the concept of alienation seems to hold less appeal for economists, it is useful for helping us reconstruct some of what Marx was after.

Actually, alienation seems to refer to at least two different concepts. The first, which has most intrigued noneconomists, describes the psychological state of workers in relation to the capitalist production process. According to Marx, capitalism, by replacing artisanship with mass-production techniques, by putting workers on assembly lines where their functions are reduced to repetitive detail rather than concern with the quality of the whole product, and by treating workers (or, rather, their labor power) as mere commodities that are bought and sold as part of the profit-making process, causes workers to lose any sense of satisfaction from their labor and any means for identifying with their output. In short, modern workers are *alienated* from the production process in ways that the medieval artisans were not.

What . . . constitutes the alienation of labour? First . . . that in his work . . . he does not . . . feel content but unhappy, does not develop freely his physical and mental energy but mortifies his body and ruins his mind. . . . Lastly, the external [alien] character of labour for the worker appears in the fact that it is not his own, but someone else's . . . that in it he belongs, not to himself, but to another.[11]

The second concept of alienation, which has more relevance to our present discussion, describes the connection between the accumulation process and the produced means of production that are made available to the economy. According to Marx, such items as plant and equipment are as much the product of labor

[11]Karl Marx, *Economic and Philosophical Manuscripts of 1844, Collected Works,* vol. 3, pages 273–74.

as are any other commodities. However, in industrial economies, the worker's job depends on the availability of factories and machinery. Thus, after he has labored to make these particular products, the worker must confront them again, this time as domineering, alien objects that hold the power to determine whether he will remain employed. The very items that the worker has made with his own hands become the means by which capitalists can control him.

Aside from the domination to which the worker is subjected by the alienated products of his own making, this form of alienation is significant because it has an inherent tendency to escalate. Accumulation, by its very nature, builds up the economy's stock of productive equipment. As this happens, workers become increasingly dependent on more and more equipment in order to remain employed. And as time passes, their dependence on the alienated products of their labor continues to grow proportionally with the economy.

In the early stages of capitalism, workers could easily find employment on their own in industries that utilized relatively few machines. But as capitalism matures, workers more and more are forced into automated factories with all the frustration and alienation that attends such work places. Here we have the seeds of the class antagonism that Marx predicted would contribute to the demise of capitalism. In other words, here we have a law of motion of capitalism.

If this interpretation of alienation is valid (and it is not entirely clear from Marx's unfinished writing on the subject), it is a problem that lies at the heart of the dynamics of capitalism as Marx saw them. The very mechanism that produces surplus value and capital accumulation must aggravate alienation, and through it, we are told, capitalism does indeed sow the seeds of its own destruction.

Thus, Marx felt that a revolution spurred by worker alienation might be one way that capitalism would die. Another would be through a spasmodic business cycle.

Marxian Crisis Theory

Marx wrote at a time when many leading economists believed that general overproduction is impossible because "supply creates its own demand." This view, dating back to Adam Smith, is now called *Say's Law* after the French economist J. B. Say, who publicized it early in the nineteenth century. The argument states that anybody who earns income from the production process must be doing so in order either to spend it on consumer goods or to invest it in a way that earns more money. In the latter case, there is an implicit or explicit demand for more production goods, such as plant and equipment. Thus, in either case, every penny earned in the production process is quickly spent so that the effective demand for any economy's output is always exactly equal to the amount it costs to produce the output. In this way, argued the classical predecessors of Marx, there can never be a general insufficiency of the demand needed to sell an economy's output. True, there can be overproduction of individual items. Industry may miscalculate and produce too many yo-yos at a time when the public would rather buy Frisbees, but such errors are quickly corrected when toy manufacturers notice unsold yo-yo inventories beginning to pile up.

However, not every economist in the early nineteenth century believed that general overproduction was impossible. There were some, including the conservative Thomas Robert Malthus and a number of early socialists, who believed that the threat of depression was very real; and the harsh facts of economic reality certainly supported them. Unfortunately, though, their analysis was confused and unsystematic, and no match for the powerful logic of the followers of Adam

Smith and J. B. Say. Among those who argued that economic crises were a real danger, a recurrent theme was that the economy tends not to give consumers enough purchasing power to buy all the available output. This idea provided the basis for the **underconsumption models** set forth by writers at both ends of the political spectrum. Malthus implied that the remedy is to provide more money to the idle rich. He felt that if those who demand goods without producing them had more money to spend, they would increase the demand without adding to the supply. The early socialists, on the other hand, argued that the proper way to deal with the problem is to pay more money to workers because their poverty forces them to spend everything they earn, whereas large portions of capitalists' profits, because they are not spent on consumption, reduce the effective demand.

Marx rejected both arguments—those that claimed overproduction is impossible as well as those that have been called the "naïve underconsumption" theories. Marx's grounds for rejection were remarkably compatible with modern ideas on the subject. He believed that general overproduction would result if those who sell inputs and receive income from the production of products decided not to use their money *at once* to demand goods or if they decided to hold on to the money itself instead of spending it. But even the capitalists' saving is *not* a deduction from demand if they use their money to buy new factories and machines instead of consumer goods.

Having established that business fluctuations can be a real problem for a profit economy and that the reasons are more complex than those offered by the naïve underconsumption model, Marx went on to propose a variety of crisis analyses of his own. Implicit in his argument was the view that there is not necessarily only one model to explain all business fluctuations. Accordingly, his analyses varied widely.

For example, one of his models emphasized the delay between the time the building of a large project, such as a railroad, produces income for construction workers (thus creating demand) and the later time when the products of such projects begin to be available (thus creating supply). At this later time, the former construction workers of a completed railroad no longer are earning the income with which to demand the goods the railroad carries.

Another of Marx's cycle models stressed the way accumulation leads to competition for workers, which in turn bids up wages and cuts into profits, causing trouble for business firms. A third model indicated that problems can arise when the timing of outputs by industries that make producers' goods does not match the needs of the industries that make consumers' goods. And still another model was a more plausible version of the underconsumption analysis.

In fact, the Marxian models covered such a wide range of cyclical relationships that there is hardly a modern theory of the business cycle that cannot find some antecedent in Marx's writings. And for this reason Marx must be considered the father of all modern cycle analyses. Yet the Marxian models were never fully worked out. Marx discussed them only briefly and unsystematically, and none ever went beyond a mere outline or hint of the full mechanism underlying the analysis.

Will the Business Cycle Kill Capitalism?

One issue in particular that has given rise to considerable speculation is Marx's views about the future of business cycles. Did he see them as growing increasingly more severe? Did he predict that capitalism would inevitably collapse in one gigantic crisis? The answers are unclear because Marx never thoroughly discussed the specific ways in which capitalism would collapse. To be sure, there are several colorful passages that paint a dramatic picture of its ruin, but these can hardly have been meant to constitute serious analysis. Here is an example from the first volume of *Capital*:

> *Along with the constantly diminishing number of magnates of capital, who usurp and monopolise all advantages . . . grows the mass of misery, oppression, slavery, degradation, exploitation; but with this too grows the revolt of the working class, a class always increasing in numbers, and disciplined, united, organised by the very mechanism of capitalist production itself. The monopoly of capital becomes a fetter upon the mode of production, which has sprung up and flourished along with, and under it. Centralisation of means of the production and socialisation of labour at last reach a point where they become incompatible with their capitalist integument. This integument is burst asunder. The knell of capitalist private property sounds. The expropriators are expropriated.[12]*

In the *Communist Manifesto* (1848) Marx and Engels mention "the commercial crises that by their periodic return put on its trial, each time more threateningly, the existence of the entire bourgeois society." And they do say that the process of recovery paves "the way for more extensive and destructive crises."

However, the *Communist Manifesto* appeared two decades before *Capital*, Marx's mature work, and we are not told how he felt about the subject at this later time. There is, though, one place in which a much older Engels specifically states that crises of increasing severity are *not* inevitable under capitalism. In 1884, writing about trends he had recently been observing (this was one year after the death of Marx and nearly 40 years after the *Communist Manifesto*), Engels said, "The period of general prosperity preceding the crisis still fails to appear. If it should fail altogether, then chronic stagnation would necessarily become the normal condition of modern industry, with only insignificant fluctuations."[13] In short, Marx was convinced that capitalism must fall. But just how that fall will occur, from what causes and in what stages, is never made clear in his writings.

Conclusion

The writings of Marx are stamped by brilliance and originality. Parts of the writings are long-winded and dull (in fact Marx told Engels he did this deliberately to make his work "weightier"), but they contain many sparkling and powerful passages. Many of Marx's ideas are still highly illuminating, even to non-Marxists, and in areas such as business-cycle analysis, almost all modern thinking stems from his, either directly or indirectly. In short, he contributed enormously to current thought within the discipline of economics as well as in politics throughout the world.

[12]Marx, *Capital*, vol. I, pages 836–37.
[13]Preface to the First German Edition (1884) of *Poverty of the Philosophy* (London: Martin Lawrence, Ltd., N.D.), page 18fn.

Summary

1. Marx agreed that capitalism had been extraordinarily productive and had contributed to general economic advancement, but he also believed that it had outlived its usefulness and had become a drag upon further progress.

2. Marx deliberately offered almost no guidance for the running of socialist economies.

3. Historical materialism, Marx's basic philosophy, asserts

that one can only understand a society from a study of its history, and that this history is determined primarily by economic conditions.

4. To Marx, the central task of the capitalist is accumulation of profits, which are then invested in ways that expand the output of the economy.

5. The purpose of Marx's value theory was to show that labor is the source of the profits accumulated by capitalists.

6. Marx denied that the objective of his value analysis was to show that capitalism robs the workers and that they deserve all the economy's output. Rather, he wished to show how the process of accumulation increases the unhappiness of workers and undermines the capitalist economy.

7. Marx is considered the father of modern analyses of business cycles because most of today's theories have their roots in Marx's writings.

Concepts for Review

Historical materialism	Value of labor power	Alienation
Marxian "commodity"	Surplus value	Underconsumption models
Marxian "value"	Marxian price–value analysis	Marx's business-cycle analysis

Questions for Discussion

1. Given how little Marx said about the actual running of a socialist (or communist) society, do you think that the economies of the Soviet Union and China are consistent or inconsistent with Marx's views, or that the two have nothing to do with each other or with Marx's intentions?

2. Do you think that, if Marxian theory is valid, labor deserves 100 percent of the national output? Why do you think Marx and Engels disagreed with this conclusion?

3. In the Middle Ages, according to Marx, the nobility were the exploiters while the serfs were the exploited. What did the medieval nobles "do for a living," and how, in Marx's view, does the answer to this question explain why GNP did not grow during the Middle Ages as it does under current economic systems?

4. In your opinion, what do you think Marx would have considered the most likely causes of the end of capitalism?

5. Some economists have suggested that many human decisions, including marriage, family size, and even suicide, can be explained to a considerable extent by the narrow economic self-interest of the decision maker. Would Marx have agreed?

Comparative Economic Systems: What Are the Choices?

41

> Every generation regards as natural the institutions to which it is accustomed.
>
> R. H. TAWNEY

These words of the British historian and economist R. H. Tawney are worth heeding as we near the end of this book, which has been geared very closely to the particular circumstances of the contemporary United States. Our current economic institutions are not eternal. No economic system is static; each is constantly growing, adapting, and evolving. Even in the relatively stable environment of the United States, the economy of the 1980s is far different from the economy of the 1880s, and by the year 2080 our economy will have changed even more.

Tawney's remark can be applied across geographical space as well as through time. The world today has a great diversity of economic systems, and this diversity seems likely to prevail in the future. There are, in fact, many ways to organize an economy other than the mixed capitalistic structure that we have focused on in this book. And no one form of economic organization is likely to be the right one for all countries for all time.

In this chapter we examine some of these *alternative economic systems* and consider the question of how a society might choose an appropriate form of economic organization. The first parts of the chapter sketch out the elements of the two major choices that must be made by every society: Should economic activity be organized through *markets*, or by government *plan*? and Should industry be *privately* or *publicly* owned? As we shall see, there are arguments on both sides of each question; and, as you might expect, different countries in different times have made different choices. In the last sections of the chapter, we therefore turn to some of the actual choices that have been made in the contemporary world. We examine, in turn, the economic structures of Sweden, France, Yugoslavia, the Soviet Union, and the People's Republic of China, looking in each case for similarities and differences among countries, and for areas in which one system has either succeeded admirably or failed miserably. Does the United States have much to learn from the experiences of these other countries? Read this chapter, and then decide.

The Challenge to Modern Capitalism

The question of choosing among economic systems is far from academic. Indeed, it has been of vital concern to people throughout the world for centuries; and it remains a live issue today. For example, about 25 years ago former Russian leader Nikita Khrushchev made his famous promise to Americans that "we will bury you." This was not a military threat nor a prediction that capitalism would perish under the weight of its own garbage; rather it was a pledge that the great productivity and growth of the Soviet economy would enable it to surpass the productive capacity of the U.S. economy. So far, the Russians have not redeemed this pledge. (See the boxed insert on pages 784–785.) But the economic competition between these two giant nations has captured the attention of the world for decades.

Many of the observers of this competition have a keen interest in its outcome. Nations of the Third World have watched attentively, wondering which economic system might be best for them. During the years since Khrushchev's declaration, a number of these nations seem to have made a choice. But many others are still teetering on the brink of indecision. Should they try to emulate the U.S. system of free markets, as, to a degree, Taiwan and Brazil have done? Should they follow the route of "democratic socialism" that is favored by many Western European nations, a route approximately traveled by Israel and India? Should they enter the Soviet sphere, and opt for a communist system with rigid state planning, as North Korea and Vietnam seem to have done? Or, finally, should they choose a more revolutionary brand of communism, following the model of Cuba?

The choices are many. And they are of the utmost importance because a nation's economic structure has a profound influence not only over its material well-being, but also over its political system, the individual rights of its citizens, its relations with other countries, and so on.

And the Third World is not the only place where the contest among alternative economic systems is going on. In recent years, several countries in Western Europe—including France, Spain, and especially Italy—have flirted with communism in a serious way, making it a distinct possibility that Europe might see its first freely elected communist government sometime during the 1980s. Most observers agree that the miserable failure of the capitalist world to perform satisfactorily during the 1970s gave Eurocommunism, as it is called, much of its momentum. On the other side of the Iron Curtain, several nations are flirting with capitalism. Yugoslavia and Hungary, in particular, rely very heavily on markets and the price system to guide their "communist" economies. And in Poland, trade unions have won the right to bargain with their employers over wages and working conditions.

Naturally, noneconomic factors play major roles in any debate over the future of a nation's economic system. Internal political considerations, for example, are probably far more important than economic analyses. Yet, to a considerable extent, the proof of the pudding will be in the eating. Demonstrated success of either free markets or state planning in solving economic problems probably will do more to sway the undecided nations than all the ideological incantations in the world.

Economic Systems: Two Important Distinctions

Economic systems can be distinguished along many lines, but two seem most important. The first is, *How is economic activity coordinated—by the market or by the plan?* The question does not, or course, demand an "either, or" answer. Rather the choice extends over an entire range, running from laissez faire to rigid central planning, with many, many gradations in between. Society must decide

Will They Bury Us?

In 1958, Soviet Premier Nikita Khrushchev made his boastful pledge about "burying" the United States economically. His optimistic mood was probably colored both by Russia's successful launching of an earth satellite and by the outstanding performance of the Soviet economy that year: real growth of almost 11 percent over 1957. With the United States simultaneously slipping into a severe recession, the ratio of Soviet GNP to American GNP jumped from 39 percent in 1957 to 44 percent in 1958 (see the accompanying chart).

No sensible statistician would extrapolate the performance of one year very far into the future. But Khrushchev was a flamboyant political leader, not a sensible statistician. By 1965, the ratio was still stalled at 44 percent and, perhaps by coincidence, Khrushchev had been ousted and was living the quiet life. As the chart shows, the Soviet/U.S. GNP ratio resumed its upward climb in the late 1960s, and by 1975 had reached 53 percent—owing in part to another serious recession in the United States.

It may be helpful to put these figures into historical perspective. According to one estimate, Russian and American GNPs were about equal on the eve of our Civil War. But, czarist Russia did not do well compared with capitalist America, and by 1913 Russian GNP had dwindled to only 39 percent of American GNP. With the enormous human and economic losses of World War I, the Russian Revolution, and the ensuing civil war, Soviet GNP fell still further—to only about 27 percent of U.S. GNP at the start of the First Five-Year Plan (1928).

Then came the beginnings of rapid economic growth in the U.S.S.R. and the Great Depression in the United States. Soviet GNP climbed swiftly to 42 percent of the U.S. level at the start of World War II, only to fall back to 29 percent after the wartime devastation. From that point, it climbed rather steadily and was still rising when Khrushchev made his famous boast.

What of the future? It is anyone's guess. A prudent long-run estimate for the U.S. growth rate to what extent it wants decisions made by individual businesses and consumers, each acting in their own self-interest, to determine their economic destiny, and to what extent it wants to persuade these businesses and consumers to act more "in the national interest." It is worth stressing that most types of planning involve some degree of *coercion*. This term is not necessarily pejorative, however; all societies, for example, coerce people into not stealing from their neighbors.

The second crucial distinction among economic systems concerns the question, *Who owns the means of production*; specifically, are they privately owned by individuals or publicly owned by the state? Again, there is a wide range of choice and, to our knowledge, there are no examples of nations at either the **capitalist** extreme where all property is privately owned or at the **socialist** extreme where no private property whatever is permitted.

For example, while most industries are privately owned in the United States, the owners face restrictions on what they can do with their capital. Owners of automobile companies must comply with environmental and safety regulations. Owners of communication and transportation companies, where these are privately owned, often have both their prices and the conditions of their services regulated by the government. And in communist Russia, where no one can own a factory, anyone who can afford it can own a car or hold a bank account. There is also a small "capitalist" sector in which, for example, peasant farmers can sell what they have grown on their small private plots of land.

There is a tendency to merge the two distinctions between economic systems

Capitalism is a method of economic organization in which private individuals own the means of production, either directly or indirectly through corporations.

Socialism is a method of economic organization in which the state owns the means of production.

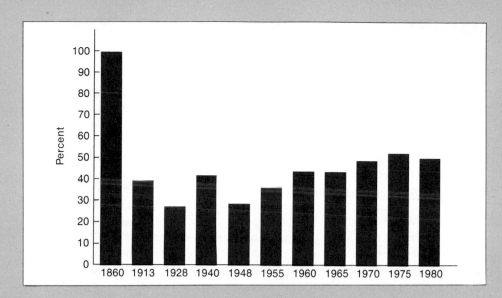

RATIO OF RUSSIAN REAL
GNP TO U.S. REAL GNP

SOURCE: Herbert Block, "Soviet
Economic Power Growth—
Achievements under Handicaps,"
*Soviet Economy in a New Perspec-
tive. A Compendium of Papers
Submitted to the Joint Economic
Committee,* Congress of the United
States, 94th Congress, 2nd Ses-
sion, October 1976. Updated to
1980 by the authors.

might be 3 percent a year, the current growth rate for potential GNP as estimated by the Council of Economic Advisers.

As for the Soviet Union, only a few years ago experts were projecting a long-term annual growth rate of 5 to 5½ percent. However, the poor performance of the Soviet economy in recent years has led these estimates to be scaled down to the 2 to 3 percent range. If the Soviet economy does manage to grow 5 percent per year while ours grows 3 percent per year, Russia will indeed "bury" us with a larger GNP by around the year 2002. (Remember, though, that Russia's population is about 20 percent larger than ours.) On the other hand, if current projections prove correct and the Russian economy grows no faster than our own, the burial will never take place.

and think of capitalist economies as those that have both a great deal of privately owned property *and* rely heavily on free markets. By the same token, socialist economies typically are thought of as heavily planned. However:

While there is an undeniable association between the degree of socialism in a country and the degree to which it plans its economy, it would be a mistake to regard these two features as equivalent.

Modern Yugoslavia, for example, provides an important instance of a country in which the means of production are socially owned but economic activity is organized mainly by markets. Closer to home, there is a great deal of state ownership in the United Kingdom, which is most assuredly a market economy. On the other hand, Germany under Hitler provided an example of a capitalist economy with rigid central planning.

Our point is not that socialist economies are no more heavily planned than capitalist ones. *In practice*, they normally are. But, *in principle*, when thinking about a society's *choice* among economic systems, it is best to keep the two distinctions separate.

The Market or the Plan? Some Issues

The choice between **planning** and reliance on **free markets** requires an understanding of just what the market accomplishes and where its strengths and weaknesses lie. Since these issues have been the focal point of much of this book, our review can be rather concise here.

What goods to produce and how much of each. In a market economy, consumers, by registering their dollar votes, determine which goods and services shall be provided and in what quantities. Items that are not wanted, or that are overproduced, will suffer a fall in price, while items that are in short supply will rise in price. These price movements act as *signals* to profit-seeking firms, which then produce larger amounts of the goods whose prices rise and less of the goods whose prices fall. This mechanism is what we call **consumer sovereignty.**

Of course, the doctrine of consumer sovereignty must be qualified in several ways when we deal with the real (as opposed to the ideal) world. For one thing, governments interfere with the price mechanism in many ways—taxing some goods and services while subsidizing others. These interferences certainly alter the bill of goods that the economy produces. For another, we have learned that in the presence of *externalities* the price system may send out false signals, leading to inappropriate levels of output for certain commodities.

How to produce each good. In a market economy, firms decide on the production technique, guided once again by the price system. Inputs that are in short supply will be assigned high prices by the market. This will encourage producers to use them sparingly. Other inputs whose supply is more abundant will be priced lower, which will encourage firms to use them.

Once again, the same two qualifications apply: Government taxes and subsidies alter relative prices, and externalities may make the price system malfunction. But on the whole, the market system has yet to meet its match as an engine of productive efficiency.

How income is distributed. The same price system that determines the levels of wages, interest rates, and profits also determines the distribution of income among individuals in a market economy. As we have stressed (especially in Chapter 34), there is no reason to expect the resulting income distribution to be "good" from an ethical point of view. And, in fact, the evidence shows that capitalist market economies produce a considerable degree of inequality. This is certainly one of capitalism's weak points, though there are many ways for the government to alter the distribution of income without destroying either free markets or private property (for example, through progressive income taxation or a negative income tax, both of which were discussed in Chapter 34).

Economic growth. The rate of economic growth depends fundamentally upon how much society decides to save and invest. In a free-market economy, these decisions are left to private firms and individuals who determine how much of their current income they will consume today and how much they will invest for the future. Once again, however, government policies can influence these choices by, for example, making investment more or less attractive through tax policy.

Business fluctuations. As we explained in Part Two, a market economy is subject to business fluctuations—periods of boom and bust, inflation and unemployment. This holds not only in capitalist market economies like the United States, but also in socialist market economies like Yugoslavia. Interestingly, the highly planned but mostly capitalist economy of France showed very little evidence of business cycle problems from 1958 until the Great Recession of the 1970s. Thus it seems that the business cycle, which Marx dubbed one of the fundamental flaws of *capitalism*, is really a problem for *market* economies, be they capitalist or socialist.

Let us now go over this list again, seeing how each question is resolved in a planned economy, and comparing this with a market economy.

What to produce and how much. Under central planning, the bill of goods that society will produce normally is not selected by consumer sovereignty. Instead, the planners decide. Depending on their particular beliefs and on the political structure of the country, their decisions may or may not be strongly influenced by consumers' desires.

Whether this is a strength or weakness of central planning depends upon your point of view. On the one hand, there is the danger that society's resources will be devoted to producing items that nobody wants. In Soviet Russia, for example, there are clearly fewer cars and more copies of Marx's *Capital* than consumers want to buy. On the other hand, consumer sovereignty can lead to some bizarre products, the kinds of things that social reformers find offensive: designer jeans, fast-food chains, low-quality television programming, and so on. But, on balance, most adherents to traditional Western values will find more to like than to dislike under consumer sovereignty. After all, who knows what is good for consumers better than consumers themselves?

How to produce. Planned economies can allow plant managers to choose a production technique, or they can let central planners do it instead. Under Soviet-style planning, plant managers have rather little discretion, and this has led to such monumental inefficiencies as production curtailments due to lack of materials, poor quality, and high production costs. No incentive system has yet been designed that can match the profit motive of competitive firms for keeping costs down.

How income is distributed. The distribution of income is always planned to some extent. Even in basically market economies like ours, the government taxes different people at different rates and pays transfer payments to others, seeking thereby to mitigate the inequality that capitalism and free markets tend to generate. Planned economies do the same thing, only more so. For instance, they may try to tamper directly with the income distribution by having the planners, rather than the market, set relative wage rates. This, however, leads to troubles similar to those mentioned in the previous paragraph. Thus, even in the Soviet Union relative wages are established more or less by supply and demand.

Economic growth. In general, planned economies have much better control over their growth rates than do unplanned ones, simply because the state can determine the volume of the investment. They therefore can, if they choose to, engineer very high growth rates—an option they often have exercised. Whether such rapid growth is a good idea, however, is another question. In Stalin's Russia and Mao's China, for example, this goal was achieved at enormous cost—some of it paid for by sacrificing current consumption, some by sacrificing personal freedom, and some by bloodshed. Furthermore, rapid growth can be achieved without planning: Some of the fastest growth rates in the postwar world have been achieved by two market economies, Japan and West Germany.

Business fluctuations. We explained in Chapter 8 that business fluctuations are not much of a problem for highly planned economies. This is because total spending in such economies is controlled tightly by the planners, and it is not permitted to get far out of line with the economy's capacity to produce. As we shall see later in this chapter, the U.S.S.R. has many serious economic problems, but the business cycle is not one of them.

The Market or the Plan? The Scoreboard

As we look back over this list, what do we find? Concerning *what to produce*, an adherent to Western values probably would give a clear edge to the market, though conceding the need to curb some of its more flagrant abuses. But, of course, much of the world does not prize individualism as dearly as we in the West do.

As to *productive efficiency*, the market mechanism is clearly superior. But when we consider the *distribution of income*, we find that all societies have decided to plan; they differ only in degree.

High growth, it seems, can be achieved with or without planning, though planned systems have an easier time of it. Here an advanced nation will pause to question whether faster is always better, and often will conclude that it is not. But among the less developed countries, the goal of rapid development is typically of paramount importance. Many of these countries also lack the savings and the financial markets needed to channel funds into their most productive uses. If so, they may have little choice but to plan.

Finally, in managing *business fluctuations*, there is no question that planned economies can do much better. The results of our scoreboard are clearly mixed. Do we, therefore, score the contest a tie? Certainly not. What we do conclude is:

Different countries—with their different political systems, value judgments, traditions, and aspirations—will score the contest differently. Some will find the market more attractive, while others will opt for the plan. Most will divide their economies into two sectors—leaving some decisions to the market mechanism and others to conscious planning.

Thus, in the United States, for example, income distribution and macroeconomic activity are substantially "planned," while other decisions are left mainly to the market.

Capitalism or Socialism?

Although the choice between capitalism and socialism seems to excite more ideological fervor, it may be much less important than the choice between the market and the plan.

If it could design an appropriate incentive structure, a socialist market economy could do just as well as a capitalist market economy in terms of producing the right set of goods in the most efficient way. However, we have emphasized the word "if" to underscore the fact that designing such an incentive system may be quite difficult under socialism. Lacking the profit motive, a socialist society must provide incentives, either material or otherwise, for its plant managers to behave in the optimal way. This has proved difficult enough. But a still deeper problem caused by the absence of the profit motive is the need to maintain inventiveness, innovation, and risk-taking in a system in which large accumulations of personal wealth are impossible. Socialist systems are noticeably low on "high rollers."

Income distribution under socialism is naturally more equal than under capitalism simply because the profits of industry do not go to a small group of stockholders but instead are dispersed among the workers or among the populace as a whole. However, if supply and demand rules the labor market, a socialist nation may have just as much inequality in the distribution of labor income as a capitalist economy does—and for the very same reasons: to attract workers into risky, or highly skilled, or difficult occupations. Indeed, students of the Soviet economy have concluded that labor incomes in the U.S.S.R. are distributed with roughly the same degree of inequality as those in the United States.

The capitalist–socialist cleavage is much more important in regard to the issue of economic growth. To oversimplify, under capitalism it is the capitalists who determine the growth rate, while under socialism it is the state. Still, government incentives can prod capitalists to invest more; and instances of both fast and slow growth can be found under both systems.

Finally, the persistence of business fluctuations in a country depends much more on whether its economy is planned or unplanned than on whether its industries are publicly or privately owned.

Socialism, Planning, and Freedom

There is, however, a *noneconomic* criterion that is of the utmost importance in choosing between capitalism and socialism, or between the market and the plan—*individual freedom.*

Planning must by necessity involve some degree of coercion; if it does not, then the plan may degenerate into wishful thinking. In the extreme case of a command economy (Soviet Russia, Nazi Germany), the abridgement of personal freedom is painfully obvious. Less rigid forms of planning involve commensurately smaller infringements of individuals rights, infringements that most people find quite tolerable. Even within a basic framework of free markets, some activities may be banned—such as prostitution and selling liquor to minors. Other economic activities may be compelled by law—safety devices in automobiles and labeling requirements on foods and drugs are just two examples. Each of these can be considered a type of planning, and each limits the freedom of some people. Yet most of these restrictions command broad public support in the United States. The doctrines of consumer sovereignty and freedom of enterprise are not absolutes.

Taxation is a still more subtle form of coercion. Most people do not view taxes as seriously impairing their personal freedom because, even though tax laws may make them pay for the privilege, they remain free to choose the courses of action that suit them best. Indeed, this is one major reason why most economists favor taxes over quotas and outright prohibitions in many instances. It is true, however, that taxation can be a very potent tool for changing individual behavior. As Chief Justice John Marshall pointed out with characteristic perspicacity, "The power to tax involves the power to destroy."

Individual freedom is also involved in the choice between capitalism and socialism. After all, under socialism there are many more restrictions on what a person can do with his or her wealth than there are under capitalism. On the other hand, the poorest people in a capitalist society may find little solace in their "freedom" if they are homeless and hungry.

Once again, it would be a mistake to paint the issue in black and white. Under extremely rigid authoritarian planning, the restrictions on individual liberties are so severe that they are probably intolerable to most people with Western values. But more moderate and relaxed forms of planning—for example, the French system discussed later in this chapter—seem quite compatible with personal freedoms. Similarly, a doctrinaire brand of socialism that bans all private property (even the clothes on your back?) would entail a major loss of liberty; but a country with a large socialized sector can be basically free. The English, for example, do not feel any less free than do Americans. So:

The real question is not *whether* we want to allow elements of socialism or planning to abridge our personal freedoms, but by *how much*.

Just as your freedom to extend your arm is limited by the proximity of your neighbor's chin, the freedom to build a factory need not extend to building it in the midst of a residential neighborhood. Just as freedom of speech does not justify yelling "Fire!" in a crowded movie theater when there is no fire, freedom of enterprise does not imply the right to monopolize trade.

A Catalog of Blueprints

Different societies have struck the balance between the market and the plan and between socialism and capitalism in different places. What follows in the rest of this chapter are rather brief descriptions of some of the alternative economic systems actually in existence today.

The catalog is ordered from the least socialized economy to the most. Thus we start with Sweden, where public ownership of the means of production is only slightly more common than it is in the United States, and work our way toward the "communist" economies of Russia and the People's Republic of China, where capitalism plays little role.

This sampling of countries brings home the point that socialism and planning are not identical. Had we ordered the countries from the least highly planned to the most, Yugoslavia would have come before France (perhaps even before Sweden), and China would have come before Russia (see Table 41–1).

Table 41–1
ECONOMIC SYSTEMS OF SELECTED COUNTRIES

Economic systems may be ranked according to the extent of socialism or the extent of central planning. As this table shows, the rankings do not always correspond. The United States, however, stands out as among the least socialistic and least planned economies in the world.

Sweden's Welfare State

The Swedish economy has been characterized as a happy marriage between capitalism and socialism. But in fact, at least as we have defined the terms, Sweden is almost as capitalistic as the United States: more than 90 percent of Swedish industry is privately owned. A more accurate statement is that:

Sweden has a capitalist market economy very much like our own, but with much more extensive government interference to ensure that the system serves two social goals of overriding importance: full employment and an equal distribution of income.

Full Employment Policy

Sweden has one of the longest and most active traditions of Keynesian macro-economic management in the world—a tradition that even predates Keynes's *General Theory of Employment, Interest, and Money* (1936). In addition to using the standard tools of monetary and fiscal policy more frequently and more vigorously than we do in the United States, the Swedes have invented a few novel tools of their own. The most important of these is the **investment reserve system.**

This system, which has been in effect since the 1950s, is based on tax incentives that induce firms to do most of their investing at times when the government thinks more spending is desirable. Specifically, firms can exempt a large portion of their profits from taxation by depositing them in special accounts at the central bank. When private demand is weak, the government "releases" these funds and offers substantial tax advantages to firms who then use them for investment. In this way, investment spending is "planned" by the government though conducted through free markets.

Judging by the results, the Swedish stabilization policy efforts seem to have borne fruit. Figure 41–1 compares the unemployment rates in Sweden and in the United States from 1960 to 1980. It is clear not only that the average rate of unemployment has been kept quite low (always below 3 percent), but also that the fluctuations have been quite restrained. However, as our discussion of the trade-off between inflation and unemployment suggests, the Swedes have paid the price for this good performance by making sacrifices on the inflation front (see Figure 41–2). Their inflation rate has typically been higher than ours.

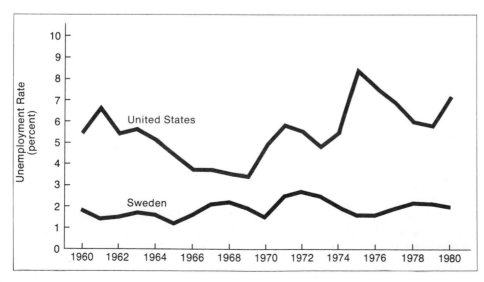

Figure 41–1
UNEMPLOYMENT IN SWEDEN AND THE UNITED STATES
As this figure indicates, Sweden's unemployment rate has been consistently lower than our own, and its fluctuations have also been less severe. Notice in particular the absence of high unemployment in Sweden during 1975 and 1976.
SOURCE: U.S. Bureau of Labor Statistics, and *Statistical Abstract of Sweden.*

Figure 41–2

INFLATION IN SWEDEN AND THE UNITED STATES
As might be expected, Sweden has paid the price for lower unemployment by having more inflation than the United States. This figure shows that inflation in Sweden has normally been higher than inflation in the United States.
SOURCE: Organization for Economic Cooperation and Development.

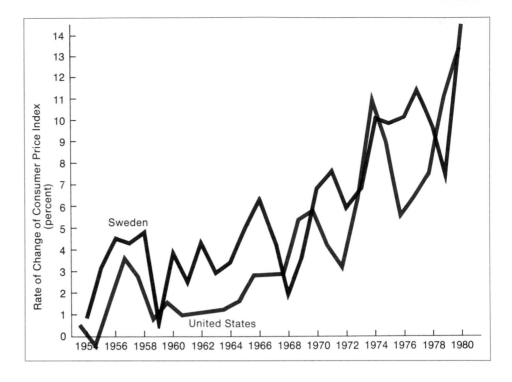

Income Distribution Policy

Sweden, as is well known, has one of the world's most comprehensive **welfare states,** with social programs that extend, quite literally, from the cradle to the grave. There are financial allowances for children, free education at all levels, a national health service, extensive benefits for the unemployed, a state retirement pension far more generous than our own social security system, and many more social welfare programs. Naturally, the heavy burden of financing these programs leads to commensurately high taxes, and in recent years more and more Swedes have objected to the oppressiveness of the tax system. These critics argue, for example, that the steeply progressive Swedish income tax is destroying incentives to work.

Swedish social welfare programs seem to be quite successful. It is really difficult to find the telltale signs of poverty, such as slums and shabby clothing, in Sweden. And it is widely agreed that Sweden has one of the most equal income distributions anywhere—a feat it has managed to accomplish while also becoming one of the richest nations in the world. Yet, here too there are problems. Absenteeism has been rising, demands for greater worker control over industry are being heard, and class antagonisms have arisen in this "classless" society.

Sweden and the United States

In many ways, the Swedish and American economic systems seem quite similar, and the apparent success of Swedish economic policy has raised the question of whether their principles can be applied here. Yet some fundamental differences exist, differences that may make it impossible to import Swedish economic policy to America. First, Sweden is a very small country whose labor unions and industries are both highly concentrated. This facilitates "consensus building" and also makes coordination easy to accomplish without formal planning. Second, Sweden is an ethnically homogeneous country. So the racial and ethnic antagonisms that underlie some of America's worst social problems are absent. Third, the Swedes care much more about full employment and much less about inflation than Americans do. They are proud of their strong record on employment and less concerned with their inability to maintain price stability. Americans might react differently to this same record.

France: Planning by Consensus[1]

The basically capitalist economy of France has developed a unique method of organizing economic activity that one expert has called "the most elaborate and detailed planning system among the advanced Western nations."[2] The system is called **indicative planning,** a name meant to suggest planning by voluntary compliance and agreement rather than by government coercion.

Under the French system, a national economic plan is hammered out and agreed to by representatives of government, industry, and labor, along with other technical experts. The aim is to achieve a good degree of *coordination* of economic activity without the need for coercion simply by passing both information and ideas back and forth among all the parties. For example, if it turned out that the production plan of the automobile industry required the use of more steel than the steel industry was expecting to sell, the participants in the plan could sit down and reconcile the differences. Was one forecast too optimistic or too pessimistic? Would government actions (such as tariffs and import quotas) render these two forecasts consistent or inconsistent?

Through negotiations like these, French planners hope that individual industries can discover potential shortages and surpluses before they arise, and thereby adjust their own plans to conform with a broad overall plan for the nation. They further hope that *participation* in the plan will lead to *voluntary compliance.* Often this is so. But when it fails, the French government does not hesitate to use a wide variety of tools—including taxes, subsidies, and price controls—to persuade businesses to abide by the plan. It has been said that "French planning may be indicative, but it is not permissive or passive."[3]

The government exercises particularly strong control over both the volume and direction of investment spending: it directly controls about half of national investment and strongly influences the rest by regulating access to the credit market.

How well has the system performed? Apparently, very well indeed. Except for the Great Recession of the mid-1970s, the French record is one of full employment and rapid growth, unbroken by recessions (see Figure 41–3). Of course, this does not prove that indicative planning has been the key to France's success. West Germany, for example, grew even faster without planning. But it does suggest that something has gone right.

Indicative Planning for the United States?

Many countries have envied the French growth record, and some have tried to emulate it. Could indicative planning be practiced successfully in the United States? There are several reasons to think that it would not work as well here. First, the U.S. government controls a much smaller fraction of total investment (perhaps 20 percent) than does the French government, and the comprehensive controls that the French government exercises over the credit market run counter to American financial practice. A second difference is that the United States does

[1] A new socialist government took office in France while this book was in production. It is too early to tell how, if at all, this will change the French system of economic planning.
[2] Gregory Grossman, *Economic Systems,* Second Edition (Englewood Cliffs, N.J.: Prentice-Hall, 1974), page 87.
[3] Egon Neuberger and William Duffy, *Comparative Economic Systems* (Boston: Allyn and Bacon, 1976), page 235.

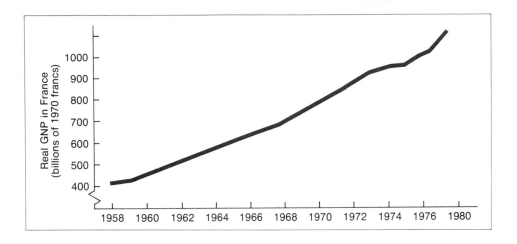

Figure 41–3
FRENCH ECONOMIC GROWTH SINCE 1958
This chart of real gross national product in France shows a remarkable absence of business fluctuations. Only the severe worldwide recession of 1974–1975 broke the upward march of real GNP in France.
SOURCE: Organization for Economic Cooperation and Development.

not have the French tradition of a close marriage between government and industry. The "old boy" network is particularly strong in France, and many of the government officials and industrialists who work together on the plan are old friends from their days as students at France's elite *écoles*. State intervention in business has long been the norm in France; here it would be a major departure. Third, planning along French lines would run afoul of America's antitrust laws. With firms sharing common forecasts and production plans, and with the government parceling out investment allotments to industries that then divide them among their constituent firms, collusion among firms is almost inevitable. This sort of cozy arrangement is widely accepted in France, where government tolerance of and even support for monopolies and cartels is traditional. But it runs counter to deeply held beliefs about American capitalism.

Workers' Management in Yugoslavia

Yugoslavia was forced by events to become the clearest illustration in the contemporary world of the fact that "socialism" need not be synonymous with "planning." A serious political rift between Tito and Stalin in the 1940s led to the ouster of Yugoslavia from the Soviet economic sphere. Up to that point, the Yugoslav economy had been built on the Soviet model, and relied very heavily on trade with the U.S.S.R.

Searching for a way out of their economic plight, the Yugoslavs embarked on a great economic experiment by passing the *Law on Worker Management of Enterprises* in 1950. This law and subsequent legislation gave to the workers of each firm the authority to make most of the decisions that are normally reserved for management. The world has watched this experiment with great interest. Nowadays there is even talk that nations as far apart ideologically as Great Britain and China may want to emulate the Yugoslav system, and experiments with **workers' management** have been made in the United States and Canada.

While Yugoslav industry is almost wholly socialistic, enterprises are *not* run by state-appointed managers following a national plan. Instead, Yugoslav managers are chosen by the workers and are expected to seek after high profits.

Subject only to the usual sorts of regulations that are found even in the United States, each firm can decide for itself *what* to produce, *how much* to produce, and by *what technique* to produce. Though there are a number of price controls, taxes, and subsidies, most commodity prices are established in free markets, and consumer sovereignty calls the tune. Firms flourish if they produce what consumers want and produce it efficiently. After paying for its nonlabor inputs, each enterprise can decide how much of its net income to invest in expansion and how much to pay out in wages to its workers.

Under workers' management, Yugoslavia has achieved a record of very good growth in total output, but a number of problems have surfaced.

For one, like other market economies, Yugoslavia is subject to the ups and downs that we call the *business cycle*. This country has had periodic bouts with stagnation, and seems plagued with both chronically high inflation and unemployment. Lately, the persistent inflation has led to greater reliance on price controls—a movement away from free markets that has been motivated not by ideology, but by desperation.

Income distribution has posed another problem. Since what is called *wages* in Yugoslavia include a share of what is called *profits* in a capitalist system, equal work in different firms is not rewarded equally. Instead, workers in the most efficient enterprises earn a bonus, and the resulting wage disparities among different firms and different regions in the country have caused social frictions.

Related to this are the twin problems of inadequate labor mobility and sluggish employment growth. In a capitalist system, the most efficient firms would expand, hiring more workers, and thus driving down their marginal productivity. Under Yugoslavia's system of worker control, this may not happen because workers in a highly profitable firm may care more about maximizing *profits per worker* than about *total* profits. Since profits per worker may well *fall* if more labor is allowed to join the enterprise, new employment opportunities may not arise very often.

While there is virtually no central planning of the Soviet variety, we would not want to leave the impression that the Yugoslav economy is totally unmanaged. This is not the case. But what planning there is, is of the French *indicative* style. As in France, the government exercises its control, often quite rigorously, through the credit market. There it influences both the overall volume of credit for investment purposes and the allocation of these funds among regions and industries.

The Soviet Economy: Historical Background

In November 1917, a determined group of Bolsheviks led by V. I. Lenin overthrew the democratic provisional government that Kerensky had established after the fall of the Czar just eight months earlier, and Russia became the first country in the world to establish a communist government. There is a great irony here in that this first triumph of communism contradicted one of the tenets of Marxian theory. Marx had prophesied that socialism would be the inevitable outgrowth of a decaying, advanced capitalist system. Instead, it came first to a land that had barely emerged from feudalism.

The Russian Revolution both surprised and dismayed the Western world, the more so since Lenin was an outspoken apostle of worldwide communist revolution. Outside support for the anticommunists helped prolong a bloody civil war between "Red" and "White" Russians, a war that Lenin's army finally won. It was out of the dire circumstances of a wartime economy that the Soviet system of state planning as we know it today emerged.

When the war was won, a pragmatic Lenin reacted to the many problems besetting detailed central planning by permitting the reintroduction of substantial amounts of both capitalist ownership and market organization under his New

Economic Policy (NEP). The NEP was a great success, especially among the peasants who were very hostile to the Communist regime, and it helped rebuild the badly battered Russian economy. After Lenin's death, there was both a fierce struggle for power within the Communist party and a vigorous policy debate over basic economic strategy. Joseph Stalin won both contests and ruthlessly set the Soviet Union on a course that it has followed, more or less, to this day.

Stalin's strategy called for single-minded application of Soviet resources to the goal of rapid *industrial* development with emphasis on *heavy* industry, particularly *armaments*.

To achieve such rapid growth and industrialization, it was necessary to limit consumption severely; so the Russian consumer was asked—or rather forced—to make sacrifices. To feed the urban laborers needed for industrial expansion, Russia's backward agricultural peasants were forced onto collective farms—at an extremely high human and economic cost. Furthermore, the starving peasants were forced to sell their food at very low prices and to work for pitifully low wages.

The events of the early Stalinist years left their mark on Soviet economic life. To this day, the Russian economy is characterized by:

- A high degree of centralization, with basic economic goals set by planners, particularly by the leaders of the Communist party. Lower levels of the hierarchy are expected to follow orders, though the methods of guaranteeing compliance are far less Draconian than in Stalin's day.

- A stress on growth, industrialization, and military power, with corresponding downgrading of consumption. While the Soviet GNP has grown quite rapidly since 1928, the Russian consumer shared little of the fruits of this growth until quite recently.

- Continuing problems in the agricultural sector, where productivity is very low and the rural peasants remain quite poor.

- A planning system based on quantity targets and quotas, which makes very little use of the price system.

In surveying almost fifty years of Soviet economic development, one expert commented that "the surprising thing about the Soviet planning system is not how much it changed since its inception, but how little."[4]

Central Planning in the Command Economy

The structure of the Russian economic system is in many ways similar to the hierarchy of a giant corporation.

At the top may be a single strongman or a ruling clique. The political leadership plays the role of chairman of the board, setting overall policy objectives, but has much more absolute authority than that of the chairman of any corporation.

Given the overall goals and priorities established by the top echelons of the Communist party, the State Planning Commission (*Gosplan*, in Russian) has responsibility for the preparation of the national economic plans (discussed below). Beneath the Gosplan are a number of ministries, which direct each industrial sector, and the various regional authorities. These bureaus oversee the

[4]Neuberger and Duffy, *Comparative Economic Systems*, page 168.

day-to-day management of the individual industries or regions within their purview. Several other layers of the hierarchy intervene as we move down the organizational pyramid. Finally, we reach the level of the enterprise. Enterprise managers in the U.S.S.R. have far less authority than do their counterparts in the United States. They are expected to carry out directives handed down from above, fill their quotas, and send information back up the hierarchical ladder. They are bureaucrats rather than entrepreneurs.

Communications within the hierarchy are almost exclusively vertical. Orders flow down from top to bottom, while data flow up from bottom to top. Since the data requirements are so immense, and the number of layers within the bureaucracy so large, the problems of accurate data transmission and processing are monumental.[5] A detailed study of the operation of a large Soviet enterprise in the 1960s found that compliance with the plan required that 44 *million* characters of information be passed up to the next highest level in a single year, and that this was only about 12 to 15 percent of the total information gathered by the enterprise. This situation led one Soviet cyberneticist, in one of those wild extrapolations, to observe that preservation of the same planning apparatus until 1980 would require the employment of every Russian adult.[6] As far as we know, the prophecy has not been fulfilled.

Markets and Prices in Soviet Economic Life

Although central planning is certainly dominant in Soviet economic life, the Russians do rely on the market mechanism for some purposes.

For instance, *given* the production target for each consumer good as set down in the plan, Soviet planners try to set prices to ration the quantity demanded down to the available quantity supplied. The result is that consumer prices often are set far above production costs, with the difference made up by the so-called *turnover tax*, the main source of government revenue. But the planners often do not succeed in equating the quantities supplied and demanded, and any visitor to the Soviet Union is struck by the frequency with which long lines appear in front of many stores. Conversely, large stocks of unwanted goods sit waiting for customers at other establishments. Consumers do exercise free choice among the available goods, but they are certainly not sovereign.

The price system is used even more extensively in the labor market. Given the plan for industrial output, Soviet planners try to set wages to attract workers to the right industries and the right regions. With some exceptions (for instance, peasants who must stay on collective farms), Soviet workers now have considerable freedom to work where they please—a far cry from the situation in Stalin's day. To provide material incentives for high productivity, many Soviet workers are paid *piece rates* rather than straight hourly wages. (Ironically, this is precisely the form of compensation that American labor unions find most objectionable and inhumane.) Partly as a result of the piece-rate system, but also because of the strong desire to direct labor to the areas assigned top priority by the plan, wage differentials in the Soviet Union are quite large. According to most observers, they are at least as large as those in the United States, and they lead to considerable inequality in the distribution of labor income. Of course, income from property is negligible in the U.S.S.R., so the overall distribution of income is more equal than ours.

---

[5]Giant corporations have a similar problem of handling and transmitting data. However, not even the largest corporation approaches the size and scope of the Soviet economy.
[6]Neuberger and Duffy, *Comparative Economic Systems*, pages 179–80.

The Five-Year and One-Year Plans

Russia's celebrated Five-Year Plans lay down the basic strategies and growth targets for Soviet economic development, but in many ways they are not as important as the less well known One-Year Plans.

Both of these documents are the responsibility of the Gosplan.

The **Five-Year Plans** set the nation's basic strategy for resource allocation: How much for investment? How much for consumption? How much for military procurement and for scientific research? They also provide guidelines for the distribution of these totals among the various industries (Will there be more cars or more refrigerators?), and they may include specific large construction projects, such as hydroelectric power plants. Much attention is paid, both in the West and in the U.S.S.R., to the numerical goals posted by these plans. Table 41–2 lists a few of the goals and actual achievements of the Tenth Five-Year Plan (1976–1980) and the Ninth Five-Year Plan (1971–1975).

But the Five-Year Plans are not detailed enough to serve as blueprints for action. This job is left to the **One-Year Plans**—enormous sets of documents covering almost every facet of Soviet economic life. In fact, One-Year Plans are so detailed and complex that any one of them is normally not completed until well into the year to which it applies. Sometimes these plans are never completed at all.

The planning procedure starts with a set of broad national goals (and some rather specific ones) handed down from the political leadership to the Gosplan. The planners then attempt to translate these goals—which are partly reflections of the current Five-Year Plan—into a set of specific directives for subordinate ministries and agencies. As the plan is passed down from one level of the hierarchy to the next, the lower level is constantly supplying the higher level with both data and suggestions for changes—changes in specific tactics, not in basic goals (which are never questioned). One perennial problem of Soviet planning is that enterprises strive to obtain low production quotas that they will find easy to meet and surpass, because their success is measured by their ability to meet the quotas. To this end, they may deliberately mislead their superiors and understate their productive capacity.

The process of give-and-take up and down the hierarchy eventually leads to a complete One-Year Plan that, the planners hope, is *internally consistent*. Consistency, however, is not often achieved. To see why, let us briefly consider one of the major problems of Soviet planning—achieving what they call **material balance.** This phrase means nothing more than equating quantity supplied and quantity demanded for each type of input—a relatively easy task for a market

Table 41–2
THE NINTH AND TENTH SOVIET FIVE-YEAR PLANS

ITEM	TENTH FIVE-YEAR PLAN (1976–1980)		NINTH FIVE-YEAR PLAN (1971–1975)	
	TARGET GROWTH RATE (1976–1980) (percent per year)	ACTUAL GROWTH RATE (1976–1979)	TARGET GROWTH RATE (percent per year)	ACTUAL GROWTH RATE (percent per year)
GNP	5.0	3.1	6.7	5.1
Industrial output	6.3	3.6	8.0	7.4
Agricultural output	4.9	2.3	4.0	2.5

SOURCE: *The Soviet Economy in 1978–1979 and Prospects for 1980,* National Foreign Assessment Center, Central Intelligence Agency, June 1980.

economy, but an impossibly difficult one for Soviet planners.

To take a simple example, suppose three industries (called A, B, and C) use ball bearings. The output targets for industries A, B, and C will then imply a corresponding need for inputs of ball bearings. This quantity (the quantity of ball bearings demanded) must, then, be equal to the output target of the ball-bearing industry (the quantity of ball bearings supplied). This seems simple enough. But the complications become apparent once it is realized that the ball-bearing industry needs inputs, too, and that some of these inputs may be the outputs of industries A, B, and C. So if, for example, the production of ball bearings is to be increased, more steel and machinery may be required; and these additional outputs will require more ball bearings as inputs; and so on and so on.

To gain an appreciation of the complexity of the task facing Soviet planners, try your hand at the following simple problem. Suppose there are only three goods—ball bearings, steel, and automobiles—and that the national plan calls for individual consumers to get no ball bearings, $\frac{1}{2}$ unit of steel, and 1 unit of automobiles. How much must each of the three industries produce to achieve material balance?

To try to answer this, you must know the input requirements of each industry. Suppose the inputs required *per unit of output* of each industry are as follows:

OUTPUT	NECESSARY INPUTS
Ball bearings (one unit)	$\frac{1}{2}$ unit of steel *plus* $\frac{1}{4}$ unit of automobiles
Steel (one unit)	$\frac{1}{4}$ unit of ball bearings *plus* $\frac{1}{4}$ unit of steel *plus* $\frac{1}{4}$ unit of automobiles
Automobiles (one unit)	$\frac{1}{3}$ unit of ball bearings *plus* $\frac{1}{2}$ unit of steel *plus* $\frac{1}{6}$ unit of automobiles

Use trial and error to figure out the necessary production levels for each industry. It will not take long to convince yourself that the problem is quite difficult.[7]

The mathematical technique devised to cope with problems like this is called *input–output analysis*,[8] and the preceding little problem is easily solved using this method. But the Russian planners face a problem of this character with, literally, tens of thousands of commodities. Not even the most sophisticated high-speed computer is capable of carrying out the necessary calculations—even if all the data were available. In short, a perfectly correct solution to the problem of material balance is impossible.

What, then, do the Russians do? In practice, input–output analysis is of little use in formulating One-Year Plans. Trial and error is the only viable approach, and planners seek to avoid as many material imbalances as they can in the time

[7] The answer is: 2 units of ball bearings, 4 units of steel, and 3 units of automobiles.
[8] Input–output analysis was discussed in Chapter 23, pages 436–437.

allotted to them. They concentrate particularly on avoiding any bottlenecks in those industries that are accorded highest priority by the political leadership. If necessary, Soviet planners will redirect scarce inputs to the high-priority sectors to make sure that production there is not interrupted. Thus Soviet spacecraft factories are unlikely to close down for lack of steel, but factories producing toasters are quite likely to.

Performance and Problems of Soviet Planning

Most observers rate the Soviet performance as quite good on growth, at least until quite recently, but quite poor on economic efficiency.

Rigorous economic planning brought the backward Soviet economy of the 1920s into the modern age very quickly. Postwar economic growth averaged about 7 percent in the 1950s and somewhat more than 5 percent in the 1960s. However, the Soviet growth rate slipped into the 3 to 4 percent range—about the same as the U.S. growth rate—during the 1970s, and is projected to be only 2 to 3 percent per year in the 1980s.

There are several reasons for this slowdown in Soviet economic growth. For one thing, part of the rapid early growth was achieved by borrowing advanced technology from the West; this obviously could not last forever. For another, the Soviet Union (like the United States) achieved part of its industrial growth through the migration of peasants to the cities. But the poor performance of Soviet agriculture has prevented the Russian government from pushing this migration as far as it has gone in the United States. A third factor was the increasing outcry of the Soviet citizenry for more and better consumer goods. Only in recent years was the regime willing to accommodate these demands, and this required cutting back on investment. Finally, the plain fact is that the Russian economic mechanism does not function very smoothly, and seems to be growing increasingly arthritic.

Both Western and Soviet observers agree that Russia's economic problems are manifold:

- We have already mentioned the tremendous *burden of information transmission*. The result is that planners are often misinformed and make correspondingly incorrect decisions. Compounding this problem, firms seeking easy quotas have an incentive to falsify information deliberately.

- The system of production targets based on physical quantities rather than on profits or sales often leads to *huge stockpiles of unwanted and inferior goods and equally huge waiting lines for other goods*. For example, since automobile factories generally have quotas stated in terms of cars, there is an almost legendary shortage of spare parts in the Soviet Union. Manufacturers simply do not want to produce things that do not help fulfill their quotas. Similarly, a manufacturer ordered to produce 10,000 pairs of shoes, but faced with a shortage of leather, may produce 10,000 pairs of children's shoes. Selling them is not his concern.

- Because government policy has generally led to shortages of most consumer goods, managers of enterprises producing these goods have been able to turn out *low-quality merchandise*, knowing that eager consumers will buy up almost anything. (See the boxed insert on page 802.)

- Concern with quotas and targets also *stifles innovation*, despite rewards for plant managers who innovate. Innovation carries risks, and Russian managers worry about not fulfilling their plan. They also realize that a brilliant production performance this year will bring with it a much tougher quota next year.

- Worries about the future unavailability of materials have led some Soviet enterprises to maintain *inventories of crucial materials at levels that would be considered ludicrous in the United States*, and sometimes even to hide this fact from the authorities.

Widely publicized reforms in 1965, following suggestions made by the Soviet economist E. Liberman (and hence dubbed "Libermanism"), attempted to deal with some of these problems by introducing the profit motive into Soviet enterprise. With managerial bonuses based on *sales* or *profits*, it was hoped that some of the adverse incentives of the quantity-oriented planning system could be avoided. The reforms have scored some measure of success, but most observers feel that they were too limited to change the basic character of Soviet industry. For many enterprises, the quantity of output is still the most important indicator of success. Furthermore, the profit motive may not produce desirable results when market prices indicate neither production costs nor values to consumers.

Revolutionary Communism: China Under Mao

Immediately after the communist takeover in 1949, the Chinese economy was patterned on the Russian model and developed with Russian economic aid and technical expertise.

Despite the subsequent tremendous political rift between the two giants of the communist world, their economic structures remain quite similar today.

In particular, China's is very much a command economy, perhaps even more so than the Soviet economy. Also, China's traditional emphasis on rapid economic growth, particularly industrial growth, is quite similar to Russia's. Finally China, like Russia, has accorded high priority to the goal of economic self-sufficiency. Until the mid-1970s, China's foreign trade was negligible.

But there were also important differences. Probably the most important of these derived from the conscious decision by Mao Tse-tung *not* to rely on material incentives to motivate the work force. Mao and the Chinese leadership looked with disdain at this "bourgeois" practice, and preferred to motivate Chinese workers by exhortation, patriotism, and, where necessary, force. Russian communism bent its socialist doctrine somewhat in order to accommodate human nature. But Chinese communism for many years seemed determined to bend human nature to accommodate Maoist doctrine—to create "the new man in the new China," an effort that now seems abandoned.

A second, less important, difference is that Chinese planning is rather less centralized than Russian planning. Local and industrial authorities have more power and discretion than they do in the U.S.S.R. In part, some decentralization probably was dictated by China's immense size and economic backwardness in 1949. Without modern communications equipment (and perhaps even *with* it), there was no way for planners in Peking to hope to control economic activity in the outlying provinces.

The Visible Absence of the Invisible Hand

Since we live in a consumer-oriented society, it is hard to imagine what everyday life is like in a society where the consumer is not king. No one disputes the fact that the consumer has not yet ascended to the throne in the Soviet Union. In the following excerpt from a 1976 article in *Time* magazine, we get a glimpse of the problems that plague the Russian consumer.

The workingman, and particularly the working woman, . . . spends an inordinate amount of time tracking down scarce consumer goods. . . . Although the capital is by far the best-supplied city in the Soviet Union, TIME Moscow Bureau Chief Marsh Clark reports that "soap, toothpaste, perfumes, detergents, toilet paper, hairpins and matches are either of inferior quality or not available at all. The soaps don't clean, the mint-flavored toothpaste is harsh and repugnant, and the perfumes smell like overripe raspberries." The shortages are so common that people join any queue they see, then ask what it is for. In Moscow recently, Clark spotted a crowd jostling about a man selling something at a table. As the eager buyers got nearer, they saw that the choice item on sale was an English-language textbook entitled *Animal Physiology.*

Along with shortages, there are bizarre examples of superabundance. Because of poorly coordinated planning and lack of inventory control, goods may suddenly appear in disproportionate profusion. Tiny commissaries on collective farms that carry only the barest necessities may suddenly receive shipments of silk neckties or Italian vermouth. A decade ago there was a glut of condoms, which Russinas casually used as bottle caps and garters; today, there is a rubber shortage, and prophylactics can scarcely be found in Moscow. . . .

Letters and editorials in the Soviet press often complain about the inferior quality of Soviet-made merchandise. . . . According to Moscow's *Literary Gazette*, the seal of quality, which indicates that an item conforms to international standards, was awarded in 1974 to only .6% of all Soviet footwear and less than 1% of clothes. *Krokodil* [a Soviet humor magazine] recently published a satirical sketch about a couple seeking to buy furniture. The sofas were all big, clumsy and "of a shade combining the colors of a country backroad in autumn and of a World War I dreadnought destroyer." The author recommended against buying these dreadnought sofas because "one mustn't scare the children with furniture."

SOURCE: "Inside Russia: A Nation of Parallel Lives," *TIME*, March 8, 1976, pages 7–8. Reprinted by permission from *TIME, The Weekly Newsmagazine*; copyright Time Inc., 1976.

Chinese economic growth under the communist regime has proceeded in fits and starts.

The immediate problem after the Maoist takeover was to lift China from the devastation of World War II, and to establish communist institutions and values in a vast and semiliterate country. With Soviet assistance, the plan was apparently quite successful.

China's next step, the **Great Leap Forward** (1958–1960), turned out to be a giant step backward. No one knows why Mao abandoned the apparently successful attempt to transplant Soviet economic planning to China, but everyone agrees that the results were disastrous. Why did the Great Leap Forward fail so miserably? First, the Great Leap's production goals were unrealistically ambitious from the start. Second, because the ideologically pure "Reds" were in Mao's favor while the technocratic "experts" were not, the means selected for carrying out the Great Leap were more romantic than rational. China's vast economic structure was supposed to be decentralized, though tightly controlled by the communist party; massive applications of brute labor were supposed to make up for China's shortages of machinery and advanced technology; and material incentives were deemphasized. In retrospect, the Greap Leap Forward seems to have achieved

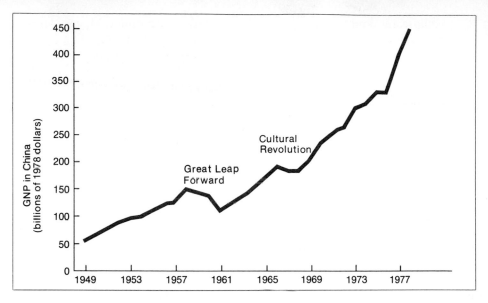

Figure 41–4
REAL GNP IN THE PEOPLE'S REPUBLIC OF CHINA
While Chinese economic statistics are notoriously inaccurate, one attempt to piece together a series of real GNP for China resulted in the data portrayed here. Other observers of China believe that the *level* of GNP is much lower than indicated here, but all agree that the general pattern shown here is about right. The Great Leap Forward and the Cultural Revolution stand out as major blemishes on the record of Chinese economic growth.
SOURCE: Central Intelligence Agency.

several things—most of them not very good for China. First, China's gross national product fell substantially (see Figure 41–4), particularly in the agricultural sector. It took years to make up for the losses of 1958–1960. Second, the ideological excesses of the period accelerated the growing schism between Russia and China. Third, it persuaded the Chinese leadership to throw out the "Reds" and bring back the "experts," signaling a return to rational economic calculation.

In large measure, China's Five-Year Plan covering 1961 to 1965 moved this giant nation back toward the Soviet model, though some elements of decentralization from the Great Leap were retained. One departure both from Soviet practice and from China's first Five-Year Plan (1953–1957), however, was the greater emphasis on agricultural development—no doubt a wise decision given China's resources. As a result, economic growth resumed.

Then, inexplicably, Mao changed China's course once again with the **Great Proletarian Cultural Revolution** (1966–1969). The "Reds" were in and the "experts" were out as never before. The infamous Red Guards (later assisted by the army) were sent out to purge rightist elements from Chinese society, organize revolutionary cadres, and spread the teachings of Chairman Mao. If anyone worried about economic productivity in this environment, it did not show. By the summer of 1967, both the Chinese economy and other elements of Chinese society were in utter disarray. Output fell again, but recovered much more quickly than it had from the Great Leap (see Figure 41–4).

Things began to change in the 1970s. The period until Mao's death in 1976 was one of consolidation and economic growth. The Chinese revolutionary fever receded and, once again, the "experts" were rehabilitated. There was a restoration of material incentives and of rational economic calculation—both of which had been considered reactionary during the Cultural Revolution. In general, there was less politics and ideology and more economic growth.

China Today

The Chinese economic system is now very much in a state of flux. The leaders who have followed Mao have shown themselves to be far less interested in doctrine and far more interested in results.

The opening of China to the West began with President Richard Nixon's visit there in 1972; it proceeded slowly at first, but in a torrent beginning in the 1970s.

The technicians and scientists who fell into disgrace under Mao's Cultural Revolution were rehabilitated, and put into positions of influence. In a startling reversal of roles, it was Mao and the revolutionaries whose wisdom was questioned.

In the early 1980s, the Chinese have welcomed Western tourism, trade, and technology as never before. Chinese managers, engineers, and economists have come to the United States and other Western nations to study modern business techniques. And perhaps most important, material incentives have been restored, and the Chinese have shown themselves willing to experiment with a wide variety of different models of economic organization. The Yugoslav system of worker management has been studied carefully. Even capitalism has been allowed back on the Chinese mainland. According to one newspaper report about China's Sichuan Province, ". . . factories are scrambling for orders, cutting prices and responding to market forces in a daring . . . experiment with the once-heretical techniques of capitalism. Profit, pure and simple, is the official motive."[9]

Still, the Chinese are proceeding gingerly, and at this writing China's economy still resembles the Soviet Union's far more than it does our own. At this point in history, it would be hazardous and imprudent to predict how the Chinese economy will evolve in the years ahead.

[9]"China Tries Capitalism, and It Works," *The New York Times*, August 14, 1980, p. D11. © 1980 by The New York Times Company. Reprinted by permission.

Summary

1. Economic systems differ in the amount of planning they do and in the extent to which they permit private ownership of property. However, socialism (state ownership of the means of production) need not go hand in hand with central planning, and capitalism need not rely on free markets. The two choices are distinct, at least conceptually.

2. Free markets seem to do a good job of selecting the bill of goods and services to be produced and at choosing the most efficient techniques for producing these goods and services. Planned systems have difficulties with both these choices.

3. Market economies, however, do not guarantee an equitable distribution of income and are often plagued by business fluctuations. In these two areas, planning seems to have clear advantages.

4. A major problem for socialism is how to motivate management to achieve maximal efficiency and to maintain inventiveness in the absence of the profit motive.

5. Individual freedom is a noneconomic goal that is of major importance in the choice among economic systems. Any elements of planning or of socialism will infringe upon the personal freedoms of some individuals. Yet complete freedom does not exist anywhere, and certain limitations on individual freedom command wide popular support.

6. The Swedish economy is almost entirely capitalistic, and there is little planning. The chief departures from the U.S. economic system are in the comprehensive ways the Swedish government intervenes to maintain full employment and in its extensive "welfare state."

7. Much more planning is done in France, which also has a rather larger socialist sector than does Sweden. But French planning differs from coercive Soviet-style planning in that it is "indicative," that is, it relies on consensus-building and on voluntary compliance.

8. Yugoslavia has a unique type of economic system called workers' management in which the managers of a firm are actually employed by the workers, who make all major decisions for themselves. While it is almost entirely socialist, the Yugoslav economy relies mainly on free markets and does very little planning.

9. Since the days of Stalin, the Soviet Union has followed a rather rigid system of central planning in which heavy industry and armaments are emphasized and consumer needs are deemphasized.

10. Russia's planning system is very bureaucratic and hierarchical; it has encountered monumental difficulties in transmitting accurate information. Goals and methods are set forth in Five-Year Plans and in even more detailed One-Year Plans.

11. While Soviet consumers are free to spend their money on what they please, there is no consumer sovereignty. Instead, it is the planners, not the consumers, who decide what will be produced. The labor market, however, operates much like it does in America—using wage rates to equate supply and demand.

12. With central planning replacing the price system, even

tasks that are rather simple for a market economy can become inordinately complex. The Soviet Union's difficulties in achieving material balance—that is, in equating supply and demand for the various inputs—illustrate this complexity.

13. The Chinese economic system has changed several times since the Communist takeover in 1949. After passing through several periods of intense revolutionary fervor and little economic progress, things seem to have normalized in China, where planning appears now to be similar to that in Russia, although somewhat less centralized. In addition, the Chinese have ended their traditional abhorrence of material incentives to motivate workers and have even flirted a bit with capitalism.

Concepts for Review

Capitalism	Sweden's investment reserve system	Material balance
Socialism	Welfare state	Material incentives
Planning	Indicative planning	Great Leap Forward
Free markets	Workers' management	Great Proletarian Cultural Revolution
Consumer sovereignty	Soviet Five-Year and One-Year Plans	

Questions for Discussion

1. Explain why the choice between capitalism and socialism is not the same as the choice between markets and central planning. Cite an example of a socialist market economy and of a planned capitalist economy.

2. If you were the leader of a small, developing country, what are some of the factors that would weigh heavily in your choice of an economic system?

3. Which type of economic system generally has the most trouble achieving each of the following goals? In each case, explain why.
   a. An equal distribution of income
   b. Adequate incentives for industrial managers
   c. Eliminating business fluctuations
   d. Balancing supply and demand for inputs

4. What are some of the advantages and disadvantages of the system of workers' management of industry as it is practiced in Yugoslavia?

5. "Both the goals and the techniques of Soviet economic planning have changed dramatically since Stalin's day." Comment.

6. If you were a Russian plant manager, what are some of the things you might do to make your life easier and more successful? (Use your imagination. Russian plant managers do!)

7. At the beginning of the chapter, we posed the question, "Does America have much to learn from the experiences of these other countries?" Given what you now know about Sweden, France, Yugoslavia, the U.S.S.R., and the People's Republic of China, what do you think?

Dissenting Opinions: Conservative, Moderate, and Radical

42

The principles that have been expounded in this book represent the mainstream view of modern economics. While they command the assent of a very large majority of American economists, there are dissenters. And these dissenters are not all fanatics and polemicists. Many of them are serious thinkers who are disturbed in one way or another by some aspects either of the modern American economy or the state of economic science, or both.

The dissent comes both from the left and the right of the mainstream of economics. On the right are the *libertarians*, who, while they agree with the portrayal of the virtues of the capitalist market economy given in this book, would no doubt insist that we have vastly overstated its vices and limited the realm of the market much too severely. To libertarians, the market rather than the state is the ultimate guarantor of freedom, and, consequently, they argue that the realm of the market should be expanded at the expense of the state. These are economic Jeffersonians who believe "that government is best that governs least." They want the government to keep its hands off the market.

Toward the left, the celebrated liberal economist and author John Kenneth Galbraith has been arguing for thirty years that most of the economics profession has been using the wrong model of the economy and, as a predictable result, has been generating policy prescriptions that look more and more absurd. Still farther to the left, a new group of *radical economists*, claiming to be the intellectual heirs of Marx, has attracted increasing numbers of adherents since its beginnings in the late 1960s. These critics claim that mainstream economists not only are asking all the wrong questions and seeking answers in all the wrong ways, but are little more than apologists for the interests of the capitalist ruling class.

The reader who has come this far will no doubt realize that the authors of this book generally ascribe to the mainstream view. But since that perspective has had a sufficiently long airing in this book, we believe it is useful now to take a brief look at the views of the dissenters. For one thing, history may yet prove that at least some of the dissenters have it right after all! In any event, it is certain that each of the critiques carries valuable lessons for mainstream economic analysis. Indeed, as we shall see, parts of each dissenting view have already been integrated into the body of standard economic analysis.

The Libertarian Credo

Libertarianism is really a philosophy rather than a system of economic thought. Libertarians prize individual freedom above all other social goals—way above them. They are willing to tolerate restrictions on individual freedom in only a very few cases; so few, in fact, that most observers find the more extreme variants of libertarian doctrine totally outlandish. Would you, for example, permit unhappy 10-year-olds to run away from home *legally*, provided only that they could support themselves? Would you sell city streets and highways to private businesses to operate for a profit? Would you permit drug companies to sell anything they want, without labeling requirements (but with legal liability for any harm done by their products)? There are libertarians who would advocate all of these measures, and many, many more.[1]

On economic matters, libertarians are usually associated with the political right wing as staunch defenders of laissez faire. But in issues concerning civil rights, legislation of morality, and protection of citizens against government coercion, their views coincide more with the political left wing. There can be no question that they fervently support civil liberties. As one outspoken libertarian put it:

The central idea of libertarianism is that people should be permitted to run their own lives as they wish. We totally reject the idea that people must be forcibly protected from themselves. A libertarian society would have no laws against drugs, gambling, pornography—and no compulsory seat belts in cars. We also reject the idea that people have an enforceable claim on others, for anything more than being left alone.[2]

The Libertarian Economics of Milton Friedman

The hallmark of libertarian economics is a belief—we might call it a *devout* belief—in the ability of free markets not only to do the tasks normally assigned to them by economists (efficient production of goods, utilization of scarce resources, and so on), but to do *almost everything.*

There is no question that the leading apostle of libertarian economics is Milton Friedman. So unquestioned is his preeminence that the libertarian school is often referred to by economists as the "Chicago School," a name acquired during the many years that Friedman taught at the University of Chicago.[3] While he is a sufficiently brilliant technical economist to have earned the Nobel Prize, he is also an irrepressible public advocate of his libertarian views. In fact, it is in this latter role (often voiced through his columns in *Newsweek* magazine) that Friedman has received the most notice, or notoriety. We might as well treat Friedman as the spokesman for all libertarian economists, for that is more or less what he is. According to Friedman:

[1]See, for example, David Friedman, *The Machinery of Freedom* (New York: Harper & Row, 1973), where each of these is advocated.

[2]David Friedman, *The Machinery of Freedom*, page xiii.

[3]He is now retired and a resident scholar at the Hoover Institution in Stanford, California. In fairness, we should note that the University of Chicago has had several other great libertarian economists on its faculty.

The kind of economic organization that provides economic freedom directly, namely, competitive capitalism, also promotes political freedom because it separates economic power from political power and in this way enables the one to offset the other.

Historical evidence speaks with one voice on the relation between political freedom and a free market. I know of no example in time or place of a society that has been marked by a large measure of political freedom, and that has not also used something comparable to a free market to organize the bulk of economic activity.[4]

We have spent many pages in this book detailing the appropriate role of government in a modern mixed capitalist society (see especially Chapters 23 and 29). Friedman would make this role much smaller, limiting it essentially to the following three tasks.

1. ***The government as umpire.*** Friedman is surely no anarchist, although some libertarians are. He recognizes that any society needs laws, and that legislation and enforcement of the law are proper roles for government in a free society. The government must, for example, enforce private contracts and adjudicate disputes.[5]

2. ***Control of natural monopoly.*** As we have noted in earlier chapters (see especially Chapters 25 and 27), some industries have such strong economies of large-scale production that it is inevitable, for technical reasons, that only one firm can survive. Telephone service, for example, probably comes close to fitting this model. Some have suggested (though others have disputed the claim) that the postal service also is a good example. In such cases, *competitive* capitalism is simply impossible, so society has only three choices:

   - Allow an unregulated private monopoly to exist.
   - Make the industry a public monopoly (as in the case of the U.S. Postal Service).
   - Allow private monopoly to exist, but regulate it carefully "in the public interest" (as we do, for example, with the telephone company).

   To Friedman, "all three are bad, so we must choose among evils." While Friedman is willing to decide which of the three alternatives is least bad on a case-by-case basis, he is skeptical that the choice typically made in America (regulated monopoly) is the best one.

3. ***Externalities.*** For reasons we have elaborated at some length in this book (see especially Chapters 29 and 31), the government must intervene to promote or protect the public welfare wherever there are beneficial or detrimental externalities. If it does not, the competitive price system will send out false signals and, as a result, will misallocate resources.
   Friedman accepts this anaysis but cautions against applying it too freely. The externalities argument, he notes, often is just an excuse for allocating to the public sector something that could be done better by the private sector. And even in such cases as the control of pollution, where government

---

[4]Reprinted from *Capitalism and Freedom* by Milton Friedman by permission of the University of Chicago Press (Chicago: University of Chicago Press, 1962), page 9.

[5]More extreme libertarians will suggest that even police protection could be a private enterprise. See, for example, Robert Nozick, *Anarchy, State, and Utopia* (New York: Basic Books, 1974), in which the state *arises from* a private system of police protection.

An Application of Libertarian Economics: The Licensing of Doctors

Your family doctor has a license to practice medicine in your state. He probably displays it prominently on the wall of his office. You probably would be worried if he did not have one. Yet libertarians like Professor Friedman think that licensing of doctors is a bad idea. He explains why in this excerpt from his celebrated book *Capitalism and Freedom.**

Offhand, the question, "Ought we to let incompetent physicians practice?" seems to admit of only a negative answer. But I want to urge that second thought may give pause.

Licensure is the key to the control that the medical profession can exercise over the number of physicians. . . . The American Medical Association is perhaps the strongest trade union in the United States. The essence of the power of a trade union is its power to restrict the number who may engage in a particular occupation.

How can it do this? The essential control is at the stage of admission to medical school. The Council on Medical Education and Hospitals of the American Medical Association approves medical schools. In almost every state in the United States, a person must be licensed to practice medicine, and to get the license, he must be a graduate of an approved school.

Control over admission to medical school and later licensure enables the profession to limit entry in two ways. The obvious one is simply by turning down many applicants. The less obvious, but probably far more important one, is by establishing standards for admission and licensure that make entry so difficult as to discourage young people from ever trying to get admission.

To avoid misunderstanding, let me emphasize that I am not saying that individual members of the medical profession . . . deliberately go out of their way to limit entry in order to raise their own incomes . . . the rationalization for restriction is that the members of the medical profession want to raise what they regard as the standards of "quality" of the profession. . . .

It is easy to demonstrate that quality is only a rationalization and not the underlying reason for restriction.

The power of the . . . American Medical Association has been used to limit numbers in ways that cannot possibly have any connection whatsoever with quality. The simplest example is their recommendation . . . that citizenship be made a requirement for the practice of medicine. I find it inconceivable to see how this is relevant to medical performance.

It is clear that licensure has been at the core of the restriction of entry and that this involves a heavy social cost. . . . Does licensure have the good effects that it is said to have?

It is by no means clear that it does raise the standards of competence in the actual practice of the profession. . . . The rise of the professions of osteopathy and of chiropractic is not unrelated to the restriction of entry into medicine. . . . These alternatives may well be of lower quality than medical practice would have been without the restrictions on entry into medicine.

More generally, if the number of physicians is less than it otherwise would be, and if they are fully occupied, as they generally are, this means that there is a smaller total of medical practice by trained physicians.

When these effects are taken into account, I am myself persuaded that licensure has reduced both the quantity and quality of medical practice. . . . I conclude that licensure should be eliminated as a requirement for the practice of medicine.

*For further discussion of this issue, see Discussion Question 3 at the end of this chapter (page 822).
SOURCE: *Capitalism and Freedom* by Milton Friedman by permission of the University of Chicago Press (Chicago: University of Chicago Press, 1962), pages 149–159.

---

intervention in the market can *in principle* improve the allocation of resources, the government may not have the knowledge it needs to correct the externality.

> *. . . the very factors that produce the market failure also make it difficult for government to achieve a satisfactory solution. Generally, it is no easier for government to identify the specific persons who are hurt and benefited than*

for market participants, no easier for government to assess the amount of harm or benefit to each. Attempts to use government to correct market failure have often simply substituted government failure for market failure. . . . The imperfect market may . . . do as well or better than the imperfect government. [6]

Beyond this short list, Friedman believes, there is little else for government to do in a free society.

Libertarian Economics and Public Policy

We began this discussion of libertarianism by giving some examples of rather extreme policy proposals made by some libertarians (though not necessarily by Milton Friedman). Yet some of Friedman's suggestions, which many people considered absurd when they were first made, have since either been incorporated into the mainstream of economic thought or have become the law of the land, or both.

For example, Friedman's was one of the first voices arguing that the system of fixed exchange rates among currencies was potentially dangerous and should be replaced by a system of floating rates, set not by governments but by supply and demand. We now have such a system. Friedman was also among the earliest advocates of the all-volunteer army. This piece of "insanity" became fact in 1973. His proposal for a negative income tax as a means to help poor people is now supported by almost all economists—be they of the left, the center, or the right—as well as by three of our last four presidents (though often in disguised form). The hostility toward the many government regulatory agencies that is now so much in vogue was present in Friedman's speeches and writings long before it became fashionable.

Yet there are many, many other issues about which the majority of economists and society as a whole continue to believe that Friedman is wrong. (See the boxed insert on page 809.) His voice continues to be one of dissent, and one that is every bit as radical as those on the far left. But that voice is irrepressible. As a *Wall Street Journal* columnist put it:

Mr. Friedman, it appears, has grown convinced that his ideas can be made to work here on earth just as marvelously as they already do in heaven. [7]

John Kenneth Galbraith: The Economist as Iconoclast

Milton Friedman is barely over 5 feet tall; John Kenneth Galbraith is about $6\frac{1}{2}$ feet tall. There the similarity ends. Friedman's reverence for the market is countered by Galbraith's irreverence about almost everything. Friedman's proposals for laissez faire are opposed by Galbraith's proposals to control almost everything.

John Kenneth Galbraith is a phenomenon in modern economics. This perpetual maverick, who has been blasting (often in ascerbic tones) what he calls "the conventional wisdom" for thirty years, was a member of the Department of

---

[6] Milton and Rose Friedman, *Free to Choose* (New York: Harcourt Brace Jovanovich, Inc., 1979), pages 214–218.

[7] Alfred L. Malabre, Jr., "The Milton Friedman Show," *The Wall Street Journal*, January 11, 1980. Reprinted by permission of *The Wall Street Journal* © Dow Jones & Company, Inc. 1978. All rights reserved.

Economics at Harvard University—the bastion of the "establishment"—until his retirement in 1975. Without a doubt the most widely read economist in the world, he is perhaps more highly regarded outside the profession than within it. Yet his fellow economists elected him president of the prestigious American Economic Association in 1972. In addition to his achievements in economics, he has been an adviser to presidents, the U.S. ambassador to India, leader of the Americans for Democratic Action, novelist, and TV personality. As one prominent economist put it:

Galbraith is . . . something special. His books are not only widely read, but actually enjoyed. He is a public figure of some significance; he shares . . . the power to shake stock prices by simply uttering nonsense. He is known and attended to all over the world. He mingles with the Beautiful People; for all I know, he may actually be a Beautiful Person himself.[8]

Galbraith began to move away from his successful career as a mainstream economist—which included a stint as a price-controller during World War II—with the publication of his book *American Capitalism* in 1952. There he argued that economists, in focusing on the interplay between supply and demand in impersonal markets, ignored the pervasiveness of **economic power,** and thereby blinded themselves to some of the most important things that were going on in the economy. He added further wrinkles to his developing view of the modern capitalist economy in his best-selling book *The Affluent Society* (1958) in which he argued that modern corporations, far from being the servants of consumer sovereignty they are supposed to be, actually *create* demand for their products through advertising.

These and other strands of Galbraithean thought were brought together in *The New Industrial State* (1967), which remains perhaps the most comprehensive statement of his views on modern capitalist enterprise. The book was, and is, quite controversial.

The Galbraithean Critique of Conventional Economic Theory

Galbraith maintains that conventional economists have squirreled themselves away in a dream world of their own creation, a world that has less and less to do with the real modern economy. In this hypothetical framework:

The best society is the one that best serves the economic needs of the individual. Wants are original with the individual; the more of these that are supplied the greater the general good. Generally speaking, the wants to be supplied are effectively translated by the market to firms maximizing profits therein. If firms maximize profits they respond to the market and ultimately to the sovereign choices of the consumer.[9]

The crucial omission from this picture, in Galbraith's view, is *power*, especially the power of the giant corporation, but also the power of big labor, government bureaucracies, and so on. Rather than being controlled by the market, he believes, the modern corporation controls, or even supplants, the market.

---

[8]Robert M. Solow, "The New Industrial State or Son of Affluence," *The Public Interest*, no. 9 (Fall 1967), page 100. Copyright © 1967 by National Affairs, Inc.

[9]J. K. Galbraith, "A Review of a Review," *The Public Interest*, Fall 1967, page 117.

By ignoring these phenomena, Galbraith claims, economists have been led into increasingly ridiculous policy positions. For example, the theory of monopoly (outlined in Chapters 25 and 28) stresses the *inefficiency* caused by its *restriction of output* in order to raise prices. Yet, as Galbraith sees the world, it is precisely the giant corporations that are *most efficient* and who produce *excessive amounts* of output. They do this by advertising campaigns that create the demand for the goods they are so adept at supplying. As another example, the focus on markets has led the vast majority of economists to oppose wage and price controls and therefore to accept the disagreeable trade-off between inflation and unemployment (see Chapter 16). Galbraith's is one of the few voices that refuses to accept this trade-off, putting his faith instead in a *permanent* system of wage–price controls.

What does the Galbraithean model of our economy look like? In the first place, according to Galbraith, our economy involves a great deal of *planning*.

In place of the market system, we must now assume that for approximately half of all economic output, there is a power or planning system . . . I cannot think that the power of the modern corporation, the purposes for which it is used or the associated power of the modern union would seem implausible or even very novel were they not in conflict with the vested doctrine.[10]

This *planning system* is run by *technocrats*: managers, engineers, accountants, lawyers, cyberneticists, even economists! The kinds of work they do, and the kinds of hierarchical structures they create, are more or less similar in corporations, nonprofit institutions, government bureaus, and even (to a limited extent) labor unions. The nature of their work is also basically the same under capitalism as it is under socialism, in market economies, or in planned economies. It is dictated not by ideology, but by the overwhelming complexity of modern technology. "The enemy of the market is not ideology but the engineer."[11]

These technocrats, whom Galbraith calls the **technostructure,** manipulate consumer demand through advertising. They also manipulate costs to a considerable degree, or else render them quite predictable through long-term contracts with labor unions and suppliers of other inputs (which are also giant corporations). And since the industrial giants can finance their own investment through retained earnings, they need not rely on the capital market. Thus, the market is bypassed.

The firm must take every feasible step to see that what it decides to produce is wanted by the consumer at a remunerative price. And it must see that the labor, materials, and equipment that it needs will be available at a cost consistent with the price it will receive. It must exercise control over what is sold. It must exercise control over what is supplied. It must replace the market with planning.[12]

The technocrats are guided by their own self-interest, not by the interests of their stockholders. In particular, they are certainly *not* interested in maximizing profits.

Instead, their primary interest is growth and expansion.

---

[10]J. K. Galbraith, "Power and the Useful Economist," *American Economic Review*, March 1973, page 4.

[11]J. K. Galbraith, *The New Industrial State* (Boston: Houghton Mifflin, 1967, and London: André Deutsch, Ltd., 1967), page 33.

[12]Galbraith, *The New Industrial State*, page 24.

If the technostructure . . . maximizes profits, it maximizes them . . . for the owners. If it maximizes growth, it maximizes opportunity for . . . advancement, promotion and pecuniary return for itself. That people should so pursue their own interest is not implausible.[13]

Apart from rapid growth, the technostructure cares about perpetuating the hierarchy of which it is a part, achieving technological triumphs, and earning enough profits both to keep stockholders satisfied and to allow it to finance its investments without borrowing.

The Galbraithean Critique of the American Economy

What are the results of this system for organizing economic activity? Not very good, according to Galbraith. First, American society is deluged with a dazzling array of private consumption goods of dubious merit:

What is called a high standard of living consists, in considerable measure, in arrangements for avoiding muscular energy, increasing sensual pleasure and for enhancing caloric intake above any conceivable nutritional requirement.[14]

Second, the nature of the system of want-creation effected by the planning system dictates that the outputs of the giant corporations will be produced in abundance while the outputs of what might be considered "competitive" industries (home building, for example) will remain puny:

That the present system should lead to an excessive output of automobiles, an improbable effort to cover the economically developed sections of the planet with asphalt, a lunar preoccupation with moon exploration, a fantastically expensive and potentially suicidal investment in missiles, submarines, bombers, and aircraft carriers, is as one would expect. These are the industries with power.[15]

Third, there is a shocking disparity between the abundant supplies of private consumption goods and the pitiful supplies of public consumption goods. The reason? Madison Avenue does not whet consumers' appetites for public goods. "The engines of mass communication, in their highest state of development, assail the eyes and ears of the community on behalf of more beer but not of more schools."[16]

Fourth, and finally, the system shows a shocking disregard for the environment, or what may be termed more generally "the quality of life":

The family which takes its mauve and cerise, air-conditioned, power-steered, and power-braked automobile out for a tour passes through cities that are badly paved, made hideous by litter, blighted buildings, billboards, and posts for wires that should long since have been put underground. They pass on to a countryside that has been rendered largely invisible by commercial art. . . . They picnic on exquisitely packaged food from a portable icebox by a polluted stream

---

[13]Galbraith, "A Review of a Review," page 113.
[14]J. K. Galbraith, as quoted by R. M. Solow, "The New Industrial State or Son of Affluence," page 107.
[15]J. K. Galbraith, "Power and the Useful Economist," page 7.
[16]J. K. Galbraith, *The Affluent Society* (Boston: Houghton Mifflin Company, 1958, and London: André Deutsch, Ltd., 1958), page 205.

and . . . spend the night at a park which is a menace to the public health and morals. Just before dozing off on an air mattress, beneath a nylon tent, amid the stench of decaying refuse, they may reflect vaguely on the curious unevenness of their blessings. Is this, indeed, the American genius?[17]

A Critique of the Critique

The typical mainstream economist's reaction to Galbraith is to ignore him. However, on occasion, the Galbraithean challenge has been met head-on.

Undoubtedly, the best of these occasions was when a prominent mainstream economist, Professor Robert Solow of M.I.T., published a scathing review of *The New Industrial State* in 1967. Solow's basic contentions were, first, that while the Galbraithean view of the economy no doubt contains some important insights (for example, modern economics pays too little attention to the giant corporation), the things that Galbraith appeals to as "facts" are really not facts at all; and second, that the Galbraithean model as a whole lacks structure and coherence. Our guess is that Solow's review of Galbraith represents the views of many economists. And since Solow is one of the few economists who can match Galbraith's wit and verbal dexterity, their debate is both lively and informative.

Has the modern corporation really preempted the market mechanism? Solow thinks not:

It is unlikely that the economic system can usefully be described either as General Motors writ larger or as the family farm writ everywhere . . . it will behave like neither extreme. . . . Galbraith's story that the industrial firm has "planned" itself into complete insulation from the vagaries of the market is an exaggeration, so much an exaggeration that it smacks of the put-on.[18]

Has advertising really robbed the consumer of his sovereignty and made him a puppet of the corporation? Solow finds the claim vaguely implausible, and wants to see evidence:

Professor Galbraith offers none; perhaps that is why he states his conclusion so confidently and so often. . . . I should think a case could be made that much advertising serves only to cancel other advertising.

If Hertz and Avis were each to reduce their advertising expenditures by half . . . what would happen to the total car rental business? Galbraith presumably believes it would shrink. People would walk more, and spend their money instead on the still-advertised deodorants. But suppose . . . that all advertising were reduced . . . Galbraith believes that in the absence of persuasion . . . total consumer spending would fall. Pending some evidence, I am not inclined to take this popular doctrine very seriously.[19]

Is the model of profit maximization, so beloved by mainstream economists, really irrelevant to modern forms of business organization? While recognizing that profit maximization cannot be a *literal* description of corporate behavior ("Most large corporations are free enough from competitive pressure to afford a donation to the Community Chest"), Solow suggests that it is still a workable *approximation*. There is, for example, an *opportunity cost* of funds even when those funds are generated by internal financing. Furthermore, managements that

[17]Galbraith, *The Affluent Society*, pages 199–200.
[18]R. M. Solow, "The New Industrial State or Son of Affluence," pages 103–104.
[19]Solow, "The New Industrial State or Son of Affluence," page 105.

stray too far from profit maximization in the pursuit of other goals, thereby depressing the value of their common stock, may find their jobs threatened by a takeover bid.

Are the outputs of the system really that bad? As Solow notes, it is hard to disagree with Galbraith's disparaging remarks about chrome-plated automobiles, pungent deodorants, and ostentatiously useless gadgets "without appearing boorish." Yet these are not the wasteful expenditures of the idle rich. It must be remembered that the median family income in the United States is not excessively high—it is currently about $25,000 per year. And by definition, fully *half* of American families earn less than this. Are they squandering their money on frivolities, or are these the things that the American people really want?

His [Galbraith's] attitudes toward ordinary consumption remind one of the Duchess who, upon acquiring a full appreciation of sex, asked the Duke if it were perhaps too good for the common people.[20]

In sum, Solow views *The New Industrial State* as strong on style and wit, but weak on substance: "A book for the dinner table not for the desk."

Not surprisingly, Galbraith was unmoved by this and other attacks, viewing them as the predictable reactions of conventional economists who see their vested interests threatened:

Neoclassical economics is not without its instinct for survival. It rightly sees the unmanaged consumer, the ultimate sovereignty of the citizen and the maximization of profits and resulting subordination of the firm to the market as the three legs of a tripod on which it stands. These are what exclude the role of power in the system. All three propositions tax the capacity for belief.[21]

The Radical Economics of the New Left

The newest of the three major challenges to mainstream economics comes from the far left. Spawned by the radical student movement of the 1960s, the "New Left" is highly critical both of contemporary capitalism as practiced in America (and elsewhere) and of contemporary economic analysis as practiced by most economists. Radical economics has grown and matured: its views are no longer circulated in leaflets handed out on street corners. They appear in the most prestigious scholarly journals and even in testimony before Congress. While the movement is too diverse to define concisely, it behooves us to take a close look at some of what the New Left has been saying.

New Left economists view themselves as the inheritors of Marxism, both of its intellectual traditions and its political activism.

Like Marx, they stress the pervasive importance of the *mode of production*, including not only its influence on economic activity, but also its effects on personal attitudes and social institutions. They write much about the *class struggle*, and leave no doubt about where they line up. Like Marx, they seek to uncover the inner *contradictions* in modern capitalism, contradictions that, they believe, will contribute to its ultimate demise. And, also like Marx, their writings are replete with stinging criticisms of both contemporary economic analysis and contemporary economic institutions, but tell us much less about the type of

[20]Solow, "The New Industrial State or Son of Affluence," page 108.
[21]J. K. Galbraith, "Power and the Useful Economist," page 5.

system they would like to see take its place.

There is also much of Galbraith in the writings of the New Left: They share his emphasis on power rather than on markets, his critique of the giant corporation, his belief that consumers are manipulated by producers, and his dismay over the outputs of the industrial system. But Galbraith is surely no radical economist, and the radical economists are not Galbraithean. They find his propensity to turn to the government to solve problems hopelessly naïve. In their view, the government is part and parcel of the corporate state—a contributor to the problem, not an instrument toward a solution.

The Shortcomings of Mainstream Economics: Point and Counterpoint

In brief, New Left economists hold that mainstream economists are asking all the wrong questions and using the wrong set of tools (economic models) to provide the answers. Let us examine their complaints one by one.[22]

Narrowness of Focus
Radicals argue that economists typically narrow their field of inquiry so much that they are incapable of addressing the important questions.

For one thing, in contrast to Marx's teachings, modern economics is *ahistorical*. It is very much based on the here and how, with scant attention paid to the origins of the current system or the directions in which it may be headed. Perhaps as a consequence of this narrow scope, mainstream economics *accepts institutions as given and (tacitly) as immutable*. Little attention is paid to how institutions change.

Orthodox economics takes the existing social system for granted, much as though it were part of the natural order of things.[23]

Amplifying the attack, the New Left chides conventional economists for their preoccupation with analysis of *marginal* changes, using the celebrated tools of marginal analysis that we have described in earlier chapters. This, they argue, makes economics incapable of dealing with the really big issues: the institution of private property, poverty and discrimination, unemployment, and alienation. For example, Professor John Gurley of Stanford University, who converted from conventional to radical economics many years ago, scoffed at a prominent economist who expressed the belief that reducing unemployment would do more good things for the distribution of income than any measure he could imagine.

Well, any radical economist can imagine a direct measure that would do even better things—expropriation of the capitalist class and turning over of ownership of capital goods and land to all the people. That, of course, sounds wild— unimaginable—to anyone who does not question the existing system.[24]

The consequence of this disciplinary narrowness, radicals contend, is that economists become, whether deliberately or unwittingly, apologists for the

[22]Another attempt to draw up a list of key tenets of the New Left, similar in spirit to what we do here, appears in Assar Lindbeck's *The Political Economy of the New Left: An Outsider's View*, Second Edition (New York: Harper & Row, 1977).
[23]Paul Sweezy, "Toward a Critique of Economics," *Monthly Review*, vol. 21, no. 8 (January 1970), page 1. Copyright © 1970 by Monthly Review, Inc. Reprinted by permission of Monthly Review Press.
[24]J. G. Gurley, "The State of Political Economics," *American Economic Review*, May 1971, page 59.

present system, supporters of the propertied class, and defenders of the status quo.

Most economists are prepared to plead guilty to the charge of disciplinary narrowness. As Yale's Nobel prize winner, James Tobin, put it:

Most contemporary economists feel ill at ease with respect to big topics— national economic organization, interpretation of economic history, relations of economic and political power, origins and functions of eonomic institutions. The terrain is unsuitable for our tools. We find it hard even to frame meaningful questions, much less to answer them.[25]

But mainstream economists tend to view their inadequacy in this area as a misdemeanor, not a felony. They point out, in their defense, that a narrow focus is imperative if progress in analysis is to be made. And they are quite proud of the achievements of economic science compared with those of the more diffuse social sciences, such as sociology and political science. They counter that radicals try to paint with such broad strokes that everything becomes necessarily superficial and imprecise. And they argue that the radicals, with their very clear political biases, are hardly in a position to question the objectivity of other economists.

Acceptance of Tastes and Motivation as Given

Just as they do with institutions, conventional economists accept the tastes of consumers and the motivations of workers and managers as given and unchangeable: "just human nature."

Radicals, on the other hand, agree with Galbraith that the consumer is manipulated; and they go on to widen the charge. Not only is the consumer bombarded by Madison Avenue, he is brainwashed in the school system, influenced by politicians, and subtly molded by other social institutions.

These institutions, furthermore, are set up for the convenience of the ruling (capitalist) class.

Economics . . . takes preferences as being exogenously determined and then shifts the burden of studying their formation and change onto "other disciplines." The New Left rejects this compartmentalization and takes the Marxian view . . . that new needs are created by the same process by which their means of satisfaction are produced.[26]

This argument is broadened further by the assertion that the need for material incentives to motivate both workers and managers is culturally acquired rather than innate, a product of capitalism rather than a cause of it. Some admire Fidel Castro's efforts to create "the new man." In Che Guevara's words:

We are doing everything possible to give work this new category of social duty and to join it to the development of technology, on the one hand, and to voluntary work on the other, based on the Marxian concept that man truly achieves his full human condition when he produces without being compelled by the physical necessity of selling himself as a commodity. . . . We will make the twenty-first-century man.[27]

[25]J. Tobin, book review of Lindbeck's *The Political Economy of the New Left*, *Journal of Economic Literature*, December 1972, page 1216.
[26]S. Hymer and F. Roosevelt, "Comment," *Quarterly Journal of Economics*, November 1972, page 649.
[27]John Gerassi, ed., *Venceremos! The Speeches and Writings of Che Guevara* (New York: Simon and Schuster, 1968), pages 394 and 400. (Copyright © 1968 by John Gerassi.)

Naturally, mainstream economists do not really believe that tastes are God-given. Everyone realizes that they are acquired, and influenced by many things. The question is: What are we to do about this? Lacking a theory of taste formation, basic economic analysis proceeds on the assumption that consumer tastes are to be respected *regardless* of how they got to be what they are. If we forsake this principle we find ourselves on some dangerous ground: If consumers do not know what's good for them, who does? Still, most economists would willingly concede that more research into taste formation would be desirable; and some are working on this right now. The radicals have no doubt pushed the profession in a healthy direction.

Obsession with Efficiency Rather Than Equality

Earlier in this book we described in some detail the fundamental trade-off between efficiency and equality. All mainstream economists appreciate and understand this principle, and a great many—in their role as private citizens—advocate greater equality. However, the New Left is quite right to complain that:

The preponderant majority of economic analysis and research is concerned with efficiency, not with equality.

Many conventional economists agree with this criticism. Such "establishment" figures as Alice M. Rivlin, head of the Congressional Budget Office, and the late Robert Aaron Gordon, a past president of the American Economic Association, have echoed these sentiments.[28]

But New Left economists do not ask simply for a change in emphasis; they also want a change in the economist's tool kit. The marginal productivity theory of income distribution, they argue, is irrelevant. They maintain that to understand the distribution of income in contemporary America, we must first understand the distribution of *power*, which is largely determined by who controls the means of production.

According to marginal-productivity theory, workers receive the marginal product of labor and capitalists receive the marginal product of capital. This conservative theory tries to justify the present distribution of income. Critics . . . claim that it explains nothing, is unrealistic and refers to nothing measurable, and confuses the product of capital with the product of the capitalist.

According to radical theory, workers produce the whole product but capitalists expropriate part of it in profits (by means of their control of all the resources and productive facilities).[29]

As a radical economist sees it, the shares of national income going to workers and to property owners are largely determined by the relative power of the two groups.[30]

Here the conventional and the radical economists part company. The conventional economist wants to know just how this "power" is measured. Are there statistical studies showing that "power" influences the distribution of income? In

---

[28]Alice M. Rivlin, "Income Distribution—Can Economists Help?" *American Economic Review*, May 1975, pages 1–15; R. A. Gordon, "Rigor and Relevance in a Changing Institutional Setting," *American Economic Review*, March 1976, pages 1–14.

[29]E. K. Hunt and Howard J. Sherman, *Economics: An Introduction to Traditional and Radical Views*, Second Edition (New York: Harper & Row, 1975), pages 249–250.

[30]Gurley, "The State of Political Economics," page 59.

short, mainstream economics treats this approach to distribution theory as rhetoric, not as science.

Myopic Concentration on Quantity Rather Than Quality

Much like Galbraith, the New Left is critical of mainstream economists' preoccupation with policies designed to increase the gross national product. They argue that a great deal of this output is no more than junk, and using society's resources to produce such things is patently irrational. They also point to the spoliation of the environment caused by modern industrial production, though at least some radicals concede that conventional economics has some solutions to these problems (see Chapter 31). And they echo Galbraith's dismay that a system that is so good at producing private consumer goods should be so pathetically bad at feeding the hungry, housing and clothing the poor, and providing public services of all kinds.

The New Left adds one further element to Galbraith's indictment. In addition to ruining the quality of the environment, capitalist production ruins human beings.

It makes them aggressive, competitive, even dehumanized, by forcing them into a rat race for material gain. In Marxian terms, workers have little voice in determining the nature of their productive activities and so become *alienated* from their work rather than being proud of their accomplishments. (See Chapter 40, especially pages 777–778.)

The answers that conventional economists have to most of these charges have already been noted in connection with our discussion of Galbraith (Refer back to pages 810–815). The new charges are those of alienation and the dehumanizing effects of capitalism. We think it is safe to say that conventional economists have never known what to make of the notion of alienation. They scratch their heads about it, but that is about all. If this is an important way in which capitalism has damaged the quality of life, then conventional economics surely has been blind to it. Like "power," however, no one has yet figured out a way to measure alienation. As to the alleged dehumanization of the labor force, this seems to be a side effect of modern industrial activity—whether that activity is conducted under capitalism or under socialism.

Naïve Conception of the State

New Left economists maintain that both mainstream economists and Galbraith hold a naïve and sentimental view of the state. In this view, government is available to set things right when the market system fails (as in the case of externalities, for example), and in so doing, government decisions are dictated by the broad public interest. By contrast:

The State, in the radical view, operates ultimately to serve the interest of the controlling class in a class society. Since the "capitalist" class fundamentally controls capitalist societies, the state functions in capitalist societies to serve that class. It does so either directly, by providing services only to members of that class, or indirectly, and probably more frequently, by helping preserve and support the system of basic institutions which support and maintain the power of that class.[31]

---

[31]D. M. Gordon, *Theories of Poverty and Underemployment* (Lexington, Mass.: D. C. Heath & Company, 1972), page 61.

This *subservience of the state to the capitalists* manifests itself in several ways. First, since capitalists are driven by competition to accumulate capital continually and to expand production, more and bigger markets are necessary on which to sell this bountiful output. As a result, capitalist nations turn to *imperialist ventures* to secure new markets. Second, in order to maintain domestic demand at high levels, the military-industrial complex promotes a *war economy*, which, if not actually at war, is continually spending inordinate sums on armaments. Third, even reforms that appear to be pro-labor, such as social welfare programs, unemployment insurance, and the like, are really intended to *"buy off" the working class* so that they will not rise up in revolt, as they imply Marx had predicted. In this view, for example, the New Deal was not motivated by a desire to help the working class, but rather by a desire to forestall the coming revolution.

Mainstream economists admit to a certain political naïvete. Yet most economists are unimpressed by the radicals' view of the state. Without denying that corporations often curry political favor, and often succeed, mainstream economists wonder how the radical model can explain progressive income taxation, inheritance taxes, antitrust legislation, equal opportunity laws, affirmative action regulations, and many, many more acts that the preponderance of the wealthy opposed bitterly at the time they were enacted. Furthermore, they point out, the policy prescriptions that conventional economists offer to improve the functioning of markets are intended as just that—as prescriptions for improvement, not as predictions about what government will actually do. Economists are not *that* naïve.

The Radical Critique of the American Economy

The economics profession is by no means the only element in contemporary American society that the New Left finds objectionable. Much of its criticism of modern industrial capitalism has already been mentioned in connection with its criticism of modern economics. Radicals dislike the great disparities in income and wealth that the system produces; they despise the discrimination against blacks and women that, they argue, capitalism promotes; they blame the system for alienating its labor force and dehumanizing people in other ways (as in the schools); they cite the irrational use of resources to produce too much private junk and too few public services; they abhor what they see as its imperialist and militaristic tendencies; and they claim that the system is unable to cope with the problem of macroeconomic instability.

Taken as a whole, this is a powerful indictment. But almost all these problems have been raised many times before by nonradical economists.

What distinguishes the radical attack from the attitudes of liberal reformers is that the radicals have a unified view of it all.

Liberals see each of these . . . problems as separate and distinct. The problems, they believe, are the results of past mistakes, inabilities, and ineptitudes or the results of random cases of individual perversity . . . liberals generally favor government-sponsored reforms designed to mitigate the many evils of capitalism. These reforms never threaten the two most important features of capitalism: private ownership of the means of production, and the free market.

Radicals, however, see each of the . . . problems . . . as the direct consequence *of private ownership of capital and the process of social decision making within the impersonal cash nexus of the market. The problems cannot be solved until their underlying causes are eliminated, but this means a fundamental, radical economic reorganization.*[32]

What Is the Radical Alternative?

What would the radicals put in place of our system of market capitalism? There are many answers, but none commands anything like universal support among members of the New Left.

Some prefer a system of rigid state planning along Soviet lines, but they are a minority. For the most part, radicals see oppression by bureaucrats of the Soviet type as little better than (and little different from) oppression by capitalists. And radicals deplore the losses of human rights that accompany totalitarianism. Another group advocates a system of market socialism, along Yugoslav lines. But this runs counter to the argument that the institution of markets is one of the root causes of America's difficulties. Others see the Israeli kibbutz system, perhaps the purest form of communism ever practiced, as a model.

In fact, the radicals' hostile attitude both toward markets *and* central planning has put them in an awkward position. As one thoughtful critic of the New Left put it:

It may be possible to make a strong case against either markets or administrative systems, but if we are against both *we are in trouble; there is hardly a third method for allocating resources and coordinating economic decisions, if we eliminate physical force.*[33]

If both the market and the plan are discarded, how is the economy to be organized? The radical viewpoint is perhaps vague, but two characteristics stand out quite clearly. First, the New Left wants a *decentralized* system, not one in which power is concentrated (either in the hands of capitalists or of commissars). Second, it wants a *participatory* system in which workers have some real control over what they do and how they do it, not one in which orders only flow from the top down. These changes, they believe, would make workers both happier and more productive. In the radical view, therefore, the trade-off between efficiency and equality can be defeated. By reforming the basic structure of society, they contend, we can achieve a more egalitarian economy which is also more productive.

[32]Hunt and Sherman, *Economics*, page 186.
[33]Assar Lindbeck, *The Political Economy of the New Left: An Outsider's View*, page 32.

Summary

1. Mainstream economic analysis is not without its dissenters—conservative, moderate, and radical.
2. The libertarian philosophy translates, in economic matters, to a defense of laissez faire and to a devout belief in the workings of markets. This is because libertarians see free markets as the best guarantor of individual freedom.
3. Libertarian economists like Milton Friedman would limit government to three basic roles: enforcement of the law, regulation of natural monopolies, and control of externalities. Some libertarians would give government even less scope than this.
4. John Kenneth Galbraith has argued for years that conventional economic analysis has accorded insufficient attention to large and powerful organizations like the modern corporation. In his view, this omission has made modern economics largely irrelevant to modern society.
5. According to Galbraith, large corporations have the power to control, or even supplant, market forces by

creating the demand for their products through advertising, and by manipulating their own costs. This "planning system" is run by technocrats, who are more interested in growth and expansion than in maximizing profits.

6. Because the modern corporation controls the market, rather than vice versa, the U.S. economy, according to Galbraith, turns out tons of consumer baubles of dubious merit but underproduces crucial goods like housing, keeps the public sector starved, and despoils the environment.

7. Mainstream economists feel that Galbraith overstates his case and substitutes assertion for fact. They doubt that the corporation can avoid the discipline of the market entirely, and are skeptical of the view that the consumer is a puppet of Madison Avenue.

8. Radical economists are the economic and political heirs of Marx, though their analysis of twentieth century capitalism bears the unmistakable stamp of Galbraith. However, they disdain Galbraith's "liberal" view of the state and view the government as an instrument of the capitalist class.

9. Radicals criticize mainstream economists for having an unduly narrow focus; for accepting consumer tastes and human nature as "givens" rather than treating them as the results of the economic system; for stressing efficiency rather than equality as an economic goal; and for concentrating on increasing the quantity of output rather than the quality of life.

10. While their critique of both economic theory and the modern economy is quite clear and forceful, radicals are much less clear about what type of system should be put in its place.

Concepts for Review

Libertarianism	New Left economics	Alienation
Economic power	Manipulation of the consumer	Liberal versus radical views of the state
Technostructure		

Questions for Discussion

1. What might a libertarian think of:
   a. laws prohibiting smoking cigarettes in public places?
   b. laws prohibiting smoking marijuana in private?
   c. compulsory seat belts in cars?
   d. speed limits on highways?
   e. censorship?

2. Explain why a libertarian would support the all-volunteer army. Explain why many who are not libertarians also support it. How are the concepts of *supply and demand* and *opportunity cost* relevant?

3. Friedman believes that the medical profession has kept doctors' fees high by making it difficult to get into medical school (see page 809). Explain his argument with a supply and demand diagram. What are the costs and benefits to society of licensing doctors? How would you go about deciding whether the benefits exceed the costs, or vice versa?

4. Friedman has advocated replacing the current system of public schools by a "voucher" plan in which the parents of each school-age child would get a voucher worth, say, $2000. These educational vouchers could be spent only on education, but could be spent in any accredited school, public or private, of the parents' choosing.[34] What do you think of this idea? How might your own elementary and secondary schooling have differed if this plan had been in effect?

[34]For a full discussion of the proposal, see Milton and Rose Friedman, *Free to Choose* (New York: Harcourt Brace Jovanovich, Inc., 1979), Chapter 6.

5. Galbraith says that about 50 percent of the American economy is in the "planning system" rather than in the competitive market. What are some industries that seem to fall under both headings?

6. Some years ago, sharp limitations were placed on cigarette advertising—including the banning of such ads from TV. Yet smoking has not fallen noticeably. How does this experience bear on Galbraith's claim that the modern corporation creates demand through advertising? Would a libertarian support the ban on TV advertising? Would a radical economist? Would you?

7. According to Galbraith, modern economic analysis rests on three assumptions: consumer sovereignty, profit maximization, and the subordination of the firm to the market. Explain what he means.

8. Discuss the divergent views of the role of the state in the economy held by (a) libertarians, (b) Galbraith, and (c) radical economists. Which do you find most appealing?

9. Discuss the radical critique of conventional economics, point by point. Where do you find room for improvement in mainstream economics?

10. Radicals blame the American economic system for inequality, alienation and dehumanization, irrational use of resources, militarism, and macroeconomic instability. In your view, which of these are valid criticisms? Do you think these criticisms are indictments of private ownership of capital, of a market system, or of industrial systems in general?

Index

infant mortality and life expectancy in, 752
per capita GNP in, 752
population growth rate in, 754
real GNP growth rate in, 754
Indicative planning, France, 793
Indifference curve(s), 345–352
consumer preference and, 347
defined, 345, 347
properties of, 348
slope of, 348–349
Indirect taxes, 553, *see also* Taxation; Taxes
"Indispensable necessity" syndrome, 37–38
Individual proprietorship, advantages of, 451
Induced investment, 145, 156
Industrial pollutants, 573–576
taxing of, 17
Industry
concentration in, *see* Concentration in industry
equilibrium of, in short and long run, 420–424
interdependence in, 436
regulation of, 497–515
Industry size, supply curve shifts and, 61
Inequality
"ideal" or optimal amount of, 653–654
market mechanism of, 646
politics and economics of, 642–643
Infant-industry argument, 725
Inferior goods, income and demand related to, 341
Inflation
aggregate demand and, 85
battle against, 4, 319–334
borrowing and, 100
cause of, 85
control through fiscal and monetary policy, 303–306
cost of, 306–307
creeping vs. galloping, 104–105
demand management and, 84
demand-side, 295–300
expansionary monetary policy and, 256–257
expected rate of, 261, 310, 329
in Germany (1923), 105
government policies and, 84
hands-off vs. restrictive policy in, 305–306
history of (1963–1970), 168
indexing and, 332
index numbers for, 108
investment vs. profits in, 103
long-term contracts and, 103–104
in macroeconomics, 75
multiplier and, 183–185
myth vs. reality in, 96–99
Phillips curve on, 300, 307–309
predictability of, 104
productivity growth in, 323–324
purchasing power and, 96–97
rate, consumer spending and, 124
rational expectations and, 310
recessionary cost of, 304–306
relative prices and, 98–99
social costs of, 96–106, 312, 332
stabilization policy and, 85

statistical measurement of, 108–110
supply-side, 172–174
supply-side tax cuts and, 319–320
in Sweden vs. United States, 792
trade-off with unemployment, 4, 209, 292–318, *see also* Ideas for Beyond the Final Exam
unemployment and, 17, 87–110
wage–price controls and, 328
wage/price ratio in, 97
Inflationary expectations, 310, 329
Inflationary gap
defined, 151
elimination of, 166–167, 301
equilibrium and, 165
full employment and, 168
inflation and, 166–167
Innovation
big business and, 525–526
vs. invention, 608
production costs and, 386
Input
derived demand curve for, 594–595
optimal quantity in, 373
Input combinations
choice of, 369–370, 775
financial information and, 375
to production indifference curve, 390–391
Input–output analysis, 436–437
in Soviet Union, 799–800
Input prices
changes, 391–392
optimal input choice and, 391
Interest, defined, 597
Interest payments, national income and, 610
Interest rates, *see also* High interest rates
behavior of, 1979–1981, 249
ceilings on, 101–102, 600
controls on, 53
exchange rates and, 735–736
expansionary monetary policy and, 254
illusion of, 3, 102–103, *see also* Ideas for Beyond the Final Exam
investment and capital related to, 596–598
market determination of, 598–600
nominal vs. real, 100–101
opportunity cost and, 544
regulation of, 103
and supply of funds, 598–600
usury laws and, 595–596
velocity of circulation and, 261
Intermediate good, defined, 77
Intermediate run, defined, 381
International financial markets, developments in since 1973, 747–748
International financial system, current features of, 746–747
International Monetary Fund (IMF), 743, 747
International monetary system, 729–749, *see also* Money
International trade, 707–728, *see also* Exchange rate(s); Foreign trade
absolute advantage in, 711, 715
comparative advantage and, 6–7, 707–728, *see also* Ideas for Beyond the Final Exam
currencies involved in, 710–711

mutual gains from, 709–710
political factors in, 710–711
quotas and tariffs in, 721
reasons for, 709
Interstate Commerce Commission, 499, 504
Invention, vs. innovation, 608
Investment (I)
capacity utilization in, 140–141
capital and interest related to, 596–598
defined, 131
demand growth in, 141
extreme variability of, 140–141
gross private domestic, 131
induced, 145, 156
inflation and, 103
spending, 177
supply-side tax cuts and, 320
tax provisions and, 141
Investment bank, 463, *see also* Bank(s)
Investment reserve system, Sweden, 791
Investment-savings coordination, 152–153
Investment schedule, graphical analysis, 156
Investment tax credit, 141, 206
"Invisible hand," 48, 52, *see also* Smith, Adam
in coordination of economic decisions, 432
in distribution of goods, 446–448
failures of, 546–547
price increases and, 441
in production planning, 447–449
regulation of, 509
Iran, oil production and pricing in, 694
Israel, 649, 707, 709
Italy, productivity growth rates in, 325

J

Japan
American imports from, 708
economic progress in, 766
productivity growth rates in, 325
wages in, 708
Jawboning, 326–327
Johnson, Lyndon B., 116, 202, 327, 643
Judgmental forecasters, 290
Justice Department, antitrust suits, 516, 521

K

Kemp-Roth tax cut plan, 320
Kennedy, John F., 92, 94, 116, 170, 327
Keynes, John Maynard, 80, 140, 150–151, 176, 467
Keynesian analysis
vs. monetarist viewpoint, 263–264, 274–290
national income determination through, 681
Keynesian model
aggregate supply curve in, 283–286
monetary policy and, 253–254
money and aggregate demand in, 252–253
money and price level in, 255–257
stabilization policy in, 284
Keynesian–monetarist debate, 263–264, 274–290
aggregate supply curve and, 283–286

definitions of, 644
in less developed countries, 753
negative income tax and, 657–661
Poverty cycle, 643
Poverty line, 643
Predatory pricing, regulation of industry
and, 505
Preferred stock, 459
Present value (of money), 612, *see also*
Money
Price(s)
marginal utility and, 339
market system and, 47
in Marxian economics, 775–776
relative, 98
Price ceilings, 498
Price change
budget line and, 347
consumer choice and, 351
demand curve and, 351
income and substitution effects of,
341–342
and misallocation of resources, 525
Price controls, 53–55, *see also* Wage–price
controls
effect of, 329
on reserves of natural resources, 692
shortages and dislocations caused by,
68–69
Price cutting, equilibrium and, 58
Price discrimination
Clayton Act and, 519
monopoly and, 528
Price/earnings (P/E) ratio, of stocks, 461
Price elasticity, *see* Elasticity of demand
Price floors, 498
Price increase
oil supply and, 700–704
public interest and, 440–441
resource depletion and, 696–700
Price index, in deflation of monetary
figures, 109–110
Price leadership, 488
Price level
aggregate demand and, 183
consumer spending and, 123
equilibrium aggregate quantity demand
and, 148
expenditure schedule and, 148
money demand and, 257
money supply and, 255–257
real GNP and, 164, 205, 294
real output and, 295
in United States, 1867–1981, 79
Price mechanism, assessment of, 445
Price/quantity decision, 394
Price/quantity historical data, 365–366
Price stickiness, 481, 493–495
Price system, resource allocation and, 545
Private enterprise, *see* Free market;
Market mechanism
Private good(s)
defined, 540
Galbraithean view, 813–814
Product distribution, 434–435, 447–448
Production
in circular flow, 113–115
efficient output selection in, 437–440
factors of, 592–615
Production costs
alternative input combinations

and, 376
innovation and, 386–387
Production function, 375–378
defined, 375
Production indifference curve(s),
389–394
characteristics of, 389
cost minimization, 391
defined, 389
input combinations in, 390–391
Production indifference maps, 389
defined, 26
Production planning
allocation of inputs in, 448–449
laissez faire and, 434
Production possibilities frontier
allocation of resources between present
and future and, 543–544
defined, 41
efficient resource allocation and,
431–432, 534–536
opportunity cost and, 42–43
Productivity
aggregate supply curve and, 163
annual rate of growth in, 514
defined, 323
equivalent, 650
Productivity growth, inflation and,
323–324
Productivity slowdowns, 325
Profit(s)
economic, 425
GNP and, 606
inflation and, 103
marginal, 400–401
in Marxian economics, 774–776
monopoly power and, 607
public opinion on, 607
risk bearing and, 607
source of, 606–609
total, 396
zero, 424–425
Profit maximization
graphical interpretation of, 399–400
marginal analysis and, 400–401
marginal cost and, 402
reality and, 395–396, 405
Profit-maximizing equilibrium, for
monopolist, 473
Profit-maximizing firm, short-run
equilibrium of, 416
Profits taxation, 608–609, *see also* Income
tax; Taxation
Progressive tax
defined, 553
Lorenz curve of, 661
Property taxes, 553, 558–559
Proportional tax, defined, 553
Proprietorships, in United States, 451
Public enterprise, efficiency in, 514
Public good(s)
defined, 540
"free-rider" problem and, 540
market performance in relation to, 540
price for, 541
Public sector, collective bargaining in, 635
Public utilities
capital use by, 379–380
as monopoly suppliers, 472
regulation of, 103
Purchasing power

erosion of, 96
in less developed countries, 753
of wages, 97
Purchasing-power parity theory, 733–735
Pure monopoly
defined, 413, 470
market mechanism and, 469–479
rarity of, 490

Q

Quantity demanded, variables in,
360–361, *see also* Demand
Quantity theory of money.
equation of exchange and, 259
modernization of, 261–263
velocity of circulation and, 258–260
Quota, defined, 719

R

Radical economics of the New Left,
815–821
Radical economists, defined, 806
Ramsey Pricing Rule, 509
Random walk, stock prices as, 465–466
Rate regulation
effect of, 503–504
marginal vs. fully distributed cost
in, 507
Rational behavior, defined, 16
Rational decision(s)
defined, 39
opportunity cost and, 39, *see also* Ideas
for Beyond the Final Exam
Rational expectations, theory of, 309–310
Rationing
for oil conservation, 702–703
in World War II, 330
Rays through origin, in graphs, 24–25, *see
also* 45° lines
Reagan, Ronald, 38, 169, 173, 202–203,
281, 292, 313, 315–316, 319–323,
326–327, 441, 492, 501, 517, 550,
563, 581
Real capital gain, defined, 456
Real GNP, *see also* Gross national product
aggregate supply curve and, 283
budget deficit and, 271
defined, 77
in demand-side inflation, 294
drop in, 140
fiscal policy and, 201
leading indicators and, 289
measurement of, 162n.
multiplier and, 184
price level and, 164, 184, 186, 205, 285,
294, 304
vs. real expenditure, 186, 201, 253
resource depletion in, 696–697
Soviet Union vs. U.S. values for, 785
stabilization policy and, 84
stagflation and, 82
unemployment and, 95
of United States for years 1879–1981, 78
Real output growth
aggregate supply curve and, 297
unemployment rate and, 298
Real rate of interest, defined, 101, *see also*
Interest rates
Recession
budget balancing and, 203
defined, 75

A 2
B 3
C 4
D 5
E 6
F 7
G 8
H 9
I 0
J 1